# WHERE ON EARTH?

## OUR WORLD AS YOU'VE NEVER SEEN IT BEFORE

**SECOND EDITION**
Senior editor Rachel Thompson
Senior art editor Rachael Grady
Senior cartographic editor Simon Mumford
US editor Karyn Gerhard
Designers Chrissy Barnard, Kit Lane
Managing editor Francesca Baines
Managing art editor Philip Letsu
Production editor Gillian Reid
Production controller Samantha Cross
Jacket designer Juthi Seth

**FIRST EDITION**
Senior editor Rob Houston
Senior art editor Philip Letsu
Senior cartographic editor Simon Mumford
Editors Helen Abramson, Steve Setford, Rona Skene
Designers David Ball, Carol Davis, Mik Gates
Researchers Helen Saunders, Suneha Dutta, Kaiya Shang
Cartography Encompass Graphics, Ed Merritt
Illustrators Adam Benton, Stuart Jackson-Carter
Creative retouching Steve Willis

Picture research Taiyaba Khatoon,
Ashwin Adimari, Martin Copeland
Jacket design Laura Brim, Natasha Rees
Jacket design development manager
Sophia M. Tampakopoulos Turner
Pre-production producer Rebekah Parsons-King
Production controller Mandy Innes
Publisher Andrew Macintyre
Art director Phil Ormerod
Associate publishing director Liz Wheeler
Publishing director Jonathan Metcalf

This American Box Set Edition, 2023
First American Edition, 2021
Published in the United States by DK Publishing,
a division of Penguin Random House LLC
1745 Broadway, 20th Floor, New York, NY 10019

Copyright © 2023 Dorling Kindersley Limited
24 25 26 27 28 10 9 8 7 6 5 4 3 2 1
001–341589–Sep/2024

All rights reserved.
Without limiting the rights under the copyright reserved above, no part of this publication may be reproduced, stored in or introduced into a retrieval system, or transmitted, in any form, or by any means (electronic, mechanical, photocopying, recording, or otherwise), without the prior written permission of the copyright owner.
Published in Great Britain by Dorling Kindersley Limited.

A catalog record for this book
is available from the Library of Congress.
Box Set ISBN 978-0-5938-4501-1
Book ISBN 978-0-7440-3670-1

DK books are available at special discounts when purchased in bulk for sales promotions, premiums, fundraising, or educational use. For details, contact: DK Publishing Special Markets, 1745 Broadway, 20th Floor, New York, NY 10019
SpecialSales@dk.com

Printed and bound in the UAE

www.dk.com

# CONTENTS

## Land, sea, and air

| | |
|---|---|
| Introduction | 6 |
| Earth's crust | 8 |
| Earthquakes | 10 |
| Mountains | 12 |
| Volcanoes | 14 |
| Ocean floor | 16 |
| Ocean in motion | 18 |
| Rivers | 20 |
| Craters and meteorites | 22 |
| Hot and cold | 24 |
| Rain and snow | 26 |
| Hurricanes | 28 |
| Biomes | 30 |
| Forests | 32 |
| Deserts | 34 |
| Ice | 36 |
| Time zones | 38 |

## Living world

| | |
|---|---|
| Introduction | 42 |
| Dinosaur fossils | 44 |
| Predators | 46 |
| Deadly creatures | 48 |
| Alien invasion | 50 |
| Bird migrations | 52 |
| Whales | 54 |
| Sharks | 56 |
| River monsters | 58 |
| Insects | 60 |
| World of plants | 62 |
| Biodiversity | 64 |
| Unique wildlife | 66 |
| Endangered animals | 68 |
| Extinct animals | 70 |

# People and planet

| | |
|---|---|
| Introduction | 74 |
| Where people live | 76 |
| Nomads | 78 |
| Young and old | 80 |
| Health | 82 |
| Pandemics | 84 |
| Poverty | 86 |
| The world's gold | 88 |
| Billionaires | 90 |
| Food production | 92 |
| Food intake | 94 |
| Literacy | 96 |
| Pollution | 98 |
| Garbage and waste | 100 |
| Clean water | 102 |
| Fossil fuels | 104 |
| Alternative energy | 106 |
| Climate change | 108 |
| Wilderness | 110 |

# Engineering and technology

| | |
|---|---|
| Introduction | 114 |
| Air traffic | 116 |
| Shipping | 118 |
| Railroads | 120 |
| Roads | 122 |
| Tallest buildings | 124 |
| Internet connections | 126 |
| Satellites and space junk | 128 |
| Armed forces | 130 |

# History

| | |
|---|---|
| Introduction | 134 |
| Fossil humans | 136 |
| Prehistoric culture | 138 |
| Ancient empires | 140 |
| Ancient wonders | 142 |
| Mummies | 144 |
| Medieval wonders | 146 |
| Medieval empires | 148 |
| Castles | 150 |
| Battlegrounds | 152 |
| The last empires | 154 |
| Revolutions | 156 |
| Shipwrecks | 158 |
| Industrial wonders | 160 |

# Culture

| | |
|---|---|
| Introduction | 164 |
| Languages | 166 |
| Holy places | 168 |
| Tourism | 170 |
| Art | 172 |
| Statues | 174 |
| Festivals | 176 |
| Television | 178 |
| Stadiums | 180 |
| Motor racing | 182 |
| Roller coasters | 184 |
| National flags | 186 |
| | |
| Index | 188 |
| Acknowledgments | 192 |

# Land, sea, and air

**Skeleton Coast, Namibia**
The Atlantic Ocean meets the edge of Africa's Namib Desert at the Skeleton Coast. Rainfall here rarely exceeds 0.39 in (10 mm) per year.

# Introduction

Earth is a planet in motion, spinning on its axis as it hurtles through space around the sun. Warmed by the sun's rays, Earth's atmosphere and oceans are always on the move, while heat from the planet's core keeps the hot rock of the interior constantly churning. All of this enables Earth's surface to teem with life.

## Churning interior

The rocks in the mantle flow in currents that rise, flow sideways, cool, and then sink. These currents can force the plates of Earth's crust apart or pull sections of the crust back down into the mantle.

**Ocean floor** splits, while mantle rock rises and creates new crust in the gap

**Continent** is dragged along by the mantle moving beneath

**Mantle** moves in slow circles, driven by the core's heat below

**Crust** is destroyed as it is dragged into the mantle by the sinking current

## Water cycle

The sun's heat evaporates sea water, causing it to become water vapor in the air. As it rises and cools, the water vapor condenses into clouds of droplets or ice crystals. As the droplets or crystals grow, they fall as rain or snow. If it falls on land, some runs off the surface to form rivers and lakes, which return water to the oceans. A lot of rain seeps through gaps in the soil and rock. It is called groundwater, and it may stay underground or trickle to the sea. This continuous circulation of water is known as the water cycle.

## Earth's structure

If we could take a slice out of Earth, we would see that the planet is made up of layers. At its heart lies a solid inner core, surrounded by a liquid outer core. Both are made mainly of heavy iron. The outer core is enclosed by a deep layer of heavy, very hot, yet solid rock called the mantle. Heat from the core drives currents rising through the mantle that keep the rock moving extremely slowly. The crust—the mantle's cool, hard shell—is made up of a number of rocky plates.

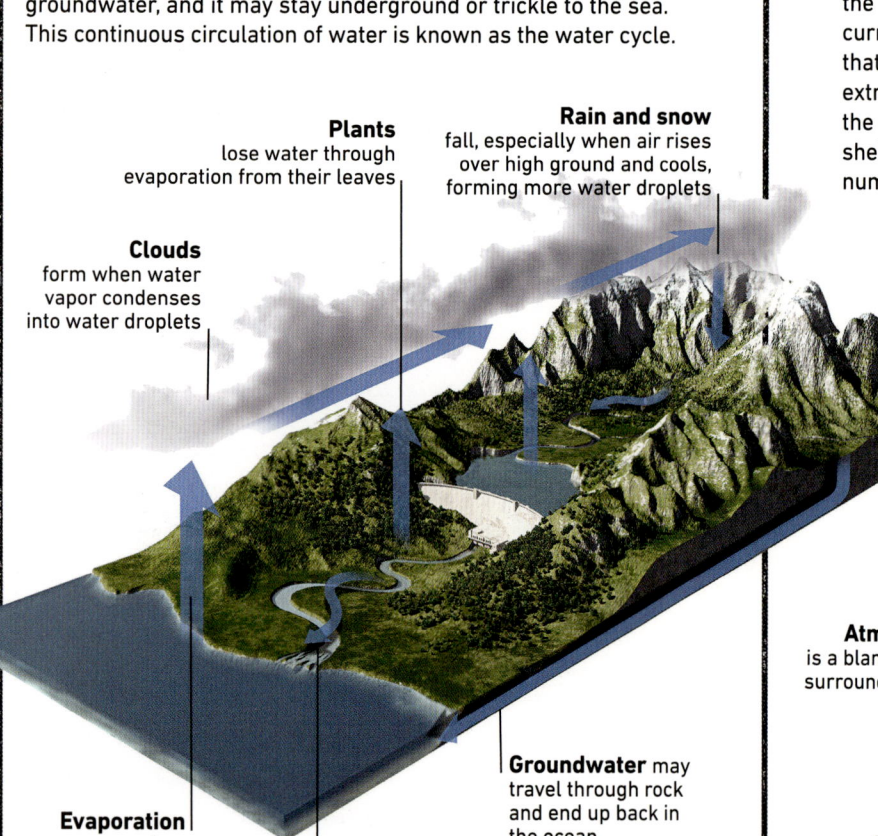

**Plants** lose water through evaporation from their leaves

**Rain and snow** fall, especially when air rises over high ground and cools, forming more water droplets

**Clouds** form when water vapor condenses into water droplets

**Evaporation** occurs when the sun heats sea water, turning it into water vapor

**Groundwater** may travel through rock and end up back in the ocean

**Rivers and streams** return water to oceans

**Atmosphere** is a blanket of gas surrounding Earth

**Mountains** form as the crust is squeezed and folded

**Clouds of water droplets** form huge swirling weather systems in the lower atmosphere

AN AVERAGE WATER MOLECULE SPENDS ABOUT 3,200 YEARS IN THE

## Land, sea, and air

### The sun's energy

In the tropics, near the equator, the sun's rays strike Earth at a steep angle, so the energy is very concentrated. But near the poles, sunlight hits the surface at a narrow angle. This spreads the sun's energy, giving a weak heating effect. The result is that polar regions are much colder than tropical zones, allowing ice to form in the Arctic and Antarctic. The difference in the solar heating at different latitudes sets bodies of air and seawater in motion, driving winds and ocean currents.

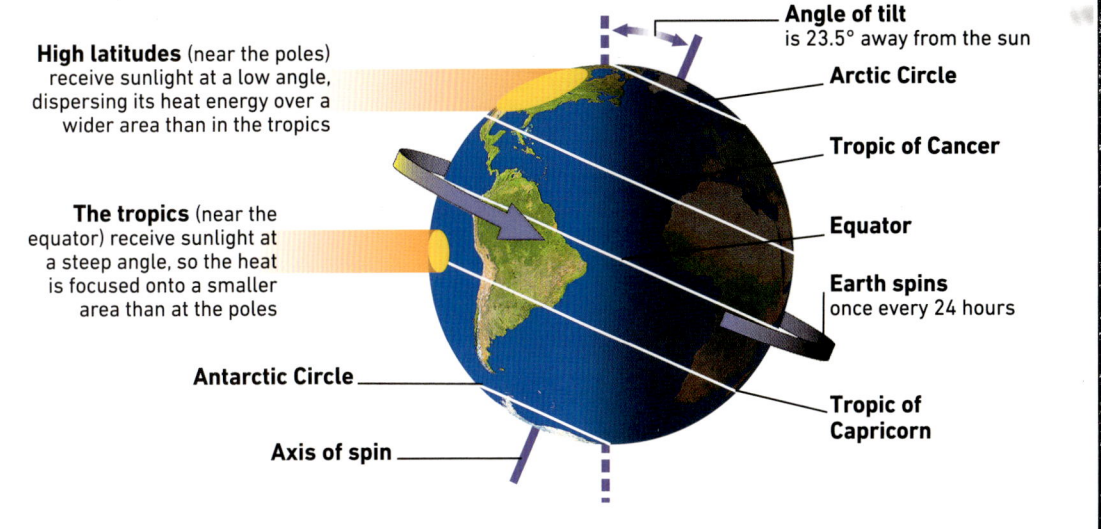

**High latitudes** (near the poles) receive sunlight at a low angle, dispersing its heat energy over a wider area than in the tropics

**The tropics** (near the equator) receive sunlight at a steep angle, so the heat is focused onto a smaller area than at the poles

**Angle of tilt** is 23.5° away from the sun

**Arctic Circle**

**Tropic of Cancer**

**Equator**

**Earth spins** once every 24 hours

**Tropic of Capricorn**

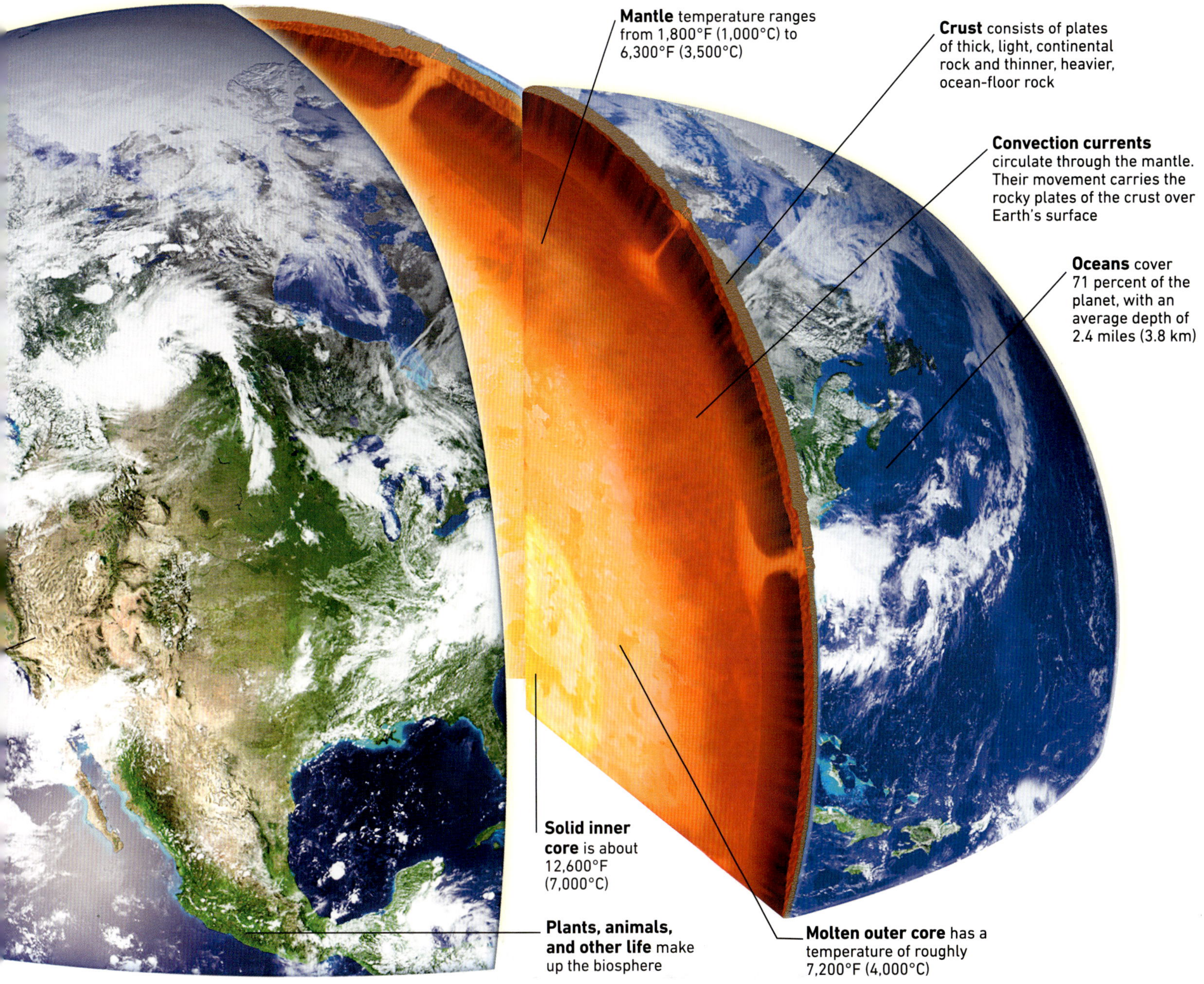

**Antarctic Circle**

**Axis of spin**

---

**Mantle** temperature ranges from 1,800°F (1,000°C) to 6,300°F (3,500°C)

**Crust** consists of plates of thick, light, continental rock and thinner, heavier, ocean-floor rock

**Convection currents** circulate through the mantle. Their movement carries the rocky plates of the crust over Earth's surface

**Oceans** cover 71 percent of the planet, with an average depth of 2.4 miles (3.8 km)

**Solid inner core** is about 12,600°F (7,000°C)

**Plants, animals, and other life** make up the biosphere

**Molten outer core** has a temperature of roughly 7,200°F (4,000°C)

OCEAN BEFORE EVAPORATION RELEASES IT INTO THE ATMOSPHERE.

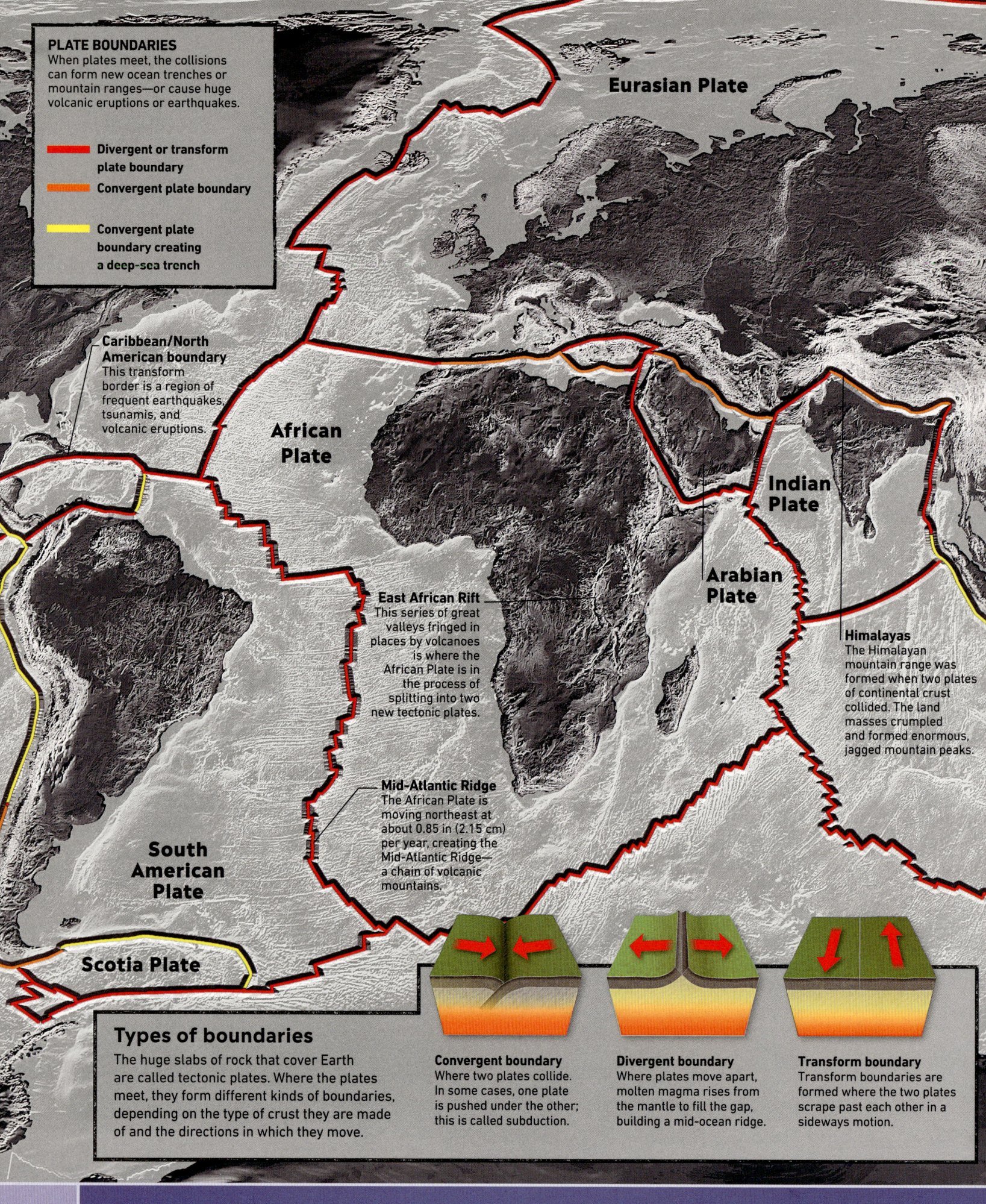

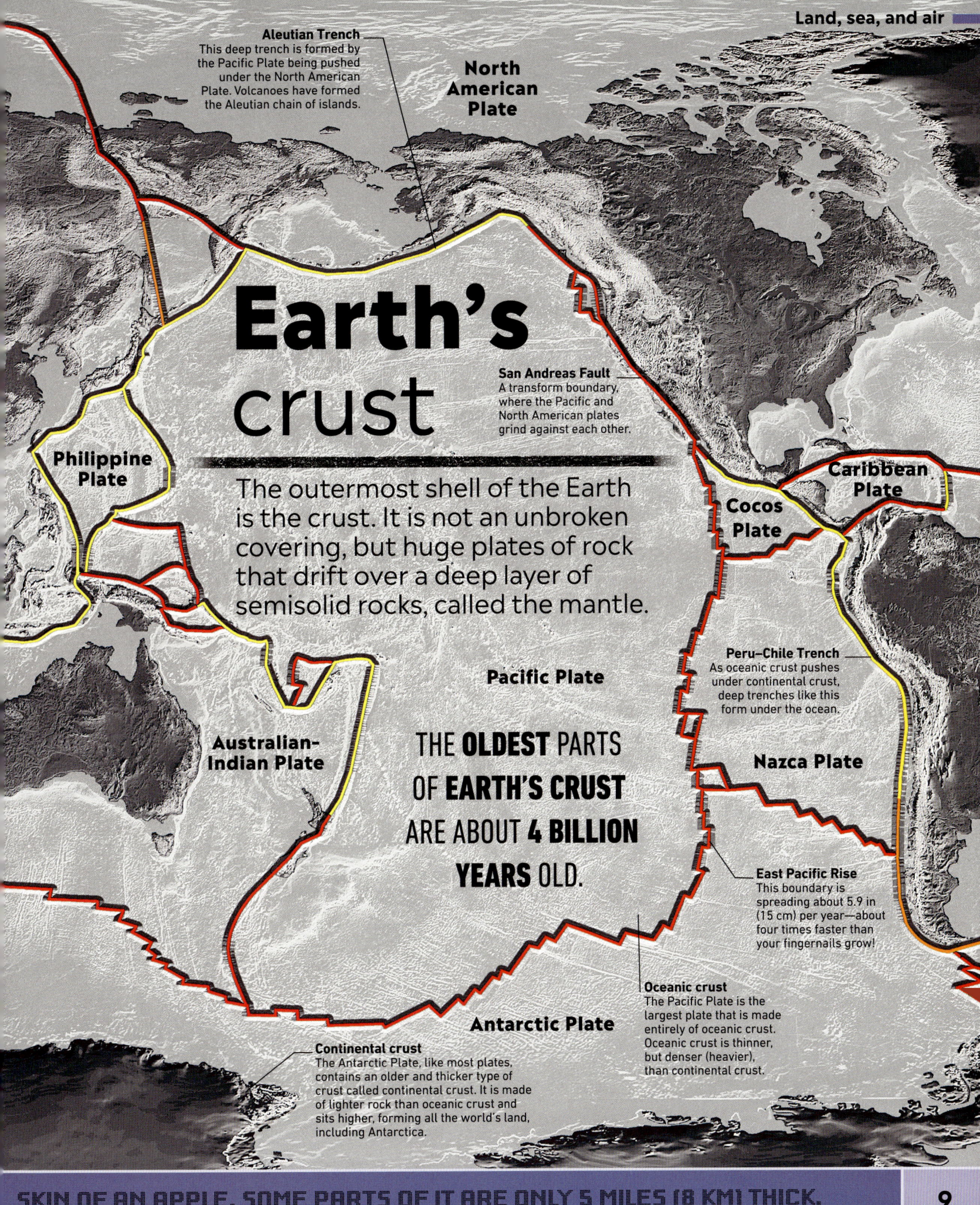

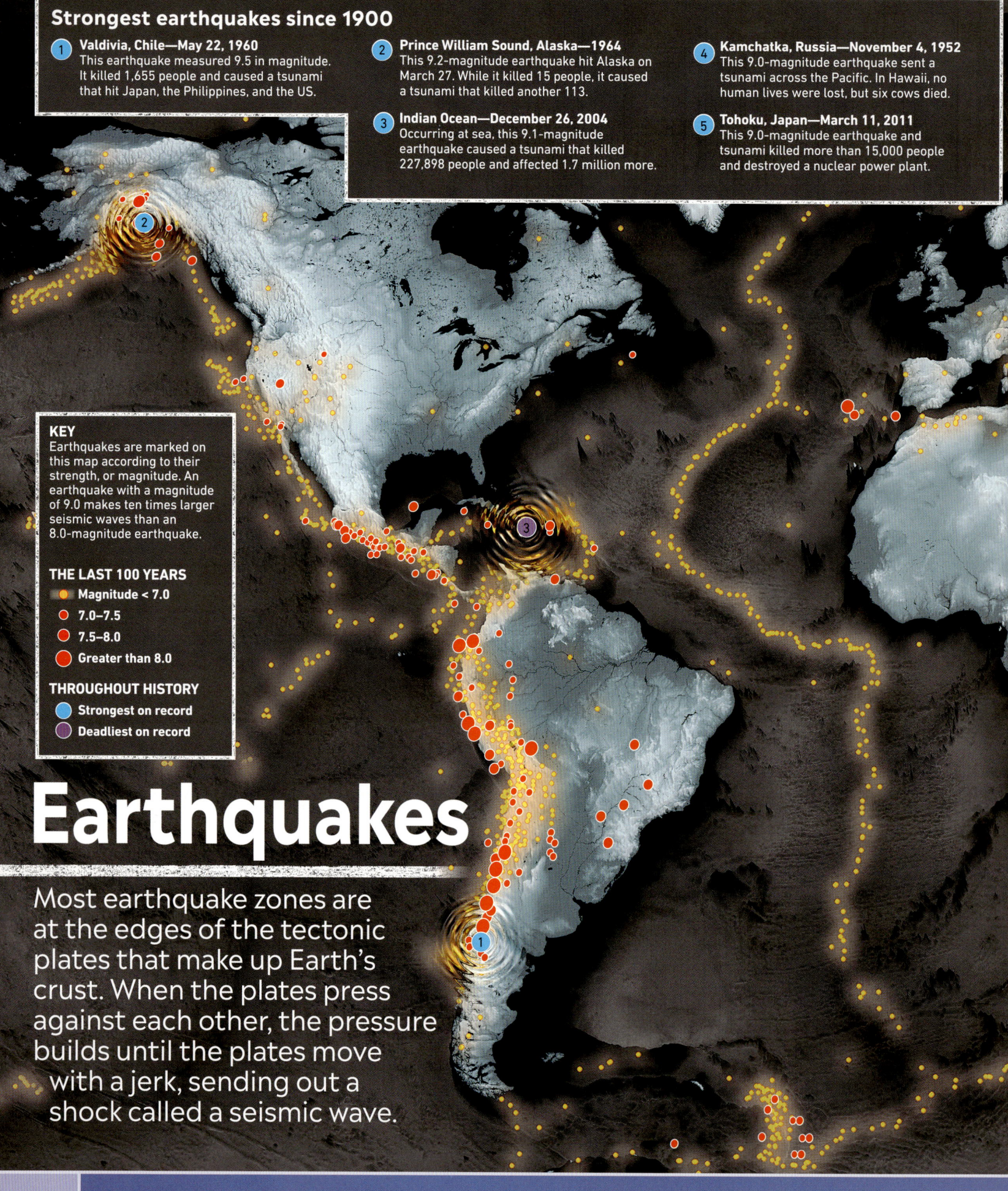

## Strongest earthquakes since 1900

**1 Valdivia, Chile—May 22, 1960**
This earthquake measured 9.5 in magnitude. It killed 1,655 people and caused a tsunami that hit Japan, the Philippines, and the US.

**2 Prince William Sound, Alaska—1964**
This 9.2-magnitude earthquake hit Alaska on March 27. While it killed 15 people, it caused a tsunami that killed another 113.

**3 Indian Ocean—December 26, 2004**
Occurring at sea, this 9.1-magnitude earthquake caused a tsunami that killed 227,898 people and affected 1.7 million more.

**4 Kamchatka, Russia—November 4, 1952**
This 9.0-magnitude earthquake sent a tsunami across the Pacific. In Hawaii, no human lives were lost, but six cows died.

**5 Tohoku, Japan—March 11, 2011**
This 9.0-magnitude earthquake and tsunami killed more than 15,000 people and destroyed a nuclear power plant.

**KEY**
Earthquakes are marked on this map according to their strength, or magnitude. An earthquake with a magnitude of 9.0 makes ten times larger seismic waves than an 8.0-magnitude earthquake.

**THE LAST 100 YEARS**
- Magnitude < 7.0
- 7.0–7.5
- 7.5–8.0
- Greater than 8.0

**THROUGHOUT HISTORY**
- Strongest on record
- Deadliest on record

# Earthquakes

Most earthquake zones are at the edges of the tectonic plates that make up Earth's crust. When the plates press against each other, the pressure builds until the plates move with a jerk, sending out a shock called a seismic wave.

THE ASTEROID IMPACT THAT WIPED OUT THE DINOSAURS 65 MILLION YEARS

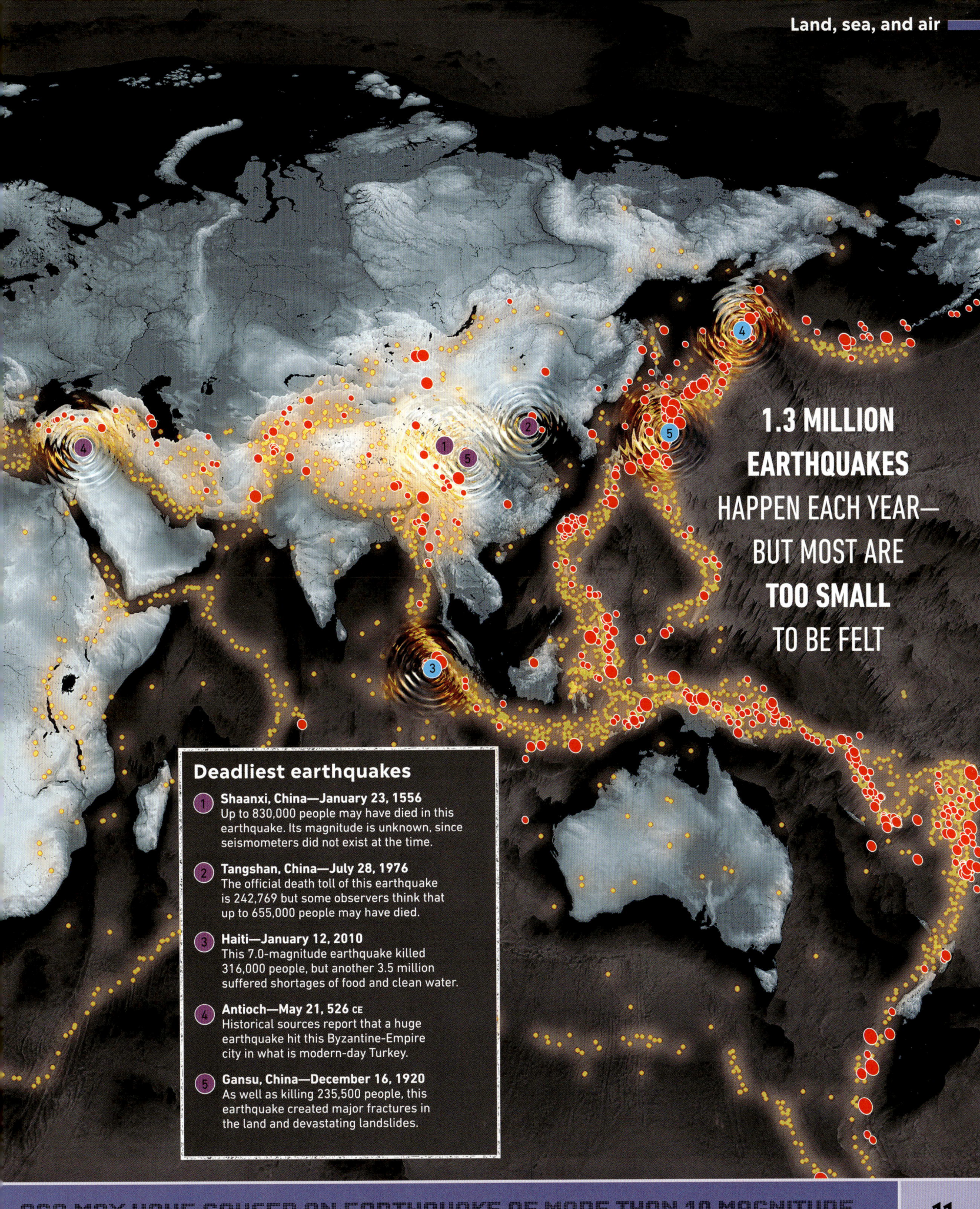

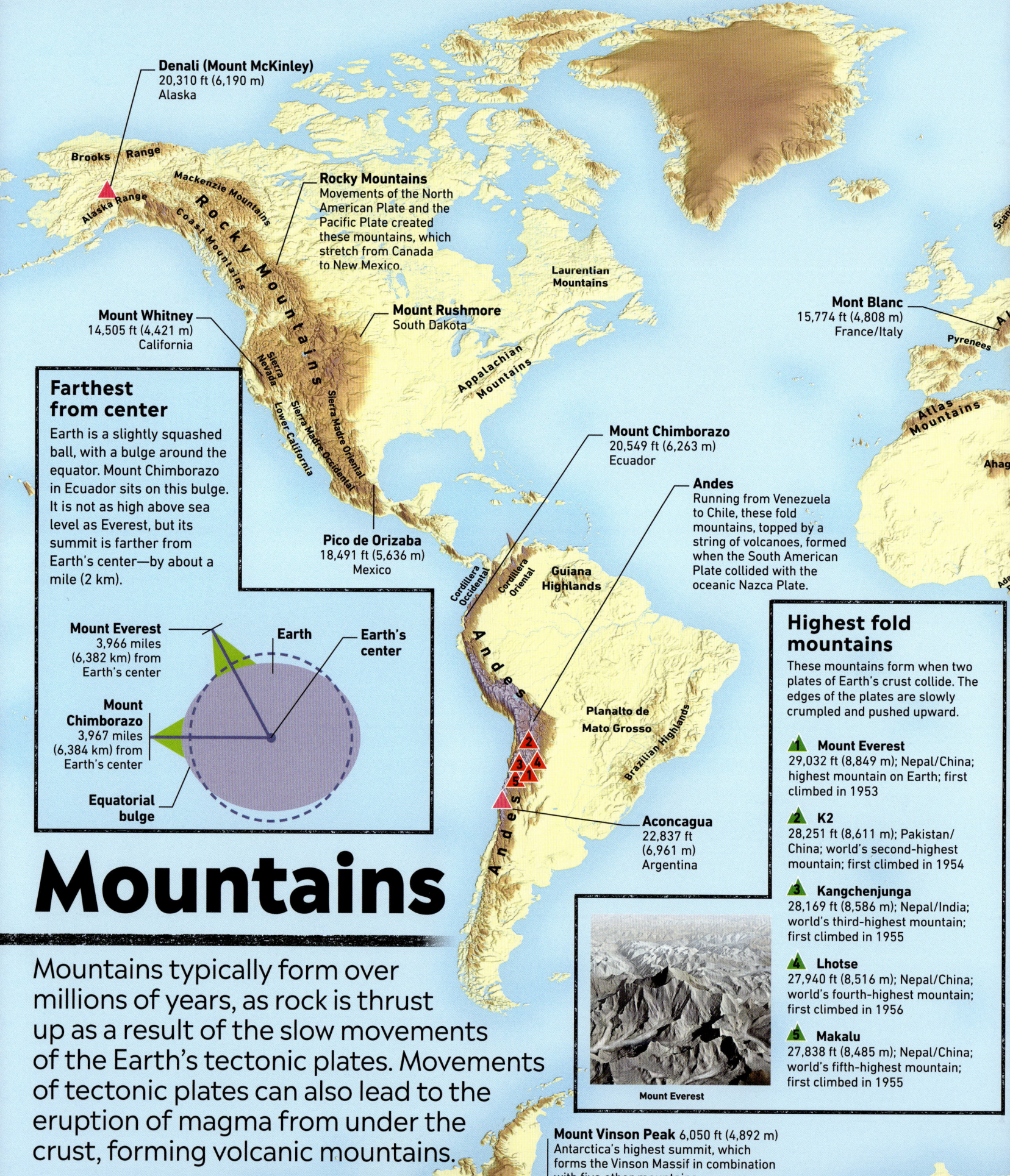

# Mountains

Mountains typically form over millions of years, as rock is thrust up as a result of the slow movements of the Earth's tectonic plates. Movements of tectonic plates can also lead to the eruption of magma from under the crust, forming volcanic mountains.

**Denali (Mount McKinley)**
20,310 ft (6,190 m)
Alaska

**Rocky Mountains**
Movements of the North American Plate and the Pacific Plate created these mountains, which stretch from Canada to New Mexico.

**Mount Whitney**
14,505 ft (4,421 m)
California

**Mount Rushmore**
South Dakota

**Mont Blanc**
15,774 ft (4,808 m)
France/Italy

**Mount Chimborazo**
20,549 ft (6,263 m)
Ecuador

**Pico de Orizaba**
18,491 ft (5,636 m)
Mexico

**Andes**
Running from Venezuela to Chile, these fold mountains, topped by a string of volcanoes, formed when the South American Plate collided with the oceanic Nazca Plate.

**Aconcagua**
22,837 ft (6,961 m)
Argentina

**Mount Vinson Peak** 6,050 ft (4,892 m)
Antarctica's highest summit, which forms the Vinson Massif in combination with five other mountains.

## Farthest from center

Earth is a slightly squashed ball, with a bulge around the equator. Mount Chimborazo in Ecuador sits on this bulge. It is not as high above sea level as Everest, but its summit is farther from Earth's center—by about a mile (2 km).

**Mount Everest** 3,966 miles (6,382 km) from Earth's center

**Mount Chimborazo** 3,967 miles (6,384 km) from Earth's center

## Highest fold mountains

These mountains form when two plates of Earth's crust collide. The edges of the plates are slowly crumpled and pushed upward.

**1 Mount Everest**
29,032 ft (8,849 m); Nepal/China; highest mountain on Earth; first climbed in 1953

**2 K2**
28,251 ft (8,611 m); Pakistan/China; world's second-highest mountain; first climbed in 1954

**3 Kangchenjunga**
28,169 ft (8,586 m); Nepal/India; world's third-highest mountain; first climbed in 1955

**4 Lhotse**
27,940 ft (8,516 m); Nepal/China; world's fourth-highest mountain; first climbed in 1956

**5 Makalu**
27,838 ft (8,485 m); Nepal/China; world's fifth-highest mountain; first climbed in 1955

Mount Everest

THE TALLEST KNOWN MOUNTAIN ANYWHERE IS OLYMPUS MONS,

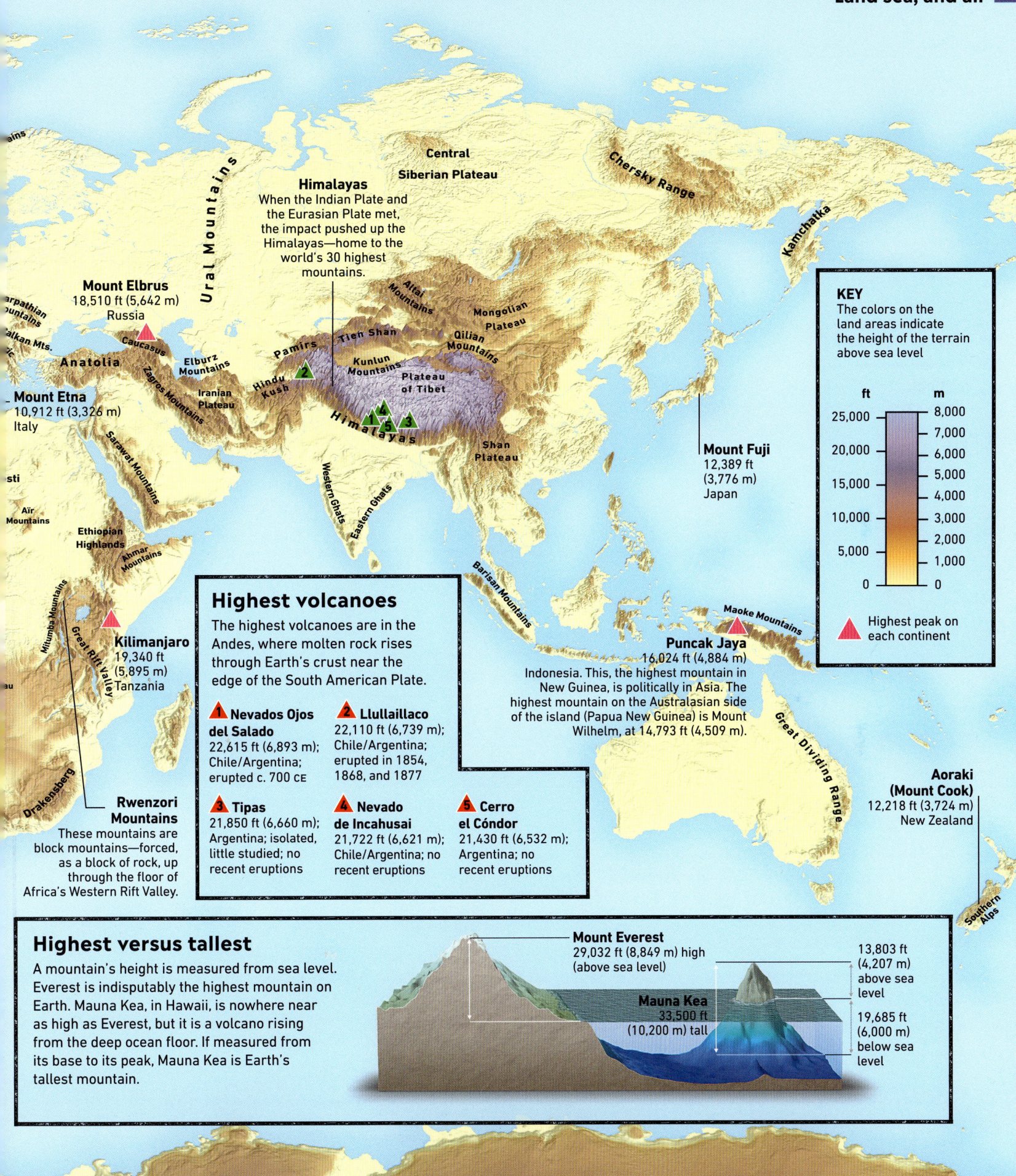

# Volcanoes

Earth's crust is made up of plates of rock that fit together like a puzzle. Most volcanoes occur where the plates meet, but some erupt in hot spots in the middle of the plates.

**Active Iceland**
Iceland has many active volcanoes, since it sits on top of the Mid-Atlantic Ridge, where magma wells up as the seabed splits apart.

**Alaska**
Alaska and the Aleutian Islands are located on the Pacific Ring of Fire.

**Hawaii**
This chain of island volcanoes has formed as Earth's crust passes over a "hot spot" in the mantle below.

### How volcanoes form
Molten rock (magma) from Earth's interior may erupt where plates pull apart, or force its way to the surface where plates collide.

Plates collide and one is pushed beneath the other

Magma forms and pushes upward

**Mid-Atlantic Ridge**
Volcanoes dot the seafloor in the middle of the Atlantic Ocean, where two plates are moving away from each other.

### Largest eruptions since 1800

1. **Tambora, Indonesia, 1815**
Tambora threw so much ash into the atmosphere that global weather was disrupted and temperatures fell.

2. **Krakatau, Indonesia, 1883**
The explosion was heard 2,850 miles (4,600 km) away. It destroyed two-thirds of the island of Krakatau.

3. **Novarupta, Alaska, 1912**
The largest volcanic blast of the 20th century marked the formation of this new volcano on the Pacific Ring of Fire.

4. **Mount Pinatubo, Philippines, 1991**
A plume of ash 250 miles (400 km) wide rose 21 miles (34 km) into the sky, blocking out the sun for days.

5. **Santa Maria, Guatemala, 1902**
The explosion formed a 0.6-mile- (1-km-) wide crater. Ash fell in San Francisco 2,500 miles (4,000 km) away.

BETWEEN 50 AND 70 VOLCANOES ERUPT EVERY YEAR, MOSTLY AROUND

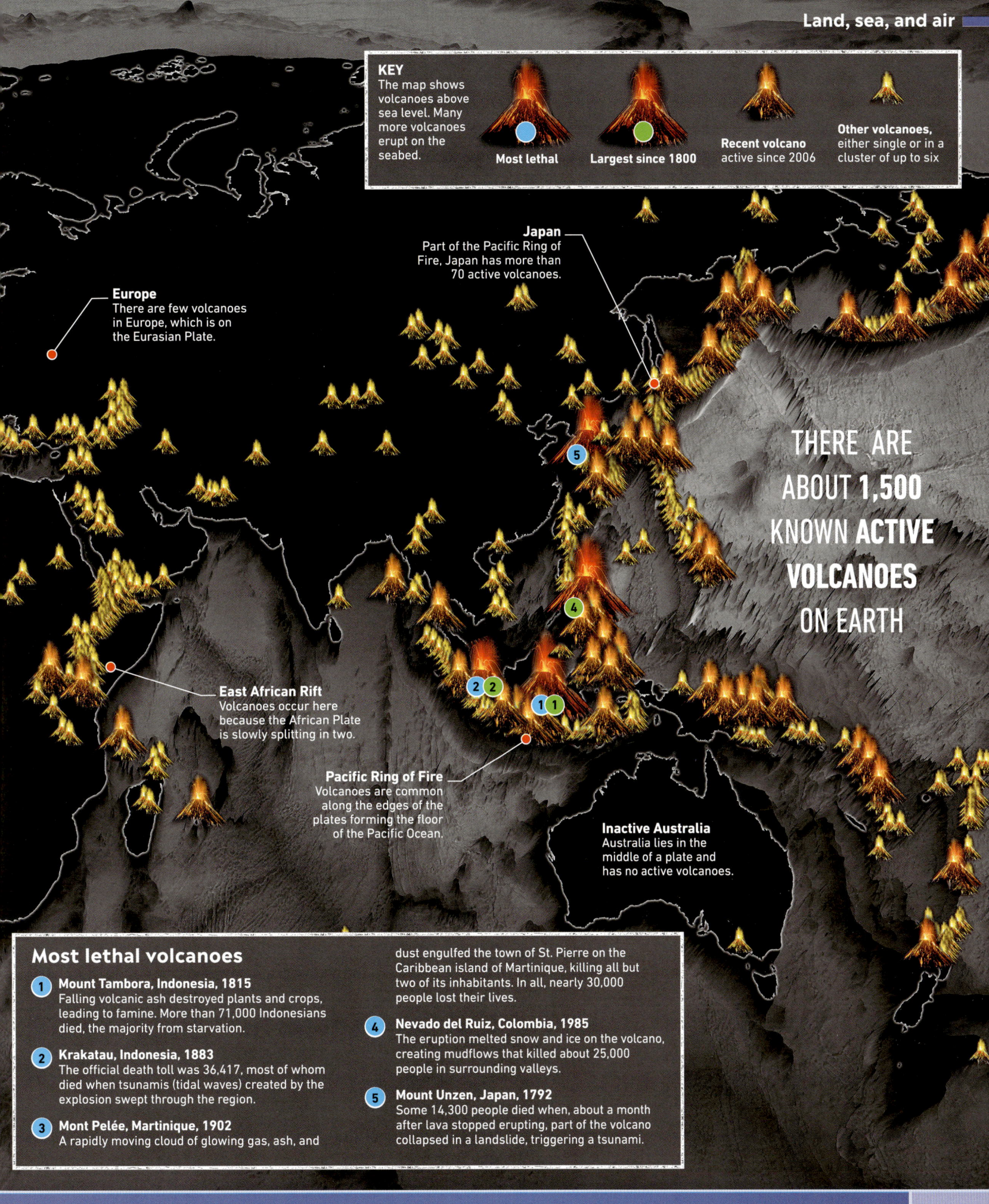

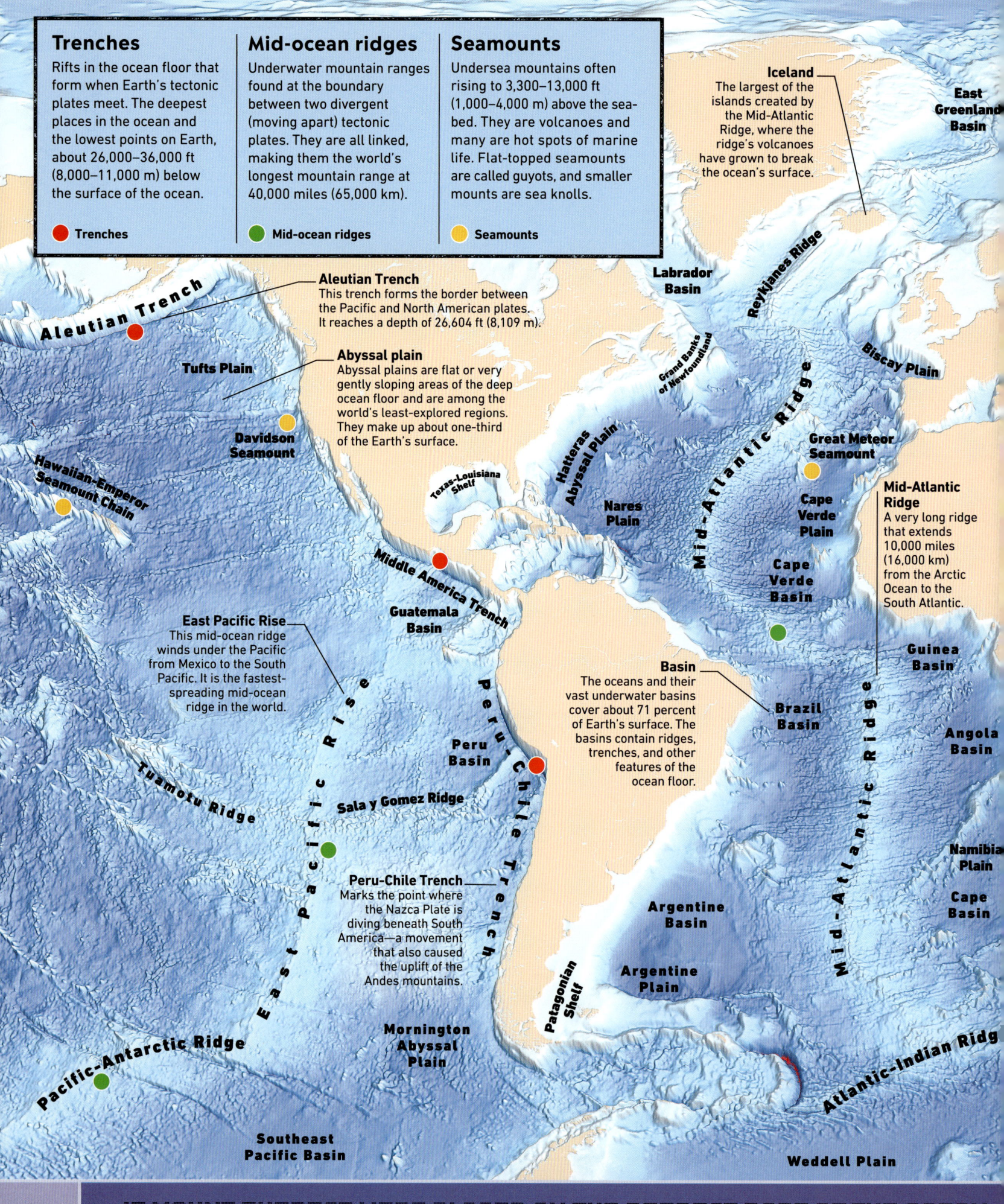

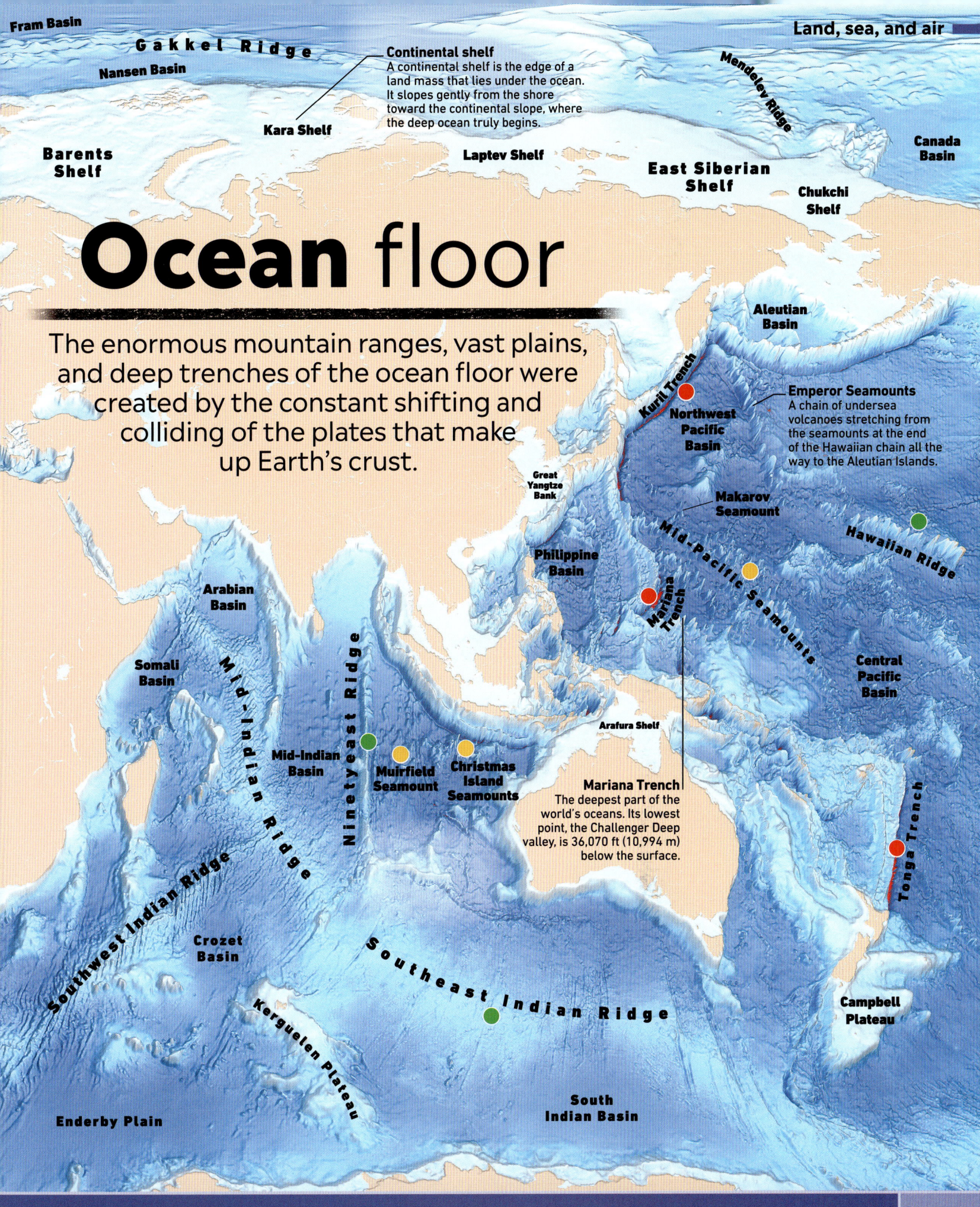

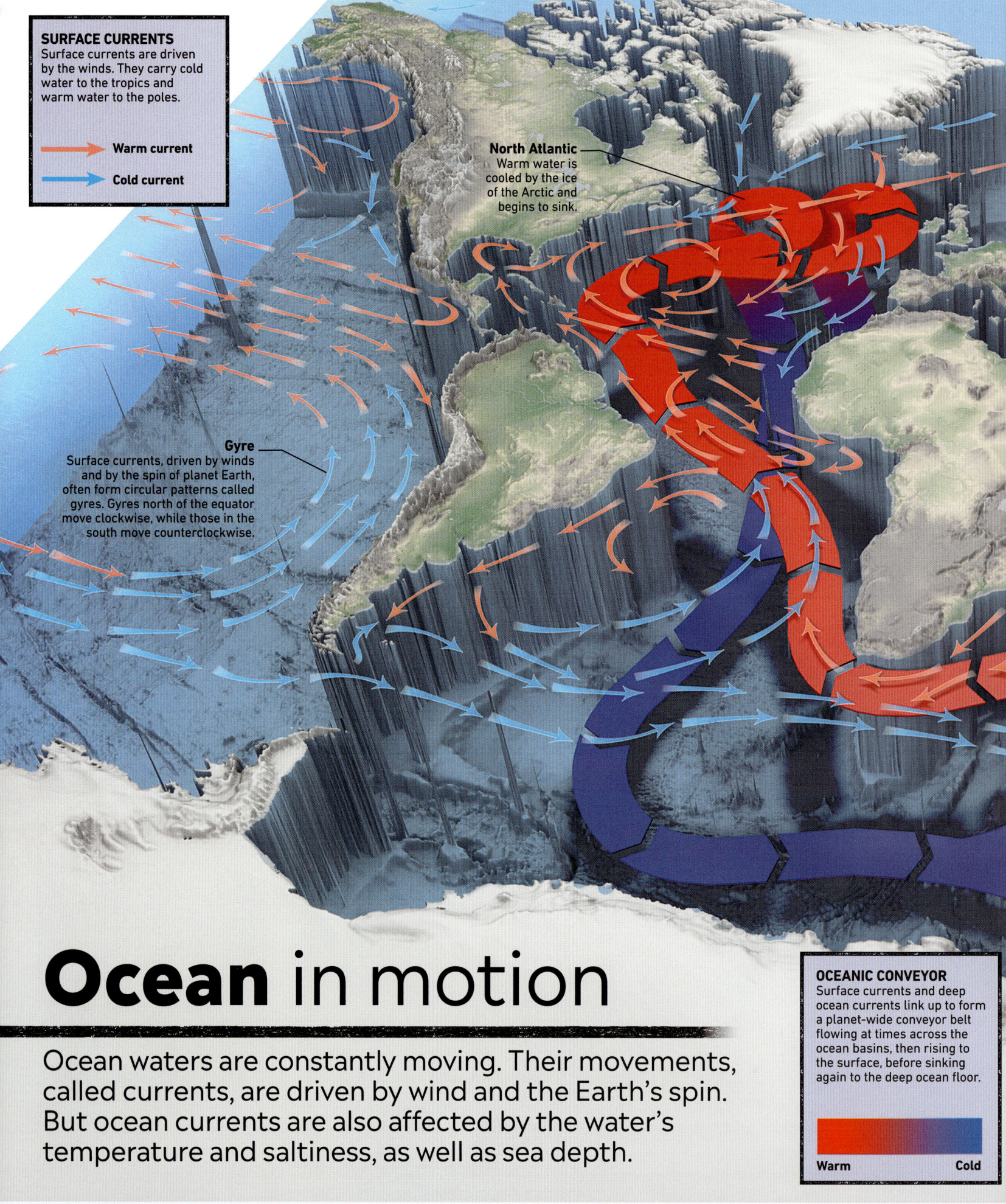

# Ocean in motion

Ocean waters are constantly moving. Their movements, called currents, are driven by wind and the Earth's spin. But ocean currents are also affected by the water's temperature and saltiness, as well as sea depth.

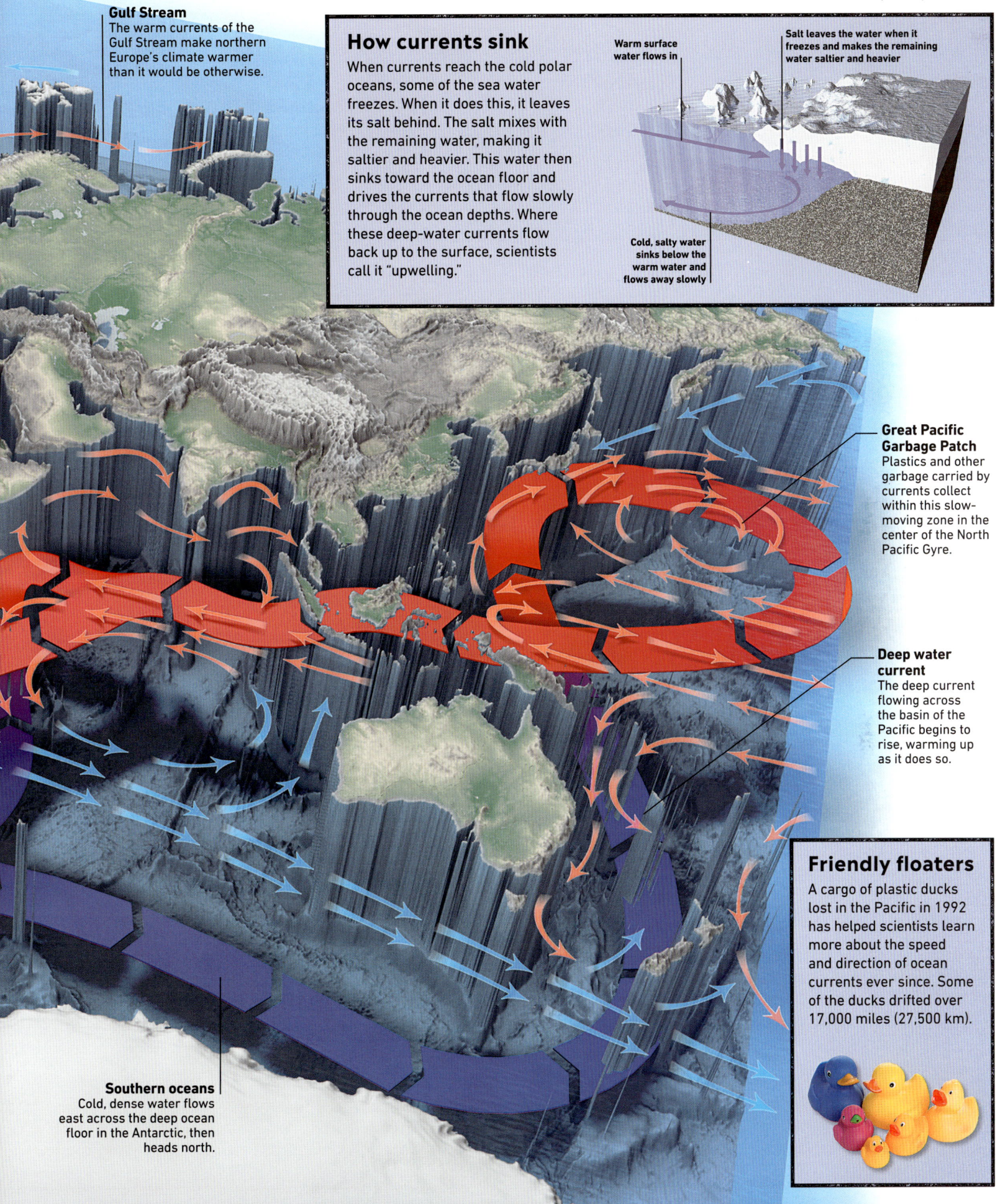

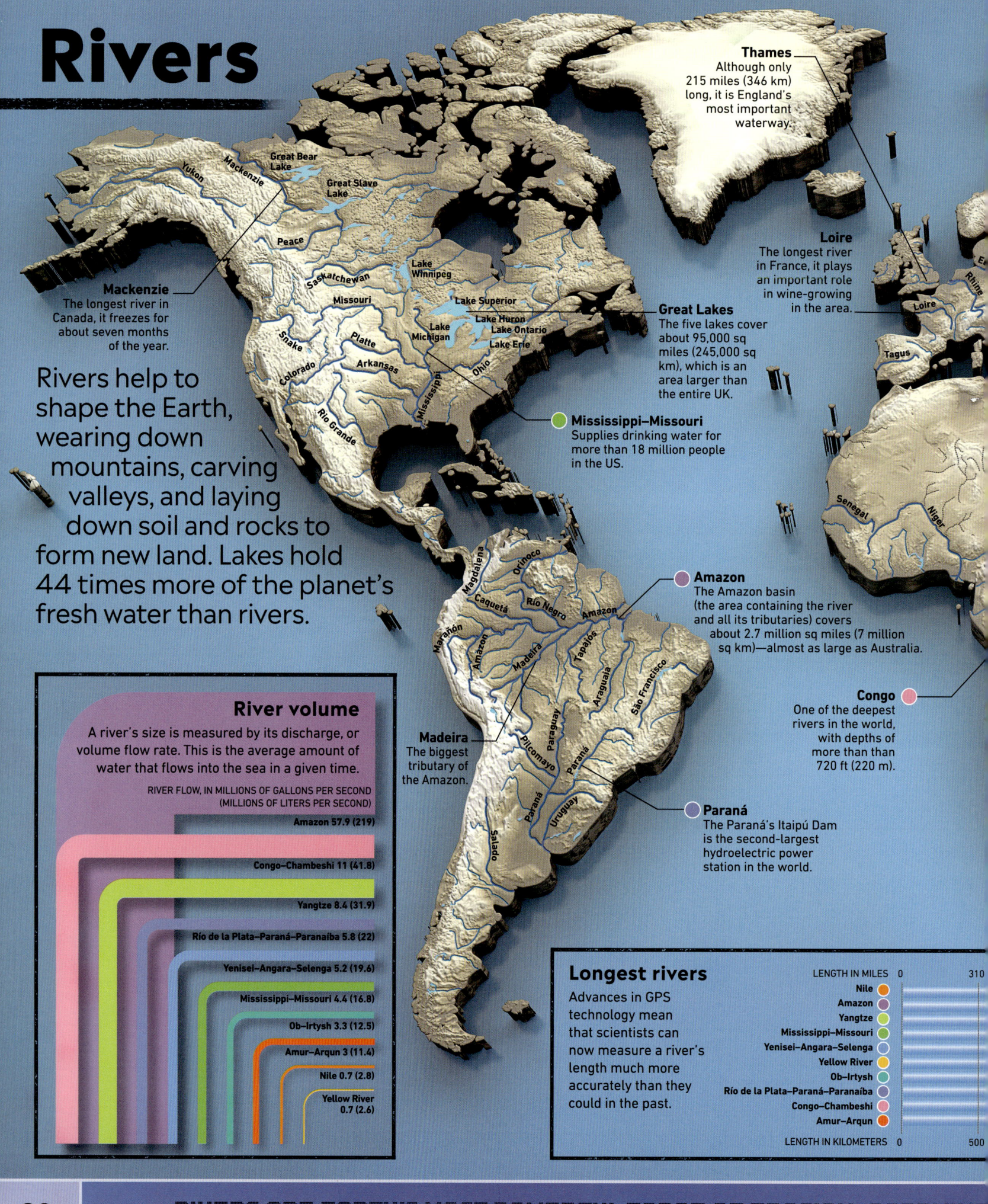

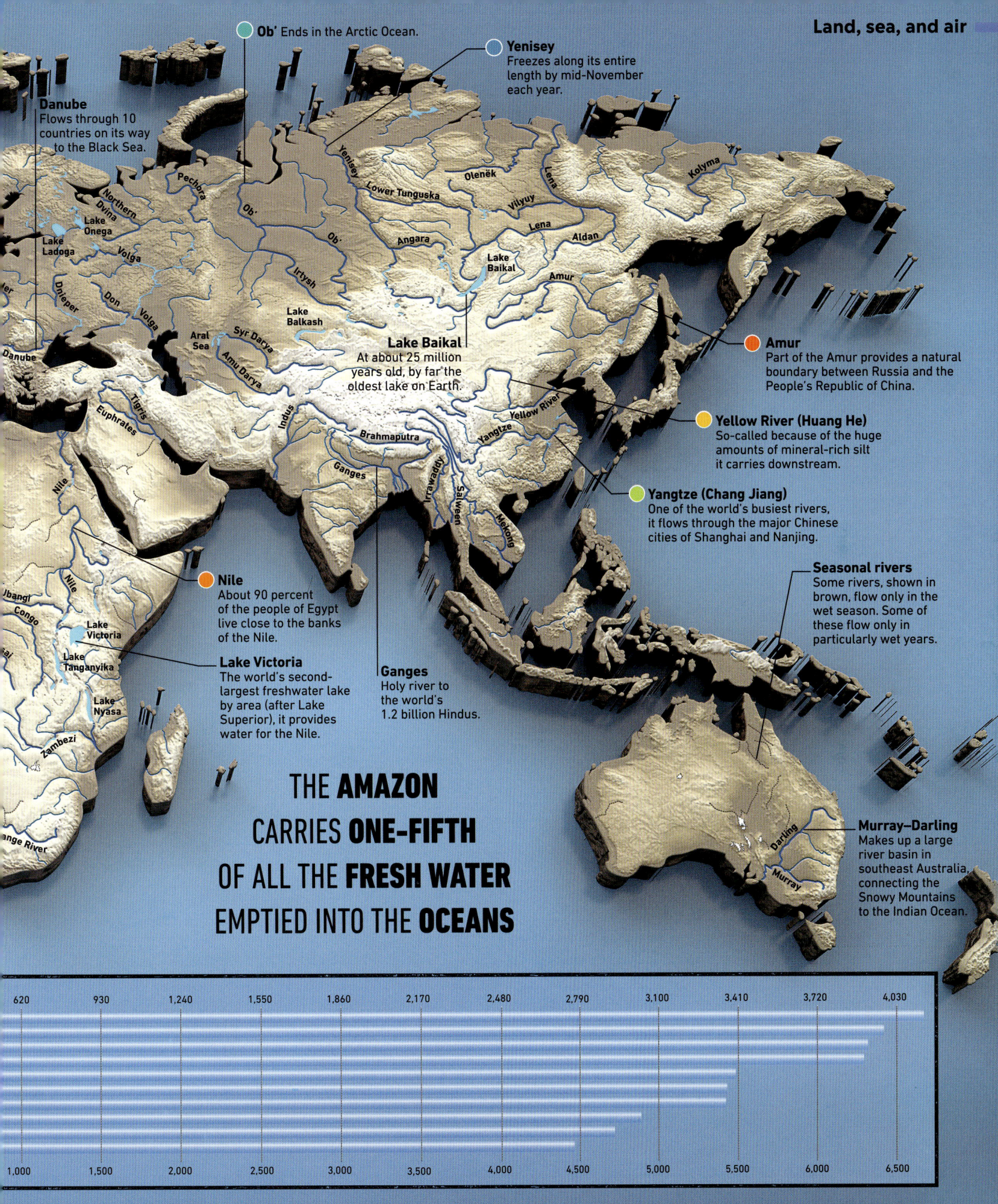

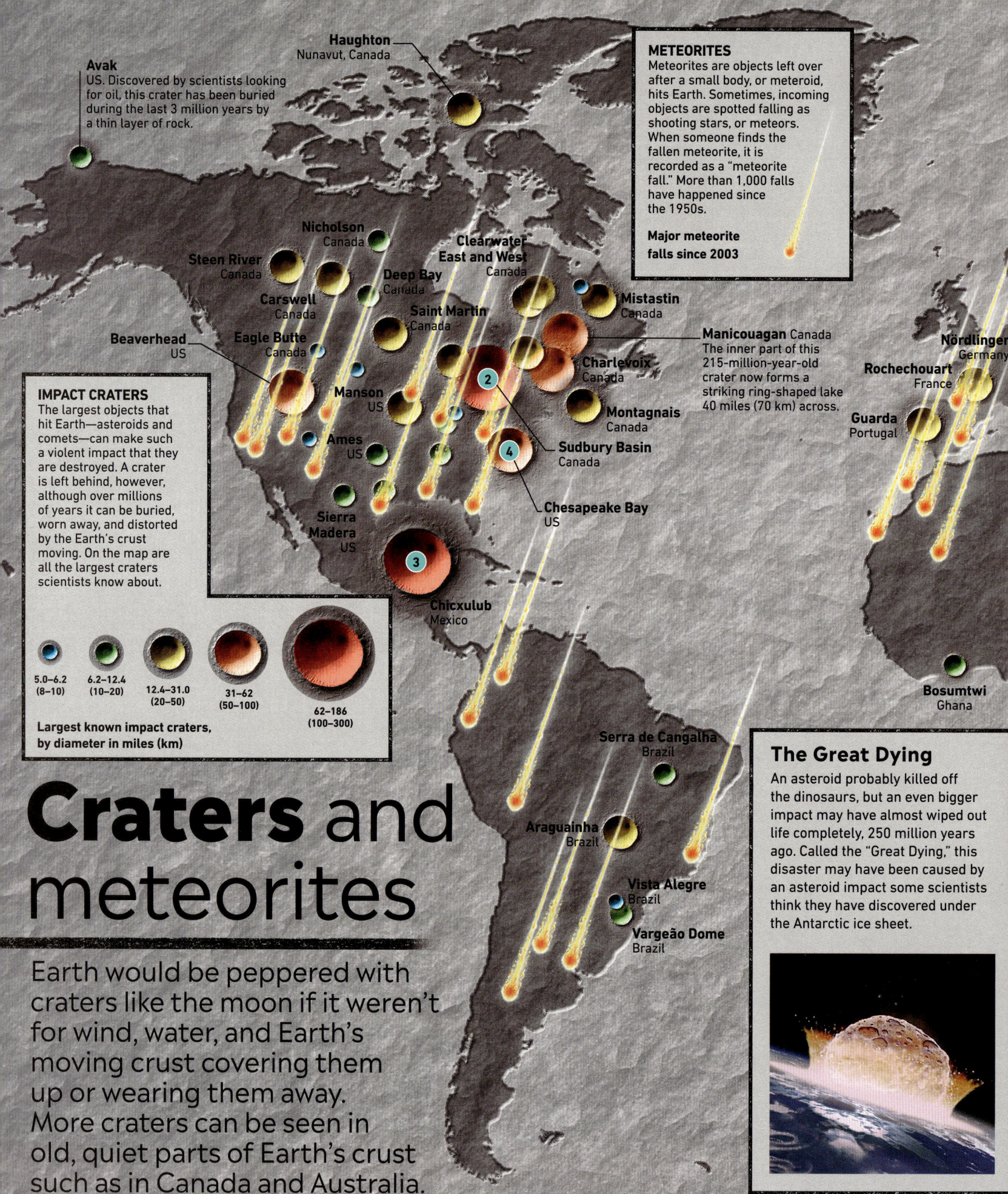

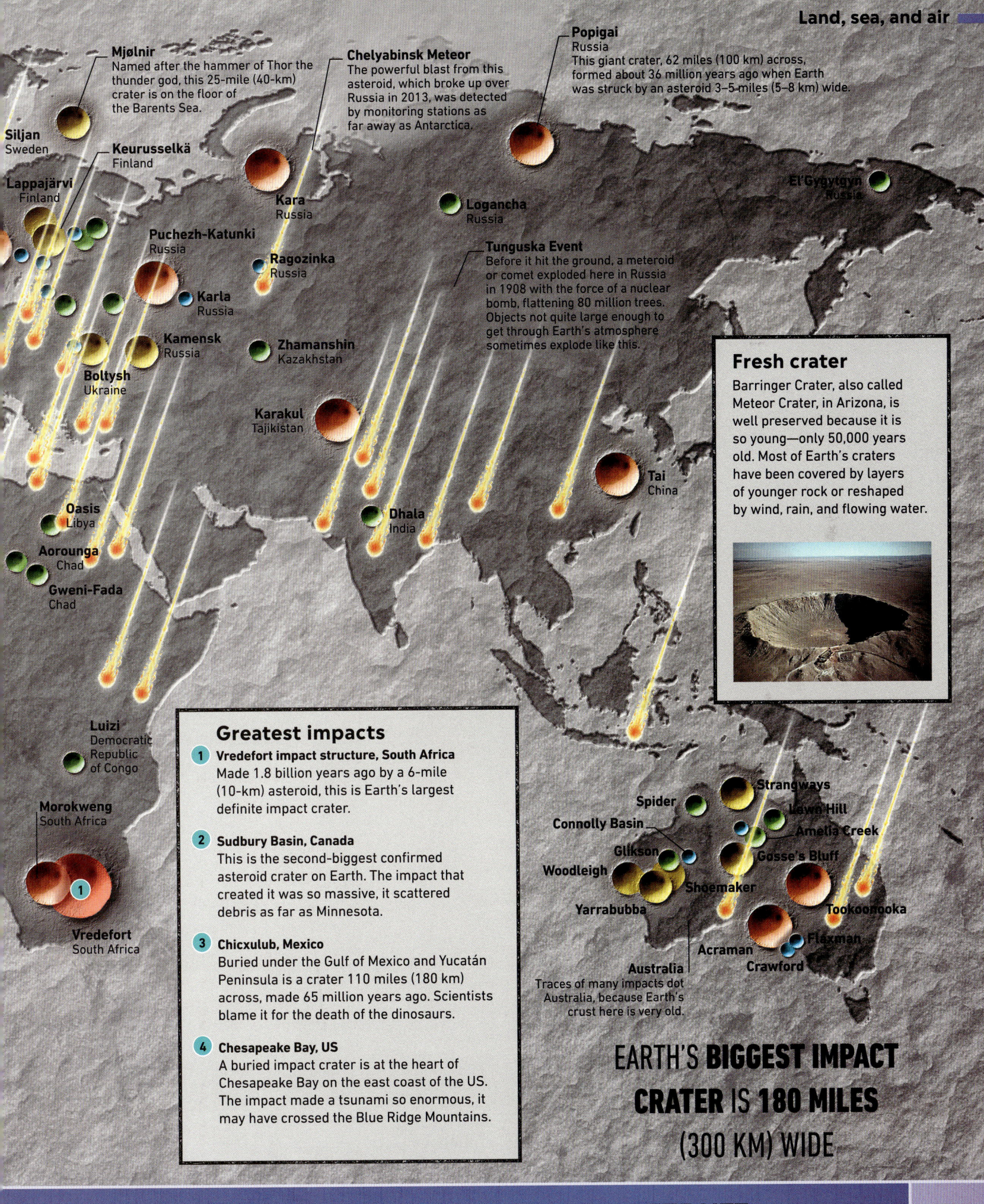

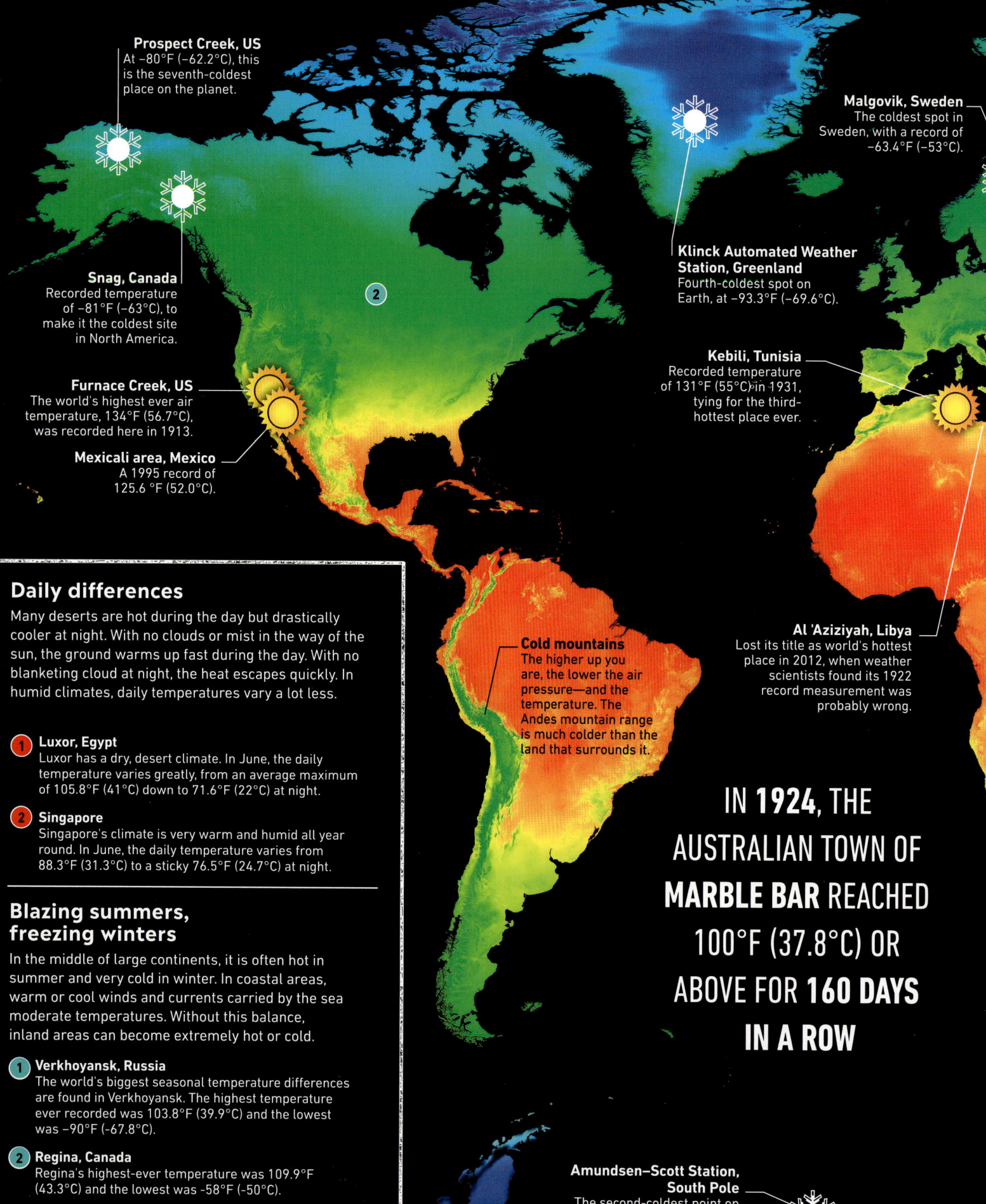

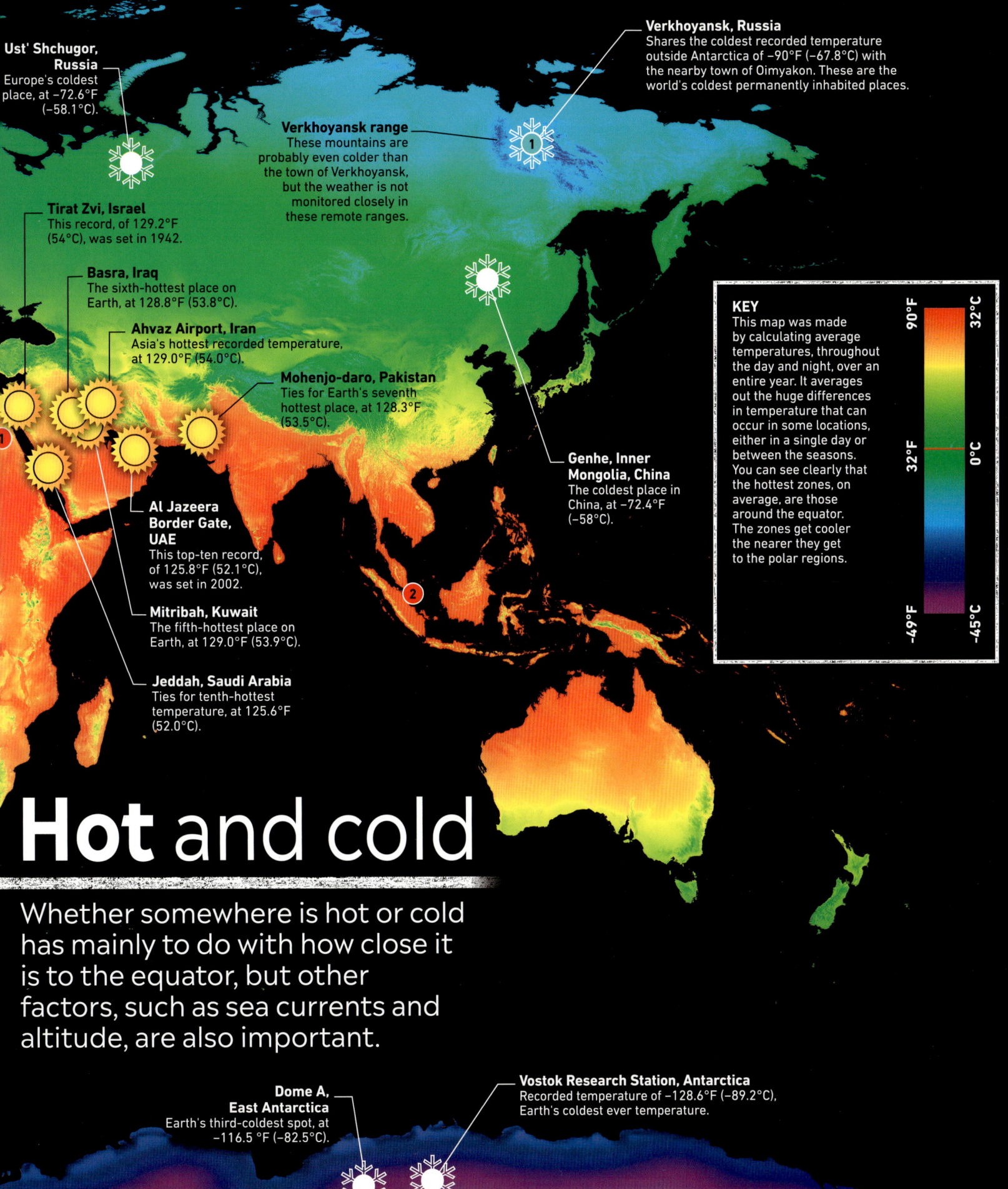

# Hot and cold

Whether somewhere is hot or cold has mainly to do with how close it is to the equator, but other factors, such as sea currents and altitude, are also important.

**Land, sea, and air**

**Ust' Shchugor, Russia** — Europe's coldest place, at −72.6°F (−58.1°C).

**Verkhoyansk, Russia** — Shares the coldest recorded temperature outside Antarctica of −90°F (−67.8°C) with the nearby town of Oimyakon. These are the world's coldest permanently inhabited places.

**Verkhoyansk range** — These mountains are probably even colder than the town of Verkhoyansk, but the weather is not monitored closely in these remote ranges.

**Tirat Zvi, Israel** — This record, of 129.2°F (54°C), was set in 1942.

**Basra, Iraq** — The sixth-hottest place on Earth, at 128.8°F (53.8°C).

**Ahvaz Airport, Iran** — Asia's hottest recorded temperature, at 129.0°F (54.0°C).

**Mohenjo-daro, Pakistan** — Ties for Earth's seventh hottest place, at 128.3°F (53.5°C).

**Al Jazeera Border Gate, UAE** — This top-ten record, of 125.8°F (52.1°C), was set in 2002.

**Mitribah, Kuwait** — The fifth-hottest place on Earth, at 129.0°F (53.9°C).

**Jeddah, Saudi Arabia** — Ties for tenth-hottest temperature, at 125.6°F (52.0°C).

**Genhe, Inner Mongolia, China** — The coldest place in China, at −72.4°F (−58°C).

**KEY**
This map was made by calculating average temperatures, throughout the day and night, over an entire year. It averages out the huge differences in temperature that can occur in some locations, either in a single day or between the seasons. You can see clearly that the hottest zones, on average, are those around the equator. The zones get cooler the nearer they get to the polar regions.

**Dome A, East Antarctica** — Earth's third-coldest spot, at −116.5°F (−82.5°C).

**Vostok Research Station, Antarctica** — Recorded temperature of −128.6°F (−89.2°C), Earth's coldest ever temperature.

NORTHWEST EUROPE WARMER WINTERS THAN PLACES FARTHER SOUTH.

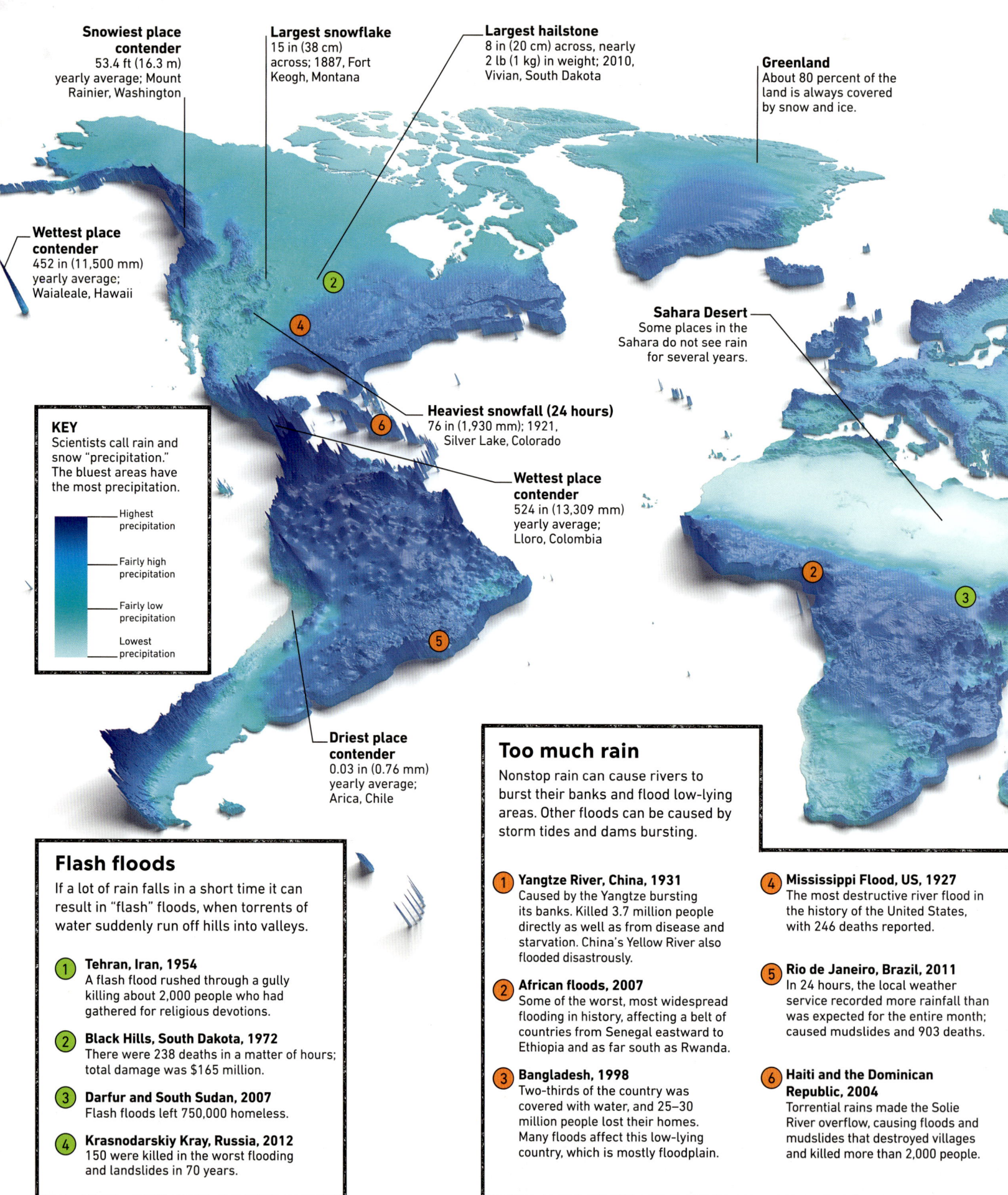

Land, sea, and air

# Rain and snow

Rainfall varies dramatically with place. Torrential rain drenches southern Asia during the monsoon season, yet some desert regions have virtually no rain at all. Near the poles, very little snow falls, but the snow rarely melts, so some land is permanently under a layer of ice.

**197 IN (5,000 MM) OF RAIN MAY FALL IN ONE PLACE DURING INDIA'S MONSOON SEASON**

**Heaviest rainfall (1 month, and 1 year)**
370 in (9,300 mm) and 905 in (22,987 mm); both 1860–61, Cherrapunji, India

**Arabian Peninsula**
As in the Sahara, there is very little rain in this largely desert region.

**Heaviest rainfall (24 hours)**
71.9 in (1,825 mm); 1966, Foc-Foc, Réunion, during Tropical Cyclone Denise

**Snowiest place contender**
49.5 ft (15 m) yearly average; Niseko, Japan

**Borneo**
Many equatorial rainforests, such as those in Borneo, have no dry season, and it rains every day.

**Australia**
This is the driest inhabited continent.

**New Zealand**
Rainfall is fairly high and is spread evenly throughout the year.

**Driest place on Earth**
0 in (0 mm) yearly average; Antarctica's Dry Valleys, which are free of snow and ice.

## Monsoon extremes

Chittagong, in Bangladesh, has almost no rain in the dry season, but its monsoon rains are torrential. Paris, in France, has much more even monthly rainfall.

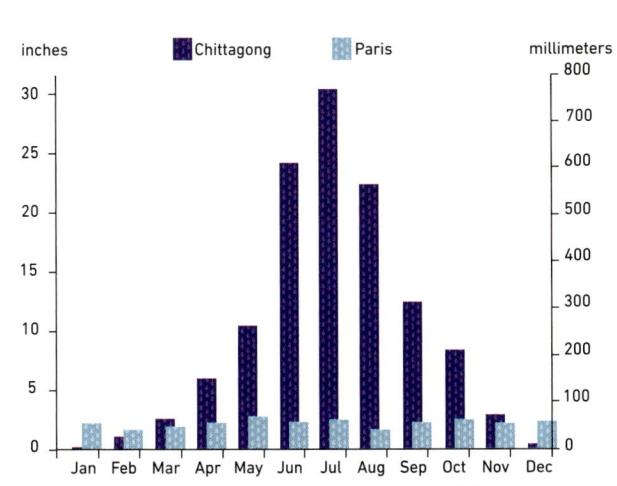

INTERIOR, HAVE NOT SEEN RAIN FOR MORE THAN 2 MILLION YEARS.

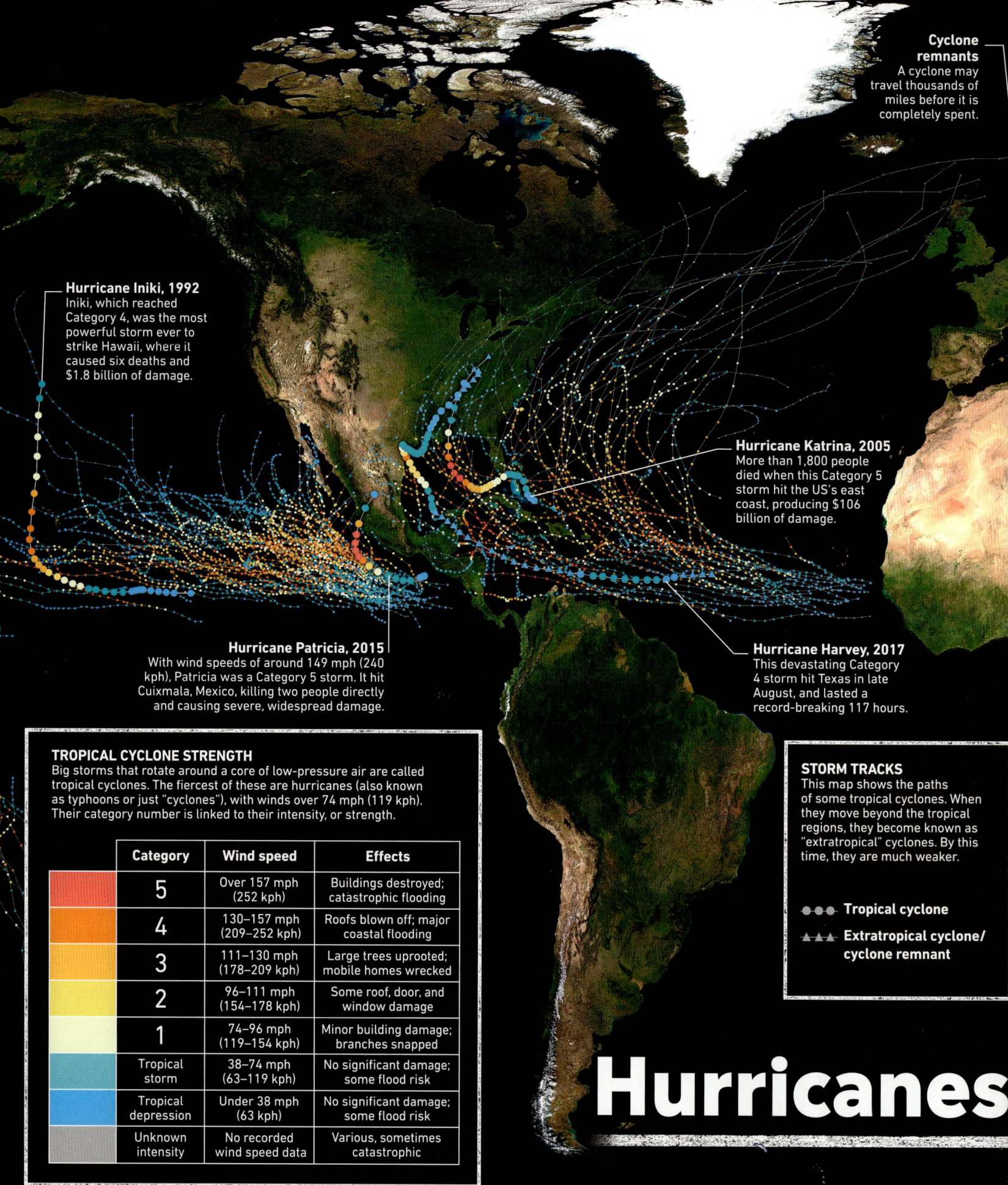

# Hurricanes

**Cyclone remnants** A cyclone may travel thousands of miles before it is completely spent.

**Hurricane Iniki, 1992** Iniki, which reached Category 4, was the most powerful storm ever to strike Hawaii, where it caused six deaths and $1.8 billion of damage.

**Hurricane Katrina, 2005** More than 1,800 people died when this Category 5 storm hit the US's east coast, producing $106 billion of damage.

**Hurricane Patricia, 2015** With wind speeds of around 149 mph (240 kph), Patricia was a Category 5 storm. It hit Cuixmala, Mexico, killing two people directly and causing severe, widespread damage.

**Hurricane Harvey, 2017** This devastating Category 4 storm hit Texas in late August, and lasted a record-breaking 117 hours.

## TROPICAL CYCLONE STRENGTH

Big storms that rotate around a core of low-pressure air are called tropical cyclones. The fiercest of these are hurricanes (also known as typhoons or just "cyclones"), with winds over 74 mph (119 kph). Their category number is linked to their intensity, or strength.

| Category | Wind speed | Effects |
|---|---|---|
| 5 | Over 157 mph (252 kph) | Buildings destroyed; catastrophic flooding |
| 4 | 130–157 mph (209–252 kph) | Roofs blown off; major coastal flooding |
| 3 | 111–130 mph (178–209 kph) | Large trees uprooted; mobile homes wrecked |
| 2 | 96–111 mph (154–178 kph) | Some roof, door, and window damage |
| 1 | 74–96 mph (119–154 kph) | Minor building damage; branches snapped |
| Tropical storm | 38–74 mph (63–119 kph) | No significant damage; some flood risk |
| Tropical depression | Under 38 mph (63 kph) | No significant damage; some flood risk |
| Unknown intensity | No recorded wind speed data | Various, sometimes catastrophic |

## STORM TRACKS

This map shows the paths of some tropical cyclones. When they move beyond the tropical regions, they become known as "extratropical" cyclones. By this time, they are much weaker.

●●● Tropical cyclone
▲▲▲ Extratropical cyclone/ cyclone remnant

TROPICAL CYCLONES ROTATE COUNTERCLOCKWISE IN THE NORTHERN

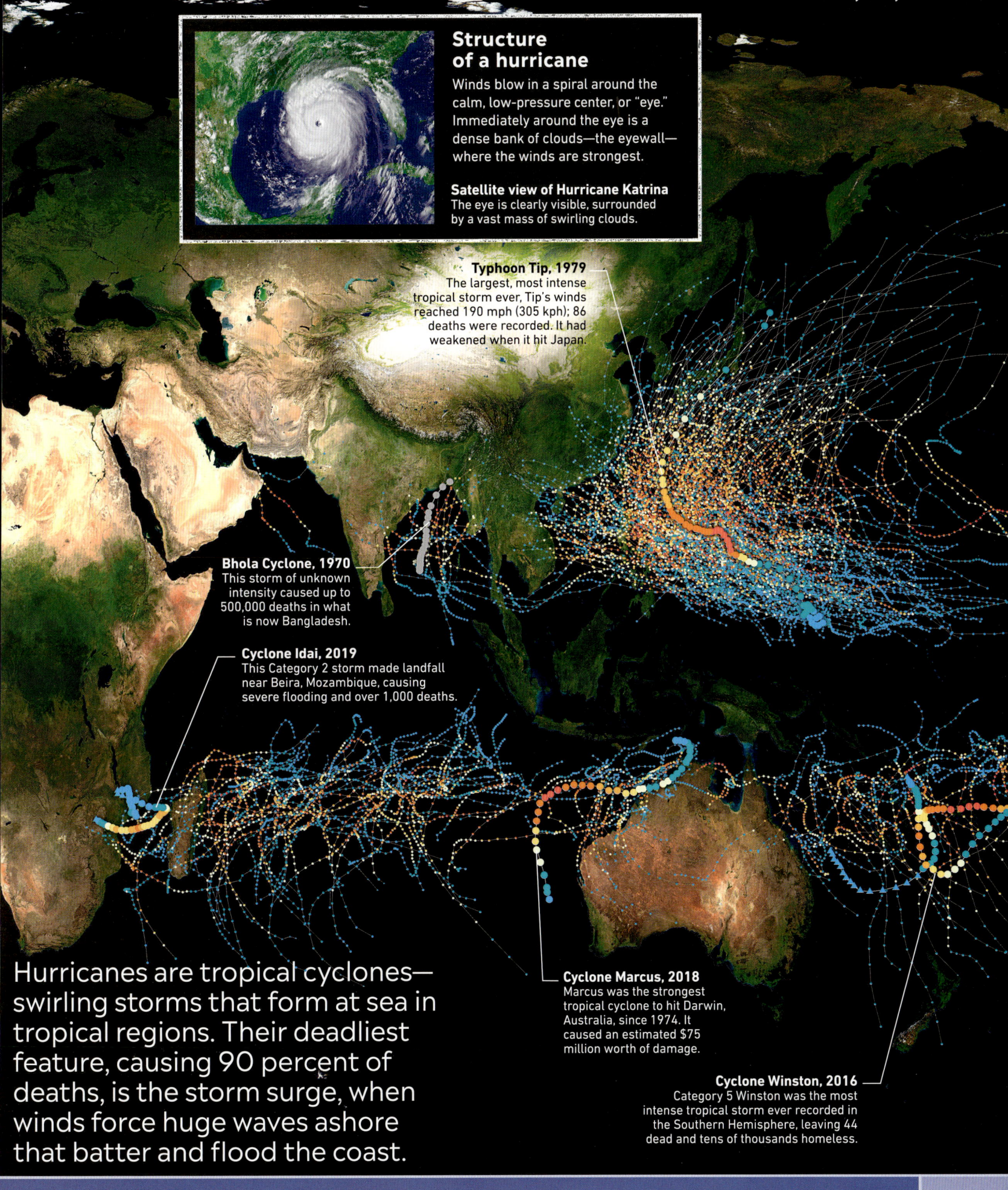

### Structure of a hurricane

Winds blow in a spiral around the calm, low-pressure center, or "eye." Immediately around the eye is a dense bank of clouds—the eyewall—where the winds are strongest.

**Satellite view of Hurricane Katrina**
The eye is clearly visible, surrounded by a vast mass of swirling clouds.

**Typhoon Tip, 1979**
The largest, most intense tropical storm ever, Tip's winds reached 190 mph (305 kph); 86 deaths were recorded. It had weakened when it hit Japan.

**Bhola Cyclone, 1970**
This storm of unknown intensity caused up to 500,000 deaths in what is now Bangladesh.

**Cyclone Idai, 2019**
This Category 2 storm made landfall near Beira, Mozambique, causing severe flooding and over 1,000 deaths.

**Cyclone Marcus, 2018**
Marcus was the strongest tropical cyclone to hit Darwin, Australia, since 1974. It caused an estimated $75 million worth of damage.

**Cyclone Winston, 2016**
Category 5 Winston was the most intense tropical storm ever recorded in the Southern Hemisphere, leaving 44 dead and tens of thousands homeless.

Hurricanes are tropical cyclones—swirling storms that form at sea in tropical regions. Their deadliest feature, causing 90 percent of deaths, is the storm surge, when winds force huge waves ashore that batter and flood the coast.

**Tropical broad-leaved moist forest**
Also known as rainforest, these warm, wet woods support a huge variety of animal and plant life.

**Tropical broad-leaved dry forest**
These areas are warm all year round but have a long dry season, and many trees lose their leaves.

**Tropical coniferous forest**
Many migrating birds and butterflies spend the winter in these warm, dense conifer forests.

**Temperate broad-leaved forest**
The most common habitat of northern Europe and home to trees that lose their leaves in winter.

**Temperate coniferous forest**
Giant trees, such as the California redwood, thrive in these regions of warm summers and cool winters.

**Boreal forest**
Also called taiga, this is the largest land biome on Earth. It is dominated by just a few types of coniferous trees.

**Savanna**
A long dry season and short rainy periods results in a grassland studded with trees and herds of grazing animals.

**Flooded savanna**
Birds are attracted to these marshy wetland areas that are flooded in the wet season but grassland at other times.

**Temperate grassland**
Also known as prairie, steppe, or pampas, many of these vast, fertile plains are now farmland.

**Mountain grassland**
The inhabitants of these remote, high habitats must adapt to the cold and the intense sunlight.

**Coral reef**
The warm, shallow waters of a reef support a huge variety of life, from sharks to tiny sea horses.

## Marine Biomes
Sea biomes are as varied as those on land. From beaches to the darkest ocean depths, living things find ways to survive and thrive.

**Mangrove**
On the shore, the mangroves' thick, tangled roots slow the water's flow and create a swamp.

TROPICAL RAINFORESTS COVER ABOUT 6 PERCENT OF THE LAND,

Land, sea, and air

**Mediterranean shrubland**
Hot, dry summers can lead to fires that actually help the biome's typical shrubby plants sprout.

**Desert and dry shrubland**
Desert inhabitants have to be able to survive on less than 10 in (250 mm) of rainfall per year.

**Arctic tundra**
A cold, dry biome where the soil stays frozen at depth. This permafrost stops trees from growing.

**Polar desert**
Too cold and dry for almost all plants. Only animals dependent on the sea, such as penguins, can live here.

A **BIOME'S PLANTS** AND **ANIMALS** FORM A **COMPLEX** AND **INTERCONNECTED** COMMUNITY

# Biomes

A biome is an area that we define according to the animals and plants that live there. They have to adapt to the biome's specific conditions such as temperature, type of soil, and the amount of light and water.

BUT ARE HOME TO NEARLY HALF OF ALL LIVING THINGS ON EARTH.

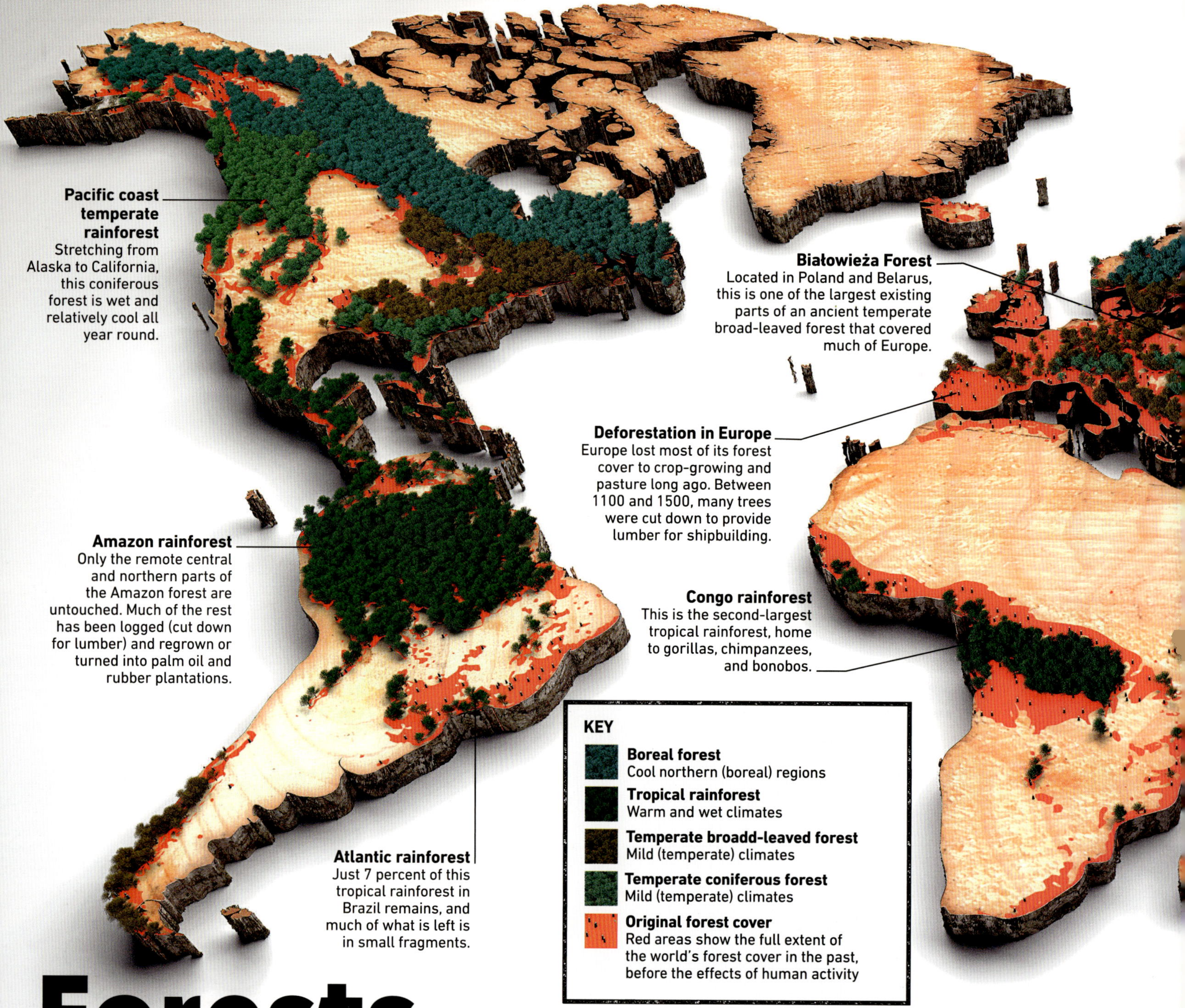

**Pacific coast temperate rainforest**
Stretching from Alaska to California, this coniferous forest is wet and relatively cool all year round.

**Białowieża Forest**
Located in Poland and Belarus, this is one of the largest existing parts of an ancient temperate broad-leaved forest that covered much of Europe.

**Deforestation in Europe**
Europe lost most of its forest cover to crop-growing and pasture long ago. Between 1100 and 1500, many trees were cut down to provide lumber for shipbuilding.

**Amazon rainforest**
Only the remote central and northern parts of the Amazon forest are untouched. Much of the rest has been logged (cut down for lumber) and regrown or turned into palm oil and rubber plantations.

**Congo rainforest**
This is the second-largest tropical rainforest, home to gorillas, chimpanzees, and bonobos.

**Atlantic rainforest**
Just 7 percent of this tropical rainforest in Brazil remains, and much of what is left is in small fragments.

**KEY**
- **Boreal forest** — Cool northern (boreal) regions
- **Tropical rainforest** — Warm and wet climates
- **Temperate broadd-leaved forest** — Mild (temperate) climates
- **Temperate coniferous forest** — Mild (temperate) climates
- **Original forest cover** — Red areas show the full extent of the world's forest cover in the past, before the effects of human activity

# Forests

Forests are vital to life on Earth. They make the air breathable, protect the soil, and preserve fresh water supplies. But they are disappearing—and while efforts are being made to slow deforestation, about 25 million acres are still lost each year.

## Types of forests

Forests differ according to climate. Each type of forest has its own distinct collection of trees, forest-floor plants, and animal life. Tropical rainforests are the most diverse—30 percent of all plant and animal species live in the Amazon alone. Some tropical forests are evergreen, while in others the trees lose their leaves in the dry season.

**Temperate broad-leaved**
Deciduous trees, such as oak and beech. Herbs, ferns, and shrubs on the forest floor.

IN 2019, AN AREA OF TROPICAL RAINFOREST ABOUT THE SIZE OF

# Land, sea, and air

**Taiga**
This vast belt of boreal forest stretches right across northern Europe and Asia. In the east, it is wilderness, but much in the west is working forest, managed for lumber and paper production.

## Disappearing forests
With the world's population growing, demand for lumber and land for farming and towns has increased the rate of forest clearance. Here you can see the decline in Borneo's forests from 1950 to 2010.

**Borneo, 1950**

**1985**

**2010**

**Japan**
Japan retains a lot of its original woodland and is the most thickly forested industrialized country.

**Borneo**
Home of most of the world's orangutans, Borneo's rainforest has declined by more than 50 percent since the mid-20th century (see above).

**New Guinea**
Two-thirds of New Guinea is largely unspoiled rainforest, with many unique species. It is at risk from logging, mining, and agriculture.

## AT CURRENT RATES OF **LOGGING**, IN **100 YEARS** WE WILL **NO LONGER** HAVE ANY **RAINFORESTS**

**Australia**
About 38 percent of Australia's forests have been lost since European settlers arrived around 200 years ago.

**New Zealand**
The remote southwest of New Zealand is home to unique temperate rainforests full of lush tree ferns.

**Tropical rainforest**
As many as 300 tree species per 2.5 acres (hectare). Often rich in forest-floor plants.

**Boreal forest**
Hardy conifers, such as larch, spruce, fir, and pine. Mosses dominate the forest floor.

**A FOOTBALL FIELD WAS DESTROYED EVERY SIX SECONDS.**

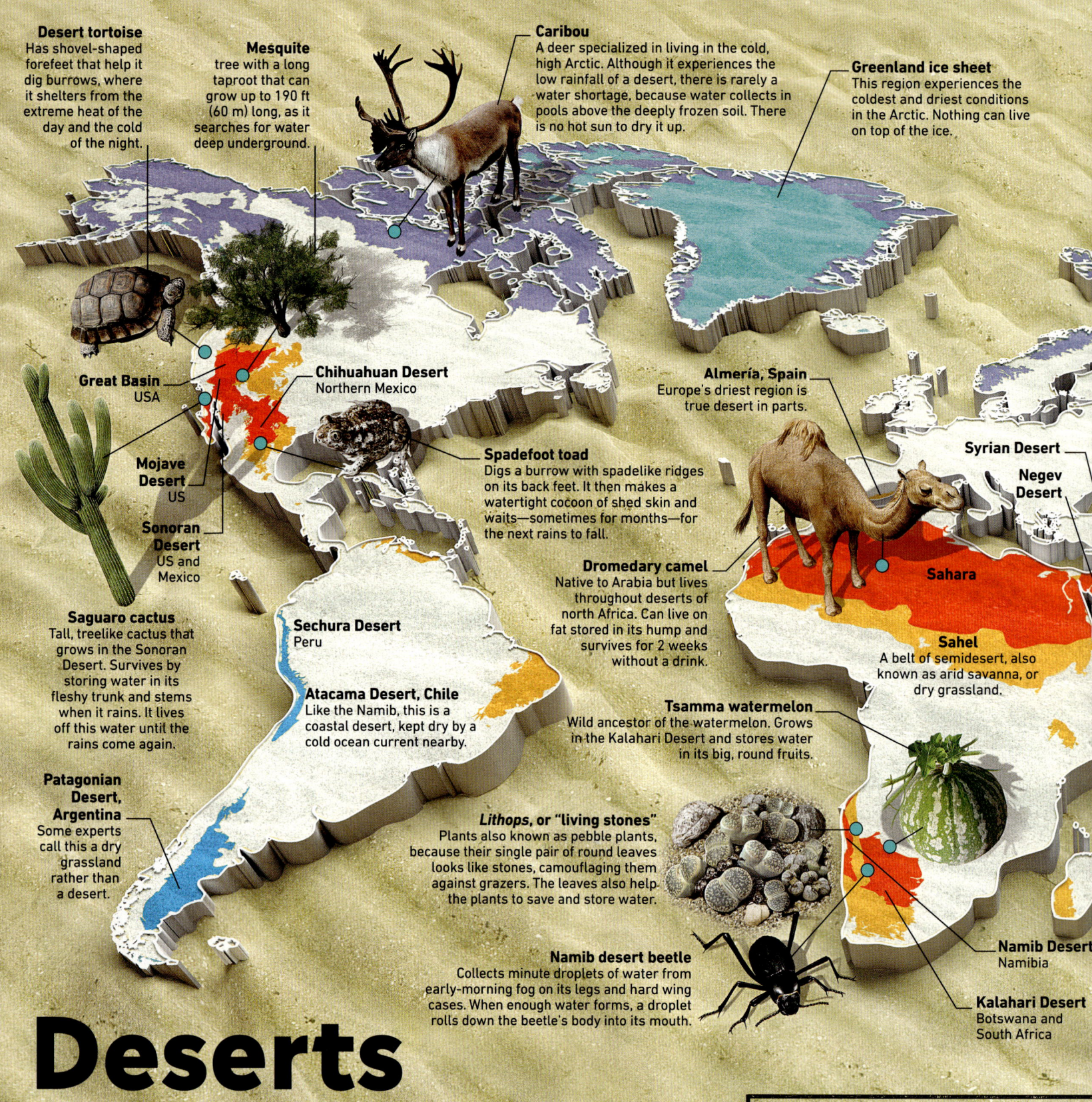

# Deserts

Deserts are found from the icy poles to the tropics. So while all deserts have low rainfall—less than 10 in (250 mm) a year, and often much less—they are not always hot. Even in hot deserts, the nights are often cold.

**Desert tortoise** Has shovel-shaped forefeet that help it dig burrows, where it shelters from the extreme heat of the day and the cold of the night.

**Mesquite** tree with a long taproot that can grow up to 190 ft (60 m) long, as it searches for water deep underground.

**Caribou** A deer specialized in living in the cold, high Arctic. Although it experiences the low rainfall of a desert, there is rarely a water shortage, because water collects in pools above the deeply frozen soil. There is no hot sun to dry it up.

**Greenland ice sheet** This region experiences the coldest and driest conditions in the Arctic. Nothing can live on top of the ice.

**Great Basin** USA

**Chihuahuan Desert** Northern Mexico

**Almería, Spain** Europe's driest region is true desert in parts.

**Syrian Desert**

**Negev Desert**

**Mojave Desert** US

**Sonoran Desert** US and Mexico

**Spadefoot toad** Digs a burrow with spadelike ridges on its back feet. It then makes a watertight cocoon of shed skin and waits—sometimes for months—for the next rains to fall.

**Dromedary camel** Native to Arabia but lives throughout deserts of north Africa. Can live on fat stored in its hump and survives for 2 weeks without a drink.

**Sahara**

**Sahel** A belt of semidesert, also known as arid savanna, or dry grassland.

**Saguaro cactus** Tall, treelike cactus that grows in the Sonoran Desert. Survives by storing water in its fleshy trunk and stems when it rains. It lives off this water until the rains come again.

**Sechura Desert** Peru

**Atacama Desert, Chile** Like the Namib, this is a coastal desert, kept dry by a cold ocean current nearby.

**Tsamma watermelon** Wild ancestor of the watermelon. Grows in the Kalahari Desert and stores water in its big, round fruits.

**Patagonian Desert, Argentina** Some experts call this a dry grassland rather than a desert.

**Lithops, or "living stones"** Plants also known as pebble plants, because their single pair of round leaves looks like stones, camouflaging them against grazers. The leaves also help the plants to save and store water.

**Namib desert beetle** Collects minute droplets of water from early-morning fog on its legs and hard wing cases. When enough water forms, a droplet rolls down the beetle's body into its mouth.

**Namib Desert** Namibia

**Kalahari Desert** Botswana and South Africa

**Antarctica** One of the most arid parts of Earth's largest desert is its Dry Valleys region (right), the only area of Antarctica not covered in thick ice, and where there is almost no snowfall. Cold, dry winds blast down from mountain peaks and turn all moisture to water vapor.

THE SAHARA TAKES UP 8 PERCENT OF THE EARTH'S LAND

Land, sea, and air

## Desert terrain

Deserts range widely in how they look. Soil forms very slowly and the land is often bare rock or gravel. Any loose, sandy soil may be blown into dunes. Sometimes, though, tough grasses or fleshy plants bind the soil together.

**Dunes, or "sand seas"**
Shifting mountains of sand can prevent plant growth.

**Rock and gravel**
Where no plants grow, the bedrock is often visible.

**Dry grassland**
Desert grasses can form soil and provide food for grazers.

**Fleshy plants**
Fleshy, water-storing plants may form thick vegetation.

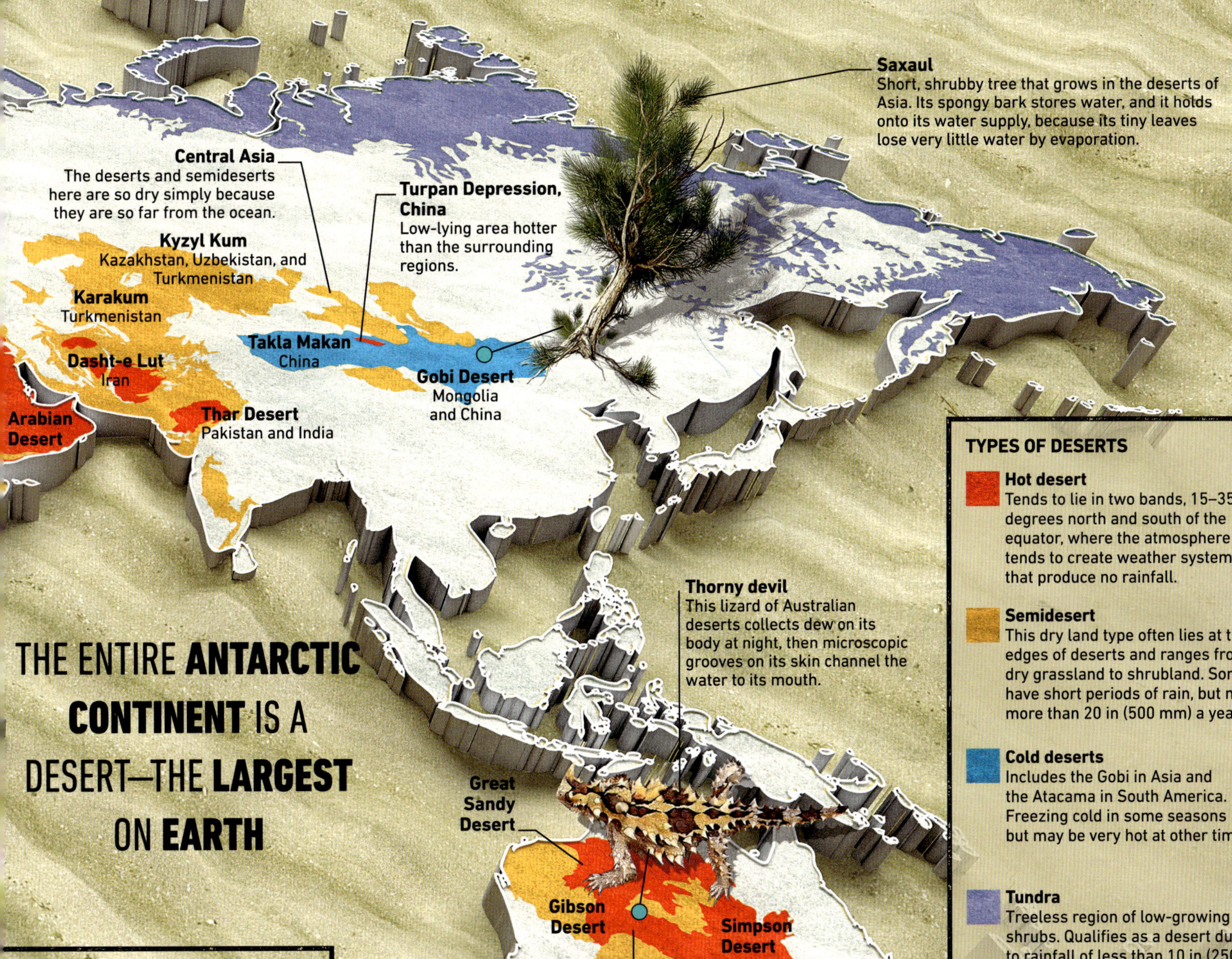

**Saxaul**
Short, shrubby tree that grows in the deserts of Asia. Its spongy bark stores water, and it holds onto its water supply, because its tiny leaves lose very little water by evaporation.

**Central Asia**
The deserts and semideserts here are so dry simply because they are so far from the ocean.

**Kyzyl Kum**
Kazakhstan, Uzbekistan, and Turkmenistan

**Karakum**
Turkmenistan

**Dasht-e Lut**
Iran

**Arabian Desert**

**Thar Desert**
Pakistan and India

**Turpan Depression, China**
Low-lying area hotter than the surrounding regions.

**Takla Makan**
China

**Gobi Desert**
Mongolia and China

**Thorny devil**
This lizard of Australian deserts collects dew on its body at night, then microscopic grooves on its skin channel the water to its mouth.

**Great Sandy Desert**

**Gibson Desert**

**Simpson Desert**

**Great Victoria Desert**

## THE ENTIRE ANTARCTIC CONTINENT IS A DESERT—THE LARGEST ON EARTH

### TYPES OF DESERTS

**Hot desert**
Tends to lie in two bands, 15–35 degrees north and south of the equator, where the atmosphere tends to create weather systems that produce no rainfall.

**Semidesert**
This dry land type often lies at the edges of deserts and ranges from dry grassland to shrubland. Some have short periods of rain, but no more than 20 in (500 mm) a year.

**Cold deserts**
Includes the Gobi in Asia and the Atacama in South America. Freezing cold in some seasons but may be very hot at other times.

**Tundra**
Treeless region of low-growing shrubs. Qualifies as a desert due to rainfall of less than 10 in (250 mm) a year, but low evaporation means there is no lack of water.

**Polar desert**
Includes the driest, coldest parts of the Arctic where few tundra plants can live, and the ice sheets on Greenland and Antarctica, where almost nothing lives at all.

AND IS ABOUT THE SAME SIZE AS THE ENTIRE UNITED STATES!

35

# Ice

Ice covers one-tenth of Earth's land surface, mostly in the polar regions. At earlier times in Earth's history, when the climate was much cooler, ice covered an area up to three times larger than it does today.

## Sea ice

Sea ice is frozen sea. It forms when the ocean's surface freezes in winter. Where it lasts year round, it may be 20 ft (6 m) thick—elsewhere it is thinner. "Pancake ice" (right) is disks of sea ice up to 4 in (10 cm) thick.

- **Summer ice** The polar sea ice cover shrinks in summer, but some sea always remains under a layer of ice.
- **Winter ice** As the weather gets colder, the polar sea ice spreads far beyond its summer limits.

## Land ice

Thick ice gradually builds up on land as old, unmelted snow is compacted by layers of fresh snow and turned into ice. Antarctica's ice sheet is up to 3 miles (4.8 km) thick.

- **Ice sheet** A vast layer of land ice that has formed over thousands or even millions of years.
- **Ice shelf** A floating extension of an ice sheet or glacier, usually hundreds of yards thick.

THE TALLEST ICEBERG EVER SEEN IN THE NORTH ATLANTIC ROSE 551 FT

## Land, sea, and air

### Glaciers and ice sheets

Glaciers are bodies of land ice that usually form on high mountains in many parts of the world. These "rivers of ice" flow slowly downhill until the end melts or meets the ocean. As they flow, they dramatically shape the landscape by carving deep valleys in the rock over which they pass. The largest glaciers are the ice sheets that cover land in polar regions, such as the Greenland and Antarctic ice sheets.

■ Glaciers

(168 M) ABOVE SEA LEVEL—HIGHER THAN A 55-STORY BUILDING!

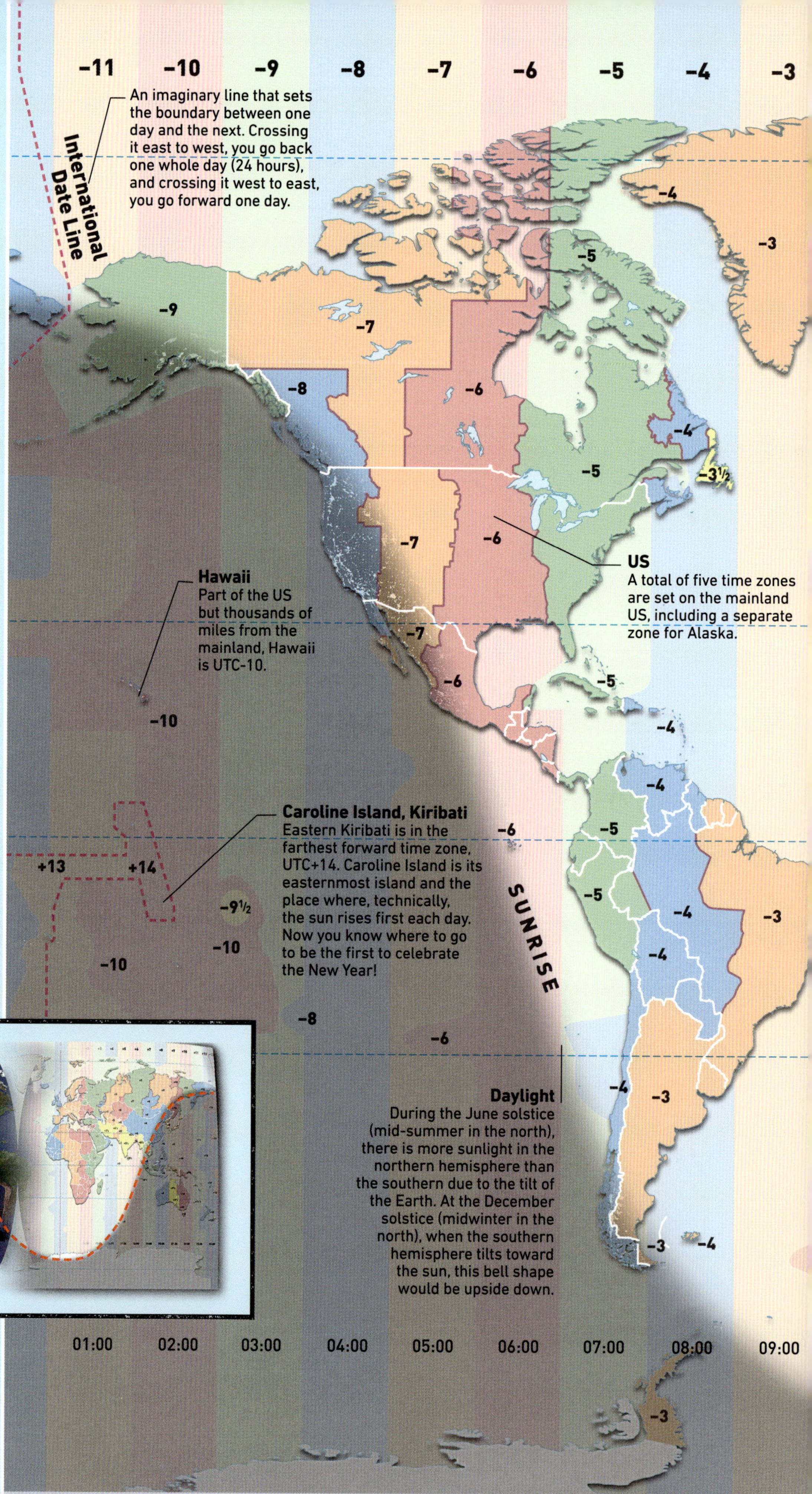

# Time zones

As Earth rotates, some of it faces the sun and the rest is in darkness. Since the sun is high in the sky at noon, noon is at different times in different places. We adjust by splitting the Earth into time zones.

## Time zones map

The map shows the time of day at 12 noon Coordinated Universal Time (UTC), the base from which all times are set. The columns are time zones labeled with the number of hours they are ahead or behind UTC. If you stood halfway between the boundaries of a time zone with your watch set to the correct time, at 12 noon the sun would be at its highest point.

-11
-10
-9
-8
-7
-6
-5
-4
-3
International Date Line
An imaginary line that sets the boundary between one day and the next. Crossing it east to west, you go back one whole day (24 hours), and crossing it west to east, you go forward one day.
-9
-7
-8
-6
-5
-4
-3
-5
-4
-3½
-7
-6
US
A total of five time zones are set on the mainland US, including a separate zone for Alaska.
Hawaii
Part of the US but thousands of miles from the mainland, Hawaii is UTC-10.
-7
-6
-5
-10
-4
Caroline Island, Kiribati
Eastern Kiribati is in the farthest forward time zone, UTC+14. Caroline Island is its easternmost island and the place where, technically, the sun rises first each day. Now you know where to go to be the first to celebrate the New Year!
+13
+14
-9½
-10
-10
-6
SUNRISE
-5
-5
-4
-3
-4
-8
-6
Daylight
During the June solstice (mid-summer in the north), there is more sunlight in the northern hemisphere than the southern due to the tilt of the Earth. At the December solstice (midwinter in the north), when the southern hemisphere tilts toward the sun, this bell shape would be upside down.
-4
-3
-3
-4
01:00
02:00
03:00
04:00
05:00
06:00
07:00
08:00
09:00
-3


### Day and night

On the globe of Earth, we can see day and night divided by a straight line from north to south. When the Earth is laid flat as on the map here, the light and dark areas form a bell shape.

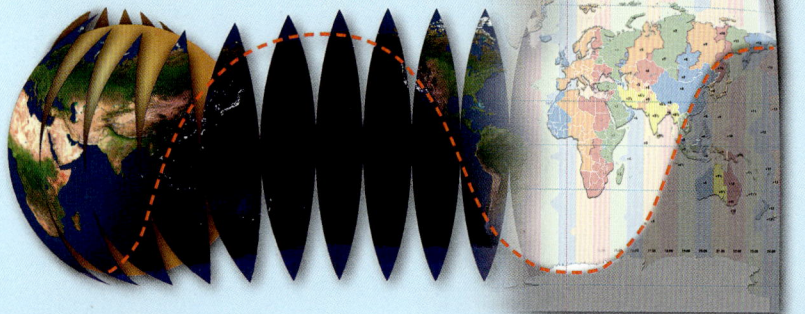

**Northern summer**
The Earth is tilted. When the North Pole tilts toward the sun and the South Pole leans away, it is summer in the northern hemisphere (northern half of the world) and winter in the southern hemisphere, as on the main map.



BEFORE TIME ZONES, LOCAL TIME WAS DECIDED BY THE TOWN TIME-

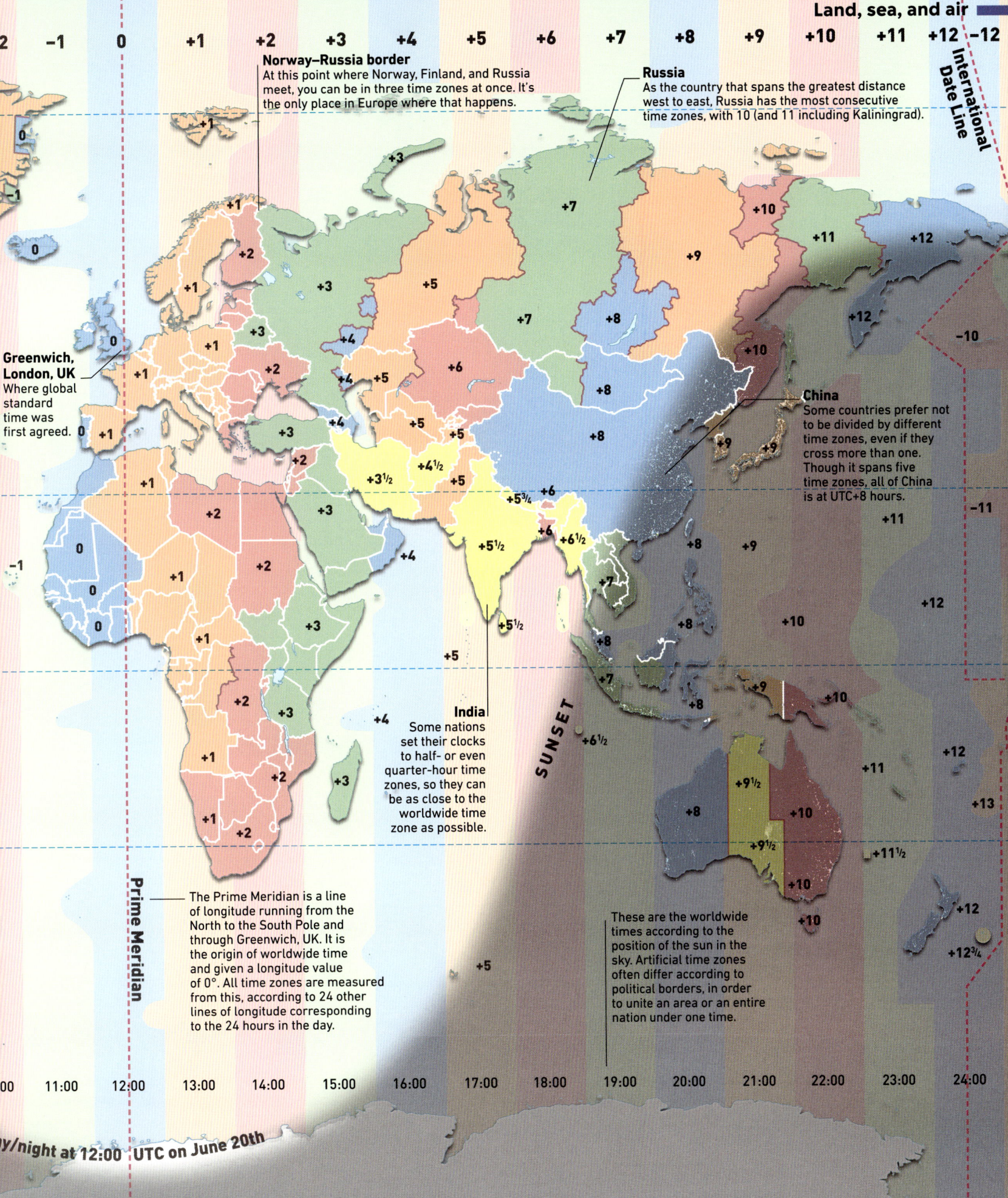

# Living world

**Humpback whales**
Two humpbacks "breach" (leap out of the water) off the coast of Alaska. During winter, humpbacks move south to warmer waters.

# Introduction

Life exists in every corner of the planet—from high mountains to deep oceans, and from blazing deserts to the freezing polar regions. Each animal's body, life cycle, and behavior is adapted to its particular habitat, because this maximizes its chances of survival. Plant species, too, have their own adaptations that help them thrive.

## Birds

The power of flight allows birds to reach the remotest islands, and some to live in different parts of the world in summer and winter, migrating between the two. There is almost nowhere on Earth that lacks birdlife. Here are their secrets.

- **Lightweight bones**
  Most bird bones are hollow, reinforced by bony struts.
- **Flight feathers**
  Wing and tail feathers provide lift and steer the bird in fight.
- **Warming feathers**
  Two layers of body feathers keep the bird's skin warm.
- **Efficient lungs**
  Bird lungs are far more efficient than mammals', giving them the oxygen they need for energetic flight.

**Bald eagle**
A North American bird of prey, the bald eagle snatches fish from lakes.

## Marine animals

Living in water gives more support than living on land, so many sea creatures survive without strong skeletons. Sea water carries clouds of microscopic life-forms and dead matter, and many sea animals can afford to give up moving from place to place, fix themselves to the seabed, and "filter feed" by grabbing these passing pieces of food.

**Coral**
Tropical coral reefs are giant growths of filter-feeding life-forms on the seabed.

- **Gills**
  Sea mammals must surface to breathe, but fish take oxygen directly from the water using their gills.
- **Smooth shape**
  Fast-moving marine animals have a streamlined body, which helps them move through the water easily.
- **Buoyancy aid**
  Some fish have an air-filled "swim bladder" to help control buoyancy.
- **Bioluminescence**
  It is dark in the ocean depths. Many deep-sea animals produce light by chemical reactions in their bodies.

## Desert cacti

The waxy, fleshy bodies of these desert plants store water. The leaves are reduced to spines, which lose less water to the air. The roots of a cactus may spread out over a wide area, to absorb as much water as possible.

**Spineless cactus**
A spineless variety of the prickly pear.

# Living world

## Polar regions

The sea in the Arctic and Antarctic is so cold, fish are in danger of freezing. Above the water it is even colder, and no large, cold-blooded animals exist. Warm-blooded animals—those able to retain body heat—predominate. Polar mammals often have two layers of fur: an underlayer of soft hairs that trap air warmed by the animal's body close to the skin, and an outer coat of coarse hairs that keeps out the fiercest gales.

**Polar bear**
This arctic mammal has a bulky, rounded body surrounded by fat and fur that keep it warm.

- **Natural antifreeze**
  Most polar fish have a chemical in their blood that prevents ice crystals from forming in the body.
- **Small extremities**
  Polar bears and Arctic foxes have small, rounded ears and muzzles that reduce heat loss.
- **Legs and feet**
  Some animals have long legs that wade through snow or broad feet that act like snowshoes.

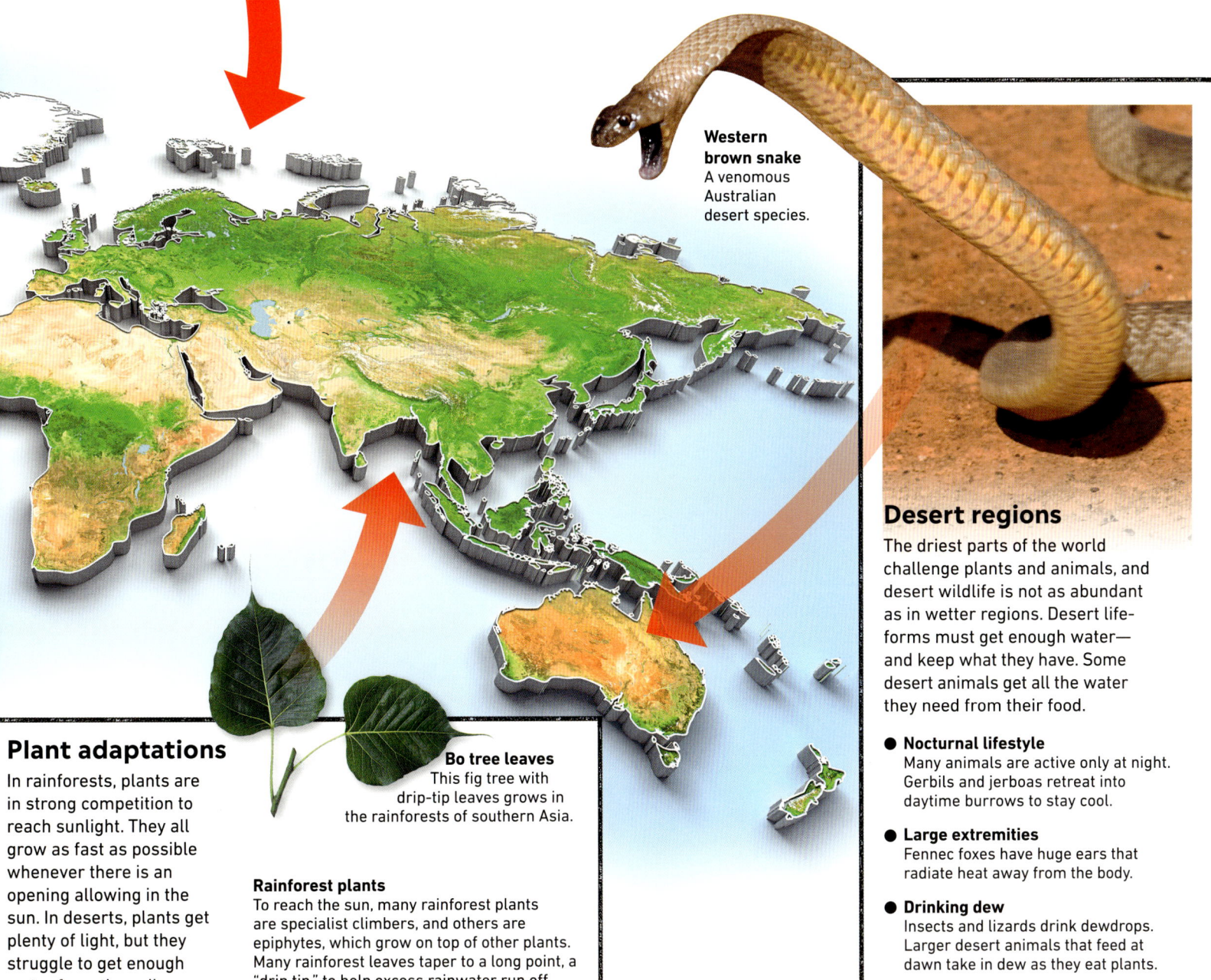

**Western brown snake**
A venomous Australian desert species.

## Plant adaptations

In rainforests, plants are in strong competition to reach sunlight. They all grow as fast as possible whenever there is an opening allowing in the sun. In deserts, plants get plenty of light, but they struggle to get enough water from the soil.

**Bo tree leaves**
This fig tree with drip-tip leaves grows in the rainforests of southern Asia.

**Rainforest plants**
To reach the sun, many rainforest plants are specialist climbers, and others are epiphytes, which grow on top of other plants. Many rainforest leaves taper to a long point, a "drip tip," to help excess rainwater run off.

## Desert regions

The driest parts of the world challenge plants and animals, and desert wildlife is not as abundant as in wetter regions. Desert life-forms must get enough water—and keep what they have. Some desert animals get all the water they need from their food.

- **Nocturnal lifestyle**
  Many animals are active only at night. Gerbils and jerboas retreat into daytime burrows to stay cool.
- **Large extremities**
  Fennec foxes have huge ears that radiate heat away from the body.
- **Drinking dew**
  Insects and lizards drink dewdrops. Larger desert animals that feed at dawn take in dew as they eat plants.

**THE MUD OF THE DEEP OCEAN FLOOR—PERHAPS UP TO 100 MILLION!**

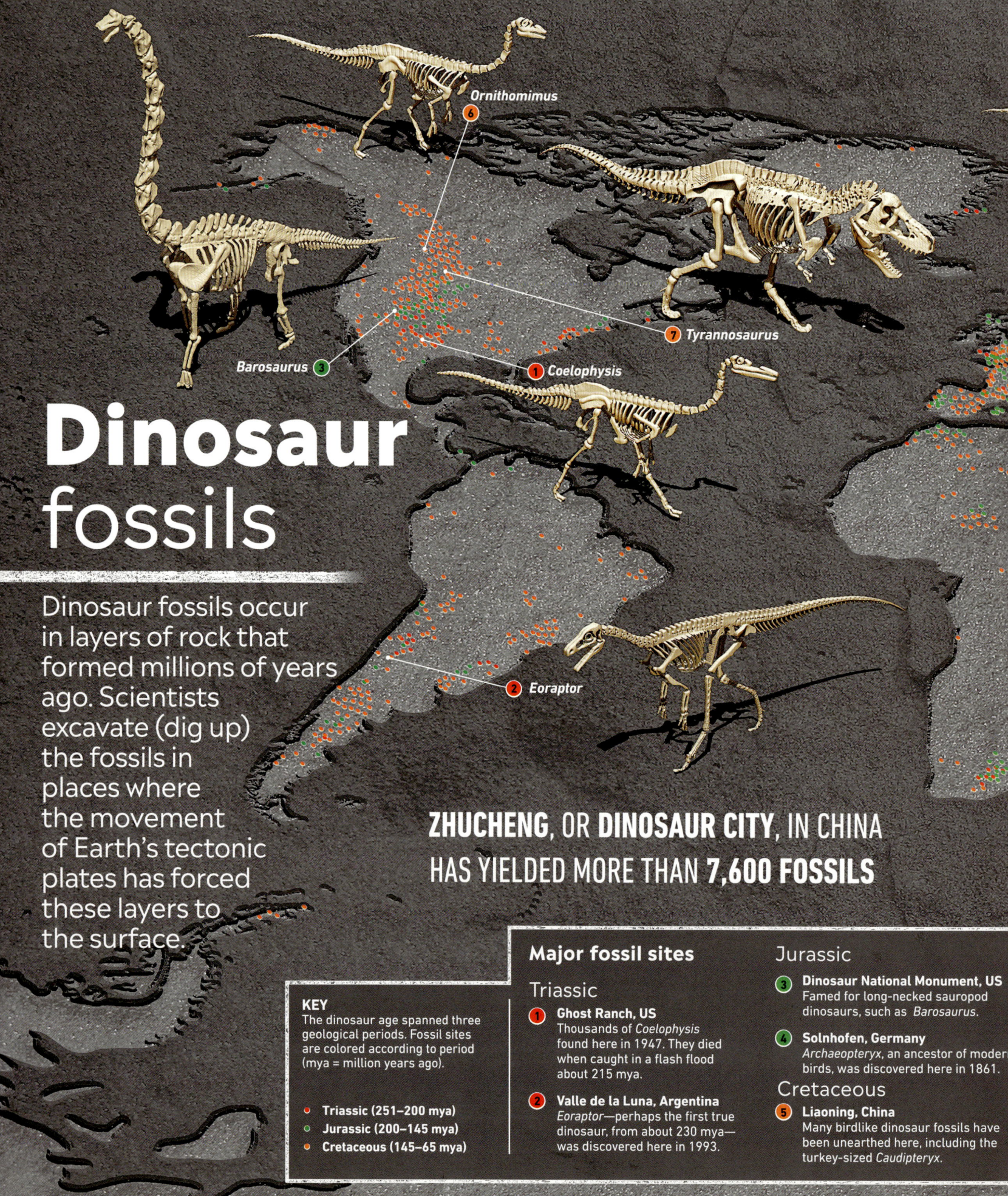

# Dinosaur fossils

Dinosaur fossils occur in layers of rock that formed millions of years ago. Scientists excavate (dig up) the fossils in places where the movement of Earth's tectonic plates has forced these layers to the surface.

**ZHUCHENG, OR DINOSAUR CITY, IN CHINA HAS YIELDED MORE THAN 7,600 FOSSILS**

**KEY**
The dinosaur age spanned three geological periods. Fossil sites are colored according to period (mya = million years ago).

- Triassic (251–200 mya)
- Jurassic (200–145 mya)
- Cretaceous (145–65 mya)

## Major fossil sites

### Triassic

**1 Ghost Ranch, US**
Thousands of *Coelophysis* found here in 1947. They died when caught in a flash flood about 215 mya.

**2 Valle de la Luna, Argentina**
*Eoraptor*—perhaps the first true dinosaur, from about 230 mya—was discovered here in 1993.

### Jurassic

**3 Dinosaur National Monument, US**
Famed for long-necked sauropod dinosaurs, such as *Barosaurus*.

**4 Solnhofen, Germany**
*Archaeopteryx*, an ancestor of modern birds, was discovered here in 1861.

### Cretaceous

**5 Liaoning, China**
Many birdlike dinosaur fossils have been unearthed here, including the turkey-sized *Caudipteryx*.

AS WELL AS BONES, NESTS, EGGS, AND TRACKS, FOSSILS INCLUDE

Living world

### Dinosaur footprints

Fossil hunters have found tracks preserved in mud and sand that later turned into rock. These tracks can tell us how dinosaurs walked, and whether they lived alone or in groups. The sites shown here are all in the US.

**Dinosaur Ridge** Colorado. Hundreds of prints unearthed when building a road.

**Dinosaur State Park** Connecticut. One of the largest track sites in North America.

**Purgatoire River site** Colorado. Giant sauropod prints left on a lake shore.

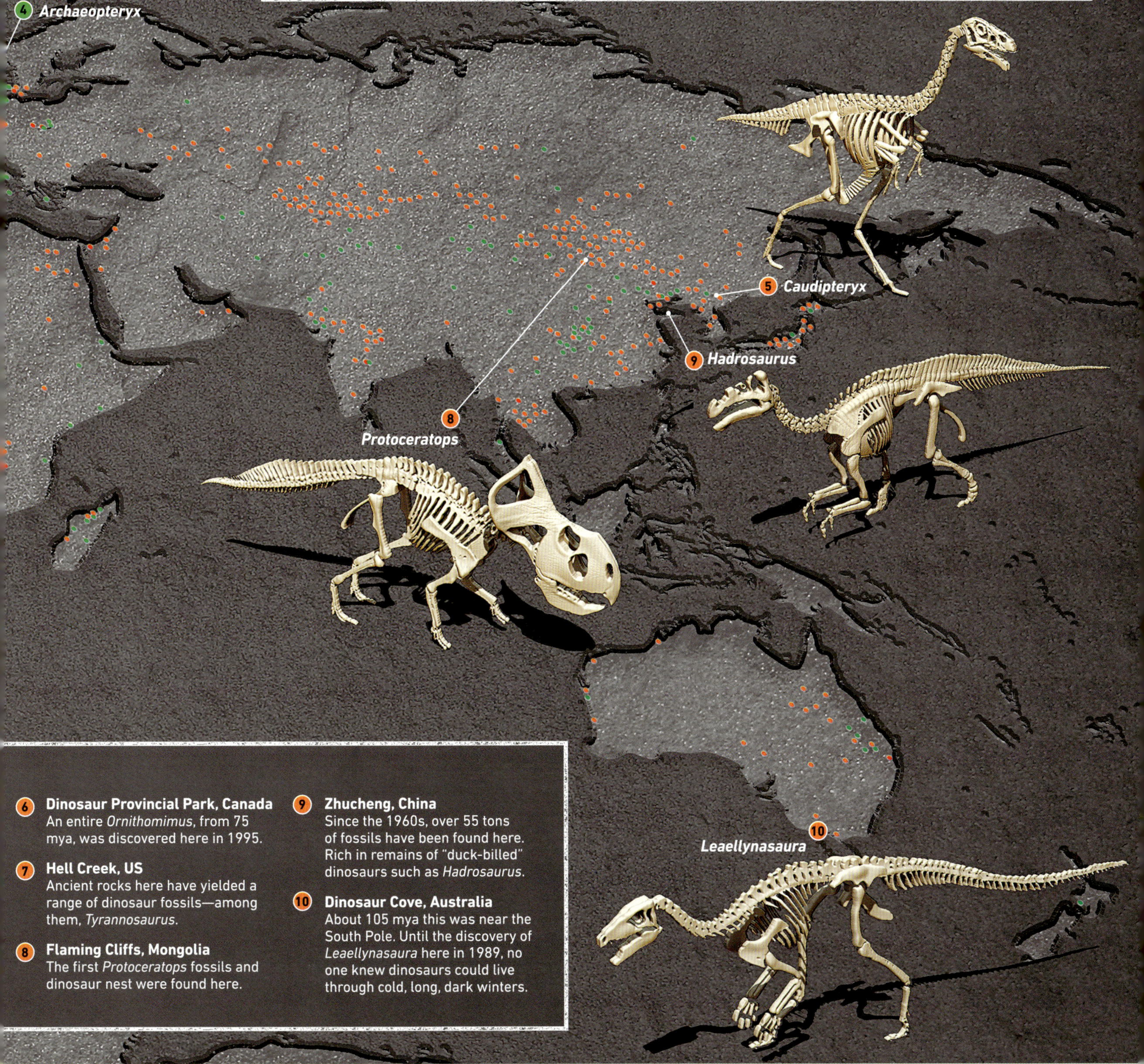

4 *Archaeopteryx*

5 *Caudipteryx*

9 *Hadrosaurus*

8 *Protoceratops*

10 *Leaellynasaura*

6 **Dinosaur Provincial Park, Canada** An entire *Ornithomimus*, from 75 mya, was discovered here in 1995.

7 **Hell Creek, US** Ancient rocks here have yielded a range of dinosaur fossils—among them, *Tyrannosaurus*.

8 **Flaming Cliffs, Mongolia** The first *Protoceratops* fossils and dinosaur nest were found here.

9 **Zhucheng, China** Since the 1960s, over 55 tons of fossils have been found here. Rich in remains of "duck-billed" dinosaurs such as *Hadrosaurus*.

10 **Dinosaur Cove, Australia** About 105 mya this was near the South Pole. Until the discovery of *Leaellynasaura* here in 1989, no one knew dinosaurs could live through cold, long, dark winters.

**TRACES OF SKIN AND FEATHERS, AND EVEN DINOSAUR POOP!**

# Predators

Found on every continent and in every ocean, predators are animals that kill and eat other creatures. With their incredible array of hunting strategies and body parts adapted for killing, they include some of the most fascinating species on the planet.

## Americas

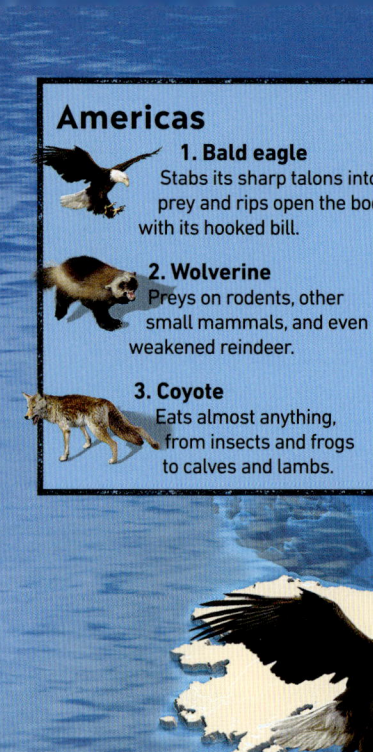

**1. Bald eagle** Stabs its sharp talons into prey and rips open the body with its hooked bill.

**2. Wolverine** Preys on rodents, other small mammals, and even weakened reindeer.

**3. Coyote** Eats almost anything, from insects and frogs to calves and lambs.

**4. Boa constrictor** A large snake, the boa coils around its prey and squeezes until the victim suffocates.

**5. Jaguar** Unable to run fast for very long, the jaguar relies on stealth to creep up on prey.

**6. Piranha** Using razor-sharp teeth, a shoal can reduce a deer to bones in minutes.

## Africa

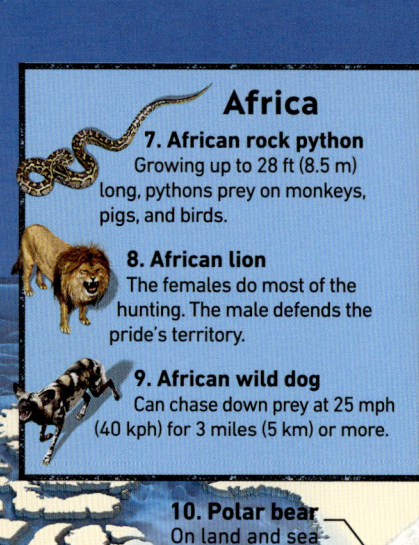

**7. African rock python** Growing up to 28 ft (8.5 m) long, pythons prey on monkeys, pigs, and birds.

**8. African lion** The females do most of the hunting. The male defends the pride's territory.

**9. African wild dog** Can chase down prey at 25 mph (40 kph) for 3 miles (5 km) or more.

## Eurasia

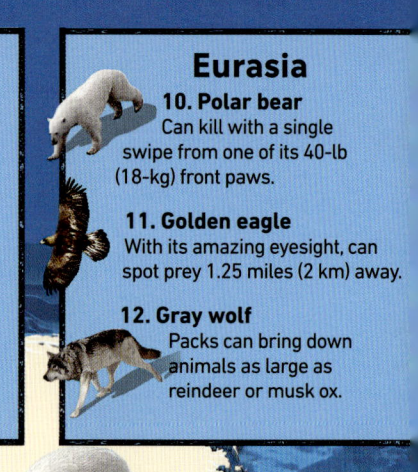

**10. Polar bear** Can kill with a single swipe from one of its 40-lb (18-kg) front paws.

**11. Golden eagle** With its amazing eyesight, can spot prey 1.25 miles (2 km) away.

**12. Gray wolf** Packs can bring down animals as large as reindeer or musk ox.

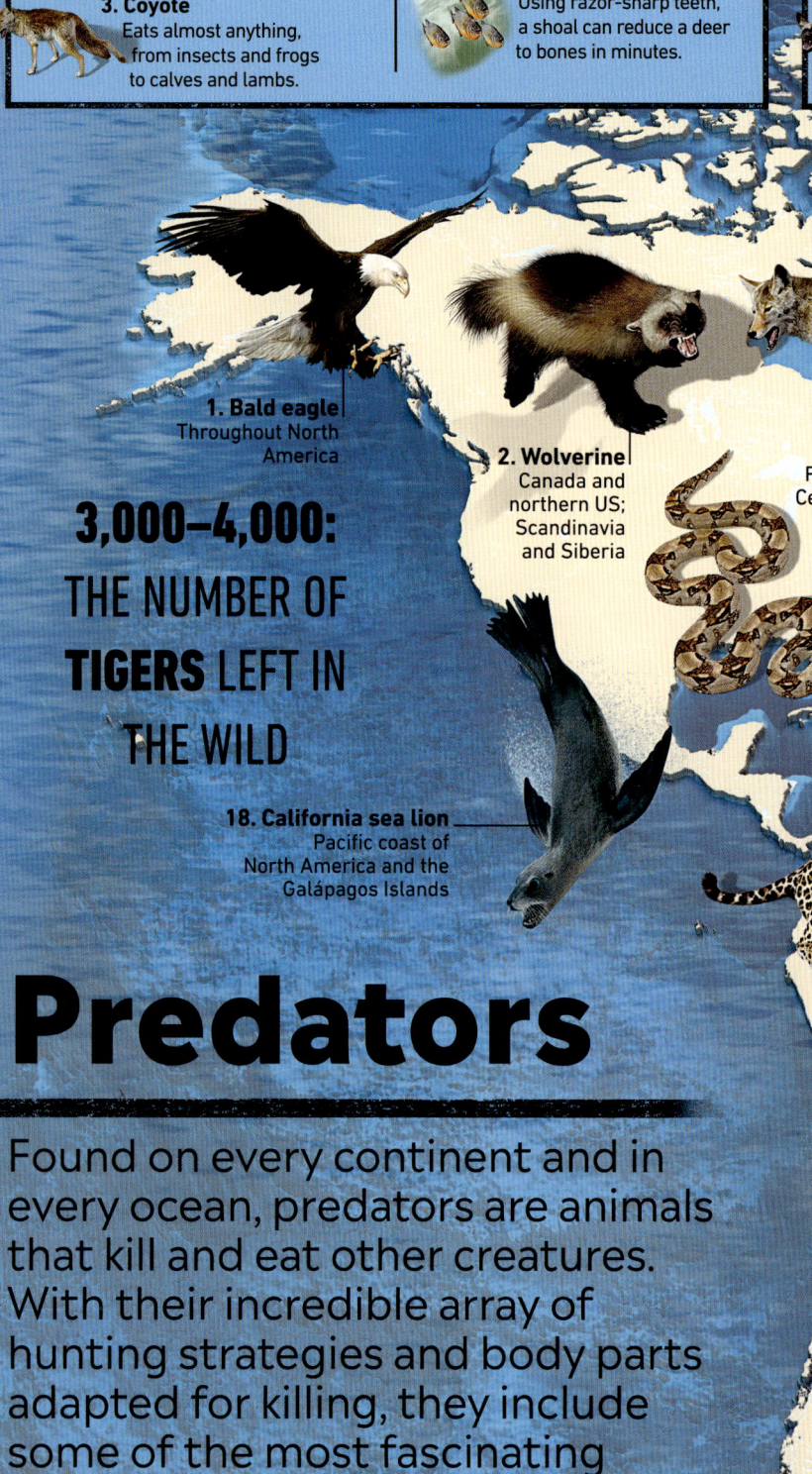

**1. Bald eagle** Throughout North America

**2. Wolverine** Canada and northern US; Scandinavia and Siberia

**3. Coyote** From Alaska to Central America

**4. Boa constrictor** From Mexico to Argentina

**5. Jaguar** Southwestern US to northern Argentina

**6. Piranha** North, central, and eastern South America

**7. African rock python** Africa, south of the Sahara

**10. Polar bear** On land and sea ice within the Arctic Circle

**11. Golden eagle** Europe, North America, northern Asia, and Africa

**18. California sea lion** Pacific coast of North America and the Galápagos Islands

**19. Killer whale (orca)** Oceans worldwide

**20. Common dolphin** Cool and warm oceans worldwide

**21. Sperm whale** Worldwide, to the edge of the polar ice

**22. Tuna** Cool and warm oceans worldwide

**23. Great white shark** Cool and warm oceans worldwide

**3,000–4,000:** THE NUMBER OF **TIGERS** LEFT IN THE WILD

WHEN A PEREGRINE FALCON DIVES ON A PIGEON AT FULL SPEED,

# Living world

**13. Eurasian lynx** Furry ear tufts gather prey noises in the dense forest, where sounds are muffled.

**14. Peregrine falcon** Dives onto prey at 200 mph (320 kph), making it the fastest animal on Earth.

**15. Eurasian badger** Eats worms, insects, birds, frogs, lizards, and small mammals, plus plants.

**16. Tiger** Camouflaged by its stripes, a tiger stalks its prey and kills with a bite to the neck.

**17. Sunda clouded leopard** For its size, this shy forest-dweller has longer canine teeth than any other cat.

## Oceans

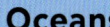
**18. California sea lion** May hunt nonstop for 30 hours, diving for up to 5 minutes at a time.

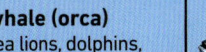
**19. Killer whale (orca)** Many hunt sea lions, dolphins, and even whales. Can snatch seals off the ice.

**20. Common dolphin** Together, dolphins can herd fish to the surface, where they are easier to catch.

**21. Sperm whale** May dive to 9,843 ft (3,000 m) deep in search of giant squid.

**22. Tuna** Able to swim at 50 mph (80 kph); hunts fish and squid near surface.

**23. Great white shark** Kills dolphins, seals, and big fish, including other sharks, with its jagged teeth.

**12. Gray wolf** Much of Asia, parts of Europe, and northern North America

**14. Peregrine falcon** Lives on every continent except Antarctica

**13. Eurasian lynx** Europe (mainly northern and eastern parts) to northern and central Asia

**16. Tiger** Parts of India, China, Siberia, and southeast Asia

**15. Eurasian badger** Europe and Asia below the Arctic Circle

**8. African lion** Africa, south of the Sahara

**17. Sunda clouded leopard** Sumatra and Borneo in southeast Asia

## Australasia

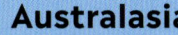
**24. Saltwater crocodile** Preys on water buffalo and cattle on land. Spends much of its life at sea, catching fish.

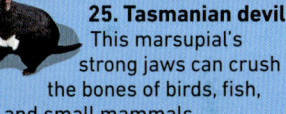
**25. Tasmanian devil** This marsupial's strong jaws can crush the bones of birds, fish, and small mammals.

**9. African wild dog** Africa, south of the Sahara

**24. Saltwater crocodile** Southeast Asia and Northern Australia

**25. Tasmanian devil** Tasmania, an island off the southeastern tip of Australia

## Food chains

A food chain shows how food energy passes from one living thing to the next. Food chains start with plants, which use sunlight to make their own food. Plants are eaten by herbivores. Predators eat herbivores and smaller predators.

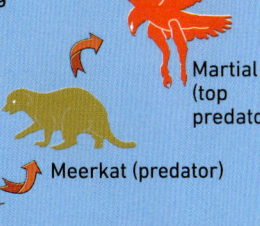

Martial eagle (top predator)

Meerkat (predator)

Imperial scorpion (predator)

Grasshopper (herbivore)

Grass

A FOOD CHAIN IN THE AFRICAN SAVANNA

**THE FORCE OF THE IMPACT MAY DECAPITATE (BEHEAD) ITS PREY!**

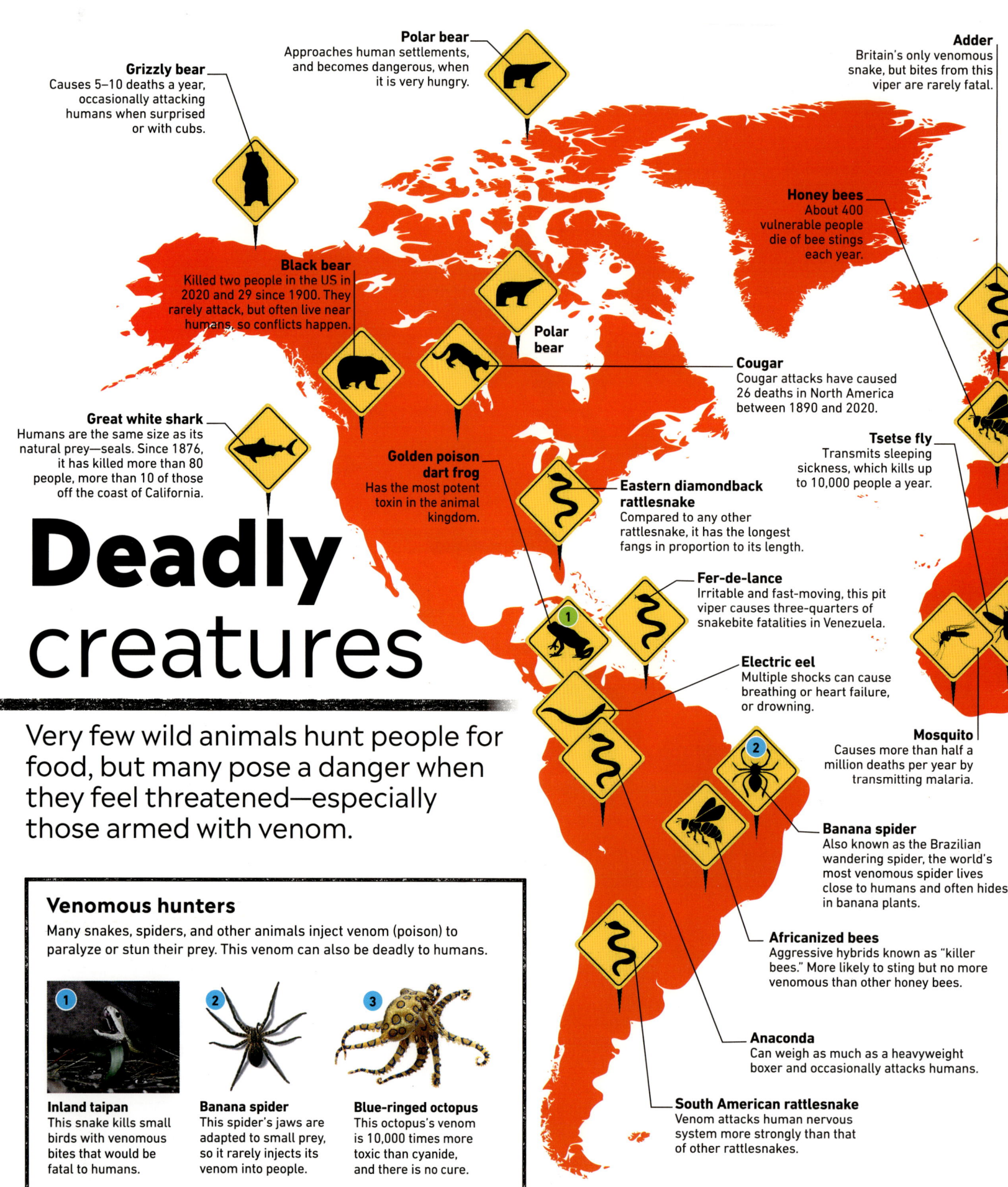

# Deadly creatures

Very few wild animals hunt people for food, but many pose a danger when they feel threatened—especially those armed with venom.

**Grizzly bear**
Causes 5–10 deaths a year, occasionally attacking humans when surprised or with cubs.

**Polar bear**
Approaches human settlements, and becomes dangerous, when it is very hungry.

**Adder**
Britain's only venomous snake, but bites from this viper are rarely fatal.

**Black bear**
Killed two people in the US in 2020 and 29 since 1900. They rarely attack, but often live near humans, so conflicts happen.

**Honey bees**
About 400 vulnerable people die of bee stings each year.

**Polar bear**

**Cougar**
Cougar attacks have caused 26 deaths in North America between 1890 and 2020.

**Great white shark**
Humans are the same size as its natural prey—seals. Since 1876, it has killed more than 80 people, more than 10 of those off the coast of California.

**Golden poison dart frog**
Has the most potent toxin in the animal kingdom.

**Tsetse fly**
Transmits sleeping sickness, which kills up to 10,000 people a year.

**Eastern diamondback rattlesnake**
Compared to any other rattlesnake, it has the longest fangs in proportion to its length.

**Fer-de-lance**
Irritable and fast-moving, this pit viper causes three-quarters of snakebite fatalities in Venezuela.

**Electric eel**
Multiple shocks can cause breathing or heart failure, or drowning.

**Mosquito**
Causes more than half a million deaths per year by transmitting malaria.

**Banana spider**
Also known as the Brazilian wandering spider, the world's most venomous spider lives close to humans and often hides in banana plants.

**Africanized bees**
Aggressive hybrids known as "killer bees." More likely to sting but no more venomous than other honey bees.

**Anaconda**
Can weigh as much as a heavyweight boxer and occasionally attacks humans.

**South American rattlesnake**
Venom attacks human nervous system more strongly than that of other rattlesnakes.

## Venomous hunters

Many snakes, spiders, and other animals inject venom (poison) to paralyze or stun their prey. This venom can also be deadly to humans.

**1. Inland taipan**
This snake kills small birds with venomous bites that would be fatal to humans.

**2. Banana spider**
This spider's jaws are adapted to small prey, so it rarely injects its venom into people.

**3. Blue-ringed octopus**
This octopus's venom is 10,000 times more toxic than cyanide, and there is no cure.

ANIMAL TOXINS ARE USEFUL. SCIENTISTS HAVE ADAPTED THE

**Living world**

# SOME VICTIMS OF **STONEFISH VENOM** SAY IT'S GOOD FOR THEIR ARTHRITIS

## Defensive poisons

Many animals use toxins (poisons) against predators. The poisons may be in spines or stings, or they may ooze from the skin.

**① Golden poison dart frog**
The skin has enough toxin to kill 10 people. It is effective against its snake predators.

**② Pufferfish**
The poison in puffers' skin and liver could kill a human, but these fish make a prized dish in Japan.

**③ Stonefish**
This fish's spines stop predators, but also endanger humans who are pricked by accident.

**Asp viper**
Causes about 90 percent of all snake bites in Italy, but only 4 percent of bites are fatal.

**European black widow spider**
Venom is 15 times stronger than a rattlesnake's.

**Fat-tailed scorpion**
Most dangerous scorpion in North Africa and the Middle East.

**Pallas's viper**
0.004 oz (0.1 gram) of venom can kill a human, but only strikes if threatened.

**Tiger**
Until recent improvements in tiger management, hunted and killed about 50 people every year in the Sundarbans mangroves of India.

**Common krait**
Most venomous land snake in Asia.

**Malayan pit viper**
Responsible for 700 snakebites annually in Malaysia.

**Pufferfish**
Eaten as *fugu* in Japan and *bok-uh* in Korea, but some parts highly poisonous. Accidents happen when untrained people catch and eat the fish.

**Puff adder**
Lives in heavily populated areas and is the most dangerous snake in Africa.

**Elephant**
Attacks people when threatened and kills nearly 300 people a year.

**African lion**
Kills 70 people a year in Tanzania, either by hunting them for food, or in defense.

**Hippopotamus**
Causes more than 300 deaths a year, sometimes by upturning boats.

**Asian cobra**
Responsible for more human deaths than any other snake.

**Komodo dragon**
Giant lizard that grows up to 10 ft (3 m) long and may, very rarely, attack and eat humans.

**Box jellyfish**
Has enough toxin to kill 60 humans, and in the Philippines 20–40 people die each year from stings.

**Lionfish**
Its venomous spines can cause severe injuries, breathing difficulties, and temporary paralysis.

**Saltwater crocodile**
Makes frequent fatal attacks on humans in New Guinea, the Solomon Islands, and Indonesia.

**Stonefish**
Venom injected by spines causes unbearable pain and death in a few hours if not treated.

**Cape buffalo**
Attacks when defending itself and kills more than 200 people a year.

**Black mamba**
Fastest snake on Earth and kills any human it bites unless the victim takes antivenom.

**Six-eyed sand spider**
There is no antivenom for its bite but (luckily) it is shy and has little contact with people.

**Blue-ringed octopus**
Enough toxin in its body to kill 26 adult humans. It can cause respiratory failure.

**Redback spider**
Also known as the Australian black widow. Deaths are rare, but bites can result in fatal complications.

**Inland taipan**
Deadliest venom of any land snake, but snake scientists are almost the only known victims. They recovered after treatment with antivenom.

**Funnel-web spider**
Its extremely toxic venom could kill a small child in 15 minutes.

**Tiger snake**
In humans, 60 percent of untreated bites result in serious poisoning or death.

**TOXIN FROM POISON DART FROGS TO PRODUCE A POTENT PAINKILLER.**

49

### How the aliens invade

**Stowaways**
Fleas and other parasites can hitch a ride via animal or human hosts. Rats, mice, and insects can travel hidden in ships' cargo. Some species sneak in when empty cargo ships take on local seawater as ballast, then pump it out at their destination. Every day, large numbers of marine organisms are transported around the globe in this way.

**Black rat**

**Introduced by humans**
Some species are deliberately introduced by humans. This can be by hunters, for meat, fur, or sport; by farmers; or for biological control, where a new species is introduced to control native pests. Some invaders are escaped pets, or plants washed out of home aquariums. A few have even been released by immigrants who introduce familiar wildlife to remind them of home!

**Cane toad**

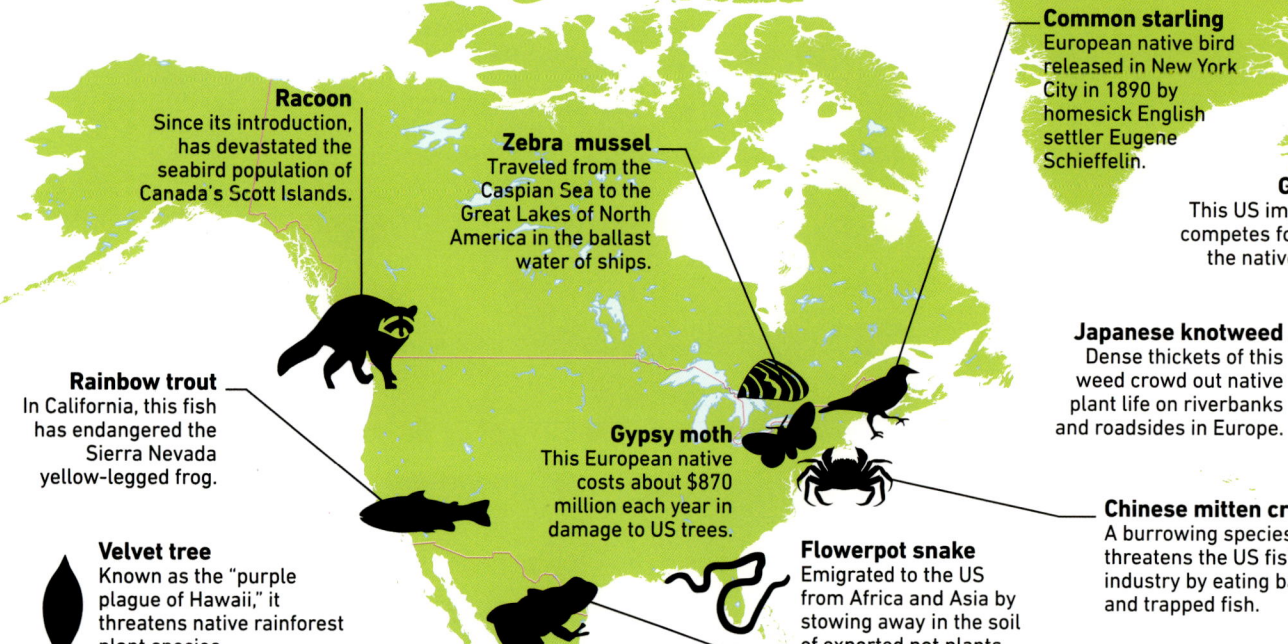

**Racoon** — Since its introduction, has devastated the seabird population of Canada's Scott Islands.

**Zebra mussel** — Traveled from the Caspian Sea to the Great Lakes of North America in the ballast water of ships.

**Common starling** — European native bird released in New York City in 1890 by homesick English settler Eugene Schieffelin.

**Stoat** — Introduced to islands off Denmark and the Netherlands, it eradicated the native water voles.

**Gray squirrel** — This US import to Britain competes for habitat with the native red squirrel.

**Rainbow trout** — In California, this fish has endangered the Sierra Nevada yellow-legged frog.

**Gypsy moth** — This European native costs about $870 million each year in damage to US trees.

**Japanese knotweed** — Dense thickets of this weed crowd out native plant life on riverbanks and roadsides in Europe.

**Velvet tree** — Known as the "purple plague of Hawaii," it threatens native rainforest plant species.

**Flowerpot snake** — Emigrated to the US from Africa and Asia by stowing away in the soil of exported pot plants.

**Chinese mitten crab** — A burrowing species that threatens the US fishery industry by eating bait and trapped fish.

**Feral pig** — In Mexico's Revillagigedo Islands, this former farm animal preys on the endangered Townsend's shearwater bird.

**American bullfrog** — Native to North America, it is now a resident of more than 40 countries.

**Fire ant** — Threatens tortoises on the Galápagos Islands by eating hatchlings and attacking adults.

**Red-vented bulbul** — A major agricultural pest in Tahiti, it feeds on fruit and vegetable crops.

**Feral goat** — Has caused serious damage to native vegetation on the Galápagos Islands.

**Africanized honey bee** — Specially bred for survival in the tropics, this "killer bee" turned out to be too aggressive and unpredictable for beekeepers.

**Red Deer** — Introduced from Europe to provide sportspeople with game.

**House mouse** — With no predators on Gough Island, non-native mice have grown to three times their usual size.

## ABOUT 90 PERCENT OF THE WORLD'S ISLANDS HAVE NOW BEEN INVADED BY RATS

# Alien invasion

Invasive species are animals or plants that enter and thrive in an environment where they are not native. Native species (plants and animals already living there) usually have no defense. The invading aliens can wipe out native species by preying on them or out-competing them.

**Living world**

**Signal crayfish**
Introduced from North America to Scandinavia for food, but carries "crayfish plague" which hits native crayfish.

**"Warty" comb jellyfish**
A recent arrival via tankers from the US, it peaked at more than 95 percent of the weight of all living things in the Black Sea.

**Chinese creeper vine**
Introduced to India in World War II to camouflage airfields, it is now a rampant weed.

**African land snail**
Brought to Taiwan as human food, it carries diseases, including meningitis.

**Small Indian mongoose**
Has destroyed seven native animal species on Japan's Amami Ōshima Island since 1979.

**Arctic fox**
Its introduction to the Aleutian Islands by fur hunters has been disastrous for ground-nesting birds.

**Brown tree snake**
Accidentally introduced, it has caused the extinction of most of Guam's native birds and lizards.

**Water hyacinth**
Kills fish and turtles in Papua New Guinea by blocking sunlight and starving the water of oxygen.

**Cane toad**
Australians are trying to control their 200 million cane toads (which were themselves introduced to control beetle crop pests) by culling and genetic engineering.

**Giant sensitive plant**
A serious weed in Thailand, it clogs irrigation systems and lowers crop yields.

**Nile perch**
This fish has contributed to the extinction of more than 200 fish species in Lake Victoria.

**Yellow crazy ants**
On Christmas Island, millions of red land crabs have been killed by these invaders.

**European rabbit**
More than 200 million rabbits overran Australia, from an original 24 released by an English immigrant for hunting.

**Brown rat**
A threat to island-nesting seabirds everywhere, it was eradicated from seven islands in Fiji in 2010.

**Polynesian rat (kiore)**
Stowed away with Māori settlers. Eats nesting seabirds.

**Common brushtail possum**
First brought to New Zealand to establish a fur trade.

**Prickly pear**
South Africa is looking at biological methods of controlling this invasive weed—for instance, by introducing the cactus moth, whose caterpillars eat it.

**Feral cat**
On the Kerguelen Islands, cats kill 1.2 million nesting seabirds every year.

**Dromedary camel**
Originally brought in for transport, there are now 1.1 million feral ("gone wild") camels in Australia.

**Northern Pacific seastar**
In Tasmania, volunteers organize "hunting days" to try to eradicate this Japanese starfish.

**Black swan**
Introduced in 1864 to New Zealand from Australia as an ornamental bird.

**Wasps**
Have reached plague proportions in the beech forests of the South Island.

**ANIMAL EXTINCTIONS THAT HAVE OCCURRED IN THE LAST 400 YEARS.**

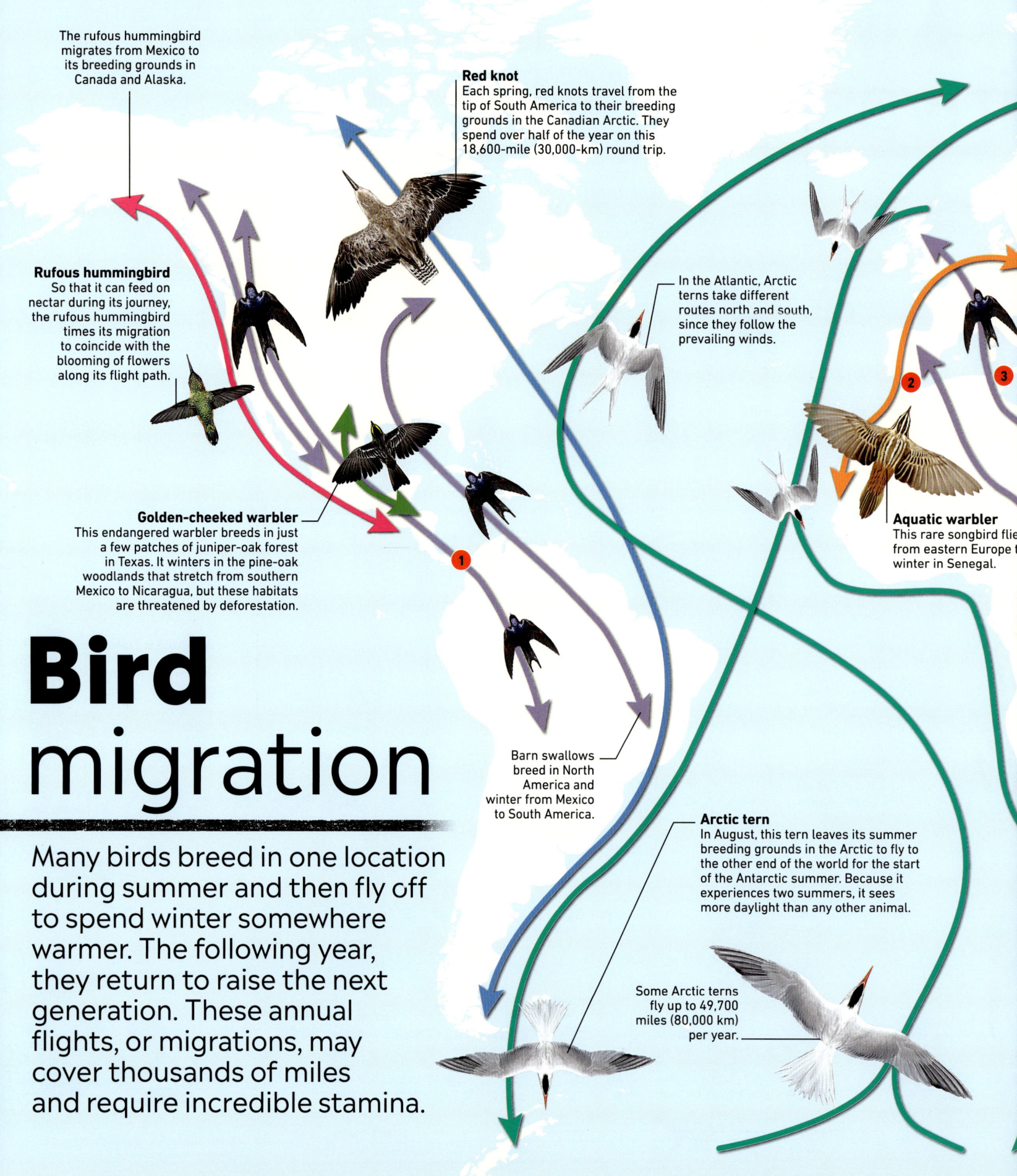

# Bird migration

Many birds breed in one location during summer and then fly off to spend winter somewhere warmer. The following year, they return to raise the next generation. These annual flights, or migrations, may cover thousands of miles and require incredible stamina.

The rufous hummingbird migrates from Mexico to its breeding grounds in Canada and Alaska.

**Rufous hummingbird**
So that it can feed on nectar during its journey, the rufous hummingbird times its migration to coincide with the blooming of flowers along its flight path.

**Red knot**
Each spring, red knots travel from the tip of South America to their breeding grounds in the Canadian Arctic. They spend over half of the year on this 18,600-mile (30,000-km) round trip.

**Golden-cheeked warbler**
This endangered warbler breeds in just a few patches of juniper-oak forest in Texas. It winters in the pine-oak woodlands that stretch from southern Mexico to Nicaragua, but these habitats are threatened by deforestation.

In the Atlantic, Arctic terns take different routes north and south, since they follow the prevailing winds.

**Aquatic warbler**
This rare songbird flies from eastern Europe to winter in Senegal.

Barn swallows breed in North America and winter from Mexico to South America.

**Arctic tern**
In August, this tern leaves its summer breeding grounds in the Arctic to fly to the other end of the world for the start of the Antarctic summer. Because it experiences two summers, it sees more daylight than any other animal.

Some Arctic terns fly up to 49,700 miles (80,000 km) per year.

IN A LIFETIME THAT CAN SPAN MORE THAN 30 YEARS, AN ARCTIC

Living world

**Red-breasted goose**
After wintering on the Black Sea coast, the red-breasted goose heads north to raise chicks on the Russian tundra.

Barn swallows that spend winter in India fly north to nest in northern Asia.

**Ferruginous duck**
This widespread duck breeds on marshes and lakes and makes relatively short migrations. Ferruginous ducks that breed in western China and Mongolia winter in India and Pakistan.

A bar-tailed godwit may travel up to 286,000 miles (460,000 km) during the course of its life.

Barn swallows of southern Africa fly to Europe to breed.

**Sociable lapwing**
In 2007, the sociable lapwing's migration route from east Africa to Kazakhstan and Russia was revealed for the first time by satellite tracking.

**Barn swallow**
Each year, huge flocks migrate between northern Australia and eastern Russia. These birds can catch insects on the wing and drink by scooping water from lakes.

## ARCTIC TERNS FLY FROM THE **ANTARCTIC** TO **GREENLAND** IN 40 DAYS

Aided by strong tailwinds at high altitude, the godwits can make the return journey to New Zealand in just over eight days.

**Bar-tailed godwit**
Bar-tailed godwits fly from New Zealand to breed in Alaska. On the return trip, one was tracked flying 7,258 miles (11,680 km) nonstop over the Pacific Ocean—the longest continuous journey ever recorded for a bird.

### Migration bottlenecks
Places that lie on the flight paths of many birds are known as migration bottlenecks. They are especially important for soaring birds such as storks and birds of prey. These birds can't fly far over water, so they rely on routes with the shortest sea crossings. Millions of birds may pass at these favorite spots.

1. **Panama**
About 3 million birds of prey use this land bridge between North and South America.

2. **Strait of Gibraltar**
Soaring birds fly to Europe from Africa on this sea crossing of only 9 miles (14 km).

3. **Sicily and Malta**
These islands are "stepping stones" for birds flying from Italy to Tunisia and Libya.

4. **Egypt**
Egypt has several bottlenecks—such as Suez, Hurghada, and Zaranik—for birds flying between Africa and Europe or Asia.

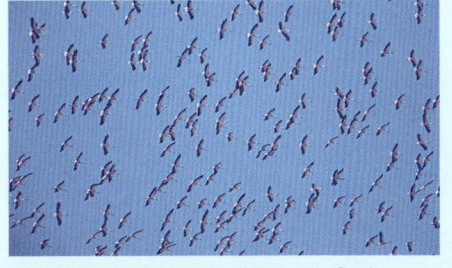

This flock of white storks flying over Spain reached Europe via the Strait of Gibraltar.

TERN MAY FLY THE EQUIVALENT OF THREE ROUND TRIPS TO THE MOON!

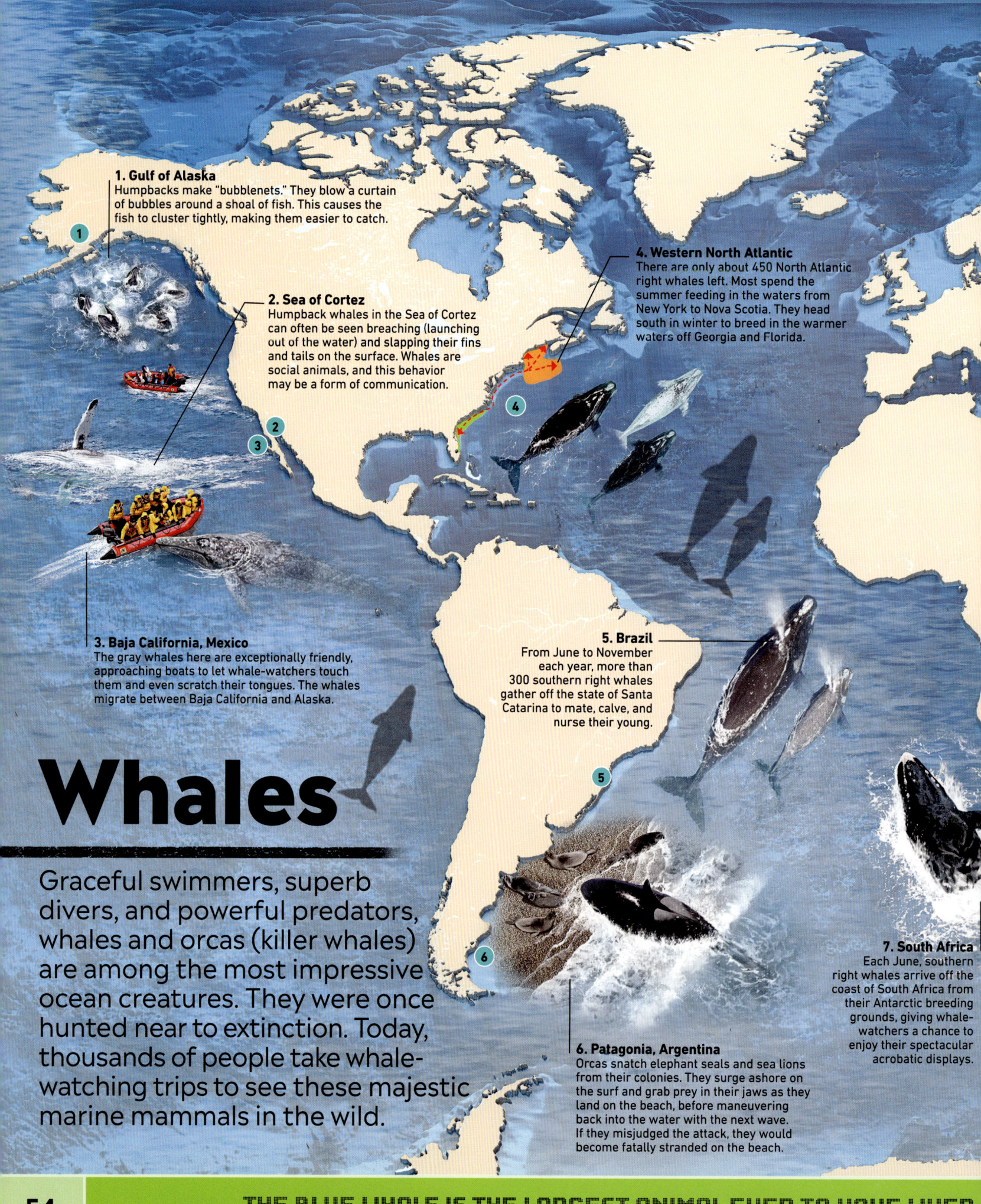

# Whales

Graceful swimmers, superb divers, and powerful predators, whales and orcas (killer whales) are among the most impressive ocean creatures. They were once hunted near to extinction. Today, thousands of people take whale-watching trips to see these majestic marine mammals in the wild.

**1. Gulf of Alaska**
Humpbacks make "bubblenets." They blow a curtain of bubbles around a shoal of fish. This causes the fish to cluster tightly, making them easier to catch.

**2. Sea of Cortez**
Humpback whales in the Sea of Cortez can often be seen breaching (launching out of the water) and slapping their fins and tails on the surface. Whales are social animals, and this behavior may be a form of communication.

**3. Baja California, Mexico**
The gray whales here are exceptionally friendly, approaching boats to let whale-watchers touch them and even scratch their tongues. The whales migrate between Baja California and Alaska.

**4. Western North Atlantic**
There are only about 450 North Atlantic right whales left. Most spend the summer feeding in the waters from New York to Nova Scotia. They head south in winter to breed in the warmer waters off Georgia and Florida.

**5. Brazil**
From June to November each year, more than 300 southern right whales gather off the state of Santa Catarina to mate, calve, and nurse their young.

**6. Patagonia, Argentina**
Orcas snatch elephant seals and sea lions from their colonies. They surge ashore on the surf and grab prey in their jaws as they land on the beach, before maneuvering back into the water with the next wave. If they misjudged the attack, they would become fatally stranded on the beach.

**7. South Africa**
Each June, southern right whales arrive off the coast of South Africa from their Antarctic breeding grounds, giving whale-watchers a chance to enjoy their spectacular acrobatic displays.

THE BLUE WHALE IS THE LARGEST ANIMAL EVER TO HAVE LIVED

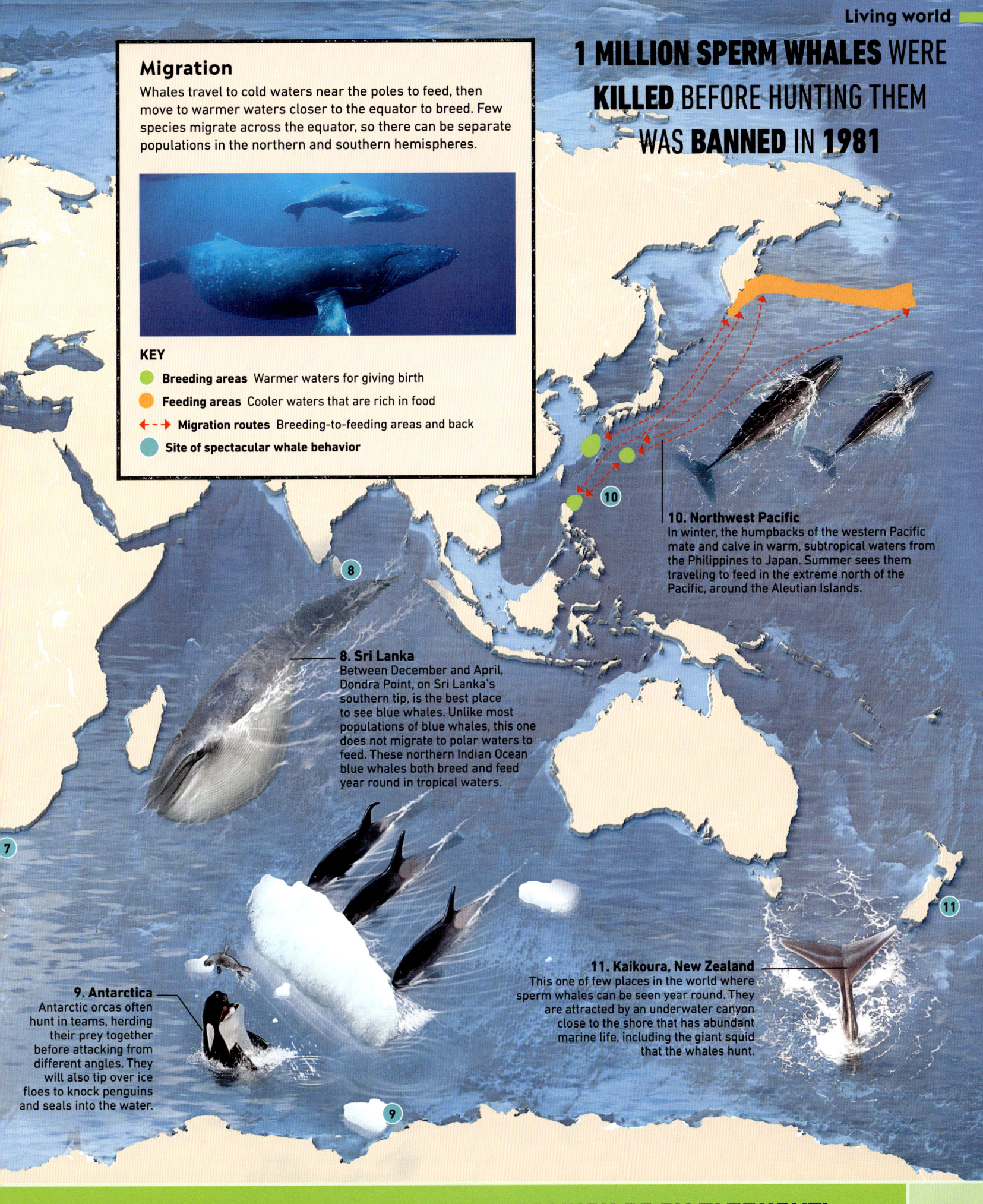

## SOME **SHARKS** GROW UP TO **30,000 TEETH** IN THEIR **LIFETIME**

### Freshwater sharks
Some shark species are found in freshwater habitats. The bull shark, for example, lives in warm coastal waters worldwide, but it sometimes swims up larger rivers and into lakes. Bull sharks are very territorial, so if they find humans swimming in their river, they may attack them.

**Mississippi River**
One bull shark reached Alton, Illinois, 1,150 miles (1,850 km) upstream.

**Potomac River**
Bull sharks up to 8 ft (2.4 m) long have been caught in the Potomac.

**Lake Nicaragua**
Bull sharks reach the lake via the San Juan River.

**Amazon River**
There have been sightings of bull sharks 1,200 miles (2,000 km) from the sea.

### Nicole
In 2003–04, a female great white shark, nicknamed Nicole, made the longest known migration by a shark. Nicole swam from Africa to Australia and back—more than 12,400 miles (20,000 km)—in 9 months. She mostly swam at the surface, but at times she reached depths of up to 3,200 ft (980 m).

Nicole's route was tracked using an electronic tag fitted to her fin.

### DISTRIBUTION OF SHARKS WORLDWIDE
Some shark species cruise almost all the world's oceans, while others have a more limited range, preferring either cooler or warmer seas.

**Whale shark**
The largest fish in the sea, reaching lengths of 40 ft (12 m) or more, the whale shark prefers warm waters. It feeds mainly on plankton.

**Basking shark**
At 30 ft (10 m) long, this is the second-largest fish. Found in temperate seas, it swims open-mouthed, filtering plankton from the water.

**Great white shark**
Found in the majority of the world's seas, the great white has made the most recorded attacks on humans. It can swim at more than 25 mph (40 kph).

**Great hammerhead shark**
Often found near tropical reefs, the great hammerhead preys on stingrays, using its hammer to pin down the fish before biting them.

**Port Jackson shark**
A reef-dweller from around southern Australia, this shark has wide, flat teeth that crush hard-shelled prey such as oysters, snails, and crabs.

**Pygmy shark**
At 8–10 in (20–25 cm) long, this is one of the smallest sharks. It hunts squid at depths of up to 6,000 ft (1,800 m) in subtropical and temperate seas.

Living world

# Sharks

Fast, powerful, and armed with razor-sharp teeth, sharks are superb predators. They are much feared, but attacks on people are relatively rare. Humans, in contrast, kill 100 million sharks per year.

**Subarctic species**
Piked dogfish inhabit temperate and cool seas, venturing as far north as the edge of the Arctic Circle.

**Ganges River**
In the Ganges and Brahmaputra, the bull shark is often mistaken for the rare Ganges shark.

**Wide distribution**
The great white shark has one of the greatest ranges of any shark species. However, it is not found in polar waters.

**Zambezi River**
Bull sharks are known to attack young hippos.

**Nicole's route**
The trip from South Africa to Australia took Nicole the great white shark 99 days. After about 3 months, she set off again on the return journey.

**Pacific angel shark**
This shark of the eastern Pacific lies on the seabed and ambushes passing fish. It is superbly camouflaged by its mottled, sandy back.

**Ornate wobbegong**
Elaborately patterned and with fleshy projections around its jaws, this shark inhabits tropical waters, mainly around the Australian coast.

**Frilled shark**
With its flat head and eellike body, this frilled shark looks very different than other sharks. It lives near the seabed in deep water.

**Longnose sawshark**
The longnose lives off southern Australia. Its snout is a long, sawlike projection edged with rows of large, sharp teeth.

**Bull shark**
This shark is one of the most dangerous to humans. It preys on sharks, rays, and other fish, as well as squid, turtles, and crustaceans.

**Piked dogfish**
Once among the most abundant sharks, the piked dogfish is now threatened as a result of overfishing. It gathers in shoals by the thousand.

DROPS OF BLOOD IN THE WATER FROM 3 MILES (5 KM) AWAY.

# Americas

**1. North American white sturgeon**
Similar to sturgeons living 100 million years ago, this fish depends heavily on its sense of smell.

**2. American paddlefish**
Takes its name from its long, paddle-shaped snout.

**3. Alligator gar**
Hides in aquatic plants to ambush its prey.

**4. Electric eel**
Generates huge electric shocks to stun prey and ward off attackers.

**5. Redtail catfish**
Stops feeding to shed its skin like a snake.

**6. Spectacled caiman**
Named after the bony ridge between its eyes.

**7. Arapaima**
The adult fish relies on air-breathing, not gills, to get oxygen. But its need to come to the surface makes it vulnerable to hunters.

**8. Amazon river dolphin**
Hunts in the murky water by sonar and uses its long snout to catch prey hiding in underwater plants. Females are normally larger than males.

# Eurasia

**9. Wels catfish**
Uses its fins to capture prey before swallowing its catch whole.

**10. Beluga sturgeon**
The world's largest river fish, it spends some of its life in salt water. Extra-large beluga no longer exist due to persistent overfishing and poaching of the species.

A LARGE **CROCODILE** CAN GO FOR MORE THAN **1 YEAR** BETWEEN **MEALS**

**North American white sturgeon** 1
20 ft (6.1 m)
Columbia River

**Alligator gar** 3
8–10 ft (2.4–3 m)
Mississippi River

**American paddlefish** 2
7 ft (2.2 m)
Mississippi River

**Redtail catfish** 5
4.3 ft (1.3 m)
Essequibo River

**Spectacled caiman** 6
8.2 ft (2.5 m)
Essequibo River

**Electric eel** 4
6.7 ft (2 m)
Orinoco River

**Marbled lungfish** 11
6.6 ft (2 m)
River Nile

**Arapaima** 7
8.2 ft (2.5 m)
Amazon River

**Amazon river dolphin** 8
8.2 ft (2.5 m)
Amazon River

**Goliath tigerfish** 12
4.9 ft (1.5 m)
Congo River

# Becoming giant

The sizes of river monsters shown here are mainly extreme historical records. It has always been rare for them to reach such sizes, but is especially so these days, since most are overfished and several are critically endangered.

# Australasia

**22. Saltwater crocodile**
The largest reptile in the world, it can kill and eat prey as large as horses and will not hesitate to kill humans who invade its territory.

**23. Freshwater crocodile**
Much smaller than its saltwater relative, it will not attack humans unless provoked.

IN ANCIENT JAPANESE FOLKLORE, A GIANT CATFISH, NAMAZU,

# Living world

### Africa

**11. Marbled lungfish** In the dry season, digs itself into a mud cocoon for up to 2 years.

**12. Goliath tigerfish** Fierce fish known to attack humans.

**13. Nile perch** When brought to live in new rivers and lakes, it can kill so many fish that it causes the extinction of native fish species.

### Asia

**14. Giant devil catfish** This rare species has sharp teeth similar to a shark's.

**15. Wallago** Human remains have been found inside its stomach.

**16. Gavial** An endangered crocodilian with a long, thin snout, good for catching fish. Rarely grows to 23 ft (7 m).

**17. Chinese giant salamander** The world's largest living amphibian.

**18. Giant freshwater stingray** Finds its prey using an electric field sensor.

**19. Kaluga** Cannibalism is common among these sturgeons of the Russian Far East.

**20. Taimen** The largest of the salmon family, also called the "Mongolian terror trout."

**21. Giant pangasius** Also known as the "dog-eating catfish." Another critically endangered fish.

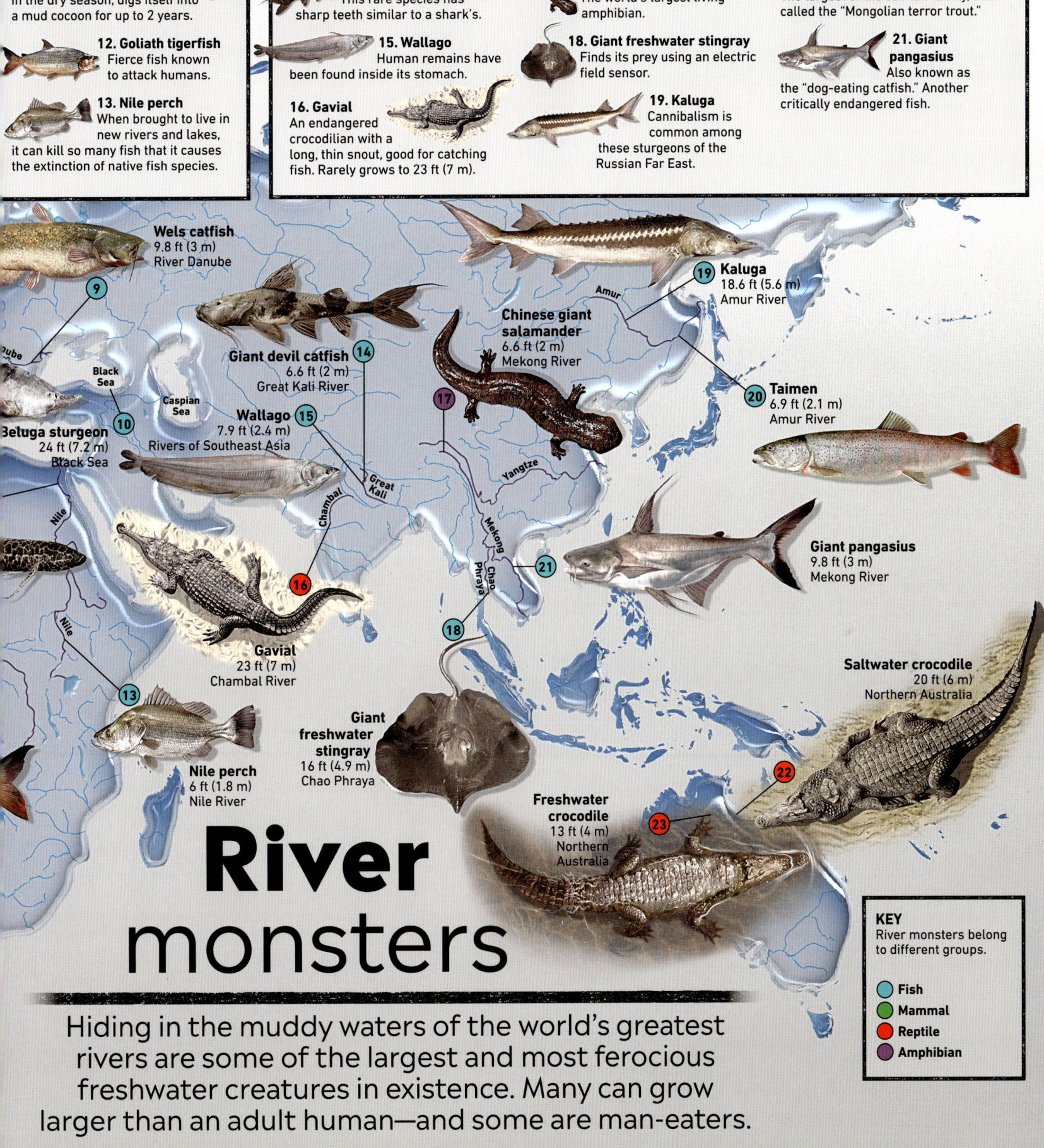

# River monsters

Hiding in the muddy waters of the world's greatest rivers are some of the largest and most ferocious freshwater creatures in existence. Many can grow larger than an adult human—and some are man-eaters.

**KEY** River monsters belong to different groups.
- Fish
- Mammal
- Reptile
- Amphibian

LIVES IN THE MUD UNDER THE SEA AND CAUSES EARTHQUAKES.

**KEY**
Some insects are found the world over, and some survive only in specific habitats and locations. The insects shown in this map are in locations where they are frequently found.

- 🟠 Insect swarms
- 🔵 Insect record-breakers

**Types of swarms**
When insects form a large group that moves as a single unit, it is called a swarm. Insects sometimes migrate in swarms, or they swarm when looking for a new home, a mate, or for food.

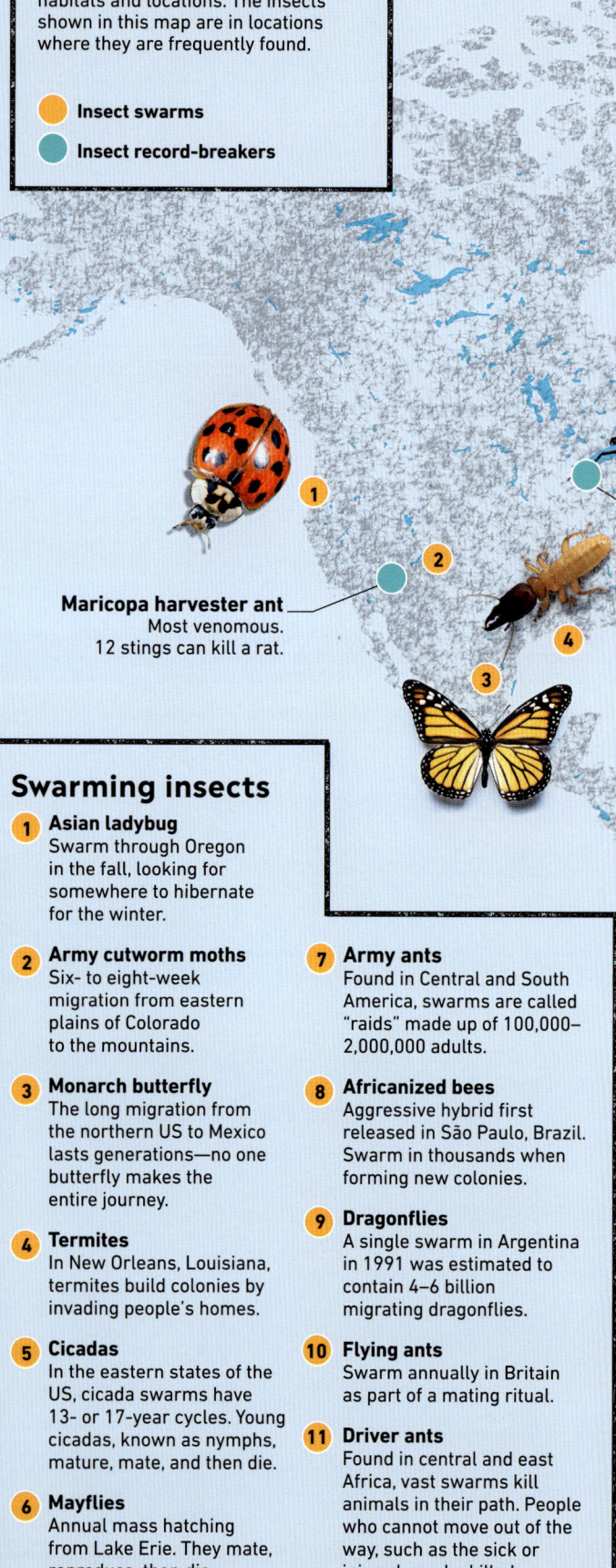

**Maricopa harvester ant**
Most venomous. 12 stings can kill a rat.

**Mayflies**
Shortest adult life. Mayflies spend most of their lives as water-living nymphs. They transform into winged adults that live just long enough to mate and lay eggs. The most extreme example is the American sand-burrowing mayfly, whose adult life lasts just a few minutes.

***Rhyniognatha***
Earliest. A 400-million-year-old fossil was found in Scotland in 1919. Scientists believe it may have been winged.

**Fairy wasp**
Smallest. 0.006 in (0.14 mm) long. Only visible under a powerful microscope.

**Termite queen**
Longest life. Can live up to 45 years.

**Goliath Beetle**
Heaviest larva. Weighs up to 3.5 oz (100 g).

## Swarming insects

1. **Asian ladybug** — Swarm through Oregon in the fall, looking for somewhere to hibernate for the winter.
2. **Army cutworm moths** — Six- to eight-week migration from eastern plains of Colorado to the mountains.
3. **Monarch butterfly** — The long migration from the northern US to Mexico lasts generations—no one butterfly makes the entire journey.
4. **Termites** — In New Orleans, Louisiana, termites build colonies by invading people's homes.
5. **Cicadas** — In the eastern states of the US, cicada swarms have 13- or 17-year cycles. Young cicadas, known as nymphs, mature, mate, and then die.
6. **Mayflies** — Annual mass hatching from Lake Erie. They mate, reproduce, then die.
7. **Army ants** — Found in Central and South America, swarms are called "raids" made up of 100,000–2,000,000 adults.
8. **Africanized bees** — Aggressive hybrid first released in São Paulo, Brazil. Swarm in thousands when forming new colonies.
9. **Dragonflies** — A single swarm in Argentina in 1991 was estimated to contain 4–6 billion migrating dragonflies.
10. **Flying ants** — Swarm annually in Britain as part of a mating ritual.
11. **Driver ants** — Found in central and east Africa, vast swarms kill animals in their path. People who cannot move out of the way, such as the sick or injured, can be killed.
12. **Mosquito swarms** — In May 2012, immense swarms of mosquitoes hatched from a lake near Mikoltsy, Belarus.
13. **Locusts** — The largest swarm recorded was in Kenya in 1954. It covered 77 sq miles (200 sq km) and involved an estimated 10 billion locusts.
14. **Midges** — The midges that form mating swarms start out as underwater larvae in lakes. Once they can fly, they take off and try to find a mate.

AT ANY ONE TIME, THERE ARE AN ESTIMATED 10 QUINTILLION

Living world

**Honey bees**
Bees swarm when they leave their hive to find a new home. Once a small number of special "scouts" have agreed on the most suitable site, the queen and the main cluster of bees fly to the new location.

**Monarch migration**
Every year, by instinct alone, millions of monarch butterflies travel up to 2,500 miles (4,000 km) from northern parts of America to warmer climates as far south as Mexico, before they return north in spring.

**Midges**
Huge swarms appear over Lake Victoria in Africa during the annual mating season, as thousands of dancing male midges try to attract females. Swarms are so big, they look like giant brown clouds.

**Froghopper**
Highest jumper. Jumps 28 in (71 cm)—150 times its own height, which is comparable to a human jumping over a 60-story building!

**Himalayan cicada**
Loudest. Calls at up to 120 decibels—as loud as an ambulance siren.

**Stink bug**
Smelliest. Toxic odor can be smelled by humans about 3.3–5 ft (1–1.5 m) away.

**Flea**
Longest jumper. Can jump more than 200 times its body length.

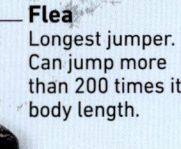

## SCIENTISTS ESTIMATE 4–20 MILLION TYPES OF INSECTS HAVE YET TO BE DISCOVERED

**Dung beetle**
Strongest. Can pull 1,141 times its own body weight—the equivalent to an average human pulling six double-decker buses full of people.

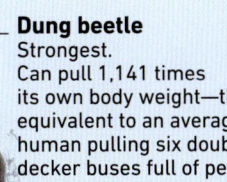

**Chan's megastick**
Longest. 22.3 in (56.7 cm). Only six specimens have ever been found, all on the island of Borneo.

**Australian tiger beetle**
Fastest runner. 5.6 mph (9 kph). Equivalent to a human running at 480 mph (770 kph).

**Giant weta**
Heaviest. Weighs up to 2.5 oz (70 g)—heavier than a sparrow.

**Horsefly**
Fastest flyer. Maximum speed recorded briefly on takeoff at 90 mph (145 kph). The next fastest are dragonflies and hawk moths, at about 30–35 mph (50–55 kph).

# Insects

We know of more than 1 million different types of insects, and more are identified every year. They have fascinating habits, and their strange appearances can be seen with the help of microscopes and special cameras.

[10,000,000,000,000,000,000] INDIVIDUAL INSECTS ALIVE.

# Living world

**Butterwort**
Boggy parts of Europe, North and South America, and Asia. Sticky hairs on its leaves trap insects.

**Monkshood**
Mountains of the northern hemisphere. Also known as aconite, it is a source of a deadly poison contained in the seeds.

**KEY**

 **Poisonous plants** Some plants contain toxic chemicals. The map shows eight of the most poisonous.

 **Carnivorous plants** These plants trap and consume insects and other small creatures.

 **Incredible plants** Four amazing plants are highlighted on the map, but there are many thousands more worldwide.

**Sundew**
Worldwide in boggy places. Traps insects with droplets of glue coating its leaves.

**Waterwheel plant**
Africa, Asia, Australia, and Europe. Freshwater plant a little like an underwater Venus flytrap.

**Deadly nightshade**
Europe, north Africa, and west Asia

**Nepenthes rajah**
Borneo. This giant pitcher plant may sometimes catch rats or lizards to eat.

**Castor oil plant**
East Africa, Mediterranean, and India. Origin of the poison ricin.

**Rosary pea**
Indonesia. Toxins are used in herbal medicines of southern India.

**Welwitschia**
Namib Desert. Has just two straplike leaves. They can grow up to 20 ft (6.2 m) long over several centuries.

# World of plants

**Rainbow plant**
Australia. Catches insects on its sticky leaves.

**Terrestrial bladderwort**
Worldwide. Grows on wet, rocky surfaces and catches tiny prey in bladderlike traps.

Scientists estimate there are at least 400,000 species of plants on Earth— and possibly many thousands more. Some parts of the world have a rich diversity of plant life; in others, such as Antarctica, plants are scarce.

1,500 YEARS, BUT IN THAT TIME IT GROWS ONLY TWO GIANT LEAVES.

# Biodiversity

Richness of different life-forms, or species, is called biodiversity. Places such as tropical rainforests are naturally high in biodiversity. Harsh environments have fewer species, but those species might be unique and equally precious.

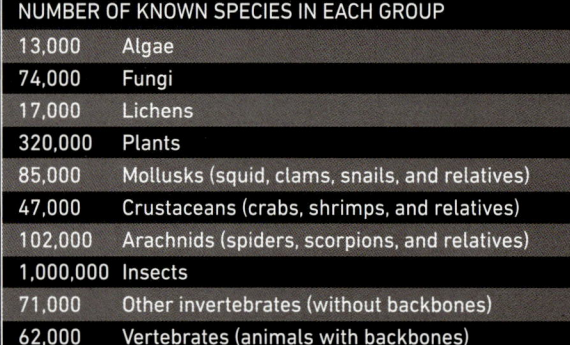

## Total number of life-forms

There are many thousands of species of vertebrate animals, such as birds and reptiles. But these numbers are dwarfed by the amazing number of other life-forms, particularly insects.

| NUMBER OF KNOWN SPECIES IN EACH GROUP | |
|---|---|
| 13,000 | Algae |
| 74,000 | Fungi |
| 17,000 | Lichens |
| 320,000 | Plants |
| 85,000 | Mollusks (squid, clams, snails, and relatives) |
| 47,000 | Crustaceans (crabs, shrimps, and relatives) |
| 102,000 | Arachnids (spiders, scorpions, and relatives) |
| 1,000,000 | Insects |
| 71,000 | Other invertebrates (without backbones) |
| 62,000 | Vertebrates (animals with backbones) |

### 70,000 weevils
Weevils form only one family of beetles, yet there are more different types than all the world's vertebrates.

Giraffe-necked weevil

*Cratosomus roddami*, a weevil

*Eupholus linnei*, a weevil

### Barren Arctic
Plants grow very slowly in the cold Canadian Arctic, so there is not a lot of food to go round. Vegetation is ground-hugging, with little variety of homes for small animals—unlike forests. Biodiversity is low.

### Rich Amazon
The Amazon is the largest and most diverse tropical forest on Earth. In general, large, continuous areas of habitat support the greatest diversity of species.

### Deserted Sahara
There are hardly any amphibians in this dry environment, but the few that survive here are uniquely adapted to the conditions. Preserving areas of pristine Sahara would ensure the survival of some rare creatures.

### Unique Atlantic Forest
What remains of the rainforest region in Brazil is not only rich in species. Because it is isolated from other rainforests, many of its species are also found nowhere else.

### KEY
This map shows the pattern of biodiversity across the world's land, combining measures of 5,700 mammal species, 7,000 amphibians, and 10,000 species of birds. This gives an overall measure, because the variety of these three groups usually mirrors the total biodiversity, including the numbers of different insects and plants. Scientists know biodiversity in the oceans is lower than on land, but it is not shown on the map.

Lowest — Highest
BIODIVERSITY (SPECIES RICHNESS)

SCIENTISTS ESTIMATE THAT GLOBAL BIODIVERSITY HAS FALLEN TO 84.6

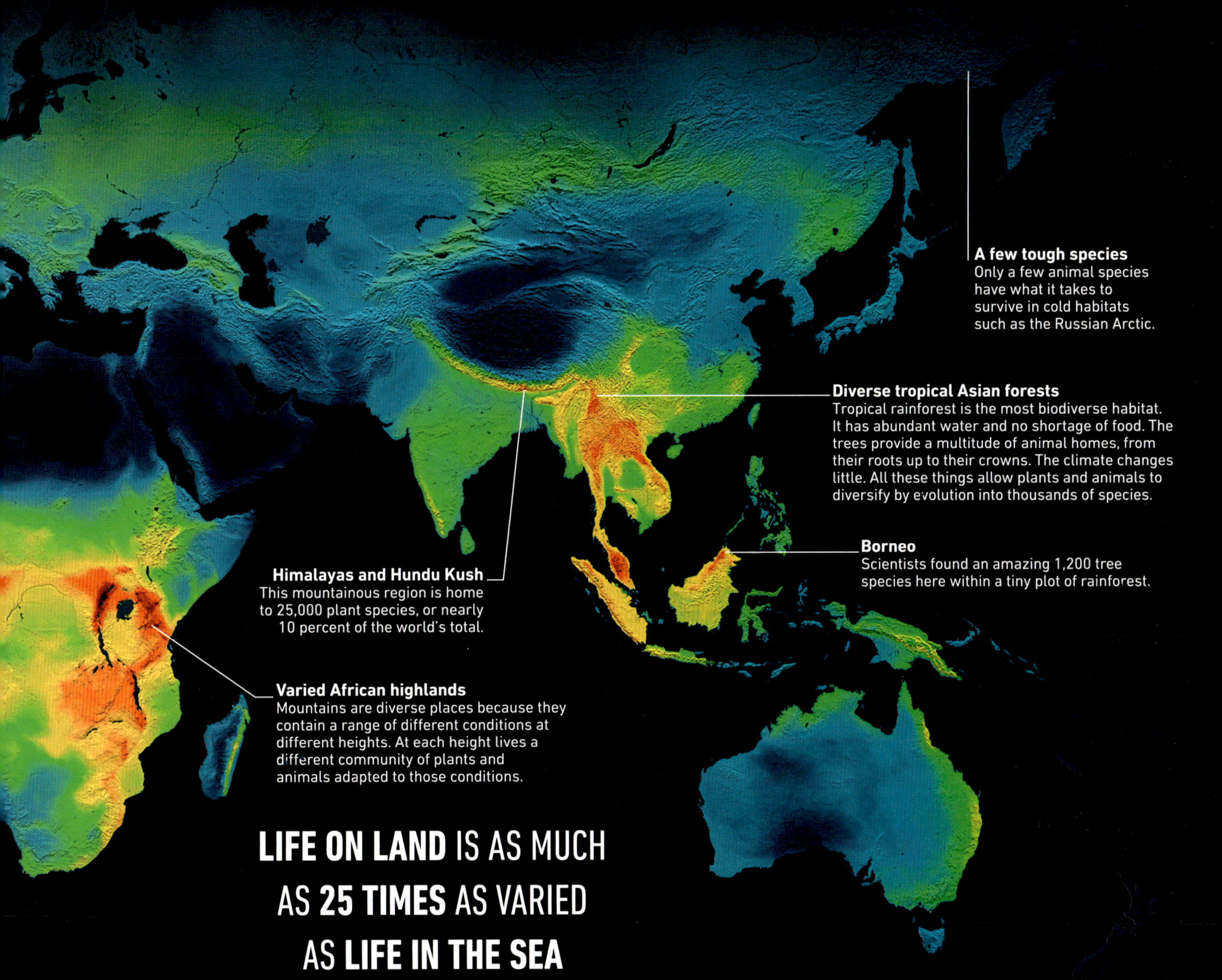

Living world

**A few tough species**
Only a few animal species have what it takes to survive in cold habitats such as the Russian Arctic.

**Diverse tropical Asian forests**
Tropical rainforest is the most biodiverse habitat. It has abundant water and no shortage of food. The trees provide a multitude of animal homes, from their roots up to their crowns. The climate changes little. All these things allow plants and animals to diversify by evolution into thousands of species.

**Borneo**
Scientists found an amazing 1,200 tree species here within a tiny plot of rainforest.

**Himalayas and Hundu Kush**
This mountainous region is home to 25,000 plant species, or nearly 10 percent of the world's total.

**Varied African highlands**
Mountains are diverse places because they contain a range of different conditions at different heights. At each height lives a different community of plants and animals adapted to those conditions.

## LIFE ON LAND IS AS MUCH AS 25 TIMES AS VARIED AS LIFE IN THE SEA

**POISON-DART FROGS**
There are 175 species in the poison-dart frog family, which lives in the tropical rainforests of Central and South America. They are all related, but each has evolved slightly differently.

Mimic poison-dart frog | Granular poison-dart frog

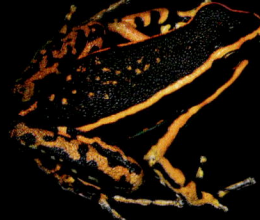
Three-striped poison-dart frog

Yellow-banded poison-dart frog

Brazil-nut poison-dart frog

Golden poison-dart frog

PERCENT OF ITS LEVEL BEFORE PEOPLE CHANGED THE LANDSCAPE.

# Unique wildlife

Some parts of the world are home to animals and plants that live nowhere else. These places are often remote islands, where life is cut off. In other cases, they are patches of unusual habitat, complete with the unique wildlife that depends on it.

**California**
A Mediterranean-type climate results in some unique forests featuring the world's largest living organism—the giant sequoia, a gigantic species of coniferous tree.

**Mexican pine-oak forests**
These forests on Mexican mountain ridges are patches of habitat not found anywhere else nearby. There are nearly 4,000 endemic plants and unique birds such as the Montezuma quail.

**Western Mediterranean**
Europe's hot spot of unique wildlife. One species of midwife toad lives only on Majorca, and Barbary macaques live only on Gibraltar and in patches of habitat in Morocco and Algeria.

**Canary Islands**
Rich in endemic plants, the Canary Islands off Africa gave their name to the bird that lives only here and on nearby Atlantic islands—the canary.

**Caribbean Islands**
Each island has its own versions of many plants and animals. This Cuban knight anole lives only on Cuba.

**Hawaii and Polynesia**
Only certain life-forms have reached these remote islands. Hawaii has no ants, but has 500 species of unique fruit flies, all evolved from a single species blown ashore 8 million years ago. Some of them are flightless and have taken up antlike lifestyles. Hawaii also has many unique plants, including the strange Hawaiian silversword, endemic to its mountaintops.

**Galápagos Islands**
These islands were made famous by Charles Darwin for their unique wildlife, including their giant tortoises.

**Tropical Andes**
Perhaps the richest region on Earth, these mountains are home to 664 species of amphibians, 450 of which are in danger of dying out. Of 1,700 bird species, 600—including this fiery-throated fruiteater—are found nowhere else.

**Atlantic Forest**
This thin strip of rainforest is cut off from the Amazon rainforest, so it has its own set of wildlife, including the endangered golden lion tamarin.

## 75 PERCENT OF THE UNIQUE PLANTS OF THE CANARY ISLANDS ARE ENDANGERED

NEARLY 7 PERCENT OF THE WORLD'S PLANTS ARE UNIQUE TO THE

# Living world

**ENDEMIC HOT SPOTS**
Scientists have shown that these regions have the greatest number of plant species living only within a small area. They call these species "endemic" to that area. In these hot spots of unique plants, scientists tend to find lots of endemic animals, too.

- Region rich in endemic species

**BIOMES**
- Tropical dry broad-leaved forest
- Tropical coniferous forest
- Temperate broad-leaved forest
- Temperate coniferous forest
- Tropical moist broad-leaved forest
- Boreal forest
- Savanna
- Flooded savanna
- Steppe
- Mountain grasslands and shrublands
- Mediterranean shrublands
- Desert and dry shrublands
- Arctic tundra
- Polar desert
- Mangroves

**Mountains of southwest China**
Each ridge of mountains has its own distinct wildlife. Endangered species, such as the Yunnan snub-nosed monkey, live only here.

**Eastern Mediterranean**
The Cedar of Lebanon lives only in a small area, including Lebanon, Israel, Palestine, and parts of Syria, Jordan, and Turkey.

**Philippines**
Of this country's 1,000 types of orchids, 70 percent grow nowhere else.

**Wallacea**
This region is named after 19th-century naturalist Alfred Russel Wallace, who noticed its unique wildlife such as the piglike babirusa.

**New Guinea**
This large island is home to many unique birds of paradise and several endemic tree kangaroos, including this species, the ursine tree kangaroo.

**Ethiopian Highlands**
These highlands are home to 30 endemic bird species and the endangered Ethiopian wolf.

**Sri lanka and Western Ghats**
This hot spot is home to 5,000 species of flowering plants, 139 mammal species, 508 birds, and 179 amphibian species.

**East Melanesia**
This string of islands has 3,000 endemic plant species and spectacular birdwing and swallowtail butterflies. This is a Ulysses swallowtail.

**Madagascar**
Ninety-eight percent of Madagascar's land mammals, 92 percent of its reptiles, 68 percent of its plants, and 41 percent of its breeding bird species exist nowhere else on Earth. All 16 mantella frogs are also endemic to the island.

**Sundaland**
Naturalists outline this region because its wildlife is distinct from next-door regions. One bizarre plant unique to Sundaland is *Rafflesia*, the stinking corpse lily.

**East African Highlands**
These islands of high ground in a sea of savanna support unusual plants such as this giant lobelia that grows on the slopes of Mount Kenya and Kilimanjaro.

**Cape region**
This is a small area of amazingly distinctive plantlife, including 6,000 endemic species such as this pincushion protea.

**Western Australia**
Like the South African Cape region, this is a "habitat island" of Mediterranean-type shrubland, full of plants found nowhere else, including the odd "kangaroo paw."

**New Caledonia**
Nothing like the strange, flightless kagu bird is found anywhere else in the world.

**TROPICAL ANDES, WHICH COVER ONLY 0.8 PERCENT OF THE LAND AREA.**

**Kittlitz's murrelet** — Alaska and Russian Far East

**Maui parrotbill** — Hawaii

**Vaquita** — Gulf of California

**Hawaiian monk seal** — Hawaii

**Iberian lynx** — Spain

**Blue iguana** — Grand Cayman Island, Caribbean

**Lamotte's roundleaf bat** — Mount Nimba (border area of Guinea, Liberia, and Côte d'Ivoire)

**Variable harlequin frog** — Costa Rica

**Short-tailed chinchilla** — Mountains on the Bolivia–Chile border

**Western gorilla** — Congo rainforest

**Glaucous macaw** — Argentina, Uruguay, Paraguay, and Brazil

**Blue-eyed black lemur** — Madagascar

**Maui parrotbill** In danger because of the loss of its forest habitat—only about 500 now survive.

**Hawaiian monk seal** Once hunted for its skin and oil, today many become tangled in fishing nets or die because of pollution.

## MORE THAN 7,000 ANIMAL SPECIES ARE CRITICALLY ENDANGERED

### In the red
Animals on the Red List—a list kept by the IUCN (International Union for the Conservation of Nature)—are in varying levels of endangerment. Those that are "critically endangered" may soon die out completely in the wild.

**Vaquita** This porpoise is the world's most endangered sea mammal; scientists estimate only about 10 are left.

**Kittlitz's murrelet** Thousands of these seabirds have been killed by sticky oil, spilled from giant tankers.

**Blue iguana** This lizard lives only on Grand Cayman Island. Numbers are increasing due to conservation.

**Variable harlequin frog** One of several harlequin frog species critically endangered due to a fungal disease.

**Short-tailed chinchilla** Hunted for its soft gray fur, this rock-dwelling rodent is now almost extinct in the wild.

**Glaucous macaw** Became rare because so many were caught and sold as pets. Only sighted twice in 100 years.

**Iberian lynx** If it dies out, it will be the first big cat species to go extinct in 10,000 years.

**Western gorilla** Many of these apes are killed for their meat, or have died from disease.

**Lamotte's roundleaf bat** This African mammal has become endangered mainly through the loss of its habitat.

**Greater bamboo lemur** Less than 100 have been spotted in 20 years of surveys.

**Blue-eyed black lemur** Like many other lemurs, this one could soon die out due to loss of its forest habitat.

**Russian sturgeon** This fish has been killed for its roe (eggs), known as caviar.

**Indian vulture** Many of these birds died after feeding on cattle that had been given drugs to help them work longer.

**Bactrian camel** Fewer than 1,000 survive in the wild.

**Irrawaddy river shark** As no one has seen this species for many years, it may be extinct in the wild.

**Sumatran orangutan** Just 15,000 of this species are left, since their forest is being cut down.

PEOPLE ARE WORKING HARD TO SAVE THE WORLD'S FEW REMAINING

Living world

# Endangered animals

Our world has thousands of species, or kinds, of animals. Many are in danger of dying out, mainly because humans are destroying their habitats, or homes. Some animals have not been seen in their habitats for 50 years or more and can be declared "extinct in the wild."

**Russian sturgeon**
Caspian, Black, and Azov seas; Ural, Volga, and Danube rivers

**Bactrian camel**
Gobi Desert of Mongolia and China

**Indian vulture**
Pakistan and India

**Sumatran orangutan**
Sumatra, Indonesia

**Greater bamboo lemur**
Madagascar

**Irrawaddy River shark**
Around the mouth of the Irrawaddy River, Myanmar

**Javan rhinoceros**
Java, Indonesia

**David's tiger butterfly**
Philippines

**Southern bluefin tuna**
These large, bony fish are dying out because too many have been caught by humans for food.

**Kakapo (owl parrot)**
These giant, flightless parrots were hunted by the first humans to settle in New Zealand. Today, only about 200 survive.

**Attenborough's long-beaked echidna**
New Guinea

**Woylie**
Western Australia

**Southern bluefin tuna**
Throughout southern oceans

**Kakapo**
Islands off the coast of New Zealand

**Javan rhinoceros**
Today, only about 50 adults survive in the remaining rainforest on Java.

**David's tiger butterfly**
One of the world's most endangered butterflies, found only in the Philippines.

**Attenborough's long-beaked echidna**
One of three critically endangered echidna (spiny anteater) species.

**Woylie**
This marsupial has recently declined dramatically and fewer than 5,000 survive in the wild.

KAKAPO—EVERY BIRD IS PROTECTED, AND EACH ONE HAS A NAME!

Living world

## Africa

**Quagga** Its very distinctive markings made it an easy target for hunters.

**Aldabra banded snail** A sudden decrease in rainfall, possibly caused by climate change, spelled extinction for this species.

**Large sloth lemur** Gorilla-sized species that died out in Madagascar about 400 years ago.

**Elephant bird** Huge flightless bird that was wiped out by hunting.

**Dodo** This flightless bird became extinct within only 100 years of humans and their domestic animals arriving on the island of Mauritius.

## Australasia

**Lesser bilby** Probably wiped out by cats and foxes.

**Eastern hare wallaby** Extinction was partly due to the introduction of cats, which hunted them.

**Desert-rat kangaroo** Thought extinct, recovered, then declared extinct again in 1994.

**King Island emu** Wiped out by sealers and their hunting dogs.

**Tasmanian wolf** Hunted and trapped by human settlers in Tasmania—its last hiding place.

**Moa** Victims of overhunting and loss of habitat.

---

**Eurasian aurochs** Extinct by 1627

**Woolly mammoth** Extinct by c. 1700 BCE

**Baiji** Last confirmed sighting in 2004

**Yunnan lake newt** Last seen in 1979

**Japanese sea lion** Last confirmed sighting in 1951

**Aldabra banded snail** (Aldabra Island, Indian Ocean) Last seen in 1997

**Large sloth lemur** Extinct by about 1600

**Dodo** (Mauritius, Indian Ocean) Extinct by 1690

**Desert-rat kangaroo** Last confirmed sighting in 1935, although sightings reported until the 1980s

**Eastern hare wallaby** Extinct by about 1890

**Lesser bilby** Reported sightings until the 1960s

**Moa** Extinct by about 1400

**King Island emu** Extinct by around 1802

**Tasmanian wolf** Presumed extinct in 1936

**ABOUT 26 PERCENT OF ALL MAMMALS ARE IN DANGER OF EXTINCTION**

TIMES FASTER THAN THE NATURAL EXTINCTION RATE.

# People and planet

**Sprawling city**
Los Angeles, California, stretches as far as the horizon in this photo taken from Mount Hollywood. The skyscrapers of downtown LA can be seen on the left.

# Introduction

Humans, together with animals and other living things, form what is called the biosphere—the living part of the world. Since modern humans first appeared in Africa about 200,000 years ago, we have colonized virtually the entire world—even hot deserts and the ice-cold Arctic. As we have done so, our impact on the biosphere has been far-reaching.

### Human impact
The human "footprint" on planet Earth is deep and broad. We have transformed the landscape—clearing forests to produce food, digging minerals and ores from the ground, and channeling and storing water to meet our needs. Our living space is concentrated into larger and larger cities, but these cities are hungry for food and energy taken from the surrounding land.

**Renewable energy**
New ways of harnessing the energy of sunlight and wind are reducing our use of fossil fuels. Unlike fossil fuels, these energy sources will never run out.

### Natural resources
Buried within Earth's crust there are limited supplies of minerals, metal ores, and fossil fuels (coal, oil, and gas). Once these reserves are exhausted, they cannot be replaced. Burning these fuels also damages Earth's atmosphere and is contributing to global warming.

### Population
For most of humanity's existence, the human population grew relatively slowly. In 10,000 BCE, there were only 1–5 million people on Earth. By 1000 BCE, after farming was invented, the population had increased to about 50 million. Since reaching the 1 billion mark in 1804, during the early Industrial Revolution, the population has expanded much more quickly than ever before.

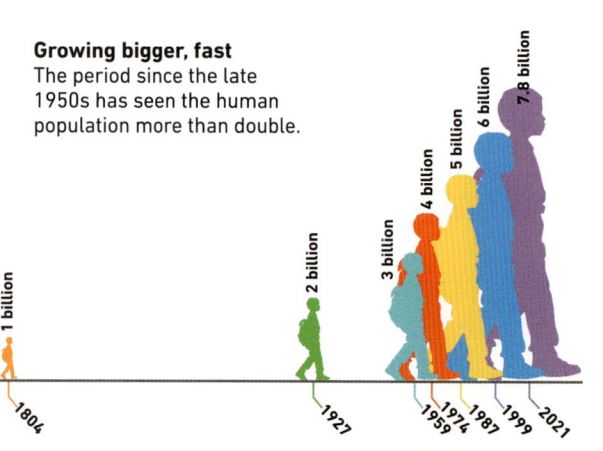

**Growing bigger, fast**
The period since the late 1950s has seen the human population more than double.

SINCE 1965, THE WORLD'S POPULATION HAS

# People and planet

**Agriculture**
In 1700 CE, about 7 percent of Earth's land area was used for growing crops and raising farm animals. Today, that figure has risen to about 50 percent.

**Pollution**
Vehicle exhaust gases, smoke and waste chemicals from factories, and oil spills all poison the environment, threatening plant and animal life.

**Conservation**
To protect the plant and animal life of unique habitats, many countries set up conservation areas, where no farming, industry, or new settlement can occur.

**Using water**
We build dams and reservoirs to store water. We need it for drinking, for use in industrial processes, and to irrigate crops and generate electricity.

## Successful species

Part of the success of humans is due to our ability to use the materials around us to give us protection and shelter. This ability opens up nearly every part of the globe for human living space, no matter how harsh the environment. Even thousands of years ago, the Inuit of the North American Arctic made coats from the fur of caribou (reindeer) and waterproof boots from seal skin. They found a way to live on the meager resources of the high Arctic.

**Inuit boat**
The *umiak* is a type of traditional open boat used by Inuit people. The frame is made of driftwood or whalebone, with a walrus- or seal-skin covering. These boats are still used, since the law allows whale hunting only with traditional Inuit tools.

DOUBLED, BUT ITS WEALTH HAS MULIPLIED BY SEVEN.

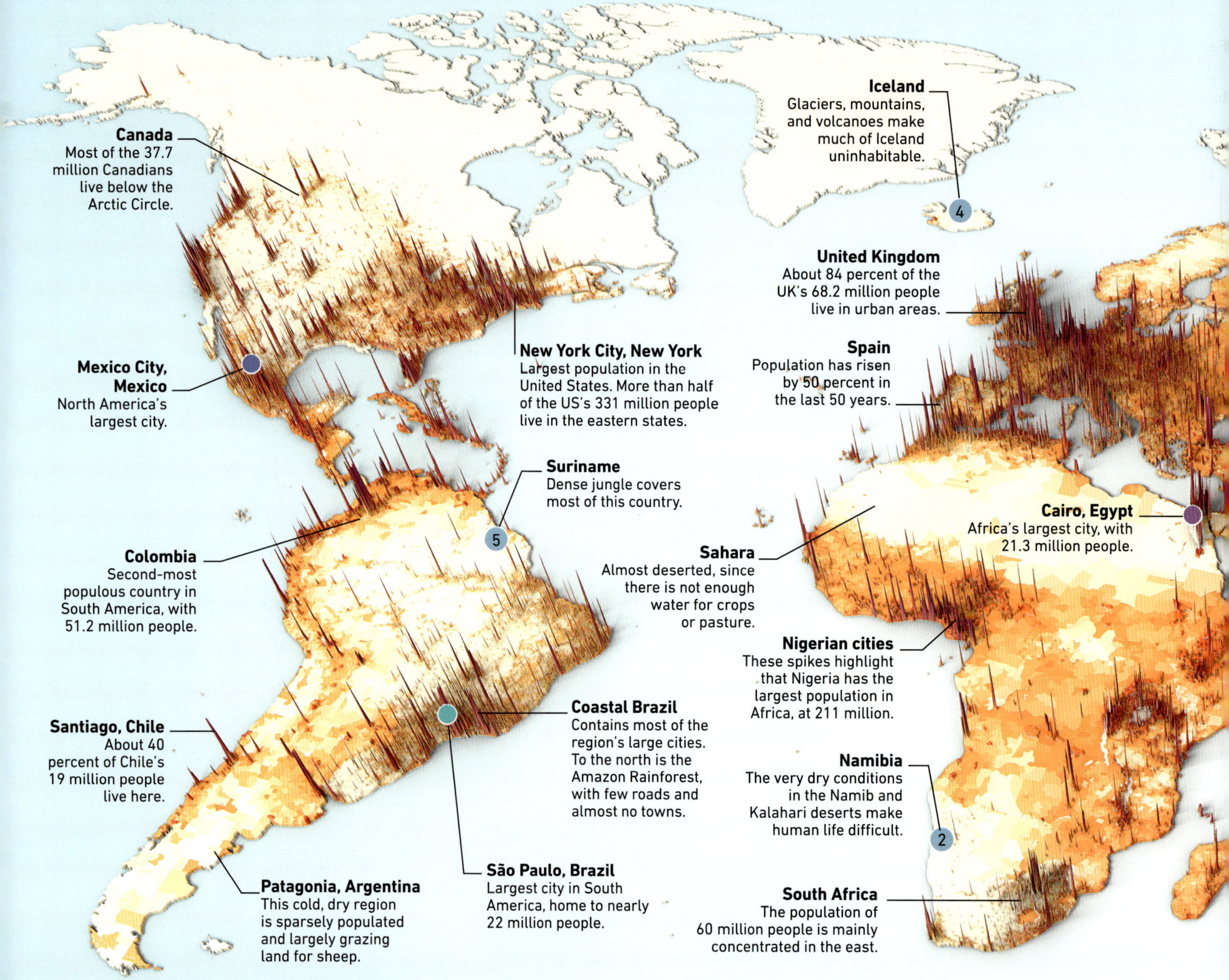

**Canada**
Most of the 37.7 million Canadians live below the Arctic Circle.

**Iceland**
Glaciers, mountains, and volcanoes make much of Iceland uninhabitable.

**United Kingdom**
About 84 percent of the UK's 68.2 million people live in urban areas.

**Mexico City, Mexico**
North America's largest city.

**New York City, New York**
Largest population in the United States. More than half of the US's 331 million people live in the eastern states.

**Spain**
Population has risen by 50 percent in the last 50 years.

**Suriname**
Dense jungle covers most of this country.

**Cairo, Egypt**
Africa's largest city, with 21.3 million people.

**Colombia**
Second-most populous country in South America, with 51.2 million people.

**Sahara**
Almost deserted, since there is not enough water for crops or pasture.

**Nigerian cities**
These spikes highlight that Nigeria has the largest population in Africa, at 211 million.

**Santiago, Chile**
About 40 percent of Chile's 19 million people live here.

**Coastal Brazil**
Contains most of the region's large cities. To the north is the Amazon Rainforest, with few roads and almost no towns.

**Namibia**
The very dry conditions in the Namib and Kalahari deserts make human life difficult.

**Patagonia, Argentina**
This cold, dry region is sparsely populated and largely grazing land for sheep.

**São Paulo, Brazil**
Largest city in South America, home to nearly 22 million people.

**South Africa**
The population of 60 million people is mainly concentrated in the east.

## Biggest cities

More than half the world's people now live in towns and cities, rather than in the countryside. Many cities have grown quickly and have been dubbed "megacities," with more than 10 million people in a metropolitan area. Below are the 10 largest.

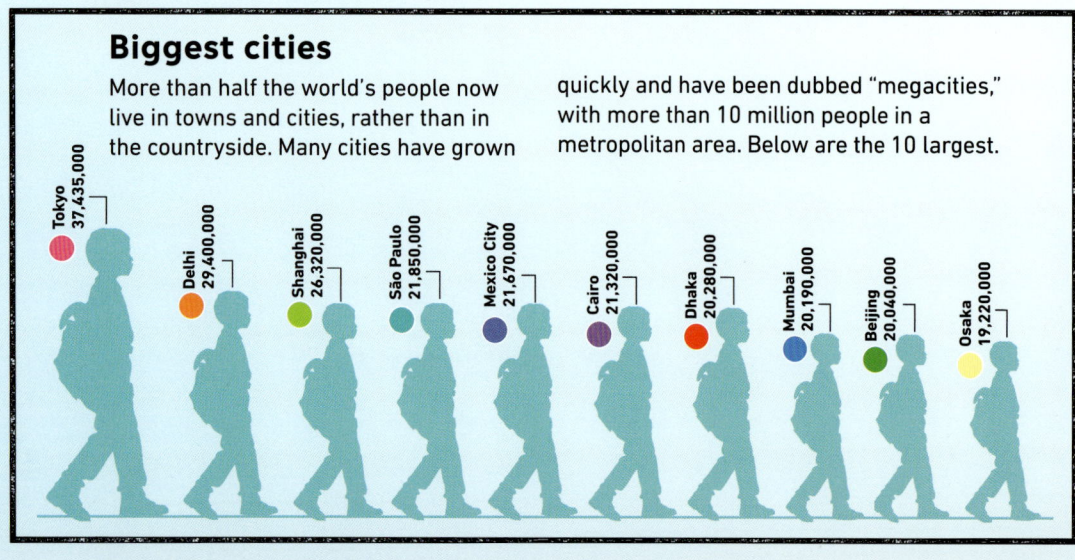

Tokyo 37,435,000
Delhi 29,400,000
Shanghai 26,320,000
São Paulo 21,850,000
Mexico City 21,670,000
Cairo 21,320,000
Dhaka 20,280,000
Mumbai 20,190,000
Beijing 20,040,000
Osaka 19,220,000

## KEY

The map shows population density, or how closely people are packed together. Denser places, such as cities, appear as red mountains.

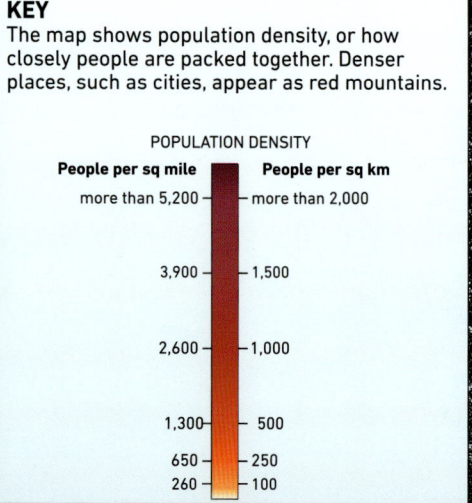

POPULATION DENSITY
People per sq mile | People per sq km
more than 5,200 | more than 2,000
3,900 | 1,500
2,600 | 1,000
1,300 | 500
650 | 250
260 | 100

**IN 1800, THE WORLD'S POPULATION WAS LESS THAN 1 BILLION PEOPLE.**

People and planet

# Where people live

The world's 7.8 billion people are not spread evenly across the globe: most live where there are natural resources and fertile land for farming. Some places are too hostile for humans to thrive.

**Siberia, Russia**
Few people live here, since the climate is too cold to grow crops. Some spikes show the location of cities based around extracting oil and gas from under the frozen tundra.

**Moscow, Russia**
Home to 12.5 million people.

**Kolkata, India**
Center of eastern India.

**Mongolia**
Little of the land is good for growing crops and many people are scattered in small communities of nomadic herdspeople.

**Shanghai, China**
China's largest city.

**Beijing**
The capital of China.

**Tokyo, Japan**
The largest city in the world since the 1960s.

**Osaka, Japan**
The second-largest city in Japan.

**Delhi, India**
India's capital sits in the densely populated Ganges River basin, home to 650 million people packed in at nearly 1,000 per sq mile (400 per sq km).

**Eastern China**
Most of China's 1.4 billion people live here.

**Manila, Philippines**
Not including its outlying districts, this is the world's most densely populated city.

**Dhaka, Bangladesh**
The world's most densely populated, continuously built-up area.

**Mumbai, India**
Fast-growing entertainment hub of India.

**Jakarta, Indonesia**
Of all Indonesia's islands, Java is by far the most crowded and contains the booming capital, Jakarta.

IN **MANILA**, PHILIPPINES, ON AVERAGE **296 PEOPLE LIVE** IN AN AREA THE SIZE OF A **SOCCER PITCH**

**Australia**
Australia's center is too dry to support farming and very few people live here.

**Melbourne, Australia**
Most of Australia's population lives on the southeastern coast, in cities including Melbourne.

**Auckland, New Zealand**
About one in three New Zealanders live here.

## Most sparsely populated countries

| | | total population | people per sq mile | people per sq km |
|---|---|---|---|---|
| 1 | Mongolia | 3,278,000 | 5.5 | 2.1 |
| 2 | Namibia | 2,541,000 | 8.0 | 3.1 |
| 3 | Australia | 25,500,000 | 8.6 | 3.3 |
| 4 | Iceland | 341,000 | 8.8 | 3.4 |
| 5 | Suriname | 587,000 | 9.7 | 3.8 |

ESTIMATES SUGGEST IT WILL BE CLOSE TO 10 BILLION BY 2060.

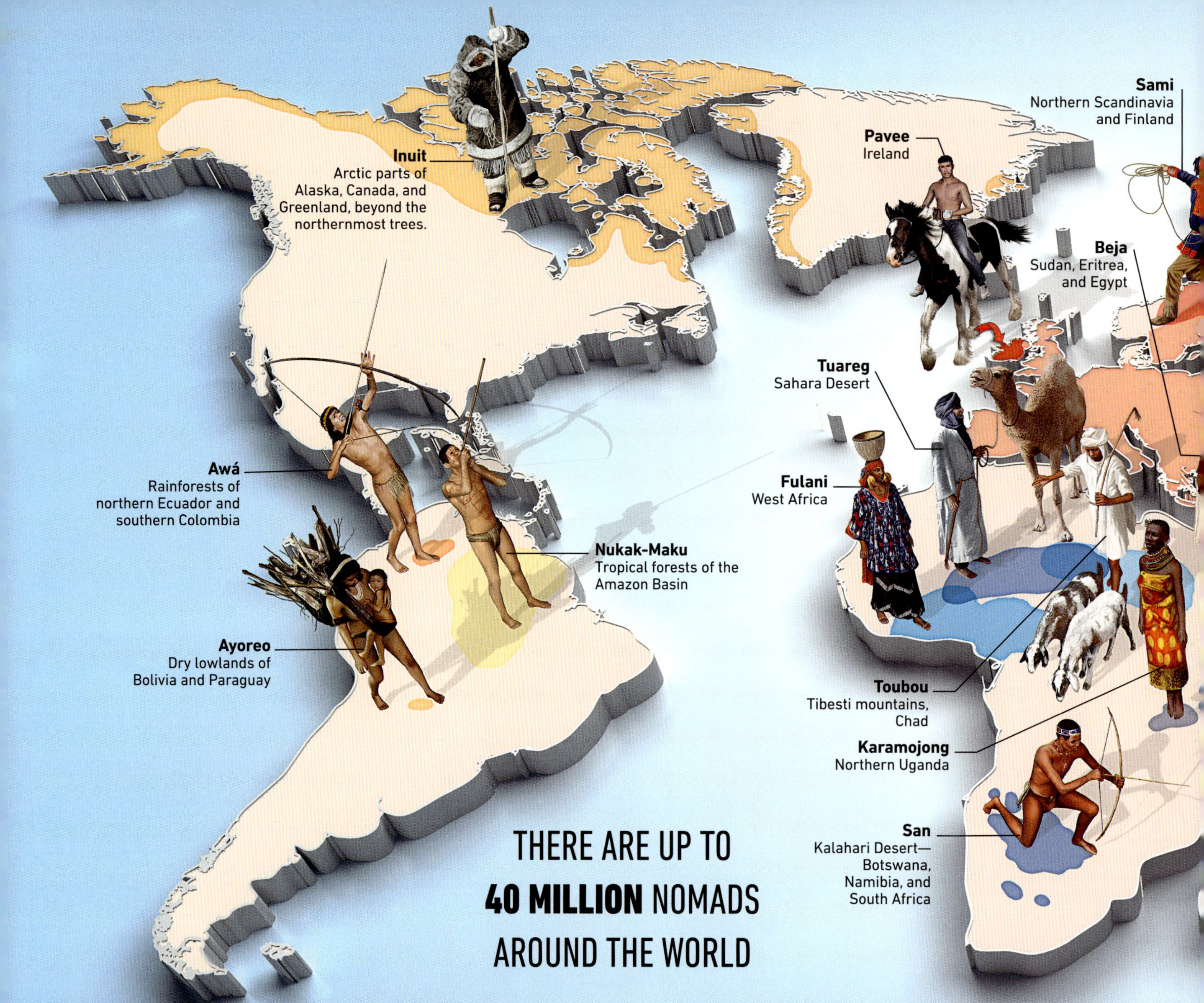

**Inuit**
Arctic parts of Alaska, Canada, and Greenland, beyond the northernmost trees.

**Pavee**
Ireland

**Sami**
Northern Scandinavia and Finland

**Beja**
Sudan, Eritrea, and Egypt

**Awá**
Rainforests of northern Ecuador and southern Colombia

**Tuareg**
Sahara Desert

**Fulani**
West Africa

**Nukak-Maku**
Tropical forests of the Amazon Basin

**Ayoreo**
Dry lowlands of Bolivia and Paraguay

**Toubou**
Tibesti mountains, Chad

**Karamojong**
Northern Uganda

**San**
Kalahari Desert—Botswana, Namibia, and South Africa

## THERE ARE UP TO 40 MILLION NOMADS AROUND THE WORLD

### Americas

**Inuit**
For 4,000 years, the Inuit have roamed the region they call Nunavut, "our land."

**Awá**
The Awá speak their own ancient language called Awa Pit.

**Nukak-Maku**
The Nukak people are expert hunters who were entirely isolated until 1988.

**Ayoreo**
The Ayoreo mix a hunter-gatherer lifestyle with agriculture.

### Europe

**Pavee, or Irish Travelers**
The Pavee have strict moral beliefs laid out in "The Travelers' Code."

**Sami**
The Sami reindeer herders and fur trappers have existed for over 5,000 years.

**Roma**
There are 2–5 million Roma worldwide, mostly in Europe.

**Nenets**
Every year, Nenets move huge herds of reindeer up to 620 miles (1,000 km).

### Africa

**Beja**
Only some Beja clans are nomadic.

**Tuareg**
In Tuareg culture, men rather than women wear the veil.

**Toubou**
The Toubou are divided into two peoples: the Teda and the Daza.

**Fulani**
The Fulani traditionally herd goats, sheep, and cattle across large areas of west Africa.

**Gabra**
These herders make their dome-shaped houses out of acacia roots and cloth.

**Afar**
The Afar live by rivers in the dry season and head for higher ground in the wet season.

**Karamojong**
This name means "the old men can walk no further."

**San**
The San are famous for being excellent trackers and hunters.

**MOST NOMADS LIVE IN DESERT, STEPPE, OR TUNDRA—DRY PLACES THAT**

People and planet

# Nomads

Nomads move home every year to find fresh pasture or hunting grounds. Some are herders, some hunter-gatherers, and others are wandering traders. Their nomadic lifestyle is quickly dying out, as many of them are settling in villages and towns.

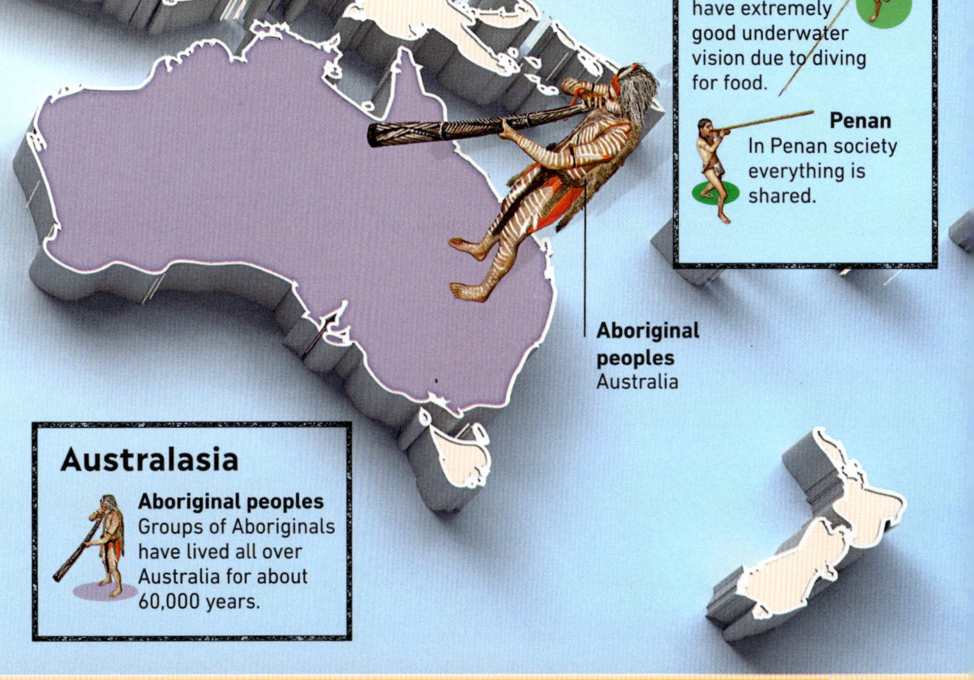

**Roma** — Central and eastern Europe

**Kazakhs** — Kazakhstan and other parts of northern central Asia

**Nenets** — Arctic Russia

**Bakhtiari** — Southwestern Iran

**Qashqai** — Southwestern Iran

**Bedouin** — The Middle East, predominantly Saudi Arabia

**Afar** — The Horn of Africa

**Gabra** — Chalbi Desert of Kenya and highlands of southern Ethiopia

**Yakut** — The Yakutia Republic, Russia

**Evenks** — Southern Siberia, Mongolia, and northeasternmost China

**Chukchi** — The Bering Strait region of Siberia

**Moken** — Southern Burma and the west coast of Thailand

**Penan** — Sarawak, Malaysia

**Aboriginal peoples** — Australia

### Asia

**Bakhtiari** — Bakhtiari means "bearer of good luck." Some still move pastures with the seasons.

**Kazakhs** — There are still many nomadic Kazakhs left in Xinjiang, China.

**Bedouin** — Bedouin are desert-dwelling wanderers known for their hospitality.

**Qashqai** — Qashqai are traditionally farmers known for their beautiful wool products.

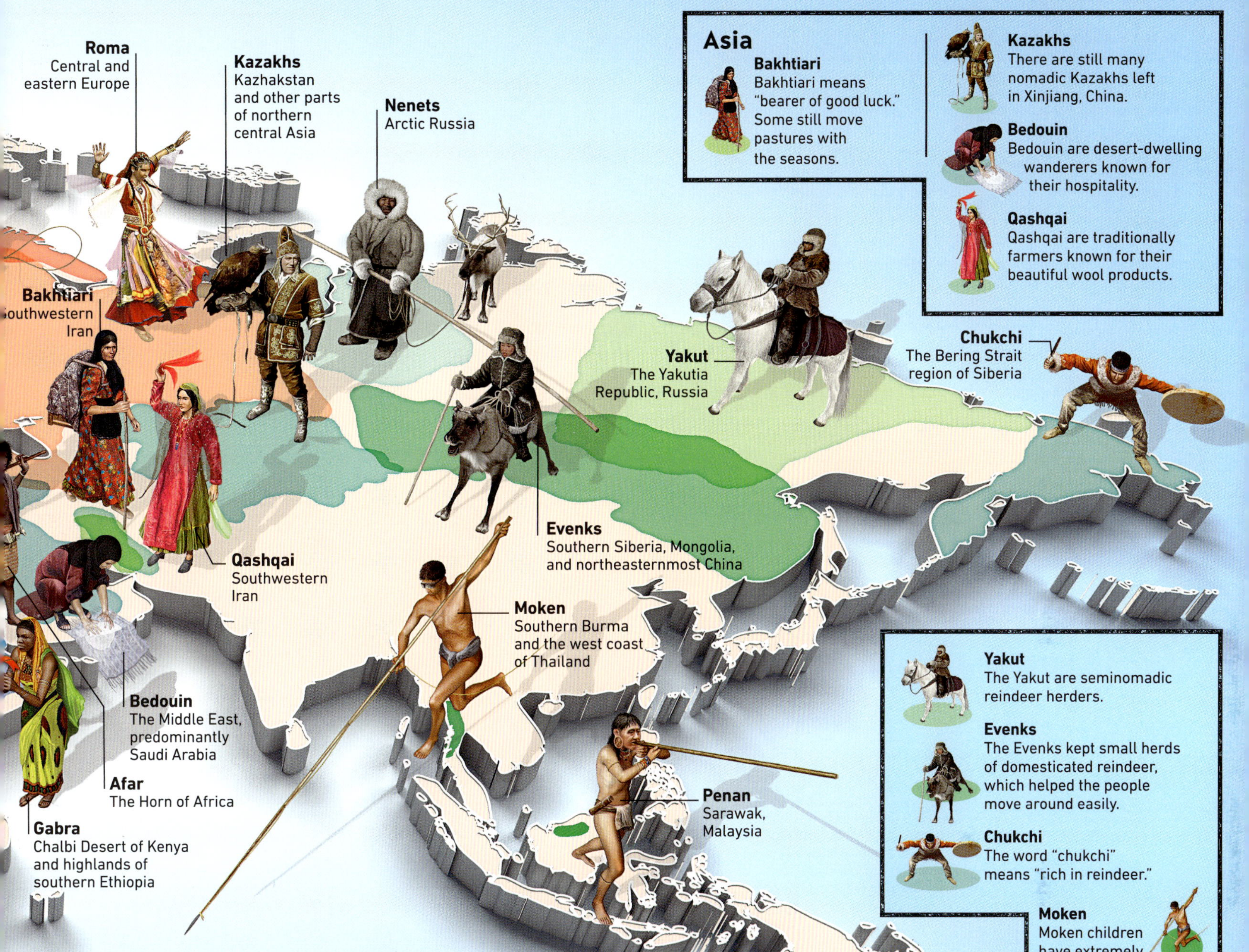

**Yakut** — The Yakut are seminomadic reindeer herders.

**Evenks** — The Evenks kept small herds of domesticated reindeer, which helped the people move around easily.

**Chukchi** — The word "chukchi" means "rich in reindeer."

**Moken** — Moken children have extremely good underwater vision due to diving for food.

**Penan** — In Penan society everything is shared.

### Australasia

**Aboriginal peoples** — Groups of Aboriginals have lived all over Australia for about 60,000 years.

DON'T PROVIDE ENOUGH FOOD FOR PEOPLE TO STAY ALL YEAR ROUND.

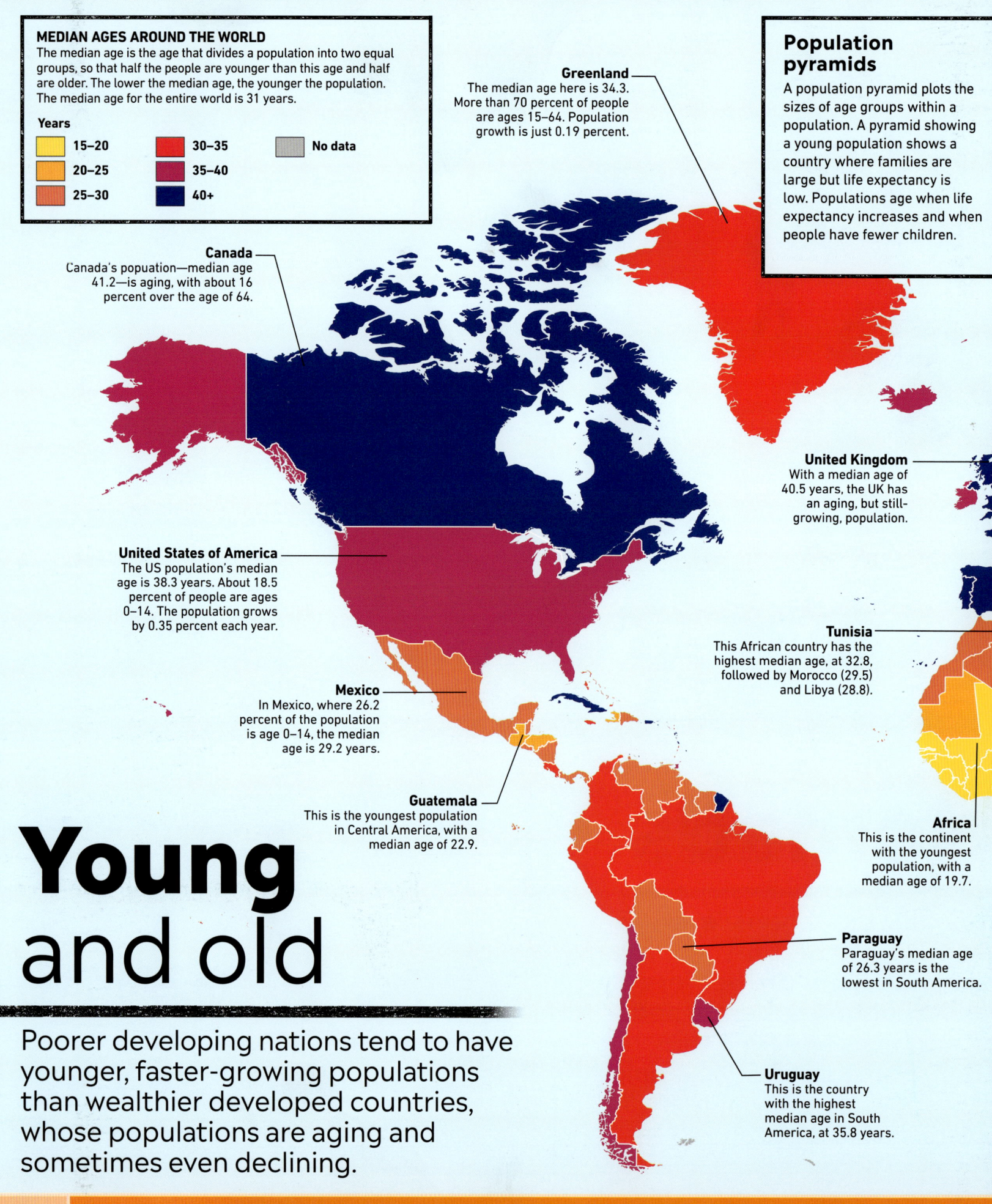

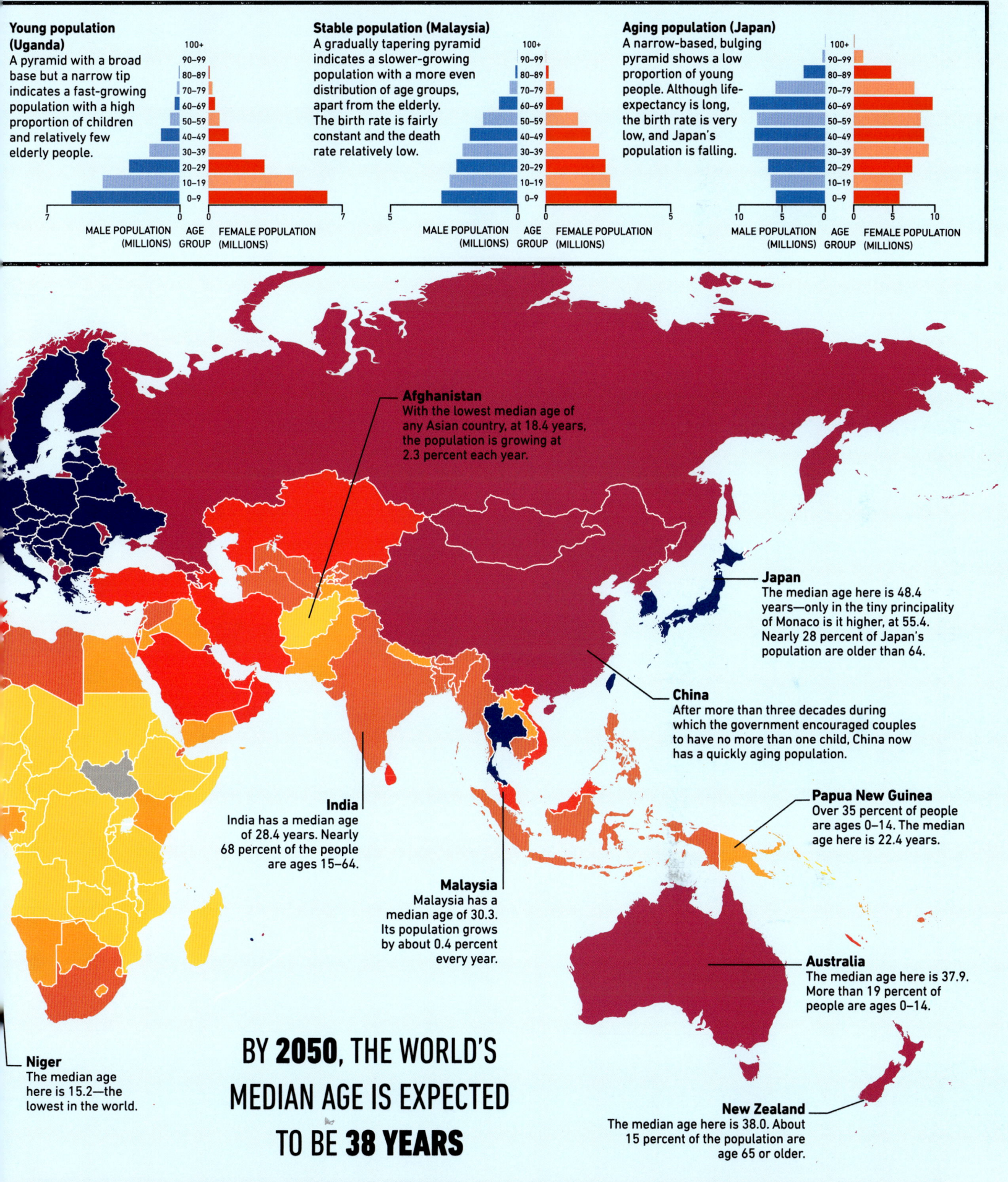

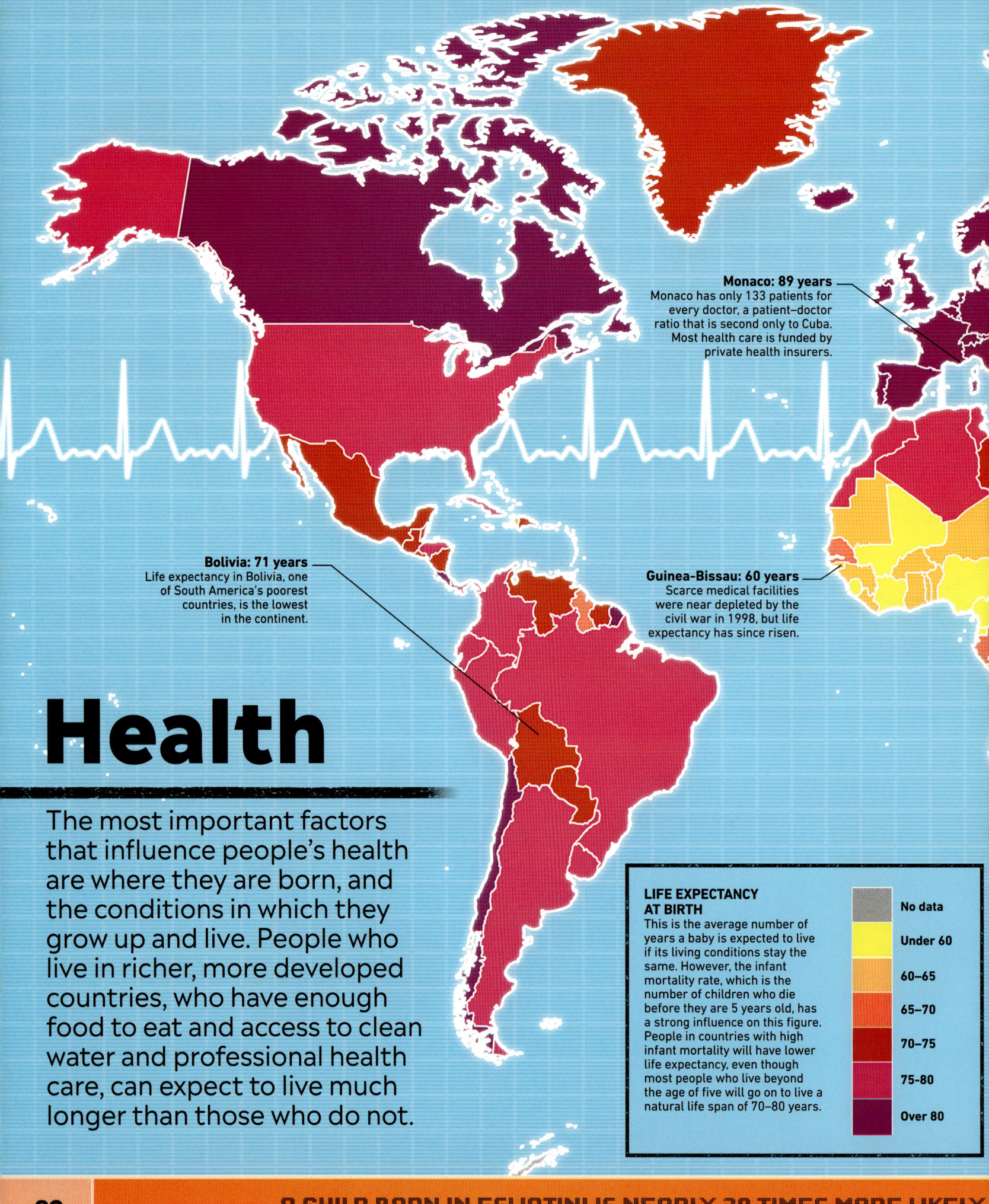

# Health

The most important factors that influence people's health are where they are born, and the conditions in which they grow up and live. People who live in richer, more developed countries, who have enough food to eat and access to clean water and professional health care, can expect to live much longer than those who do not.

**Monaco: 89 years**
Monaco has only 133 patients for every doctor, a patient–doctor ratio that is second only to Cuba. Most health care is funded by private health insurers.

**Bolivia: 71 years**
Life expectancy in Bolivia, one of South America's poorest countries, is the lowest in the continent.

**Guinea-Bissau: 60 years**
Scarce medical facilities were near depleted by the civil war in 1998, but life expectancy has since risen.

**LIFE EXPECTANCY AT BIRTH**
This is the average number of years a baby is expected to live if its living conditions stay the same. However, the infant mortality rate, which is the number of children who die before they are 5 years old, has a strong influence on this figure. People in countries with high infant mortality will have lower life expectancy, even though most people who live beyond the age of five will go on to live a natural life span of 70–80 years.

- No data
- Under 60
- 60–65
- 65–70
- 70–75
- 75–80
- Over 80

A CHILD BORN IN ESWATINI IS NEARLY 30 TIMES MORE LIKELY

People and planet

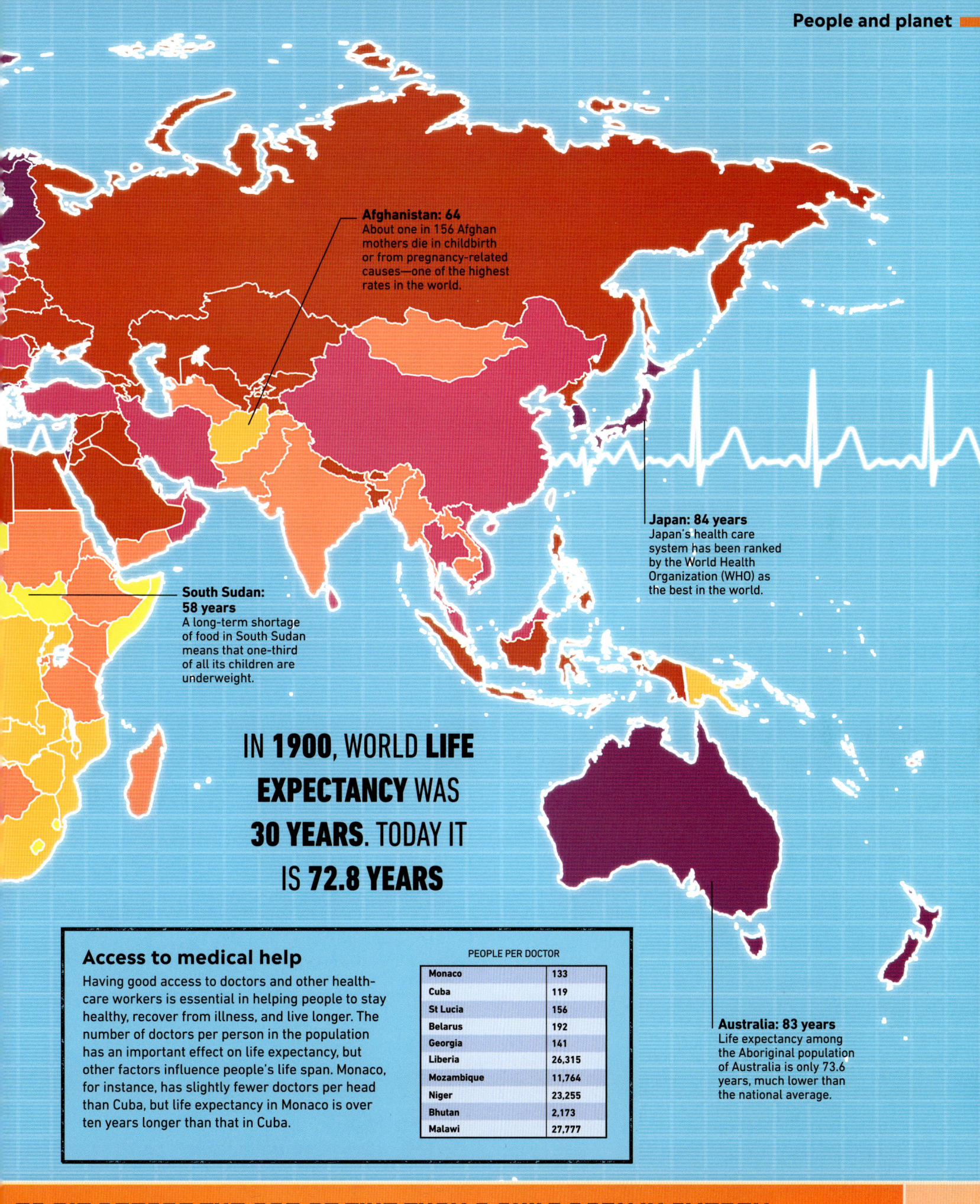

**Afghanistan: 64**
About one in 156 Afghan mothers die in childbirth or from pregnancy-related causes—one of the highest rates in the world.

**Japan: 84 years**
Japan's health care system has been ranked by the World Health Organization (WHO) as the best in the world.

**South Sudan: 58 years**
A long-term shortage of food in South Sudan means that one-third of all its children are underweight.

IN **1900**, WORLD **LIFE EXPECTANCY** WAS **30 YEARS**. TODAY IT IS **72.8 YEARS**

**Australia: 83 years**
Life expectancy among the Aboriginal population of Australia is only 73.6 years, much lower than the national average.

### Access to medical help

Having good access to doctors and other health-care workers is essential in helping people to stay healthy, recover from illness, and live longer. The number of doctors per person in the population has an important effect on life expectancy, but other factors influence people's life span. Monaco, for instance, has slightly fewer doctors per head than Cuba, but life expectancy in Monaco is over ten years longer than that in Cuba.

| | PEOPLE PER DOCTOR |
|---|---|
| Monaco | 133 |
| Cuba | 119 |
| St Lucia | 156 |
| Belarus | 192 |
| Georgia | 141 |
| Liberia | 26,315 |
| Mozambique | 11,764 |
| Niger | 23,255 |
| Bhutan | 2,173 |
| Malawi | 27,777 |

TO DIE BEFORE THE AGE OF FIVE THAN A CHILD BORN IN SWEDEN.

83

### Infecting germs
Many infectious diseases are caused by microscopic living organisms. They live and multiply inside our bodies and can pass from human to human by touch, through blood or saliva, and through the air.

### Bubonic plague bacteria
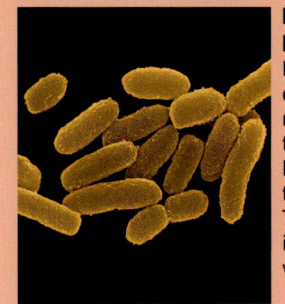
Bacteria are single-celled organisms that multiply by dividing into two again and again. Millions could fit on the head of a pin. Today, many bacterial infections can be treated with antibiotics.

### Flu virus
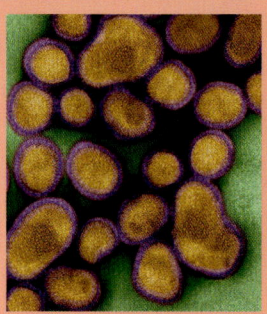
Viruses are very simple organisms far smaller even than bacteria. They spread by invading and taking over cells in the body. Viruses are unharmed by antibiotics, but the body can be fortified against them with a vaccine.

The Black Death ravaged Britain in 1348–50.

Troops returning home from Asia at the end of World War I brought the Spanish Flu back with them.

In August 1918, a second wave of Spanish Flu crossed the Atlantic and hit the port city of Freetown, Sierra Leone.

**3 Spanish Flu**
This infection was called "Spanish Flu" because people first thought it began in Spain. However, it actually was first reported at a training camp for American soldiers in the United States. The disease spread quickly when infected soldiers traveled to Europe to fight in World War I. It is estimated to have killed 20–50 million people.

**4 Freetown**
According to some studies, HIV began its spread through the human population in Cameroon.

# Pandemics

Infectious diseases—illnesses that pass between people—can spread rapidly. Many people become ill, causing a local disaster called an epidemic. When this effect becomes global, we call it a pandemic.

**KEY**
This map shows the spread of three of history's most lethal pandemics—in ancient times, the Middle Ages, and modern times.

 **Plague of Justinian** Bubonic plague, 541–42 CE

 **Black Death** Bubonic plague, 1346–55 CE

 **Spanish Flu** Influenza, 1918–20

SPANISH FLU MAY HAVE KILLED UP TO 50 MILLION PEOPLE.

**People and planet**

## Superbugs and new viruses

Bacteria and viruses change fast. "Superbug" bacteria become immune to antibiotics, while scientists try to develop vaccines against new viruses. Today, air travel can spread infection worldwide in days, so the fear of a fast-spreading pandemic is greater than ever. Here are five recent cases of new viruses.

**1 Hong Kong Flu, 1968–69**
In 2 years, Hong Kong Flu caused about 1 million deaths. The virus killed about 34,000 people in the United States alone.

**2 Avian (Bird) Flu, Hong Kong, 1997–present**
This virus first appeared in humans in Hong Kong, through contact with infected poultry. It has killed hundreds of people since then.

**3 H1N1 ("Swine Flu"), Mexico City, 2009–10**
This new flu developed from viruses of birds, pigs, and humans. Up to 575,400 people died in the first year of this pandemic.

**4 HIV, west–central Africa, 1981–present**
This virus causes AIDS—an often-fatal disease of the body's defenses. It now infects more than 30 million people worldwide.

### Black Death
In the 14th century, an outbreak of bubonic plague spread from Asia across Europe, causing devastation along the way. It caused some 50 million deaths—about half in Europe, where 25 percent of the population was killed.

Constantinople (Istanbul)

Some experts think the Plague of Justinian began not in Ethiopia, but in Central Asia.

The Black Death passed along sea trade routes, since the bacteria that caused the disease lived in fleas, which lived on ships' rats.

### Plague of Justinian
At its height, during the rule of the Emperor Justinian (ruler of the Byzantine, or Eastern Roman, Empire), this disease killed at least 25 million people. It may have started in Ethiopia, then spread along trade routes through northern Egypt and Constantinople (modern-day Istanbul) into Europe.

### COVID-19

**5 Dec 2019–present**
First identified in Wuhan, China, in late 2019, this fast-spreading virus can cause severe respiratory problems; up to 2.6 million deaths were reported in the first year of the pandemic. Vaccines have now been developed to help protect against the disease.

Spanish Flu was brought to New Zealand in 1918 by soldiers returning home from fighting in World War I in Europe.

**UP TO 2,000 PEOPLE STILL SUFFER FROM PLAGUE EACH YEAR**

**THAT'S MORE THAN THE TOTAL NUMBER OF DEATHS DURING WORLD WAR I.**

# Poverty

## The poverty line

A poverty line is the minimum level of income thought to be enough for a person to live on. It is the least amount needed to provide basic necessities: food, clothing, health care, and shelter. The cost of living is different around the world, so the poverty line varies from country to country.

### PEOPLE ON LESS THAN $1.90 A DAY

The international extreme poverty line of $1.90 income a day is a global measure of absolute poverty. This amount was set by the World Bank in 2015, and will be updated when necessary to reflect the cost of living. The map shows the percentage of each country's people earning less than $1.90 a day.

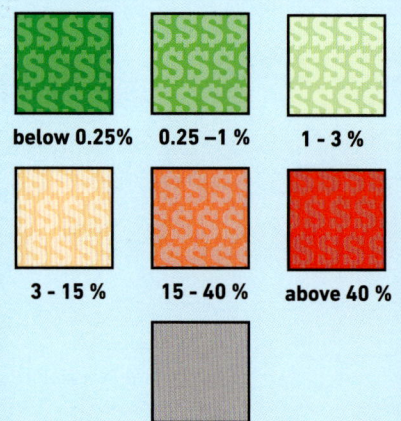

- below 0.25%
- 0.25 – 1 %
- 1 – 3 %
- 3 – 15 %
- 15 – 40 %
- above 40 %
- No data

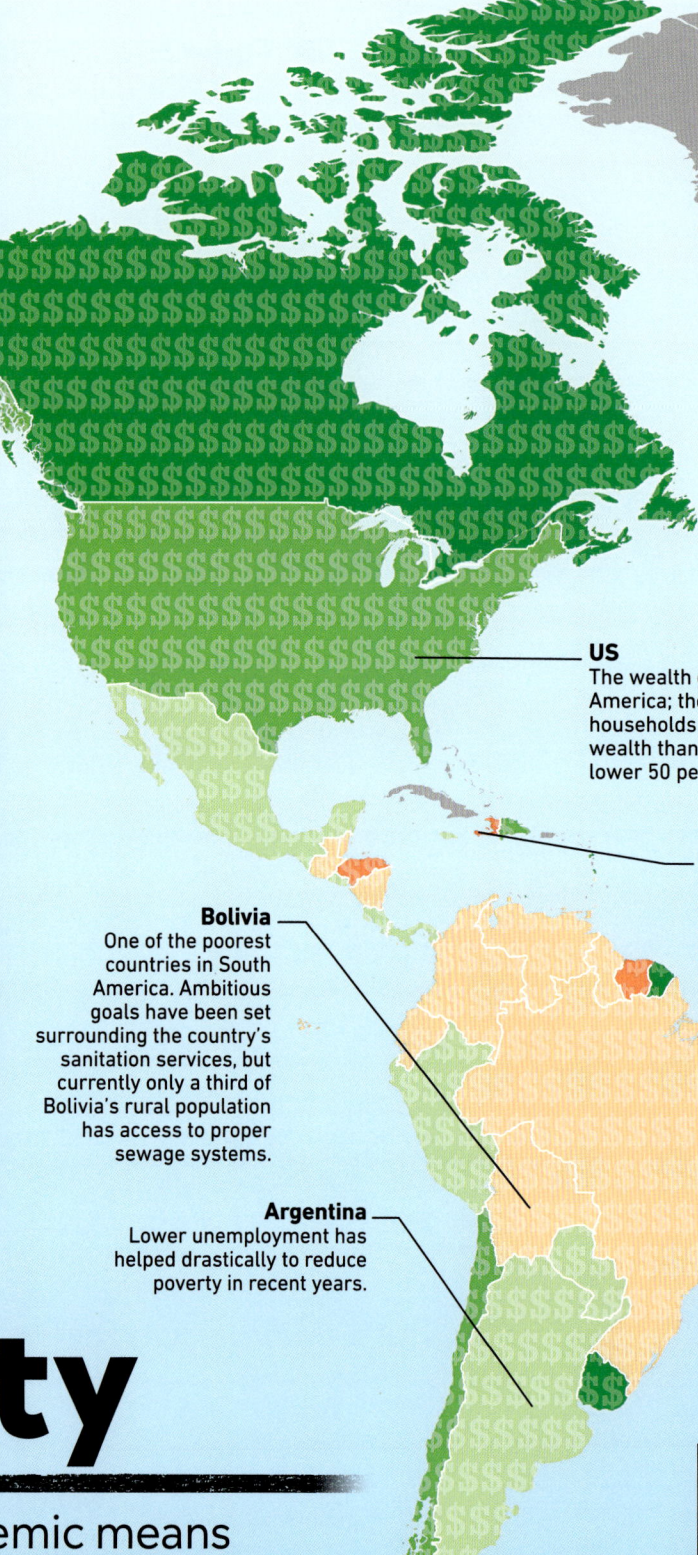

**Morocco** — Income inequality here is the highest in North Africa.

**US** — The wealth gap is huge in America; the top 1 percent of US households hold 15 times more wealth than the entirety of the lower 50 percent.

**Haiti** — The most cases of extreme poverty in the western hemisphere. Haiti's economy was severely affected by a 2010 earthquake, and is still yet to recover.

**Bolivia** — One of the poorest countries in South America. Ambitious goals have been set surrounding the country's sanitation services, but currently only a third of Bolivia's rural population has access to proper sewage systems.

**Liberia** — One of the poorest countries in the world. An estimated 64 percent of the population lives below the $1.90-a-day line.

**Ghana** — While the overall poverty rate has gone down sharply over the last 30 years, poverty in the north of the country has changed little.

**Argentina** — Lower unemployment has helped drastically to reduce poverty in recent years.

The COVID-19 pandemic means that global poverty is expected to rise for the first time since 2000. Sub-Saharan Africa has by far the most cases of extreme poverty—half of the countries in this region have a poverty rate higher than 35%.

## Inequality

In many countries, the gap between rich and poor is widening. Tax, special benefits for the lowest earners, and free education, among other things, can help reduce this. These charts show how much of a country's overall wealth the richest people own. The countries shown here are those with a very large gap between rich and poor, and those where the gap is less noticeable.

MORE THAN 24% OF THE WORLD'S POPULATION LIVED ON LESS THAN

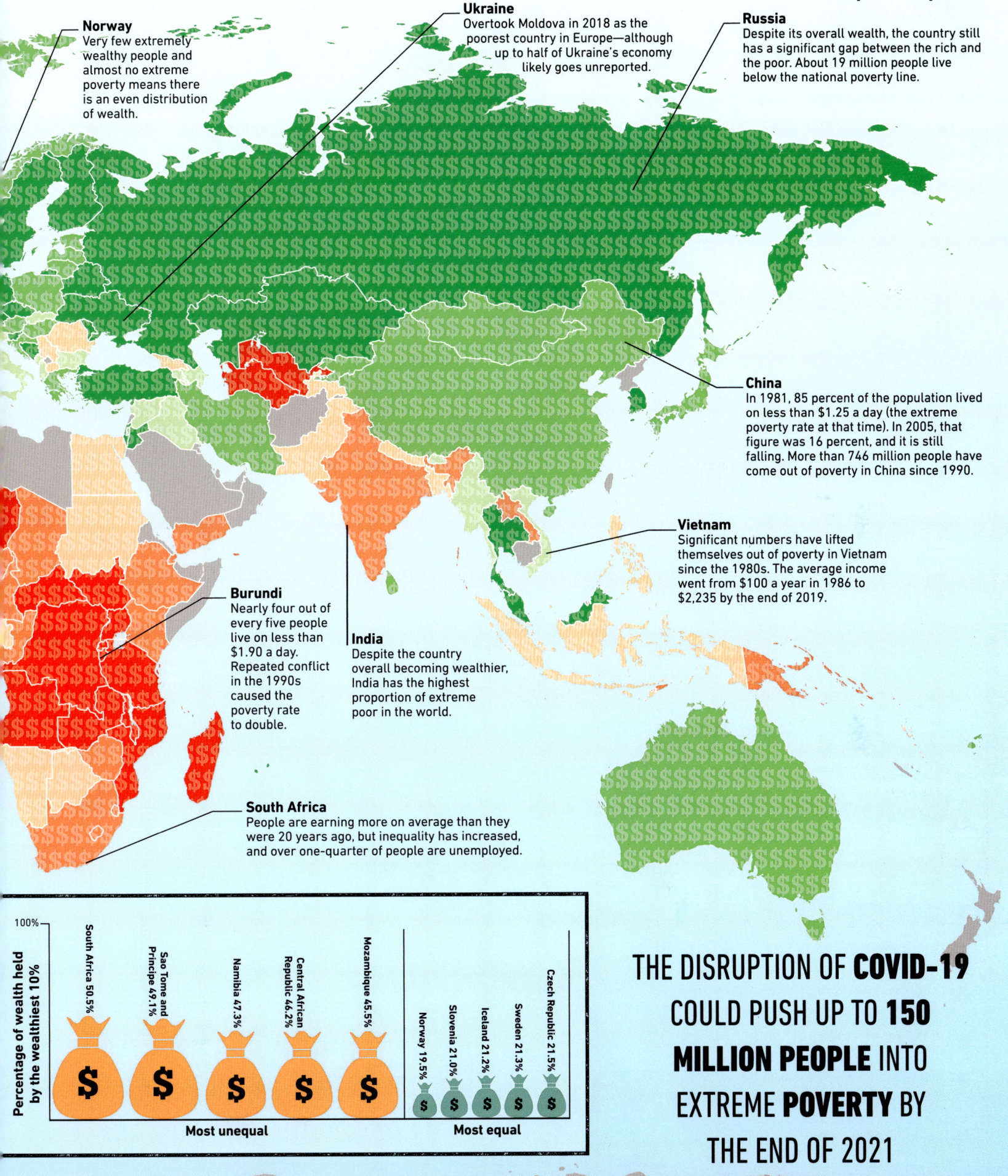

# The world's gold

Beautiful, rare, and highly prized, gold has been mined since ancient Egyptian times. Sometimes a discovery of gold led to a "gold rush," with thousands of people flocking to the site in the hope of making their fortune.

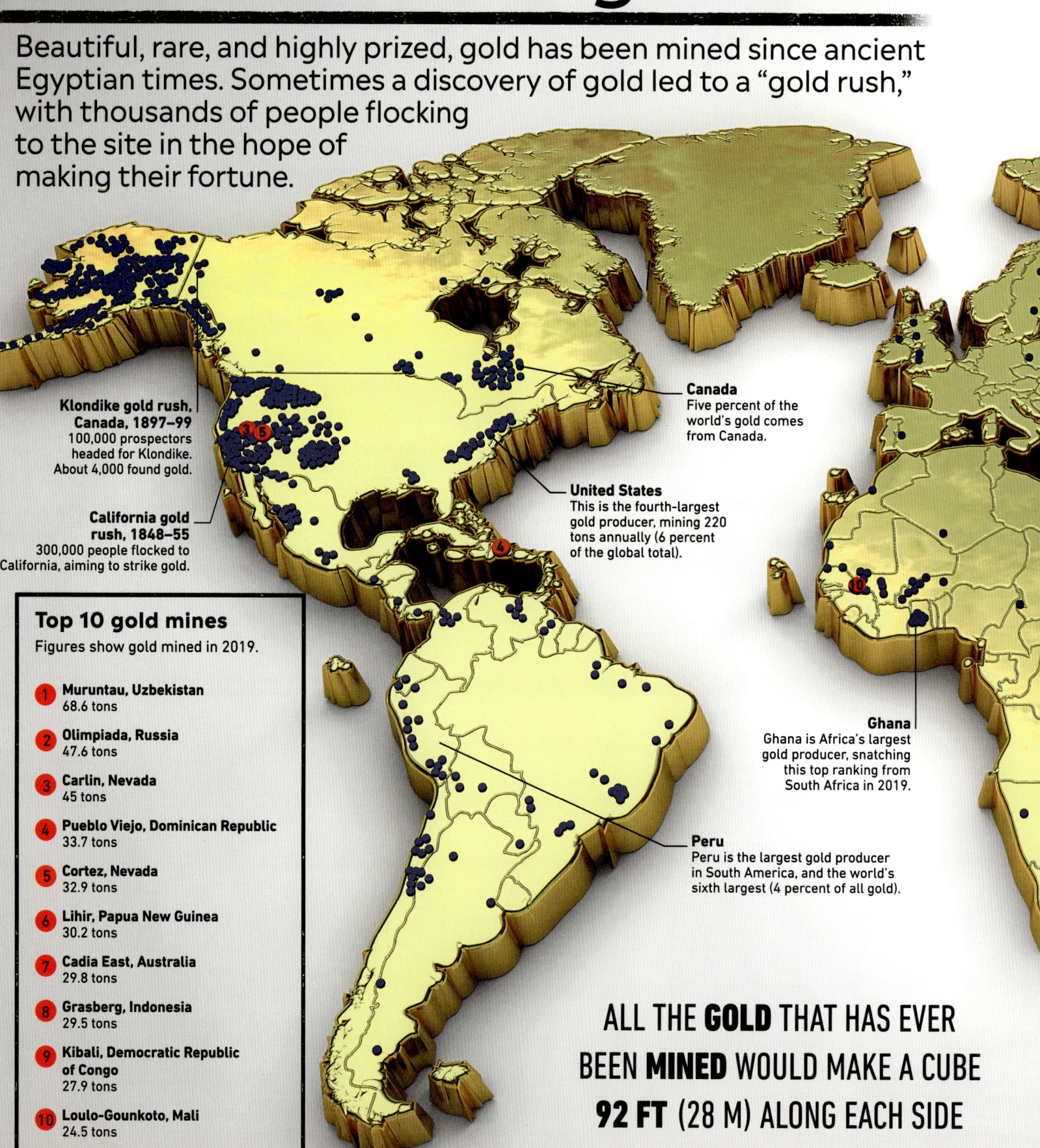

**Klondike gold rush, Canada, 1897–99**
100,000 prospectors headed for Klondike. About 4,000 found gold.

**California gold rush, 1848–55**
300,000 people flocked to California, aiming to strike gold.

**Canada**
Five percent of the world's gold comes from Canada.

**United States**
This is the fourth-largest gold producer, mining 220 tons annually (6 percent of the global total).

**Ghana**
Ghana is Africa's largest gold producer, snatching this top ranking from South Africa in 2019.

**Peru**
Peru is the largest gold producer in South America, and the world's sixth largest (4 percent of all gold).

### Top 10 gold mines
Figures show gold mined in 2019.

1. **Muruntau, Uzbekistan** — 68.6 tons
2. **Olimpiada, Russia** — 47.6 tons
3. **Carlin, Nevada** — 45 tons
4. **Pueblo Viejo, Dominican Republic** — 33.7 tons
5. **Cortez, Nevada** — 32.9 tons
6. **Lihir, Papua New Guinea** — 30.2 tons
7. **Cadia East, Australia** — 29.8 tons
8. **Grasberg, Indonesia** — 29.5 tons
9. **Kibali, Democratic Republic of Congo** — 27.9 tons
10. **Loulo-Gounkoto, Mali** — 24.5 tons

ALL THE **GOLD** THAT HAS EVER BEEN **MINED** WOULD MAKE A CUBE **92 FT** (28 M) ALONG EACH SIDE

FOUND IN AUSTRALIA IN 1869, "WELCOME STRANGER" WAS THE BIGGEST

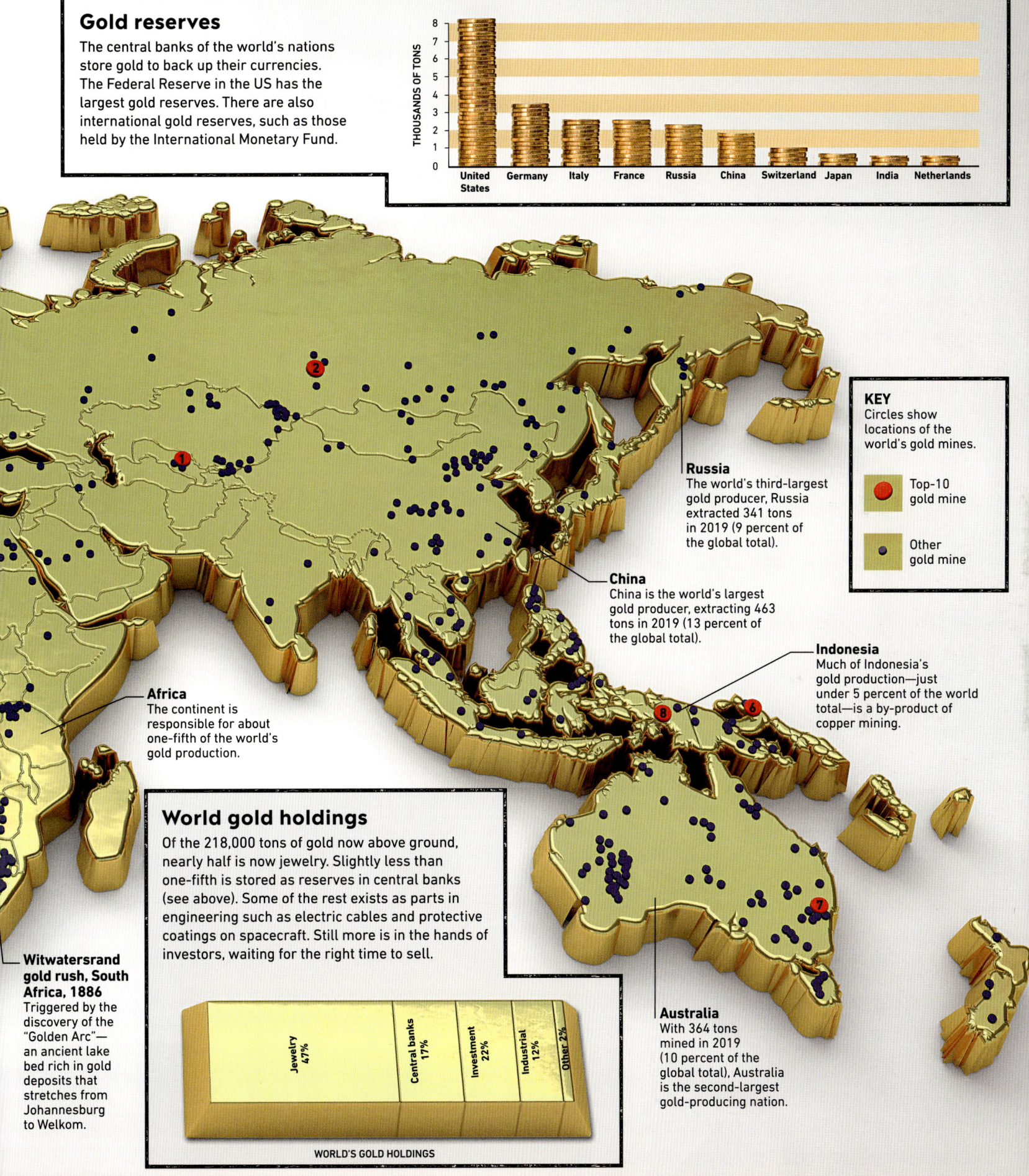

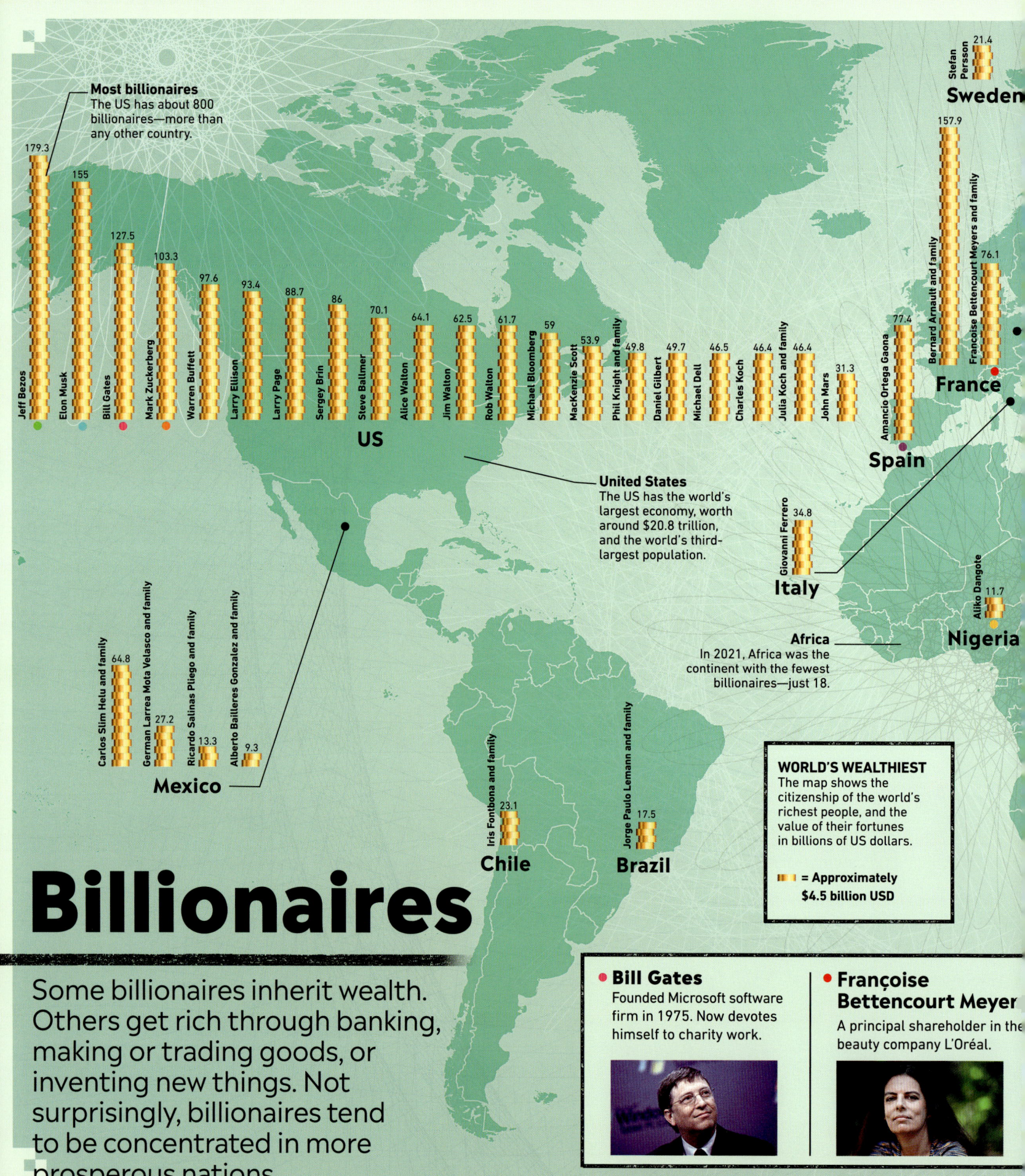

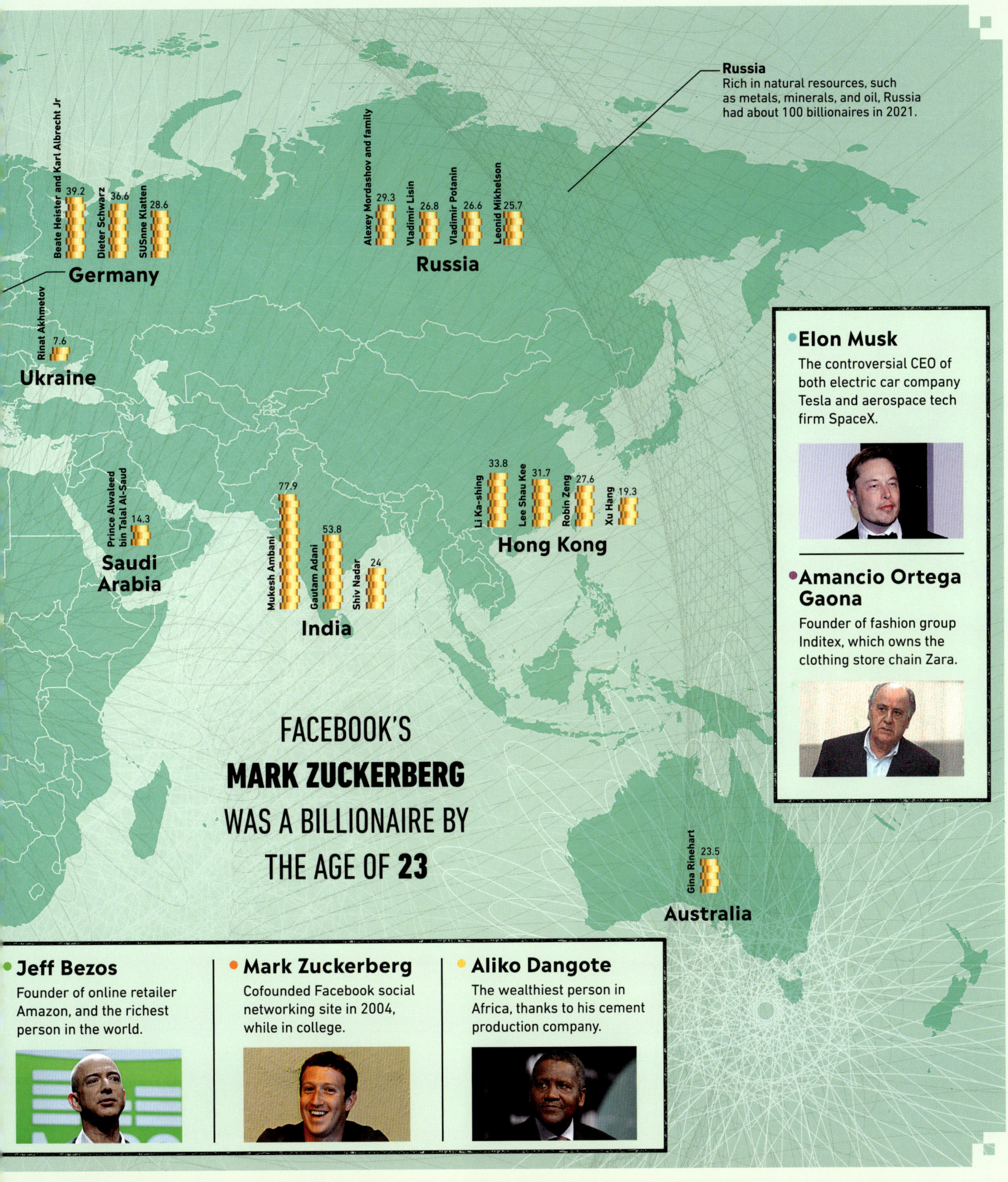

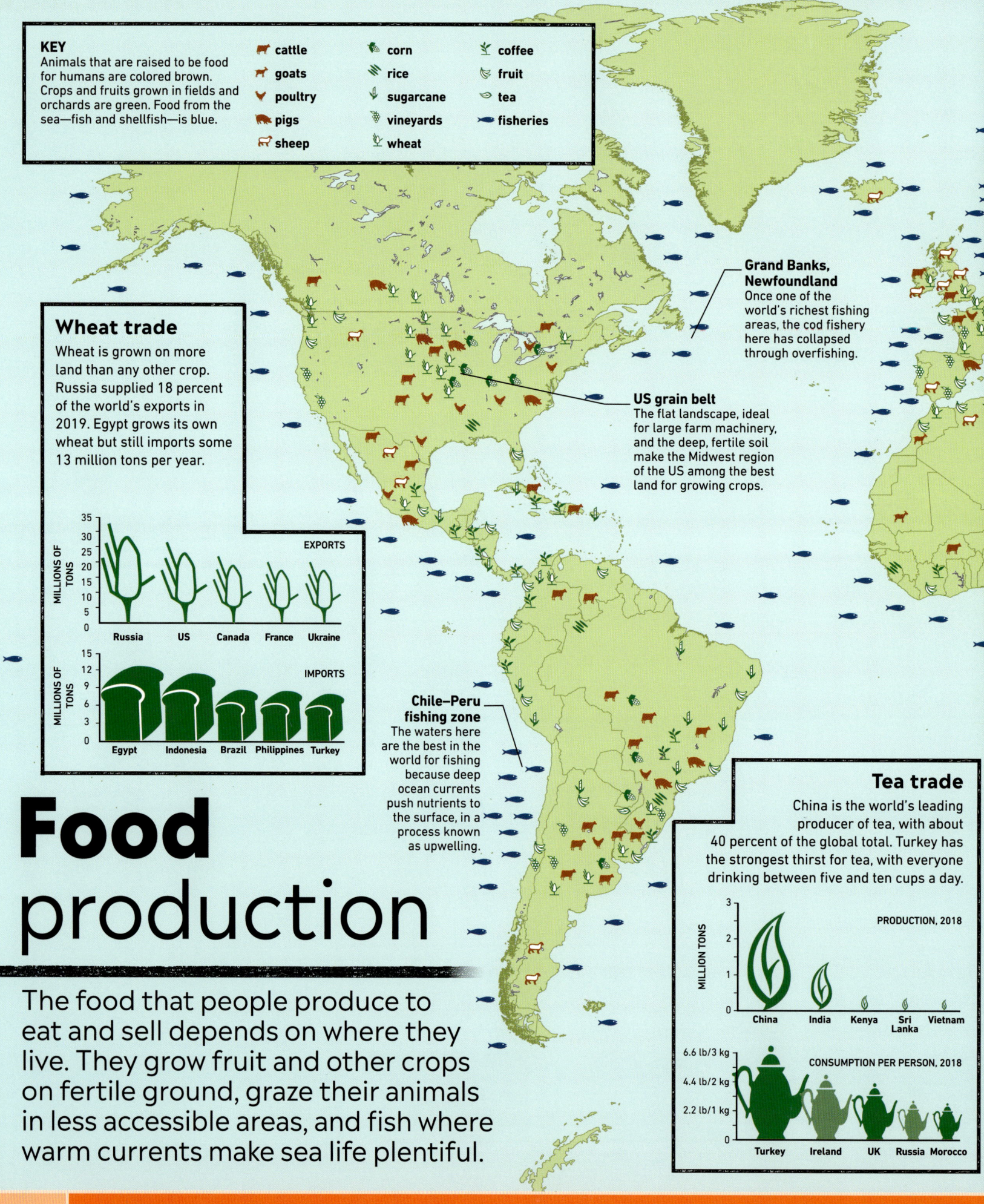

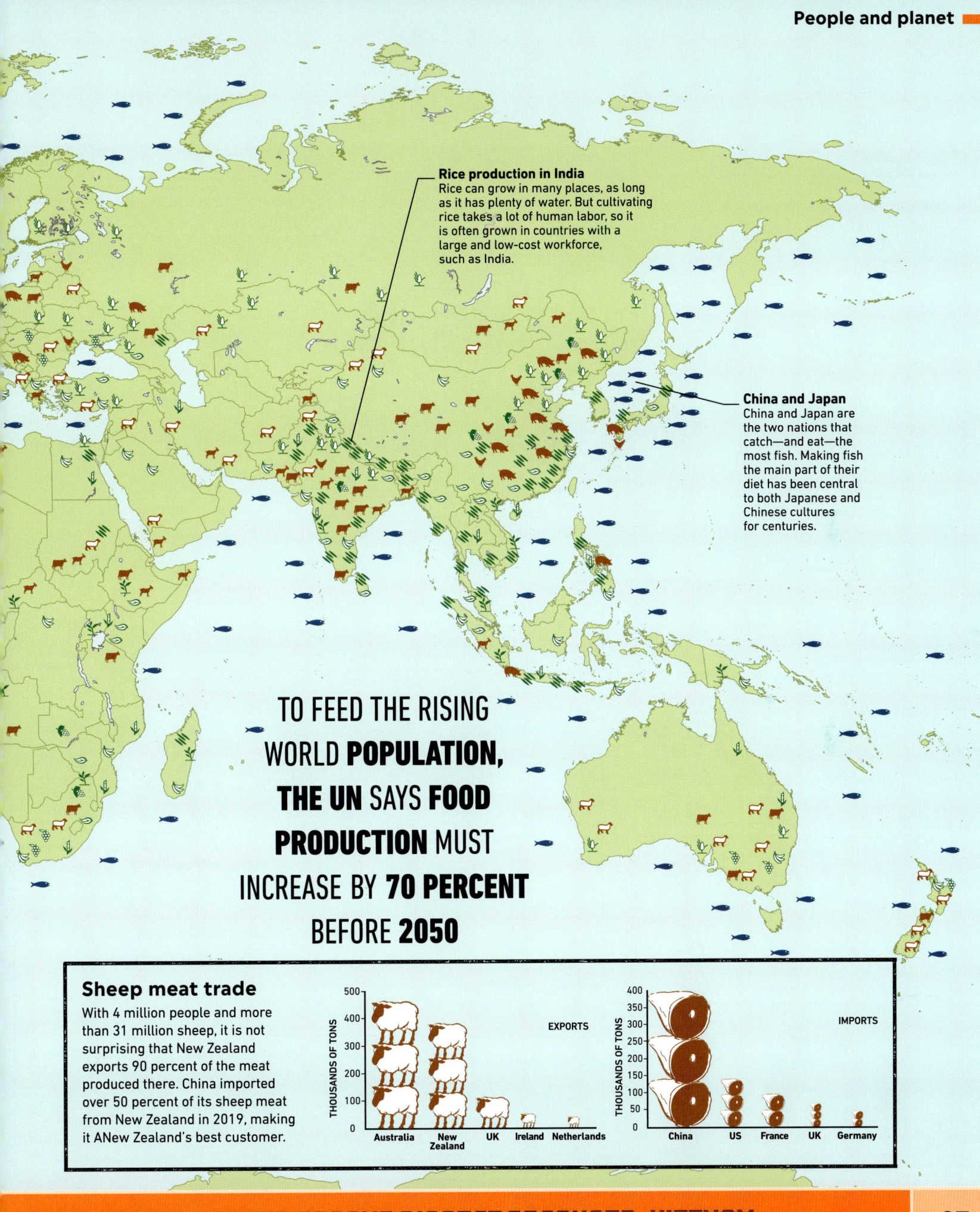

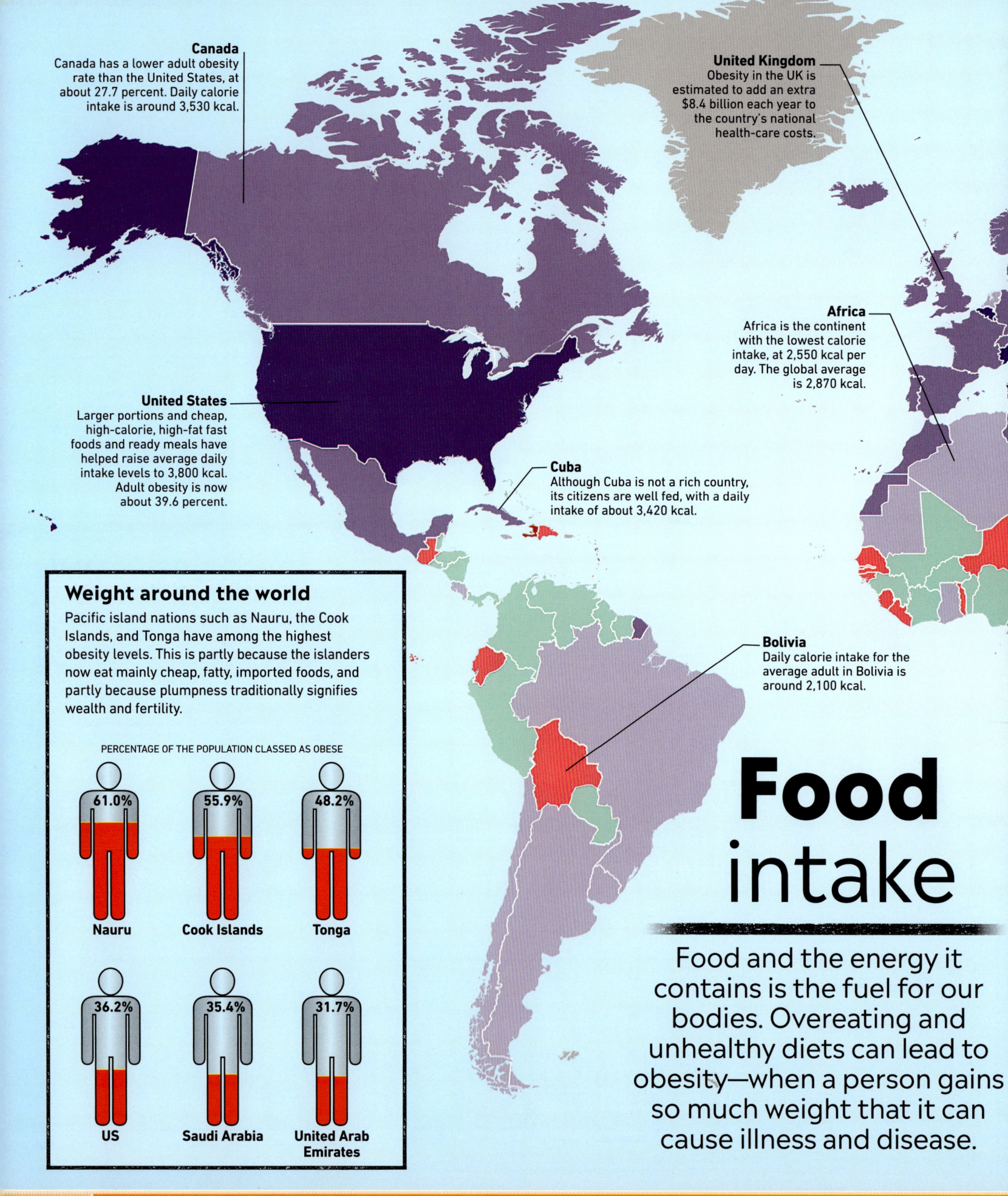

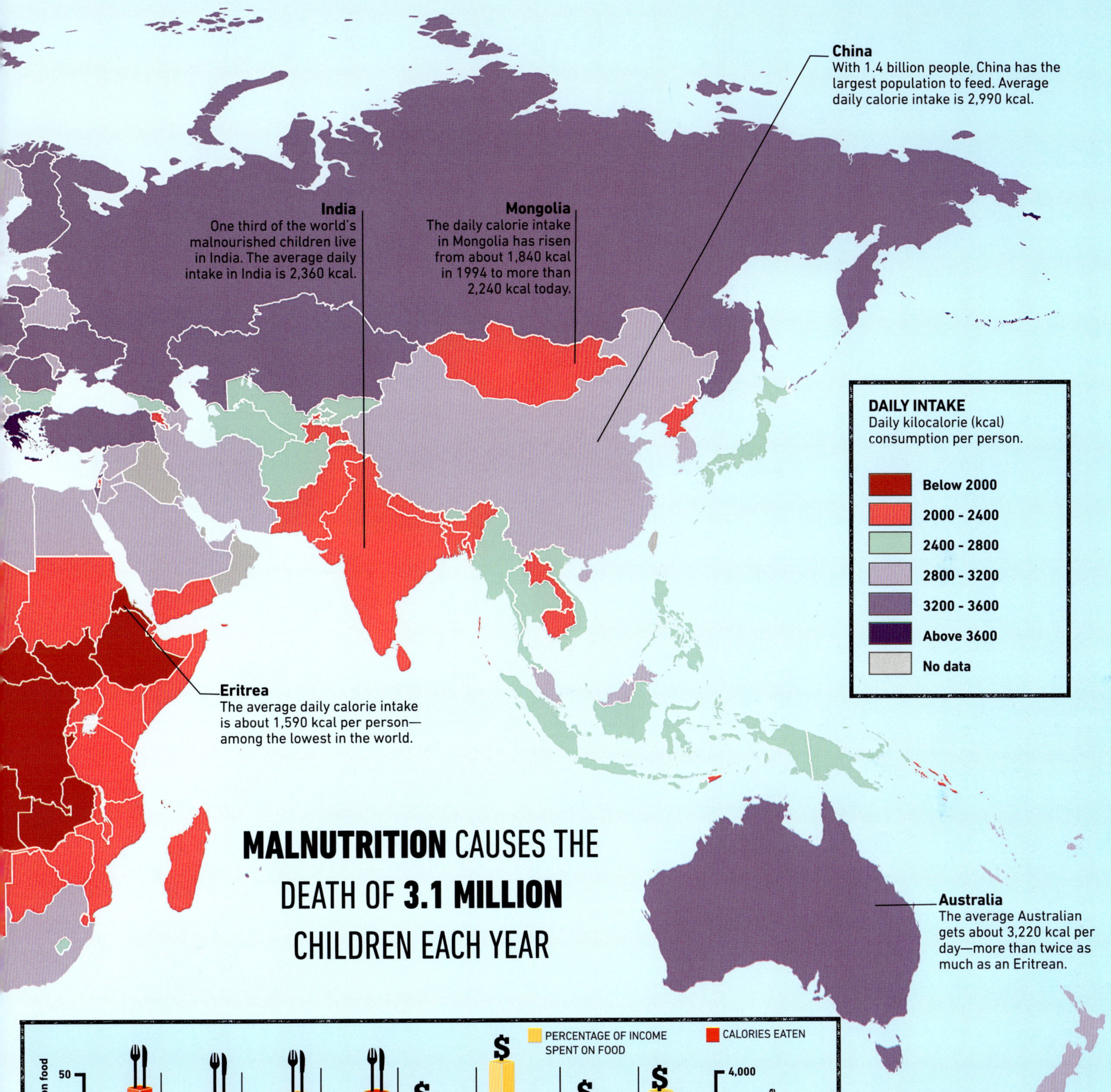

China
With 1.4 billion people, China has the largest population to feed. Average daily calorie intake is 2,990 kcal.
India
One third of the world's malnourished children live in India. The average daily intake in India is 2,360 kcal.
Mongolia
The daily calorie intake in Mongolia has risen from about 1,840 kcal in 1994 to more than 2,240 kcal today.
DAILY INTAKE
Daily kilocalorie (kcal) consumption per person.
Below 2000
2000 - 2400
2400 - 2800
2800 - 3200
3200 - 3600
Above 3600
No data
Eritrea
The average daily calorie intake is about 1,590 kcal per person—among the lowest in the world.
Australia
The average Australian gets about 3,220 kcal per day—more than twice as much as an Eritrean.


**MALNUTRITION** CAUSES THE DEATH OF **3.1 MILLION** CHILDREN EACH YEAR

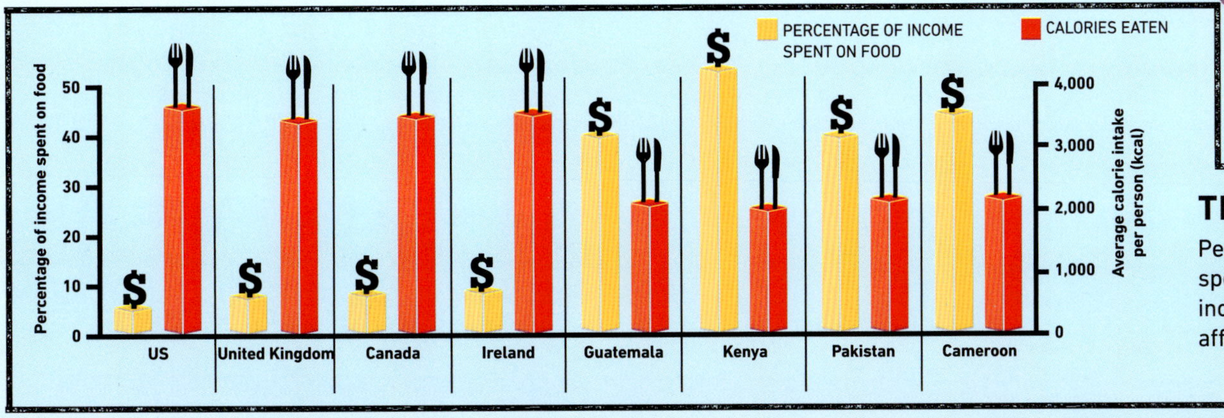

PERCENTAGE OF INCOME SPENT ON FOOD
CALORIES EATEN
Percentage of income spent on food
0
10
20
30
40
50
Average calorie intake per person (kcal)
0
1,000
2,000
3,000
4,000
US
United Kingdom
Canada
Ireland
Guatemala
Kenya
Pakistan
Cameroon


## The cost of food

People in poor countries have to spend a greater proportion of their income on food, so they cannot afford a high-calorie intake.

THE WORLD—THAT'S 8.9 PERCENT OF THE TOTAL POPULATION.

# Literacy

**Canada**
About 16 percent of Canadians struggle to pass basic literary tests.

**Europe**
Although most countries in Europe have very high literacy rates, more than 55 million adults classed as "literate" still lack basic reading and writing skills.

**United States**
About 21 percent of adults in the US are classed as "functionally illiterate."

**Mauritania**
Little more than half of Mauritania's population—52.1 percent—can read and write.

**Chad**
Just 23.3 percent of people in Chad are literate—the world's lowest literacy rate.

**Brazil**
Just over nine out of every ten Brazilians are literate.

## Going to secondary school

Wealthy nations can afford to provide secondary education for all children, but governments in poorer countries cannot offer every child a place. This is particularly true in Africa south of the Sahara. In Niger, for example, only 24 percent of children go to secondary school.

PERCENTAGE OF SECONDARY-SCHOOL-AGE CHILDREN ENROLLED IN SCHOOL

(France, Japan, Sweden, New Zealand, Seychelles, Burundi, Burkina Faso, Mozambique, Niger, Central African Republic)

Literacy—being able to read and write—is an essential life skill. Being literate makes it easier for people to learn, make the most of their abilities, and get better jobs. High levels of illiteracy make it difficult for nations to develop and become wealthier.

**IN DEVELOPING COUNTRIES, 200 MILLION PEOPLE AGES 15–24 HAVE NOT COMPLETED PRIMARY SCHOOL**

ABOUT 61 MILLION PRIMARY-AGE CHILDREN WORLDWIDE WERE RECEIVING

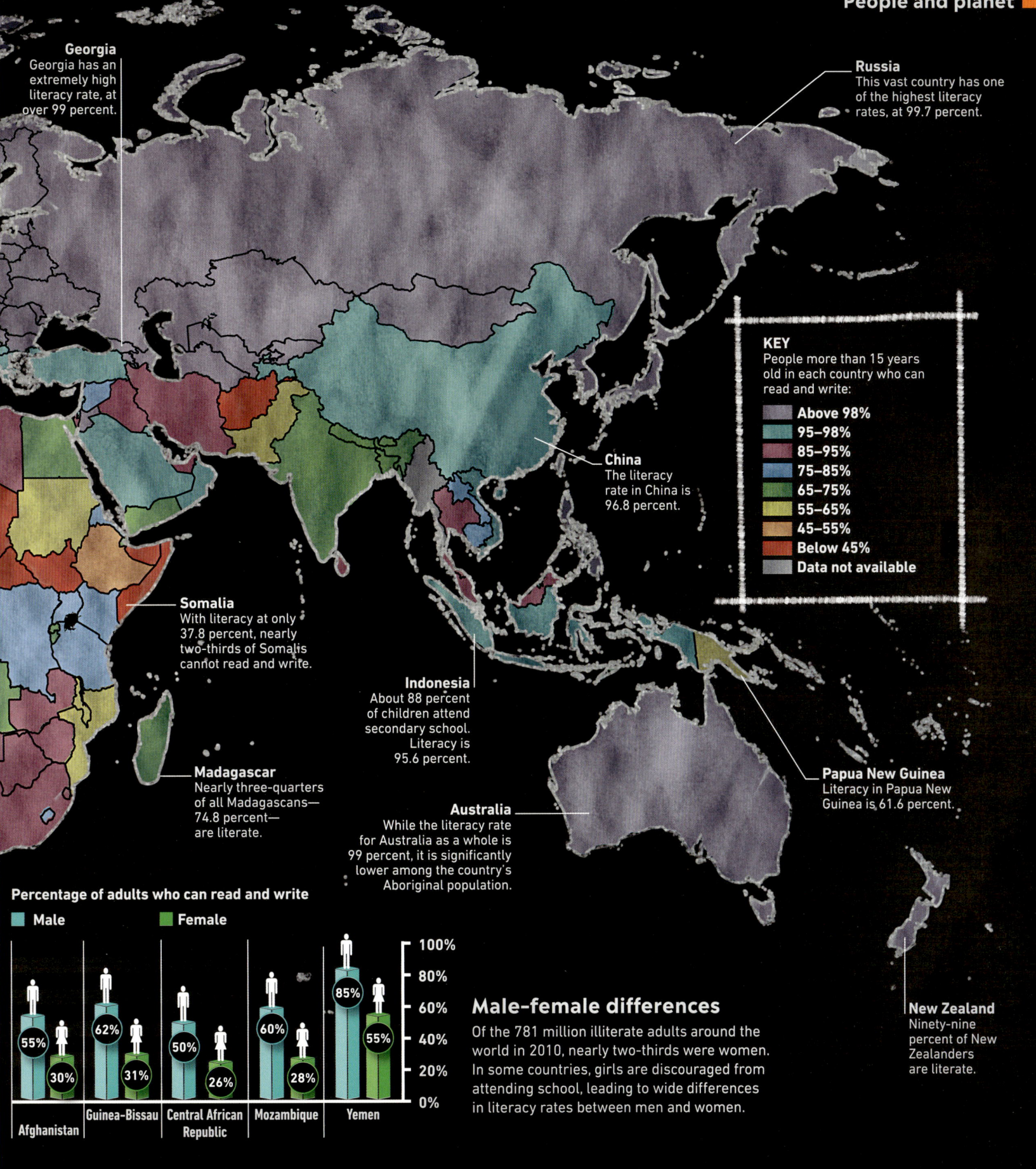

# Pollution

Oil spills, industrial waste, and radiation leaks from nuclear power stations cause harm to people and the environment. Carbon dioxide gas ($CO_2$) produced by transportation and industry is adding to global warming.

## Biggest oil spills

Oil spills—when oil escapes into the environment—cause devastation to wildlife and are difficult and costly to clean up.

**1. Gulf War oil spill, Persian Gulf, 1991**
*330,000–1,322,000 tons*
Iraqi forces opened valves on Kuwaiti oil wells and pipes, causing a 100-mile (160-km) slick.

**2. Lakeview gusher, California 1910-11**
*1,212,000 tons*
An oil well erupted like a geyser, spilling out oil for over a year until it naturally died down.

**3. Deepwater Horizon, Gulf of Mexico, 2010**
*740,000 tons*
A deep-sea oil spill occurred when an explosion destroyed the Deepwater Horizon drilling rig.

**4. Ixtoc 1 oil spill, Gulf of Mexico, USA, 1979–80**
*454,000–480,000 tons*
The Ixtoc 1 drilling platform collapsed after an explosion. The spill continued for 9 months.

**5. *Atlantic Empress*, Trinidad and Tobago, 1979**
*287,000 tons*
The largest oil spill from a ship. The tanker *Atlantic Empress* hit another ship, killing 26 crew.

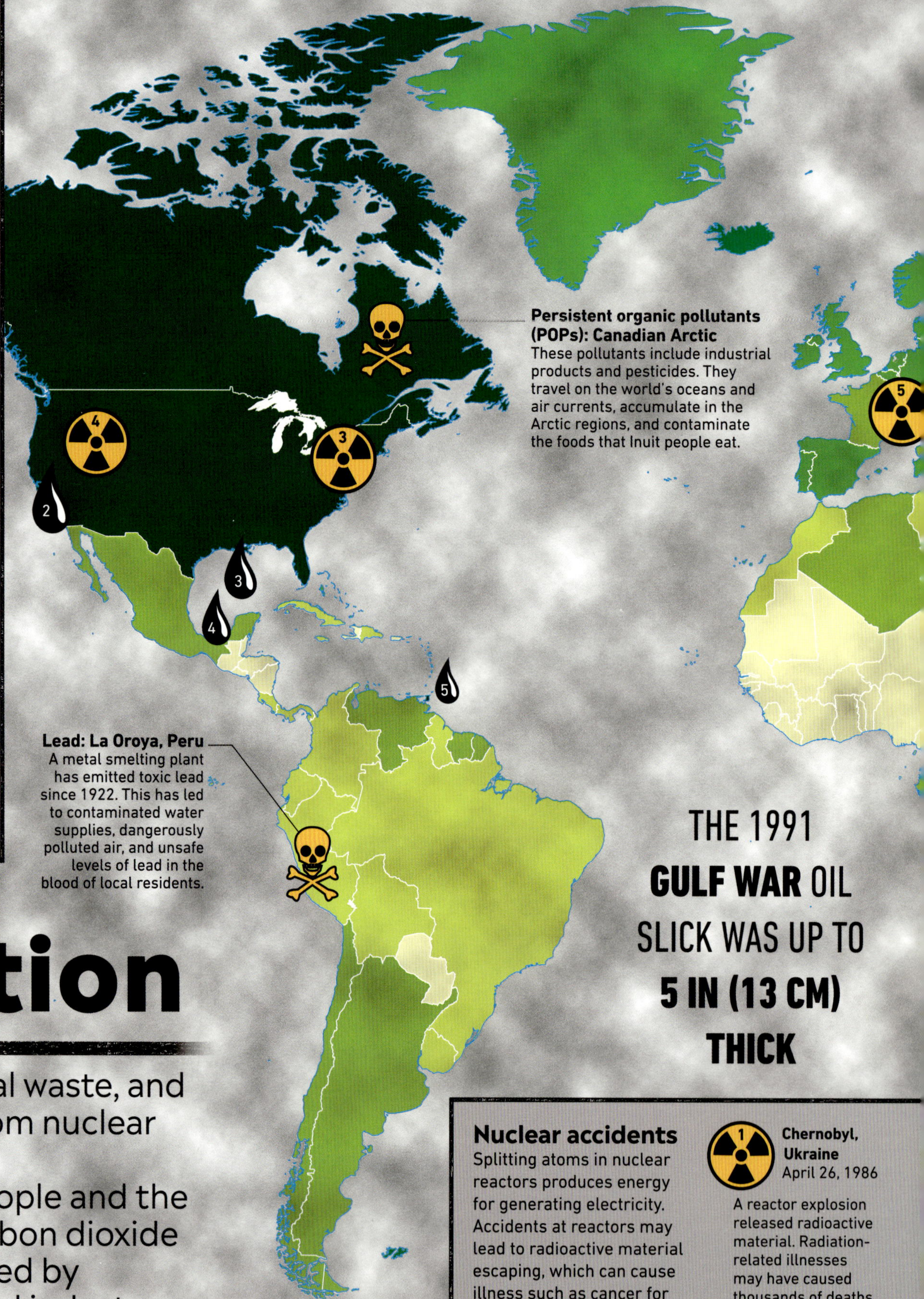

**Persistent organic pollutants (POPs): Canadian Arctic**
These pollutants include industrial products and pesticides. They travel on the world's oceans and air currents, accumulate in the Arctic regions, and contaminate the foods that Inuit people eat.

**Lead: La Oroya, Peru**
A metal smelting plant has emitted toxic lead since 1922. This has led to contaminated water supplies, dangerously polluted air, and unsafe levels of lead in the blood of local residents.

THE 1991 **GULF WAR** OIL SLICK WAS UP TO **5 IN (13 CM)** THICK

## Nuclear accidents

Splitting atoms in nuclear reactors produces energy for generating electricity. Accidents at reactors may lead to radioactive material escaping, which can cause illness such as cancer for many years.

**1. Chernobyl, Ukraine** April 26, 1986
A reactor explosion released radioactive material. Radiation-related illnesses may have caused thousands of deaths.

RADIOACTIVE WASTE FROM NUCLEAR REACTORS CAN REMAIN DANGEROUS

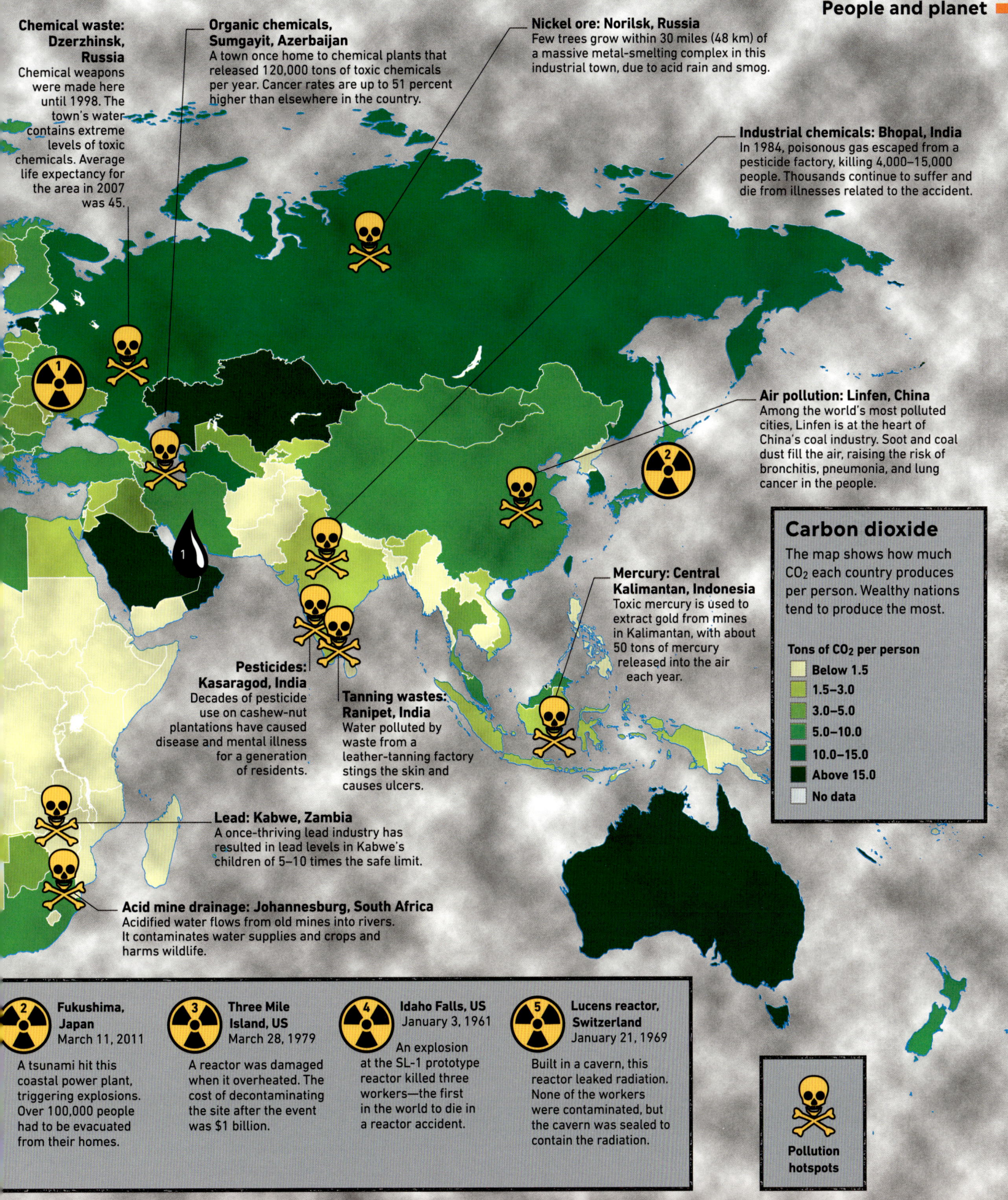

# Garbage and waste

As living standards improve worldwide and cities grow, so does the amount of garbage that people produce. Most waste goes to garbage dumps, which are expensive, use up a lot of land, and are harmful to the environment. Recycling is one way of helping to stop the global garbage heap from growing any bigger.

**KEY**
The world's five largest garbage dumps, or landfills, labeled with the amount of waste dumped in them every day.

**Puente Hills—Los Angeles, California**
Approximately 11,350 tons per day.

**Apex—Las Vegas, Nevada**
Approximately 11,600 tons per day.

**Greenland**
Currently Greenland produces 30% more waste than it can process, though two new garbage-to-energy incinerators are due to open in 2021 and 2022.

**Western Pacific Garbage Patch**
A lot of discarded litter ends up in rivers, which take it to the sea, where circular currents called gyres collect it into vast patches in the ocean surface waters. This patch is the largest of these oceanic rubbish dumps.

**North Atlantic Garbage Patch**
The North Atlantic Garbage Patch measures hundreds of miles across. It shifts by as much as 990 miles (1,600 km) north and south with the seasons.

**Bordo Poniente Landfill—Nezahualcoyotl, Mexico**
Over 13,200 tons per day.

**Gabon**
Less wealthy countries, such as Gabon, produce less garbage because people buy less overall, they buy proportionally more local produce without plastic packaging, and do more recycling.

**South Pacific Garbage Patch**
So far, the South Pacific Gyre appears to contain less plastic waste than other ocean garbage patches.

**South Atlantic Garbage Patch**
The first evidence of a South Atlantic Garbage Patch was discovered in 2011. Most plastic particles in ocean garbage patches are too small to be seen with the naked eye.

**Top of the recycling table**
Only a handful of countries currently recycle more than half their waste; Germany tops this list, recycling 56.1% of all waste in 2019. This figure is a rapid increase from 1991, when the country recycled only 3% of its garbage.

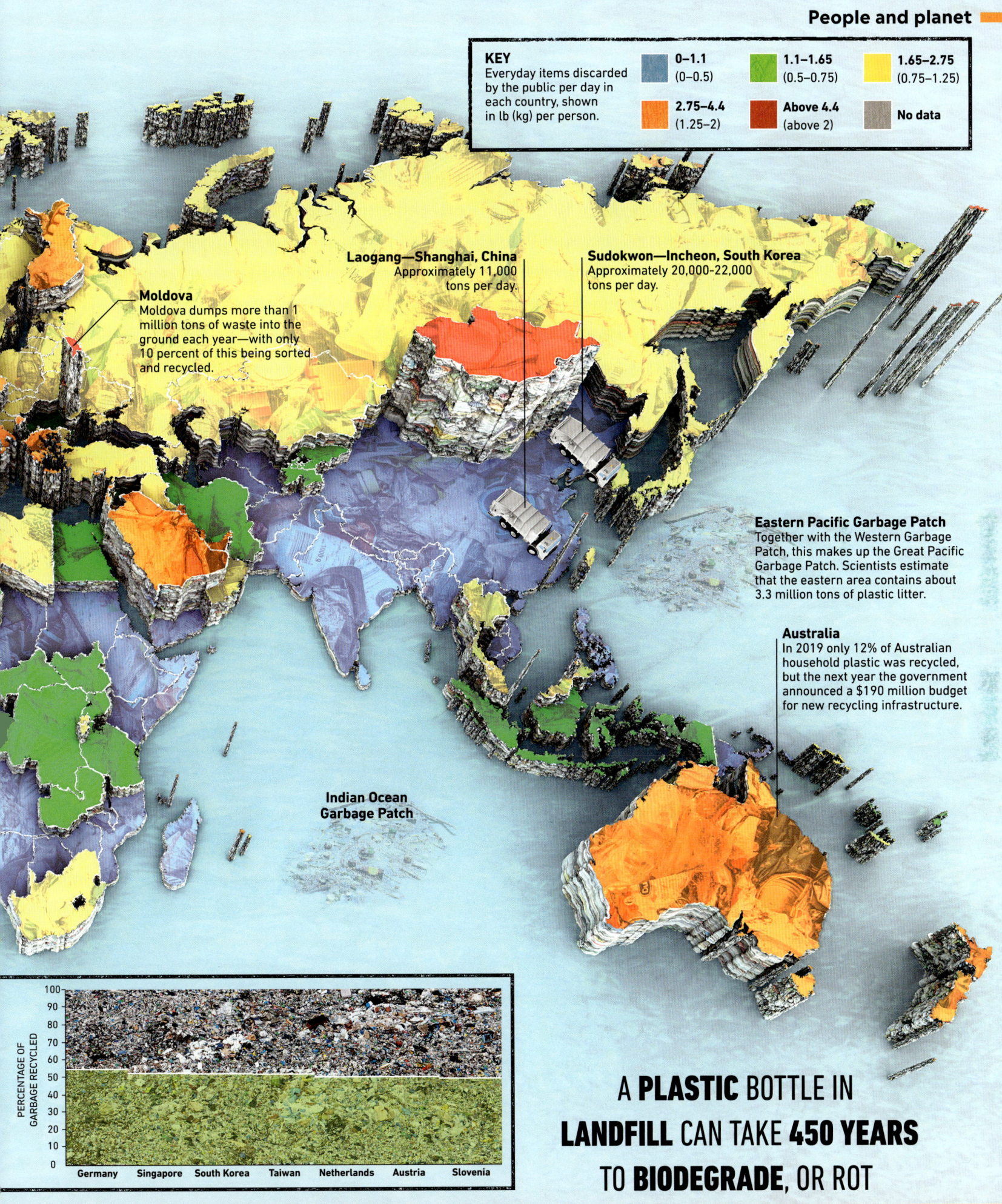

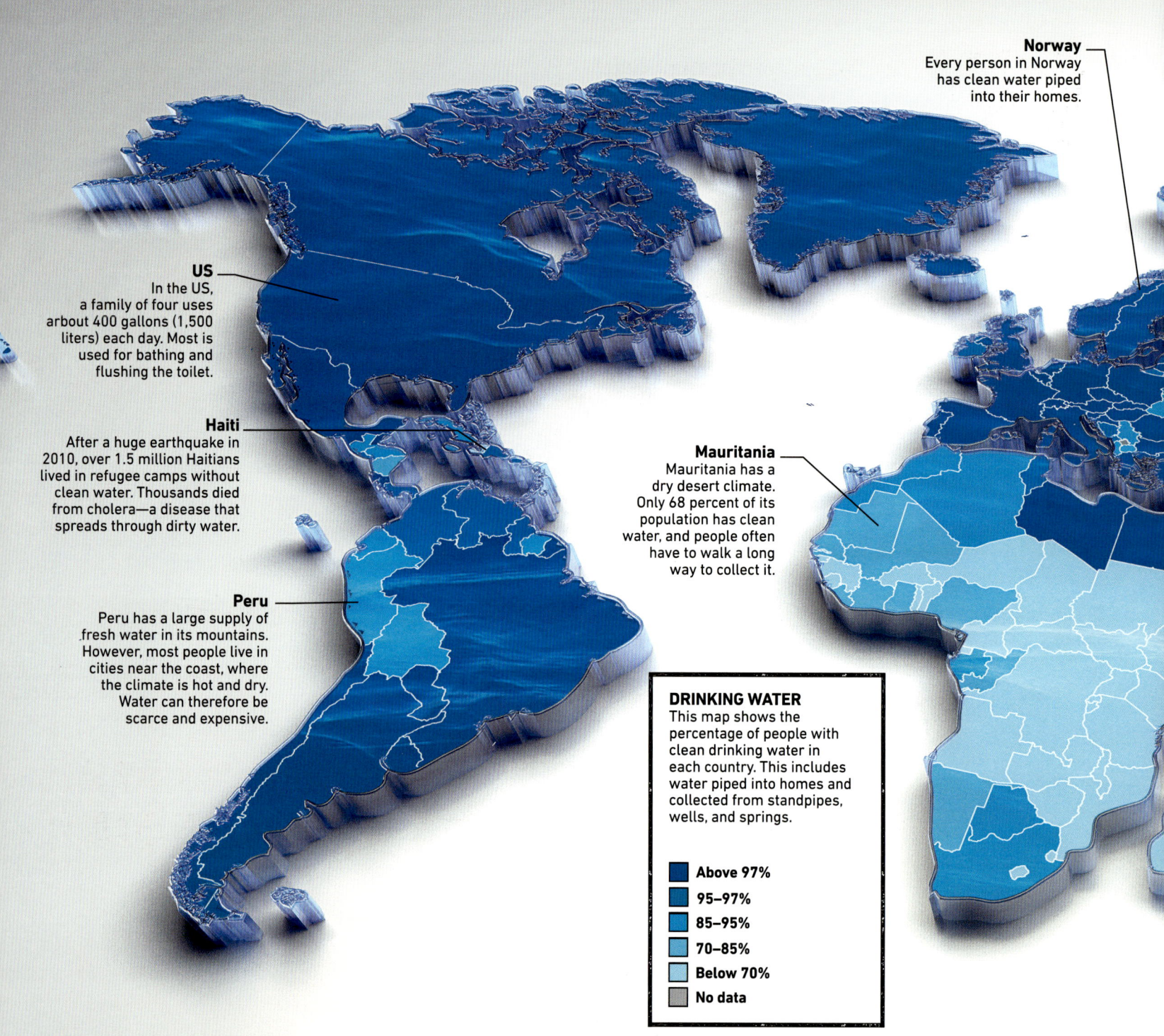

**Norway**
Every person in Norway has clean water piped into their homes.

**US**
In the US, a family of four uses arbout 400 gallons (1,500 liters) each day. Most is used for bathing and flushing the toilet.

**Haiti**
After a huge earthquake in 2010, over 1.5 million Haitians lived in refugee camps without clean water. Thousands died from cholera—a disease that spreads through dirty water.

**Mauritania**
Mauritania has a dry desert climate. Only 68 percent of its population has clean water, and people often have to walk a long way to collect it.

**Peru**
Peru has a large supply of fresh water in its mountains. However, most people live in cities near the coast, where the climate is hot and dry. Water can therefore be scarce and expensive.

**DRINKING WATER**
This map shows the percentage of people with clean drinking water in each country. This includes water piped into homes and collected from standpipes, wells, and springs.

- Above 97%
- 95–97%
- 85–95%
- 70–85%
- Below 70%
- No data

# Clean water

The tap in your home may give you an instant supply of clean drinking water. However, millions of people around the world must get their water from a standpipe or a well. For one in three people, their sources of water are contaminated and unsafe to drink.

**Thirsty crops**
Growing crops in dry climates is by far the thirstiest human activity. It uses much more water than is used in people's homes and dominates water use in many countries. That's why parts of central Asia, where farmers water fields of cotton, top this list of overall water consumers.

IN DEVELOPING COUNTRIES, 70 PERCENT OF INDUSTRIAL WASTE IS

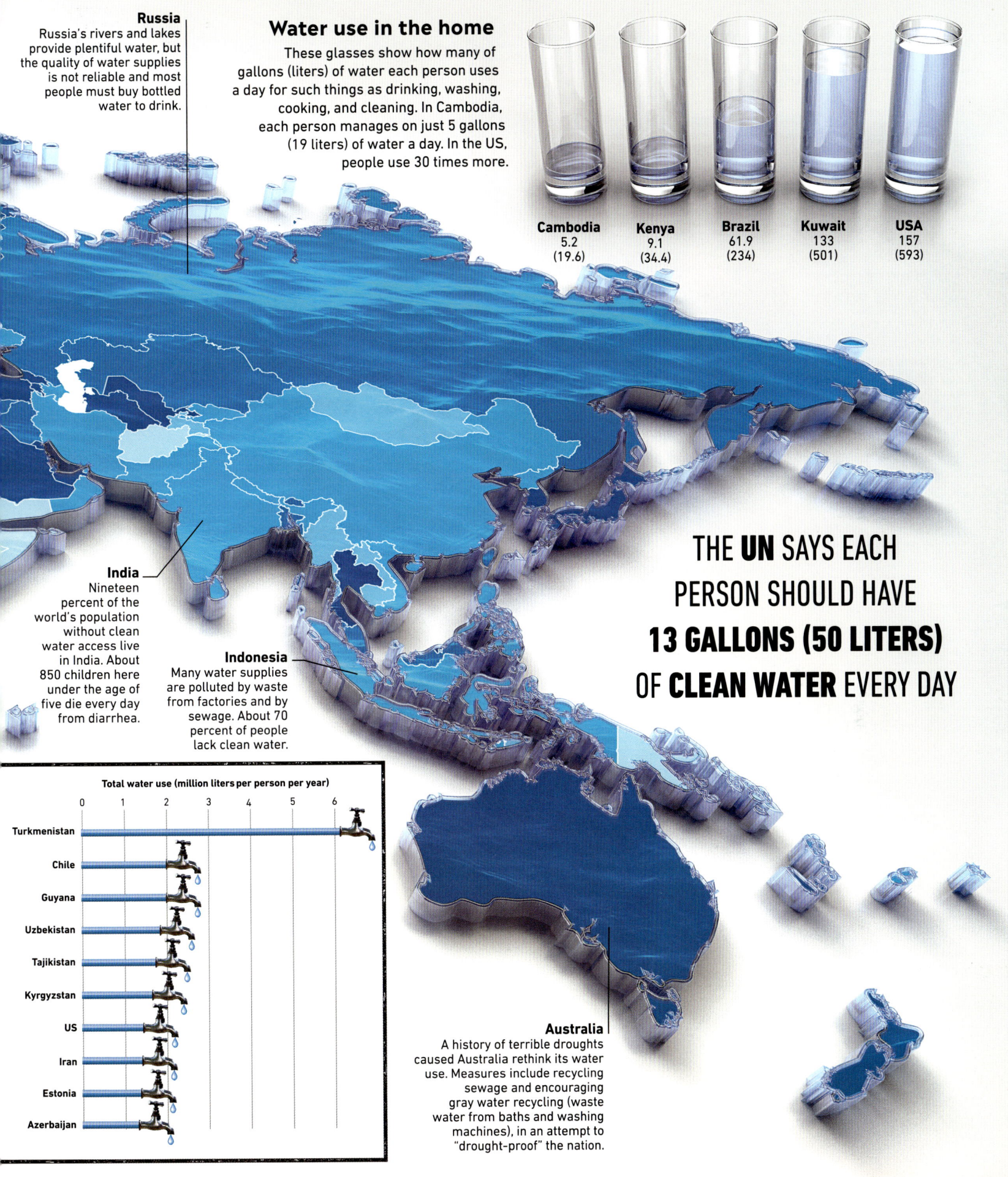

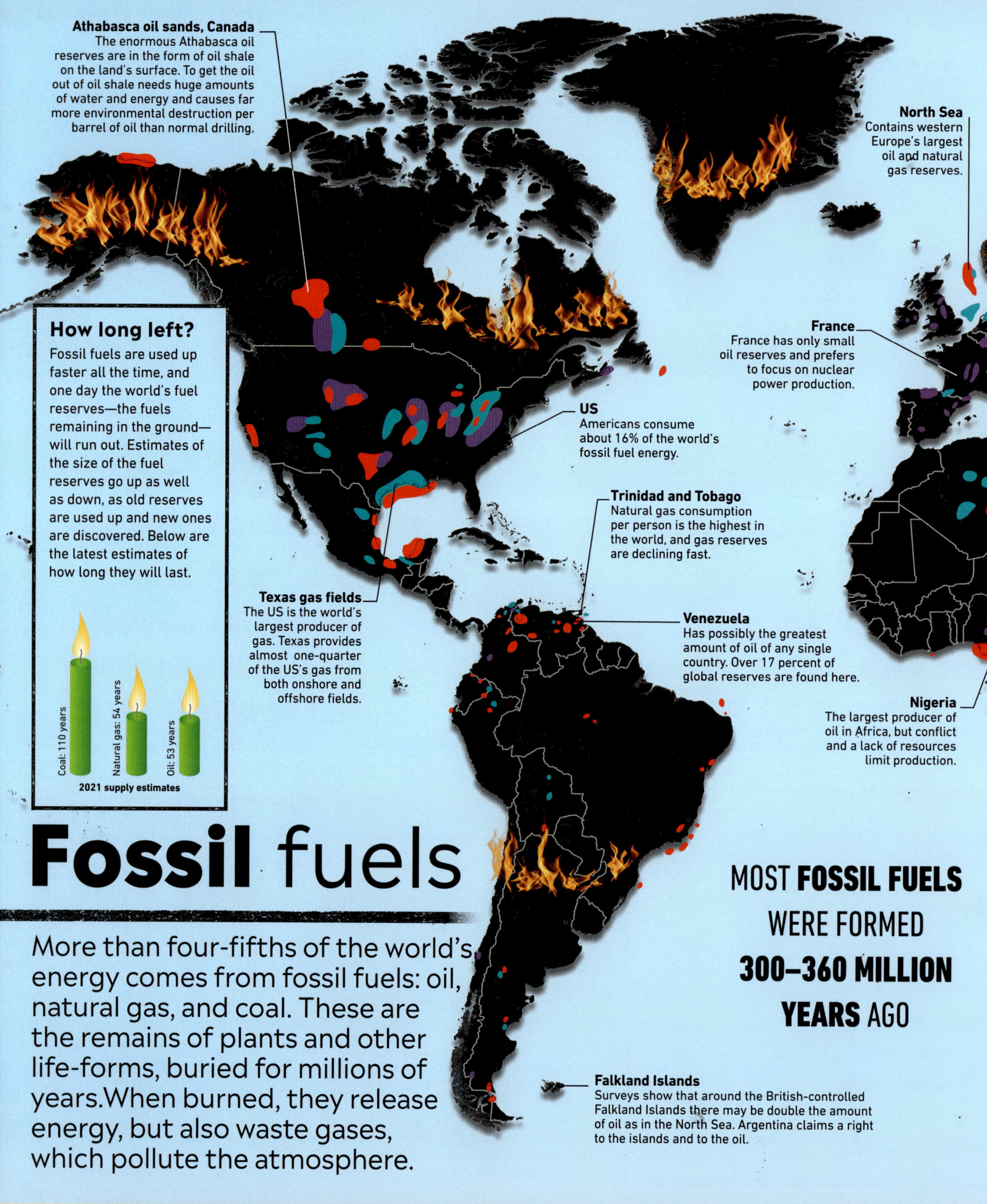

# Fossil fuels

More than four-fifths of the world's energy comes from fossil fuels: oil, natural gas, and coal. These are the remains of plants and other life-forms, buried for millions of years. When burned, they release energy, but also waste gases, which pollute the atmosphere.

**MOST FOSSIL FUELS WERE FORMED 300–360 MILLION YEARS AGO**

## How long left?

Fossil fuels are used up faster all the time, and one day the world's fuel reserves—the fuels remaining in the ground—will run out. Estimates of the size of the fuel reserves go up as well as down, as old reserves are used up and new ones are discovered. Below are the latest estimates of how long they will last.

Coal: 110 years
Natural gas: 54 years
Oil: 53 years
2021 supply estimates

**Athabasca oil sands, Canada**
The enormous Athabasca oil reserves are in the form of oil shale on the land's surface. To get the oil out of oil shale needs huge amounts of water and energy and causes far more environmental destruction per barrel of oil than normal drilling.

**North Sea**
Contains western Europe's largest oil and natural gas reserves.

**France**
France has only small oil reserves and prefers to focus on nuclear power production.

**US**
Americans consume about 16% of the world's fossil fuel energy.

**Texas gas fields**
The US is the world's largest producer of gas. Texas provides almost one-quarter of the US's gas from both onshore and offshore fields.

**Trinidad and Tobago**
Natural gas consumption per person is the highest in the world, and gas reserves are declining fast.

**Venezuela**
Has possibly the greatest amount of oil of any single country. Over 17 percent of global reserves are found here.

**Nigeria**
The largest producer of oil in Africa, but conflict and a lack of resources limit production.

**Falkland Islands**
Surveys show that around the British-controlled Falkland Islands there may be double the amount of oil as in the North Sea. Argentina claims a right to the islands and to the oil.

104 FROM THE LATE 2ND CENTURY CE, THE ROMANS IN BRITAIN MINED

People and planet

**Russia**
Has the world's largest natural gas reserves and second-largest coal reserves. Three times as much gas is consumed in Russia as coal.

**FUEL RESERVES**
Fossil fuels form in intense underground conditions as remains of dead organisms are compressed over millions of years. Oil and natural gas are found trapped in underground spaces and are extracted by drilling. Coal can be mined at the surface or deep underground. The map shows areas where there are significant oil, gas, and coal fields.

- Oil field
- Gas field
- Coal field

**China**
Largest producer of coal in the world, though it has the fourth-largest coal reserves.

**The Middle East**
Richest oil region on Earth—contains almost half the world's oil reserves.

**Ghawar oil field, Saudi Arabia**
Produces more oil than any other single oil field, contributing more than half of Saudi Arabia's vast oil production since 1938.

### Top fuel consumers

In 2007, China overtook the US as the largest burner of fossil fuels, mostly coal. However, because there are fewer people in the US, the average American burns more than twice as much fuel as the average Chinese citizen.

**Australia**
One of the world's top exporters of coal. Coal consumption per person is the highest in the world.

**Top gas consumer**
United States

**Top coal consumer**
China

**Top oil consumer**
United States

Oil refinery, New Orleans, Louisiana

COAL ON A LARGE SCALE TO HEAT HOUSES THROUGH UNDERFLOOR PIPES.

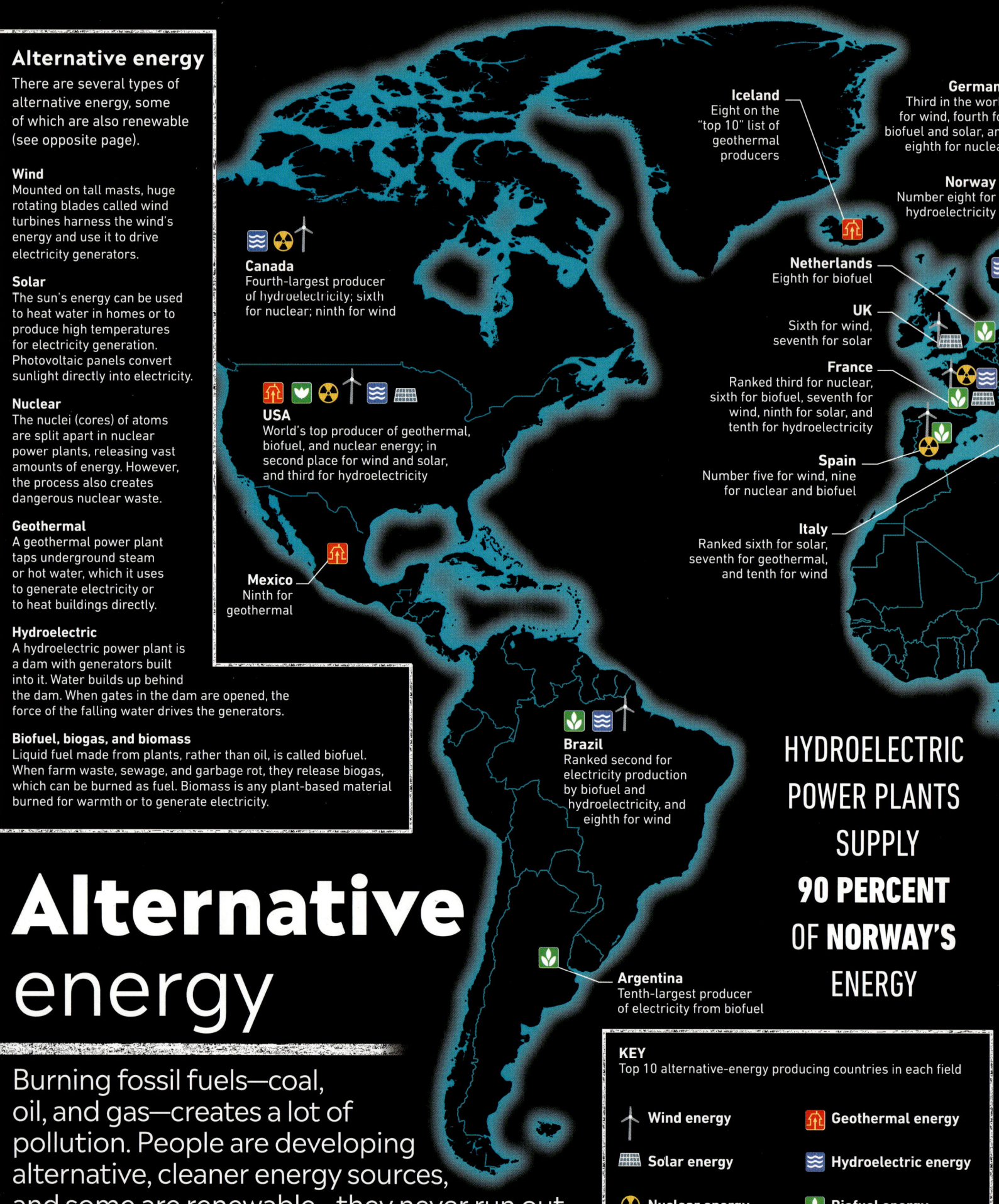

# Alternative energy

Burning fossil fuels—coal, oil, and gas—creates a lot of pollution. People are developing alternative, cleaner energy sources, and some are renewable—they never run out.

## Alternative energy

There are several types of alternative energy, some of which are also renewable (see opposite page).

**Wind**
Mounted on tall masts, huge rotating blades called wind turbines harness the wind's energy and use it to drive electricity generators.

**Solar**
The sun's energy can be used to heat water in homes or to produce high temperatures for electricity generation. Photovoltaic panels convert sunlight directly into electricity.

**Nuclear**
The nuclei (cores) of atoms are split apart in nuclear power plants, releasing vast amounts of energy. However, the process also creates dangerous nuclear waste.

**Geothermal**
A geothermal power plant taps underground steam or hot water, which it uses to generate electricity or to heat buildings directly.

**Hydroelectric**
A hydroelectric power plant is a dam with generators built into it. Water builds up behind the dam. When gates in the dam are opened, the force of the falling water drives the generators.

**Biofuel, biogas, and biomass**
Liquid fuel made from plants, rather than oil, is called biofuel. When farm waste, sewage, and garbage rot, they release biogas, which can be burned as fuel. Biomass is any plant-based material burned for warmth or to generate electricity.

**Canada** — Fourth-largest producer of hydroelectricity; sixth for nuclear; ninth for wind

**USA** — World's top producer of geothermal, biofuel, and nuclear energy; in second place for wind and solar, and third for hydroelectricity

**Mexico** — Ninth for geothermal

**Brazil** — Ranked second for electricity production by biofuel and hydroelectricity, and eighth for wind

**Argentina** — Tenth-largest producer of electricity from biofuel

**Iceland** — Eight on the "top 10" list of geothermal producers

**Germany** — Third in the world for wind, fourth for biofuel and solar, and eighth for nuclear

**Norway** — Number eight for hydroelectricity

**Netherlands** — Eighth for biofuel

**UK** — Sixth for wind, seventh for solar

**France** — Ranked third for nuclear, sixth for biofuel, seventh for wind, ninth for solar, and tenth for hydroelectricity

**Spain** — Number five for wind, nine for nuclear and biofuel

**Italy** — Ranked sixth for solar, seventh for geothermal, and tenth for wind

**HYDROELECTRIC POWER PLANTS SUPPLY 90 PERCENT OF NORWAY'S ENERGY**

**KEY**
Top 10 alternative-energy producing countries in each field
- Wind energy
- Solar energy
- Nuclear energy
- Geothermal energy
- Hydroelectric energy
- Biofuel energy

ICELAND IS A VOLCANIC ISLAND. CURRENTLY, ABOUT 90 PERCENT

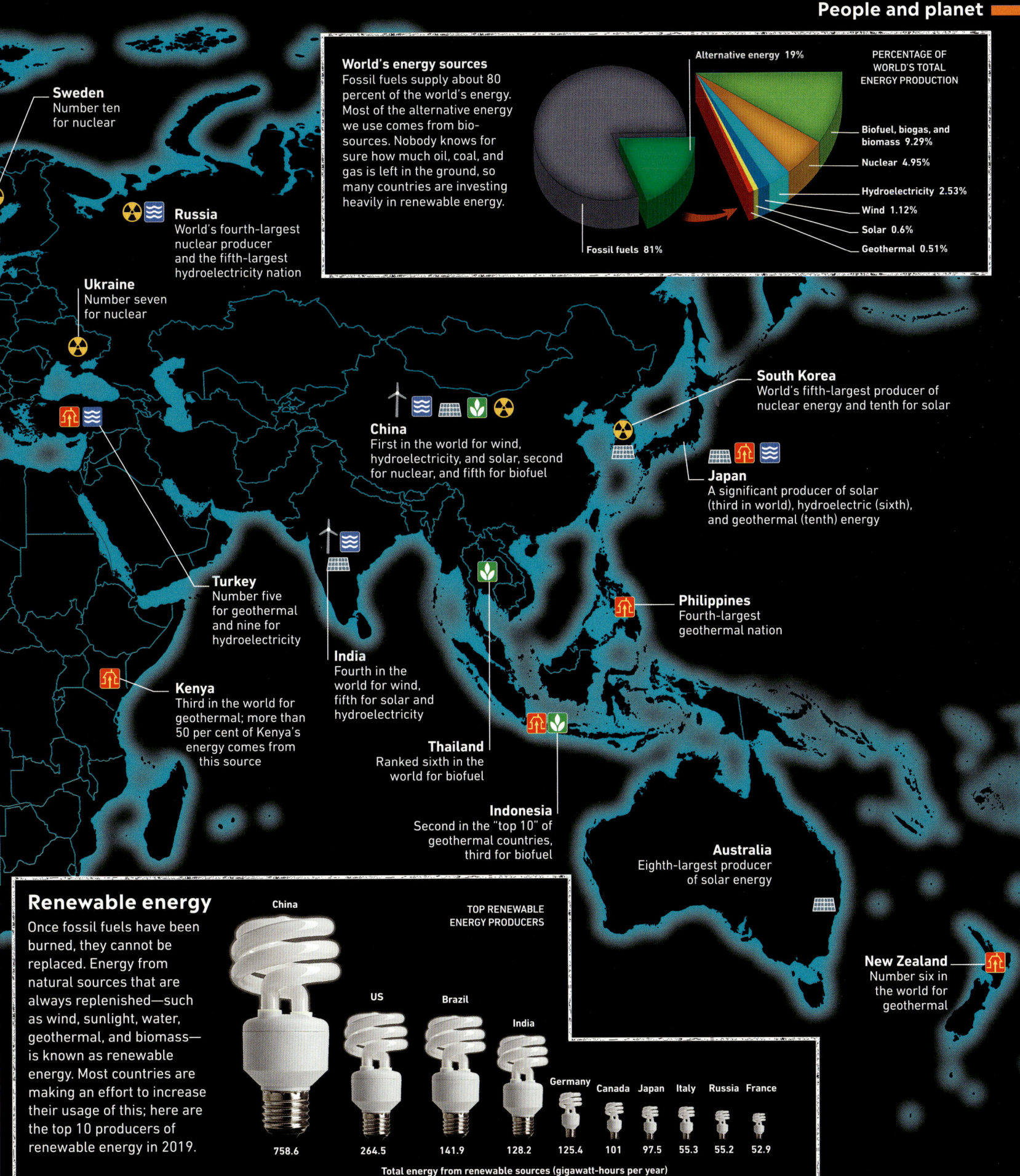

# Climate change

Earth's climate has been warming and cooling for millions of years. But in the last century, the planet has been warming rapidly. Scientists widely accept that this warming is linked with carbon dioxide and other gases released by human industry, transportation, and other activities. The gases trap outgoing heat in Earth's atmosphere, warming the planet.

**Glacier National Park, Montana**
In this center of climate change research, the glaciers have been retreating since the end of the Little Ice Age—a cool period ending in 1850. The shrinking has accelerated recently and experts think it is due to artificial global warming.

**Greenland ice sheet**
In an average summer, ice melts on about 20 percent of the surface of Greenland's ice sheet. At one point in the summer of 2012, scientists observed that 97 percent of the surface was melting.

**Warming oceans**
Satellite measurements show that the Southern Ocean is warming by 0.4°F (0.2°C) per decade—much more rapidly than other oceans.

**GLACIER NATIONAL PARK, MONTANA, NOW HAS ONLY 25 GLACIERS. IN 1910, THERE WERE 150**

**TEMPERATURE CHANGE**
This map, produced by scientists at NASA, shows the 5-year average global temperature for the years 2013–17, compared to temperatures for the years 1950–80. Regions that are hotter in 2013–17 than they were in the earlier period are shaded red. Those that are now colder appear blue.

°Fahrenheit: -3 -2 -1 0 1 2 3
°Celsius: -2 -1 0 1 2

● Other evidence of climate change

ALL SEVEN OF THE YEARS FROM 2014 TO 2020 RANK AS THE

People and planet

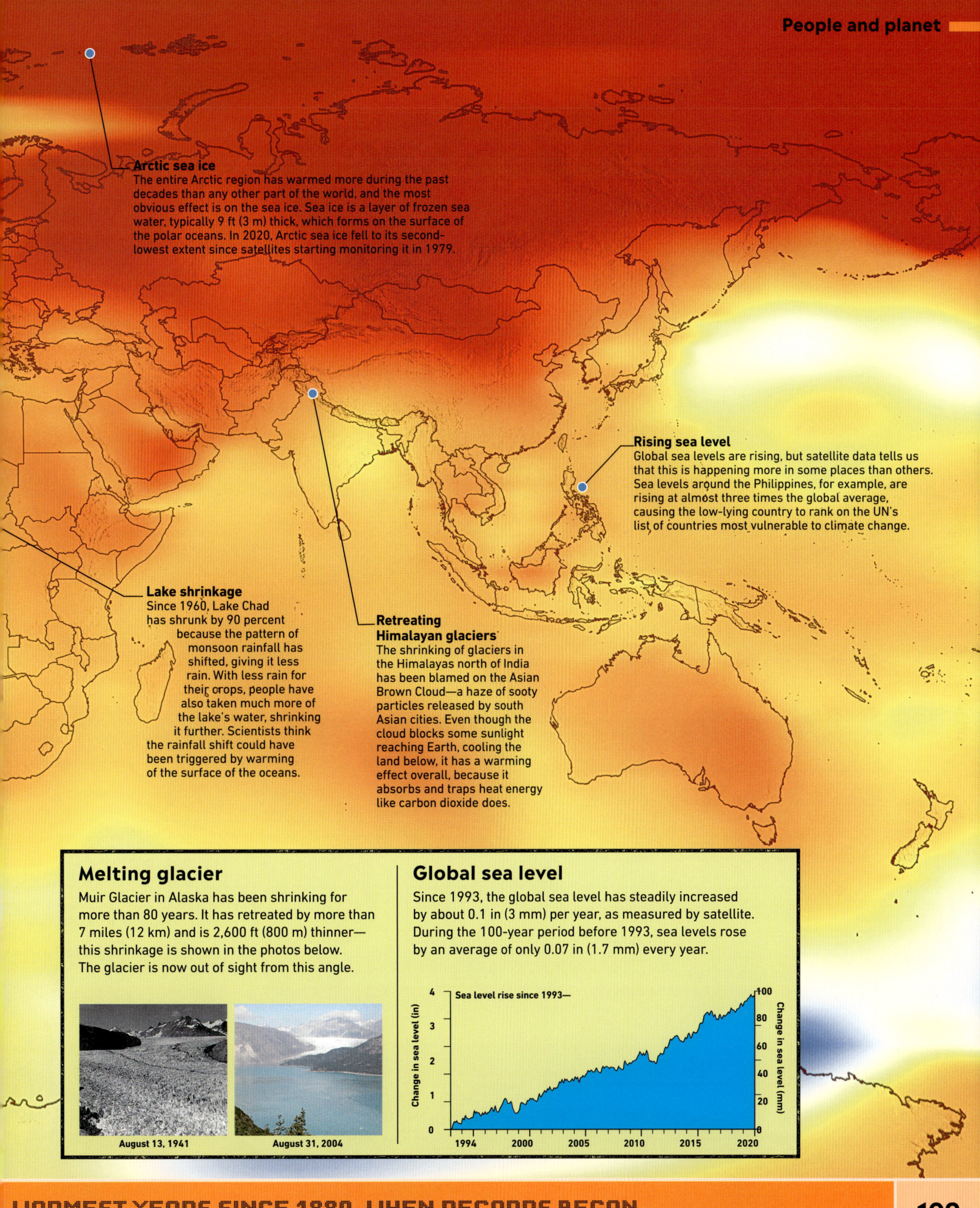

**Arctic sea ice**
The entire Arctic region has warmed more during the past decades than any other part of the world, and the most obvious effect is on the sea ice. Sea ice is a layer of frozen sea water, typically 9 ft (3 m) thick, which forms on the surface of the polar oceans. In 2020, Arctic sea ice fell to its second-lowest extent since satellites starting monitoring it in 1979.

**Rising sea level**
Global sea levels are rising, but satellite data tells us that this is happening more in some places than others. Sea levels around the Philippines, for example, are rising at almost three times the global average, causing the low-lying country to rank on the UN's list of countries most vulnerable to climate change.

**Lake shrinkage**
Since 1960, Lake Chad has shrunk by 90 percent because the pattern of monsoon rainfall has shifted, giving it less rain. With less rain for their crops, people have also taken much more of the lake's water, shrinking it further. Scientists think the rainfall shift could have been triggered by warming of the surface of the oceans.

**Retreating Himalayan glaciers**
The shrinking of glaciers in the Himalayas north of India has been blamed on the Asian Brown Cloud—a haze of sooty particles released by south Asian cities. Even though the cloud blocks some sunlight reaching Earth, cooling the land below, it has a warming effect overall, because it absorbs and traps heat energy like carbon dioxide does.

## Melting glacier
Muir Glacier in Alaska has been shrinking for more than 80 years. It has retreated by more than 7 miles (12 km) and is 2,600 ft (800 m) thinner—this shrinkage is shown in the photos below. The glacier is now out of sight from this angle.

August 13, 1941
August 31, 2004

## Global sea level
Since 1993, the global sea level has steadily increased by about 0.1 in (3 mm) per year, as measured by satellite. During the 100-year period before 1993, sea levels rose by an average of only 0.07 in (1.7 mm) every year.

WARMEST YEARS SINCE 1880, WHEN RECORDS BEGAN.

109

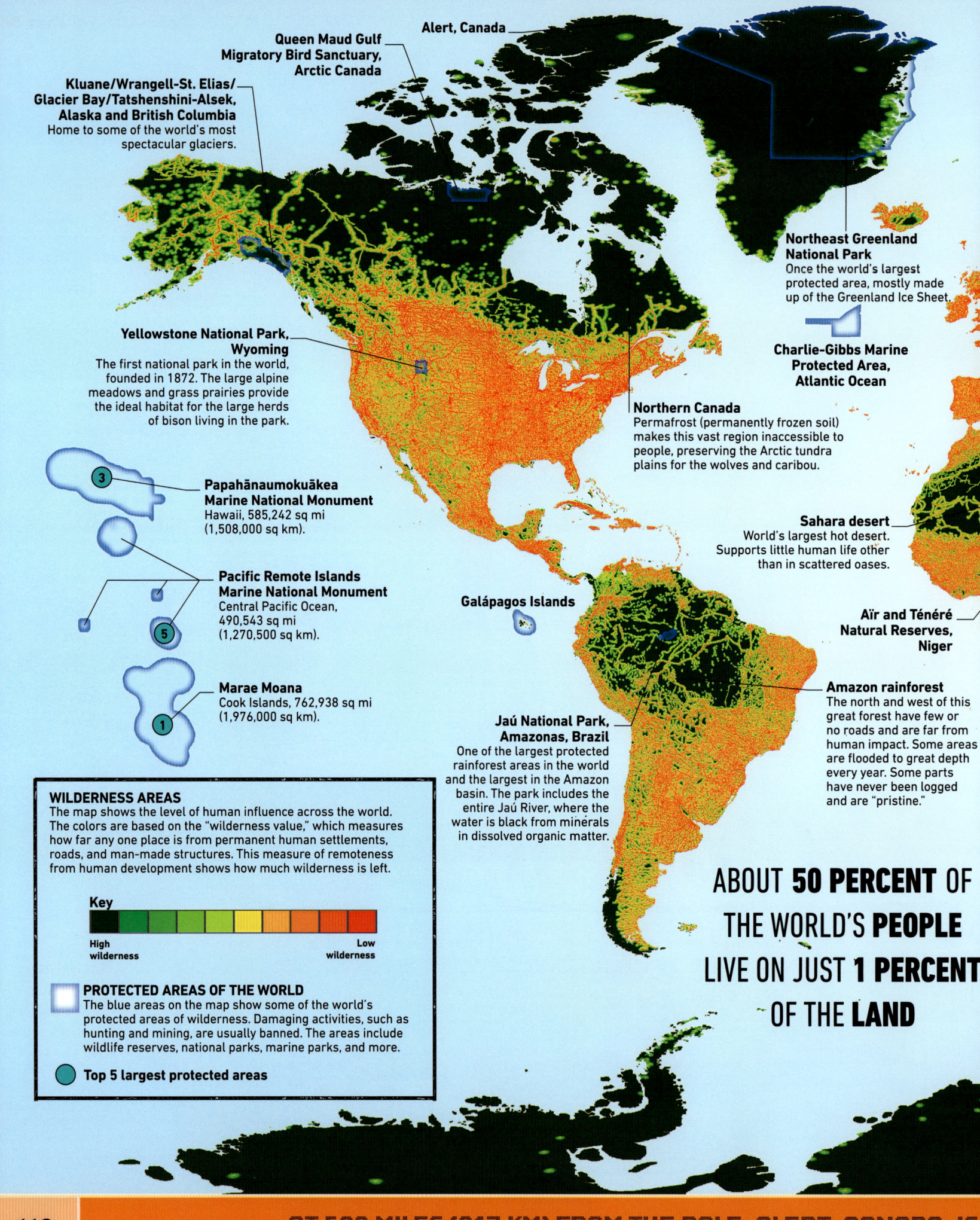

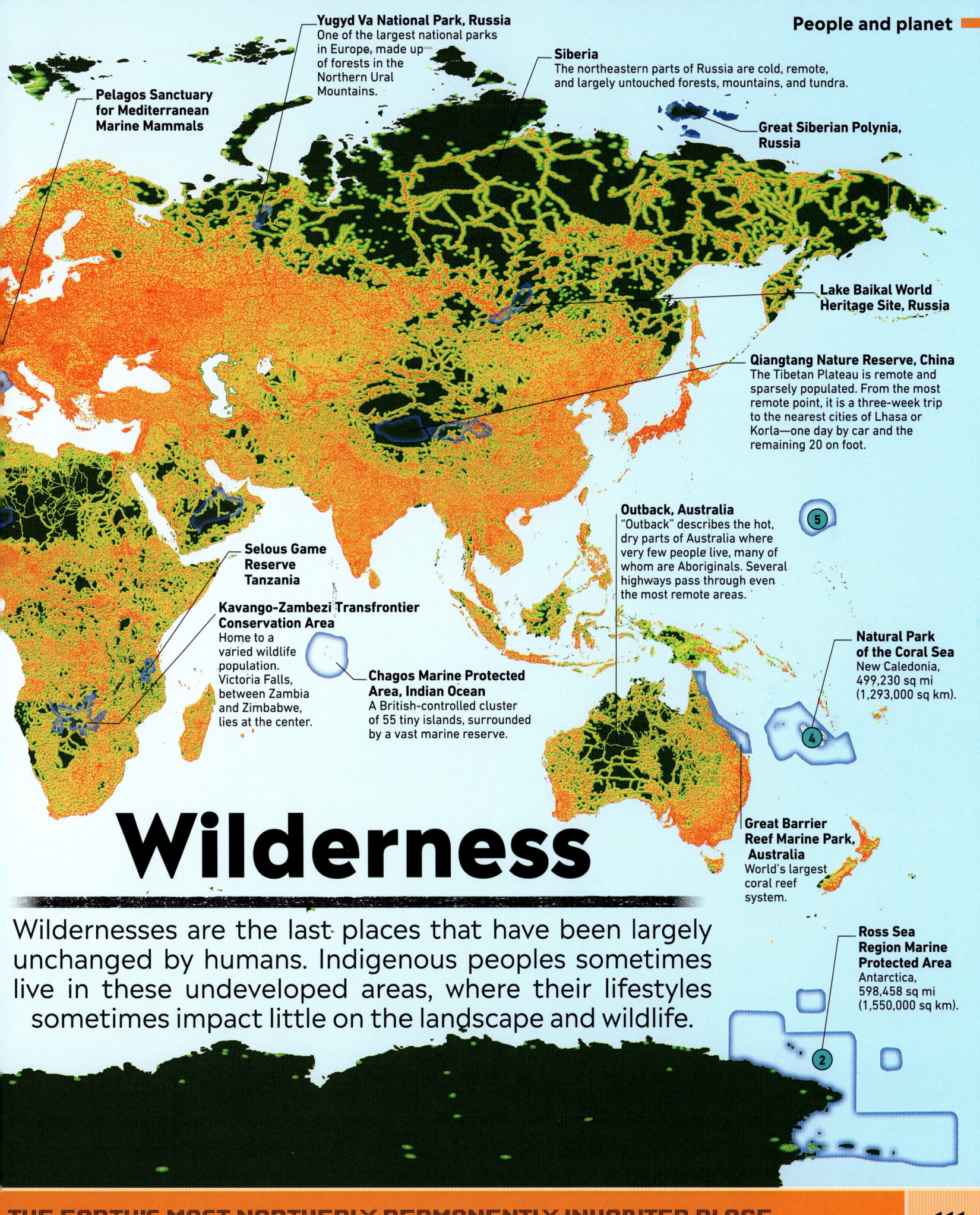

# Wilderness

**People and planet**

**Pelagos Sanctuary for Mediterranean Marine Mammals**

**Yugyd Va National Park, Russia** One of the largest national parks in Europe, made up of forests in the Northern Ural Mountains.

**Siberia** The northeastern parts of Russia are cold, remote, and largely untouched forests, mountains, and tundra.

**Great Siberian Polynia, Russia**

**Lake Baikal World Heritage Site, Russia**

**Qiangtang Nature Reserve, China** The Tibetan Plateau is remote and sparsely populated. From the most remote point, it is a three-week trip to the nearest cities of Lhasa or Korla—one day by car and the remaining 20 on foot.

**Selous Game Reserve Tanzania**

**Kavango-Zambezi Transfrontier Conservation Area** Home to a varied wildlife population. Victoria Falls, between Zambia and Zimbabwe, lies at the center.

**Chagos Marine Protected Area, Indian Ocean** A British-controlled cluster of 55 tiny islands, surrounded by a vast marine reserve.

**Outback, Australia** "Outback" describes the hot, dry parts of Australia where very few people live, many of whom are Aboriginals. Several highways pass through even the most remote areas.

**Natural Park of the Coral Sea** New Caledonia, 499,230 sq mi (1,293,000 sq km).

**Great Barrier Reef Marine Park, Australia** World's largest coral reef system.

**Ross Sea Region Marine Protected Area** Antarctica, 598,458 sq mi (1,550,000 sq km).

Wildernesses are the last places that have been largely unchanged by humans. Indigenous peoples sometimes live in these undeveloped areas, where their lifestyles sometimes impact little on the landscape and wildlife.

THE EARTH'S MOST NORTHERLY PERMANENTLY INHABITED PLACE.

# Engineering and technology

**Reaching for the sky**
The Burj Khalifa, the world's tallest building, can be seen in the distance in this view of fog-bound Dubai, the largest city in the United Arab Emirates.

# Introduction

Engineering and technology enable humans to achieve amazing feats. We build skyscrapers that reach toward the clouds, bridges that span great canyons, and tunnels that pierce mountains and travel under the sea. Our computer networks and transportation systems keep people and places connected. We can even explore other planets.

## World in motion

Transportation has shrunk our world. Thanks to jet airliners, superhighways, and high-speed rail routes, we can go on long-distance journeys that would have been unthinkable just a few decades ago. This transportation revolution began with the invention of the railroad at the start of the 19th century, and it has continued at speed ever since.

**Train collects** electricity from power cables suspended above the track.

**High-speed electric locomotive**
Launched in 1999, the Velaro is now in service in Germany, Spain, France, the UK, China, Russia, Belgium, Turkey, and the Netherlands. It is powered by electricity and can reach speeds of more than 218 mph (350 kph).

## Shrinking technology

Few, if any, areas of technology have advanced faster than computing. ENIAC, developed by the US Army in 1946, was the first general-purpose programmable electronic computer. ENIAC contained more than 100,000 components. Since then, electronic components have become smaller and smaller. A modern laptop computer is controlled by a tiny microchip that may be etched with more than a billion components.

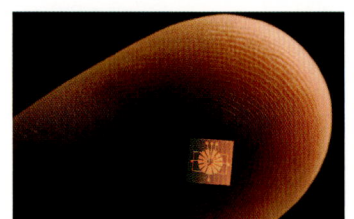

**Modern marvel**
This tiny computer, just 0.04 in (1 mm) square, is implanted into the eye to help people with the disease glaucoma.

**Enormous ancestor**
ENIAC weighed 33 tons and occupied an entire room. Operators programmed ENIAC by plugging and unplugging cables and adjusting switches.

FUGAKU WAS CROWNED THE WORLD'S FASTEST COMPUTER IN 2020, AND

# Engineering and technology

**Early steam engine**
Puffing Billy is the world's oldest surviving steam locomotive. Built in 1813 to haul coal in northern England, it had a top speed of about 6 mph (10 kph).

**Coal** carried in the tender was burned to heat water in the boiler and produce steam to drive the wheels.

**Bullet-shaped nose** enables locomotive to cut through the air more easily, increasing speed.

## Construction

A steel-and-concrete building revolution began in the late 19th century. Frames made of steel girders allowed taller structures to be built, and the invention of reinforced concrete—concrete with steel rods set into it—introduced an amazingly strong, durable new material. Together, steel and reinforced concrete gave birth to the modern skyscraper, changing the face of the world's cities.

- **Ancient concrete**
  The Romans were experts in building with concrete. It was used in the construction of the Colosseum and the Pantheon in Rome.

- **World's oldest skycraper city?**
  Shibam, in Yemen, has about 500 high-rise apartment buildings made of mud brick, most dating from the 16th century.

- **First steel-framed skyscraper**
  Completed in 1885, the innovative 10-story Home Insurance Building in Chicago, Illinois, used a steel frame to support the walls.

- **Reinforced first**
  The first skyscraper built with reinforced concrete was the 15-story Ingalls Building, in Cincinnati, Ohio, erected in 1903.

**Manhattan, then and now**
The Brooklyn Bridge spans New York's East River. The view across to Manhattan Island has changed dramatically since the bridge opened in 1883, and it now bristles with skyscrapers.

## Infrastructure

The built and engineered systems that we rely on every day—from sewers and telecommunication networks to power lines, railroads, and roads—are collectively known as infrastructure. Without such systems, our modern way of life would be impossible.

- **First telephone exchange**
  The first commercial exchange to connect callers was built in New Haven, Connecticut, in 1878.

- **Intercity railroad**
  Opened in 1830, the Manchester to Liverpool route in England was the first intercity railroad.

**Ulm–Stuttgart autobahn, 1950**
Germany was a pioneer of the freeway, or autobahn, in the 1930s. Cars did not clog the roads until much later!

CAN PERFORM OVER 442 QUADRILLION CALCULATIONS PER SECOND!

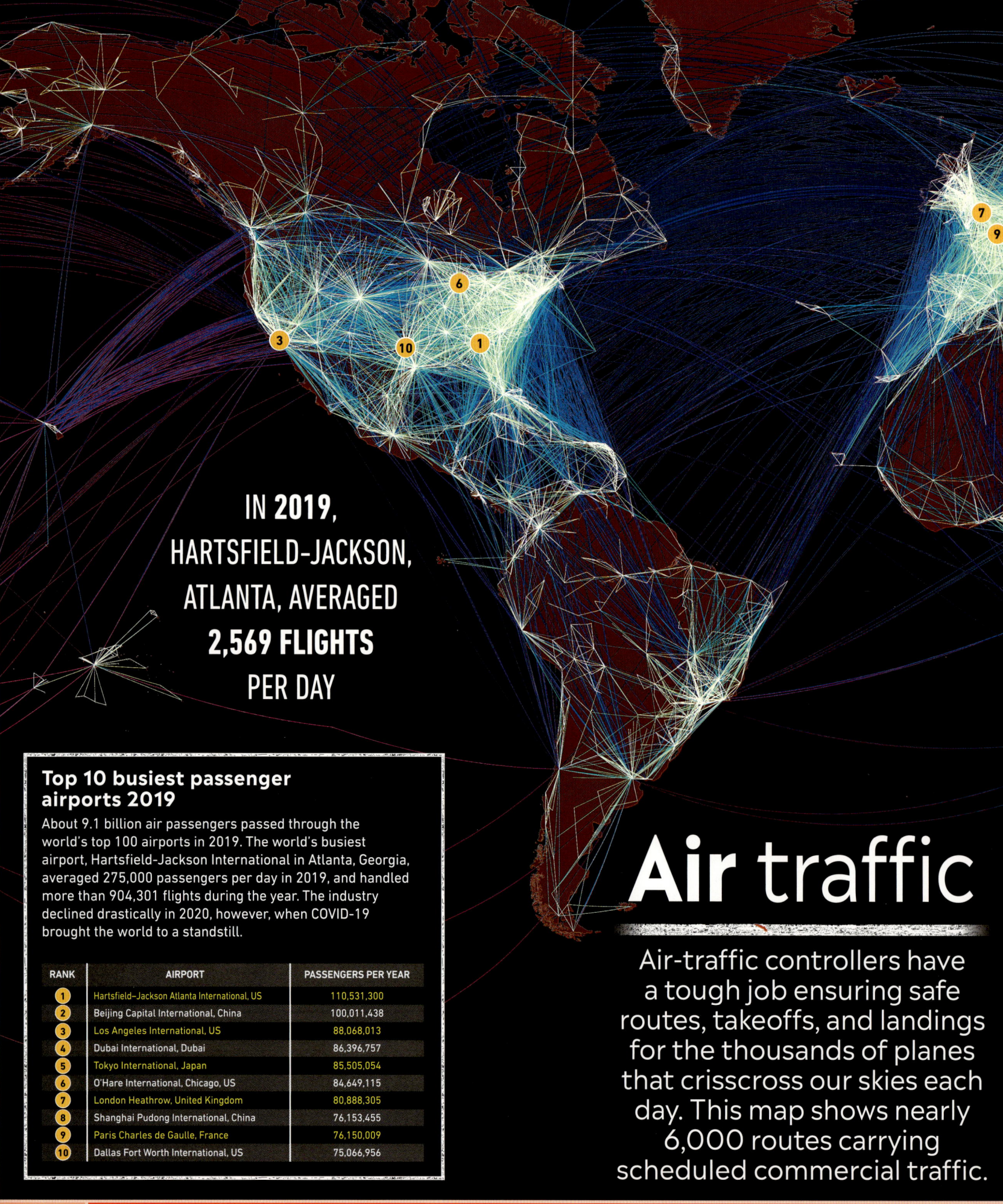

# Air traffic

Air-traffic controllers have a tough job ensuring safe routes, takeoffs, and landings for the thousands of planes that crisscross our skies each day. This map shows nearly 6,000 routes carrying scheduled commercial traffic.

**IN 2019, HARTSFIELD-JACKSON, ATLANTA, AVERAGED 2,569 FLIGHTS PER DAY**

## Top 10 busiest passenger airports 2019

About 9.1 billion air passengers passed through the world's top 100 airports in 2019. The world's busiest airport, Hartsfield-Jackson International in Atlanta, Georgia, averaged 275,000 passengers per day in 2019, and handled more than 904,301 flights during the year. The industry declined drastically in 2020, however, when COVID-19 brought the world to a standstill.

| RANK | AIRPORT | PASSENGERS PER YEAR |
|---|---|---|
| 1 | Hartsfield–Jackson Atlanta International, US | 110,531,300 |
| 2 | Beijing Capital International, China | 100,011,438 |
| 3 | Los Angeles International, US | 88,068,013 |
| 4 | Dubai International, Dubai | 86,396,757 |
| 5 | Tokyo International, Japan | 85,505,054 |
| 6 | O'Hare International, Chicago, US | 84,649,115 |
| 7 | London Heathrow, United Kingdom | 80,888,305 |
| 8 | Shanghai Pudong International, China | 76,153,455 |
| 9 | Paris Charles de Gaulle, France | 76,150,009 |
| 10 | Dallas Fort Worth International, US | 75,066,956 |

WORLDWIDE, THERE WERE 38.3 MILLION FLIGHT DEPARTURES

# Engineering and technology

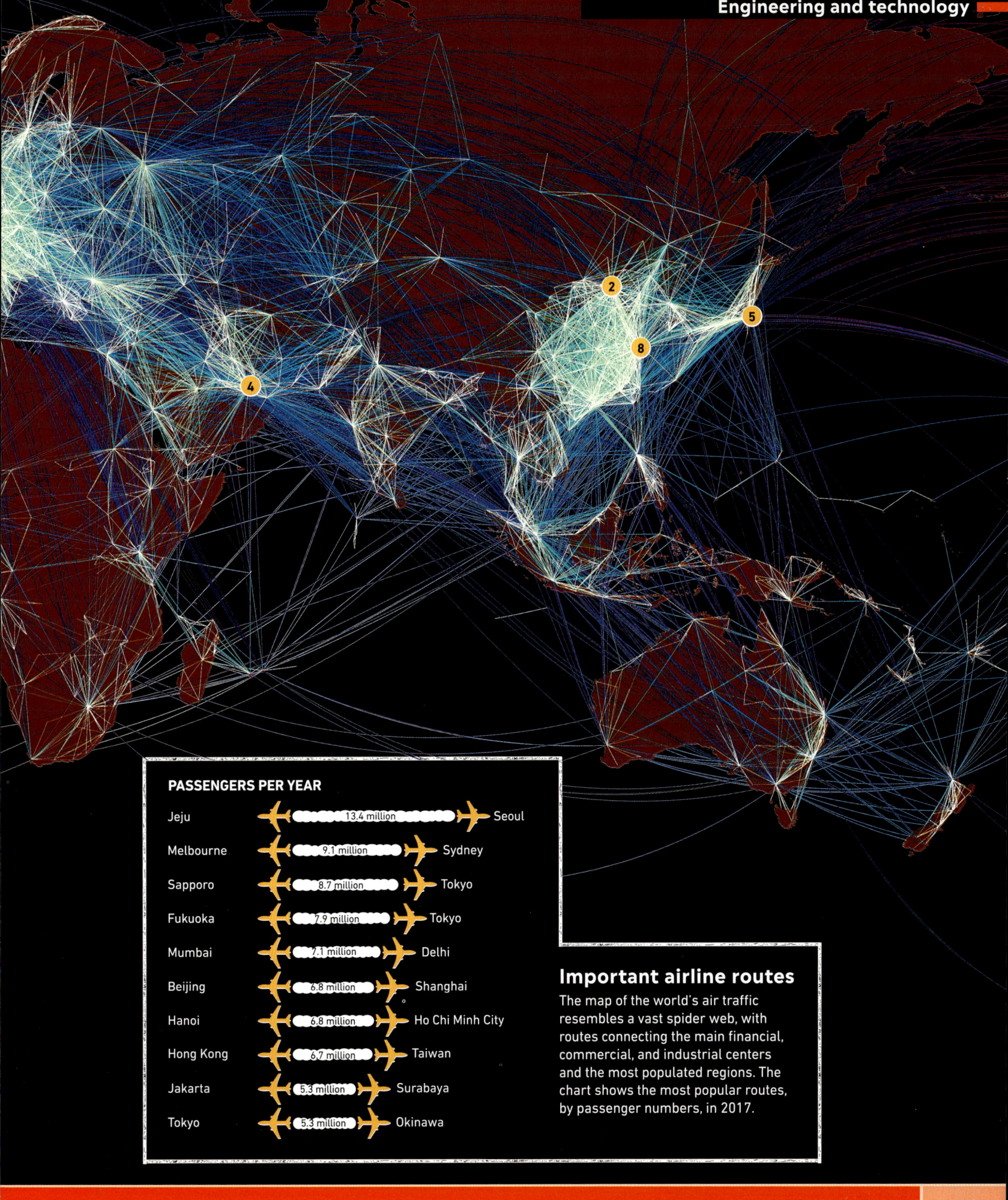

**PASSENGERS PER YEAR**

| From | Passengers | To |
|---|---|---|
| Jeju | 13.4 million | Seoul |
| Melbourne | 9.1 million | Sydney |
| Sapporo | 8.7 million | Tokyo |
| Fukuoka | 7.9 million | Tokyo |
| Mumbai | 7.1 million | Delhi |
| Beijing | 6.8 million | Shanghai |
| Hanoi | 6.8 million | Ho Chi Minh City |
| Hong Kong | 6.7 million | Taiwan |
| Jakarta | 5.3 million | Surabaya |
| Tokyo | 5.3 million | Okinawa |

## Important airline routes

The map of the world's air traffic resembles a vast spider web, with routes connecting the main financial, commercial, and industrial centers and the most populated regions. The chart shows the most popular routes, by passenger numbers, in 2017.

IN 2019, IT IS PREDICTED THAT THERE WILL BE 51.71 MILLION IN 2030.

**SHIPPING ROUTES**
The map shows the main shipping routes of the world and how busy they are. It is based on information from a study by scientists who used GPS technology to monitor the journeys of 16,363 cargo ships over a year.

- Over 3,000 journeys
- 1,001–3,000
- 501–1,000
- 101–500
- 25–100
- Less than 25

Los Angeles
Long Beach

PACIFIC OCEAN

**Panama Canal**
The canal, opened in 1914, connects the Pacific and Atlantic oceans. It is the world's busiest route, with about 14,000 ships passing through it each year.

ATLANTIC OCEAN

# Shipping

Most countries need to sell the goods they produce and import the things they need. Shipping plays an essential role in world trade, carrying food, fuel, chemicals, and manufactured goods between markets.

**MORE THAN 80 PERCENT OF GLOBAL TRADE IS CARRIED BY SEA**

MOVING CARGO BY SHIP IS ABOUT TWICE AS ENERGY EFFICIENT

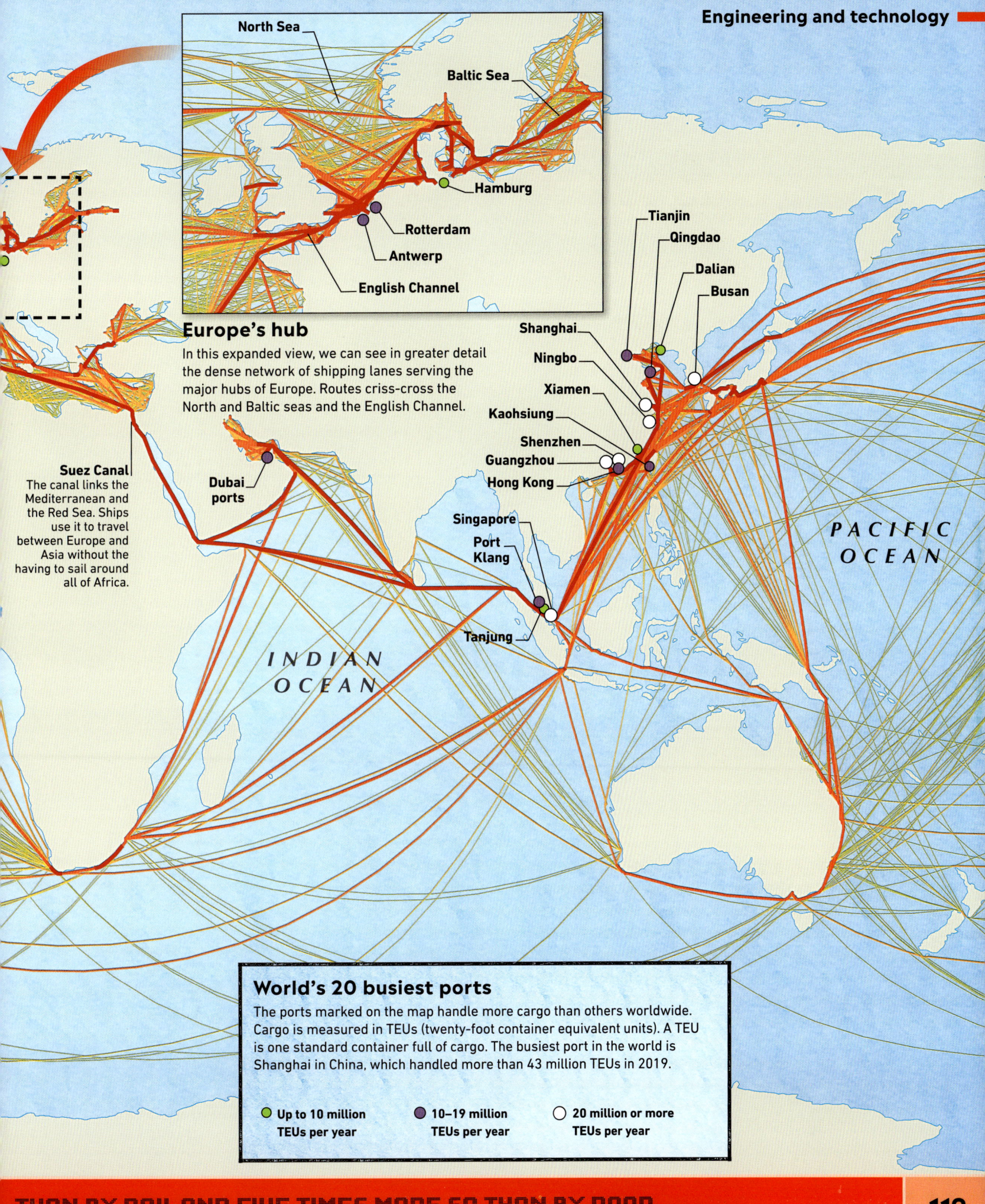

# Railroads

In the early 19th century, railroads began to change the world radically by opening up new opportunities for travel and trade. Today, with roads gridlocked by traffic, modern railroads are making a comeback.

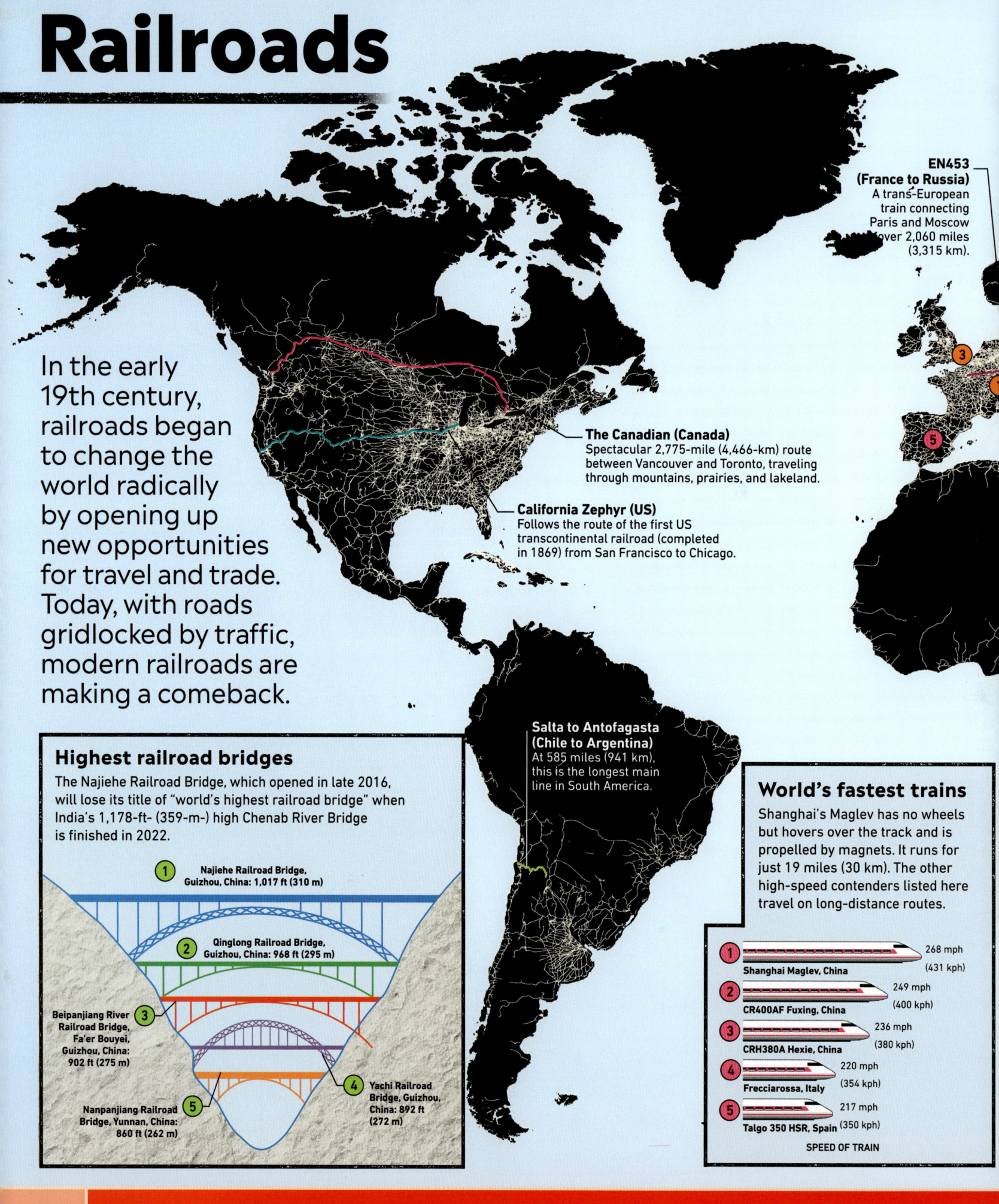

**EN453 (France to Russia)**
A trans-European train connecting Paris and Moscow over 2,060 miles (3,315 km).

**The Canadian (Canada)**
Spectacular 2,775-mile (4,466-km) route between Vancouver and Toronto, traveling through mountains, prairies, and lakeland.

**California Zephyr (US)**
Follows the route of the first US transcontinental railroad (completed in 1869) from San Francisco to Chicago.

**Salta to Antofagasta (Chile to Argentina)**
At 585 miles (941 km), this is the longest main line in South America.

## Highest railroad bridges

The Najiehe Railroad Bridge, which opened in late 2016, will lose its title of "world's highest railroad bridge" when India's 1,178-ft- (359-m-) high Chenab River Bridge is finished in 2022.

1. Najiehe Railroad Bridge, Guizhou, China: 1,017 ft (310 m)
2. Qinglong Railroad Bridge, Guizhou, China: 968 ft (295 m)
3. Beipanjiang River Railroad Bridge, Fa'er Bouyei, Guizhou, China: 902 ft (275 m)
4. Yachi Railroad Bridge, Guizhou, China: 892 ft (272 m)
5. Nanpanjiang Railroad Bridge, Yunnan, China: 860 ft (262 m)

## World's fastest trains

Shanghai's Maglev has no wheels but hovers over the track and is propelled by magnets. It runs for just 19 miles (30 km). The other high-speed contenders listed here travel on long-distance routes.

1. Shanghai Maglev, China — 268 mph (431 kph)
2. CR400AF Fuxing, China — 249 mph (400 kph)
3. CRH380A Hexie, China — 236 mph (380 kph)
4. Frecciarossa, Italy — 220 mph (354 kph)
5. Talgo 350 HSR, Spain — 217 mph (350 kph)

SPEED OF TRAIN

**THE WORLD'S FIRST HIGH-SPEED RAIL SYSTEM OPENED IN JAPAN**

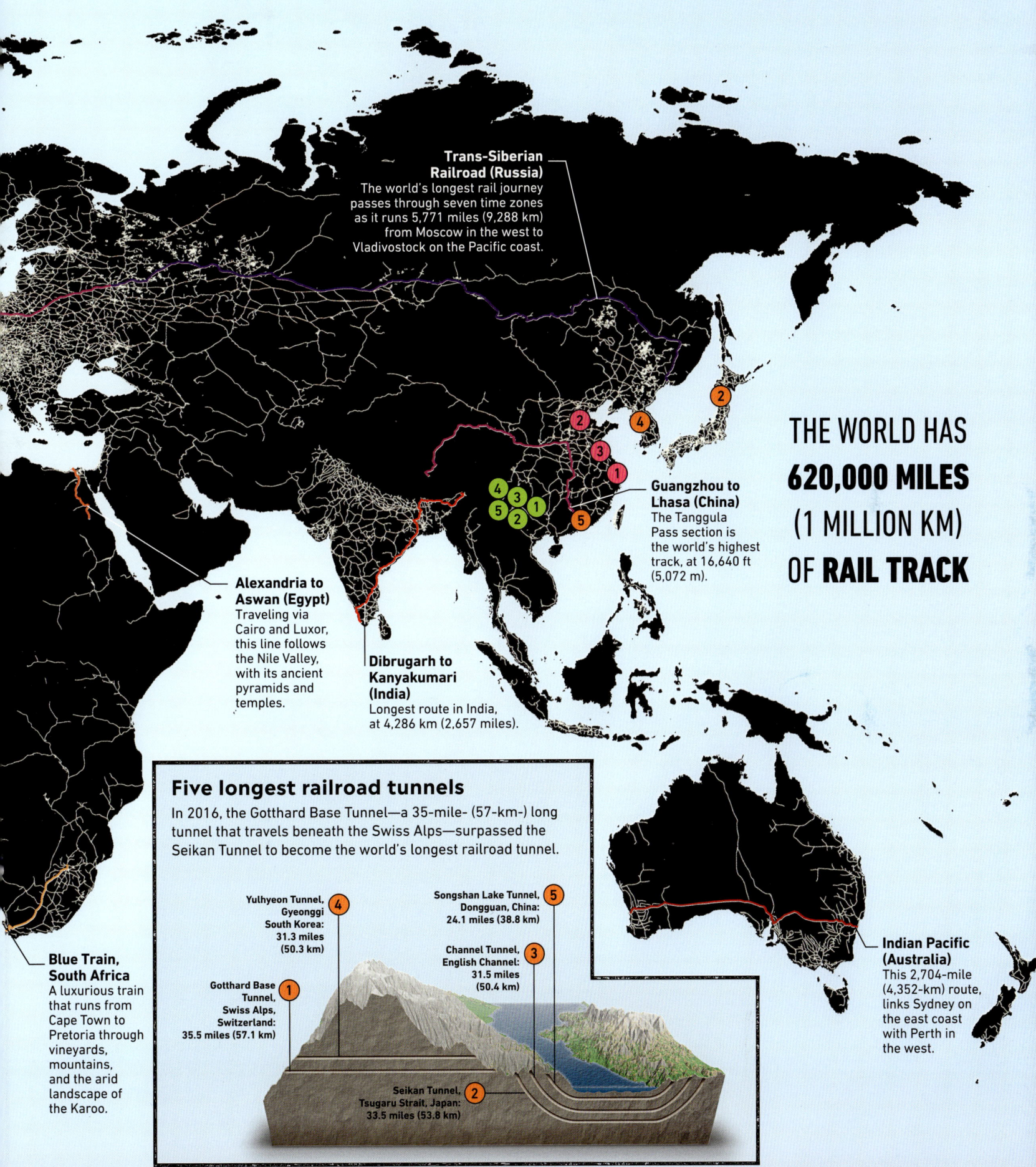

# Roads

The planet is now more accessible by road than it has ever been. There are about 65 million miles (104 million km) of roads on Earth, from multilane urban freeways to seasonal ice roads made from frozen lakes and seas.

## Mountain roads and passes

**① Trollstigen, Norway**
This dramatic road's name means "Trolls' ladder." It has 11 hairpin bends, which wind up the steep mountainside.

**② Stelvio Pass, Italy**
One of the highest roads in the Alps, its 60 hairpin bends provide a challenge for both drivers and bicyclers.

**③ Khardung La, India**
This famously high mountain pass in the Ladakh part of Kashmir was built in 1976 and opened to motor vehicles in 1988.

**④ Semo La, Tibet, China**
Possibly the highest vehicle-accessible pass in the world, it was reliably measured in 1999 at 18,258 ft (5,565 m).

**⑤ Irohazaka Winding Road**
Each of the 48 hairpin turns on this route in Japan is labeled with one of the 48 characters of the Japanese alphabet.

**Dempster Highway Extension**
An ice road built on the frozen Mackenzie River and Arctic Ocean, it provides a winter route to the isolated community of Tuktoyaktuk.

**Tibbit to Contwoyto Winter Road**
An ice road built over frozen lakes, it is open for about 10 weeks from late January each year.

**Pacific Coast Highway**
This world-famous route hugs the California coast from Orange County in the south to the forests of giant redwood trees in the north.

**Bonn–Köln Autobahn**
Built in 1932, it was the first road designed exclusively for cars, with divided lanes and no intersections with other roads.

**Cabot Trail**
Looping around the northern tip of Cape Breton Island, Nova Scotia, and named after 16th-century Italian explorer, John Cabot.

**Route 66**
A 2,448-mile (3,940-km) road that follows the historic route taken by migrants to California during the Great Depression.

**Natchez Trace Parkway**
A route used by Native Americans and their animals for thousands of years before the modern road was built.

**Darién Gap, Panama**
A stretch of rainforest that breaks the Pan-American Highway's route.

**Pan-American Highway**
About 29,800 miles (48,000 km) long, it runs through 18 countries, from Alaska to the southern tip of Argentina.

**Yungas Road, Bolivia**
A single-track mountain road heavily used by trucks but with unprotected sheer drops of 1,970 ft (600 m). Up to 300 travelers are killed on the route every year.

## World's busiest roads

**① Ontario Highway 401, Canada**
The busiest highway in North America—more than 440,000 vehicles pass through the Toronto section every day. It is also one of the widest in the world—some sections of the route have 18 lanes.

**② Interstate 405, California**
Runs north from the city of Irvine in Orange County to San Fernando, a route that is known as the northern segment of the San Diego Freeway. This freeway is the busiest and most congested in the US, carrying up to 379,000 vehicles a day.

HIGHWAY 401, ONTARIO, CANADA

**FRANCE HAS NEARLY 620,000 MILES (1 MILLION KM) OF PAVED ROADS.**

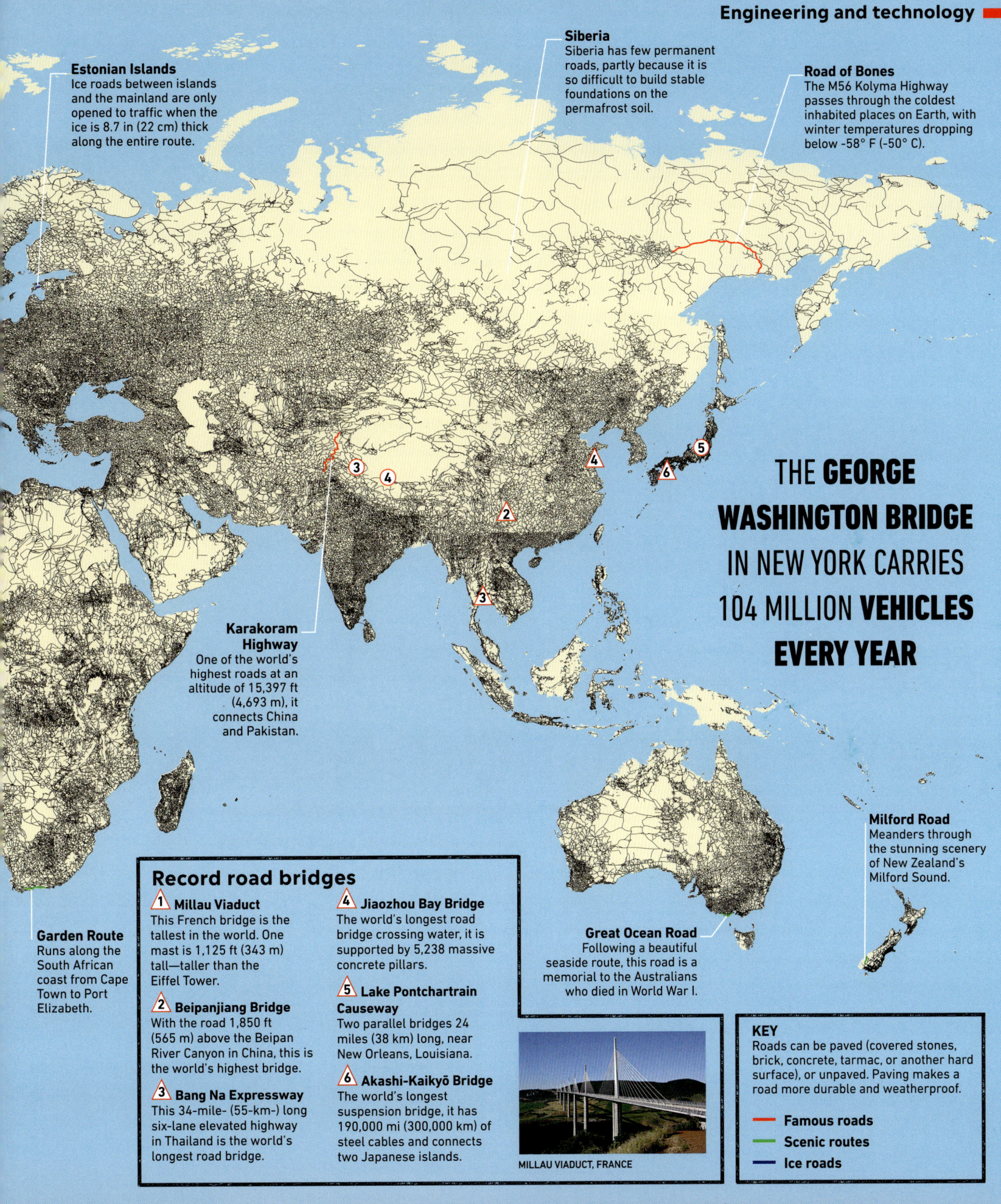

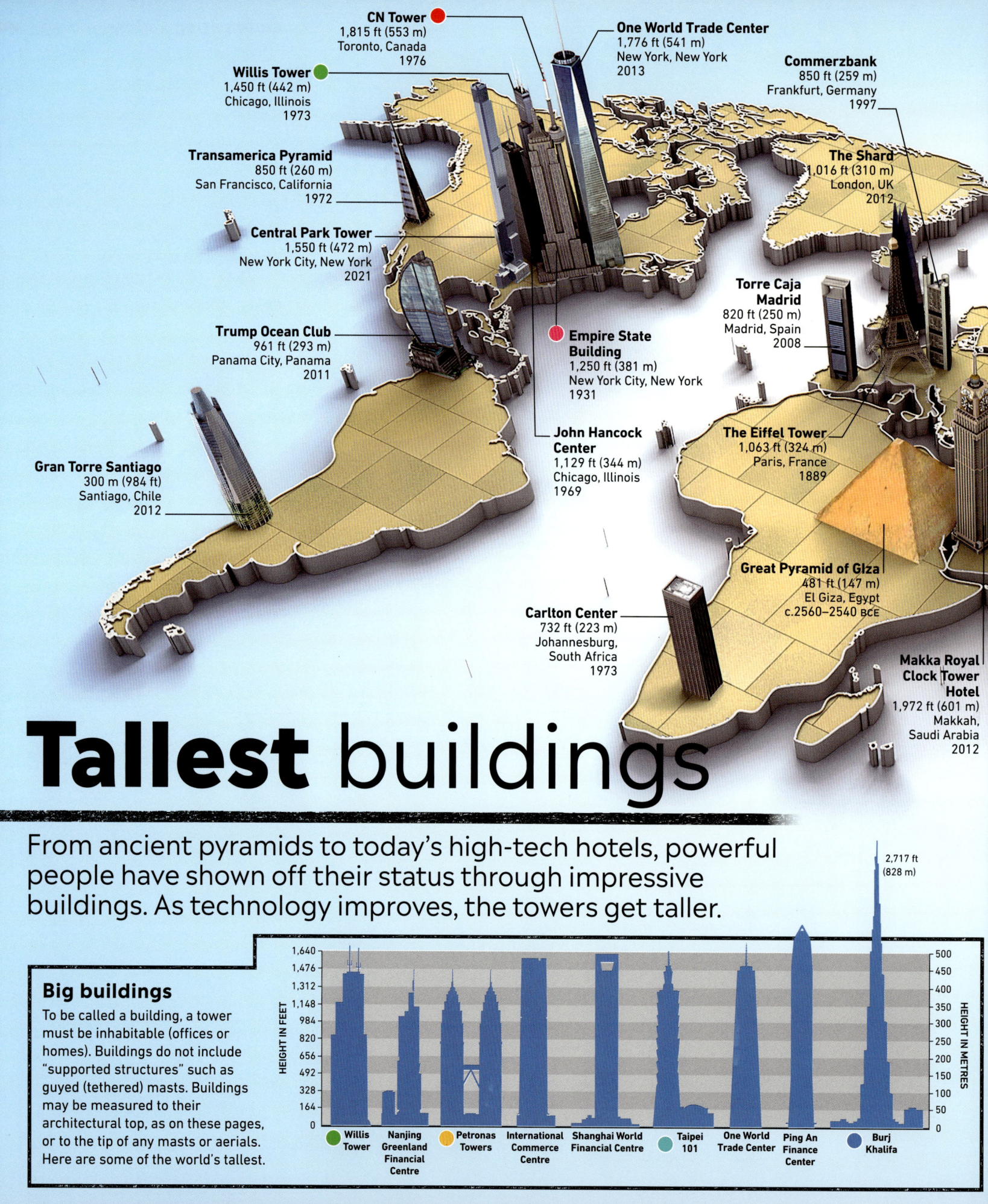

# Tallest buildings

From ancient pyramids to today's high-tech hotels, powerful people have shown off their status through impressive buildings. As technology improves, the towers get taller.

## Big buildings

To be called a building, a tower must be inhabitable (offices or homes). Buildings do not include "supported structures" such as guyed (tethered) masts. Buildings may be measured to their architectural top, as on these pages, or to the tip of any masts or aerials. Here are some of the world's tallest.

NEW YORK'S CHRYSLER BUILDING WAS THE WORLD'S TALLEST FOR JUST

**Engineering and technology**

## THE BURJ KHALIFA HAS **163** FLOORS LINKED BY **57** DOUBLE-DECKER LIFTS

● **Ostankino Tower**
1,770 ft (540 m)
Moscow, Russia
1967

● **Mercury City Tower**
1,112 ft (339 m)
Moscow, Russia
2012

● **Oriental Pearl Tower**
1,535 ft (468 m)
Shanghai, China
1994

**International Commerce Center**
1,588 ft (484 m)
Hong Kong
2010

**Shanghai World Financial Center**
1,614 ft (492 m)
Shanghai, China
2008

**Shanghai Tower**
2,073 ft (632 m)
Shanghai, China
2014

**Tianjin CTF Finance Center**
1,739 ft (530 m)
Tianjin, China
2018

**Ping An Finance Center**
1,965 ft (599 m)
Shenzhe, China
2017

**Milad Tower**
1,427 ft (435 m)
Tehran, Iran
2007

**Burj Khalifa**
2,717 ft (828 m)
Dubai, UAE
2010

● **Tokyo Sky Tree**
2,080 ft (634 m)
Tokyo, Japan
2011

**Taipei 101**
1,670 ft (509 m)
Taipei, Taiwan
2004

**Lotte World Tower**
1,820 ft (555 m)
Seoul, South Korea
2017

**Petronas Towers**
1,483 ft (452 m)
Kuala Lumpur, Malaysia
1998

● **Canton Tower**
1,969 ft (600 m)
Guangzhou, China
2010

**Q1**
1,060 ft (323 m)
Gold Coast, Australia
2005

### Unsupported towers
Unlike buildings, these structures don't contain offices, homes, or stores. They are observation and communications towers.

● **Tokyo Sky Tree**
This communications tower overtook the Canton Tower in 2011 to become the world's tallest.

● **Canton Tower**
Canton is the former name of Guangzhou, where this tower was completed in 2010.

● **CN Tower**
More than 2 million people visit this tower's glass-floored observation deck every year.

● **Ostankino Tower**
This broadcasting tower was the world's first free-standing structure over 1,640 ft (500 m) tall.

● **Oriental Pearl Tower**
There are 11 spheres in the design of this TV tower, which has 15 observation levels.

### Record-breaking buildings
The record for the tallest building (a structure that must be inhabitable) is a fiercely contested prize. These five have all won it.

● **Burj Khalifa, 2010–present**
This building has broken all records, including the tallest building and tallest unsupported structure.

● **Taipei 101, 2004–10**
The world's tallest building until the Burj Khalifa was built, Taipei 101 has 101 floors above ground.

● **Petronas Towers, 1998–2004**
These office blocks were the tallest buildings until 2004. They are still the tallest twin towers.

● **Willis Tower, 1973–98**
Formerly known as the Sears Tower, this 108-story skyscraper towers above Chicago.

● **Empire State Building, 1931–72**
This was the first building in the world to have more than 100 stories—it has 102. It was the tallest building for 40 years.

ONE YEAR, UNTIL THE EMPIRE STATE BUILDING WAS FINISHED IN 1931.

# Internet connections

The Internet has revolutionized the way we live our lives. At the click of a mouse, we can instantly exchange news, ideas, and images with people on the other side of the world, and we can buy or sell goods without having to leave our homes.

### The Internet in a minute

Today, there are more than three times as many computers, phones, and other devices connected to the Internet as there are people in the world. As a result, an incredible amount of Internet activity can occur in just one minute.

- 4.7 million videos viewed
- 4.1 million Google searches
- 59 million messages sent
- 347,222 stories viewed
- 764,000 hours of Netflix watched
- $1.1 million in online sales

**THERE ARE 4.54 BILLION INTERNET USERS**

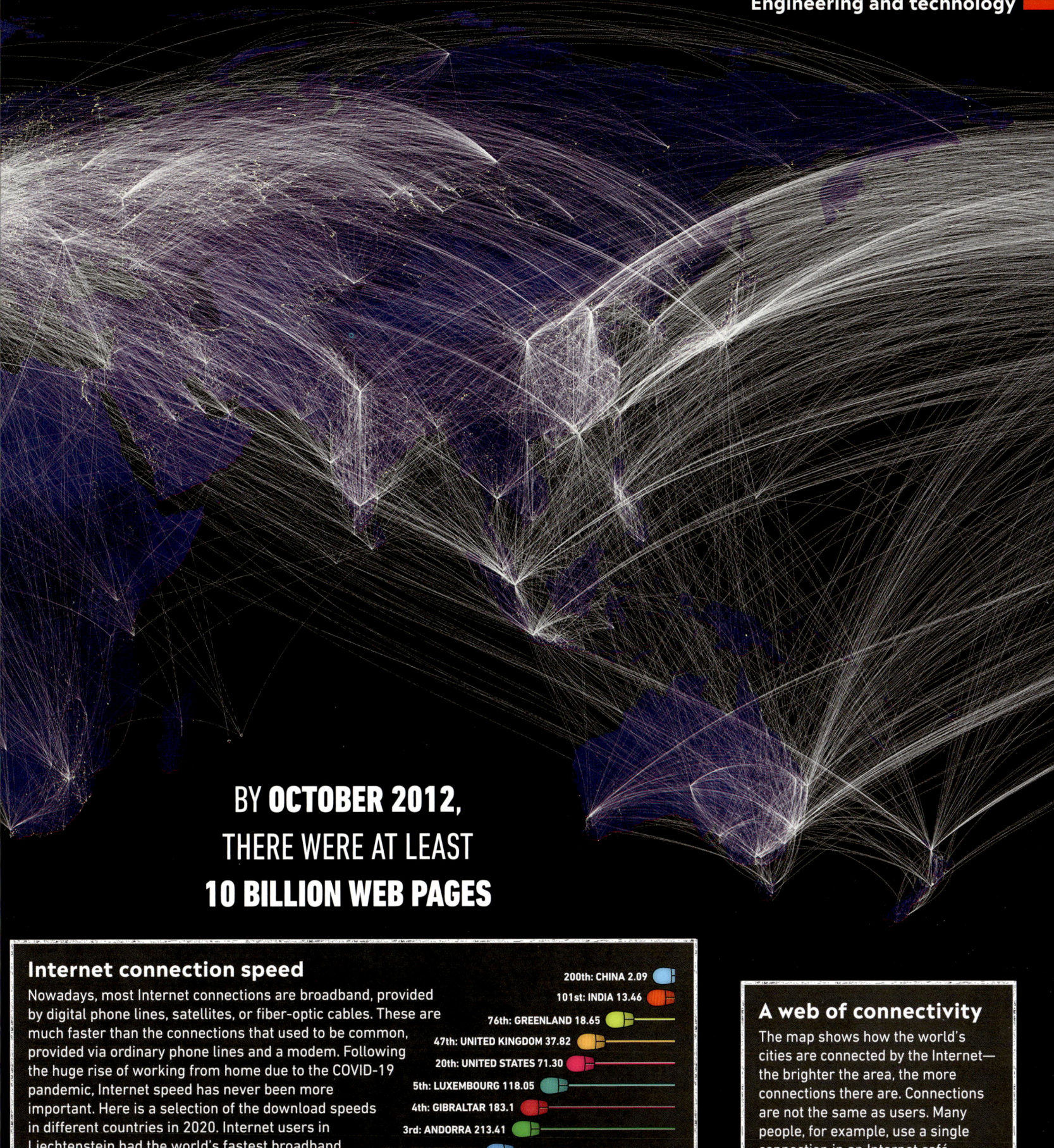

## BY **OCTOBER 2012**, THERE WERE AT LEAST **10 BILLION WEB PAGES**

### Internet connection speed

Nowadays, most Internet connections are broadband, provided by digital phone lines, satellites, or fiber-optic cables. These are much faster than the connections that used to be common, provided via ordinary phone lines and a modem. Following the huge rise of working from home due to the COVID-19 pandemic, Internet speed has never been more important. Here is a selection of the download speeds in different countries in 2020. Internet users in Liechtenstein had the world's fastest broadband, with an average peak download speed of just under 230 megabits per second.

200th: CHINA 2.09
101st: INDIA 13.46
76th: GREENLAND 18.65
47th: UNITED KINGDOM 37.82
20th: UNITED STATES 71.30
5th: LUXEMBOURG 118.05
4th: GIBRALTAR 183.1
3rd: ANDORRA 213.41
2nd: JERSEY 218.37
1st: LIECHTENSTEIN 229.98

PEAK CONNECTION SPEED (MEGABITS PER SECOND) AND WORLD RANKING

### A web of connectivity

The map shows how the world's cities are connected by the Internet—the brighter the area, the more connections there are. Connections are not the same as users. Many people, for example, use a single connection in an Internet café.

——— Lines represent Internet connections between cities

**WORLDWIDE – WELL OVER HALF THE POPULATION.**

# Satellites and space junk

The first satellite, *Sputnik 1*, was launched by the Soviet Union in 1957. Since then, thousands of satellites and millions of other objects have accumulated around Earth, creating a serious hazard for space travel.

**Geosynchronous ring**
This ring-shaped concentration of satellites appears more than 22,200 miles (35,700 km) above Earth's equator. It exists because it is extremely useful for a satellite to "hover" above a point on Earth's turning surface.

**High-speed danger**
The pattern of spots shows the strikes collected during the entire NASA Space Shuttle program, from 1983–2002. The vast majority of space debris is less than 0.5 in (1 cm) across and includes specks of solid rocket fuel and flakes of paint. But even dust acts like tiny bullets at speeds of up to 26,000 mph (42,000 kph).

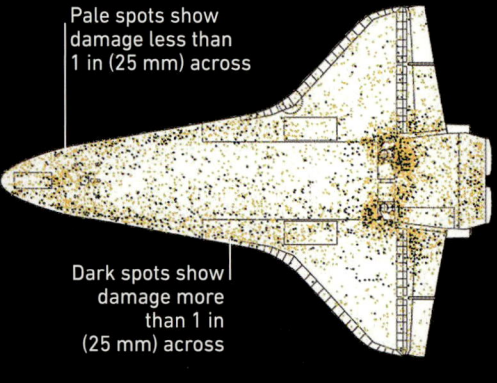

Pale spots show damage less than 1 in (25 mm) across

Dark spots show damage more than 1 in (25 mm) across

**Engineering and technology**

## AT LEAST 10 MILLION PIECES OF ARTIFICIAL DEBRIS ARE NOW IN EARTH ORBIT

**KEY**
The image shows 22,300 objects monitored by the ESA Space Debris team by radar and telescopes.

- Satellites—mostly dead. About 2,300 operational
- Spent rockets
- Mission waste (nuts, gloves, lost items)
- Debris from explosions and collisions

**Low Earth Orbit**
This region is full of orbiting spacecraft, but also full of waste material ejected from spacecraft during missions and countless pieces of debris from collisions.

**GPS (Global Positioning System) satellite**
One of 31 forming a network, the GPS satellites orbit in one of six orbits. Each orbit is at a different angle to ensure they cover the entire surface of Earth. Someone on the ground is in contact with at least six of them at any one time.

### How high are satellites?

Most objects launched into space are in Low Earth Orbit (LEO). At the lowest LEOs (99 miles / 160 km) objects circle Earth in 87 minutes at 17,470 mph (28,100 kph). Certain orbits are particularly useful. Image-taking satellites use polar sun-synchronous orbits, which pass the equator at the same local time on every pass, so the shadows are the same.

**Geosynchronous orbit**
22,236 miles (35,786 km)
Satellites at this height orbit at the same speed as Earth turns, so they stay in the same spot over Earth's surface.

**GPS satellites**
12,600 miles (22,200 km)
Objects orbit once every 12 hours, or twice a day.

**Hubble Space Telescope**
345 miles (555 km)

**Polar sun-synchronous satellites**
373–497 miles (600–800 km)

1,244 miles (2,000 km)

**International Space Station**
255 miles (410 km)

HIGH EARTH ORBIT ZONE | MEDIUM EARTH ORBIT ZONE | LOW EARTH ORBIT ZONE

SPACE WALK IN 1965, ORBITED FOR A MONTH AT 17,000 MPH (28,000 KPH).

# Armed forces

A FEW **COUNTRIES**, SUCH AS **LIECHTENSTEIN** AND **COSTA RICA**, HAVE **NO MILITARY FORCES**

**USA**
The USA spends almost $934 billion per year on its armed forces—more than the next seven-biggest spending countries added together.

**UK**
In 2010, the UK spent $56 billion on its armed forces, making it the world's fifth-biggest military spender.

**France**
France holds the world's third-largest nuclear arsenal, with 300 active warheads.

**Israel**
All Israeli men and women must serve for 2 to 3 years in their armed forces. Israel is the only country to make service for women mandatory.

**Egypt**
All Egyptian men between 18 and 30 must serve in the army for 1 to 3 years.

**Brazil**
Brazil's armed forces are the largest in South America. The army takes an active role in education, health care, and the construction of roads and railroads.

**KEY**
The total amount of military expenditure by all the countries of the world in 2010 was $1.83 trillion, which is equivalent to $235 for every person on the planet—almost double what was spent per capita in 2001. The map shows the total number of military vehicles, hardware, and weapons held by selected major countries.

- Up to 10 large warships (including aircraft carriers, cruisers, destroyers, frigates, and corvettes)
- Up to 10 submarines
- Up to 500 combat-capable aircraft
- Up to 1,000 main battle tanks
- Up to 500 nuclear warheads

Almost all countries have a military—an organized force of soldiers and weapons that defends the country against threats from outside or within. Many countries believe that a large, well-equipped military will discourage others from attacking.

**Sky-high warfare**
Armed forces are increasingly using unmanned drones for surveillance or to launch missiles. Drones are controlled remotely from the ground, so air crew is not risked during missions.

THE US HAS 4 PERCENT OF THE WORLD'S POPULATION BUT

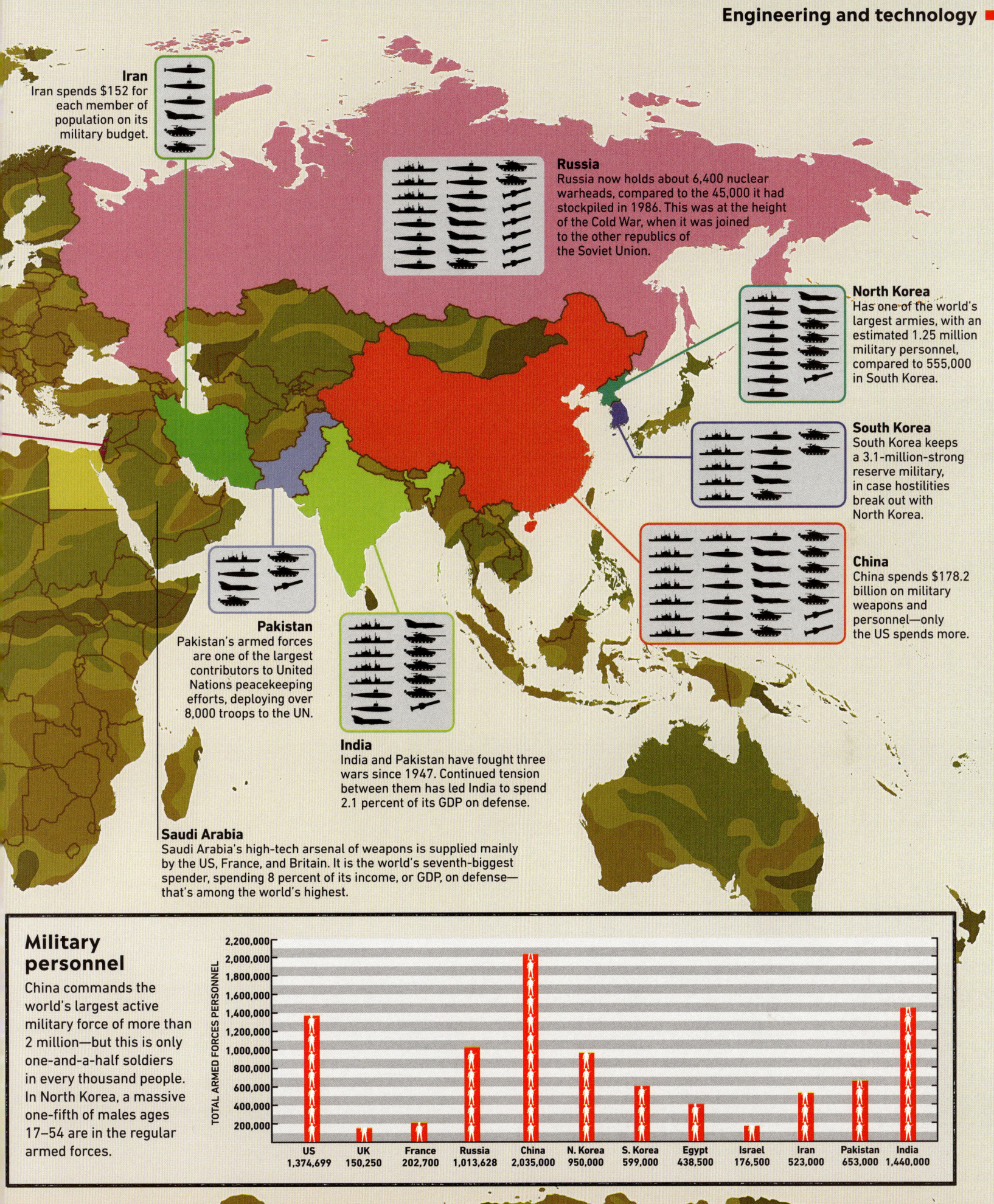

# History

**Easter Island statues**
The giant statues, or *moai*, on this small Pacific island stand up to 33 ft (10 m) tall. They were carved with stone tools, mainly between 1250 and 1500, by the Polynesian people who settled the island.

# Introduction

Human history is crammed full of incidents, from civilizations rising and falling as wars are fought and lost, to revolutions sweeping away the past to begin again. There has also been great architecture and many important innovations, from the first stone tools that enabled people to hunt animals to radio telescopes that can "see" into deep space.

**The Great Sphinx**
This statue at Giza, in Egypt, has a human head on a lion's body. It is thought to have been made about 4,500 years ago.

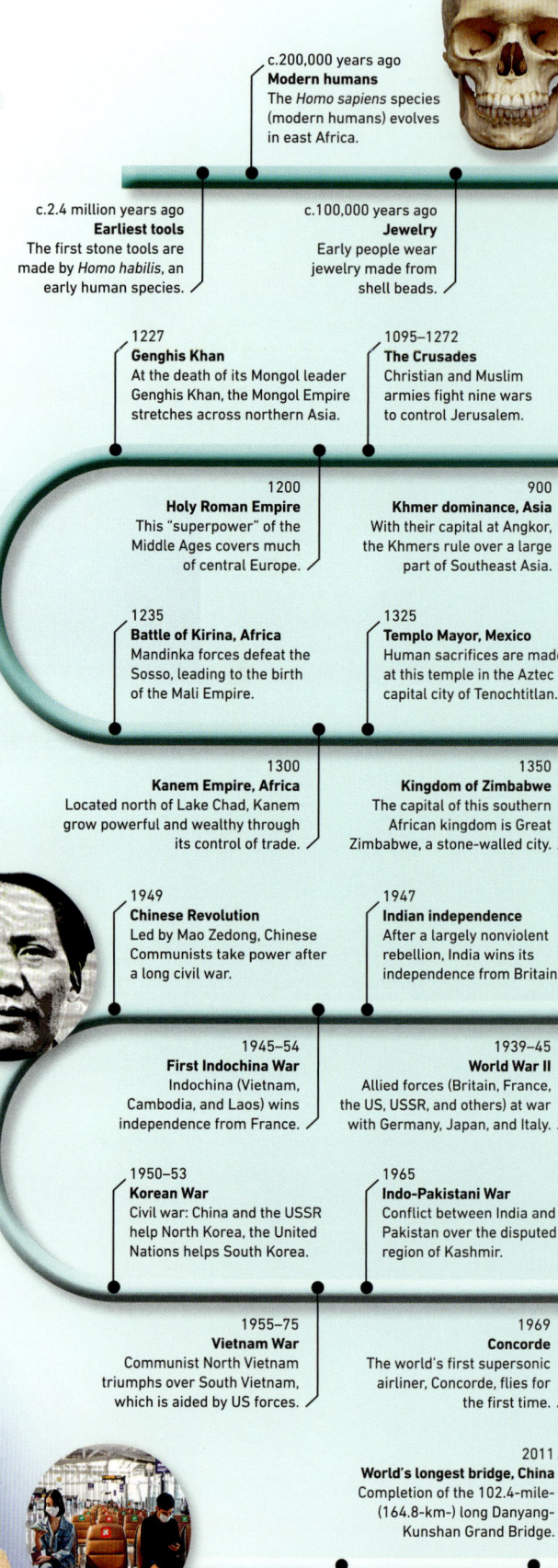

**c.200,000 years ago**
**Modern humans**
The *Homo sapiens* species (modern humans) evolves in east Africa.

**c.2.4 million years ago**
**Earliest tools**
The first stone tools are made by *Homo habilis*, an early human species.

**c.100,000 years ago**
**Jewelry**
Early people wear jewelry made from shell beads.

**1227**
**Genghis Khan**
At the death of its Mongol leader Genghis Khan, the Mongol Empire stretches across northern Asia.

**1095–1272**
**The Crusades**
Christian and Muslim armies fight nine wars to control Jerusalem.

**1200**
**Holy Roman Empire**
This "superpower" of the Middle Ages covers much of central Europe.

**900**
**Khmer dominance, Asia**
With their capital at Angkor, the Khmers rule over a large part of Southeast Asia.

**1235**
**Battle of Kirina, Africa**
Mandinka forces defeat the Sosso, leading to the birth of the Mali Empire.

**1325**
**Templo Mayor, Mexico**
Human sacrifices are made at this temple in the Aztec capital city of Tenochtitlan.

**1300**
**Kanem Empire, Africa**
Located north of Lake Chad, Kanem grow powerful and wealthy through its control of trade.

**1350**
**Kingdom of Zimbabwe**
The capital of this southern African kingdom is Great Zimbabwe, a stone-walled city.

**1949**
**Chinese Revolution**
Led by Mao Zedong, Chinese Communists take power after a long civil war.

**1947**
**Indian independence**
After a largely nonviolent rebellion, India wins its independence from Britain.

**1945–54**
**First Indochina War**
Indochina (Vietnam, Cambodia, and Laos) wins independence from France.

**1939–45**
**World War II**
Allied forces (Britain, France, the US, USSR, and others) at war with Germany, Japan, and Italy.

**1950–53**
**Korean War**
Civil war: China and the USSR help North Korea, the United Nations helps South Korea.

**1965**
**Indo-Pakistani War**
Conflict between India and Pakistan over the disputed region of Kashmir.

**1955–75**
**Vietnam War**
Communist North Vietnam triumphs over South Vietnam, which is aided by US forces.

**1969**
**Concorde**
The world's first supersonic airliner, Concorde, flies for the first time.

**2011**
**World's longest bridge, China**
Completion of the 102.4-mile- (164.8-km-) long Danyang-Kunshan Grand Bridge.

**2020**
**COVID-19**
Outbreak of a newly discovered coronavirus causes a global pandemic, with up to 2.6 million deaths in the first year.

**2011**
**"Arab Spring"**
Revolution and protest sweep through Egypt, Libya, and other Arab countries.

# History

**c.90,000 years ago — Burial rites**
People begin burying their dead along with meaningful objects such as beads.

**c.3200 BCE — Pirámide Mayor, Peru**
Built by the Norte Chico civilization at Caral, the most ancient city in the Americas.

**1450 BCE — New Kingdom of Egypt**
Egypt's empire stretches north to Syria and south to Nubia (modern Sudan).

**490 BCE — First Persian Empire**
Persia rules territory from the edge of India to Egypt and Greece, linking East with West.

**265 BCE — Mauryan Empire, Asia**
Under Ashoka, the Mauryan Empire extends over almost all of the Indian subcontinent.

**c.40,000 years ago — First music and art**
Music is played on simple flutes, and figurines are carved from stone.

**c.2589–2500 BCE — Pyramids of Giza, Egypt**
Vast tombs are built for the Egyptian pharaohs Khufu, Khafre, and Menkaure.

**c.700 BCE — Olmec civilization**
Mexico's Olmec culture reaches its peak. It will influence the later Mayan and Aztec cultures.

**323 BCE — Macedonian Empire**
King Alexander the Great of Macedonia rules lands from Greece to the edge of India.

**264–146 BCE — Punic Wars**
Three wars erupt between Rome and Carthage, North Africa. Rome emerges victorious.

**750 — Umayyad Caliphate**
The second of four great Islamic dynasties, with its capital in Damascus (Syria).

**650 — Huari Empire, Peru**
The highly organized Huari, in Peru, conquer and control much of the Andean region.

**c.300 CE — Mayan culture, Central America**
Established by 1000 BCE, Mayan civilization is now at its height. It will last until 1697 CE.

**100 CE — Pyramid of the Sun, Mexico**
One of two huge stepped pyramids is built in the city of Teotihuacán.

**87 BCE — Han Dynasty, China**
A time of prosperity in China and an expansion of territories ruled by China.

**700 — Tihuanaco, Peru/Bolivia**
This strong state is centered on a bustling city beside Lake Titicaca in the Andes.

**555 — Byzantine power**
Byzantine rule extends over North Africa and the eastern part of the old Roman Empire.

**117 CE — Roman supremacy**
Rome now controls much of Europe, north Africa, and the Middle East.

**80 CE — Colosseum, Rome**
Opening of the stadium in Rome where gladiators fought to the death.

**214 BCE — Great Wall of China**
Construction begins of this vast defensive wall along China's northern border.

*Colosseum, Rome*

**1453 — Fall of Constantinople**
The capital of the Byzantine Empire falls to invading Muslim Ottoman forces.

**1500 — Songhai power, Africa**
The Songhai control the Niger Valley, west to Senegal and east to Agades (modern Niger).

**1532 — Battle of Cajamarca, Peru**
Spanish invaders defeat the Inca forces of Atahualpa, leading to 300 years of Spanish rule.

**1683 — Battle of Vienna**
Ottoman expansion finally halts with a defeat by the Holy Roman Empire.

**1450 — Machu Picchu, Peru**
A secret hilltop city of the Incas, who will dominate northern South America.

**1500 — Ming Dynasty, China**
After throwing out the Mongols, China restores its culture and expands its borders.

**1519 — Aztec rule, Mexico**
The Aztecs now rule more than 25 million people. In 1521, they are conquered by the Spanish.

**1642–51 — English Civil War**
Parliamentarians defeat Royalists, leading to the execution of King Charles I.

**1690 — Mughal Empire, India**
Under Aurangzeb, the Islamic Mughal Empire of India is at its most powerful.

**1922 — Height of British Empire**
Britain's empire now covers more than 20 percent of the world's land area.

**1914–18 — World War I**
Britain, France, the US, and other allies battle Germany, Austria-Hungary, and Turkey.

**1880–1902 — Boer Wars, Africa**
Two wars are fought between Dutch Boer settlers in South Africa and Britain.

**1819–30 — South American independence**
Independence from Spain for Colombia, Peru, Bolivia, Ecuador, and Venezuela.

**1789–99 — French Revolution**
Overthrow of the French monarchy in a bloody revolution. France becomes a republic.

**1917 — Russian Revolution**
Revolt against rule by Tsar Nicholas II; Russia becomes Communist.

**1912 — Sinking of the *Titanic***
More than 1,500 people die when this luxury liner hits an iceberg and sinks.

**1861–65 — American Civil War**
War between the southern Confederate states and the Union states of the north.

**1799–1815 — Napoleonic era**
France, led by Napoleon Bonaparte, is the dominant military power in Europe.

**1775–83 — American Revolutionary War**
With the help of France and other countries, the US wins independence from Britain.

**1980 — Very Large Array**
In New Mexico, this giant radio astronomy observatory is completed.

**Sydney Opera House**
Opened in 1973, this arts venue in Sydney, Australia, was designed by Danish architect Jørn Utzon.

**1994 — End of Apartheid**
South Africa's official segregation policy, Apartheid, ends and equality is reached for Black South Africans.

**1989–1991 — End of Communist bloc**
Communist regimes in many countries of eastern Europe are overthrown.

ONLY VIRUS TO BE ERADICATED THROUGH VACCINATION.

### Australopithecus

*Australopithecus* hominins evolved about 4.2 million years ago in east Africa. Six species are known. One species, called *A. afarensis*, may be the ancestor of humans. Fossils show that it was up to 5 ft (1.5 m) tall and had a relatively small brain. Crucially, it could walk upright.

### Paranthropus

The three *Paranthropus* species had a bony crest on top of the skull to anchor strong chewing muscles. *P. boisei* is nicknamed "nutcracker man" because of its massive jaws and cheek teeth.

**Neander Valley, Germany**
A partial skeleton of *H. neanderthalensis* found in a cave here in 1856 was the first fossil to be identified as human remains.

**Laetoli, Tanzania**
Footprints of at least two *Australopithecus afarensis* individuals were discovered here, preserved in volcanic ash.

**Olduvai Gorge, Tanzania**
Stone tools and fossils of *P. boisei* and *H. habilis* were found here.

**South Africa**
Finds include *Australopithecus*, *Paranthropus*, *H. habilis*, and *H. sapiens* fossils.

# Fossil humans

Fossil discoveries have helped scientists to piece together the story of human evolution. Modern humans—*Homo sapiens*—and their ancestors are called hominins. *Sahelanthropus tchadensis*, the first hominin, was an apelike animal that appeared in Africa about 7 million years ago. Later hominin species left Africa and spread out around the world.

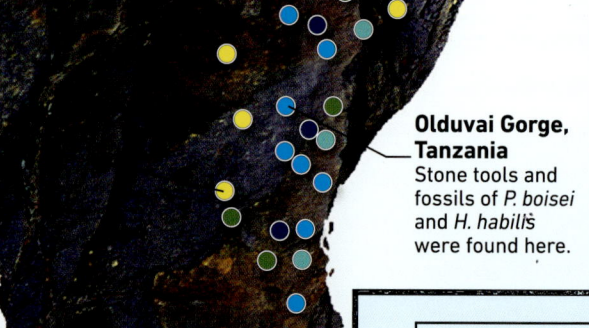

Apelike
*Australopithecus*—
six species

4 million years ago

136    HOMO SAPIENS EVOLVED ABOUT 200,000 YEARS AGO. THE EARLIEST

# History

## *Homo*—meet the family

We and our extinct relatives belong to the *Homo* genus. A second Latin word, such as *sapiens*, completes each species' name.

**Homo habilis**
(2.4–1.4 million years ago)
*H. habilis* ("Handy man") is thought to have been the first hominin species to make stone tools.

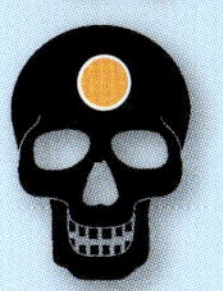

**Homo georgicus**
(1.8 million years ago)
Known only from a single fossil site in Georgia, this may have been the first hominin to leave Africa.

**Homo ergaster**
(1.9–1.5 million years ago)
As tall as modern humans and with a similar build, it looked very different than its apelike ancestors.

**Homo erectus**
(1.8 million–200,000 years ago)
Along with *H. ergaster*, *H. erectus* ("Upright man") is known to have used stone hand-axes.

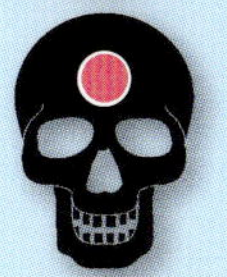

**Homo antecessor**
(1.2 million–500,000 years ago)
Around 780,000 years ago, *H. antecessor* became the first hominin to reach western Europe.

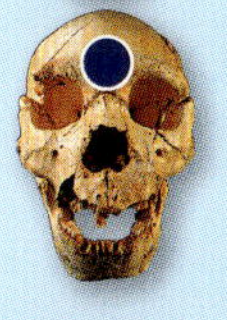

**Homo heidelbergensis**
(600,000–250,000 years ago)
With a big brain and a muscular body, this species could hunt large animals and make complex tools.

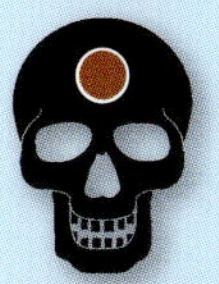

**Homo floresiensis**
(95,000–17,000 years ago)
Nicknamed "Hobbit", *H. floresiensis* was tiny—just over 3 ft 3 in (1 m) tall. It lived until very recently.

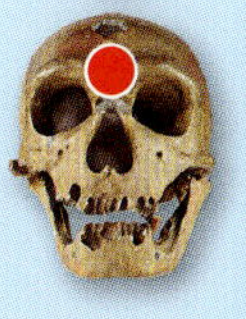

**Homo neanderthalensis, or Neanderthals**
(200,000–30,000 years ago)
This successful species was skilled at hunting, made and used stone tools, and buried its dead.

**Zhoukoudian Caves, China**
Some of the most important fossils of *H. erectus* were found in these limestone caves 30 miles (50 km) from Beijing.

**Flores, Indonesia**
*H. floresiensis* remains are known from just one cave on this island.

**Java, Indonesia**
The earliest known human fossils in East Asia—of *Homo erectus*—come from this island.

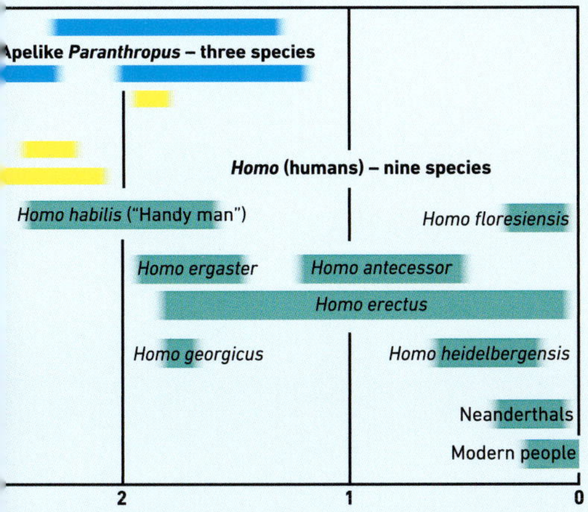

## Family tree

This chart shows the "family tree" of hominins from *Australopithecus* onward. Scientists are still working to understand the relationships between different hominin species.

- Apelike *Paranthropus* – three species
- *Homo* (humans) – nine species
  - Homo habilis ("Handy man")
  - Homo floresiensis
  - Homo ergaster
  - Homo antecessor
  - Homo erectus
  - Homo georgicus
  - Homo heidelbergensis
  - Neanderthals
  - Modern people

KNOWN FOSSILS, FROM ETHIOPIA, ARE 195,000 YEARS OLD.

137

# Prehistoric culture

Music, art, religion, and technology all began so long ago, we can't be certain of exactly when. There are clues to early culture, however, such as ritual burial sites, which archaeologists can date.

### Earliest music
Music, like art, is much older than writing, since bone flutes and other musical instruments have been made and played for more than 40,000 years.

◆ Early instrument site

**Antler flute, Hohle Fels, Germany, 43,000 years ago**

### First jewelry
People wore jewelry more than 100,000 years ago in sites as distant as Israel and South Africa.

◆ Early jewelry site

**Shell beads, Balzi Rossi, Italy**

Map locations:
- East Wenatchee, Washington, US
- Horseshoe Canyon paintings, Utah, US
- Clovis, New Mexico, US
- Salado, Texas, US
- Walker, Minnesota, US
- Cactus Hill, Virginia, US
- Wicklow Pipes, Ireland
- Shell bead necklace, Cro-Magnon, France
- Lascaux Caves, France
- Altamira and El Castillo caves, Spain. El Castillo features the oldest known paintings, made 40,800 years ago, possibly by Neanderthals
- Lady of Brassempouy carving, France
- Ivory horse figurine, Lourdes, France
- Shell beads, Grotte des Pidgeons, Morocco
- Algerian Sahara
- Serra de Capivara paintings, Brazil
- Cueva de las Manos paintings, Argentina
- Cueva del Milodon, Chile

## Changes in stone tools

**2.4 million years ago**
The earliest tools, called the Oldowan tool kit, were made by an early human species called "Handy man," or *homo habilis*, in Africa. Oldowan-style tools in Europe and Asia are much younger, made by later types of humans, including Neanderthals.

● Oldowan site

**1.8 million years ago**
The Acheulean tool kit of our later ancestors, such as *Homo erectus*, included a new invention—the hand ax, with a finely chiseled edge.

● Acheulean site

**200,000 years ago**
Mousterian tools spanned the Middle Stone Age (ended around 40,000 BCE) and included lots of specialized shapes for different jobs.

● Mousterian site

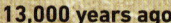

**13,000 years ago**
The earliest stone tools discovered in America are from the 13,000-year-old "Clovis" people.

● Clovis site

THE FIRST KNOWN SEWING NEEDLE DATES BACK ABOUT 25,000 YEARS.

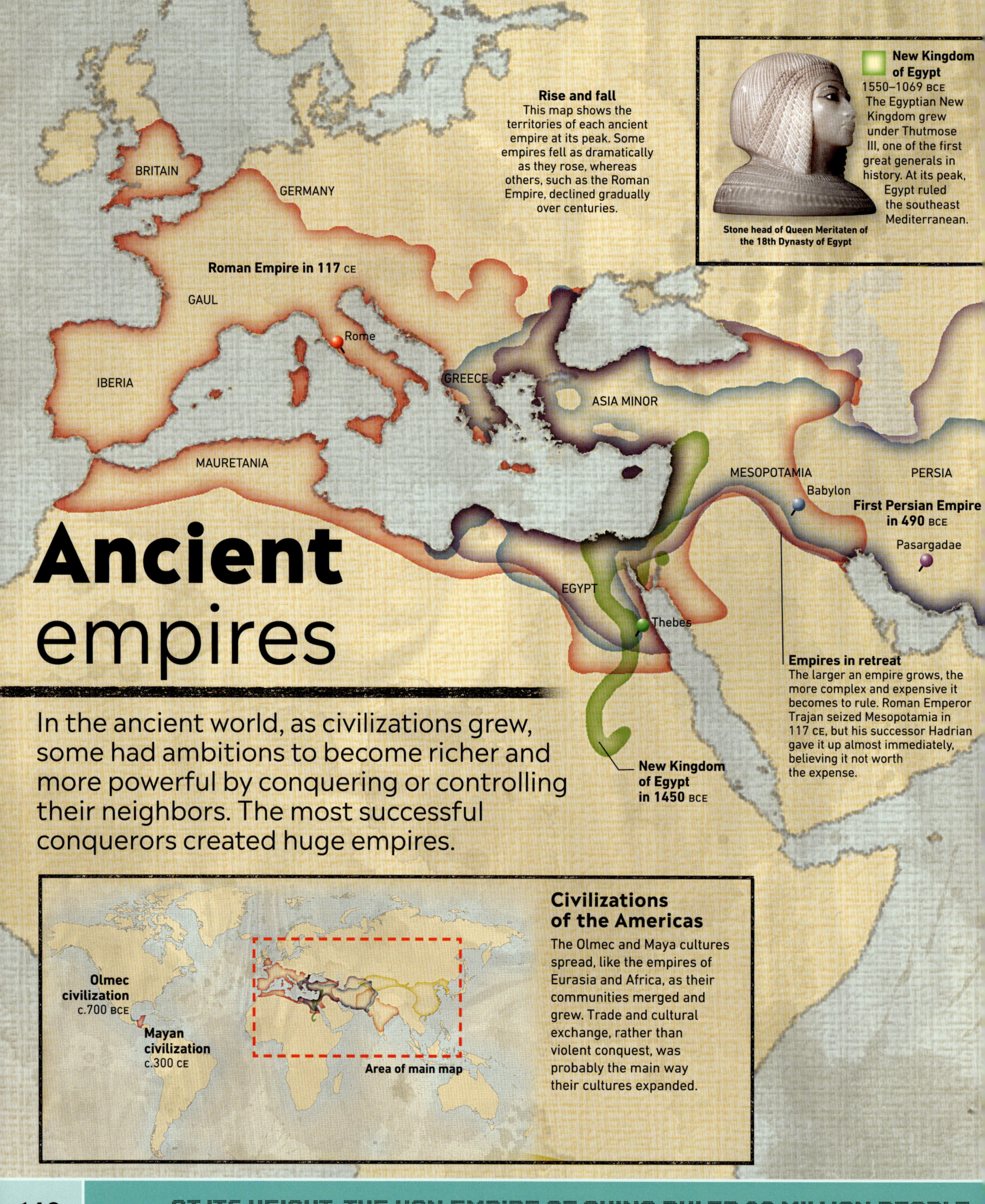

# History

**Olmec civilization**
1500–400 BCE
The first major culture in Central America, the Olmecs lived in what is now Mexico. They were expert farmers and traded all over the region. They developed one of the first writing systems in the Americas.

*Olmec stone mask*

**First Persian Empire**
550–336 BCE
Cyrus the Great and his army conquered huge swathes of central Asia and grabbed enormous wealth from the kingdoms they conquered. Cyrus's successor, Darius I, built cities, roads, and even a canal from the Nile river to the Red Sea.

*Ornate Persian silver bowl*

**Empire of Alexander the Great**
330–323 BCE
Alexander was a general from Macedon, a kingdom north of Greece. At its height, his empire covered most of the world known to Greeks. For centuries after his death, the Greek culture that he introduced continued to dominate the eastern Mediterranean and western Asia.

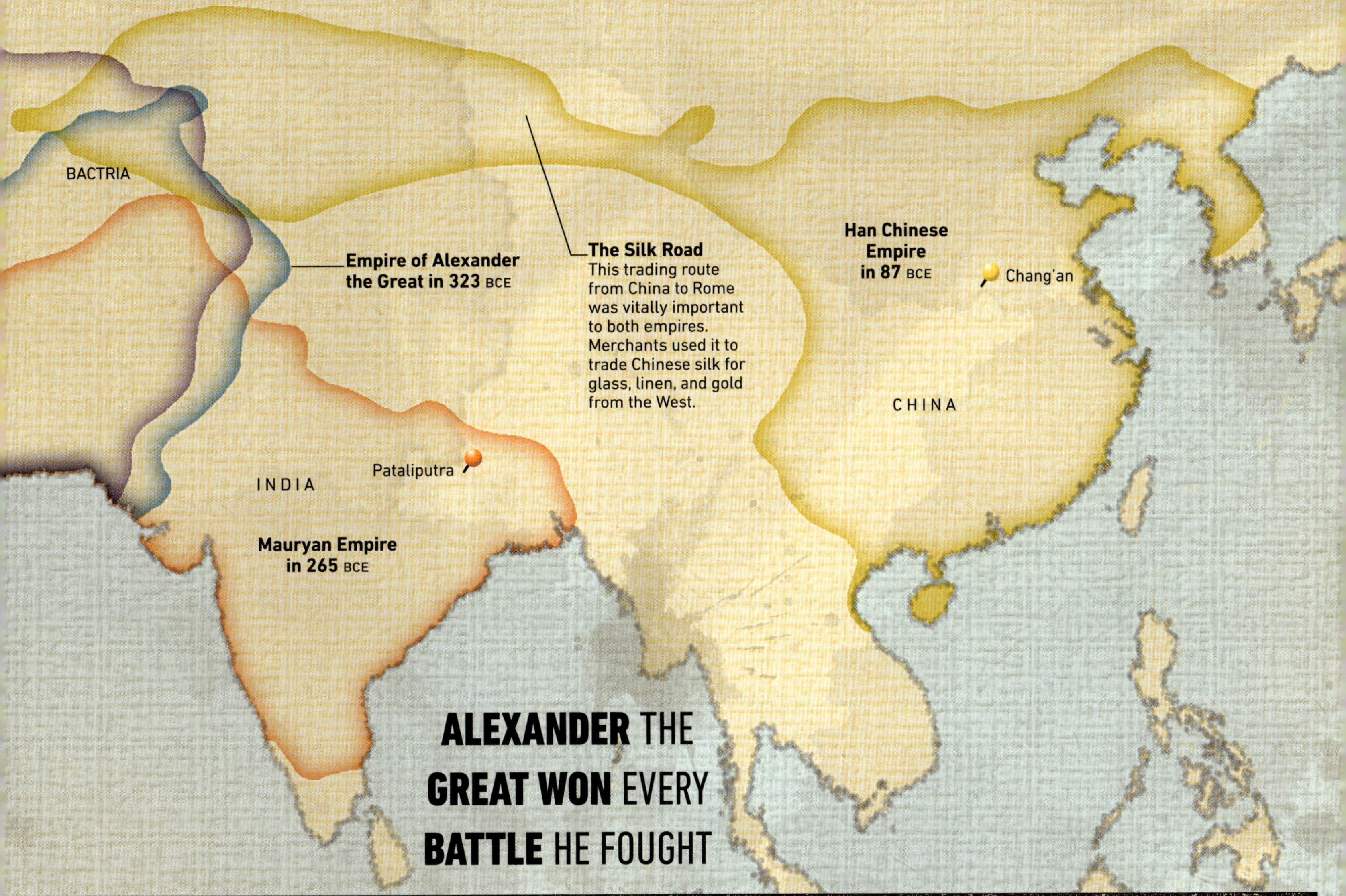

*Coin showing Alexander the Great's head*

BACTRIA

**Empire of Alexander the Great in 323 BCE**

**The Silk Road**
This trading route from China to Rome was vitally important to both empires. Merchants used it to trade Chinese silk for glass, linen, and gold from the West.

**Han Chinese Empire in 87 BCE**

Chang'an

CHINA

INDIA

Pataliputra

**Mauryan Empire in 265 BCE**

## ALEXANDER THE GREAT WON EVERY BATTLE HE FOUGHT

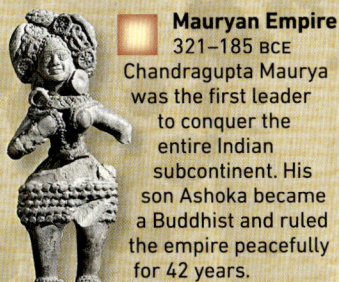

**Mauryan Empire**
321–185 BCE
Chandragupta Maurya was the first leader to conquer the entire Indian subcontinent. His son Ashoka became a Buddhist and ruled the empire peacefully for 42 years.

*Mauryan figure*

**Han Empire**
206–220 CE
The four centuries of Han rule are often called the Golden Age of Ancient China. It was an era of peace and prosperity in which China became a major world power.

*Han pot*

**Roman Empire**
27 BCE–476 CE
One of history's most influential civilizations, Rome controlled much of Europe, western Asia, and north Africa. Many roads, aqueducts, and canals built by the Romans are still in use today.

*Head of Emperor Claudius*

**Mayan civilization**
500–900 CE
One of the most advanced cultures of the ancient world, the Maya developed an accurate yearly calendar based on their sophisticated understanding of astronomy.

*Mayan statuette*

MORE THAN ONE-QUARTER OF THE WORLD'S POPULATION AT THE TIME.

# Ancient wonders

Ancient Greek travelers and authors such as Herodotus, Antipater, and Philo of Byzantium praised the architectural marvels of the age in their writings. The buildings and statues they described became known as the "Seven Wonders of the World." Today, we recognize many other amazing structures that architects, masons, and sculptors of the past built with relatively simple tools.

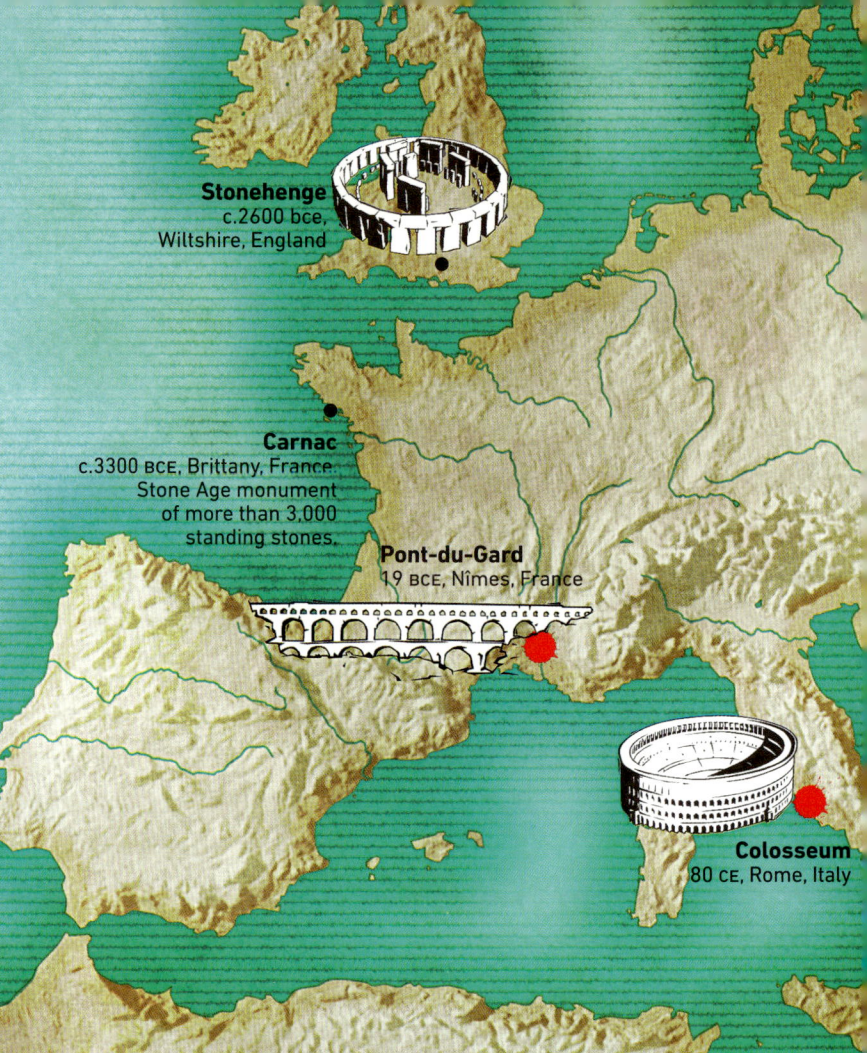

**Stonehenge** c.2600 BCE, Wiltshire, England

**Carnac** c.3300 BCE, Brittany, France. Stone Age monument of more than 3,000 standing stones.

**Pont-du-Gard** 19 BCE, Nîmes, France

**Colosseum** 80 CE, Rome, Italy

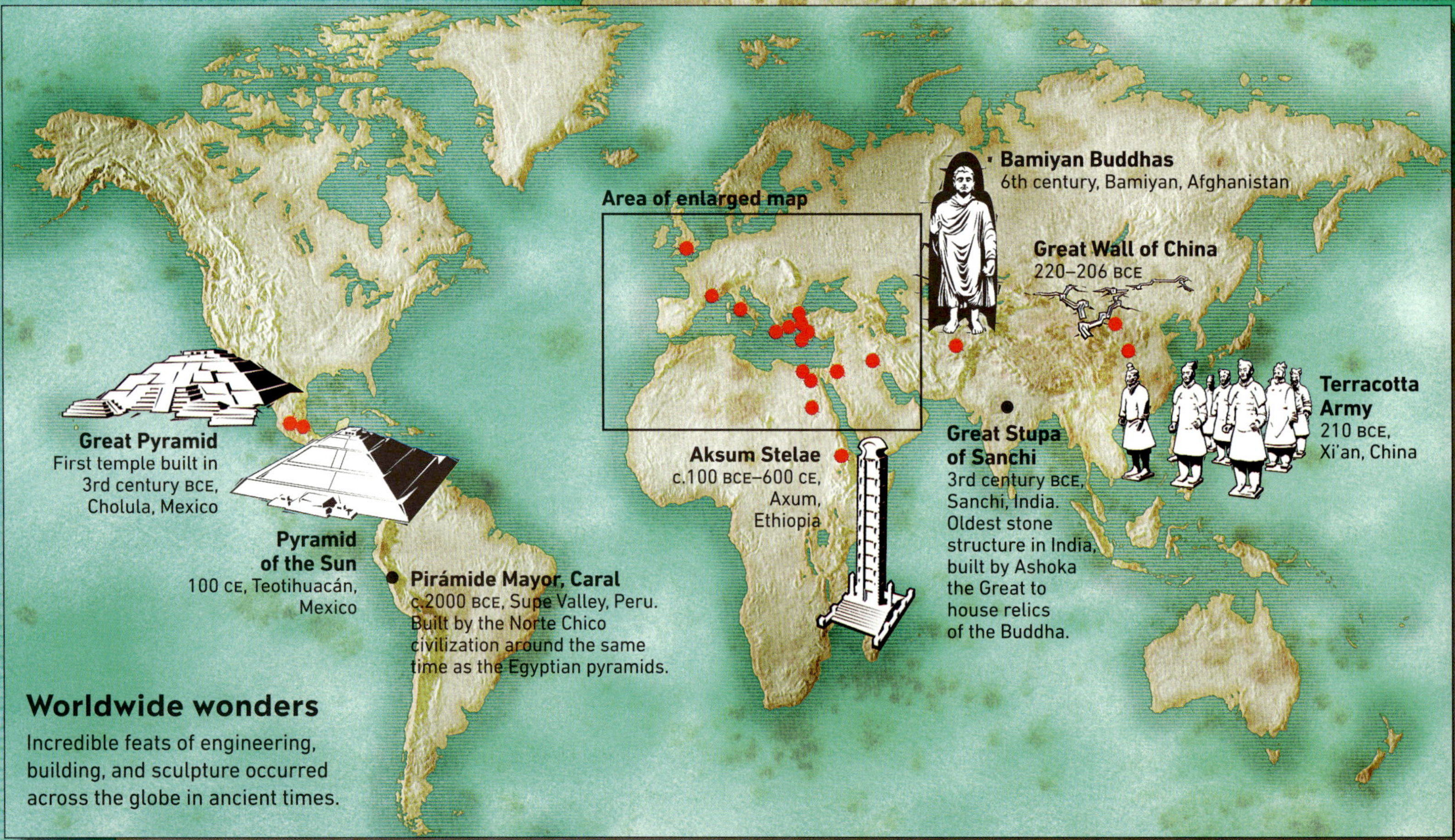

**Bamiyan Buddhas** 6th century, Bamiyan, Afghanistan

**Great Wall of China** 220–206 BCE

**Terracotta Army** 210 BCE, Xi'an, China

**Great Stupa of Sanchi** 3rd century BCE, Sanchi, India. Oldest stone structure in India, built by Ashoka the Great to house relics of the Buddha.

**Aksum Stelae** c.100 BCE–600 CE, Axum, Ethiopia

**Great Pyramid** First temple built in 3rd century BCE, Cholula, Mexico

**Pyramid of the Sun** 100 CE, Teotihuacán, Mexico

**Pirámide Mayor, Caral** c.2000 BCE, Supe Valley, Peru. Built by the Norte Chico civilization around the same time as the Egyptian pyramids.

**Worldwide wonders**
Incredible feats of engineering, building, and sculpture occurred across the globe in ancient times.

THE COLOSSEUM IN ROME COULD HOLD MORE THAN 50,000 SPECTATORS.

# History

## Seven Wonders of the World

Only the pyramids at Giza still stand. Earthquakes destroyed the Hanging Gardens, the Colossus, and the Pharos; flooding and fire ruined the Mausoleum and the Statue of Zeus. The Temple of Artemis was wrecked by the Goths.

**Pyramids of Giza**
Built as tombs for the pharaohs Khufu, Khafre, and Menkaure.

**Hanging Gardens of Babylon**
Nebuchadnezzar II built these lush, terraced gardens for his wife, Amytis.

**Mausoleum at Halicarnassus**
Tomb of Persian governor Mausolus, famed for its size and lavish carvings.

**Temple of Artemis**
Dedicated to the Greek goddess of hunting, chastity, and childbirth.

**Colossus of Rhodes**
Vast bronze-and-iron statue, 105 ft (32 m) tall, of the Greek sun-god Helios.

**Pharos of Alexandria**
A fire at the top of this huge lighthouse was visible from 30 miles (50 km) away.

**Statue of Zeus in Olympia**
The sculptor Phidias built this 43-ft (13-m) statue of the king of the gods.

## Other ancient wonders

These wonders didn't make the Seven Wonders list, mainly because they were unknown to the Greeks. Some of them were built during later periods.

**Colosseum**
Stadium where gladiators fought to the death.

**Hagia Sofia**
Enormous, richly decorated church, later a mosque.

**Petra**
A city hewn out of rock. Capital of the Nabataeans.

**Temples of Abu-Simbel**
Two temples built to honor the pharaoh Rameses II.

**Pont-du-Gard**
Roman aqueduct that carried water to Nîmes.

**Acropolis**
Greek citadel that includes the Parthenon Temple.

**Great Pyramid**
World's largest pyramid, now with a church on top.

**Pyramid of the Sun**
Steep steps up the side led to a temple on the top.

**Stonehenge**
Prehistoric monument with a circle of enormous stones.

**Bamiyan Buddhas**
Huge statues chiseled into a cliff; destroyed in 2001.

**Great Wall of China**
Once ran for 3,889 miles (6,259 km) along China's northern border.

**Terracotta Army**
8,000 life-size warriors entombed with the first emperor of China.

**Aksum Stelae**
A group of memorial obelisks carved from huge blocks of stone.

**Hagia Sofia** 532–537 CE, Istanbul, Turkey

**Acropolis** 5th century BCE, Athens, Greece

**Temple of Artemis** Reconstructed in c.550 BCE, Ephesus, Turkey

**Mausoleum at Halicarnassus** 351 BCE, Bodrum, Turkey

**Statue of Zeus** 430 BCE, Olympus, Greece

**Pharos of Alexandria** c.280 BCE, Alexandria, Egypt

**Colossus of Rhodes** 292–280 BCE, Rhodes, Greece

**Hanging Gardens of Babylon** c.600 BCE, Hillah, central Iraq

**Petra** 4th century BCE, Jordan

**Pyramids of Giza** c.2589–2500 BCE, Cairo, Egypt

**Temples of Abu-Simbel** c.1257 BCE, Abu-Simbel, Egypt

**THE GREAT PYRAMID OF GIZA COULD WEIGH AS MUCH AS 716 MILLION TONS**

THE ARENA COULD BE FLOODED TO STAGE MOCK SEA BATTLES.

## Famous mummies

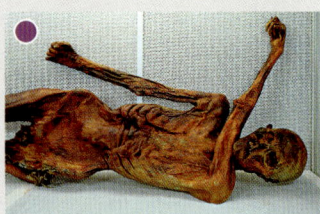

**Ötzi the Iceman**
About 5,300 years ago, a traveler died when caught in a snowstorm in the Alps. His body became buried in the snow and then froze. In 1991, the corpse was discovered on top of a glacier.

**Pharaoh Tutankhamun**
The mummy of Tutankhamun was found in a tomb in the Valley of the Kings in 1922. It wore a gold mask and lay inside a nest of three gold cases. The tomb, which had been sealed for 3,200 years, contained statues, furniture, and jewelry.

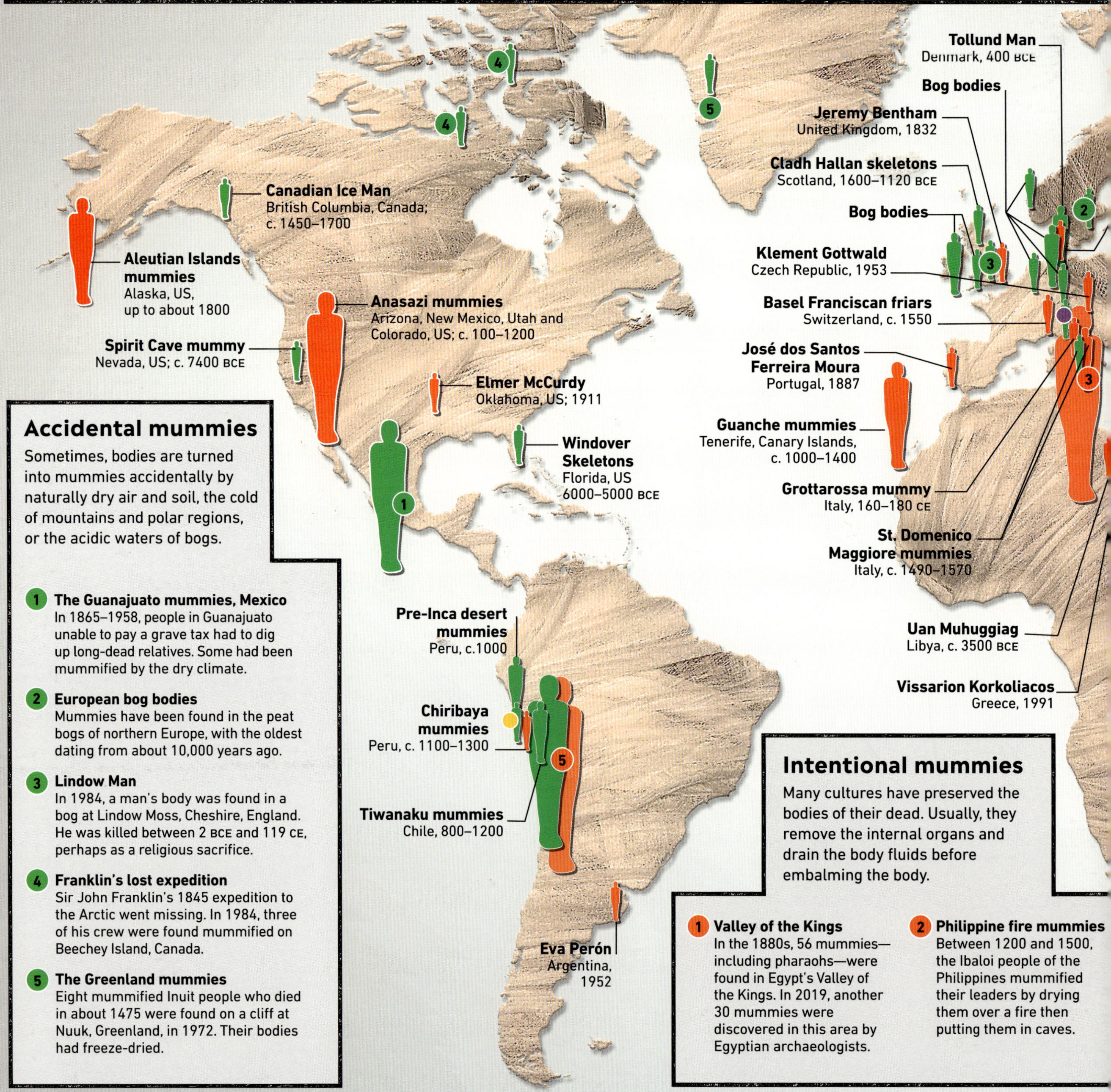

### Map labels

- **Tollund Man** — Denmark, 400 BCE
- **Bog bodies**
- **Jeremy Bentham** — United Kingdom, 1832
- **Cladh Hallan skeletons** — Scotland, 1600–1120 BCE
- **Bog bodies**
- **Klement Gottwald** — Czech Republic, 1953
- **Basel Franciscan friars** — Switzerland, c. 1550
- **José dos Santos Ferreira Moura** — Portugal, 1887
- **Guanche mummies** — Tenerife, Canary Islands, c. 1000–1400
- **Grottarossa mummy** — Italy, 160–180 CE
- **St. Domenico Maggiore mummies** — Italy, c. 1490–1570
- **Uan Muhuggiag** — Libya, c. 3500 BCE
- **Vissarion Korkoliacos** — Greece, 1991
- **Canadian Ice Man** — British Columbia, Canada; c. 1450–1700
- **Aleutian Islands mummies** — Alaska, US, up to about 1800
- **Anasazi mummies** — Arizona, New Mexico, Utah and Colorado, US; c. 100–1200
- **Spirit Cave mummy** — Nevada, US; c. 7400 BCE
- **Elmer McCurdy** — Oklahoma, US; 1911
- **Windover Skeletons** — Florida, US 6000–5000 BCE
- **Pre-Inca desert mummies** — Peru, c.1000
- **Chiribaya mummies** — Peru, c. 1100–1300
- **Tiwanaku mummies** — Chile, 800–1200
- **Eva Perón** — Argentina, 1952

## Accidental mummies

Sometimes, bodies are turned into mummies accidentally by naturally dry air and soil, the cold of mountains and polar regions, or the acidic waters of bogs.

1. **The Guanajuato mummies, Mexico**
In 1865–1958, people in Guanajuato unable to pay a grave tax had to dig up long-dead relatives. Some had been mummified by the dry climate.

2. **European bog bodies**
Mummies have been found in the peat bogs of northern Europe, with the oldest dating from about 10,000 years ago.

3. **Lindow Man**
In 1984, a man's body was found in a bog at Lindow Moss, Cheshire, England. He was killed between 2 BCE and 119 CE, perhaps as a religious sacrifice.

4. **Franklin's lost expedition**
Sir John Franklin's 1845 expedition to the Arctic went missing. In 1984, three of his crew were found mummified on Beechey Island, Canada.

5. **The Greenland mummies**
Eight mummified Inuit people who died in about 1475 were found on a cliff at Nuuk, Greenland, in 1972. Their bodies had freeze-dried.

## Intentional mummies

Many cultures have preserved the bodies of their dead. Usually, they remove the internal organs and drain the body fluids before embalming the body.

1. **Valley of the Kings**
In the 1880s, 56 mummies—including pharaohs—were found in Egypt's Valley of the Kings. In 2019, another 30 mummies were discovered in this area by Egyptian archaeologists.

2. **Philippine fire mummies**
Between 1200 and 1500, the Ibaloi people of the Philippines mummified their leaders by drying them over a fire then putting them in caves.

History

# Mummies

Mummies—the preserved bodies of the dead—have been found the world over. Many were made deliberately, while others formed naturally. More recently, some countries have mummified their leaders.

**THE PALERMO CATACOMBS CONTAIN ABOUT 8,000 MUMMIES**

## Juanita the Ice Maiden
In 1995, an Inca girl aged 11–15 was found on Mount Ampato, Peru. The discoverers named her Juanita, or the "Ice Maiden." She was sacrificed to the gods about 530 years ago. The cold had preserved her skin, organs, blood, and stomach contents.

### MUMMY DISCOVERIES WORLDWIDE
Some mummies are discovered singly, often in remote locations such as in peat bogs or on high mountains. Other finds involve larger numbers of mummies—for example, in communal graves, tombs, caves, or catacombs.

- Accidental mummies
- Intentional mummies

Number of mummies: 0–19, 20–39, 40–59, 60–79, 80–99, 100–119, 120–139, 140+

## Map Locations

- **James Hepburn, 4th Earl of Bothwell** — Denmark, 1578
- **Charles Eugène de Croÿ** — Estonia, 1702
- **Vladimir Lenin** — Russia, 1924
- **Georgi Dimitrov** — Bulgaria, 1949
- **bnitz Girl** — ...
- **Valley of the Golden Mummies** — Egypt, 332 BCE–395 CE
- **Maronite mummies** — Lebanon, 1283
- **Chehrabad Salt Mine mummies** — Iran, 4th century BCE–4th century CE
- **Iufaa and family** — Egypt, c. 500 BCE
- **Saqqara mummies** — Egypt, 640 BCE
- **Nubian mummies** — Sudan, 250–1400
- **Tarim mummies** — China, 1800–200 BCE
- **Siberian Ice Maiden** — Russia, c. 400 BCE
- **Pazyryk ice mummies** — Mongolia, c. 700–200 BCE
- **Mao Zedong** — China, 1976
- **Xin Zhui** — China, c. 150 BCE
- **Ho Chi Minh** — Vietnam, 1969
- **Mummy monk "Luang Phor Daeng"** — Thailand, c. 1985
- **Vu Khac Minh and Vu Khac Truong** — Vietnam, c. 1600–1700
- **Chiang Kai-shek and Chiang Ching-kuo** — Taiwan, 1975 and 1988
- **Buddhist self-mummified nun and monks** — Taiwan, 1680–1830
- **Fujiwara clan mummies** — Japan, 1128–1189
- **Kim Il-Sung and Kim Jong-il** — North Korea, 1994 and 2011
- **Korean mummies** — South Korea, c. 1350–1500
- **Lost mummies of New Guinea** — Papua New Guinea, up to 1950s

## 3 Mummies of Palermo
In 1599, Christian monks in Palermo, Sicily, began to mummify their dead and stored them in catacombs. Later, rich people paid the monks to mummify their bodies.

## 4 Self-mummified monks
From 1680–1830, some Buddhist monks in Japan mummified themselves. They starved, drank special tea to make their body toxic to maggots, and then were sealed alive in a stone tomb.

## 5 Chinchorro mummies
The Chinchorro, who lived in what is now Chile and Peru, were the first people known to make mummies. Their oldest mummies date from as early as 5000 BCE.

MUMMIFICATION, THEY PULLED THE BRAIN OUT THROUGH THE NOSE.

145

# History

## AT ITS PEAK, THE MONGOL EMPIRE RULED OVER 100 MILLION PEOPLE

**Mongol Empire in 1227 CE**

**Mongol Empire**
1206–1368
Founded by Genghis Khan in 1206. Numerous violent conquests led to the largest continuous land empire in history.

*Mongol horde helmet*

Karakorum

**Ming China in 1500 CE**
Beijing

**Ming China**
1368–1644
Founded by Zhu Yuanzhang, the leader of an uprising that overthrew the Mongols. A socially stable era during which the Grand Canal and the Great Wall were rebuilt.

**Mughal Empire in 1690 CE**
Shahjahanabad (Old Delhi)

*Mughal sword*

**Khmer Empire in 900 CE**
Angkor

**Holy Roman Empire**
962–1806
One of the longest-lasting empires in history, this was a Christian state with no capital. In 1356 Frankfurt became the home of imperial elections.

**Byzantine Empire**
330–1453
Evolved from the Eastern Roman Empire. A Christian, Greek-speaking empire that preserved both Roman and Greek cultures.

*Byzantine necklace pendant*

**Mughal Empire**
1526–1857
The Mughals brought centralized government, education, and religious tolerance to south Asia.

**Khmer Empire**
802–1400s
A Hindu and Buddhist empire influenced by Indian culture. Architecture of the empire reached its height with the construction of the temple at the capital, Angkor.

**Aztec Empire**
1428–1521
From their capital built on artificial islands on a lake, the Aztecs, who called themselves Mexica, conquered most of modern-day Mexico.
*Statue of Aztec god of death*

**Inca Empire**
1438–1536
The largest empire of pre-Spanish Americas. Incas worshipped Inti, the sun-god, and were skilled at building cities high up in the Andes mountains.

**Songhai Empire**
1375–1591
Rose up in the wake of the declining Mali Empire. The city of Timbuktu became a center of Islamic learning.
*Songhai coin*

**Chimú culture**
c.850–1470
Skilled in pottery, textiles, and metalwork. Territory covered coastal regions by the Andes mountains. Conquered by the rival Inca Empire in 1470.

**Umayyad Caliphate**
661–1031
The second of four great Muslim dynasties of the Arab caliphate, meaning "kingdom."

**Kanem Empire**
700–1387
One of the most powerful African empires. The main religion became Islam during the second dynasty under the rule of the Sayfawa.

**Huari Empire**
540–1100
The first of the New World powers to use large cities to run the empire and to live in, rather than just for religious ceremonies.
*Huari wooden figure*

**Tihuanaco Empire**
400–950
Began as a small town on the shores of Lake Titicaca on the border of Peru and Bolivia before rapidly expanding to the surrounding areas.

**Ottoman Empire**
1299–1922
Sometimes called the "Turkish Empire," a long-lasting Islamic state with the wealthy city of Constantinople (modern-day Istanbul) as its capital.

PEOPLE AND ENEMY PRISONERS EACH YEAR TO APPEASE THE GODS.

149

# Castles

From castles and forts to walled cities, rulers and nations throughout history have tried to build impregnable structures to keep their enemies at bay and strengthen their grip on power.

**KEY**
Flags pinpoint some of the world's most impressive fortifications.

 Selected castles, forts, citadels, and fortified cities

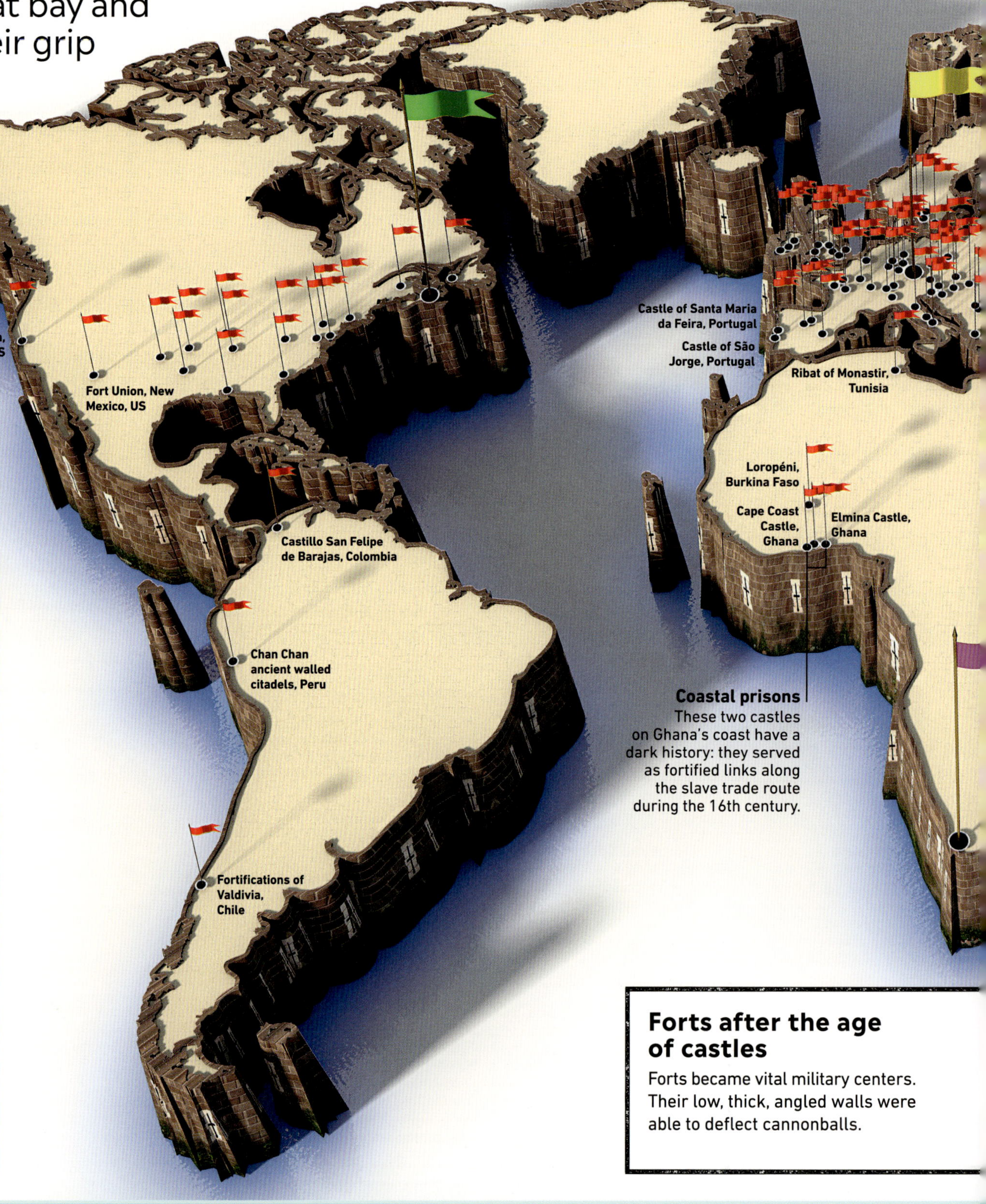

- Fort Columbia, Washington, US
- Fort Union, New Mexico, US
- Castle of Santa Maria da Feira, Portugal
- Castle of São Jorge, Portugal
- Ribat of Monastir, Tunisia
- Loropéni, Burkina Faso
- Cape Coast Castle, Ghana
- Elmina Castle, Ghana
- Castillo San Felipe de Barajas, Colombia
- Chan Chan ancient walled citadels, Peru
- Fortifications of Valdivia, Chile

### European castles
Most were fortified residences of nobles or monarchs; others were purely defensive.

**Burghausen, Germany** Europe's longest castle complex, consisting of a main castle and inner courtyard protected by five outer courtyards.

**Krak des Chevaliers, Syria** This 12th-century crusader castle has an outer wall with 13 towers separated from the inner wall and keep by a moat.

### Coastal prisons
These two castles on Ghana's coast have a dark history: they served as fortified links along the slave trade route during the 16th century.

### Forts after the age of castles
Forts became vital military centers. Their low, thick, angled walls were able to deflect cannonballs.

150 THE OTTOMAN TURKS BESIEGED THE FORTIFIED TOWN OF CANDIA,

# History

## Asian castles
Castles in Asia reflect local building styles and look different than those in Europe, but they served the same purpose.

**Himeji, Japan** Built as a fort in 1333, Himeji was then rebuilt several times between the 14th and 17th centuries. It has 83 buildings protected by 85-ft- (26-m-) high walls and 3 moats, and is Japan's largest castle.

**Mehrangarh Fort, India** This fort, 400 ft (122 m) above the city of Jodhpur, hides several palaces within its walls. Built by the ruler Rao Jodha in 1459, it is entered through a series of seven gates.

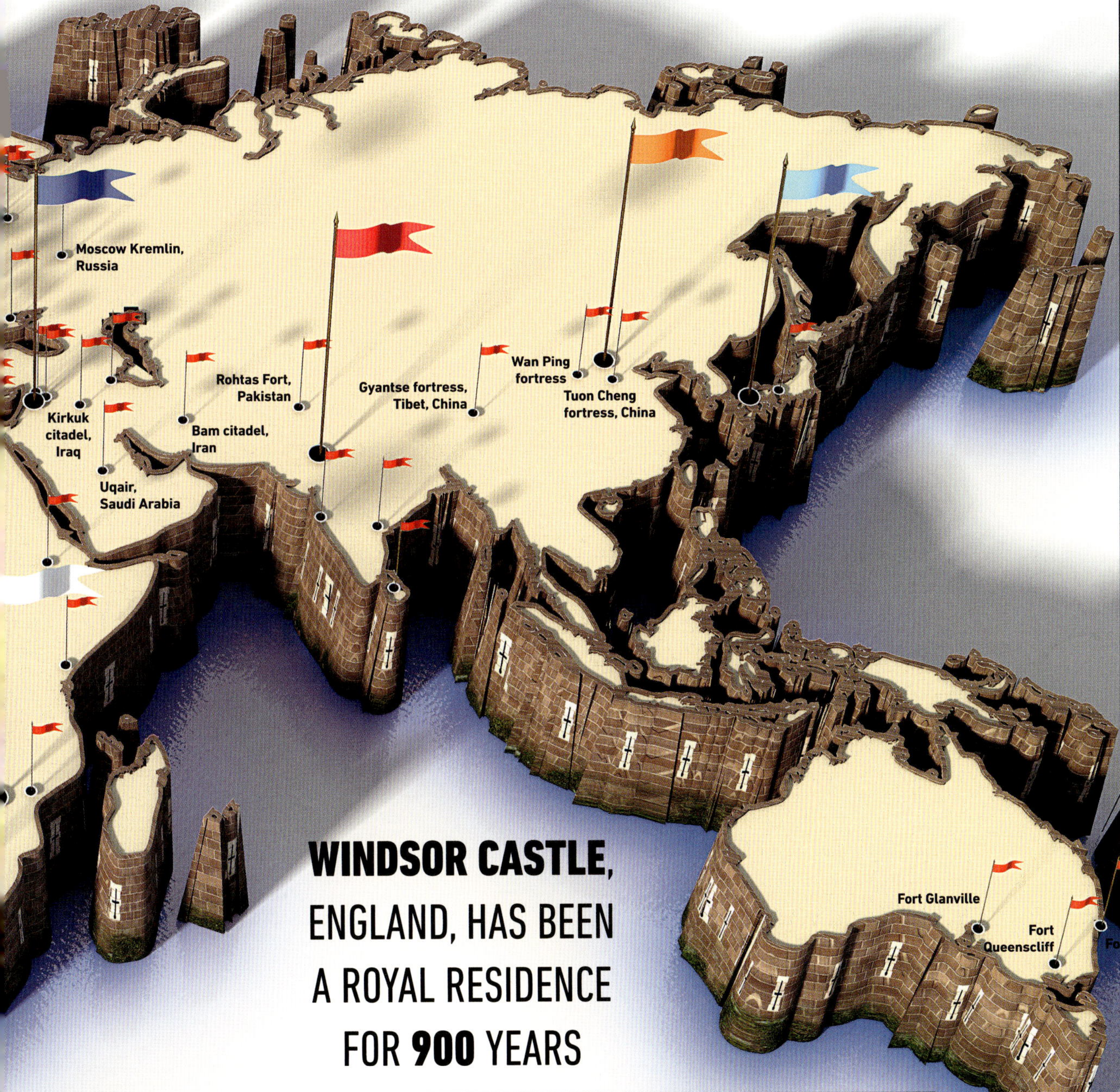

## Fortified cities
Cities surrounded by defensive walls, often incorporating a castle or royal residence.

**Forbidden City, China** The former imperial palace in Beijing has 980 buildings ringed by a wall and a 171-ft- (52-m-) wide moat.

**Great Zimbabwe** Once the capital of the Kingdom of Zimbabwe, the stone walls of this royal city were built without using mortar.

Moscow Kremlin, Russia
Kirkuk citadel, Iraq
Rohtas Fort, Pakistan
Bam citadel, Iran
Uqair, Saudi Arabia
Gyantse fortress, Tibet, China
Wan Ping fortress
Tuon Cheng fortress, China
Fort Glanville
Fort Queenscliff
Fort Denison

**WINDSOR CASTLE, ENGLAND, HAS BEEN A ROYAL RESIDENCE FOR 900 YEARS**

**Fort Independence, US** This star-shaped fort, completed in 1851, defended the harbor of Boston. Guns were mounted on its five pointed bastions.

**Castle of Good Hope, South Africa** A star fort built by the Dutch East India Company in 1666–79 to protect Dutch settlers on the Cape of Good Hope.

CRETE, FOR OVER 21 YEARS BEFORE IT SURRENDERED IN 1669.

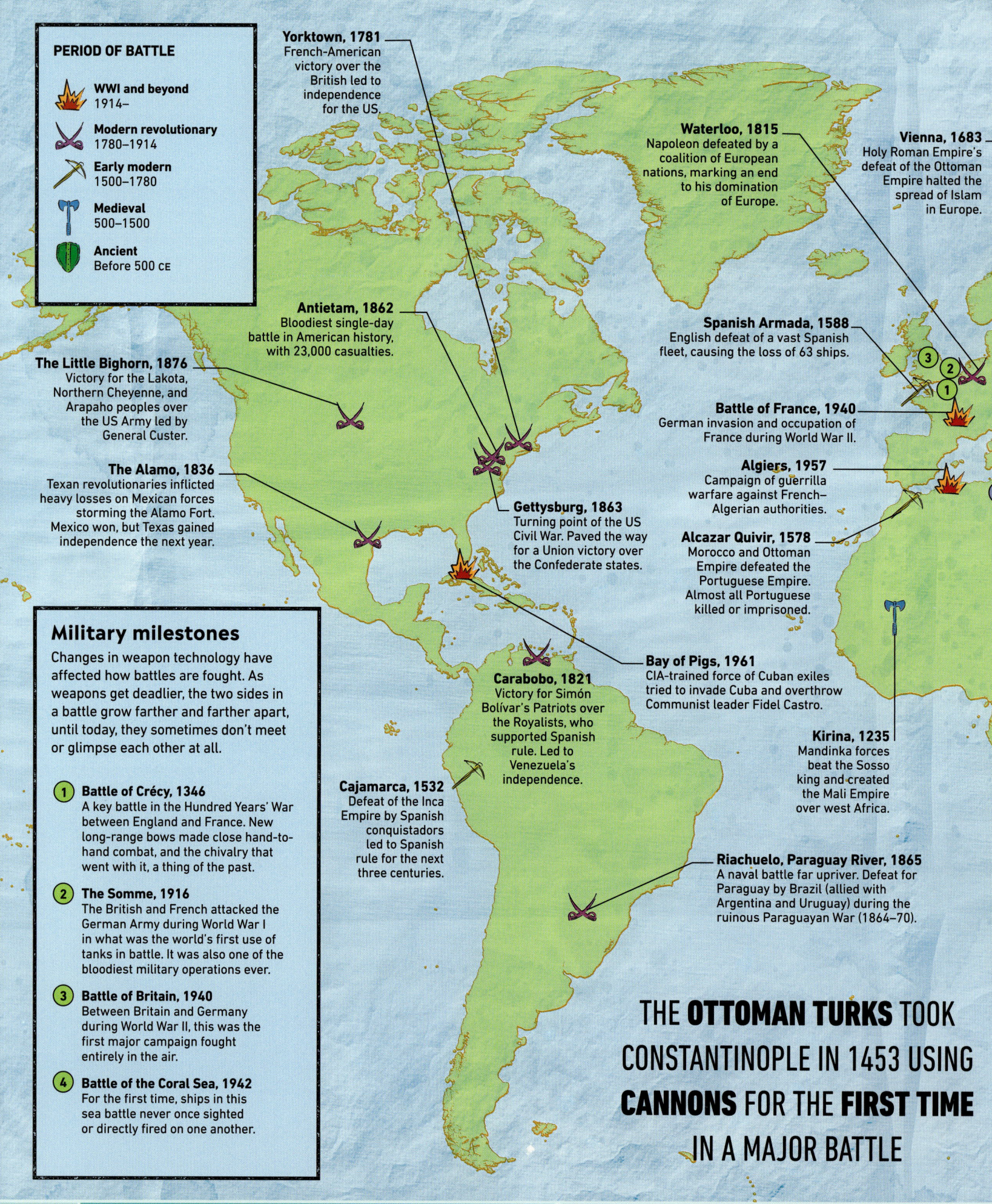

## PERIOD OF BATTLE

- WWI and beyond 1914–
- Modern revolutionary 1780–1914
- Early modern 1500–1780
- Medieval 500–1500
- Ancient Before 500 CE

**Yorktown, 1781** French-American victory over the British led to independence for the US.

**Waterloo, 1815** Napoleon defeated by a coalition of European nations, marking an end to his domination of Europe.

**Vienna, 1683** Holy Roman Empire's defeat of the Ottoman Empire halted the spread of Islam in Europe.

**Antietam, 1862** Bloodiest single-day battle in American history, with 23,000 casualties.

**Spanish Armada, 1588** English defeat of a vast Spanish fleet, causing the loss of 63 ships.

**The Little Bighorn, 1876** Victory for the Lakota, Northern Cheyenne, and Arapaho peoples over the US Army led by General Custer.

**Battle of France, 1940** German invasion and occupation of France during World War II.

**The Alamo, 1836** Texan revolutionaries inflicted heavy losses on Mexican forces storming the Alamo Fort. Mexico won, but Texas gained independence the next year.

**Algiers, 1957** Campaign of guerrilla warfare against French–Algerian authorities.

**Gettysburg, 1863** Turning point of the US Civil War. Paved the way for a Union victory over the Confederate states.

**Alcazar Quivir, 1578** Morocco and Ottoman Empire defeated the Portuguese Empire. Almost all Portuguese killed or imprisoned.

**Bay of Pigs, 1961** CIA-trained force of Cuban exiles tried to invade Cuba and overthrow Communist leader Fidel Castro.

**Carabobo, 1821** Victory for Simón Bolívar's Patriots over the Royalists, who supported Spanish rule. Led to Venezuela's independence.

**Kirina, 1235** Mandinka forces beat the Sosso king and created the Mali Empire over west Africa.

## Military milestones

Changes in weapon technology have affected how battles are fought. As weapons get deadlier, the two sides in a battle grow farther and farther apart, until today, they sometimes don't meet or glimpse each other at all.

1. **Battle of Crécy, 1346** A key battle in the Hundred Years' War between England and France. New long-range bows made close hand-to-hand combat, and the chivalry that went with it, a thing of the past.

2. **The Somme, 1916** The British and French attacked the German Army during World War I in what was the world's first use of tanks in battle. It was also one of the bloodiest military operations ever.

3. **Battle of Britain, 1940** Between Britain and Germany during World War II, this was the first major campaign fought entirely in the air.

4. **Battle of the Coral Sea, 1942** For the first time, ships in this sea battle never once sighted or directly fired on one another.

**Cajamarca, 1532** Defeat of the Inca Empire by Spanish conquistadors led to Spanish rule for the next three centuries.

**Riachuelo, Paraguay River, 1865** A naval battle far upriver. Defeat for Paraguay by Brazil (allied with Argentina and Uruguay) during the ruinous Paraguayan War (1864–70).

**THE OTTOMAN TURKS TOOK CONSTANTINOPLE IN 1453 USING CANNONS FOR THE FIRST TIME IN A MAJOR BATTLE**

AFTER THE BLOODY BATTLE OF KALINGA, INDIAN EMPEROR ASHOKA

# History

## Sieges
Not strictly a battle, a siege is a military blockade of a city or fortress. The aim is to conquer the city by waiting for those inside to surrender. Sometimes, the side laying siege attacks to speed things up.

**1. Siege of Carthage 149–146 BCE** — One of the longest sieges in history. The Romans surrounded Carthage (in modern Tunisia) and waited 3 years for its surrender, then enslaved the Carthaginian population.

**2. Capture of Jerusalem, 1099** — During the Crusader wars between Christians and Muslims, the Muslim defenders of Jerusalem lost control when the Christians built two enormous siege engines (towers on wheels) and scaled the walls.

**Austerlitz, 1805** — With smaller forces, the French Empire crushed Russia and Austria. One of Napoleon's greatest victories.

**Actium, 31 BCE** — Rome declared war on Antony and Cleopatra of Egypt. The Roman victory led to the beginning of the Roman Empire.

**Thermopylae, 480 BCE** — Vastly outnumbered Greek forces held the Persian Emperor Xerxes at bay for a vital 3 days.

**Stalingrad, 1942–43** — Long siege of this Soviet city caused immense suffering on both sides and eventually led to crippling defeat for Nazi Germany.

**Fall of Constantinople, 1453** — After a 4-month siege, Byzantine Empire fell to the invading Ottoman Empire.

**Badger Mouth, 1211** — Mongol ruler Genghis Khan's victory over the Jin Dynasty of China. One of history's bloodiest battles.

**Huai-Hai, 1948** — Final major fight in Chinese Civil War that led to the Communist takeover of China.

**Battle of Inchon, 1950** — A clear victory for the United Nations against North Korean forces in the Korean War.

**Battle of Phillora, 1965** — One of the largest tank battles of the Indo-Pakistani War. Decisive victory for Indian Army.

**Iwo Jima, 1945** — The US captured this island as a way of possibly invading Japan. More than 21,000 Japanese died.

**Wuhan, 1938** — Soviet and revolutionary Chinese forces totaling 1,100,000 troops and 200 aircraft failed to stop Japan from capturing the city.

**Omdurman, 1898** — Small British and Egyptian forces massacred a huge, but ill-equipped, Sudanese Army.

**El Alamein, 1942** — Major tank battle of World War II. British-led victory over Axis Powers (Italy and Germany).

**Dien Bien Phu, 1954** — Viet Minh communist revolutionaries besieged and defeated the French to end the First Indochina War. The next year began another 20 years of fighting in Vietnam.

**Kalinga, 262–261 BCE** — The Mauryan Empire under Ashoka the Great fought the republic of Kalinga. At least 100,000 Kalingans were killed.

**Isandlwana, 1879** — Crushing victory for the Zulu nation over the British, despite relying mainly on spears and cowhide shields.

**Surabaya, 1945** — Heaviest battle of the Indonesian Revolution against the British and Dutch. Celebrated as Heroes' Day in Indonesia.

**Coral Sea, 1942** — World War II naval battle between Japan and the US and Australia. The battle was the first time aircraft carriers engaged each other.

# Battlegrounds

At one time, armies met in formation on a single field of battle and fought for one to several days. By the 20th century, long-range weapons had changed warfare. Battlefields in places became theaters of war the size of countries.

# The last empires

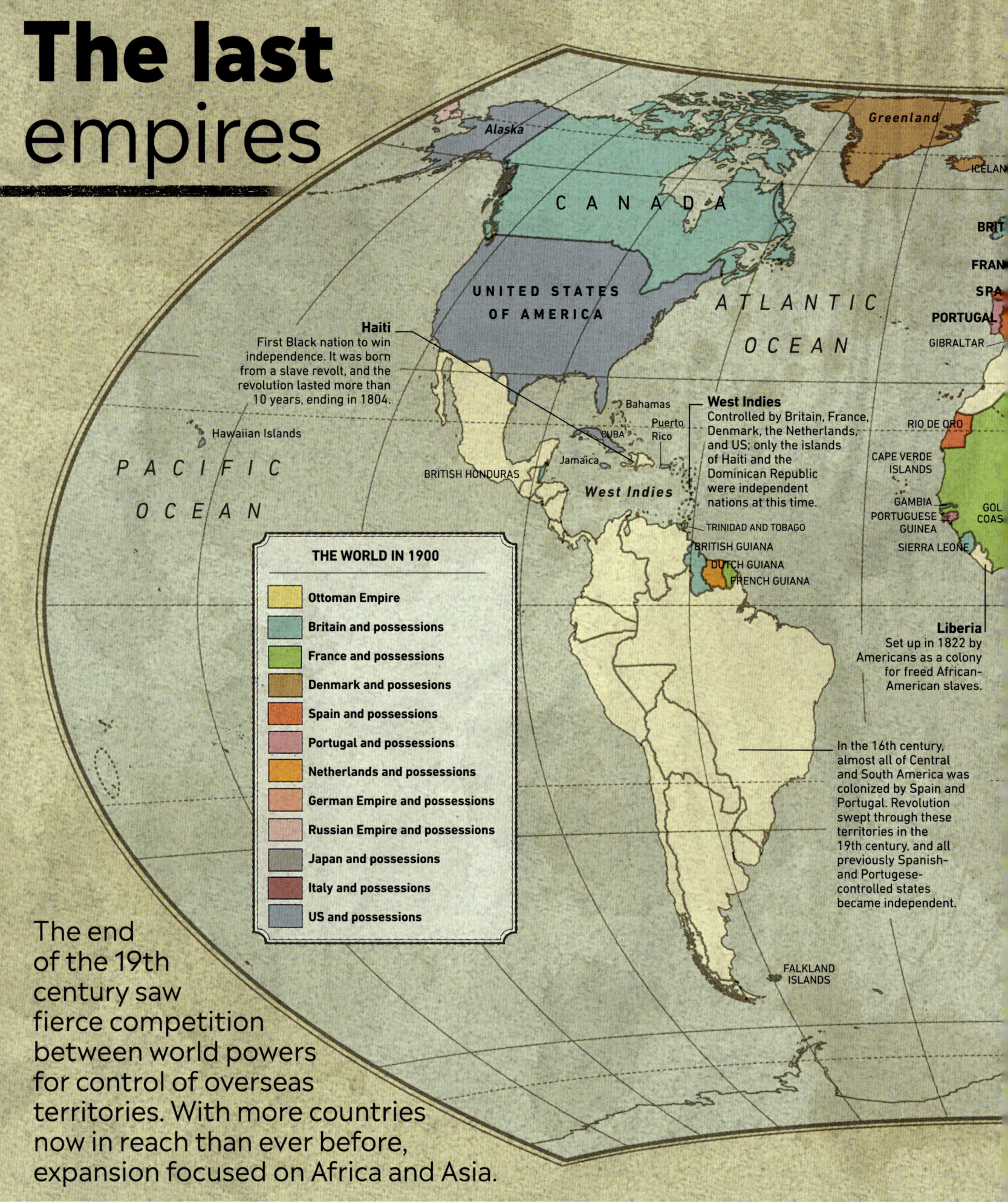

Haiti
First Black nation to win independence. It was born from a slave revolt, and the revolution lasted more than 10 years, ending in 1804.

West Indies
Controlled by Britain, France, Denmark, the Netherlands, and US; only the islands of Haiti and the Dominican Republic were independent nations at this time.

**THE WORLD IN 1900**
- Ottoman Empire
- Britain and possessions
- France and possessions
- Denmark and possesions
- Spain and possessions
- Portugal and possessions
- Netherlands and possessions
- German Empire and possessions
- Russian Empire and possessions
- Japan and possessions
- Italy and possessions
- US and possessions

Liberia
Set up in 1822 by Americans as a colony for freed African-American slaves.

In the 16th century, almost all of Central and South America was colonized by Spain and Portugal. Revolution swept through these territories in the 19th century, and all previously Spanish- and Portugese-controlled states became independent.

The end of the 19th century saw fierce competition between world powers for control of overseas territories. With more countries now in reach than ever before, expansion focused on Africa and Asia.

154 — AT ITS HEIGHT IN 1922, THE BRITISH EMPIRE CONTROLLED

# History

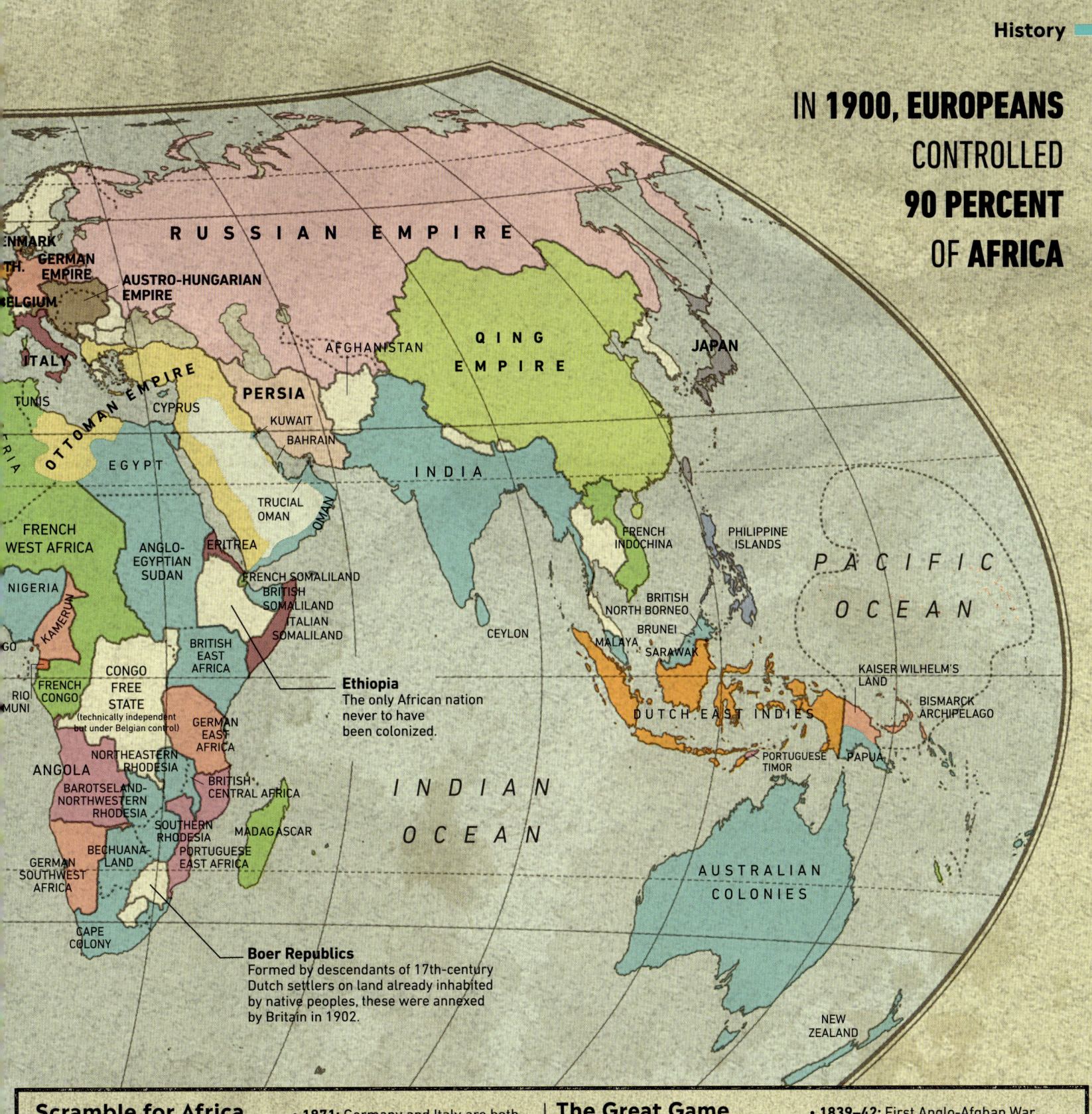

**IN 1900, EUROPEANS CONTROLLED 90 PERCENT OF AFRICA**

**Ethiopia**
The only African nation never to have been colonized.

**Boer Republics**
Formed by descendants of 17th-century Dutch settlers on land already inhabited by native peoples, these were annexed by Britain in 1902.

## Scramble for Africa
The Atlantic slave trade, in which Africans were forcibly sold to people in the Americas, ended in the mid-19th century. European powers colonized Africa for economic, political, and religious reasons, scrambling to claim territory before their rivals.

- **1871:** Germany and Italy are both unified. No more territory available for expansion of empires in Europe.
- **1884–85:** Berlin Conference, where European powers decide rules on carving up Africa.
- **1900:** Only a handful of regions are still independent states. Britain rules 30 percent of Africa's population.

## The Great Game
In the 1830s, Britain feared Russia was planning on invading British-ruled India through controlling India's neighbor, Afghanistan. The "Great Game" was the rivalry for power in Asia between the British and Russian empires.

- **1839–42:** First Anglo-Afghan War. Terrible defeat at Kabul for the British.
- **1878–80:** Second Anglo-Afghan War. Russia is defeated and Britain withdraws but takes control of Afghanistan's foreign affairs.
- **1907:** Russia and Britain sign a peace treaty in the face of the German threat of expansion in the Middle East.

**ALMOST ONE-QUARTER OF THE WORLD'S POPULATION AND LAND.**

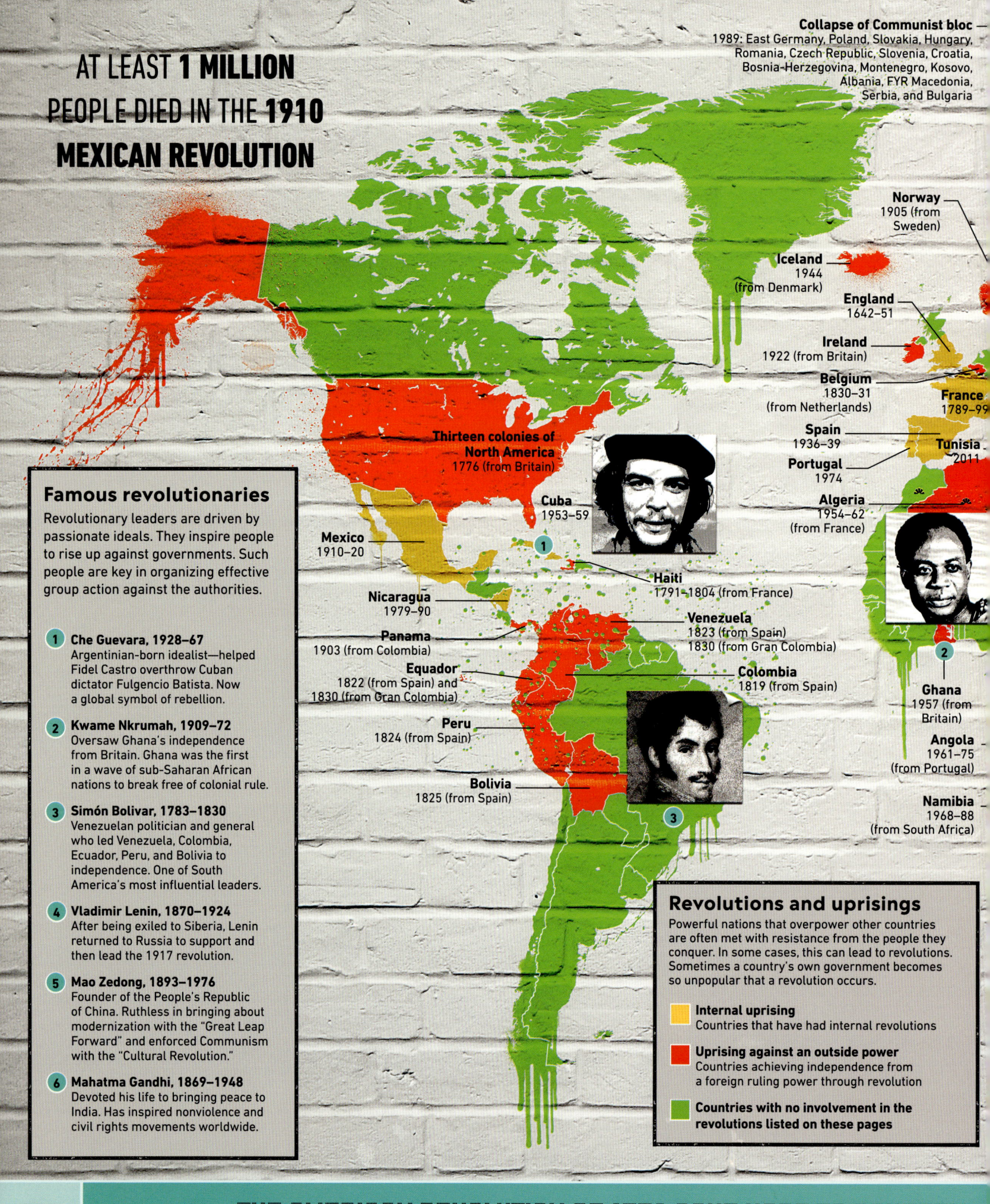

# History

# Revolutions

People all over the world have risen up against oppressive rulers. Revolutions can be sudden or lengthy, bloody or peaceful, but have one thing in common: they are all an attempt to change the way a country is ruled.

**Lithuania** 1989 (from USSR)
**Finland** 1917 (from Russia)
**Estonia** 1989 (from USSR)
**Latvia** 1989 (from USSR)
**Belarus** 1989 (from USSR)
**Ukraine** 1989 (from USSR)
**Moldova** 1989 (from USSR)
**Georgia** 1989 (from USSR)
**Armenia** 1989 (from USSR)
**Greece** 1821–32 (from Ottoman Empire)
**Libya** 2011
**Egypt** 2011
**Iraq** 2014–17
**Syria** From 2011
**Iran** 1979
**Azerbaijan** 1989 (from USSR)
**Turkmenistan** 1989 (from USSR)
**Uzbekistan** 1989 (from USSR)
**Kazakhstan** 1989 (from USSR)
**Kyrgyzstan** 1989 (from USSR)
**Tajikistan** 1989 (from USSR)
**Afghanistan** 1996
**Russia** 1917
**Korea** 1945 (from Japan)
**China** 1949
**Vietnam** 1975 (Socialist Republic of Vietnam created after war between North and South Vietnam)
**Myanmar (Burma)** 1962
**Philippines** 1896–98 (from Spain)
**Laos** 1975 (from USSR)
**Cambodia** 1979 (Khmer Rouge)
**Papua New Guinea** 1975 (from Australia)
**Eritrea** 1961–91 (from Ethiopia)
**Yemen** 2011
**India** 1947 (from Britain)
**Singapore** 1965 (from Malaysia)
**South Sudan** 2011 (from Sudan)
**Somalia** 1986–92
**Kenya (Mau Mau)** 1952–60 (from Britain)
**Indonesia** 1945–49 (from the Netherlands)
**East Timor** 1975 (from Portugal) and 2002 (from Indonesia)
**Democratic Republic of the Congo** 1997
**Rwanda** 1961 (from Belgium)
**Madagascar** 1960 (from France)
**South Africa** 1994

### Collapse of Communism

The USSR was a Communist state that incorporated Russia and 14 other Soviet republics (some of the red areas on the map). The USSR also had great influence over several other European states that collectively were known as the "Communist bloc" (some of the yellow map areas). In 1989, revolution spread through all these states, and in 1991 the USSR was dissolved.

▼ **Fall of communism** Indicates countries in which Communism collapsed in 1989–91

### Arab Spring

The "Arab Spring" revolutions and protests swept through the Arab world in 2011. As the map shows, in some countries rulers were forced out, while in others there were failed uprisings. The Arab Spring was the first uprising where protestors used social media to coordinate their actions. Not all of the movements were successful, however; the uprising in Tunisia led to a number of improvements, but many of the other countries are still marked by unrest.

**Arab Spring** Indicates countries involved in the Arab Spring

STRICKEN EUROPE AND INSPIRED THE 1789–99 FRENCH REVOLUTION.

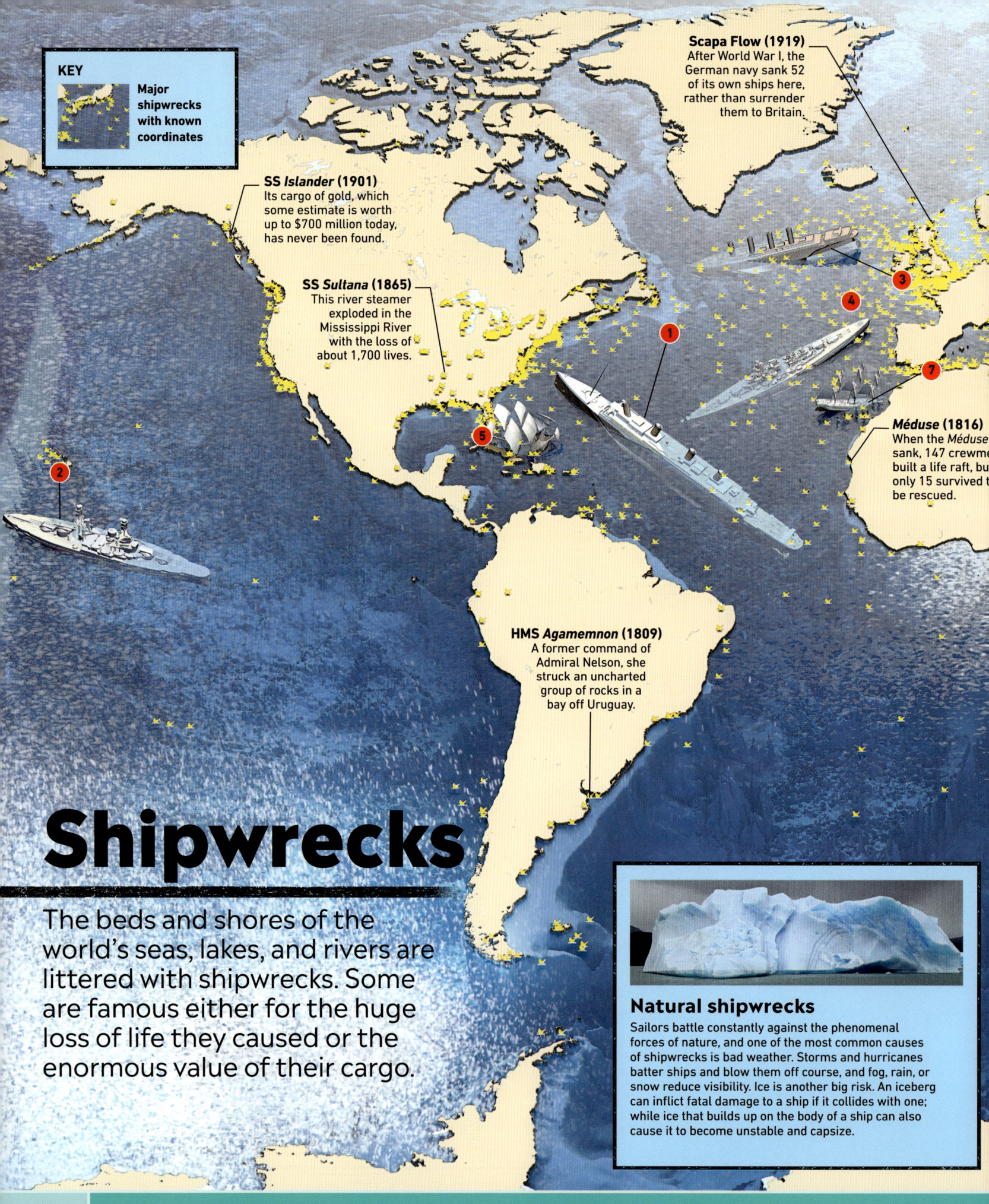

**KEY** — Major shipwrecks with known coordinates

**Scapa Flow (1919)** After World War I, the German navy sank 52 of its own ships here, rather than surrender them to Britain.

**SS *Islander* (1901)** Its cargo of gold, which some estimate is worth up to $700 million today, has never been found.

**SS *Sultana* (1865)** This river steamer exploded in the Mississippi River with the loss of about 1,700 lives.

***Méduse* (1816)** When the *Méduse* sank, 147 crewmen built a life raft, but only 15 survived to be rescued.

**HMS *Agamemnon* (1809)** A former command of Admiral Nelson, she struck an uncharted group of rocks in a bay off Uruguay.

# Shipwrecks

The beds and shores of the world's seas, lakes, and rivers are littered with shipwrecks. Some are famous either for the huge loss of life they caused or the enormous value of their cargo.

### Natural shipwrecks

Sailors battle constantly against the phenomenal forces of nature, and one of the most common causes of shipwrecks is bad weather. Storms and hurricanes batter ships and blow them off course, and fog, rain, or snow reduce visibility. Ice is another big risk. An iceberg can inflict fatal damage to a ship if it collides with one; while ice that builds up on the body of a ship can also cause it to become unstable and capsize.

ONE OF THE WORLD'S LARGEST WRECKS IS THE AMOCO CADIZ, WHICH

# History

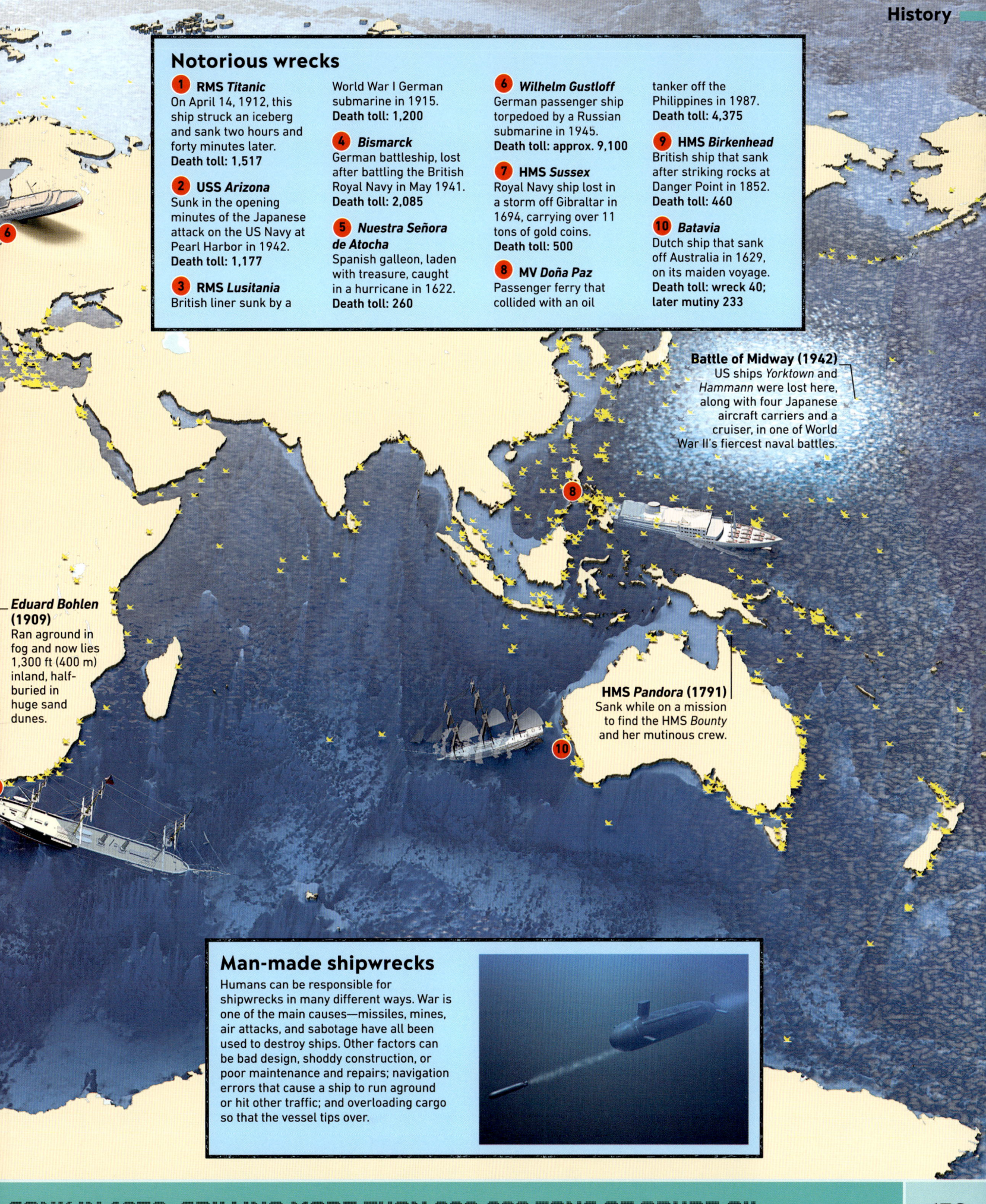

## Notorious wrecks

**1. RMS *Titanic*** On April 14, 1912, this ship struck an iceberg and sank two hours and forty minutes later. Death toll: 1,517

**2. USS *Arizona*** Sunk in the opening minutes of the Japanese attack on the US Navy at Pearl Harbor in 1942. Death toll: 1,177

**3. RMS *Lusitania*** British liner sunk by a World War I German submarine in 1915. Death toll: 1,200

**4. *Bismarck*** German battleship, lost after battling the British Royal Navy in May 1941. Death toll: 2,085

**5. *Nuestra Señora de Atocha*** Spanish galleon, laden with treasure, caught in a hurricane in 1622. Death toll: 260

**6. *Wilhelm Gustloff*** German passenger ship torpedoed by a Russian submarine in 1945. Death toll: approx. 9,100

**7. HMS *Sussex*** Royal Navy ship lost in a storm off Gibraltar in 1694, carrying over 11 tons of gold coins. Death toll: 500

**8. MV *Doña Paz*** Passenger ferry that collided with an oil tanker off the Philippines in 1987. Death toll: 4,375

**9. HMS *Birkenhead*** British ship that sank after striking rocks at Danger Point in 1852. Death toll: 460

**10. *Batavia*** Dutch ship that sank off Australia in 1629, on its maiden voyage. Death toll: wreck 40; later mutiny 233

**Battle of Midway (1942)** US ships *Yorktown* and *Hammann* were lost here, along with four Japanese aircraft carriers and a cruiser, in one of World War II's fiercest naval battles.

**Eduard Bohlen (1909)** Ran aground in fog and now lies 1,300 ft (400 m) inland, half-buried in huge sand dunes.

**HMS Pandora (1791)** Sank while on a mission to find the HMS *Bounty* and her mutinous crew.

## Man-made shipwrecks

Humans can be responsible for shipwrecks in many different ways. War is one of the main causes—missiles, mines, air attacks, and sabotage have all been used to destroy ships. Other factors can be bad design, shoddy construction, or poor maintenance and repairs; navigation errors that cause a ship to run aground or hit other traffic; and overloading cargo so that the vessel tips over.

**SANK IN 1978, SPILLING MORE THAN 220,000 TONS OF CRUDE OIL.**

# Industrial wonders

The Industrial Revolution of the 18th and 19th centuries saw remarkable advances in technology and materials. This led to extraordinary design and engineering feats, the likes of which had never been seen before.

**Golden Gate Bridge**
San Francisco, California, 1937. World-famous steel bridge and longest suspension bridge in the world when built.

**Boeing Everett Factory**
Everett, Washington, 1968. Aircraft assembly building and the largest building in the world.

**Great Belt Fixed Link**
Denmark, 1997. Connects islands of Zealand and Funen. Comprises two bridges and a railroad tunnel.

**Bell Rock Lighthouse**
Inchcape, Scotland, 1810. Oldest surviving lighthouse at sea.

**The Langeled Pipeline**
2006. Undersea pipeline pumping Norwegian natural gas to Britain.

**London Sewage System**
Late 19th century. Declared an engineering triumph for successfully diverting raw sewage away from the Thames.

**Hibbing Taconite Company Mine**
Hibbing, Minnesota, 1895. One of the world's largest iron ore mines.

**Lockheed SR-71 Blackbird**
Beale, California, 1964. Fastest manned jet aircraft.

**Channel Tunnel**
Folkestone, UK—Calais, France, 1994. International undersea train tunnel.

**Hoover Dam**
Nevada/Arizona, 1936. Largest concrete structure ever built at the time of construction.

**Guggenheim Museum**
New York, New York, 1959. Architectural and design feat.

**Graf Zeppelin**

**Guggenheim Museum**
Bilbao, Spain, 1997. Important work of modern architecture.

**WM Keck Observatory**
Mauna Kea, Hawaii, 1993 and 1996. Second-largest optical telescopes on Earth.

**Concorde**

**Sagrada Familia**
Barcelona, Spain, 1882–current. Huge church designed by Antoni Gaudí, considered a masterpiece, and still under construction.

**Very Large Array**
Socorro, New Mexico, 1973–80. Astronomical observatory made up of 27 radio antennas arranged in a Y-shape.

**Panama Canal**
1914. 48 miles (77 km) long. Among the most difficult engineering projects in history.

**Large Hadron Collider**
Geneva, Switzerland, 1998–2008. Giant scientific instrument for testing particles.

**Itaipu Dam**
Brazil/Paraguay, 1984. The second-largest dam in the world.

**San Alfonso del Mar swimming pool**
Algarrobo, Chile, 2006. 0.6 mile (1 km) long and 115 ft (35 m) deep. Second-largest swimming pool in the world.

### Industrial pioneers

1. **First transatlantic cable, Canada–Ireland, 1858**
Cable that transported messages from one end to the other. The first of its kind to be laid across the Atlantic, meaning messages could be received in a matter of minutes.

2. **Transcontinental Railroad, California–Nebraska, 1869**
Connected the east coast railroads of the US with the Pacific coast for the first time. Considered to be one of the greatest technological feats of the 19th century.

3. **Home Insurance Building, Chicago, Illinois, 1885**
First ever steel-framed building, and first tall building to be supported by a fireproof metal frame. Although not very tall, the technology used made it the first "skyscraper."

FRENCH ENGINEER ALBERT MATHIEU PUT FORWARD A PROPOSAL

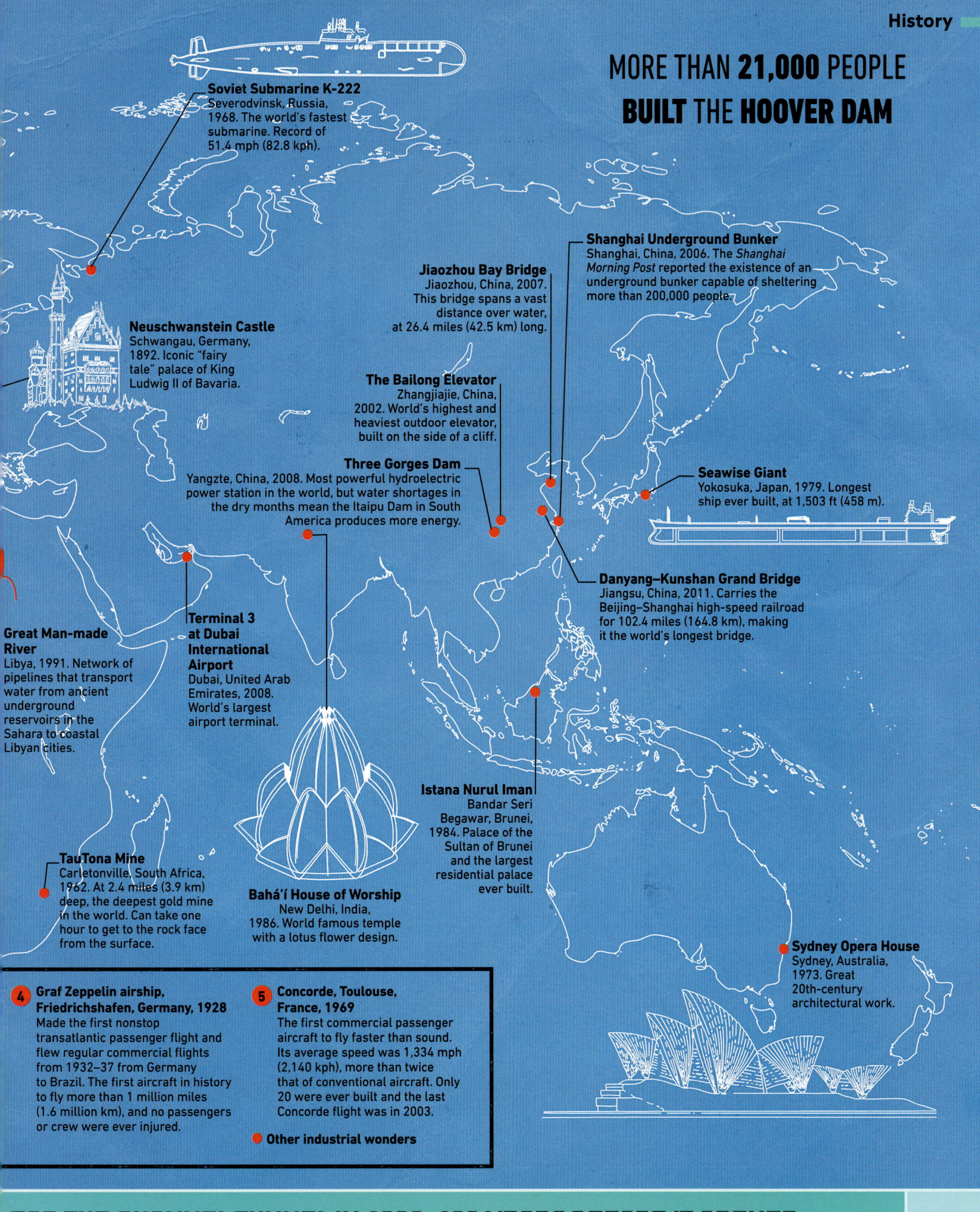

## Culture

**Holi Festival, Jodhpur, India**
During the Hindu spring festival of Holi—known as the Festival of Colors—people throw pigments and colored water over each other.

# Introduction

The word "culture" is a broad idea, and includes the values, beliefs, and behavior of a society, or group of people. Culture includes many things, including customs, language, religion, music, art, food, and clothing. Some points of culture are traditional, having survived virtually unchanged for centuries. Others are short-lived, such as fashion styles and trends in pop music.

### Modern culture

Today's culture is fast-moving and ever-changing, thanks in part to the instant communication offered by the Internet. But long before the Internet, the migration of people around the world began introducing people to cultures different from their own. Global broadcasting then accelerated this effect in the 20th century. The cultural contact often creates a fusion (uniting) of different cultural styles, especially in the fields of music, fashion, and cooking.

**Live performances**
Huge crowds watch singers, such as Beyoncé (right), perform live, just as they have always done. But today the "live" audience can number many millions, with most following remotely via Internet-based platforms like YouTube or Spotify.

**Stadium spectators**
For many sports fans, being part of a passionate, noisy, banner-waving stadium crowd makes them feel an important part of the event.

**Headdress,** called a *kiritam*, varies in size and design, according to the character being portrayed.

**Hand gestures** (known as *mudra*) are the dancer's main way of telling the story.

**Noble-hearted** characters always have green faces; dark red signifies a treacherous nature.

**Kathakali dancer**
Indian kathakali dancers enact stories from two epic poems, the *Ramayana* and the *Mahabarata*. Dealing with the constant struggle between good and evil, dances end with the destruction of a demon.

**Heroes** always wear red jackets

**Dancer's skirt** is made up of many layers of white cotton.

DRAGON DANCES ARE TRADITIONAL PERFORMANCES IN CHINESE

# Culture

## Traditional culture

Older people can pass culture on to the next generation, enabling a society's traditions to be preserved for many years. The *Ramayana*, a Hindu poem written in the 5th or 4th century BCE, tells the story of Rama and Sita, and their battle against the demon-king Ravana. Over many generations, the *Ramayana* and its values have been kept alive in India and southern Asia through writing, story telling, painting, sculpture, festivals, music, and dance.

**Literature**
The *Ramayana* was originally written in Sanskrit, the language of Hinduism and ancient Indian literary texts.

**Sculpture**
The great warrior Rama, holding his bow, stands next to his wife Sita. Both hold up their right hands in blessing.

**Festival**
At the Hindu festival of Diwali, people light lamps to commemorate Rama's return from exile and his victory over Ravana.

**Painting**
In this scene from the *Ramakien*, a Thai version of the *Ramayana*, the monkey god Hanuman uses his body as a bridge for Rama to cross.

**Music**
Musicians in Bali, Indonesia, provide accompaniment to kecak dancers, who perform parts of the *Ramayana*.

CULTURE, BELIEVED TO DRIVE AWAY EVIL SPIRITS AND BRING GOOD LUCK.

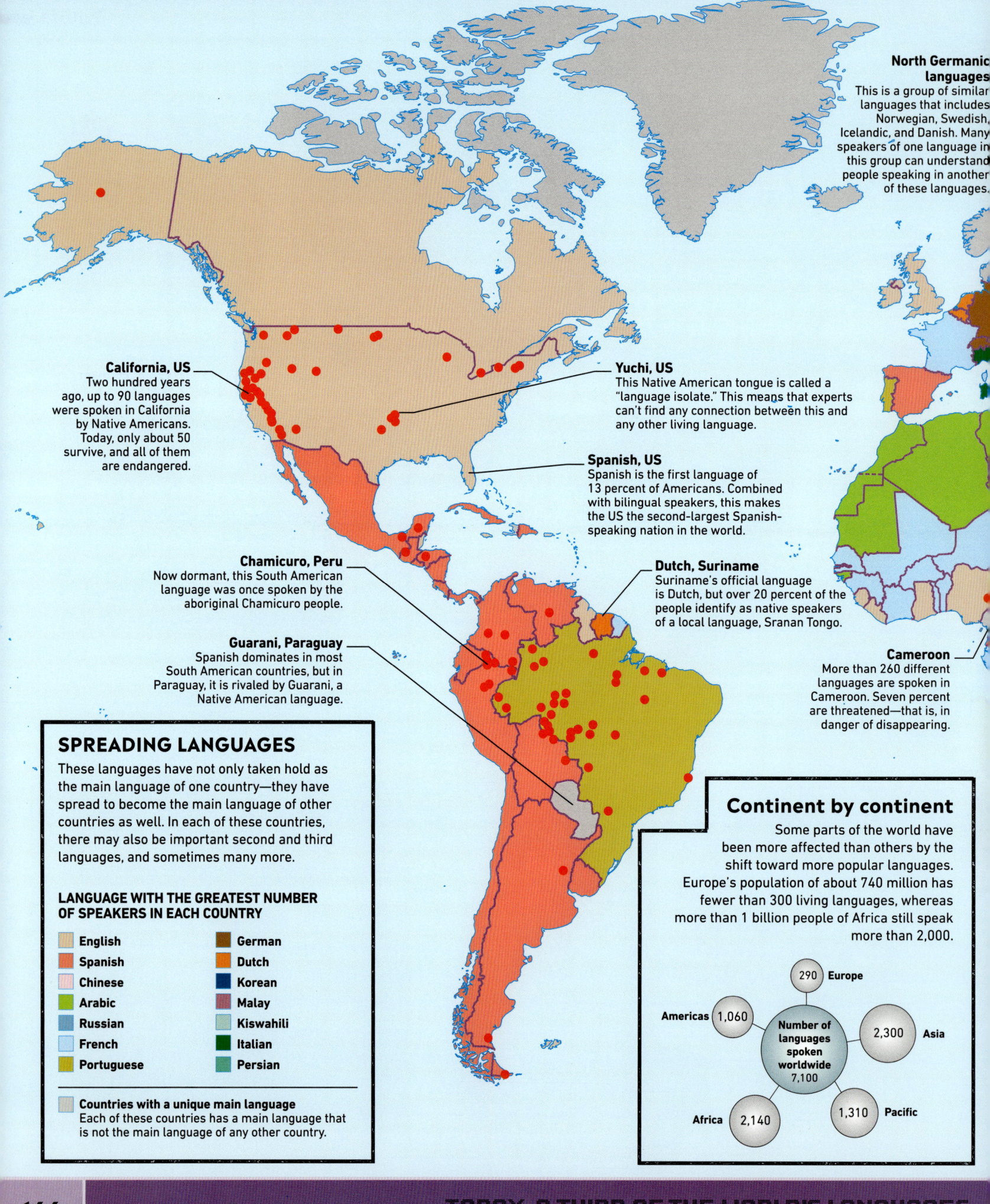

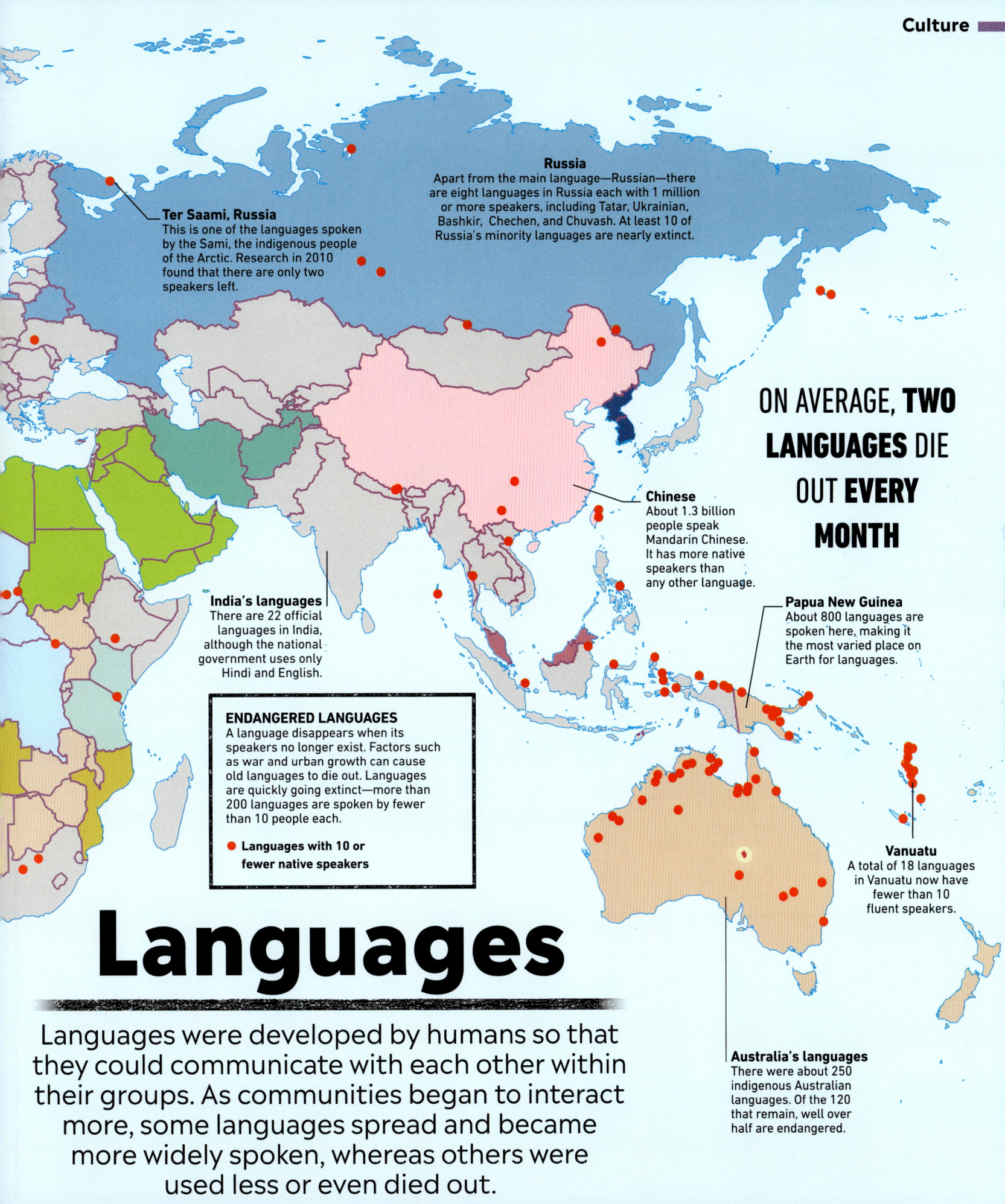

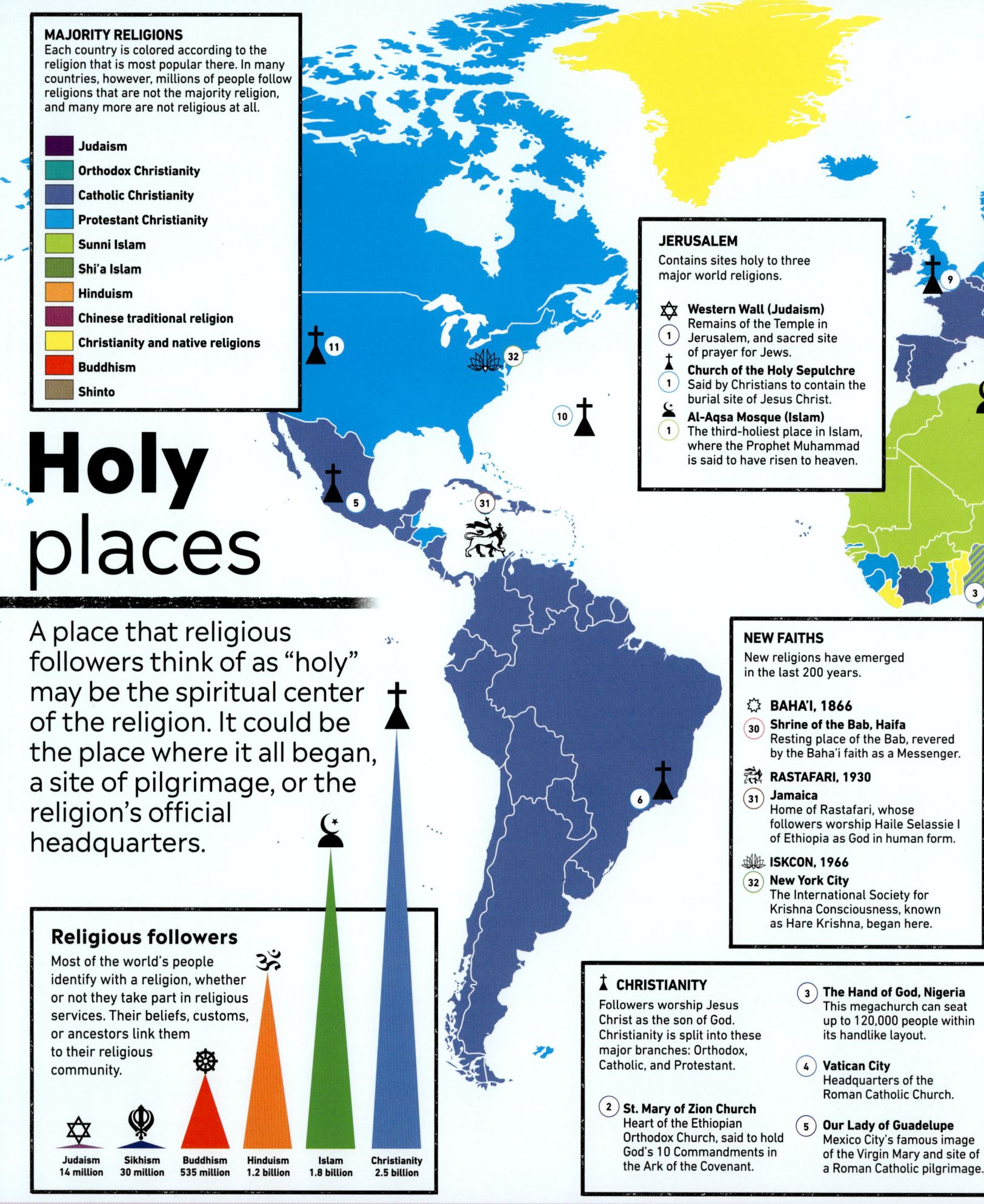

Culture

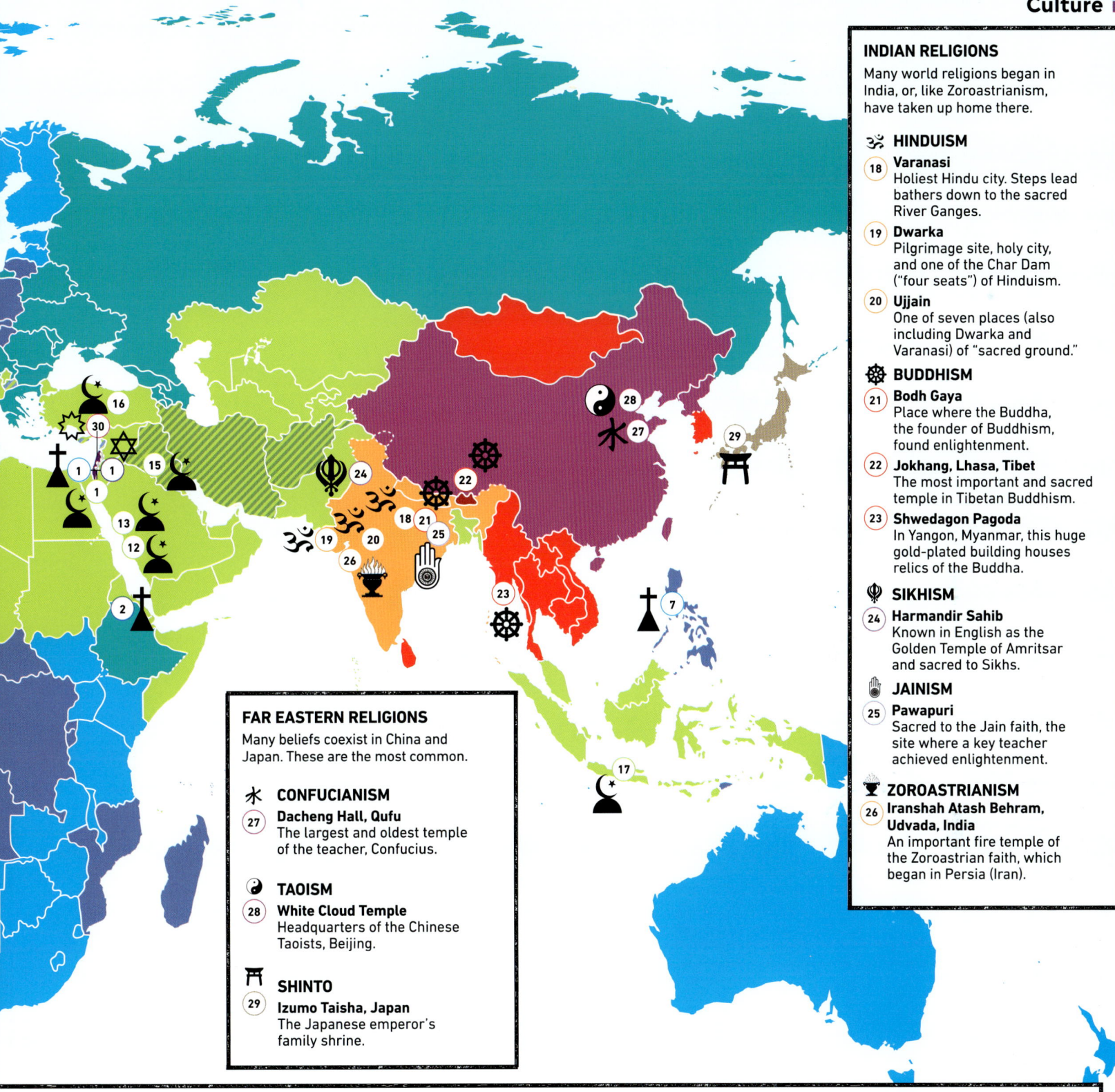

**INDIAN RELIGIONS**
Many world religions began in India, or, like Zoroastrianism, have taken up home there.

🕉 **HINDUISM**
- 18 **Varanasi** Holiest Hindu city. Steps lead bathers down to the sacred River Ganges.
- 19 **Dwarka** Pilgrimage site, holy city, and one of the Char Dam ("four seats") of Hinduism.
- 20 **Ujjain** One of seven places (also including Dwarka and Varanasi) of "sacred ground."

☸ **BUDDHISM**
- 21 **Bodh Gaya** Place where the Buddha, the founder of Buddhism, found enlightenment.
- 22 **Jokhang, Lhasa, Tibet** The most important and sacred temple in Tibetan Buddhism.
- 23 **Shwedagon Pagoda** In Yangon, Myanmar, this huge gold-plated building houses relics of the Buddha.

☬ **SIKHISM**
- 24 **Harmandir Sahib** Known in English as the Golden Temple of Amritsar and sacred to Sikhs.

🖐 **JAINISM**
- 25 **Pawapuri** Sacred to the Jain faith, the site where a key teacher achieved enlightenment.

🔥 **ZOROASTRIANISM**
- 26 **Iranshah Atash Behram, Udvada, India** An important fire temple of the Zoroastrian faith, which began in Persia (Iran).

**FAR EASTERN RELIGIONS**
Many beliefs coexist in China and Japan. These are the most common.

氺 **CONFUCIANISM**
- 27 **Dacheng Hall, Qufu** The largest and oldest temple of the teacher, Confucius.

☯ **TAOISM**
- 28 **White Cloud Temple** Headquarters of the Chinese Taoists, Beijing.

⛩ **SHINTO**
- 29 **Izumo Taisha, Japan** The Japanese emperor's family shrine.

- 6 **Our Lady of Aparecida, São Paulo, Brazil** Eight million Catholic pilgrims a year visit this celebrated statue of the Virgin Mary.
- 7 **San Agustin Church, Manila** The Philippines' oldest church, dating from 1607.
- 8 **All Saint's Church, Germany** In Wittenberg, Martin Luther began Protestantism by nailing his ideas on the church door.
- 9 **Canterbury Cathedral** Place of pilgrimage and world center of the Anglican Protestant Church.
- 10 **St. Peter's Church** The oldest Anglican church outside Britain, in Bermuda.
- 11 **Salt Lake Temple** Largest center of worship of the Church of Jesus Christ of Latter-day Saints, known as the Mormon Church.

☪ **ISLAM**
Muslims, followers of Islam, believe in one god and that Muhammad (570–632 CE) is His prophet. This religion split into Sunni and Shi'a faiths early on.

- 12 **Makkah** Sacred to all Muslims as Muhammad's birthplace.
- 13 **Medinah** The burial site of Islam's prophet, Muhammad.
- 14 **Kairouan, Tunisia** Fourth city of Sunni Islam, and seat of Islamic learning.
- 15 **Najaf, Iraq** Third city of Shi'a Muslims. Features the tomb of their first imam, Imam Ali.
- 16 **Konya, Turkey** Home of Sufi mystic Rumi, whose followers perform the "Whirling Dervish" dance.
- 17 **Demak Great Mosque** One of Indonesia's oldest mosques, built in the 15th century.

2019 FOR THE KUMBH MELA FESTIVAL, HELD EVERY FOUR YEARS.

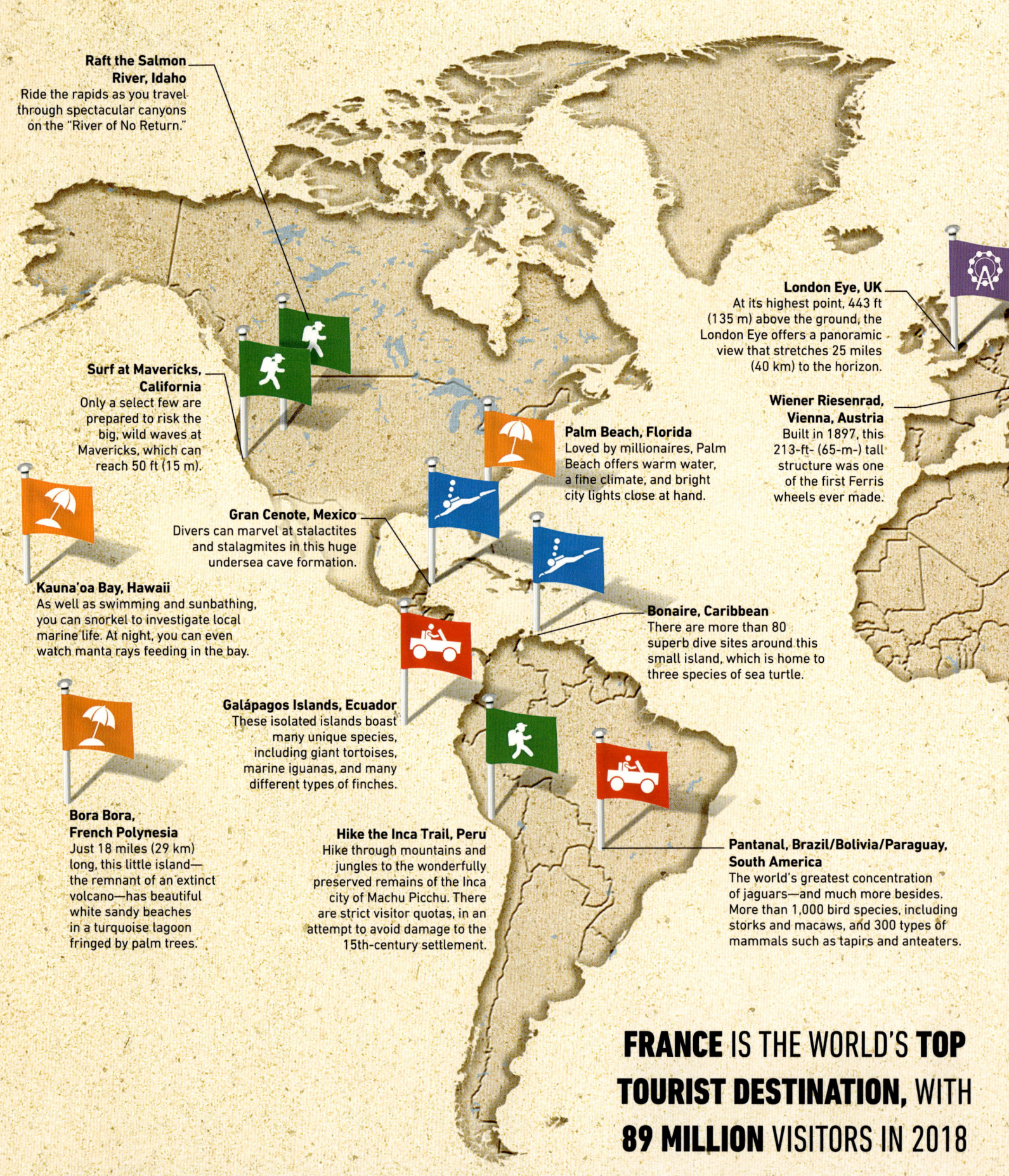

Culture

## KEY

 **Adventure destinations** These spots are for those who like their holidays thrill-packed, offering extreme activities such as white-water rafting, skydiving, surfing, and trekking in remote regions.

 **World's top big wheels** Why not take a city break and ride one of the world's amazing observation wheels? Watch the world turn and take in the incredible views from the top.

 **Best diving and snorkeling sites** Take the plunge and immerse yourself in the magical worlds of coral reefs and undersea caverns. Be careful not to touch the coral, though, as it's easily damaged.

 **Top 5 Beaches** Relax, stretch out, and catch some rays on a sandy shore somewhere. Can't decide where to go? No worries—we've done the hard work for you and picked the best of the bunch.

 **Top 5 Safari sites** Get right up close to nature on a safari. See wild animals in their natural habitats, experience incredible animal migrations, and marvel at unique species.

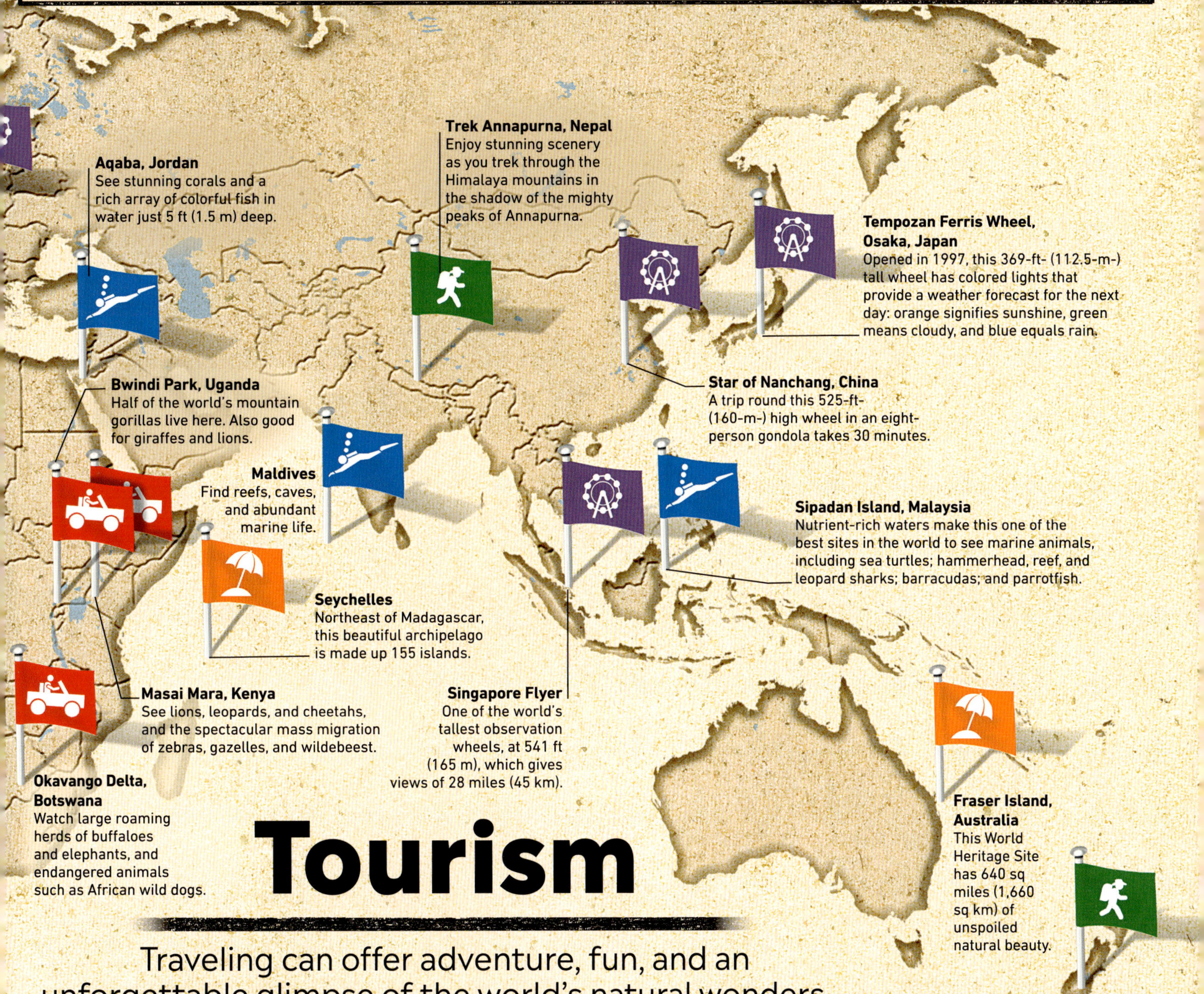

**Aqaba, Jordan** See stunning corals and a rich array of colorful fish in water just 5 ft (1.5 m) deep.

**Trek Annapurna, Nepal** Enjoy stunning scenery as you trek through the Himalaya mountains in the shadow of the mighty peaks of Annapurna.

**Tempozan Ferris Wheel, Osaka, Japan** Opened in 1997, this 369-ft- (112.5-m-) tall wheel has colored lights that provide a weather forecast for the next day: orange signifies sunshine, green means cloudy, and blue equals rain.

**Bwindi Park, Uganda** Half of the world's mountain gorillas live here. Also good for giraffes and lions.

**Star of Nanchang, China** A trip round this 525-ft- (160-m-) high wheel in an eight-person gondola takes 30 minutes.

**Maldives** Find reefs, caves, and abundant marine life.

**Sipadan Island, Malaysia** Nutrient-rich waters make this one of the best sites in the world to see marine animals, including sea turtles; hammerhead, reef, and leopard sharks; barracudas; and parrotfish.

**Seychelles** Northeast of Madagascar, this beautiful archipelago is made up 155 islands.

**Masai Mara, Kenya** See lions, leopards, and cheetahs, and the spectacular mass migration of zebras, gazelles, and wildebeest.

**Singapore Flyer** One of the world's tallest observation wheels, at 541 ft (165 m), which gives views of 28 miles (45 km).

**Okavango Delta, Botswana** Watch large roaming herds of buffaloes and elephants, and endangered animals such as African wild dogs.

**Fraser Island, Australia** This World Heritage Site has 640 sq miles (1,660 sq km) of unspoiled natural beauty.

# Tourism

Traveling can offer adventure, fun, and an unforgettable glimpse of the world's natural wonders—but it's important to consider the environmental impact of tourism, too. In 2020, the industry was severely affected by the COVID-19 pandemic.

**Skydive in Queenstown, New Zealand** Step out of a plane 15,000 ft (4,500 m) above Queenstown and freefall for 60 seconds, until a pull on the ripcord opens your parachute and you float gently to the ground.

**Edward Hopper**
1882–1967; US.
Hopper painted in the Realist style, which tries to show things as they are in real life. Hopper used simple colors and often painted solitary, lonely-looking people.

**Andy Warhol**
1928–1987; US.
Warhol pioneered Pop Art—the "pop" refers to popular culture. His art used familiar images of famous people and everyday items such as soup cans. Warhol took his inspiration from advertising, TV, and comic strips.

**Edvard Munch**
1863–1944; Norway.
Munch was an Expressionist artist. Expressionists tried to express feelings in their work, rather than portray people and objects accurately. Munch's most famous painting is *The Scream* (1893), which shows a person with an agonized expression.

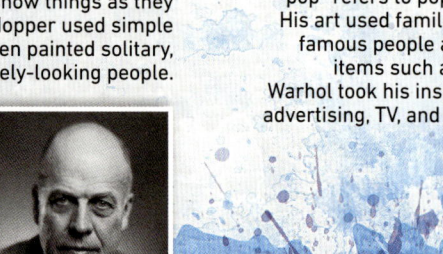

**Thomas Gainsborough**
1727–88; England.
Founder of the 18th-century British Landscape school, Gainsborough also made portraits. *Mr. and Mrs. Andrews* (1750; right) is an early masterpiece.

**Claude Monet**
1840–1926; France.
Impressionists such as Monet painted their view of brief moments in time.

**Frida Kahlo**
1907–1954; Mexico.
Frida Kahlo began painting after she was badly injured in an accident. She is best known for her self-portraits. Her work used bold, bright colors and was influenced by Mexican folk art.

**Pablo Picasso**
1881–1973; Spain.
Among many other things, this famous artist was a founder of Cubism—a style that used shapes to depict people and objects, often showing them from multiple viewpoints at the same time.

**Victor Meirelles**
1832–1903; Brazil.
Meirelles' religious and military paintings and depictions of episodes from Brazilian history won him fame and praise in the 19th century. His painting *The First Mass in Brazil* (1860; right) still appears in primary-school history books in Brazil.

**Eugène Delacroix**
1798–1863; France.
Delacroix was one of the Romantics, who stressed imagination and emotion. *Liberty Leading the People* (1830; above) marks the overthrow of Charles X of France in 1830.

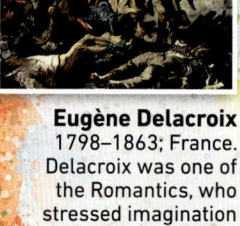

# Art

People the world over value art because it allows them to express their emotions and their culture, record history and everyday life, and explore what it means to be human. The works of the world's great artists often sell for huge sums of money.

**Sculpture**
13th century–present; Nigeria.
The people of the Kingdom of Benin, in what is now Nigeria, sculptured bronze heads and figures. They also made masks out of wood, bronze, and ivory. The tradition continues: on the right is a wooden mask of the late 20th century.

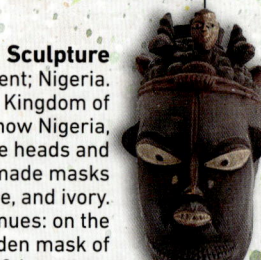

IN NOVEMBER 2017, LEONARDO DA VINCI'S "SALVATOR MUNDI" WAS AUCTIONED

Culture

**Marc Chagall**
1887–1985; Russia.
Chagall produced Expressionist and Cubist paintings, and also stained-glass windows. He is known for his paintings of village scenes and of lovers floating in the air.

**Yue Minjun**
Born 1962; China.
Based in Beijing, Yue Minjun is best known for his oil paintings, which show him frozen with laughter in various poses and in different settings. He has also represented himself in sculptures, watercolor paintings, and prints. He first exhibited his work in 1987; by 2007, he had sold 13 paintings for more than $1 million each.

**Tamara de Lempicka**
1898–1980; Poland.
In the 1920s and 1930s, de Lempicka was the most famous painter in the Art Deco style, which featured geometric shapes and intense, bright colors. She lived a flamboyant life and associated with the rich and famous.

**Caravaggio**
1571–1610; Italy.
Caravaggio was one of the Baroque artists, who revolutionized art by painting realistic rather than idealized people and scenes. He is one of the most influential painters in art history.

**Katsushika Hokusai**
1760–1849; Japan.
Hokusai is perhaps the most famous Japanese printmaker. His wood-block prints included seascapes, such as *The Great Wave off Kanagawa* (1831; above), and scenes from everyday life.

**Basawan**
c.1580–1600; India.
A painter of miniature scenes, Basawan illustrated the *Akbarnama* (right)—the official chronicle of Akbar, the third Mughal Emperor.

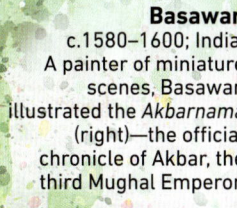

**Willie Bester**
Born 1956; South Africa.
Bester's collages and sculptures use recycled material and objects found in scrapyards and flea markets. His 1992 *Tribute to Biko* (above) commemorates Stephen Biko, who campaigned for racial equality in South Africa.

**Yannima Tommy Watson**
1935–2017; Australia.
Despite starting painting only in 2001, when he was in his mid-60s, Tommy Watson rapidly became one of Australia's foremost Aboriginal artists. His paintings relate to the stories of the Dreamtime—the creation period in Aboriginal mythology.

**IT IS ESTIMATED THAT PICASSO PRODUCED ABOUT 148,000 WORKS OF ART DURING HIS LIFETIME**

FOR $450 MILLION, MAKING IT THE MOST EXPENSIVE PAINTING EVER SOLD.

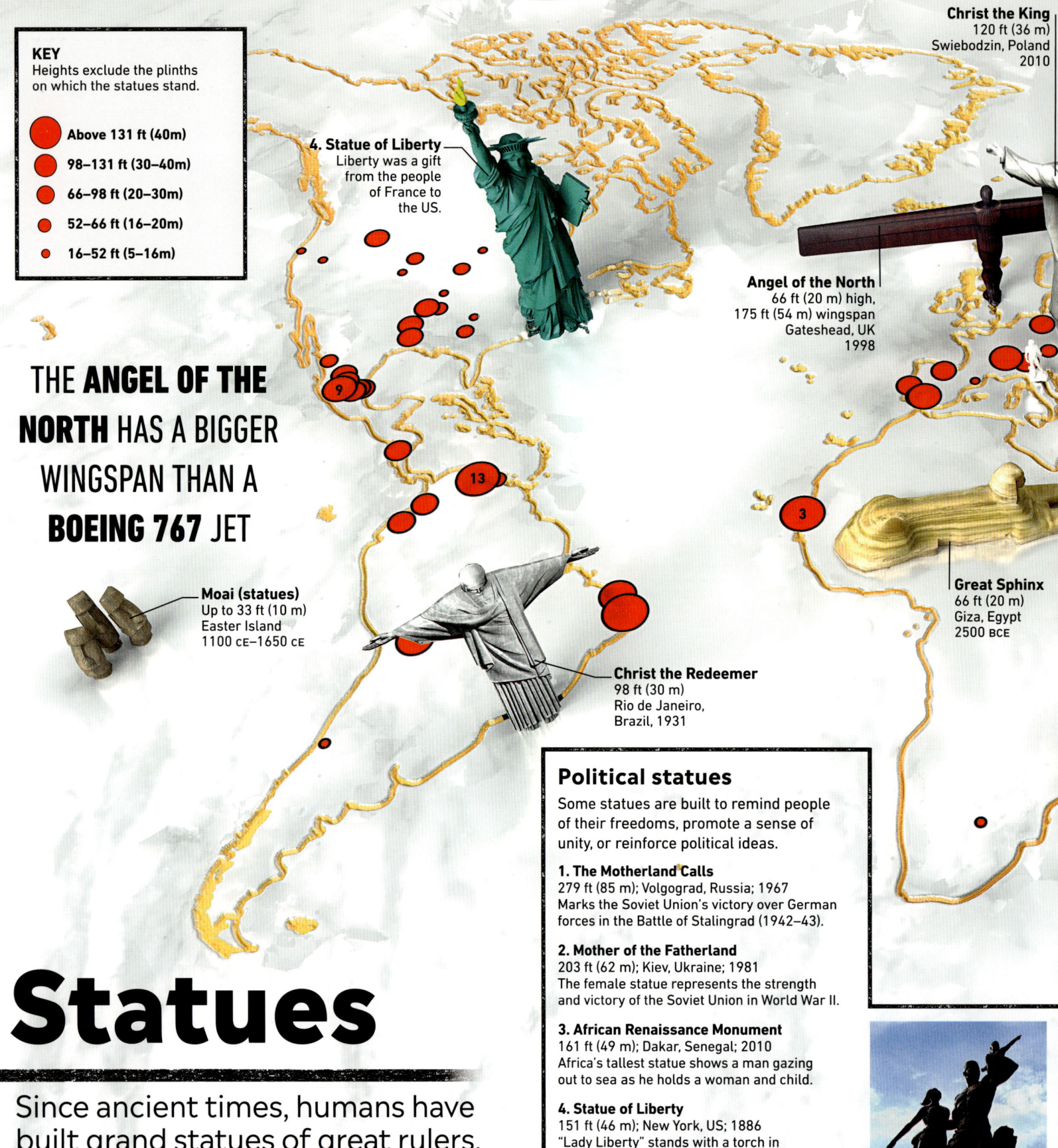

# Statues

Since ancient times, humans have built grand statues of great rulers, heroic figures, and gods and goddesses. We are still doing it, and statues today are getting bigger and bigger.

**KEY**
Heights exclude the plinths on which the statues stand.

- Above 131 ft (40m)
- 98–131 ft (30–40m)
- 66–98 ft (20–30m)
- 52–66 ft (16–20m)
- 16–52 ft (5–16m)

THE **ANGEL OF THE NORTH** HAS A BIGGER WINGSPAN THAN A **BOEING 767** JET

**Moai (statues)**
Up to 33 ft (10 m)
Easter Island
1100 CE–1650 CE

**4. Statue of Liberty**
Liberty was a gift from the people of France to the US.

**Christ the Redeemer**
98 ft (30 m)
Rio de Janeiro, Brazil, 1931

**Christ the King**
120 ft (36 m)
Swiebodzin, Poland
2010

**Angel of the North**
66 ft (20 m) high,
175 ft (54 m) wingspan
Gateshead, UK
1998

**Great Sphinx**
66 ft (20 m)
Giza, Egypt
2500 BCE

## Political statues

Some statues are built to remind people of their freedoms, promote a sense of unity, or reinforce political ideas.

**1. The Motherland Calls**
279 ft (85 m); Volgograd, Russia; 1967
Marks the Soviet Union's victory over German forces in the Battle of Stalingrad (1942–43).

**2. Mother of the Fatherland**
203 ft (62 m); Kiev, Ukraine; 1981
The female statue represents the strength and victory of the Soviet Union in World War II.

**3. African Renaissance Monument**
161 ft (49 m); Dakar, Senegal; 2010
Africa's tallest statue shows a man gazing out to sea as he holds a woman and child.

**4. Statue of Liberty**
151 ft (46 m); New York, US; 1886
"Lady Liberty" stands with a torch in one hand and a stone tablet in the other.

**5. Juche Tower statues**
98 ft (30 m); Pyongyang, North Korea; 1982
Three figures represent a peasant, an industrial worker, and an intellectual.

African Renaissance Monument

THE STATUE OF LIBERTY IN NEW YORK CONTAINS

Culture

**1. The Motherland Calls**
The statue beckons fighters to come to the defense of their nation.

**The Statue of Unity**
597 ft (182 m)
Gujurat, India; 2018
The world's tallest statue, depicting India's first Deputy Prime Minister.

**Spring Temple Buddha**
420 ft (128 m)
Lushan, China; 2002
Named after the nearby Tianrui hot spring.

## Religious statues

Many religious movements use statues to inspire belief and to aid worship.

Guanyin, Hainan, China

**11. Buddha**
381 ft (116 m); Monywa, Myanmar; 2008
Depicts the Buddha standing. World's third-tallest statue.

**12. Guanyin**
354 ft (108 m); Sanya, Hainan, China; 2005
Represents the goddess Guanyin blessing the world.

**13. Virgin of Peace**
154 ft (47 m) Trujillo, Venezuela; 1983
The Virgin Mary, mother of Jesus, is shown holding a dove of peace in her hand.

**14. Shiva**
143 ft (44 m); Chitapol, Kathmandu, Nepal; 2012
Hindu god Shiva stands with a trident in his left hand. His right hand offers a blessing.

**15. Murugan**
141 ft (43 m); Batu Caves, Gombak, Malaysia; 2006
Statue stands by a cave shrine to the Hindu god Murugan.

## Historical statues

Nations often use statues to celebrate famous people from their past. If a controversial figure has been chosen, this can lead to the statue being defaced or even toppled by the public.

**6. Yan Di and Huang Di**
348 ft (106 m); Zhengzhou, China; 2007
Shows the heads of two legendary kings regarded as the early founders of the Chinese nation.

**7. Peter the Great**
315 ft (96 m); Moscow, Russia; 1997
Erected to celebrate 300 years of the Russian Navy, which Tsar Peter I founded.

**8. Guan Yu**
200 ft (61 m); Yucheng, Shanxi, China; 2010
Statue of the general Guan Yu (160–219), later deified as Chinese god of war, at his birthplace.

**9. José Maria Morelos**
131 ft (40 m); Janitzio, Michoacán, Mexico; 1934
Mexico's rebel leader in the War of Independence (1810–21), fist clenched.

**10. Genghis Khan**
131 ft (40 m); Tsonjin Boldog, Mongolia; 2007
This statue depicts the famous Mongol leader (ruled 1206–1227) mounted on a horse.

Peter the Great

30 TONS OF COPPER AND 125 TONS OF STEEL.

Culture

**Wife-Carrying World Championships**
*Sonkajärvi*, Finland
Male entrants carry their wives over an obstacle course. The winner receives his wife's weight in beer.

**Baltai**
*Tatarstan*, Russia
*Baltai* means "feast of honey." The festival marks the start of the mowing season and is celebrated by decorating a bear with birch leaves.

**Chinese New Year**
Called the Spring Festival in China, since it marks the end of winter, this festival typically involves street processions with lanterns and Chinese dragons. Families clean their houses to sweep away bad fortune and welcome in the New Year. The festival is celebrated in all countries with significant populations of Chinese people.

 Locations with important Chinese New Year celebrations

Rijeka, Croatia

Patras, Greece

Limassol, Cyprus

Beijing

**Boryeong Mud Festival**
*Boryeong*, South Korea
At this mucky festival, which dates from 1998, people cover each other in mud. The mud is said to contain minerals that are good for the skin.

**Ghost Festival**, China
Part of "Ghost Month," when the ghosts and spirits of dead ancestors are said to emerge from the underworld.

Asakusa district, Tokyo

**Awa Odori**
*Tokushima*, Japan
Awa Odori began in 1586, when Tokushima's residents decided to celebrate their town's new castle. Today, more than 1 million tourists visit to watch performers in traditional dress dance in the streets.

Kolkata, India

Goa, India

**Janmashtami**
*Mumbai*, India
Marks the birthday of the Hindu god Krishna. Boys and men clamber to the top of a pole, trying to smash a clay pot full of curd and spill its contents. Krishna is said to have stolen curd from pots as a boy.

Philippines

Singapore

Indonesia

**Esala Maha Perahera**
*Kandy*, Sri Lanka
The 10-day "Festival of the Tooth" celebrates the Tooth Relic of the Lord Buddha. Dancers, acrobats, and fire performers gather in Kandy. On the last night, an elegantly dressed elephant carries the tooth.

**Bendigo Easter Festival**
*Bendigo*, Australia
Dating from 1871, this is Australia's longest continuously running festival. During the festival's Easter procession, the *Sun Loong*, the longest imperial dragon in the world, dances through the streets of Bendigo.

Mauritius

**Incwala**
*Eswatini*
At the "Festival of the first fruits," the king eats pumpkins and other fruits. People dance and sing in his honor and to bring blessings on the harvest.

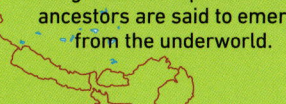

**World parties**
Some festivals draw people from far and wide. They may be messy, such as Tomatina (left), or involve unusual competitions, such as wife-carrying.

 Key world party sites

Sydney, Australia

**Prickly Pear Festival**
*Mandela Bay*, South Africa
This is a day for celebrating (and eating!) traditional foods such as ginger beer, pancakes, potjiekos, bunnychow, and fish braai.

**Te Matatini**
*New Zealand*
A Māori dance festival in which performers come together from all over New Zealand to compete in the national finals. *Te Matatini* means "many faces."

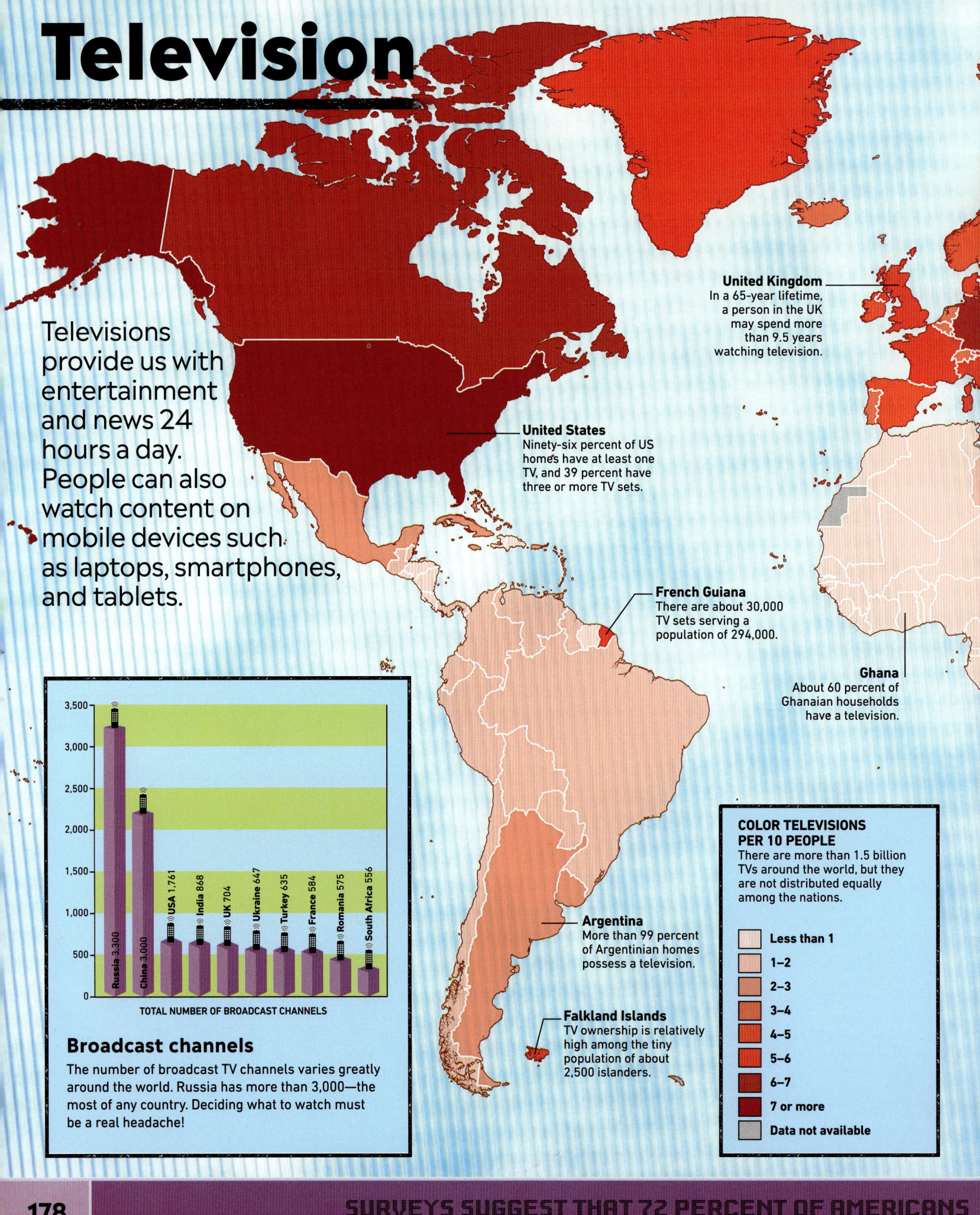

Culture

## Hours per week
Experts say that watching more than 2 hours of TV per day (14 hours per week) can be bad for your health, yet in many countries, people watch twice that.

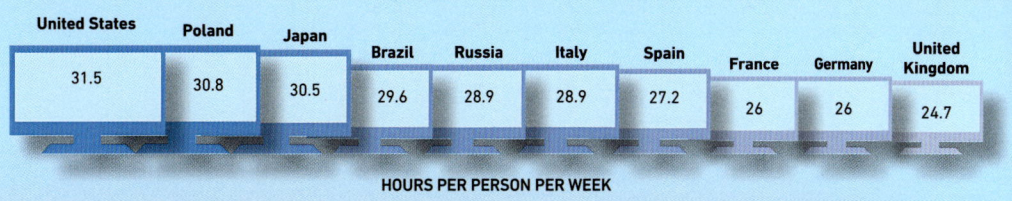

| United States | Poland | Japan | Brazil | Russia | Italy | Spain | France | Germany | United Kingdom |
|---|---|---|---|---|---|---|---|---|---|
| 31.5 | 30.8 | 30.5 | 29.6 | 28.9 | 28.9 | 27.2 | 26 | 26 | 24.7 |

HOURS PER PERSON PER WEEK

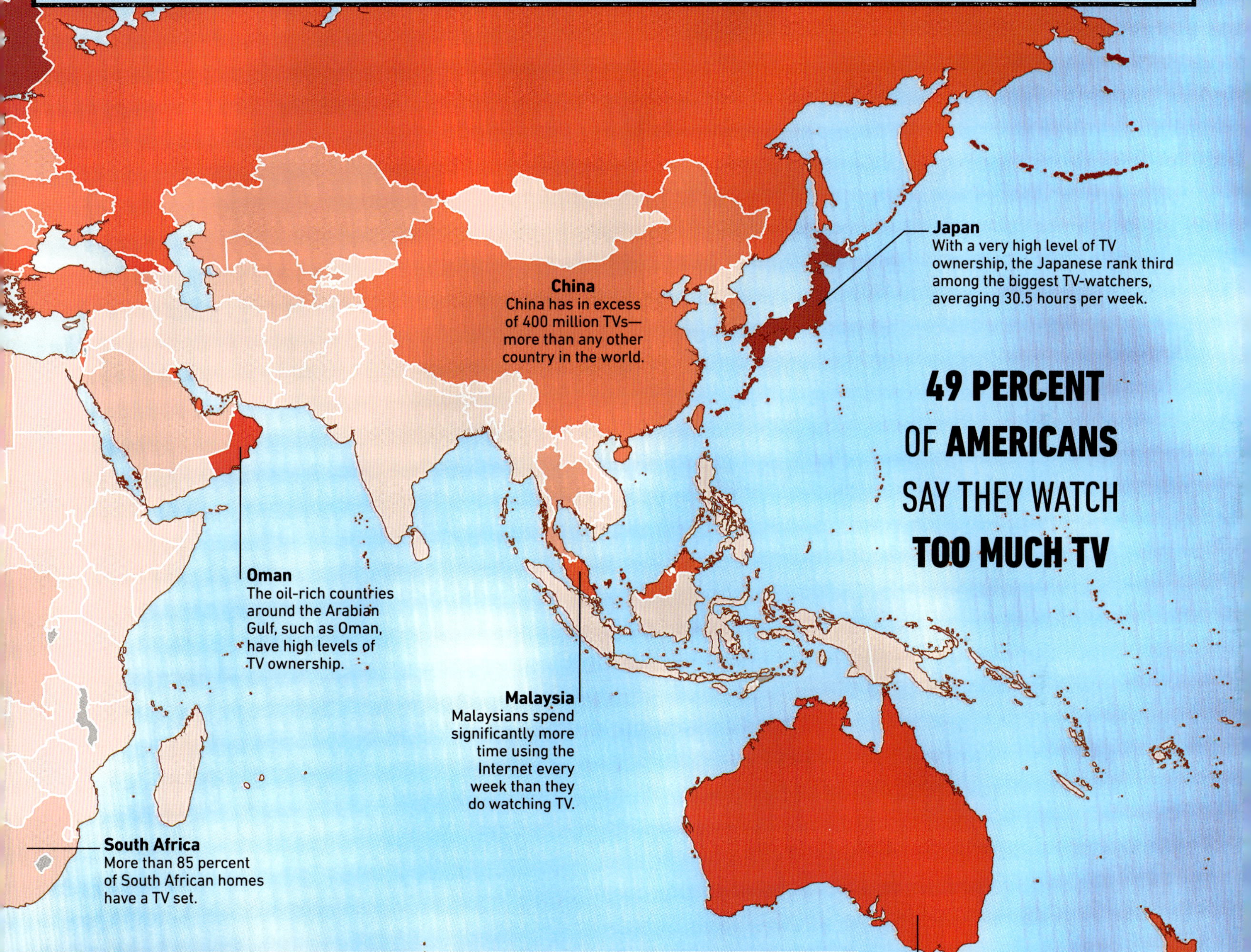

**Japan**
With a very high level of TV ownership, the Japanese rank third among the biggest TV-watchers, averaging 30.5 hours per week.

**China**
China has in excess of 400 million TVs—more than any other country in the world.

## 49 PERCENT OF AMERICANS SAY THEY WATCH TOO MUCH TV

**Oman**
The oil-rich countries around the Arabian Gulf, such as Oman, have high levels of TV ownership.

**Malaysia**
Malaysians spend significantly more time using the Internet every week than they do watching TV.

**South Africa**
More than 85 percent of South African homes have a TV set.

**Australia**
In 2017, Australian homes had an average of 6.4 screens per household.

## Content streaming
"Terrestrial" channels reach your TV via an aerial on your home, while extra channels can be broadcast by satellite or sent through cables. Paying for cable TV has become steadily less popular with the rise of television streaming services such as Netflix, however, which involve playing video content over an Internet connection. Since the content isn't live, viewers can choose exactly what they want to watch, and when. In 2020, the streaming subscription market grew by a massive 37 percent.

REGULARLY WATCH TELEVISION WHILE EATING DINNER.

### Americas

**1** Los Angeles Memorial Coliseum
California, US. Capacity 93,607; opened 1921

**2** Rose Bowl
Pasadena, California, US. Capacity 92,542; opened 1922

**3** Dodgers Stadium
California, US. Capacity 56,000; opened 1962

**4** Estadio Monumental "U"
Lima, Peru. Capacity 80,093; opened 2000

**5** Bell Center
Montreal, Canada. Capacity 21,273; opened 1996

**6** Beaver Stadium
Pennsylvania, US. Capacity 106,572; opened 1960

**7** Madison Square Garden
New York, US. Capacity 22,292; opened 1968

**8** Arthur Ashe Stadium
New York, US. Capacity 23,200; opened 1997

**9** Ohio Stadium
Ohio, US. Capacity 102,329; opened 1922

**10** Neyland Stadium
Tennessee, US. Capacity 102,455; opened 1921

**11** Sanford Stadium
Georgia, US. Capacity 92,746; opened 1929

**12** Bryant–Denny Stadium
Alabama, US. Capacity 101,821; opened 1929

**13** Tiger Stadium
Louisiana, US. Capacity 92,542; opened 1924

**14** Darrell K. Royal—Texas Memorial Stadium
Texas, US. Capacity 100,119; opened 1924

**Michigan Stadium**
Ann Arbor, Michigan. Capacity 114,804; opened 1926. Nicknamed "The Big House," this is the largest stadium in the US. It is home to the Michigan Wolverines American football team.

**Camp Nou**
Barcelona, Spain. Capacity 99,354; opened 1957. The largest stadium in Europe and 12th largest in the world.

**KEY**
The colors show capacity (numbers of spectators).
- 🔴 110,000 and above
- 🟣 100,000–109,999
- 🟠 90,000–99,999
- 🟡 80,000–89,999
- 🔵 Fewer than 80,000

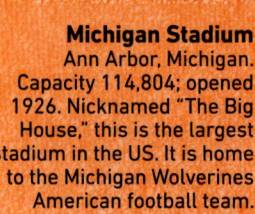

**Estádio Azteca**
Mexico City, Mexico. Capacity 87,523; opened 1961. This huge soccer stadium is the official home of the Mexican national team. The Azteca and the Estádio Maracanã are the only stadiums in the world to have hosted two FIFA World Cup soccer finals.

**Estádio do Maracanã**
Rio de Janeiro, Brazil. Capacity 82,238; opened 1950. Built for the 1950 football FIFA World Cup, the Maracanã was the world's largest stadium at the time, with room for nearly 200,000 people. Capacity was greatly reduced in the 1990s after part of the stadium collapsed. It served as the venue for the opening and closing ceremonies of the 2016 Summer Olympics and Paralympics.

# Stadiums

Stadiums and arenas are among the largest and most impressive buildings on the planet. They not only enable us to experience the thrills and drama of competition between the best sports players, teams, and athletes, but also host pop concerts and other shows.

### Europe

**15** Millennium Stadium
Cardiff, UK. Capacity 74,500; opened 1999

**16** Wembley Stadium
London, UK. Capacity 90,000; opened 2007

**17** Allianz Arena
Munich, Germany. Capacity 69,901; opened 2005

**18** Estádio Santiago Bernabéu
Madrid, Spain. Capacity 85,454; opened 1947

# THE RECORD FOR THE LOUDEST CROWD ROAR OF 142.2 DECIBELS WAS SET AT ARROWHEAD STADIUM, KANSAS CITY, MISSOURI, DURING A FOOTBALL GAME IN 2014

Culture

**Rungrado May Day Stadium**
Pyongyang, North Korea. Capacity 150,000; opened 1989. Said to look like a magnolia blossom, the stadium is used for sports and military parades.

### Record crowd sizes
Crowds were even larger before the modern safety-conscious era, and standing and overcrowding were common. The largest-ever crowds at sports events are below.

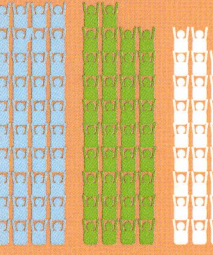

- Soccer: 199,854. Maracanã Stadium, Brazil. Brazil vs Uruguay, World Cup Final, July 1950.
- Wrestling: 190,000. May Day Stadium, North Korea. Pro-Wrestling event, April 1995.
- Soccer: 149,415 (plus 20,000 without tickets). Hampden Park, Scotland. Scotland vs England, 1937.
- Soccer: 135,000. Estádio da Luz, Portugal. Benfica vs Porto, January 1987.

**FNB Stadium (Soccer City)**
Johannesburg, South Africa. Capacity 94,736; opened 1989. Nicknamed "The Calabash" because it looks like the African pot of the same name, the FNB is the largest stadium in Africa. The stadium played host to the 2010 FIFA World Cup.

### Asia

**19** **Azadi Stadium**
Tehran, Iran. Capacity 100,000; opened 1971

**20** **Salt Lake Stadium**
Kolkata, India. Capacity 120,000; built 1984

**21** **Lumpinee Boxing Stadium**
Bangkok, Thailand. Capacity 9,500; opened 1956

**22** **Beijing National Stadium ("Bird's Nest")**
China. Capacity: 80,000; opened 2008

**23** **Gwangmyeong Velodrome**
South Korea. Capacity 30,000; opened 2006

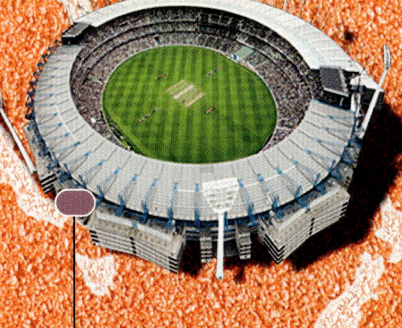

**Melbourne Cricket Ground**
Victoria, Australia. Capacity 100,018; opened 1854. This stadium holds the record for the highest floodlight towers of any sporting venue. It is known to locals as "The G."

THE BRISTOL MOTOR SPEEDWAY, TENNESSEE, ON AUGUST 23, 2008.

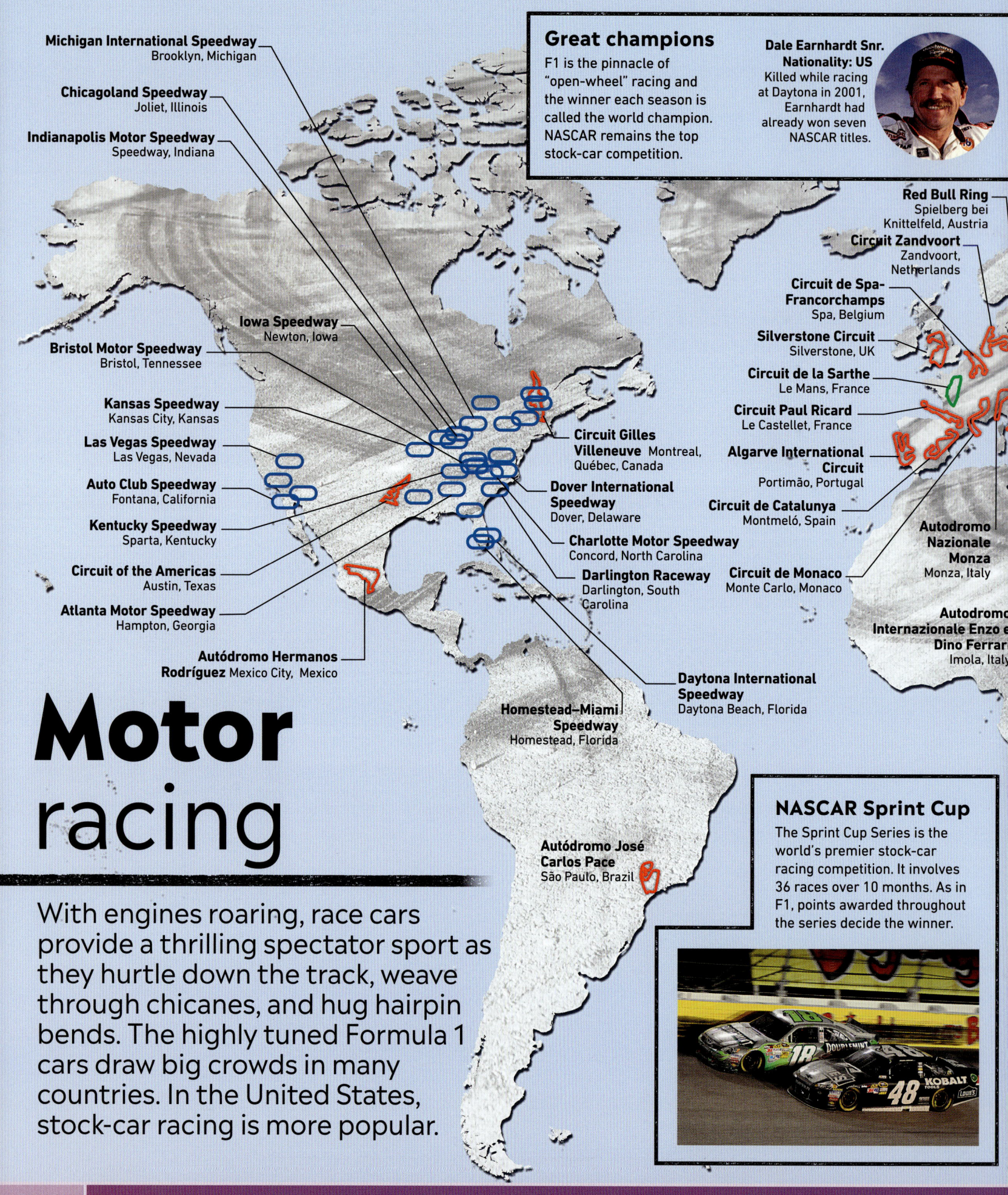

# Culture

**Michael Schumacher**
Nationality: German
Seven-time F1 World Champion with 91 Grand Prix wins. He suffered a severe skiing accident in 2013 and has been receiving treatment ever since.

**Ayrton Senna**
Nationality: Brazilian
Three-time F1 World Champion. Fifth-most-successful driver of all time in terms of F1 race wins (41). Died in an accident at the 1994 San Marino Grand Prix.

**Lewis Hamilton**
Nationality: British
Jointly tied with Shumacher for the most World Championship titles, and holds the record outright for the most ever F1 wins.

## A FORMULA 1 STEERING WHEEL COSTS ABOUT $32,000

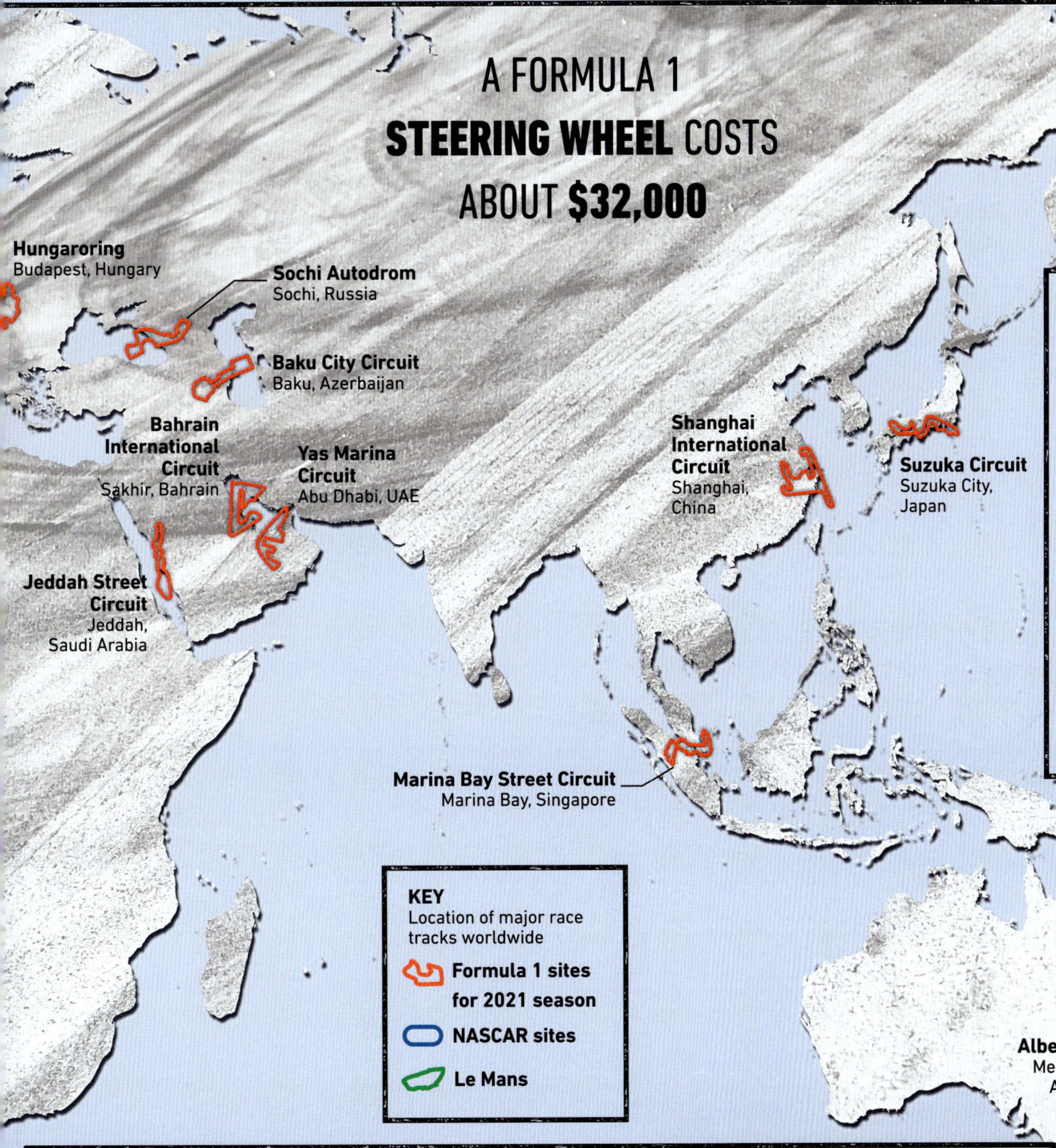

**Hungaroring** — Budapest, Hungary

**Sochi Autodrom** — Sochi, Russia

**Baku City Circuit** — Baku, Azerbaijan

**Bahrain International Circuit** — Sakhir, Bahrain

**Yas Marina Circuit** — Abu Dhabi, UAE

**Jeddah Street Circuit** — Jeddah, Saudi Arabia

**Shanghai International Circuit** — Shanghai, China

**Suzuka Circuit** — Suzuka City, Japan

**Marina Bay Street Circuit** — Marina Bay, Singapore

**Albert Park** — Melbourne, Australia

### Le Mans
The French town of Le Mans hosts the world's toughest endurance race. Teams of three drivers keep their sports cars racing for 24 hours, grabbing what food and rest they can between two-hour stints behind the wheel.

**KEY**
Location of major race tracks worldwide
- Formula 1 sites for 2021 season
- NASCAR sites
- Le Mans

### Formula 1 (F1)
In the annual F1 World Championship, ultra high-performance "open-wheel" race cars compete in a series of Grand Prix races worldwide. Cars finishing in the top-10 positions in each race win points. At the season's end, trophies are awarded for the driver and manufacturer with the most points.

**BUT FORMULA 1 TYRES LAST A MAXIMUM OF 200 KM (125 MILES).**

# Roller coasters

**Leviathan**
Canada's Wonderland, Ontario
92 mph (148 kph)
306 ft (93 m) high
5,486 ft (1,672 m) long

**Top Thrill Dragster**
Cedar Point, Ohio
120 mph (193 kph); 420 ft (128 m) high
2,800 ft (853 m) long

**Intimidator 305**
Kings Dominion, Virginia
90 mph (145 kph)
305 ft (93 m) high
5,100 ft (1,554 m) long

**Colossus**
Thorpe Park, England
45 mph (72 kph);
100 ft (30 m) high
2,789 ft (850 m) long

**Millennium Force**
Cedar Point, Ohio
93 mph (150 kph)
310 ft (94 m) high
6,595 ft (2,010 m) long

**Superman: Escape from Krypton**
Six Flags Magic Mountain, California
100 mph (161 kph)
415 ft (126 m) high
1,235 ft (376 m) long

**Vortex**
Carowinds, North Carolina
50 mph (80 kph)
90 ft (27 m) high
2,040 ft (622 m) long

**Fury 325**
Carowinds, North Carolina
95 mph (153 kph)
325 ft (99 m) high
6,602 ft (2,012 m) long

**Alpengeist**
Busch Gardens, Florida
67 mph (107 kph)
195 ft (59 m) high
3,828 ft (1,148 m) long

**Apocalypse**
Six Flags America, Maryland
55 mph (89 kph)
100 ft (30 m) high
2,900 ft (884 m) long

**Red Force**
Ferrari Land, Spain
112 mph (180 kph)
367 ft (112 m) high
2,890 ft (880 m) long

**Kingda Ka**
Six Flags Great Adventure, New Jersey
128 mph (206 kph)
456 ft (139 m) high
3,118 ft (950 m) long

**Ultimate**
Lightwater Valley, UK
50 mph (80 kph)
107 ft (33 m) high
7,442 ft (2,268 m) long

**Montezum**
Hopi Hari, Brazil
64 mph (103 kph)
139 ft (42 m) high
3,380 ft (1,030 m) long

**Colossos**
Heide-Park, Soltau, Germany
75 mph (102 kph)
197 ft (60 m) high
4,409 ft (1,344 m) long

**Tower of Terror**
Gold Reef City, South Africa
59 mph (95 kph)
112 ft (34 m) high
328 ft (100 m) long

**Kingda Ka**
This ride goes from 0–128 mph (206 kph) in 3.5 seconds, catapulting riders as high as a 45-story building.

**ROLLER COASTERS AROUND THE WORLD**
Numbers indicate ranking from 1–5.

- Red: Fastest
- Green: Highest
- Blue: Longest
- Black: Unranked

Breakneck speeds, hair-raising twists and turns, stomach-churning drops—roller coasters can satisfy even hardened thrill-seekers. This map shows some of the world's biggest and best coasters.

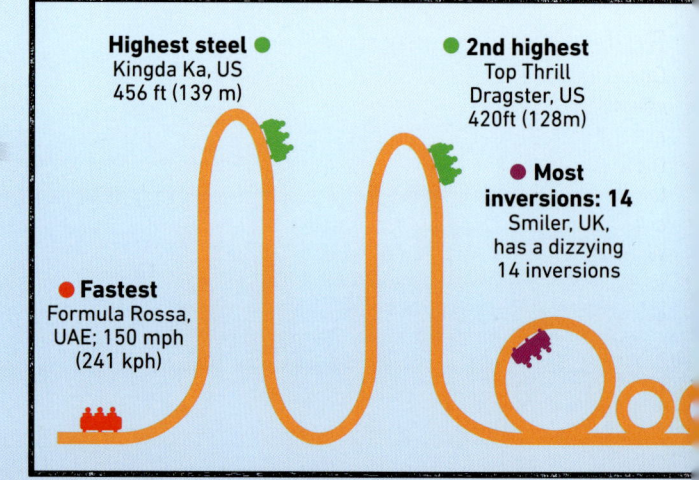

**Highest steel** — Kingda Ka, US — 456 ft (139 m)

**2nd highest** — Top Thrill Dragster, US — 420 ft (128 m)

**Most inversions: 14** — Smiler, UK, has a dizzying 14 inversions

**Fastest** — Formula Rossa, UAE; 150 mph (241 kph)

SIX FLAGS MAGIC MOUNTAIN PARK, AT VALENCIA, CALIFORNIA,

# Culture

## Flying roller coasters
These coasters—such as Manta at SeaWorld in Florida (right)—make you feel as though you are flying. The cars run on the underside of the track. Riders start in a seated position, but as the ride starts they are rotated to face the ground.

**Formula Rossa**
Ferrari World, UAE
150 mph (241 kph)
171 ft (52 m) high
6,791 ft (2,070 m) long

**Do-Dodonpa**
Fuji-Q Highland, Japan
107 mph (172 kph); 171 ft (52 m) high;
3,901 ft (1,189 m) long

**Steel Dragon 2000**
Nagashima Spa Land, Japan
95 mph (153 kph)
318 ft (97 m) high
8,133 ft (2,437 m) long

**Dinoconda**
China Dinosaurs Park, China
80 mph (128 kph); 249 ft (76 m) high
3,471 ft (1,058 m) long

**Ten Inversion Roller Coaster**
Chimelong Paradise, China
45 mph (72 kph); 100 ft (30 m) high 2,789 ft (850 m) long

**Fujiyama**
Fuji-Q Highland, Japan
81 mph (130 kph)
260 ft (70 m) high
6,709 ft (2,045 m) long

**Takabisha**
Fuji-Q Highland, Japan
62 mph (100 kph)
141 ft (43 m) high
3,281 ft (1,000 m) long

**DC Rivals Hypercoaster**
Warner Bros. Movie World, Queensland, Australia; 71.5 mph (115 kph); 4,593 ft (1,400 m) long; 202 ft (61.6 m) high

## 18 MPH (29 KPH): SPEED OF THE WORLD'S OLDEST COASTER, LEAP THE DIPS

## Roller coaster records
Opened in 1902, the world's oldest coaster is the wooden Leap-the-Dips, at Lakemont Park, Pennsylvania. Since then, coasters have become taller, longer, faster—and scarier! Today's coasters are usually made of steel. Wood is less flexible than steel, so wooden coasters tend to be less complex and extreme than steel ones.

- **Steepest drop** TMNT Shellraiser, US 121.5 degrees
- **Highest G-force** Tower of Terror, South Africa 6.3G

## 4-D roller coasters
Fourth-dimension (4-D) coasters, such as China's Dinoconda, give theme parks an extra level of thrills. The seats on a 4-D coaster can rotate forward or backward, so as the riders hurtle along the track they also spin in a full circle. Eejanaika (below) is a 4-D ride at Japan's Fuji-Q Highland theme park.

HAS 19 ROLLER COASTERS—MORE THAN ANY OTHER THEME PARK.

# National flags

**NORTH AMERICA**

| CANADA | UNITED STATES OF AMERICA | MEXICO | BELIZE | COSTA RICA | EL SALVADOR | GUATEMALA | HONDURAS |

**SOUTH AMERICA**

| GRENADA | HAITI | JAMAICA | ST KITTS & NEVIS | ST LUCIA | ST VINCENT & THE GRENADINES | TRINIDAD & TOBAGO | COLOMBIA |

**AFRICA**

| URUGUAY | CHILE | PARAGUAY | ALGERIA | EGYPT | LIBYA | MOROCCO | TUNISIA |

| LIBERIA | MALI | MAURITANIA | NIGER | NIGERIA | SENEGAL | SIERRA LEONE | TOGO |

| BURUNDI | DJIBOUTI | ERITREA | ETHIOPIA | KENYA | RWANDA | SOMALIA | SUDAN |

| NAMIBIA | SOUTH AFRICA | ESWATINI (formerly SWAZILAND) | ZAMBIA | ZIMBABWE | COMOROS | MADAGASCAR | MAURITIUS |

       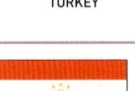

| LUXEMBOURG | NETHERLANDS | GERMANY | FRANCE | MONACO | ANDORRA | PORTUGAL | SPAIN |

| POLAND | SLOVAKIA | ALBANIA | BOSNIA & HERZEGOVINA | CROATIA | KOSOVO (disputed) | NORTH MACEDONIA | MONTENEGRO |

**ASIA**

| LATVIA | LITHUANIA | CYPRUS | MALTA | RUSIA | ARMENIA | AZERBAIJAN | GEORGIA | TURKEY |

| QATAR | SAUDI ARABIA | UNITED ARAB EMIRATES | YEMEN | IRAN | KAZAKHSTAN | KYRGYZSTAN | TAJIKISTAN |

| CHINA | MONGOLIA | NORTH KOREA | SOUTH KOREA | TAIWAN | JAPAN | MYANMAR (BURMA) | CAMBODIA |

**AUSTRALASIA & OCEANIA**

| SINGAPORE | MALDIVES | AUSTRALIA | NEW ZEALAND | PAPUA NEW GUINEA | FIJI | SOLOMON ISLANDS | VANUATU |

A SOVEREIGN STATE IS A COUNTRY INDEPENDENT OF OTHER STATES, AND

# OF ALL THE FLAGS OF THE WORLD'S **195 SOVEREIGN STATES**, ONLY **NEPAL'S** HAS MORE THAN **FOUR SIDES**

**WITH ITS OWN GOVERNMENT SYSTEM AND A PERMANENT POPULATION.**

# Index

## A
Abu-Simbel 143
Abyssal plains 16
acid rain 99
Acropolis 143
adaptations 42–43
Afghanistan 83, 97, 142, 143, 155
Africa 26, 78, 80, 86, 89, 90, 94, 155
age profile 80–81
agriculture 75, 92–93, 102
air pollution 98–99
air travel 85, 116–17, 160–61
aircraft, military 130–31
airports, busiest 116
Aksum stelae 142–43
Alaska 10, 14, 32, 40–41, 54
Aleutian Trench 9, 16
Alexander the Great 135, 141
algae 64
Algeria 24
alternative energy 74, 106–07
aluminum 100–01
Amazon Rainforest 32, 64, 110
Amazon, River 20, 21, 56
American Civil War 135, 152
Amoco Cadiz 158–59
Amur-Arqun 20, 21
ancient civilizations 140–43, 152–53
Andes 12, 24, 66–67
animals see wildlife
Antarctica 7, 26–27, 34–35, 36–37, 55
Antioch 11
ants 60
apartheid, end of 135
Arab Spring 134, 157
arachnids 48–49, 64
arapaimas 58
architecture
  castles 150–51
  medieval 146–47
  modern era 160–61
  tallest buildings 124–25
Arctic 7, 31, 36, 64, 65, 74, 75
Arctic terns 52–53
Argentina 13, 44, 54, 86, 106, 178
USS *Arizona* 159
armed forces 130–31, 152–53
art 164, 165, 172–75
  prehistoric 135, 138–39
Artemis, Temple of 143
Ashoka, Emperor 152–53
asteroid impact 10, 22
Atacama Desert 34
Atlanta 116
atmosphere 6, 104, 108
Australia
  culture 167, 173, 177, 179, 181
  land 22, 24, 27, 29, 33
  living world 45, 67
  people 77, 83, 89, 92, 95, 103, 107
Australopithecus 136–37
Austria 101
autobahns 115, 122
Aztec Empire 135, 146, 148, 149

## B
Baikal, Lake 21
Bali 165
Bamiyan Buddhas 142, 143
Bangladesh 26, 27, 29, 77
Barringer Crater 23
Basawan 173
basins, oceanic 16
Batavia 159
battlegrounds 152–53
beaches 170–71
bees 48, 60, 61
beetles 60, 61
Beijing 76, 77, 116, 117, 151, 181
Belarus 32, 83
Belgium 179
Bester, Willie 173
Bettencourt Meyers, Françoise 90
Bezos, Jeff 91
Bhola Cyclone 29
Bhutan 83
big wheels 170–71
billionaires 90–91
biodiversity 64–65
biofuel, biogas, and biomass 106–07
bioluminescence 42
biomes 30–31, 67
biosphere 7, 74
Bird Flu 85
birds 42, 46–53, 68–71
HMS *Birkenhead* 159
Bismarck 159
Black Death 84, 85
blue whales 54–55
bog bodies 144
Bolivar, Simón 156
Bolivia 82, 86, 94, 135, 156
boreal forests 30, 33
Borneo 27, 33, 65
Borobudar, Java 147
boundaries, plate 8–9
boxing 181
Brazil 10, 26, 54, 76, 92, 96, 103, 106, 107, 130, 172, 176, 180, 181, 183
bridges 115, 120, 123, 135, 161
Britain, Battle of 152
British Empire 135, 154–55
broadband 127
Brooklyn Bridge 115
bubonic plague 84, 85
Buddhism 168, 169
Burghausen 150
burial sites 135, 139, 144–45
Burj Khalifa 112–13, 124, 125
Burundi 87
butterflies 60, 61, 69, 70
Byzantine Empire 135, 149

## C
Cajamarca, Battle of 135, 152
California 32, 50, 66
calories, daily intake of 94–95
Cairo 76
Cambodia 103
Cameroon 95, 166
Canada
  culture 177, 179, 180
  land 22, 24
  living world 44
  people 80, 88, 92, 94, 96, 98, 104, 106, 107, 110
Canary Islands 66
Cape Town 117
Caravaggio 173
carbon dioxide 99, 108
cargo 118–19
Carnival 176–77
carnivorous plants 60–61
Carthage, Siege of 153
Castle of Good Hope 151
castles 150–51
Central African Republic 97
Cerro el Cóndor 13
Chad 96
Chagall, Marc 173
Channel Tunnel 160–61
channels, TV 178
chemical pollution 98–99
Chesapeake Bay 23
Chicago 116
Chicxulub 23
Chile 10, 12, 13, 92, 145
Chimborazo, Mount 12
Chimu Empire 148, 149
China
  armed forces 131
  culture 167, 169, 173, 175, 177, 178, 179
  history 134, 137, 142, 143, 151, 156
  land 11, 12, 25, 26
  living world 44–45, 67
  people 77, 81, 87, 89, 93, 95, 97, 99, 101, 105, 107
Chinese New Year 177
Christianity 148, 168–69
Chrysler Building 124
cicadas 60, 61
cities, biggest 76–77
civilizations 134, 140–41, 148–49
climate change 98, 108–09
clothing 164
clouds 6
coal 104–05, 106, 107
coffee 92–93
cold deserts 35
Colombia 15, 135, 156
colonialism 154–55
Colosseum 135, 142–43
Colossus of Rhodes 143
Columbus, Christopher 146
Communism, collapse of 135, 157
computer technology 114, 126–27
Concorde 134, 161
concrete 115
Congo-Chambeshi 20
conservation 75, 110–11
Constantinople, Fall of 135, 153
construction 115, 124–25
continental crust 9
continental shelf 17
convection currents 7
convergent boundaries 8
Coordinated Universal Time (UTC) 38
coral/coral reefs 30, 42, 111
Coral Sea, Battle of the 152, 153
core, Earth's 6, 7
cost of living 86–87
Costa Rica 130
COVID-19 85, 86, 134
craters 22–23
Crécy, Battle of 152
Cretaceous Period 44–45
cricket 181
crocodiles 49, 58–59
crops 92–3
Crusades 134, 153
crust, Earth's 6, 7, 8–9
crustaceans 64
Cuba 66, 83, 94, 152, 156
culture 162–87
  prehistoric 138–39
currencies 89
currents, ocean 18–19
cycling 181
cyclones 28–29

## D
Dallas 116
dance 164–65
Dangote, Aliko 91
Darfur 26
day and night 38
deep water currents 19
deforestation 32–33
Delacroix, Eugène 172
Delhi 76, 77, 117
Democratic Republic of Congo 106
Denmark 166, 179
deserts 4–5, 24, 31, 34–35
  life in 42–43, 64
  nomads 78, 79

188

# Index

Dhaka 76, 77
dinosaurs 10, 22, 44–45
divergent boundaries 8
diving and snorkelling 70–71
Diwali 165
doctors, per capita 83
Dominican Republic 26
MV Doña Paz 159
dragonflies 60
drones, unmanned 130
droughts 103
Dubai 112–13
dunes 35

## E

Earnhardt, Dale Snr. 182
Earth
   interior of 6
   rotation of 7, 38
   structure of 6–7
earthquakes 8, 10–11
East African Rift 8, 15
East Melanesia 67
East Pacific Rise 9, 16
Easter Island 132–33, 174, 176
Ecuador 12, 135, 156
education 96–97
Egypt 24, 53, 92, 130, 131
   ancient 134, 135, 140, 143, 144–45
El Salvador 106
Emperor Seamounts 17
Empire State Building 125
empires
   ancient 140–41
   colonial 154–55
   medieval 148–49
endemic hot spots 67
energy
   alternative 74, 106–07
   resources and consumption 74, 104–05
ENIAC 114
Eritrea 95
erosion 20
Eswatini 82–83, 177
Ethiopia 67, 155
   empire 148
Europe, literacy in 96
Everest, Mount 12, 13, 16
extinctions 10, 22, 50–51, 68, 69, 70–71

## F

Falkland Islands 104, 178
fashion 164
fault lines 9
festivals 162–63, 165, 176–77
Finland 177, 179
fish 46, 47
   dangerous 48–49
   river 58–59
fishing industry 92, 93
flags 186–87
flash floods 26
fleas 50, 61
flooded savanna 30
floods 26
floral kingdoms 62
flu viruses 84–85
food
   cookery 164
   cost of 95
   intake 94–95
   production 92–93
   supplies 82
food chains 47
football (soccer) 180–81
footprint, human 74–75
footprints, dinosaur 45
Forbidden City, Beijing 151
forests 30, 32–33, 110–11
Formula 1 (F1) 182–83
Fort Independence, Boston 151
fossil fuels 74, 104–05, 106, 107
fossils 44–45, 136–37
France 89, 92, 104, 106, 122, 130, 131, 154–55, 172, 178, 179
Frankfurt 116
freeways 115, 122
French Guiana 178
French Revolution 135
freshwater creatures 56, 58–59
Fukuoka 117
fungi 64

## G

Gabon 100
Gainsborough, Thomas 172
Galápagos Islands 50, 66
Gandhi, Mahatma 156
Gansu earthquake 11
garbage patches 19, 100–01
gas 104–05, 106, 107
Gates, Bill 90
gender differences 97
Genghis Khan 134, 149, 175
Georgia 83, 97
geosynchronous orbit 128, 129
geothermal energy 106–07
Germany 44, 89, 101, 106, 107, 115, 136, 151, 154–55, 178, 179, 180, 183
Ghana 86, 88, 156, 178
   ancient 148
giant catfish 58–59
Gibraltar 53
glaciers 37, 108–09, 110
global warming 98, 108–09
gold 88–89
GPS satellites 129
Graf Zeppelin airship 161
grasslands 30, 35
Great Dying 10, 22
Great Game 155
Great Lakes 20
Great Sphinx 134, 174–75
Great Stupa of Sanchi 142
Great Wall of China 135, 142, 143
great white sharks 48, 56–57
Great Zimbabwe 134, 148, 151
Greeks, ancient 142, 143, 153

Greenland 24, 53, 80, 110
   ice sheet 34, 109
Greenwich Mean Time (GMT) 39
Guatemala 14, 80, 95
Guevara, Che 156
Guinea-Bissau 82, 97
Gulf Stream 19
Gulf War 98
Guyana 80, 103
gyres 18, 19, 100

## H

habitats
   and adaptations 42–43
   destruction of 68–69
   unusual 66–67
Hagia Sofia 143
Haiti 11, 26, 86, 102
Halincarnassus, Mausoleum at 143
Hamilton, Lewis 183
Han Empire 135, 141
Hanging Gardens of Babylon 143
Harvey, Hurricane 28
Hawaii 13, 14, 28, 38, 66
health 82–85, 98–99
Himalayas 8, 13, 65, 109
Himeji 151
Hinduism 168, 169
history 132–61, 174–75
HIV/AIDS 85
Hokusai, Katsushika 173
Holi Festival 162–63
Holy Roman Empire 135, 149, 152
Homo genus 134, 136–37
Hong Kong 116, 117, 127
Hong Kong Flu 85
Hoover Dam 161
Hopper, Edward 172
Huari Empire 135, 148, 149
Hubble Space Telescope 129
humans
   early 136–37
   impact of 74–75
hurricanes 28–29
hydroelectric energy 106–07

## I

ice 7, 36–37
ice sheets 36, 37, 108, 110
icebergs 37, 158
Iceland 14, 16, 77, 87, 106–07, 166
Idai, Cyclone 29
impact craters 22–23
Inca Empire 148, 149
income, per capita 86–87
India
   armed forces 131
   culture 162–63, 164–65, 167, 173, 177, 178, 181
   history 134, 142, 151, 152–53, 157
   land 12, 27, 39
   people 77, 81, 87, 89, 93, 95, 99, 103, 107
Indian Ocean 10

indigenous peoples 78–79, 111
Indo-Pakistani War 134, 153
Indochina War, First 134, 153
Indonesia 14, 15, 89, 97, 99, 103, 107, 137
Industrial Revolution 160
industrial waste/accidents 98–99
industrial wonders 160–61
inequality 86–87
infectious diseases 84–85
information technology 126–27
infrastructure 115, 120–23
Iniki, Hurricane 28
insects 48–51, 60–61, 64
International Date Line 38
International Monetary Fund 89
International Space Station 129
International Union for Conservation (IUNC) 68
Internet connections 126–27, 164
Inuit 75, 78
invasive species 50–51
invertebrates 64
Iran 26, 131, 181
Iraq 25, 103
Ireland 95, 179
Islam 148, 168, 169
Israel 25, 130, 131
Italy 89, 92, 106, 154–55, 173, 179

## J

Japan
   culture 169, 173, 177, 179
   history 145, 151, 154–55
   land 10, 15, 27, 29, 33
   people 77, 81, 83, 89, 92, 93, 99, 107
Jeju 117
Jerusalem 153, 168
jewelry, first 135, 138
Johannesburg 117, 181
Juanita the Ice Maiden 145
Judaism 168
Jurassic Period 44

## K

K2 12
Kahlo, Frida 172
kakapo (owl parrot) 68–69
Kalinga, Battle of 152–53
Kamchatka earthquake 10
Kanem Empire 134, 149
Kangchenjunga 12
Kathakali dancers 164–65
Katrina, Hurricane 28, 29
Kazakhstan 103
Kenya 92, 95, 103, 107
Khmer Empire 149
Kiribati 38
Kolkata 77
Korean War 134, 153
Krak des Chevaliers 150
Krakatau 14, 15
Kuwait 25, 101, 103
Kyrgyzstan 103

## L

Lalibela 147
lakes 6, 20–21, 109
land ice 36
landfill 100, 101
languages 164, 166–67
Large Hadron Collider 160
Le Mans 183
lead pollution 98–99
Leaning Tower of Pisa 147
Lempicka, Tamara de 173
Lenin, Vladimir 156
Lhotse 12
Liberia 83, 86, 155
Liberty, Statue of 174–75
Libya 24
lichens 64
Liechtenstein 130
life on Earth 6, 7, 40–71
life expectancy 82–83
Lindow Man 144
literacy 96–97
literature 165
livestock 92–93
Llullaillaco 13
locusts 60
London 116
Los Angeles 72–73, 116
Low Earth Orbit (LEO) 129
RMS Lusitania 159
Luxor 24

## M

Macedonian Empire 135, 141
Machu Picchu 135, 146
Madagascar 67, 97
Makalu 12
Malawi 83
Malaysia 81, 175, 179
Mali 134, 148, 176
malnutrition 94–95
Malta 53
mammals 46–51, 68–71
mangrove 30
Manila 77
mantle 6, 7
Mao Zedung 134, 156
Marble Bar 24
Marcus, Cyclone 29
Mariana Trench 17
marine animals 42, 48–49, 54–57
marine biomes 30
Mars 12–13
Martinique 15
Mauna Kea 13
Mauritania 96, 102
Mauryan Empire 135, 141, 153
Mayan civilization 135, 140, 141, 146
mayflies 60
median age 80–81
medical care 82, 83
medieval age 146–49, 152–53
Mehrangarh Fort, Jodhpur 151
Meirelles, Victor 172
Melbourne 117
mercury, toxic 99
meteorites 22–23
Mexico 24, 28, 54, 66, 76, 80, 98, 106, 142, 144, 172, 175, 176, 180
Mexico City 76, 180
Mid-Atlantic Ridge 8, 14, 16
mid-ocean ridges 16–17
Middle East, oil 105
midges 60, 61
migration
    animals 170–71
    birds 52–53
    human 78–79, 164
    insects 60, 61
    sharks 48, 49
    whales 55
military forces 130–31
minerals 74
mines, gold 88
Ming Dynasty 135, 149
Mississippi–Missouri 20, 26, 56
mollusks 64
Monaco 82, 83
monarch butterflies 60, 61
Monet, Claude 172
Mongol Empire 134, 149
Mongolia 45, 77, 95, 175, 178
monsoon 27
Morocco 80, 86
mosquitoes 60
moths 60
motor racing 182–83
mountains 6, 12–13, 16–17, 122
Mozambique 83, 97
Mughal Empire 135, 149
Mumbai 76, 77, 117
mummies 144–45
Munch, Edvard 172–73
music 135, 138, 164, 165
Musk, Elon 91
Myanmar (Burma) 175

## N

Namib Desert 4–5, 34
Namibia 4–5, 77, 87
NASCAR sites 182
national parks 110–11
native species 50–51
natural resources 74, 102–05
Nauru 94
Neanderthals 136, 137
Nepal 12, 175, 187
Netherlands 89, 92, 101, 154–55, 179
Nevado de Incahusai 13
Nevado del Ruiz 15
Nevados Ojos de Salado 13
New Caledonia 67
New York City 76, 115, 174
New Zealand 27, 33, 55, 81, 93, 97, 177
nickel 99
Niger 83
Nigeria 100, 104, 172
night and day 38
Nile, River 20
Nkrumah, Kwame 156
nomads 78–79
Norte Chico civilization 135
North Korea 131, 174, 181
North Sea 104
Norway 39, 87, 101, 102, 106, 107, 166, 172, 179
Novarupta 14
nuclear energy 106–07
nuclear waste/accidents 98–99
nuclear weapons 130–31
Nuestra Señora de Atocha 159

## O

Ob-Irtysh 20–21
obesity 94
ocean floor 6, 16–17
oceanic crust 9
oceans 7
    and climate change 108–09
    conservation 110–11
    currents 18–19, 24–25
    life in 42, 47, 48–49, 54–57
    pollution 19, 98, 100–01
oil
    resources 104–05, 106, 109
    spills 98, 158–59
Olduvai Gorge 136
Olmec civilization 135, 140, 141
Olympus Mons 12–13
Oman 179
Ortega Gaona, Amancio 91
Osaka 76, 117
Ottoman Empire 149, 152–55
Ötzi the Iceman 144

## P

Pacific Ring of Fire 14, 15
paintings 139, 165, 172–73
Pakistan 12, 25, 92, 95, 131
Palermo 145
Panama 53
Panama Canal 118, 160
pandemics 84–85
Papua New Guinea 33, 67, 81, 97, 167
Paraguay 166
Paraná 20
Paranthropus 136–37
parasites 50
Paris 27, 116
passengers, air 116–17
passes, mountain 122
Patagonian Desert 34
Patricia, Hurricane 28
Pelée, Mont 15
peregrine falcons 46–47
Persian Empire, First 135, 141
Persian Gulf 98
Peru 88, 92, 98, 102, 135, 142, 145, 152, 156, 166, 176
Peru-Chile Trench 9, 16
pesticides 98–99
pests 50–51
Petra 143

Petronas Towers 124, 125
Pharos of Alexandria 143
Philippines 14, 67, 77, 107, 144
Picasso, Pablo 172, 173
Pinatubo, Mount 14
plague 84–85
plants 6, 7, 62–63
    adaptations 42–43
    biodiversity 64–65
    biomes 30–31
    invasive species 50–51
    unique 66–67
plastic waste 100–01
plate tectonics see tectonic plates
poison-dart frogs 48–49, 65
Poland 32, 173, 174
polar regions 7, 36–37
    deserts 31, 35
    life in 43
pollution 75, 98–99, 104, 108
Polynesia 66
Pont-du-Gard 142, 143
pop music 164, 180
population
    age profile 80–81
    distribution 76–77, 110–11
    and food supplies 93
    growth 74–75
ports, busiest 119
Portugal 154, 181
pottery 139
poverty 86–87
predators 46–47
prehistory 136–39
Prime Meridian 39
Prince William Sound 10
Puffing Billy 115
pyramids 142–43, 146

## R

radioactive waste 98–99
railroads 114–15, 120–21, 160
rainfall 5, 6, 26–27
rainforests 32–33, 43, 64, 65
Ramayana 164–65
rats 50
recycling 74, 100–01, 103
Red List (IUCN) 68
religion 168–69, 175, 176–77
renewable energy 74, 106–07
reptiles 43, 46–51, 58–59
Réunion 27, 29
revolutions 152–53, 156–57
rice production 93
Rio de Janeiro 26, 117, 176, 180
Rio de la Plata 20
rivers 6, 20–21
river monsters 58–59
roads 115, 122–23
Rocky Mountains 12
roller coasters 184–85
Romania 178
Romans 115, 135, 141, 153
rubbish 100–01

# Index

Russia
  armed forces 131
  culture 167, 173, 174, 175, 177
  history 135, 154–55, 156, 157
  land 10, 24, 25, 26, 39
  people 87, 89, 91, 92, 97, 99, 103, 105, 107
Ruwenzori Mountains 13

## S
safaris 170–71
Sahara Desert 34–35, 64, 110
St. Peter's Basilica, Rome 147
salt 19
San Andreas Fault 9
Santa Maria volcano 14
São Paulo 76, 117
Sapporo 117
satellites 128–29
Saudi Arabia 94, 105, 131
savanna 30
Schumacher, Michael 183
Scramble for Africa 155
sculpture 139, 165, 172, 174–75
sea ice 36, 109
sea levels 108–09
sea transportation 118–19
seamounts 16–17
secondary education 96
seismic waves 10
semideserts 35
Senegal 26, 174
Senna, Ayrton 183
Seoul 117
Seven Wonders of the World 142–43
Shaanxi earthquake 11
Shanghai 76, 77, 117, 119
sharks 46, 47, 48, 56–57
sheep 93
Shinto 168, 169
shipping routes 118–19
shipwrecks 158–59
shrubland 31
Sicily 53, 145
sieges 153
Sikhism 168, 169
Singapore 24
skyscrapers 112–13, 115, 124–25, 160
slave trade 155
snakes 43, 46–51
snow 6, 26–27
solar energy 74, 106–07
Solomon Islands 101
Somalia 25, 97
Somme, Battle of the 134–35, 152
Songhai Empire 149
South Africa 55, 67, 87, 89, 99, 136, 151, 173, 177, 178, 179, 181
South Korea 101, 131, 177, 181
South Sudan 26, 83, 123,
space debris 128–29
Space Shuttle 128
Spain 106, 107, 154, 166, 172, 176, 177, 180, 183

Spanish flu 84, 85
speedway 182
sperm whales 55
spiders 48–49
sport 180–83
Sri Lanka 55, 67, 177
stadiums 164, 180–81
statues 174–75
steam engines 115
Stone Age 138–39
Stonehenge 142, 143
streaming 179
submarines 130–31
Sudbury Basin 23
Suez Canal 119
sun, energy from 7
Sundaland 67
superbugs 85
surface currents 18
Suriname 77, 103, 166
HMS *Sussex* 159
swarms 60–61
Sweden 24, 83, 87, 101, 107, 166, 179
Swine Flu 85
Switzerland 89, 99, 100–01, 179
Sydney 117
Sydney Opera House 135, 161
Syria 151

## T
Taipei 101, 117, 124, 125
Tajikistan 103
Tambora 14, 15
Tangshan earthquake 11
tanks, battle 130–31
Tanzania 25, 136
tea trade 92
tectonic plates 8–9, 10, 12, 14, 16, 17
telecommunications 115, 126–27, 160
television 178–79
temperate biomes 30, 32
temperatures 24–25, 108–09
termites 60
Terracotta Army 142, 143
Thailand 107, 181
Thanksgiving 176–77
time zones 38–39
Tip, Typhoon 29
Tipas 13
RMS *Titanic* 135, 159
Tiwanaku Empire 148, 149
Tohoku earthquake 10
Tokyo 76, 77, 116, 117
Tonga 94
tools, early 134, 138
tourism 170–71
towers, unsupported 125
trade 118–19
trains 114–15, 120
transform boundaries 8
transportation 114–23
trenches, ocean 8, 9, 16–17
Triassic Period 44
Trinidad and Tobago 98, 104
tropical cyclones 28–29

tropical forests 30, 33, 64, 65
tsunamis 8
tundra 31, 35, 78, 110
Tunisia 24, 176
tunnels, longest rail 121
Turkey 11, 178, 181
Turkmenistan 103
Tutankhamun 144

## U
Uganda 81
Ukraine 98, 107, 174
Umayyad Caliphate 135, 149
United Arab Emirates 94, 112–13
United Kingdom
  armed forces 130, 131
  culture 172, 174–75, 176, 178, 179, 180, 181
  history 135, 152, 154–55
  people 92, 94, 95
  time zone 38
United States
  armed forces 130, 131
  culture 166, 172, 176, 178–79, 180, 182
  history 151, 152, 153, 158, 160
  land 23, 24, 26, 28, 38
  living world 44–45
  people 76, 80, 86, 88, 89, 91, 92, 94, 95, 96, 98, 99, 101, 102, 103, 104, 105, 106, 107
Unzen, Mount 15
Uruguay 80
USSR 157
Uzbekistan 103

## V
Valdivia earthquake 10
Vanuatu 167
vegetation
  biomes 30–31
  deserts 34–35
  forests 32–33
  wilderness 110–11
Velaro 114–15
Venezuela 104, 106, 135, 156, 175
venom
  animals 48–49, 65
  plants 62–63
Verkhoyansk 24, 25
vertebrates 64
Very Large Array 135, 160
Victoria, Lake 21
Vienna, Battle of 135, 152
Vietnam 87, 93, 134
viruses 84–85
volcanoes 8, 13, 14–15
Vredefort impact structure 23

## W
Wallacea 67
warfare 130–31, 152–53
Warhol, Andy 172
warships 130–31

wasps 60
waste 100–01
water
  clean 82, 102–03
  human consumption 102, 103
  pollution 98–99
  use of 75, 102
water cycle 6
Watson, Yannima Tommy 173
wealth 75, 86–91
weapons 130–31
weather 6
weevils 64
weight 94–95
Welwitschia 60–61
whales 40–41, 46, 47, 54–55
wheat 92
wilderness 100–11
wildlife
  adaptations 42–43
  biodiversity 64–65
  conservation 110–11
  deadly 48–49
  deserts 34–35
  endangered 66, 68–69
  extinct 44–45
  invasive species 50–51
  marine 42, 48–49, 54–57
  predators 46–47
  unique 66–67
  see also specific types
Wilhelm Gustloff 159
Willis Tower 124, 125
wind energy 74, 106–07
Windsor Castle 151
Winston, Cyclone 29
world parties 177
World War I 134–35, 152, 153, 158
World War II 134, 152, 153, 159
wrestling 181

## Y
Yangtze River 20, 21, 26
Yellow River 20, 21
Yemen 97
Yenisei-Angara-Selenga 20, 21
Yue Minjun 173

## Z
Zambia 99
Zeus, statue in Olympia 143
Zhoukoudian Caves 137
Zhucheng 44, 45
Zimbabwe 134, 148, 151
Zuckerberg, Mark 91

# Acknowledgments

Dorling Kindersley would like to thank: Caitlin Doyle for proofreading, Helen Peters for indexing, Haisam Hussein, Anders Kjellberg, Peter Minister, Martin Sanders, and Surya Sarangi for illustration, Deeksha Miglani and Surbhi N. Kapoor for research, and David Roberts for cartographic assistance.

**The publisher would like to thank the following for their kind permission to reproduce their photographs:**

(Key: a-above; b-below/bottom; c-center; f-far; l-left; r-right; t-top)

**2 Andy Biggs:** www.andybiggs.com (tc). **Corbis:** Alaska Stock (tr). **3 Corbis:** Floris Leeuwenberg (ftr); SOPA / Pietro Canali (tl). **Getty Images:** Art Wolfe (tr). **Sebastian Opitz:** (tc). **4–5 Andy Biggs:** www.andybiggs.com. **22 Getty Images:** Mark Garlick (br). **23 Corbis:** Charles & Josette Lenars (cr). **24–25 Robert J. Hijmans:** Hijmans, R.J, S.E. Cameron, J.L. Parra, P.G. Jones and A. Jarvis, 2005. Very high resolution interpolated climate surfaces for global land areas. International Journal of Climatology 25: 1965–1978 (base-map data). **26–27 Robert J. Hijmans:** Hijmans, R.J, S.E. Cameron, J.L. Parra, P.G. Jones and A. Jarvis, 2005. Very high resolution interpolated climate surfaces for global land areas. International Journal of Climatology 25: 1965–1978 (base-map data). **28–29 Adam Sparkes:** Data of the tropical cyclones projected by Adam Sparkes. Base image: NASA Goddard Space Flight Center Image by Reto Stöckli (land surface, shallow water, clouds). Enhancements by Robert Simmon (ocean color, compositing, 3D globes, animation). Data and technical support: MODIS Land Group; MODIS Science Data Support Team; MODIS Atmosphere Group; MODIS Ocean Group Additional data: USGS EROS Data Center (topography); USGS Terrestrial Remote Sensing Flagstaff Field Center (Antarctica); Defense Meteorological Satellite Program (city lights). **29 NOAA:** (tc). **30 Dorling Kindersley:** Rough Guides (tl, tr). **Shutterstock:** Edwin van Wier (crb). **31 Dreamstime.com:** (tc). **PunchStock:** Digital Vision / Peter Adams (tr). **35 NASA:** Goddard Space Flight Center, image courtesy the NASA Scientific Visualization Studio, (bl). **36 Dorling Kindersley:** Rough Guides / Tim Draper (bl). **Dreamstime.com:** Darryn Schneider (tr). **40–41 Corbis:** Alaska Stock. **42 Alamy Images:** Martin Strmiska (bl). Getty Images: Werner Van Steen (c). **43 NHPA / Photoshot:** Ken Griffiths (cr). **45 Corbis:** Science Faction / Louie Psihoyos (tr). Dorling Kindersley: Christian Williams (tc). **48 Alamy Images:** National Geographic Image Collection (bl). **Dorling Kindersley:** Courtesy of the Weymouth Sea Life Centre (bc). **49 Dreamstime.com:** Francesco Pacienza (tr). **53 Corbis:** Roger Tidman (bc). **55 Corbis:** Paul Souders (ca). **56 Corbis:** Minden Pictures / Mike Parry (cl); National Geographic Society / Ben Horton (tc). **60 Dorling Kindersley:** Courtesy of the Natural History Museum, London (cra, c). **Getty Images:** Visuals Unlimited, Inc. / Alex Wild (cr). **61 Alamy Images:** Premaphotos (tl). **Corbis:** Visuals Unlimited / Robert & Jean Pollock (tr). **Getty Images:** Mint Images / Frans Lanting (tc). Photoshot: Gerald Cubitt (br). **62–63 Dreamstime.com:** Jezper. **62 Alamy Images:** Tim Gainey (bc); John Glover (br). FLPA: Imagebroker / Ulrich Doering (cb). **Getty Images:** Shanna Baker (clb); Alessandra Sarti (bl). **64 Dorling Kindersley:** Courtesy of Oxford University Museum of Natural History (clb). **64–65 Dr. Clinton N. Jenkins:** Data: IUCN Red List of Threatened Species / www.iucnredlist.org / BirdLife International; Processing: Clinton Jenkins / SavingSpecies.org; Design & Render; Félix Pharand–Deschênes / Globaia.org. **66 Dorling Kindersley:** Rough Guides (cl). **67 Corbis:** Ocean (crb). **Dorling Kindersley:** Roger and Liz Charlwood (crb/New Caledonia). **72–73 Corbis:** SOPA / Pietro Canali. **74–75 Getty Images:** Doug Allan. **75 Corbis:** Aurora Photos / Bridget Besaw (tl); Frank Lukasseck (ftl); Minden Pictures / Ch'ien Lee (tc); John Carnemolla (tr). **76–77 Center for International Earth Science Information Network (CIESIN):** Columbia University; International Food Policy Research Institute (IFPRI); The World Bank; and Centro Internacional de Agricultura Tropical (CIAT). **84 Corbis:** Dennis Kunkel Microscopy, Inc. / Visuals Unlimited (tc); Dr. Dennis Kunkel Microscopy / Visuals Unlimited (tr). **85 Dreamstime.com:** Lukas Gojda (cr). **89 Dreamstime.com:** Cammeraydave (tr). **90 Getty Images:** AFP / Martin Bureau (br). James Leynse (bc). **91 Corbis:** epa / Justin Lane (bl); Kim Kulish (cra); epa / Mario Guzman (br). **Getty Images:** AFP (cr); Bloomberg / Wei Leng Tay (bc). (bc). **93 Dreamstime.com:** Kheng Guan Toh (br). **101 Corbis:** Peter Adams (bl). **105 Corbis:** Shuli Hallak (bc). **107 Dreamstime.com:** Milosluz (bc). **108–109 NASA:** Goddard Space Flight Center Scientific Visualization Studio. **109 NASA:** 1941 photo taken by Ulysses William O. Field; 2004 photo taken by Bruce F. Molnia. Courtesy of the Glacier Photograph Collection, National Snow and Ice Data Center / World Data Center for Glaciology. (bl). **110–111 UNEP–WCMC:** Dataset derived using the Digital Chart of the World 1993 version and methods based on the Australian National Wilderness Inventory (Lesslie, R. and Maslen, M. 1995. National Wilderness Inventory Handbook. 2nd edn, Australian Heritage Commission. Australian Government Publishing Service, Canberra) (base-map data). **112–113 Sebastian Opitz. 114–115 Dreamstime.com:** Dmitry Mizintsev (c). **114 Corbis:** (bc); Science Faction / Louie Psihoyos (br). **115 Corbis:** Bettmann (crb); Cameron Davidson (br). **Dorling Kindersley:** Courtesy of The Science Museum, London (tc). **Getty Images:** Three Lions (bc). **116–117 Michael Markieta:** www.spatialanalysis.ca. **118–119 Prof. Dr. Bernd Blasius:** Journal of the Royal Society Interface, The complex network of global cargo ship movements, p1094, 2010 (base-map data). **122 Getty Images:** Radius Images (bc). **126–127 Chris Harrison** (base-map). **128–129 ESA. 128 NASA:** Columbia Accident Investigation Report, (bc). **129 ESA:** (cra). **NASA:** Image created by Reto Stockli with the help of Alan Nelson, under the leadership of Fritz Hasle (br). **130 Corbis:** DoD (br). **132–133 Getty Images:** Art Wolfe. **134 Corbis:** Radius Images (bl). **Getty Images:** (cr). **Dreamstime.com:** Kawee Srital On (cb). **135 Corbis:** Sodapix / Bernd Schuler (b). **136–137 Corbis:** W. Cody. **137 Science Photo Library:** MSF / Javier Trueba (crb). **138 akg-images:** Oronoz (clb/Mousterian Tool). **Dorling Kindersley:** The American Museum of Natural History (bl); Natural History Museum, London (cl, clb). **Getty Images:** AFP (tc); De Agostini (tr). **139 akg-images:** Ulmer Museum (bc). **Getty Images:** De Agostini (crb). **141 Dorling Kindersley:** Courtesy of the University Museum of Archaeology and Anthropology, Cambridge (tl); Ancient Art / Judith Miller (bc/Urn); Alan Hills and Barbara Winter / The Trustees of the British Museum (tc); Stephen Dodd / The Trustees of the British Museum (tr). **Getty Images:** De Agostini (bl). **144 Alamy Images:** Ancient Art & Architecture Collection Ltd (tc). **Getty Images:** Copper Age (tl). Rex Features: (tr). **148 Dorling Kindersley:** © The Board of Trustees of the Armouries (tr); The Wallace Collection, London (cb). **149 Dorling Kindersley:** © The Board of Trustees of the Armouries (cla); Lennox Gallery Ltd / Judith Miller (cra); William Jamieson Tribal Art / Judith Miller (br); Courtesy of the Royal Armories (tc); The Trustees of the British Museum (cb); Peter Wilson / CONACULTA–INAH–MEX. Authorized reproduction by the Instituto Nacional de Antropología e Historia (clb). **150 Corbis:** Walter Geiersperger (cl); Robert Harding World Imagery / Michael Jenner (clb). **151 Alamy Images:** Peter Titmuss (bc). **Corbis:** Design Pics / Keith Levit (cra). **Dreamstime.com:** (bl). Getty Images: AFP (cr). **156 Corbis:** Bettmann (cb, cra). **Getty Images:** (c). **157 Corbis:** Bryan Denton (bl); Peter Turnley (cr). Getty Images: AFP (ca); (c); (clb). **159 Dreamstime.com:** (bc). **162–163 Corbis:** Floris Leeuwenberg. **164 Getty Images:** Redferns / Tabatha Fireman (c). **Dreamstime.com:** Constantin Sava (bl). **165 Alamy Images:** Hemis (br). **Corbis:** Godong / Julian Kumar (tr). **Dreamstime.com:** F9photos (cr); Teptong (crb). **Getty Images:** Philippe Lissac (tc). **172 Alamy Images:** GL Archive (tr); The Art Archive (cb). **Corbis:** Bettmann (cl, cr); Oscar White (cla); The Gallery Collection (crb). **Dorling Kindersley:** Philip Keith Private Collection / Judith Miller (br). Getty Images: De Agostini (cra, cra/Gainsborough); Stringer / Powell (tc). **172–173 123RF.com. 173 Corbis:** (cl, cr, cb); Contemporary African Art Collection Limited (clb). **Getty Images:** AFP (bc); (tl, tr); (cla). **174 Corbis:** In Pictures / Barry Lewis (br). **175 Corbis:** JAI / Michele Falzone (cra). **Dorling Kindersley:** Rough Guides (bc); Surya Sankash Sarangi (c). **176 Dorling Kindersley:** Alex Robinson (br). **177 Corbis:** Jose Fuste Raga (br). **178–179 Dreamstime.com:** Luminis (background image). **179 Dreamstime.com:** Mathayward (bl). **180 Alamy Images:** Aerial Archives (cl). **Getty Images:** (ca). **180–181 Getty Images:** AFP (cb); (ca). **181 Corbis:** Arcaid / John Gollings (br). **Getty Images:** (ca). **182 Corbis:** GT Images / George Tiedemann (tr); Icon SMI / Jeff Vest (br). **182–183 Dreamstime.com:** Eugenesergeev (tyre tracks on the map). **183 Getty Images:** (tl, tc, cr, bc). **Dreamstime.com:** Marco Canoniero (tr). **184 Alamy Images:** David Wall (tr). **Dreamstime.com:** Anthony Aneese Totah Jr (c). **Getty Images:** AFP (cl). **185 Alamy Images:** G.P.Bowater (tr); Philip Sayer (tc). Getty Images: AFP (br)

All other images © Dorling Kindersley
For further information see: www.dkimages.com

# DK WHERE ON EARTH?
## ATLASES

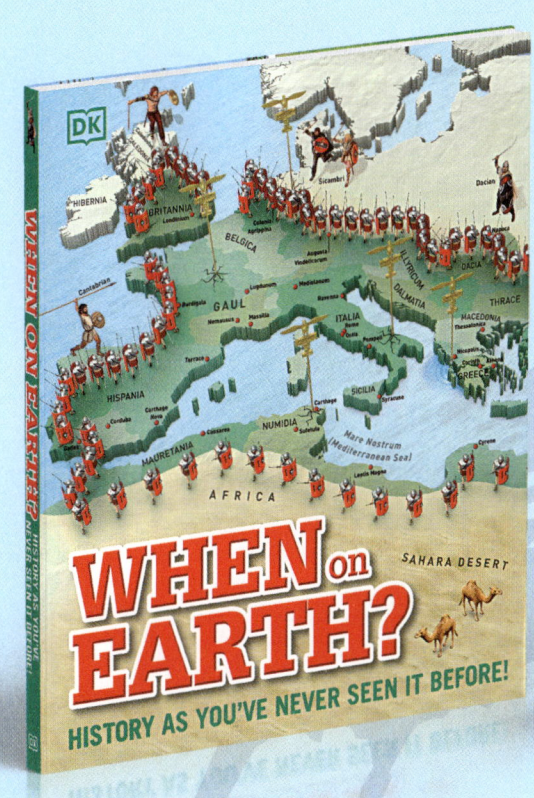
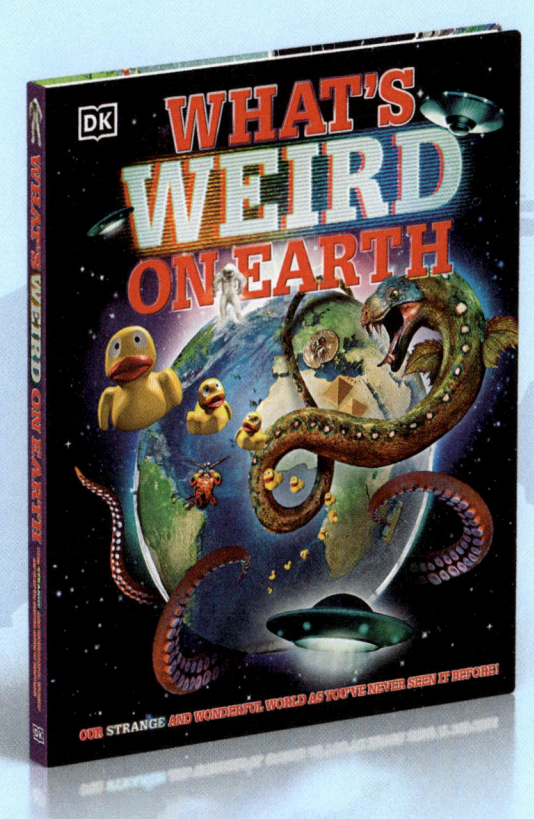

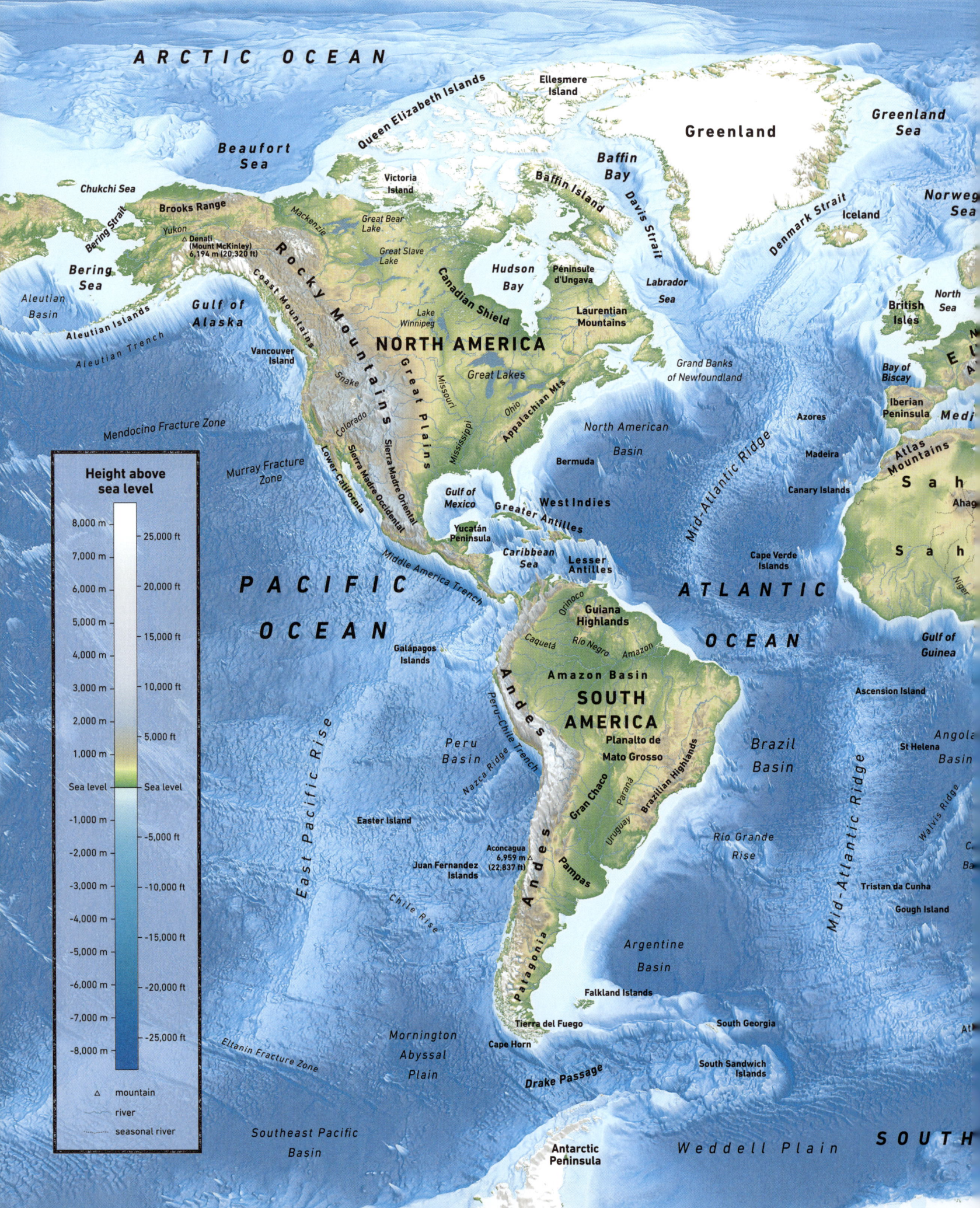

# DK WHERE ON EARTH? ATLAS

**DK London**
**Senior editor** Chris Hawkes
**Senior art editor** Rachael Grady
**Editors** Tom Booth, Anna Fischel, Anna Limerick
**US editor** Jenny Siklos
**Designers** David Ball, Chrissy Barnard, Mik Gates, Spencer Holbrook, Kit Lane
**Illustrators** Adam Benton, Stuart Jackon-Carter, Jon@kja-artists
**Cartography** Simon Mumford, Encompass Graphics

**Jacket editor** Claire Gell
**Jacket designer** Mark Cavanagh
**Jacket design development manager** Sophia MTT
**Picture research** Jayati Sood

**Producer, pre-production** Nadine King, Rob Dunn
**Senior producer** Gary Batchelor

**Managing editor** Francesca Baines
**Managing art editor** Philip Letsu
**Publisher** Andrew Macintyre
**Publishing director** Jonathan Metcalf
**Associate publishing director** Liz Wheeler
**Art director** Karen Self

This American Box Set Edition, 2024
First American Edition, 2017
Published in the United States by DK Publishing,
a division of Penguin Random House LLC
1745 Broadway, 20th Floor, New York, NY 10019

Copyright © 2017, 2024 Dorling Kindersley Limited
A Penguin Random House Company
24 25 26 27 28 10 9 8 7 6 5 4 3 2 1
001–341589–Sep/2024

All rights reserved.
No part of this publication may be reproduced, stored in or introduced into a retrieval system, or transmitted, in any form, or by any means (electronic, mechanical, photocopying, recording, or otherwise), without the prior written permission of the copyright owner.

A catalog record for this book
is available from the Library of Congress.
Box Set ISBN 978-0-5938-4501-1
Book ISBN 978-1-4654-5864-3

DK books are available at special discounts when purchased in bulk for sales promotions, premiums, fund-raising, or educational use. For details, contact: DK Publishing Special Markets, 1745 Broadway, 20th Floor, New York, NY 10019 SpecialSales@dk.com

Printed and bound in the UAE

www.dk.com

# CONTENTS

## Early Earth
| | |
|---|---|
| Introduction | 6 |
| 500–380 million years ago | 8 |
| 300–220 million years ago | 10 |
| 180–80 million years ago | 12 |
| 40 million years ago–Present day | 14 |

## North America
| | |
|---|---|
| Countries and borders | 18 |
| Landscape | 20 |
| Fascinating facts | 22 |
| Population | 24 |
| The Grand Canyon | 26 |
| Famous landmarks | 28 |
| Climate | 30 |
| Wildlife | 32 |
| By night | 34 |

## South America
| | |
|---|---|
| Countries and borders | 38 |
| Landscape | 40 |
| Fascinating facts | 42 |

| | |
|---|---|
| Population | 44 |
| Amazon Basin | 46 |
| Famous landmarks | 48 |
| Climate | 50 |
| Wildlife | 52 |
| By night | 54 |

## Africa

| | |
|---|---|
| Countries and borders | 58 |
| Landscape | 60 |
| Fascinating facts | 62 |
| Population | 64 |
| The Great Rift Valley | 66 |
| Famous landmarks | 68 |
| Climate | 70 |
| Wildlife | 72 |
| By night | 74 |

## Europe

| | |
|---|---|
| Countries and borders | 78 |
| Landscape | 80 |
| Fascinating facts | 82 |
| Population | 84 |
| The Alps | 86 |
| Famous landmarks | 88 |
| Climate | 90 |
| Wildlife | 92 |
| By night | 94 |

## Asia

| | |
|---|---|
| Countries and borders | 98 |
| Landscape | 100 |
| Fascinating facts | 102 |
| Population | 104 |
| The Himalayas | 106 |
| Famous landmarks | 108 |
| Climate | 110 |
| Wildlife | 112 |
| By night | 114 |

## Australia and Oceania

| | |
|---|---|
| Countries and borders | 118 |
| Landscape | 120 |
| Fascinating facts | 122 |
| Population | 124 |
| New Zealand | 126 |
| Famous landmarks | 128 |
| Climate | 130 |
| Wildlife | 132 |

## Polar regions

| | |
|---|---|
| Antarctica | 136 |
| The Arctic | 138 |

## The oceans

| | |
|---|---|
| Pacific Ocean | 142 |
| Atlantic Ocean | 144 |
| Indian Ocean | 146 |

## Reference

| | |
|---|---|
| Countries of the world | 150 |
| Glossary | 156 |
| Index | 158 |
| Acknowledgements | 160 |

Kangaroo

The South Pole

# EARLY EARTH

**Under attack**
Rock and debris from space crashed into Earth's surface during its early formation, turning it molten and triggering volcanic activity.

# Early Earth

Earth's formation started shortly after the birth of the Sun, 4.6 billion years ago. A star exploding in nearby space caused a vast amount of interstellar dust to collapse in on itself. This formed our Sun, and over time the rest of the surrounding debris clumped together into planets. As these grew larger, their steadily increasing gravity pulled them into spheres. One of these was our planet, Earth, a rocky ball with a molten metal core, and a thin shell, called a crust, at its surface.

The layered interior structure of Earth emerged early in its evolution. Heat from Earth's molten core forced the crust, which is made up of large slabs of rock called tectonic plates, to move constantly. As these plates shunted around and crashed into each other, they caused earthquakes and fiery volcanoes, formed mountain ranges and entire continents, and helped create the conditions in which life could emerge.

This illustration shows the sequence of Earth's formation—from small fragments of rock and dust sticking together, to a planet with its own atmosphere.

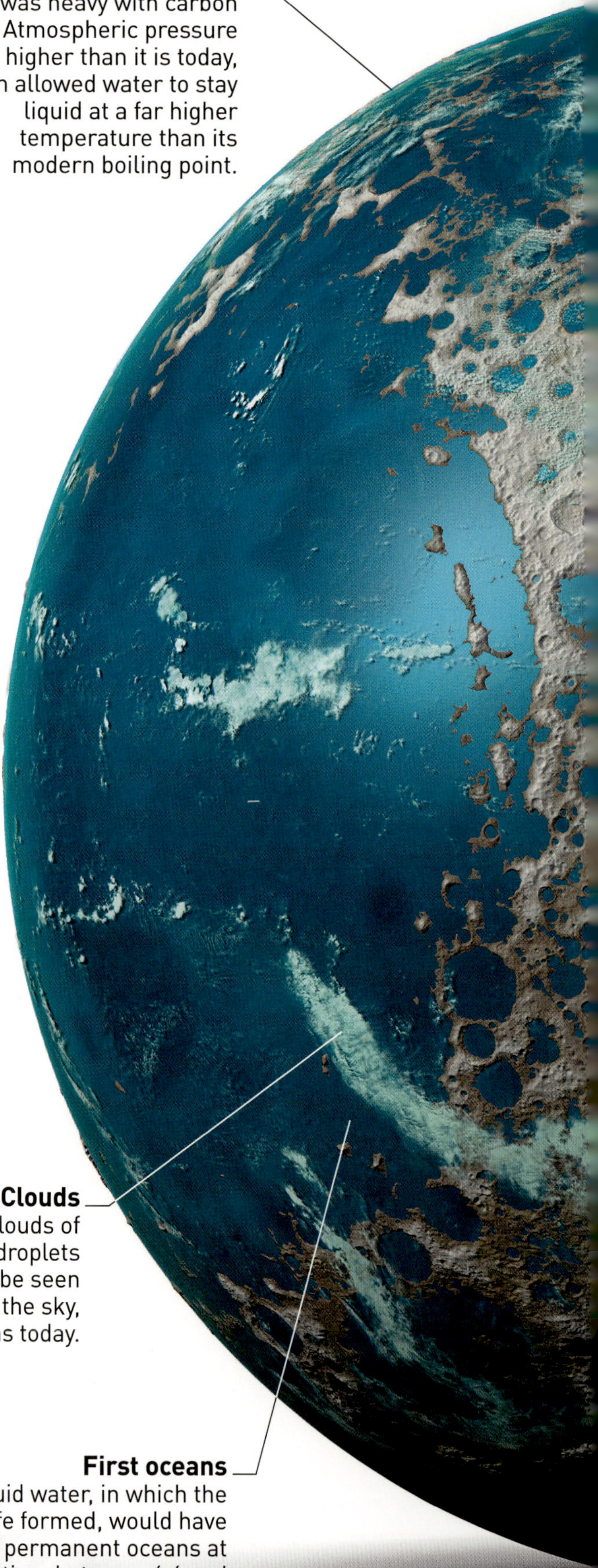

**Atmosphere**
The air was heavy with carbon dioxide. Atmospheric pressure was higher than it is today, which allowed water to stay liquid at a far higher temperature than its modern boiling point.

**Clouds**
Clouds of water droplets could be seen in the sky, much as today.

**First oceans**
Liquid water, in which the first life formed, would have become permanent oceans at some time between 4.4 and 4.2 billion years ago.

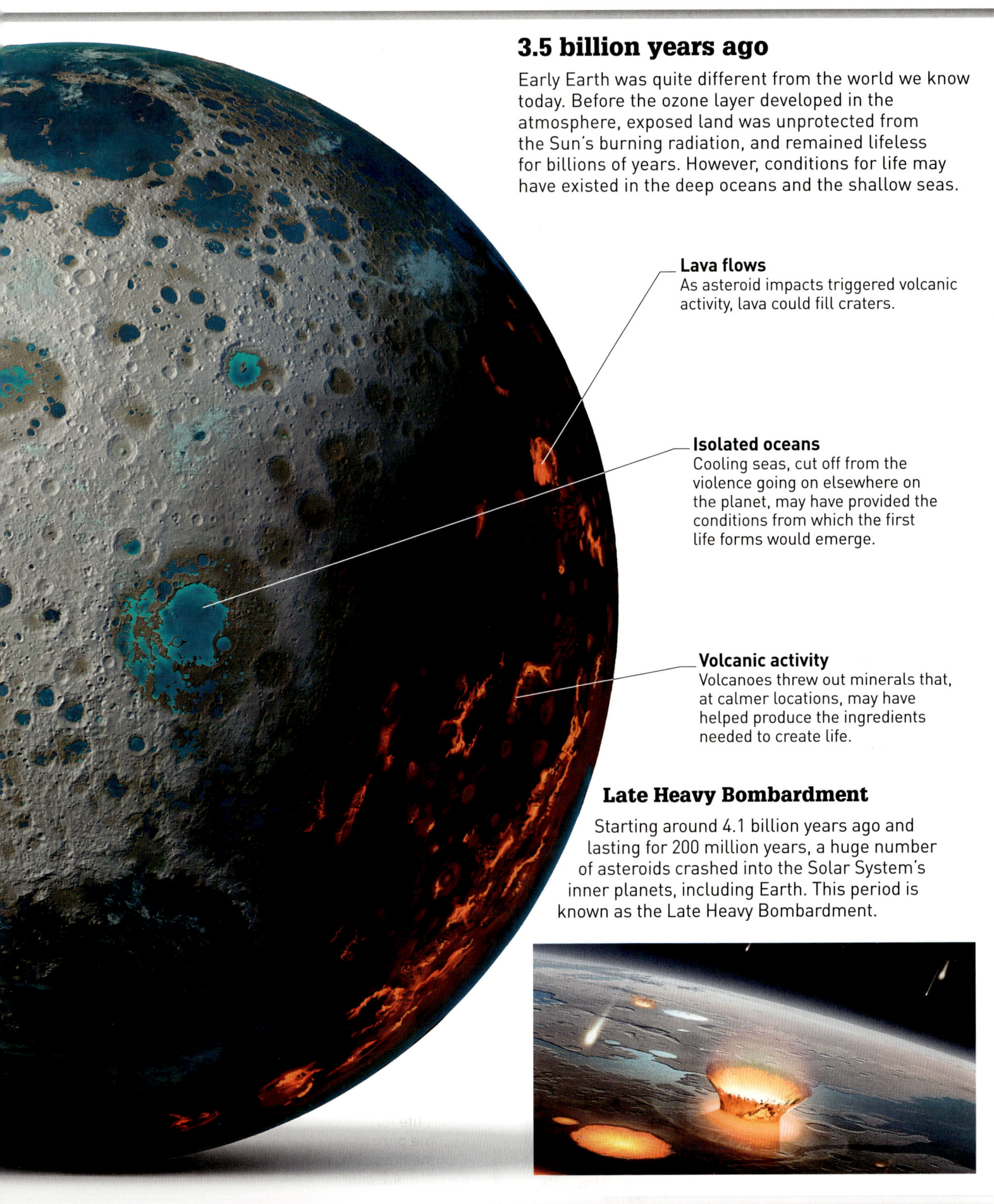

## 3.5 billion years ago

Early Earth was quite different from the world we know today. Before the ozone layer developed in the atmosphere, exposed land was unprotected from the Sun's burning radiation, and remained lifeless for billions of years. However, conditions for life may have existed in the deep oceans and the shallow seas.

**Lava flows**
As asteroid impacts triggered volcanic activity, lava could fill craters.

**Isolated oceans**
Cooling seas, cut off from the violence going on elsewhere on the planet, may have provided the conditions from which the first life forms would emerge.

**Volcanic activity**
Volcanoes threw out minerals that, at calmer locations, may have helped produce the ingredients needed to create life.

**Late Heavy Bombardment**
Starting around 4.1 billion years ago and lasting for 200 million years, a huge number of asteroids crashed into the Solar System's inner planets, including Earth. This period is known as the Late Heavy Bombardment.

BACTERIA, ARE THOUGHT TO HAVE EMERGED 3.5 BILLION YEARS AGO.

EARLY EARTH

### 500 million years ago
By this stage of Earth's history two major continents had formed. The largest, Gondwana, was mainly tropical. Laurentia (now North America) had also drifted from the polar regions to the tropics and sat on the Equator. Temperatures were mild across the globe, but cooling.

**In the water**
Many life forms developed in the warm, shallow seas, including marine invertebrates such as *Hallucigenia*, a worm with limbs.

*Hallucigenia*

### 420 million years ago
Continents continued to shift. Avalonia (now split across present-day southern Britain and Canada) moved north to collide with Laurentia. Siberia headed north and Gondwana south, taking most of present-day Australia and Antarctica into the southern hemisphere. Sea levels started to rise.

The giant continent of Gondwana sat on the tropics
*Reverse view*

*Reverse view*

**Lifeless land**
Carbon dioxide levels in the atmosphere were 15 times higher than today, and no animals could survive on land.

**Early algae**

There was no land vegetation, but many types of algae (plant-like oganisms that live in the sea) had appeared and diversified.

**Animals**
Millipedes, such as the one below, were the first known oxygen-breathing animals on land.

8  THE FIRST INSECTS ARE THOUGHT TO HAVE

## In the water
The first coral reefs and fish appeared. *Guiyu oneiros* remains dating back to 419 million years ago have been found in Yunnan province, China.

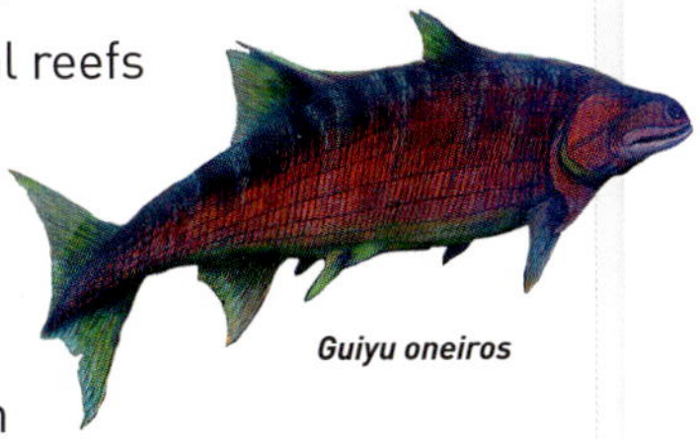

*Guiyu oneiros*

## 380 million years ago
Laurentia and Baltica collided, closing up the Iapetus Ocean and forming the continent of Eurasia. The collision created the Appalachian-Caledonide Mountain Range, which extended from Scandinavia to the Appalachian Mountains in North America. Gondwana rotated clockwise, approaching Eurasia.

## In the water
The "Age of Fish" saw a variety of lobe-finned fish and jawed predators. Placoderms (armored fish) included the mighty *Dunkleosteus*.

*Dunkleosteus*

SIBERIA

BALTICA

GONDWANA

EURASIA

SIBERIA

GONDWANA

*Reverse view*

## Plants
The tiny, but upright, *Cooksonia* was one of the first plants to colonize land. It was short, had branching stems, and lived in damp habitats.

*Cooksonia*

## Fish with legs
The first tetrapods (four-legged animals) developed. The earliest were like fish with legs, such as *Ichthyostega*.

*Ichthyostega*

*Archaeopteris*

## Plants
The landmasses turned green as woody, spore-bearing plants such as *Archaeopteris*, a treelike plant with ferny leaves, created major forests and swamps.

 EVOLVED AROUND 480 MILLION YEARS AGO.

EARLY EARTH

## 300 million years ago
By 300 million years ago, Eurasia had merged with Gondwana to form the supercontinent Pangea, which extended from high in the northern hemisphere to the South Pole, where ice caps spread. Siberia collided with eastern Europe, creating the Ural Mountains.

### In the water
Fish and aquatic tetrapods, such as *Microbrachis* ("tiny limbs"), shared the seas with corals, crinoids (sea lilies), and brachiopods (mollusks).

*Microbrachis*

## 250 million years ago
All the continents were absorbed into the giant supercontinent Pangea. Global sea levels fell, while, in Siberia, massive volcanic eruptions poured out ash and gases, poisoning both the atmosphere and the oceans. Such events led to a global mass extinction.

*Reverse view*

### Animals
The shelled egg evolved, so tetrapods, such as *Ophiacodon*, could lay eggs on land without them drying out.

*Ophiacodon*

### Plants
Lush swamps dominated by tree ferns laid the foundations for rich deposits of coal, and provided a habitat for arthropods, such as winged insects.

*Reverse view*

### Animals
About 70 percent of land species became extinct, including *Dimetrodon*.

*Dimetrodon*

10    AROUND 250 MILLION YEARS AGO, A MASS EXTINCTION WIPED

*Helicoprion*

**In the water**
Falling sea levels exposed reefs. An estimated 95 percent of marine species died out in the mass extinction—*Helicoprion* was one of the few survivors.

## 220 million years ago
Pangea was at its largest—it extended from pole to pole—and sea levels had lowered. The supercontinent moved north, rotating counterclockwise. New life forms, including dinosaurs, started to evolve on the land.

**In the water**
Marine reptiles included turtles, frogs, crocodiles, and dolphinlike ichthyosaurs, such as *Mixosaurus*. Corals and mollusks also evolved new forms.

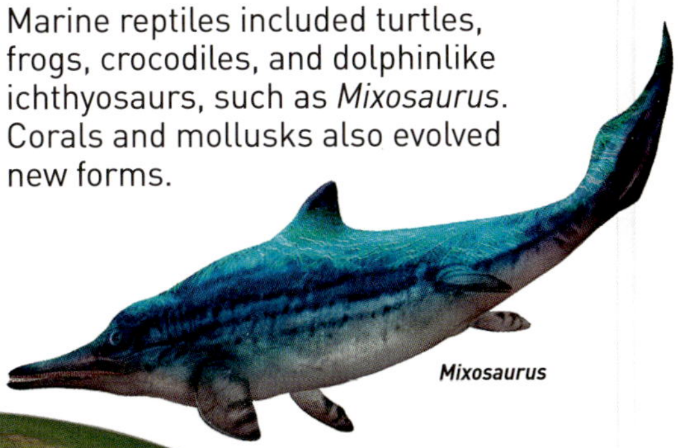

*Mixosaurus*

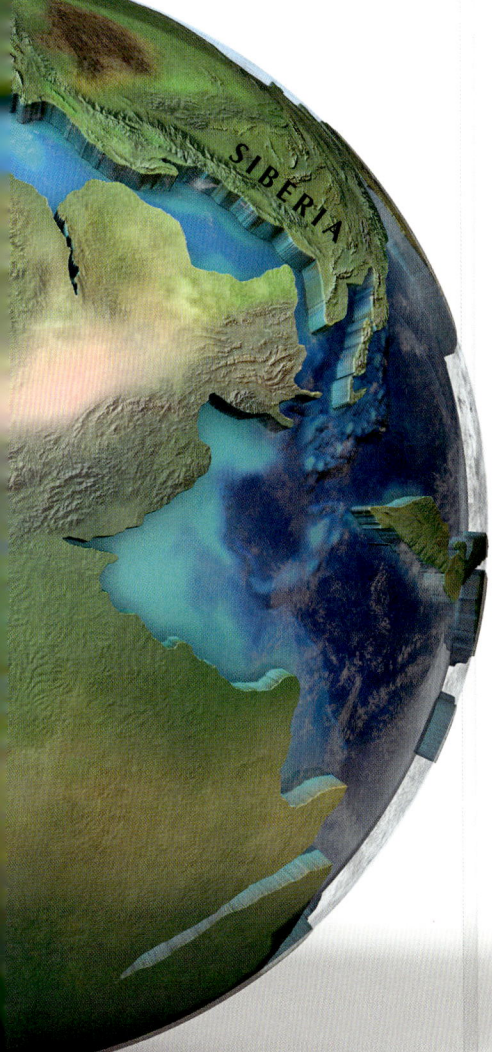

PANGEA

*Reverse view*

**Plants**
Half of all plant species died out. *Glossopteris*, widespread for 50 million years, declined, as did conifers, horsetails, and ferns.

*Glossopteris*

**Animals**
The first flies evolved, and early archosaurs (ruling reptiles), such as *Euparkeria*, paved the way for dinosaurs.

*Euparkeria*

*Dicroidium*

**Plants**
Vegetation adapted to the dry climate. Flora included conifers and the seed fern *Dicroidium*, which was distributed throughout Pangea.

OUT WELL OVER HALF OF ALL KNOWN PLANT AND ANIMAL SPECIES.

## 180 million years ago

The supercontinent Pangea separated into Laurasia in the north and Gondwana in the south, divided by the ever-growing Tethys Ocean. The climate was warm with no evidence of glaciation.

### In the water
The oceans were full of fish and marine reptiles, such as *Ichthyosaurus*, as well as bivalves (such as mussels), starfish, and sea urchins.

*Ichthyosaurus*

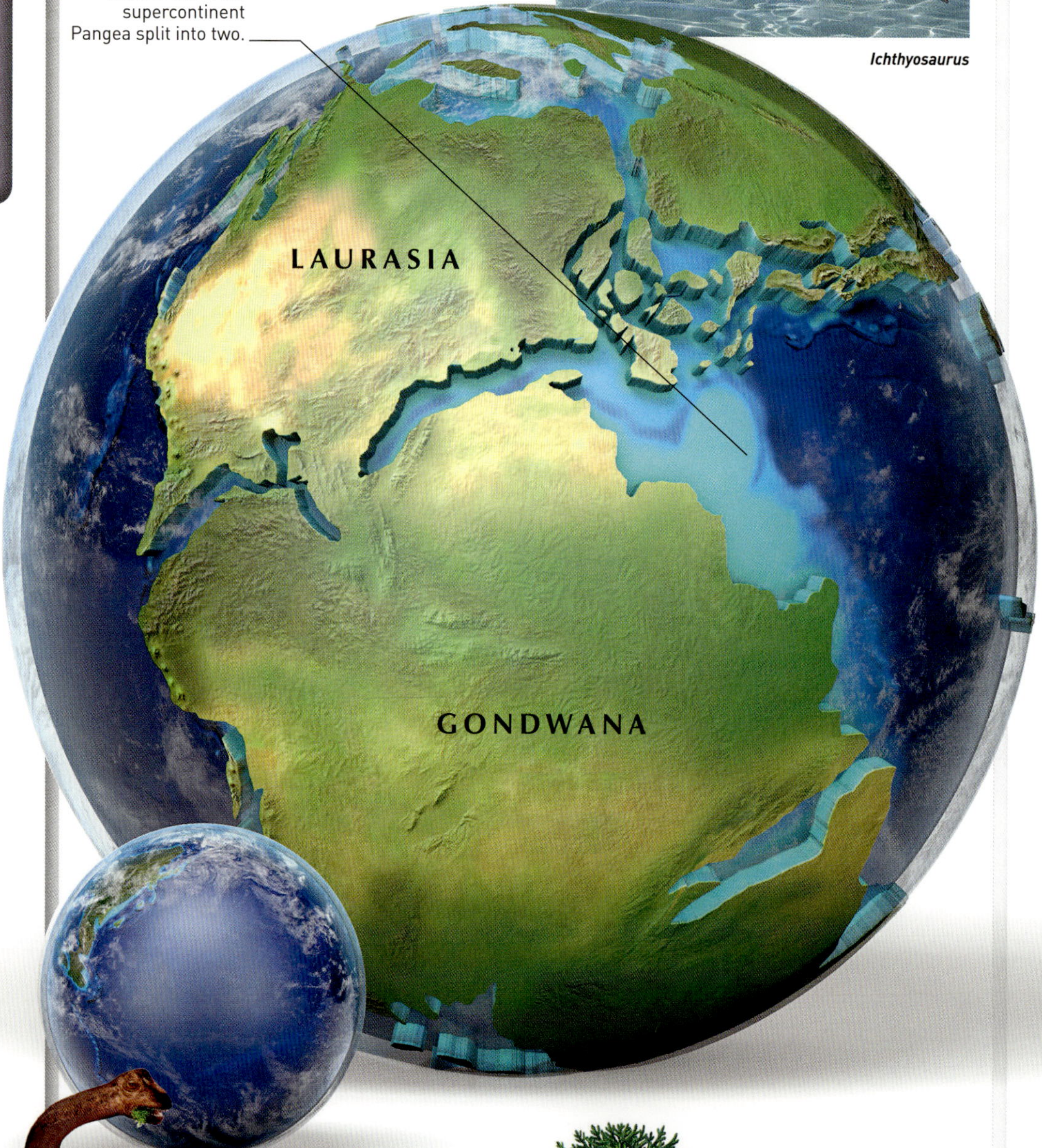

Tethys Ocean—formed when the supercontinent Pangea split into two.

LAURASIA

GONDWANA

*Reverse view*

### Animals
Dinosaurs dominated the land during this period. Among them was the giant, plant-eating *Barapasaurus*.

*Barapasaurus*

### Plants
Conifers, ginkgo, and monkey puzzle trees, dominated Laurasia. There were also ferns and palmlike cycads further south in tropical regions.

Monkey puzzle tree

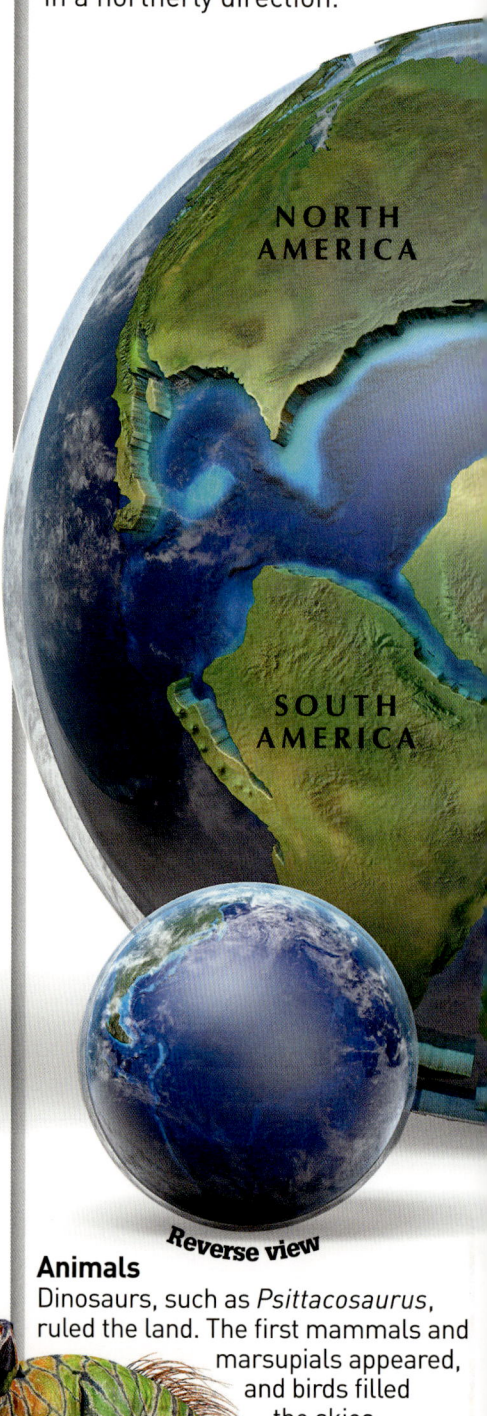

## 120 million years ago

Today's oceans began to take shape. The South Atlantic Ocean opened up as Africa and South America split apart, splintering Pangea further. North America was still attached to Europe, but India separated from western Australia and started to move in a northerly direction.

NORTH AMERICA

SOUTH AMERICA

*Reverse view*

### Animals
Dinosaurs, such as *Psittacosaurus*, ruled the land. The first mammals and marsupials appeared, and birds filled the skies.

*Psittacosaurus*

MODERN-DAY MAMMAL GROUPS BEGAN TO

### In the water
*Archelon* (giant sea turtles) and other sea reptiles flourished. New species of strangely coiled creatures called ammonoids thrived, as did sea snails and anemones.

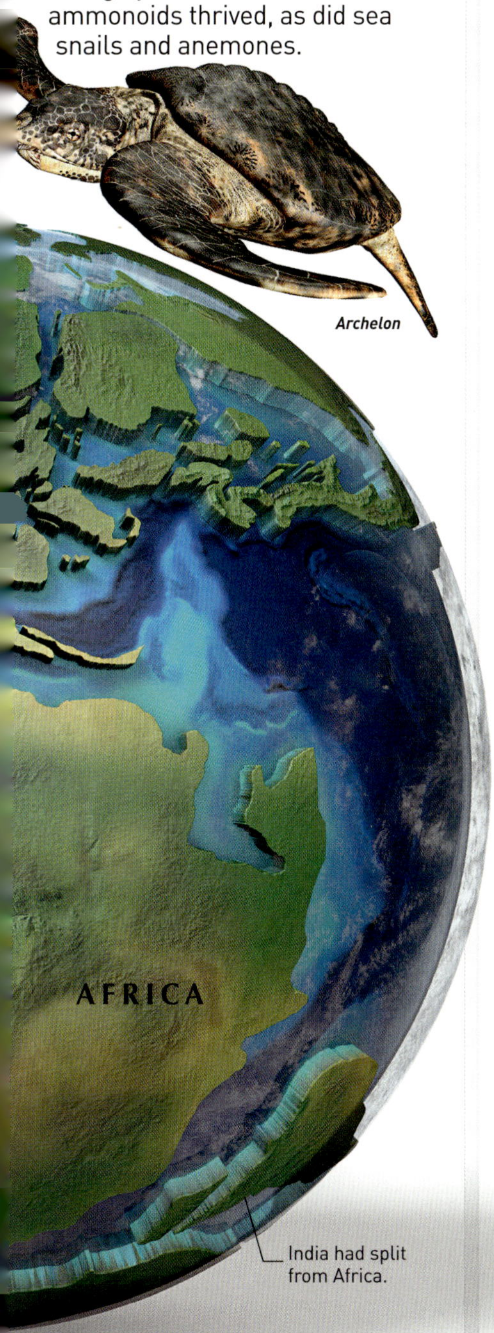

*Archelon*

### 80 million years ago
High sea levels flooded much of North America and created a seaway that extended from the Gulf of Mexico to the newly forming Atlantic Ocean. By 65 million years ago, India had collided with Asia, causing volcanic eruptions. An asteroid had hit Mexico, causing a mass extinction.

### In the water
New types of shellfish continued to evolve and peculiar sea reptiles, such as the long-necked *Albertonectes*, came into being.

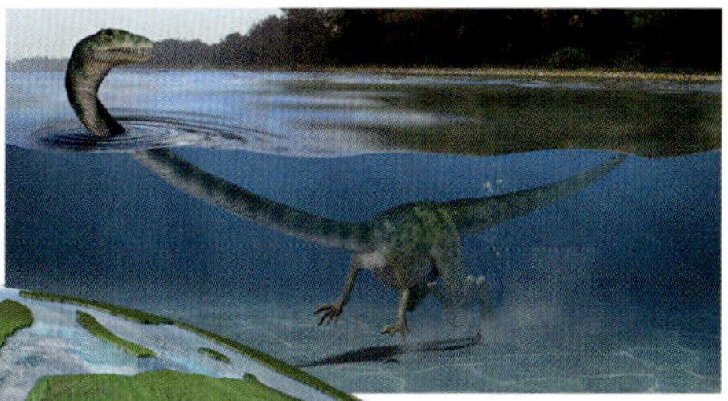

*Albertonectes*

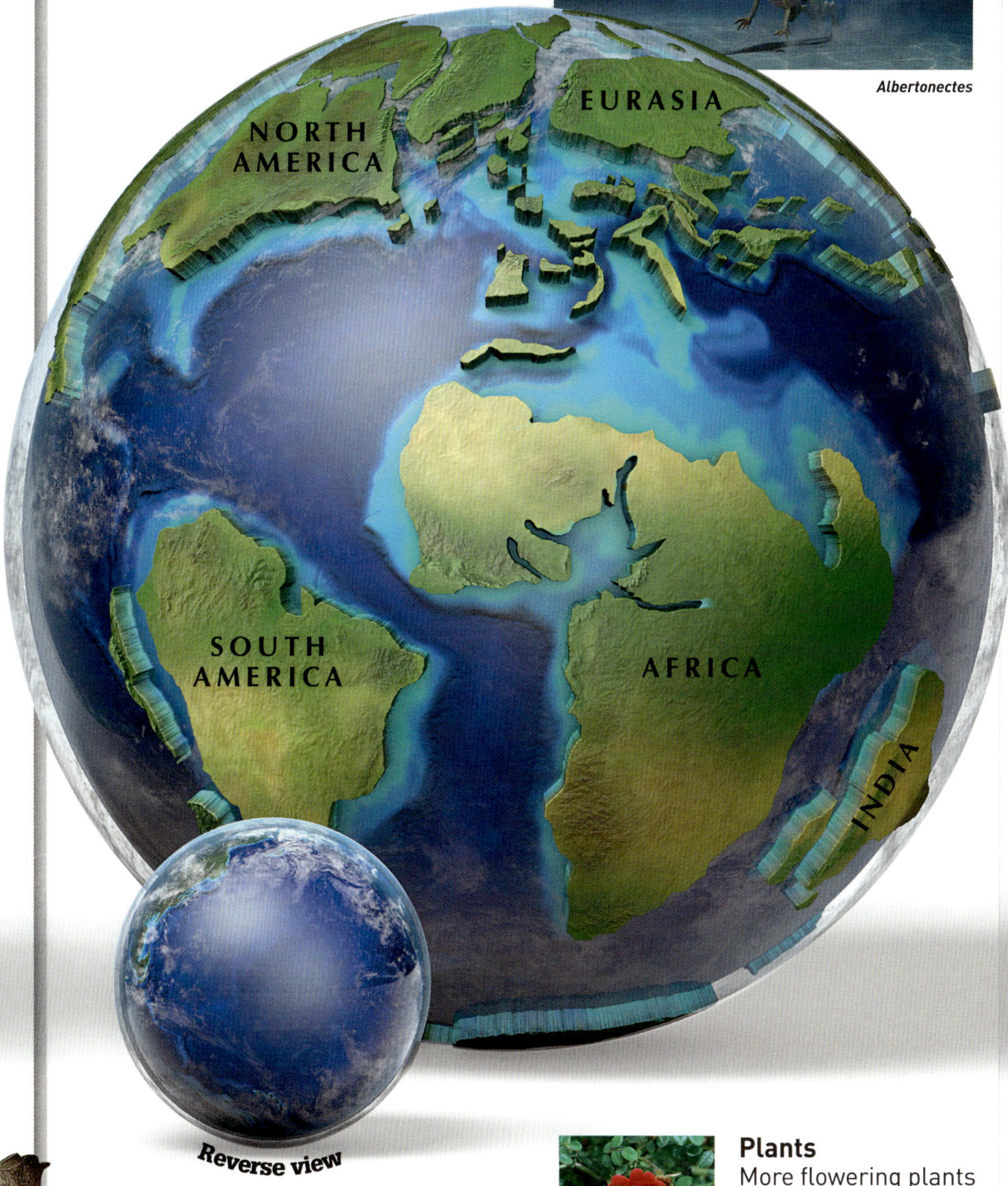

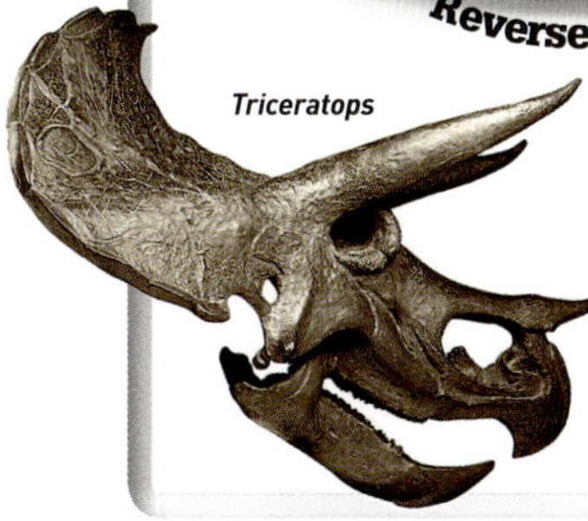

India had split from Africa.

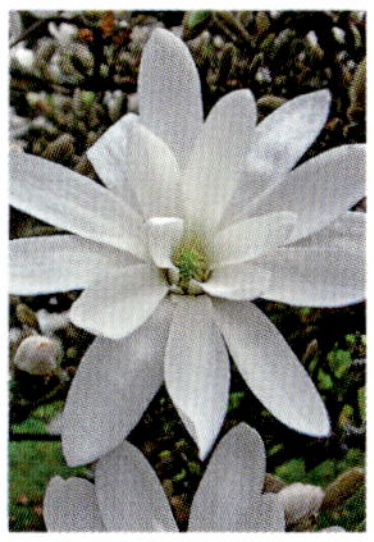

*Reverse view*

*Triceratops*

### Plants
The first angiosperms (flowering plants), such as magnolia, colonized the land, evolving alongside pollinating insects, including bees.

### Animals
New dinosaurs evolved, including *Triceratops*. Snakes, ants, and termites also emerged.

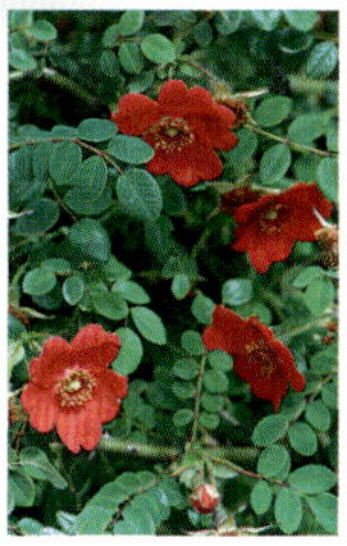

### Plants
More flowering plants started to appear on land. Conifers and palmlike cycads spread, thanks to the success of their seed-bearing cones.

DIVERGE ABOUT 120 MILLION YEARS AGO.

13

### 40 million years ago
North and South America were separate, and Antarctica split away from Australia. These isolated landmasses saw animals and plants develop independently. Mountain ranges, such as the Rocky Mountains and the Himalayas, formed along plate margins, and the closing of the Tethys Ocean forced up the Alps.

**In the water**
Single-celled plankton were at their most diverse and coral reefs grew. At the other end of the size scale, *Basilosaurus* was an early whale.

*Basilosaurus*

*Reverse view*

**Animals**
Moths, butterflies, birds, and bats flew above new mammals, such as rhinos, camels, and early horses, like *Protorohippus*.

*Protorohippus*

**Plants**
Grasslands expanded across the continents, and flowering plants and conifers were joined by deciduous trees, such as the beech.

### 50,000–18,000 years ago
Part of a cycle of ice ages, ocean levels fell and rose as glaciers advanced and retreated. India nudged further into Asia, Australia into Indonesia, and Africa and the Middle East into Europe and Asia. France and England were joined until rising sea levels created the English Channel.

*Woolly mammoth*

*Reverse view*

**Animals**
Giant mammals evolved, such as the woolly mammoth, with its thick fur coat for protection.

**Bottlenose dolphin**

### In the water
Aquatic mammals such as dolphins shared the seas with plankton species that adapted to successive changes in the water temperature.

### Present day
The last ice age ended and giant mammals became extinct around 12,000 years ago. By that time, humans had started to make their mark on the world. Human activity has triggered global warming and has affected natural cycles of glaciation. The consequences of this could have a major impact on life on Earth.

### In the water
Coral reefs provide a habitat for up to a quarter of all marine species. Marine life is still diverse, with an estimated 2 million species living in the oceans.

**Fish at coral reef**

*Reverse view*

### Plants
Steppe (grassland too dry for trees to grow) plant types expanded. Much land was tundra—so cold, dry, and windy, that only the hardiest plants grew.

**Zebra**

### Animals
The land today is home to an estimated 6 million species of animal, including the zebra.

### Plants
Tropical rain forests are home to about 40,000 known plant species, from tiny mosses to towering mahogany and kapok trees.

EL CASTILLO, SPAIN, AROUND 40,000 YEARS AGO.

# NORTH AMERICA

**North America from space**
North America is a huge continent that dominates the northern half of Earth's western hemisphere. From space, the Great Lakes and the Rocky Mountains are clearly visible.

# NORTH AMERICA

## North American Free Trade Agreement

Established in 1994, the North American Free Trade Association, also known as NAFTA, is an agreement signed by the United States, Canada, and Mexico. Its aim is to increase the flow of trade between the three countries.

**Alaska**
The United States bought Alaska from Russia for $7.2 million in 1867.

**United States of America**
The United States is a country made up of 50 states.

**Hawaii**
The volcanic Pacific islands became the United States' 50th state in 1959.

## FAST FACTS

**Total land area:** 9,358,340 sq miles (24,238,000 sq km)

**Total population:** 576 million

**Number of countries:** 23

**Largest country:** Canada—3,855,103 sq miles (9,984,670 sq km)

**Smallest country:** St. Kitts and Nevis—101 sq miles (261 sq km)

**Largest country population:** United States of America—321 million

18 — NORTH AMERICA IS THE THIRD LARGEST AND THE FOURTH

# Countries and borders

The continent of North America is dominated by Canada, the second largest country in the world, and the United States of America, the richest. The seven countries of Central America have struggled with the problems of poverty and war in the past, but have experienced peace and economic recovery in recent years.

**Greenland**
Although part of Denmark, Greenland has been self-governing since 1979. It is the world's largest island.

**Canada**
North America's largest country, Canada gained its independence from the United Kingdom in 1931 and has 10 provinces.

**KEY**
● Capital city
● Major city

**US-Mexico border**
This border is the most frequently crossed international border in the world.

**Dividing line**
Panama's border with Colombia marks the divide between North and South America.

MOST POPULATED CONTINENT IN THE WORLD.

## NORTH AMERICA

### 1. Denali
At 20,321 ft (6,194 m), Denali, located in south-central Alaska, is the highest peak in North America. Denali means "tall" or "high" in Kokuyon, the language used by the people who live in the area that surrounds the mountain.

### 4. Greenland

**Western Cordillera**
A system of parallel mountain ranges that extends along the continent's western coast.

# Landscape

North America lies between the Atlantic Ocean to the east and the Pacific Ocean to the west, and stretches from the Arctic in the north to just short of the equator in the south. The continent is also home to Greenland, the world's largest island.

BEFORE THE ISTHMUS OF PANAMA FORMED 20 MILLION YEARS

**FAST FACTS**

**① Highest point:** Denali, Alaska, United States of America—20,321 ft (6,194 m)

**② Longest river:** Mississippi River, United States—3,700 miles (5,960 km)

**③ Largest lake:** Lake Superior—32,151 sq miles (83,270 sq km)

**④ Largest island:** Greenland— 822,700 sq miles (2,130,800 sq km)

Greenland—a permanent ice sheet covers four-fifths of the island.

**Canadian Shield** A raised, flat plateau of land that contains thousands of lakes.

**Appalachian Mountains** Formed around 400 million years ago, this is one of the world's oldest mountain ranges.

**Caribbean Islands** These are made up of over 7,000 islands, islets, reefs, and cays (low banks of reef, coral, rock, or sand).

**Great Plains** A vast, flat, fertile area created by retreating glaciers during the last Ice Age.

**Isthmus of Panama** At its narrowest, the Isthmus of Panama—an isthmus is a narrow strip of land with sea on either side—is just 31 miles (50 km) wide.

**KEY** The colors on the map represent the height of the land in relation to sea level.

| ELEVATION | |
|---|---|
| Feet | Meters |
| above 26,247 | above 8,000 |
| 22,965 | 7,000 |
| 19,685 | 6,000 |
| 16,404 | 5,000 |
| 13,123 | 4,000 |
| 9,842 | 3,000 |
| 6,560 | 2,000 |
| 3,280 | 1,000 |
| Sea level 0 | 0 Sea level |

AGO, NORTH AND SOUTH AMERICA WERE SEPARATED BY OCEAN.

# Fascinating facts

**Largest lake: Lake Superior, United States/Canada**—32,151 sq miles (83,270 sq km)

## Deepest lake
Great Slave Lake, Canada—
**2,014 ft (614 m) deep**

**Longest tunnels**

 **Railroad tunnel** Mount Macdonald Tunnel, British Columbia, Canada—9.1 miles (14.7 km)

 **Subway tunnel** Angrignon–Honoré-Beaugrand (Line 1 Green), Montreal Metro, Canada—13.7 miles (22.1 km)

 **Road tunnel** Ted Williams Extension, Boston, United States—2.6 miles (4.2 km)

**Number of time zones 10**

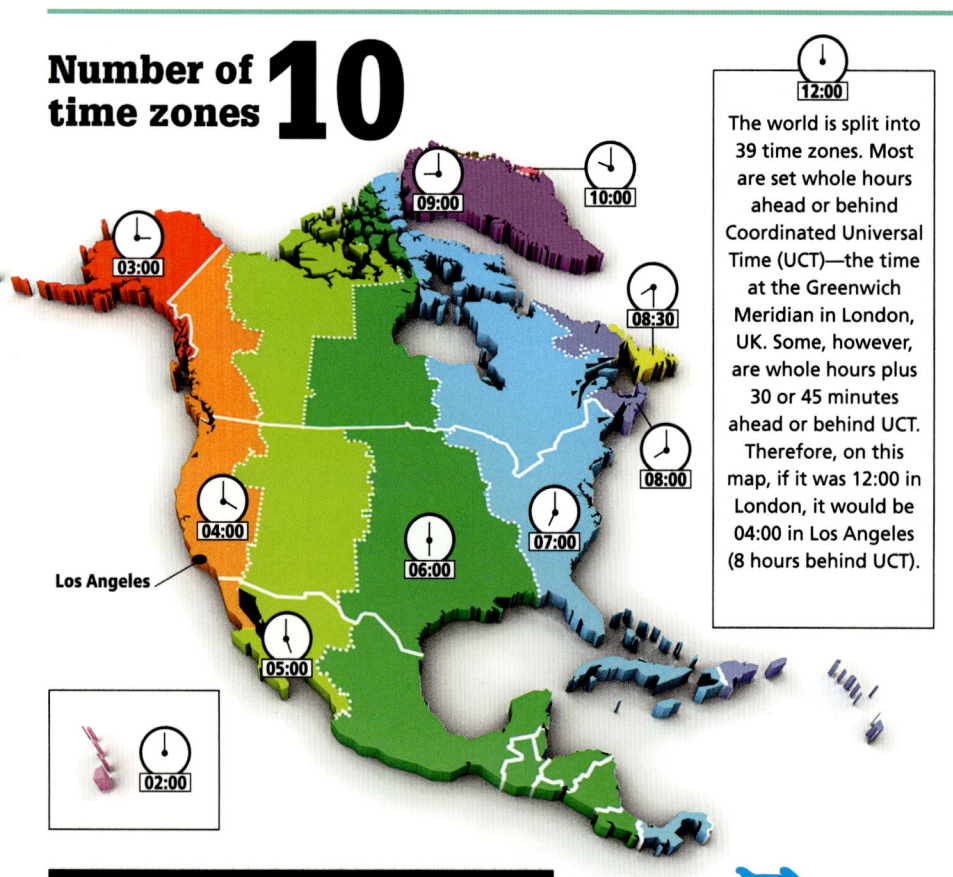

The world is split into 39 time zones. Most are set whole hours ahead or behind Coordinated Universal Time (UCT)—the time at the Greenwich Meridian in London, UK. Some, however, are whole hours plus 30 or 45 minutes ahead or behind UCT. Therefore, on this map, if it was 12:00 in London, it would be 04:00 in Los Angeles (8 hours behind UCT).

## Most active volcano
Kilauea, Hawaii

**Official languages 7**
Amerindian languages • **Creole** • Danish (Greenland) • **Dutch** • English • **French** • Spanish

 **Busiest airport**
Hartsfield-Jackson Atlanta International Airport, Atlanta—**101,489,887 passengers per year**

## Fastest train
North America's fastest train is the **Acela Express**, in the US, which can reach speeds of up to **150 mph (240 km/h)**

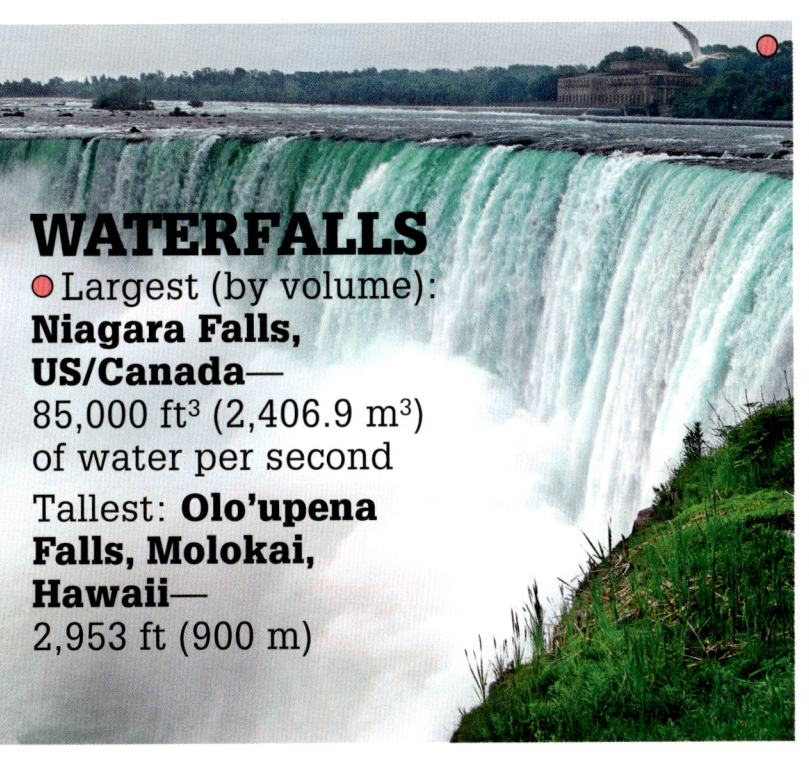

# WATERFALLS
- **Largest (by volume): Niagara Falls, US/Canada**—85,000 ft³ (2,406.9 m³) of water per second
- **Tallest: Olo'upena Falls, Molokai, Hawaii**—2,953 ft (900 m)

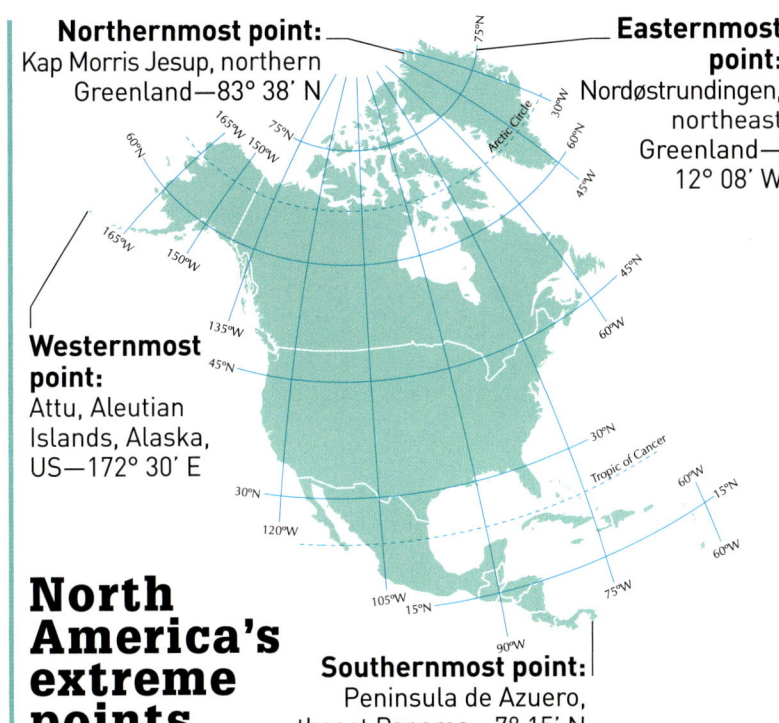

## North America's extreme points

**Northernmost point:** Kap Morris Jesup, northern Greenland—83° 38' N

**Easternmost point:** Nordøstrundingen, northeast Greenland—12° 08' W

**Westernmost point:** Attu, Aleutian Islands, Alaska, US—172° 30' E

**Southernmost point:** Peninsula de Azuero, southeast Panama—7° 15' N

# Longest coastline
Canada—**125,567 miles (202,080 km)**

# Longest bridge
Lake Pontchartrain Causeway, Louisiana — **23.89 miles (38.442 km)**

# Tallest bridge
Royal Gorge Bridge, Colorado — **955 ft (291 m)**

## BIGGEST GLACIER
Bering Glacier, Alaska

# Tallest buildings

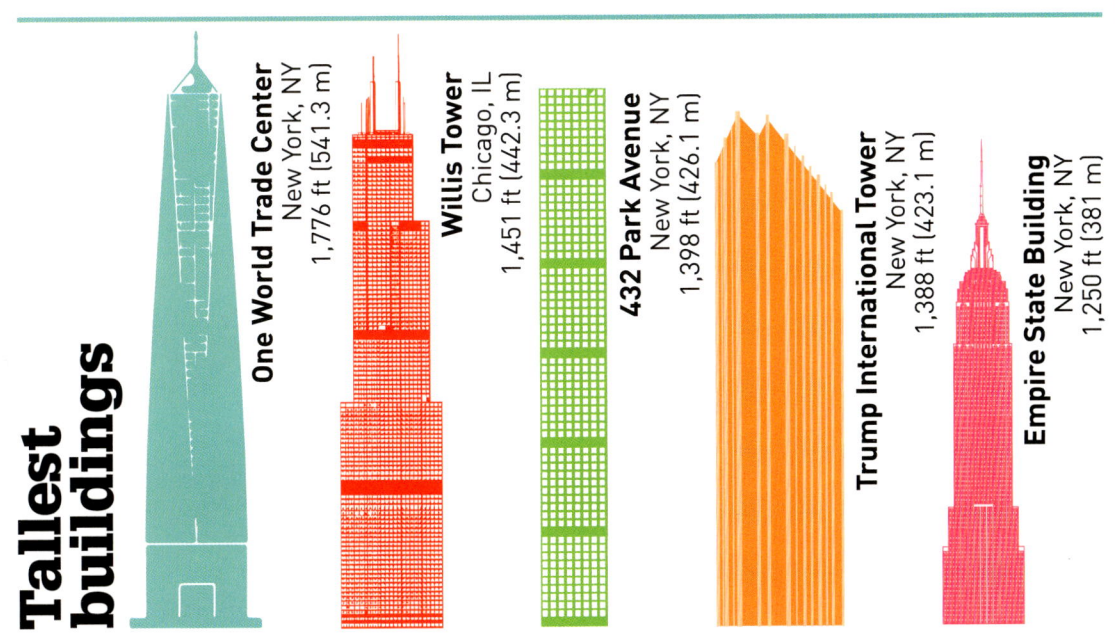

- **One World Trade Center** New York, NY — 1,776 ft (541.3 m)
- **Willis Tower** Chicago, IL — 1,451 ft (442.3 m)
- **432 Park Avenue** New York, NY — 1,398 ft (426.1 m)
- **Trump International Tower** New York, NY — 1,388 ft (423.1 m)
- **Empire State Building** New York, NY — 1,250 ft (381 m)

# Most visited cities (Visitors per year)

- **New York, US** — 12.27 million
- **Los Angeles, US** — 5.2 million
- **Miami, US** — 4.52 million
- **Toronto, Canada** — 4.18 million
- **Vancouver, Canada** — 3.76 million

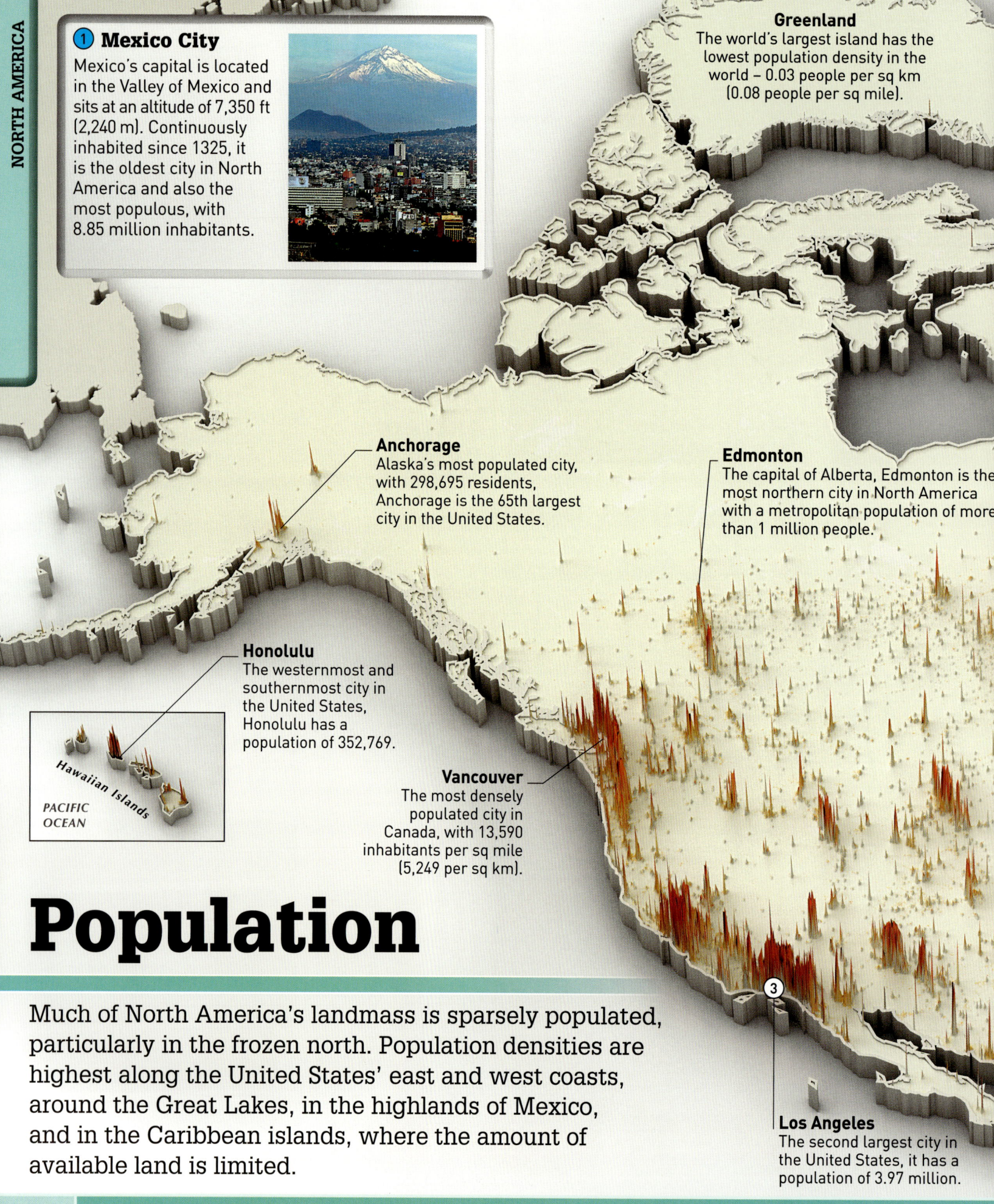

## NORTH AMERICA

**① Mexico City**
Mexico's capital is located in the Valley of Mexico and sits at an altitude of 7,350 ft (2,240 m). Continuously inhabited since 1325, it is the oldest city in North America and also the most populous, with 8.85 million inhabitants.

**Greenland**
The world's largest island has the lowest population density in the world – 0.03 people per sq km (0.08 people per sq mile).

**Anchorage**
Alaska's most populated city, with 298,695 residents, Anchorage is the 65th largest city in the United States.

**Edmonton**
The capital of Alberta, Edmonton is the most northern city in North America with a metropolitan population of more than 1 million people.

**Honolulu**
The westernmost and southernmost city in the United States, Honolulu has a population of 352,769.

**Vancouver**
The most densely populated city in Canada, with 13,590 inhabitants per sq mile (5,249 per sq km).

**Los Angeles**
The second largest city in the United States, it has a population of 3.97 million.

# Population

Much of North America's landmass is sparsely populated, particularly in the frozen north. Population densities are highest along the United States' east and west coasts, around the Great Lakes, in the highlands of Mexico, and in the Caribbean islands, where the amount of available land is limited.

NINE OF NORTH AMERICA'S 10 MOST DENSELY POPULATED

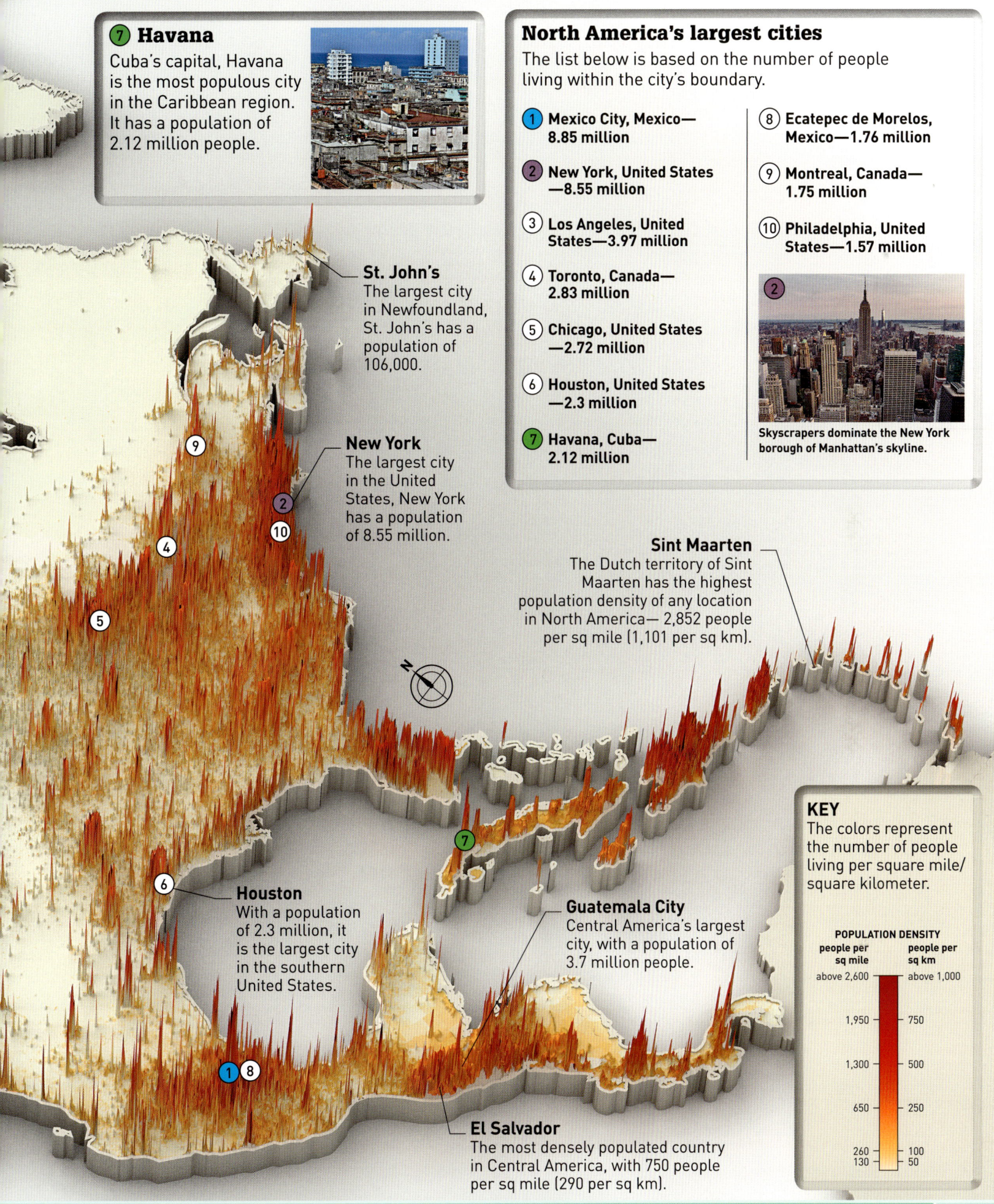

### 7 Havana
Cuba's capital, Havana is the most populous city in the Caribbean region. It has a population of 2.12 million people.

### North America's largest cities
The list below is based on the number of people living within the city's boundary.

1. Mexico City, Mexico—8.85 million
2. New York, United States—8.55 million
3. Los Angeles, United States—3.97 million
4. Toronto, Canada—2.83 million
5. Chicago, United States—2.72 million
6. Houston, United States—2.3 million
7. Havana, Cuba—2.12 million
8. Ecatepec de Morelos, Mexico—1.76 million
9. Montreal, Canada—1.75 million
10. Philadelphia, United States—1.57 million

Skyscrapers dominate the New York borough of Manhattan's skyline.

**St. John's**
The largest city in Newfoundland, St. John's has a population of 106,000.

**New York**
The largest city in the United States, New York has a population of 8.55 million.

**Sint Maarten**
The Dutch territory of Sint Maarten has the highest population density of any location in North America— 2,852 people per sq mile (1,101 per sq km).

**Houston**
With a population of 2.3 million, it is the largest city in the southern United States.

**Guatemala City**
Central America's largest city, with a population of 3.7 million people.

**El Salvador**
The most densely populated country in Central America, with 750 people per sq mile (290 per sq km).

### KEY
The colors represent the number of people living per square mile/square kilometer.

**POPULATION DENSITY**

| people per sq mile | people per sq km |
|---|---|
| above 2,600 | above 1,000 |
| 1,950 | 750 |
| 1,300 | 500 |
| 650 | 250 |
| 260 | 100 |
| 130 | 50 |

TERRITORIES ARE LOCATED IN THE CARIBBEAN.

**NORTH AMERICA**

# The Grand Canyon

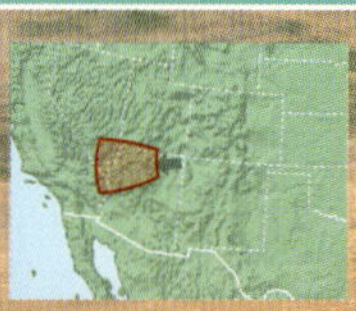

Formed over millions of years by the flow of the Colorado River, the Grand Canyon is a steep-sided canyon in the state of Arizona. It is 277 miles (446 km) long, 18 miles (29 km) wide at its widest point, and reaches a depth of 6,093 ft (1,857 m).

**Granite Gorge**
The most-visited section of the Grand Canyon, it is the starting point for the majority of rafting trips through the canyon along the Colorado River.

Grand Canyon Village

Grand Canyon

Granit

Grand Canyon Lodge

Colorado River

Bright Angel Canyon

Walhalla Plateau

Cape Royal

Granite Gorge

Desert View

Colorado River

Painted

**South Rim**
Approximately 90 percent of tourists catch their first dramatic glimpse of the Grand Canyon from here.

**Painted Desert**
Starting at the eastern edge of the Grand Canyon, the Painted Desert is 7,500 sq miles (19,425 sq km). It is named for its multi-colored layers of rock, which range from gray to purple, and from orange to pink.

THE FIRST EUROPEAN TO SEE THE GRAND CANYON WAS GARCIA

## NORTH AMERICA

### ● Chichen Itza
The largest and most famous Mayan site, Chichen Itza, Mexico, was a major urban center between 750 and 1200 CE. The highlight of the site is the El Castillo pyramid, whose four sides are made up of 365 steps (one for each day of the solar year).

### Illulisat Icefjord
Located 220 miles (350 km) north of the Arctic Circle, the area's many icebergs have made Illulisat a popular tourist destination.

**Illulisat Icefjord,** *Greenland*

**Mount Shishaldin,** *Alaska, United States*

### Mount Shishaldin
The highest mountain peak on the Aleutian Islands (9,373 ft/2,857 m), Mount Shishaldin is the most symmetrical cone-shaped volcano on Earth.

**Ninstints,** *British Columbia, Canada*

**The Bow,** *Calgary, Canada*

**Mount Rushmore,** *South Dakota, United States*

**Space Needle,** *Seattle, United States*

**Old Faithful,** *Wyoming, United States*

**Mauna Loa,** *Hawaii, United States*

*Hawaiian Islands*

PACIFIC OCEAN

**Redwood National Park,** *California, United States*

### Golden Gate Bridge
When it opened in 1937, it had the longest main span (4,200 ft/1,280 m) of any suspension bridge in the world.

**Hoover Dam,** *Nevada-Arizona, United States*

**Chaco Canyon,** *New Mexico, United States*

**Golden Gate Bridge,** *San Francisco, United States*

**Hollywood Sign,** *Los Angeles, United States*

## The **United States** is the world's **second-** most-visited country.

**KEY**
○ Landmark location

28 — THE ZOCALO, MEXICO CITY'S MAIN SQUARE, IS NORTH AMERICA'S MOST-

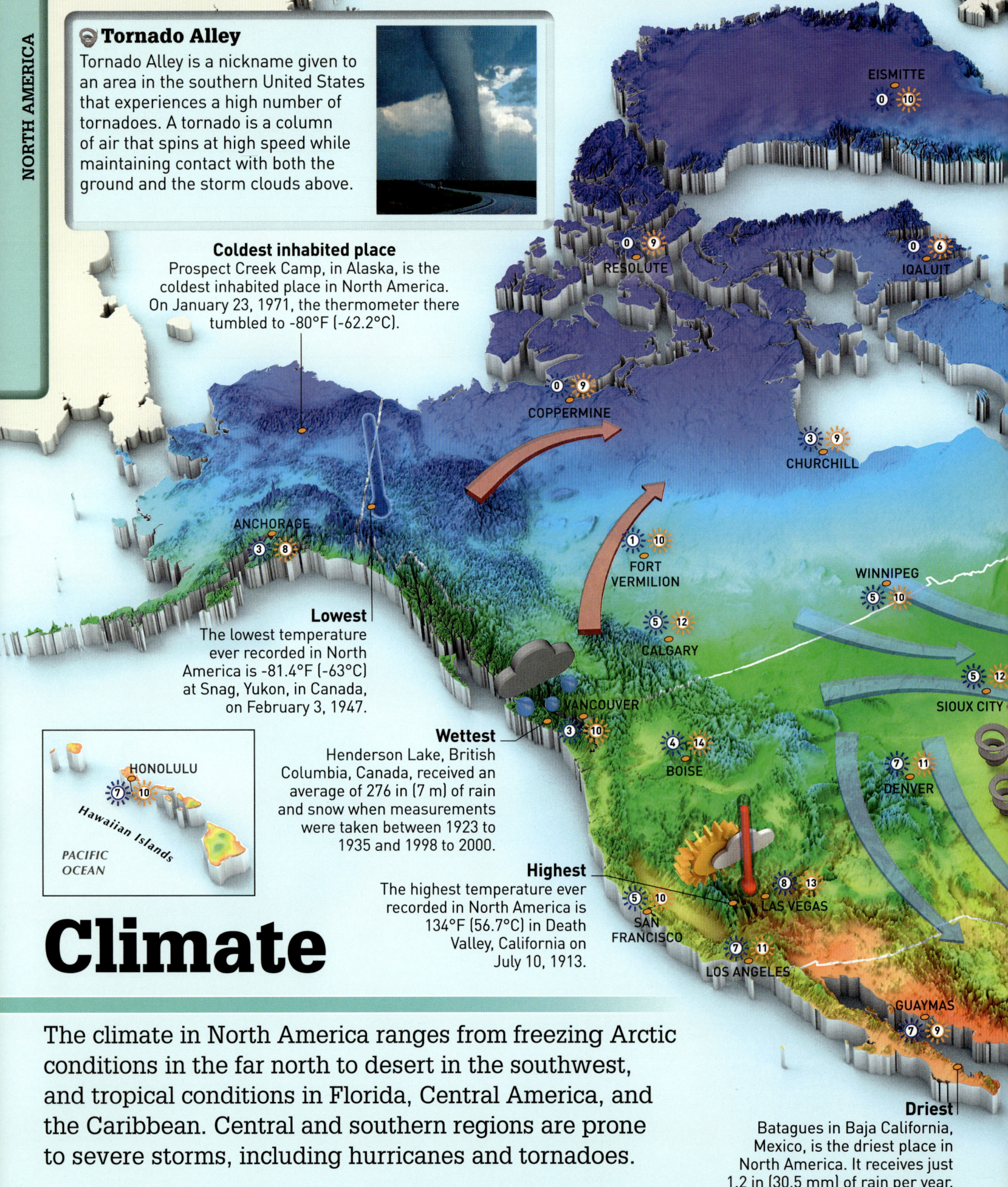

# NORTH AMERICA

### Tornado Alley
Tornado Alley is a nickname given to an area in the southern United States that experiences a high number of tornadoes. A tornado is a column of air that spins at high speed while maintaining contact with both the ground and the storm clouds above.

### Coldest inhabited place
Prospect Creek Camp, in Alaska, is the coldest inhabited place in North America. On January 23, 1971, the thermometer there tumbled to -80°F (-62.2°C).

### Lowest
The lowest temperature ever recorded in North America is -81.4°F (-63°C) at Snag, Yukon, in Canada, on February 3, 1947.

### Wettest
Henderson Lake, British Columbia, Canada, received an average of 276 in (7 m) of rain and snow when measurements were taken between 1923 to 1935 and 1998 to 2000.

### Highest
The highest temperature ever recorded in North America is 134°F (56.7°C) in Death Valley, California on July 10, 1913.

### Driest
Batagues in Baja California, Mexico, is the driest place in North America. It receives just 1.2 in (30.5 mm) of rain per year.

# Climate

The climate in North America ranges from freezing Arctic conditions in the far north to desert in the southwest, and tropical conditions in Florida, Central America, and the Caribbean. Central and southern regions are prone to severe storms, including hurricanes and tornadoes.

30    IN 1998-99, A WORLD RECORD 95 FT (29 M) OF SNOW FELL ON THE

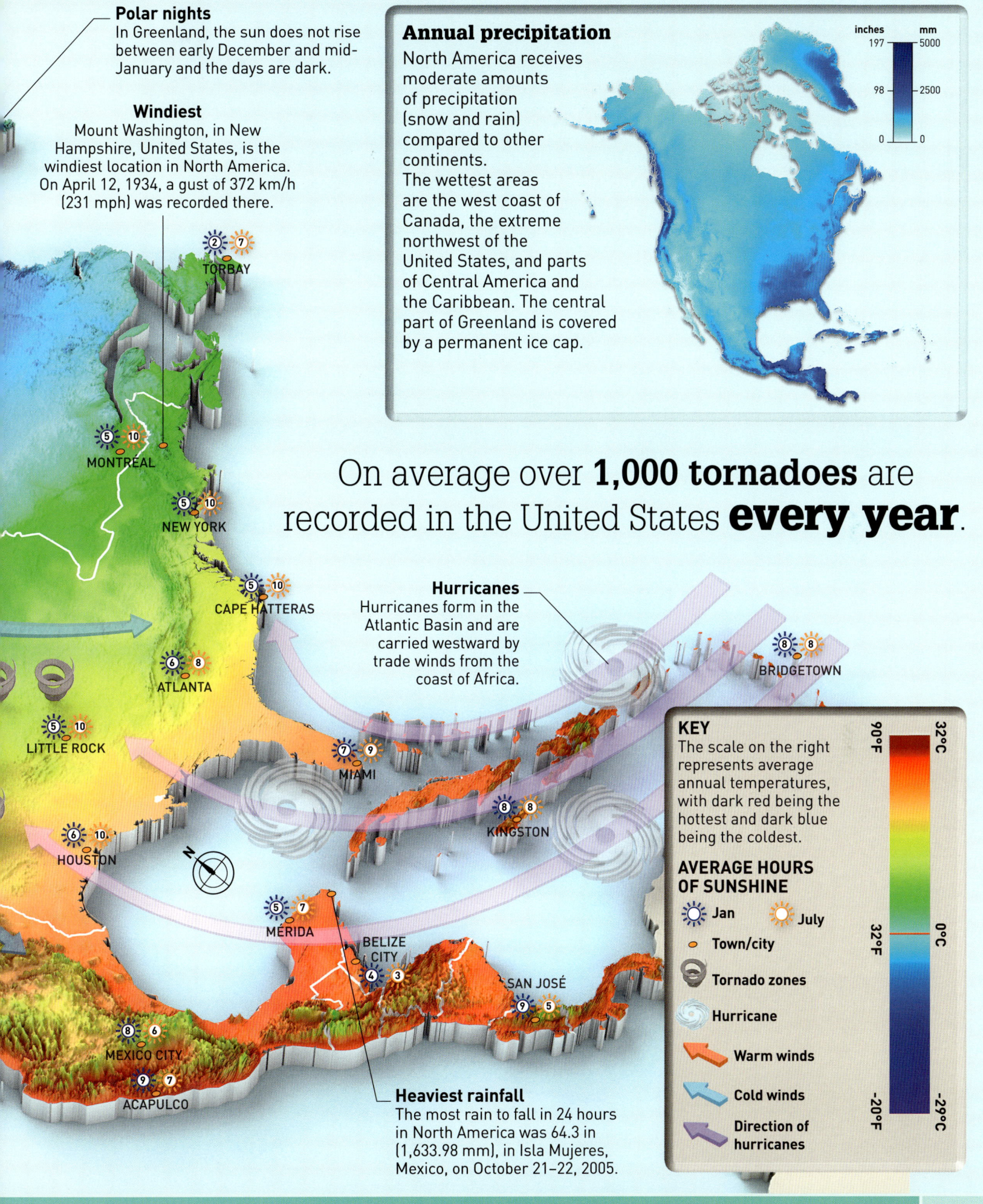

# NORTH AMERICA

## BIOMES
North America has a number of different biomes—large geographical areas of distinctive plant and animal groups—from deciduous forests in the south to tundra in the far north.

- Ice
- Tundra
- Boreal forest/Taiga
- Temperate coniferous forest
- Temperate broadleaf forest
- Temperate grassland
- Mediterranean
- Tropical coniferous forest
- Tropical broadleaf forest
- Tropical dry broadleaf forest
- Tropical, sub-tropical grassland
- Desert
- Flooded grassland
- Mangrove

**Walrus** — This mammal uses its tusks to haul its enormous 3,000 lb (1,500 kg) body out of the water.

**Harbor seal** — This common seal slows its heartbeat when swimming underwater.

**Musk ox** — Gets its name from the strong odor males emit during the rutting season.

**Ringed seal** — This seal can hold its breath underwater for 45 minutes.

**Snowy owl** — An unusual owl because it hunts by day.

**American black bear** — Short, non-retractable claws make it an excellent tree-climber.

**American bison** — North America's largest land mammal, it can weigh up to 1 ton (907 kg).

**Antelope** — The fastest land animal in North America, the antelope can reach speeds of 55 mph (88.5 km/h).

**Elk** — Male elk clash antlers in battle for mating rights.

**Arctic ground squirrel** — This squirrel doubles its weight during summer to prepare for a seven-month hibernation.

**Steller sea lion** — The largest sea lion species. Male bulls can be 2,205 lb (1,000 kg).

**Dall sheep** — This sheep has thick, curled horns that stop growing in the winter.

**Gray wolf** — Wolf pairs can track prey for up to 50 miles (80 km).

**Striped skunk** — This mammal's foul-smelling oil can be smelled up to 1 mile (1.6 km) away.

**Coyote** — A nocturnal canine that will eat whatever it finds.

**Hawaiian monk seal** — The only species of seal native to Hawaii. It is highly endangered.

**Great white shark** — A streamlined swimmer with powerful jaws that contain seven rows of knifelike teeth.

**Golden eagle** — North America's largest bird of prey can reach speeds of 200 mph (320 km/h) in a vertical dive.

**Bighorn sheep** — The horns of a male can weigh more than its whole skeleton.

NORTH AMERICA IS HOME TO 457 SPECIES OF MAMMALS, 4,000

# Wildlife

A diverse array of animals roams North America's lands and waters. The contrasting biomes—from freezing tundra in the north to tropical rain forest in the south—provide a remarkable range of habitats for countless species to survive and thrive.

**Gray seal**
Two fur layers and blubber help this seal keep warm in freezing water.

**Starnosed mole**
Nose tentacles help this mole identify food.

**Raccoon**
Dextrous front paws help this mammal snatch fish from rivers and pick snacks from the trash.

**River otter**
Webbed feet and sleek body make this playful mammal an excellent swimmer.

### ● Oldest and largest
Situated above a dormant (inactive) volcano, and boasting more than half of the world's great geysers, Yellowstone, in Wyoming, became the world's first national park in 1872. This has helped preserve the landscape from human exploitation, and protect its animal herds from poachers.

**Beaver**
Powerful jaws help this rodent fell trees and build dams in deep water.

**Lemon shark**
A stocky shark that lives in groups in tropical coastal waters.

**Rattlesnake**
Highly venomous, this snake grows new "rattle" segments when it sheds its skin.

**American alligator**
This extremely territorial and powerful predator can be 13 ft (4 m) long.

**Magnificent frigatebird**
An agile flier with long wings and a forked tail.

**Caribbean reef shark**
This shark lives on reefs, and can dive to 1,250 ft (380 m).

**Prairie dog**
A rodent that lives in underground towns on grasslands.

**Olive Ridley sea turtle**
A solitary, open-ocean dweller; females return to land to lay eggs.

**American crocodile**
The largest crocodile species, it lives in brackish (slightly salty) water.

ARACHNIDS (SPIDERS AND SCORPIONS), 914 BIRDS, AND 662 REPTILES.

NORTH AMERICA

### Canada
Despite its vast size (only the Russian Federation is larger), almost 90 percent of Canada is uninhabitable. The cold temperatures in the country's frozen north are too extreme for humans to live there.

### Hawaii
With 953,000 people, Oʻahu is the most populous of Hawaii's main islands.

PACIFIC OCEAN

Hawaiian Islands

### California
The Los Angeles-Long Beach-Anaheim area is the most densely populated region in the United States.

# By night

This image of North America at night provides a fascinating insight into where people live. The major urban areas are found in the eastern half of the United States, California, and central Mexico, but much of the northern half of the continent is uninhabited.

34     OF THE 50 STATES THAT MAKE UP THE UNITED STATES,

**Greenland**
This vast island has only 13 towns with a population of more than 1,000 people. The largest is Nuuk, which has a population of 16,500.

**Canada**
An estimated 90 percent of Canada's population live within 100 miles (160 km) of the US border.

**Great Lakes**
Towns and cities frame the shores of the Great Lakes, which are clearly visible in this image.

**District of Columbia**
Over 600,000 people live in an area of just 68 sq miles (177 sq km).

**Mexico**
Over half the country's 123.2 million population live in a small band of land in the center of the country.

**Costa Rica**
Has an urban population of 76.8 percent—the highest in Central America.

## Caribbean islands
Although some of North America's most densely populated territories can be found in the Caribbean region, some of the islands are also home to ever-growing rural populations.

● **Cayman Islands**—Along with Anguilla, Bermuda, and Sint Maarten, this is one of four North American territories with an entirely urban population.

● **Haiti**—A consequence of the devastating 2010 earthquake, the number of people living in towns increased by 3.78 percent between 2010 and 2015.

● **Montserrat**—Only 9 percent of this volcanic island's population live in an urban environment.

● **Trinidad and Tobago**—Fewer people live in towns here than anywhere else in North America.

**KEY**
Illuminated areas on the map reflect urban, built-up areas and roads, in contrast to rural regions.
- Rural area
- Urban area

MAINE HAS THE LOWEST URBAN POPULATION (38.7 PERCENT).

# SOUTH AMERICA

**Mountains and forests**
The Andes mountain range and the mighty Amazon rain forest dominate South America, which runs from the Caribbean Sea in the north to the Tierra del Fuego in the south.

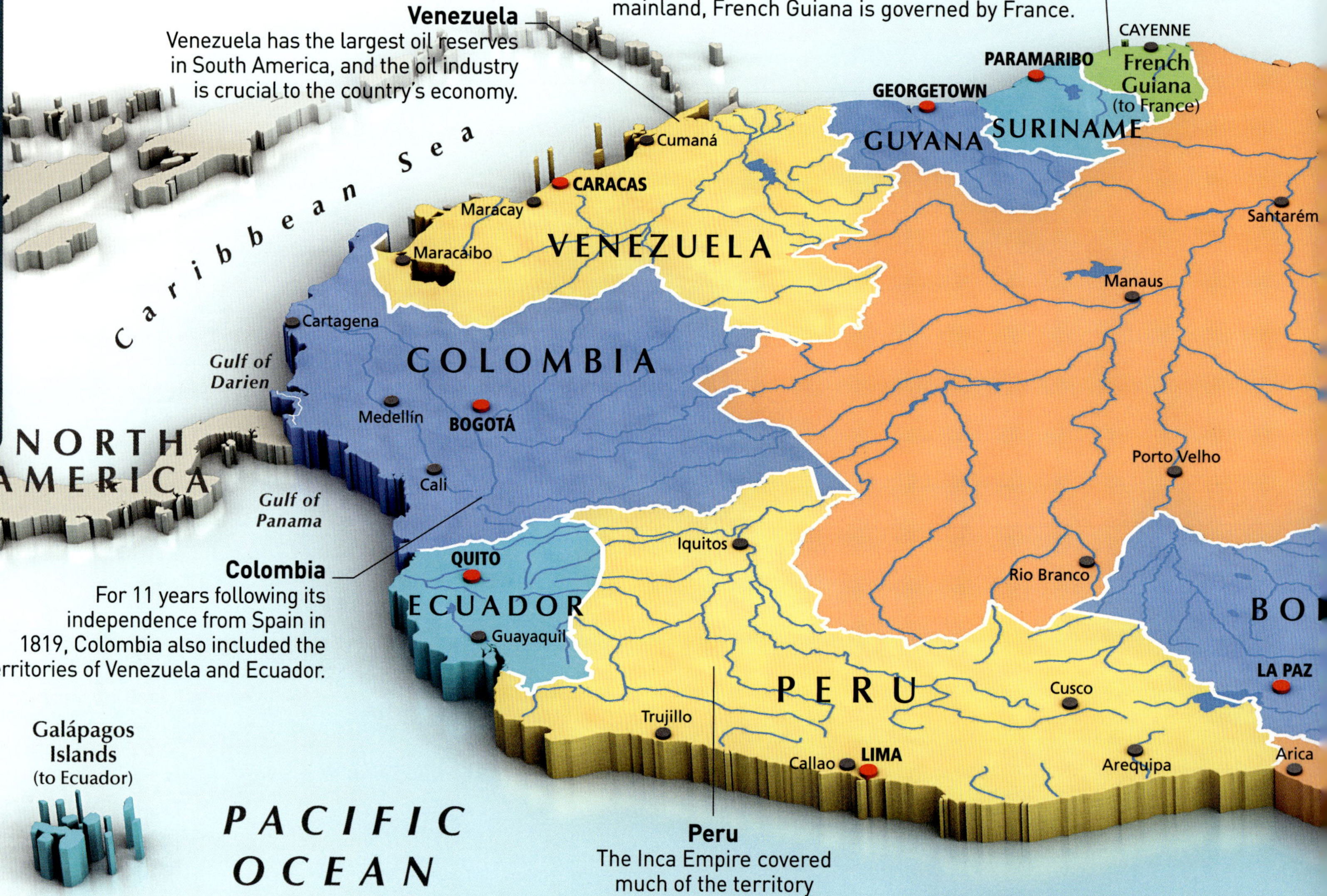

ATLANTIC OCEAN

**Venezuela**
Venezuela has the largest oil reserves in South America, and the oil industry is crucial to the country's economy.

**French Guiana**
The only remaining colony on the South American mainland, French Guiana is governed by France.

**Colombia**
For 11 years following its independence from Spain in 1819, Colombia also included the territories of Venezuela and Ecuador.

**Peru**
The Inca Empire covered much of the territory of modern Peru. It was overthrown by Spanish soldiers led by Francisco Pizarro in 1533.

# Countries and borders

For centuries, most of South America was under Spanish or Portuguese rule. Although the majority of countries became independent in the early 19th century, the languages and cultures of their past rulers have shaped the lives of people living there today.

### Simón Bolívar
Popularly known as "the Liberator," Simón Bolívar (1783–1830) was a Venezuelan military leader who played a major role in the continent's uprising against the Spanish Empire. His ideas—and dream of creating a united continent—continue to inspire many South Americans even today.

# Landscape

South America boasts an extraordinary range of landscapes, from the tropical forests on the northern coast to the icy fjords of Tierra del Fuego. The Andes mountains extend along the west coast, while the Amazon Basin dominates the heart of the continent. To the south lie the grasslands of the Pampas.

**The Orinoco**
This river flows in a vast arc through Venezuela, passing through the flat Llanos, where it creates vast floodplains during the rainy season.

**Guiana Highlands**
The tablelike mountains of the Guiana Highlands are surrounded by cliffs that rise up to 1,300 ft (400 m).

**The Colombian Andes**
The Andes separate into three ranges in Colombia. Two of the country's great rivers, the Río Magdalena and the Río Cauca, have their sources here.

**Galápagos Islands**
This isolated group of volcanic islands is home to a number of unique animal species.

**The Andes**
Spanning 4,350 miles (7,000 km) along the western side of South America, the Andes is the longest mountain range on Earth.

**The Altiplano**
The second highest plain in the world, the Altiplano, in Bolivia, has an average altitude of 12,303 ft (3,750 m).

**③ Lake Titicaca**
South America's largest lake, Lake Titicaca is the highest navigable body of water in the world, with an elevation of 12,500 ft (3,800 m). It is home to the Uros people, who live on floating islands made from reeds. One island even houses a meeting hall and a school.

40    LOCATED AT THE MOUTH OF THE AMAZON, ILHA DE

MARAJO IS THE WORLD'S LARGEST RIVER ISLAND.

# Fascinating facts

## BIGGEST GLACIER
Brüggen Glacier, Chile —488 sq miles (1,265 sq km) and 41 miles (66 km)

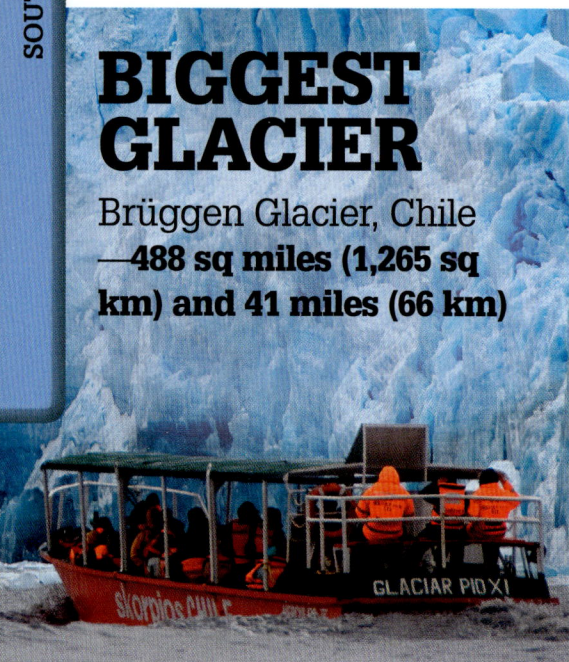

**Number of time zones** 4

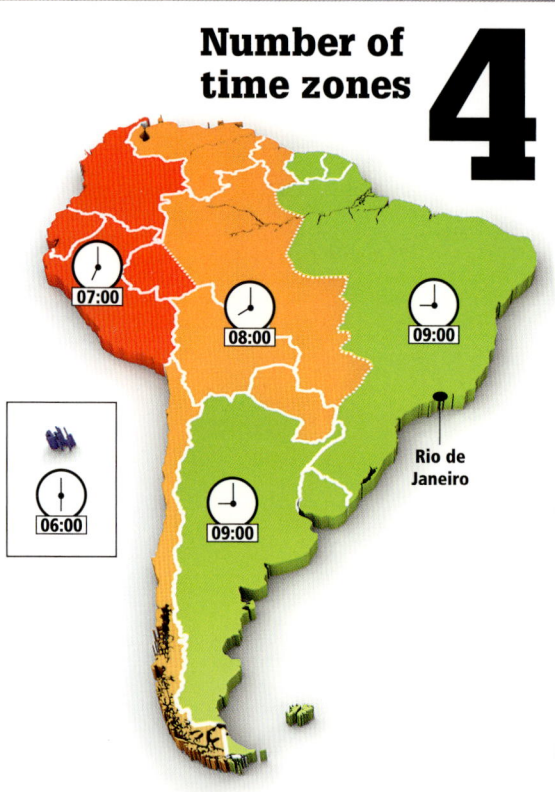

The world is split into 39 time zones. Most are set whole hours ahead or behind Coordinated Universal Time (UCT)—the time at the Greenwich Meridian in London, UK. Some, however, are whole hours plus 30 or 45 minutes ahead or behind UCT. Therefore, on this map, if it was 12:00 in London, it would be 09:00 in Rio de Janeiro, Brazil (3 hours behind UCT).

## COUNTRY WITH THE MOST NEIGHBORS

### Brazil (10)
French Guiana, **Suriname,** Guyana, **Venezuela,** Colombia, **Peru,** Bolivia, **Paraguay,** Argentina, **Uruguay**

## Longest tunnels

**Railroad tunnel**
Cuajone–El Sargento tunnel, Peru— 9.1 miles (14.72 km)

**Road tunnel**
Fernando Gomez Martinez tunnel, Colombia—2.86 miles (4.6 km)

**Number of official languages** 5
Portuguese ▪ Spanish ▪ English ▪ Dutch ▪ French

## Longest coastline

Brazil—**4,655 miles (7,491 km)**

## Most active volcano
Villarrica, Chile

## Busiest airport

Biggest airport São Paulo-Guarulhos Airport, Brazil—passengers in 2015: **35.96 million**

Tallest:
**Angel Falls, Venezuela** —3,212 ft (979 m)

Largest (by volume):
**Iguazú Falls, Brazil— Argentina—** 62,012 ft³ (1,756 m³) of water per second

## Tallest buildings

- **Gran Torre** Santiago, Chile 984 ft (300 m)
- **Parque Central Complex, East Tower** Caracas, Venezuela 738 ft (225 m)
- **Parque Central Complex, West Tower** Caracas, Venezuela 738 ft (225 m)
- **Torre Colpatria** Bogotá, Colombia 643 ft (196 m)
- **Titanium La Portada** Santiago, Chile 636 ft (194 m)

## Most visited cities (Visitors per year)

- Lima, Peru — 4.03 million
- São Paulo, Brazil — 2.3 million
- Buenos Aires, Argentina — 2.02 million
- Rio de Janeiro, Brazil — 1.37 million
- Bogotá, Colombia — 1.26 million

## South America's extreme points

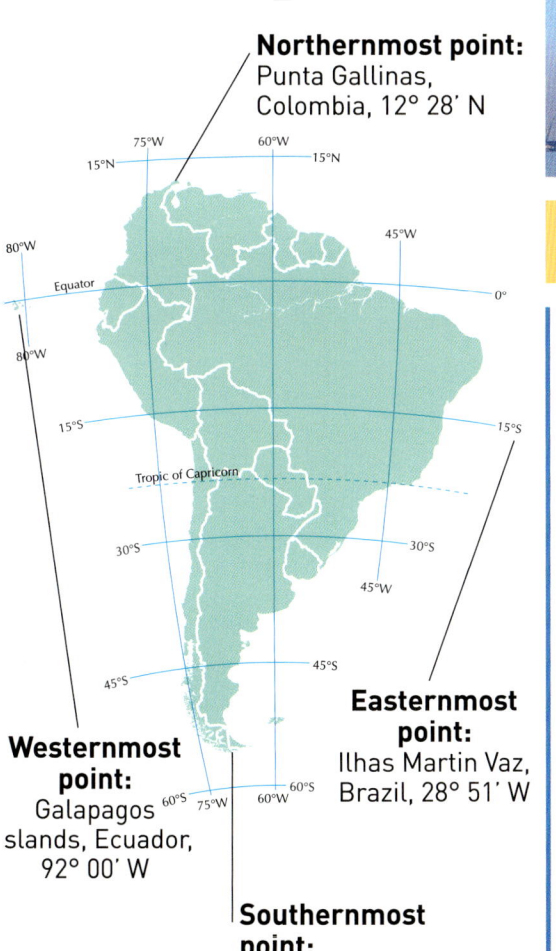

- **Northernmost point:** Punta Gallinas, Colombia, 12° 28' N
- **Westernmost point:** Galapagos Islands, Ecuador, 92° 00' W
- **Easternmost point:** Ilhas Martin Vaz, Brazil, 28° 51' W
- **Southernmost point:** Cape Horn, Chile, 55° 59' S

## Longest bridge

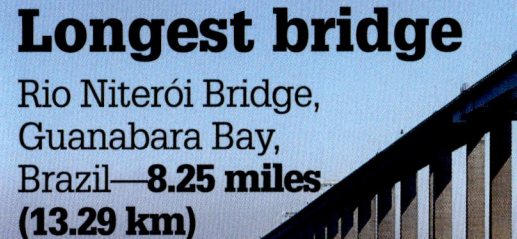

Rio Niterói Bridge, Guanabara Bay, Brazil—**8.25 miles (13.29 km)**

## Lowest point

Laguna del Carbón, Santa Cruz, Argentina—**-344 ft (-104.9 m)**

This is the seventh-lowest point on Earth's surface.

## Landlocked countries 2—Bolivia and Paraguay

## Highest mountains

1. **Aconcagua** Argentina 22,831 ft (6,959 m)
2. **Ojos del Salado** Argentina/Chile 22,572 ft (6,880 m)
3. **Bonete** Argentina 22,546 ft (6,872 m)
4. **Monte Pissis** Argentina 22,224 ft (6,774 m)
5. **Mercedario** Argentina 22,205 ft (6,768 m)

# Population

SOUTH AMERICA

**KEY**
The colors represent the number of people living per square mile/square kilometer.

**POPULATION DENSITY**

| people per sq mile | people per sq km |
|---|---|
| above 2,600 | above 1,000 |
| 1,950 | 750 |
| 1,300 | 500 |
| 650 | 250 |
| 260 | 100 |
| 130 | 50 |

**Colombia**
South America's second-most densely populated country is Colombia, with 41 people per sq km (106 people per sq mile).

**Paramaribo**
240,000 people live in the capital of Suriname, about half the country's population.

**French Guiana**
This French overseas department is home to 244,118 people.

**The Amazon**
The river provides the only means of transport here, and many towns and villages are found on its riverbanks.

**Ecuador**
15.9 million people live in Ecuador. It is the most densely populated country in South America, with 145 people per sq mile (56 people per sq km).

**Iquitos**
More than 400,000 people live in the largest city on the Peruvian section of the Amazon River. Iquitos can only be reached by boat or plane.

**Lima**
8.9 million people live in Lima, the capital of Peru. Its population has almost doubled since 1980.

**São Paulo**
The discovery of gold near São Paulo in the 1690s attracted settlers from around the world. Today, South America's largest city is a bustling business center, with a population of 12 million.

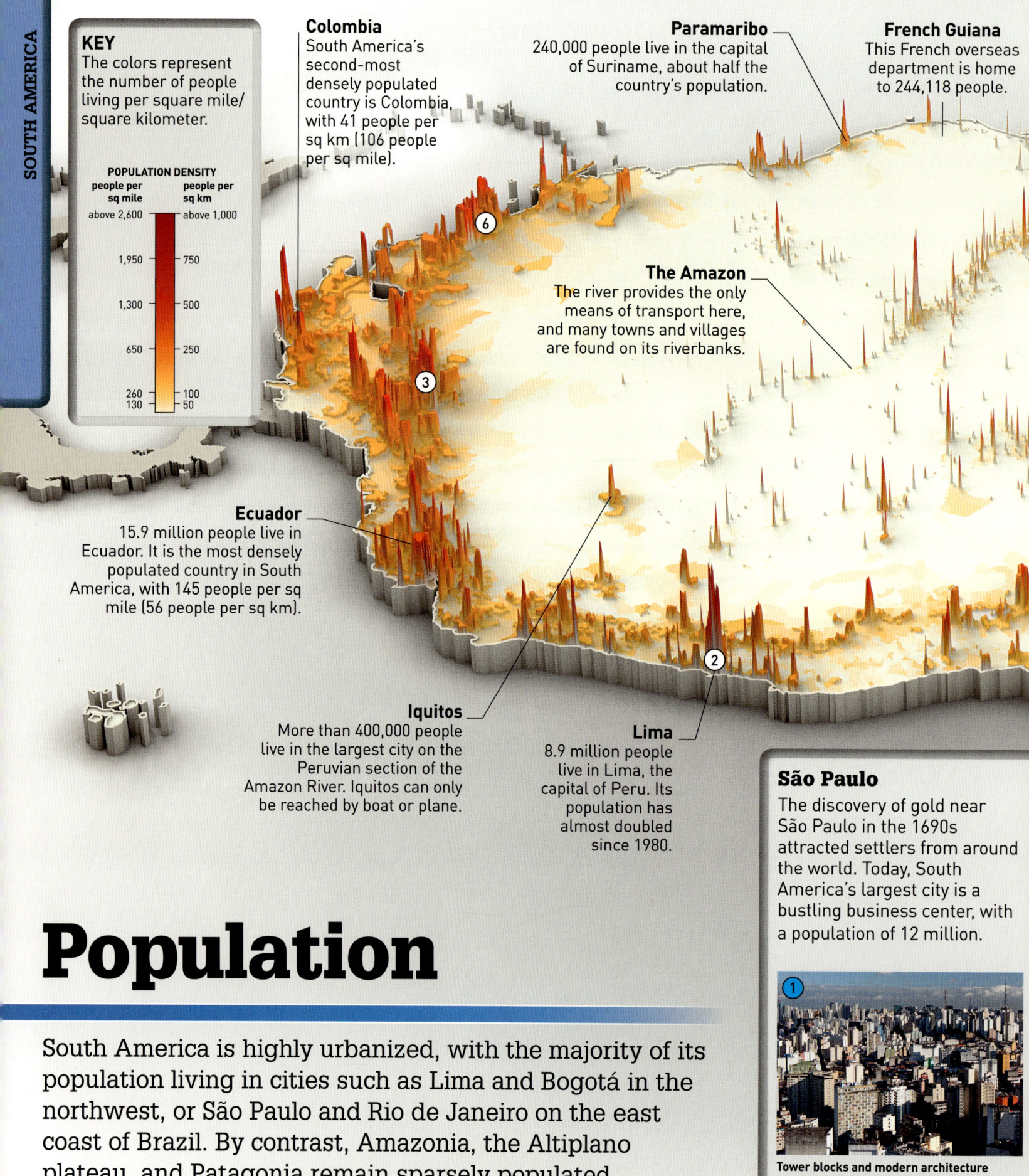

Tower blocks and modern architecture dominate downtown São Paulo.

South America is highly urbanized, with the majority of its population living in cities such as Lima and Bogotá in the northwest, or São Paulo and Rio de Janeiro on the east coast of Brazil. By contrast, Amazonia, the Altiplano plateau, and Patagonia remain sparsely populated.

BRAZIL IS THE FIFTH LARGEST COUNTRY IN THE WORLD—

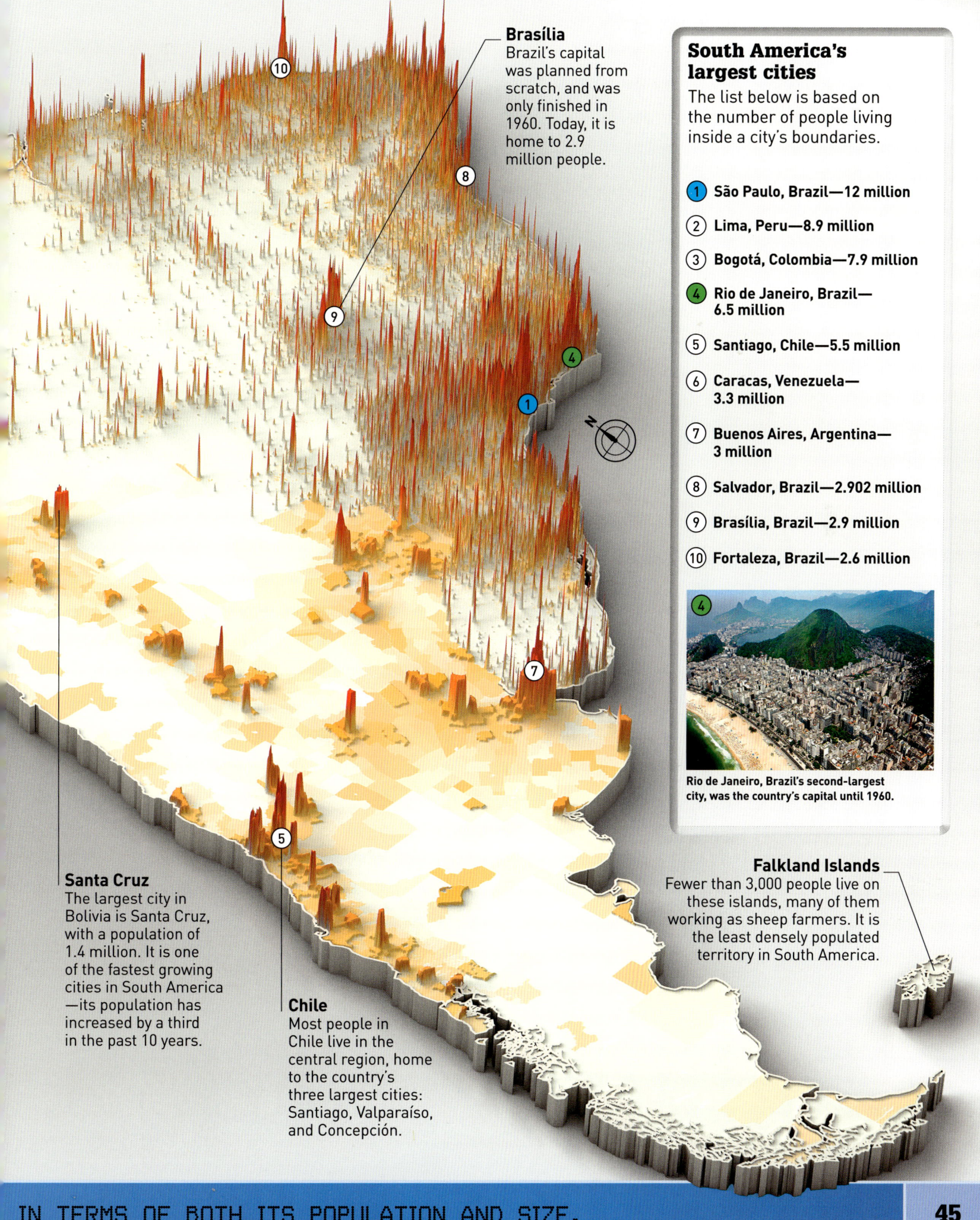

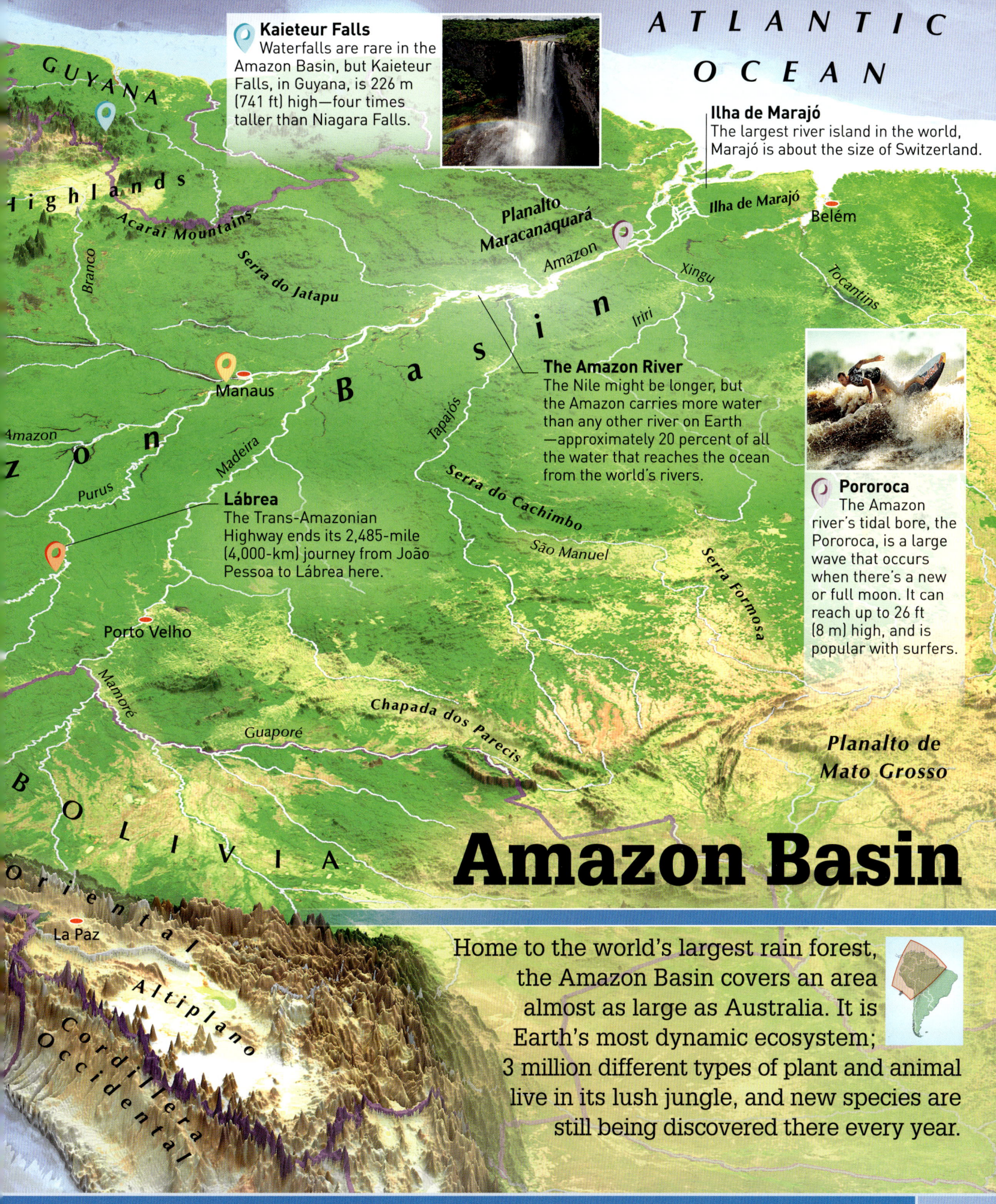

# Amazon Basin

**Kaieteur Falls**
Waterfalls are rare in the Amazon Basin, but Kaieteur Falls, in Guyana, is 226 m (741 ft) high—four times taller than Niagara Falls.

**Ilha de Marajó**
The largest river island in the world, Marajó is about the size of Switzerland.

**The Amazon River**
The Nile might be longer, but the Amazon carries more water than any other river on Earth—approximately 20 percent of all the water that reaches the ocean from the world's rivers.

**Pororoca**
The Amazon river's tidal bore, the Pororoca, is a large wave that occurs when there's a new or full moon. It can reach up to 26 ft (8 m) high, and is popular with surfers.

**Lábrea**
The Trans-Amazonian Highway ends its 2,485-mile (4,000-km) journey from João Pessoa to Lábrea here.

Home to the world's largest rain forest, the Amazon Basin covers an area almost as large as Australia. It is Earth's most dynamic ecosystem; 3 million different types of plant and animal live in its lush jungle, and new species are still being discovered there every year.

RAINFALL ANNUALLY. MOST OF IT FALLS BETWEEN NOVEMBER AND MAY.

SOUTH AMERICA

**Angel Falls**
At 3,212 ft (979 m), Angel Falls is the world's tallest waterfall—more than twice the height of the Empire State Building.

**Presidential Palace,** *Suriname*

**Coro historic town,** *Venezuela*

**Angel Falls,** *Venezuela*

**Teatro Amazonas,** *Brazil*

**Castillo San Felipe de Barajas,** *Colombia*

**Santa Barbara Church,** *Colombia*

**San Agustín Archaeological Park,** *Colombia*

**Jesuit missions,** *Bolivia*

**El Panecillo Statue,** *Ecuador*

**Giant tortoise**
11 species of giant tortoise live on the Galápagos Islands. Many live for more than 100 years.

**Machu Picchu,** *Peru*

**Tiwanaku,** *Bolivia*

**Giant tortoise,** *Galápagos*

**Chan Chan,** *Peru*

**Sacred city of Caral-Supe,** *Peru*

**Wak'a Wallamarka,** *Peru*

**Nazca Lines,** *Peru*

**Chan Chan**
The largest pre-Columbian city in the Americas, Chan Chan was built by the Chimu people in around 850 CE. Many of the city's walls have crumbled over time, but several statues have survived.

**Nazca Lines**
Hundreds of geometric patterns cover the Nazca Desert. About 70 of them are images of animals, but they can only be seen in full from an aircraft.

**Christ the Redeemer**
Looking down from the summit of Mount Corcovado onto Rio de Janeiro, Christ the Redeemer is one of the continent's best-loved landmarks. Finished in 1931, the 128-ft (39-m) tall statue took five years to build.

# Famous landmarks

South America is home to an incredible wealth of cultural sites, ranging from the Inca ruins of Machu Picchu to the modern architecture of Brasília. It also boasts awe-inspiring natural wonders, such as Venezuela's Angel Falls and the glaciers of Chile and Argentina.

● The giant statue of Jesus Christ towers over Brazil's second city, Rio de Janeiro.

48 THE CUEVA DE LAS MANOS IS A CAVE IN ARGENTINA COVERED WITH

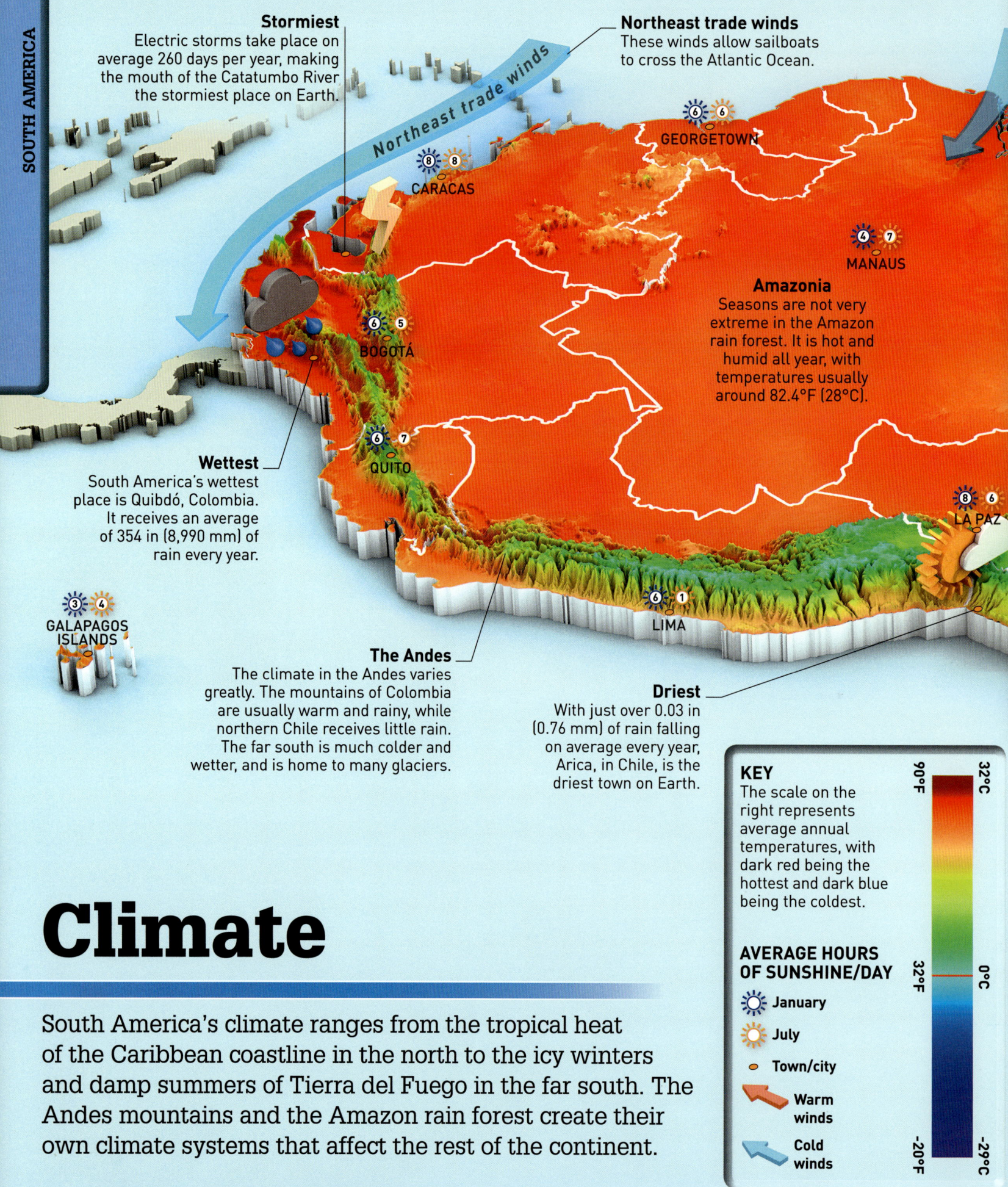

# Climate

South America's climate ranges from the tropical heat of the Caribbean coastline in the north to the icy winters and damp summers of Tierra del Fuego in the far south. The Andes mountains and the Amazon rain forest create their own climate systems that affect the rest of the continent.

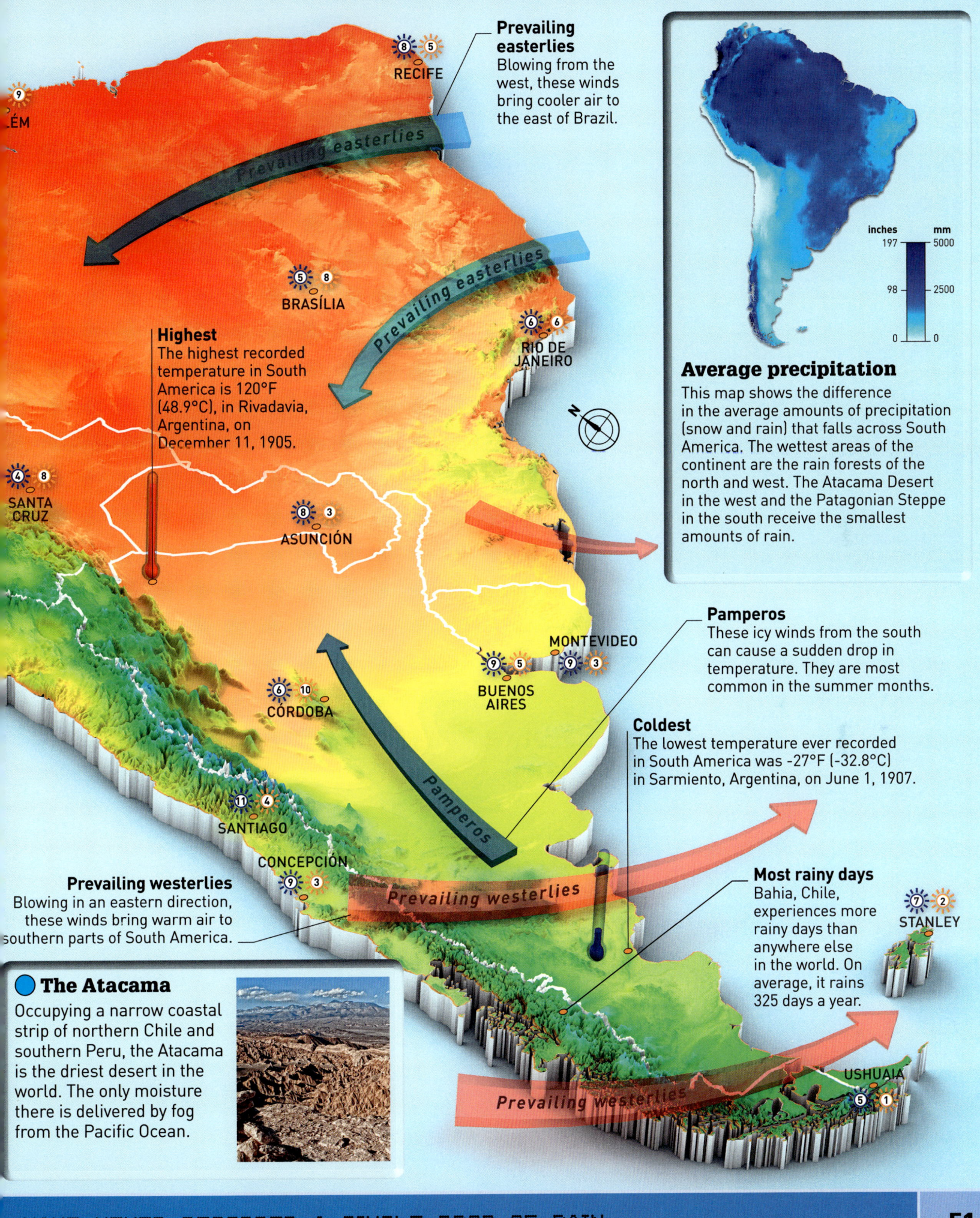

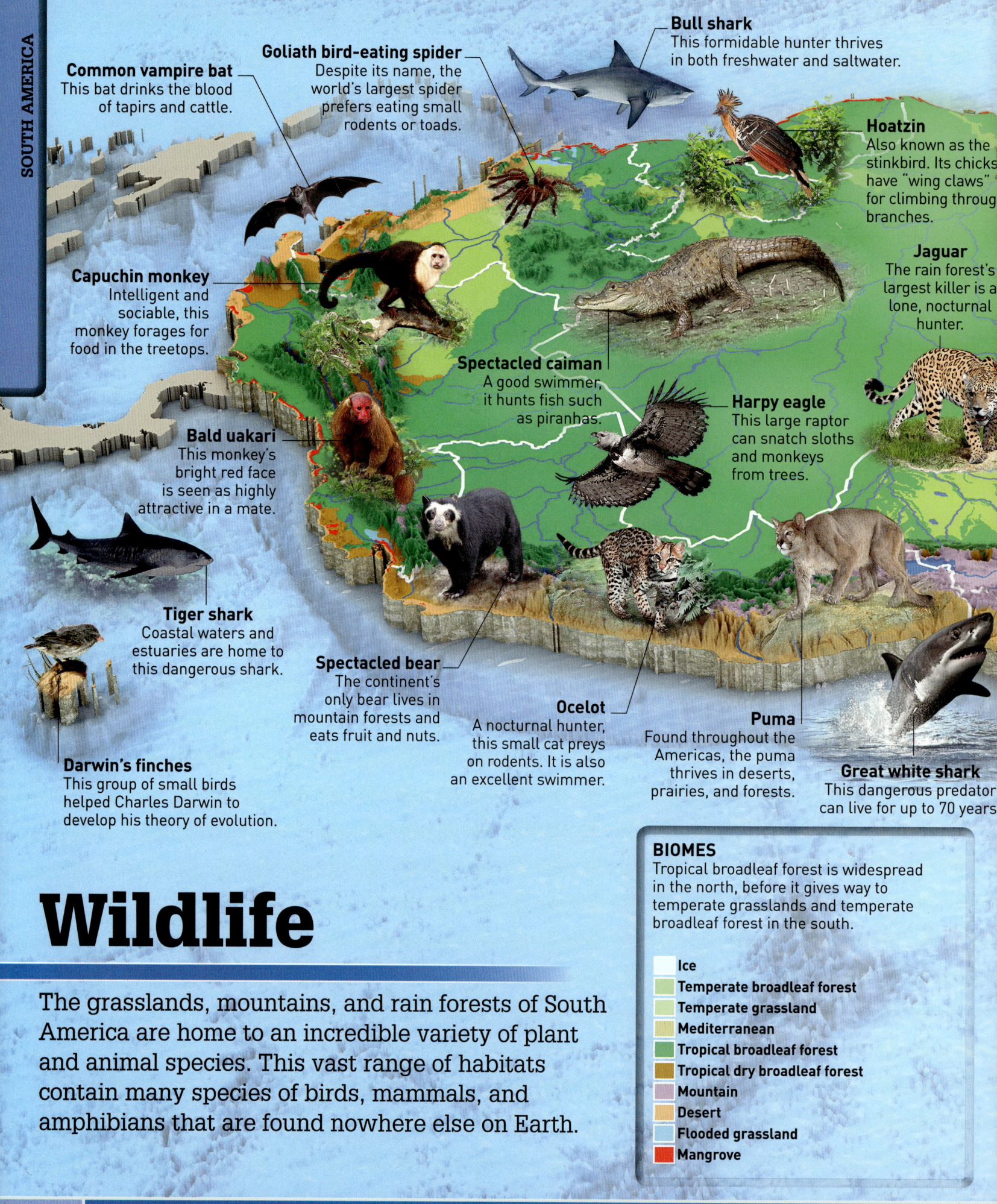

SOUTH AMERICA

**Common vampire bat** — This bat drinks the blood of tapirs and cattle.

**Goliath bird-eating spider** — Despite its name, the world's largest spider prefers eating small rodents or toads.

**Bull shark** — This formidable hunter thrives in both freshwater and saltwater.

**Hoatzin** — Also known as the stinkbird. Its chicks have "wing claws" for climbing throug branches.

**Capuchin monkey** — Intelligent and sociable, this monkey forages for food in the treetops.

**Jaguar** — The rain forest's largest killer is a lone, nocturnal hunter.

**Bald uakari** — This monkey's bright red face is seen as highly attractive in a mate.

**Spectacled caiman** — A good swimmer, it hunts fish such as piranhas.

**Harpy eagle** — This large raptor can snatch sloths and monkeys from trees.

**Tiger shark** — Coastal waters and estuaries are home to this dangerous shark.

**Spectacled bear** — The continent's only bear lives in mountain forests and eats fruit and nuts.

**Ocelot** — A nocturnal hunter, this small cat preys on rodents. It is also an excellent swimmer.

**Puma** — Found throughout the Americas, the puma thrives in deserts, prairies, and forests.

**Great white shark** — This dangerous predator can live for up to 70 years.

**Darwin's finches** — This group of small birds helped Charles Darwin to develop his theory of evolution.

**BIOMES**
Tropical broadleaf forest is widespread in the north, before it gives way to temperate grasslands and temperate broadleaf forest in the south.

- Ice
- Temperate broadleaf forest
- Temperate grassland
- Mediterranean
- Tropical broadleaf forest
- Tropical dry broadleaf forest
- Mountain
- Desert
- Flooded grassland
- Mangrove

# Wildlife

The grasslands, mountains, and rain forests of South America are home to an incredible variety of plant and animal species. This vast range of habitats contain many species of birds, mammals, and amphibians that are found nowhere else on Earth.

THE JAGUAR IS AN EXCELLENT SWIMMER AND HAS EVEN

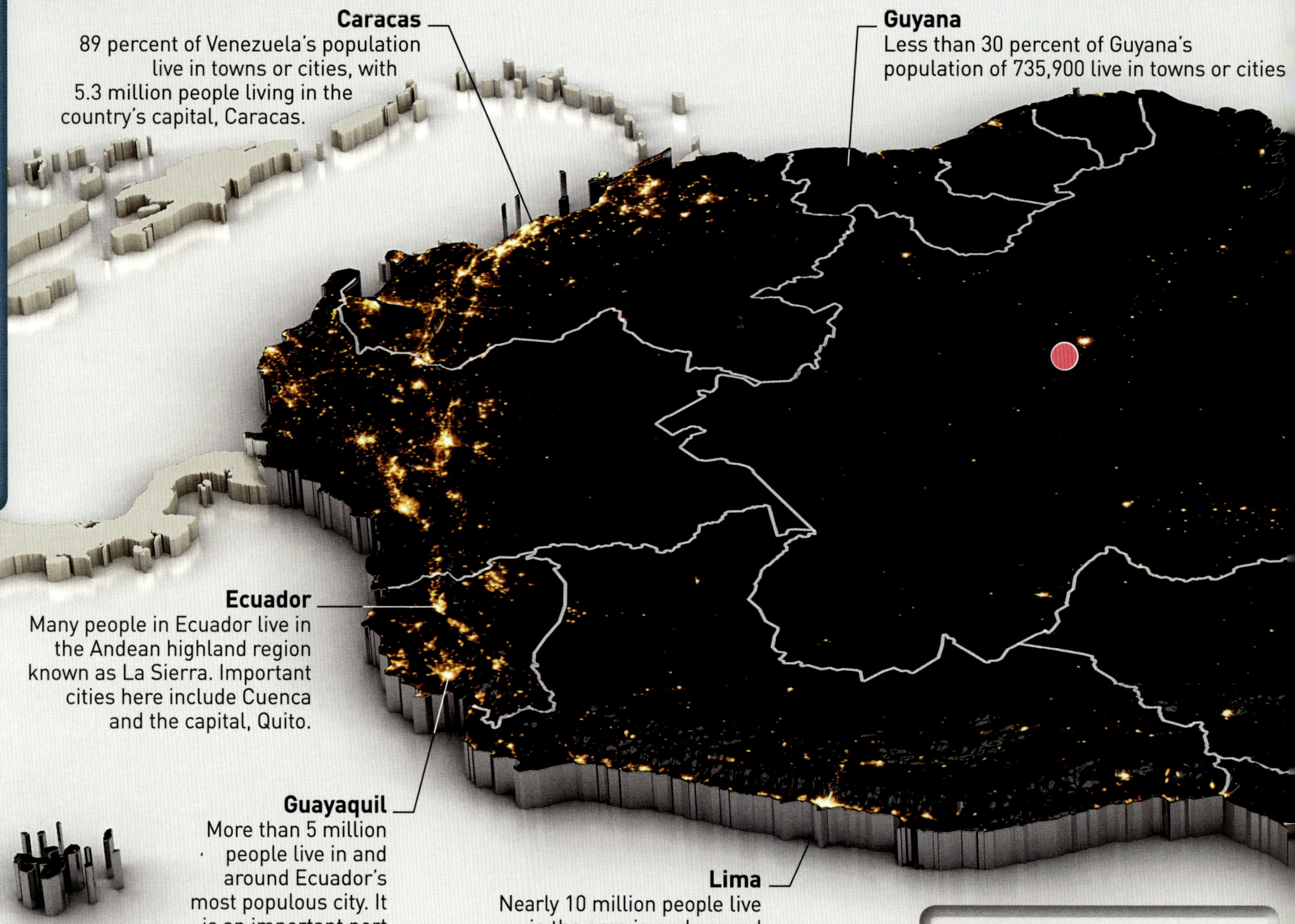

SOUTH AMERICA

**Caracas**
89 percent of Venezuela's population live in towns or cities, with 5.3 million people living in the country's capital, Caracas.

**Guyana**
Less than 30 percent of Guyana's population of 735,900 live in towns or cities

**Ecuador**
Many people in Ecuador live in the Andean highland region known as La Sierra. Important cities here include Cuenca and the capital, Quito.

**Guayaquil**
More than 5 million people live in and around Ecuador's most populous city. It is an important port and business centre.

**Lima**
Nearly 10 million people live in the area in and around the Peruvian capital.

Almost **one half** of South America's population lives **in Brazil**.

# By night

The brightly lit urban areas of Ecuador, Colombia, and Venezuela dominate the northwest of the continent. The cities of southeast Brazil, meanwhile, contrast sharply with the dark expanses of Amazonia, in which only occasional dots of light mark the rain forest's few settlements.

● **Manaus**
Located at the heart of the Amazon rain forest, Manaus, with a population of 2 million, is the largest city in Amazonia. This lively port made its wealth in the 19th century through the rubber trade.

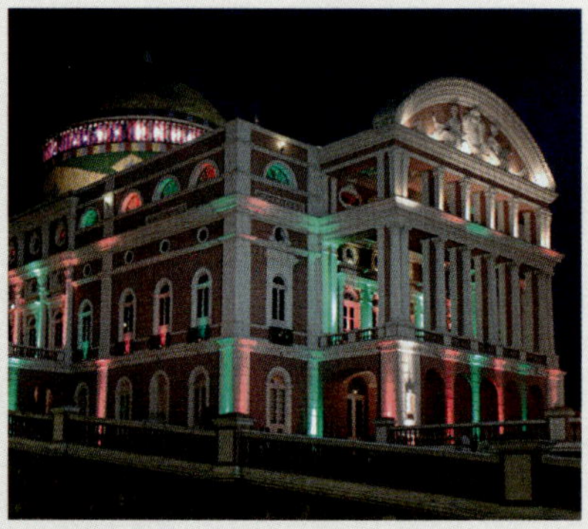

The opera house in Manaus is one of the grandest buildings in Amazonia.

SURINAME IS SOUTH AMERICA'S MOST SPARSELY POPULATED COUNTRY,

# AFRICA

**Africa from space**
The Equator splits Africa between the northern and southern hemispheres. It is bordered by the Mediterranean, the Red Sea, and the Atlantic and Indian Oceans.

# Countries and borders

Africa's different kingdoms were brutally split up between European nations in the 19th century. After World War Two, struggle for independence, as well as civil wars, created new nations, re-drawn borders, and disputed territories.

**Algeria**
Algeria is Africa's largest country, and more than 80 percent of it is made up of the Sahara Desert. Its main cities are all in the north.

**Liberia**
Claiming independence as early as 1847, it became a new home to many African-American former slaves.

**Nigeria**
It is known as the "Giant of Africa" for its large population (186 million) and booming economy (the 20th largest in the world).

**KEY**
- 🔴 Capital city
- ⚫ Major city

## FAST FACTS

**Total land area:**
11,712,409 sq miles (30,335,000 sq km)

**Total population:**
1.1 billion

**Number of countries:** 53

**Largest country:**
Algeria—919,595 sq miles (2,381,741 sq km)

**Smallest country:**
Seychelles—176 sq miles (455 sq km)

**Largest country population:**
Nigeria—186 million

**KEY**
The colors on the map represent the height of the land in relation to sea level.

**ELEVATION**

| Feet | Meters |
|---|---|
| above 26,247 | above 8,000 |
| 22,965 | 7,000 |
| 19,685 | 6,000 |
| 16,404 | 5,000 |
| 13,123 | 4,000 |
| 9,842 | 3,000 |
| 6,560 | 2,000 |
| 3,280 | 1,000 |
| Sea level 0 | 0 Sea level |

**Niger River**
From its source in the Guinea Highlands, the Niger flows north, into the desert, and then back south, before flowing into the Gulf of Guinea.

**Low-lying coasts**
Mangroves, swamps, and sandy beaches line much of West Africa's coast.

**Sahel**
The dry grasslands of the Sahel are slowly turning into desert due to drought and human activity.

# Landscape

Africa has many extreme landscapes. Deserts spread across the north and south, while rain forests dominate the continent's tropical central and western parts. The land rises toward the east, culminating in the Ethiopian Highlands and the Great Rift Valley region, home to Africa's largest lakes and mountains.

**FAST FACTS**

**1 Highest point:**
Kilimanjaro—19,341 ft (5,895 m)

**2 Longest river:**
Nile—4,160 miles (6,695 km)

**3 Largest lake:**
Lake Victoria—26,828 sq miles (69,484 sq km)

**4 Largest island:**
Madagascar—229,345 sq miles (594,000 sq km)

THE CONGO BASIN, DRAINED BY THE CONGO RIVER, CONTAINS THE

# Fascinating facts

AFRICA

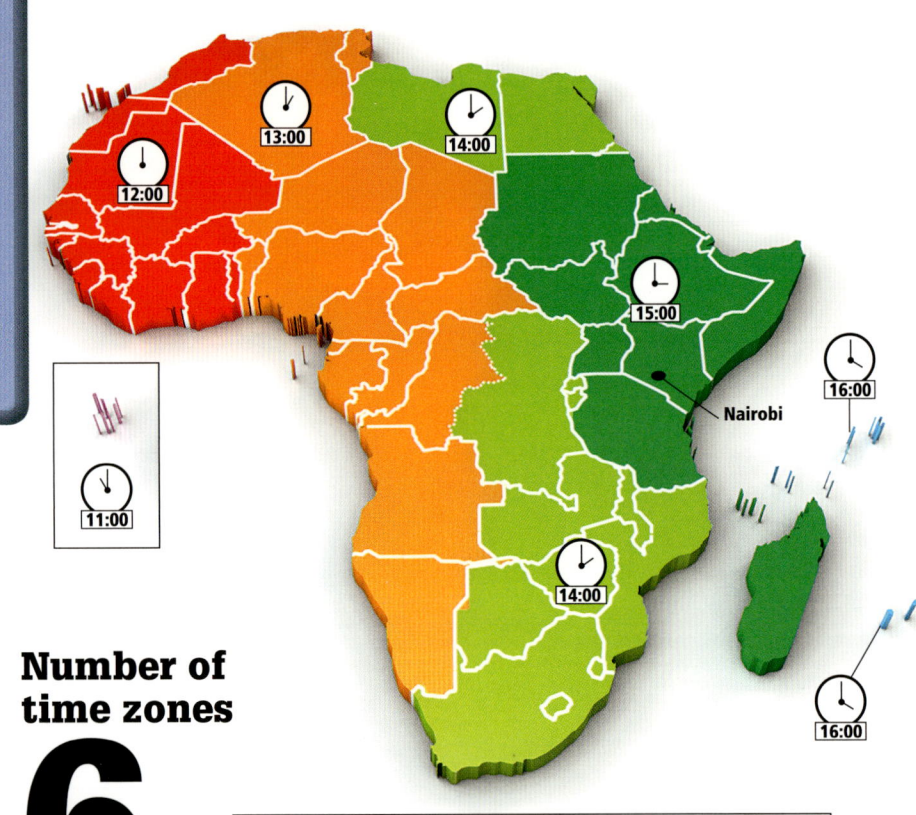

**Number of time zones**
# 6

The world is split into 39 time zones. Most are set whole hours ahead or behind Coordinated Universal Time (UCT)—the time at the Greenwich Meridian in London, UK. Some, however, are whole hours plus 30 or 45 minutes ahead or behind UCT. Therefore, on this map, if it was 12:00 in London, it would be 15:00 in Nairobi, Kenya (3 hours ahead of UCT).

## COUNTRIES WITH THE MOST NEIGHBORS

### Tanzania (8)
Burundi, **Democratic Republic of Congo**, Kenya, **Malawi**, Mozambique, **Rwanda**, Uganda, **Zambia**

### Zambia (8)
Angola, **Botswana**, Democratic Republic of Congo, **Malawi**, Mozambique, **Namibia**, Tanzania, **Zimbabwe**

## LONGEST BRIDGE
**6th October Bridge**, **Cairo**, **Egypt**— 12.7 miles (20.5 km)

# 16 LANDLOCKED COUNTRIES
Botswana ▪ **Burkina Faso** ▪ Burundi ▪ **Central African Republic** ▪ Chad ▪ **Ethiopia** ▪ Lesotho ▪ **Malawi** ▪ Mali ▪ **Niger** ▪ Rwanda ▪ **South Sudan** ▪ Eswatini ▪ **Uganda** ▪ Zambia ▪ **Zimbabwe**

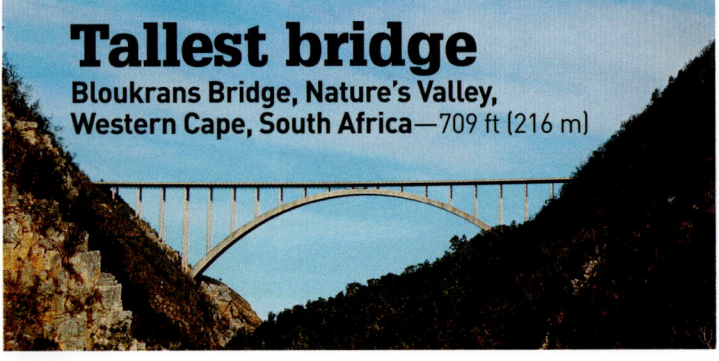

## Tallest bridge
Bloukrans Bridge, Nature's Valley, Western Cape, South Africa—709 ft (216 m)

**Number of languages spoken**
more than **2,000**

# LAKES

- **Largest: Lake Victoria**, Uganda / Tanzania / Kenya— 26,828 sq miles (69,484 sq km)

**Deepest: Lake Tanganyika**, Burundi / Democratic Republic of Congo / Tanzania / Zambia—4,823 ft (1,470 m) deep

# WATERFALLS

Tallest: **Tugela Falls**, South Africa— 3,110 ft (948 m)

- Largest (by volume): **Victoria Falls**, Zimbabwe / Zambia— 38,422 ft³ (1,088 m³) of water per second

**LONGEST COASTLINE** Madagascar—3,000 miles (4,828 km)

**Busiest airport** O.R. Tambo International, Johannesburg, South Africa—**19.164 million passengers per year**

**Longest railroad line**
The Blue Train, Pretoria–Cape Town, South Africa— 994 miles (1,600 km)

**Longest subway system**
Cairo Metro, Egypt— 48 miles (78 km)

# AFRICA'S EXTREME POINTS

**Northernmost point:** Jalta, Tunisia 37° 31′ N

**Easternmost point:** Raas Xaafuun, Somalia 51° 24′ E

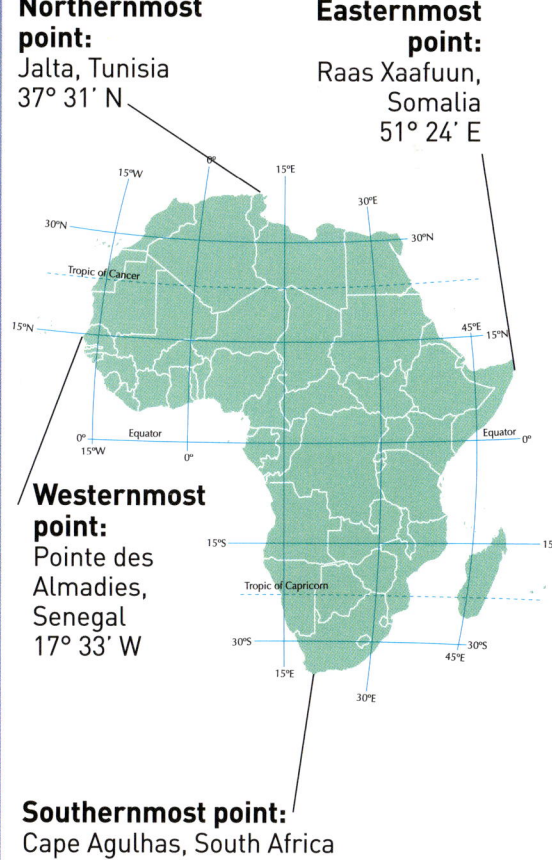

**Westernmost point:** Pointe des Almadies, Senegal 17° 33′ W

**Southernmost point:** Cape Agulhas, South Africa 34° 52′ S

## Most visited cities (Visitors per year)

- Johannesburg, S. Africa — 3.6 million
- Cairo, Egypt — 1.5 million
- Cape Town, S. Africa — 1.4 million
- Casablanca, Morocco — 1.1 million
- Durban, S. Africa — 0.8 million

## Most active volcano
Nyamuragira, **Democratic Republic of Congo**

# LOWEST POINT
**Lake 'Assal, Djibouti**— 512 ft (156 m) below sea level

# AFRICA

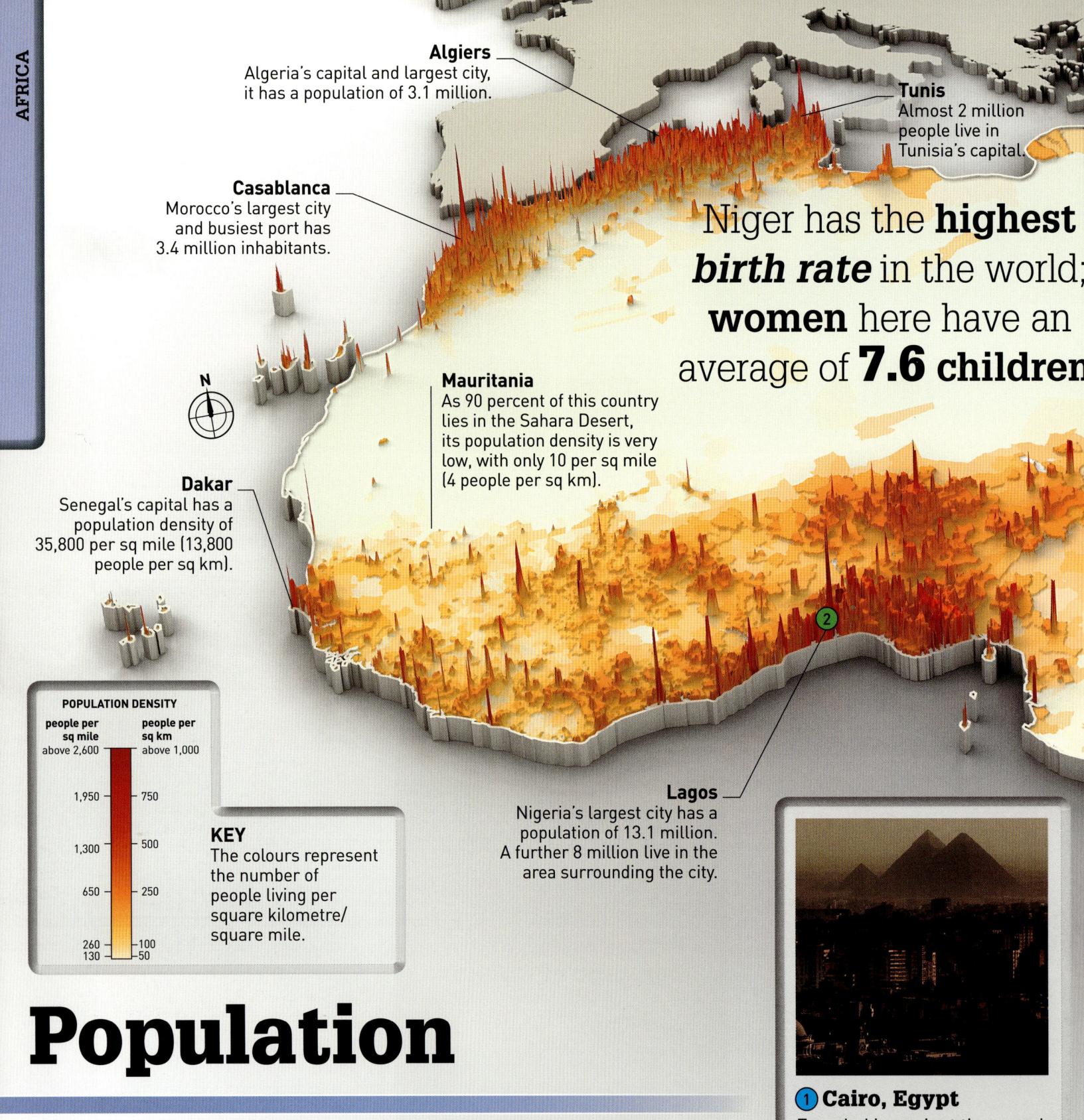

**Algiers** — Algeria's capital and largest city, it has a population of 3.1 million.

**Tunis** — Almost 2 million people live in Tunisia's capital.

**Casablanca** — Morocco's largest city and busiest port has 3.4 million inhabitants.

Niger has the **highest birth rate** in the world; **women** here have an average of **7.6 children**

**Mauritania** — As 90 percent of this country lies in the Sahara Desert, its population density is very low, with only 10 per sq mile (4 people per sq km).

**Dakar** — Senegal's capital has a population density of 35,800 per sq mile (13,800 people per sq km).

**Lagos** — Nigeria's largest city has a population of 13.1 million. A further 8 million live in the area surrounding the city.

**POPULATION DENSITY**

| people per sq mile | people per sq km |
|---|---|
| above 2,600 | above 1,000 |
| 1,950 | 750 |
| 1,300 | 500 |
| 650 | 250 |
| 260 | 100 |
| 130 | 50 |

**KEY** The colours represent the number of people living per square kilometre/ square mile.

# Population

Africa, the birthplace of our earliest human ancestors, is the second-most populous continent in the world (after Asia). But because the continent is so large, its average population density is low—only half that of Europe. In reality, some regions are very crowded, while others, like the Sahara, are almost deserted.

**① Cairo, Egypt**
Founded in ancient times and Egypt's capital since 1168, Cairo is Africa's largest city, with 18.7 million inhabitants. Greater Cairo sprawls in all directions, and includes the famous pyramids at Giza.

THE WORLD'S FIRST HOMININS (EARLY HUMANS) APPEARED IN

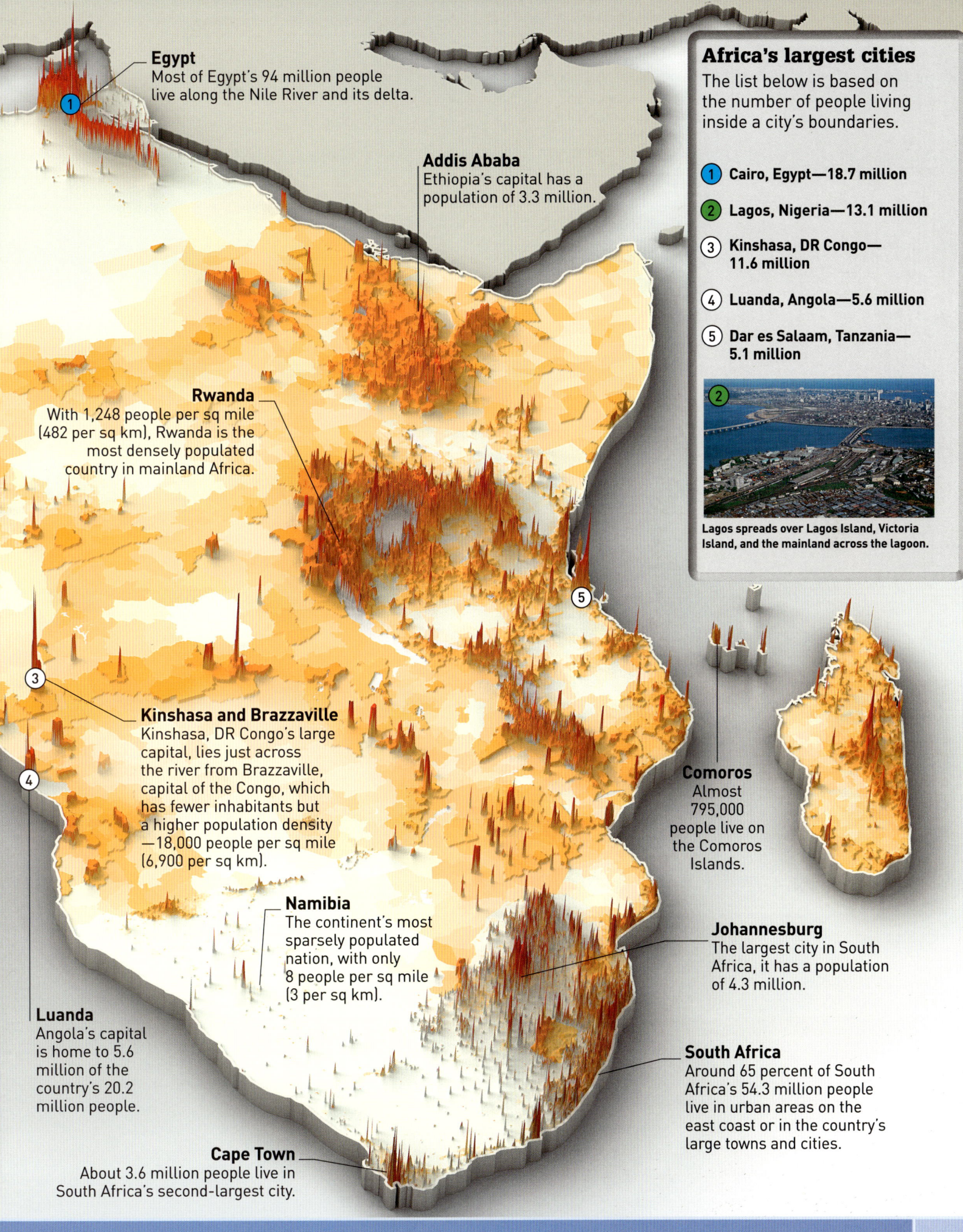

# AFRICA

**Red Sea**
Formed when the African and Arabian plates split apart, and still widening, this salty sea can reach over 30°C (86°F). Its coral reefs are teeming with fish.

**Rwenzori Mountains**
The snow-capped peaks of this range in the Western Rift Valley include Mount Stanley, Africa's third highest mountain at 16,762 ft (5,109 m).

**Lake Victoria**
Africa's largest lake lies on the plateau located between the Great Rift Valley's eastern and western branch. At its widest, it measures 209 miles (337 km) across.

**Western Rift Valley**
The western branch of the Great Rift Valley is characterized by deep lakes and high mountain ranges.

**Lake Tanganyika**
The longest of the Rift Valley's many lakes, Tanganyika is also the world's second deepest lake, at 4,710 ft (1,436 m).

IN THE FUTURE, THE LAND EAST OF THE RIFT WILL FORM A NEW

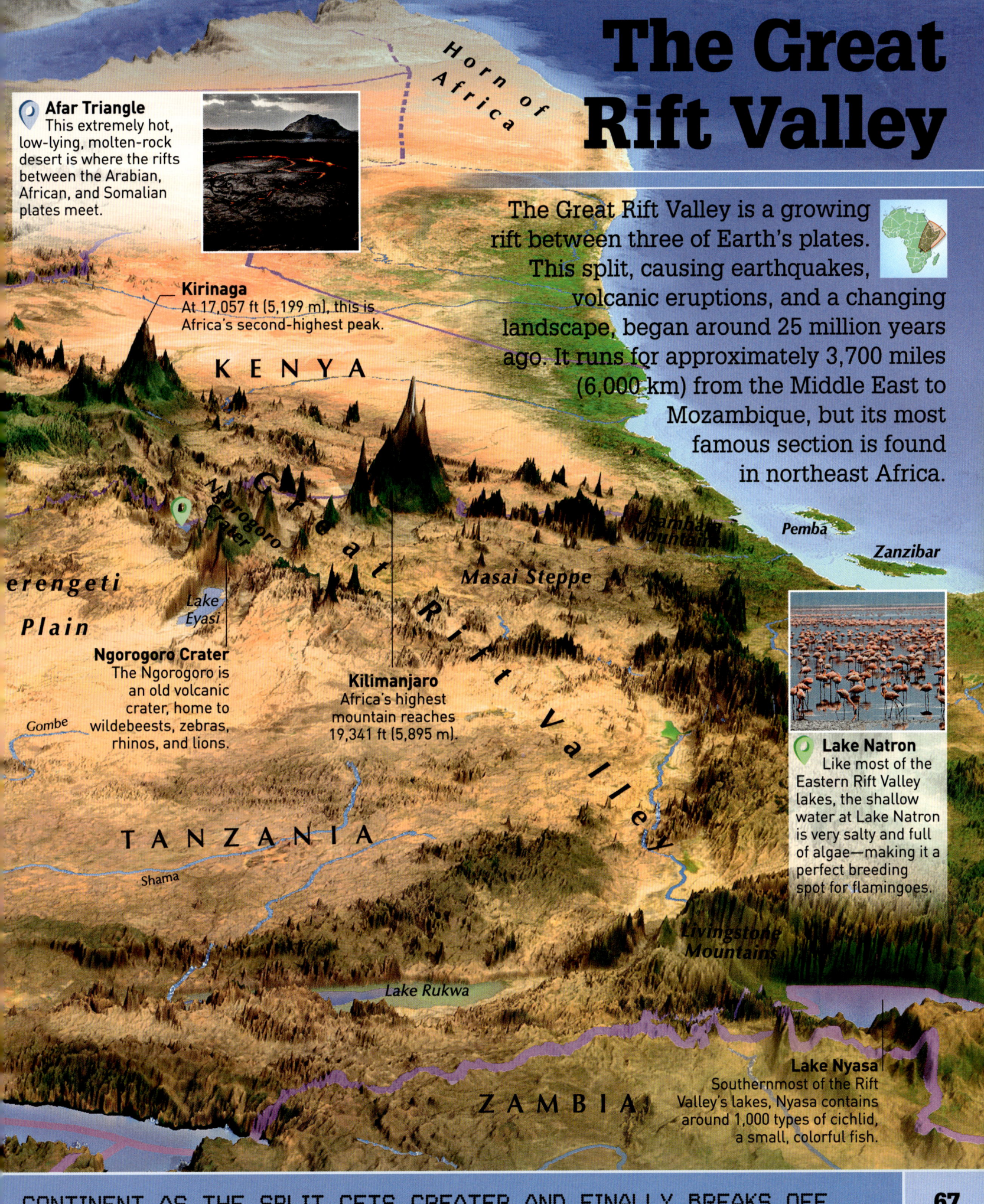

# The Great Rift Valley

**Afar Triangle**
This extremely hot, low-lying, molten-rock desert is where the rifts between the Arabian, African, and Somalian plates meet.

The Great Rift Valley is a growing rift between three of Earth's plates. This split, causing earthquakes, volcanic eruptions, and a changing landscape, began around 25 million years ago. It runs for approximately 3,700 miles (6,000 km) from the Middle East to Mozambique, but its most famous section is found in northeast Africa.

**Kirinaga**
At 17,057 ft (5,199 m), this is Africa's second-highest peak.

**Ngorogoro Crater**
The Ngorogoro is an old volcanic crater, home to wildebeests, zebras, rhinos, and lions.

**Kilimanjaro**
Africa's highest mountain reaches 19,341 ft (5,895 m).

**Lake Natron**
Like most of the Eastern Rift Valley lakes, the shallow water at Lake Natron is very salty and full of algae—making it a perfect breeding spot for flamingoes.

**Lake Nyasa**
Southernmost of the Rift Valley's lakes, Nyasa contains around 1,000 types of cichlid, a small, colorful fish.

CONTINENT AS THE SPLIT GETS GREATER AND FINALLY BREAKS OFF.

## AFRICA

**Roman towns** — Timgad is one of North Africa's many ancient Roman settlements. *Timgad, Algeria*

**Leptis Magna** ancient Roman site, *Libya*

**Desert stop-offs** — Trading centers that served travelers crossing the Sahara Desert in the 11th and 12th centuries.

**Koutoubia Mosque,** *Marrakesh, Morocco*

**Great pyramid** — The oldest of Giza's three pyramids was built over 4,500 years ago.

**Afzejare Arch,** *Acacus Mountains, Libya*

**Guelta d'Archei,** *Chad*

**Ancient Ksour of Ouadane,** *Mauritania*

**Koutammakou** — The mud-tower houses (takienta) of the Batammariba tribe have become a symbol of Togo.

**Agadez Mosque,** *Niger*

**Guelta d'Archei** — The most famous desert pool in the Sahara, it has been a resting place for travelers and their camels for thousands of years.

**Island of Gorée,** *Senegal*

**Great Mosque,** *Djenné, Mali*

**Koutammakou,** *Togo*

**Osun-Osogbo Sacred Grove,** *Nigeria*

**Dzanga-Sangha Special Reserve,** *Central African Republic*

**Stone circles of Senegambia,** *Senegal and The Gambia*

**Greater Accra forts,** *Ghana*

**Kisantu Cathedral,** *Democratic Rep. of Congo*

**Grim reminder** — Gorée, an island off the coast of Senegal's capital, Dakar, was the largest slave-trading center in Africa between the 15th and 19th centuries.

**Sacred Grove** — The Yoruba people of Nigeria once prayed to their many gods in sacred places in the forest. This grove, honoring the river goddess Osun, is one of the last left.

# Famous landmarks

Africa boasts breathtaking natural beauty and ancient archeological wonders. It is home to the rich wildlife of the Serengeti and the thunderous waters of Victoria Falls. Towering minarets, ancient pyramids, and monumental mud-brick architecture reflect the continent's rich cultural history.

● **Great Mosque, Djenné**
Djenné was one of the great cities of the rich Mali Empire, one of Africa's medieval kingdoms, and its mosque was a famous center of learning. Built of sun-baked bricks made of sand and earth, it was reconstructed in 1907.

FISH RIVER CANYON IS AFRICA'S BIGGEST CANYON: 100 MILES (160 KM)

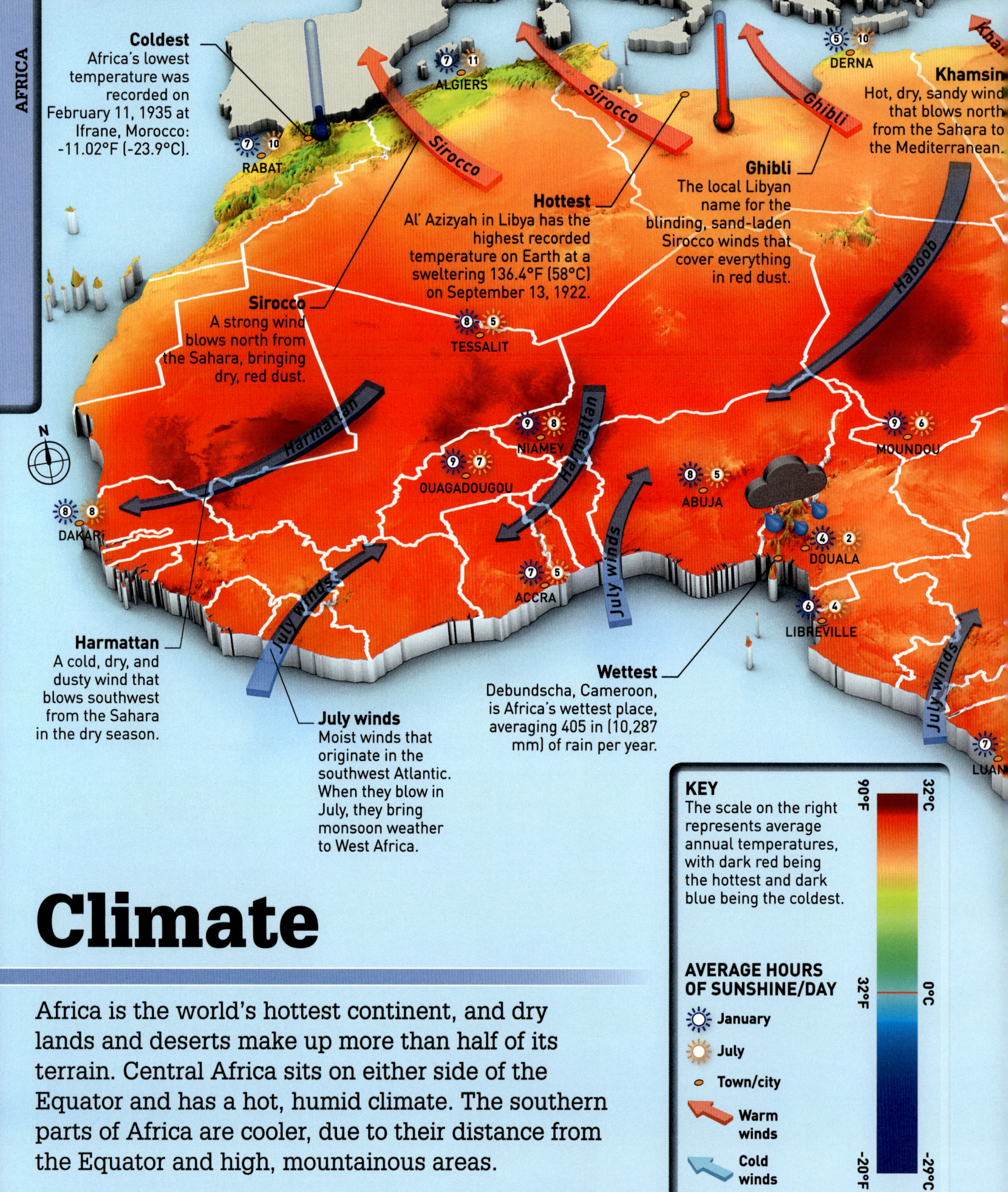

# Climate

Africa is the world's hottest continent, and dry lands and deserts make up more than half of its terrain. Central Africa sits on either side of the Equator and has a hot, humid climate. The southern parts of Africa are cooler, due to their distance from the Equator and high, mountainous areas.

STORMS HAVE CARRIED SAND FROM THE SAHARA DESERT AS

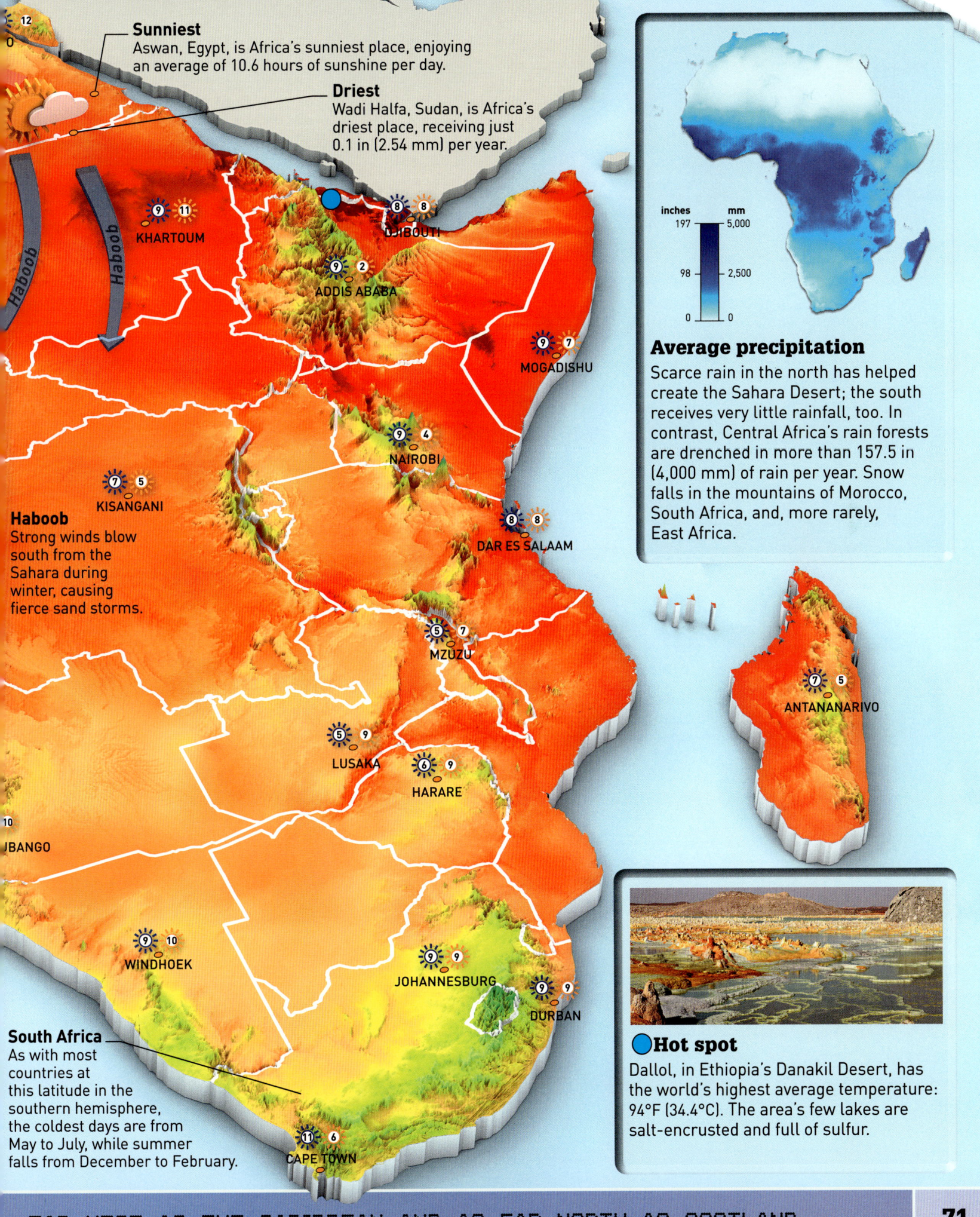

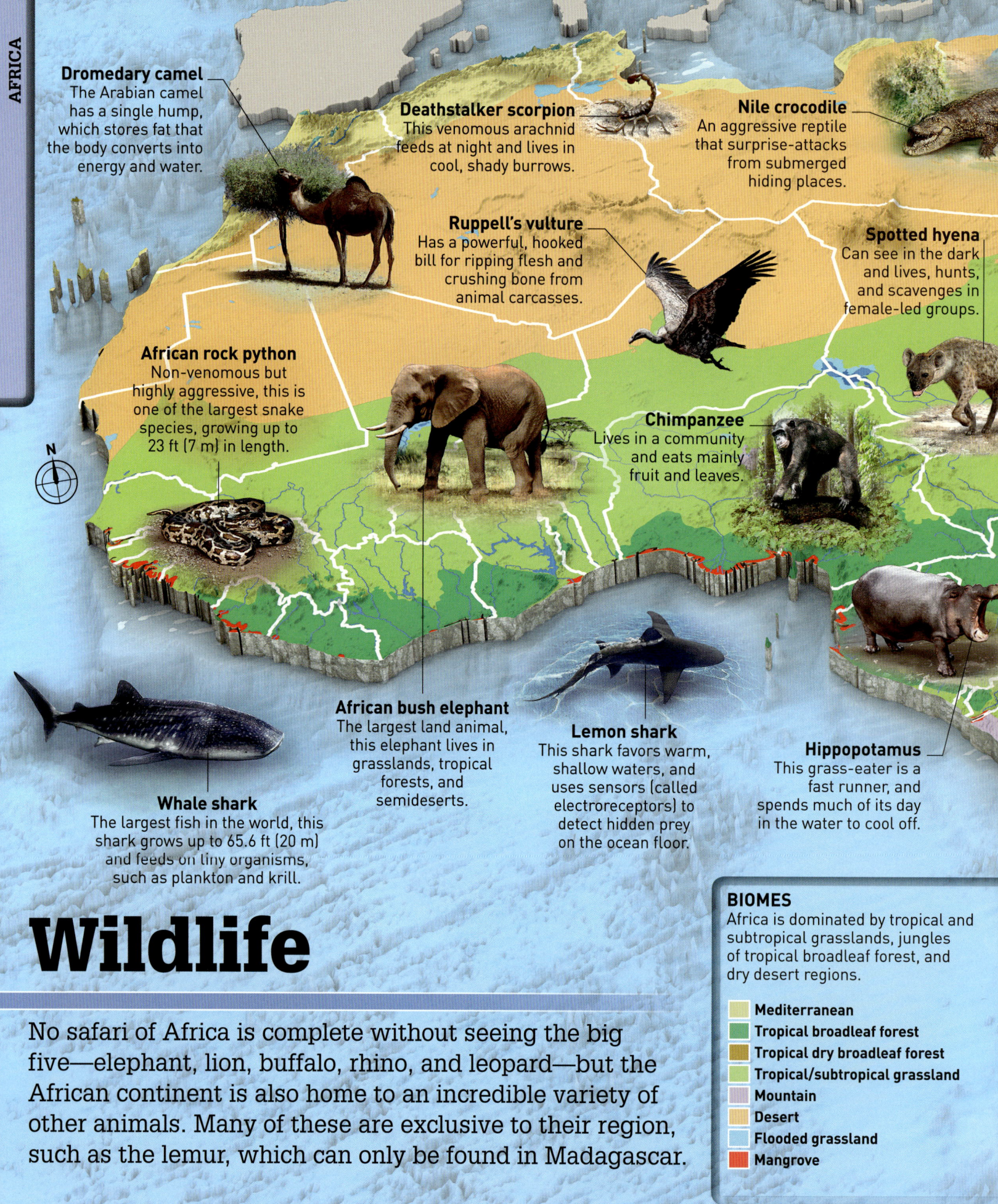

# Wildlife

No safari of Africa is complete without seeing the big five—elephant, lion, buffalo, rhino, and leopard—but the African continent is also home to an incredible variety of other animals. Many of these are exclusive to their region, such as the lemur, which can only be found in Madagascar.

**BIOMES**
Africa is dominated by tropical and subtropical grasslands, jungles of tropical broadleaf forest, and dry desert regions.

- Mediterranean
- Tropical broadleaf forest
- Tropical dry broadleaf forest
- Tropical/subtropical grassland
- Mountain
- Desert
- Flooded grassland
- Mangrove

MADAGASCAR IS FAMOUS FOR ITS UNIQUE ANIMALS; 97 PERCENT OF

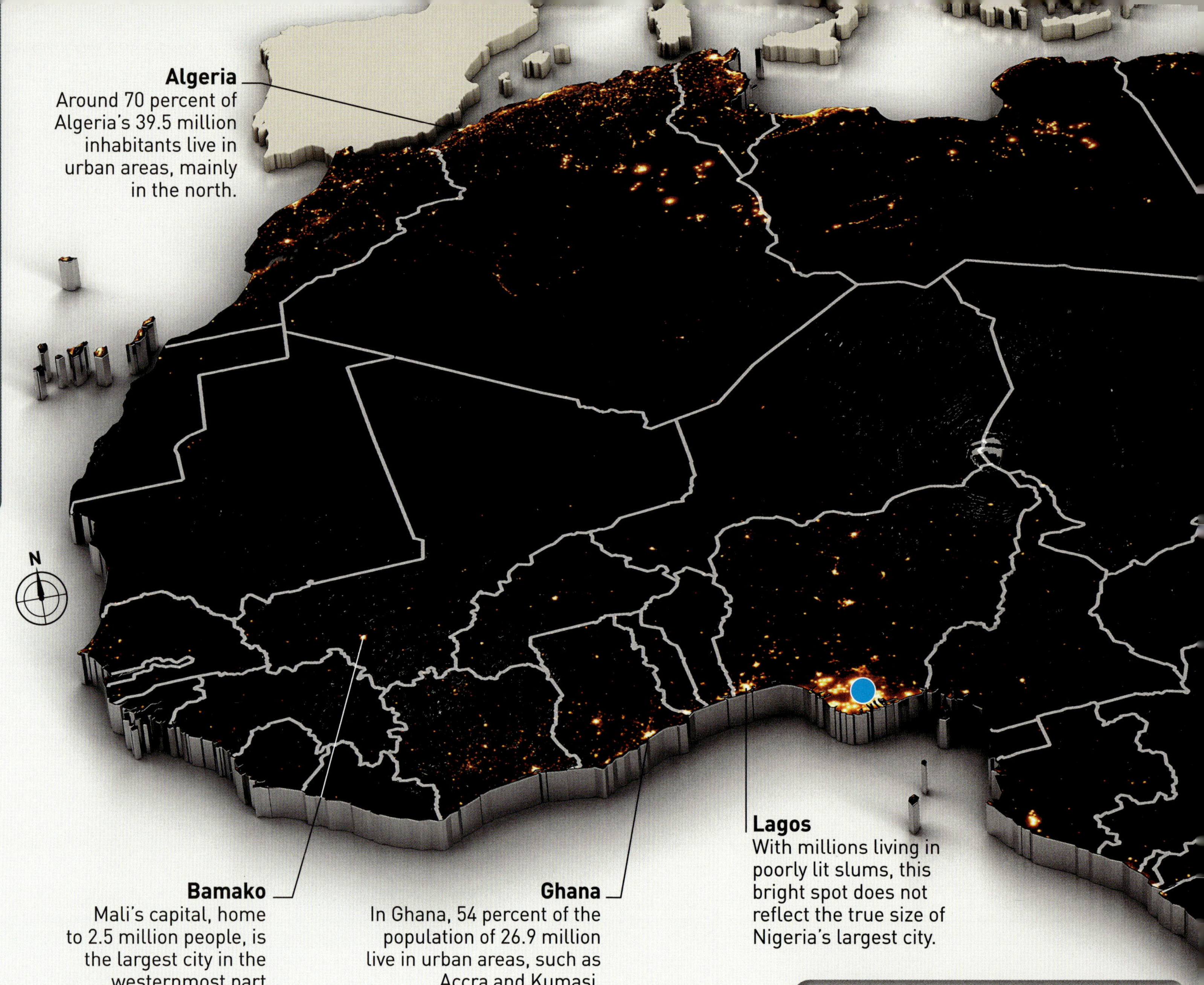

## AFRICA

**Algeria**
Around 70 percent of Algeria's 39.5 million inhabitants live in urban areas, mainly in the north.

**Bamako**
Mali's capital, home to 2.5 million people, is the largest city in the westernmost part of West Africa.

**Ghana**
In Ghana, 54 percent of the population of 26.9 million live in urban areas, such as Accra and Kumasi.

**Lagos**
With millions living in poorly lit slums, this bright spot does not reflect the true size of Nigeria's largest city.

# By night

The speed at which cities grow in population is very high in Africa. But here, not all densely populated places show up at night—poorer areas do not have street lights, lit-up store windows, or even electric indoor lights. Most dark areas, however, are desert, jungle, or savanna.

● **Niger Delta oil fields**
Much of the strong glow in Nigeria's Niger Delta comes from the many oil fields, with their open gas flares, big refineries, and busy ports.

74　　SOUTH SUDAN HAS THE FASTEST-GROWING POPULATION OF ANY

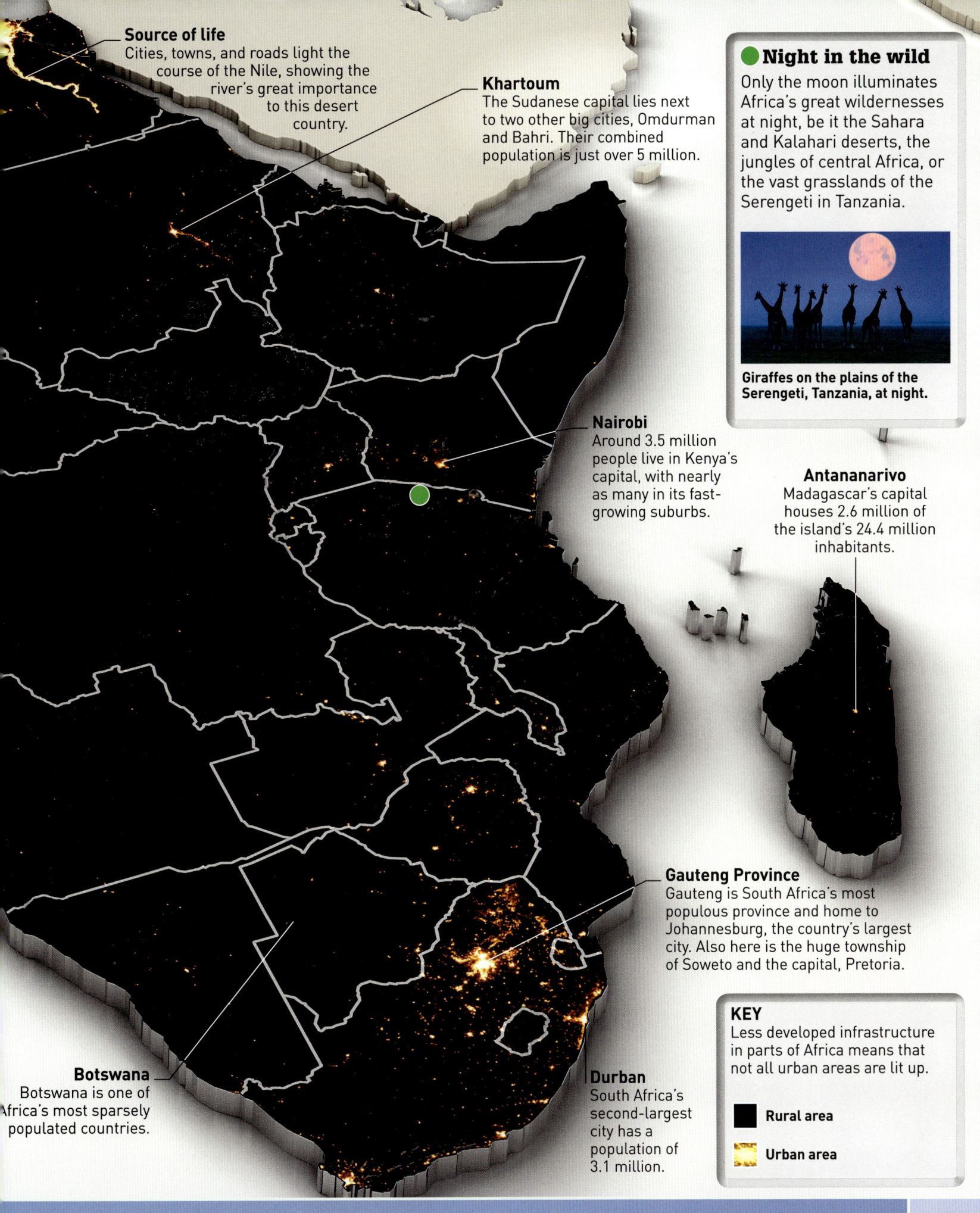

**Source of life**
Cities, towns, and roads light the course of the Nile, showing the river's great importance to this desert country.

**Khartoum**
The Sudanese capital lies next to two other big cities, Omdurman and Bahri. Their combined population is just over 5 million.

### Night in the wild
Only the moon illuminates Africa's great wildernesses at night, be it the Sahara and Kalahari deserts, the jungles of central Africa, or the vast grasslands of the Serengeti in Tanzania.

Giraffes on the plains of the Serengeti, Tanzania, at night.

**Nairobi**
Around 3.5 million people live in Kenya's capital, with nearly as many in its fast-growing suburbs.

**Antananarivo**
Madagascar's capital houses 2.6 million of the island's 24.4 million inhabitants.

**Gauteng Province**
Gauteng is South Africa's most populous province and home to Johannesburg, the country's largest city. Also here is the huge township of Soweto and the capital, Pretoria.

**Botswana**
Botswana is one of Africa's most sparsely populated countries.

**Durban**
South Africa's second-largest city has a population of 3.1 million.

### KEY
Less developed infrastructure in parts of Africa means that not all urban areas are lit up.

- Rural area
- Urban area

COUNTRY ON EARTH; IT IS GROWING BY 3.92 PERCENT EVERY YEAR.

# EUROPE

**Europe from space**
The European continent lies in the northern hemisphere and has an eastern land border with Asia. The distinctive "boot" of Italy is clearly visible in this image.

# Countries and borders

The borders of European countries have changed many times over history, as conquering armies advanced and defeated ones retreated. In the 20th century, two world wars shook the continent, and conflict and political change continue to shape the continent's borders.

**United Kingdom**
It is formed of England, Scotland, Wales, and Northern Ireland.

**Andorra**
The small principality was formed in is bordered by France to the north and by Spain to the south.

## FAST FACTS

**Total land area:**
4,053,300 sq miles
(10,498,000 sq km)

**Total population:**
743 million

**Number of countries:** 46

**Largest country:**
Russia (European section) — 1,527,350 sq miles (3,955,818 sq km)

**Smallest country:**
Vatican City—0.17 sq miles (0.44 sq km)

**Largest country population:**
Russia (European section)— 110 million

THE VATICAN CITY, THE WORLD'S SMALLEST COUNTRY (POPULATION:

EUROPE

# Landscape

Despite its small size, the continent of Europe has an incredibly diverse landscape. To the northwest, east, and south, it is enclosed by mountains. In between, lies the North European Plain, which stretches 2,485 miles (4,000 km) from eastern England to the Ural Mountains in Russia.

**FAST FACTS**

① **Highest point:**
Mount Elbrus, Russia—18,510 ft (5,642 m)

② **Longest river:**
Volga, Russia—2,291 miles (3,688 km)

③ **Largest lake:**
Lake Ladoga, Russia—7,100 sq miles (18,390 sq km)

④ **Largest island:**
Britain (England, Wales, and Scotland)—88,745 sq miles (229,848 sq km)

③ Europe's largest lake, Ladoga lies close to the city of St. Petersburg, in Russia.

80    EUROPE HAS A HIGHER RATIO OF COAST TO LANDMASS

# Fascinating facts

## Landlocked countries—14

**Andorra** • Austria • **Belarus** • Czechia • **Hungary** • Liechtenstein • **Luxembourg** • North Macedonia • **Moldova** • San Marino • **Serbia** • Slovakia • **Switzerland** • Vatican City

## Number of languages

# 39

There are 39 official European languages and many more regional languages and dialects.

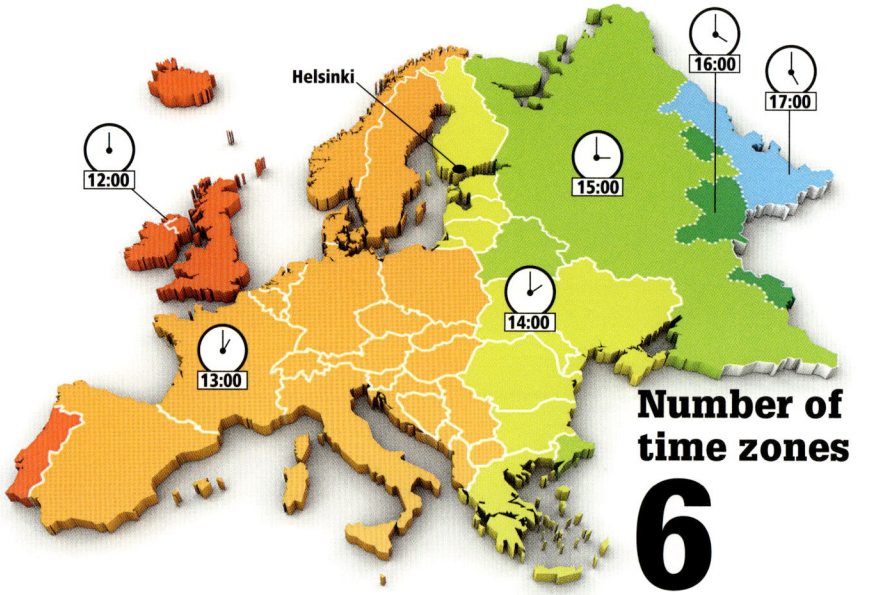

### Number of time zones

# 6

The world is split into 39 time zones. Most are set whole hours ahead or behind Coordinated Universal Time (UCT)—the time at the Greenwich Meridian in London, UK. Some, however, are whole hours plus 30 or 45 minutes ahead or behind UCT. Therefore, on this map, if it was 12:00 in London, it would be 14:00 in Helsinki, Finland (2 hours ahead of UCT).

## Deepest lake

Hornindalsvattnet, Norway—
**1,686 ft (514 m)**

## Fastest train

Europe's fastest train is the **Frecciarossa 1000** in **Italy**, which can reach speeds of up to **249 mph (400 km/h)**

### Tallest buildings

- **Federation Tower** — Moscow, Russia — 1,226 ft (373.7 m)
- **OKO: South Tower** — Moscow, Russia — 1,162 ft (354.1 m)
- **Mercury City Tower** — Moscow, Russia — 1,112 ft (338.8 m)
- **The Shard** — London, United Kingdom — 1,016 ft (309.6 m)
- **Eurasia** — Moscow, Russia — 1,013 ft (308.9 m)

# WATERFALLS

- **Tallest:**
**Vinnufossen, Norway**—2,821 ft (860 m)

**Largest (by volume): Dettifoss, Iceland**—7,063 ft³ (200 m³) of water per second

The falls are 328 ft (100 m) wide

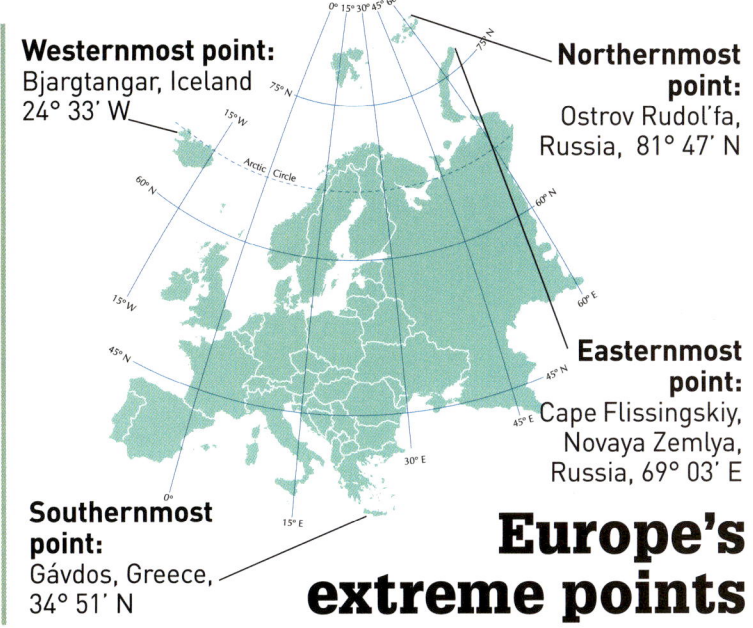

**Westernmost point:** Bjargtangar, Iceland 24° 33' W

**Northernmost point:** Ostrov Rudol'fa, Russia, 81° 47' N

**Easternmost point:** Cape Flissingskiy, Novaya Zemlya, Russia, 69° 03' E

**Southernmost point:** Gávdos, Greece, 34° 51' N

## Europe's extreme points

 **Busiest airport** Heathrow Airport, London, UK: **74,985 million passengers per year**

## Longest tunnels

 **Railroad tunnel** Gotthard Base Tunnel, Switzerland—35.5 miles (57.09 km)

 **Subway line** Serpukhovsko line, Moscow, Russia—25.8 miles (41.5 km)

 **Road tunnel** Laerdal, Norway—15.2 miles (24.53 km)

# Longest bridge
Vasco da Gama, Lisbon, Portugal  **10.68 miles (17.185 km)**

# Biggest glacier
**Severny Island** ice cap—northern island of the Novaya Zemlya archipelago in Russia—**7,915 sq miles (20,500 sq km)**

## Longest coastline

**Norway**
15,626 miles (25,148 km)

## Most active volcano
Mount Etna, Italy

# Highest mountains

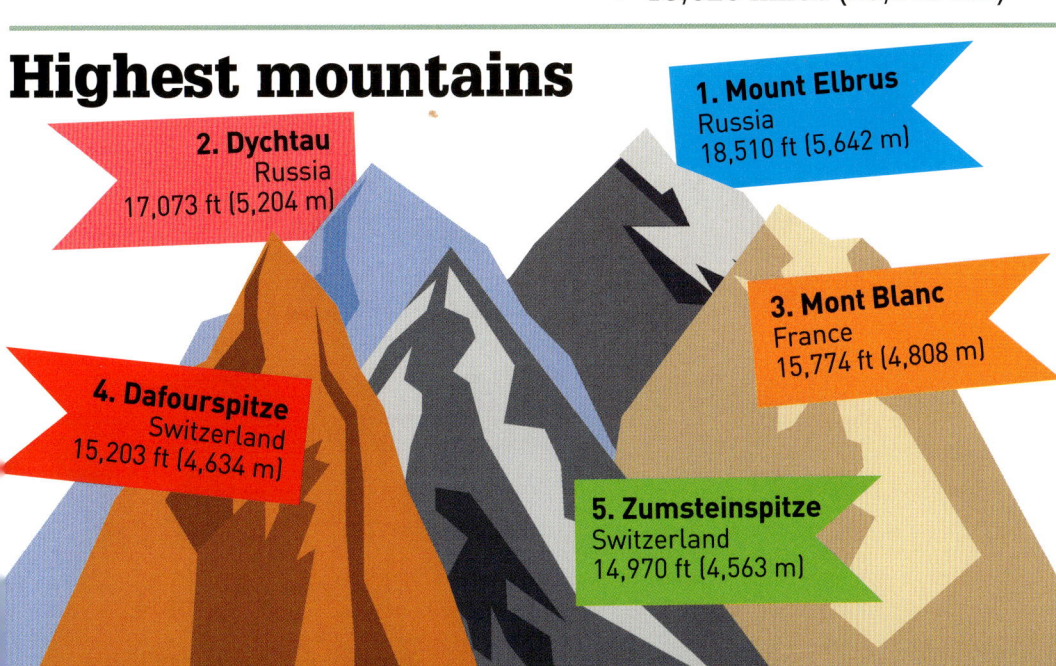

**1. Mount Elbrus** Russia 18,510 ft (5,642 m)

**2. Dychtau** Russia 17,073 ft (5,204 m)

**3. Mont Blanc** France 15,774 ft (4,808 m)

**4. Dafourspitze** Switzerland 15,203 ft (4,634 m)

**5. Zumsteinspitze** Switzerland 14,970 ft (4,563 m)

# Tallest bridge
Millau Viaduct, France—bridge deck is **886 ft (270 m)** above the ground

# Population

Europe is the world's second-most densely populated continent (after Asia), with an average of 188 per sq mile (73 people per sq km). The majority of Europe's population live in the northern half of the continent.

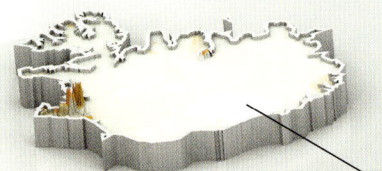

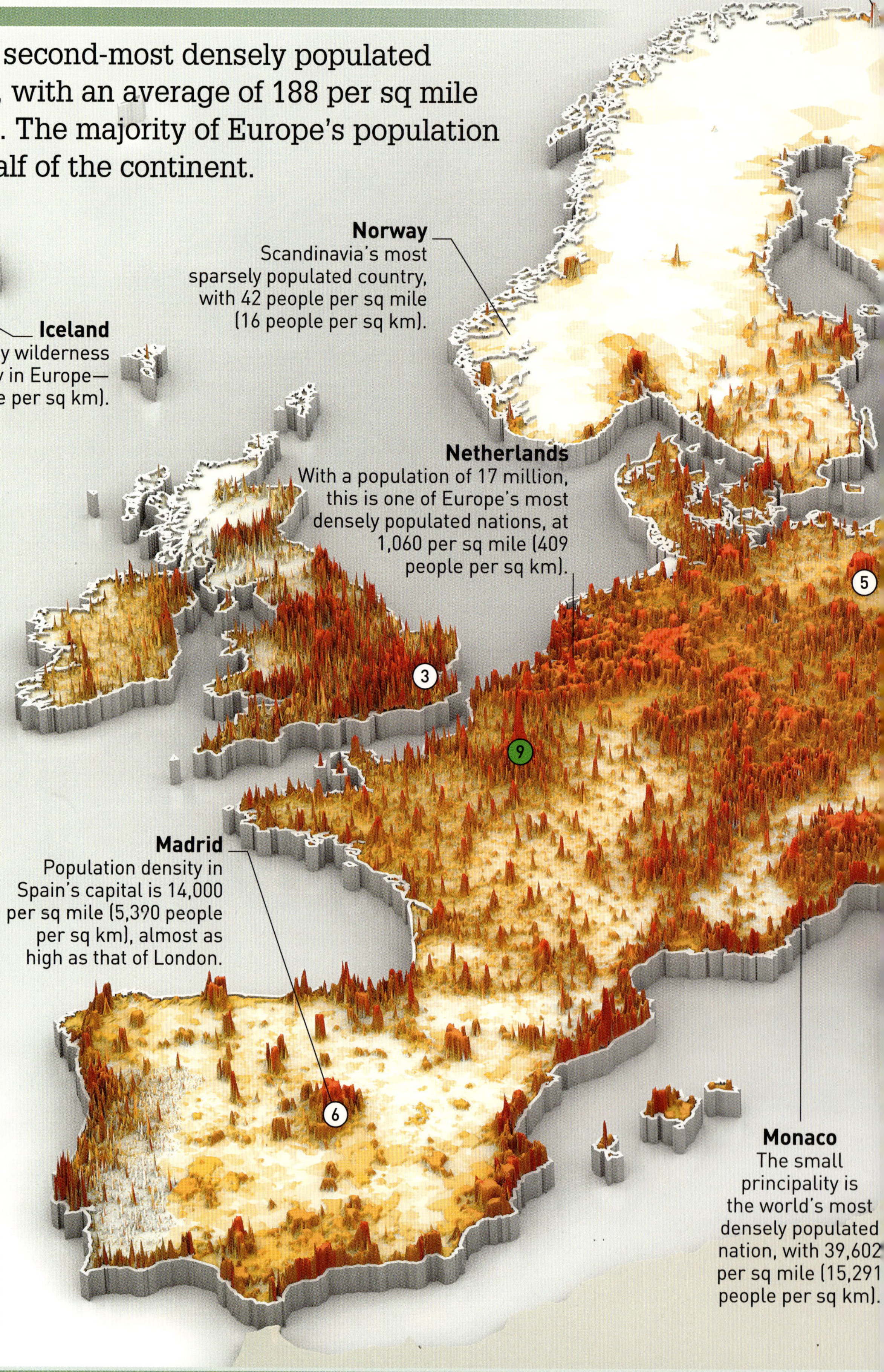

**Iceland**
This island of volcanoes and icy wilderness has the lowest population density in Europe—8 people per sq mile (3 people per sq km).

**Murmansk, Russia**
The largest city north of the Arctic Circle. It has 299,000 inhabitants.

**Norway**
Scandinavia's most sparsely populated country, with 42 people per sq mile (16 people per sq km).

**Netherlands**
With a population of 17 million, this is one of Europe's most densely populated nations, at 1,060 per sq mile (409 people per sq km).

**Madrid**
Population density in Spain's capital is 14,000 per sq mile (5,390 people per sq km), almost as high as that of London.

**Monaco**
The small principality is the world's most densely populated nation, with 39,602 per sq mile (15,291 people per sq km).

## Europe's largest cities

The list below is based on the number of people living inside a city's boundaries.

1. Istanbul, Turkey—14.7 million
2. Moscow, Russia—12.3 million
3. London, United Kingdom—8.7 million
4. St. Petersburg, Russia—5.2 million
5. Berlin, Germany—3.6 million
6. Madrid, Spain—3.1 million
7. Kyiv, Ukraine—2.9 million
8. Rome, Italy—2.87 million
9. Paris, France—2.2 million
10. Minsk, Belarus—1.9 million

The Eiffel Tower dominates the skyline of Paris, France's most populous city.

OF THE WORLD'S 10 MOST DENSELY POPULATED LOCATIONS, FOUR

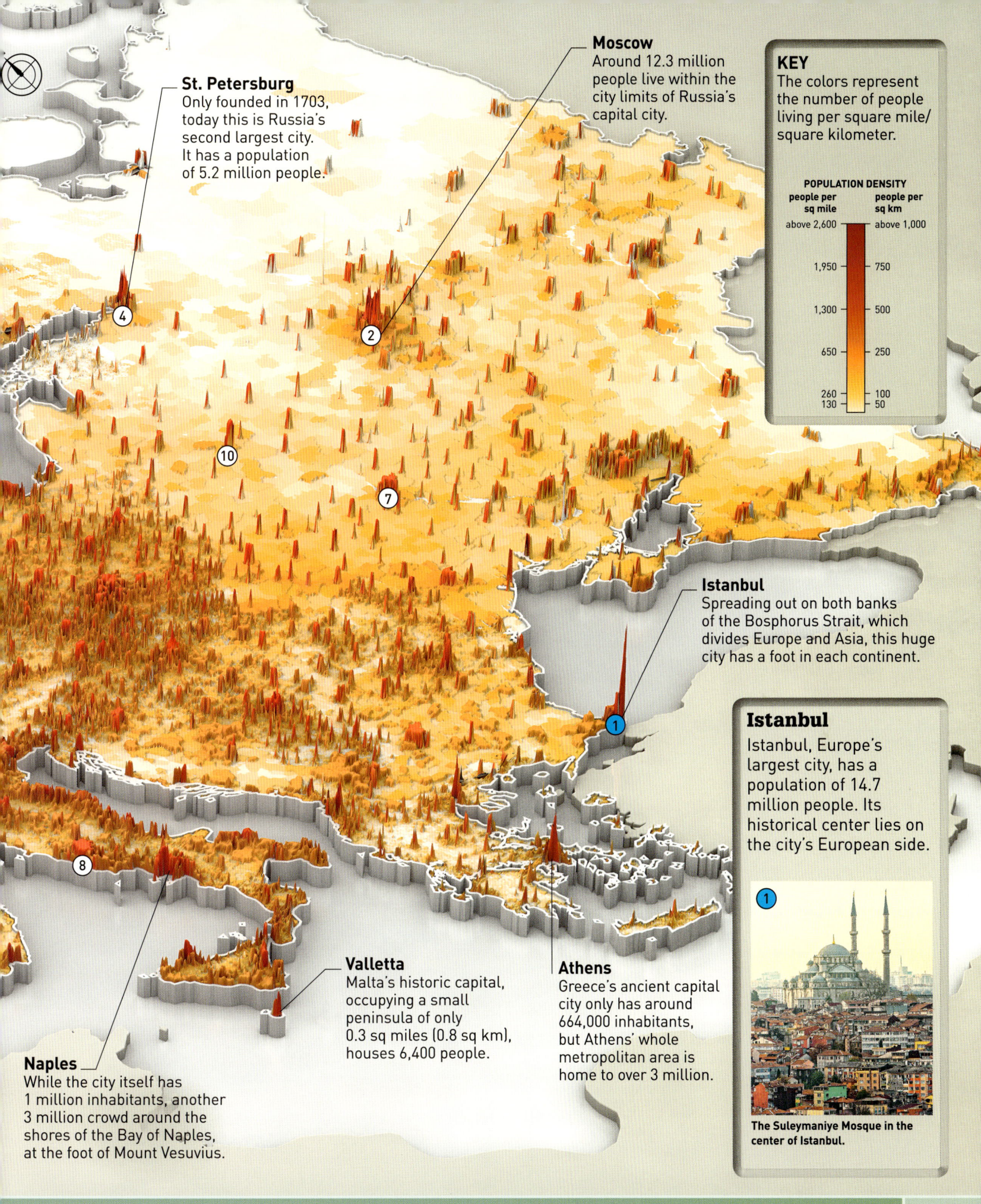

**St. Petersburg**
Only founded in 1703, today this is Russia's second largest city. It has a population of 5.2 million people.

**Moscow**
Around 12.3 million people live within the city limits of Russia's capital city.

**KEY**
The colors represent the number of people living per square mile/square kilometer.

**POPULATION DENSITY**

| people per sq mile | people per sq km |
|---|---|
| above 2,600 | above 1,000 |
| 1,950 | 750 |
| 1,300 | 500 |
| 650 | 250 |
| 260 | 100 |
| 130 | 50 |

**Istanbul**
Spreading out on both banks of the Bosphorus Strait, which divides Europe and Asia, this huge city has a foot in each continent.

**Istanbul**
Istanbul, Europe's largest city, has a population of 14.7 million people. Its historical center lies on the city's European side.

The Suleymaniye Mosque in the center of Istanbul.

**Valletta**
Malta's historic capital, occupying a small peninsula of only 0.3 sq miles (0.8 sq km), houses 6,400 people.

**Athens**
Greece's ancient capital city only has around 664,000 inhabitants, but Athens' whole metropolitan area is home to over 3 million.

**Naples**
While the city itself has 1 million inhabitants, another 3 million crowd around the shores of the Bay of Naples, at the foot of Mount Vesuvius.

(MONACO, GIBRALTAR, THE VATICAN CITY, AND MALTA) ARE IN EUROPE.

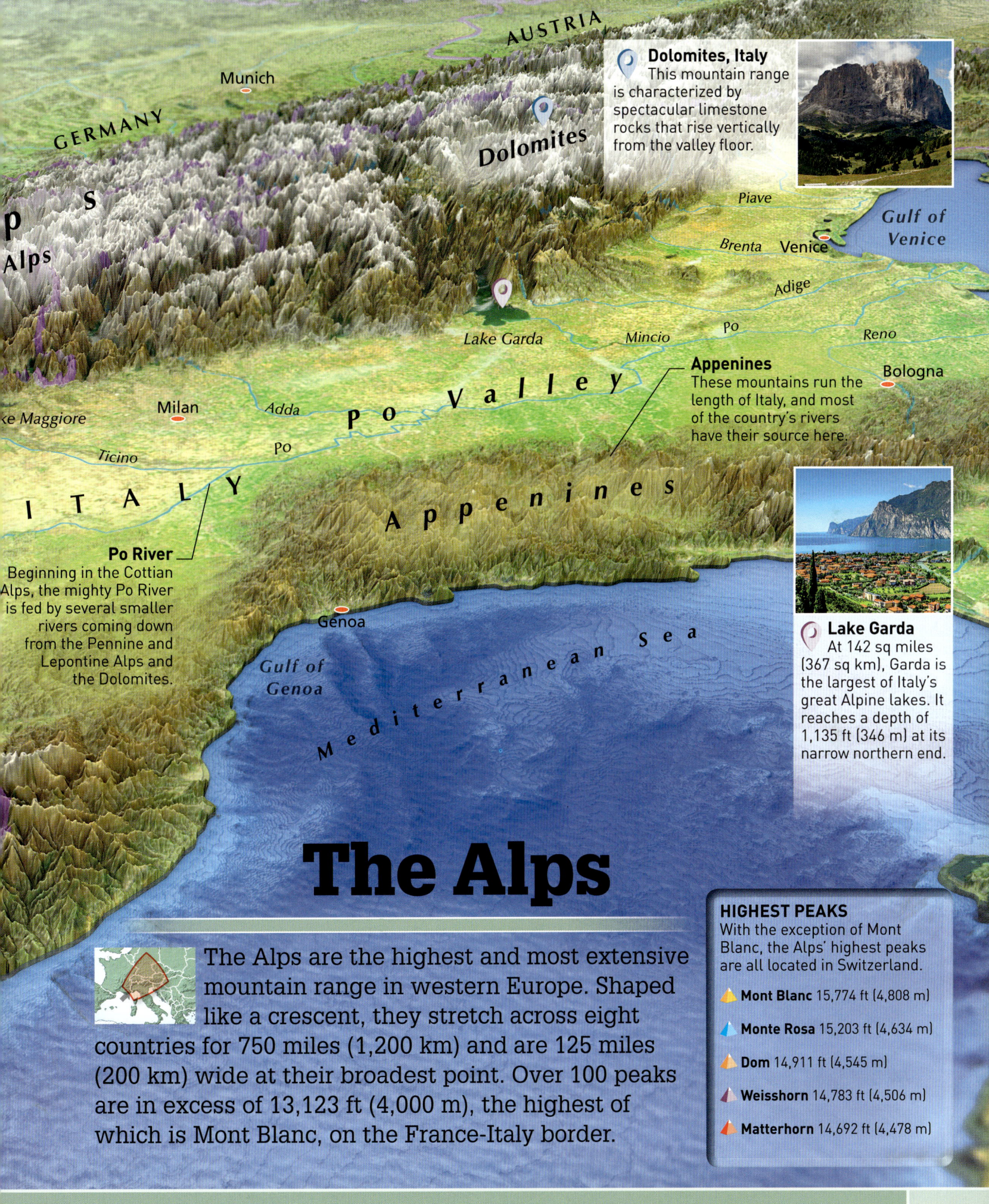

**Dolomites, Italy**
This mountain range is characterized by spectacular limestone rocks that rise vertically from the valley floor.

**Appenines**
These mountains run the length of Italy, and most of the country's rivers have their source here.

**Po River**
Beginning in the Cottian Alps, the mighty Po River is fed by several smaller rivers coming down from the Pennine and Lepontine Alps and the Dolomites.

**Lake Garda**
At 142 sq miles (367 sq km), Garda is the largest of Italy's great Alpine lakes. It reaches a depth of 1,135 ft (346 m) at its narrow northern end.

# The Alps

The Alps are the highest and most extensive mountain range in western Europe. Shaped like a crescent, they stretch across eight countries for 750 miles (1,200 km) and are 125 miles (200 km) wide at their broadest point. Over 100 peaks are in excess of 13,123 ft (4,000 m), the highest of which is Mont Blanc, on the France-Italy border.

**HIGHEST PEAKS**
With the exception of Mont Blanc, the Alps' highest peaks are all located in Switzerland.

- Mont Blanc 15,774 ft (4,808 m)
- Monte Rosa 15,203 ft (4,634 m)
- Dom 14,911 ft (4,545 m)
- Weisshorn 14,783 ft (4,506 m)
- Matterhorn 14,692 ft (4,478 m)

VISITORS COME TO SKI, HIKE, AND EXPLORE THERE EVERY YEAR.

# Famous landmarks

From prehistoric monuments and Roman ruins to medieval town centers, Gothic cathedrals, and Baroque palaces, Europe has a wealth of architectural treasures from across the ages. Some of its most famous landmarks are natural formations, often protected as national parks.

**United Kingdom**
The 29 UNESCO heritage sites in England, Scotland, Wales, and Northern Ireland include Stone Age monuments, castles, and feats of Victorian engineering.

## Landscapes
Europe has 468 national parks. Some are precious habitats or areas of natural beauty, while others contain particular geological formations.

- Iceland's Thingvellir National Park lies at the meeting point between the North American and Eurasian plates.
- Giant's Causeway, Northern Ireland, is made of basalt columns in different formations, some like giant honeycombs.

**France**
Among France's many famous landmarks, 42 are UNESCO World Heritage Sites.

**Moorish Alhambra**
Many of Spain's landmarks show the country's Arabic heritage, such as the Alhambra palace and gardens in Granada.

Landmarks shown: Thingvellir National Park, Iceland; Drottningholm Palace, Sweden; Urnes Stave Church, Norway; Edinburgh Castle, Scotland; Kronborg Castle, Helsingør, Denmark; Giant's Causeway, Northern Ireland; Stonehenge, England; Kinderdijk-Elshout Windmills, Netherlands; Big Ben, London, England; Charlottenburg Palace, Berlin, Germany; Aachen Cathedral, Germany; Brú na Bóinne, Ireland; Eiffel Tower, Paris, France; Hôtel de Ville, Brussels, Belgium; Chartres Cathedral, France; Rhaetian Railway, Switzerland; Palais des Papes, Avignon, France; Leaning Tower of Pisa, Italy; Sagrada Familia, Barcelona, Spain; Toledo Cathedral, Spain; Torre de Belém, Lisbon, Portugal; Alhambra, Granada, Spain.

OF EUROPE'S MANY LANDMARKS, 453 ARE DESIGNATED UNESCO WORLD

EUROPE

# Climate

Europe's climate varies from subtropical in the south to polar in the north. Western and north-western parts have a mild, generally humid climate, while central and eastern Europe has a humid climate with cool summers.

**Polar easterlies**
Prevailing winds that bring dry, cold air southward from the North Pole.

**Prevailing westerlies**
Blowing in a northeastern direction, these winds bring warm air to western parts of Europe.

**Cloudiest**
Glasgow, in the United Kingdom, is Europe's cloudiest city. It averages only 1,203 hours of sunshine a year.

**Mistral**
A strong, cold wind that blows hardest in winter and spring.

**Hottest**
The highest temperature recorded in Europe is 122°F (50°C), in Seville, Spain, on August 4, 1881.

**Sirocco winds**
Hot air from Africa creates storms over the sea, bringing cloud, fog, and rain to northern Mediterranean locations.

90    ON JULY 7, 1889, 8.1 IN (205.7 MM) OF RAIN FELL AT THE CITY

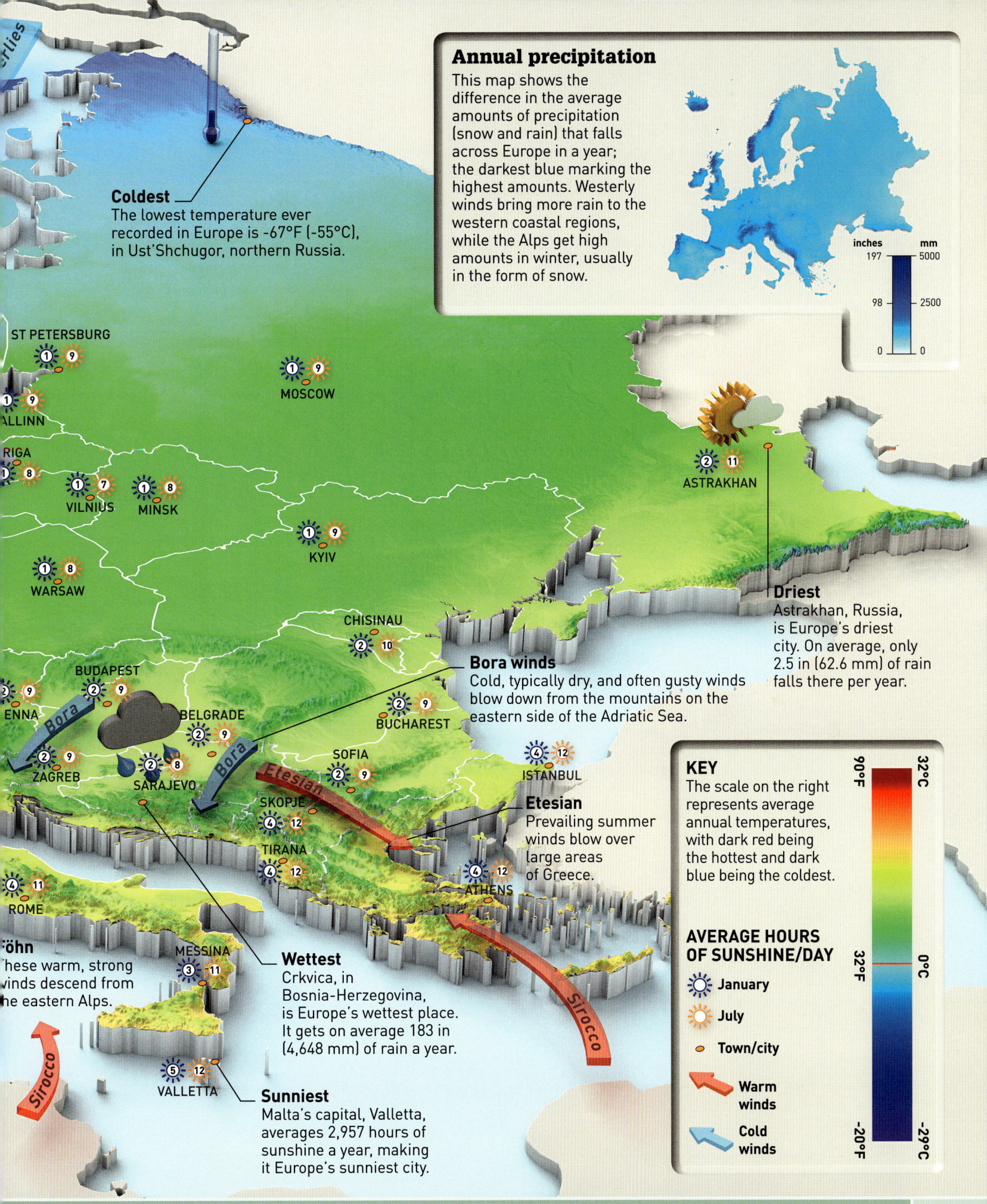

# Wildlife

In densely populated Europe there is not much wilderness left for animals to thrive in, but nature reserves and some species' ability to adapt mean that the continent's wildlife is still surprisingly varied.

**Humpback whale** In winter, Arctic waters provide rich feeding grounds for these migrating whales.

**Reindeer** Both male and female reindeer have antlers.

**Eurasian lynx** Large padded paws prevent this big cat from sinking through the snow.

**Arctic fox** Thick, white winter fur keeps this fox warm and camouflaged in snow and ice.

**Moose** This giant of the forest is commonly seen in Scandinavia and the Baltic states.

**Capercaillie** A bird famous for its spectacular courting ritual.

**Red deer** Scotland has its own subspecies of this large deer, which is common throughout the continent.

**Roe deer** Small and graceful, this deer is widespread throughout Europe.

**Irish hare** Modern farming practices threaten this shy, nocturnal creature.

**Gray wolf** The largest of the dog family, wolves live in family packs in isolated, forested areas of Europe.

**Badger** Big groups live in setts (tunnels and underground chambers).

**Basking shark** To feed, this gigantic shark simply keeps its mouth wide open as it swims.

**Pine marten** Hollow trees make good homes for this member of the weasel family.

**Alpine marmot** These rodents hibernate in burrows for up to nine months.

**Golden eagle** This huge raptor picks and patrols huge territories in less populated areas across Europe.

**Pyrenean chamois** Close to extinction, as its skin was used for chamois gloves and polishing cloths, the numbers have recovered.

**European bee eater** Male birds offer the best insect morsels to the female during courtship.

**Barbary macaque** A 300-strong colony of Barbary macaques live on the Rock of Gibraltar.

**Iberian lynx** Only around 400 remain of the endangered Spanish lynx.

# By night

This image photo of Europe at night shows where people live. The west of the continent is densely populated; the north and east are relatively uninhabited.

**Iceland**
Reykjavík is almost the only bright spot, and is home to two-thirds of the country's population.

**Scandinavia**
The relatively small populations of the large Scandinavian countries are concentrated in the main southern coastal cities.

**Northwest England**
The triangle formed by the cities of Liverpool, Manchester, and Birmingham is densely populated.

**Mega metropolitan area**
Urban areas of Belgium, the Netherlands, Luxembourg, and Germany's Rhine-Ruhr form a continuous built-up zone.

**London**
Europe's third-largest city has a population density of 14,290 people per sq mile (5,518 per sq km).

● **Urban Monaco**
The small principality of Monaco, squeezed into an area of only 0.78 sq miles (2 sq km), is all city. Every one of its 30,581 inhabitants lives in an urban environment.

**Paris**
About 20 percent of France's 62.8 million inhabitants live in the Paris metropolitan area.

**Industrial hub**
Milan and Turin, two of Italy's major industrial and economic centres are home to a combined 6.57 million people.

**Lisbon**
Just over one-quarter (26.2 percent) of Portugal's 10.8 million inhabitants live in the metropolitan area of Lisbon.

**Madrid**
Madrid is Spain's largest metropolitan area and 6.3 million people live here.

ALBANIA IS THE COUNTRY WITH THE FASTEST GROWING

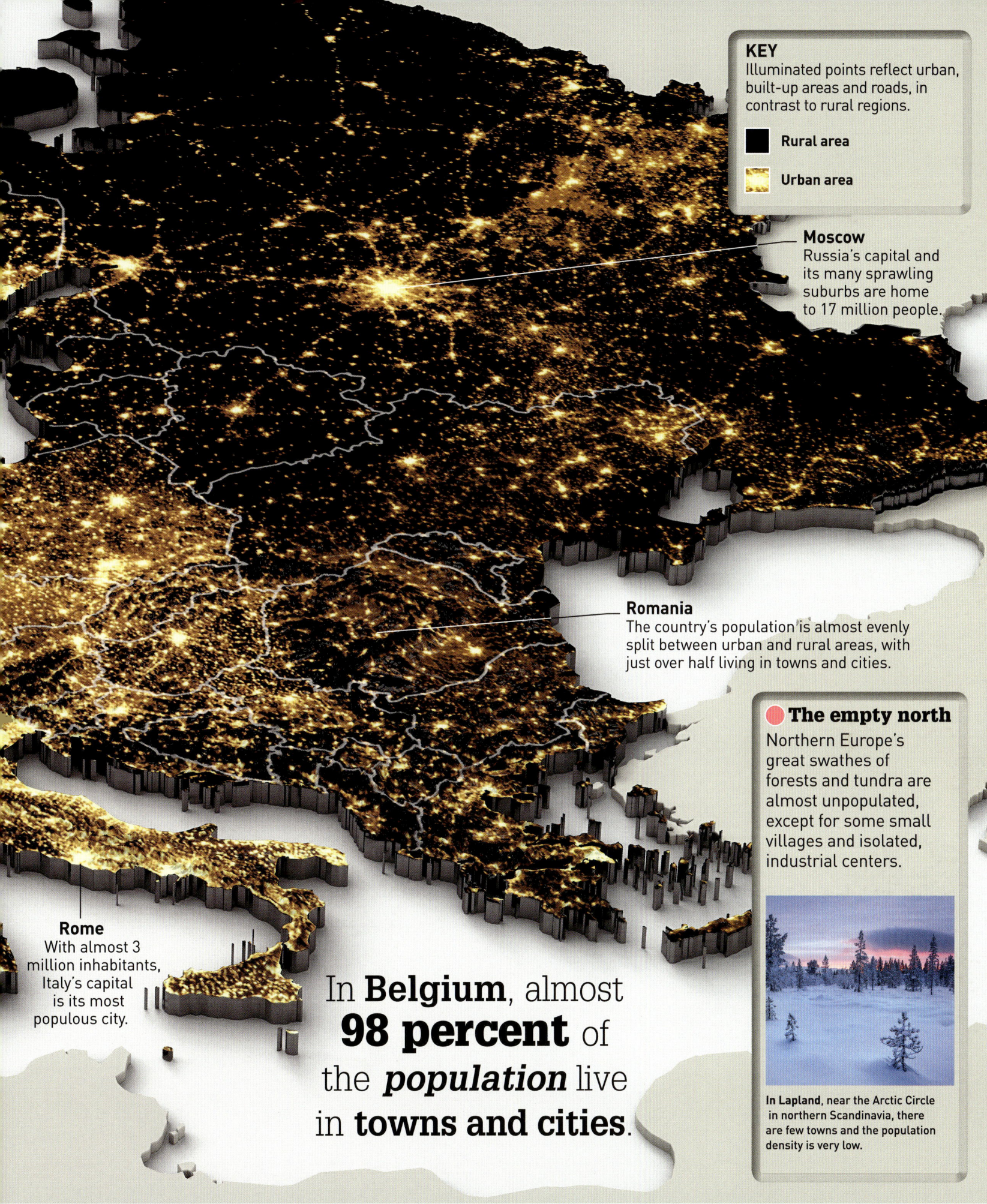

# ASIA

**Mighty continent**
Asia extends from the Arctic Ocean in the north to the Indian Ocean in the south, and from the Pacific Ocean in the east, to the Ural Mountains, the Suez Canal, the Bosphorus Strait, and the Caucasus Mountains in the west.

## FAST FACTS

**Total land area:** 16,837,143 sq miles (43,608,000 sq km)

**Total population:** 4.4 billion

**Number of countries:** 49

**Largest country:** Russia — 6,601,668 sq miles (17,098,242 sq km)

**Smallest country:** Maldives — 115 sq miles (298 sq km)

**Largest country population:** China — 1.37 billion

Streets packed with people are a common sight in China's cities.

**Russia** Three-quarters of Russia lies in Asia, making it the continent's largest country.

**Israel** The State of Israel was established in 1948.

**India** With a population of 1.27 billion, India is the world's largest democracy.

**Indonesia** The world's largest island nation, Indonesia is made up of more than 13,000 islands.

# Countries and borders

The vast continent of Asia includes two giant nations—China and India, each with a population of more than a billion people and with rapidly growing economies. To the north is the world's biggest country by area—Russia. To the west lie the countries of the Middle East, today the centre of the Islamic world.

# Landscape

**ASIA**

**Dead Sea** A salt lake bordering Israel, the West Bank, and Jordan. At 1,286 ft (392 m) below sea level, it is the lowest land point on Earth's surface.

**West Siberian Plain** One of the largest plains in the world, it is a vast system of marshes.

**Indian Shield** Its collision with the Eurasian Plate has created the Himalayas, the world's tallest mountain system.

**Indonesian islands** Indonesia is the most volcanic country in the world. It is home to 147 volcanoes, 76 of which are active.

### FAST FACTS

① **Highest point:** Mount Everest, Nepal/Tibet, China—29,029 ft (8,848 m)

② **Longest river:** Yangtze, China—3,964 miles (6,380 km)

③ **Largest lake:** Caspian Sea—143,243 sq miles (371,000 sq km)

④ **Largest island:** Borneo—288,869 sq miles (748,168 sq km)

**Borneo** is the largest island in Asia, and the third-largest island in the world.

Asia covers approximately 30 percent of Earth's land area and makes up the eastern portion of the Eurasian supercontinent (with Europe lying to the west). It is made up of five different landscapes: mountain systems, plateaus, plains, steppes (large areas of unforested grassland), and deserts.

ASIA

# Fascinating facts

**Number of time zones**
# 16

The world is split into 39 time zones. Most are set whole hours ahead or behind Coordinated Universal Time (UCT)—the time at the Greenwich Meridian in London, UK. Some, however, are whole hours plus 30 or 45 minutes ahead or behind UCT. Therefore, on this map, if it was 12:00 in London, it would be 17:30 in Mumbai, India (5½ hours ahead of UCT).

# 13 Landlocked countries
Afghanistan ▪ Armenia ▪ Azerbaijan ▪ Belarus ▪ Bhutan ▪ Kazakhstan ▪ Kyrgyzstan ▪ Laos ▪ Mongolia ▪ Nepal ▪ Tajikistan ▪ Turkmenistan ▪ Uzbekistan

## Fastest train
Shanghai Maglev Train, China—
**267.2 mph (430 km/h)**

## Longest tunnels

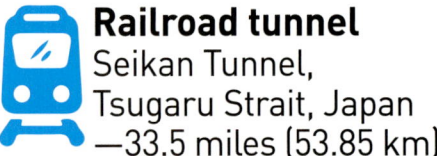 **Railroad tunnel** Seikan Tunnel, Tsugaru Strait, Japan—33.5 miles (53.85 km)

 **Subway line** Guangzhou Metro Line 3, Guangzhou, China—37.5 miles (60.4 km)

 **Road tunnel** Xishan Tunnel, Shanxi, China—8.5 miles (13.6 km)

 **Longest coastline** Indonesia— 33,999 miles (54,716 km)

 **Busiest airport** Beijing International Airport, China—**90.203 million** passengers per year

## Tallest buildings

- Burj Khalifa, Dubai, UAE — 2,715 ft (828 m)
- Shanghai Tower, Shanghai, China — 2,073 ft (632 m)
- Makkah Royal Clock Tower, Mecca, Saudi Arabia — 1,971 ft (601 m)
- Taipei 101, Taipei, Taiwan — 1,670 ft (509 m)
- Shanghai World Finance Centre, Shanghai, China — 1,614 ft (492 m)

## Biggest glacier
Fedchenko Glacier, Tajikistan—
48 miles (77 km) long

The Fedchenko Glacier is the longest glacier in the world outside of the polar regions

# WATERFALLS

Tallest:
**Hannoki Falls, Toyama, Japan**—1,640 ft (500 m)

Largest (by volume):
**Chutes de Khone, Laos**—410,000 ft³ (11,610 m³) of water per second

## Deepest lake

Lake Baikal, Russia—

**5,387 ft (1,642 m)**

Lake Baikal is the deepest lake in the world

## Most active volcano

Mount Merapi, Indonesia

## Asia's extreme points

**Northernmost point:** Mys Articesku, Russia—81° 12' N

**Easternmost point:** Mys Dezhneva, Russia—169° 40' W

**Southernmost point:** Pulau Panama, Indonesia—11' S

**Westernmost point:** Bozca Adasi, Turkey—26° 2' E

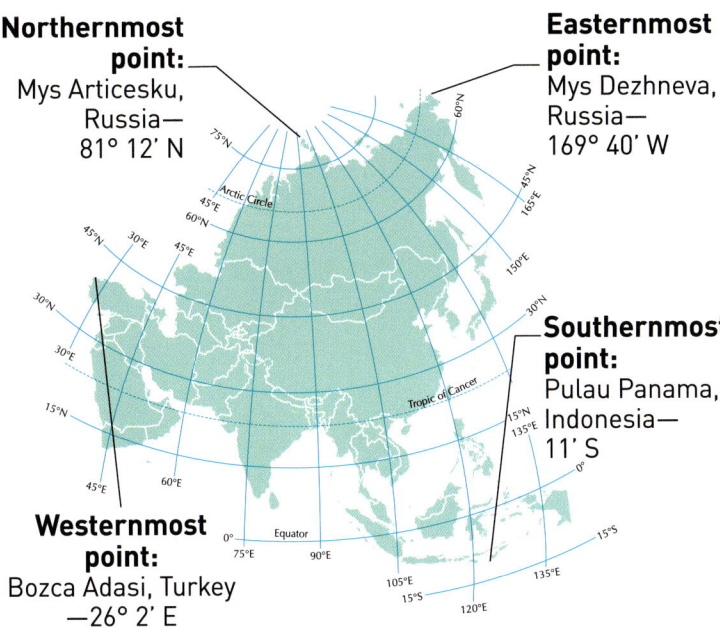

## Highest mountains

1. **Mount Everest** Nepal/Tibet, China — 29,029 ft (8,848 m)
2. **K2** China/Pakistan — 28,251 ft (8,611 m)
3. **Kangchenjunga** India/Nepal — 28,169 ft (8,586 m)
4. **Lhotse** Nepal/Tibet, China — 27,940 ft (8,516 m)
5. **Makalu** Nepal/Tibet, China — 27,838 ft (8,485 m)

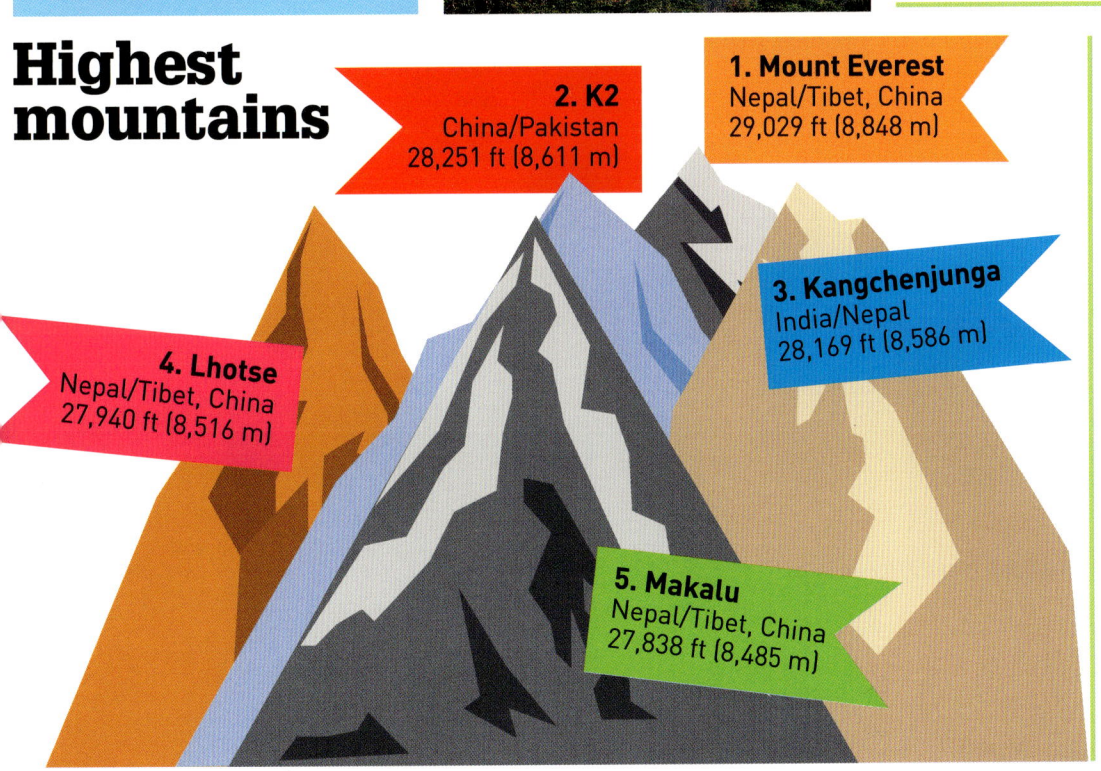

## Most visited cities (Visitors per year)

- **Bangkok, Thailand** 18.24 million
- **Singapore** 11.88 million
- **Kuala Lumpur, Malaysia** 11.12 million
- **Seoul, South Korea** 10.35 million
- **Hong Kong** 8.66 million

## Tallest bridge

Duge Beipan River Bridge, Liupanshui, Guizhou, China —**1,854 ft (535 m)**

The world's three tallest bridges are all in Asia:
- Duge Beipan River Bridge—1,854 ft (565 m)
- Sidu River Bridge—1,627 ft (496 m)
- Puli Bridge—1,591 ft (485 m)

## Longest bridge
Danyang–Kunshan Grand Bridge (Beijing–Shanghai high-speed railroad) —**102.4 miles (164.8 km)**

This is the longest bridge of any type in the world

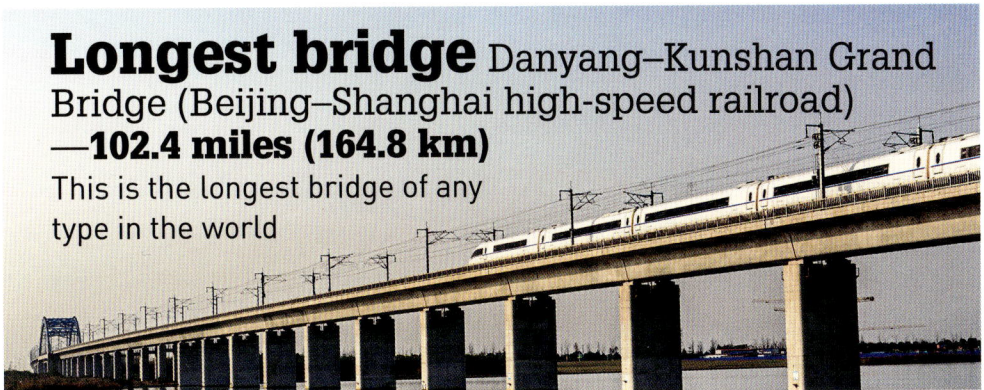

ASIA

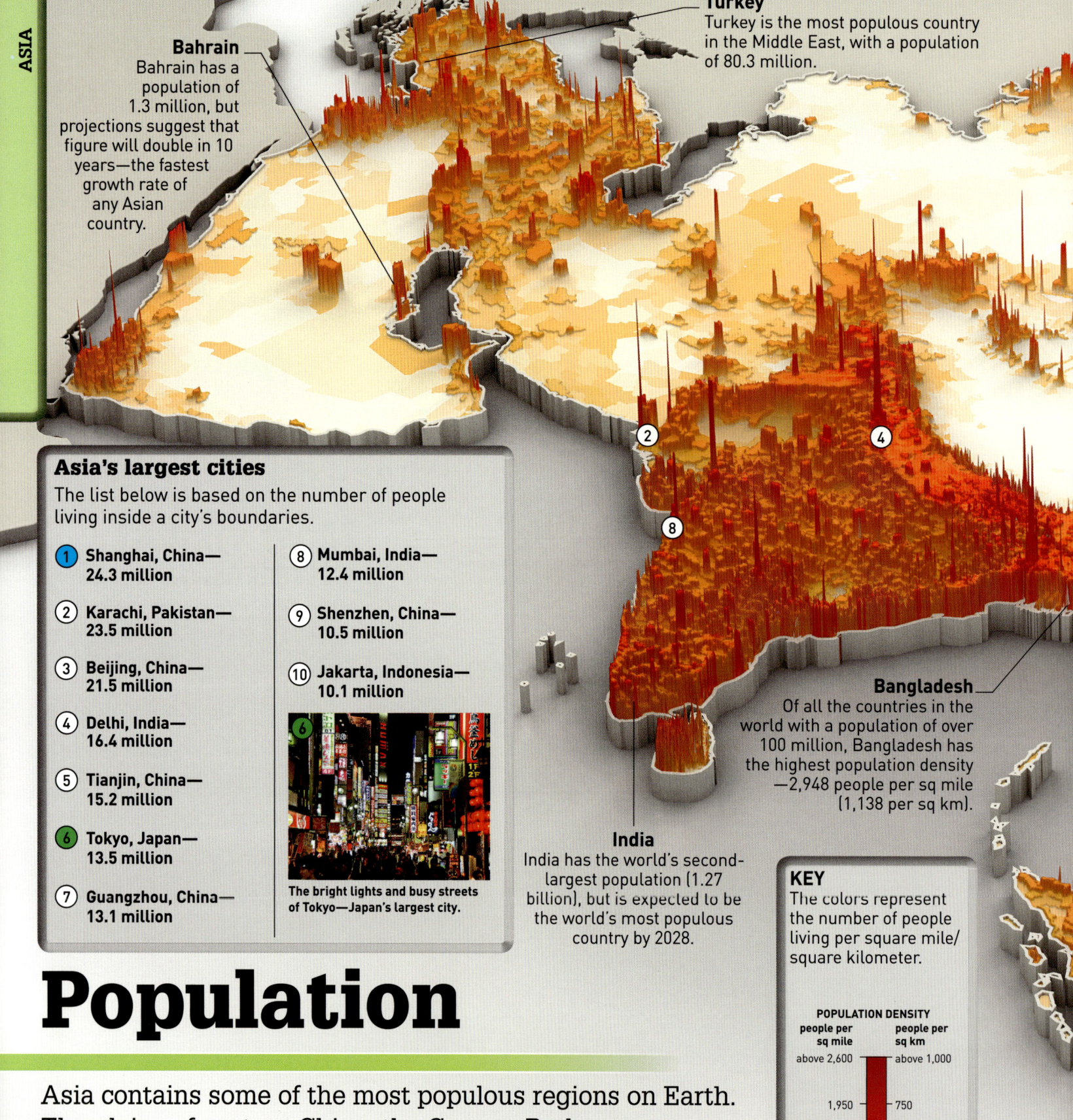

**Turkey**
Turkey is the most populous country in the Middle East, with a population of 80.3 million.

**Bahrain**
Bahrain has a population of 1.3 million, but projections suggest that figure will double in 10 years—the fastest growth rate of any Asian country.

**Bangladesh**
Of all the countries in the world with a population of over 100 million, Bangladesh has the highest population density —2,948 people per sq mile (1,138 per sq km).

**India**
India has the world's second-largest population (1.27 billion), but is expected to be the world's most populous country by 2028.

### Asia's largest cities
The list below is based on the number of people living inside a city's boundaries.

1. Shanghai, China— 24.3 million
2. Karachi, Pakistan— 23.5 million
3. Beijing, China— 21.5 million
4. Delhi, India— 16.4 million
5. Tianjin, China— 15.2 million
6. Tokyo, Japan— 13.5 million
7. Guangzhou, China— 13.1 million
8. Mumbai, India— 12.4 million
9. Shenzhen, China— 10.5 million
10. Jakarta, Indonesia— 10.1 million

The bright lights and busy streets of Tokyo—Japan's largest city.

### KEY
The colors represent the number of people living per square mile/ square kilometer.

**POPULATION DENSITY**

| people per sq mile | people per sq km |
|---|---|
| above 2,600 | above 1,000 |
| 1,950 | 750 |
| 1,300 | 500 |
| 650 | 250 |
| 260 | 100 |
| 130 | 50 |

# Population

Asia contains some of the most populous regions on Earth. The plains of eastern China, the Ganges-Brahmaputra rivers in India, Japan, and the Indonesian island of Jakarta all have very high population densities. By contrast, Siberia and the Plateau of Tibet are virtually uninhabited.

OVER HALF OF ASIA'S POPULATION OF 4.5 BILLION LIVES IN

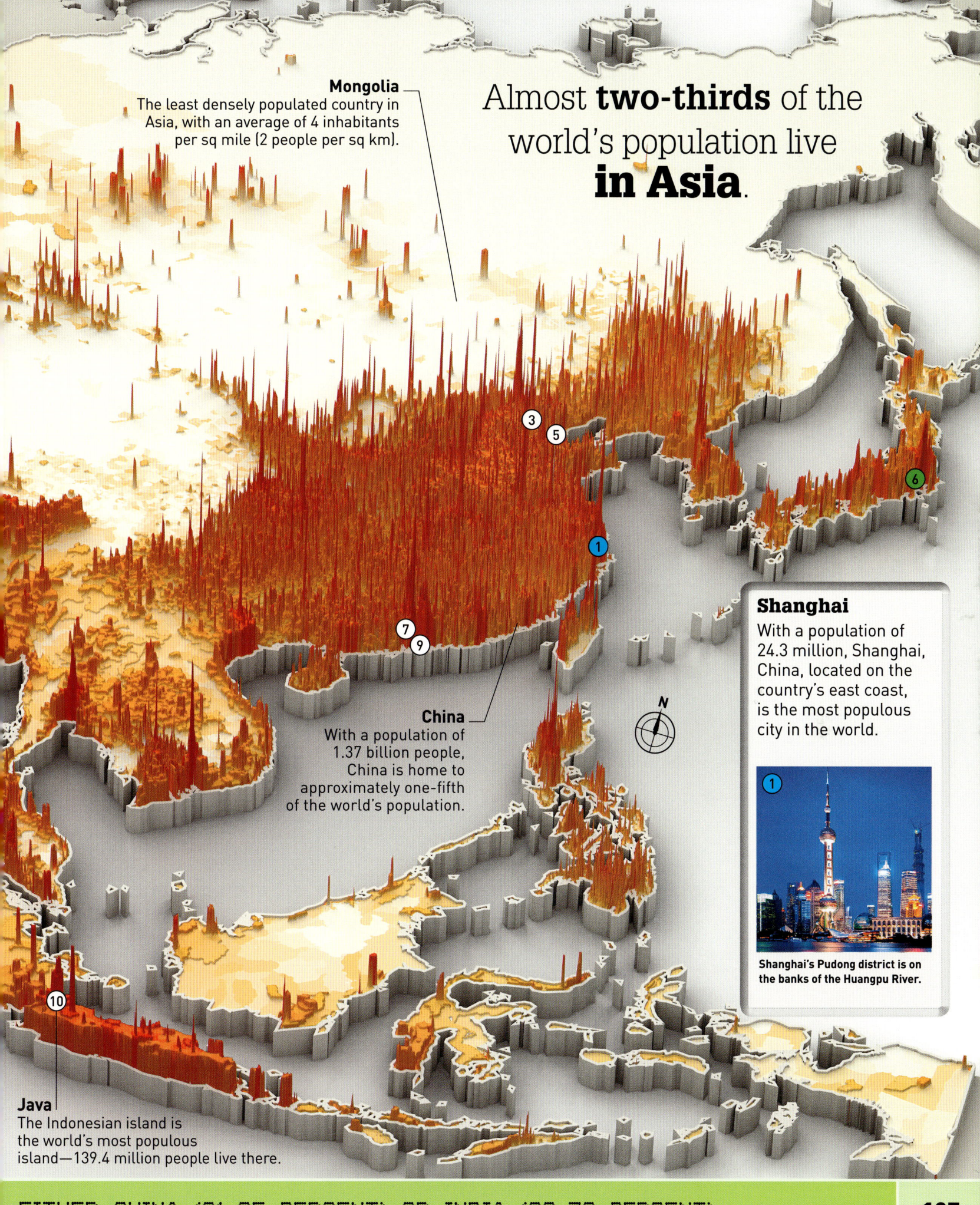

ASIA

**Karakoram Range**
This vast mountain range lies to the west of the Himalayas and contains the highest concentration of peaks over 26,247 ft (8,000 m) on Earth.

**Kathmandu**
The capital city of Nepal, Kathmandu has a population of 1.18 million people and is a gateway for tourism in the Himalayas.

**Taklamakan Desert**
A lifeless, sand-shifting desert, the famed Silk Road passed along its northern and southern fringes.

**Mount Everest**
Situated on the border between Nepal and Tibet, China, Mount Everest is the world's tallest mountain at 29,029 ft (8,848 m).

**The Ganges**
The Ganges is the most sacred river of the Hindu religion. It rises in the Himalayas, and flows through India and Bangladesh to the Bay of Bengal.

**Siwalik Range**
An outer range of the Himalayas that extends more than 1,000 miles (1,600 km) from east to west.

**Bhutan**
The small Himalayan kingdom only opened its borders to foreigners in 1974.

**Thimphu**
At 8,688 ft (2,648 m), Thimphu, in Bhutan, is the third-highest capital city in the world, after La Paz (Bolivia) and Quito (Ecuador).

106 — THE HIMALAYAS ARE STILL RISING AT A RATE OF 0.25 IN (4 MM) PER

# The Himalayas

The Himalayas is the world's highest mountain range. It runs in an arc 1,500 miles (2,400 km) long, spread across five countries: Pakistan, India, Nepal, Bhutan, and China. It is also the source of some of the region's major rivers, including the mighty Ganges and Brahmaputra rivers.

**Plateau of Tibet**
The world's largest and highest plateau, it contains the largest amount of ice found outside the poles.

**Tsangpo Gorge**
With an average depth of 16,400 ft (5,000 m), Tsangpo Gorge, in Tibet, China, is the deepest canyon in the world.

**HIGHEST PEAKS**
The Himalayas is home to more than 110 mountains over 24,000 ft (7,300 m). The top five are:

- **Mount Everest** 29,029 ft (8,848 m)
- **Kangchenjunga** 28,169 ft (8,586 m)
- **Lhotse** 27,940 ft (8,516 m)
- **Makalu** 27,765 ft (8,462 m)
- **Cho Oyu** 26,905 ft (8,201 m)

**Brahmaputra River**
One of Asia's major rivers, it cuts through China, Bhutan, India, and Bangladesh before flowing into the Bay of Bengal.

**Makkah Royal Clock Tower** The tower contains the world's largest clock face.

**Dome of the Rock** The world's oldest-standing Islamic monument, it dates to the seventh century CE.

**Fortress of Nisa** The fortress forms part of an ancient city that was totally destroyed by an earthquake in the first decade BCE.

- Dome of the Rock, Jerusalem, Israel
- Ziggurat of Ur, Nasiriyah, Iraq
- Makkah Royal Clock Tower, Mecca, Saudi Arabia
- Fortress of Nisa, Turkmenistan
- Citadel of Herat, Afghanistan
- Mausoleum of Khoja Ahmed Yasui, Turkestan, Kazakhstan
- Shah-i-Zinda Mausoleum, Samarkand, Uzbekistan
- Great Mosque of Sana'a, Yemen
- Persepolis, Marvdasht, Iran
- Burj Khalifa, Dubai, UAE
- Badshahi Mosque, Lahore, Pakistan
- Potala Palace, Lhasa, Tibet, China

**Citadel of Herat** Dates back to 330 BCE, when Alexander the Great arrived in Herat with his army.

- Gateway of India, Mumbai, India
- Taj Mahal, Agra, India
- Meenakshi Amman Temple, Madurai, India
- Bagan, Myanmar

**Burj Khalifa** Standing at 2,715 ft (828 m), the Burj Khalifa in Dubai, UAE, is the tallest manmade structure in the world. Completed in 2009, it has 163 floors (including the world's highest observation deck on the 148th floor), 57 elevators, and eight escalators.

**Meenakshi Amman Temple** This Hindu temple lies at the heart of the ancient Indian city of Madurai.

**Taj Mahal** The white-marble mausoleum (a building that covers a burial chamber) attracts 8 million visitors a year.

**Petronas Towers** At 1,483 ft (452 m), they are the world's tallest twin towers.

# Famous landmarks

Asia is a continent of huge contrasts. It was the birthplace of some of the earliest human civilizations, has been a hub for many of the world's great religions, such as Islam, Hinduism, and Buddhism, and, today, is the site of some of the world's most amazing modern architecture.

**KEY**
○ Landmark location

CHINA IS THE MOST VISITED COUNTRY IN ASIA.

ASIA

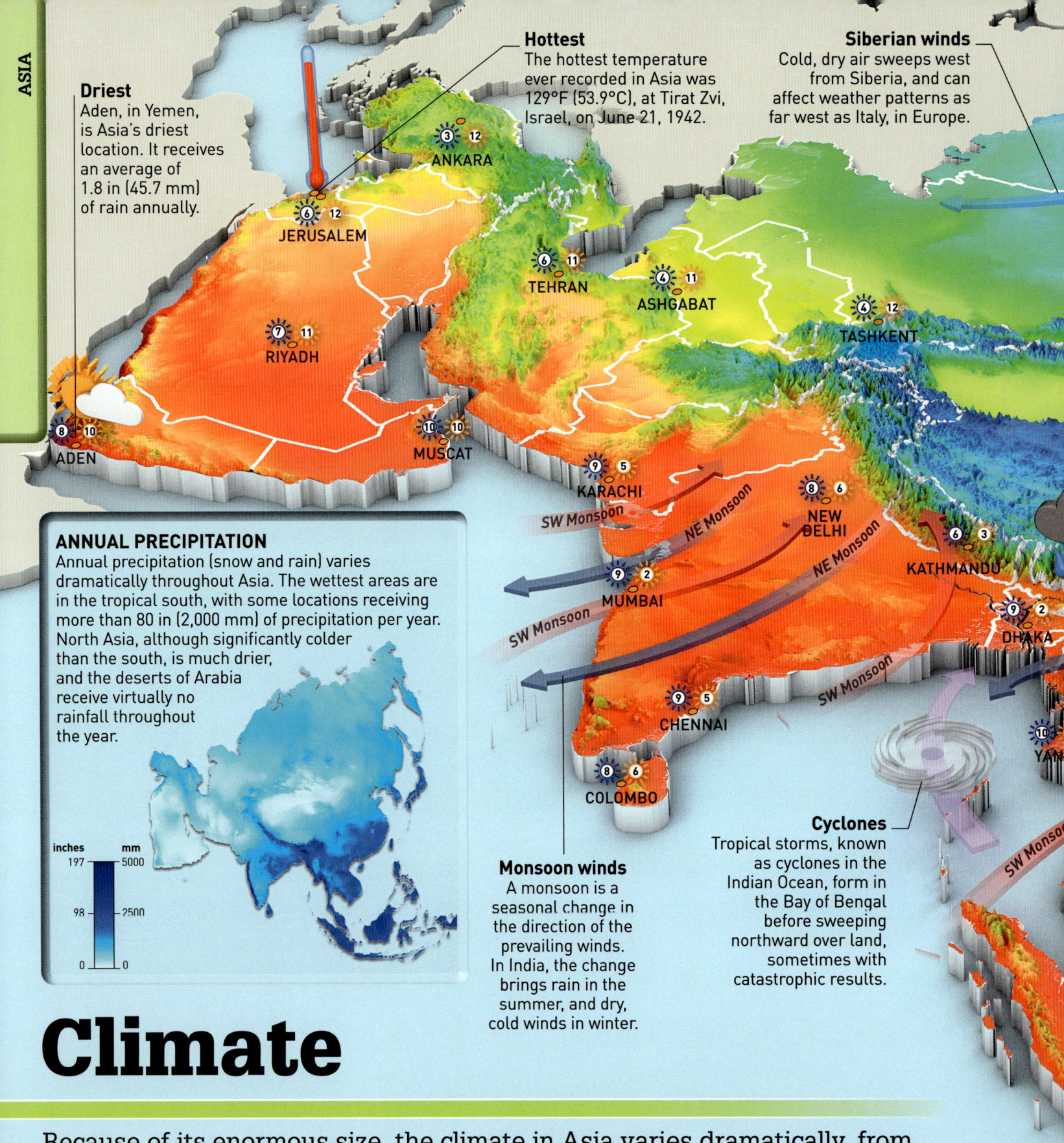

**Driest**
Aden, in Yemen, is Asia's driest location. It receives an average of 1.8 in (45.7 mm) of rain annually.

**Hottest**
The hottest temperature ever recorded in Asia was 129°F (53.9°C), at Tirat Zvi, Israel, on June 21, 1942.

**Siberian winds**
Cold, dry air sweeps west from Siberia, and can affect weather patterns as far west as Italy, in Europe.

**ANNUAL PRECIPITATION**
Annual precipitation (snow and rain) varies dramatically throughout Asia. The wettest areas are in the tropical south, with some locations receiving more than 80 in (2,000 mm) of precipitation per year. North Asia, although significantly colder than the south, is much drier, and the deserts of Arabia receive virtually no rainfall throughout the year.

**Monsoon winds**
A monsoon is a seasonal change in the direction of the prevailing winds. In India, the change brings rain in the summer, and dry, cold winds in winter.

**Cyclones**
Tropical storms, known as cyclones in the Indian Ocean, form in the Bay of Bengal before sweeping northward over land, sometimes with catastrophic results.

# Climate

Because of its enormous size, the climate in Asia varies dramatically, from the polar cold of the north, to the dry, desert environments of the southwest and center, and the hot, humid conditions of the tropical south. The continent is home to some of the coldest, hottest, driest, and wettest places on Earth.

110 LIFE IN ASIA IS CRITICALLY DEPENDENT ON MONSOON RAINS. A WEAK

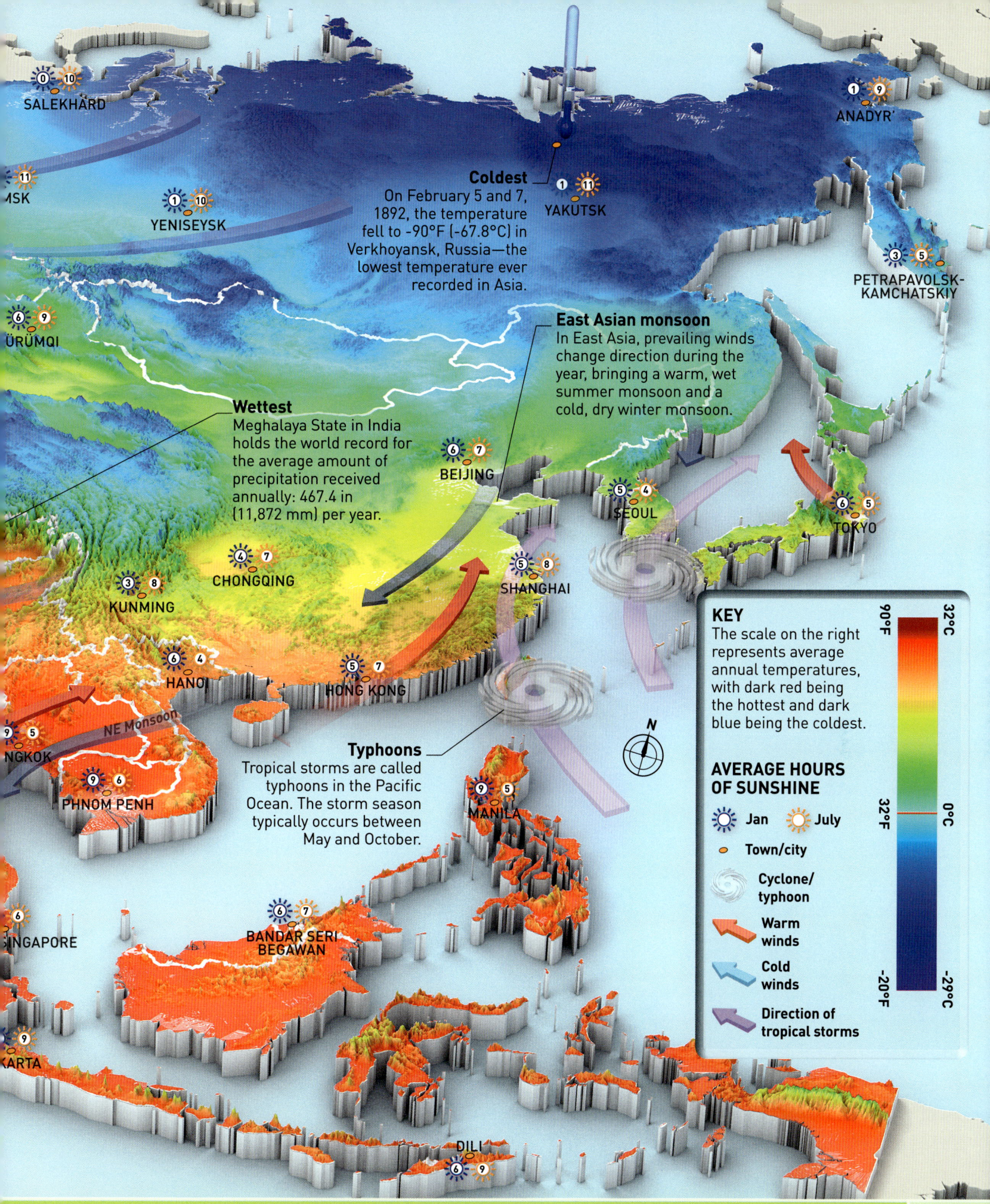

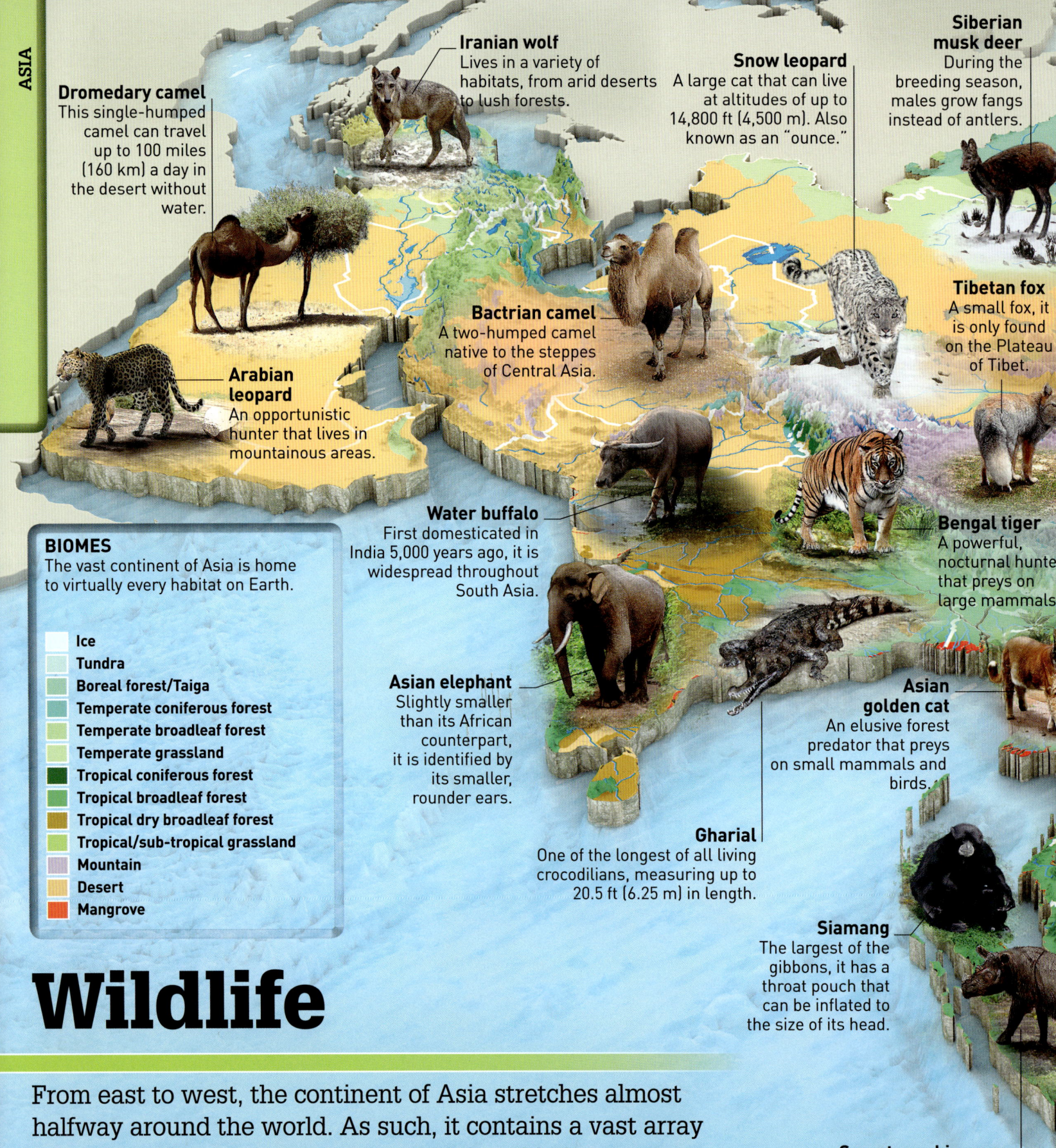

# Wildlife

From east to west, the continent of Asia stretches almost halfway around the world. As such, it contains a vast array of habitats, from Arctic tundra and high, cold plateaus, to barren deserts and damp, lush rain forests. The continent's array of wildlife is as vast and varied as the landscape itself.

ASIA

**KEY**
Illuminated areas on the map reflect urban, built-up areas and roads, in contrast to rural regions.

■ Rural area
▨ Urban area

**Trans-Siberian Railway**
Bright lights mark a dotted line across Siberia, showing the route of the Trans-Siberian Railway.

**Arabian Peninsula**
A large portion of the Arabian Peninsula is an area of desert known as the "Empty Quarter."

**Oman**
This country had the fastest rate of urbanization in Asia over the past five years (8.54 percent).

**● Hong Kong**
Hong Kong has a population of 7.35 million, making it the 21st largest city in Asia, but the city is the fourth most densely populated territory on Earth, with a staggering 17,294 inhabitants per sq mile (6,682 per sq km).

**Indus Valley**
This river valley in northern Pakistan is home to some of the country's largest cities, including Lahore and Islamabad.

**India**
Home to 1.27 billion people, but only 32.7 percent of the population live in towns or cities.

**Bangkok**
Almost one-sixth of Thailand's 68.2 million people live in or around the country's capital, Bangkok.

# By night

This satellite image of Asia at night shows how the continent's huge population is concentrated in small pockets of land. India, northern China, the southern Korean peninsula, and Japan are densely populated, whereas Siberia and Central Asia are virtually empty.

**Singapore**
One of three territories in Asia —along with Hong Kong and Macau—in which the entire population live in an urban environment.

ASIA IS HOME TO THREE OF THE WORLD'S FIVE MOST DENSELY

**Tokyo-Yokohama**
38 million people live in and around the cities of Tokyo and Yokohama.

**North Korea**
Almost 61 percent of North Korea's population of 25.1 million live in an urban environment, but electricity shortages in the country mean few lights shine at night.

**Philippines**
The National Capital Region of the Philippines, which includes Manila, the country's capital, is home to 12.9 million people.

🔴 **Sri Lanka**
Only 18.4 percent of Sri Lanka's 22 million population live in towns and cities—the lowest figure of any Asian country.

POPULATED TERRITORIES: MACAU, HONG KONG, AND BAHRAIN.

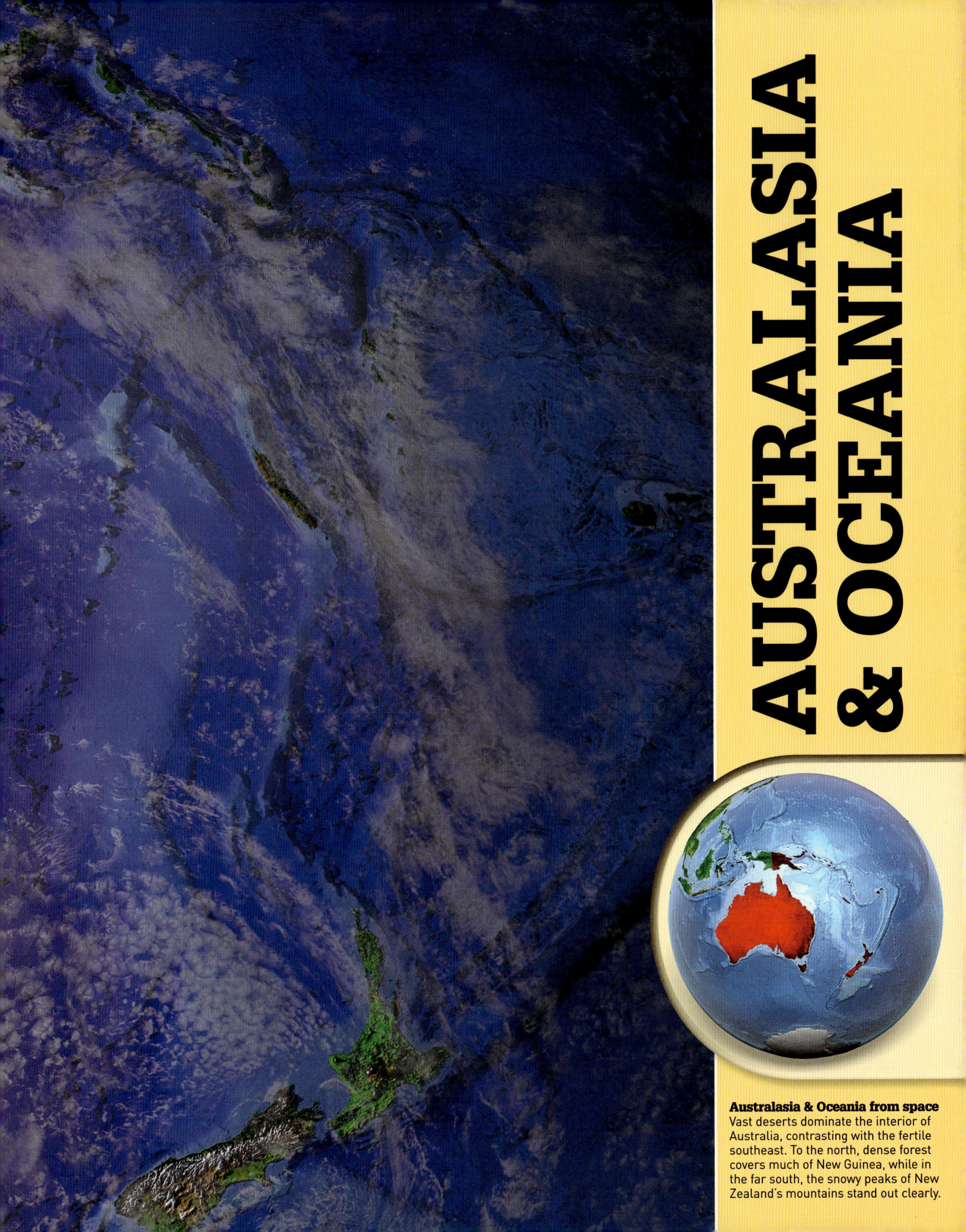

# AUSTRALASIA & OCEANIA

**Australasia & Oceania from space**
Vast deserts dominate the interior of Australia, contrasting with the fertile southeast. To the north, dense forest covers much of New Guinea, while in the far south, the snowy peaks of New Zealand's mountains stand out clearly.

# AUSTRALASIA AND OCEANIA

**PACIFIC OCEAN**

**KEY**
- 🔴 Capital city
- ⚫ Major city

Wake Island (to US)

**Marshall Islands**
Conquered during World War Two, these islands belonged to the United States until 1986.

**MARSHALL ISLANDS**

MAJURO ATOLL

Northern Mariana Islands (to US)

HAGÅTÑA

Guam (to US)

*Philippine Sea*

PALIKIR

TARA ATO K

**MICRONESIA**

NAURU

NGERULMUD

**PALAU**

*Bismarck Sea*

HONIARA

**SOLOMON ISLANDS**

**PAPUA NEW GUINEA**

PORT MORESBY

*Solomon Sea*

**VANUATU**

PORT V

**ASIA**

**New Caledonia**
One of the three groups of islands in the Pacific Ocean that are controlled by France. The others are French Polynesia and Wallis and Futuna.

NOUM

New Caledonia (to France)

*Arafura Sea*

*Coral Sea*

Cairns

*Gulf of Carpentaria*

Darwin

Townsville

*Joseph Bonaparte Gulf*

**NORTHERN TERRITORY**

**QUEENSLAND**

Brisbane

*Timor Sea*

Alice Springs

Lord Howe Island (to Australia)

**AUSTRALIA**

**NEW SOUTH WALES**

Sydney

**SOUTH AUSTRALIA**

**CANBERRA**

AUSTRALIAN CAPITAL TERRITORY

**WESTERN AUSTRALIA**

Adelaide

**VICTORIA**

Melbourne

*Tasman Sea*

*Great Australian Bight*

**TASMANIA**

Hobart

Perth

**Australia**
Canberra was chosen to be Australia's capital city in 1908. The country is made up of eight states.

N

118    THE BRITISH MONARCH, QUEEN ELIZABETH II, IS ALSO

**Kiribati**
This group of 33 tiny islands is spread over a vast area of the Pacific Ocean. Kiribati was a British colony from 1915 until it gained its independence in 1979.

**● Nauru**
The Republic of Nauru is the world's smallest island nation, with a total area of 8 sq miles (21 sq km) and a population of just 9,591. The oval-shaped island is surrounded by sandy beaches and a coral reef.

**New Zealand**
Most New Zealanders have European ancestors, but about 15 percent of the population belong to the Maori community. The Maoris arrived in New Zealand in about 1300.

**French Polynesia**
Tahiti is the largest island in French Polynesia. Many people work in tourism and pearl-farming.

# Countries and borders

Australasia is dominated by Australia and New Zealand, two former British colonies that, in recent years, have built new relations with other Pacific nations, such as Japan. Oceania includes the many islands of the Pacific Ocean, whose communities rely increasingly on tourism.

**FAST FACTS**

**Total land area:**
3,285,049 sq miles (8,508,238 sq km)

**Total population:**
39.7 million

**Number of countries:** 14

**Largest country:**
Australia—2,988,901 sq miles (7,741,220 sq km)

**Smallest country:**
Nauru— 8.1 sq miles (21 sq km)

**Largest country population:**
Australia—22.9 million

HEAD OF STATE OF AUSTRALIA AND NEW ZEALAND.

### 3 Lake Eyre

With an area of 3,700 sq miles (9,583 sq km), Lake Eyre is the largest lake in Australasia and Oceania. During the dry season, much of the lake evaporates, leaving behind a thick salt crust.

Lake Eyre sometimes turns pink because of a type of algae in the water.

### Marshall Islands

A group of 34 scattered atolls (low-lying islands made of coral reefs) in the Pacific Ocean. The average height of each island is only 6.6 ft (2 m) above sea level.

### New Guinea

The world's second-largest island after Greenland, New Guinea is dominated by the New Guinea Highlands.

### Kimberley Plateau

Rocky gorges and sandstone hills dominate this isolated region of Western Australia.

### Great Dividing Range

These mountains divide the fertile coastal plains from the dry interior.

### Southern Alps

These young mountains are growing rapidly as the Australian and Pacific plates move toward one another.

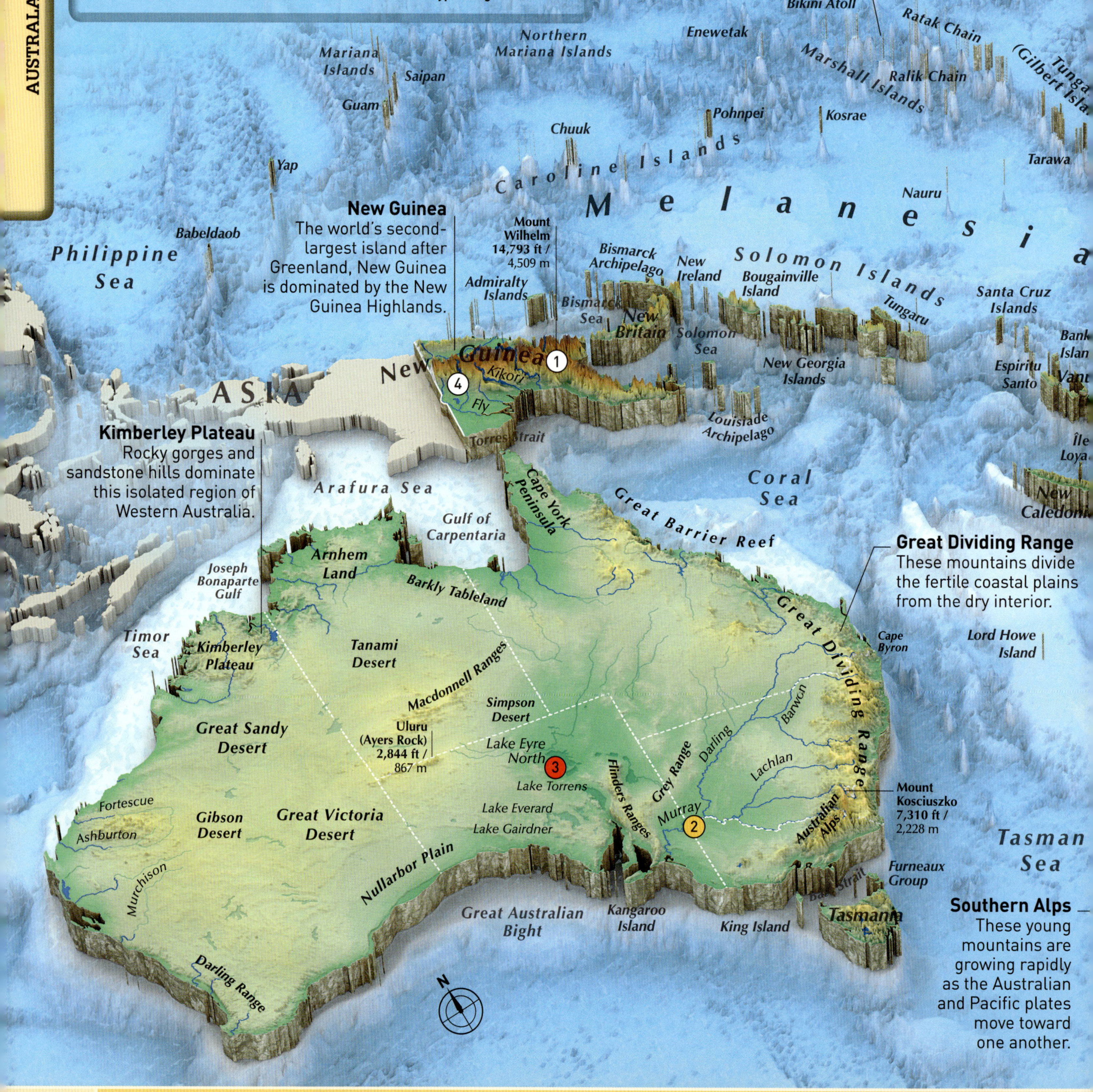
Micr
Bikini Atoll
Ratak Chain
Tunga (Gilbert Isla
Enewetak
Northern Mariana Islands
Mariana Islands
Saipan
Guam
Marshall Islands
Ralik Chain
Kosrae
Pohnpei
Chuuk
Tarawa
Yap
Caroline Islands
Nauru
Melanesia
Mount Wilhelm 14,793 ft / 4,509 m
Babeldaob
Philippine Sea
Bismarck Archipelago
New Ireland
Solomon Islands
Bougainville Island
Santa Cruz Islands
Admiralty Islands
Bismarck Sea
Tungaru
New Britain
Solomon Sea
Bank Islan
New Guinea
Kikori
Fly
Espiritu Santo
Vanu
New Georgia Islands
ASIA
Louisiade Archipelago
Île Loya
Torres Strait
Coral Sea
New Caledon
Arafura Sea
Cape York Peninsula
Great Barrier Reef
Gulf of Carpentaria
Arnhem Land
Joseph Bonaparte Gulf
Barkly Tableland
Great Dividing Range
Cape Byron
Lord Howe Island
Timor Sea
Kimberley Plateau
Tanami Desert
Macdonnell Ranges
Simpson Desert
Barwon
Great Sandy Desert
Uluru (Ayers Rock) 2,844 ft / 867 m
Lake Eyre North
Darling
Lachlan
Lake Torrens
Flinders Ranges
Grey Range
Mount Kosciuszko 7,310 ft / 2,228 m
Fortescue
Gibson Desert
Great Victoria Desert
Lake Everard
Murray
Ashburton
Lake Gairdner
Australian Alps
Tasman Sea
Nullarbor Plain
Furneaux Group
Murchison
Bass Strait
Great Australian Bight
Kangaroo Island
King Island
Tasmania
Darling Range
N



SOME OF THE OLDEST ROCKS ON EARTH–DATING BACK 4.4

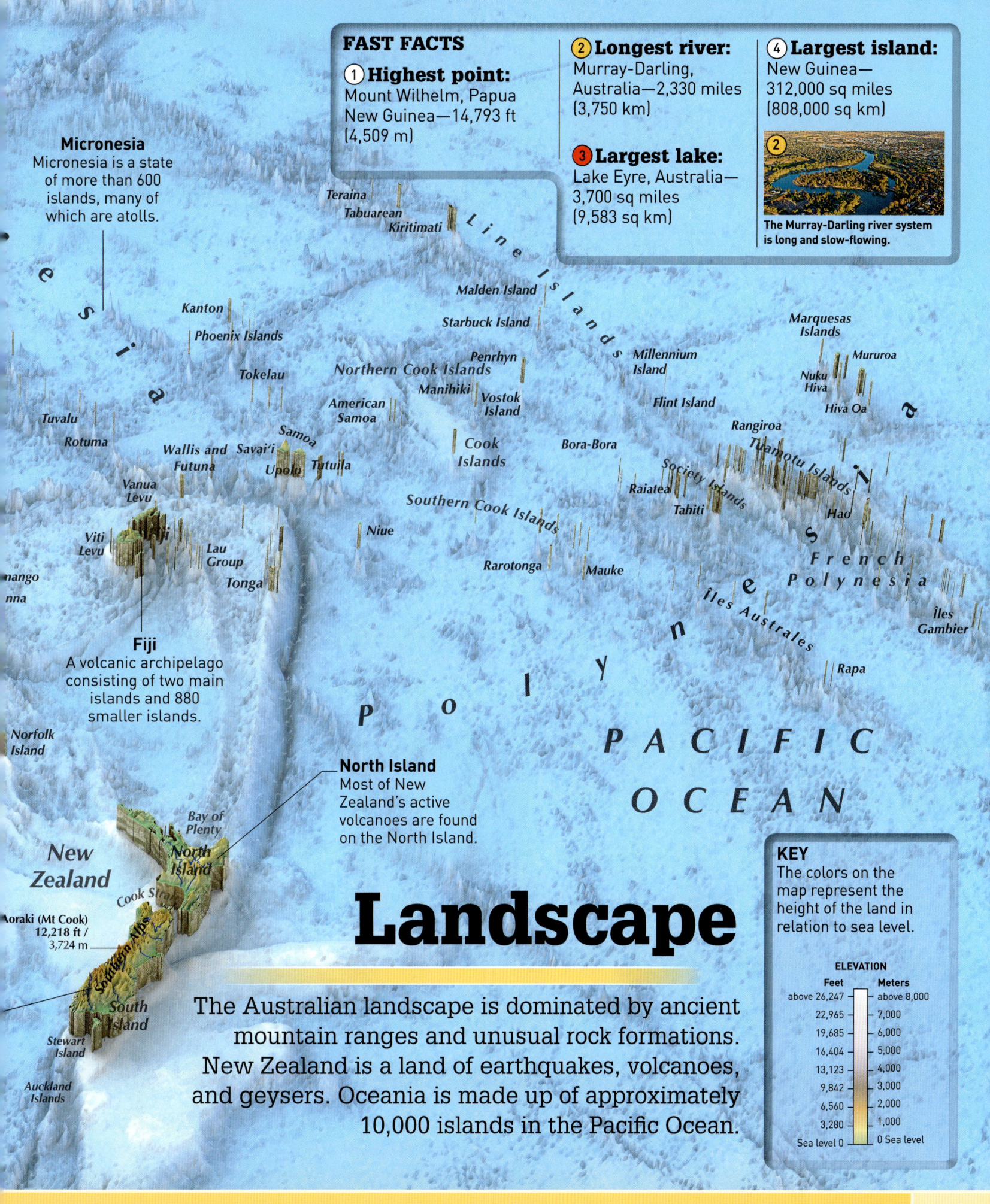

# Landscape

**FAST FACTS**

**① Highest point:** Mount Wilhelm, Papua New Guinea—14,793 ft (4,509 m)

**② Longest river:** Murray-Darling, Australia—2,330 miles (3,750 km)

**③ Largest lake:** Lake Eyre, Australia—3,700 sq miles (9,583 sq km)

**④ Largest island:** New Guinea—312,000 sq miles (808,000 sq km)

The Murray-Darling river system is long and slow-flowing.

**Micronesia** — Micronesia is a state of more than 600 islands, many of which are atolls.

**Fiji** — A volcanic archipelago consisting of two main islands and 880 smaller islands.

**North Island** — Most of New Zealand's active volcanoes are found on the North Island.

The Australian landscape is dominated by ancient mountain ranges and unusual rock formations. New Zealand is a land of earthquakes, volcanoes, and geysers. Oceania is made up of approximately 10,000 islands in the Pacific Ocean.

**KEY** — The colors on the map represent the height of the land in relation to sea level.

**ELEVATION**

| Feet | Meters |
|---|---|
| above 26,247 | above 8,000 |
| 22,965 | 7,000 |
| 19,685 | 6,000 |
| 16,404 | 5,000 |
| 13,123 | 4,000 |
| 9,842 | 3,000 |
| 6,560 | 2,000 |
| 3,280 | 1,000 |
| Sea level 0 | 0 Sea level |

BILLION YEARS—HAVE BEEN FOUND IN WESTERN AUSTRALIA.

# Fascinating facts

**AUSTRALASIA AND OCEANIA**

## COUNTRY WITH THE MOST NEIGHBORS

**Papua New Guinea**
1—Indonesia

## LONGEST TUNNELS

**Railroad tunnel**
Kaimai Tunnel, North Island, New Zealand—5.5 miles (8.85 km)

**Road tunnel**
Airport Link, Brisbane, Australia—4.16 miles (6.7 km)

## Number of time zones
**11**

The world is split into 39 time zones. Most are set whole hours ahead or behind Coordinated Universal Time (UCT) – the time at the Greenwich Meridian in London, UK. Some, however, are whole hours plus 30 or 45 minutes ahead or behind UCT. Therefore, on this map, if it was 12:00 in London, it would be 22:00 in Sydney, Australia (10 hours ahead of UCT).

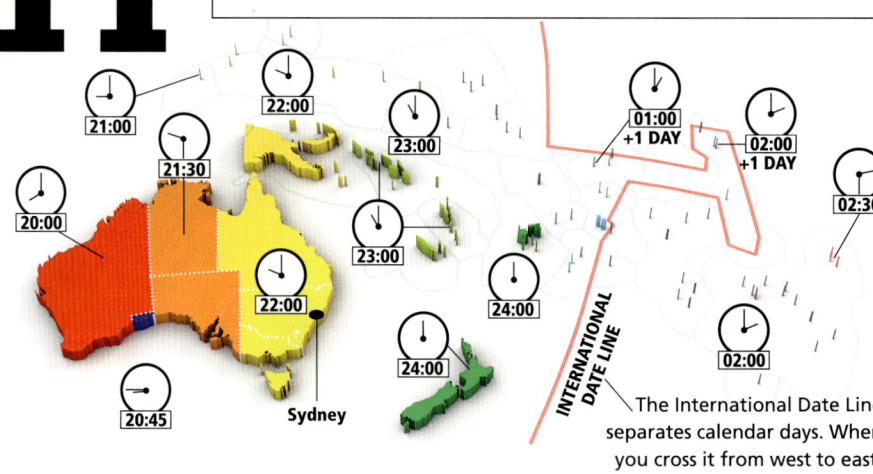

The International Date Line separates calendar days. When you cross it from west to east, you move ahead one day.

**Longest coastline**
Australia—16,006.5 miles (25,760 km)

**Busiest port**
Port Hedland, Western Australia—**537,927 kilotons of cargo per year,** making it the eighth-busiest port in the world

## Fastest train
Tilt Train, Australia—130.5 mph (210 km/h)

## Tallest buildings

Q1
Gold Coast, Australia
1,060 ft (323 m)

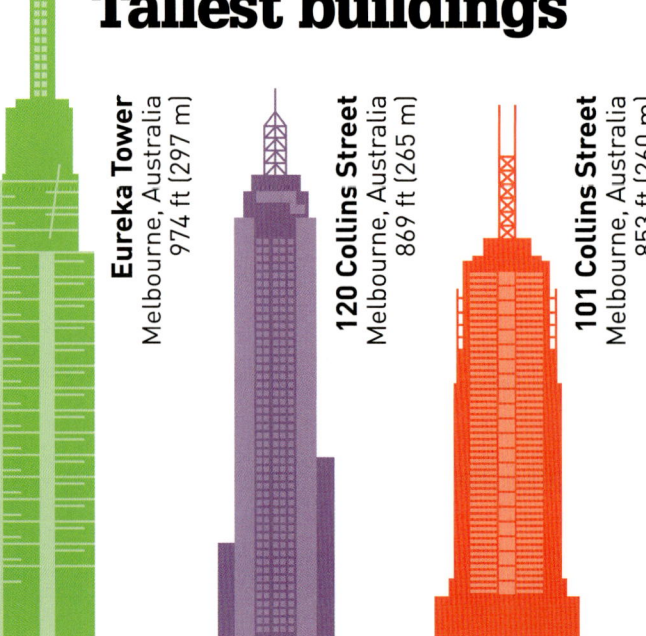

Eureka Tower
Melbourne, Australia
974 ft (297 m)

120 Collins Street
Melbourne, Australia
869 ft (265 m)

101 Collins Street
Melbourne, Australia
853 ft (260 m)

Prima Pearl
Melbourne, Australia
833 ft (254 m)

 **Busiest airport** Sydney Airport, Sydney, Australia—**39.7 million passengers per year**

# BRIDGES

**Longest bridge:** Macleay River Bridge, Australia — **2 miles (3.2 km)**

● **Tallest bridge:** Mohaka Viaduct, Raupunga, New Zealand — **312 ft (95 m)**

# WATERFALLS

**Highest: Browne Falls, New Zealand**— 2,744 ft (836 m)

**Largest (by volume): Huka Falls, Taupo, New Zealand**— 7,769 ft$^3$ (220 m$^3$) of water per second

# LAKES

**Largest lake:** Lake Eyre, Australia — **3,700 sq miles (9,583 sq km)**

● **Deepest lake:** Lake Hauroko, New Zealand — **1,516 ft (462 m)**

## Most visited cities (Visitors per year)

- Sydney, Australia — 2.853 million
- Melbourne, Australia — 2.166 million
- Auckland, NZ — 1.965 million
- Christchurch, NZ — 1.732 million
- Brisbane, Australia — 1.066 million

## Highest mountains

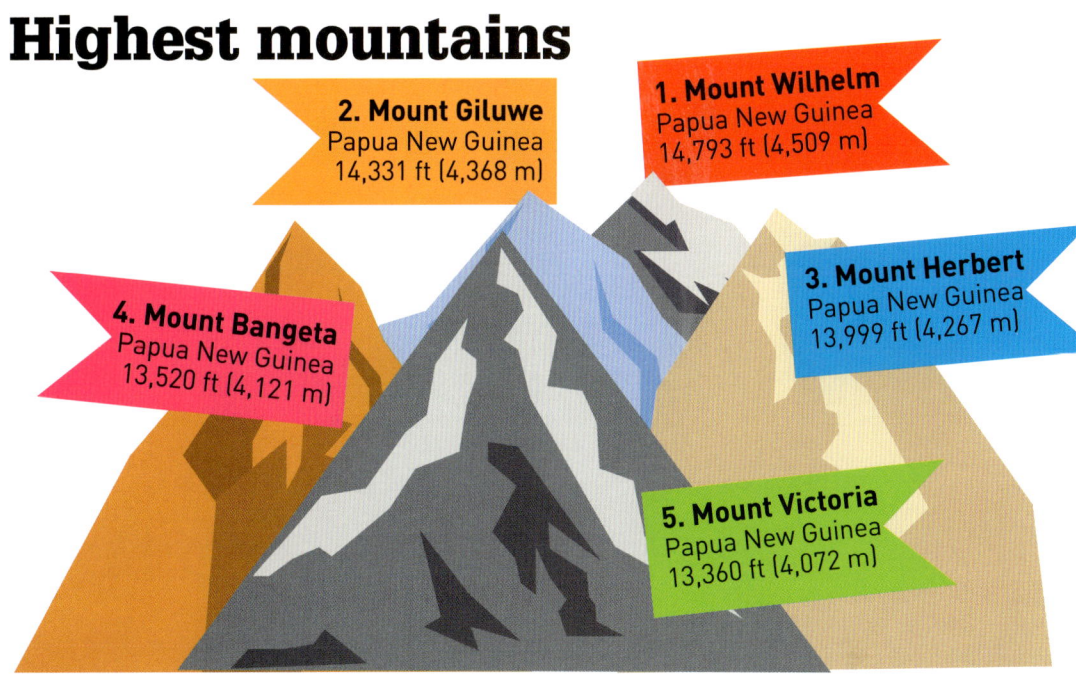

1. **Mount Wilhelm** Papua New Guinea 14,793 ft (4,509 m)
2. **Mount Giluwe** Papua New Guinea 14,331 ft (4,368 m)
3. **Mount Herbert** Papua New Guinea 13,999 ft (4,267 m)
4. **Mount Bangeta** Papua New Guinea 13,520 ft (4,121 m)
5. **Mount Victoria** Papua New Guinea 13,360 ft (4,072 m)

# TALLEST VOLCANO
Mount Giluwe, Papua New Guinea — **14,331 ft (4,368 m)**

# BIGGEST GLACIER
Tasman Glacier, New Zealand — **17 miles (27 km) long, with an area of 39 sq miles (101 sq km)**

## Australasia and Oceania's extreme points

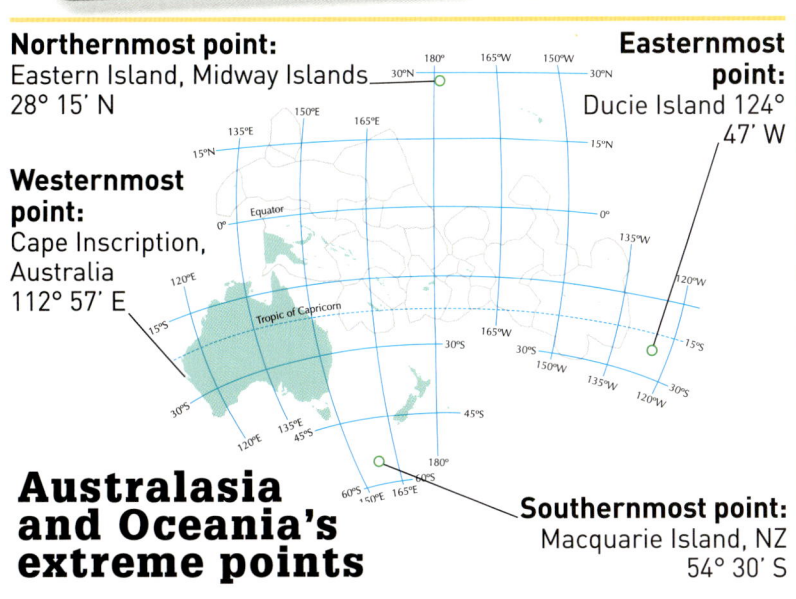

**Northernmost point:** Eastern Island, Midway Islands 28° 15' N

**Westernmost point:** Cape Inscription, Australia 112° 57' E

**Easternmost point:** Ducie Island 124° 47' W

**Southernmost point:** Macquarie Island, NZ 54° 30' S

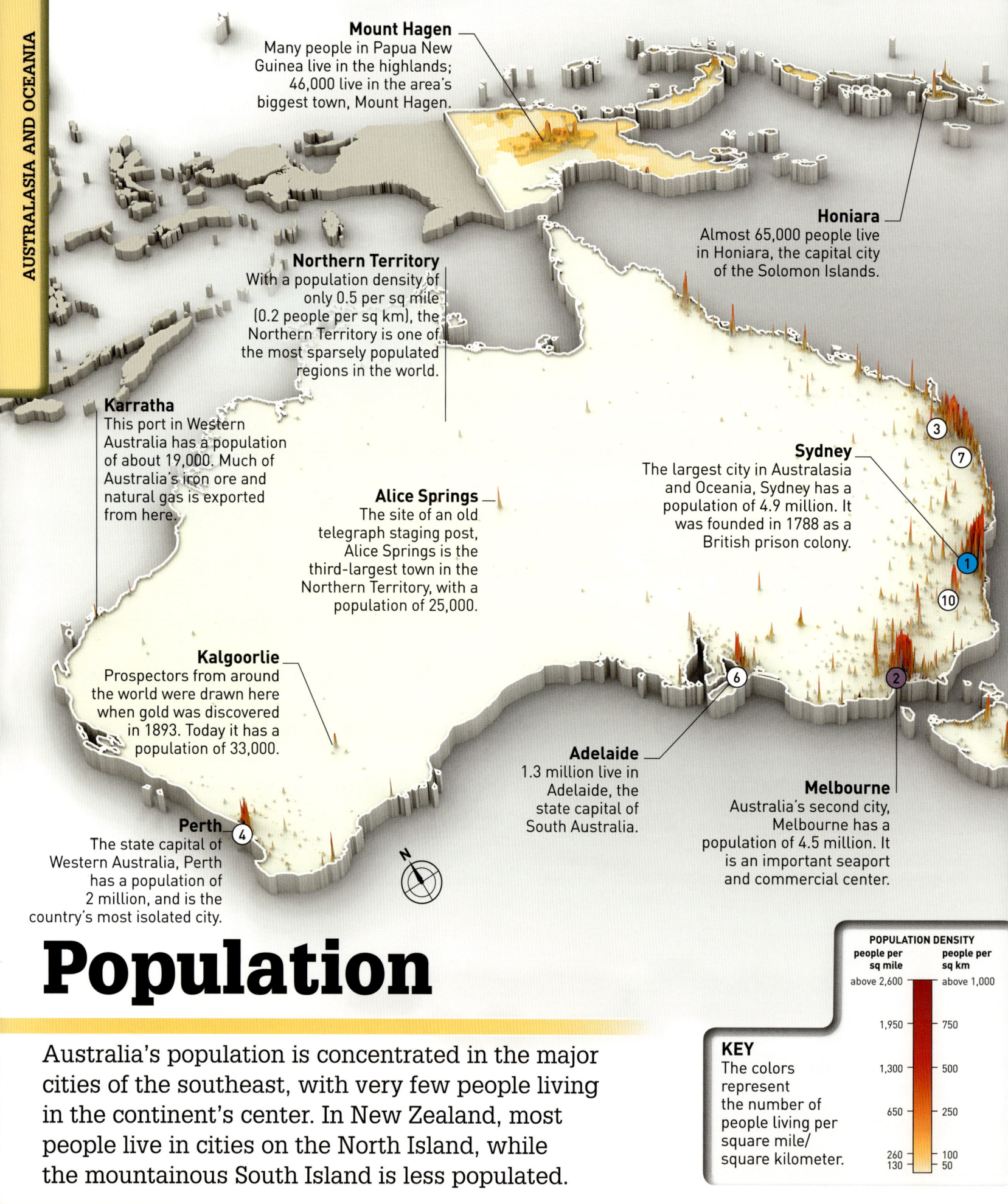

## AUSTRALASIA AND OCEANIA

**Mount Hagen**
Many people in Papua New Guinea live in the highlands; 46,000 live in the area's biggest town, Mount Hagen.

**Honiara**
Almost 65,000 people live in Honiara, the capital city of the Solomon Islands.

**Northern Territory**
With a population density of only 0.5 per sq mile (0.2 people per sq km), the Northern Territory is one of the most sparsely populated regions in the world.

**Karratha**
This port in Western Australia has a population of about 19,000. Much of Australia's iron ore and natural gas is exported from here.

**Sydney**
The largest city in Australasia and Oceania, Sydney has a population of 4.9 million. It was founded in 1788 as a British prison colony.

**Alice Springs**
The site of an old telegraph staging post, Alice Springs is the third-largest town in the Northern Territory, with a population of 25,000.

**Kalgoorlie**
Prospectors from around the world were drawn here when gold was discovered in 1893. Today it has a population of 33,000.

**Adelaide**
1.3 million live in Adelaide, the state capital of South Australia.

**Melbourne**
Australia's second city, Melbourne has a population of 4.5 million. It is an important seaport and commercial center.

**Perth**
The state capital of Western Australia, Perth has a population of 2 million, and is the country's most isolated city.

# Population

Australia's population is concentrated in the major cities of the southeast, with very few people living in the continent's center. In New Zealand, most people live in cities on the North Island, while the mountainous South Island is less populated.

**KEY**
The colors represent the number of people living per square mile/ square kilometer.

**POPULATION DENSITY**

| people per sq mile | people per sq km |
|---|---|
| above 2,600 | above 1,000 |
| 1,950 | 750 |
| 1,300 | 500 |
| 650 | 250 |
| 260 | 100 |
| 130 | 50 |

AUSTRALIA IS THE WORLD'S SIXTH-LARGEST COUNTRY

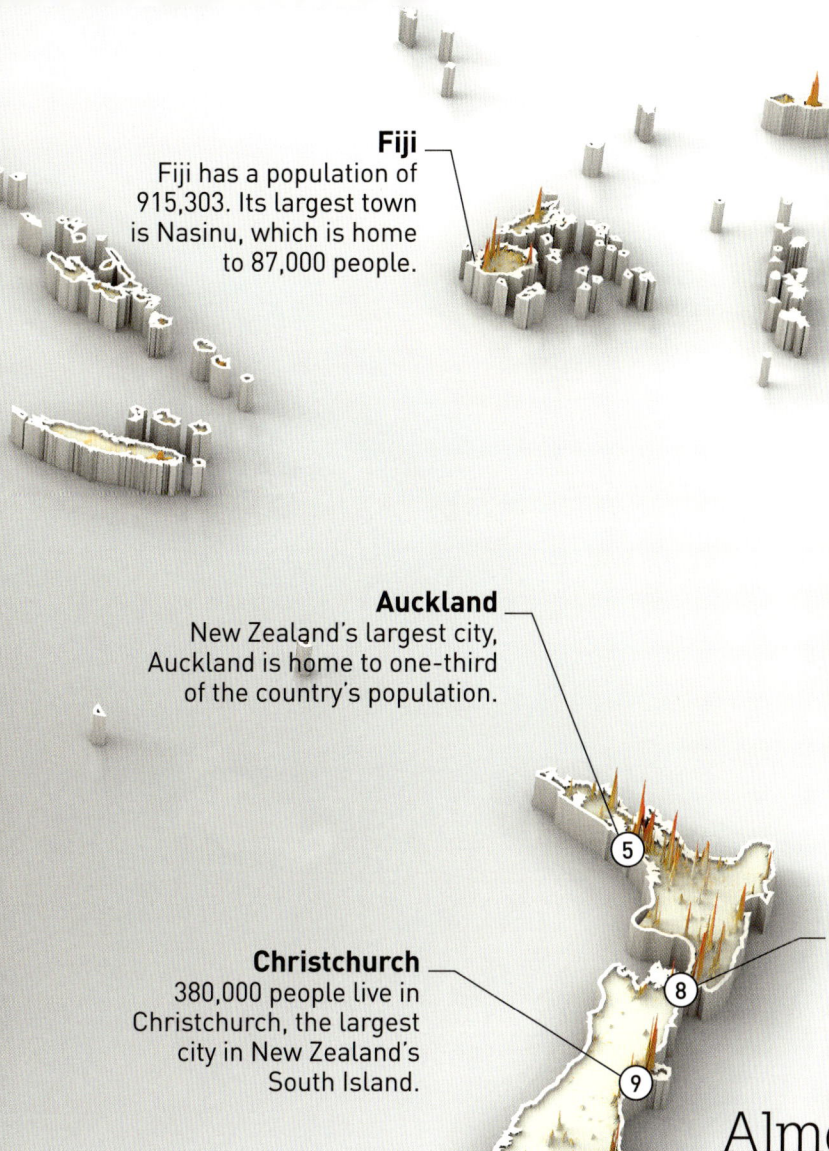

**Fiji**
Fiji has a population of 915,303. Its largest town is Nasinu, which is home to 87,000 people.

**Auckland**
New Zealand's largest city, Auckland is home to one-third of the country's population.

**Christchurch**
380,000 people live in Christchurch, the largest city in New Zealand's South Island.

**Wellington**
New Zealand's capital, Wellington has a population of 400,000 and is the country's second-largest city.

### Australasia and Oceania's largest cities

The list below is based on the number of people living inside a city's boundaries.

1. Sydney, Australia—4.9 million
2. Melbourne, Australia—4.5 million
3. Brisbane, Australia—2.3 million
4. Perth, Australia—2 million
5. Auckland, New Zealand—1.4 million
6. Adelaide, Australia—1.3 million
7. Gold Coast, Australia—530,000
8. Wellington, New Zealand—400,000
9. Christchurch, New Zealand—389,000
10. Canberra, Australia—380,000

Melbourne is the capital city of the Australian state of Victoria.

## Almost **one in three** Australians were born **outside** the country.

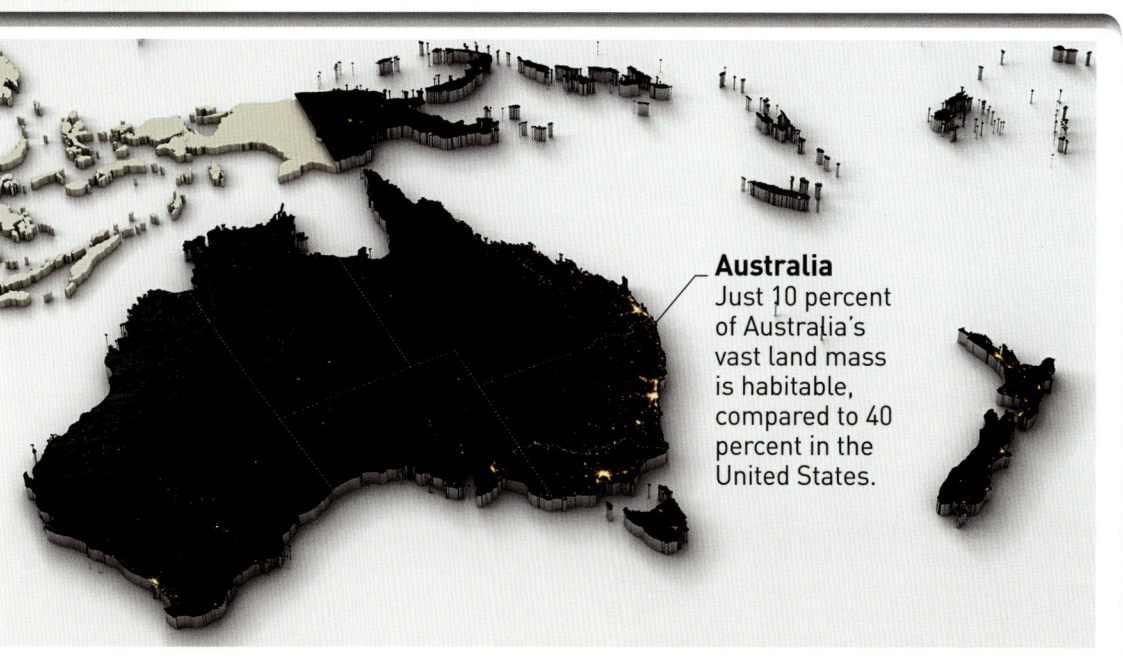

**BY NIGHT**
The brightly lit cities of southeastern Australia shine brightly, and Sydney, Melbourne, and Brisbane are easy to spot. In contrast, the country's interior is shrouded in darkness. Auckland and Wellington are two of the bright points on New Zealand's North Island, with only Christchurch standing out on South Island.

**KEY**
■ Rural area
▨ Urban area

**Australia**
Just 10 percent of Australia's vast land mass is habitable, compared to 40 percent in the United States.

# New Zealand

Almost one-third of New Zealand has been set aside as protected national park. Among its incredible range of landscapes are the towering peaks of the Southern Alps, and the geysers and hot springs of North Island.

**Mount Aspiring National Park**
Soaring peaks, alpine lakes, and dense forests make this one of the country's most beautiful national parks.

**Queenstown**
One of the biggest tourist resorts in the South Island, Queenstown attracts lovers of extreme sports, such as bungee jumping and white-water rafting.

**Fiordland National Park**
Fourteen beautiful fjords cut their way through rugged mountain scenery in this remote wilderness. The fjords are home to fur seals, dolphins, and penguins.

*Tasman Sea*

*Fiordland*  *Southe...*

Livingstone Mountains
Lak Wakat
Queensto
Kepler Mountains
Lake Te Anau
Te Anau
Takitimu Mountains
Hunter Mountains
Kaherekoau Mts
Cameron Mts

Resolution Island

Te Waewae Bay

**Southland**
South Island's most southerly region is sparsely populated, with only 7.4 people per sq mile (2.9 people per sq km).

*Tasman Sea*

Puysegur Point

**Milford Sound**
This 10-mile (16-km) long fjord is one of the highlights of the Fiordland National Park. The surrounding mountains are very popular with hikers.

**Lake Te Anau**
With a depth of up to 1,368 ft (417 m), Lake Te Anau contains the largest amount of freshwater in Australasia and Oceania. It is a popular destination for fishing and water sports.

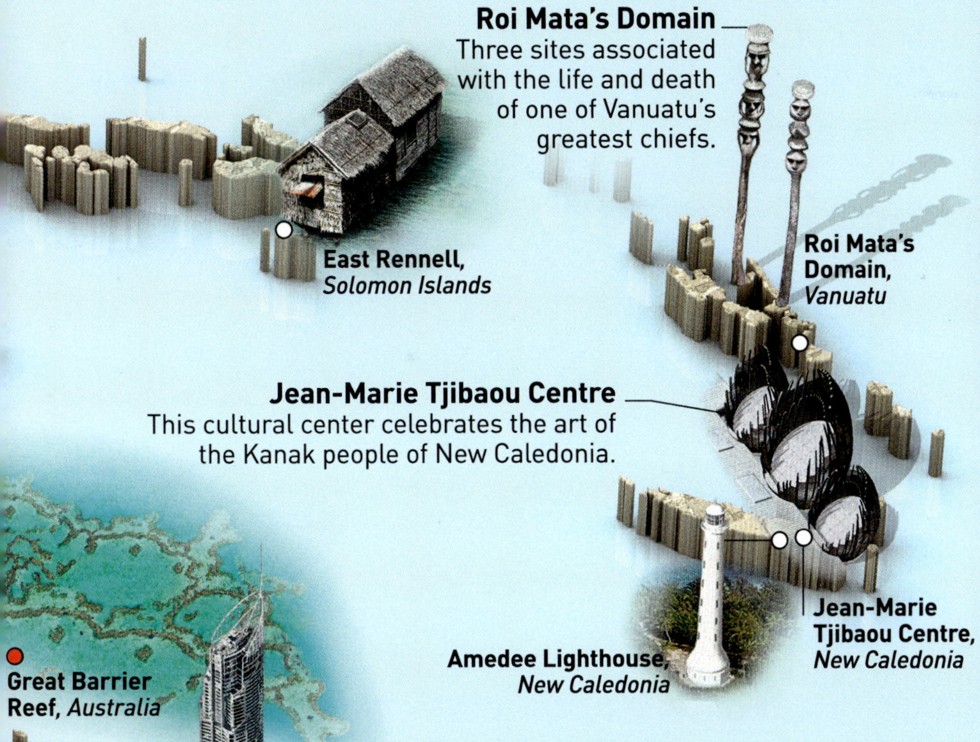

# Famous landmarks

The rock formations of the Australian Outback and the dramatic scenery of New Zealand's fjordland are just two of the region's many natural wonders. The region is also home to some iconic modern architecture, such as the Sydney Opera House.

The *roof* of the **Sydney Opera House** is covered with **1,056,006** *ceramic tiles*.

**Roi Mata's Domain**
Three sites associated with the life and death of one of Vanuatu's greatest chiefs.

**East Rennell,** Solomon Islands

**Roi Mata's Domain,** Vanuatu

**Jean-Marie Tjibaou Centre**
This cultural center celebrates the art of the Kanak people of New Caledonia.

**Amedee Lighthouse,** New Caledonia

**Jean-Marie Tjibaou Centre,** New Caledonia

## The Great Barrier Reef

One of the natural wonders of the world, the Great Barrier Reef stretches for 2,600 km (1,600 miles) along the northeastern coast of Australia. The reef is made of coral, which is built by billions of tiny creatures over hundreds of years. It is home to about 1,500 species of fish, 14 species of sea snake, and more than 3,000 different types of mollusc.

**Great Barrier Reef,** Australia

**Q1 Tower,** Gold Coast, Australia

**Byron Bay Lighthouse,** New South Wales

**Sydney Opera House,** Sydney, Australia

**Royal Exhibition Building,** Melbourne, Australia

**Twelve Apostles National Park,** Victoria

**Port Arthur Historic Site,** Tasmania

**Sky Tower,** Auckland, New Zealand

**Mount Ngauruhoe,**
This active volcano is situated at the heart of New Zealand's oldest national park.

**Mount Ngauruhoe,** Tongariro National Park, New Zealand

**Milford Sound,** Te Wahipounamu, New Zealand

**Moeraki Boulders,** Hampden, New Zealand

**KEY**
○ Landmark location

FROM SYDNEY TO PERTH ON THE TRANS-AUSTRALIAN RAILWAY.

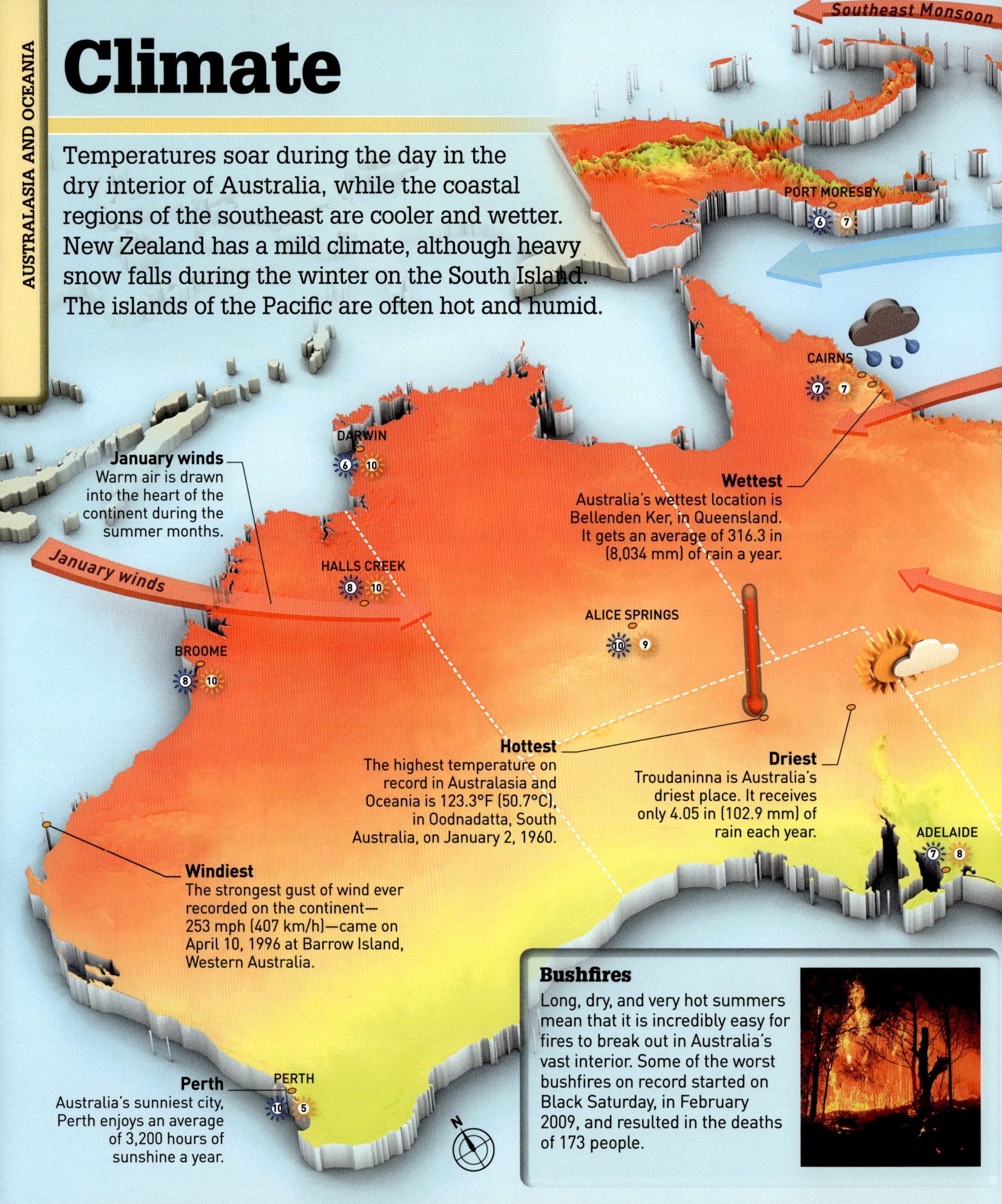

# Climate

Temperatures soar during the day in the dry interior of Australia, while the coastal regions of the southeast are cooler and wetter. New Zealand has a mild climate, although heavy snow falls during the winter on the South Island. The islands of the Pacific are often hot and humid.

**January winds**
Warm air is drawn into the heart of the continent during the summer months.

**Wettest**
Australia's wettest location is Bellenden Ker, in Queensland. It gets an average of 316.3 in (8,034 mm) of rain a year.

**Hottest**
The highest temperature on record in Australasia and Oceania is 123.3°F (50.7°C), in Oodnadatta, South Australia, on January 2, 1960.

**Driest**
Troudaninna is Australia's driest place. It receives only 4.05 in (102.9 mm) of rain each year.

**Windiest**
The strongest gust of wind ever recorded on the continent—253 mph (407 km/h)—came on April 10, 1996 at Barrow Island, Western Australia.

**Perth**
Australia's sunniest city, Perth enjoys an average of 3,200 hours of sunshine a year.

**Bushfires**
Long, dry, and very hot summers mean that it is incredibly easy for fires to break out in Australia's vast interior. Some of the worst bushfires on record started on Black Saturday, in February 2009, and resulted in the deaths of 173 people.

130 IN MAY 2015, THE RESIDENTS OF GOULBURN, NSW, AUSTRALIA, AWOKE

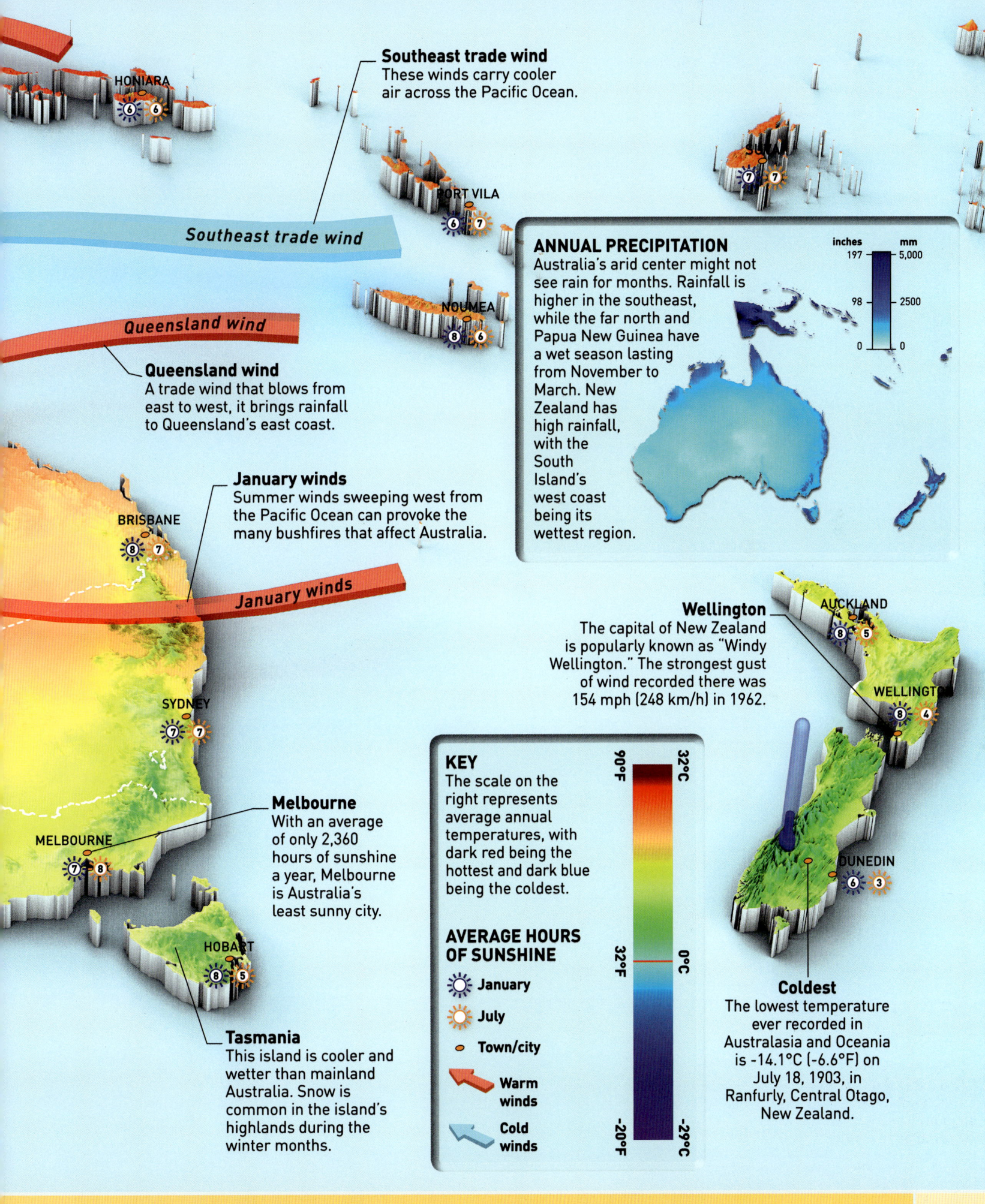

## AUSTRALASIA AND OCEANIA

### BIOMES
Deserts and temperate broadleaf forest are dominant in Australia, while the mountain habitat of the Southern Alps dominates New Zealand.

- Temperate broadleaf forest
- Temperate grassland
- Mediterranean
- Tropical broadleaf forest
- Tropical dry broadleaf forest
- Tropical/subtropical grassland
- Mountain
- Desert
- Mangrove

**Sir David's echidna** This spiny anteater, named for British naturalist Sir David Attenborough, is critically endangered.

**Southern cassowary** Its hornlike crest helps this bird push head-first through vegetation.

**Queen Alexandra birdwing butterfly** The world's largest butterfly, it has a wingspan of up to 12 in (31 cm).

**Cuscus** This possum uses its strong tail to climb through trees.

**Clownfish** This fish hides among the poisonous tentacles of the sea anemone.

**Saltwater crocodile** The largest of the reptiles, this crocodile drowns its prey by rolling it in the water.

**Frilled lizard** When threatened, this lizard opens a flap of skin to warn off predators.

**Black flying fox** This fruit bat's wingspan reaches up to 6.6 ft (2 m).

**Dingo** Descended from prehistoric domestic dogs, dingoes are widespread throughout Australia.

**Cockatoo** These noisy parrots gather in flocks that can include several hundred birds.

**Wallaby** Like their larger cousin, the kangaroo, wallabies carry their young in pouches.

**Blue-spotted stingray** Hiding patiently on the seabed, this ray ambushes passing snails and crabs.

**Kangaroo** These animals are marsupials, meaning that females nurture their young in pouches.

**Spiny anteater** One of the few mammals to lay eggs, the spiny anteater is protected by sharp spines.

**Dwarf bearded dragon** This small lizard lives off insects, invertebrates, and small mammals.

**Wombat** This marsupial lives in complex burrows that can be up to 660 ft (200 m) long.

**Inland taipan** The most venomous land snake in the world, its prey includes rats and other small mammals.

**Western brown snake** This fast-moving snake preys on mice and lizards.

**Redback spider** A bite from this spider can cause pain, sickness, and convulsions.

**Emu** Australia's largest bird can reach up to 6.2 ft (1.9 m) in height. Its shaggy plumage resembles hair.

**Tiger snake** This extremely venomous snake preys on frogs, lizards, birds, and small mammals.

**Numbat** This marsupial rips open termite nests with its powerful front teeth and claws.

### Poisonous snakes
Some of the world's most dangerous snakes live in Australia. The eastern brown snake causes the most deaths, followed by the western brown snake, and the tiger snake.

The eastern brown snake can be extremely aggressive.

**132** AUSTRALIA IS HOME TO AROUND 300,000 WILD CAMELS—DESCENDANTS OF

# Wildlife

Australia and New Zealand are home to some weird and wonderful animals, among them egg-laying mammals, marsupials, and flightless birds. The seas of Oceania, meanwhile, are home to turtles, dolphins, and an extraordinary range of tropical fish.

**Fijian monkey-faced bat** This bat can only be found on Fiji, but is endangered due to habitat loss.

**Coconut crab** The largest land-living crab in the world uses its pincers to pierce coconut shells.

**Banded sea krait** The coral reef provides a hunting ground for this highly venomous sea snake.

**Giant manta ray** To feed, this ray pulls in water through its mouth, collecting up to 66 lb (30 kg) of plankton each day.

The **platypus** has a pair of **venomous spurs** on its hind legs.

**Koala** Eucalyptus leaves provide the koala with its staple diet.

**Green turtle** This turtle feeds on seagrasses and is found throughout the region's seas.

**Kiwi** This nocturnal, flightless bird preys on earthworms and other invertebrates.

**Regent bowerbird** The male's plumage is glossy black and gold, while the female's is drab olive-brown.

**Dusky dolphin** Highly acrobatic, these dolphins can be found in the coastal waters around New Zealand.

**Lyrebird** During courtship, the male displays an extraordinary repertoire of songs.

**Kakapo** This large, flightless parrot lives off seeds and fruit.

**Duck-billed platypus** With its webbed feet and paddlelike tail, the platypus is well equipped for its semi-aquatic life.

**New Zealand sea lion** This highly endangered sea lion preys on crabs and penguins in the seas around New Zealand's South Island.

**Kookaburra** Known for its laughing call, the kookaburra eats mice and small reptiles.

**Tasmanian devil** The size of a small dog, this ferocious marsupial feeds on animal carcasses.

CAMELS BROUGHT TO THE COUNTRY IN THE 19TH CENTURY.

# POLAR REGIONS

**Extreme cold**
The North and South Poles are the northernmost and southernmost points on Earth. The climate there is extremely harsh, with temperatures rarely rising above 32°F (0°C).

ANTARCTICA

**Vinson Massif**
Part of a large mountain range by the Ronne Ice Shelf, this massif contains Antarctica's highest peak, Mount Vinson, at 16,050 ft (4,892 m).

**South Pole Station**
The Amundsen-Scott research station is located at the Geographical South Pole. First opened in 1956, it can house up to 200 researchers.

**Southern elephant seal**
The largest of all seals, males can be over 20 ft (6 m) long and weigh up to 8,800 lb (4,000 kg).

**Antarctic minke whale**
This small whale lives in groups of two to four.

**Antarctic ice fish**
A type of anti-freeze in its blood enables this fish to survive in ice-cold water.

**Wandering albatross**
With the largest wingspan of any bird—up to 11.5 ft (3.5 m)—it spends most of its life in flight at sea.

**Snowy sheathbill**
This bird does not swim, so it steals fish, and eggs or chicks, from penguins.

**South polar skua**
Up to 21 in (53 cm) tall, this large bird breeds in Antarctica before returning to a life on the oceans.

**Antarctic toothfish**
Growing up to 5.6 ft (1.7 m) long, this fish feeds on squid, crabs, shrimp, and smaller fish.

**Leopard seal**
This fierce, sharp-toothed predator hunts other seals, penguins, and fish.

# Antarctica

Earth's southernmost continent is the coldest region in the world, with temperatures reaching as low as -135.8°F (-93.2°C). Despite the harsh conditions, the continent is home to a number of animals. However, climate change is a threat to both Antarctica's animals and landscape.

**Ross Ice Shelf**
This enormous layer of floating ice is over 370 miles (600 km) long. About 90 percent of its ice lies underwater.

ANTARCTICA CONTAINS ABOUT 90 PERCENT OF THE WORLD'S ICE. IF

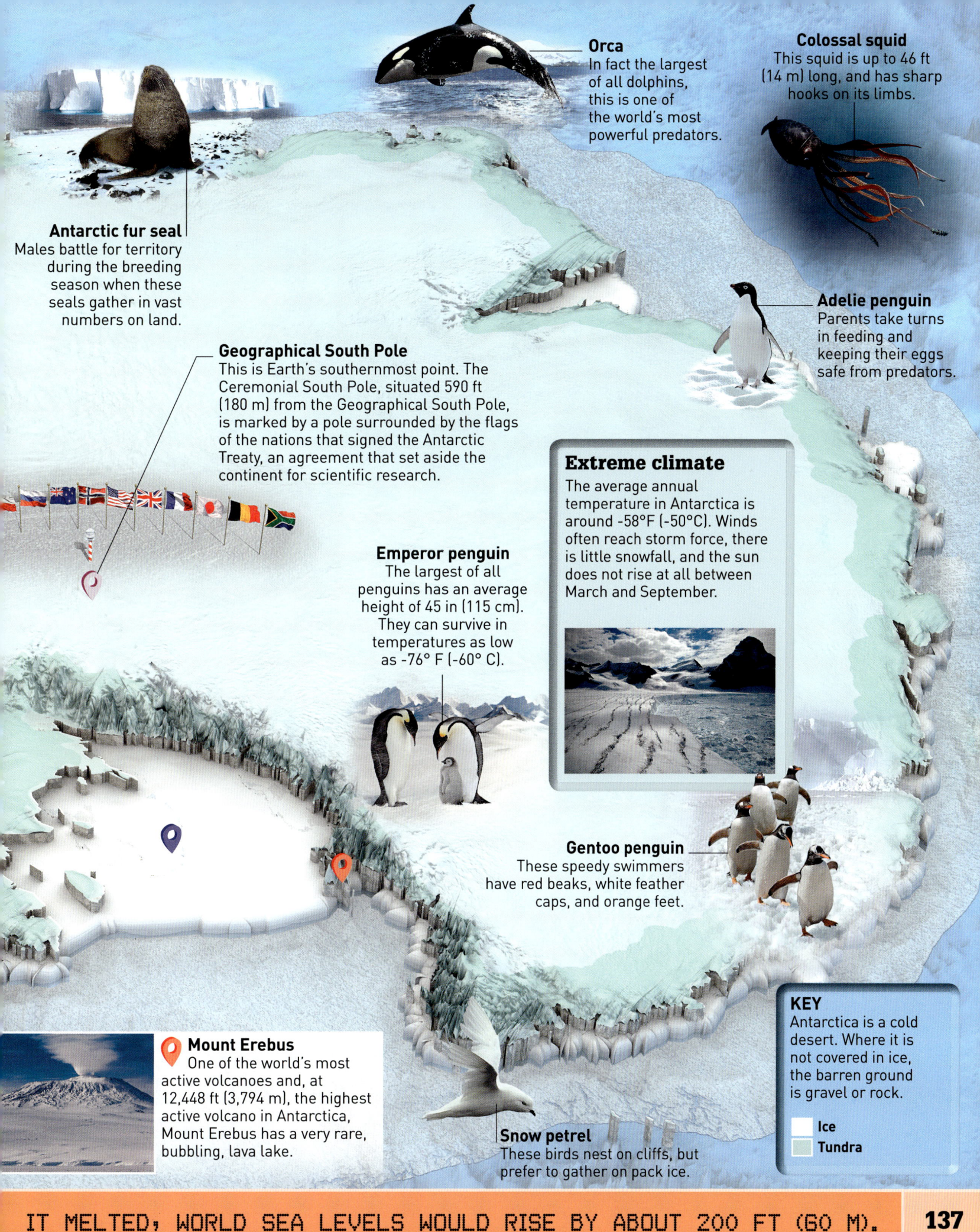

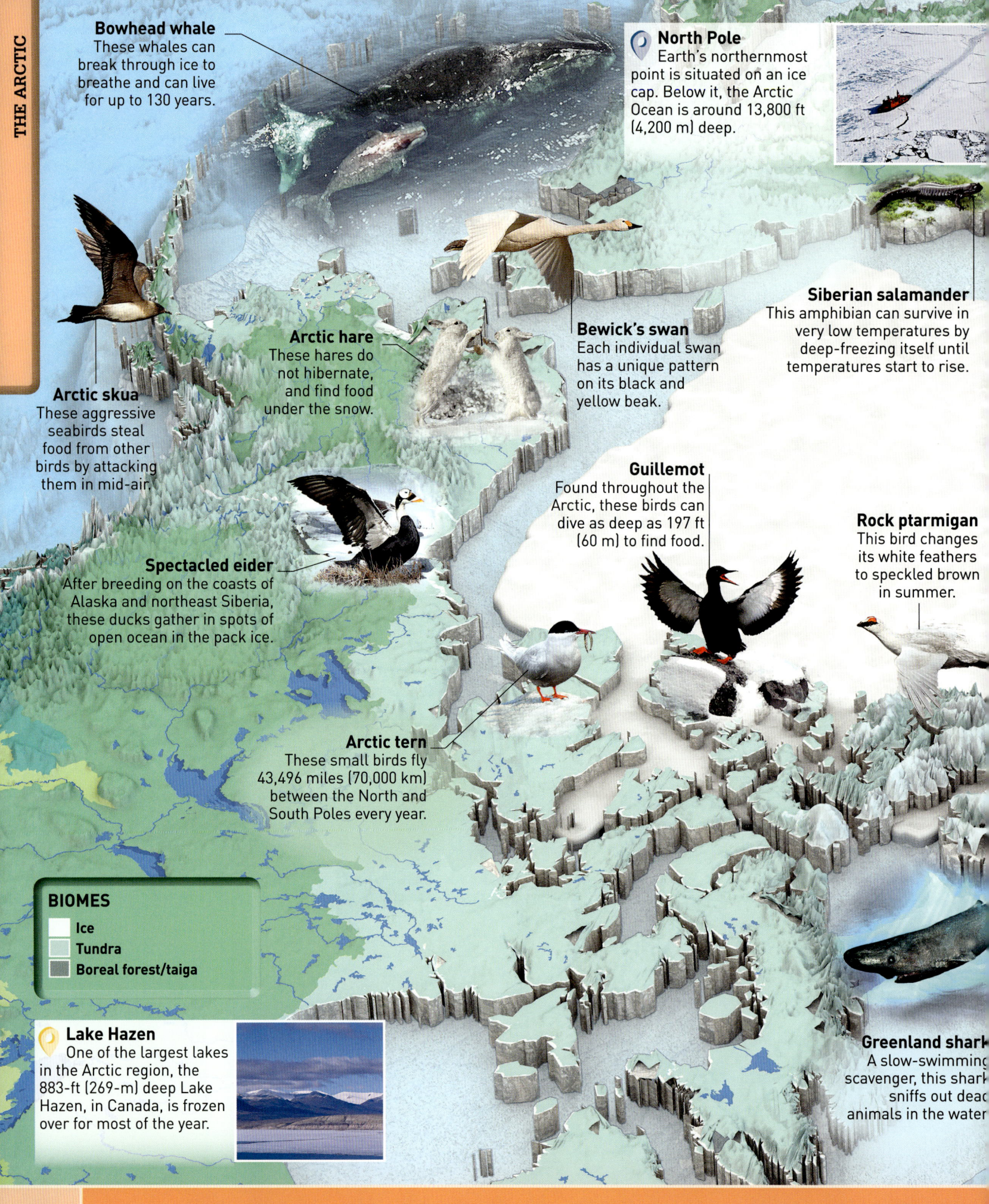

# The Arctic

Unlike Antarctica, the Arctic is not a continent, but the area of frozen waters surrounding the North Pole. It includes the northernmost parts of three continents—North America, Europe, and Asia. Many different animals have made a home in this inhospitable region.

**Yenisei**
The Yenisei river in Russia is the largest river to flow out into the Arctic Ocean. Its 31-mile (50-km) wide estuary is frozen for long parts of the year.

**Siberian crane**
This bird easily snips off roots and catches fish with its saw-edged beak.

**Beluga whale**
White in color, is small whale peaks in clicks and whistles.

**Ermine**
This mammal's coat turns from brown to white in winter for camouflage.

**Porbeagle shark**
This shark grows up to 8.2 ft (2.5 m) in length and feeds on squid and fish.

**Spiny dogfish**
This fish is one of the most numerous species of shark in the world.

**Brent goose**
Unlike other geese, the Brent flies in long lines instead of in a V-shape.

**Narwhal**
The tusks of this small whale can grow to 9.8 ft (3 m).

**Lemming**
Soft, warm fur helps this rodent stay active through the winter.

**Polar bear**
A powerful predator, this bear roams over land and pack ice to find prey.

**Bluntnose sixgill shark**
This fast-swimming shark has six gills instead of the five normal in most sharks.

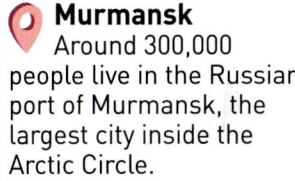

**Puffin**
60 percent of the world's puffins live in Iceland.

**Murmansk**
Around 300,000 people live in the Russian port of Murmansk, the largest city inside the Arctic Circle.

COVERS CHANGES SIGNIFICANTLY FROM WINTER TO SUMMER.

# THE OCEANS

**Mighty seas**
Oceans cover approximately 71 percent of Earth's surface and contain 97 percent of the water found on our planet.

# Pacific Ocean

The Pacific is by far the world's largest ocean. At its widest point (stretching from Colombia to Indonesia), it extends for 12,300 miles (19,800 km)—almost halfway around the world. The deepest trenches on Earth can be found here, along with massive volcanoes that rise up from the ocean's floor.

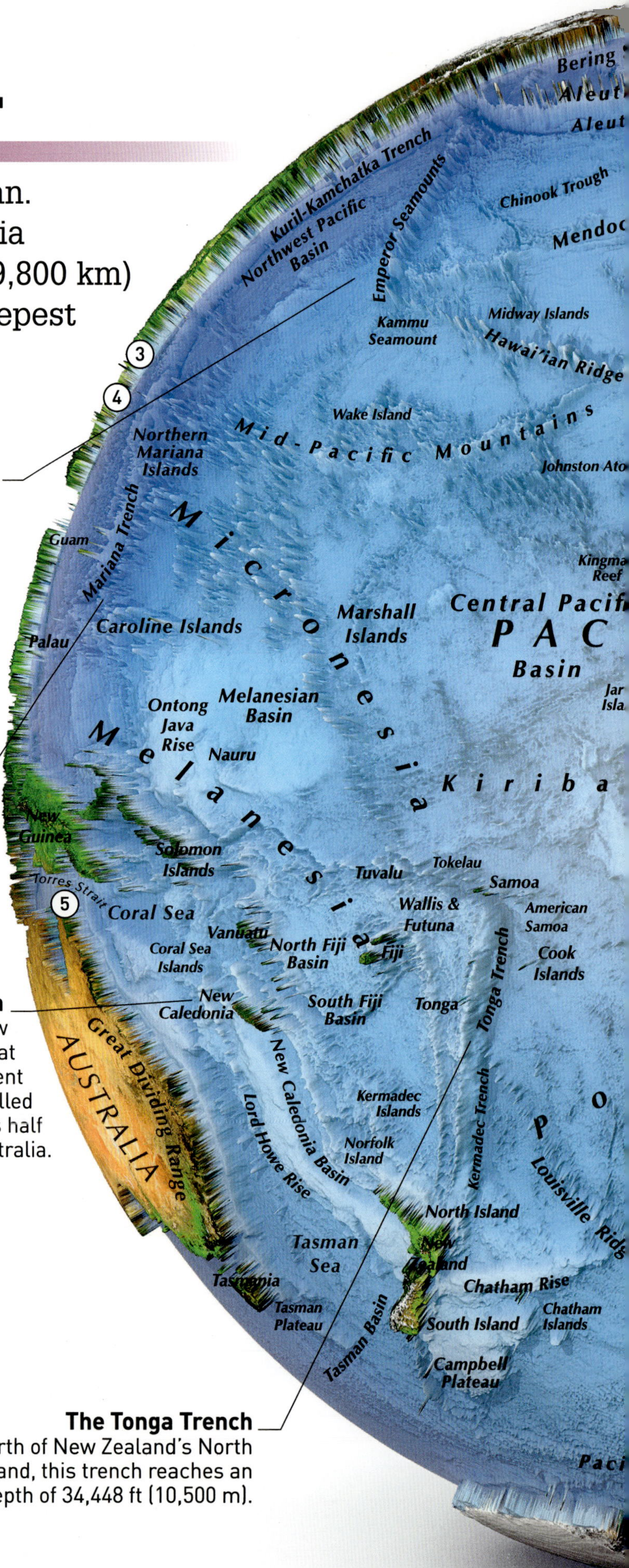


**The Emperor Seamounts**
These underwater mountains extend northwest from Hawaii. Each mount is named after a Japanese emperor.

**Mariana Trench**
The lowest point on Earth, its deepest point lies almost 7 miles (11 km) beneath the ocean's surface.

**New Caledonia**
This island and New Zealand are all that remain of an ancient continent called Zealandia that was half the size of Australia.

**The Tonga Trench**
Lying north of New Zealand's North Island, this trench reaches an average depth of 34,448 ft (10,500 m).

**FAST FACTS**

**Total area:**
60,060,893 sq miles (155,557,000 sq km)

**Coastline:**
84,297 miles (135,663 km)

**Average depth:**
13,025 ft (3,970 m)

**Lowest point:**
Challenger Deep, Mariana Trench—35,840 ft (10,924 m)

**Major access points:**

1. Panama Canal
2. Strait of Magellan
3. Tsugaru Strait
4. Tsushima
5. Torres Straits

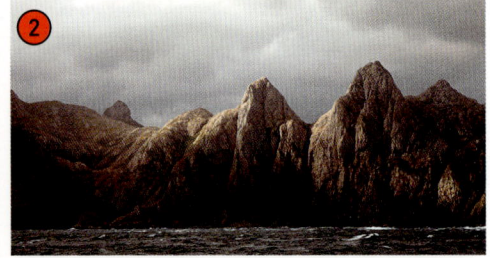

The Strait of Magellan, in southern Chile/Argentina, connects the Pacific and Atlantic Oceans.



ALL SEVEN OF THE EARTH'S CONTINENTS COULD

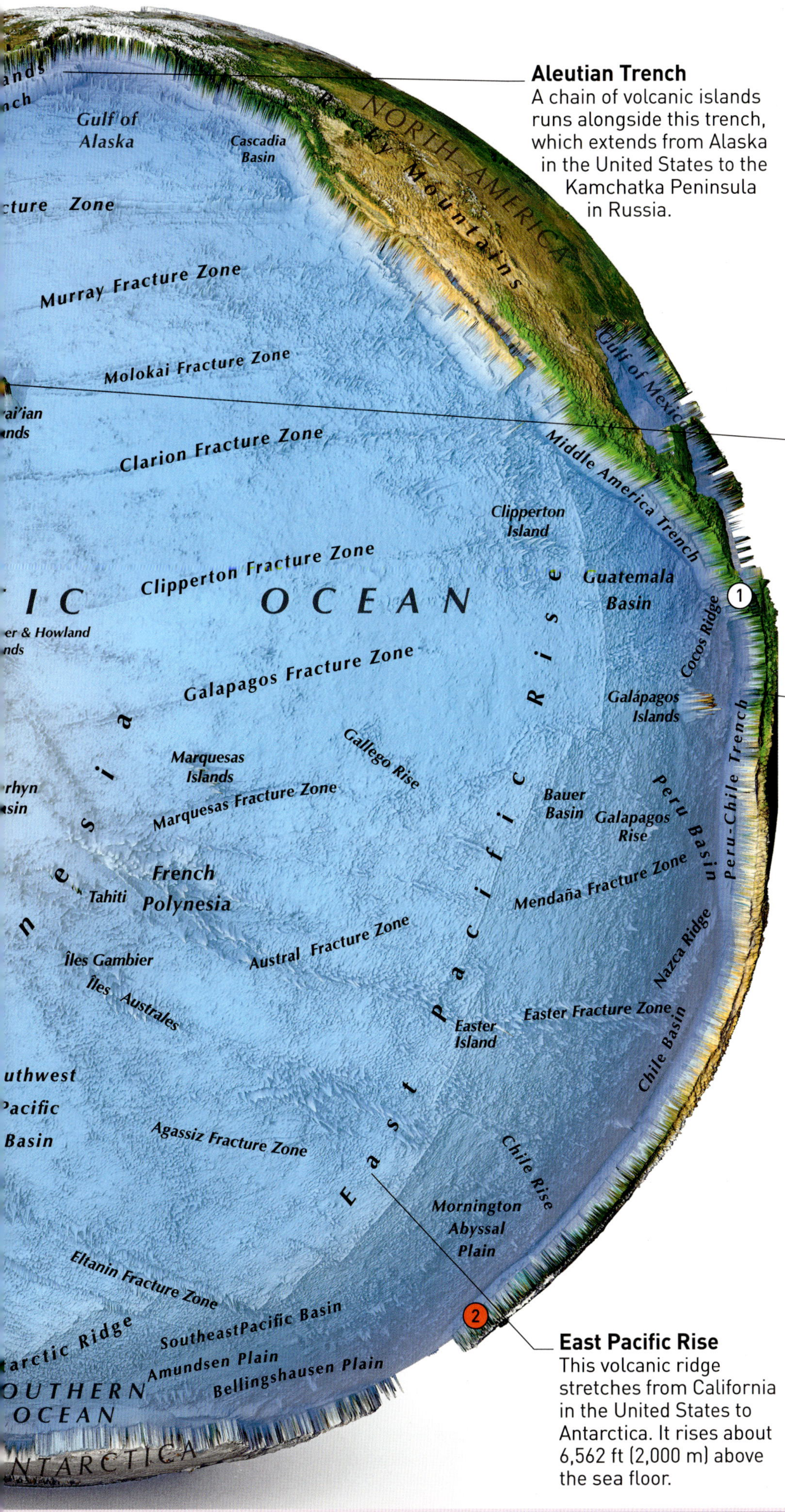


**Aleutian Trench**
A chain of volcanic islands runs alongside this trench, which extends from Alaska in the United States to the Kamchatka Peninsula in Russia.

# The **Pacific Ocean** contains ***just over half*** of all the world's **seawater**.

**Mauna Loa**
Measuring 29,500 ft (9,000 m) in height from the ocean floor to its summit, the world's largest active volcano looms over Hawaii.

**Peru-Chile Trench**
This 3,660-mile (5,900-km) long trench is the longest in the Pacific Ocean. It follows the line of the Andes Mountains.

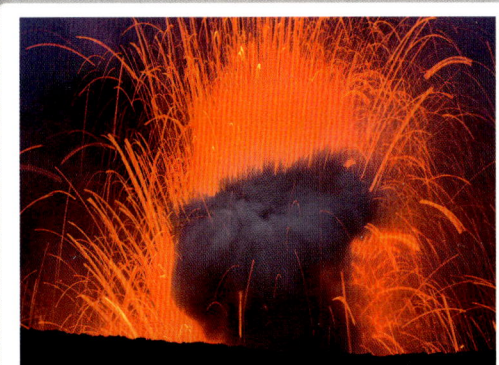

## Ring of Fire

The Pacific Ocean is surrounded by a band of volcanoes called the Ring of Fire. This ring extends from New Zealand to South America and contains more than three-quarters of the world's volcanoes, including Mount Fuji, in Japan, and Mount St. Helens in the United States.

**East Pacific Rise**
This volcanic ridge stretches from California in the United States to Antarctica. It rises about 6,562 ft (2,000 m) above the sea floor.

EASILY FIT INTO THE PACIFIC BASIN.

# Atlantic Ocean

The Atlantic is the world's second-largest ocean. It stretches from the Arctic to the Antarctic, separating Europe and Africa from the Americas. The Atlantic Ocean covers about one-fifth of the planet's surface, is home to some of the world's richest fishing waters, and contains a plentiful supply of gas and oil.

## FAST FACTS

**Total area:**
29,637,974 sq miles (76,762,000 sq km)

**Coastline:**
69,510 miles (111,866 km)

**Average depth:**
11,962 ft (3,646 m)

**Lowest point:**
Milwaukee Deep, Puerto Rico Trench—28,232 ft (8,605 m)

**Major access points:**
1. English Channel
2. Panama Canal
3. Straits of Florida
4. Strait of Gibraltar
5. Strait of Magellan

The Panama Canal, one of the world's busiest waterways, connects the Pacific and Atlantic Oceans.

**Puerto Rico Trench**
This trench stretches for 497 miles (800 km) and contains the Atlantic Ocean's deepest point.

**Mid-Atlantic Ridge**
This underwater mountain range runs for about 10,000 miles (16,000 km) along the ocean floor.

**Amazon Fan**
Mud and clay from the Amazon River have settled on the ocean floor, forming a mound of sediment 502,000 sq miles (1.3 million sq km) in size.

**Icebergs**
The icebergs of the Antarctic are usually much larger than those found in the Arctic. They can reach lengths of up to 50 miles (80 km).

THE FIRST PERSON TO FLY ACROSS THE ATLANTIC WAS

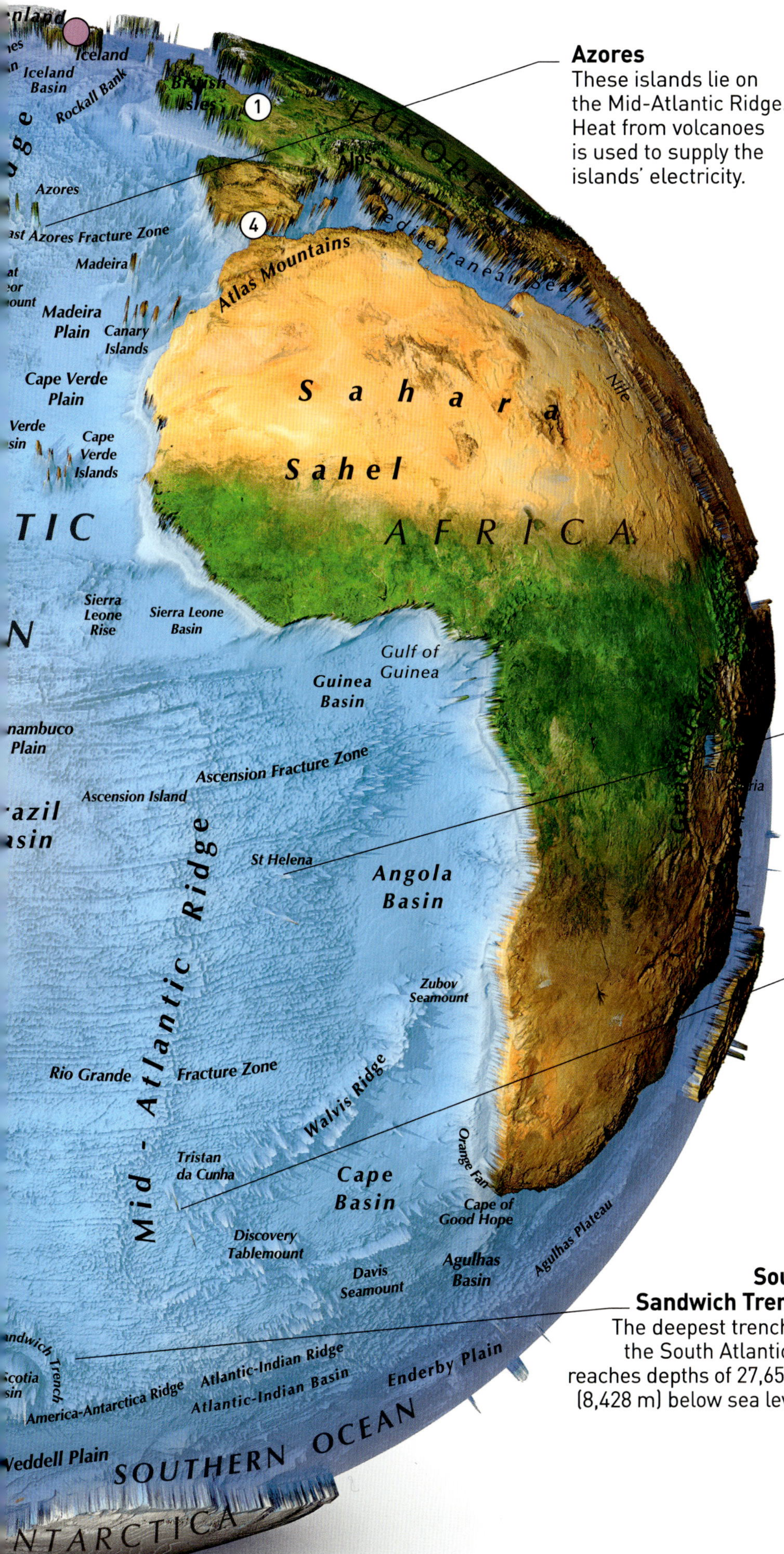


**Azores**
These islands lie on the Mid-Atlantic Ridge. Heat from volcanoes is used to supply the islands' electricity.

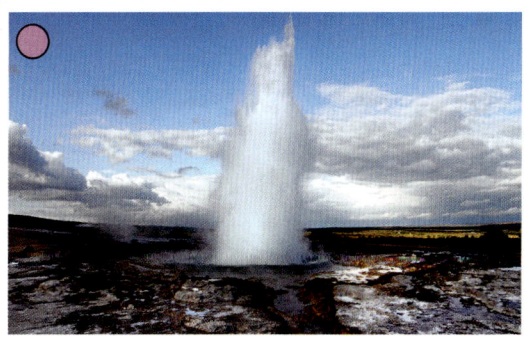

**Iceland**
With an area of 39,769 sq miles (103,000 sq km), Iceland is the largest of the islands that lie on the Mid-Atlantic Ridge. It is home to more than 100 volcanoes, many of which are still active, as well as to many geysers and hot springs.

**Saint Helena**
This tiny volcanic island has an area of just 47 sq miles (122 sq km). It has been under British control since 1676.

**Tristan da Cunha**
Lying 1,250 miles (2,000 km) from the nearest inhabited land (Saint Helena), this is the most isolated group of inhabited islands in the world. Just over 250 people live there.

**South Sandwich Trench**
The deepest trench in the South Atlantic, it reaches depths of 27,651 ft (8,428 m) below sea level.

The ***Atlantic*** is **widening** by up to **3.9 in** (10 cm) every year as its ***continental plates*** move **slowly** apart.

CHARLES LINDBERGH IN 1927. IT TOOK HIM 33.5 HOURS.

## THE OCEANS

# Indian Ocean

The Indian Ocean is the smallest of the world's major oceans, but it provides important sea routes connecting the Middle East, Africa, and East Asia, with Europe and the Americas. As with the Pacific Ocean, its warm waters are dotted with coral atolls and islands. Around one-fifth of the world's population live on its shores.

### FAST FACTS

**Total area:**
26,469,620 sq miles (68,556, 000 sq km)

**Coastline:**
41,337 miles (66,526 km)

**Average depth:**
12,274 ft (3,741 m)

**Lowest point:**
Diamantina Deep, Java Trench— 23,812 ft (7,258 m)

**Major access points:**
① Bab El Mandeb
② Strait of Hormuz
③ Strait of Malacca
④ Suez Canal
⑤ Torres Straits

**Satellite view of the Strait of Hormuz, with the United Arab Emirates on the left of the image.**

**Mid-Indian Ridge**
Heading southeast from the Gulf of Aden, this ridge meets the Southwest Indian Ridge mid-ocean.

**Seychelles**
This group of 115 islands lies 1,130 miles (1,819 km) to the north of Madagascar. It forms part of the Mascarene Plateau.

**Southwest Indian Ridge**
This ridge connects the Mid-Indian Ridge to the Mid-Atlantic Ridge.

**Prince Edward Islands**
These two small islands are the peaks of volcanoes that extend 3 miles (5 km) from the sea bed.

NONE OF THE MALDIVES, A GROUP OF ABOUT 1,200 ISLANDS SOUTH

**The Ganges Fan**
Two of the world's great rivers—the Ganges and the Brahmaputra—flow into the Indian Ocean here. Sediment from the rivers collects in a huge fan shape in the Bay of Bengal.

**Indian Ocean tsunami**
On December 26, 2004, an earthquake (the third largest ever recorded) off the coast of Sumatra, Indonesia, triggered a tsunami (a huge wave that destroys everything in its path). It had catastrophic consequences for many countries bordering the Indian Ocean, when waves of up to 100 ft (30 m) high left as many as 230,000 people dead.

**Java Trench**
The Indian Ocean's only major trench runs for 1,600 miles (2,570 km) south of the Indonesian islands of Java and Sumatra.

**Ninety East Ridge**
This ridge is named for the line of longitude it follows. At 3,100 miles (5,000 km), it is the world's longest sea ridge, and also its straightest.

**Kerguelen Plateau**
Only a few uninhabited islands remain of what was once a small continent.

**Southern Ocean**
The Indian, Pacific, and Atlantic Oceans come together in the seas around Antarctica.

The **Indian Ocean** is the world's **warmest**. Water temperatures reach **82.4°F (28°C)** in its **eastern** parts.

# REFERENCE

**Night and day**
While Asia, the Middle East, and East Africa are bathed in sunlight, in Europe and West Africa, the lights continue to shine in the dark hours before dawn.

# Countries of the world

This section includes 195 of the world's countries. With the exception of Taiwan and the Vatican City, all of them are member states of the United Nations.

\* denotes official language

## NORTH AND CENTRAL AMERICA

### CANADA
**North America**
**Capital:** Ottawa
**Population:** 35.1 million / 9 people per sq mile (4 people per sq km)
**Total area:** 3,855,103 sq miles (9,984,670 sq km)
**Languages:** English*, French*, Punjabi, Italian, German, Cantonese, Inuktitut
**Currency:** Canadian dollar = 100 cents

### UNITED STATES OF AMERICA
**North America**
**Capital:** Washington, DC
**Population:** 324 million / 85 people per sq mile (33 people per sq km)
**Total area:** 3,796,742 sq miles (9,833,517 sq km)
**Languages:** English, Spanish
**Currency:** US dollar = 100 cents

### MEXICO
**North America**
**Capital:** Mexico City
**Population:** 123.2 million / 162 people per sq mile (63 people per sq km)
**Total area:** 758,449 sq miles (1,964,375 sq km)
**Languages:** Spanish*, Nahuatl, Mayan
**Currency:** Mexican peso = 100 centavos

### BELIZE
**Central America**
**Capital:** Belmopan
**Population:** 347,370 / 39 people per sq mile (15 people per sq km)
**Total area:** 8,867 sq miles (22,966 sq km)
**Languages:** English*, English Creole, Spanish, Mayan, Garifuna (Carib)
**Currency:** Belizean dollar = 100 cents

### COSTA RICA
**Central America**
**Capital:** San José
**Population:** 4.8 million / 243 people per sq mile (94 people per sq km)
**Total area:** 19,730 sq miles (51,100 sq km)
**Languages:** Spanish*, English
**Currency:** Costa Rican colón = 100 céntimos

### EL SALVADOR
**Central America**
**Capital:** San Salvador
**Population:** 6.1 million / 750 people per sq mile (290 people per sq km)
**Total area:** 8,124 sq miles (21,041 sq km)
**Languages:** Spanish*, Nawat
**Currency:** US dollar = 100 cents

### GUATEMALA
**Central America**
**Capital:** Guatemala City
**Population:** 15.2 million / 362 people per sq mile (140 people per sq km)
**Total area:** 42,042 sq miles (108,889 sq km)
**Languages:** Spanish*, indigenous languages
**Currency:** Quetzal = 100 centavos

### HONDURAS
**Central America**
**Capital:** Tegucigalpa
**Population:** 8.9 million / 206 people per sq mile (79 people per sq km)
**Total area:** 43,278 sq miles (112,090 sq km)
**Languages:** Spanish*, Indigenous languages
**Currency:** Lempira = 100 centavos

### NICARAGUA
**Central America**
**Capital:** Managua
**Population:** 6 million / 119 people per sq mile (46 people per sq km)
**Total area:** 50,336 sq miles (130,370 sq km)
**Languages:** Spanish*, Miskito
**Currency:** Córdoba = 100 centavos

### PANAMA
**Central America**
**Capital:** Panama City
**Population:** 3.7 million / 127 people per sq mile (49 people per sq km)
**Total area:** 29,120 sq miles (75,420 sq km)
**Languages:** Spanish*, English Creole, Indigenous languages including Ngabere
**Currency:** Balboa = 100 centesimos

### ANTIGUA AND BARBUDA
**West Indies**
**Capital:** St. John's
**Population:** 92,436 / 540 people per sq mile (209 people per sq km)
**Total area:** 171 sq miles (443 sq km)
**Languages:** English*, Antiguan Creole
**Currency:** Eastern Caribbean dollar = 100 cents

### THE BAHAMAS
**West Indies**
**Capital:** Nassau
**Population:** 324,600 / 61 people per sq mile (23 people per sq km)
**Total area:** 5,359 sq miles (13,880 sq km)
**Languages:** English*, English Creole, French Creole
**Currency:** Bahamian dollar = 100 cents

### BARBADOS
**West Indies**
**Capital:** Bridgetown
**Population:** 290,600 / 1,750 people per sq mile (676 people per sq km)
**Total area:** 166 sq miles (430 sq km)
**Languages:** English*, Bajan (Barbadian English)
**Currency:** Barbados dollar = 100 cents

### CUBA
**West Indies**
**Capital:** Havana
**Population:** 11 million / 256 people per sq mile (99 people per sq km)
**Total area:** 42,803 sq miles (110,860 sq km)
**Languages:** Spanish*
**Currency:** Cuban peso = 100 centavos

### DOMINICA
**West Indies**
**Capital:** Roseau
**Population:** 73,607 / 254 people per sq mile (98 people per sq km)
**Total area:** 290 sq miles (751 sq km)
**Languages:** English*, French Creole
**Currency:** East Caribbean dollar = 100 cents

### DOMINICAN REPUBLIC
**West Indies**
**Capital:** Santo Domingo
**Population:** 10.5 million / 559 people per sq mile (216 people per sq km)
**Total area:** 18,792 sq miles (48,670 sq km)
**Languages:** Spanish*
**Currency:** Dominican Republic peso = 100 centavos

### GRENADA
**West Indies**
**Capital:** St. George's
**Population:** 111,000 / 836 people per sq mile (323 people per sq km)
**Total area:** 133 sq miles (344 sq km)
**Languages:** English*, French Patois
**Currency:** East Caribbean dollar = 100 cents

### HAITI
**West Indies**
**Capital:** Port-au-Prince
**Population:** 10.5 million / 979 people per sq mile (378 people per sq km)
**Total area:** 10,714 sq miles (27,750 sq km)
**Languages:** French*, French Creole*
**Currency:** Gourde = 100 centimes

### JAMAICA
**West Indies**
**Capital:** Kingston
**Population:** 3 million / 613 people per sq mile (237 people per sq km)
**Total area:** 4,243 sq miles (10,991 sq km)
**Languages:** English*, English Creole
**Currency:** Jamaican dollar = 100 cents

### SAINT KITTS AND NEVIS
**West Indies**
**Capital:** Basseterre
**Population:** 52,329 / 519 people per sq mile (201 people per sq km)
**Total area:** 101 sq miles (261 sq km)
**Language:** English*
**Currency:** Eastern Caribbean dollar = 100 cents

### SAINT LUCIA
**West Indies**
**Capital:** Castries
**Population:** 164,464 / 692 people per sq mile (267 people per sq km)
**Total area:** 238 sq miles (616 sq km)
**Languages:** English*, French Creole
**Currency:** Eastern Caribbean dollar = 100 cents

### SAINT VINCENT AND THE GRENADINES
**West Indies**
**Capital:** Kingstown
**Population:** 102,350 / 682 people per sq mile (263 people per sq km)
**Total area:** 150 sq miles (389 sq km)
**Languages:** English*, English Creole
**Currency:** Eastern Caribbean dollar = 100 cents

### TRINIDAD AND TOBAGO
**West Indies**
**Capital:** Port-of-Spain
**Population:** 1.2 million / 606 people per sq mile (234 people per sq km)
**Total area:** 1,980 sq miles (5,128 sq km)
**Languages:** English*, Caribbean Hindustani, French, Spanish
**Currency:** Trinidad and Tobago dollar = 100 cents

## SOUTH AMERICA

### COLOMBIA
**South America**
**Capital:** Bogotá
**Population:** 46.7 million / 106 people per sq mile (41 people per sq km)
**Total area:** 439,736 sq miles (1,138,910 sq km)
**Languages:** Spanish*, Amerindian languages, English Creole
**Currency:** Colombian peso = 100 centavos

### GUYANA
**South America**
**Capital:** Georgetown
**Population:** 735,900 / 9 people per sq mile (3 people per sq km)
**Total area:** 83,000 sq miles (214,969 sq km)
**Languages:** English*, English Creole, Indigenous languages, Indian languages
**Currency:** Guyana dollar = 100 cents

### SURINAME
**South America**
**Capital:** Paramaribo
**Population:** 585,800 / 9 people per sq mile (4 people per sq km)
**Total area:** 63,251 sq miles (163,820 sq km)
**Languages:** Dutch*, English, Sranan Tongo
**Currency:** Suriname dollar = 100 cents

### VENEZUELA
**South America**
**Capital:** Caracas
**Population:** 30.9 million / 88 people per sq mile (34 people per sq km)
**Total area:** 352,143 sq miles (912,050 sq km)
**Languages:** Spanish*, numerous indigenous languages
**Currency:** Bolivar fuerte = 100 centimos

SOUTH SUDAN IS THE WORLD'S NEWEST COUNTRY. IT BECAME A

## BOLIVIA
*South America*
**Capital:** Sucre (judicial); La Paz (administrative)
**Population:** 10.8 million / 26 people per sq mile (10 people per sq km)
**Total area:** 424,165 sq miles (1,098,581 sq km)
**Languages:** Spanish*, Quechua*, Aymara*
**Currency:** Boliviano = 100 centavos

## ECUADOR
*South America*
**Capital:** Quito
**Population:** 15.9 million / 145 people per sq mile (56 people per sq km)
**Total area:** 109,484 sq miles (283,561 sq km)
**Languages:** Spanish*, Quechua*, other indigenous languages
**Currency:** US dollar = 100 cents

## PERU
*South America*
**Capital:** Lima
**Population:** 30.7 million / 62 people per sq mile (24 people per sq km)
**Total area:** 496,225 sq miles (1,285,216 sq km)
**Languages:** Spanish*, Quechua*, Aymará*, other indigenous languages
**Currency:** New sol = 100 centimos

## BRAZIL
*South America*
**Capital:** Brasília
**Population:** 204.3 million / 62 people per sq mile (24 people per sq km)
**Total area:** 3,287,957 sq miles (8,515,770 sq km)
**Languages:** Portuguese*, German, Italian, Spanish, Polish, Japanese
**Currency:** Real = 100 centavos

## ARGENTINA
*South America*
**Capital:** Buenos Aires
**Population:** 43.4 million / 40 people per sq mile (16 people per sq km)
**Total area:** 1,073,518 sq miles (2,780,400 sq km)
**Languages:** Spanish*, Italian, English, German, French, Indigenous languages
**Currency:** Argentine Peso = 100 centavos

## URUGUAY
*South America*
**Capital:** Montevideo
**Population:** 3.4 million / 70 people per sq mile (27 people per sq km)
**Total area:** 68,036 sq miles (176,215 sq km)
**Languages:** Spanish*, Portuñol
**Currency:** Uruguayan peso = 100 centesimos

## CHILE
*South America*
**Capital:** Santiago
**Population:** 17.5 million / 60 people per sq mile (23 people per sq km)
**Total area:** 291,932 sq miles (756,102 sq km)
**Languages:** Spanish*, Indigenous languages
**Currency:** Chilean peso = 100 centavos

## PARAGUAY
*South America*
**Capital:** Asunción
**Population:** 6.9 million / 44 people per sq mile (17 people per sq km)
**Total area:** 157,048 sq miles (406,752 sq km)
**Languages:** Spanish*, Guaraní*
**Currency:** Guaraní = 100 centimos

# AFRICA

## ALGERIA
*North Africa*
**Capital:** Algiers
**Population:** 39.5 million / 43 people per sq mile (17 people per sq km)
**Total area:** 919,595 sq miles (2,381,740 sq km)
**Languages:** Arabic*, Tamazight*, French
**Currency:** Algerian dinar = 100 santeems

## LIBYA
*North Africa*
**Capital:** Tripoli
**Population:** 6.5 million / 10 people per sq mile (4 people per sq km)
**Total area:** 679,362 sq miles (1,759,540 sq km)
**Languages:** Arabic*, Berber languages
**Currency:** Libyan dinar = 1,000 dirhams

## MOROCCO
*North Africa*
**Capital:** Rabat
**Population:** 33.7 million / 196 people per sq mile (76 people per sq km)
**Total area:** 172,414 sq miles (446,550 sq km)
**Languages:** Arabic*, Tamazight*, French
**Currency:** Moroccan dirham = 100 santim

## TUNISIA
*North Africa*
**Capital:** Tunis
**Population:** 11.1 million / 176 people per sq mile (68 people per sq km)
**Total area:** 63,170 sq miles (163,610 sq km)
**Languages:** Arabic*, French, Berber
**Currency:** Tunisian dinar = 1,000 millimes

## BURUNDI
*Central Africa*
**Capital:** Bujumbura
**Population:** 10.7 million / 996 people per sq mile (384 people per sq km)
**Total area:** 10,745 sq miles (27,830 sq km)
**Languages:** Kirundi*, French*, Kiswahili
**Currency:** Burundi franc = 100 centimes

## DJIBOUTI
*East Africa*
**Capital:** Djibouti
**Population:** 828,324 / 92 people per sq mile (36 people per sq km)
**Total area:** 8,958 sq miles (23,200 sq km)
**Languages:** French*, Arabic*, Somali, Afar
**Currency:** Djibouti franc = 100 centimes

## EGYPT
*North Africa*
**Capital:** Cairo
**Population:** 88.5 million / 229 people per sq mile (88 people per sq km)
**Total area:** 386,660 sq miles (1,001,450 sq km)
**Languages:** Arabic*, French, English
**Currency:** Egyptian pound = 100 piastres

## ERITREA
*East Africa*
**Capital:** Asmara
**Population:** 5.9 million / 130 people per sq mile (50 people per sq km)
**Total area:** 45,406 sq miles (117,600 sq km)
**Languages:** Tigrinya*, Arabic*, English*, Tigre, Afar, Bilen, Kunama, Nara
**Currency:** Nafka = 100 cents

## ETHIOPIA
*East Africa*
**Capital:** Addis Ababa
**Population:** 102.3 million / 235 people per sq mile (91 people per sq km)
**Total area:** 426,373 sq miles (1,104,300 sq km)
**Languages:** Amharic*, Oromo, Tigrinya
**Currency:** Ethiopian birr = 100 santim

## KENYA
*East Africa*
**Capital:** Nairobi
**Population:** 45.5 million / 208 people per sq mile (80 people per sq km)
**Total area:** 224,081 sq miles (580,367 sq km)
**Languages:** Kiswahili*, English*
**Currency:** Kenya shilling = 100 cents

## RWANDA
*Central Africa*
**Capital:** Kigali
**Population:** 12.9 million / 1,269 people per sq mile (490 people per sq km)
**Total area:** 10,169 sq miles (26,338 sq km)
**Languages:** French*, Kinyarwanda*, English
**Currency:** Rwandan franc = 100 centimes

## SOMALIA
*East Africa*
**Capital:** Mogadishu
**Population:** 10.8 million / 44 people per sq mile (17 people per sq km)
**Total area:** 246,199 sq miles (637,657 sq km)
**Languages:** Somali*, Arabic*, English, Italian
**Currency:** Somali shilling = 100 cents

## SOUTH SUDAN
*East Africa*
**Capital:** Juba
**Population:** 12.5 million / 50 people per sq mile (19 people per sq km)
**Total area:** 248,777 sq miles (644,329 sq km)
**Languages:** English*, Arabic, Dinka, Nuer
**Currency:** South Sudanese pound = 100 piasters

## SUDAN
*East Africa*
**Capital:** Khartoum
**Population:** 36.7 million / 51 people per sq mile (20 people per sq km)
**Total area:** 718,723 sq miles (1,861,484 sq km)
**Languages:** Arabic*, English*, Nubian, Fur
**Currency:** Sudanese pound = 100 piastres

## TANZANIA
*East Africa*
**Capital:** Dodoma
**Population:** 52.5 million / 144 people per sq mile (55 people per sq km)
**Total area:** 365,755 sq miles (947,300 sq km)
**Languages:** English*, Swahili*, Sukuma, Chagga, Nyamwezi, Hehe, Makonde
**Currency:** Tanzanian shilling = 100 cents

## UGANDA
*East Africa*
**Capital:** Kampala
**Population:** 38.3 million / 412 people per sq mile (159 people per sq km)
**Total area:** 93,065 sq miles (241,038 sq km)
**Languages:** English*, Luganda
**Currency:** Uganda shilling = 100 cents

## BENIN
*West Africa*
**Capital:** Porto-Novo
**Population:** 10.4 million / 239 people per sq mile (92 people per sq km)
**Total area:** 43,483 sq miles (112,622 sq km)
**Languages:** French*, Fon, Bariba, Yoruba, Adja, Houeda, Somba
**Currency:** West African CFA franc = 100 centimes

## BURKINA FASO
*West Africa*
**Capital:** Ouagadougou
**Population:** 18.9 million / 179 people per sq mile (69 people per sq km)
**Total area:** 105,869 sq miles (274,200 sq km)
**Languages:** French*, various languages belonging to the Sudanic family
**Currency:** West African CFA franc = 100 centimes

## CAPE VERDE
*Atlantic Ocean*
**Capital:** Praia
**Population:** 545,993 / 351 people per sq mile (135 people per sq km)
**Total area:** 1,557 sq miles (4,033 sq km)
**Languages:** Portuguese*, Portuguese Creole
**Currency:** Cape Verde escudo = 100 centavos

## IVORY COAST
*West Africa*
**Capital:** Yamoussoukro
**Population:** 23.7 million / 190 people per sq mile (74 people per sq km)
**Total area:** 124,504 sq miles (322,463 sq km)
**Languages:** French*, Dioula
**Currency:** West African CFA franc = 100 centimes

## THE GAMBIA
*West Africa*
**Capital:** Banjul
**Population:** 2 million / 458 people per sq mile (177 people per sq km)
**Total area:** 4,363 sq miles (11,300 sq km)
**Languages:** English*, Mandinka, Fula, Wolof
**Currency:** Dalasi = 100 butut

## GHANA
*West Africa*
**Capital:** Accra
**Population:** 26.9 million / 292 people per sq mile (113 people per sq km)
**Total area:** 92,098 sq miles (238,533 sq km)
**Languages:** English*, Asante, Ewe, Fante, Boron
**Currency:** Cedi = 100 pesewas

## GUINEA
*West Africa*
**Capital:** Conakry
**Population:** 12.1 million / 128 people per sq mile (49 people per sq km)
**Total area:** 94,925 sq miles (245,857 sq km)
**Languages:** French*, Fulani, Malinke, Soussou
**Currency:** Guinea franc = 100 centimes

## GUINEA BISSAU
*West Africa*
**Capital:** Bissau
**Population:** 1.8 million / 124 people per sq mile (49 people per sq km)
**Total area:** 13,948 sq miles (36,125 sq km)
**Languages:** Portuguese*, West African Crioulo
**Currency:** West African CFA franc = 100 centimes

## LIBERIA
*West Africa*
**Capital:** Monrovia
**Population:** 4.3 million / 101 people per sq mile (39 people per sq km)
**Total area:** 43,000 sq miles (111,370 sq km)
**Languages:** English*
**Currency:** Liberian dollar = 100 cents

## MALI
*West Africa*
**Capital:** Bamako
**Population:** 17.5 million / 37 people per sq mile (14 people per sq km)
**Total area:** 478,764 sq miles (1,240,000 sq km)
**Languages:** French*, Bambara, Peul, Dogon
**Currency:** West African CFA franc = 100 centimes

MEMBER STATE OF THE UNITED NATIONS ON JULY 14, 2011.

### MAURITANIA
*West Africa*
**Capital:** Nouakchott
**Population:** 3.7 million / 9 people per sq mile (4 people per sq km)
**Total area:** 397,953 sq miles (1,030,700 sq km)
**Languages:** Arabic*, Hassaniyah Arabic, Pulaar, Soninke
**Currency:** Ouguiya = 5 khoums

### NIGER
*West Africa*
**Capital:** Niamey
**Population:** 18.6 million / 38 people per sq mile (15 people per sq km)
**Total area:** 489,189 sq miles (1,267,000 sq km)
**Languages:** French*, Hausa, Djerma
**Currency:** West African CFA franc = 100 centimes

### NIGERIA
*West Africa*
**Capital:** Abuja
**Population:** 186 million / 522 people per mile km (201 people per sq km)
**Total area:** 356,667 sq miles (923,768 sq km)
**Languages:** English*, Hausa, Yoruba, Ibo
**Currency:** Naira = 100 kobo

### SENEGAL
*West Africa*
**Capital:** Dakar
**Population:** 14.3 million / 188 people per sq mile (73 people per sq km)
**Total area:** 75,955 sq miles (196,722 sq km)
**Languages:** French*, Wolof, Pulaar
**Currency:** West African CFA franc = 100 centimes

### SIERRA LEONE
*West Africa*
**Capital:** Freetown
**Population:** 6 million / 217 people per sq mile (84 people per sq km)
**Total area:** 27,669 sq miles (71,740 sq km)
**Languages:** English*, Mende, Temne, Krio
**Currency:** Leone = 100 cents

### TOGO
*Western Africa*
**Capital:** Lomé
**Population:** 7.8 million / 356 people per sq mile (137 people per sq km)
**Total area:** 21,925 sq miles (56,785 sq km)
**Languages:** French*, Ewe, Mina, Kabye
**Currency:** West African CFA franc = 100 centimes

### CAMEROON
*Central Africa*
**Capital:** Yaoundé
**Population:** 23.7 million / 130 people per mile (50 people per sq km)
**Total area:** 183,567 sq miles (475,440 sq km)
**Languages:** English*, French*, Bamileke, Fang, Fulani
**Currency:** Central African CFA franc = 100 centimes

### CENTRAL AFRICAN REPUBLIC
*Central Africa*
**Capital:** Bangui
**Population:** 5.4 million / 23 people per sq mile (9 people per sq km)
**Total area:** 240,535 sq miles (622,984 sq km)
**Languages:** French*, Sangho, Banda, Gbaya
**Currency:** CFA franc =100 centimes

### CHAD
*Central Africa*
**Capital:** N'Djaména
**Population:** 13 million / 27 people per sq mile (10 people per sq km)
**Total area:** 495,752 sq miles (1,284,000 sq km)
**Languages:** French*, Arabic*, Sara, Maba
**Currency:** Central African CFA franc = 100 centimes

### CONGO
*Central Africa*
**Capital:** Brazzaville
**Population:** 4.8 million / 36 people per sq mile (14 people per sq km)
**Total area:** 132,046 sq miles (342,000 sq km)
**Languages:** French*, Monokutuba, Mikongo, Lingala
**Currency:** Central African CFA franc = 100 centimes

### CONGO, DEM. REP.
*Central Africa*
**Capital:** Kinshasa
**Population:** 79.4 million / 88 people per sq mile (34 people per sq km)
**Total area:** 905,355 sq miles (2,344,858 sq km)
**Languages:** French*, Tshiluba, Kikongo, Lingala, Kingwana
**Currency:** Congolese Franc = 100 centimes

### EQUATORIAL GUINEA
*Central Africa*
**Capital:** Malabo
**Population:** 759,451 / 70 people per sq mile (27 people per sq km)
**Total area:** 10,830 sq miles (28,051 sq km)
**Languages:** Spanish*, Fang, Bubi
**Currency:** Central African CFA franc = 100 centimes

### GABON
*Central Africa*
**Capital:** Libreville
**Population:** 1.7 million / 16 people per sq mile (6 people per sq km)
**Total area:** 103,346 sq miles (267,667 sq km)
**Languages:** French*, Fang, Myene, Bapounou, Nzebi
**Currency:** Central African CFA franc = 100 centimes

### SÃO TOMÉ AND PRINCIPE
*West Africa*
**Capital:** São Tomé
**Population:** 197,541 / 531 people per sq mile (204 people per sq km)
**Total area:** 372 sq miles (964 sq km)
**Languages:** Portuguese*, Forro
**Currency:** Dobra = 100 centimos

### ANGOLA
*Southern Africa*
**Capital:** Luanda
**Population:** 25.7 million / 54 people per sq mile (21 people per sq km)
**Total area:** 481,351 sq miles (1,246,700 sq km)
**Languages:** Portuguese*, Umbundu, Kimbundu, Kikongo
**Currency:** Kwanza = 100 centimos

### BOTSWANA
*Southern Africa*
**Capital:** Gaborone
**Population:** 2.2 million / 10 people per sq mile (4 people per sq km)
**Total area:** 224,607 sq miles (581,730 sq km)
**Languages:** English*, Setswana, Shona, San, Khoikhoi, Ndebele
**Currency:** Pula = 100 thebe

### COMOROS
*Indian Ocean*
**Capital:** Moroni
**Population:** 780,972 / 905 people per sq mile (349 people per sq km)
**Total area:** 863 sq miles (2,235 sq km)
**Languages:** Arabic*, French*, Comoran*
**Currency:** Comoros franc = 100 centimes

### LESOTHO
*Southern Africa*
**Capital:** Maseru
**Population:** 2 million / 171 people per sq mile (66 people per sq km)
**Total area:** 11,720 sq miles (30,355 sq km)
**Languages:** Sesotho*, English*, Zulu
**Currency:** Loti = 100 lisente

### MADAGASCAR
*Indian Ocean*
**Capital:** Antananarivo
**Population:** 24.4 million / 108 people per sq mile (42 people per sq km)
**Total area:** 226,658 sq miles (587,041 sq km)
**Languages:** French*, Malagasy*
**Currency:** Malagasy ariary = 5 iraimbilanja

### MALAWI
*Southern Africa*
**Capital:** Lilongwe
**Population:** 18.6 million / 407 people per sq mile (157 people per sq km)
**Total area:** 45,747 sq miles (118,484 sq km)
**Languages:** English*, Chichewa*, Chinyanja, Chiyao
**Currency:** Malawi kwacha = 100 tambala

### MAURITIUS
*Indian Ocean*
**Capital:** Port Louis
**Population:** 1.4 million / 1,778 people per sq mile (686 people per sq km)
**Total area:** 788 sq miles (2,040 sq km)
**Languages:** English, French, French Creole
**Currency:** Mauritian rupee = 100 cents

### MOZAMBIQUE
*Southern Africa*
**Capital:** Maputo
**Population:** 26 million / 84 people per sq mile (32 people per sq km)
**Total area:** 308,642 sq miles (799,380 sq km)
**Languages:** Portuguese*, Emakhuwa, Xichangana
**Currency:** Metical = 100 centavos

### NAMIBIA
*Southern Africa*
**Capital:** Windhoek
**Population:** 2.4 million / 8 people per sq mile (3 people per sq km)
**Total area:** 318,261 sq miles (824,292 sq km)
**Languages:** English*, Oshiwambo languages, Nama, Afrikaans
**Currency:** Namibian dollar = 100 cents

### SEYCHELLES
*Indian Ocean*
**Capital:** Victoria
**Population:** 93,200 / 531 people per sq mile (205 people per sq km)
**Total area:** 176 sq miles (455 sq km)
**Languages:** Seychellois Creole*, English*, French*
**Currency:** Seychelles rupee = 100 cents

### SOUTH AFRICA
*Southern Africa*
**Capital:** Pretoria (administrative)
**Population:** 54.3 million / 115 people per sq mile (45 people per sq km)
**Total area:** 470,693 sq miles (1,219,090 sq km)
**Languages:** IsiZulu*, IsiXhosa*, Afrikaans*, English*
**Currency:** Rand = 100 cents

### ESWATINI (SWAZILAND)
*Southern Africa*
**Capital:** Mbabane
**Population:** 1.5 million / 224 people per sq mile (86 people per sq km)
**Total area:** 6,704 sq miles (17,364 sq km)
**Languages:** Siswati*, English*
**Currency:** Lilangeni = 100 cents

### ZAMBIA
*Southern Africa*
**Capital:** Lusaka
**Population:** 15.5 million / 53 people per sq mile (21 people per sq km)
**Total area:** 290,587 sq miles (752,618 sq km)
**Languages:** English*, Bemba, Nyanja, Tonga
**Currency:** Zambian kwacha = 100 ngwee

### ZIMBABWE
*Southern Africa*
**Capital:** Harare
**Population:** 14.5 million / 96 people per sq mile (37 people per sq km)
**Total area:** 150,872 sq miles (390,757 sq km)
**Languages:** Shona*, Ndebele*, English
**Currency:** US dollar = 100 cents

## EUROPE

### ICELAND
*Northwest Europe*
**Capital:** Reykjavík
**Population:** 335,900 / 8 people per sq mile (3 people per sq km)
**Total area:** 39,768 sq miles (103,000 sq km)
**Languages:** Icelandic*, English
**Currency:** Icelandic króna = 100 aurar

### DENMARK
*Northern Europe*
**Capital:** Copenhagen
**Population:** 5.4 million / 325 people per sq mile (125 people per sq km)
**Total area:** 16,639 sq miles (43,094 sq km)
**Languages:** Danish*, Faroese, Inuit
**Currency:** Danish krone = 100 øre

### FINLAND
*Northern Europe*
**Capital:** Helsinki
**Population:** 5.5 million / 42 people per sq mile (16 people per sq km)
**Total area:** 130,559 sq miles (338,145 sq km)
**Languages:** Finnish*, Swedish, Sami
**Currency:** Euro = 100 cents

### NORWAY
*Northern Europe*
**Capital:** Oslo
**Population:** 5.3 million / 42 people per sq mile (16 people per sq km)
**Total area:** 125,021 sq miles (323,802 sq km)
**Languages:** Norwegian* (Bokmål and Nynorsk), Sami, Finnish
**Currency:** Norwegian krone = 100 øre

### SWEDEN
*Northern Europe*
**Capital:** Stockholm
**Population:** 9.9 million / 57 people per sq mile (22 people per sq km)
**Total area:** 173,860 sq miles (450,295 sq km)
**Languages:** Swedish*, Finnish, Sami
**Currency:** Swedish krona = 100 öre

## BELGIUM
*Northwest Europe*
**Capital:** Brussels
**Population:** 11.3 million / 874 people per sq mile (338 people per sq km)
**Total area:** 11,787 sq miles (30,528 sq km)
**Languages:** Dutch*, French*, German*, Flemish
**Currency:** Euro = 100 cents

## LUXEMBOURG
*Northwest Europe*
**Capital:** Luxembourg
**Population:** 582,300 / 583 people per sq mile (225 people per sq km)
**Total area:** 998 sq miles (2,586 sq km)
**Languages:** French*, German*, Luxembourgish*, Portuguese
**Currency:** Euro = 100 cents

## NETHERLANDS
*Northwest Europe*
**Capital:** Amsterdam/The Hague
**Population:** 17 million / 1,060 people per sq mile (409 people per sq km)
**Total area:** 16,040 sq miles (41,543 sq km)
**Languages:** Dutch*, Frisian
**Currency:** Euro = 100 cents

## IRELAND
*Northwest Europe*
**Capital:** Dublin
**Population:** 4.9 million / 181 people per sq mile (70 people per sq km)
**Total area:** 27,133 sq miles (70,273 sq km)
**Languages:** English*, Irish*
**Currency:** Euro = 100 cents

## UNITED KINGDOM
*Northwest Europe*
**Capital:** London
**Population:** 64.4 million / 685 people per sq mile (264 people per sq km)
**Total area:** 94,058 sq miles (243,610 sq km)
**Languages:** English*, Welsh
**Currency:** Pound sterling = 100 pence

## FRANCE
*Western Europe*
**Capital:** Paris
**Population:** 62.8 million / 295 people per sq mile (114 people per sq km)
**Total area:** 212,935 sq miles (551,500 sq km)
**Languages:** French*, Provencal, Breton, Catalan, Basque, Corsican
**Currency:** Euro = 100 cents

## MONACO
*Southern Europe*
**Capital:** Monaco
**Population:** 30,581 / 39,602 people per sq mile (15,291 people per sq km)
**Total area:** 0.77 sq miles (2 sq km)
**Languages:** French*, Italian, Monégasque, English
**Currency:** Euro = 100 cents

## ANDORRA
*Southwest Europe*
**Capital:** Andorra la Vella
**Population:** 85,580 / 474 people per sq mile (183 people per sq km)
**Total area:** 181 sq miles (468 sq km)
**Languages:** Catalan*, Spanish, French, Portuguese
**Currency:** Euro = 100 cents

## PORTUGAL
*Southwest Europe*
**Capital:** Lisbon
**Population:** 10.8 million / 281 people per sq mile (109 people per sq km)
**Total area:** 35,556 sq miles (92,090 sq km)
**Languages:** Portuguese*, Mirandese
**Currency:** Euro = 100 cents

## SPAIN
*Southwest Europe*
**Capital:** Madrid
**Population:** 48.6 million / 249 people per sq mile (96 people per sq km)
**Total area:** 195,125 sq miles (505,370 sq km)
**Languages:** Castilian Spanish*, Catalan*, Galician*, Basque*
**Currency:** Euro = 100 cents

## AUSTRIA
*Central Europe*
**Capital:** Vienna
**Population:** 8.7 million / 269 people per sq mile (104 people per sq km)
**Total area:** 32,383 sq miles (83,871 sq km)
**Languages:** German*, Turkish, Serbian, Croatian, Slovene, Hungarian (Magyar)
**Currency:** Euro = 100 cents

## GERMANY
*Northern Europe*
**Capital:** Berlin
**Population:** 81 million / 588 people per sq mile (227 people per sq km)
**Total area:** 137,847 sq miles (357,022 sq km)
**Languages:** German*
**Currency:** Euro = 100 cents

## LIECHTENSTEIN
*Central Europe*
**Capital:** Vaduz
**Population:** 37,937 / 614 people per sq mile (237 people per sq km)
**Total area:** 62 sq miles (160 sq km)
**Languages:** German*, Alemannish dialect, Italian
**Currency:** Swiss franc = 100 centimes

## SLOVENIA
*Central Europe*
**Capital:** Ljubljana
**Population:** 2 million / 256 people per sq mile (99 people per sq km)
**Total area:** 7,827 sq miles (20,273 sq km)
**Languages:** Slovene*, Serbo-Croat
**Currency:** Euro = 100 cents

## SWITZERLAND
*Central Europe*
**Capital:** Bern
**Population:** 8.2 million / 515 people per sq mile (199 people per sq km)
**Total area:** 15,937 sq miles (41,277 sq km)
**Languages:** German*, French*, Italian*, Romansch*
**Currency:** Swiss franc = 100 centimes

## ITALY
*Southern Europe*
**Capital:** Rome
**Population:** 62 million / 533 people per sq mile (206 people per sq km)
**Total area:** 116,348 sq miles (301,340 sq km)
**Languages:** Italian*, German, French, Slovene
**Currency:** Euro = 100 cents

## MALTA
*Southern Europe*
**Capital:** Valletta
**Population:** 415,196 / 3,403 people per sq mile (1,314 people per sq km)
**Total area:** 122 sq miles (316 sq km)
**Languages:** Maltese*, English
**Currency:** Euro = 100 cents

## SAN MARINO
*Southern Europe*
**Capital:** San Marino
**Population:** 33,285 / 1,413 people per sq mile (546 people per sq km)
**Total area:** 24 sq miles (61 sq km)
**Language:** Italian*
**Currency:** Euro = 100 cents

## VATICAN CITY
*Southern Europe*
**Capital:** Vatican City
**Population:** 1000 / 5,886 people per sq mile (2,273 people per sq km)
**Total area:** 0.17 sq miles (0.44 sq km)
**Languages:** Italian*, Latin*
**Currency:** Euro = 100 cents

## CZECHIA
*Central Europe*
**Capital:** Prague
**Population:** 10.6 million / 348 people per sq mile (134 people per sq km)
**Total area:** 30,450 sq miles (78,867 sq km)
**Languages:** Czech*, Slovak,
**Currency:** Czech koruna = 100 halers

## HUNGARY
*Central Europe*
**Capital:** Budapest
**Population:** 9.9 million / 276 people per sq mile (106 people per sq km)
**Total area:** 35,918 sq miles (93,028 sq km)
**Languages:** Hungarian*
**Currency:** Forint = 100 fillér

## POLAND
*Northern Europe*
**Capital:** Warsaw
**Population:** 38.5 million / 319 people per sq mile (123 people per sq km)
**Total area:** 120,728 sq miles (312,685 sq km)
**Languages:** Polish*, Silesian
**Currency:** Zloty = 100 groszy

## SLOVAKIA
*Central Europe*
**Capital:** Bratislava
**Population:** 5.5 million / 291 people per sq mile (112 people per sq km)
**Total area:** 18,933 sq miles (49,035 sq km)
**Languages:** Slovak*, Hungarian (Magyar), Romany
**Currency:** Euro = 100 cents

## ALBANIA
*Southeast Europe*
**Capital:** Tirana
**Population:** 3 million / 270 people per sq mile (104 people per sq km)
**Total area:** 11,100 sq miles (28,748 sq km)
**Languages:** Albanian*, Greek, Macedonian
**Currency:** Lek = 100 qindarkas

## BOSNIA AND HERZEGOVINA
*Southeast Europe*
**Capital:** Sarajevo
**Population:** 3.9 million / 197 people per sq mile (76 people per sq km)
**Total area:** 19,767 sq miles (51,197 sq km)
**Languages:** Bosnian*, Croatian*, Serbian*
**Currency:** Marka = 100 pfenigs

## CROATIA
*Southeast Europe*
**Capital:** Zagreb
**Population:** 4.5 million / 206 people per sq mile (80 people per sq km)
**Total area:** 21,851 sq miles (56,594 sq km)
**Languages:** Croatian*, Serbian, Hungarian
**Currency:** Kuna = 100 lipa

## NORTH MACEDONIA
*Southeast Europe*
**Capital:** Skopje
**Population:** 2.1 million / 212 people per sq mile (82 people per sq km)
**Total area:** 9,928 sq miles (25,713 sq km)
**Languages:** Macedonian*, Albanian, Turkish
**Currency:** Macedonian denar = 100 deni

## MONTENEGRO
*Southern Europe*
**Capital:** Podgorica
**Population:** 644,578 / 121 people per sq mile (47 people per sq km)
**Total area:** 5,322 sq miles (13,812 sq km)
**Languages:** Montenegrin*, Serbian, Bosnian, Albanian
**Currency:** Euro = 100 cents

## SERBIA
*Southern Europe*
**Capital:** Belgrade
**Population:** 7.1 million / 238 people per sq mile (92 people per sq km)
**Total area:** 29,913 sq miles (77,474 sq km)
**Languages:** Serbian*, Hungarian
**Currency:** Serbian dinar = 100 para

## CYPRUS
*Southeast Europe*
**Capital:** Nicosia
**Population:** 1.2 million / 336 people per sq mile (130 people per sq km)
**Total area:** 3,751 sq miles (9,250 sq km)
**Languages:** Greek*, Turkish*, English
**Currency:** Euro = 100 cents

## BULGARIA
*Southeast Europe*
**Capital:** Sofia
**Population:** 7.2 million / 168 people per sq mile (65 people per sq km)
**Total area:** 42,811 sq miles (110,879 sq km)
**Languages:** Bulgarian*, Turkish, Roma
**Currency:** Lev = 100 stotinki

## GREECE
*Southeast Europe*
**Capital:** Athens
**Population:** 10.7 million / 210 people per sq mile (81 people per sq km)
**Total area:** 50,949 sq miles (131,957 sq km)
**Languages:** Greek*
**Currency:** Euro = 100 cents

## BELARUS
*Eastern Europe*
**Capital:** Minsk
**Population:** 9.6 million / 120 people per sq mile (46 people per sq km)
**Total area:** 80,154 sq miles (207,600 sq km)
**Languages:** Belarussian*, Russian*
**Currency:** New Belarussian rouble = 100 copecks

## ESTONIA
*Northeast Europe*
**Capital:** Tallinn
**Population:** 1.3 million / 74 people per sq mile (29 people per sq km)
**Total area:** 17,463 sq miles (45,228 sq km)
**Languages:** Estonian*, Russian
**Currency:** Euro = 100 cents

## LATVIA
*Northeast Europe*
**Capital:** Riga
**Population:** 2 million / 80 people per sq mile (31 people per sq km)
**Total area:** 24,938 sq miles (64,589 sq km)
**Languages:** Latvian*, Russian
**Currency:** Euro = 100 cents

### LITHUANIA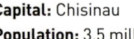
*Northeast Europe*
**Capital:** Vilnius
**Population:** 2.8 million / 111 people per sq mile (43 people per sq km)
**Total area:** 25,213 sq miles (65,300 sq km)
**Languages:** Lithuanian*, Russian
**Currency:** Euro = 100 cents

### MOLDOVA
*Southeast Europe*
**Capital:** Chisinau
**Population:** 3.5 million / 268 people per sq mile (103 people per sq km)
**Total area:** 13,070 sq miles (33,851 sq km)
**Languages:** Moldovan*, Romanian, Russian
**Currency:** Moldovan leu = 100 bani

### ROMANIA
*Southeast Europe*
**Capital:** Bucharest
**Population:** 21.6 million / 235 people per sq mile (91 people per sq km)
**Total area:** 91,699 sq miles (237,500 sq km)
**Languages:** Romanian*, Hungarian, Romany
**Currency:** Romanian leu = 100 bani

### UKRAINE
*Eastern Europe*
**Capital:** Kyiv
**Population:** 44.2 million / 190 people per sq mile (73 people per sq km)
**Total area:** 233,031 sq miles (603,550 sq km)
**Languages:** Ukrainian*, Russian
**Currency:** Hryvnia = 100 kopiykas

### RUSSIA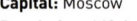
*Europe/Asia*
**Capital:** Moscow
**Population:** 142.4 million 22 people per sq mile / (8 people per sq km)
**Total area:** 6,601,668 sq miles (17,098,242 sq km)
**Languages:** Russian*, Tatar
**Currency:** Russian Rouble = 100 kopeks

## ASIA

### KAZAKHSTAN
*Central Asia*
**Capital:** Nur-Sultan
**Population:** 18.4 million / 15 people per sq mile (6 people per sq km)
**Total area:** 1,052,090 sq miles (2,724,900 sq km)
**Languages:** Kazakh*, Russian
**Currency:** Tenge = 100 tiin

### ARMENIA
*Southwest Asia*
**Capital:** Yerevan
**Population:** 3.1 million / 270 people per sq mile (104 people per sq km)
**Total area:** 11,484 sq miles (29,743 sq km)
**Languages:** Armenian*, Russian, Kurdish
**Currency:** Dram = 100 luma

### AZERBAIJAN
*Southwest Asia*
**Capital:** Baku
**Population:** 9.8 million / 293 people per sq mile (113 people per sq km)
**Total area:** 33,436 sq miles (86,600 sq km)
**Languages:** Azeri*, Russian
**Currency:** Manat = 100 qopiks

### GEORGIA
*Southwest Asia*
**Capital:** Tbilisi
**Population:** 4.9 million / 182 people per sq mile (70 people per sq km)
**Total area:** 26,911 sq miles (69,700 sq km)
**Languages:** Georgian*, Russian
**Currency:** Lari = 100 tetri

### TURKEY
*Asia/Europe*
**Capital:** Ankara
**Population:** 80.3 million / 265 people per sq mile (103 people per sq km)
**Total area:** 302,535 sq miles (783,562 sq km)
**Languages:** Turkish*, Kurdish
**Currency:** Turkish lira = 100 kurus

### ISRAEL
*Southwest Asia*
**Capital:** Jerusalem (disputed)
**Population:** 8.2 million / 1,023 people per sq mile (395 people per sq km)
**Total area:** 8,019 sq miles (20,770 sq km)
**Languages:** Hebrew*, Arabic, English
**Currency:** Shekel = 100 agorot

### JORDAN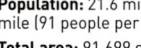
*Southwest Asia*
**Capital:** Amman
**Population:** 8.2 million / 143 people per sq mile (55 people per sq km)
**Total area:** 34,495 sq miles (89,342 sq km)
**Languages:** Arabic*
**Currency:** Jordanian dinar = 1,000 fils

### LEBANON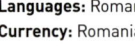
*Southwest Asia*
**Capital:** Beirut
**Population:** 6.2 million / 1,544 people per sq mile (596 people per sq km)
**Total area:** 4,015 sq miles (10,400 sq km)
**Languages:** Arabic*, French, Armenian, Assyrian
**Currency:** Lebanese pound = 100 piastres

### SYRIA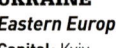
*Southwest Asia*
**Capital:** Damascus
**Population:** 17.2 million / 241 people per sq mile (93 people per sq km)
**Total area:** 71,498 sq miles (185,180 sq km)
**Languages:** Arabic*, Kurdish, Armenian, Circassian, Aramaic
**Currency:** Syrian pound = 100 piastres

### BAHRAIN
*Southwest Asia*
**Capital:** Manama
**Population:** 1.3 million / 4,590 people per sq mile (1,772 people per sq km)
**Total area:** 293 sq miles (720 sq km)
**Languages:** Arabic*, English, Urdu, Farsi
**Currency:** Bahraini dinar = 1,000 fils

### IRAN
*Southwest Asia*
**Capital:** Tehran
**Population:** 82.8 million / 130 people per sq mile (50 people per sq km)
**Total area:** 636,372 sq miles (1,648,195 sq km)
**Languages:** Farsi (Persian)*, Azeri, Gilaki, Balochi, Mazandarani, Kurdish, Arabic
**Currency:** Iranian rial = 10 tomans

### IRAQ
*Southwest Asia*
**Capital:** Baghdad
**Population:** 38.2 million / 226 people per sq mile (87 people per sq km)
**Total area:** 169,235 sq miles (438,317 sq km)
**Languages:** Arabic*, Kurdish*, Armenian, Assyrian, Turkic languages
**Currency:** Iraqi dinar = 100 fils

### KUWAIT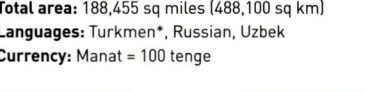
*Southwest Asia*
**Capital:** Kuwait City
**Population:** 2.8 million / 407 people per sq mile (157 people per sq km)
**Total area:** 6,880 sq miles (17,820 sq km)
**Languages:** Arabic*, English
**Currency:** Kuwaiti dinar = 1,000 fils

### OMAN
*Southwest Asia*
**Capital:** Muscat
**Population:** 3.4 million / 28 people per sq km (11 people per sq mile)
**Total area:** 119,499 sq miles (309,500 sq km)
**Languages:** Arabic*, Baluchi
**Currency:** Omani rial = 1000 baizas

### QATAR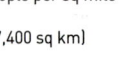
*Southwest Asia*
**Capital:** Doha
**Population:** 2.3 million / 514 people per sq mile (198 people per sq km)
**Total area:** 4,473 sq miles (11,586 sq km)
**Languages:** Arabic*
**Currency:** Qatar riyal = 100 dirhams

### SAUDI ARABIA
*Southwest Asia*
**Capital:** Riyadh
**Population:** 28.1 million / 34 people per sq mile (13 people per sq km)
**Total area:** 830,000 sq miles (2,149,690 sq km)
**Languages:** Arabic*
**Currency:** Saudi riyal = 100 halalas

### UNITED ARAB EMIRATES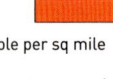
*Southwest Asia*
**Capital:** Abu Dhabi
**Population:** 5.9 million / 183 people per sq mile (71 people per sq km)
**Total area:** 32,278 sq miles (82,600 sq km)
**Languages:** Arabic*, Farsi, English, Indian and Pakistani languages
**Currency:** UAE dirham = 100 fils

### YEMEN
*Southwest Asia*
**Capital:** Sanaa
**Population:** 27.4 million / 134 people per sq mile (52 people per sq km)
**Total area:** 203,850 sq miles (527,968 sq km)
**Languages:** Arabic*
**Currency:** Yemeni rial = 100 fils

### AFGHANISTAN
*Central Asia*
**Capital:** Kabul
**Population:** 32 million / 129 people per sq mile (50 people per sq km)
**Total area:** 251,827 sq miles (652,230 sq km)
**Languages:** Persian*, Pashto*, Uzbek, Turkmen
**Currency:** Afghani = 100 puls

### KYRGYZSTAN
*Central Asia*
**Capital:** Bishkek
**Population:** 5.7 million / 74 people per sq mile (29 people per sq km)
**Total area:** 77,202 sq miles (199,951 sq km)
**Languages:** Krygyz*, Russian*, Uzbek
**Currency:** Som = 100 tyiyn

### TAJIKISTAN
*Central Asia*
**Capital:** Dushanbe
**Population:** 8.3 million / 149 people per sq mile (58 people per sq km)
**Total area:** 55,637 sq miles (144,100 sq km)
**Languages:** Tajik*, Russian
**Currency:** Somoni = 100 diram

### TURKMENISTAN
*Central Asia*
**Capital:** Ashgabat
**Population:** 5.3 million / 28 people per sq mile (11 people per sq km)
**Total area:** 188,455 sq miles (488,100 sq km)
**Languages:** Turkmen*, Russian, Uzbek
**Currency:** Manat = 100 tenge

### UZBEKISTAN
*Central Asia*
**Capital:** Tashkent
**Population:** 29.5 million / 171 people per sq mile (66 people per sq km)
**Total area:** 172,741 sq miles (447,400 sq km)
**Languages:** Uzbek*, Russian
**Currency:** Som = 100 tiyin

### CHINA
*East Asia*
**Capital:** Beijing
**Population:** 1.37 billion / 370 people per sq mile (143 people per sq km)
**Total area:** 3,705,960 sq miles (9,596,960 sq km)
**Languages:** Mandarin*, Wu, Cantonese, Xiang, Min, Hakka, Gan
**Currency:** Yuan (Renminbi) = 100 fen

### MONGOLIA
*East Asia*
**Capital:** Ulaanbaatar
**Population:** 3 million / 4 people per sq mile (2 people per sq km)
**Total area:** 603,909 sq miles (1,566,116 sq km)
**Languages:** Khalkha Mongolian*, Kazakh, Chinese, Russian
**Currency:** Tögrög = 100 möngös

### NORTH KOREA
*East Asia*
**Capital:** Pyongyang
**Population:** 25.1 million / 539 people per sq mile (208 people per sq km)
**Total area:** 46,540 sq miles (120,538 sq km)
**Languages:** Korean*
**Currency:** North Korean won = 100 chon

### SOUTH KOREA
*East Asia*
**Capital:** Seoul
**Population:** 50.9 million / 1,322 people per sq mile (510 people per sq km)
**Total area:** 38,502 sq miles (99,720 sq km)
**Languages:** Korean*
**Currency:** South Korean won = 100 jeon

### TAIWAN
*East Asia*
**Capital:** Taipei
**Population:** 22.5 million / 1,620 people per sq mile (625 people per sq km)
**Total area:** 13,892 sq miles (35,980 sq km)
**Languages:** Mandarin Chinese*, Taiwanese (Min), Hakka Chinese
**Currency:** Taiwan dollar = 100 cents

### JAPAN
*East Asia*
**Capital:** Tokyo
**Population:** 127.7 million / 868 people per sq mile (335 people per sq km)
**Total area:** 145,914 sq miles (377,915 sq km)
**Languages:** Japanese
**Currency:** Yen = 100 sen

NEPAL'S FLAG IS THE ONLY NATIONAL FLAG IN THE WORLD

### INDIA
*South Asia*
**Capital:** New Delhi
**Population:** 1.27 billion / 1,001 people per sq mile (386 people per sq km)
**Total area:** 1,269,219 sq miles (3,287,263 sq km)
**Languages:** Hindi*, English*, Urdu, Bengali, Marathi, Telugu, Tamil, Kannada, other
**Currency:** Indian rupee = 100 paise

### SRI LANKA
*South Asia*
**Capital:** Colombo
**Population:** 22.2 million / 876 people per sq mile (338 people per sq km)
**Total area:** 25,332 sq miles (65,610 sq km)
**Languages:** Sinhalese*, Tamil, English
**Currency:** Sri Lanka rupee = 100 cents

### MALDIVES
*Indian Ocean*
**Capital:** Malé
**Population:** 393,000 / 3,415 people per sq mile (1,319 people per sq km)
**Total area:** 115 sq miles (298 sq km)
**Languages:** Dhivehi*, English
**Currency:** Rufiyaa = 100 laari

### PAKISTAN
*South Asia*
**Capital:** Islamabad
**Population:** 202 million / 657 people per sq mile (254 people per sq km)
**Total area:** 307,374 sq miles (796,095 sq km)
**Languages:** Urdu*, Punjabi, Sindhi, Pashtu, Balochi
**Currency:** Pakistani rupee = 100 paise

### BANGLADESH
*South Asia*
**Capital:** Dhaka
**Population:** 169 million / 2,948 people per sq mile (1,138 people per sq km)
**Total area:** 57,321 sq miles (148,460 sq km)
**Languages:** Bengali*, Urdu, Chakma
**Currency:** Taka = 100 poisha

### BHUTAN
*South Asia*
**Capital:** Thimphu
**Population:** 741,919 / 50 people per sq mile (19 people per sq km)
**Total area:** 14,824 sq miles (38,394 sq km)
**Languages:** Dzongkha*, Sharchhopka, Lhotshamkha
**Currency:** Ngultrum = 100 chetrum

### NEPAL
*South Asia*
**Capital:** Kathmandu
**Population:** 29 million / 510 people per sq mile (197 people per sq km)
**Total area:** 56,827 sq miles (147,181 sq km)
**Languages:** Nepali*, Maithili, Bhojpuri
**Currency:** Nepalese rupee = 100 paise

### CAMBODIA
*Southeast Asia*
**Capital:** Phnom Penh
**Population:** 15.7 million / 225 people per sq mile (87 people per sq km)
**Total area:** 69,898 sq miles (181,035 sq km)
**Languages:** Khmer*, French, Chinese, Vietnamese, Cham
**Currency:** Riel = 100 sen

### LAOS
*Southeast Asia*
**Capital:** Vientiane
**Population:** 7 million / 77 people per sq mile (30 people per sq km)
**Total area:** 91,428 sq miles (236,800 sq km)
**Languages:** Lao*, various local dialects, French
**Currency:** New kip = 100 att

### MYANMAR (BURMA)
*Southeast Asia*
**Capital:** Nay Pyi Taw
**Population:** 56.9 million / 218 people per sq mile (84 people per sq km)
**Total area:** 261,228 sq miles (676,578 sq km)
**Languages:** Burmese*
**Currency:** Kyat = 100 pyas

### THAILAND
*Southeastern Asia*
**Capital:** Bangkok
**Population:** 68.2 million / 344 people per sq mile (133 people per sq km)
**Total area:** 198,117 sq miles (513,120 sq km)
**Languages:** Thai*, Burmese
**Currency:** Baht = 100 satangs

### VIETNAM
*Southeast Asia*
**Capital:** Hanoi
**Population:** 95.3 million / 745 people per sq mile (288 people per sq km)
**Total area:** 128,565 sq miles (333,212 sq km)
**Languages:** Vietnamese*, Chinese, Khmer
**Currency:** Dông = 10 hao = 100 xu

### BRUNEI
*Southeast Asia*
**Capital:** Bandar Seri Begawan
**Population:** 429,646 / 193 people per sq mile (75 people per sq km)
**Total area:** 2,226 sq miles (5,765 sq km)
**Languages:** Malay*, English, Chinese
**Currency:** Brunei dollar = 100 cents

### EAST TIMOR
*Southeast Asia*
**Capital:** Dili
**Population:** 1.2 million / 210 people per sq mile (81 people per sq km)
**Total area:** 3,756 sq miles (14,874 sq km)
**Languages:** Tetum*, Indonesian, Portuguese*
**Currency:** US dollar = 100 cents

### INDONESIA
*Southeast Asia*
**Capital:** Jakarta
**Population:** 258 million / 351 people per sq mile (135 people per sq km)
**Total area:** 735,358 sq miles (1,904,569 sq km)
**Languages:** Bahasa Indonesia*, more than 700 other languages are used
**Currency:** Rupiah = 100 sen

### MALAYSIA
*Southeast Asia*
**Capital:** Kuala Lumpur
**Population:** 31 million / 243 people per sq mile (94 people per sq km)
**Total area:** 127,355 sq miles (329,847 sq km)
**Languages:** Bahasa Malaysia*, Chinese*, English, Tamil
**Currency:** Ringgit = 100 sen

### PHILIPPINES
*Southeast Asia*
**Capital:** Manila
**Population:** 102.6 million / 886 people per sq mile (342 people per sq km)
**Total area:** 115,830 sq miles (300,000 sq km)
**Languages:** Filipino*, English*, Cebuano
**Currency:** Philippine Peso = 100 centavos

### SINGAPORE
*Southeast Asia*
**Capital:** Singapore
**Population:** 5.8 million / 21,552 people per sq mile (8,321 people per sq km)
**Total area:** 269 sq miles (697 sq km)
**Languages:** Malay*, Mandarin*, English*, Tamil*
**Currency:** Singapore dollar = 100 cents

## AUSTRALASIA AND OCEANIA

### FIJI
*Australasia and Oceania*
**Capital:** Suva
**Population:** 915,303 / 130 people per sq mile (50 people per sq km)
**Total area:** 7,055 sq miles (18,274 sq km)
**Languages:** Fijian*, English*, Hindi, Urdu, Tamil, Telegu
**Currency:** Fijian dollar = 100 cents

### KIRIBATI
*Australasia and Oceania*
**Capital:** Tarawa Atoll
**Population:** 106,925 / 342 people per sq mile (132 people per sq km)
**Total area:** 313 sq miles (811 sq km)
**Languages:** English*, Kiribati
**Currency:** Australian dollar = 100 cents

### MARSHALL ISLANDS
*Australasia and Oceania*
**Capital:** Majuro Atoll
**Population:** 73,376 / 1,050 people per sq mile (405 people per sq km)
**Total area:** 70 sq miles (181 sq km)
**Languages:** Marshallese*, English*
**Currency:** US dollar = 100 cents

### MICRONESIA
*Australasia and Oceania*
**Capital:** Palikir
**Population:** 104,700 / 490 people per sq mile (189 people per sq km)
**Total area:** 271 sq miles (702 sq km)
**Languages:** English, Trukese, Pohnpeian, Mortlockese, Kosrean
**Currency:** US dollar = 100 cents

### NAURU
*Australasia and Oceania*
**Capital:** No official capital
**Population:** 9,591 / 1,183 people per sq mile (457 people per sq km)
**Total area:** 8 sq miles (21 sq km)
**Languages:** Nauruan*, English, Kiribati, Chinese
**Currency:** Australian dollar = 100 cents

### PALAU
*Australasia and Oceania*
**Capital:** Ngerulmud
**Population:** 21,347 / 121 people per sq mile (47 people per sq km)
**Total area:** 177 sq miles (459 sq km)
**Languages:** Palauan, English*, Sonsorolese*
**Currency:** US dollar = 100 cents

### PAPUA NEW GUINEA
*Australasia and Oceania*
**Capital:** Port Moresby
**Population:** 6.8 million / 38 people per sq mile (15 people per sq km)
**Total area:** 178,703 sq miles (462,840 sq km)
**Languages:** Tok Pisin*, English*, Hiri Motu*, over 800 native languages
**Currency:** Kina = 100 toea

### SAMOA
*Australasia and Oceania*
**Capital:** Apia
**Population:** 198,930 / 182 people per sq mile (70 people per sq km)
**Total area:** 1,093 sq miles (2,831 sq km)
**Languages:** Samoan*, English
**Currency:** Tala = 100 sene

### SOLOMON ISLANDS
*Australasia and Oceania*
**Capital:** Honiara
**Population:** 635,000 / 57 people per sq mile (22 people per sq km)
**Total area:** 11,157 sq miles (28,896 sq km)
**Languages:** English*, Melanesian Pidgin, 120 indigenous languages
**Currency:** Solomon Islands dollar = 100 cents

### TONGA
*Australasia and Oceania*
**Capital:** Nuku'alofa
**Population:** 106,500 / 366 people per sq mile (141 people per sq km)
**Total area:** 288 sq miles (747 sq km)
**Languages:** Tongan*, English
**Currency:** Pa'anga = 100 seniti

### TUVALU
*Australasia and Oceania*
**Capital:** Funafuti Atoll
**Population:** 10,900 / 1,086 people per sq mile (419 people per sq km)
**Total area:** 10 sq miles (26 sq km)
**Languages:** Tuvaluan*, English*, Kiribati
**Currency:** Australian/Tuvaluan dollar = 100 cents

### VANUATU
*Australasia and Oceania*
**Capital:** Port Vila
**Population:** 277,600 / 59 people per sq mile (23 people per sq km)
**Total area:** 4,706 sq miles (12,189 sq km)
**Languages:** Bislama*, English*, French*
**Currency:** Vatu

### AUSTRALIA
*Australasia and Oceania*
**Capital:** Canberra
**Population:** 22.8 million / 8 people per sq mile (3 people per sq km)
**Total area:** 2,988,902 sq miles (7,741,220 sq km)
**Languages:** English*, Mandarin, Greek, Arabic, Italian, Aboriginal languages
**Currency:** Australian dollar = 100 cents

### NEW ZEALAND
*Australasia and Oceania*
**Capital:** Wellington
**Population:** 4.5 million / 43 people per sq mile (17 people per sq km)
**Total area:** 103,799 sq miles (268,838 sq km)
**Languages:** English*, Maori*
**Currency:** New Zealand dollar = 100 cents

THAT IS NOT SQUARE OR RECTANGULAR IN SHAPE.

# Glossary

**Alkaline**
Describes something that contains high levels of salts, such as a lake.

**Amerindian**
The peoples native to America, who lived there long before the arrival of European explorers and settlers.

**Amphibious**
Term used to describe a cold-blooded animal that is able to live both on land and in water, such as frogs, toads, and salamanders.

**Aquatic**
Animal or plant that lives in water.

**Arachnid**
Type of animal, such as a spider or a scorpion, that has a two-part body and four pairs of legs.

**Archipelago**
A group, or chain, of islands.

**Arthropod**
An animal without a backbone but with a hard outer shell, and with legs that can bend in many places, such as crabs, spiders, and centipedes.

**Asteroid**
A small body of rock or metal that circles the Sun, mainly between the orbits of Mars and Jupiter.

**Atmosphere**
The layer of gases, including oxygen and nitrogen, that surrounds Earth and protects us from radiation and debris coming in from space.

**Atoll**
A circular, or horseshoe-shaped, coral reef enclosing a shallow area of water (lagoon).

**Biome**
A large area that has a particular climate, type of vegetation, and species of animals living in it.

**Birth rate**
The number of children born in an area, usually measured in the number of live births per 1,000 individuals within a population, or the average number of children per woman in that area.

**Boreal forest**
A type of coniferous forest—see taiga.

**Broadleaf forest**
A type of forest that can be temperate (with trees such as oak) or tropical (with various types of palm trees).

**Caldera**
A huge crater in a volcano, often formed by the collapse of the volcano's cone during an eruption.

**Canyon**
A steep valley that has been carved through rock by a river.

**Civil war**
A war between people living in the same country, because of political, religious, or racial differences.

**Climate**
What the weather is usually like, over a long time, in a specific area.

**Climate change**
When the climate is changing, due to Earth's atmosphere getting hotter because of human activity, such as pollution. Higher temperatures will affect weather systems, which in turn will affect the people, animals, and plants living in an area.

**Coniferous**
A type of tree or shrub, such as pine or fir, that has needles instead of leaves. They are found in both temperate and boreal forests.

**Continent**
One of the seven large landmasses on Earth: North America, South America, Europe, Africa, Asia, Australasia and Oceania, and Antarctica.

**Crust**
The hard, thin, outer shell of Earth.

**Deciduous forest**
A type of broadleaf forest found in temperate regions.

**Deforestation**
The cutting down of trees for timber or to clear the land for farming or for roads. It can lead to soil erosion.

**Delta**
A low-lying, fan-shaped area at a river mouth, usually where it flows into the sea. It is formed by layers of sediment brought along by the river.

**Democracy**
A system of ruling a country in which the people have a say, usually in the form of voting for who will be the country's leader (such as a president or prime minister).

**Desert**
A very arid (dry) region that has little or no precipitation. Some are cold deserts, such as the barren areas of rock and ice in the Arctic and Antarctic.

**Dictatorship**
The rule of a country by a person who often came to, or held on to, power without the vote of their people; the opposite of democracy.

**Disputed territory**
An area, or country, that wants to be independent from another, but that has not been officially recognized by the original nation, or the United Nations (UN).

**Diversity**
The variety of plants and animals in an ecosystem; or of different people living in an area.

**Dormant**
Describes a volcano which is not extinct, but that has not erupted for a long time, although is likely to do so in the future.

**Ecosystem**
How all living things in an area interact with each other, the climate, and the various habitats there.

**Elevation**
The height of land above sea level.

**Endemic**
An animal or plant that is native and particular to one specific area.

**Equator**
The 0° line of latitude. It divides Earth into the northern and southern hemispheres.

**Erosion**
The wearing down of the land surface by running water, waves, ice, wind, and weather.

**Evolution**
How animals and plants change and develop over a long time, in order to adapt and survive.

**Extinct**
Refers to an animal that no longer exists, due to overhunting or loss of habitat.

**Fjord**
A long, narrow, and deep inlet of sea situated between steep, coastal mountain sides.

**Geyser**
A fountain of hot water that erupts regularly as underground streams come into contact with hot rocks.

**Glaciation**
When ice sheets and glaciers grow and how that changes the landscape.

**Glacier**
A mass of ice made up of compacted and frozen snow, which moves slowly down a mountain, eroding and depositing rocks as it flows.

**Gravity**
The pulling force that attracts objects to each other—it keeps us on Earth, and planets in their orbits.

**Habitat**
The environment or place in which an animal or plant normally lives.

**Hemisphere**
The northern hemisphere is the half of Earth that sits above the Equator; the southern hemisphere is the half of the globe that falls below it.

**Hominin**
Humans, including the very first type of human ancestor, that first appeared in Africa about 7 million years ago.

**Hurricane**
A violent, tropical storm, also known as a cyclone in the Indian Ocean, and as a typhoon in the Pacific Ocean.

# Glossary

**Iceberg**
A large, floating mass of ice that has broken off from a glacier, or ice shelf, with most of its body underwater.

**Ice sheet**
A permanent layer of ice that covers large areas of land, such as in Antarctica or Greenland.

**Ice shelf**
A permanent layer of ice that floats on water, but which is partly attached to land.

**Inca empire**
A powerful ancient empire located in the Andes mountains of South America, which was conquered by the Spanish in the 16th century.

**Indigenous**
A plant, animal, or people native to a geographical area.

**Infrastructure**
A term used to describe the things that make a country or region function, such as roads, transportation, communications, schools, and industry.

**Interstellar**
Means "between stars."

**Invertebrate**
Animals that do not have a backbone, such as insects, crabs, and worms.

**Isthmus**
A narrow strip of land with water on either side that connects two larger landmasses.

**Lagoon**
A shallow stretch of coastal salt-water that is partly sheltered behind a barrier, such as a sandbank or coral reef; see atoll.

**Latitude**
A series of imaginary lines that run parallel to the Equator, measured in degrees north or south of it. The Equator is 0°, the North Pole 90°N, and the South Pole 90°S.

**Longitude**
As latitude, but giving the distance for how far east or west something is from 0° longitude in Greenwich, London, in the United Kingdom.

**Mammal**
Warm-blooded animals that give birth to babies that feed on milk.

**Mangrove**
Trees and shrubs that grow along muddy shores and riverbanks, often in salty water, and with many of their roots exposed.

**Marsupial**
A type of mammal, such as a kangaroo, that keeps its young in a pouch on its stomach until they can take care of themselves.

**Mayan empire**
An ancient civilization in South America that existed from around 2,000 BCE to the 16th century, when they were conquered by the Spanish.

**Metropolitan area**
The built-up, often densely populated area surrounding a city, including suburbs and nearby urban areas.

**Migration**
The movement of animals or people from one place to another, often to find food or to breed.

**Molten**
Rock or metal that has been heated to liquid form; lava is molten rock.

**Monsoon**
A seasonal wind in South and East Asia that brings heavy rains.

**Montane**
The type of biome (climate, plants, and wildlife) found in mountains.

**Nomad**
People who move around a region to find fresh pasture for their herds.

**Oasis**
A fertile, green area in a desert that usually gets its water from underground sources.

**Peninsula**
A thin strip of land that sticks out from the mainland into the ocean.

**Plain**
A flat, low-lying region of land.

**Plateau**
A flat area of land on a highland.

**Population density**
Describes how crowded or sparsely populated an area is, based on how many people live per square mile or square kilometer—it is worked out by dividing a country's (or city's) population by its area.

**Precipitation**
The moisture that falls from the atmosphere onto Earth, in the form of rain, snow, hail, or sleet.

**Prevailing winds**
Commonly occurring winds that blow in the same direction, and which influence the climate of a particular region.

**Rain forest**
Dense forests growing in tropical zones, with high rainfall, temperature, and humidity.

**Rift valley**
A long depression in Earth's crust, formed by the sinking of rocks between two faults or plates.

**River basin**
The land into which water (usually in the form of rivers) gathers.

**Rural**
Relating to unbuilt areas, usually countryside; the opposite of urban.

**Sea ice**
The ice that forms when ocean water in the polar regions freezes.

**Steppe**
Large areas of dry grassland in the northern hemisphere—especially in southeast Europe and central Asia.

**Subcontinent**
A large landmass that is part of a continent, such as India (subcontinent) in Asia (continent).

**Subtropical**
An area or climate that is nearly tropical, located to the north or south of the tropics.

**Taiga**
The Russian word for a coniferous forest.

**Tectonic plates**
Huge interlocking plates that make up Earth's surface. A plate boundary is the point at which plates meet, and where earthquakes often occur.

**Temperate**
The mild, variable climate found in areas between the tropics and cold polar regions.

**Tetrapod**
Any vertebrate (animal that has a spine) with four limbs (arms or legs).

**Time zone**
The world is split into 39 different time zones. Most are set whole hours ahead or behind Coordinated Universal Time (UTC)—the time at the Greenwich Meridian in London, UK. Some, however, are whole hours plus 30 or 45 minutes ahead or behind UTC.

**Trade wind**
A prevailing wind that blows toward the Equator, either from northeast or southeast.

**Trench**
A deep valley in the ocean floor, formed when tectonic plates collide.

**Tributary**
A stream or small river that feeds into a larger one.

**Tropical**
Referring to the climate or biomes in the areas just north and south of the Equator. These areas are characterized by heavy rainfall, high temperatures, and no clearly defined seasons.

**Tundra**
A biome in the very cold, northern parts of Europe, North America, and Asia, in which the ground never thaws beneath the surface (called permafrost).

**United Nations (UN)**
An organization of 193 states that work together to keep peace in the world, and make it better for all people who live here.

**UNESCO**
Part of the UN, UNESCO works for peace by helping people understand each other through their cultures. They have made a list of heritage sites that should be protected, ranging from natural landscapes to historic buildings.

**Urban**
Built up; relating to living in a town or a city.

**Urbanization**
A term that refers to both the growth of towns and cities, and to the number of people that move from rural to urban areas.

# Index

**A**
Afghanistan 98, 108
Africa 13–15, 56–75
Alaska 18, 20, 23, 24, 28, 30
Albania 79, 89, 94–95
Aleutian Islands 28
Algeria 58, 64, 68, 74
Alps 86–87, 90–91, 92
Amazon River and Basin 40–41, 44, 46–47, 50, 53, 54, 144
Andes 40, 46, 49, 50
Angel Falls 42, 48
Angola 59, 65
Antarctica 136–137, 147
Arctic 138–139
Argentina 39, 43, 48–49, 51, 55
Asia 95–115
Atacama Desert 51
Atlantic Ocean 12–13, 144–145
Australasia 116–133
Australia 118, 120, 122–123, 124, 125, 128–133
Austria 78–79, 89

**B**
Bahrain 98, 104
Baikal, Lake 103, 113
Bangladesh 98, 104
Barbados 19, 29
Belarus 79, 89
Belgium 78, 88, 94, 95
Bhutan 98, 106
biomes 32, 52, 72, 93, 112, 132
Blanc, Mont 86
Bolívar, Simón 38
Bolivia 39, 40, 45, 48–49
Borneo 100, 101, 113
Bosnia & Herzegovina 79, 89, 91
Botswana 59, 69, 75
Brahmaputra River 107, 147
Brazil 39, 41, 42, 43, 44–45, 48–49, 51, 54, 55
bridges 23, 28, 43, 62, 83, 103, 123
Buenos Aires, Argentina 55
buildings 23, 28, 29, 43, 48–49, 82, 88–89, 102, 108–109, 122, 128–129
Bulgaria 79, 89
Burma see Myanmar
bushfires 130

**C**
Cairo, Egypt 62, 63, 64
Cambodia 99, 109
Cameroon 58, 70
Canada 18–25, 28–35
Caribbean 19, 21, 29, 31, 33, 35
Cayman Islands 19, 35
Central African Republic 59, 68
Central America 16–35
Chad 58, 68
Chichen Itza, Mexico 28
Chile 39, 42, 43, 45, 49, 50, 51, 55
China 98, 99, 101, 102, 103, 104, 105, 108–109
cities
    Africa 63, 64, 65, 74–75
    Americas 23, 24–25, 43, 44–45, 54
    Arctic 139
    Asia 103, 104, 106, 114, 115
    Australasia 123, 124–125
    Europe 84–85, 94–95
climate 30–31, 50–51, 70–71, 90–91, 110–111, 130–131, 137
Colombia 38, 40, 43, 44, 48, 50
Colorado River 26–27
Comoros Islands 65
Congo Basin 60–61
Congo River 69
Croatia 79, 89
Cuba 19, 25, 29
Czechia 78–79, 89

**D**
Danube River 81
Dead Sea 100
Democratic Republic of Congo 59, 63, 65, 69
Denali 20
Denmark 78, 88
deserts 26–27, 51, 60–61, 67, 68, 70–71, 106, 114
Djibouti 59, 63
Dominican Republic 19, 29
Dubai, UAE 108

**E**
early earth 4–15
Ecuador 38, 44, 48, 54
Egypt 59, 62, 63, 64, 65, 68–69, 71
El Salvador 19, 25
Elbrus, Mount 81
Erebus, Mount 137
Estonia 79, 89
Ethiopia 58–59, 61, 65, 69, 71
Europe 76–95
European Union 79
Everest, Mount 106

**F**
Falkland Islands 39, 45
Fiji 119, 121, 125, 133
Finland 78–79, 88–89
Fish River Canyon 68–69
France 78, 83, 84, 86, 88, 94
French Guiana 38, 44
French Polynesia 119

**G**
Galápagos Islands 40, 48
Gambia, The 58, 68
Ganges River 106, 147
Germany 78, 88, 94
Ghana 58, 59, 68, 74
glaciers 23, 42, 83, 86, 102, 123, 127
Grand Canyon 26–27
Great Barrier Reef 129
Great Rift Valley 61, 66–67
Greece 79, 81, 85, 89, 91
Greenland 18–19, 20–21, 24, 28–29, 31, 34–35
Guatemala 19, 25
Guyana 38, 54

**H**
Haiti 19, 35
Havana, Cuba 25
Hawaii 18, 22, 24, 28, 32, 34, 143
Himalayas 14, 100, 106–107
Hong Kong 103, 109, 114
Hungary 79, 89
hurricanes 31

**I**
icebergs 144
Iceland 80, 83, 84, 88, 94, 145
India 98, 100, 104, 108, 110–111
Indian Ocean 110, 146–147
Indonesia 98–99, 100–101, 102, 103, 104–105, 109
Iran 98, 108
Iraq 98, 108
Ireland 78, 88, 92
Israel 98, 108, 110
Istanbul, Turkey 85
Italy 78–79, 82, 83, 85, 87, 88–89, 94–95

**J**
Japan 99, 101, 102, 103, 104, 109, 113, 115

**K**
Karakorum Range 106
Kathmandu, Nepal 106
Kazakhstan 98, 108
Kenya 59, 69, 75
Kilimanjaro, Mount 61, 67
Kiribati 119

**L**
Lagos, Nigeria 64, 74
lakes 22, 35, 40, 59, 63, 66, 67, 80, 82, 86, 87, 103, 120, 123, 126, 127, 137, 138
languages 22, 42, 62, 82
Laos 99, 103

158

# Index

Lapland 95
Latvia 79, 89
Liberia 58
Libya 58, 68, 70
Lithuania 79, 89
Luxembourg 78, 94

## M

Madagascar 59, 63, 69, 72–73, 75
Malawi 59, 69
Malaysia 99, 103, 108–109
Maldives 98, 146–147
Mali 58, 68, 74
Malta 79, 85, 91
Manaus, Brazil 54
Marshall Islands 118, 120
Mauna Loa 143
Mauritania 58, 64, 68
Mexico 18–19, 24, 25, 28, 29, 30–31, 35
Micronesia 121
Moldova 79, 89
Monaco 78, 84, 94
Mongolia 99, 105, 109
monsoons 110, 111
Montenegro 79, 89
Montserrat 19, 35
Morocco 58, 64, 68, 70
mountains
  Africa 61, 66, 67, 69
  Americas 20–21, 28, 40–41, 43, 46, 50
  Asia 100, 103, 106–107
  Australasia 120–121, 123, 126–127
  early 9, 10, 14
  Europe 80–81, 83, 86–87
  Polar 136
  underwater 142, 144
Murmansk, Russia 139
Myanmar (Burma) 98, 108

## N

Namib Desert 61
Namibia 59, 65, 69
Nauru 118, 119
Nepal 98, 106
Netherlands 78, 84, 88, 94
New Caledonia 118, 129, 142
New Guinea 99, 101, 118, 120, 121
  *see also* Papua New Guinea
New York 23, 25, 29
New Zealand 119, 121, 123, 124, 125, 126–127, 129, 131, 133, 142
Niagara Falls 23, 29
Niger 58, 64, 68
Niger River 60, 74
Nigeria 58, 64, 65, 68, 74
Nile River 61, 72, 75
North America 12–14, 16–35
North Korea 99, 115
North Macedonia 79, 89
Norway 78, 82, 83, 84, 88

## O

Oceania 116–133
oceans 140–147
Okavango Delta 61
Oman 98, 114
Orinoco River 40

## P

Pacific Ocean 111, 142–143
  Oceania 116–133
Painted Desert 26–27
Pakistan 98, 104, 108, 114
Palau 118, 128
Panama 19, 21
Panama Canal 29, 144
Pangea 10–12
Papua New Guinea 118, 123, 124, 128, 131
Paraguay 39, 49
Patagonia 41, 55
Peru 38, 43, 44, 46, 48, 49, 54
Philippines 99, 109, 113, 115
Poland 79, 89
Polar regions 134–139
Portugal 78, 83, 88, 94
Prince Edward Islands 146

## R

railroads 22, 42, 63, 82, 83, 102, 103, 115, 122, 128
rain forests 46–47, 50, 53, 60–61, 113
Red Sea 66
Riga, Latvia 89
Ring of Fire 143
Rio de Janeiro, Brazil 39, 45, 48
rivers 26–27, 40, 44, 46–47, 60, 61, 69, 81, 87, 106, 107, 139, 147
Romania 79, 89, 90–91, 95
Russia 79, 80, 81, 82, 83, 84–85, 89, 91, 95, 99, 103, 109, 111, 139
Rwanda 59, 65

## S

Sahara Desert 60–61, 68, 70–71
Saint Helena 145
São Paulo, Brazil 44
Saudi Arabia 98, 108
Senegal 58, 64, 68
Serbia 79, 89
Serengeti 73, 75
Seychelles 59, 146
Shanghai, China 105
Siberia 8, 10, 100–101, 110–111, 112–113, 115
Singapore 99, 103, 114–115
Sint Maarten 25
Slovakia 79, 89
Slovenia 79, 89
Solomon Islands 118, 120, 124, 129
South Africa 59, 62, 63, 65, 69, 71, 75
South America 12–14, 36–55
South Korea 99, 103, 109
South Sudan 59, 74–75
Southern Ocean 147
Spain 78, 84, 88, 90, 92, 94
Sri Lanka 98, 115
storms 30, 31, 110, 111
Strait of Hormuz 146
Strait of Magellan 41, 142
Sudan 59, 69, 71, 75
Suriname 38, 44, 48, 54–55
Sweden 78, 88
Switzerland 78, 83, 86, 88

## T

Table Mountain 69
Taiwan 99, 102
Tajikistan 98, 102
Taklimakan Desert 106
Tanganyika, Lake 63, 66
Tanzania 59, 62, 65, 69, 75
Thailand 99, 103, 109, 114–115
Tibet, Plateau of 106–107, 112
Tierra del Fuego 41
time zones 22, 42, 62, 82, 102, 122
Titicaca, Lake 40
Togo 58, 68
tornadoes 30, 31
Trinidad and Tobago 19, 35
Tristan da Cunha 145
tsunami 147
Tunisia 58, 64
Turkey 79, 85, 98, 104
Turkmenistan 98, 108

## U

Ukraine 79, 89
Uluru (Ayers Rock) 128
United Kingdom 78, 80, 88, 90, 92, 94
United States of America 18–35
Ural Mountains 10, 81
Uruguay 39, 49, 55
Uzbekistan 98, 108

## V

Vanuatu 118, 120, 129
Vatican City 78–79
Venezuela 38, 42, 43, 45, 48, 54
Victoria, Lake 59, 63, 66
Victoria Falls 63, 69
Vietnam 99, 109
volcanoes 22, 28, 42, 63, 81, 83, 103, 123, 127, 129, 137
  early 7, 10
  oceans and 143, 145, 147

## W

waterfalls 23, 29, 42, 47, 48, 63, 69, 83, 103, 123
wildlife 32–33, 52–53, 72–73, 92–93, 112–113, 132–133, 136–139
  early 8–15

## Y Z

Yellowstone Park 33
Yemen 98, 108, 110
Zambia 59, 62, 69
Zimbabwe 59, 69

# Acknowledgments

The publisher would like to thank the following for their kind permission to reproduce their photographs:

(Key: a-above; b-below/bottom; c-center; f-far; l-left; r-right; t-top)

4-5 Science Photo Library: Mark Garlick. 6 Science Photo Library: Richard Bizley (bl). 7 Science Photo Library: Mark Garlick (br). 8 123RF.com: Tolga Tezcan / tolgatezcan (bc); Oleg Znamenskiy / znm (bl). 9 Dr. Brian Choo: (tl). Dorling Kindersley: Natural History Museum, London (br, bl); Royal Museum of Scotland, Edinburgh (bc). 11 Dorling Kindersley: Natural History Museum, London (br); Jon Hughes (tr); Swedish Museum of Natural History (bl). Science Photo Library: Christian Darkin (tl). 12 Dorling Kindersley: Jon Hughes (bl). 13 Dorling Kindersley: Natural History Museum, London (bc). Dreamstime.com: Mr1805 (tl). 14 Alamy Stock Photo: Kostyantyn Ivanyshen / Stocktrek Images, Inc. (bl). Dorling Kindersley: Natural History Museum, London (tc). Dreamstime.com: Roberto Caucino / Rcaucino (bc); Digitalstormcinema (br). 15 Getty Images: Robert Postma / First Light (bl). 21 PunchStock: Peter Adams (cra). 22 Dreamstime.com: Bryan Busovicki (cr); Paul Lemke (tl). 23 123RF.com: bennymarty (cr). Dreamstime.com: Harryfn (tl). 24 Dreamstime.com: Rafael Ben-ari (tc). 25 123RF.com: Kan Khampanya (cra). Alamy Stock Photo: Kike Calvo / Vwpics (tc). 26 Getty Images: Carol Polich Photo Workshops (bc). 27 Alamy Stock Photo: Danita Delimont (tc); Henk Meijer (tr); Colleen Miniuk-Sperry (cr). Getty Images: Bloomberg (bc). 28 Alamy Stock Photo: IF204 (tc). 29 123RF.com: ishtygashev (cr). 30 Alamy Stock Photo: Iuliia Bycheva (tc). 33 123RF.com: Menno Schaefer (cr). 34 Getty Images: Chris Moore - Exploring Light Photography (tc). 35 Alamy Stock Photo: Reynold Mainse / Perspectives (cra); Martin Shields (ca). Dreamstime.com: Altinosmanaj (cr). Getty Images: Walter Bibikow (c). 38 Alamy Stock Photo: Mary Evans Picture Library (br). 39 Alamy Stock Photo: Yadid Levy (cr). 41 Dreamstime.com: Paweł Opaska (cr). 42 Alamy Stock Photo: Barbagallo Franco / hemis.fr (tl); Francisco Negroni (tr). Dreamstime.com: Olegmj (br). 43 Dreamstime.com: Achilles Moreaux / Almor67 (c). 44 Dreamstime.com: King Ho Yim (br). 45 Alamy Stock Photo: David Davis Photoproductions (crb). 46 123RF.com: Matyas Rehak (bc). Alamy Stock Photo: HUGHES Herve / hemis.fr (br). Dreamstime.com: André Costa (tl); Rosendo Francisco Estevez Rodriguez (cl). Getty Images: Alex Robinson (tc). 47 Alamy Stock Photo: Roger Bacon (cra); Lee Dalton (tc). 48 Dreamstime.com: Renato Machado / Froogz (br). 49 Dreamstime.com: Paura (cr). 51 123RF.com: steba (cr). 53 Dreamstime.com: Igor Terekhov / Terex (cra). 55 Dreamstime.com: piccaya (cra). 59 Alamy Stock Photo: F. Schneider / Arco Images GmbH (br). Dreamstime.com: Demerzel21 (cra). 61 Alamy Stock Photo: frans lemmens (cra). Getty Images: Peter Adams (br). 62 Dreamstime.com: Evgeniy Fesenko (cr); Marcin Okupniak (bl). Getty Images: Danita Delimont (crb). 63 Dreamstime.com: Mwitacha (tl). Getty Images: Richard Roscoe / Stocktrek Images (cb); Westend61 (tr). 64 Getty Images: Alex Saberi / National Geographic (crb). 65 Alamy Stock Photo: Hutchison / Hutchison Archive / Eye Ubiquitous (cr). 66 Alamy Stock Photo: Nigel Pavitt (tl); Jan Wlodarczyk (tc). Dreamstime.com: Dmitry Kuznetsov (bc). 67 Alamy Stock Photo: david tipling (cr). Getty Images: Harri Jarvelainen Photography (ca). 68 Getty Images: Peter Adams (br). 69 Getty Images: Westend61 (cra). 71 Alamy Stock Photo: Richard Roscoe / Stocktrek Images (crb). 73 Alamy Stock Photo: Eyal Bartov (cra). 74 Getty Images: George Steinmetz (crb). 75 Alamy Stock Photo: Konrad Wothe (cra). 80 Dreamstime.com: Danil Nikonov (bl). 81 Alamy Stock Photo: Zoonar / Julialine (crb). 82 Alamy Stock Photo: Martin Plöb (bl). Dreamstime.com: Rostislav Glinsky (cb). 83 123RF.com: Alexander Baron (tl). Dreamstime.com: Ebastard129 (crb). 84 123RF.com: Luciano Mortula (bl). 85 123RF.com: Stefan Holm (br). 86 123RF.com: jakezc (bl); myrtilleshop (tl). Dreamstime.com: Claudio Giovanni Colombo (tc); Reinhardt (tr). 87 123RF.com: Santi Rodriguez Fontoba (tr); Janos Gaspar (cr). 88 123RF.com: Aitor Munoz Munoz (bl); Alexey Stiop (clb). 89 123RF.com: Roman Babakin (crb); dr. Le Thanh Hung (br). 93 Alamy Stock Photo: David & Micha Sheldon (tr). 94 Dreamstime.com: Palaine (cl). 95 Getty Images: simonbyrne (crb). 98 Alamy Stock Photo: Foto 28 (cb). 100 Dreamstime.com: Noracarol (cb). 102 Dreamstime.com: Michal Knitl (br); Yinan Zhang (cra). 103 Alamy Stock Photo: EPA (tc). Getty Images: Edward L. Zhao (br). 104 Dreamstime.com: Simone Matteo Giuseppe Manzoni (cb). 105 123RF.com: Jiang Yifan / bassphoto (crb). 106 Dreamstime.com: Bayon (tr); Daniel Boiteau (clb). Getty Images: Holly Wilmeth (bc). 107 Alamy Stock Photo: Stefan Auth (bc); Jian Liu (cra). 108 123RF.com: sophiejames (c). 109 Dreamstime.com: Sean Pavone (crb). 113 Getty Images: Barry Kusuma (crb). 114 Dreamstime.com: Nohead Lam (c). 115 Alamy Stock Photo: Matthew Williams-Ellis (br). 119 Getty Images: UniversalImagesGroup (tr). 120 Alamy Stock Photo: Ingo Oeland (tc). 121 Alamy Stock Photo: Excitations (tr). 122 Alamy Stock Photo: Fullframe Photographics / redbrickstock.com (bl). 123 Alamy Stock Photo: Simon Browitt (tl). Dreamstime.com: Gábor Kovács / Kovgabor79 (tr). Getty Images: Raimund Linke / Photodisc (br). 125 Dreamstime.com: Chu-wen Lin (cra). 126 Alamy Stock Photo: Bhaskar Krishnamurthy (br). Dreamstime.com: Rawpixelimages (bc). 127 Alamy Stock Photo: Tui De Roy (bc); John Rendle NZ (crb). Dreamstime.com: Dmitry Pichugin (tr). 129 Alamy Stock Photo: Norbert Probst (cra). 130 Alamy Stock Photo: Horizon (br). 132 Dreamstime.com: Kristian Bell (br). 134-135 Alamy Stock Photo: Adam Burton. 136 Alamy Stock Photo: John Higdon (br). Getty Images: Galen Rowell (tc); Gordon Wiltsie (tl). 137 Alamy Stock Photo: Dan Leeth (bl). Dreamstime.com: Staphy (c). 138 Alamy Stock Photo: JTB Photo (bc). Getty Images: Per Breiehagen (tr). 139 123RF.com: Irina Borsuchenko / vodolej (br); Aleksei Ruzhin (tl). 140-141 Alamy Stock Photo: H. Mark Weidman Photography. 142 Alamy Stock Photo: Mark Hannaford / John Warburton-Lee Photography (bl). 143 Alamy Stock Photo: Kevin Schafer (crb). 144 Dreamstime.com: Richardpross (bl). 145 Dreamstime.com: Naten (tr). 146 Getty Images: Stocktrek Images (bl). 147 Getty Images: Jim Holmes / Perspectives (tr)

**Climate data**
Hijmans, R. J., S. E. Cameron, J. L. Parra, P. G. Jones and A. Jarvis, 2005. Very high resolution interpolated climate surfaces for global land areas.

**Population data**
Center for International Earth Science Information Network—CIESIN—Columbia University. 2016. Gridded Population of the World, Version 4 (GPWv4): Population Density. Palisades, NY: NASA Socioeconomic Data and Applications Center (SEDAC).

**Paleogeography globes**
Derived from original maps produced by Colorado Plateau Geosystems Inc.

**Landsat satellite data for feature spread 3D models**
These data are distributed by the Land Processes Distributed Active Archive Center (LP DAAC), located at USGS/EROS, Sioux Falls, SD. http://lpdaac.usgs.gov

**Nighttime**
Data courtesy Marc Imhoff of NASA GSFC and Christopher Elvidge of NOAA NGDC. Image by Craig Mayhew and Robert Simmon, NASA GSFC.

**Wildlife biomes data**
WWF Terrestrial Ecoregions of the World (TEOW). Olson, D. M., Dinerstein, E., Wikramanayake, E. D., Burgess, N. D., Powell, G. V. N., Underwood, E. C., D'Amico, J. A., Itoua, I., Strand, H. E., Morrison, J. C., Loucks, C. J., Allnutt, T. F., Ricketts, T. H., Kura, Y., Lamoreux, J. F., Wettengel, W. W., Hedao, P., Kassem, K. R. 2001. Terrestrial ecoregions of the world: a new map of life on Earth. Bioscience 51(11):933-938.

**All other images © Dorling Kindersley Limited**

# DK WHERE ON EARTH? ATLASES

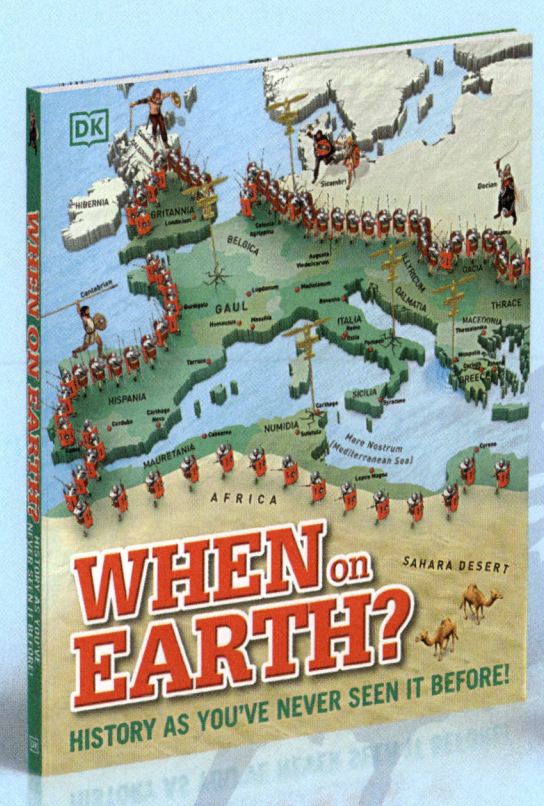

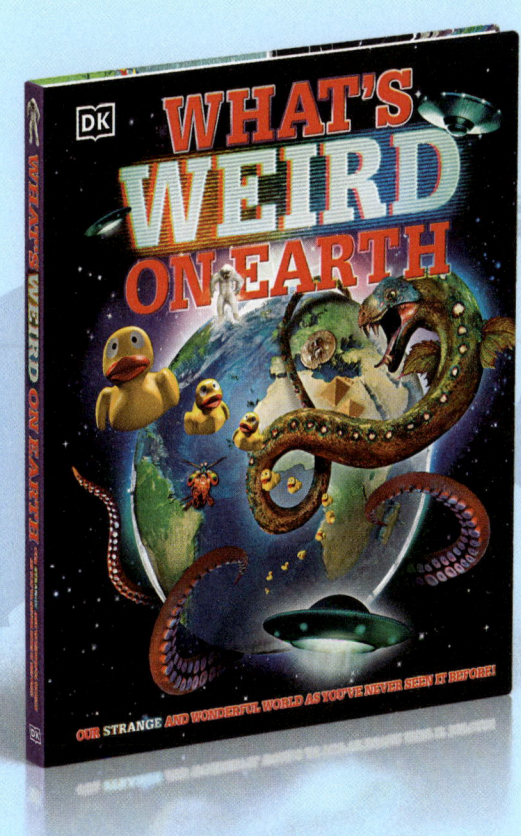

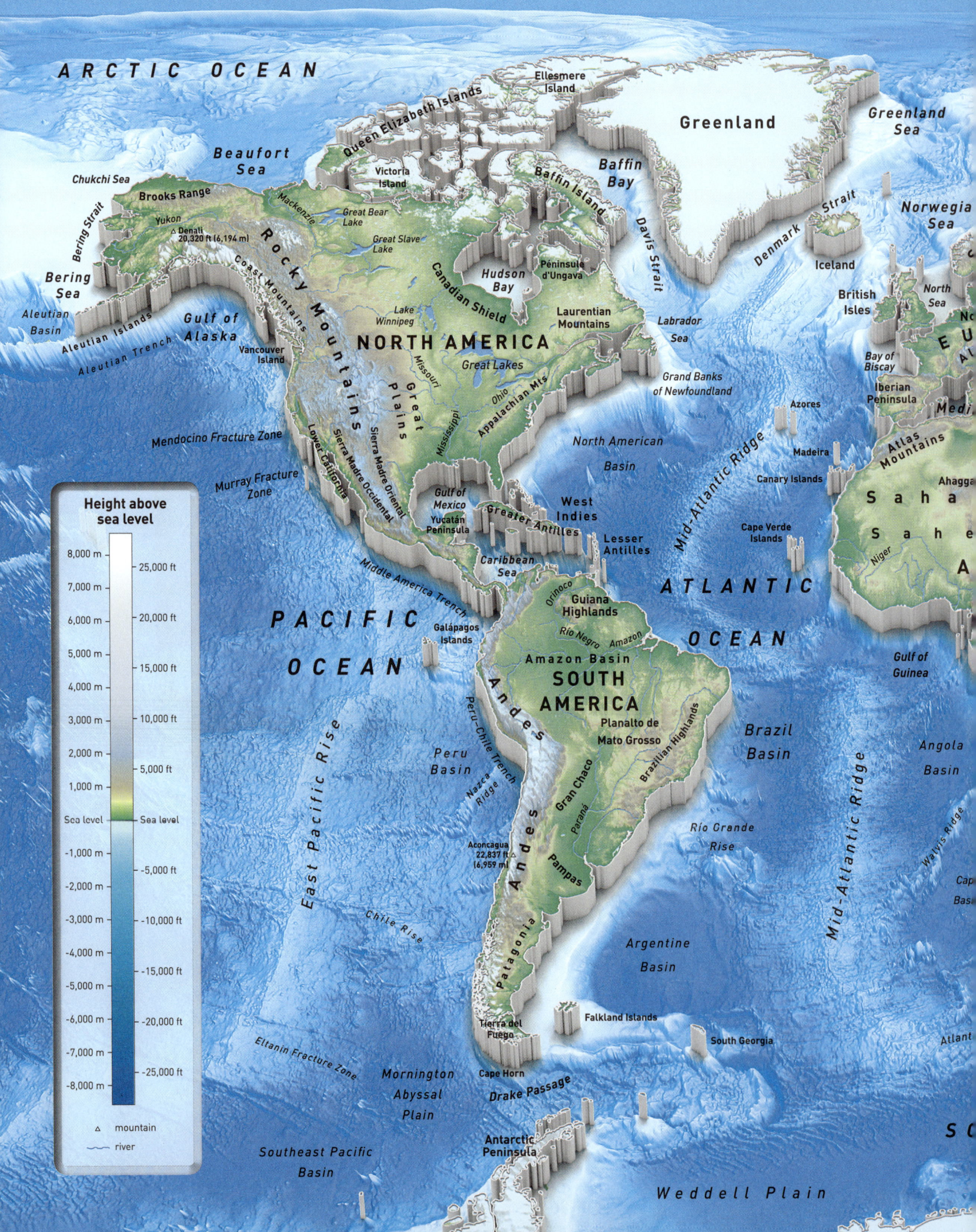

# DK SMITHSONIAN
# DINOSAUR
## & OTHER PREHISTORIC CREATURES
# ATLAS

**Written by** Chris Barker and Darren Naish
**Consultant** Darren Naish

# CONTENTS

## Rise of the dinosaurs

| | |
|---|---|
| Timeline of Earth | 8 |
| Early life | 10 |
| Triassic world | 12 |
| Jurassic world | 14 |
| Cretaceous world | 16 |
| What is a dinosaur? | 18 |

## North America

| | |
|---|---|
| *Coelophysis* | 22 |
| *Stegosaurus* | 24 |
| Three against one | 26 |
| *Allosaurus* | 28 |
| *Ceratosaurus* | 30 |
| *Diplodocus* | 32 |
| *Corythosaurus* | 34 |
| *Albertosaurus* | 36 |
| *Ankylosaurus* | 38 |
| *Tyrannosaurus* | 40 |
| Daylight attack | 42 |
| *Triceratops* | 44 |
| *Pachycephalosaurus* | 46 |
| Fossil finds | 48 |

*Yutyrannus*

*Coelophysis*

## South America
| | |
|---|---|
| *Herrerasaurus* | 52 |
| *Chilesaurus* | 54 |
| *Giganotosaurus* | 56 |
| Fighting it out | 58 |
| *Argentinosaurus* | 60 |
| *Carnotaurus* | 62 |
| Fossil finds | 64 |

## Africa
| | |
|---|---|
| *Mesosaurus* | 92 |
| *Lystrosaurus* | 94 |
| *Giraffatitan* | 96 |
| *Spinosaurus* | 98 |
| A fish dinner | 100 |
| Fossil finds | 102 |

## Australia and Antarctica
| | |
|---|---|
| *Cryolophosaurus* | 122 |
| A welcome discovery | 124 |
| *Muttaburrasaurus* | 126 |
| *Leaellynasaura* | 128 |
| Fossil finds | 130 |

## Europe
| | |
|---|---|
| *Plateosaurus* | 68 |
| Muddy swamps | 70 |
| *Ophthalmosaurus* | 72 |
| *Archaeopteryx* | 74 |
| *Iguanodon* | 76 |
| *Baryonyx* | 78 |
| *Polacanthus* | 80 |
| *Pelecanimimus* | 82 |
| *Hatzegopteryx* | 84 |
| Today's catch | 86 |
| Fossil finds | 88 |

## Asia
| | |
|---|---|
| *Shunosaurus* | 106 |
| *Psittacosaurus* | 108 |
| *Yutyrannus* | 110 |
| Surprise attack | 112 |
| *Microraptor* | 114 |
| *Velociraptor* | 116 |
| Fossil finds | 118 |

## After the dinosaurs
| | |
|---|---|
| *Titanoboa* | 134 |
| *Gastornis* | 136 |
| *Basilosaurus* | 138 |
| *Smilodon* | 140 |
| Woolly mammoth | 142 |
| Hunting in the grasslands | 144 |
| *Varanus priscus* | 146 |

**Polacanthus**

**Hatzegopteryx**

**Giraffatitan**

## Reference
| | |
|---|---|
| Fossilization | 150 |
| Early fossils and hunters | 152 |
| Mass extinctions | 154 |
| Glossary | 156 |
| Index | 158 |
| Acknowledgments | 160 |

# Foreword

My adventures as a paleontologist have taken me to many exciting places at home, in the UK, and abroad, and led to the discovery of new species. Working with teams of colleagues, I named the new dinosaurs *Eotyrannus*, *Xenoposeidon*, *Mirischia*, and *Vectaerovenator*, and the pterosaurs *Vectidraco* and *Eurazhdarcho*. One of the things that interests me most about dinosaurs, giant marine reptiles, and other ancient animals is that every one of them has a unique history, just as animals do today.

In this book, you'll meet a huge variety of creatures that lived on our planet in the prehistoric past, mostly during the "age of the dinosaurs," around 235–66 million years ago. The stories about them here focus on where animals once lived and what this can tell us about them.

Wild animals today live in specific areas, known as "ranges," which provide them with what they need to survive. Imagine a forest-dwelling, fruit-eating animal such as an orangutan. It cannot live anywhere but in a forest, and that must be a forest with the right kind of fruit trees. Some animals still live in the lands of their ancestors, while others have broadened their range, driven by factors such as climate and the slow shift of continents. In some cases, animals can discover new habitats by swimming or flying.

How our planet changed over millions of years, and how animals adapted to those changes, are exciting ideas. Exploring them will help us to

picture prehistoric species as the living animals they once were. Using the latest and most up-to-date maps, this book shows the ranges ancient animals might have had, and what the world looked like when they were alive. In many cases, our knowledge is incomplete, and the true ranges of these animals have yet to be properly discovered.

I hope that this book inspires you to be interested in Earth's fascinating prehistoric past and perhaps to make scientific discoveries yourself if you're lucky enough to have the opportunity.

Dr. Darren Naish

## Understanding the locator globes

Earth's landmasses have changed over time, so alongside every main map showing when and where the prehistoric animal lived, you will also find a globe to show you this area relative to modern-day Earth.

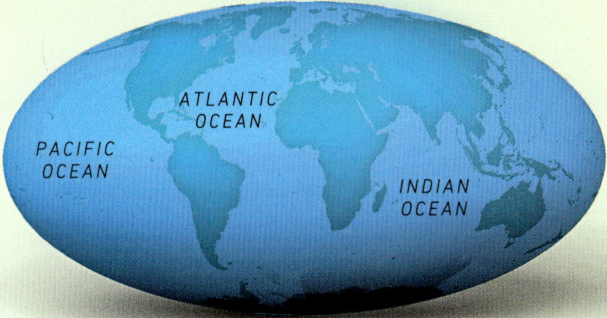

The first layer is the modern-day map of Earth, outlining three major oceans.

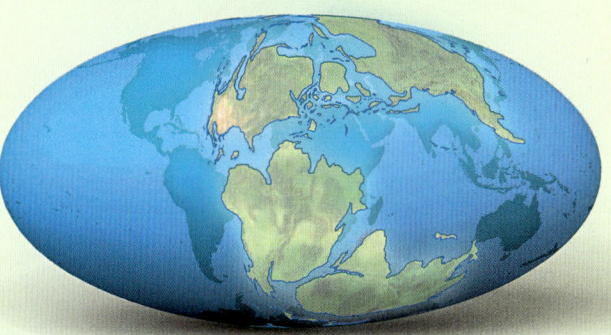

This second, light-green layer shows what Earth's landmass would have looked like when the profiled animal lived.

The third, dark-green layer represents the specific region shown in the larger map featured on the pages.

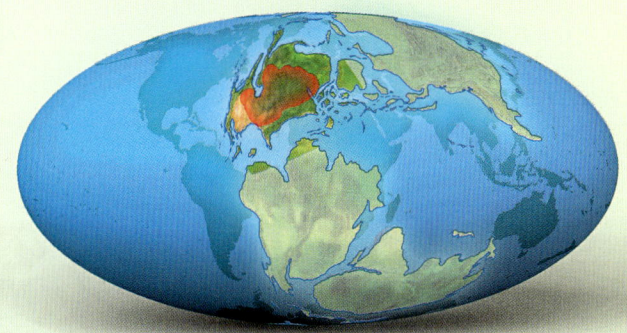

The final layer in red locates the roaming range of the profiled animal, as reflected on the larger map.

# RISE OF THE DINOSAURS

**Triassic encounter**
Alarmed by the appearance of the fearsome meat-eating reptile *Postosuchus*, a group of *Coelophysis* scurry frantically around. Another reptile, *Desmatosuchus*, moves wisely in the other direction.

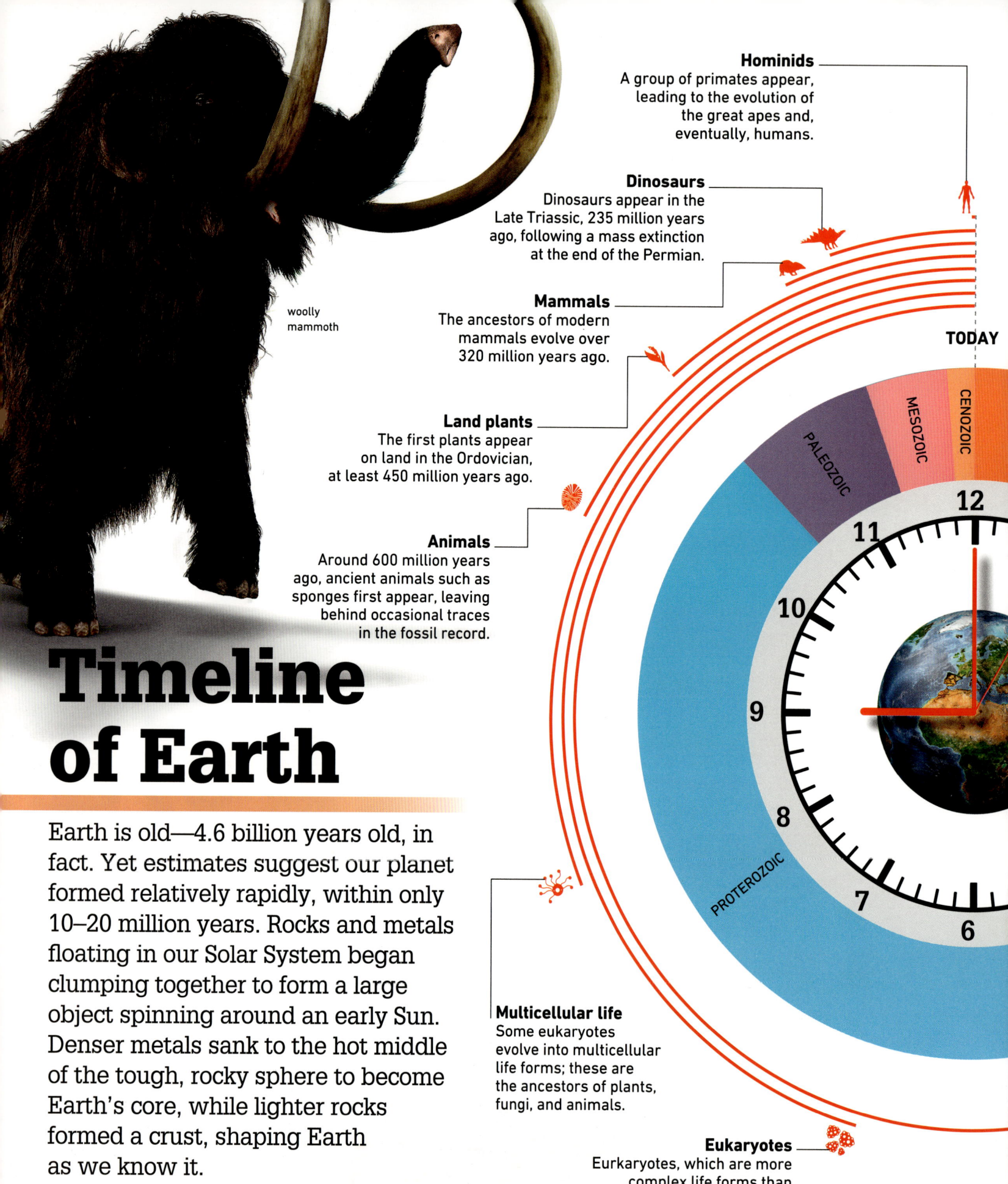

**Hominids**
A group of primates appear, leading to the evolution of the great apes and, eventually, humans.

**Dinosaurs**
Dinosaurs appear in the Late Triassic, 235 million years ago, following a mass extinction at the end of the Permian.

**Mammals**
The ancestors of modern mammals evolve over 320 million years ago.

**Land plants**
The first plants appear on land in the Ordovician, at least 450 million years ago.

**Animals**
Around 600 million years ago, ancient animals such as sponges first appear, leaving behind occasional traces in the fossil record.

**Multicellular life**
Some eukaryotes evolve into multicellular life forms; these are the ancestors of plants, fungi, and animals.

**Eukaryotes**
Eurkaryotes, which are more complex life forms than prokaryotes, evolve over two billion years ago.

woolly mammoth

# Timeline of Earth

Earth is old—4.6 billion years old, in fact. Yet estimates suggest our planet formed relatively rapidly, within only 10–20 million years. Rocks and metals floating in our Solar System began clumping together to form a large object spinning around an early Sun. Denser metals sank to the hot middle of the tough, rocky sphere to become Earth's core, while lighter rocks formed a crust, shaping Earth as we know it.

# Earth over time

Some scientists describe the formation of Earth in terms of a 12-hour clock. This makes it easier to understand the scale and huge leaps of geological time. The clock starts at midnight, with the formation of Earth, with each hour representing roughly 375 million years. Some periods last several hours, and others barely a second.

**Prokaryotes**
The first forms of life evolve over 3.5 billion years ago, as simple single-celled organisms.

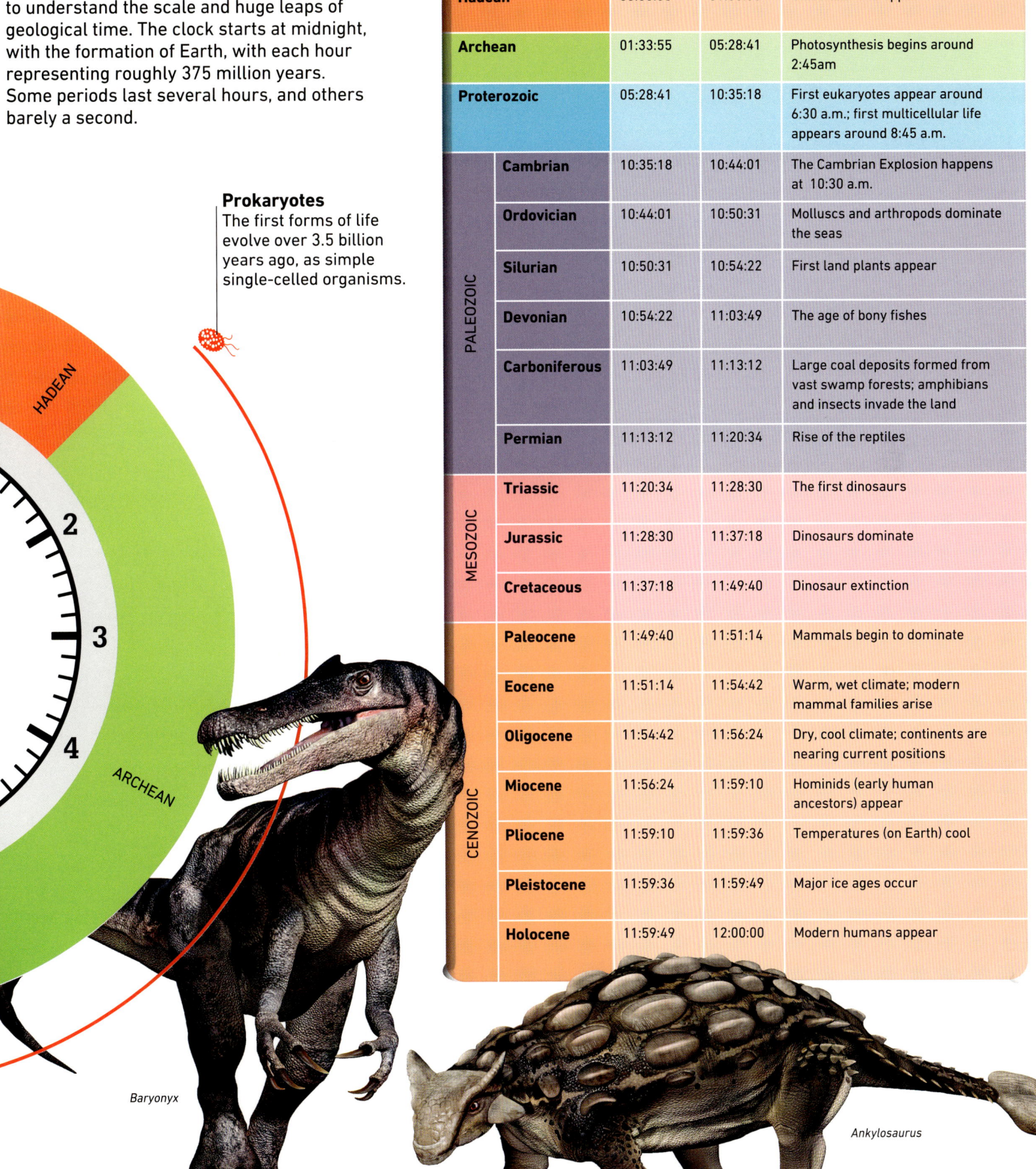

*Baryonyx*

*Ankylosaurus*

| Geological time | | Begins | Ends | Major events |
|---|---|---|---|---|
| **Hadean** | | 00:00:00 | 01:33:55 | Unicellular life appears |
| **Archean** | | 01:33:55 | 05:28:41 | Photosynthesis begins around 2:45am |
| **Proterozoic** | | 05:28:41 | 10:35:18 | First eukaryotes appear around 6:30 a.m.; first multicellular life appears around 8:45 a.m. |
| PALEOZOIC | **Cambrian** | 10:35:18 | 10:44:01 | The Cambrian Explosion happens at 10:30 a.m. |
| | **Ordovician** | 10:44:01 | 10:50:31 | Molluscs and arthropods dominate the seas |
| | **Silurian** | 10:50:31 | 10:54:22 | First land plants appear |
| | **Devonian** | 10:54:22 | 11:03:49 | The age of bony fishes |
| | **Carboniferous** | 11:03:49 | 11:13:12 | Large coal deposits formed from vast swamp forests; amphibians and insects invade the land |
| | **Permian** | 11:13:12 | 11:20:34 | Rise of the reptiles |
| MESOZOIC | **Triassic** | 11:20:34 | 11:28:30 | The first dinosaurs |
| | **Jurassic** | 11:28:30 | 11:37:18 | Dinosaurs dominate |
| | **Cretaceous** | 11:37:18 | 11:49:40 | Dinosaur extinction |
| CENOZOIC | **Paleocene** | 11:49:40 | 11:51:14 | Mammals begin to dominate |
| | **Eocene** | 11:51:14 | 11:54:42 | Warm, wet climate; modern mammal families arise |
| | **Oligocene** | 11:54:42 | 11:56:24 | Dry, cool climate; continents are nearing current positions |
| | **Miocene** | 11:56:24 | 11:59:10 | Hominids (early human ancestors) appear |
| | **Pliocene** | 11:59:10 | 11:59:36 | Temperatures (on Earth) cool |
| | **Pleistocene** | 11:59:36 | 11:59:49 | Major ice ages occur |
| | **Holocene** | 11:59:49 | 12:00:00 | Modern humans appear |

# Early life

The origins of life are shrouded in mystery. Evidence suggests that it evolved roughly half a billion years after Earth's creation.

### STEPPING STONES TO LIFE
The development of life was probably a gradual, multistep process, as molecules (groups of atoms) assembled and developed a structure and the ability to reproduce themselves. Some scientists have suggested life originated in the deep sea, in vents near volcanoes that spew hot, chemical-rich water.

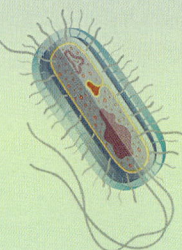

**Life appears**
Four billion years ago in the Hadean, organisms made of a single cell, called prokaryotes, were the first life forms to appear.

**Sun power**
Around 3.5 billion years ago during the Archean, early organisms began producing energy from the Sun's light—a process we know today as photosynthesis.

**Eukaryotes**
Complex, single-celled organisms, called eukaryotes, evolved more than 2 billion years ago in the Proterozoic.

**Multicellular life**
Around 1.7 billion years ago in the Proterozoic, some eukaryotes became multicellular organisms. These are the ancestors of plants and animals.

Cambrian Earth / Reverse view

### CAMBRIAN PERIOD (541–485 MYA)
The Cambrian Explosion occurred 541 million years ago and refers to the huge and rapid diversification of life that saw most of the modern animal groups emerge. These animals began developing new lifestyles, with many swimming or burrowing in the ancient oceans. Features such as eyes also evolved for the first time.

**PLANET EARTH**
A global supercontinent, known as Pannotia, was breaking up into smaller plates. Fluctuating sea levels led to a succession of "ice ages."

**TYPES OF LIFE**
**Animals**: Many ocean-dwelling invertebrate animals were successful, including arthropods and mollusks.
**Plants**: Plants had yet to evolve.

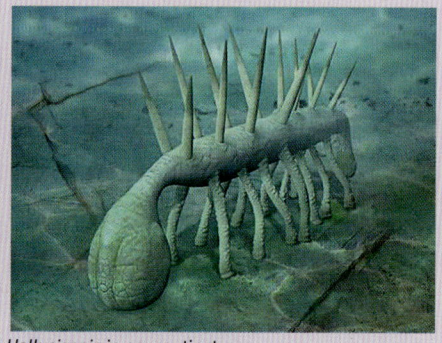

*Hallucigenia* is now extinct

Ordovician Earth / Reverse view

### ORDOVICIAN PERIOD (485–443 MYA)
Arthropods and mollusks continued to thrive during the Ordovician, while new types of fish also evolved. However, by the end of this period, a mass extinction—possibly caused by cooling temperatures—wiped out many marine habitats.

Silurian Earth / Reverse view

### SILURIAN PERIOD (443–419 MYA)
Fish continued to diversify after the extinction event, sharing a habitat with giant sea scorpions. On land, early plants developed tissue with the ability to transport water and began to colonize areas next to lakes and streams.

*Reverse view*

## DEVONIAN PERIOD
## (419–358 MYA)

The "Age of Fishes" took place during the Devonian, with species evolving into many different shapes and sizes. The placoderms were the top predators—huge, armored fish with bone-crunching bites. However, these creatures would not survive at the end of this period.

**PLANET EARTH**
The supercontinent Gondwana made up much of the Southern Hemisphere and was starting to collide with the continent of Euramerica. This was the start of the creation of the supercontinent known as Pangea.

**TYPES OF LIFE**
**Animals**: The first insects explored the land. Meanwhile, fish such as *Tiktaalik* began showing features seen in later four-legged semi-aquatic animals such as *Acanthostega*.

*Tiktaalik*

**Plants**: Moss forests and plants with primitive roots began to take hold of the land, and by the Late Devonian, the oldest-known trees had emerged.

Impression of extinct *Archaeopteris* trees

*Reverse view*

## CARBONIFEROUS PERIOD
## (358–298 MYA)

The invasion of the land took hold during the Carboniferous, creating lush forests teeming with wildlife. These forests grew so quickly that billions of tons of their remains were buried, forming the coal we use today. Insects also grew huge due to the air's high oxygen levels.

**PLANET EARTH**
Pangea had formed by the Carboniferous, with all but a few Asian subcontinents colliding to form the giant landmass. In the south, ice sheets spread across several places by the end of the period.

**TYPES OF LIFE**
**Animals**: Sharks thrived in the sea, while giant arthropods, some up to 6.5 ft (2 m) long, patrolled the land. Amphibians, such as *Amphibamus*, were now diverse and common, while the first reptiles also evolved, looking very similar to the lizards of today. Reptiles would continue to diversify throughout the period.

*Amphibamus*

**Plants**: Huge, dense forests, some filled with plants that reached as tall as 98 ft (30 m), covered large parts of Carboniferous Pangea.

Carboniferous forests resembled this modern swamp

*Reverse view*

## PERMIAN PERIOD
## (298–252 MYA)

The Carboniferous Rainforest Collapse at the end of the previous era left behind huge, dry, desertlike areas. These harsher conditions meant amphibians were no longer as widespread. Reptiles, on the other hand, were better adapted to the arid environment.

**PLANET EARTH**
All the continents had collided to form Pangea. The period inherited an ice age from the Carboniferous, but became gradually warmer and drier.

**TYPES OF LIFE**
**Animals**: Both reptiles and a group of animals called synapsids (right) dominated much of the food chain, and included large herbivores and carnivores. However, these would be severely affected by the huge mass extinction at the end of the period, probably caused by the release of volcanic gases.

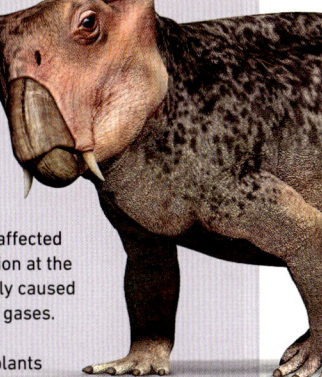
*Lystrosaurus*

**Plants**: Seed-producing plants such as conifers and cycads made up much of the plant life.

Artwork of the End Permian extinction event

**11**

# Triassic world
## 252–201 MYA

Throughout much of the Triassic, life on Earth was still recovering from the devastating mass extinction at the end of the Permian. Dinosaurs first appeared around 15 million years after the extinction, but were small and rare parts of the ecosystem, living on a single vast supercontinent known as Pangea.

Reverse view

**Planet Earth**
At this time, the land formed a single vast continent known as Pangea, which began splitting apart in the Late Triassic.

**Long reach**
The long neck of *Plateosaurus* allowed the animal to reach tall plants, which it cut up with its leaf-shaped back teeth.

**Early dinosaur battle**
In this Late Triassic depiction, a small group of hungry young *Liliensternus* attempt to bring down a *Plateosaurus* much larger than themselves. Despite their advantage in numbers, this is a risky venture for the predators.

# Environment

The shape of the continent affected the global climate, making life during the Triassic very different from modern times.

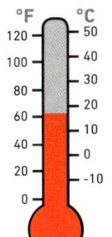

**CLIMATE**
The average Triassic temperature was about 62.6°F (17°C)—with the interior of Pangea receiving hardly any rain. However, the oceans kept life on the coasts cooler and wetter.

**PLANTS**
Many plants took a long time to recover from the Permian mass extinction, but ferns, ginkgos, and conifers survived. Flowering plants had not yet evolved.

Fern

# Animals

Lacking competitors, the survivors of the mass extinction were briefly successful. However, new animal groups began to evolve, some of which would dominate Earth for millions of years.

**INVERTEBRATES**
Insects began to develop into a much larger range of species throughout the Triassic. They included cockroaches, flies, and aquatic species. In the sea, modern, stony corals began to appear.

Fossil cockroach

**FIRST DINOSAURS**
During the Late Triassic, approximately 235 million years ago, the first dinosaurs evolved. They were small, carnivorous creatures that ran around on two legs.

**OTHER LAND REPTILES**
Predatory relatives of modern crocodiles and alligators sat at the top of the food chain. Turtles also began to evolve, while pterosaurs took to the sky.

*Mixosaurus*, a small ichthyosaur

**MARINE REPTILES**
A diverse range of marine reptiles evolved in the Triassic, including ichthyosaurs, plesiosaurs, nothosaurs, and shell-crushing placodonts. Some, such as the nothosaurs and placodonts, would die out at the end of the Triassic, while others continued to prosper in the Mesozoic seas.

*Proganochelys* turtles date from the Triassic

**Heavier herbivores**
The first large plant-eating dinosaurs, such as this *Plateosaurus,* belonged to a group called sauropodomorphs. These animals moved on two legs.

**Larger predators**
By the Late Triassic, bigger 16-ft (5-m) long theropods such as *Liliensternus* began to evolve, These dinosaurs were capable of attacking large prey.

# Jurassic world
## 201–145 MYA

As the supercontinent of Pangea split into two separate landmasses—Laurasia and Gondwana—both climate and life on Earth changed. With longer coastlines creating more moisture and warm, humid conditions, plants spread fast and new species developed in lush environments. Dinosaurs dominated on land and grew even bigger.

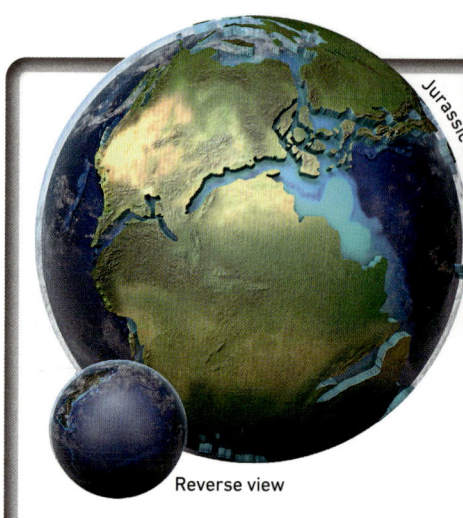
Reverse view

**Planet Earth**
The Atlantic Ocean began to appear, as the moving continents and the advancing Tethys Ocean slowly separated North America from Africa.

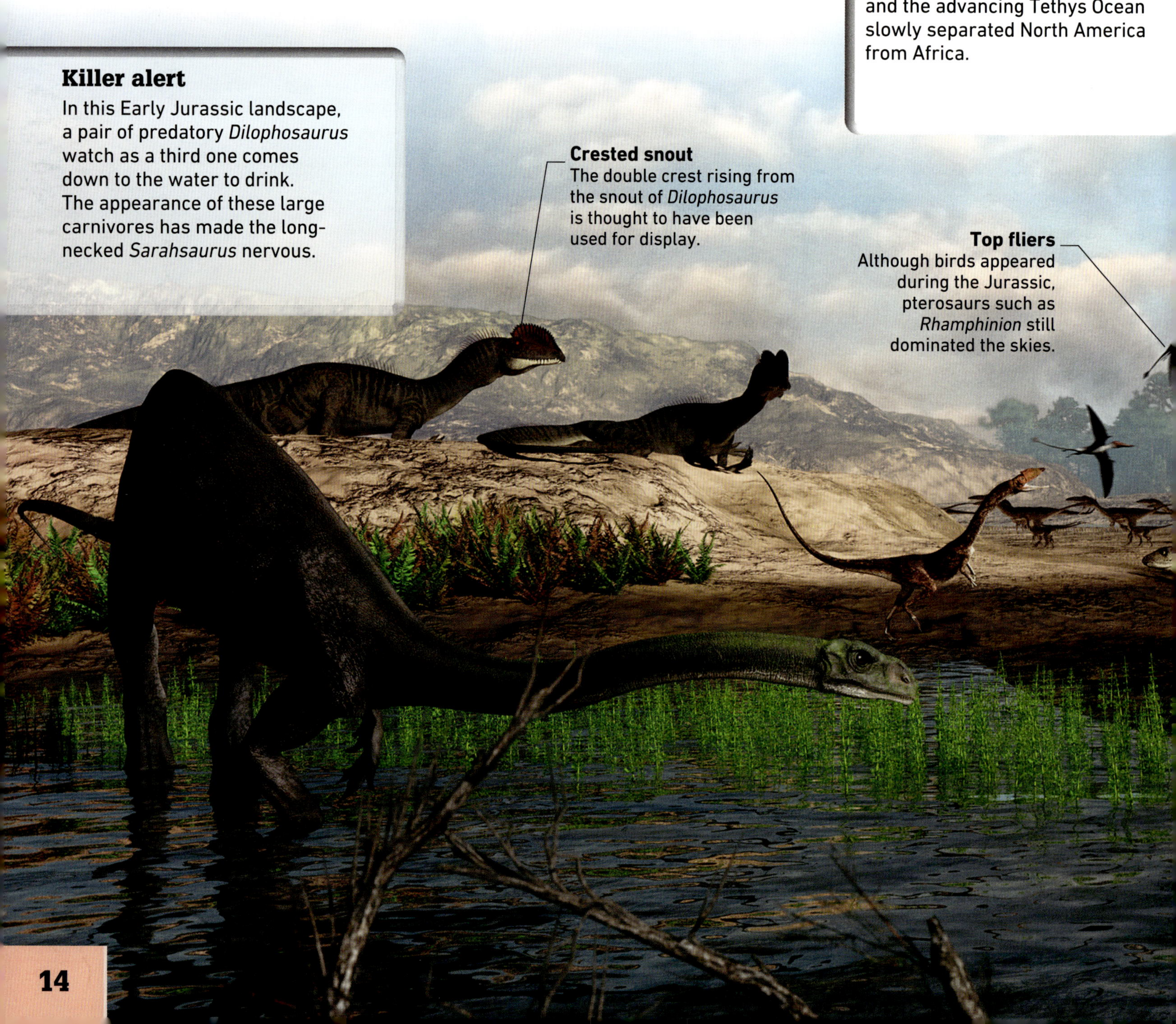

**Killer alert**
In this Early Jurassic landscape, a pair of predatory *Dilophosaurus* watch as a third one comes down to the water to drink. The appearance of these large carnivores has made the long-necked *Sarahsaurus* nervous.

**Crested snout**
The double crest rising from the snout of *Dilophosaurus* is thought to have been used for display.

**Top fliers**
Although birds appeared during the Jurassic, pterosaurs such as *Rhamphinion* still dominated the skies.

## Environment

A mass extinction at the end of the Triassic allowed dinosaurs to flourish, while the increasing coastlines brought climate change.

**CLIMATE**
With a warm climate averaging 61.7°F (16.5°C), there were no ice caps at the poles. An increase in coastlines produced more moisture in the air, which fell as rain, creating humid habitats perfect for plants. All these plants increased oxygen levels in the air.

**PLANTS**
Jurassic Earth still had no flowering plants and was instead dominated by forests of conifers and ginkgos, as well as by ferns and cycads. This plant life sustained the large herbivorous dinosaurs.

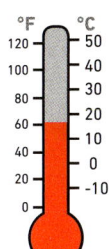
Cycad

## Animals

With many Triassic reptiles now extinct, the dinosaurs took over, introducing new lifestyles. The number of dinosaur species grew rapidly, with many variations in size and shape.

**MARINE ANIMALS**
Invertebrates such as ammonites and belemnites, cousins of modern-day octopuses and squids, flourished in the warm Jurassic seas.

**LAND INVERTEBRATES**
Insects thrived in the forests, the smaller ones surviving the arrival of new predators—birds—better than the larger ones.

**GIANT DINOSAURS**
Armored stegosaurs and large theropods were weighing in at the multiton mark, but it was the sauropods that became truly huge.

**MARINE REPTILES**
Ichthyosaurs, plesiosaurs, and crocodilian relatives, such as toothy *Dakosaurus*, hunted in the oceans.

*Dakosaurus*

**LAND ANIMALS**
The first birds appeared during the Jurassic, evolving from a branch of theropods. Lizards scurried around in the undergrowth. Early mammal relatives also evolved, but they would remain in the shadow of dinosaurs for a long time to come.

*Cylindroteuthis*

**Triassic relic**
The small *Coelophysis*, one of the earliest-known theropods, may have survived into the Jurassic.

**Synapsids**
Small animals belonging to a group known as synapsids lived in the Jurassic. They are the relatives of modern mammals.

# Cretaceous world
## 145–66 MYA

By the end of the Cretaceous, drifting landmasses had split up into the continents we see today. Dinosaurs remained the dominant large animals on land, while new bird and mammal species evolved. However, an 8.7-mile (14-km) wide asteroid would collide with Earth, closing this period with a mass extinction that wiped out 75 percent of all species.

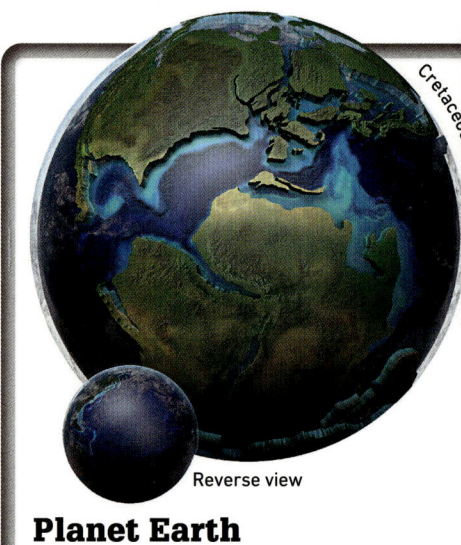

**Planet Earth**
During the Cretaceous, the expanding Atlantic Ocean pushed North America away from Africa, while Gondwana split into South America, Antarctica, and India.

**Tyrant lizard**
By the Late Cretaceous, tyrannosaurs such as *Lythronax* were the top carnivores of the northern hemisphere.

# Environment

The fragmenting continents and high sea levels created a wide variety of new environments, which sped up the evolution of new species.

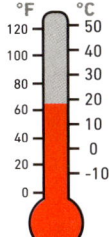

### CLIMATE
The cooling temperatures of the Late Jurassic continued into the Cretaceous but soon rose again. The climate was generally warm for the remainder of the period, perhaps due to increased volcanic activity. The average temperature was 64.4°F (18°C).

### PLANTS
Flowering plants evolved in the Cretaceous and rapidly spread across the globe. Grasses also evolved, but were not as widespread as today. Other plants seen throughout the Mesozoic, such as conifers and ferns, continued to thrive.

Flowering plant

# Animals

The changing world saw animal life become more diverse as it took advantage of new habitats and food sources. The now separated continents isolated animals from one another and, as they learned to survive in different habitats, new species evolved.

### LAND INVERTEBRATES
With the appearance of flowers, bees and other pollinating insects evolved to feed on the nectar.

### MAMMALS
The relatives of modern mammals began to adopt different lifestyles, such as meat eating and semiaquatic foraging.

### DINOSAURS
Dinosaurs still ruled the land, with giant predators—including feathered theropods such as *Dakotaraptor*—and even bigger plant eaters. Birds became even more varied.

*Eomaia*

### MARINE LIFE
Modern forms of marine life, such as sharks and bony fish, became common, and some reached huge sizes. Ichthyosaurs, however, became extinct by the Late Cretaceous and were replaced by mosasaurs.

*Iberomesornis*

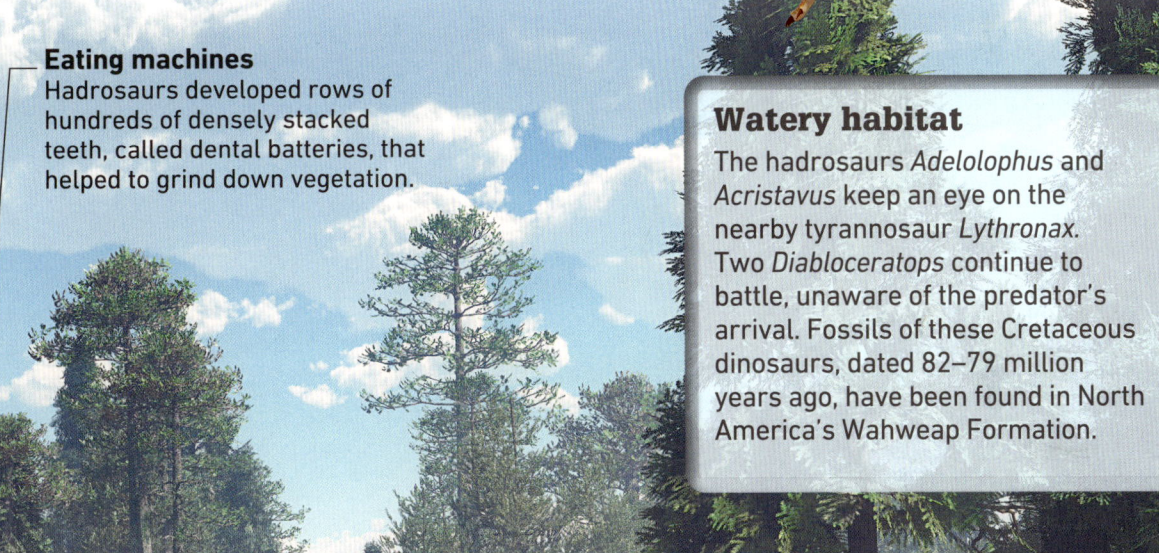

### Eating machines
Hadrosaurs developed rows of hundreds of densely stacked teeth, called dental batteries, that helped to grind down vegetation.

### Watery habitat
The hadrosaurs *Adelolophus* and *Acristavus* keep an eye on the nearby tyrannosaur *Lythronax*. Two *Diabloceratops* continue to battle, unaware of the predator's arrival. Fossils of these Cretaceous dinosaurs, dated 82–79 million years ago, have been found in North America's Wahweap Formation.

# What is a dinosaur?

Dinosaurs evolved from small reptiles about 240 million years ago. Based on shared features observed in their bones, this family tree shows the main dinosaur groups. However, with exciting discoveries continually being made, this tree may change over time.

### Saurischians
These are called "lizard-hipped" dinosaurs, though not all of them had hip bones like those of a lizard. They had long neck bones and often a large claw on each hand.

*Coelophysis*

### Early relatives
The dinosaurs belong to a larger group of reptiles called dinosauriforms, which includes their closest relatives. These reptilian cousins first appeared 245 million years ago, but do not share all dinosaur traits.

**Dinosaur cousin**
The tiny Triassic reptile *Marasuchus* was related to the dinosaurs and looked like them in many ways, but was not a direct ancestor.

*Psittacosaurus*

### Ornithischians
The "bird-hipped" ornithischian dinosaurs had backward-pointing hip bones similar to those of birds. They also had an extra bone, the predentary, in the lower jaw.

### What is *not* a dinosaur?
The Mesozoic world was full of amazing reptiles that flourished both on land and in the ocean, but not all of them were dinosaurs. These other creatures, which are often confused with dinosaurs, include the marine reptiles, the crocodilians and their relatives, and flying pterosaurs.

**Ocean-dwelling animal**
This Late Jurassic ichthyosaur was a fast swimmer and fed on squid and fish.

*Stenopterygius*     *Hatzegopteryx*

### Theropods
The dinosaurs that would eventually give rise to birds were bipedal—they walked on two legs. Many theropods were predators, but some ate plants.

*Tyrannosaurus*

### Sauropodomorphs
Although early species were bipedal, most members of this group walked on four legs and had a distinctive long neck and tail. Some became gigantic.

*Diplodocus*

### Pachycephalosaurs
These bipedal plant eaters had heads made for combat, with flattened or dome-shaped skulls up to 10 in (25 cm) thick. This feature helped to protect the brain from heavy blows.

*Pachycephalosaurus*

### Ceratopsians
With some of the largest skulls of any land animal, the horned ceratopsians ranged from small bipeds to multiton quadrupeds.

*Triceratops*

### Ornithopods
Some of these hugely successful herbivores had showy crests for display and hundreds of plant-crushing teeth.

*Corythosaurus*

### Stegosaurs
With plates and spikes running down their backs and tails, and occasionally protruding from their shoulders, these large herbivores were excellent defenders.

*Stegosaurus*

### Ankylosaurs
Wide bodies, various plates, spikes, and tail clubs armed the herbivorous ankylosaurs against predators.

*Ankylosaurus*

**Cerapoda**

**Thyreophorans**

## Walking tall
Many dinosaurs evolved limbs that were set under the body to support their weight and allow them to walk upright.

The sprawling limbs of lizards do not support their weight, so their bellies touch the ground.

A crocodilian can lift its body in a "high walk" on straighter legs, but this uses a lot of energy.

All dinosaurs stood tall on straight legs and had a hinged ankle, so walking took less effort.

19

# NORTH AMERICA

**Muddy battle**
Two *Allosaurus* take down a towering *Diplodocus*. Alongside some of the largest and most ferocious animals that ever lived, they roamed the continent now known as North America.

**220 MYA**

**Supercontinent**
At this time, all the continents were joined in a supercontinent called Pangea, enabling *Coelophysis* to travel across a lot of the globe.

**Up north**
Many *Coelophysis* fossils have been found in North America.

PANGEA

**Far and wide**
*Coelophysis* also roamed modern-day South America and Africa. Their remains are often found in ancient floodplains.

**Fragile arms**
Although long, this dinosaur's arms were rather weak and weren't very useful for tackling big prey.

**The inside truth**
When bones were first found in the stomach of an adult *Coelophysis* specimen, experts thought this dinosaur was a cannibal. However, it turned out these bones were actually from a different reptile.

Remains of a small reptile

COELOPHYSIS LIVED AT THE SAME TIME

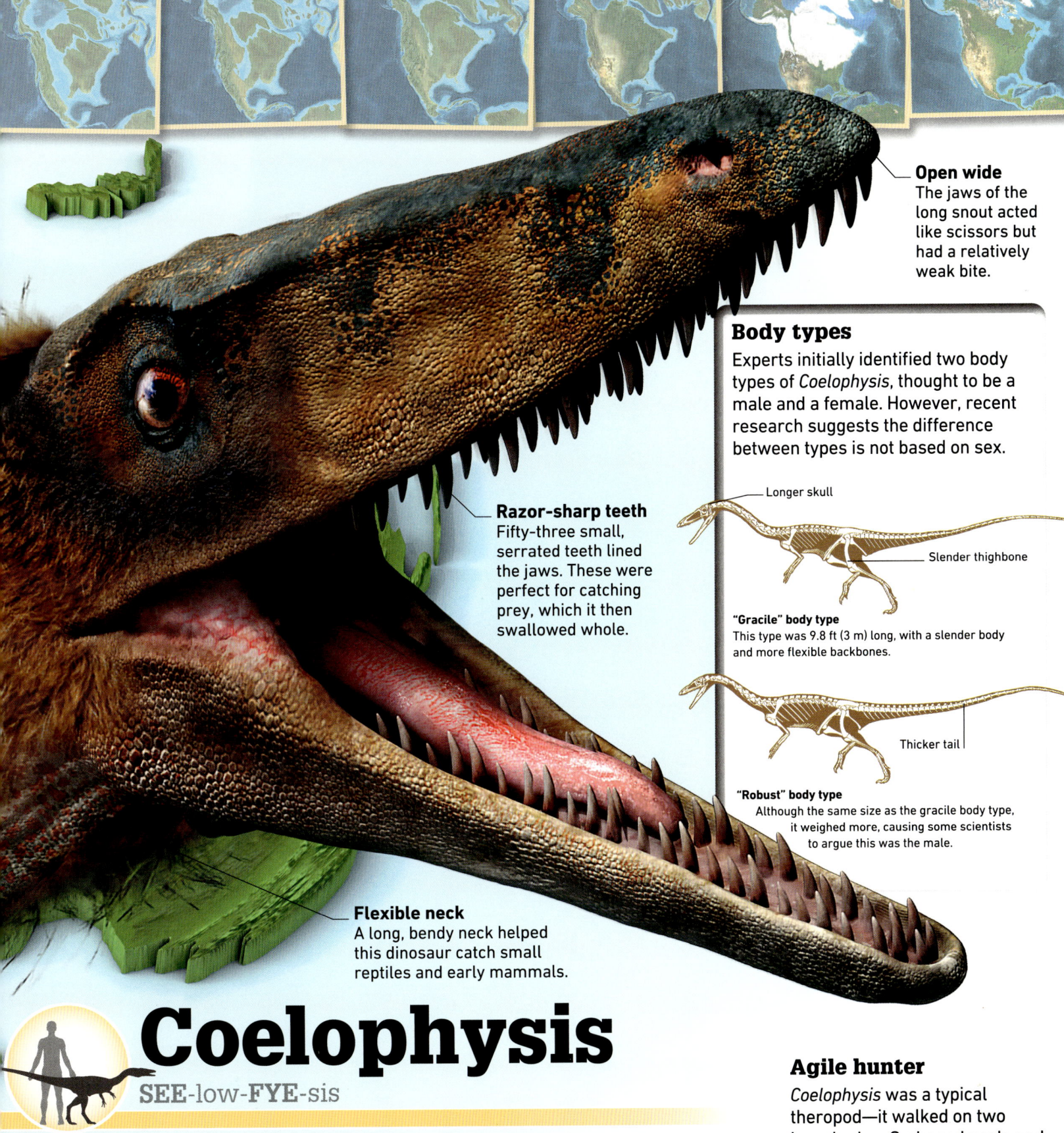

**Open wide**
The jaws of the long snout acted like scissors but had a relatively weak bite.

**Body types**
Experts initially identified two body types of *Coelophysis*, thought to be a male and a female. However, recent research suggests the difference between types is not based on sex.

— Longer skull
— Slender thighbone

**"Gracile" body type**
This type was 9.8 ft (3 m) long, with a slender body and more flexible backbones.

Thicker tail

**"Robust" body type**
Although the same size as the gracile body type, it weighed more, causing some scientists to argue this was the male.

**Razor-sharp teeth**
Fifty-three small, serrated teeth lined the jaws. These were perfect for catching prey, which it then swallowed whole.

**Flexible neck**
A long, bendy neck helped this dinosaur catch small reptiles and early mammals.

# Coelophysis
SEE-low-FYE-sis

**Agile hunter**
*Coelophysis* was a typical theropod—it walked on two legs, had an S-shaped neck, and had a long tail for balance. With excellent eyesight, it probably hunted small, agile prey.

From modern-day North America to Africa, *Coelophysis* fossils are spread far and wide. This 3-ft (2-m) long dinosaur is also one of the earliest to roam the planet, living 220–190 million years ago. Over a thousand specimens have been identified, including the remains of juveniles.

AS MASSIVE, LAND-DWELLING RELATIVES OF TODAY'S CROCODILES.

# Stegosaurus
STEG-oh-SORE-us

Instantly recognizable with its spiked tail and plated back, the 29.5-ft (9-m) long, 6.5-ton *Stegosaurus* is one of the most famous Jurassic dinosaurs. It ate its way through much of North America and some parts of Europe.

**Fossils in Portugal**
At this time, Europe and North America were joined by a land bridge. In fact, *Stegosaurus* remains have been identified in Portugal.

## Plated plant eater
Living 155–151 million years ago, *Stegosaurus* is perhaps best known for its dorsal plates. However, scientists still aren't certain what they were for. Some experts think they were for display, as they were too high on the body to be used for defense. Others argue the plates helped regulate its body temperature.

**Decorative plates**
Covered in keratin (material that forms birds' beaks), the plates might have been brightly colored.

### Brainy myth
The 19th-century American paleontologist Othniel Charles Marsh thought that an expansion of the spinal cord near the hips of *Stegosaurus* housed a secondary brain. This is not true, and this space probably contained nerves that controlled muscular movement.

The site of the incorrectly proposed "hip brain."

A *Stegosaurus* brain was about the same size as a small dog's.

## Three against one

Grazing in the Late Jurassic sun, a *Stegosaurus* finds itself cornered by three *Allosaurus*. The smaller plated dinosaur may be outnumbered, but its flexible, spiked tail can inflict deadly wounds. The outcome is far from certain.

**150 MYA**

**Eye horns**
Small horns above the eyes were perhaps used to attract mates.

**Serrated teeth**
Almost 80 teeth lined the jaws, perfect for slicing through flesh.

### Open wide
Experts are uncertain of how *Allosaurus* bit its prey. It could open its mouth a massive 79 degrees and had a strongly built skull, yet the force of its bite was not exceptional. Some scientists believe it used its upper jaw like a hatchet to make long, slashing wounds.

### Violent behavior
Marks on some *Allosaurus* fossils indicate rivalry with dangerous dinosaurs. One specimen in particular shows evidence of an aggressive infection in its hip bone, courtesy of a *Stegosaurus* spike puncturing the bone.

3-D image of an *Allosaurus* skull

# Allosaurus
al-oh-**SORE**-us

Averaging 30 ft (9 m) in length, this prime predator was a common theropod that patrolled much of North America and parts of Europe 156–144 million years ago. With its serrated teeth, large claws, and powerful leg muscles, this carnivore was built for the hunt.

ANALYSIS OF NECK MUSCLES SHOWED THAT *ALLOSAURUS*

**150 MYA**

**Strange horn**
*Ceratosaurus* is Greek for "horn lizard."

**Nose-y predator**
Analysis of a *Ceratosaurus* brain reveals this dinosaur had a good sense of smell.

**Bony skin**
*Ceratosaurus* had osteoderms running down the middle of the neck, back, and tail. These are small bones embedded in the skin, similar to those seen in crocodiles today (above), and were perhaps used in display.

**Toothy predator**
This ferocious, toothy hunter roamed North America around 150–144 million years ago. *Ceratosaurus*' teeth were proportionally longer than those of other Jurassic predators. They helped it slice deeply into flesh, perfect for catching smaller herbivorous dinosaurs.

**Fierce bite**
*Ceratosaurus* could deliver fast, slashing bites.

**Long tail**
The tail contained roughly around 50 vertebrae.

CERATOSAURUS

**Wetland specialist**
Unlike other bipedal dinosaurs of the time, *Ceratosaurus* were commonly found around water sources.

E U R O P E

**European dinosaurs**
Bones have been found in Europe, supporting the idea that a land bridge once existed between the two continents.

**Nasal horn**
The 6-in (15-cm) tall horn that adorned *Ceratosaurus* is somewhat of a mystery. Juveniles had smaller horns, supporting the idea that this adaptation was used once they were old enough to compete for mating rights.

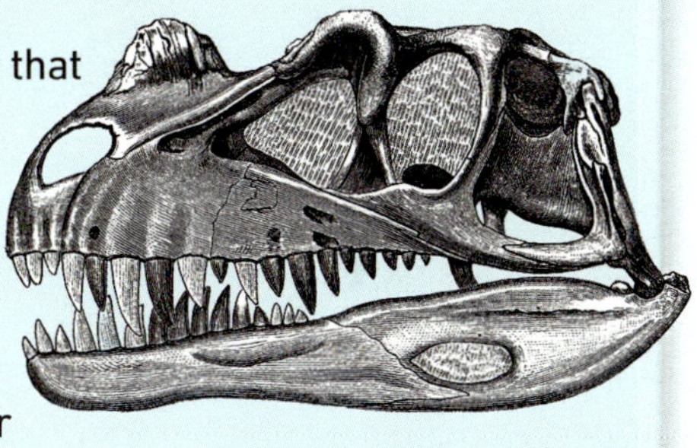

Early illustration of *Ceratosaurus* skull

**Spiked and dangerous**
*Ceratosaurus* was one of the few meat-eating dinosaurs to have small, bony scales covering the top of its body.

# Ceratosaurus
ser-**AT**-oh-**SORE**-us

**Small arms**
Probably too small for catching prey, this dinosaur's arms might have helped it to get up from the ground.

This rare Jurassic predator had to compete for food and space with larger dinosaurs, such as the more common *Allosaurus*. At a terrifying 23 ft (7 m) long, its most striking features were the horns above its eyes and snout.

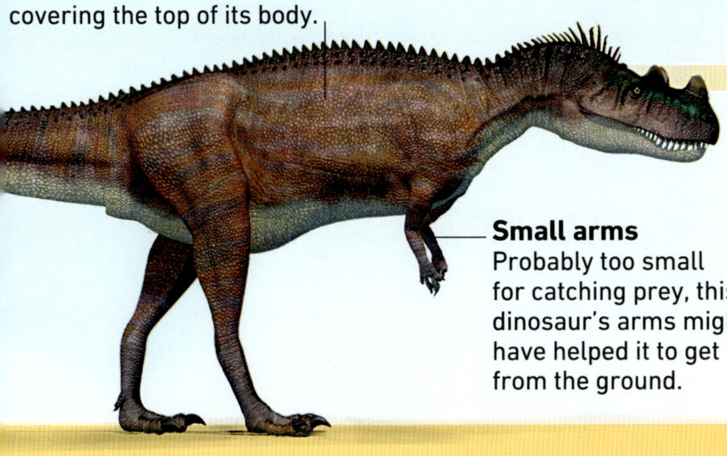

WAS ONE OF THE RARE CARNIVOROUS DINOSAURS TO POSSESS HORNS.

150 MYA

**Small head**
Relative to its incredible size, the skull of *Diplodocus* was tiny—only 24 in (60 cm) long, or about the size of a horse's head. As a result, this dinosaur also had a small brain, which occupied a fist-sized cavity at the back of the skull.

Fossilized *Diplodocus* skull

**Giant plant eater**
With its long neck and whiplike tail, *Diplodocus* is easily recognizable. Yet, despite its size, this plant-eating dinosaur was relatively lightweight, weighing between 11 and 17 tons.

**Peglike teeth**
*Diplodocus* consumed up to 73 lb (33 kg) of leaves and ferns daily. Its hard-working teeth fell out and were replaced monthly.

# Diplodocus
dip-**LOD**-oh-kuss

Growing to 108 ft (33 m) in length, *Diplodocus* was one of the longest dinosaurs that ever lived. This massive Jurassic herbivore marched throughout the area that is now North America 150–145 million years ago, searching for plants to help fuel its bulky body.

ONE ADULT *DIPLODOCUS* WOULD HAVE BEEN ABOUT THE

**SAME LENGTH AS THREE SCHOOL BUSES LINED UP END TO END.** 33

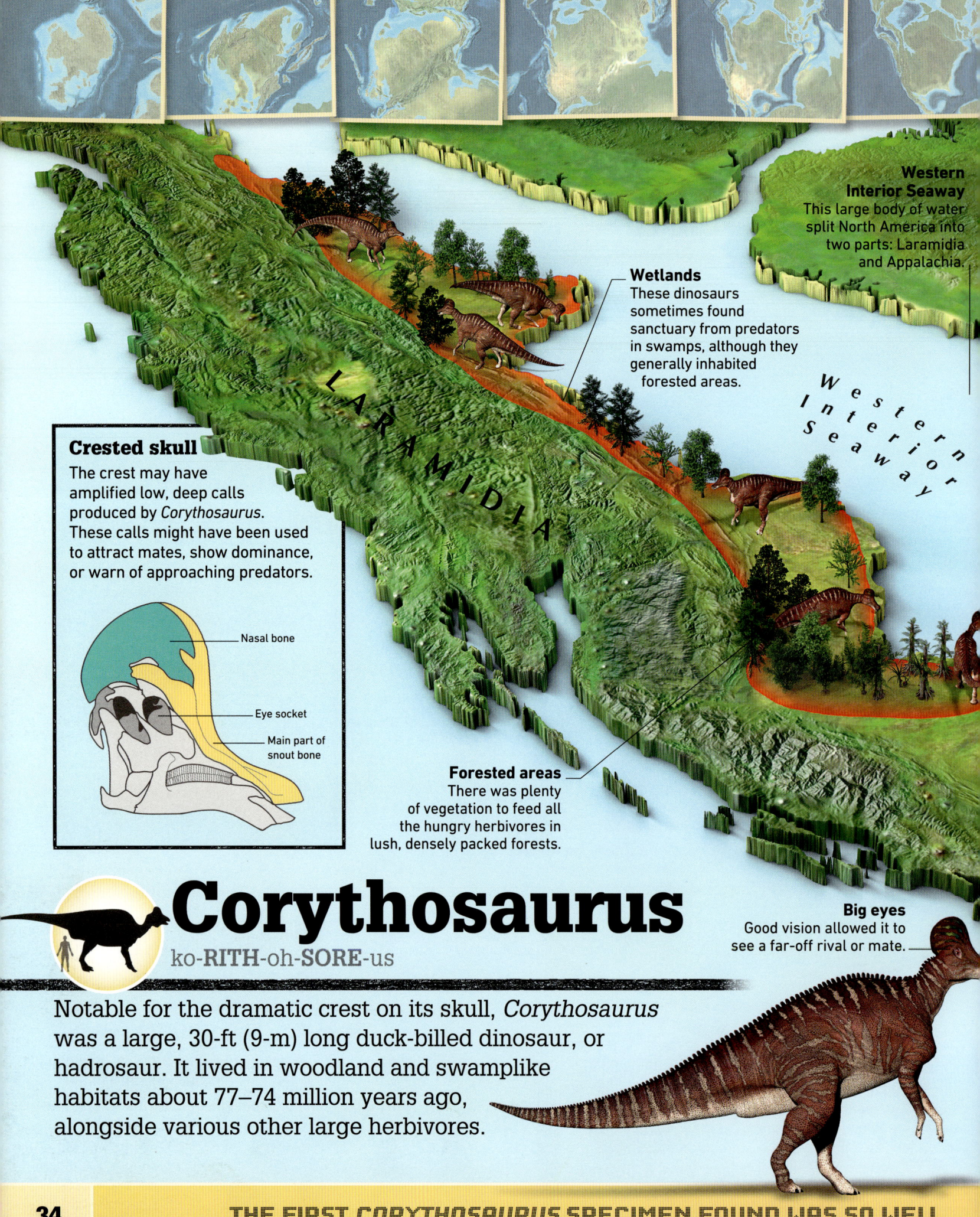

**Western Interior Seaway**
This large body of water split North America into two parts: Laramidia and Appalachia.

**Wetlands**
These dinosaurs sometimes found sanctuary from predators in swamps, although they generally inhabited forested areas.

**Crested skull**
The crest may have amplified low, deep calls produced by *Corythosaurus*. These calls might have been used to attract mates, show dominance, or warn of approaching predators.

- Nasal bone
- Eye socket
- Main part of snout bone

**Forested areas**
There was plenty of vegetation to feed all the hungry herbivores in lush, densely packed forests.

# Corythosaurus
ko-**RITH**-oh-**SORE**-us

**Big eyes**
Good vision allowed it to see a far-off rival or mate.

Notable for the dramatic crest on its skull, *Corythosaurus* was a large, 30-ft (9-m) long duck-billed dinosaur, or hadrosaur. It lived in woodland and swamplike habitats about 77–74 million years ago, alongside various other large herbivores.

75 MYA

APPALACHIA

### Herbivore heaven
Many large herbivores lived at this time in North America, including other hadrosaurs. So it is likely that *Corythosaurus* specialized in eating specific plants, so as not to be in direct competition with these dinosaurs for food.

### Narrow beak
*Corythosaurus* had a slimline beak that was adapted to a more selective feeding habit than other hadrosaurs.

### Growing crest
Baby *Corythosaurus* were born without a crest. But, as this dinosaur grew, a crest gradually appeared and became larger with age.

### Healthy diet
Conifer needles, seeds, and fruits have been found in the ribcage of one specimen. It would have fed on these just before it died.

PACIFIC OCEAN  ATLANTIC OCEAN  INDIAN OCEAN

**PRESERVED, YOU COULD SEE TRACES OF ITS SKIN.**

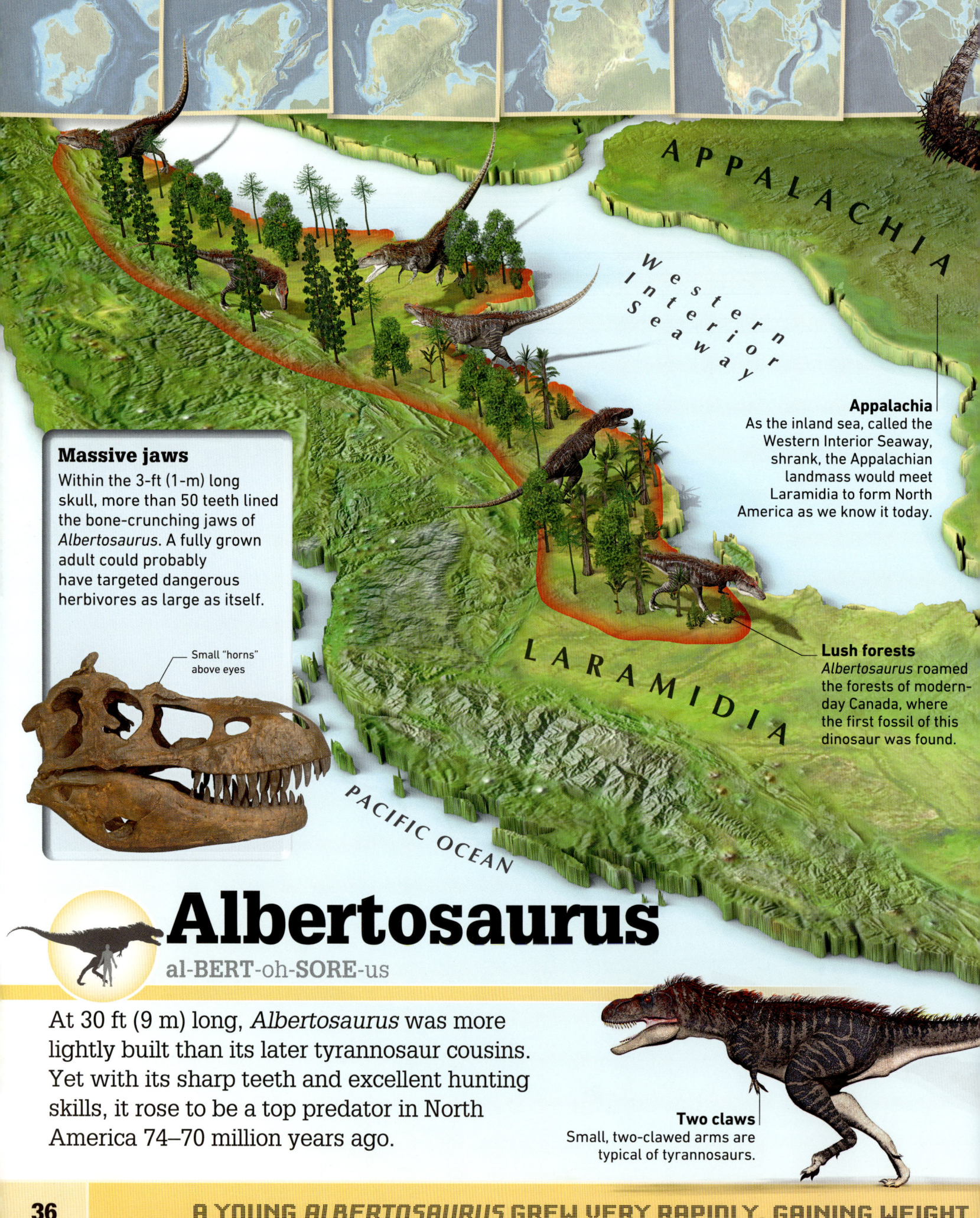

**Massive jaws**
Within the 3-ft (1-m) long skull, more than 50 teeth lined the bone-crunching jaws of *Albertosaurus*. A fully grown adult could probably have targeted dangerous herbivores as large as itself.

Small "horns" above eyes

**Appalachia**
As the inland sea, called the Western Interior Seaway, shrank, the Appalachian landmass would meet Laramidia to form North America as we know it today.

**Lush forests**
*Albertosaurus* roamed the forests of modern-day Canada, where the first fossil of this dinosaur was found.

# Albertosaurus
al-BERT-oh-SORE-us

At 30 ft (9 m) long, *Albertosaurus* was more lightly built than its later tyrannosaur cousins. Yet with its sharp teeth and excellent hunting skills, it rose to be a top predator in North America 74–70 million years ago.

**Two claws**
Small, two-clawed arms are typical of tyrannosaurs.

A YOUNG *ALBERTOSAURUS* GREW VERY RAPIDLY, GAINING WEIGHT

**Feathery debate**
Some experts argue that large tyrannosaurs such as *Albertosaurus* possessed feathers.

**Predator poop**
Scientists have found and studied fossilized tyrannosaur droppings to find out more about these predators. Being meat eaters, food passed through the gut very rapidly. Some droppings contained finely ground bone and even undigested muscle tissue.

**Long legs**
This leggy predator could easily travel long distances.

**Dewclaw**
The small first digit, or dewclaw, was set high on the leg and never touched the ground.

**Sore jaw**
Some *Albertosaurus* jawbones show holes that could have been caused by infection.

70 MYA

PACIFIC OCEAN · ATLANTIC OCEAN · INDIAN OCEAN

AT A MAXIMUM RATE OF MORE THAN 4.5 LB (AROUND 2 KG) A WEEK.

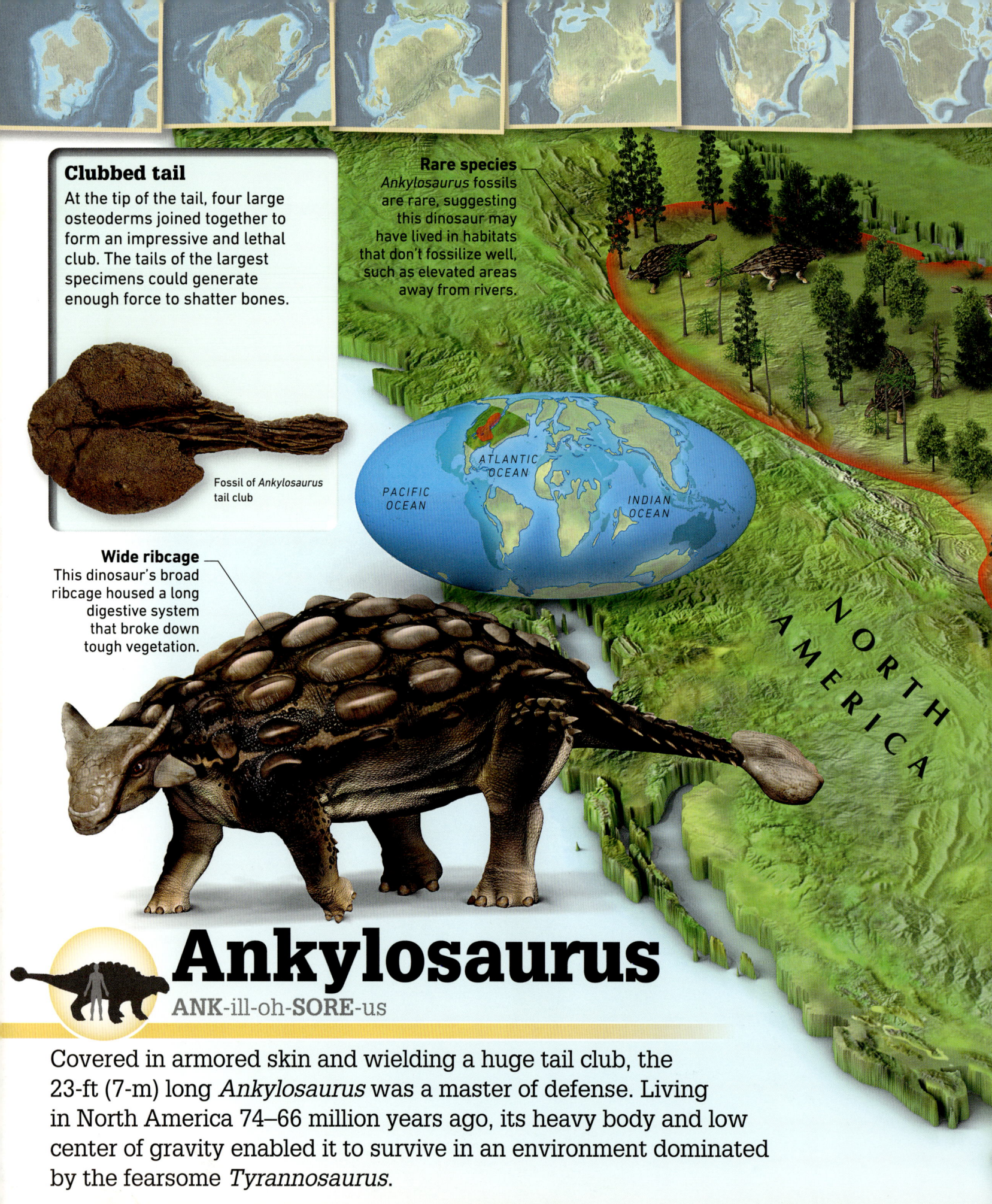

### Clubbed tail
At the tip of the tail, four large osteoderms joined together to form an impressive and lethal club. The tails of the largest specimens could generate enough force to shatter bones.

Fossil of *Ankylosaurus* tail club

### Rare species
*Ankylosaurus* fossils are rare, suggesting this dinosaur may have lived in habitats that don't fossilize well, such as elevated areas away from rivers.

### Wide ribcage
This dinosaur's broad ribcage housed a long digestive system that broke down tough vegetation.

# Ankylosaurus
ANK-ill-oh-SORE-us

Covered in armored skin and wielding a huge tail club, the 23-ft (7-m) long *Ankylosaurus* was a master of defense. Living in North America 74–66 million years ago, its heavy body and low center of gravity enabled it to survive in an environment dominated by the fearsome *Tyrannosaurus*.

ANKYLOSAURUS HAD A LARGE, MUSCULAR, AND FLEXIBLE TONGUE.

**67 MYA**

**Drying sea**
This dinosaur lived on the western shore of the Western Interior Seaway, which was rapidly drying up.

**Tough opponent**
With its bones that grew in the skin and covered the neck, back, and tail—known as osteoderms—*Ankylosaurus* could withstand the toughest enemies. This plant eater's head was also incredibly strong, with bones fused together that increased the skull's strength, protecting the dinosaur's brain.

**Club injuries**
Possible bone infections have been found on some *Ankylosaurus* clubs, but it's difficult to tell if these were the result of combat.

**Bony plates**
Hundreds of armor plates of various sizes protected the body of *Ankylosaurus*.

**Nasal cavity**
The complex airways on the snout are likely to have helped retain water and control body temperature.

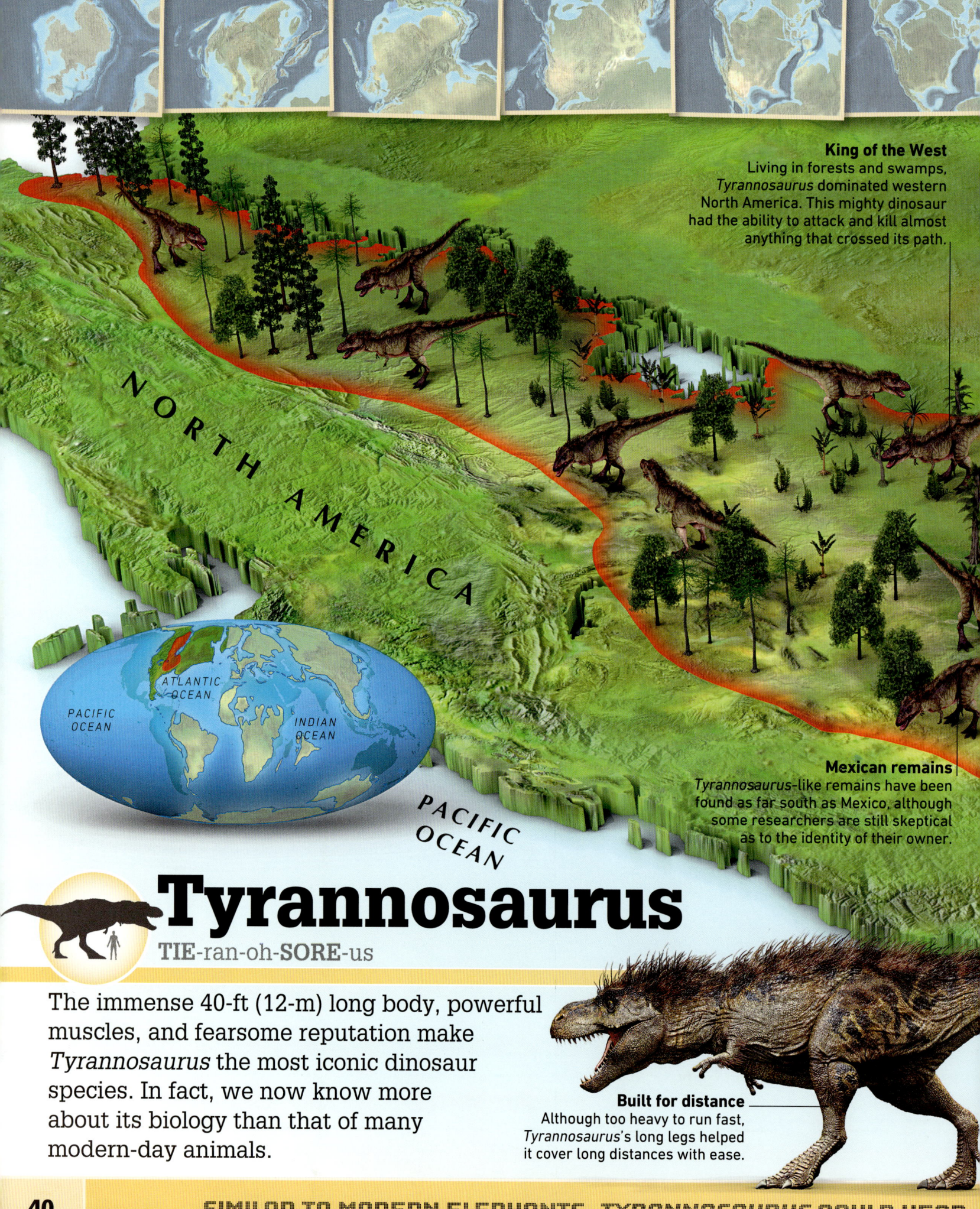

**King of the West**
Living in forests and swamps, *Tyrannosaurus* dominated western North America. This mighty dinosaur had the ability to attack and kill almost anything that crossed its path.

**Mexican remains**
*Tyrannosaurus*-like remains have been found as far south as Mexico, although some researchers are still skeptical as to the identity of their owner.

# Tyrannosaurus
TIE-ran-oh-SORE-us

The immense 40-ft (12-m) long body, powerful muscles, and fearsome reputation make *Tyrannosaurus* the most iconic dinosaur species. In fact, we now know more about its biology than that of many modern-day animals.

**Built for distance**
Although too heavy to run fast, *Tyrannosaurus*'s long legs helped it cover long distances with ease.

SIMILAR TO MODERN ELEPHANTS, *TYRANNOSAURUS* COULD HEAR

## Prime predator
Around 67–66 million years ago, the 6.5-ton *Tyrannosaurus* dominated North America. Incredibly agile, it could turn twice as fast compared to other large theropods. Its large brain also allowed it to quickly process information about its surroundings.

## Bone breaker
*Tyrannosaurus* was the strongest biting organism to ever live on land. Its long, banana-shaped teeth and formidable jaws could shatter the bones of its prey, then inflict enough damage to break up a carcass into bite-sized pieces.

*Tyrannosaurus* skull

## Eagle eyes
Similar to a modern-day eagle, *Tyrannosaurus* had exceptional vision. This dinosaur could see a long way in front, giving it the advantage when attacking prey.

Bald eagle

### Balancing act
The stiff tail helped this large dinosaur balance its very heavy head.

### Lethal bite
Sharp teeth could crunch through the tough hide of its prey.

### Sharp claws
These pointed claws were very strong and provided a steady foothold.

VERY DEEP SOUNDS THAT HAD TRAVELED OVER MANY MILES.

**Daylight attack**
*Tyrannosaurus* wasn't fast, but its forward-facing eyes and relatively large brain allowed it to execute an ambush perfectly. Here, the carnivorous predator attempts to bring down the herbivore *Triceratops* as it tries to flee.

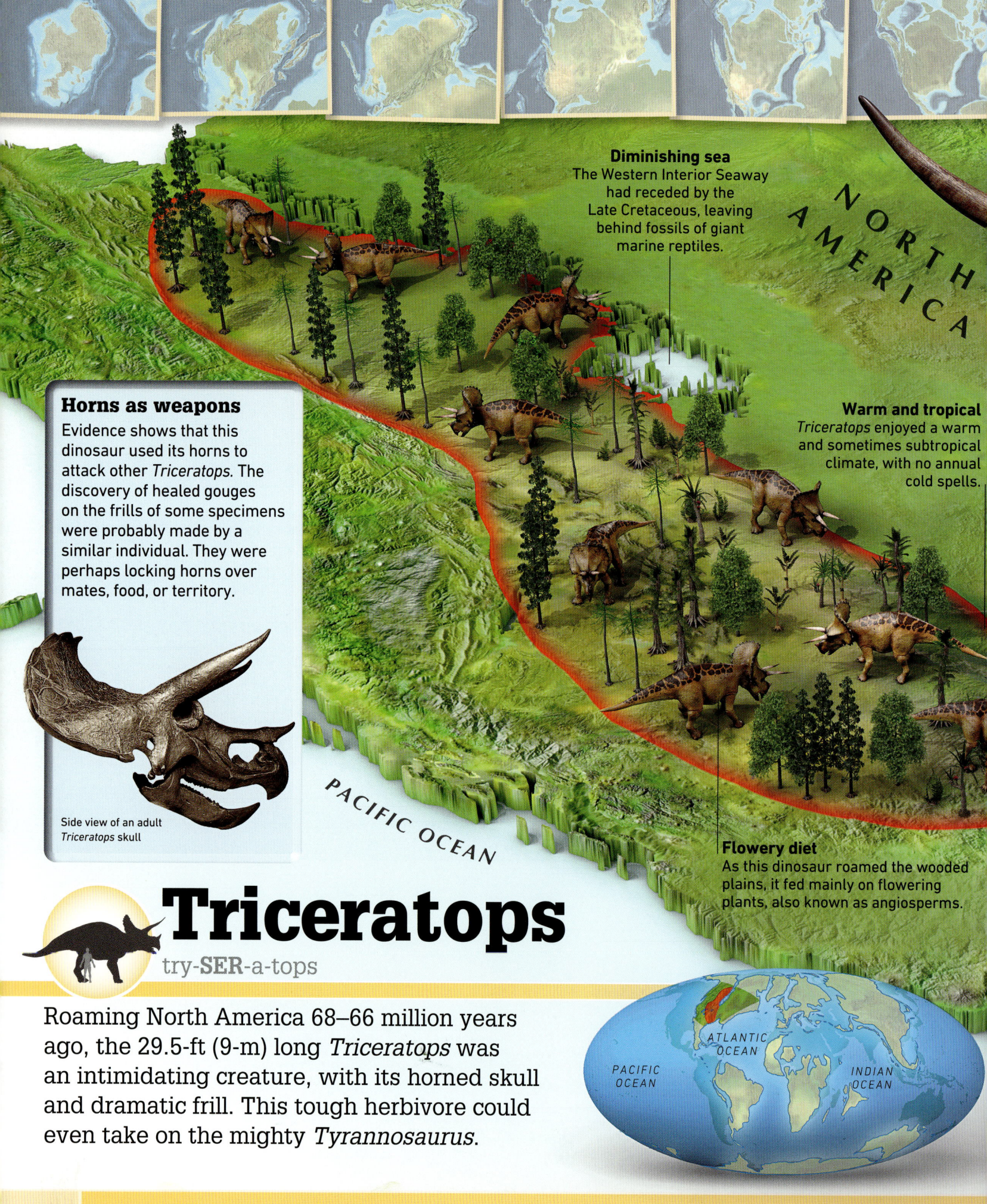

**Diminishing sea**
The Western Interior Seaway had receded by the Late Cretaceous, leaving behind fossils of giant marine reptiles.

**Warm and tropical**
*Triceratops* enjoyed a warm and sometimes subtropical climate, with no annual cold spells.

**Flowery diet**
As this dinosaur roamed the wooded plains, it fed mainly on flowering plants, also known as angiosperms.

**Horns as weapons**
Evidence shows that this dinosaur used its horns to attack other *Triceratops*. The discovery of healed gouges on the frills of some specimens were probably made by a similar individual. They were perhaps locking horns over mates, food, or territory.

Side view of an adult *Triceratops* skull

# Triceratops
try-**SER**-a-tops

Roaming North America 68–66 million years ago, the 29.5-ft (9-m) long *Triceratops* was an intimidating creature, with its horned skull and dramatic frill. This tough herbivore could even take on the mighty *Tyrannosaurus*.

WHEN FIRST FOUND IN 1887, TRICERATOPS HORNS WERE

**Pointed horns**
The two brow horns could reach 4 ft (1.3 m) long, with sharp tips and strong bony cores.

**Impressive frill**
The neck frill was made of solid bone and covered in scaly skin. It was surrounded by bony spikes.

**Changing with age**
Many *Triceratops* fossils have been found, from full-grown adults to tiny juveniles. Using these finds, scientists have discovered that as they grew older, the horns changed shape, the frill became smoother, and the nose horn fused to the skull bones.

**Sturdy stance**
Bulky limb muscles helped to support its weight.

**Big beak**
This dinosaur had a sharp, parrot-like beak.

THOUGHT TO BELONG TO AN EXTINCT BISON.

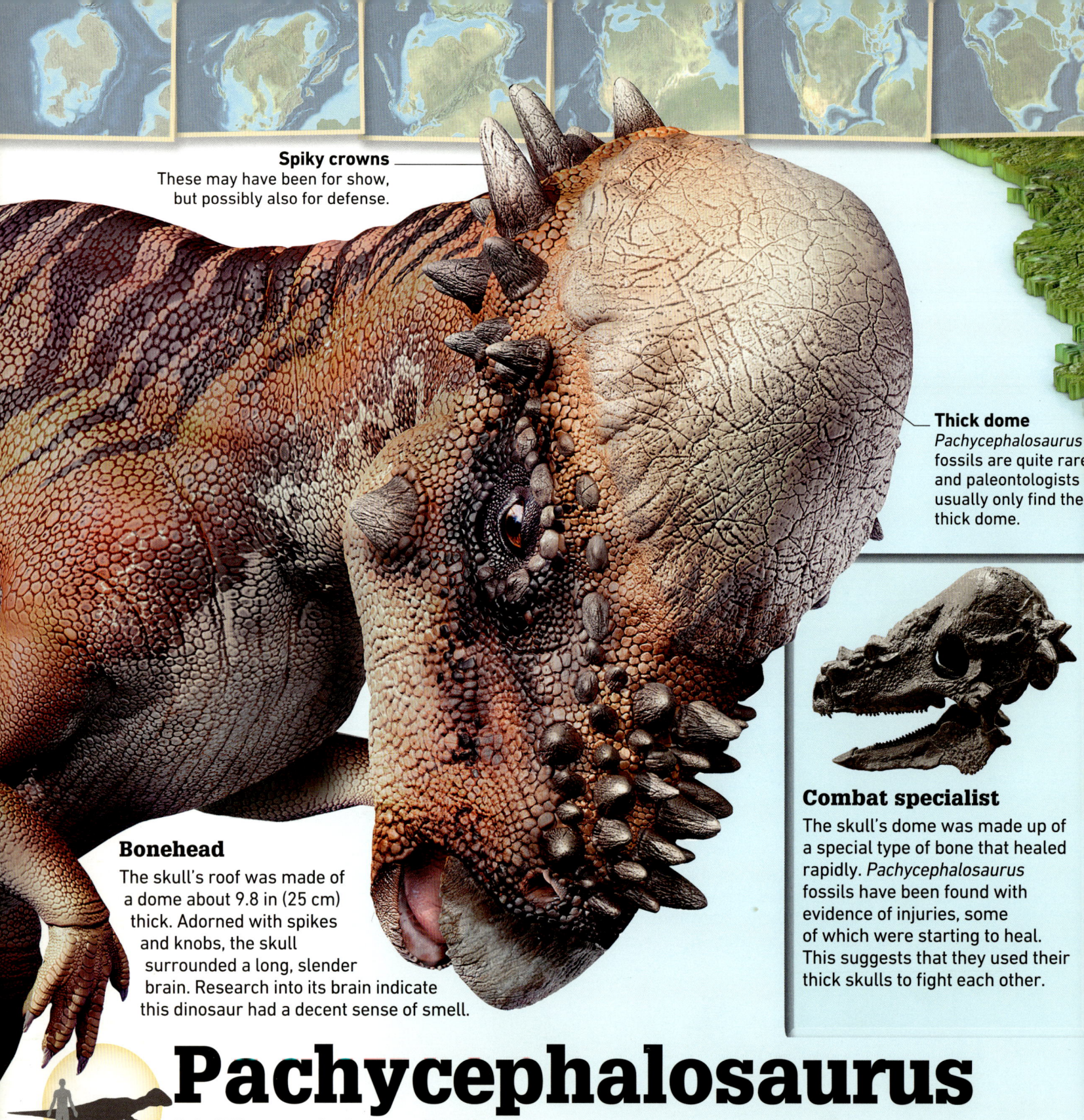

**Spiky crowns**
These may have been for show, but possibly also for defense.

**Thick dome**
*Pachycephalosaurus* fossils are quite rare and paleontologists usually only find the thick dome.

**Bonehead**
The skull's roof was made of a dome about 9.8 in (25 cm) thick. Adorned with spikes and knobs, the skull surrounded a long, slender brain. Research into its brain indicate this dinosaur had a decent sense of smell.

**Combat specialist**
The skull's dome was made up of a special type of bone that healed rapidly. *Pachycephalosaurus* fossils have been found with evidence of injuries, some of which were starting to heal. This suggests that they used their thick skulls to fight each other.

# Pachycephalosaurus
PACK-ee-sef-ah-low-SORE-us

Weighing around half a ton and at 16.5 ft (5 m) in length, the thick, dome-headed *Pachycephalosaurus* is instantly recognizable. It lived 72–66 million years ago in the area we now know as North America, just before the extinction event that killed the dinosaurs.

COMPLETE PACHYCEPHALOSAURUS SKELETON.

# Fossil finds
## North America

Throughout the history of fossil hunting, North America has been one of the best places to find dinosaur bones. From northwestern Alaska and the remotest parts of Canada to fossil-rich rock formations in Mexico, this vast continent is a treasure trove for paleontologists.

**Bay of Fundy, Nova Scotia, Canada**
The 200 million-year-old rocks found here preserve evidence of a mass extinction that left dinosaurs dominating the land.

**South Hadley, Massachusetts**
In 1802, 12-year-old Pliny Moody discovered a slab of rock with strange marks. These were the first officially recognized dinosaur tracks. The three-toed prints were probably those of a theropod.

**Dinosaur Valley State Park, Texas**
The trackway along the Paluxy River, once an ancient ocean shoreline, preserved hundreds of footprints of giant sauropods and theropods.

**Ornithomimus**
This feathery theropod was named in the late 19th century during the "Bone Wars"—a bitter fossil hunting rivalry between Edward Cope and Othniel Marsh.

**Cerro del Pueblo Formation, Mexico**
Various plant-eating dinosaurs have been found here, including ornithopods and ceratopsids.

### Major fossil sites

- **Horseshoe Canyon Formation, Alberta, Canada (Cretaceous)**
  Major find: *Albertosaurus*

- **Dinosaur Park Formation, Alberta, Canada (Cretaceous)**
  Major find: *Corythosaurus*

- **Hell Creek Formation, Montana (Cretaceous)**
  Major finds: *Tyrannosaurus, Ankylosaurus, Pachycephalosaurus*

- **Morrison Formation, Utah (Jurassic)**
  Major finds: *Stegosaurus, Diplodocus, Allosaurus, Ceratosaurus*

- **Chinle Formation, New Mexico (Triassic)**
  Major find: *Coelophysis*

Dinosaur bones in the rocks from the Morrison Formation in Utah.

FOSSILS THAT IT HAS BEEN NAMED DINOSAUR NATIONAL MONUMENT.

# SOUTH AMERICA

**Horns and teeth**
Few carnivores looked more formidable than *Carnotaurus*, with its bull-like horns and spiky teeth. This animal terrorized regions of South America around 70 million years ago.

# Herrerasaurus
her-air-ah-**SORE**-us

231 MYA

One of the earliest dinosaurs to evolve, around 231 million years ago, *Herrerasaurus* stalked an area dominated by floodplains in the supercontinent of Gondwana. At 20 ft (6 m) long, it was a large, carnivorous predator.

**Flexible jaw**
A joint in the lower jaw of *Herrerasaurus* allowed the front portion to move a little, helping it to grip struggling, live prey—similar to some modern lizards. Elasticlike ligaments created this flexibility, probably allowing the jaw to absorb shock during biting.

Model of *Herrerasaurus* skull

**Long hands**
Three elongated, clawed fingers were useful for grasping prey. The outer two fingers were buried in the soft tissues of each hand.

**Uncertain ancestry**
Because of its great age and unusual anatomy, the position of *Herrerasaurus* in the dinosaur family tree is still uncertain. Recent research places it as closely related to sauropods, while older research generally suggests theropod ancestry.

THE SKULL BONES OF ONE INDIVIDUAL SHOW BITE MARKS THAT

**Bird-beaked**
A keratin beak covering the front of the jaws was perfect for biting off low-lying vegetation.

**Strange skeleton**
*Chilesaurus* possessed hind legs similar to those of a theropod. Its teeth were spatulate—flat and blunt, perfect for biting and chewing plant matter. Although this dinosaur looked like a carnivore in some ways, it certainly did not have the knifelike teeth of meat eaters such as the fearsome Cretaceous predator *Tyrannosaurus*.

Reconstruction of *Chilesaurus* skeleton

**Receding sea**
Dropping sea levels exposed more land for *Chilesaurus* to inhabit.

**Volcanic activity**
At this time, volcanic eruptions in the region may have killed or injured some *Chilesaurus*, as they weren't the quickest to escape.

**Balancing act**
The long tail of the *Chilesaurus* helped to balance its body on its small legs.

# Chilesaurus
chi-le-**SORE**-us

A 10-ft (3-m) long herbivore, *Chilesaurus* roamed South America around 150 million years ago. Experts have struggled to find a place for it in the dinosaur family tree. Its body outline is similar to a carnivore, yet its birdlike hips look similar to an ornithischian dinosaur, such as *Stegosaurus*.

CHILESAURUS DIEGOSUAREZI—ITS FULL NAME—WAS NAMED AFTER

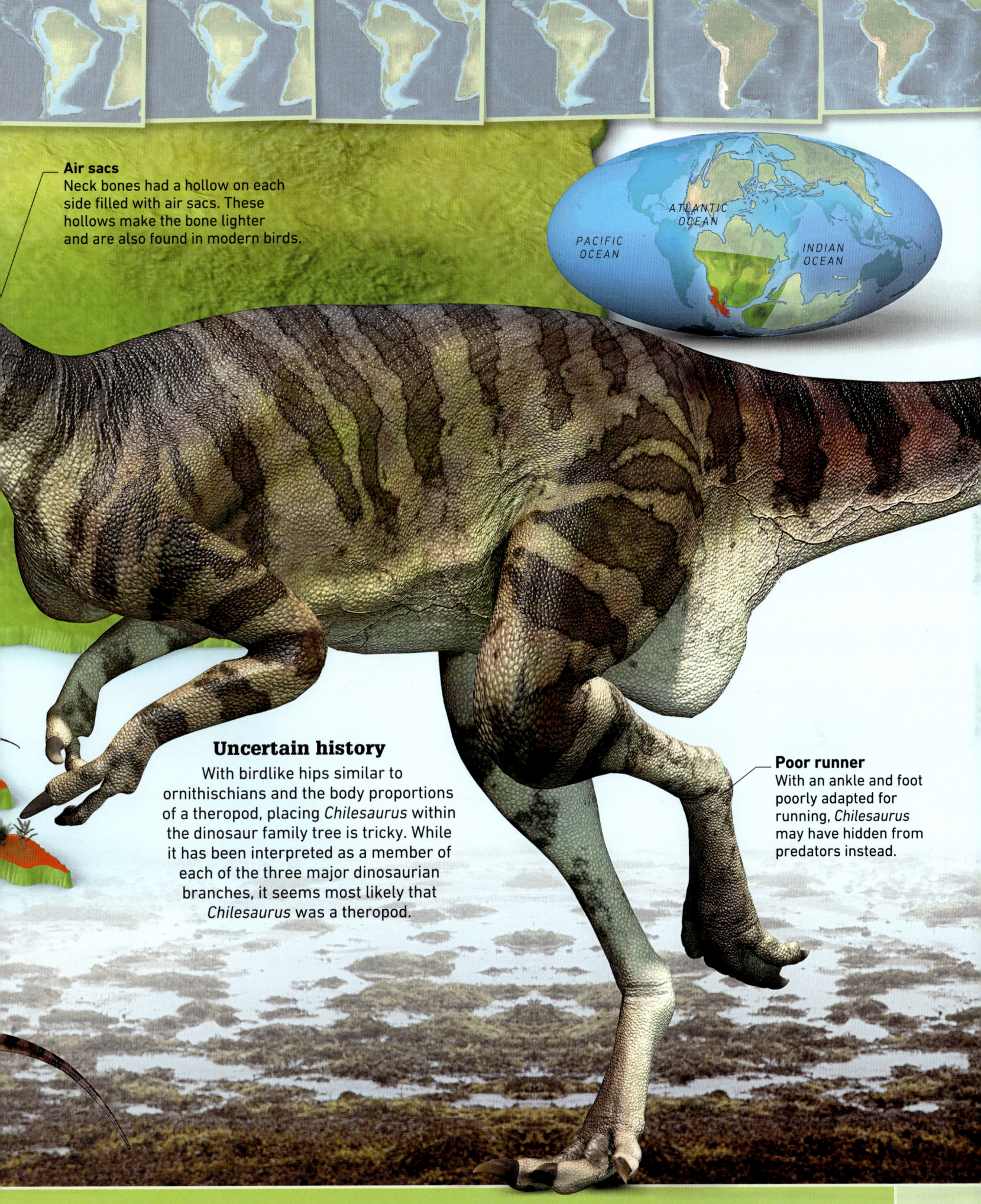

**Air sacs**
Neck bones had a hollow on each side filled with air sacs. These hollows make the bone lighter and are also found in modern birds.

**Uncertain history**
With birdlike hips similar to ornithischians and the body proportions of a theropod, placing *Chilesaurus* within the dinosaur family tree is tricky. While it has been interpreted as a member of each of the three major dinosaurian branches, it seems most likely that *Chilesaurus* was a theropod.

**Poor runner**
With an ankle and foot poorly adapted for running, *Chilesaurus* may have hidden from predators instead.

THE 7-YEAR-OLD WHO DISCOVERED ITS FOSSILS, DIEGO SUAREZ.

**100 MYA**

AFRICA

SOUTH AMERICA

PACIFIC OCEAN

**Shifting land**
At this time, Africa had fully separated from South America, and the Atlantic Ocean had started to form.

### Big tooth
*Giganotosaurus* and its cousins are carcharodontosaurids, which means "shark-toothed lizards." Their thin, sawlike teeth—6 in (15 cm) long and made to slice through flesh—were set in a skull almost 6.5 ft (2 m) long.

**Vanished rivers**
Much of the rock where *Giganotosaurus* fossils were found revealed signs of complex river systems.

**Hunting ground**
*Giganotosaurus* is likely to have hunted among conifer forests and flowering plants.

**Rising Andes**
Rapid sea floor spreading in the Atlantic and Pacific Oceans helped to push up the Andes Mountains in this region.

# Giganotosaurus
GEEG-ah-NOTE-ih-SORE-us

In 1993, amateur fossil hunter Rubén Carolini alerted local scientists to an exposed leg bone he had found in the southernmost part of South America. Little did he know then that the bone belonged to one of the largest carnivores ever to walk the Earth—and one that ruled at the very top of the food chain.

*GIGANOTOSAURUS* WEIGHED 17,700 LB (8,000 KG), WHICH IS EQUIVALENT

### Giant killers
About 100 million years ago, a group of allosaurs began to grow to huge sizes, perhaps because they had few competitors and plenty of large prey. These hunters included the 40-ft (12-m) long *Giganotosaurus*.

### Steady temperature
The body temperature of *Giganotosaurus* remained steady—some experts think this is why it grew so rapidly.

### Three claws
This dinosaur's arm bones have not yet been found, but it probably had three fingers like other allosaurs.

### Walking pace
It was once thought that *Giganotosaurus* could run quickly, but modern research suggests that it probably kept to a fast walk.

### Quick bite
*Giganotosaurus* did not have especially powerful jaws but could make rapid bites, one after another.

TO 125 ADULT PEOPLE OF AVERAGE SIZE.

### Fighting it out
There are advantages to being a giant. Even though the smaller *Ekrixinatosaurus* was the first to find the carcass, *Giganotosaurus* has muscled its way in to take over the spoils. If it survives, *Ekrixinatosaurus* will have to wait for any scraps left behind.

**Holding up**
The largest of the bones that made up the spine and tail, called vertebrae, was 5 ft (1.6 m) high and helped prevent the body from sagging.

**Continents apart**
At the time, South America and North America were not connected as they are today.

**Dry climate**
Evidence from fossil sites suggests that *Argentinosaurus* probably lived in an arid environment.

**Argentinian fossils**
*Argentinosaurus* gets its name from the country where its fossils were first discovered—modern-day Argentina.

**Dinosaur nursery**
In 1997, in the southern tip of South America, a large sauropod nesting ground was found. The dinosaurs had dug the ground and laid 15–34 eggs. This revealed that dinosaurs such as *Argentinosaurus* nested together.

**Long reach**
The long neck may have helped *Argentinosaurus* to browse efficiently without using up too much energy moving around.

**Digestion**
Plant matter was probably broken down by bacteria in the gut to release its energy.

Sauropod egg fragments

BULKY *ARGENTINOSAURUS* COULD ONLY AMBLE ALONG AT A SLOW

**Supporting skeleton**
One of the heaviest land animals ever to exist, *Argentinosaurus* needed strongly built legs. This formed a natural supportive arch for its body, putting the least possible stress on the joints.

**South American giant**
*Argentinosaurus* is known only from an incomplete skeleton found in Argentina. Based on this, scientists have worked out that it would have weighed around 88 tons—or about the same as six fire engines.

**Heavy muscles**
Bulky triceps muscles at the back of the forelimbs helped support the dinosaur's weight as it roamed around.

# Argentinosaurus
ARE-jen-teen-oh-SORE-us

One of the colossal sauropods known as titanosaurs, *Argentinosaurus* was possibly the largest animal to ever walk the Earth. Reaching 115 ft (35 m) in length, this herbivore roamed South America 90 million years ago. This giant ate a lot, probably 235–500 lb (106–230 kg) of food every day—that's as heavy as 30–65 bricks!

PACE, ACHIEVING A TOP SPEED OF NO MORE THAN 5 MPH (8 KM/H).

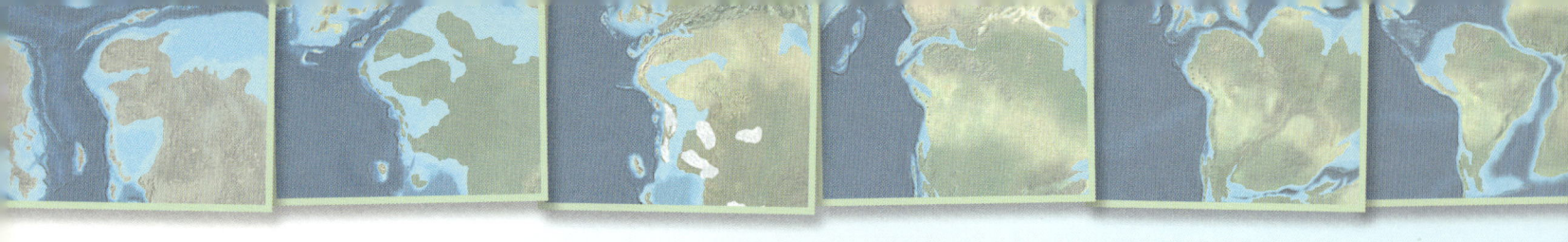

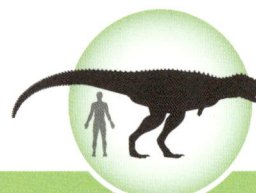

# Carnotaurus

car-noe-**TOR**-us

A 26-ft (8-m) long predator, *Carnotaurus* was a threatening presence in Late Cretaceous South America, around 70 million years ago. Named after the ancient Greek for "meat-eating bull," this fast-running dinosaur was armed with a horned skull, sharp teeth, and a decent sense of smell.

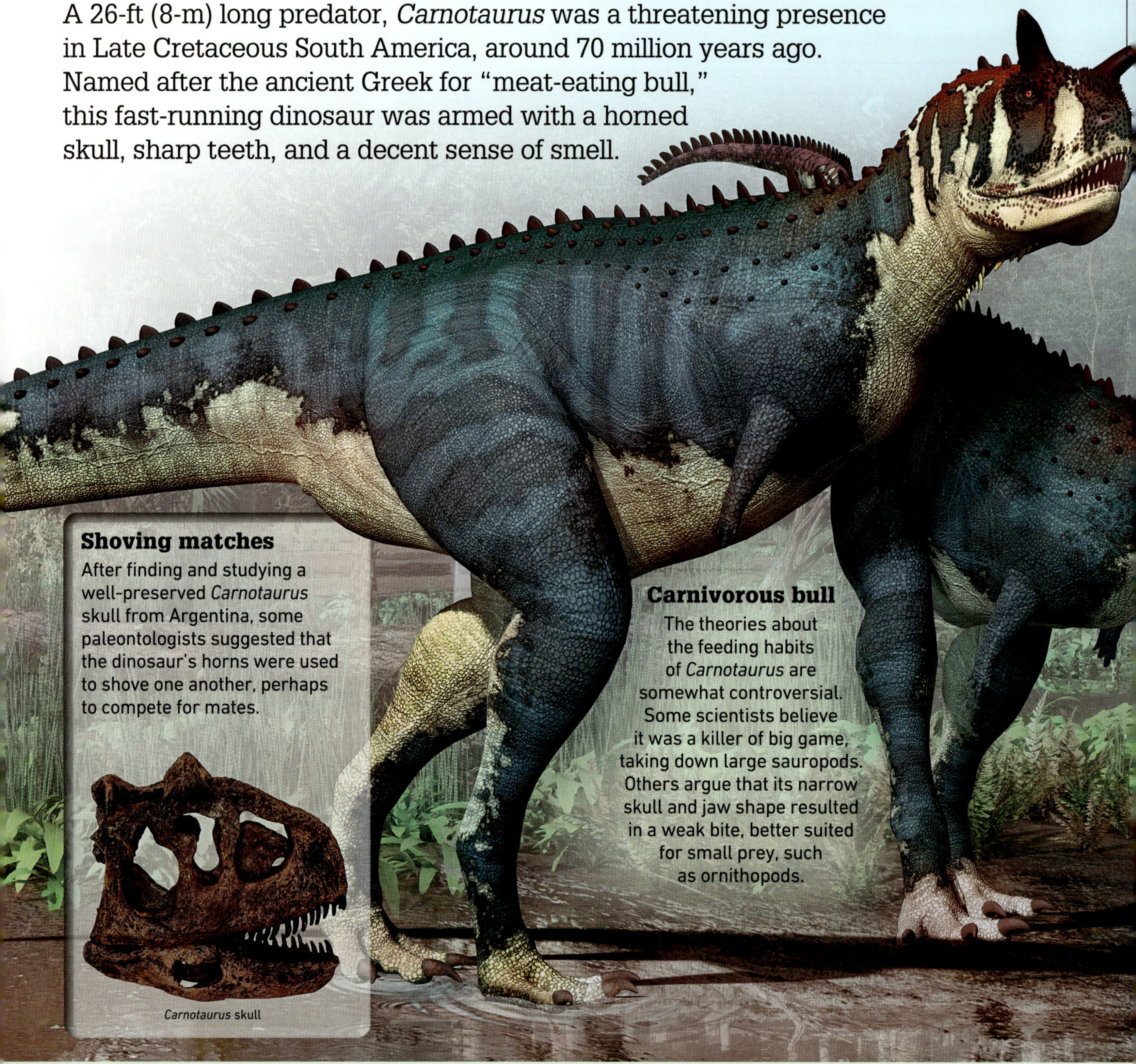

**Horned beast**
Two 6-in (15-cm) long, cone-shaped horns protruded above each eye socket.

**Carnivorous bull**
The theories about the feeding habits of *Carnotaurus* are somewhat controversial. Some scientists believe it was a killer of big game, taking down large sauropods. Others argue that its narrow skull and jaw shape resulted in a weak bite, better suited for small prey, such as ornithopods.

### Shoving matches

After finding and studying a well-preserved *Carnotaurus* skull from Argentina, some paleontologists suggested that the dinosaur's horns were used to shove one another, perhaps to compete for mates.

*Carnotaurus* skull



FOSSILIZED SKIN IMPRESSIONS HAVE SHOWN LARGE, BUMPY

# Fossil finds
## South America

**Eoraptor**
One of the earliest dinosaurs known, this 3-ft (1-m) long animal was found in the rocky landscape of the Ischigualasto Formation in Argentina. *Eoraptor* probably hunted small reptiles.

**Itapecuru Group, Brazil**
Dinosaur remains from sauropods and theropods have been found at this site in Maranhão state.

**Girón Formation, Colombia**
One of the rare Jurassic sauropods to be found outside Argentina was excavated here.

**Vilquechico Group, Peru**
Dinosaur tracks have been found at this site just to the north of Lake Titicaca.

Fossils of some of the earliest and largest dinosaurs ever have been unearthed in South America. However, with the dense Amazon rainforest, South America can be a challenging place to search for fossils. The southern parts of the continent yield the most finds.

**KEY**
● Dinosaur fossil site

THE ONLY DINOSAUR GROUP NOT YET FOUND IN SOUTH AMERICA ARE THE

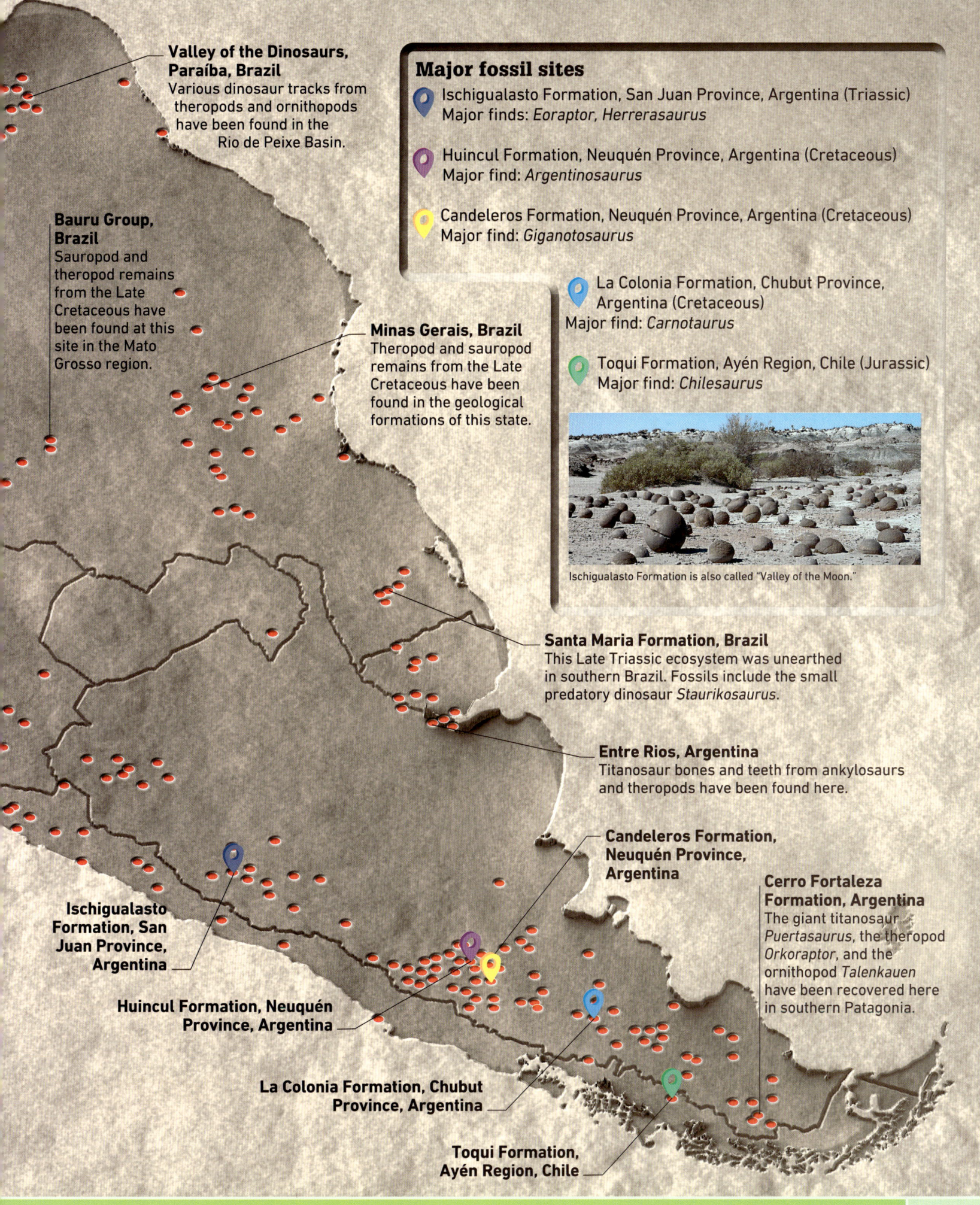

# EUROPE

**Ancient bird**
Crow-sized and the oldest-known bird, *Archaeopteryx* had a bony tail, clawed wings, and toothed jaws. Living in the dry, sparse landscape of Late Jurassic Europe, it could fly only short distances.

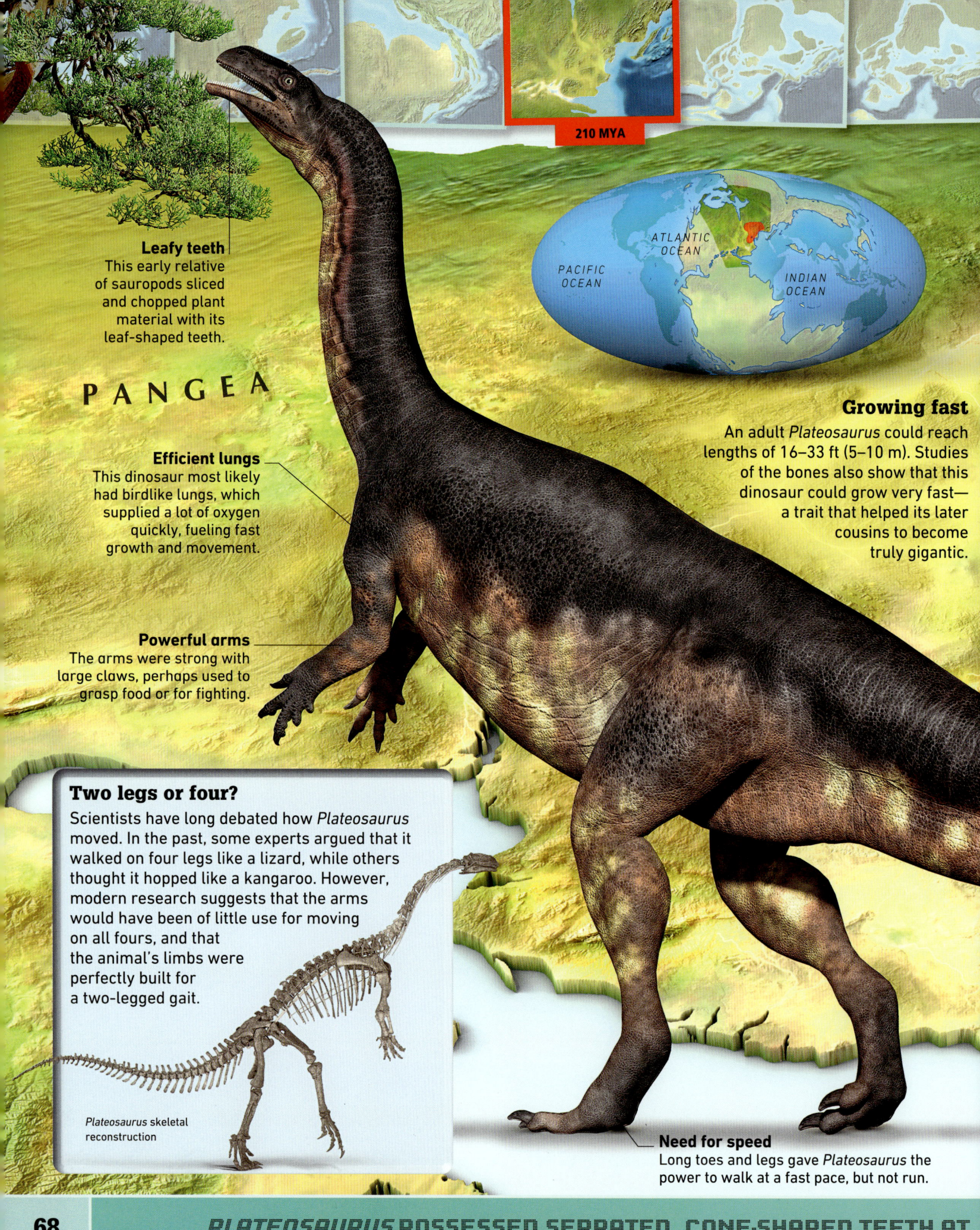

210 MYA

**Leafy teeth**
This early relative of sauropods sliced and chopped plant material with its leaf-shaped teeth.

PANGEA

**Efficient lungs**
This dinosaur most likely had birdlike lungs, which supplied a lot of oxygen quickly, fueling fast growth and movement.

**Growing fast**
An adult *Plateosaurus* could reach lengths of 16–33 ft (5–10 m). Studies of the bones also show that this dinosaur could grow very fast—a trait that helped its later cousins to become truly gigantic.

**Powerful arms**
The arms were strong with large claws, perhaps used to grasp food or for fighting.

### Two legs or four?
Scientists have long debated how *Plateosaurus* moved. In the past, some experts argued that it walked on four legs like a lizard, while others thought it hopped like a kangaroo. However, modern research suggests that the arms would have been of little use for moving on all fours, and that the animal's limbs were perfectly built for a two-legged gait.

*Plateosaurus* skeletal reconstruction

**Need for speed**
Long toes and legs gave *Plateosaurus* the power to walk at a fast pace, but not run.

PLATEOSAURUS POSSESSED SERRATED, CONE-SHAPED TEETH AT

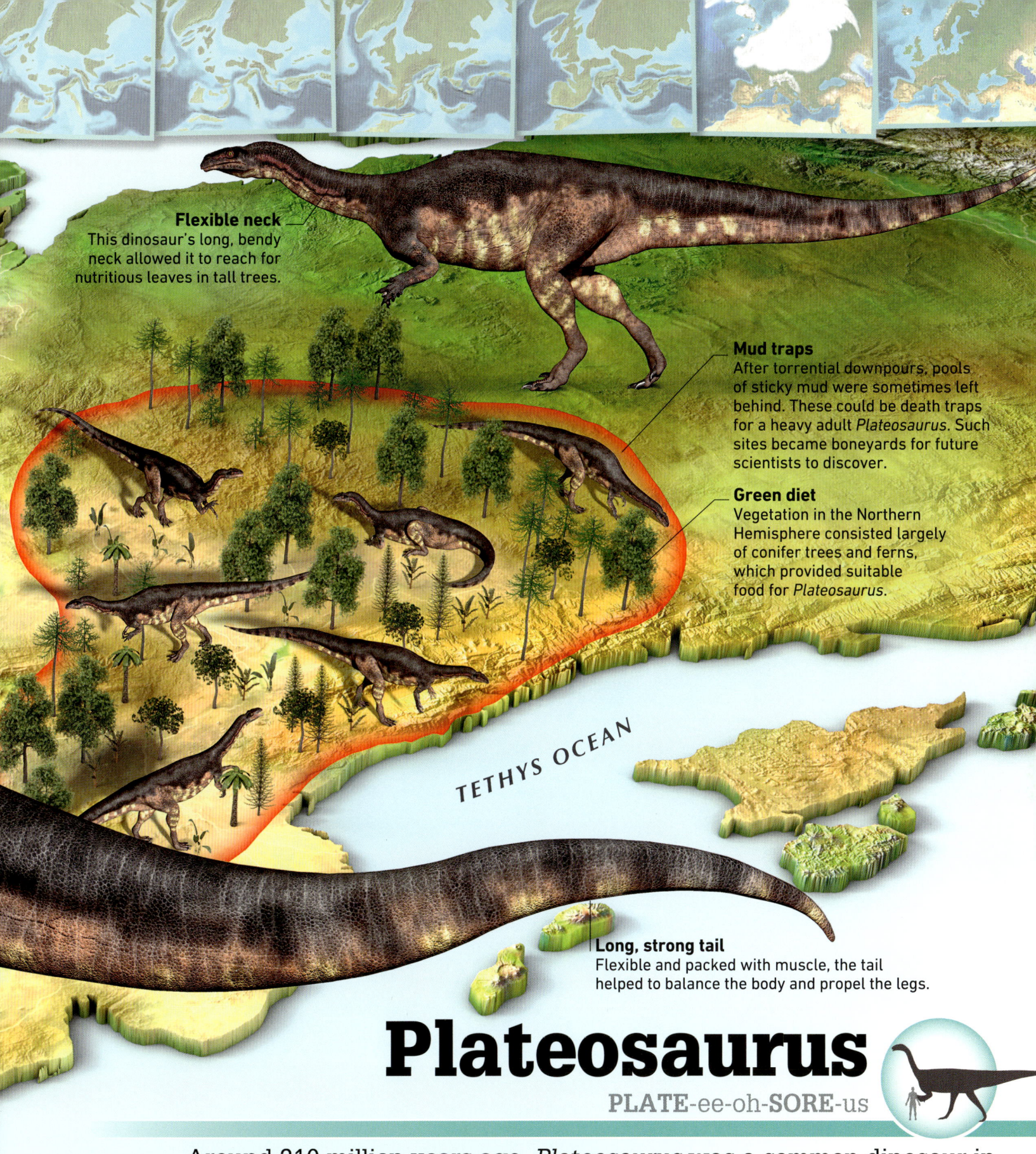

**Flexible neck**
This dinosaur's long, bendy neck allowed it to reach for nutritious leaves in tall trees.

**Mud traps**
After torrential downpours, pools of sticky mud were sometimes left behind. These could be death traps for a heavy adult *Plateosaurus*. Such sites became boneyards for future scientists to discover.

**Green diet**
Vegetation in the Northern Hemisphere consisted largely of conifer trees and ferns, which provided suitable food for *Plateosaurus*.

TETHYS OCEAN

**Long, strong tail**
Flexible and packed with muscle, the tail helped to balance the body and propel the legs.

# Plateosaurus
PLATE-ee-oh-SORE-us

Around 210 million years ago, *Plateosaurus* was a common dinosaur in the supercontinent of Pangea. With so many well-preserved skeletons discovered in what is now Europe, experts have learned a great deal about this fascinating herbivore, including its diet and anatomy.

**Muddy swamps**
Pterosaurs swoop by two *Plateosaurus* making their way through a swamp, while a prehistoric turtle stays at a safe distance. Millions of years later, the tracks left behind by these dinosaurs will be preserved, as the mud solidifies into fossil footprints.

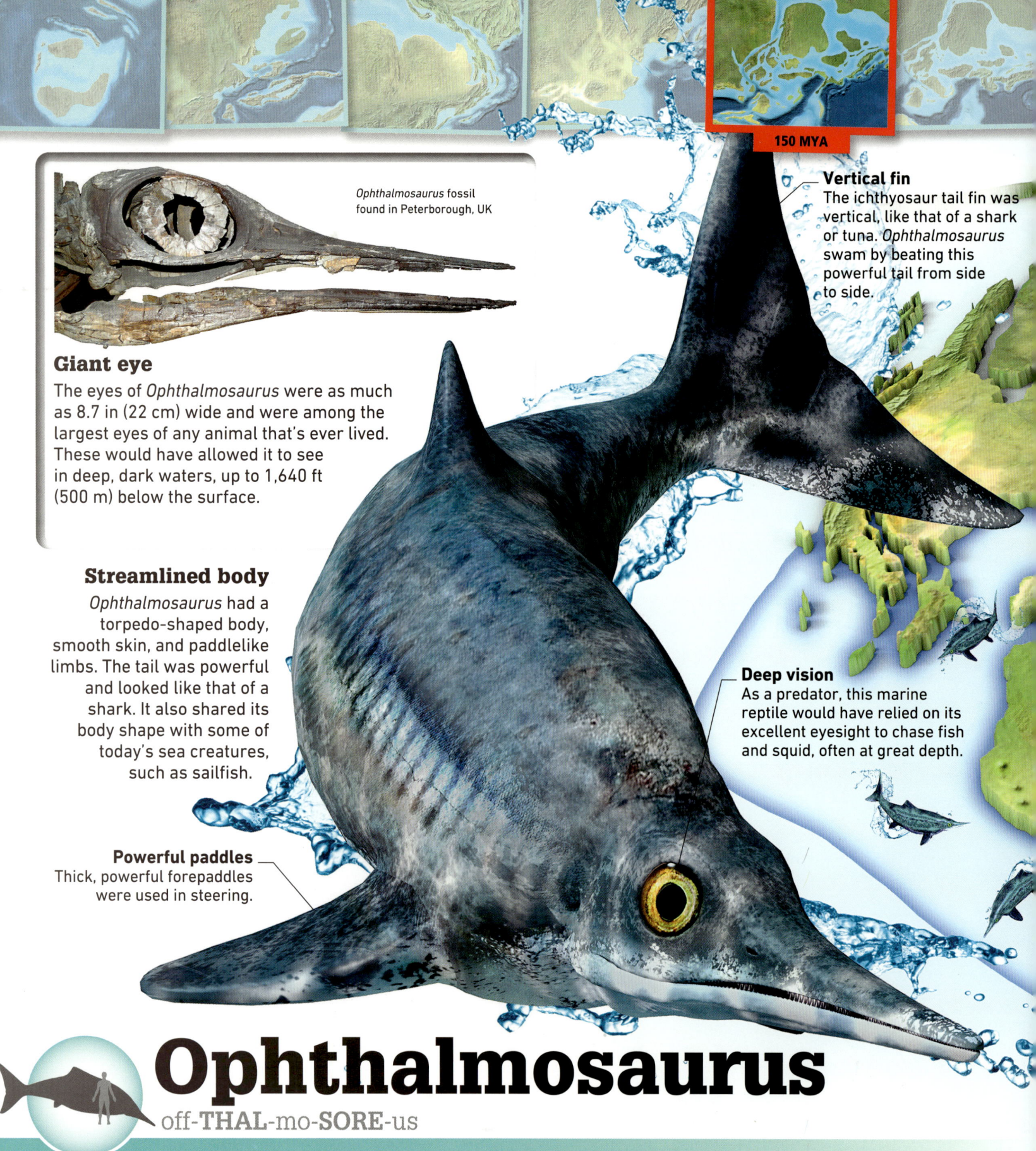

*Ophthalmosaurus* fossil found in Peterborough, UK

150 MYA

### Giant eye
The eyes of *Ophthalmosaurus* were as much as 8.7 in (22 cm) wide and were among the largest eyes of any animal that's ever lived. These would have allowed it to see in deep, dark waters, up to 1,640 ft (500 m) below the surface.

### Vertical fin
The ichthyosaur tail fin was vertical, like that of a shark or tuna. *Ophthalmosaurus* swam by beating this powerful tail from side to side.

### Streamlined body
*Ophthalmosaurus* had a torpedo-shaped body, smooth skin, and paddlelike limbs. The tail was powerful and looked like that of a shark. It also shared its body shape with some of today's sea creatures, such as sailfish.

### Deep vision
As a predator, this marine reptile would have relied on its excellent eyesight to chase fish and squid, often at great depth.

### Powerful paddles
Thick, powerful forepaddles were used in steering.

# Ophthalmosaurus
off-THAL-mo-SORE-us

This Jurassic animal is not a dinosaur, but belongs to a group called ichthyosaurs. Descended from lizardlike land animals, *Ophthalmosaurus* was 20 ft (6 m) long and swam in seas worldwide 150 million years ago.

IN 1874, THE BRITISH SCIENTIST HENRY SEELEY NAMED THIS ANIMAL

### Early bird

Some scientists think that *Archaeopteryx* is the oldest known bird. It inherited its long, bony tail and toothed jaws from theropod dinosaurs. Research has led to a greater understanding of the origins of birds, as well as the evolution of dinosaurs.

### Upright claw

The second toe was held off the ground, like its later cousin *Velociraptor*, perhaps to keep it sharp for attacking prey or climbing trees.

### Flight muscles

The small, light breastbone suggests that the muscles used in flight must have been small.

### Taking to the air

The shape of the wing bones suggests *Archaeopteryx* was capable of some form of flight. Recent analysis has revealed that it could fly over short distances in bursts, similar to modern-day pheasants, shown here.

150 MYA

ANALYSIS OF A SET OF BONES IN THE EYE, CALLED THE SCLERAL

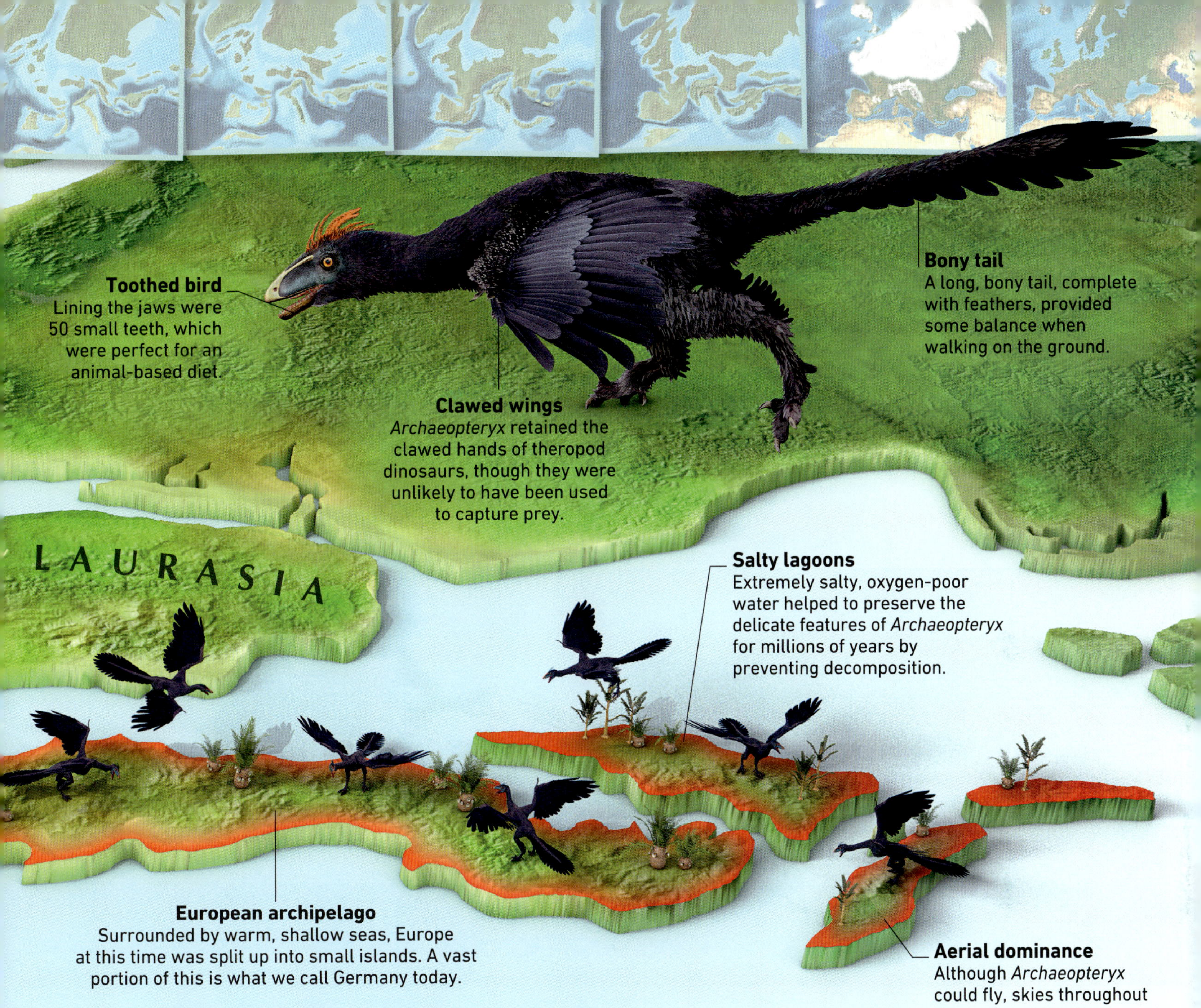

**Toothed bird**
Lining the jaws were 50 small teeth, which were perfect for an animal-based diet.

**Bony tail**
A long, bony tail, complete with feathers, provided some balance when walking on the ground.

**Clawed wings**
*Archaeopteryx* retained the clawed hands of theropod dinosaurs, though they were unlikely to have been used to capture prey.

LAURASIA

**Salty lagoons**
Extremely salty, oxygen-poor water helped to preserve the delicate features of *Archaeopteryx* for millions of years by preventing decomposition.

**European archipelago**
Surrounded by warm, shallow seas, Europe at this time was split up into small islands. A vast portion of this is what we call Germany today.

**Aerial dominance**
Although *Archaeopteryx* could fly, skies throughout the region at this time were dominated by several types of pterosaurs.

# Archaeopteryx
ar-kee-OP-ter-ix

First discovered in Germany in 1861, the exquisitely preserved fossils of *Archaeopteryx* revealed a crow-sized animal that could fly, although not very well. It inhabited the wooded islands of Late Jurassic Europe, 151–146 million years ago.

**Fossilized feather**
Studies of this fossilized *Archaeopteryx* feather have shown that it was black and had a structure just like that of modern bird feathers. This would have helped the animal to fly short distances.

RING, SUGGESTS *ARCHAEOPTERYX* WAS ACTIVE DURING THE DAY.

**Plant diet**
Horsetails, ferns, and low-lying conifer branches may have all nourished the bulky *Iguanodon*.

**Scaly skin**
*Iguanodon* was covered with tough skin that protected it from infections and scratches.

**Plant predator**
A sharp beak and iguanalike teeth, from which *Iguanodon* gets its name, helped to grind up plant food.

**Important find**
In 1822, Mary Mantell bought some fossil teeth, which she gave to her husband Gideon. Scientists first believed these teeth belonged to a big lizard, but later realized that they were from a huge reptile very different from modern lizards. In 1878, complete *Iguanodon* skeletons were found in Belgium.

# Iguanodon
ig-WAH-no-don

In 1825, *Iguanodon* became famous as one of the first dinosaurs to be formally named. This plant-eating, heavyweight ornithopod roamed areas of Europe 125 million years ago. Studies of its thick bones suggest that adults could reach lengths of 33 ft (10 m) and weigh up to 4.5 tons.

**Fused wrist**
The bones of the wrist were fused together, helping *Iguanodon* bear weight on its front limbs.

FROM THE UK RESEMBLES LIVING CROCODILIANS AND BIRDS.

**British icon**
The first *Baryonyx* fossil was found in Surrey, in the south of England.

125 MYA

**Wetland habitat**
The many rivers and lakes found in Europe during the Early Cretaceous provided a home for *Baryonyx*, allowing it to coexist with other large predators.

**Iberian hunter**
Fossils have been found as far as Spain.

# Baryonyx
bah-ree-ON-ix

The 26-ft (8-m) long *Baryonyx* evolved to exploit a different habitat to other theropods: water. Its long skull and conical teeth were perfect for catching slippery fish at the edges of rivers and lakes across a wide area of Europe 125 million years ago.

**Bipedal locomotion**
Typical of two-legged theropods, *Baryonyx* balanced its body over its hind legs.

78 — ALTHOUGH MOST *BARYONYX* BONES ARE UNEARTHED IN EUROPE,

**Toothy grin**
Sixty-four small teeth lined the lower jaw—more than the average theropod.

EUROPE

**Muscular tail**
Like many other theropods, the long, powerful tail provided the balance needed to walk and run.

**Hunting strategies**
The details of the predatory lifestyle of *Baryonyx* are still debated. However, most experts describe this dinosaur as a "generalist" predator, exploiting prey in both water and land, including thick-scaled fish and juvenile dinosaurs.

**Stomach contents**
The scales of the fish *Scheenstia* were found in the stomach of the original *Baryonyx* specimen. This led to the view that this dinosaur and its cousins ate a variety of organisms and differed from other theropods in including fish in their diet.

**Robust arms**
Paleontologists still question how the heavily built arms were used. They may have been used to catch fish or open their carcasses.

**Heavy claw**
The function of the 10-in (25-cm) claw is unclear. It is most commonly thought to be a tool for hooking fish out of water, much like a grizzly bear does today.

Fossil of *Baryonyx* thumb claw

SOME NORTH AFRICAN FOSSILS MAY ALSO BELONG TO THIS DINOSAUR.

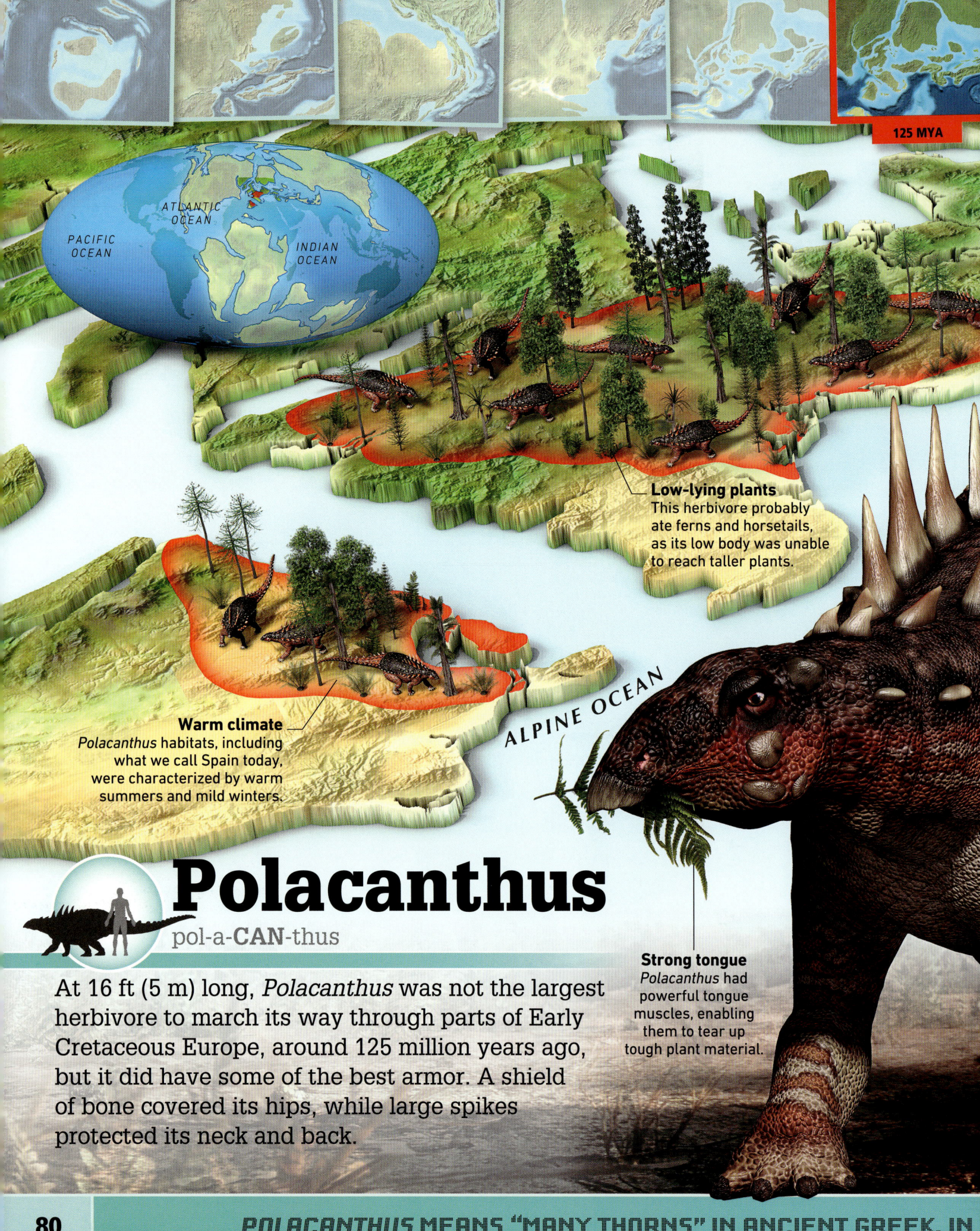

**Low-lying plants**
This herbivore probably ate ferns and horsetails, as its low body was unable to reach taller plants.

**Warm climate**
*Polacanthus* habitats, including what we call Spain today, were characterized by warm summers and mild winters.

**Strong tongue**
*Polacanthus* had powerful tongue muscles, enabling them to tear up tough plant material.

# Polacanthus
pol-a-**CAN**-thus

At 16 ft (5 m) long, *Polacanthus* was not the largest herbivore to march its way through parts of Early Cretaceous Europe, around 125 million years ago, but it did have some of the best armor. A shield of bone covered its hips, while large spikes protected its neck and back.

POLACANTHUS MEANS "MANY THORNS" IN ANCIENT GREEK, IN

**EUROPE**

**Shallow seas**
Waterways separated western Europe from the rest of the Eurasian continent.

**Long guts**
The broad hips suggest it had long intestines to digest plant material.

**Hip shield**
A single, fused sheet of bone covered the upper surface of the hip region to protect the hip bones and thigh muscles.

**Unarmed**
*Polacanthus* and its closest cousins lacked a tail club, but small spikes along the tail may have been enough to deter predators.

**Blood supply**
The plates and spikes have shown imprints of blood vessels, which may have supplied growing tissue with blood.

**Armored beast**
Bones called osteoderms grew directly from the skin of *Polacanthus* and many of its cousins. Smaller osteoderms known as ossicles grew around them, sometimes forming plates of armor that protected them from predators.

Ossicles   Osteoderms

Small part of fossilized *Polacanthus* skin

**Rare creature**
Not much is known of *Polacanthus* because fossils are rare. While some bones from parts of continental Europe have been assigned to this dinosaur, it is mainly known from fossils found in the UK. From these, there is enough material to reconstruct this animal as a wide, armored herbivore.

REFERENCE TO THE SPIKY ARMOR COVERING MUCH OF ITS BODY.

81

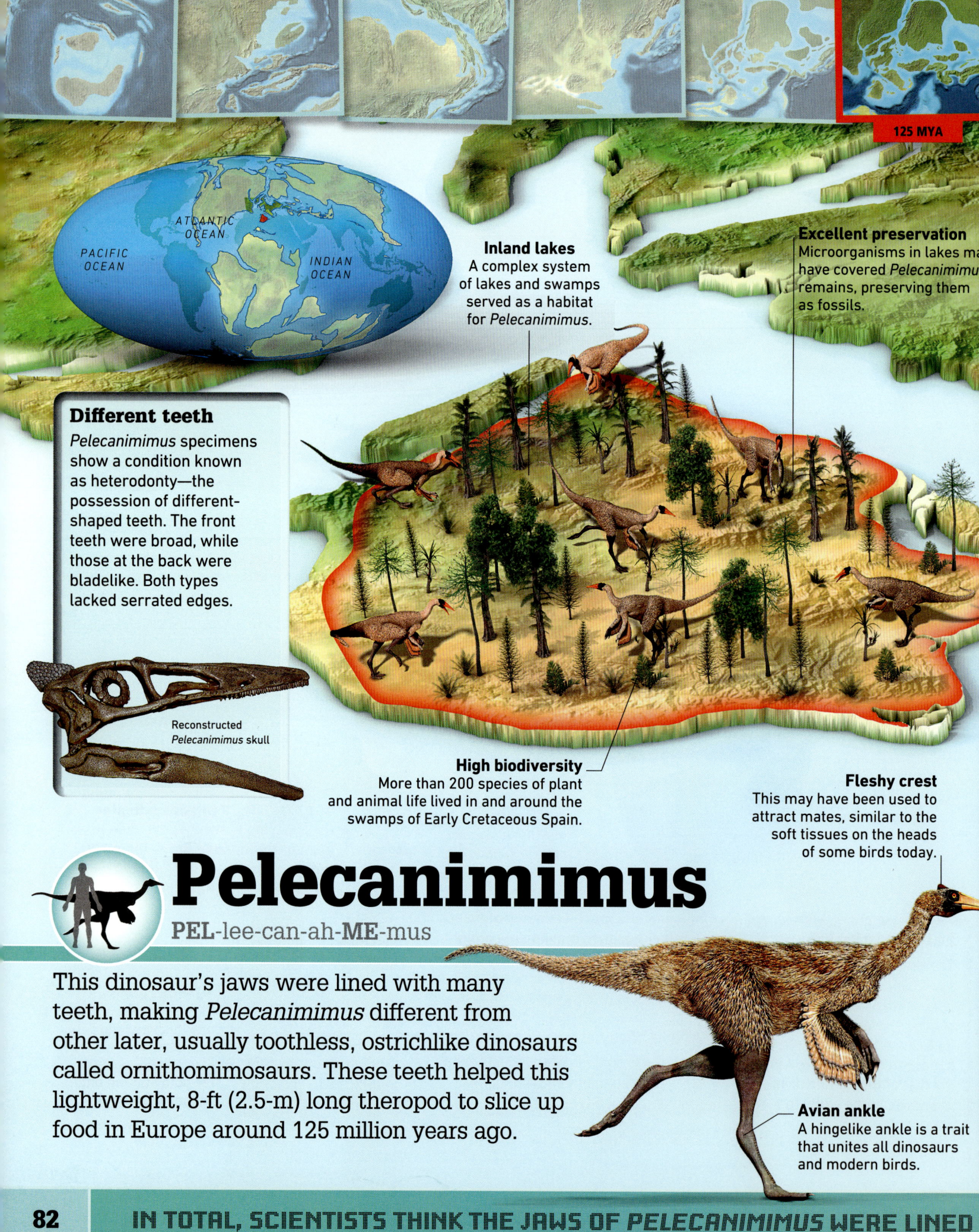

125 MYA

**Inland lakes**
A complex system of lakes and swamps served as a habitat for *Pelecanimimus*.

**Excellent preservation**
Microorganisms in lakes may have covered *Pelecanimimus* remains, preserving them as fossils.

**Different teeth**
*Pelecanimimus* specimens show a condition known as heterodonty—the possession of different-shaped teeth. The front teeth were broad, while those at the back were bladelike. Both types lacked serrated edges.

Reconstructed *Pelecanimimus* skull

**High biodiversity**
More than 200 species of plant and animal life lived in and around the swamps of Early Cretaceous Spain.

**Fleshy crest**
This may have been used to attract mates, similar to the soft tissues on the heads of some birds today.

# Pelecanimimus
PEL-lee-can-ah-ME-mus

This dinosaur's jaws were lined with many teeth, making *Pelecanimimus* different from other later, usually toothless, ostrichlike dinosaurs called ornithomimosaurs. These teeth helped this lightweight, 8-ft (2.5-m) long theropod to slice up food in Europe around 125 million years ago.

**Avian ankle**
A hingelike ankle is a trait that unites all dinosaurs and modern birds.

IN TOTAL, SCIENTISTS THINK THE JAWS OF *PELECANIMIMUS* WERE LINED

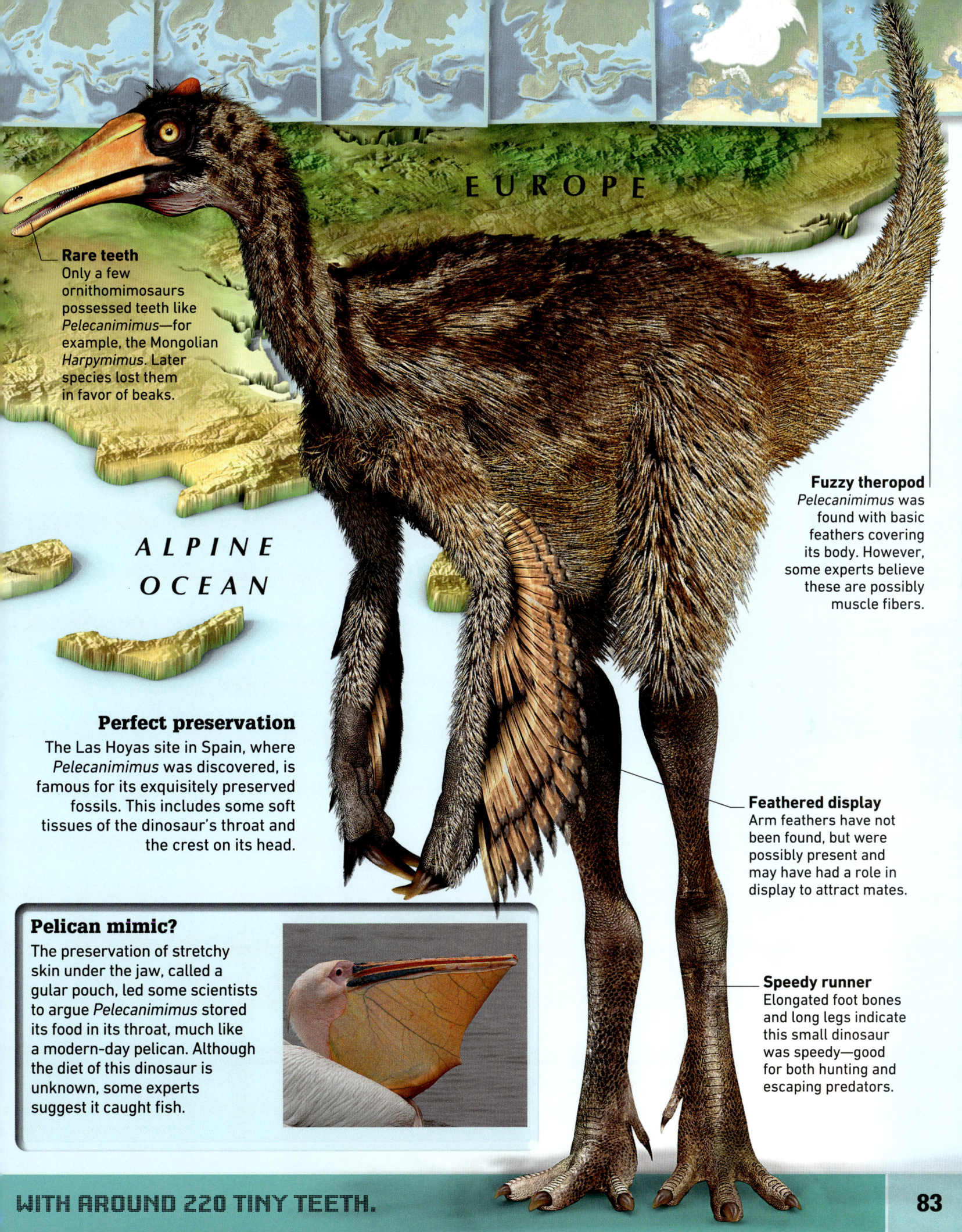

**Rare teeth**
Only a few ornithomimosaurs possessed teeth like *Pelecanimimus*—for example, the Mongolian *Harpymimus*. Later species lost them in favor of beaks.

EUROPE

ALPINE OCEAN

**Fuzzy theropod**
*Pelecanimimus* was found with basic feathers covering its body. However, some experts believe these are possibly muscle fibers.

**Perfect preservation**
The Las Hoyas site in Spain, where *Pelecanimimus* was discovered, is famous for its exquisitely preserved fossils. This includes some soft tissues of the dinosaur's throat and the crest on its head.

**Feathered display**
Arm feathers have not been found, but were possibly present and may have had a role in display to attract mates.

**Pelican mimic?**
The preservation of stretchy skin under the jaw, called a gular pouch, led some scientists to argue *Pelecanimimus* stored its food in its throat, much like a modern-day pelican. Although the diet of this dinosaur is unknown, some experts suggest it caught fish.

**Speedy runner**
Elongated foot bones and long legs indicate this small dinosaur was speedy—good for both hunting and escaping predators.

WITH AROUND 220 TINY TEETH.

**Giant of the skies**
Although its bones were thick and heavy, this pterosaur was light for its size and could definitely fly. *Hatzegopteryx* could walk and run on the ground, too.

**Huge wings**
Wing membranes stretched from the tips of the fourth fingers to the body and leg.

**Wing supports**
The wing was mostly supported by long hand bones and an elongated, thick fourth finger that extended to the tip of the wing.

# Hatzegopteryx
HAT-zeg-OP-ter-ix

Of all the flying reptiles known as pterosaurs, *Hatzegopteryx* was the biggest. Taking to the skies around 70 million years ago, it had a wingspan of around 33 ft (10 m) and stood 10 ft (3 m) tall at the shoulder. With its thick neck and storklike jaws, it could catch prey the size of a human.

**Skull crest**
A bony crest probably ran along the top of the skull and upper jaw.

**Toothless**
The group of pterosaurs to which *Hatzegopteryx* belonged did not have teeth.

HATZEGOPTERYX HAD A SKULL MEASURING AROUND 10 FT (3 M)

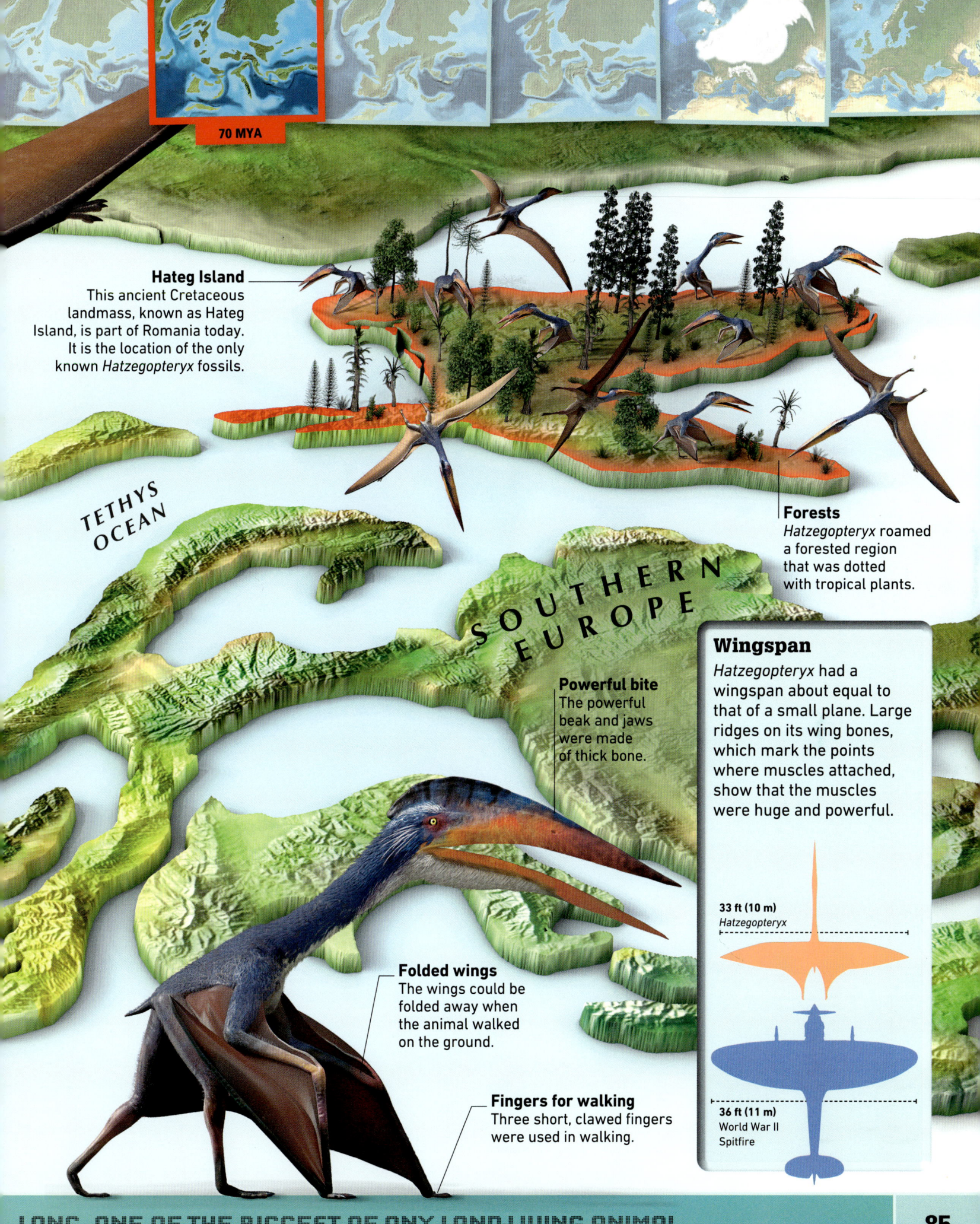

**Today's catch**

*Hatzegopteryx* was not a dinosaur but a flying reptile, or pterosaur. It was one of the largest pterosaurs ever, with a wingspan of 33 ft (10 m) and a skull around 6.5 ft (2 m) long. Its powerful neck and strong jaws allowed it to grab and swallow prey such as this turkey-sized dinosaur.

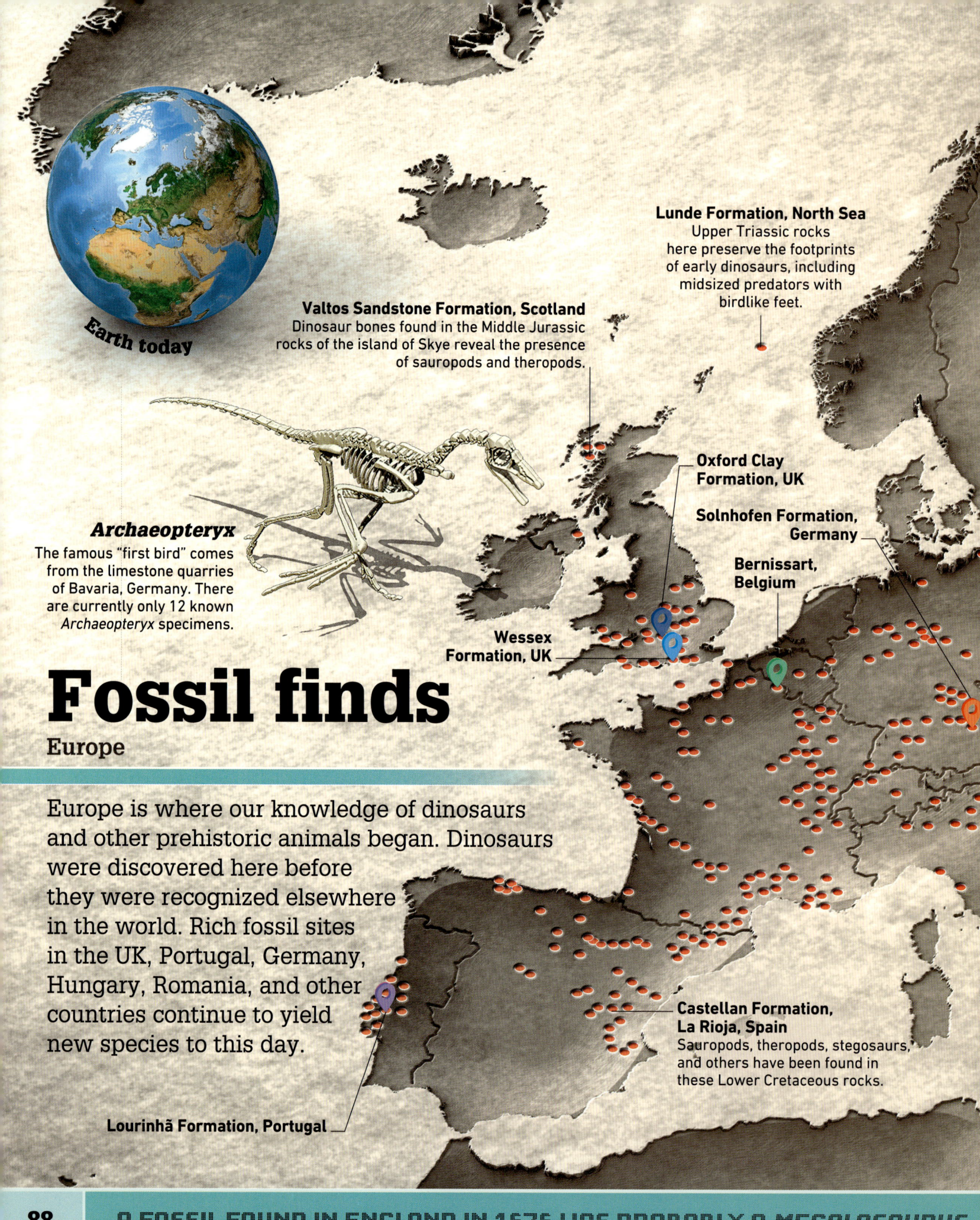

# Fossil finds
## Europe

Europe is where our knowledge of dinosaurs and other prehistoric animals began. Dinosaurs were discovered here before they were recognized elsewhere in the world. Rich fossil sites in the UK, Portugal, Germany, Hungary, Romania, and other countries continue to yield new species to this day.

**Earth today**

**Valtos Sandstone Formation, Scotland**
Dinosaur bones found in the Middle Jurassic rocks of the island of Skye reveal the presence of sauropods and theropods.

**Lunde Formation, North Sea**
Upper Triassic rocks here preserve the footprints of early dinosaurs, including midsized predators with birdlike feet.

**Archaeopteryx**
The famous "first bird" comes from the limestone quarries of Bavaria, Germany. There are currently only 12 known *Archaeopteryx* specimens.

**Oxford Clay Formation, UK**

**Solnhofen Formation, Germany**

**Bernissart, Belgium**

**Wessex Formation, UK**

**Castellan Formation, La Rioja, Spain**
Sauropods, theropods, stegosaurs, and others have been found in these Lower Cretaceous rocks.

**Lourinhã Formation, Portugal**

A FOSSIL FOUND IN ENGLAND IN 1676 WAS PROBABLY A *MEGALOSAURUS*

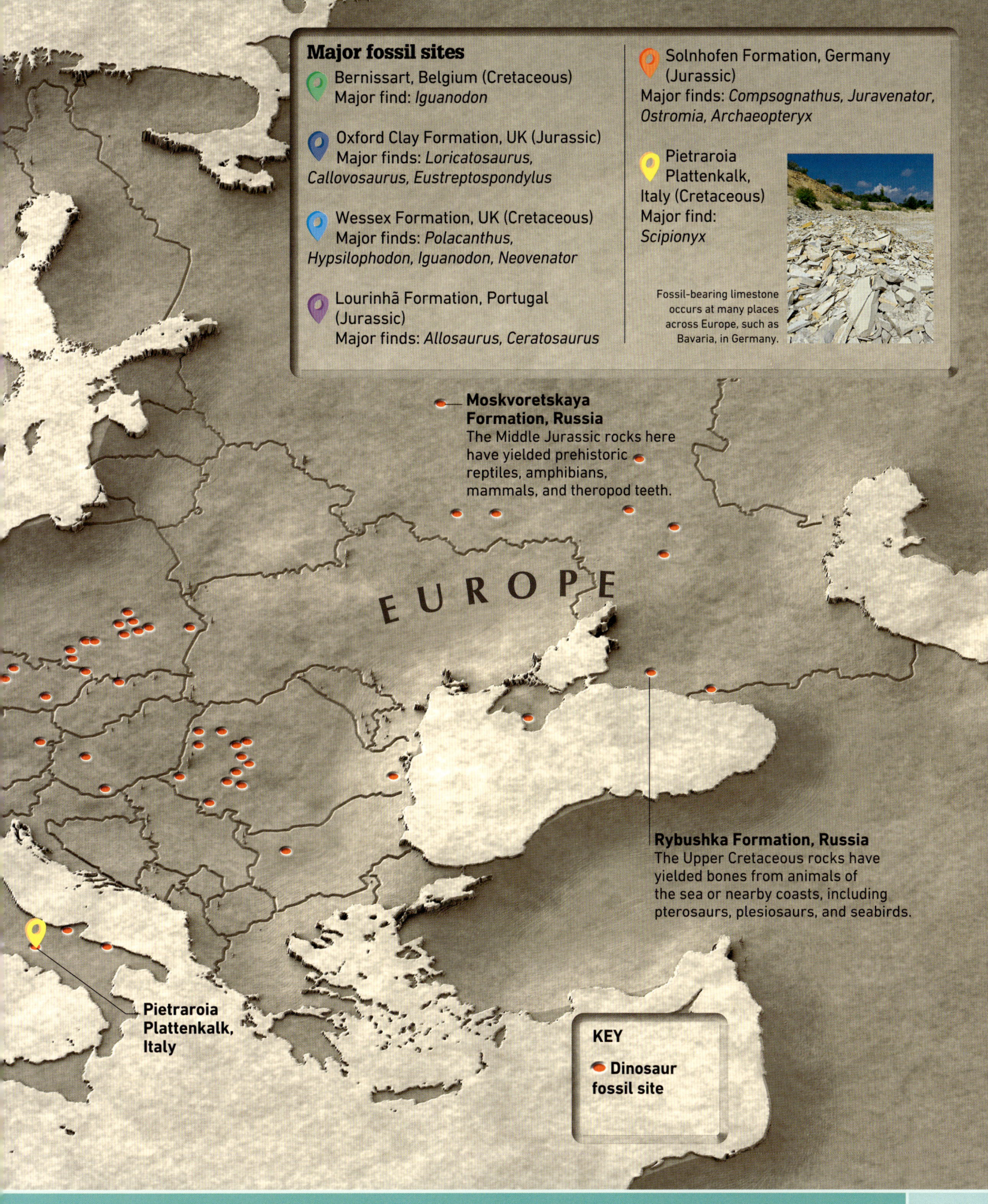

# AFRICA

**Aquatic predators**
Three slender *Mesosaurus* swirl above a Pangean lake bed, their needlelike teeth ready to snatch prey. These swimming reptiles lived in cool, fresh waters around 290 million years ago.

290 MYA

WESTERN PANGEA

PACIFIC OCEAN · ATLANTIC OCEAN · INDIAN OCEAN

**Cool lagoons**
*Mesosaurus* lived in cool, salty lagoons or lakes across western Pangea.

**Plant life**
At this time, the land in the area nearby was covered in forest, mostly formed of the tree-sized plant *Glossopteris*.

**Ice Age**
*Mesosaurus* lived in the Permian world before dinosaurs existed and when parts of Earth were in the grip of an Ice Age.

*Mesosaurus* skull

**Needle teeth**
*Mesosaurus* was equipped with long jaws lined with many thin, needlelike teeth. Too delicate to handle large prey, these teeth were most likely used to grab small, swimming crustaceans, the ancestors of today's shrimp and crabs.

**Lake-dwelling lizard**
*Mesosaurus* was one of the earliest aquatic reptiles, inhabiting the ancient supercontinent Pangea around 290 million years ago. It lived a semiaquatic lifestyle, spending much of its time searching for food in cool lakes.

**Buoyant bones**
Dense ribs may have helped with buoyancy.

92 THE DISCOVERY OF *MESOSAURUS* FOSSILS ON TWO SEPARATE

# Mesosaurus
mee-so-SORE-us

At 3 ft (1 m) long, *Mesosaurus* was not a dinosaur but an ancient swimming reptile that lived in lakes. Fossil finds in southern Africa and South America show that these two areas were joined when this creature was alive.

**Built-in paddle**
The long, deep tail could be used like a paddle when swimming.

**High nostrils**
The nostrils sat high up, close to the eyes.

**Webbed feet**
*Mesosaurus* had webbed fingers and toes to help it swim.

EASTERN PANGEA

**250 MYA**

# Lystrosaurus
LIS-trow-SORE-us

This pudgy herbivore lived in Pangea 250 million years ago, during the Late Permian and Early Triassic. Several species are known, most of which were 3–6 ft (1–2 m) long. *Lystrosaurus* is not a dinosaur but belonged to a group called the dicynodont therapsids, a group closely related to mammals.

**Hardy survivor**
*Lystrosaurus* was tough and could survive in harsh, dry places. Although fossils have only been found in the northern and southern parts of Pangea, it probably lived throughout this region.

**Sprawling gait**
Unlike most modern mammals, the limbs of *Lystrosaurus* stuck out sideways from its body, like those of a reptile.

**Burrow dweller**
Fossils show that *Lystrosaurus* took shelter in burrows, probably to escape the heat of the day and cold of the night. It may have used its hands and beak when digging.

**Broad body**
Like all dicynodonts, *Lystrosaurus* had a broad, barrel-shaped body. Its large guts helped it digest tough plant food.

THIS THERAPSID'S TWO TUSKLIKE CANINE TEETH

# Giraffatitan
ji-**RAF**-a-**TIE**-tan

An African giant, *Giraffatitan* towered over most other Late Jurassic dinosaurs. This 66-ft (20-m) long herbivore held its head 39 ft (12 m) above the ground, allowing it to access vegetation almost no other plant eater could reach.

**150 MYA**

**Andes forming**
The formation of the Andes Mountains was underway at this time, with oceanic plates moving under South America.

**Long neck**
The number of bones in the neck of *Giraffatitan* is still unknown, but has been estimated at around 13—almost twice as many as a giraffe. Some researchers believe small muscles in the neck helped to pump blood to the head.

*Giraffatitan* neck bone fossil

**Long-limbed**
*Giraffatitan*'s arms were longer than its legs, providing extra height when feeding.

TO FUEL ITS BODY,

**Shearing bite**
Wear on the teeth suggests it stripped leaves off branches rather than cutting them.

**Tendaguru ecosystem**
Found in the Tendaguru beds of Tanzania, *Giraffatitan* lived in conifer-rich inland habitats 154–142 million years ago. Nearer the coast, saltwater lagoons could be found, but offered little in terms of food for these giants.

AFRICA

**Major discovery**
An expedition to Tendaguru between 1909 and 1913 uncovered 248 tons of dinosaur bones, including those of *Giraffatitan*.

**Absent Atlantic Ocean**
At this time, South America and Africa were still joined. However, they were starting to move apart, gradually breaking up this ancient landmass.

**Air sacs**
A complex system of air sacs in the vertebrae lightened the neck.

**Heavyweight herbivore**
Recent estimates for the mass of *Giraffatitan* suggest it weighed around 33 tons—the equivalent of around five modern-day African elephants.

TETHYS OCEAN

**Supporting tail**
The tail's muscles attached to its thighs enabled it to walk quickly.

GIRAFFATITAN ATE UP TO 243 LB (110 KG) OF PLANT MATTER EACH DAY.

# Spinosaurus
SPINE-oh-SORE-us

The largest known theropod at 50 ft (15 m) long, *Spinosaurus* patrolled the floodplains of North Africa 90–75 million years ago. The first specimen found was lost during World War II, so this predator long remained shrouded in mystery. Recent finds have allowed paleontologists to reconstruct this remarkable creature.

**Fossil finds**
*Spinosaurus* mainly ate fish. Most of the other fossils found in modern-day North Africa have been carnivores. Very few plant-eating dinosaurs have been unearthed in this area.

**Tall tail**
The *Spinosaurus* tail was deep, unlike those of other theropods, and was potentially useful for chasing prey underwater. However, experts have doubted this style of hunting. Instead, the tall tail could have been used for display.

**Nasal crest**
A small, fanlike crest on the snout might have been used for display.

**Broad bones**
The neck bones of *Spinosaurus* and its close cousins were broad, perhaps limiting side-to-side movements.

**Long jaw**
The skull was around 6 ft (2 m) long, with large teeth at the front to help skewer slippery prey.

**Short legs**
This animal may have had relatively short legs.

ON *SPINOSAURUS*'S BACK MEASURED MORE THAN 6 FT (2 M).

### A fish dinner
An unlucky lungfish has been snared by a sail-backed *Spinosaurus* prowling the riverbanks for prey. This dinosaur will take its catch to a more secluded area, a safe distance from the watchful eyes of the crocodilelike *Elosuchus*.

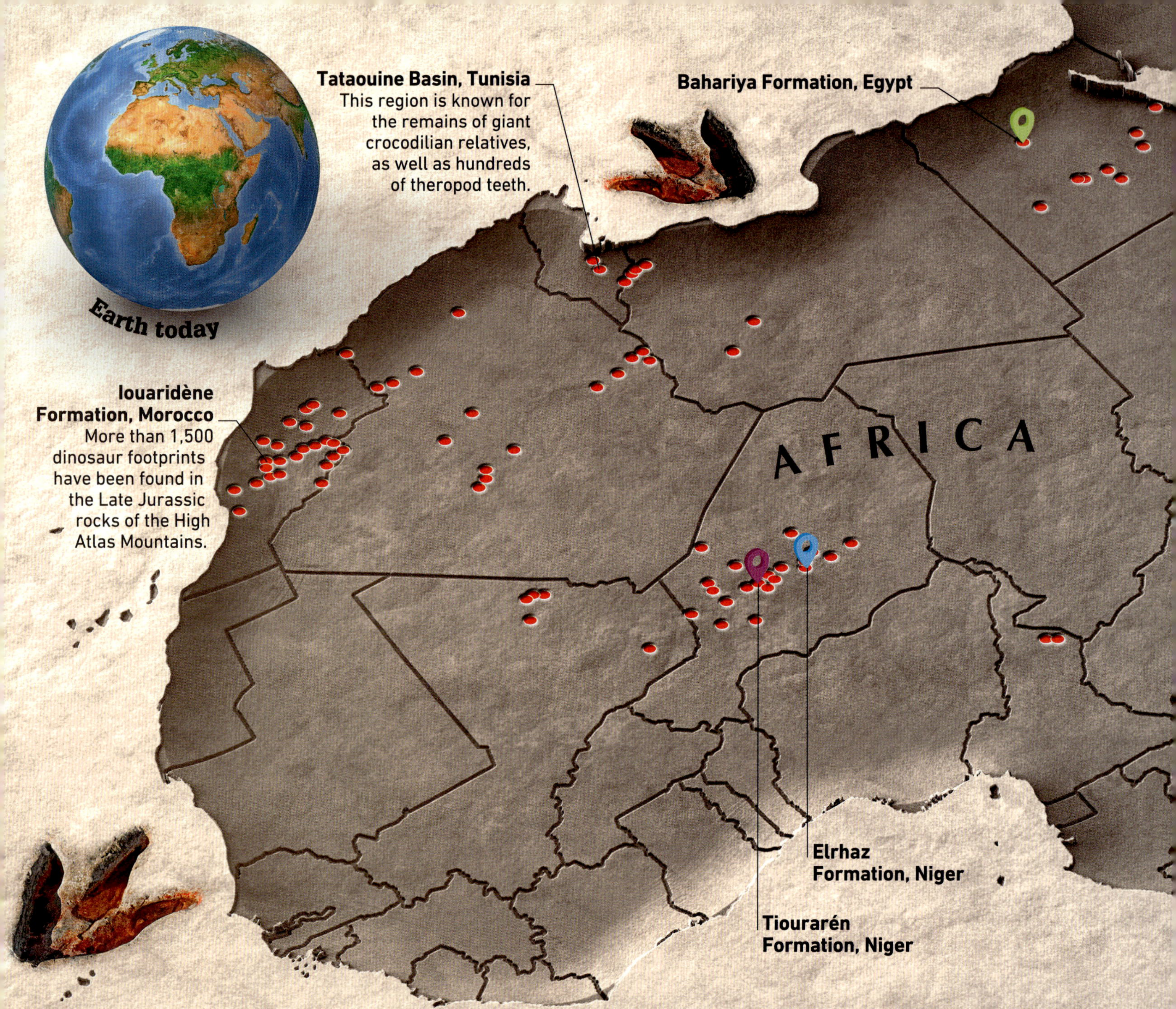

**Earth today**

**Tataouine Basin, Tunisia**
This region is known for the remains of giant crocodilian relatives, as well as hundreds of theropod teeth.

**Bahariya Formation, Egypt**

**Iouaridène Formation, Morocco**
More than 1,500 dinosaur footprints have been found in the Late Jurassic rocks of the High Atlas Mountains.

AFRICA

**Elrhaz Formation, Niger**

**Tiouarén Formation, Niger**

## Major fossil sites

- Bahariya Formation, Egypt (Cretaceous). Major finds: *Paralititan, Aegyptosaurus, Spinosaurus, Carcharodontosaurus*
- Tiouarén Formation, Niger (Jurassic). Major finds: *Jobaria, Afrovenator*
- Elrhaz Formation, Niger (Cretaceous). Major finds: *Suchomimus, Nigersaurus, Ouranosaurus*
- Bushveld Sandstone Formation, South Africa (Triassic). Major find: *Massospondylus*
- Upper Kirkwood Formation, South Africa (Cretaceous). Major finds: *Nqwebasaurus, Paranthodon*
- Tendaguru Formation, Tanzania (Jurassic). Major finds: *Giraffatitan, Kentrosaurus, Elaphrosaurus*

Chalk rock formations in the fossil-rich White Desert, near Bahariya Oasis, Egypt.

THE FIRST RECOGNIZED AFRICAN DINOSAUR FOSSILS, BELONGING

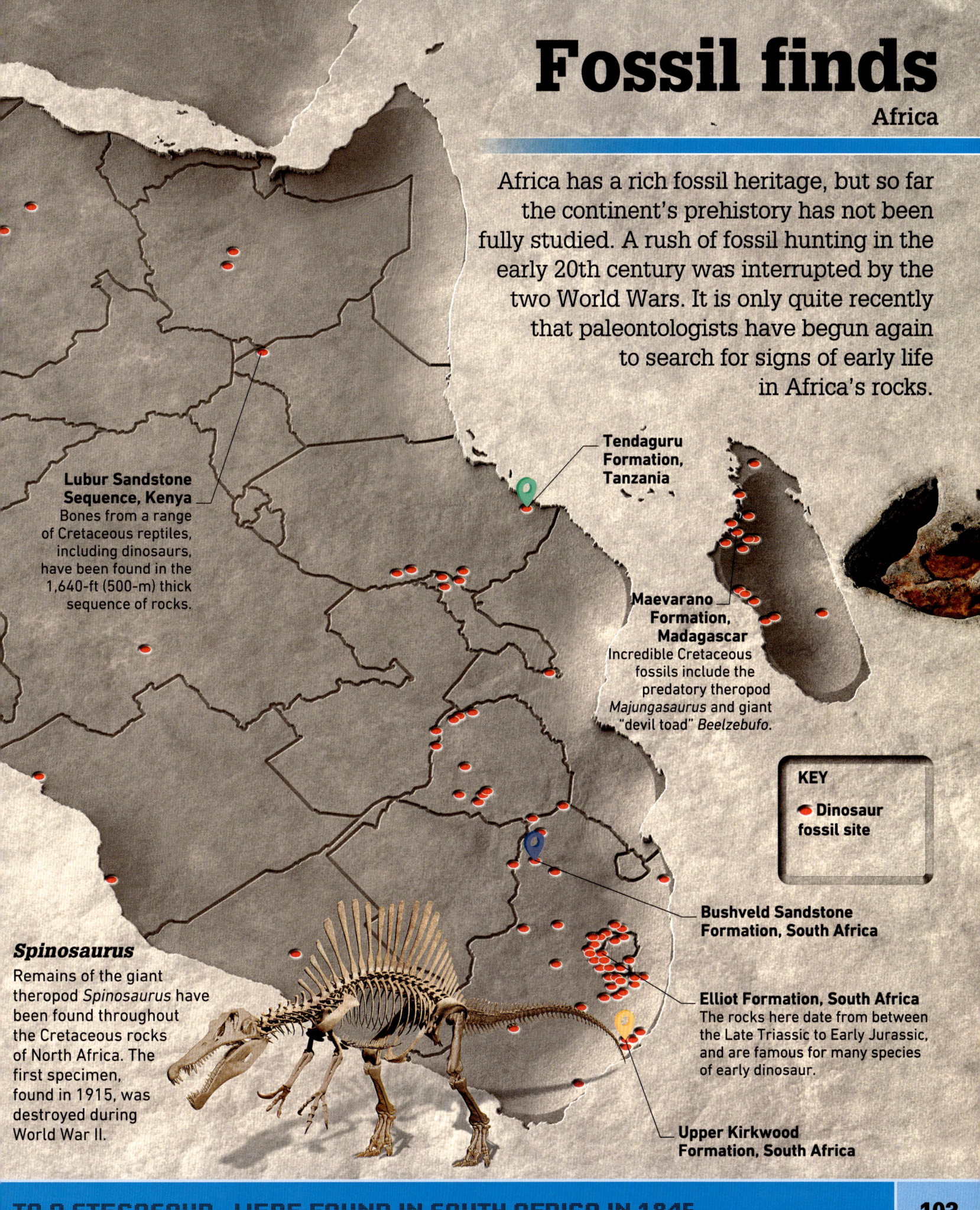

# Fossil finds
## Africa

Africa has a rich fossil heritage, but so far the continent's prehistory has not been fully studied. A rush of fossil hunting in the early 20th century was interrupted by the two World Wars. It is only quite recently that paleontologists have begun again to search for signs of early life in Africa's rocks.

**Lubur Sandstone Sequence, Kenya**
Bones from a range of Cretaceous reptiles, including dinosaurs, have been found in the 1,640-ft (500-m) thick sequence of rocks.

**Tendaguru Formation, Tanzania**

**Maevarano Formation, Madagascar**
Incredible Cretaceous fossils include the predatory theropod *Majungasaurus* and giant "devil toad" *Beelzebufo*.

**KEY**
● Dinosaur fossil site

**Bushveld Sandstone Formation, South Africa**

**Elliot Formation, South Africa**
The rocks here date from between the Late Triassic to Early Jurassic, and are famous for many species of early dinosaur.

**Upper Kirkwood Formation, South Africa**

**Spinosaurus**
Remains of the giant theropod *Spinosaurus* have been found throughout the Cretaceous rocks of North Africa. The first specimen, found in 1915, was destroyed during World War II.

# ASIA

**Parrot lizard**
A small dinosaur that resembled a parrot, *Psittacosaurus* came complete with a beak and quills. This plant eater was a common forest-dweller in Early Cretaceous Asia.

**170 MYA**

LAURASIA

TETHYS OCEAN

**Dominant herbivore**
*Shunosaurus* was a very common animal in this region. In a place called Dashanpu quarry, in modern-day China, 90 percent of all the dinosaur material found belong to this sauropod.

**Lush forest**
This habitat was rich in trees that surrounded large lakes.

**Spiky tail**
*Shunosaurus* roamed the area we now call China 170–160 million years ago. This dinosaur also possessed an interesting tail, with a small, spiked club at its end. Some experts think it was used for defense.

**Low browser**
The relatively short neck probably meant *Shunosaurus* foraged for plants close to the forest floor because it couldn't reach as far as its longer-necked cousins, such as *Diplodocus*.

TEN *SHUNOSAURUS* WERE FOUND AT JUST ONE SITE, HAVING

# Shunosaurus
SHOO-noe-SORE-us

A 33-ft (10-m) long body may sound huge, but *Shunosaurus* was small compared to its giant sauropod cousins. Weighing around 3.5 tons, this dinosaur would wander through open plains and forests in search of plants to eat.

**Tail weapon**
A double row of 2-in (5-cm) tall spikes, called osteoderms, which lined the tail's club, might have scared off some hungry Jurassic predators.

**Built to eat plants**
The tall skull and long teeth of this sauropod has led some paleontologists to suggest the jaws acted like garden shears, slicing through branches.

*Shunosaurus* skeleton

**Growing up**
Leg bone analysis by scientists suggests that *Shunosaurus* continued to grow even once it had reached adulthood.

DROWNED IN A FLASH FLOOD.

120 MYA

ARCTIC OCEAN

**Tail quills**
These structures may be related to the feathers of today's birds.

**Big-brained**
A large brain suggests *Psittacosaurus* may have been capable of pretty complex behaviors, such as caring for their young.

**Cheek horns**
Prominent horns on the cheeks grew with age, which suggests they might have been used for attracting a mate.

**Family life**
Hundreds of individual *Psittacosaurus* specimens have been unearthed, ranging from tiny babies to full-grown adults. One was even found next to 34 hatchlings, suggesting that this dinosaur cared for its young.

PACIFIC OCEAN · ATLANTIC OCEAN · INDIAN OCEAN

JUVENILES APPEAR TO HAVE

# Psittacosaurus
SIT-ack-oh-SORE-us

An early relative of *Triceratops*, *Psittacosaurus* grew to 7 ft (2 m) in length and roamed the woodlands of modern-day Asia 125–100 million years ago. Based on 400 known specimens, nine species of this dinosaur have been identified.

**Adaptable herbivore**
*Psittacosaurus* species lived in a range of habitats over their 20-million-year evolution, from cool forests to arid deserts.

**Large range**
Fossils have been found as far north as modern-day Siberia, and south through China and Mongolia.

**Early Cretaceous Asia**
Modern-day India was not part of Asia at this time. It would later crash into Asia to form the Himalayas.

**Perfect preservation**
Study of this well-preserved specimen from China has shown that some *Psittacosaurus* species had a brown back and pale belly. This was a form of camouflage called "countershading."

Tail quills
Well-preserved bones
Stomach contents

**Parrot beak**
The name *Psittacosaurus* means "parrot lizard" and refers to its parrotlike beak. The beak would have been used to slice off vegetation, which would then have been shredded by its small, sharp teeth.

FORMED LARGE GROUPS, PERHAPS FOR PROTECTION FROM PREDATORS.

## Fuzzy predator
At the top of the food chain, *Yutyrannus* probably preyed upon the diverse fauna found in Early Cretaceous Asia, which included small ornithischians such as *Psittacosaurus*.

**Big skull**
Filled with thick, banana-shaped teeth, the 35-in (90-cm) long skull was similar to that of later tyrannosaurs.

**Fuzzy coat**
The feathers that covered the body were long, hairlike, and formed a dense coat.

**Three-clawed hands**
Both the arms and claws were proportionally larger than those seen in later tyrannosaurs and may have helped to catch prey.

**Heavy tyrannosaur**
Weighing around a ton, *Yutyrannus* was substantially larger than most early tyrannosaurs.

**Feeding aid**
The large feet might have been used to pin down carcasses while *Yutyrannus* tore chunks of meat off them with its teeth.

120 MYA

110   A DISTINCTIVE CREST RAN ALONG

# Yutyrannus

you-tie-RAN-us

The 30-ft (9-m) long tyrannosaur *Yutyrannus* lived in Cretaceous Asia, around 125 million years ago. It is notable for the long, shaggy coat of feathers that covered its body, making it one of the largest dinosaurs known to possess plumage.

**PACIFIC OCEAN**

**Dry seasons**
While the area was generally humid and wet, there is evidence that over time water levels dropped and the region became drier.

**Vast continent**
The range over which *Yutyrannus* is thought to have roamed covers large parts of what is now China.

**Diverse plants**
The diverse plant life, including conifer trees and various smaller plants, helped sustain a huge range of animals for *Yutyrannus* to prey upon.

ASIA

**Long tail**
As in other tyrannosaurs, the heavy tail helped with balance.

**Feathered tyrant**
Paleontologists believe that *Yutyrannus*'s feathers—some of which grew as long as 8 in (20 cm)—may have helped regulate its temperature. With average air temperatures during this time around 50°F (10°C), feathers would have kept it warm in the winter months.

Reconstructed face of *Yutyrannus*

YUTYRANNUS'S SNOUT, WHICH MAY HAVE BEEN USED FOR DISPLAY.

111

**Surprise attack**
A large *Yutyrannus* launches out of its hiding place and sinks its serrated teeth into the flesh of the herbivore *Beipiaosaurus*. Two *Psittacosaurus* use the commotion to escape toward the safety of the forest.

**Folding wrist**
The wings folded at the wrist, which prevented them from being damaged by trailing them on the ground.

**Shiny plumage**
Studies of pigments in fossilized *Microraptor* feathers revealed that it had shimmering black plumage. In fact, the feathers would look much like those of modern birds, such as starlings.

**Powered flight**
*Microraptor* appears to have been capable of taking off from the ground for short bursts of flight.

**Mixed diet**
Living around 120 million years ago, *Microraptor* had a varied diet. The fossilized stomach contents of several of these dinosaurs show that it ate small mammals, fish, and a type of extinct bird.

**Tail feathers**
These long feathers may have been used for display rather than flight, perhaps to attract partners.

120 MYA

114 DINOSAUR EXPERTS HAVE DISCOVERED MORE THAN

# Microraptor
my-CROW-rap-ter

One of the smallest known dinosaurs, this little predator weighed about 2 lb (1 kg) and was around 30 in (80 cm) long. *Microraptor* had four "wings" and was fully feathered, with extra-long arm and leg feathers. Its fossils have all been found in modern-day China.

**Airborne**
*Microraptor* had a wingspan of roughly 28 in (70 cm), wide enough for it to take to the air.

**Preservation**
There was volcanic activity across this area of eastern Asia. The volcanic ash preserved the soft tissue, such as feathers, in fossils.

**Cool climate**
The climate of this region of Asia was cool, with temperatures around 50°F (10°C).

**Tiny teeth**
*Microraptor* teeth had both serrated and unserrated edges, as well as ridged surfaces for gripping prey.

300 FOSSILS OF *MICRORAPTOR* AND ITS CLOSEST COUSINS.

ARCTIC OCEAN

**Razor teeth**
Below its upturned snout, this dinosaur's jaws were filled with sharp, meat-slicing teeth.

**Killer claw**
Located on the second toe of each foot, the 2.5-in (6.5-cm) claw was held off the ground, which kept it sharp. It might have been used to pin down struggling prey, while the rest of the foot provided grip.

Fossilized *Velociraptor* claw

**Foldable wrist**
The birdlike wrist could bend to stop long feathers from dragging on the ground.

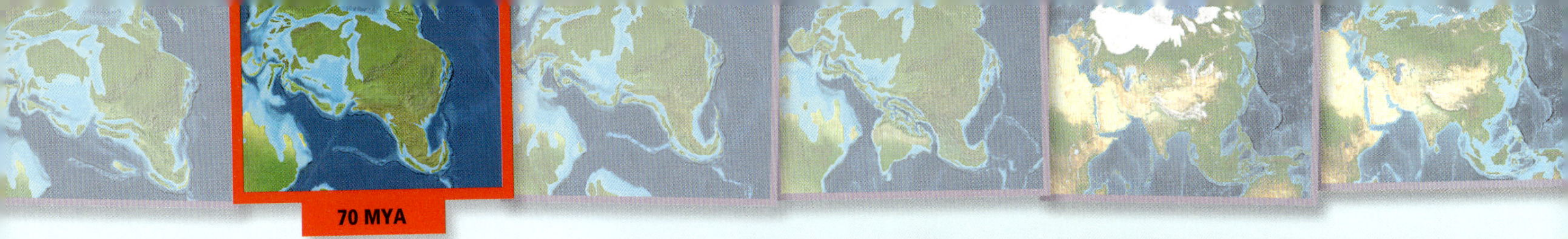

# Velociraptor
veh-loss-ih-**RAP**-tor 

Of all the predatory tools used by the 6.5-ft (2-m) long *Velociraptor*, none is more famous than its "killer claws." Prowling parts of what is today Mongolia and China, this dinosaur used these deadly weapons to tackle prey.

**Little rain**
In *Velociraptor*'s inland range, rain clouds would have been rare, creating a dry and dusty environment.

**Large eyes**
Good eyesight gave *Velociraptor* an advantage when detecting small prey.

**Athletic body**
*Velociraptor* had a lean body that was built for speed and agility rather than strength.

**Dry habitat**
This was a dry region of ever-changing sand dunes. Water was scarce, and *Velociraptor* may have only found water in rare oases or temporary rivers.

**Fine feathers**
*Velociraptor* probably possessed extensive plumage, as remains of its close cousins have been discovered bearing feathers.

**Mongolian hunter**
Living 74–70 million years ago, *Velociraptor* was a small but deadly predator. It had more than 60 teeth lining its jaws, which were more serrated on one side than the other. This helped tear through tough muscle.

**Trapped in time**
One *Velociraptor* specimen was found to have died fighting—its skeleton locked in combat with the herbivore *Protoceratops*. The wrestling dinosaurs may have been killed and buried by a collapsing sand dune.

OF ONE *VELOCIRAPTOR*—A REMNANT OF ITS LAST MEAL.

# Fossil finds
## Asia

The quality of the preservation of fossils from certain locations in Asia is nothing short of breathtaking. Key finds range from soft tissues, such as feathers and skin pigments, to whole nurseries of baby dinosaurs.

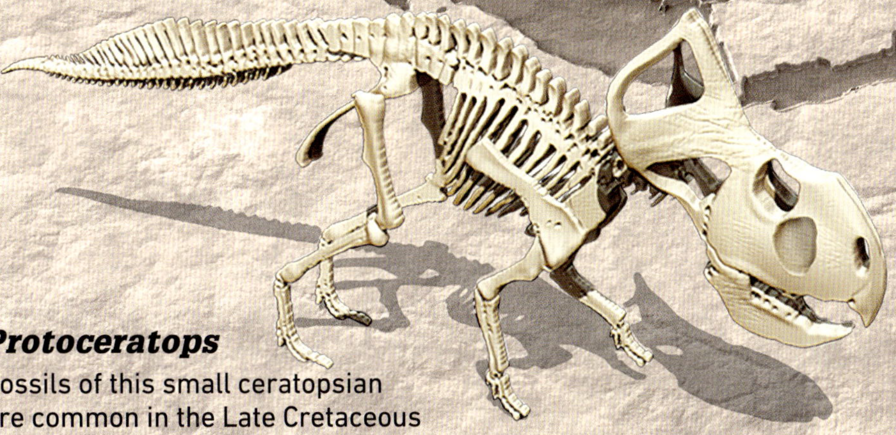

**Djadochta Formation, Gobi Desert, Mongolia**

**Yuliangze Formation, Jiliu Province, China**

**Amur River Region, Russia**

**Kitadani Formation, Fukui Province, Japan**
A variety of Cretaceous dinosaur remains have been found here.

**Yixian Formation, Liaoning Province, China**

**Nemegt Formation, Gobi Desert, Mongolia**

**Laijia Formation, China.** Numerous dinosaur egg fossils were uncovered here.

**Dashanpu Formation, Sichuan, China** Sauropod remains dating back to the Jurassic have been found at this site.

**Lufeng Formation, Yunnan, China** These early Jurassic rocks preserved many sauropodomorphs (long-necked plant eaters) and theropod species.

**Sao Khua Formation, Thailand**

### Major fossil sites

Bostobinskaya Formation, Kazakhstan (Cretaceous).
Major finds: *Arstanosaurus, Batyrosaurus*

Ilek Formation, Siberia, Russia (Cretaceous).
Major finds: *Sibirotitan, Psittacosaurus*

Nemegt Formation, Gobi Desert, Mongolia (Cretaceous).
Major finds: *Tarbosaurus, Avimimus, Conchoraptor, Zanabazar, Deinocheirus, Saichania, Saurolopus, Nemegtosaurus*

Djadochta Formation, Gobi Desert, Mongolia (Cretaceous).
Major finds: *Oviraptor, Citipati, Velociraptor, Byronosaurus, Plesiohadros, Protoceratops*

Amur River Region, Russia (Cretaceous).
Major find: *Kundurosaurus*

Yuliangze Formation, Jiliu Province, China (Cretaceous).
Major finds: *Charonosaurus, Wulagasaurus*

Yixian Formation, Liaoning Province, China (Cretaceous).
Major finds: *Beipiaosaurus, Microraptor, Psittacosaurus*

Xinminbao Group, Gansu, China (Cretaceous).
Major finds: *Gobititan, Equijubus, Microceratus, Archaeoceratops*

Lameta Formation, India (Cretaceous).
Major finds: *Indosuchus, Jainosaurus, Isisaurus*

Sao Khua Formation, Thailand (Cretaceous).
Major find: *Phuwiangosaurus*

### Protoceratops
Fossils of this small ceratopsian are common in the Late Cretaceous rocks of Mongolia. It lacked the horns seen in some of its cousins, but had a large neck frill.

This skeleton of feathered theropod *Microraptor* from the Early Cretaceous was found in Liaoning Province, China.

**THE ROCKS OF CHINA, IS ONE OF THE BEST FOSSIL SITES IN THE WORLD.**

# AUSTRALIA AND ANTARCTICA

**Giant plant eater**
A massively built herbivore with a uniquely shaped snout, *Muttaburrasaurus* foraged for food 100 million years ago. This dinosaur roamed a large section of the country that we call Australia today.

**Small brain**
Research suggests theshape of the brain was more similar to that of earlier theropods than to the brain of its later cousins. As a result, this dinosaur possibly had mainly simple behaviors.

170 MYA

**Predator potential**
Experts noted that the original *Cryolophosaurus* specimen was probably a subadult. So when fully grown, these dinosaurs were larger than 23 ft (7 m) in length and capable of tackling large prey.

**Serrated teeth**
Although it probably couldn't bite through bone, its sharp, bladelike teeth were perfect for tearing through flesh

# Cryolophosaurus
CRY-uh-LOF-uh-SORE-us

Early Jurassic predatory theropods didn't get much bigger than the 23-ft (7-m) long *Cryolophosaurus*. Most famous for its distinctive crest, it was Antarctica's top predator and hunted in forests 170 million years ago.

**A welcome discovery**
It has been a good summer for this *Cryolophosaurus*. Making the most of the warmer temperatures and sunshine, it has found the carcass of a *Glacialisaurus* in a lake. The energy it will get from eating its meal will be invaluable, as a long, cold winter lies ahead.

# Muttaburrasaurus
MOO-tah-BUH-ruh-SORE-us

110 MYA

This 26-ft (8-m) long herbivore is one of the better-known dinosaurs found in the fossil-poor rocks of Australia. It lived 112–100 million years ago, in the southeastern regions of the supercontinent Gondwana.

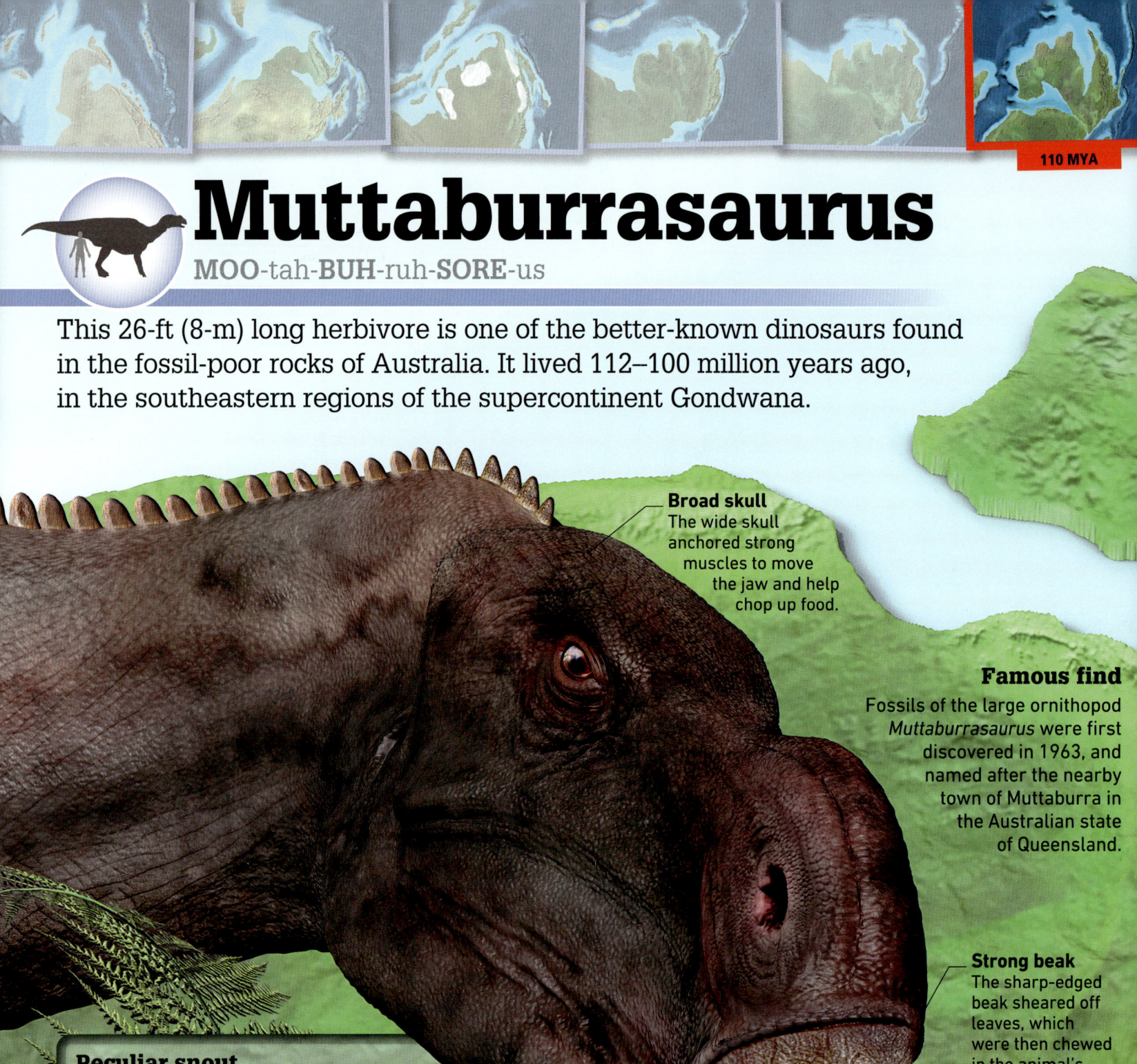

**Broad skull**
The wide skull anchored strong muscles to move the jaw and help chop up food.

**Famous find**
Fossils of the large ornithopod *Muttaburrasaurus* were first discovered in 1963, and named after the nearby town of Muttaburra in the Australian state of Queensland.

**Strong beak**
The sharp-edged beak sheared off leaves, which were then chewed in the animal's large cheeks.

**Peculiar snout**
The bones of this dinosaur's snout formed a hollow crest. Some experts think this amplified calls, while others think it was topped with an inflatable sac, as seen in some modern seals.

Inflatable sac

Male hooded seal

**Cretaceous diet**
Ferns and cycads were the likely diet of this herbivore.

SOME *MUTTABURRASAURUS* FOSSILS ARE PRESERVED

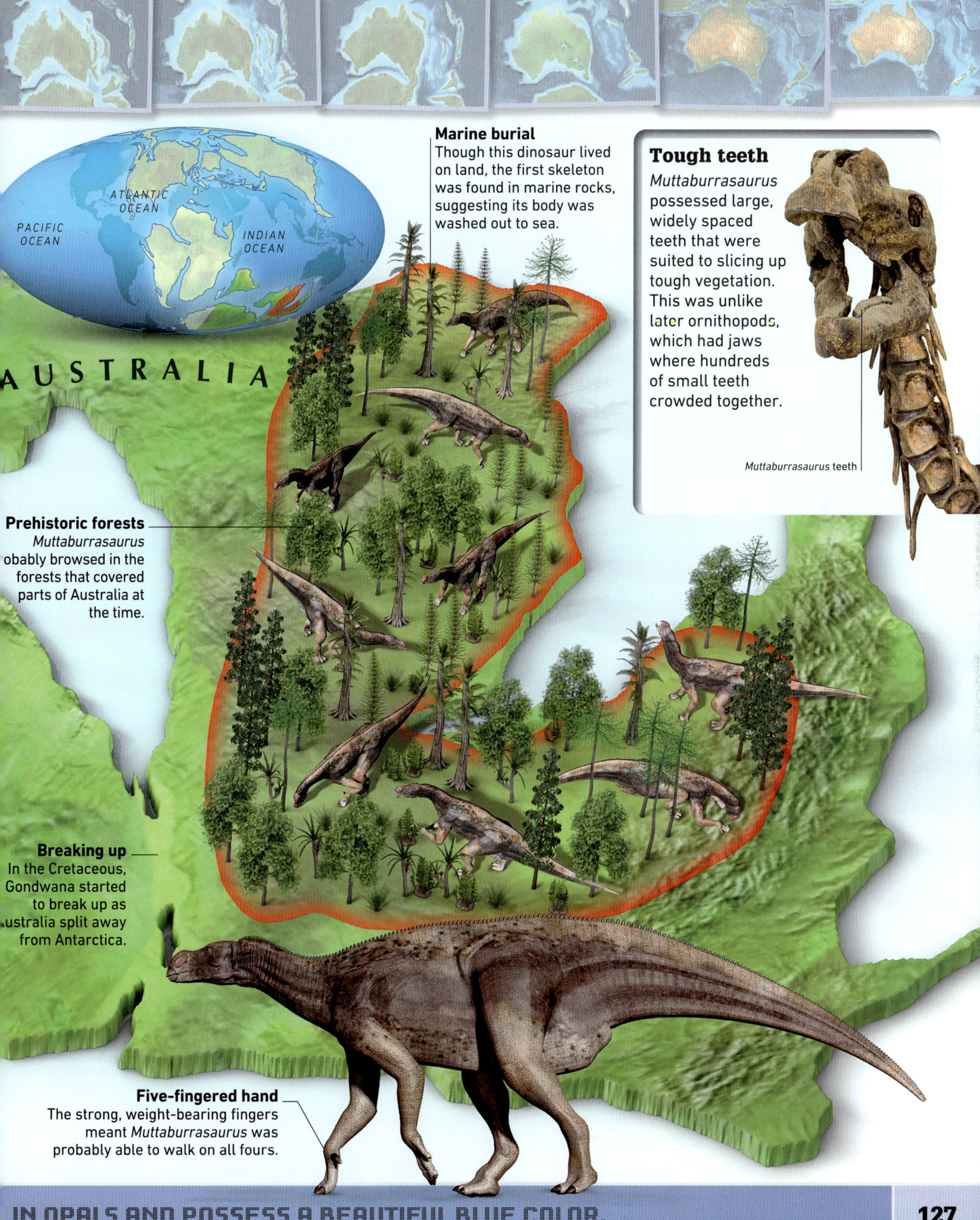

**Marine burial**
Though this dinosaur lived on land, the first skeleton was found in marine rocks, suggesting its body was washed out to sea.

**Tough teeth**
*Muttaburrasaurus* possessed large, widely spaced teeth that were suited to slicing up tough vegetation. This was unlike later ornithopods, which had jaws where hundreds of small teeth crowded together.

*Muttaburrasaurus* teeth

**Prehistoric forests**
*Muttaburrasaurus* probably browsed in the forests that covered parts of Australia at the time.

**Breaking up**
In the Cretaceous, Gondwana started to break up as Australia split away from Antarctica.

**Five-fingered hand**
The strong, weight-bearing fingers meant *Muttaburrasaurus* was probably able to walk on all fours.

IN OPALS AND POSSESS A BEAUTIFUL BLUE COLOR.

**Excellent vision**
Large eyes might have helped *Leaellynasaura* to see well in the darker winter months.

**Feathered body**
Featherlike structures might have kept it warm during the long, cold, and dark days.

**Polar specialist**
Scientists can't agree how severe winter conditions were in Early Cretaceous Australia. However, with average air temperatures ranging between 2°F (-6°C) and 59°F (15°C), some believe *Leaellynasaura* could have made burrows for winter shelter.

**Dinosaur Cove**
Although relatively few fossil discoveries have been made in Australia, Dinosaur Cove in southeastern Australia has yielded some important finds. These include the country's first dinosaur fossil in 1903 and *Leaellynasaura* in 1989.

# Leaellynasaura
lee-ELL-in-ah-SORE-uh

A small dinosaur with one of the longest tails proportional to its body, the 8-ft (2.5-m) long *Leaellynasaura* scurried around the forests that would later become Australia. These agile herbivores would have experienced long periods of darkness because, 120–110 million years ago, this region was very close to the South Pole.

ACTUALLY THOSE OF JUVENILES, AND THAT ADULTS GREW LARGER.

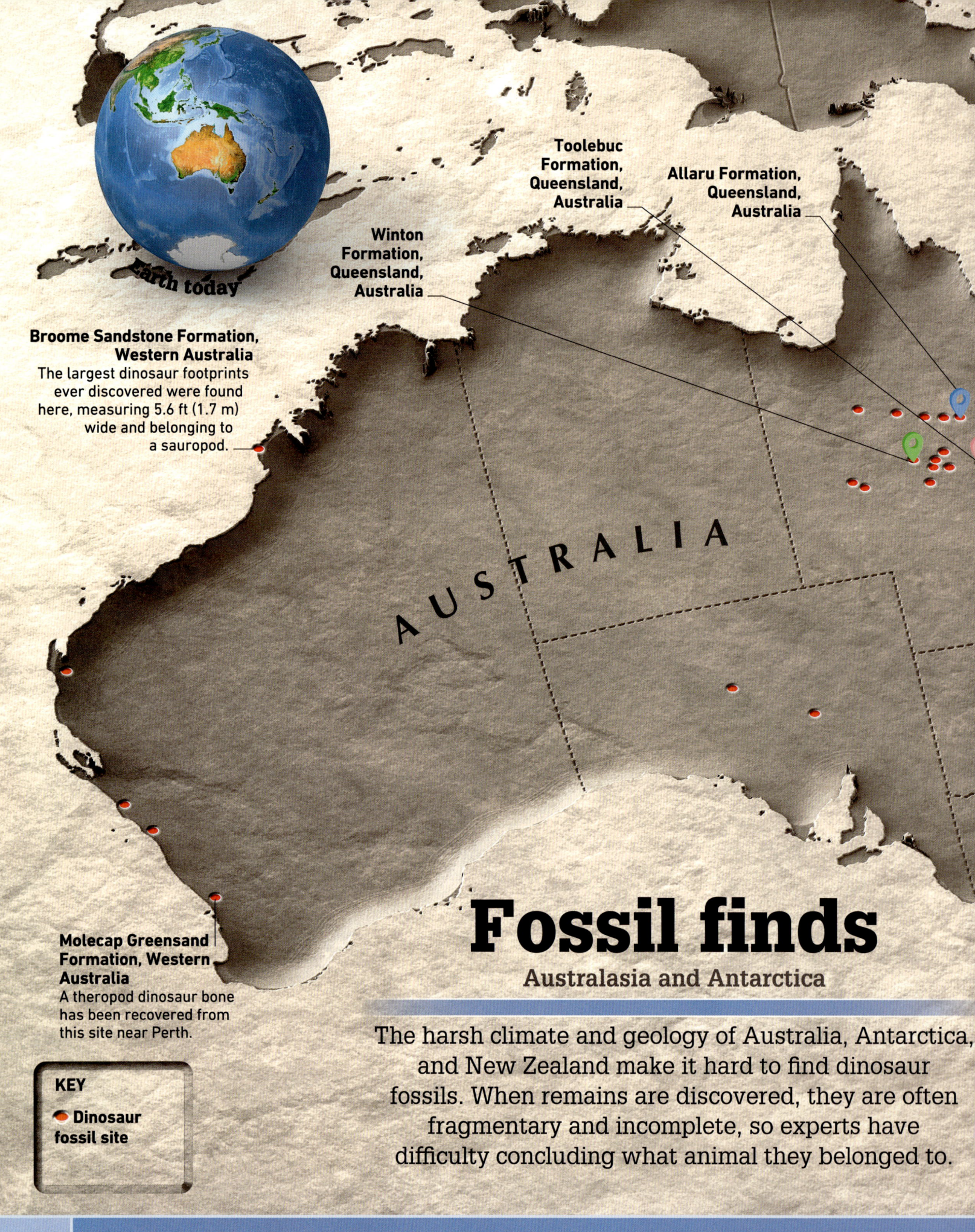

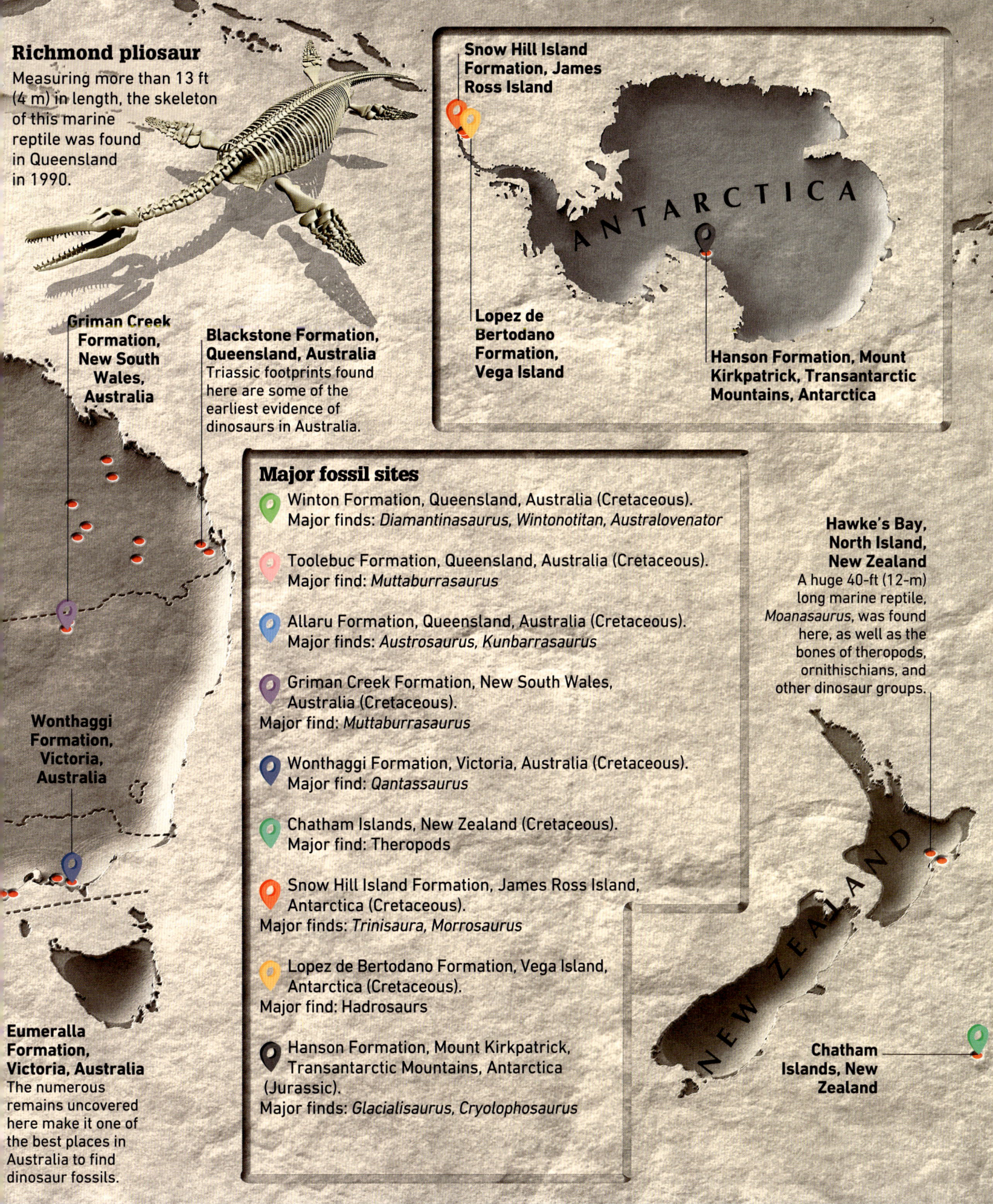

**Richmond pliosaur**
Measuring more than 13 ft (4 m) in length, the skeleton of this marine reptile was found in Queensland in 1990.

**Snow Hill Island Formation, James Ross Island**

**Lopez de Bertodano Formation, Vega Island**

**Hanson Formation, Mount Kirkpatrick, Transantarctic Mountains, Antarctica**

**Griman Creek Formation, New South Wales, Australia**

**Blackstone Formation, Queensland, Australia**
Triassic footprints found here are some of the earliest evidence of dinosaurs in Australia.

### Major fossil sites

- Winton Formation, Queensland, Australia (Cretaceous). Major finds: *Diamantinasaurus, Wintonotitan, Australovenator*
- Toolebuc Formation, Queensland, Australia (Cretaceous). Major find: *Muttaburrasaurus*
- Allaru Formation, Queensland, Australia (Cretaceous). Major finds: *Austrosaurus, Kunbarrasaurus*
- Griman Creek Formation, New South Wales, Australia (Cretaceous). Major find: *Muttaburrasaurus*
- Wonthaggi Formation, Victoria, Australia (Cretaceous). Major find: *Qantassaurus*
- Chatham Islands, New Zealand (Cretaceous). Major find: Theropods
- Snow Hill Island Formation, James Ross Island, Antarctica (Cretaceous). Major finds: *Trinisaura, Morrosaurus*
- Lopez de Bertodano Formation, Vega Island, Antarctica (Cretaceous). Major find: Hadrosaurs
- Hanson Formation, Mount Kirkpatrick, Transantarctic Mountains, Antarctica (Jurassic). Major finds: *Glacialisaurus, Cryolophosaurus*

**Hawke's Bay, North Island, New Zealand**
A huge 40-ft (12-m) long marine reptile, *Moanasaurus*, was found here, as well as the bones of theropods, ornithischians, and other dinosaur groups.

**Wonthaggi Formation, Victoria, Australia**

**Eumeralla Formation, Victoria, Australia**
The numerous remains uncovered here make it one of the best places in Australia to find dinosaur fossils.

**Chatham Islands, New Zealand**

IN OPAL, GIVING THEM SPARKLING, MULTICOLORED HUES.

# AFTER THE DINOSAURS

**Still a dangerous world**
Even without *Tyrannosaurus* around, prehistoric life could still be dangerous. Here, an ancestor of Australia's red kangaroo flees from the claws of *Varanus priscus*, a giant monitor lizard.

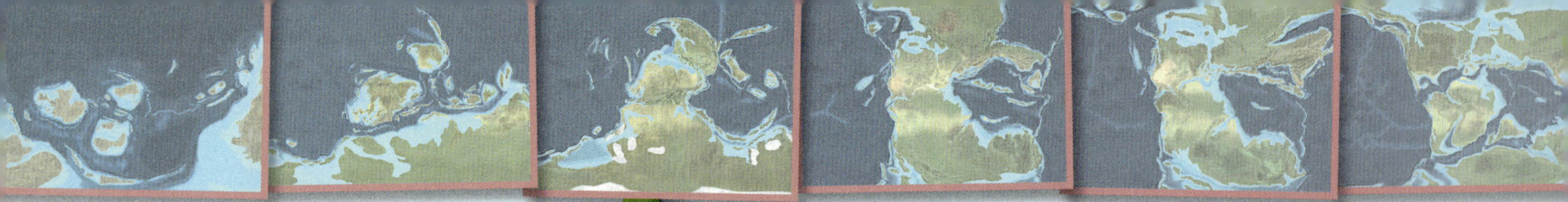

**Snake in a coal mine**
Along with numerous fossil animals, including mammals, *Titanoboa* was found at a site in modern-day Colombia that is located within a working coal mine.

**Surrounding sea**
Colombia was once surrounded and partially covered by shallow seas.

SOUTH AMERICA

**Recreating a giant**
Although the only fossils yet found of *Titanoboa* are skull fragments and some vertebrae, scientists have been able to build up an image of what the huge snake looked like. The sculptor Kevin Hockley created the full-sized model seen below, which shows *Titanoboa* gulping down a crocodilelike reptile.

**Hungry predator**
Feeding on fish and reptiles, *Titanoboa* inhabited a small, swampy region.

PACIFIC OCEAN

**Slow mover**
Like modern boas, *Titanoboa* probably moved slowly, using its belly muscles in wavelike motions to crawl along.

# Titanoboa
TIE-tan-o-BO-a

**Water dweller**
*Titanoboa* may have spent most of its time in water, which would have helped support its weight.

Sixty million years ago, in the part of South America that is now Colombia, hot swampy jungles were home to the biggest snake ever. *Titanoboa* was related to modern boa constrictors, but at a gigantic 40 ft (12 m) long, it far exceeded them in size.

ATLANTIC OCEAN
PACIFIC OCEAN
INDIAN OCEAN

TITANOBOA WAS ESTIMATED TO BE NEARLY TWICE AS LONG AND

**60 MYA**

### Forested world
When *Titanoboa* was alive, South America was covered in thick tropical forest, as were the other continents. Jungles stretched from pole to pole and global temperatures were high. Earth was in what we now call a "greenhouse" phase, perhaps because volcanic gases had warmed up the atmosphere.

### Crushing power
Powerful muscles would have enabled *Titanoboa* to suffocate large prey by squeezing it in its coils.

### Heavyweight
*Titanoboa* weighed more than 2,425 lb (1,100 kg), its body was 3 ft (1 m) wide, and its head was 16 in (40 cm) long.

### Fish catcher
The slim, curved, pointed teeth suggest that *Titanoboa* caught large fish.

### Massive jaws
Like nearly all snakes, *Titanoboa* could open its jaws wide enough to swallow prey whole. It had a long, broad skull with loosely hinged jaw bones.

Hinge

Jaw

In a snake, a hinge joint allows the jaws to open very wide.

Ligament

A ligament joining the two sides of the jaws stretches as the snake opens its mouth.

**FOUR TIMES HEAVIER THAN THE LARGEST MODERN-DAY BOA.**

**Flexible neck**
A bendy neck allowed *Gastornis* to look in all directions.

**Tropical land**
Dense, tropical forests covered most of North America during the time that *Gastornis* was alive.

**Atlantic land bridge**
Europe and North America were connected, enabling animals to move between the two areas via modern-day Greenland.

*Gastornis* skull and neck

**Gigantic bill**
Experts once believed that *Gastornis* must have used its enormous, powerful bill for tearing meat or crunching bones. It is now thought to be more likely that the bill was used for breaking branches, cracking nuts, and opening fruit.

**Fur or feathers?**
*Gastornis* is often pictured with shaggy, hairlike plumage, but it may have had normal feathers like a duck.

**Walk, don't run**
This hefty bird could run, but it was not built for speed. Its thick, heavy leg bones were more suited to walking.

**Duck relative**
*Gastornis* was long thought to belong to the group of birds that includes modern rails and cranes. Experts now consider it likely to have been a giant relative of ducks, geese, and swans.

A LANDSLIDE NEAR SEATTLE IN 2009 UNCOVERED A ROCK WITH

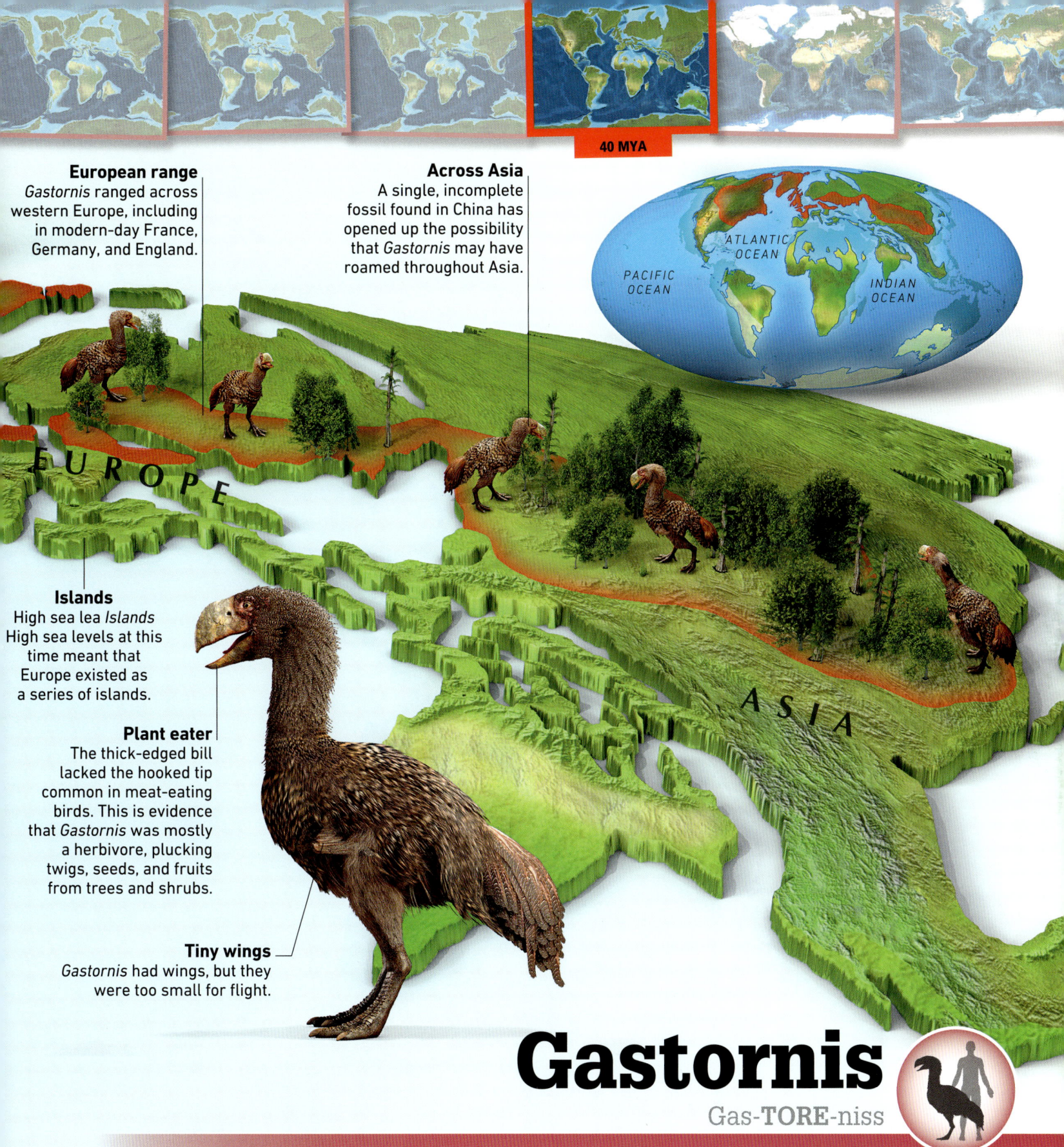

**European range**
*Gastornis* ranged across western Europe, including in modern-day France, Germany, and England.

**Across Asia**
A single, incomplete fossil found in China has opened up the possibility that *Gastornis* may have roamed throughout Asia.

**Islands**
High sea lea *Islands* High sea levels at this time meant that Europe existed as a series of islands.

**Plant eater**
The thick-edged bill lacked the hooked tip common in meat-eating birds. This is evidence that *Gastornis* was mostly a herbivore, plucking twigs, seeds, and fruits from trees and shrubs.

**Tiny wings**
*Gastornis* had wings, but they were too small for flight.

# Gastornis
Gas-**TORE**-niss

After the mass extinction event that wiped out the dinosaurs, new kinds of birds evolved. One of them, *Gastornis*, was an enormous flightless bird that lived across Europe and North America 56–40 million years ago. Standing 6.5 ft (2 m) tall, it had a deep skull and a massive bill.

HUGE FOSSIL FOOTPRINTS, THOUGHT TO BE THOSE OF *GASTORNIS*.

**Life in water**
Adapted for underwater life, the ear and skull bones of *Basilosaurus* allowed for sensitive underwater hearing.

**Complex teeth**
Unlike modern whales, *Basilosaurus* had teeth of several different shapes. Those in the front were simple and conical, while the teeth farther back were triangular and jagged, helping this hunter to tear up its prey.

Conical teeth
Triangular teeth

ATLANTIC OCEAN

**Coasts of North America**
*Basilosaurus* was common in the Atlantic Ocean along the warm coastal waters of the modern-day United States.

**Surface predator**
Studies of its jaws show that *Basilosaurus* was a predator with a very powerful bite. It mostly lived in warm, shallow seas and swam in the surface waters of North America, North Africa, Europe, and Asia.

# Basilosaurus
BASS-ill-oh-SORE-us

One of the largest known animals of its time, *Basilosaurus* was a whale very unlike those of today. It had a body up to 59 ft (18 m) long and tiny hind limbs with knees, ankles, and toes. This predator hunted fish and other marine mammals 40–34 million years ago.

**Long body**
*Basilosaurus* had a long, flexible body. Early illustrations imagined it as snakelike, but this is believed to be incorrect.

BASILOSAURUS MEANS "KING LIZARD," BECAUSE THE ANIMAL WAS

**40 MYA**

**One of many**
*Basilosaurus* lived alongside a number of other early whales in the Tethys Ocean.

**Flexible flippers**
The pectoral fins of *Basilosaurus* were more flexible than those of modern whales—both the elbow and wrist were mobile.

**India on the move**
At this time, India had moved a long way across the Indian Ocean, but had not yet collided with Asia.

**Fluked tail**
The tail bones of *Basilosaurus* show that it had horizontal tail flukes, like modern whales. It swam by moving its tail up and down.

ORIGINALLY THOUGHT TO BE A REPTILE INSTEAD OF A MAMMAL.

**La Brea Tar Pits**
Thousands of *Smilodon* fossils come from this site in modern-day Los Angeles, where both the cats and their prey were trapped in natural pits of sticky tar.

**East to west habitat**
*Smilodon* ranged across the area that is the United States today, from Pennsylvania in the east to California in the west.

**Killer canines**
*Smilodon*'s giant upper canine teeth were once thought to have been used for stabbing. Experts now think *Smilodon* used them to deliver a precise killing bite to the throat of its prey.

**Stumpy tail**
The short tail was like that of a modern lynx or bobcat.

**Sharp blades**
Curved and very sharp, the upper canines could be up to 11 in (28 cm) long.

**Sturdy legs**
Unlike most cats, *Smilodon* was not a fast runner. Its legs were short, thick, and muscular.

SMILODON NEEDED TO OPEN ITS JAWS BY ABOUT 120 DEGREES TO

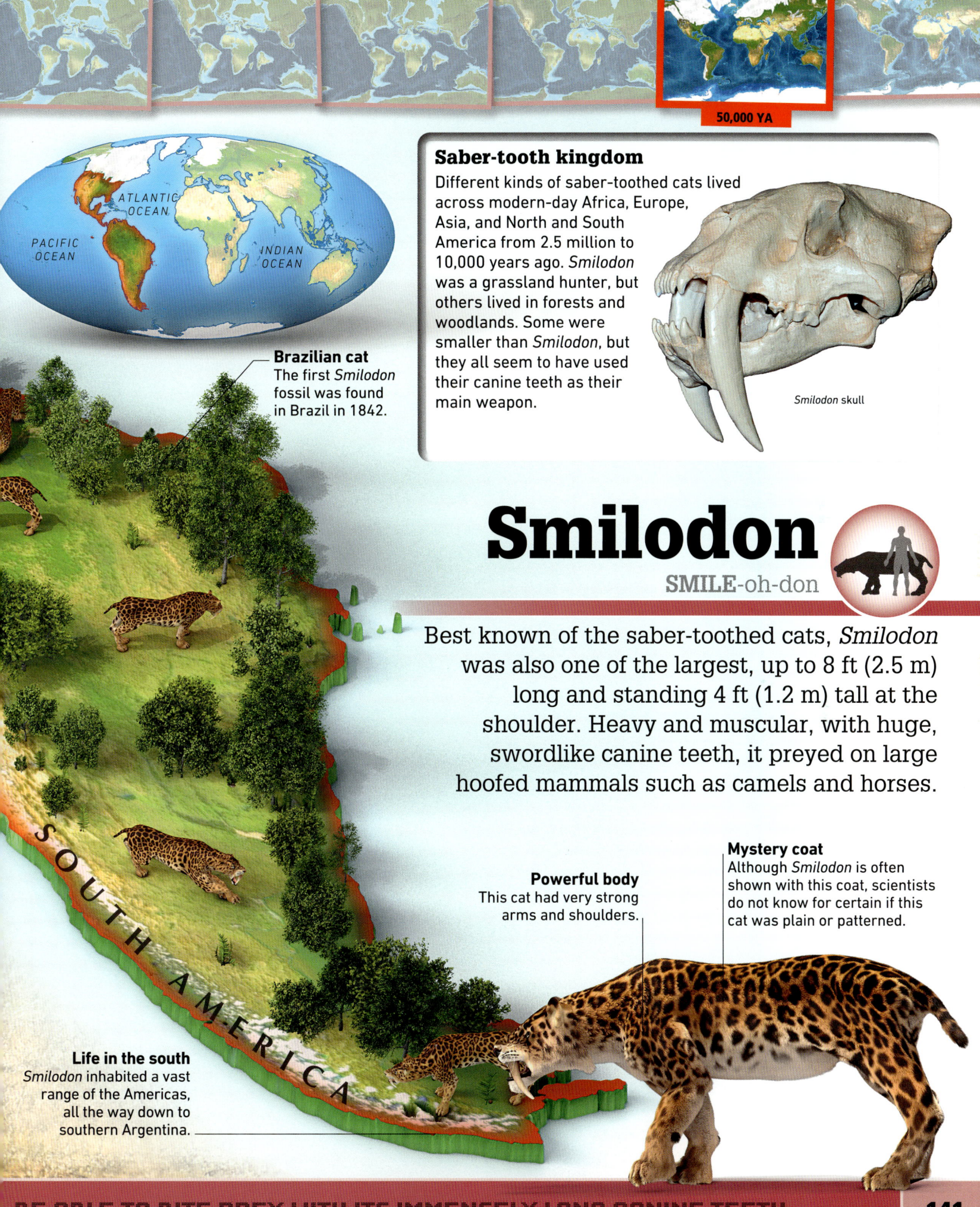

50,000 YA

### Saber-tooth kingdom
Different kinds of saber-toothed cats lived across modern-day Africa, Europe, Asia, and North and South America from 2.5 million to 10,000 years ago. *Smilodon* was a grassland hunter, but others lived in forests and woodlands. Some were smaller than *Smilodon*, but they all seem to have used their canine teeth as their main weapon.

*Smilodon* skull

**Brazilian cat**
The first *Smilodon* fossil was found in Brazil in 1842.

# Smilodon
SMILE-oh-don

Best known of the saber-toothed cats, *Smilodon* was also one of the largest, up to 8 ft (2.5 m) long and standing 4 ft (1.2 m) tall at the shoulder. Heavy and muscular, with huge, swordlike canine teeth, it preyed on large hoofed mammals such as camels and horses.

**Mystery coat**
Although *Smilodon* is often shown with this coat, scientists do not know for certain if this cat was plain or patterned.

**Powerful body**
This cat had very strong arms and shoulders.

**Life in the south**
*Smilodon* inhabited a vast range of the Americas, all the way down to southern Argentina.

BE ABLE TO BITE PREY WITH ITS IMMENSELY LONG CANINE TEETH.

### Cave paintings
Early humans illustrated woolly mammoths on European cave walls with a shoulder hump, domed head, and shaggy coat. They are sometimes shown fighting or raising their trunk.

### Out of Africa
Fossils show that mammoths originated in Africa, before spreading across Asia and Europe.

### Coat color
Genetic studies show that woolly mammoths were probably dark or sometimes blonde.

### Massive tusks
Huge, curved tusks could grow as long as 13 ft (4 m).

### Well-known giant
Many woolly mammoths have been discovered frozen in ice with their skin and hair preserved. As a result, scientists know more about this animal than any other Ice Age animal.

WOOLLY MAMMOTHS WERE

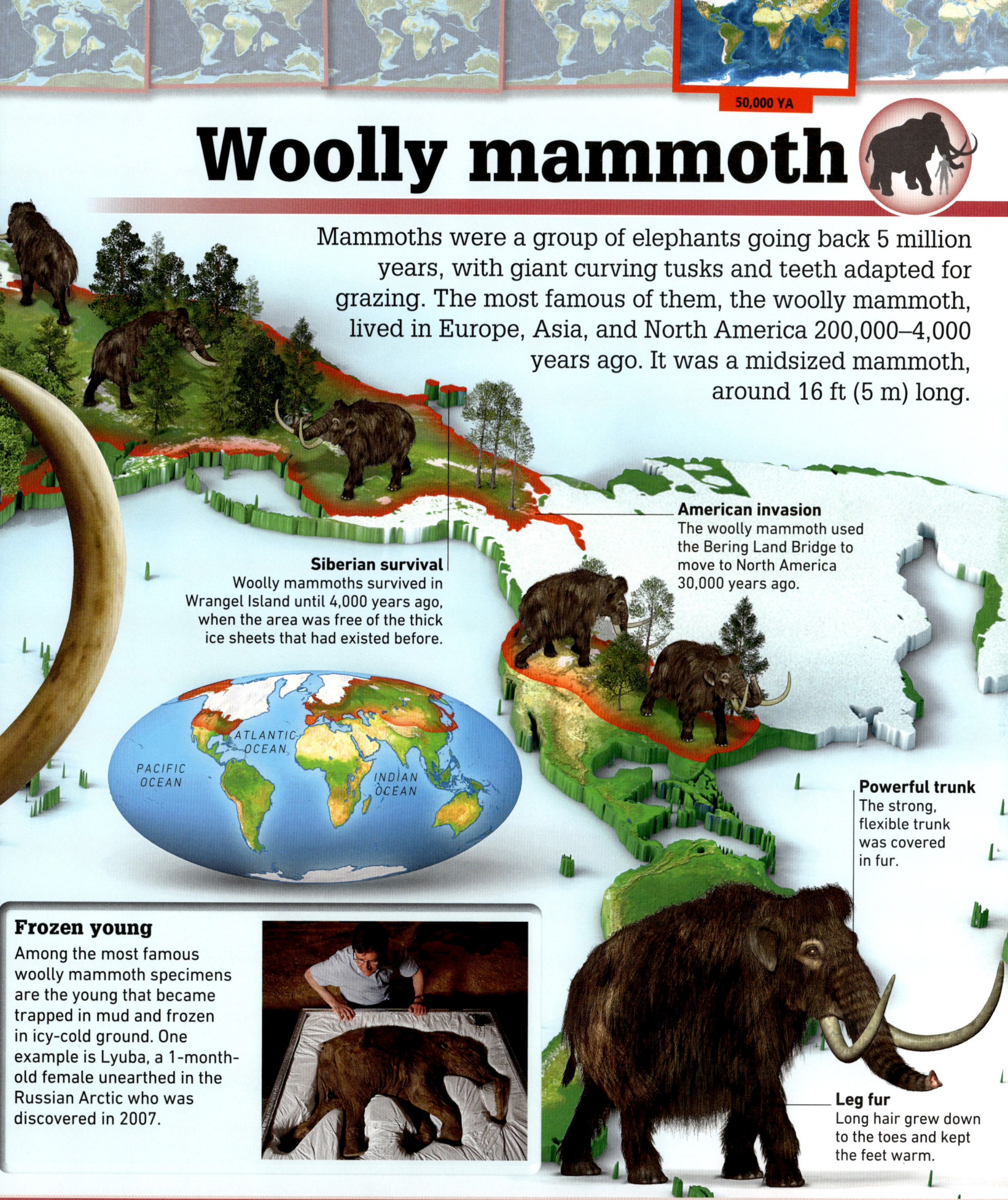

# Woolly mammoth

Mammoths were a group of elephants going back 5 million years, with giant curving tusks and teeth adapted for grazing. The most famous of them, the woolly mammoth, lived in Europe, Asia, and North America 200,000–4,000 years ago. It was a midsized mammoth, around 16 ft (5 m) long.

**American invasion**
The woolly mammoth used the Bering Land Bridge to move to North America 30,000 years ago.

**Siberian survival**
Woolly mammoths survived in Wrangel Island until 4,000 years ago, when the area was free of the thick ice sheets that had existed before.

**Powerful trunk**
The strong, flexible trunk was covered in fur.

**Frozen young**
Among the most famous woolly mammoth specimens are the young that became trapped in mud and frozen in icy-cold ground. One example is Lyuba, a 1-month-old female unearthed in the Russian Arctic who was discovered in 2007.

**Leg fur**
Long hair grew down to the toes and kept the feet warm.

STILL ALIVE WHEN THE EGYPTIAN PYRAMIDS WERE BEING BUILT.

**Hunting in the grasslands**
Unlike some other mammoths that lived in warm habitats, woolly mammoths were cold-climate specialists. Evidence from tools, damaged bones, and ancient art shows that humans hunted this 9.8-ft (3-m) tall shaggy elephant everywhere it roamed.

# Varanus priscus
vah-RAN-us PRISS-cuss

Between 1.6 million and 50,000 years ago, what is known as Australia today was home to many spectacularly gigantic animals. Among these was the 20-ft (6-m) long monitor lizard *Varanus priscus*, originally known by the name *Megalania*.

**Bony crest**
Unlike other monitor lizards, *Varanus priscus* had a raised bony crest on the top of its skull.

**Plain or patterned**
The lizard's scaly skin could have been plain or boldly marked with spots and stripes.

**Toxic bite**
The jaws probably had deadly venom glands.

### Giant monitor lizard
*Varanus priscus* probably resembled the monitor lizards of today—large, long-necked predators. Its huge size meant that it could tackle big prey, such as the giant kangaroos and bear-sized relatives of wombats that shared its habitat.

ESTIMATED TO WEIGH 4,190 LB

**Weighty tail**
Some experts think that *Varanus priscus* had a shorter, chunkier tail than monitor lizards today.

**Large landmass**
During the Pleistocene, sea levels were lower than today, meaning Australia was bigger and connected by land to New Guinea.

**Shared habitat**
Before the species died out, *Varanus priscus* was thought to have briefly lived alongside Australia's first human settlers.

**Big claws**
Long, curved claws tipped the fingers and toes and would have delivered raking wounds on the bodies of prey.

**A wide range**
Fossils of *Varanus priscus* have been found right across the eastern half of Australia, from Cape York Peninsula in the north to Melbourne in the south.

**Reptile relatives**
The largest lizard species alive today—the Komodo dragon—roamed alongside *Varanus priscus* in prehistoric Australia. Today, Komodo dragons are restricted to just a few Indonesian islands, but would have previously occupied a much larger range.

(1,900 KG), *VARANUS PRISCUS* IS THE BIGGEST EVER KNOWN LAND LIZARD.

# REFERENCE

**Remarkable specimen**
The impressions of feathers can be clearly seen in this beautifully preserved *Archaeopteryx* fossil. With every new find, experts discover more about the prehistoric world.

# Fossilization

We know a lot about ancient dinosaurs, mammoths, and other extinct animals thanks to the remains we call fossils. But how do the remnants of a once-living plant, animal, or other organism become a fossil? The process requires a very specific set of conditions.

## A slow process

Fossilization is a gradual process. Bones, leaves, and other remains can take thousands or millions of years to become fossilized. These four stages show how a dinosaur fossil forms, from the animal's death and preservation to its eventual discovery.

**Rising oceans**
Changes in sea levels can result in areas that were once dry land to become flooded by seawater.

**Fossilized flora**
Complete trees only become fossils under unusual circumstances, but leaves, seeds, cones, and fruit are more often preserved.

**Violent lives**
Some dinosaurs, even this *Tyrannosaurus*, may have been killed by other predators, only for their fossils to be discovered millions of years later.

**Safe skeleton**
Still conditions and few scavengers make some lakes and seas the ideal place for fossils to form.

**Sediment builds**
New layers of sediment constantly build up on seafloors, causing new fossils to form.

**Sunken remains**
A dead creature in the water will eventually sink to the bottom and may become buried in the sediment.

**Uncovering the past**
Millions of fossils await discovery. Every year, fossil hunters and paleontologists uncover many more.

Recently formed soft layers of sand and mud

Compressed, hardened sediment layers

Old, flattened rock layers

**Death and decay**
When an animal dies, its remains are usually eaten by scavengers. Some animals, however, end up in places where they become preserved, such as in a lake or ocean.

**Buried in mud**
If the remains are quickly buried by sand or mud, they can be preserved from scavengers. Most fossils form on lakebeds and seafloors.

**Time passes**
More sediment piles on top as time passes. Millions of years later, rising sea levels flood the area with sea water. The remains flatten and harden into fossils.

**Fossil discovery**
Layers of rock move and are worn away as continents shift and water and wind erode the land. Some fossils eventually become exposed.

# Fossil types

Fossils form in several different ways. Many fossils are the hard parts of animals or plants that have been buried, preserved, and turned to stone. More rarely, the soft parts can be preserved. Sometimes, the impressions that animal feet or shells have made in the ground may become fossilized.

**Soft parts**
Dead animals can be buried so quickly that scavengers do not destroy the soft parts. This skin of this coelacanth fossil is visible. In some fossils, even muscles and organs remain.

**Tough remains**
The most familiar fossils are of hard remains. These include the preserved bones and teeth of dinosaurs such as this *Triceratops*, mammals, and the tough outer shells of other creatures like mollusks.

**Stuck in amber**
Trees release a sticky liquid resin that fossilizes into amber. This substance is capable of preserving insects, such as this fly. Fruit, hair, and feathers can also be preserved in amber.

**Trace fossils**
Animals often leave traces of their activity on sand, soil, or mud. If covered quickly by sediment, these impressions can be fossilized. Here, we can see dinosaur footprints in the Morrison Formation, Colorado.

**Mold and cast**
This trilobite (an ancient sea creature) was buried in mud that turned to rock, preserving a mold of the animal's shape. Over time, more mud filled the mold and hardened to create a cast with the same shape as the trilobite.

# Early fossils and hunters

People have found fossils since the beginning of human existence, although they did not always understand what they were. It was not until the 18th century that experts realized fossils were the remains of ancient living things.

## Unknown objects

Before paleontologists started to study fossils, people struggled to explain what they were and where they came from. Some people thought they were plants or animals that had been turned instantly to stone. Others created stories about how they were formed. The Ancient Chinese, for example, thought that dinosaur fossils were the bones of dragons.

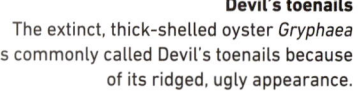

**Devil's toenails**
The extinct, thick-shelled oyster *Gryphaea* is commonly called Devil's toenails because of its ridged, ugly appearance.

## Mary Anning

One of the most important early fossil collectors was Mary Anning of Lyme Regis in southern England. In the early 19th century, Anning discovered the first complete fossil remains of the marine reptiles called plesiosaurs and ichthyosaurs, as well as the first pterosaur. She wrote about her findings to the leading experts of the day.

**Pioneering scientist**
Mainly self-taught, Anning kept detailed notes about her remarkable discoveries. She also sold fossils to make a living.

## Finding fossils

Our knowledge of dinosaurs and other prehistoric animals has grown with the discovery of fossils. From their finds, scientists can piece together a fossilized animal to learn about its appearance. However, early attempts to do this were based on incomplete fossils and resulted in mistakes. For example, it took decades before experts confirmed that *Velociraptor* had feathers.

## The first paleontologists

The earliest paleontologists of the 17th and 18th centuries were confronted with new kinds of animals unlike anything they had seen before. They already had studied the anatomy and biology of living animals, which helped them to understand the fossils they were examining.

**Georges Cuvier**
Known as the "father of paleontology," French naturalist Georges Cuvier was an expert on animal anatomy and an important early expert in interpreting the remains of fossils.

## Bone wars
During the late 19th century, people rushed to discover new fossils, especially those of the giant dinosaurs, and have them shipped to museums. In the United States, rival teams led by the scientists Othniel Marsh (standing in the middle, above) and Edward Cope raced to get to new sites first. This period is known as the "Bone Wars."

## Modern techniques
Advances in technology have allowed experts today to piece together fossils using computers. Information from X-rays and Computerized Tomography (CT) scans is combined to build up images of the insides of fossils. As a result, paleontologists have a greater understanding of ancient animal anatomy and biology. Once a digital model exists, experts can examine the fossil without the need to handle the physical object.

**Computer modeling**
Fossils can now be moved around and examined in digital space rather than in the real world. This is especially useful for large, heavy fossils. This researcher is creating a digital image of a dinosaur's foot and claw.

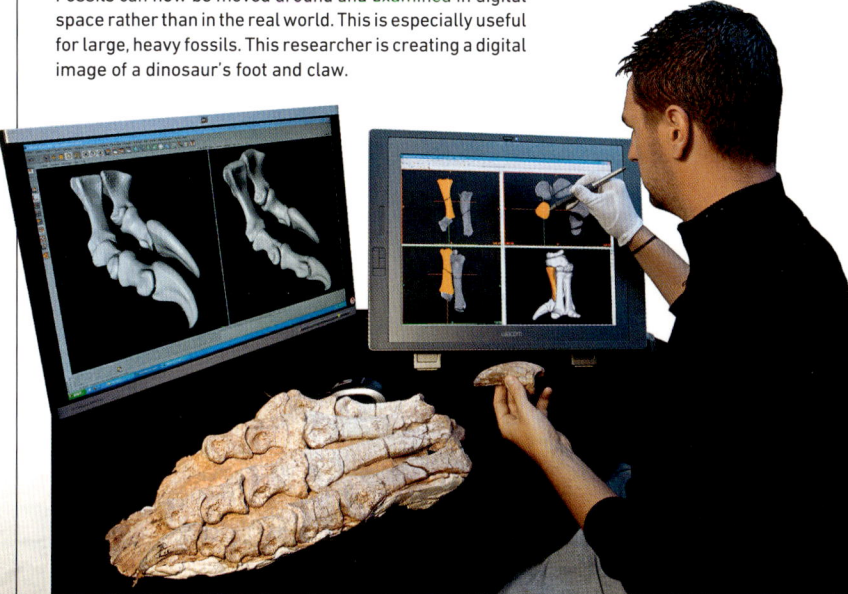

**Dinosaur dig**
The techniques used to take fossils out of the ground have not changed much over the years. Paleontologists require great skill and strong tools to dig up fossils. Here, two experts painstakingly unearth fossils of a prehistoric elephant in Indonesia.

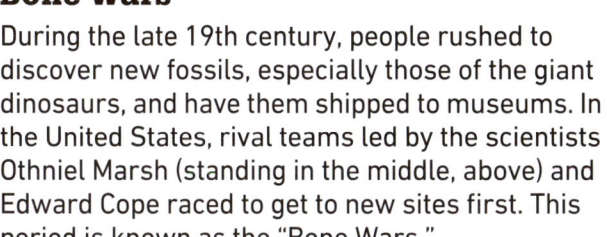

# Mass extinctions

On five occasions, major disasters have caused large numbers of living things to disappear entirely, including whole groups of plants and animals. These disasters are called mass extinction events. Their causes vary, from dramatic climate change to the impact of a comet, or a combination of factors.

## End Ordovician

One of the most devastating mass extinction events was at the end of the Ordovician, about 443 million years ago. Around 85 percent of all ocean-dwelling animals became extinct, including crustaceanlike trilobites. The main cause of this event was probably a sudden cooling of the planet, which resulted in a huge drop in sea levels and a loss of coastal habitats.

*Echinarachnius*
Some ocean animals, such as this modern sea urchin, evolved in the Ordovician and survived.

## End Permian

The largest mass extinction event of all happened 252 million years ago at the end of the Permian. Around 96 percent of animal species died out. The event was so catastrophic that it has been called "The Great Dying." In the seas, many invertebrate groups disappeared. On land, insect and vertebrate groups also became extinct. The cause of the event was probably the release of massive quantities of basalt and volcanic gases in modern-day Siberia.

*Xenacanthus*
The Permian extinction was devastating. The sharklike *Xenacanthus* was one of the few species to survive.

## End Devonian

The Devonian mass extinction occurred around 358 million years ago. This extreme extinction event led to the loss of 70–80 percent of the world's animal species. Its cause is uncertain, but some possible explanations include changing sea levels, a cooling climate, and the impact of a comet.

*Pterichthyodes*
Numerous fish were affected by this extinction. *Pterichthyodes* is a member of the extinct group called placoderms.

*Oxynoticeras*
In the oceans, shelled ammonites became extinct during this period. Ammonite shells are among the most abundant of Mesozoic fossils, and hundreds of species are known.

## End Cretaceous

The most famous extinction happened 65.5 million years ago at the end of the Cretaceous. Because the symbol for Cretaceous is K and the symbol for the following Paleogene is Pg, the event is often called the K-Pg event. About 80 percent of animal species died out, including marine invertebrates and all dinosaurs except birds. The impact of an asteroid or comet was probably the main reason for the extinction, but changing climates caused by volcanic gas may have also contributed.

## End Triassic

Around 201 million years ago, the end of the Triassic was marked by another mass extinction event. Around half of all animals died out, including giant amphibians, reef-building invertebrates, and many mollusks and marine reptiles. This extinction involved two or three episodes that happened over 18 million years. Major changes in climate—both rapid warming and cooling—is thought to be the main factor behind the extinction. This dangerous climatic pattern was most likely caused by high volcanic activity creating an increase in the release of volcanic gases. The extinction of several major reptile groups probably allowed dinosaurs to rise to dominance in the Jurassic.

*Plateosaurus*
Several groups of dinosaurs such as primitive sauropodomorphs, which includes *Plateosaurus*, were badly affected by the extinction.

## Current extinction

We are in the early stages of a sixth mass extinction. This time, it is not geological events or rocks from space that are killing things, but humans. We are destroying wild space, polluting landscapes, changing the climate, and eating living things into extinction. Unless changes are made, huge numbers of living things will disappear forever.

**Battered Earth**
Giant rocks from space have collided with Earth on many occasions, sometimes with catastrophic effect. 65.5 million years ago, an object 6.2 miles (10 km) wide crashed into the Gulf of Mexico, causing a huge explosion.

# Glossary

**Ammonite**
An extinct marine mollusk with a coiled shell and long tentacles.

**Amphibian**
A vertebrate animal that emerges from an egg as a tadpole and lives in water before changing into an air-breathing adult, such as a frog or a newt. Amphibians can live both on land and in water.

**Ankylosaurid**
A type of ankylosaur with a bony tail club that the animal used as a weapon.

**Ankylosaurs**
A group of dinosaurs that have armored bodies covered in bony plates.

**Archosaurs**
A group of reptiles that included dinosaurs, as well as the extinct relatives of crocodiles and alligators and pterosaurs. Today, the group includes modern crocodilians and birds.

**Arid**
Having little or no rainfall. Often used to describe a very dry environment.

**Azhdarchids**
A group of huge pterosaurs, common in the Late Cretaceous.

**Binocular vision**
The ability to see an object with two eyes, as humans do. Like us, an animal with binocular vision can see in 3-D.

**Biped**
An animal that moves on two legs.

**Browse**
To feed on the leaves of trees and shrubs.

**Cambrian**
A period in the Paleozoic Era that began 541 million years ago and ended 485 million years ago.

**Carboniferous**
A period in the Paleozoic Era that began 358 million years ago and ended 298 million years ago.

**Carnivore**
An animal that eats meat.

**Cenozoic Era**
The era that followed the Mesozoic, or the "age of the dinosaurs," which started 66 million years ago and continues in the present day.

**Ceratopsians**
A group of plant-eating dinosaurs, including *Triceratops*, that often had horns on their heads or bony frills at the back of the skull.

**Conifer**
A type of tree, often evergreen, with small, tough, needlelike leaves.

**Cretaceous**
A period of the Mesozoic Era that began 145 million years ago and ended 66 million years ago.

**Crocodilian**
An archosaur in the same group as modern crocodiles, alligators, caimans, and gharials, as well as their closest extinct relatives.

**Crurotarsans**
A group of reptiles that includes the crocodilians, as well as their extinct relatives.

**Cycad**
A type of tropical plant that has a broad crown of leaves and looks like, but is not related to, palm trees.

**Dental battery**
The arrangement of small, interlocking teeth, seen in some herbivorous dinosaurs that helped grind up tough plant matter.

**Devonian**
A period in the Paleozoic Era that began 419 million years ago and ended 358 million years ago.

**Display**
Behavior by an animal to pass on information to another. Display is commonly used in courtship or to ward off intruders. For example, *Cryolophosaurus*'s crest may have been used to attract potential mates.

**Ecosystem**
A community of living organisms that interact with each other and with their surrounding environment in a particular way.

**Environment**
The natural surroundings of an animal or a plant.

**Era**
A long span of geological time, such as the Mesozoic, that marks a particular division in the history of life. Eras are often made up of several shorter divisions of time called periods.

**Evolution**
The process by which animals and plants gradually change over time.

**Extinction**
The permanent dying out of a species, leaving no remaining individuals anywhere on Earth. Sometimes, several species or groups have become extinct at the same time.

**Fern**
A primitive type of nonflowering plant with leafy fronds and long stems that grows in damp places.

**Flightless**
Lacking the ability to fly. The term is used for animals belonging to a group of birds or insects in which the majority of species are capable of flight.

**Floodplain**
A flat area beside a river where sediment, carried by the water, has been deposited during high tides or seasonal floods.

**Fossil**
The preserved remains or traces of a prehistoric animal or plant that has been rapidly buried and turned to stone. Trace fossils can include tracks and footprints, nests, and droppings.

**Fossilization**
The process by which living plants or animals turn into fossils.

**Ginkgo**
A tall, nonflowering tree with semicircular leaves.

**Hadrosaurs**
A group of plant-eating dinosaurs that evolved complex sets of teeth, called dental batteries, especially adapted for browsing.

**Herbivore**
An animal that eats only plants.

**Heterodont**
Describing an animal that possesses two or more differently shaped sets of teeth in its jaws, such as sharp teeth for cutting and molars for chewing.

**Horsetail**
An ancient, water-loving plant that dates back to the Devonian period. It has an upright stem and thin leaves and produces spores instead of seeds.

**Ichthyosaur**
A prehistoric marine reptile that resembled a modern dolphin.

**Jurassic**
A period of the Mesozoic Era when dinosaurs dominated the land. It began 201 million years ago and ended 145 million years ago.

**Keratin**
A tough, fibrous protein that makes up hair, claws, horns, scales, and feathers.

**Lagoon**
A shallow body of salty water, often separated from the ocean by a coral reef.

**Marginocephalians**
A group of dinosaurs that included horned animals such as *Triceratops* and the massively thick-skulled *Pachycephalosaurus*.

**Marine reptile**
A reptile that lives in the ocean. The term also refers to plesiosaurs, ichthyosaurs, and mosasaurs, many of which became extinct at the end of the Cretaceous.

# Glossary

**Mass extinction**
An event or series of events that causes many types of life to die out within a short geological timespan.

**Mesozoic Era**
An era that spans from the Triassic, 252 million years ago, to the Cretaceous, 66 million years ago. It is sometimes referred to as the "age of the dinosaurs."

**Mosasaurs**
A group of large to gigantic ocean-going lizards that lived in oceans worldwide during the Cretaceous. They had paddles, tail-fins, and scaly bodies.

**Nodosaurid**
A type of ankylosaur that was covered in spikes and had bony shields over its hips, but did not have the tail club typical of the ankylosaurid group.

**Omnivore**
An animal that eats both plants and meat.

**Optic lobes**
Parts of the brain that process what an animal sees, such as shapes.

**Ordovician**
A period in the Paleozoic Era that began 485 million years ago and ended 443 million years ago.

**Organism**
A living thing.

**Ornithischian**
Belonging to one of the two major groups of dinosaurs. They are also known as "bird-hipped" dinosaurs.

**Ornithomimosaurs**
A group of dinosaurs that looked similar to modern ostriches and were adapted for running. Ornithomimosaurs possessed a beak, and most were toothless.

**Ornithopods**
A group of ornithischian (bird-hipped) dinosaurs that have birdlike feet. They include *Iguanodon* and the hadrosaurs.

**Osteoderms**
Bony plates embedded in the skin, making up the armor of some dinosaurs, including *Ankylosaurus*, and seen in modern animals such as crocodiles and alligators.

**Pachycephalosaurs**
A group of herbivorous dinosaurs with thick, domed skulls.

**Paleogene**
A period of the Cenozoic Era, starting 66 million years ago and ending 23 million years ago.

**Paleontologist**
A scientist who studies fossils and looks for evidence of ancient life.

**Paleozoic**
The era that came before the "age of the dinosaurs," starting 541 million years ago and ending 252 million years ago.

**Pangea**
A supercontinent made up of all of Earth's land surfaces joined together. It had formed by the Late Paleozoic Era.

**Period**
A unit of geological time that is part of an era.

**Permian**
A period in the Paleozoic Era that began 298 million years ago and ended 252 million years ago.

**Plesiosaurs**
A group of prehistoric marine reptiles that lived during the Mesozoic Era. All plesiosaurs had four winglike paddles and a short tail. Many had long, flexible necks, while others had short necks and long jaws.

**Precambrian**
A huge span of time that came before the Paleozoic Era and includes the Hadean, Archean, and Proterozoic periods. It started at the creation of Earth, 4.6 billion years ago, and ended at the Cambrian, 541 million years ago.

**Predator**
An animal that hunts and eats other animals.

**Prey**
An animal that is hunted as food by another animal.

**Prosauropod**
A commonly used name for one of several species of early, long-necked, plant-eating dinosaurs. The prosauropods did not form a true scientific group.

**Pterosaurs**
The family of flying reptiles found throughout the Mesozoic Era.

**Quadruped**
An animal that moves around on all four limbs.

**Rauisuchians**
A group of meat-eating archosaurs that moved on four legs and were mostly very large. They were the leading predators of the Triassic.

**Reptiles**
A group of animals that include turtles, lizards, crocodiles, snakes, dinosaurs, and pterosaurs.

**Saurischian**
Belonging to one of the two major groups of dinosaurs. Saurischians are often referred to as "lizard-hipped" dinosaurs.

**Sauropod**
The group of mostly gigantic, four-legged, long-necked dinosaurs that includes *Diplodocus* and *Brachiosaurus*. They evolved from the earlier sauropodomorphs known as prosauropods.

**Sauropodomorphs**
The large group of saurischian dinosaurs that includes the prosauropods and sauropods.

**Scavenger**
An animal that lives on the remains of dead animals and other scraps.

**Sclerotic ring**
A ring of bone embedded in the eyeball of some vertebrate animals that supports the eye.

**Silurian**
A period in the Paleozoic Era that began 443 million years ago and ended 419 million years ago.

**Spatulate**
Having a broad, flat end. The term is often used to describe the teeth of herbivorous animals.

**Species**
A particular type of organism that is able to breed with other individuals of the same kind.

**Stegosaurs**
A group of dinosaurs that often possessed broad plates or spines along their backs and tails.

**Supercontinent**
A gigantic landmass made up of several continents that have collided together.

**Territory**
The region of an animal's habitat that it defends from rival animals, usually of its own kind.

**Tetrapod**
A vertebrate animal with four limbs, or descends from ancestors that had four limbs. Today's snakes and whales are tetrapods.

**Theropod**
One of the two major groups of saurischian (lizard-hipped) dinosaurs. Theropods are often carnivorous and bipedal, and include modern-day birds.

**Thyreophorans**
A group of dinosaurs that includes the armored ankylosaurs and stegosaurs.

**Titanosaurs**
A group of sauropod dinosaurs that were often of immense size. Some of the titanosaurs were the largest land animals ever to exist.

**Triassic**
A period of the Mesozoic Era that began 252 million years ago and ended 201 million years ago.

**Tyrannosaurids**
A group of large, meat-eating theropods that included *Tyrannosaurus rex*. Predators of this kind evolved in the Late Cretaceous and had huge jaws adapted for bone-crunching bites.

**Vegetation**
Plant material.

**Vertebrae**
The bones forming the backbone of a vertebrate animal.

**Vertebrate**
An animal—such as a dinosaur, mammal, bird, and fish—with a backbone made up of vertebrae.

# Index

Page numbers in **bold** type refer to main entries

## A
*Acristavus* 16–17
*Adelolophus* 16–17
air sacs 55, 97, 126
*Albertosaurus* **36–37**, 49
*Allosaurus* 20–21, 26–27, **28–29**, 49, 89
ammonites 154
Andes Mountains 56, 96
ankles 19, 55, 82
*Ankylosaurus* 19, **38–39**, 49
Anning, Mary 152
Antarctica 16, 95, 122, 123, 127
Appalachia 34, 36
aquatic reptiles 91, 92, 98
*Archaeopteryx* 66–67, **74–75**, 88, 89, 148–149
Archean Era 8–9
Argentina 53, 60, 64, 65, 141
*Argentinosaurus* **60–61**, 65
armored skin 24, 38, 39, 81
arms 68, 76, 96
 theropods 22, 31, 57, 63, 79, 123
asteroids 16, 154, 155
Atlantic Ocean 14, 16, 56, 97, 137, 138
Australia 123, 126, 127, 128, 129, 146, 147

## B
*Baryonyx* **78–79**
*Basilosaurus* **138–139**
beaks 54, 95, 128, 137
 duck bills 35
 parrotlike 45, 109, 126
*Beipiaosaurus* 112–113
Belgium 77, 89
Bering Land Bridge 143
birds 14–15, 55, 74, 108, 114, 137
body temperature 25, 57, 111
brains 25, 32, 41, 108, 122

Brazil 64, 65, 141
Brown, Barnum 48
burrows 94, 129

## C
calls 34, 126
Cambrian Period 9, 10
camouflage 109
Canada 36, 48–49
Carboniferous Period 9, 11
carcharodontosaurids 56
*Carnotaurus* 50–51, **62–63**, 65
Carolini, Rubén 56
cats 140–141
Cenozoic Era 8–9
ceratopsians 19
*Ceratosaurus* **30–31**, 49, 89
*Chilesaurus* **54–55**, 65
China 95, 106, 111, 117, 152
 fossil finds 109, 115, 118–119
claws 37, 52, 147
 theropods 29, 36, 41, 52, 57, 74, 79, 110, 116
climate change 154–155
club tails 38, 39
coats 141, 142
*Coelophysis* 6–7, 15, **22–23**, 49
Colombia 64, 134
Cope, Edward 49, 153
*Corythosaurus* **34–35**, 49
crests 32, 84, 146
 ornithopods 34, 35
 theropods 82, 99, 123, 126
Cretaceous Period 9, 16–17, 154
crocodilians 18, 19
*Cryolophosaurus* **122–123**, 124–125, 131
Cuvier, Georges 152

## D
Dashanpu Formation, China 106, 119
defenses 25, 38, 46, 76, 106
*Desmatosuchus* 6–7
Devonian Period 9, 11, 154

*Diabloceratops* 17
dicynodont therapsids 94
digestive system 38, 60, 94
digital models 153
*Dilophosaurus* 14–15
Dinosaur Cove, Australia 129
Dinosauriforms 18
*Diplodocus* 20–21, **32–33**, 49
dorsal plates 25, 32
droppings 37

## E
eggs 60
Egypt 102
*Ekrixinatosaurus* 58–59
elephants 97, 143
*Elosuchus* 100
England 77, 78
Eocene Period 9
*Eoraptor* 64, 65
eukaryotes 8, 10
Euramerica 11
extinctions 10–11, 137, 154–155
eyes 34, 41, 72, 117, 129

## F
feathers 37, 75, 83 108, 111, 114, 117, 129, 136
feet 55, 83, 93, 123
fingers 52, 85, 127
fins 72, 73
flight 75, 114, 137
footprints 151
fossils 150–151, 152–153
 Africa 102–103
 Asia 118–119
 Australasia and Antarctica 130–131
 Europe 88–89
 North America 48–49
 South America 64–65
frills 45
fur 136, 143

## G
*Gastornis* **136–137**
Germany 75, 88, 89
*Giganotosaurus* **56–57**, 58–59, 65
*Giraffatitan* **96–97**, 102
*Glacialisaurus* 124–125, 131
Gondwana 11, 14, 16, 73, 123, 127
gular pouch 83
guts 37, 60, 81, 94

## H
Hadean Era 8–9
hadrosaurs 17, 34, 35
hair 142
hands 52, 94, 110, 127
*Harpymimus* 83
Hateg Island 85
*Hatzegopteryx* **84–85**, 86–87
hearing 138
*Herrerasaurus* **52–53**, 65
Himalayan Mountains 109
Hispanic Corridor 73
Hockley, Kevin 134
Holocene Period 9
horns 28, 31, 62, 108
 *Triceratops* 44, 45
humans 8, 144, 147

## I
ice ages 10, 11, 92, 142–143
ichthyosaurs 18, 72, 152
*Iguanodon* **76–77**, 89
India 16, 109, 119, 139
invertebrates 10, 13, 15, 17
 extinctions 154–155
Iran 118
Italy 89

## JK
jaws 52, 54, 85, 92, 135
 marine animals 73, 138
 theropods 28, 36, 41, 57, 63, 82, 98, 99
Jurassic Period 9, 14–15
K-Pg event 154

# Index

Kazakhstan 119
Kenya 103

## L

Laramidia 34, 36
Laurasia 14, 73
*Leaellynasaura* **128–129**
legs 19, 136, 140
  ornithopods 45, 47, 76
  sauropods 68, 96
  theropods 37, 40, 78, 83, 99
*Liliensternus* 12–13
lizards 19, 147
*Lystrosaurus* **94–95**
*Lythronax* 16–17

## MN

Madagascar 103
mammals 8, 17, 94
mammoths 142–143, 144–145
Mantell, Gideon and Mary 77
*Marasuchus* 18
Marginocephallans 19
Marsh, Othniel 25, 49, 153
mass extinctions 10–11, 137, 154–155
meat eaters 52, 62, 79, 122
  tyrannosaurs 37, 41, 110
*Megalania* 146
*Mesosaurus* 90–91, **92–93**
Mesozoic Era 8–9
Mexico 40, 48–49
*Microraptor* **114–115**, 119
Miocene Period 9
Mongolia 109, 117, 119
monitor lizard 132–133, 146–147
Morocco 102
Morrison Formation 29, 48–49, 151
multicellular life 8, 10
muscles 28, 61, 63, 135
*Muttaburrasaurus* 120–121, **126–127**, 131
*Nanuqsaurus* 48
necks 23, 55, 99, 137
  sauropods 33, 60, 69, 96, 106
nests 60
New Zealand 131
Niger 102
noses 30, 31, 39, 93, 99, 126

## O

Oligocene Period 9
*Ophthalmosaurus* **72–73**
Ordovician Period 9, 10, 154
ornithischians 18, 54, 82, 83, 110
*Ornithomimus* 49
ornithopods 19, 77, 127
Osborn, H. F. 48
osteoderms 30, 38, 39, 81, 107

## P

*Pachycelphalosaurus* 19, **46–47**, 49
paddles 72, 93
Paleocene Period 9
paleontologists 152–153
Paleozoic Era 8–9
Pangea 11, 12, 22, 69, 92
Pannotia 10
*Pelecanimimus* **82–83**
Permian Period 9, 11, 154
Peru 64
placoderms 154
plant eaters 44, 47, 54, 80–81, 136
  ornithopods 35, 77, 126
  sauropods 13, 32, 61, 68, 96, 107
plant life 33, 63, 92, 111
*Plateosaurus* 12–13, **68–69**, 70–71
plates 25, 39, 81
Pleistocene Period 9, 147
plesiosaurs 152
Pliocene Period 9
*Polacanthus* **80–81**, 89
Portugal 25, 89
*Postosuchus* 6–7
prokaryotes 9, 10
Proterozoic Era 8–9
*Protoceratops* 117, 119
*Psittacosaurus* **104–105**, **108–109**, 110, 112–113, 119
pterosaurs 18, 70–71, 75, 84, 86, 152

## QR

quills 108
reptiles 11, 13, 15, 18, 147
*Rhamphinion* 14

Rocky Mountains 47
Russia 89, 118–119

## S

saber-tooth cats 141
*Sarahsaurus* 14–15
saurischians 18
sauropods 19
*Saurosuchus* 53
scales 24, 31, 77, 146
sea levels 10, 34, 36, 39, 44, 47, 54, 63, 137, 147, 150, 154
sharks 56, 72
*Shunosaurus* **106–107**
Silurian Period 9, 10
skulls 32, 44, 46, 84, 135
  ornithopods 34, 126
  theropods 28, 62, 98, 99, 110
*Smilodon* **140–141**
snakes 134
South Africa 95, 102
Spain 78, 80, 82, 83, 88
speed 63, 68, 83, 117, 128
spikes 24, 46, 76, 81, 106, 107
spines 32, 60, 98
*Spinosaurus* **98–99**, 100–101, 102, 103
*Stegosaurus* 19, **24–25**, 26–27, 49
swamp habitats 34, 40, 70, 82
synapsids 11, 15

## T

tails 24, 47, 53, 54, 108, 128
  clubbed 38, 39
  nondinosaurs 139, 140, 147
  sauropods 33, 69, 97, 106
  theropods 29, 30, 41, 63, 75, 79, 111
Tanzania 97, 102
teeth 54, 84, 92, 95, 127, 151
  nondinosaurs 135, 138, 140
  sauropods 32, 68, 97, 107
  theropods 23, 28, 30, 41, 53, 56, 79, 82, 83, 98, 116, 122
Tendaguru Formation, Tanzania 97, 102
Thailand 119
theropods 19
thyreophorans 19
*Titanoboa* **134–135**

tongues 38, 80
Triassic Period 9, 12–13, 155
*Triceratops* 42–43, **44–45**, 151
trilobites 151, 154
tropical habitats 44, 135, 136
Tunisia 102
tusks 95, 142
*Tyrannosaurus* 15–16, 37, **40–41**, 42–43, 48, 49, 110

## UV

United Kingdom 88, 89
United States of America 138, 140
  fossils in 29, 48–49, 153
*Varanus priscus* 132–133, **146–147**
*Velociraptor* 74, **116–117**, 119, 152
venom 146
vertebrae 60, 97, 98, 128
volcanoes 53, 54, 115, 128, 154–155

## W

water-dwelling dinosaurs 31, 99, 134, 138
Western Interior Seaway 34, 36, 39, 44, 47
wetland habitats 31, 34, 78, 85
whales 138–139
wings 74, 84–85, 114–115, 137
wingspans 85, 86, 115
woolly mammoth **142–143**, 144–145
wrists 77, 114, 116

## XY

X-rays 153
*Yutyrannus* **110–111**, 112–113

# Acknowledgments

**Dorling Kindersley would like to thank:**
Sarah Edwards, Vicky Richards, and Jenny Sich for editorial assistance; Kit Lane and Shahid Mahmood for design assistance; Elizabeth Wise for the index; Caroline Stamps for proofreading.

**Smithsonian Enterprises:**
Kealy Gordon, Product Development Manager; Ellen Nanney, Senior Manager, Licensed Publishing; Jill Corcoran, Director, Licensed Publishing; Brigid Ferraro, Vice President, Consumer and Education Products; Carol LeBlanc, Senior Vice President, Consumer and Education Products

**Reviewer for the Smithsonian:**
Matthew T. Miller, Museum Technician (Collections Volunteer Manager), Department of Paleobiology, National Museum of Natural History

**The publisher would like to thank the following for their kind permission to reproduce their photographs:**
(Key: a-above; b-below/bottom; c-centre; f-far; l-left; r-right; t-top)

**6-7 James Kuether**. **11 Alamy Stock Photo:** Angela DeCenzo (bc). **Science Photo Library:** Chris Butler (br). **12-13 James Kuether:** (b). **13 Getty Images:** Albert Lleal / Minden Pictures (ca). **Science Photo Library:** Jaime Chirinos (cr). **14-15 James Kuether:** (b). **16-17 James Kuether:** (b). **18 Dorling Kindersley:** James Kuether (cl). **20-21 James Kuether. 22-147 plants by Xfrog, www.xfrog.com:** (Trees, bushes on maps). **22 Dorling Kindersley:** State Museum of Nature, Stuttgart (bc). **25 Dorling Kindersley:** Senckenberg Nature Museum, Frankfurt (cr). **26-27 James Kuether**. **28 Alamy Stock Photo:** age fotostock (bl). **29 123RF.com:** Dave Willman / dcwcreations (br). **30 Getty Images:** Francesco Tomasinelli / AGF / UIG (cla). **31 iStockphoto.com:** ivan-96 (cr). **32 Science Photo Library:** Natural History Museum, London (bl). **36 Dorling Kindersley:** Natural History Museum, London (clb). **38 Dorling Kindersley:** Royal Tyrrell Museum of Palaeontology, Alberta, Canada (cla). **41 Dorling Kindersley:** The American Museum of Natural History (crb). **Dreamstime.com:** Peter.wey (br). **42-43 James Kuether. 44 Dorling Kindersley:** Natural History Museum, London (clb). **46 Dorling Kindersley:** Oxford Museum of Natural History (cr). **49 Alamy Stock Photo:** William Mullins (br). **52 Science Photo Library:** Millard H. Sharp (bl). **54 Getty Images:** Eitan Abramovich / AFP (clb). **56 Getty Images:** Independent Picture Service / UIG (clb). **58-59 James Kuether**. **60 Alamy Stock Photo:** Rebecca Jackrel (br). **62 www.skullsunlimited.com:** (bl). **63 Depositphotos Inc:** AndreAnita (br). **65 Getty Images:** Photograph by Michael Schwab (cr). **68 Dorling Kindersley:** (tl). **70-71 James Kuether**. **72 Alamy Stock Photo:** World History Archive (cla). **74 Alamy Stock Photo:** John MacTavish (br). **75 Getty Images:** Robert Clark / National Geographic (br). **76 Alamy Stock Photo:** The Natural History Museum (bl). **79 Alamy Stock Photo:** Arco Images GmbH (bl). **Dorling Kindersley:** Natural History Museum, London (br). **81 The Trustees of the Natural History Museum, London:** (br). **82 www.eofauna.com:** (clb). **83 Alamy Stock Photo:** Biosphoto (bc). **86-87 Studio 252MYA:** Julio Lacerda. **89 Getty Images:** Olaf Kruger (cra). **92 Alamy Stock Photo:** The Bookworm Collection (bl). **94 123RF.com:** Vladimir Blinov / vblinov (b). **Science Photo Library:** Mauricio Anton (bl). **96 Reuters:** Reinhard Krause (br). **97 123RF.com:** Barisic Zaklina (crb). **98 Alamy Stock Photo:** World History Archive (cl). **100-101 Davide Bonadonna**. **102 Alamy Stock Photo:** Mike P Shepherd (br). **107 Alamy Stock Photo:** The Natural History Museum (bl). **109 Dorling Kindersley:** Natural History Museum, London (br); Senckenberg Gesellshaft Fuer Naturforschugn Museum (bc). **111 Alamy Stock Photo:** Goran Bogicevic (br). **112-113 James Kuether**. **114 Alamy Stock Photo:** Lou-Foto (cl). **116 Science Photo Library:** Dirk Wiersma (br). **117 Louie Psihoyos ©psihoyos.com:** (br). **119 Alamy Stock Photo:** Martin Shields (br). **120-12 James Kuether**. **123 Getty Images:** Kazuhiro Nogi / AFP (cra). **124-125 James Kuether**. **126 Getty Images:** Morales (bl). **127 Alamy Stock Photo:** Richard Cummins (cra). **129 Science Photo Library:** Peter Menzel (crb). **134 Getty Images:** Michael Loccisano (cl). **137 Richtr Jan:** (crb). **138 Alamy Stock Photo:** Roland Bouvier (clb). **141 Alamy Stock Photo:** Scott Camazine (cra). **142 Alamy Stock Photo:** Granger Historical Picture Archive (cl). **143 Rex by Shutterstock:** Matt Dunham / AP (bc). **147 123RF.com:** Andrey Gudkov (br). **151 123RF.com:** Camilo Maranchón García (bl); W.Scott McGill (cb). **Dorling Kindersley:** Natural History Museum, London (tr); Royal Tyrrell Museum of Palaeontology, Alberta, Canada (c); Natural History Museum (br). **152 Alamy Stock Photo:** Pictorial Press Ltd (cra). **Getty Images:** James Thompson / Underwood Archives (bl). **152-153 Alamy Stock Photo:** Reynold Sumayku (b). **153 Alamy Stock Photo:** Science History Images (tl). **Science Photo Library:** Pascal Goetgheluck (cr). **154-155 Science Photo Library:** Mark Garlick (b). **155 123RF.com:** Vladimir Salman (cra)

All other images © Dorling Kindersley
For further information see:
**www.dkimages.com**

# DK WHERE ON EARTH? ATLASES

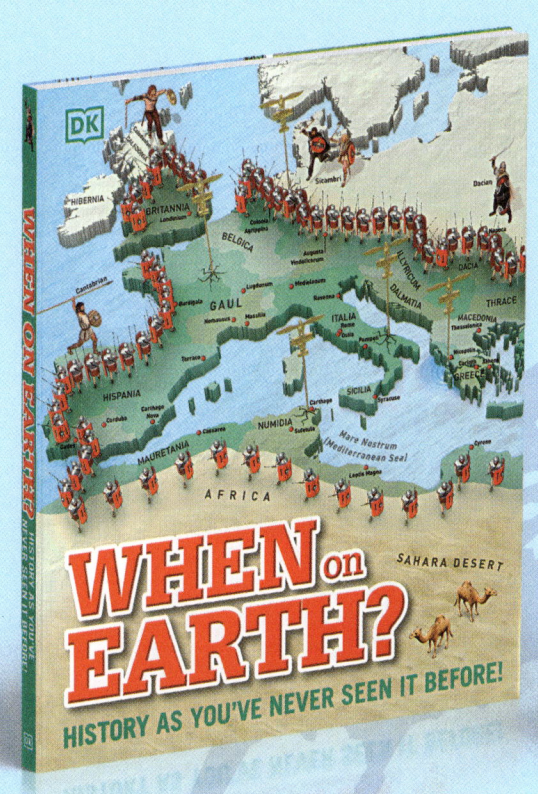

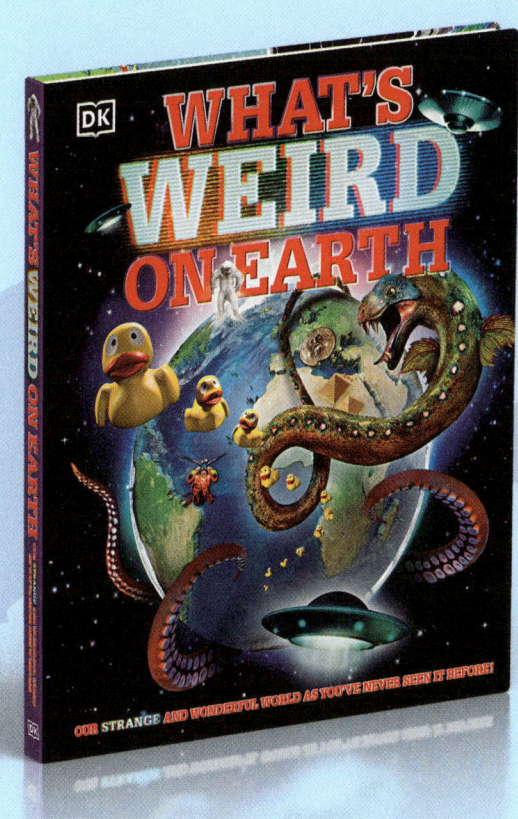

# ANIMAL ATLAS

# ANIMAL ATLAS

Derek Harvey

**Senior Editor** Jenny Sich
**Senior Art Editor** Rachael Grady
**Senior Cartographic Editor** Simon Mumford
**Senior Contributing Editors** Ashwin Khurana, Anna Streiffert-Limerick
**Editor** Kelsie Besaw
**US Editor** Megan Douglass
**Designers** Vanessa Hamilton, Elaine Hewson, Greg McCarthy, Lynne Moulding
**Illustrators** Jon @ KJA Artists, Adam Brackenbury, Adam Benton, Arran Lewis, Kit Lane
**Creative Retoucher** Steve Crozier
**Managing Editor** Francesca Baines
**Managing Art Editor** Philip Letsu
**Production Editor** Gillian Reid
**Production Controller** Sian Cheung
**Jacket Designers** Akiko Kato, Tanya Mehrotra
**DTP Designer** Rakesh Kumar
**Design Development Manager** Sophia MTT
**Picture Research** Myriam Megharbi, Sneha Murchavade, Sakshi Saluja
**Publisher** Andrew Macintyre
**Associate Publishing Director** Liz Wheeler
**Art Director** Karen Self
**Publishing Director** Jonathan Metcalf

This American Box Set Edition, 2024
First American Edition, 2021
Published in the United States by DK Publishing,
a division of Penguin Random House LLC
1745 Broadway, 20th Floor, New York, NY 10019

Copyright © 2021, 2024 Dorling Kindersley Limited
24 25 26 27 28 10 9 8 7 6 5 4 3 2 1
001–341589–Sep/2024

All rights reserved. Without limiting the rights under the copyright reserved above, no part of this publication may be reproduced, stored in or introduced into a retrieval system, or transmitted, in any form, or by any means (electronic, mechanical, photocopying, recording, or otherwise), without the prior written permission of the copyright owner.
Published in Great Britain by Dorling Kindersley Limited

A catalog record for this book
is available from the Library of Congress.
Box Set ISBN 978-0-5938-4501-1
Book ISBN 978-0-7440-2779-2

DK books are available at special discounts when purchased in bulk for sales promotions, premiums, fund-raising, or educational use.
For details, contact: DK Publishing Special Markets,
1745 Broadway, 20th Floor, New York, NY 10019
SpecialSales@dk.com

Printed and bound in the UAE

www.dk.com

# CONTENTS

## A WORLD OF ANIMALS

| | |
|---|---|
| Amazing animals | 10 |
| Where animals live | 12 |
| Global origins | 14 |
| Under threat | 16 |
| Melting ice | 18 |
| Conservation | 20 |

## INVERTEBRATES

| | |
|---|---|
| Invertebrate facts | 24 |
| Giant Pacific octopus | 26 |
| European lobster | 28 |
| Postman butterfly | 30 |
| Plant pollinator | 32 |
| Tarantulas | 34 |
| Common starfish | 36 |

## FISH

| | |
|---|---|
| Fish facts | 40 |
| Sea lamprey | 42 |
| Great white shark | 44 |
| Shallow waters | 46 |
| Steephead parrotfish | 48 |
| Red-bellied piranha | 50 |

## AMPHIBIANS

| | |
|---|---|
| Amphibian facts | 54 |
| Mudpuppy | 56 |
| Mossy frog | 58 |
| Strawberry poison frog | 60 |
| Common toad | 62 |

## REPTILES

| | |
|---|---|
| Reptile facts | 66 |
| Galápagos giant tortoises | 68 |
| Crocodilians | 70 |
| Chameleons | 72 |
| Armored lizard | 74 |
| Green anaconda | 76 |
| Venomous snakes | 78 |

## BIRDS

| | |
|---|---|
| Bird facts | 82 |
| Ostriches | 84 |
| Changing colors | 86 |
| Emperor penguin | 88 |
| Snowy owl | 90 |
| Osprey | 92 |
| A committee of vultures | 94 |
| Blue-and-yellow macaw | 96 |
| Barn swallow | 98 |

## MAMMALS

| | |
|---|---|
| Mammal facts | 102 |
| Egg-laying mammals | 104 |
| Koala | 106 |
| Armadillos | 108 |
| Brown-throated sloth | 110 |
| Elephants | 112 |
| Eurasian red squirrel | 114 |
| Desert rodent | 116 |
| Star-nosed mole | 118 |
| Lemurs | 120 |
| Japanese macaque | 122 |
| Great apes | 124 |
| Orangutans | 126 |
| Indian flying fox | 128 |
| Tiger | 130 |
| Lion | 132 |
| Stealthy lynx | 134 |
| Gray wolf | 136 |
| Bears | 138 |
| Honey badger | 140 |
| Zebras | 142 |
| Rhinos | 144 |
| Hippos | 146 |
| Moose | 148 |
| Humpback whale | 150 |
| Unicorns of the sea | 152 |
| | |
| Glossary | 154 |
| Index | 156 |
| Acknowledgments | 158 |

# Foreword

This atlas of animals is about the living world, from the freezing poles to the tropical equator, from the highest mountain to the deepest sea. But this is no ordinary atlas because it shows where the animals live, as well as what they look like, and the forests, deserts, and oceans that are their homes.

Our planet is a very special part of our solar system: it is the only one with life, and its breathtaking variety should fill us all with wonder. Animals of one kind or another survive almost everywhere on its surface, whether on land or underwater. Scientists have described more than 1.5 million species, and reckon there are many times this number still waiting to be discovered. Some, like the humpback whale or the osprey, range so far and wide that they span the entire globe. Others, like giant tortoises in the Galápagos Islands, live in less space than a single sprawling city. But all animals only succeed in places that supply what they need to survive and produce their babies, and many have very particular requirements. This means that koalas only live in Australia, where they eat eucalyptus leaves and nothing else, and parrotfish only swim in tropical coastal seas where they can munch on coral.

The animals in this book completely depend upon these wild places, but wilderness—the forests, grasslands, even unspoiled oceans—is disappearing. Since humans started building their civilizations

5,000 years ago, nearly two-thirds of the wilderness has gone. Cities have replaced trees, water and air have become polluted, and some animals have been hunted so much that very few are left. Many species have disappeared completely along with the wilderness, and others have been left threatened with extinction. This book tells the story of some of them—but also explains what is being done around the world to help. Today, more people than ever are concerned about the future of planet Earth and its extraordinary variety of animals. These animals are what make our world such an amazing place—we must look after them.

**Derek Harvey**

**Endangered animals**

Where you see the panel below, it means the animals plotted on the maps are assessed by the International Union for Conservation of Nature (IUCN, see p.20) as being near threatened, vulnerable, endangered, or critically endangered. If there is no panel, or a species isn't listed, that means the animal is of least concern (not currently at risk) or has not been assessed by the IUCN.

**ANIMALS IN DANGER**

Lion
- IUCN status: vulnerable
- Population estimate: 20,000–32,000

**Status** — The IUCN category shows how endangered the animal is thought to be.

**Population trend** — An arrow indicates whether the number of animals is rising, falling, or stable.

**Population number** — The number given is a rough estimate. For some species, the number of animals remaining is not known.

# A WORLD OF ANIMALS

# Amazing animals

Earth is teeming with life. Even places inhospitable to humans, such as the deepest oceans or hottest deserts, are alive with extraordinary animals. Wherever on the planet animals live, they have adapted to survive in their habitats.

**Birds**
Warm-blooded bodies and the power of flight mean that feathered birds have reached more parts of the world than any other group of land-living backboned animals, other than humans.

**Reptiles**
Like fish and amphibians, reptiles are cold-blooded, relying on the sun to warm their scaly bodies. They include crocodilians, turtles, lizards, and snakes.

## Variety of life

Animals are classified into major groups with shared characteristics: invertebrates, fish, amphibians, reptiles, birds, and mammals. Some of these groups contain more species than others, but all are represented around the world. Some are more widespread than others, too: invertebrates exist almost everywhere, but reptiles do not inhabit the coldest places and amphibians do not reach remote islands.

Polar bear
Golden eagle
Bee hummingbird
Marine iguana
King cobra
Adélie penguin
Antarctic krill
Housefly
Common toad

**Mammals**
Humans are warm-blooded mammals, but we share this group with thousands of other species. All mammalian mothers produce milk to feed their babies and most mammals are covered in fur.

**Fish**
Half of all vertebrate species (animals with a backbone) are fish. Half live in saltwater oceans and half in freshwater lakes and rivers. They typically have a scaly body, fins for swimming, and gills for breathing underwater.

Sailfish

Ladybug

**Invertebrates**
These animals without a backbone make up the biggest animal group. They include worms, snails, insects, and many more. They live in every place capable of supporting animals.

Cheetah

Monarch butterfly

Oarfish

**Amphibians**
With their moist, scaleless skins, amphibians are mainly found in wet, freshwater habitats. They include frogs, toads, salamanders, newts, and worm-shaped caecilians.

California sea lion

Red-eyed tree frog

## NEW SPECIES

Every year, scientists discover and name new species of animals found across the world, from forests to coral reefs. As exciting as these finds are, experts believe that approximately 90 percent of animal and plant species on Earth remain unknown. Listed below are some of the most recent amazing discoveries.

**Wasp mantis**
Found in the Peruvian Amazon in South America, this praying mantis has a body shape that makes it look like a stinging wasp. First described in 2019, it even moves and walks like a wasp, which helps to keep danger away.

**Wakanda fairy wrasse**
This purple-and-blue fish from an East African coral reef reminded the scientists who first described it of the outfit worn by Marvel's Black Panther. So in 2019 they named it Wakanda, after the superhero's fictional African kingdom.

**Mini frogs**
Scientists who discovered three tiny Madagascan frogs, each smaller than a fingernail, described them in 2019. The three species are some of the smallest frogs found in the world and were called *Mini mum*, *Mini scule* and *Mini ature*.

**Salazar's pit viper**
As fans of the Harry Potter books, the scientists who described this Indian snake in 2020 had a good option to name it. The venomous pit viper was named after the character Salazar Slytherin, who—in the story—could communicate with snakes.

**Alor Myzomela**
Sadly, by the time they are named some new species are already under threat of extinction. Described in 2019, this striking bird—a honeyeater—located in eucalyptus forests on the Indonesian island of Alor is threatened by deforestation.

# Biomes

The same type of habitat, such as a desert or tropical rainforest, can occur in different parts of the world. These habitats—called biomes—look alike, even though different animals may live there. Each color on this map represents a different land biome.

### Tundra
Close to the poles, conditions are so cold that the ground is frozen for much of the year, so few trees can grow. This open landscape, home to animals such as Arctic hares, is called the tundra.

### Mediterranean woodland

Woodland trees with thick, leathery leaves grow in places with warm, dry summers and mild winters, such as in the Mediterranean home of the asp viper, as well as in southern Africa and southern Australia.

### Taiga
Covering the largest land area is a stretch of cold, northern forest called taiga. It is dominated by evergreen coniferous trees, and is home to many animals, such as the wolverine, which range widely south of the Arctic.

### Temperate forest
Much of the forest in this temperate zone has trees that are deciduous, growing leaves in the mild summers and losing them in cold winters. North American porcupines and other animals that live here must cope with seasonal changes.

### Temperate grassland
Grasslands usually grow when conditions are too dry for forest but too wet for desert. Temperate grasslands—home of the prairie chicken—are warm in summer and cold in winter, but stay green all year.

### Tropical grassland
In the tropics, many grasslands are at their greenest during the rainy season. In places such as Africa, they support some of the biggest herds of hoofed mammals, including wildebeest, zebras, and giraffes.

## Ocean habitats

Conditions in ocean habitats are affected mainly by depths: animals living in deeper waters must cope with higher pressures, colder temperatures, and perpetual darkness.

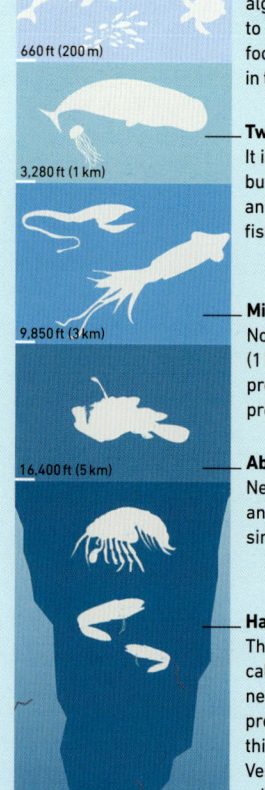

**Sunlit zone** — 660 ft (200 m)
Here there is enough sunlight for algae—the "plants" of the ocean—to grow and support the underwater food chain. Most ocean life is found in the sunlit zone.

**Twilight zone** — 3,280 ft (1 km)
It is too dark for algae to grow here, but just enough light reaches for animals to see. Many predatory fish live in the twilight zone.

**Midnight zone** — 9,850 ft (3 km)
No light reaches below 3,280 ft (1 km), so many animals here produce their own light through a process called bioluminescence.

**Abyssal zone** — 16,400 ft (5 km)
Near the cold, dark ocean floor, animals mostly rely on food sinking down from above.

**Hadal zone** — 32,800 ft (10 km)
The ocean floor contains cracks called trenches that descend to nearly 32,800 ft (10 km). The pressures and temperatures in this zone are at their most extreme. Very specialized animals have adapted to live here.

A WORLD OF ANIMALS | 13

# Where animals live

The world is made up of a variety of different habitats, from magnificent tropical forests and freezing, treeless tundras on land to colorful, sunlit coral reefs of the seas and cold, dark ocean depths. Each habitat has its own unique climate and supports its own ecosystem of plant and animal life.

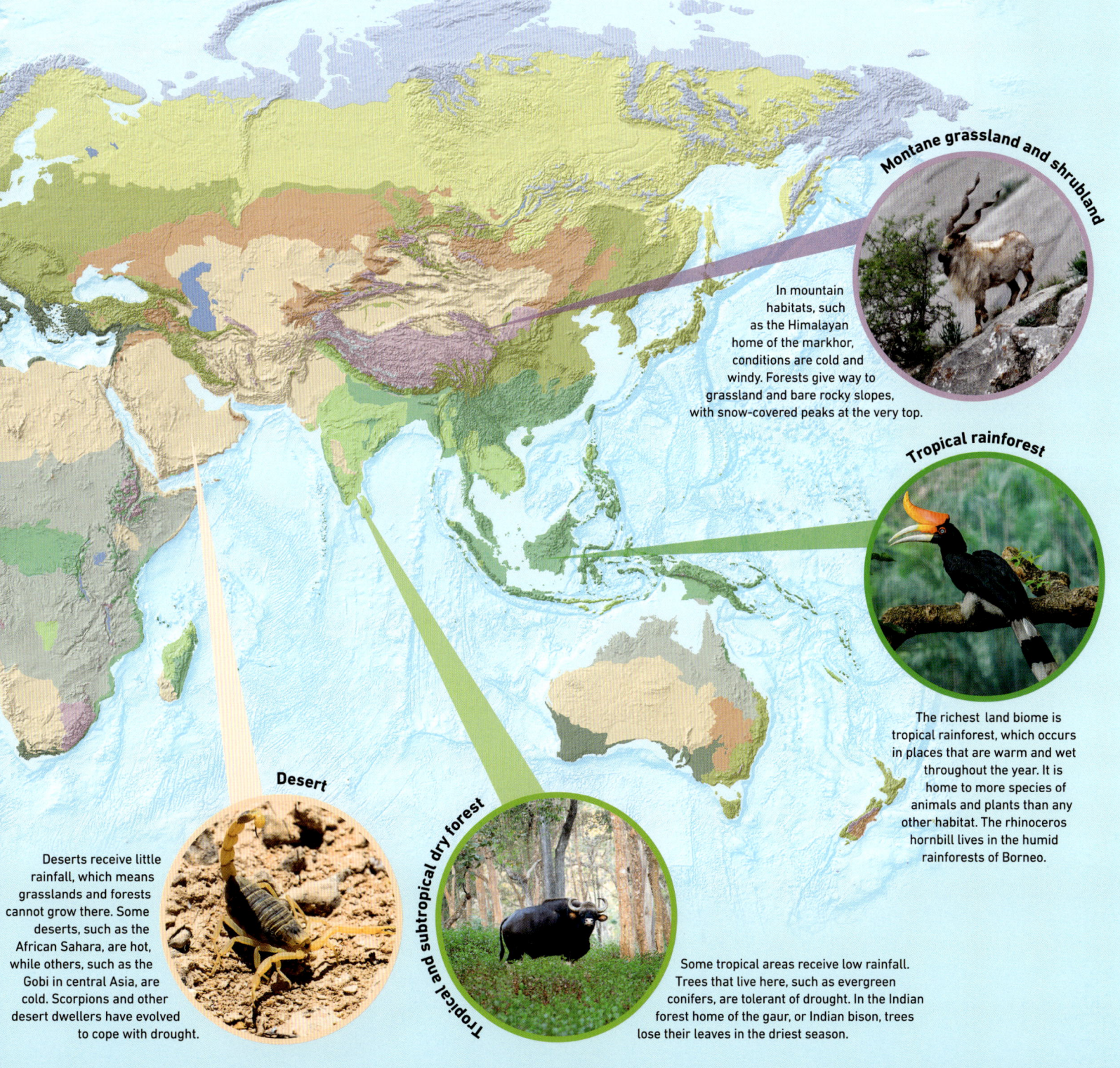

**Montane grassland and shrubland**

In mountain habitats, such as the Himalayan home of the markhor, conditions are cold and windy. Forests give way to grassland and bare rocky slopes, with snow-covered peaks at the very top.

**Tropical rainforest**

The richest land biome is tropical rainforest, which occurs in places that are warm and wet throughout the year. It is home to more species of animals and plants than any other habitat. The rhinoceros hornbill lives in the humid rainforests of Borneo.

**Desert**

Deserts receive little rainfall, which means grasslands and forests cannot grow there. Some deserts, such as the African Sahara, are hot, while others, such as the Gobi in central Asia, are cold. Scorpions and other desert dwellers have evolved to cope with drought.

**Tropical and subtropical dry forest**

Some tropical areas receive low rainfall. Trees that live here, such as evergreen conifers, are tolerant of drought. In the Indian forest home of the gaur, or Indian bison, trees lose their leaves in the driest season.

# Global origins

Over million of years, Earth has changed dramatically. Continents have split apart and crashed into each other, and large regions have flooded to create smaller islands. This has had an impact on where animals live today, sometimes leaving close cousins in different parts of the world.

## Changing Earth
Earth's outer layer, the crust, is split into tectonic plates, which move very slowly, carrying the land masses with them. Over billions of years, this slow movement has changed Earth's surface beyond recognition. This globe shows how Earth looked 300 million years ago, when the land was joined in two supercontinents called Gondwana and Laurasia.

North and South America more than 2.8 million years ago

### Separated by sea
The Atlantic and Pacific oceans were once connected by a tropical ocean called the Central American Seaway. This body of water separated the continents of North and South America.

## Continental collision
Today, North and South America are joined by a narrow strip of land that formed 2.8 million years ago. Before this, animals on each continent were separated. When these two land masses collided, it created a passage for some animals to move across. Some animals from the north, including pumas, traveled south, and some from the south, such as armadillos, ventured north.

*Puma*

*Armadillo*

*Suriname toad*

## Separated by flooding

Earth has experienced many ice ages, when large parts of the globe were covered with ice. When temperatures increased, melting ice caused sea levels to rise. Lots of islands around the world, like Sumatra and Borneo in Indonesia, formed in this way. In the process, animals there separated and evolved into different species, including the graceful pitta in Sumatra and blue-banded pitta in Borneo.

### Emerging islands
When sea levels were lower, Sumatra, Borneo, and neighboring islands were part of one land mass called the Sunda Shelf. With rising sea levels, much of the region became submerged (seen in a lighter color), leaving behind islands.

**The Sunda Shelf in Southeast Asia about 20,000 years ago**

*Graceful pitta*

*Blue-banded pitta*

*African clawed frog*

ASIA

EUROPE

AFRICA

AUSTRALASIA AND OCEANIA

## Splitting up

South America and Africa were once joined, but started to drift apart 100 million years ago, separating animals. This explains why some animals are related, even with the vast Atlantic between them. One example is the Pipidae amphibians, which include South American Suriname toads and African clawed frogs.

### New ocean
The matching shapes of South America and Africa is a clue that they were once joined. Volcanic activity in this area caused tectonic plates to move, pushing apart these land masses.

**South America and Africa about 95 million years ago**

# Under threat

All around the world, animals are in decline and many species are facing extinction. As the human population grows bigger—using more space, eating more food, and polluting the environment—it becomes harder for animals to survive.

### Biodiversity hot spots
Some places on Earth are especially rich in plant and animal species. These biodiversity hot spots are highly vulnerable to threats such as deforestation and climate change because many of the species that live there are found nowhere else in the world. This map shows some of the world's most important hot spots, on land and in the sea.

### Amazon rainforest
The Amazon rainforest is a biodiversity hot spot containing thousands of species of insects, birds, and other animals, in a huge variety of different habitats. However, this spectacular South American region is under threat, mainly from the farming industry, which is clearing land for grazing cattle and to grow animal feed.

### Rich habitat
The bright, airy canopy of the rainforest is so different from the dense vegetation growing underneath, they are like two separate habitats—with different species of animals living in each.

### Many species
The Amazon rainforest is teeming with countless different creatures, from jaguars, anteaters, and colorful birds to tiny insects and not-so-tiny spiders. Many of the plant and animal species in this rich habitat rely on other species for things like food, shelter, and protection.

### Declining wilderness
Since the Industrial Revolution, when humans started burning more fuel for energy and clearing habitats on a scale greater than ever before, wild animals have lost more than 50 percent of their living space. The wilderness has been converted to cities, farms, roads, and other developments.

### Deforestation
Trees are felled to clear land for crops and livestock, or to develop buildings, dams, and open up mines. Their timber is also sold to make products, such as paper. An estimated 15 billion trees are cut down each year, resulting in the loss of forest habitats for animals and plants.

### Climate change
Burning fossil fuels, such as coal, releases carbon dioxide and other greenhouse gases into the atmosphere. The increasing levels of these gases is causing the world to warm up, threatening habitats on land and in the oceans, including the vital polar ice habitat of penguins.

### Building on the wilderness
When humans build towns, cities, and roads, they are carving up the wilderness to leave smaller and smaller patches of natural habitat. Some animals, such as predators that are high up in the food chain, need large areas in which to roam. They cannot survive in the isolated patches of habitat that remain.

### Poaching
Many kinds of wild animals are hunted for their meat, or because their bodies supply something that is considered valuable. Elephants have long been targeted for their ivory tusks, and rhinoceroses for their horns. This is illegal but it still takes place, driving some species to the edge of extinction.

### Overfishing
Some fish are under threat because so many are taken out of the ocean that their numbers cannot recover. Other species are caught up in nets and discarded as unwanted bycatch. The sharks pictured here have been targeted for their fins, considered a delicacy in some countries.

**AN AREA OF RAINFOREST ALMOST THE SIZE OF SWITZERLAND WAS LOST DURING 2019 ALONE**

**26%** **OF MAMMALS ARE THREATENED BY EXTINCTION**

### Melting ice
Climate change is heating up the Arctic quicker than anywhere else in the world. As sea ice melts, polar bears move onto land with limited access to seals, their primary food source. Without seals, polar bears are at real risk of starvation. If nothing is done, the global population of polar bears could halve to 10,000 by 2050.

# Conservation

Despite the threats that animals face, habitats are being saved and species brought back from the edge of extinction. Conservation schemes safeguard wildlife, by protecting wild areas or breeding rare species.

## Conservation in action

Today, national parks in Madagascar are helping protect the critically endangered greater bamboo lemur—one of the world's rarest primates. Reduced habitat destruction, daily monitoring, and local educational programs have been instituted to help save this rare species. This is just one example of how organizations all over the world have worked to save species since the 1960s.

**Distinctive tufts**
The greater bamboo lemur is recognizable by the white tufts around its ears.

**Rainforest reliance**
This species relies on rainforest where giant bamboo grows. The bamboo, which makes up 95 percent of its diet, is being lost in forest clearance.

## IUCN Red List

A global body called the International Union for the Conservation of Nature (IUCN) keeps a Red List of Threatened Species. Each of the more than 120,000 species listed is assigned a threat level in order to figure out which ones need help most urgently.

 **Least concern**
Unlikely to face extinction in the near future

 **Near threatened**
Close to a threat of extinction in the near future

 **Vulnerable**
Faces a high risk of extinction in the wild

 **Endangered**
Faces a very high risk of extinction in the wild

 **Critically endangered**
Faces an extremely high extinction risk in the wild

 **Extinct in the wild**
Survives only in captivity or far outside its natural range

 **Extinct**
Very likely that the last individual has died

## Species saved

Conservationists have used different methods to protect species from threats and help them recover, including setting aside protected wild areas, stopping hunting, or taking animals into captivity so they can breed safely there. Many species that were once on the brink of extinction have been saved, and today the populations of many of those species are growing.

**Flying high**
With a wingspan of 10 ft (3 m), the California condor soars to heights of up to 15,000 ft (4,600 m). It is the biggest flying bird in North America.

**California condor**
Hunting and lead poisoning helped drive North America's biggest bird of prey to extinction in the wild in 1978. But captive breeding increased numbers, and birds could be released back into protected areas.

**Blue whale**
Once relentlessly hunted, the blue whale became one of the world's rarest species as its numbers plunged in the early 1900s. It is still endangered but, since a hunting ban in 1966, whale populations are now increasing.

**A horse apart**
Its stocky body, high mane, white nose, and shorter legs set the Przewalski's horse apart from domesticated horses.

**Przewalski's horse**
The world's only truly wild species of horse was hunted to extinction but survived in zoos, and today it is the focus of a captive breeding program. In the 1990s, some were released back into their wild habitat in Mongolia.

**Mauritius kestrel**
In the 1970s, deforestation and introduced animals, such as mongooses and cats, meant that this island bird of prey was down to just four individuals—making it the world's rarest bird. They were taken into captivity for breeding, which has raised the population to hundreds.

**100,000 NATIONAL PARKS AND WILDLIFE RESERVES EXIST IN THE WORLD TODAY**

**12% OF EARTH'S LAND IS PROTECTED**

**Sea otter**
The thick, protective fur of the sea otter made this animal a target for hunters: it was hunted until there were just a thousand or so individuals left. A hunting ban and better protection of the seas helped it recover.

### Extinction in the wild

For some species in captivity, there is no true wild for them to return to. The last wild Père David's deer probably died in China more than 200 years ago, but some animals survived in a hunting park and were brought to England. The fenced herds alive today are all descended from these.

# INVERTEBRATES

# Invertebrate facts

Tiny animals without backbones first appeared more than 600 million years ago. These early invertebrates lived in water, and many still do. Today, the diversity of invertebrates found throughout the world is staggering, from squids and starfish to worms and spiders.

## INVERTEBRATE TYPES

There are around 35 main groups of species in the animal kingdom. Just one of these groups, the vertebrates, contains all the fish, amphibians, reptiles, birds, and mammals. The other 34 groups are invertebrates—animals without an internal, jointed skeleton. Six of the main invertebrate groups are shown here.

**Sponges**
These primitive ocean organisms cannot move, and gather food by filtering it from the water.

**Cnidarians**
From jellyfish and anemones to corals, these sea creatures all have stinging tentacles to catch small prey.

**Echinoderms**
With their "spiny skin," these marine animals include starfish, sea cucumbers, and sea urchins.

**Mollusks**
From slugs to squids, mollusks live in damp habitats or in the sea. Many have a hard shell.

**Worms**
Found in water and on land, some—such as earthworms—are made up of many identical, soft-skinned segments.

**Arthropods**
With their tough outer skeletons and jointed legs, arthropods include insects, spiders, and crabs.

## ALMOST 97% OF ALL ANIMALS ARE INVERTEBRATES.

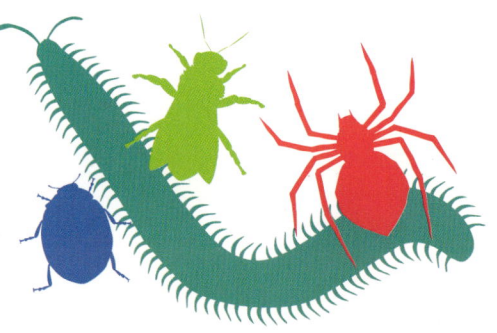

## INVERTEBRATE NUMBERS

There are approximately 1.3 million known invertebrate species, but there could be many millions more. The vast majority of invertebrates belong to two groups: arthropods and mollusks.

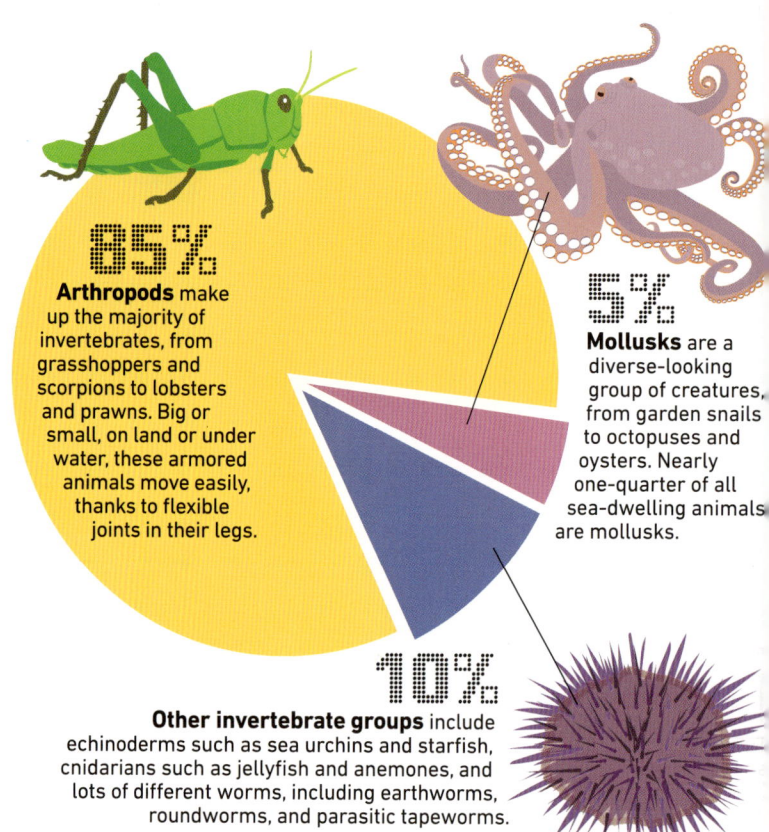

**85%**
**Arthropods** make up the majority of invertebrates, from grasshoppers and scorpions to lobsters and prawns. Big or small, on land or under water, these armored animals move easily, thanks to flexible joints in their legs.

**5%**
**Mollusks** are a diverse-looking group of creatures, from garden snails to octopuses and oysters. Nearly one-quarter of all sea-dwelling animals are mollusks.

**10%**
**Other invertebrate groups** include echinoderms such as sea urchins and starfish, cnidarians such as jellyfish and anemones, and lots of different worms, including earthworms, roundworms, and parasitic tapeworms.

## EXTREME HABITATS

Some invertebrates can withstand—and even thrive—in incredibly hostile conditions, from barren, icy Antarctica to vast, unexplored regions thousands of feet below the ocean's surface.

**Antarctic midges** are insects that measure only ⅜ in (1 cm), yet are the largest native land animal in Antarctica. They live at temperatures of 5°F (-15°C), spending nine months of the year frozen solid.

**Tube worms**, a type of marine segmented worm, live on the Pacific Ocean seafloor near hydrothermal vents—volcanic areas where sections of Earth's crust are moving apart. They grow up to 10 ft (3 m).

## BODY SHAPES
Invertebrate body shapes fall into three main categories based on symmetry.

**Bilateral symmetry**
Many insects, from ladybugs to butterflies, have two halves that mirror each other.

**Radial symmetry**
Invertebrates such as starfish have several lines of symmetry around a central point.

**No symmetry**
Invertebrates like sponges have no lines of symmetry. They have irregular body shapes.

## SMART OCTOPUS
The coconut octopus uses tools, such as discarded coconuts or clam shells, to hide in while watching for prey such as crabs. Living on sandy bottoms in bays or lagoons in the western Pacific Ocean, this clever creature, which extends to about 6 in (15 cm), is also able to pick up and carry these tools more than 66 ft (20 m).

## BIGGEST INVERTEBRATE

**COLOSSAL SQUIDS** LIVE IN THE SOUTHERN OCEAN, AND CAN REACH **40 FT** (12 M) LONG.

## SMALLEST INVERTEBRATE
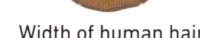
Rotifer | Width of human hair

**ROTIFERS** ARE AMONG THE WORLD'S SMALLEST ANIMALS AT **0.001 IN** (0.05 MM) LONG.

## FASTEST INSECT
The fastest insect relative to its body size is the tiger beetle. This ½ in- (1.4 cm-) long animal covers 120 times its body length in just a single second.

 **USAIN BOLT OLYMPIC SPRINTER:** 5 BODY LENGTHS IN ONE SECOND

 This long-legged creature runs so fast it temporarily goes blind from the speed.

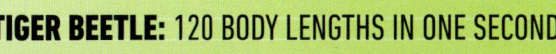 **TIGER BEETLE:** 120 BODY LENGTHS IN ONE SECOND

## HIGHEST JUMPER

THE TINY **FROGHOPPER** CAN LEAP MORE THAN **23 IN** (60 CM) IN THE AIR. THAT'S THE EQUIVALENT OF A **HUMAN JUMPING 630 FT** (190 M), OR A **40-STORY BUILDING!**

## HIGH LIFE

THE **MOUNT EVEREST JUMPING SPIDER** LIVES UP TO **22,000 FT** (6,700 M) ABOVE SEA LEVEL, ON THE SLOPES OF **MOUNT EVEREST**.

## LONGEST MIGRATION
THE **GLOBE SKIMMER DRAGONFLY** MIGRATES **4,400 MILES** (7,080 KM) THROUGH THE AIR **WITHOUT LANDING**.

## BIGGEST SWARM
The desert locust gathers in swarms of up to 8 billion. Living in parts of the Middle East, Asia, and Africa, they are known to destroy crops.

# Giant Pacific octopus

Weighing as much as two grown men, the giant Pacific octopus is the largest of all octopus species, and one of the biggest ocean predators without a backbone. It is an agile, intelligent hunter, capable of catching prey as big as sharks.

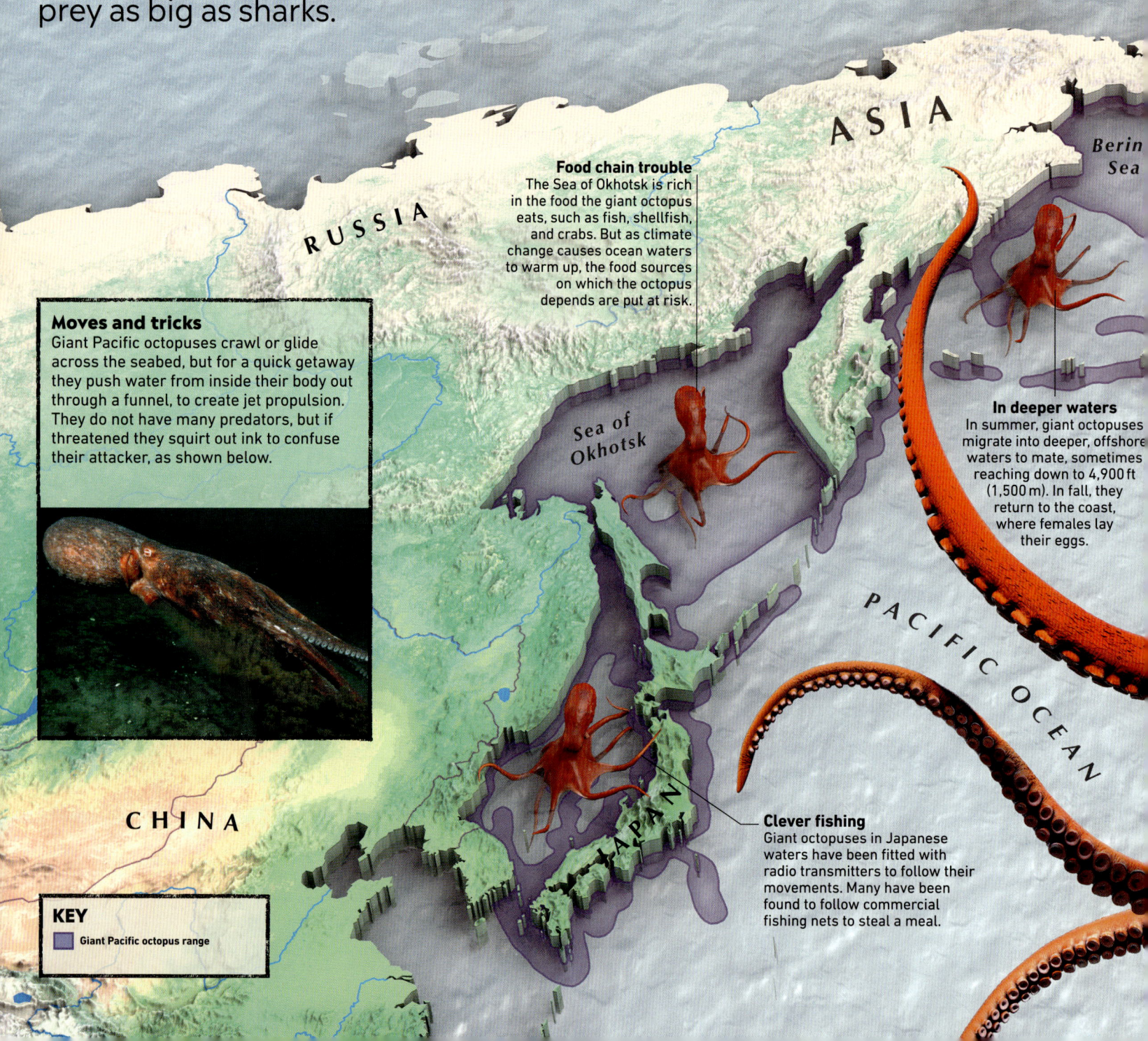

**Food chain trouble**
The Sea of Okhotsk is rich in the food the giant octopus eats, such as fish, shellfish, and crabs. But as climate change causes ocean waters to warm up, the food sources on which the octopus depends are put at risk.

**Moves and tricks**
Giant Pacific octopuses crawl or glide across the seabed, but for a quick getaway they push water from inside their body out through a funnel, to create jet propulsion. They do not have many predators, but if threatened they squirt out ink to confuse their attacker, as shown below.

**In deeper waters**
In summer, giant octopuses migrate into deeper, offshore waters to mate, sometimes reaching down to 4,900 ft (1,500 m). In fall, they return to the coast, where females lay their eggs.

**Clever fishing**
Giant octopuses in Japanese waters have been fitted with radio transmitters to follow their movements. Many have been found to follow commercial fishing nets to steal a meal.

**KEY**
- Giant Pacific octopus range

INVERTEBRATES | 27

## Cold-water hunter

A big, speedy predator, the giant Pacific octopus thrives in the cold, oxygen-rich waters around the northern rim of the Pacific Ocean, mostly in areas that are rarely deeper than 1,640 ft (500 m). The octopus grabs prey with its arms, then uses its beak to inject venom into the prey. This immobilizes the prey and softens its flesh, which the octopus then can lick out with its rasping tongue.

### Octopus nursery
Each female octopus lays up to 100,000 eggs in an underwater cave or crevice. She guards the eggs, which hang in clutches, until they hatch about six months later and she dies. The tiny hatchlings then spend about two months drifting among the ocean's plankton, before descending to the seabed, where they develop into adult shape and size.

**Fleshy body**
The thick, wrinkly skin of a giant Pacific octopus covers a soft, fleshy body that can squeeze through the smallest gaps. This is useful for catching prey hiding in crevices or escaping enemies on a rocky reef.

**Northern range**
Furthest north, most giant octopuses live in shallower waters. Many live in coastal reefs and some may even drift into the intertidal zone by the shore.

**Accidental catch**
In the rich fishing waters of the northeast Pacific, giant Pacific octopuses risk being caught in nets cast for cod and flatfish. It is the octopus species most commonly landed as a bycatch here.

**Strong arms**
Octopuses have eight arms that carry two rows of large suckers for gripping prey. Each arm can have more than 500 suckers in total.

A **GIANT PACIFIC OCTOPUS** CAN WEIGH **400 LB** (180 KG) AND ITS LONG ARMS CAN **SPAN UP TO 20 FT** (6 M)

# European lobster

Lobsters are crustaceans, a group of invertebrates with armor-like, jointed exoskeletons protecting their soft bodies. One of the largest lobster species, the European lobster lives in shallow coastal seas across most of Europe and northern Africa.

**North Sea**
The North Sea is the biggest expanse of shallow continental waters in the northeast Atlantic. It is rich in lobsters' favorite food, such as crabs, starfish, and sea urchins.

**Long antennae**
Lobsters use their antennae to feel their way around on the seabed in murky, dark waters.

**The Azores**
This group of small volcanic islands marks the westernmost part of the European lobster's territory.

**Uneven-sized claws**
The fatter claw of a lobster is stronger for slow crushing, while the slimmer one is better for faster cutting. Both are used for breaking up food or in self-defense.

**Warmer waters**
Like many European marine species, the European lobster reaches the southern limits of its range in the waters off the coast of Morocco in northwest Africa. It cannot tolerate the warmer tropical seas further south.

**Lobster movements**
Most lobsters migrate into deeper waters to spawn, but one of the most spectacular migrations happens every fall off the coast of the United States, when huge numbers of spiny lobsters move in single file over the seabed to reach their spawning grounds.

**KEY**
European lobster range

INVERTEBRATES | 29

ARCTIC OCEAN

### Life on the seabed
A lobster needs water to help support its weighty body, which is far too heavy for the lobster to move around on rocky shores or beaches. Lobsters mostly crawl across the seabed, where they live in crevices or burrows. When needed, they escape by quickly swimming backwards. Even a big lobster might be swept away by strong currents in deeper water, so they don't go too far offshore.

### Norwegian Sea
Warm ocean currents flowing up from the tropical Atlantic into the Norwegian Sea help keep waters ice-free, so lobsters live as far north as the Arctic Circle.

Baltic Sea

### Coastal crustacean
Like many other marine animals, the European lobster stays mainly in coastal seas. Lobsters are fished for food, but despite some local overfishing, especially in the North Sea, the overall population is stable.

### Black Sea
Rivers flowing into the cool Black Sea make it less salty than the ocean. European lobsters can survive here, but in fewer numbers and only in western areas.

EUROPE

Black Sea

Crete

Mediterranean Sea

### Salty environment
A warm climate evaporates water from the Mediterranean Sea and makes it slightly saltier than the Atlantic Ocean. Lobsters can take these conditions, and range widely across this region.

### Eastern Mediterranean
The Mediterranean Sea reaches a depth of over 16,400 ft (5,000 m) in the middle. Lobsters keep to shallower coastal waters, ranging as far east as the Greek island of Crete.

AFRICA

FEMALE EUROPEAN LOBSTERS CAN LIVE UP TO THE AGE OF 70

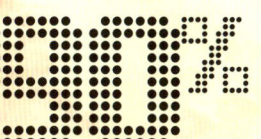
OVERFISHING IN THE NORTH SEA HAS MADE LOBSTER NUMBERS THERE DROP BY 90%

### Caterpillar diet

Postman butterflies become poisonous very early in their life. Their caterpillars eat leaves of passion vines, which contain toxic cyanide. The poison stays in their bodies without harming them, even as they turn into butterflies. Adults also only feed on passion vines, but on the nectar and pollen of its flowers.

### Guiana Highlands

In this area of tabletop mountains rising steeply from rainforests, the butterflies have little or no white in their color pattern—similar to those of the Andean mountains.

### Central America

In the rainforests from Guatemala to Panama, postman butterflies have red bands on their forewings and white bands, sometimes tinged with yellow, on their hind wings.

### Andes

High up in the mountain valleys and foothills of the northern Andes range, the butterflies' hind wings have less white; some have no white in their pattern at all.

### Regional colors

Some species of butterfly have many different varieties according to where they live. The postman butterfly, for example, has more than 20 variations. Some of these are shown on this map, in the areas where they live.

# Postman butterfly

The postman butterfly lives in varied habitats from Central to South America. Across its range, its exact pattern of red, black, and white varies from place to place. A flash of color from any postman butterfly is a sign that it is poisonous, so helps keep predatory birds away.

THERE ARE ABOUT **20,000** **SPECIES OF BUTTERFLY** IN THE **WORLD**

**AT NIGHT,** POSTMAN BUTTERFLIES GATHER TO **SLEEP IN GROUPS** KNOWN AS **COMMUNAL ROOSTS**

## Amazon Basin
Across the lowlands of the great Amazon River Basin, local postman butterflies often live along rivers and streams. Here, they have white patches on their forewings, sometimes broken into spots.

## Wings at rest
Like most day-flying butterflies, postman butterflies rest with their wings raised so their tips almost touch. Flapping their wings helps spread a scent that deters predators.

## Master mimics
Closely related to the postman butterfly, the red postman (above) is a separate species, but matches the local color pattern of the postman wherever it lives alongside it. As they are both poisonous, this mimicry reinforces the warning for potential predators and helps both species survive.

**KEY**
Postman butterfly range

## Wetlands
In Brazil's Pantanal wetlands, the postman lives near water. Here it has white stripes on the hindwings, looking more like those along Brazil's southwest coast and in Central America.

## Sucking nectar
Butterflies have a flexible tube called a proboscis for drinking liquid nectar from flowers. Usually kept coiled up, it unrolls when the butterfly is ready to feed.

Passion flower

## Wing pattern
The colors of the postman butterfly come from tiny pigmented scales that cover the surface of the two pairs of wings. Its wingspan can measure up to 3 in (7.5 cm).

### Plant pollinator
Bees are essential for keeping our planet green. They transfer pollen from flower to flower, pollinating many crops that we depend on for food. This mining bee is busy harvesting pollen from an apple blossom tree in Wisconsin. But climate change is affecting bee behavior, and intensive farming and pesticides are destroying bee habitats, such as wildflower meadows, trees, and hedgerows.

THE OLDEST **MEXICAN** RED-KNEED TARANTULA IS KNOWN TO **HAVE** LIVED FOR **28** YEARS

**GOLIATH** TARANTULA **FANGS** CAN GROW UP TO **1½ IN** (3.8 CM)

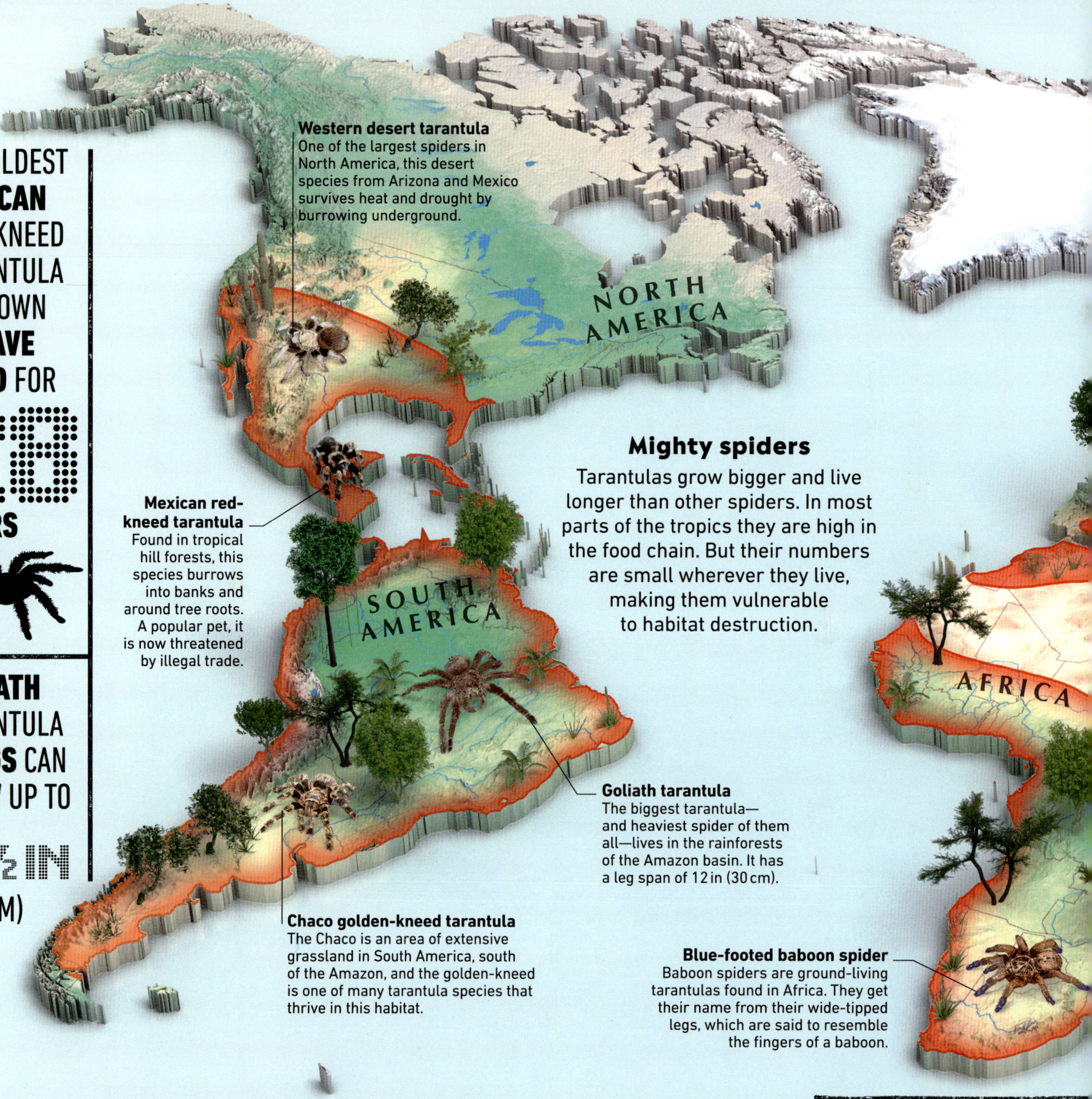

**Western desert tarantula**
One of the largest spiders in North America, this desert species from Arizona and Mexico survives heat and drought by burrowing underground.

**Mexican red-kneed tarantula**
Found in tropical hill forests, this species burrows into banks and around tree roots. A popular pet, it is now threatened by illegal trade.

**Mighty spiders**
Tarantulas grow bigger and live longer than other spiders. In most parts of the tropics they are high in the food chain. But their numbers are small wherever they live, making them vulnerable to habitat destruction.

**Goliath tarantula**
The biggest tarantula—and heaviest spider of them all—lives in the rainforests of the Amazon basin. It has a leg span of 12 in (30 cm).

**Chaco golden-kneed tarantula**
The Chaco is an area of extensive grassland in South America, south of the Amazon, and the golden-kneed is one of many tarantula species that thrive in this habitat.

**Blue-footed baboon spider**
Baboon spiders are ground-living tarantulas found in Africa. They get their name from their wide-tipped legs, which are said to resemble the fingers of a baboon.

# Tarantulas

Many big spiders are called "tarantulas," but all true tarantulas have fat hairy bodies and belong to a family called the theraphosids. Found in all warm parts of the world, there are nearly 1,000 species: the smallest is no bigger than your thumb, but the biggest can span a large dinner plate with its legs.

**Venomous fangs**
Spiders use their fangs to inject venom that disables their prey. Tarantula venom can be deadly to small creatures, but is usually no more serious to a human than a bee sting.

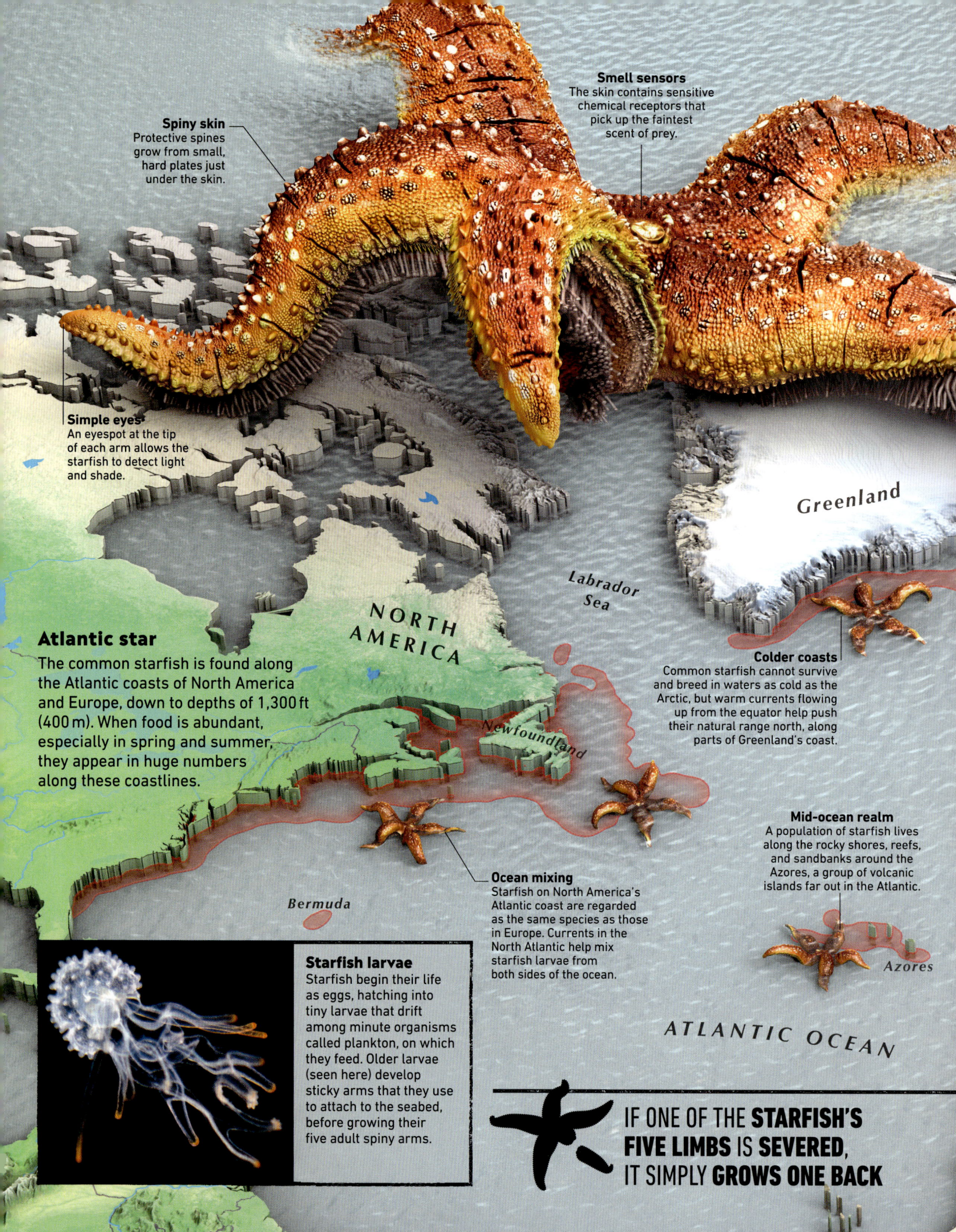

# Common starfish

Along with sea cucumbers and urchins, the common starfish belongs to a group of animals called echinoderms, which live only in the ocean. Like many marine animals commonly spotted on or near the seashore, the starfish actually spends most of its life in deeper waters, as it needs to be underwater to spawn.

**Many tiny feet**
Like other echinoderms, starfish move from place to place using tiny sucker-like tube feet. The underside of their arms is covered in hundreds of these feet, which bend from side to side to push the animal slowly along the seafloor.

**Norwegian fjords**
Norway's long coastline is carved by narrow, deep inlets called fjords. The muddy and sandy bottoms of these coastal habitats are full of common starfish.

**Northern delights**
Even along the Kola Peninsula, above the Arctic Circle, warm currents keep waters ice-free. Here, starfish feed on the plentiful scallop-beds.

**Colors**
The skin of the common starfish is usually orange, but some are in shades of brown or purple.

**North Sea water**
The North Sea is slightly less salty than the open ocean because many rivers flow into it. Common starfish still thrive here, even in river estuaries.

**The Baltic Sea**
The common starfish is one of the few echinoderms that can survive in the very low salt levels of the Baltic.

**Mussels on the menu**
The common starfish preys on lots of different invertebrates, but has a special liking for two-shelled mollusks, such as mussels. They pull the shells apart with their arms, then stick their extendable stomach through the opening to digest the meat inside.

**KEY**
 Common starfish range

# FISH

# Fish facts

Fish evolved more than 500 million years ago, and were the first animals to evolve a backbone. They can be found in a variety of places, from vast oceans to small freshwater lakes. Some fish live on bright coral reefs, while others lurk thousands of feet deeper in pitch-black oceanic trenches.

## WHAT IS A FISH?

**Vertebrates**
The typical fish skeleton consists of a spinal column, skull, ribs, and fin supports.

**Cold-blooded**
Fish may swim in warm or cold water, but their bodies are the same temperature as the water they live in.

**Breathe with gills**
Gills located on the side of a fish contain blood that absorbs oxygen from the water.

**Scaly skin**
Most fish are covered in protective, overlapping plates called scales. Some fish do not have scales.

**Live in water**
Some fish swim in salty oceans, others need fresh water to survive. Some move between the two.

## FISH TYPES

**ESTIMATED NUMBER OF FISH SPECIES:**  35,660

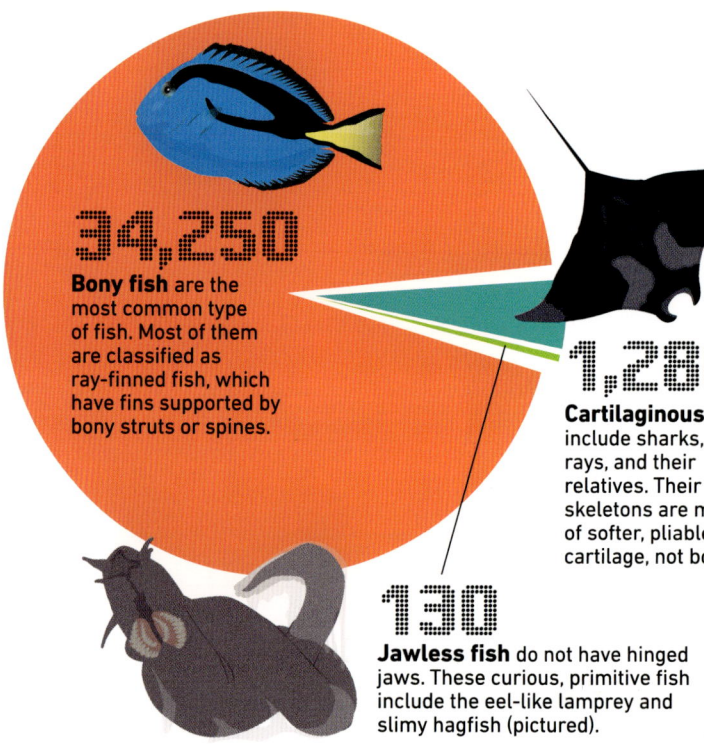

**34,250**
**Bony fish** are the most common type of fish. Most of them are classified as ray-finned fish, which have fins supported by bony struts or spines.

**1,280**
**Cartilaginous fish** include sharks, rays, and their relatives. Their skeletons are made of softer, pliable cartilage, not bone.

**130**
**Jawless fish** do not have hinged jaws. These curious, primitive fish include the eel-like lamprey and slimy hagfish (pictured).

THE **GULF CORVINA** IS THE LOUDEST FISH—WITH A CALL OF **202** DECIBELS, IT'S **LOUDER THAN A PLANE TAKING OFF!**

## EXTREME HABITATS

Some fish have evolved to survive in the most inhospitable conditions, from the frozen Arctic to dried-up riverbeds.

**Arctic cod** can survive in sub-zero temperatures, using an antifreeze protein in their blood. This allows them to find food beneath the ice in polar regions, without any competition.

**Mudskippers** are found in the Indian and Pacific oceans, but they actually prefer the land—and even climb trees! They can keep breathing on land for up to two days at a time.

**Lungfish** live in rivers and lakes in Africa, Australia, and South America. During dry seasons, they burrow into mud, before cocooning themselves in a mucus that traps life-saving moisture.

## LONGEST MIGRATION

**DORADO CATFISH** MIGRATE **7,200** MILES (11,600 KM) INLAND, FROM THE ANDES TO THE AMAZON AND BACK.

# SWIMMING LIKE A FISH

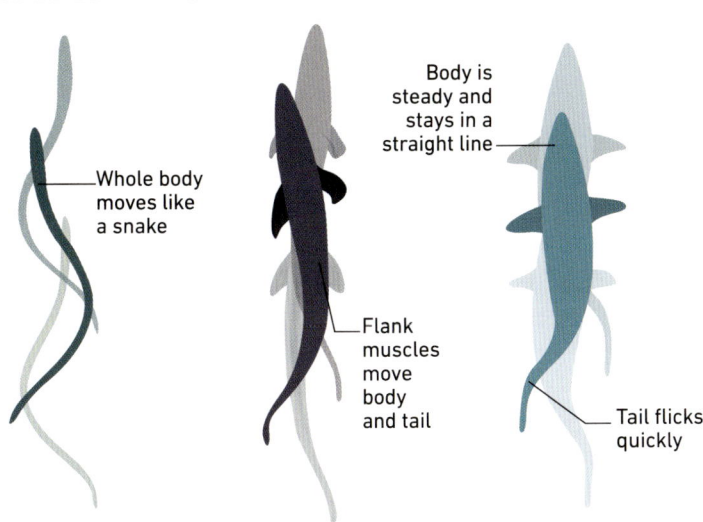

**Side to side**
Long, thin fish, such as eels, propel themselves using a series of fast S-shaped movements through the water.

**Body and tail**
Many fish, including salmon, swim with the help of their body and tail, using their powerful flank muscles to move forward.

**Strong tail**
The fastest fish, from tuna to sharks, maintain a straight, streamlined body, while their flank muscles flick their tail from side to side.

# ENDEMIC SPECIES

Some fish are native to a specific habitat and do not stray from there—they are endemic to that region. This is because these fish have evolved to adapt in that area only, and they cannot survive for long anywhere else.

**Coelacanths** were thought to be extinct for 65 million years, but in 1938 scientists discovered them off the coast of southeastern Africa. Since then, an Indonesian coelacanth has also been found.

**Elephantnose fish** are a curious-looking freshwater species native to western and central Africa. They are found in slow-moving rivers and muddy pools.

# DEEPEST FISH

Record-breaking human free diver **702 ft (214 m)**

At the bottom of the Pacific Ocean is the Mariana Trench, the deepest oceanic trench in the world. Incredibly, some fish survive in this cold, dark, and lonely place, including the Mariana snailfish—a pink, slimy species that looks like an oversize tadpole.

**MARIANA SNAILFISH CAN REACH DEPTHS OF 23,000 FT (7,010 M)**

# SMALLEST FISH

**PAEDOCYPRIS PROGENETICA IS THE SMALLEST-KNOWN FISH, WITH FEMALES MEASURING JUST 5/16 IN (7.9 mm).**

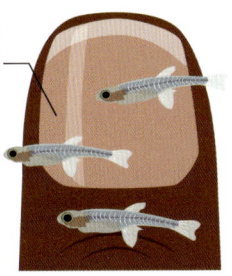
Adult fingernail

# BIGGEST FISH

**WHALE SHARKS GROW 40 FT (12 M) LONG—ABOUT THE SAME LENGTH AS A BUS.**

# SMART FISH

Found in the Indian and Pacific oceans, the reef-dwelling tuskfish can use a rock to smash open shellfish, making it the first wild fish observed using tools.

# FASTEST FISH

Named for their spectacular dorsal fin, sailfish would easily win a race against the fastest human swimmer. They live in the warm Atlantic and Indo-Pacific waters.

MICHAEL PHELPS **OLYMPIC SWIMMER** AT **4.7 MPH (7.6 KPH)**

**SAILFISH** AT **70 MPH (113 KPH)**

# Sea lamprey

The sea lamprey is a jawless fish—instead of jaws it has a sucker filled with teeth, which it uses to feed on the blood of other fishes. It grows up as a larva in the rivers and lakes of North America and Europe, then lives its adult life in the salty North Atlantic Ocean, before returning to freshwater habitats to breed and die.

### Northern waters
Sea lampreys can be found all across the North Atlantic, from the frigid waters of Greenland to the balmy latitudes of Spain and Florida, USA. While most adults live in the ocean, some make the Great Lakes of North America their home all year round.

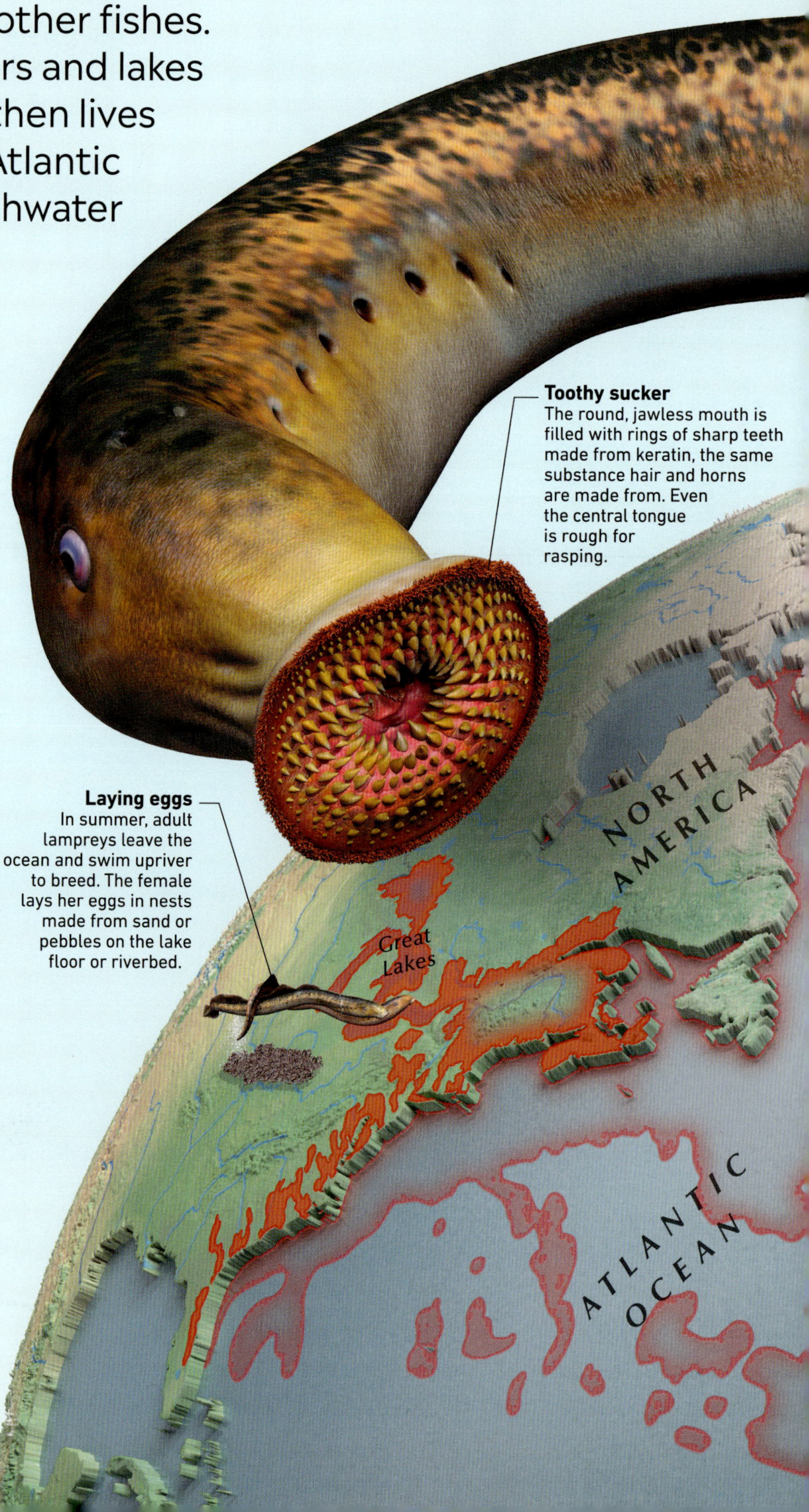

**Toothy sucker**
The round, jawless mouth is filled with rings of sharp teeth made from keratin, the same substance hair and horns are made from. Even the central tongue is rough for rasping.

**Laying eggs**
In summer, adult lampreys leave the ocean and swim upriver to breed. The female lays her eggs in nests made from sand or pebbles on the lake floor or riverbed.

**Lamprey larvae**
Sea lamprey eggs hatch into young called larvae. The larvae burrow into gravel on the riverbed, leaving their heads exposed. They filter feed on tiny particles swept into their mouth by tiny microscopic hairs called cilia. This larval phase can last for up to three years.

**Feeding on blood**
Adult lampreys clamp onto other fish with their sucker-like mouths to feed. They use their horny teeth and tongue to cut a hole in the prey's skin, swallowing its blood as food. The lamprey's saliva stops the blood clotting so it keeps flowing, often until the victim dies.

FISH | 43

 ONE **SPAWNING** FEMALE SEA LAMPREY MAY LAY UP TO **300,000 EGGS**

THE **LENGTH** OF A **SEA LAMPREY** CAN BE UP TO  (1.2 M)

**KEY**
- Sea lamprey marine range
- Sea lamprey freshwater range

**Tail fin**
A tail fin and two dorsal fins running along the back help stabilize the body when swimming. Unlike most jawed fishes, lampreys have a skeleton made of cartilage, not bone, and no paired fins.

**Feeding at sea**
Most mature adult sea lampreys feed at sea, where they consume the blood of other fishes, such as cod and herring, or even marine mammals, such as dolphins.

**Long-distance swimmers**
Sea lampreys can travel long distances into the open ocean in search of food, and may descend to depths of 2½ miles (4 km).

**Freshwater larvae**
The larvae of sea lampreys spend their time in freshwater rivers and lakes. When they reach maturity they swim down river and out toward the open ocean.

**Mediterranean lampreys**
Lampreys in the Mediterranean Sea spawn in the rivers of southern Europe.

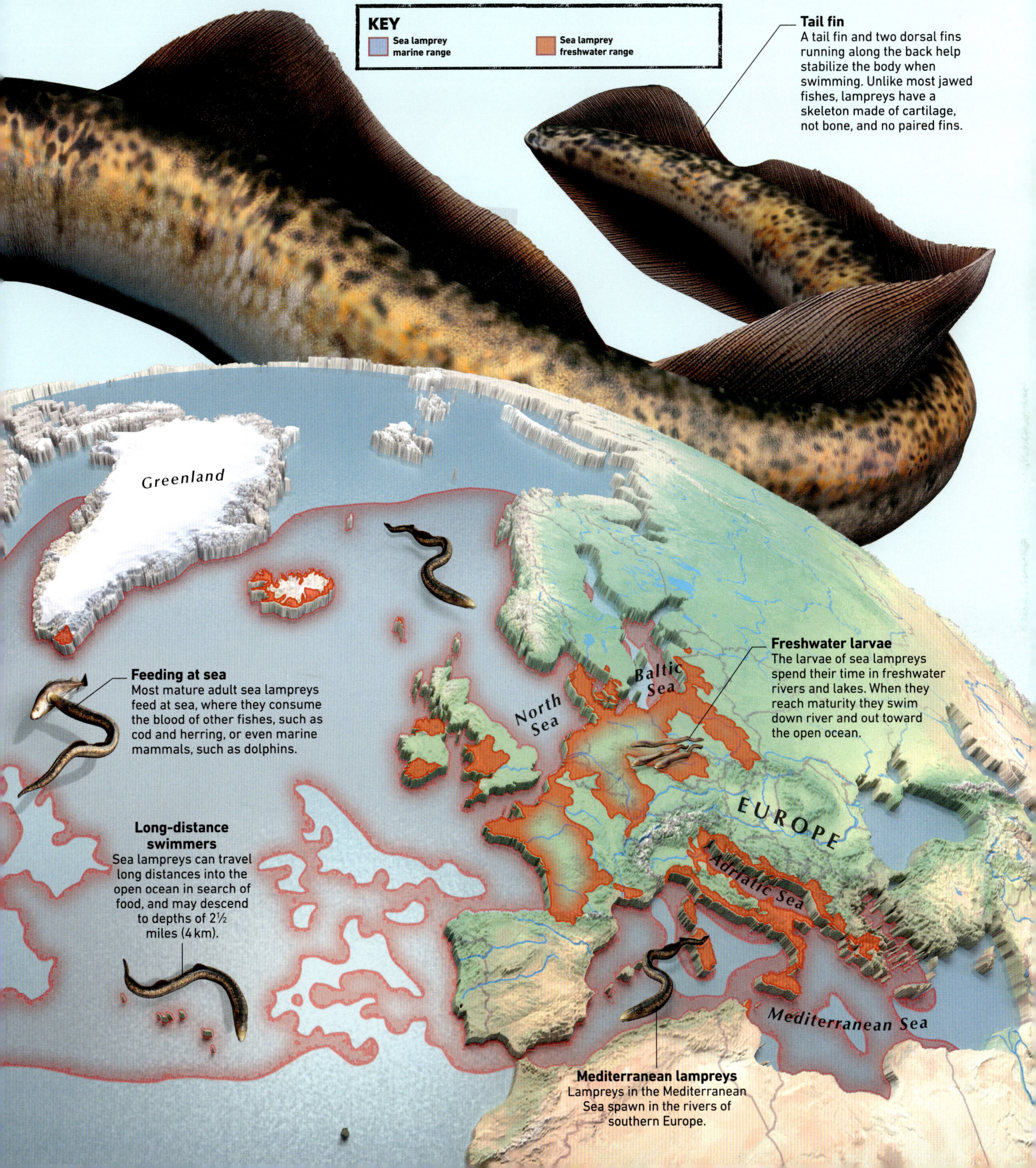

# Great white shark

Armed with razor-sharp teeth and a sleek body shaped like a torpedo, the great white shark is a fast, formidable predator. This wanderer roams throughout the world's oceans, but returns to the coast to hunt marine mammals such as seals, dolphins, and even small whales.

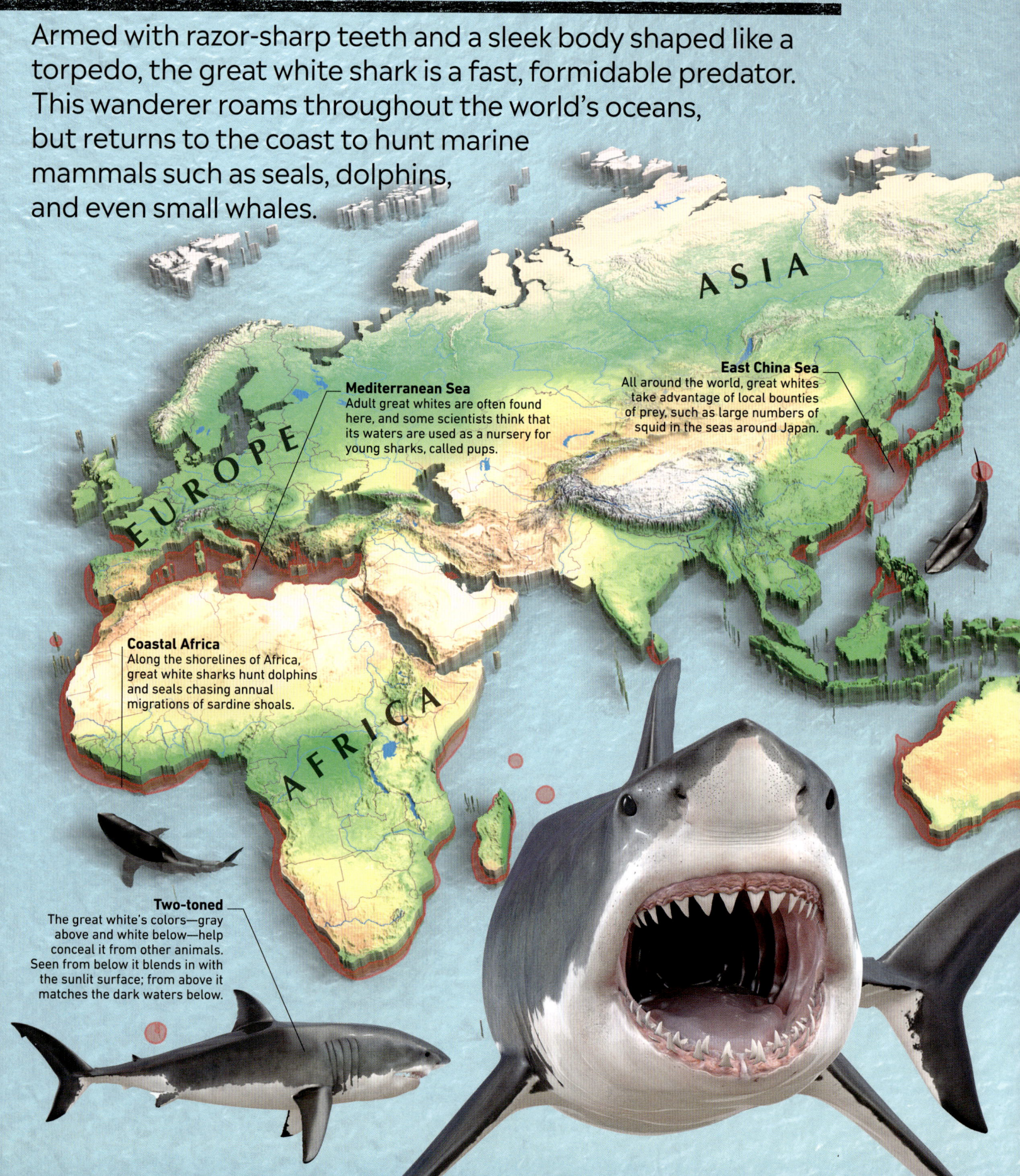

**Mediterranean Sea**
Adult great whites are often found here, and some scientists think that its waters are used as a nursery for young sharks, called pups.

**East China Sea**
All around the world, great whites take advantage of local bounties of prey, such as large numbers of squid in the seas around Japan.

**Coastal Africa**
Along the shorelines of Africa, great white sharks hunt dolphins and seals chasing annual migrations of sardine shoals.

**Two-toned**
The great white's colors—gray above and white below—help conceal it from other animals. Seen from below it blends in with the sunlit surface; from above it matches the dark waters below.

## ANIMALS IN DANGER
Great white shark
⚠ IUCN status: vulnerable
⚠ Population estimate: unknown

### KEY
▭ Great white shark range

### Tracking sharks
Little is known about the exact movements of great whites, but they can be followed by fitting them with tracking devices. These transmit signals to satellites, which send information back to Earth about the animal's location. Such studies show they travel thousands of miles across the oceans.

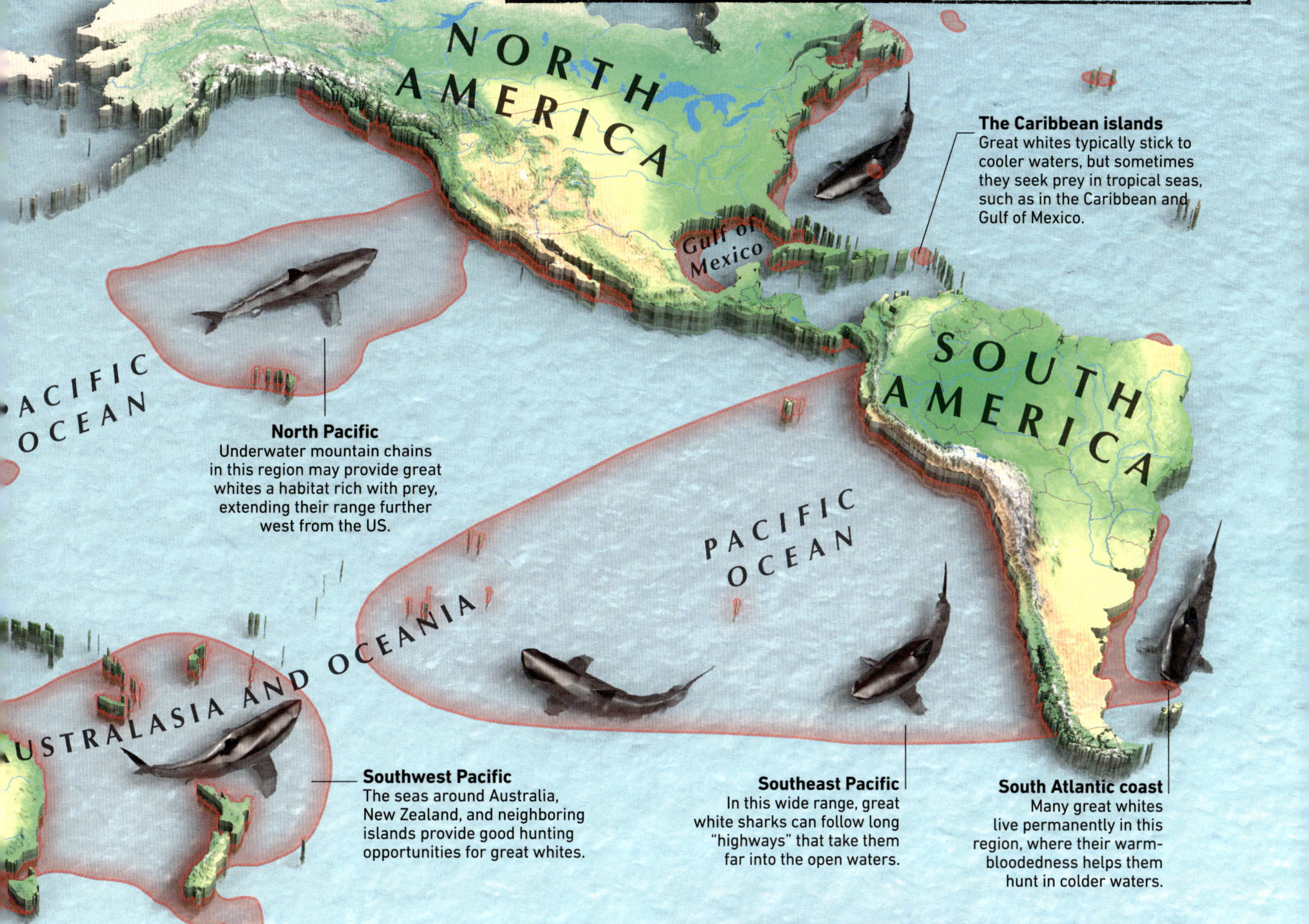

### The Caribbean islands
Great whites typically stick to cooler waters, but sometimes they seek prey in tropical seas, such as in the Caribbean and Gulf of Mexico.

### North Pacific
Underwater mountain chains in this region may provide great whites a habitat rich with prey, extending their range further west from the US.

### Southwest Pacific
The seas around Australia, New Zealand, and neighboring islands provide good hunting opportunities for great whites.

### Southeast Pacific
In this wide range, great white sharks can follow long "highways" that take them far into the open waters.

### South Atlantic coast
Many great whites live permanently in this region, where their warm-bloodedness helps them hunt in colder waters.

## Long-distance wanderer
The great white shark is the world's widest-ranging fish and can be found in most oceans, but is found most often in the ranges shown on this map. Unusually for a fish, it maintains a high body temperature, helping it survive in colder waters and chase down warm-blooded mammals.

### Ruthless killer
Once a great white shark sights a target near the water's surface, it moves in quickly for the kill. It attacks its prey, such as this sea lion, with a single ferocious bite—and in the process can breach the surface in spectacular fashion. It then lets the victim bleed to death before starting to feed.

 A GREAT WHITE SHARK CAN HAVE UP TO **300 TEETH**

## Shallow waters

In the sunlit waters of the Maldives in the Indian Ocean, blacktip reef sharks are rounding up their prey. Forcing the fish into ever denser shoals, they nudge them into shallow water close to the shore before moving in to take a bite. These agile hunters are found in all shallow tropical seas, particularly around coral reefs and lagoons.

### Slimy blanket
While it sleeps, a steephead parrotfish produces slime from its skin to build up a cocoon around it. This shield takes around an hour to make, and protects the fish from predators and also serves as a barrier to infectious parasites.

### Diversity hot spot
The stunning coral reefs between the Philippines and Papua New Guinea have the highest diversity of marine animals in the world. Known as the Coral Triangle, this region covers 2¼ million sq miles (6 million sq km) and is also home to 75 percent of all coral species.

### The Philippines
The warm, shallow waters around the Philippines represent the northernmost reach of the Coral Triangle, a region known for its diverse coral reefs and fish species.

### White-sand islands
Many tiny islands in the western Pacific are surrounded by white beaches made of sand produced by the poop of thousands of coral-eating parrotfish.

### Papua New Guinea
Islands off the coast of this country have some of the richest reefs anywhere on Earth.

AUSTRALASIA

SOLOMON ISLANDS

### Indo-Pacific beauty
The steephead parrotfish is scattered throughout parts of the Indian Ocean to the Pacific islands of Polynesia. This species' showy colors help them recognize their own kind in crowded, reef-dwelling communities. It also uses its beak to break the rocky coral, digesting its softer flesh and pooping the rocky parts as white sand.

**PARROTFISH HAVE A SET OF TEETH IN THEIR THROAT TO GRIND DOWN ROCKY CORAL**

### Northwest Australia
Coral reefs on the narrow continental shelf around this region extend the range of Indo-Pacific fish, such as the steephead parrotfish, into the fringes of the Indian Ocean.

### Head hump
Only males of the steephead parrotfish develop a head hump, but all youngsters have the potential to do so. This is because younger females can change their sex and turn into males.

INDIAN OCEAN

# Steephead parrotfish

Around one-fifth of the world's fish live on tropical coral reefs. Many of these beautiful species, including the steephead parrotfish, are dependent upon coral for their survival, finding shelter in their nooks and crannies. This parrotfish, however, is also known for its unique ability to eat the tough coral using its strong, parrotlike beak.

**Island reefs**
A scattering of volcanic islands circled by coral reefs provide habitats for reef fish, such as the steephead parrotfish, to live further east in the Pacific Ocean.

**Eastern limit**
The steephead parrotfish, like many Indo-Pacific reef fishes, has the easternmost limit of its range in Tahiti and some islands of Polynesia. Beyond this point, the island reefs are too sparsely scattered for the parrotfish to reach.

**Breeding colors**
Like other parrotfish, adult steephead parrotfish have a very different pattern compared with juveniles. Younger fish are dark brown with horizontal yellow stripes. They change color when they get mature enough to breed.

**KEY** — Steephead parrotfish range

**RED-BELLIED PIRANHAS "BARK" TO WARN OFF OTHER FISH**

**KEY**
■ Red-bellied piranha range

**White waters**
Most red-bellied piranhas live in the cloudier, sediment-heavy "white waters" closer to the Amazon's mouth, where the river drains into the Atlantic.

Branco · Rio Negro · Amazon · Madeira · Japa · Amazon Basin · Purus · Guapor · Andes

**Steady waters**
Red-bellied piranhas prefer the lower section of rivers, which are wider, deeper, and move more slowly. They are less likely to be found in the narrower and faster-flowing sections nearer the river's source.

**Shoaling**
Piranhas are often feared as blood-thirsty fish that attack big prey in frenzied shoals. But studies have shown that shoaling, as with other fish species, is more a way of protecting themselves from predators. Plenty of Amazon animals, such as giant otters, eat piranhas as prey.

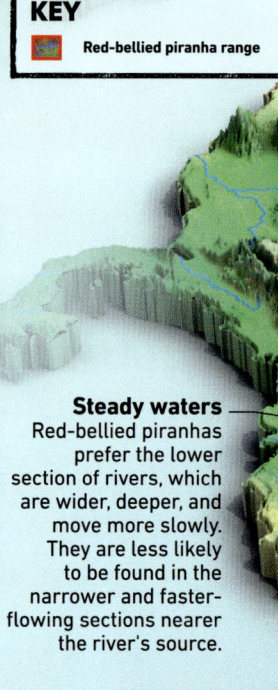

**Carnivorous fish**
Found in rivers, streams, lakes, and flooded forests, the red-bellied piranha is known for its vicious appetite. In reality it usually hunts fish and other small aquatic animals, and avoids anything bigger. Only in the dry season, when pools run low and hungry piranhas are forced together, may piranhas attack bigger land animals that stumble into the waters.

# Red-bellied piranha

The rivers running through the Amazon Basin in northern South America are home to the biggest diversity of freshwater fish in the world, including 38 species of piranha. Among them is the red-bellied piranha—a fish with a fearsome reputation.

**Red bellies**
This species is recognizable for its red belly and silvery body.

**Tocantins**
Many of the rivers that are home to the red-bellied piranha empty into the Amazon. But the Tocantins River empties directly into the Atlantic, so populations of piranhas are cut off from those of the Amazon.

**Flowing south**
In the southernmost part of their range, red-bellied piranhas live in the Paraná and Paraguay rivers, which flow through South America's open grasslands and drain into the Atlantic Ocean.

SOME PIRANHAS HAVE A **BITE FORCE** EQUAL TO **30** TIMES THEIR OWN BODY WEIGHT

**Sharp teeth**
The teeth are arranged in a single row in the upper and lower jaws, and have sharp, bladelike edges for puncturing and cutting through the flesh of animal prey.

## PIRANHA RELATIVES

**Pacu**
A giant relative of the piranhas, the pacu has strong jaws for cracking seeds and nuts that fall into the waters when the Amazon is flooded during the rainy season.

**Neon tetra**
Tetras are tiny relatives of the piranhas that eat small invertebrates. Many, such as the neon tetra, are brightly colored—making them popular in aquariums.

**Freshwater hatchetfish**
Small piranha relatives called hatchetfishes swim near the surface and prey on insects. Their muscular bodies help them jump from the water to escape danger.

**African tiger fish**
Close cousins of the piranhas live across the Atlantic in African rivers. Some, such as the African tiger fish, are also sharp-toothed meat-eaters.

**Congo tetra**
The brightly colored Congo tetra lives in Africa. These ancestors of piranha relatives first evolved when South America and Africa were joined.

# AMPHIBIANS

# Amphibian facts

The first amphibians evolved from fish and moved on to land amore than 300 million years ago. Today, most amphibians move between land and water. They are found throughout the world, and most commonly in moist, freshwater habitats like woodlands and rainforests.

## WHAT IS AN AMPHIBIAN?

**Vertebrates**
Like their fish ancestors, all amphibians have an internal skeleton made of bone.

**Cold-blooded**
The body temperature of amphibians fluctuates with that of the air and water around them.

**Lay eggs**
Most amphibians lay soft eggs, but some give birth to live young.

**Aquatic young**
The young hatch and stay for a time as tadpoles in water, eventually turning into amphibious adults.

**Moist skin**
Water passes through an amphibian's thin, moist skin, allowing it to breathe under water.

## AMPHIBIAN TYPES

**ESTIMATED NUMBER OF AMPHIBIAN SPECIES:**  8,250

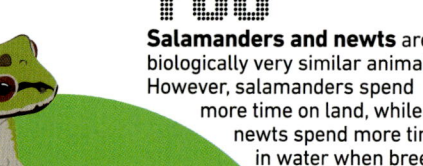

**760**
**Salamanders and newts** are biologically very similar animals. However, salamanders spend more time on land, while newts spend more time in water when breeding

**7,280**
**Frogs and toads** are the largest group of amphibians. Scientifically, frogs and toads belong to the same animal group, but frogs typically have smoother skin.

**210**
**Caecilians** are small, snakelike amphibians with no limbs and tentacles on their heads. They spend most of their lives underground, eating insects and worms. Some species live in water and have a tail fin for swimming.

## EXTREME HABITATS

These unique amphibians can withstand the toughest conditions, from icy winters to the darkest caves.

**Water-holding frogs** have adapted to harsh Australian deserts. They burrow underground and form a waxy cocoon from layers of skin, which retains moisture necessary for survival.

**Olms** are blind, aquatic salamanders that live in the caves of Slovenia and Croatia. They have excellent smell and hearing, which is helpful when foraging for food, such as snails.

**Crab-eating frogs** are able to tolerate saltier habitats than other amphibians. Native to Southeast Asia, this frog mainly eats insects, but it also preys on crabs, hence its name.

NEARLY **50%** OF ALL **AMPHIBIANS** ARE **THREATENED**, DUE TO WATER **POLLUTION**, HABITAT **DESTRUCTION**, AND THE INTRODUCTION OF **INVASIVE** SPECIES.

# FROG LIFE CYCLE

Most frogs undergo a dramatic physical change from a newborn to an adult through several distinct stages—a process known as metamorphosis.

**1. Frog spawn**
After frogs mate, the female lays the eggs in water as a clump called frog spawn. Clear jelly protects the black dot in the middle, which will become the tadpole.

**2. Tadpoles**
After about 10 days, tadpoles begin to move inside the eggs, before hatching. Over the next nine weeks, they will develop the ability to swim and eat.

**3. Froglet**
After about nine weeks, the tadpole starts to resemble a frog, with hind and front legs and a pointed head. The long tail will also shorten to a mere stub.

**4. Frog**
At 12 weeks, it is almost a fully formed frog and can leave the water. When it is an adult, it can mate and have young of its own.

## BIGGEST AMPHIBIAN

THE **SOUTH CHINA GIANT SALAMANDER** CAN GROW **6 FT** (1.8 M) LONG—ABOUT THE LENGTH OF **FOUR DOMESTIC CATS.**

## SMALLEST AMPHIBIAN

**PAEDOPHRYNE AMAUENSIS,** A FROG FROM PAPUA NEW GUINEA, IS NO BIGGER THAN A FLY, UP TO **5/16 IN** (7.7 MM) LONG.

 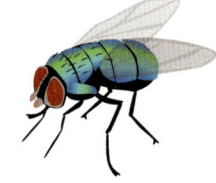

## ISLAND FROGS

Some frogs live on only one island, where the conditions—from the weather and habitat to food—are just right.

**Solomon Island leaf frogs** resemble the color and shape of leaves on the Solomon Islands in the South Pacific. Curiously, they hatch from eggs as fully developed frogs.

**Gardiner's Seychelles frogs** are one of the tiniest frogs in the world, growing to just 3/8 in (1 cm). Living in the Seychelles, off the eastern edge of Africa, their habitat is threatened by wildfires.

## VENOMOUS AMPHIBIANS

Of all the amphibians, caecilians are probably the most mysterious because they are hard to find in their burrows. However, some experts think these curious creatures, such as the giant caecilian, could have venomous saliva. There are only very few known venomous amphibians, such as Brazil's Greening's frog.

Giant caecilian

## HIGHEST AMPHIBIAN

**BOULENGER'S LAZY TOADS** LIVE **17,290 FT** (5,270 M) HIGH, IN **GURUDONGMAR LAKE**, INDIA.

## ONE GIANT LEAP

Growing up to 6 in (15 cm), American bullfrogs can leap 20 times their own body length, often pouncing on prey such as insects, fish, and even snakes. They live in freshwater ponds, lakes, and marshes in parts of North America.

The American bullfrog is the largest frog in North America.

## OTHER SALAMANDERS

**Japanese giant salamander**
This is one of the biggest amphibians—up to 4½ ft (1.4 m) long. It lives in cold mountain streams and gets almost all its oxygen directly through its wrinkled skin.

**Amphiuma**
Only found in North America, this aquatic salamander, with its tiny limbs and eel-like body, has both gills and lungs, but the gills are hidden under flaps of skin.

**Mushroom-tongued salamander**
This tiny salamander is one of nearly 500 species from the Central American tropics that lack lungs and breathe only through their skin.

**Fire salamander**
This air-breathing salamander from European forests is unusual in giving birth to live young—as aquatic larvae—rather than laying eggs.

**Great crested newt**
Newts are land salamanders that return to water to breed, changing their appearance by developing smoother skin and tail fins.

# Mudpuppy

Salamanders are amphibians shaped like lizards, with long tails and short legs. The mudpuppy is a salamander that lives on river- and lake beds in North America. They get their unusual name because it was once thought they barked like a dog, but in fact their sound is more like a squeak.

**Lake living**
The common mudpuppy is one of eight species of mudpuppies found in the wettest parts of the United States and Canada—mainly in the Great Lakes and the rivers that flow from them. It lurks among the mud and silt, hiding during the day and emerging at night to feed.

**Swamp dweller**
In the warm, wet swamps of southern Louisiana, many mudpuppies are yellower than elsewhere in the US and youngsters often venture out of water into woodland leaf litter.

**Organs for breathing**
During their life cycle, most amphibians go through a big change called metamorphosis, where their aquatic larva turns into an air-breathing adult. But in some salamanders, such as the mudpuppy, this process is incomplete. The adults keep their gills, allowing them to continue breathing underwater.

Blood-filled gills allow the mudpuppy to breathe underwater

Long lungs for breathing air

AMPHIBIANS | 57

THERE ARE MORE THAN **760** **SALAMANDER SPECIES** IN THE WORLD

 LIKE ALL OTHER AMPHIBIANS, **MUDPUPPIES** TAKE IN SOME **OXYGEN** DIRECTLY **THROUGH THEIR SKIN**

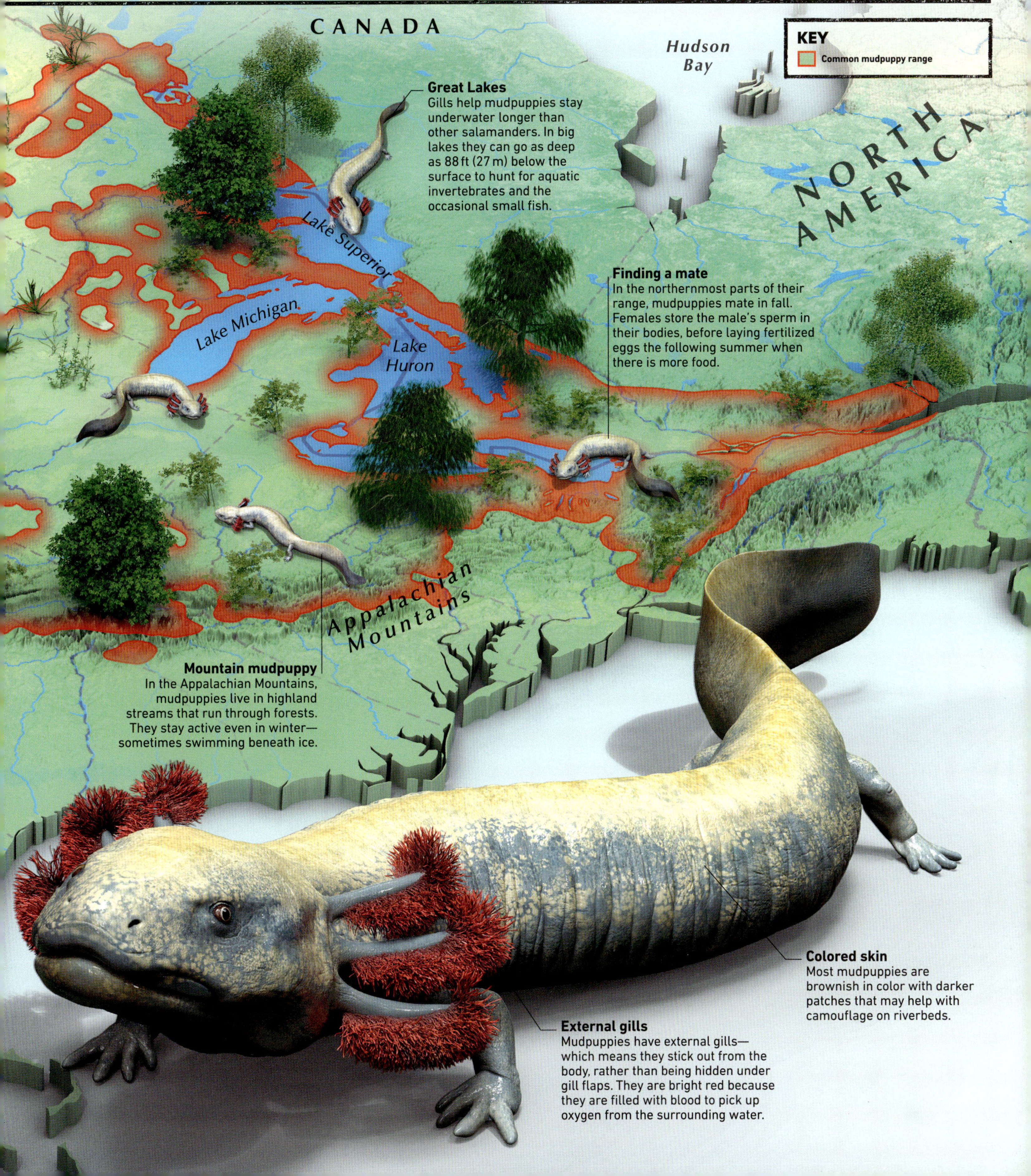

CANADA

Hudson Bay

NORTH AMERICA

**KEY**
Common mudpuppy range

**Great Lakes**
Gills help mudpuppies stay underwater longer than other salamanders. In big lakes they can go as deep as 88 ft (27 m) below the surface to hunt for aquatic invertebrates and the occasional small fish.

Lake Superior
Lake Michigan
Lake Huron

**Finding a mate**
In the northernmost parts of their range, mudpuppies mate in fall. Females store the male's sperm in their bodies, before laying fertilized eggs the following summer when there is more food.

Appalachian Mountains

**Mountain mudpuppy**
In the Appalachian Mountains, mudpuppies live in highland streams that run through forests. They stay active even in winter—sometimes swimming beneath ice.

**Colored skin**
Most mudpuppies are brownish in color with darker patches that may help with camouflage on riverbeds.

**External gills**
Mudpuppies have external gills—which means they stick out from the body, rather than being hidden under gill flaps. They are bright red because they are filled with blood to pick up oxygen from the surrounding water.

### Mossy frog
The Vietnamese mossy frog lives in the rainforest-covered mountains of northern Vietnam. Its mottled green skin, covered in bumps and ridges, blends in with the wet moss that lines the river banks and caves of the frog's forest habitat. It breeds in water-filled tree holes, laying its eggs above the waterline, safe from predators below.

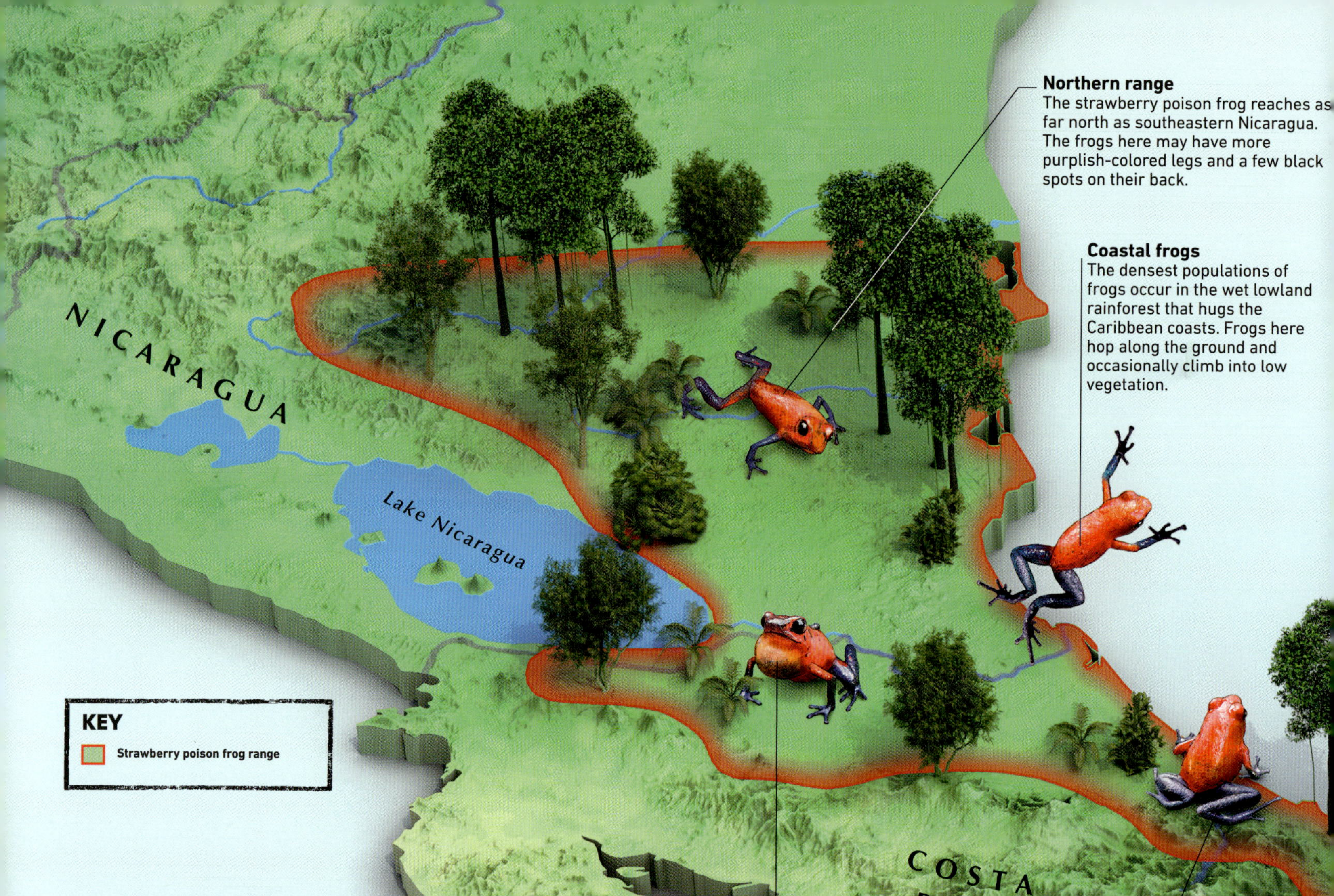

### Northern range
The strawberry poison frog reaches as far north as southeastern Nicaragua. The frogs here may have more purplish-colored legs and a few black spots on their back.

### Coastal frogs
The densest populations of frogs occur in the wet lowland rainforest that hugs the Caribbean coasts. Frogs here hop along the ground and occasionally climb into low vegetation.

**KEY**
— Strawberry poison frog range

### Rainforest frog
Mountains running through Central America keep many different lowland animal species apart on either side. The strawberry poison frog lives in the eastern forest along the Caribbean coast. These frogs are small: adults are only about ¾ in (2 cm) long. Most are bright red with blue or black legs—but in some places colors vary.

### Calling out
Strawberry frogs live on plants near the forest floor. The males use their low, buzzing call to defend their tiny territories and attract females.

### Blue jeans
Most strawberry poison frogs have red bodies and blue legs, earning them the nickname "blue jeans" frogs. In the south of their range some mainland frogs are grayish or yellow.

### Plant pool
Strawberry poison frogs are careful parents. They lay their eggs on forest leaves. When they hatch, the tadpoles are carried on the mother's back to a pool of water in a bromeliad plant, where they turn into frogs.

### Color varieties
The strawberry poison frog comes in more than 100 different colored varieties called morphs. Most of these varieties occur on tiny islands off the Central American coast, where frogs are cut off from those on the mainland. They have different colors because their populations have been separated for thousands of years and have evolved to look different.

Color morphs of the strawberry poison frog

# Strawberry poison frog

Most amphibians rely on poisons to defend themselves. Glands in their skin ooze chemicals that can be irritating or even deadly. The strawberry poison frog from Central America excels at defending itself in this way—and warns off enemies with its bright colors.

THIS FROG GETS ITS **POISON** FROM THE **ANTS IT EATS**

THERE ARE **200** SPECIES OF **POISON FROGS** IN THE AMERICAS

**Island frogs**
The tiny islands of Bocas del Toro off the Caribbean coast of Panama are home to many different colors of strawberry poison frogs (see panel below).

**Poison skin**
The skin is moistened by secretions from two types of gland: one produces mucus and makes it slimy, the other oozes poison that tastes repulsive to predators.

# Common toad

Amphibians need moisture to survive, but some are tolerant of a range of different habitats. The common toad, one of more than 600 toad species across the world, is the most widespread in Europe. It lives equally well in forests, alpine meadows, and dry sand dunes.

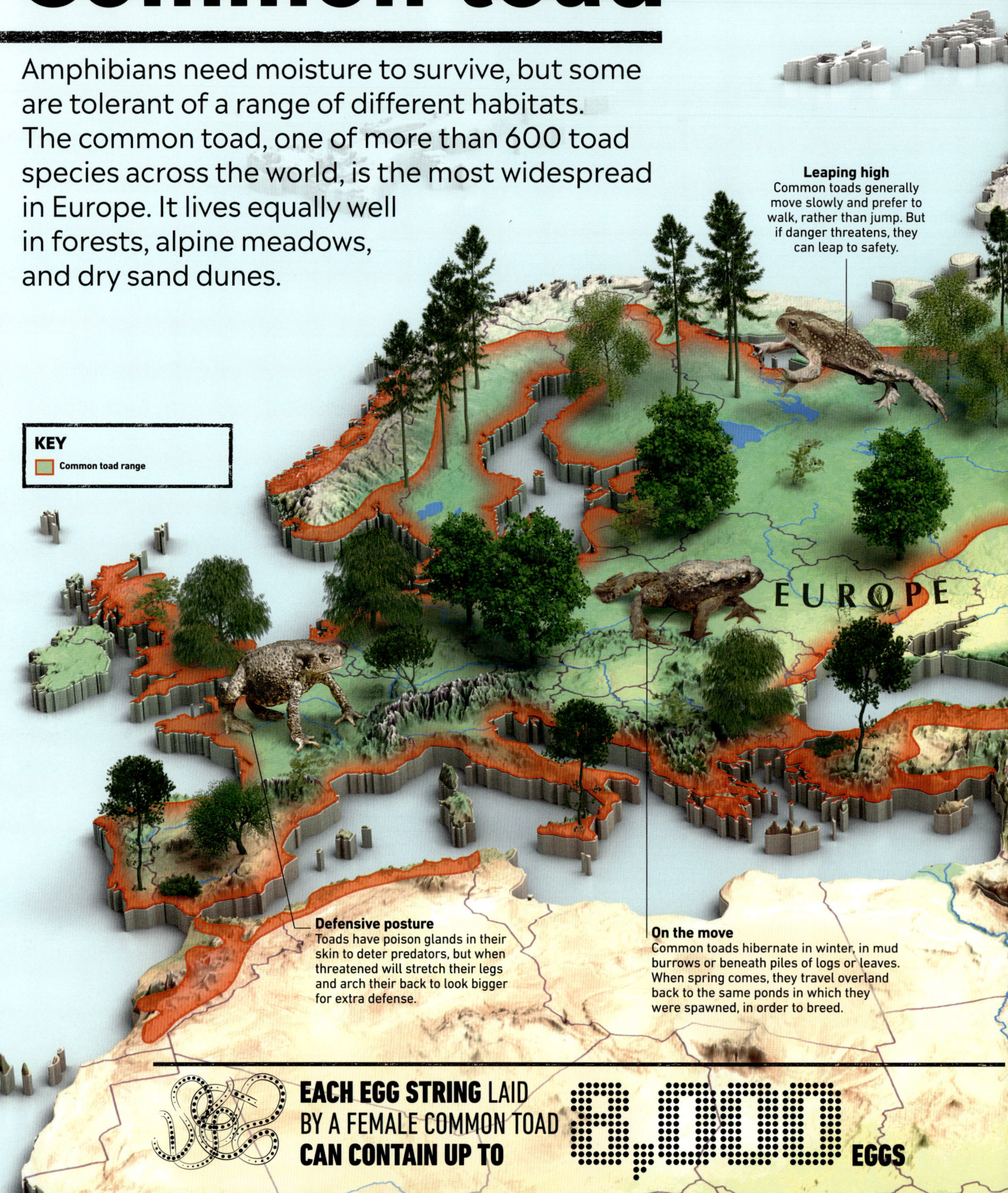

**KEY**
Common toad range

**Leaping high**
Common toads generally move slowly and prefer to walk, rather than jump. But if danger threatens, they can leap to safety.

**Defensive posture**
Toads have poison glands in their skin to deter predators, but when threatened will stretch their legs and arch their back to look bigger for extra defense.

**On the move**
Common toads hibernate in winter, in mud burrows or beneath piles of logs or leaves. When spring comes, they travel overland back to the same ponds in which they were spawned, in order to breed.

**EACH EGG STRING** LAID BY A FEMALE COMMON TOAD **CAN CONTAIN UP TO 8,000 EGGS**

AMPHIBIANS | 63

### Breeding pools
Like most amphibians, toads lay their eggs in pools of water. The female common toad lays her eggs in two long strings, each up to 16 ft (5 m) long. The eggs will hatch into aquatic larvae, or tadpoles.

### Mass migration
Each springtime, large numbers of common toads emerge from hibernation and travel to their breeding pools. In some places, special toad-crossing tunnels have been built to help them cross roads safely.

### Mating toads
When mating in ponds, the male toad grabs the larger female around the waist just behind her front legs and then fertilizes the strings of eggs as they are released into the water.

ASIA

### Temperate belt
The common toad is found throughout much of Europe—in the temperate belt south of the cold polar regions and north of hotter Africa and Asia. It lives most of its life away from water, hiding in damp, shady places, returning to the water only to breed.

### Bulging eyes
The large eyes of a common toad give it good night vision. Common toads are most active at night, using the cover of darkness to hunt for prey.

### Tongue attack
The toad catches invertebrate prey, such as slugs, snails, and spiders, with a long, sticky-tipped tongue that shoots out of its mouth at lightning speed.

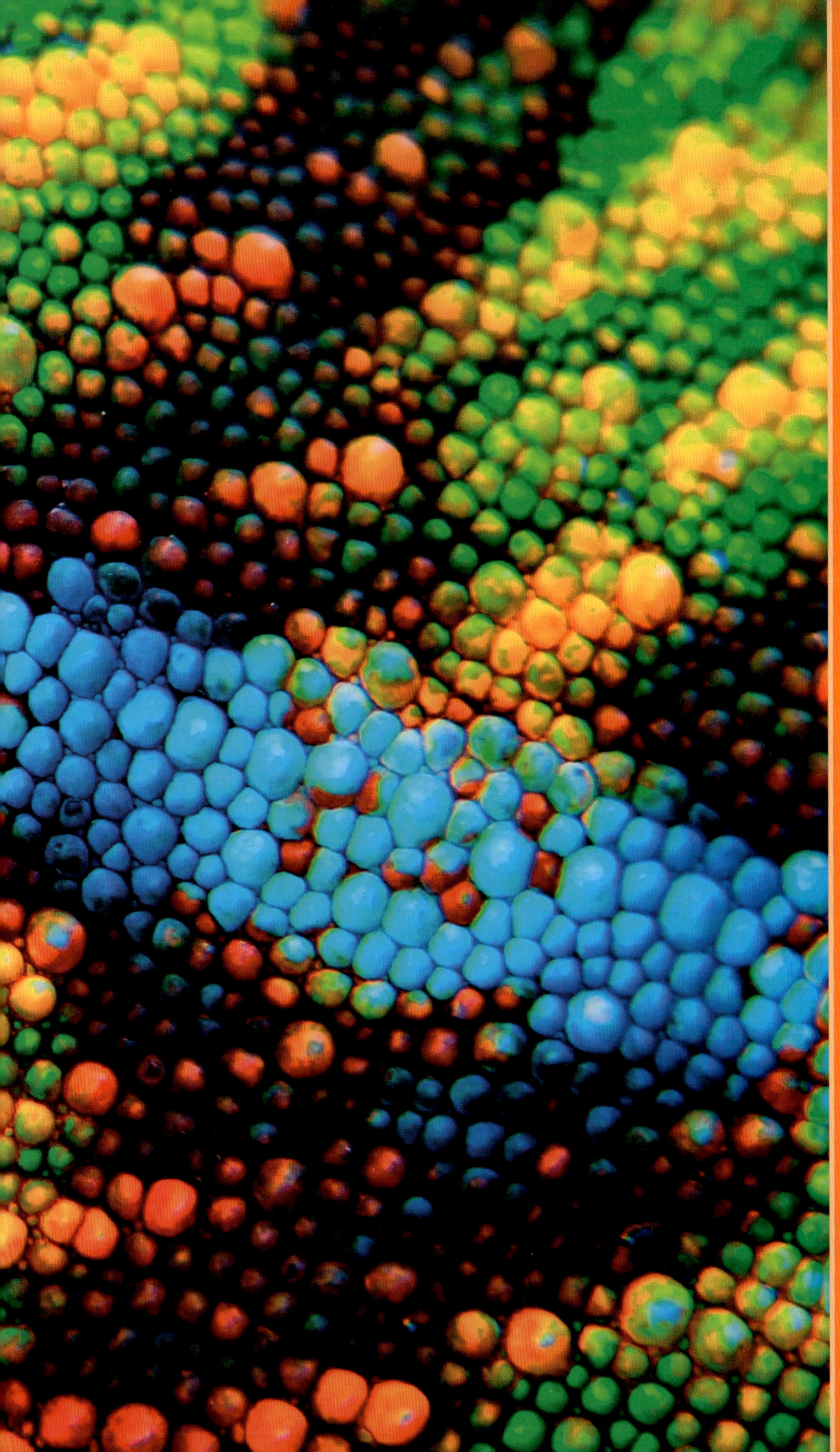

# REPTILES

# Reptile facts

Scaly and cold-blooded, reptiles first appeared around 310 million years ago and were the first backboned animals that could live entirely on land. From desert snakes to migrating sea turtles, reptiles today are scattered throughout the world, except the very coldest habitats.

## WHAT IS A REPTILE?

**Vertebrates**
From slithery snakes to giant tortoises, all reptiles are supported by a bony skeleton.

**Cold-blooded**
The body temperature of all reptiles changes depending on their environment.

**Lay eggs**
Most reptiles, from crocodiles to lizards, lay soft, leathery, and waterproof eggs.

**Live young**
Some snakes and lizards do not lay eggs like most other reptiles, but instead give birth to live young.

**Scaly skin**
Reptilian skin is covered in protective scales, or in some cases, horny plates.

## REPTILE TYPES

**ESTIMATED NUMBER OF REPTILE SPECIES:**  11,340

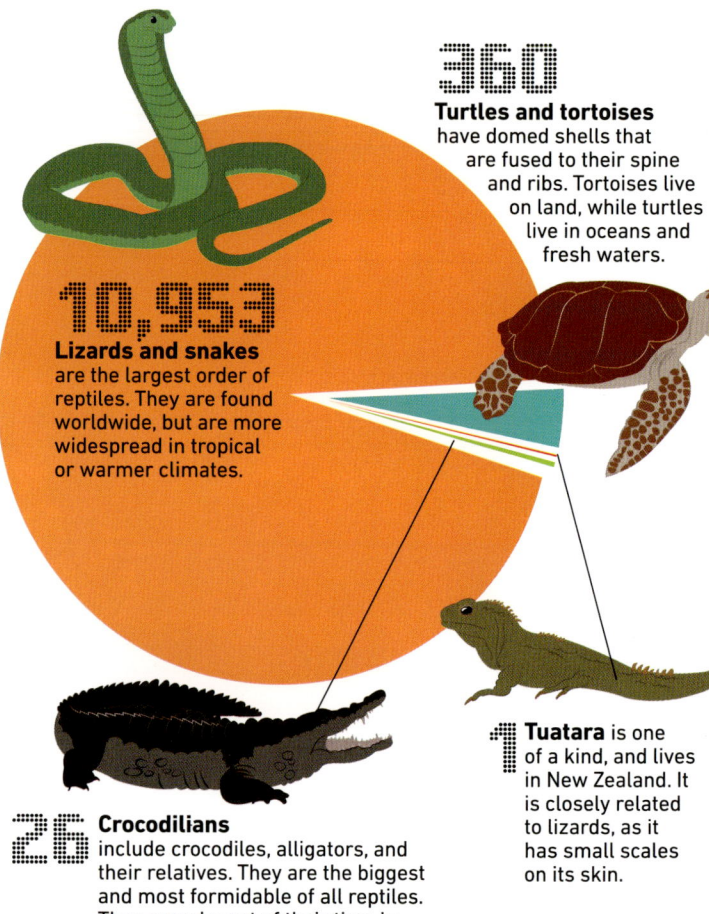

**360 Turtles and tortoises** have domed shells that are fused to their spine and ribs. Tortoises live on land, while turtles live in oceans and fresh waters.

**10,953 Lizards and snakes** are the largest order of reptiles. They are found worldwide, but are more widespread in tropical or warmer climates.

**26 Crocodilians** include crocodiles, alligators, and their relatives. They are the biggest and most formidable of all reptiles. They spend most of their time in water, although some hunt on land.

**1 Tuatara** is one of a kind, and lives in New Zealand. It is closely related to lizards, as it has small scales on its skin.

## EXTREME HABITATS

From the freezing Arctic to underground burrows in the desert, some reptiles survive and thrive in the most incredible ways.

**Common European adders** are the only snake species found within the Arctic Circle. Its huge range also extends from temperate woodlands to the European Alps 9,840 ft (3,000 m) high.

**Gopher tortoises** survive the intense heat and cold of the American Mojave Desert by burrowing underground with their sharp claws. They spend up to 95 percent of their lives in these burrows.

**Sea snakes** are the best-adapted reptile for life in water. All true sea snakes give birth to live young, without ever coming ashore to lay eggs. They live mainly in tropical oceans.

## LONGEST MIGRATION

**LEATHERBACK TURTLES** CAN TRAVEL **12,750** MILES (20,500 KM) FROM THEIR **INDONESIAN** BREEDING GROUND TO FEED OFF THE PACIFIC COAST OF **THE USA**.

# BIGGEST GATHERING

EACH **SPRING** INSIDE THE SNAKE DENS OF NARCISSE, **MANITOBA, CANADA**, **75,000** **RED-SIDED GARTER SNAKES** CONGREGATE IN A MATING FRENZY, WITH UP TO **100 MALES** VYING FOR **EVERY FEMALE**.

# SMALLEST REPTILE

— Coin

THE **VIRGIN ISLANDS DWARF SPHAERO** IS ONLY **5/8 IN** (1.6 CM) LONG.

# OLDEST REPTILE

BORN IN **1832**, THE **OLDEST-LIVING LAND ANIMAL** IS A **SEYCHELLES GIANT TORTOISE** CALLED **JONATHAN**.

# LONGEST REPTILE

THE **RETICULATED PYTHON** OF SOUTHEAST ASIA HAS SET THE RECORD-BREAKING LENGTH OF **33 FT** (10 M).

# FASTEST REPTILE

In a reptilian race between the fastest snake and swiftest lizard, the lizard would easily cross the finish line first.

**FASTEST SNAKE:** SIDEWINDER AT **18 MPH** (28 KPH)

**FASTEST LIZARD:** BEARDED DRAGON AT **25 MPH** (40 KPH)

# SNAKE MOTION

A snake can move in four main ways. Some species can switch between styles of moving, depending on the surface.

**Straight**
Scales along a snake's belly provide traction on the ground for it to propel itself in a line, using the muscles around its long ribcage.

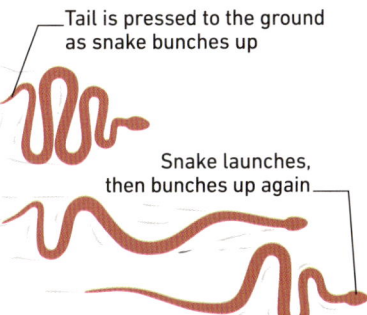

- Tail is pressed to the ground as snake bunches up
- Snake launches, then bunches up again

**Concertina**
To get a good grip on a smooth surface, a snake can bunch up before pulling its back end up and launching itself forward.

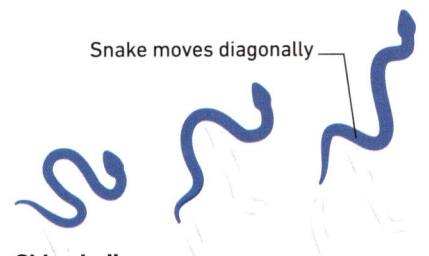

Snake moves diagonally

**Sidewinding**
In open spaces such as sandy deserts, some snakes fling their head sideways through the air, with the rest of the body following.

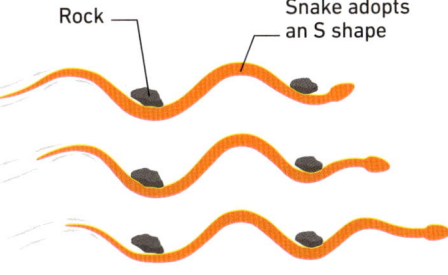

Rock — Snake adopts an S shape

**Serpentine**
This common style involves a snake pushing itself off a bump on a surface or an object, and continuing forward in a wavy motion.

# HIGHEST-LIVING REPTILE

THE **RED TAIL TOAD-HEADED LIZARD** HAS BEEN SEEN AT **17,390 FT** (5,300 M). IT LIVES IN THE QIANGTANG PLATEAU IN NORTHERN TIBET.

# SMART REPTILE

The mugger crocodile in India has been observed using sticks to lure birds, such as egrets or herons, who may be looking to build a nest. It waits motionless and partially submerged, then snaps up its unsuspecting prey when it is close enough.

### Shell shape and diet

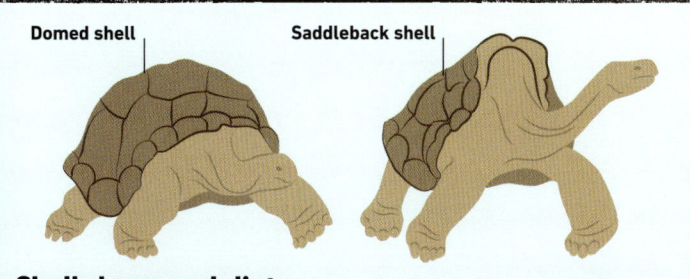

On wetter islands with plenty of ground plants to graze, the shells of Galápagos giant tortoises are dome-shaped. But on drier islands, tortoises have evolved raised shells – called saddlebacks – and long necks. This helps them reach tall cactuses that grow higher from the ground.

### Lonesome George

In 1971, scientists found the only surviving Pinta Island giant tortoise. The rest of its kind had died out, due to the overgrazing by goats introduced to the island. Named Lonesome George, this tortoise became a symbol of conservation, living out his life in captivity. He died in 2012.

*Isla Santa Cruz*

**Santa Cruz giant tortoise**
The dome-shelled giant tortoises of Santa Cruz live in separate populations on this island, and studies suggest that they might be different species.

*Galápagos Islands*

*Isla Santa Fe*

**San Cristóbal giant tortoise**
Animals introduced to this island, such as dogs and donkeys, drove San Cristóbal tortoises almost to extinction, but better control measures and captive breeding are helping to save the species.

*Isla San Cristóbal*

### Island giants

The Galápagos Islands erupted from the ocean more than three million years ago. Tortoises landed on their shores after floating across the waters from South America. With no natural predators, they evolved into giants and, as they adapted to the different conditions and food sources on each island, into separate species. Seven of these are shown on this map.

**Española giant tortoise**
On one of the oldest and most barren of the Galápagos Islands, Española tortoises have especially high-saddled shells to help them reach up to nibble on the scarce food growing here, such as cactuses.

*Isla Española*

*Isla Santa Maria*

# Galápagos giant tortoises

Tortoises are slow-moving reptiles with a heavy, protective shell. Some of the biggest tortoises on Earth live on the rugged, volcanic Galápagos Islands far out in the Pacific Ocean. Each island is home to its own species.

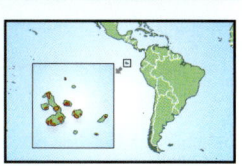

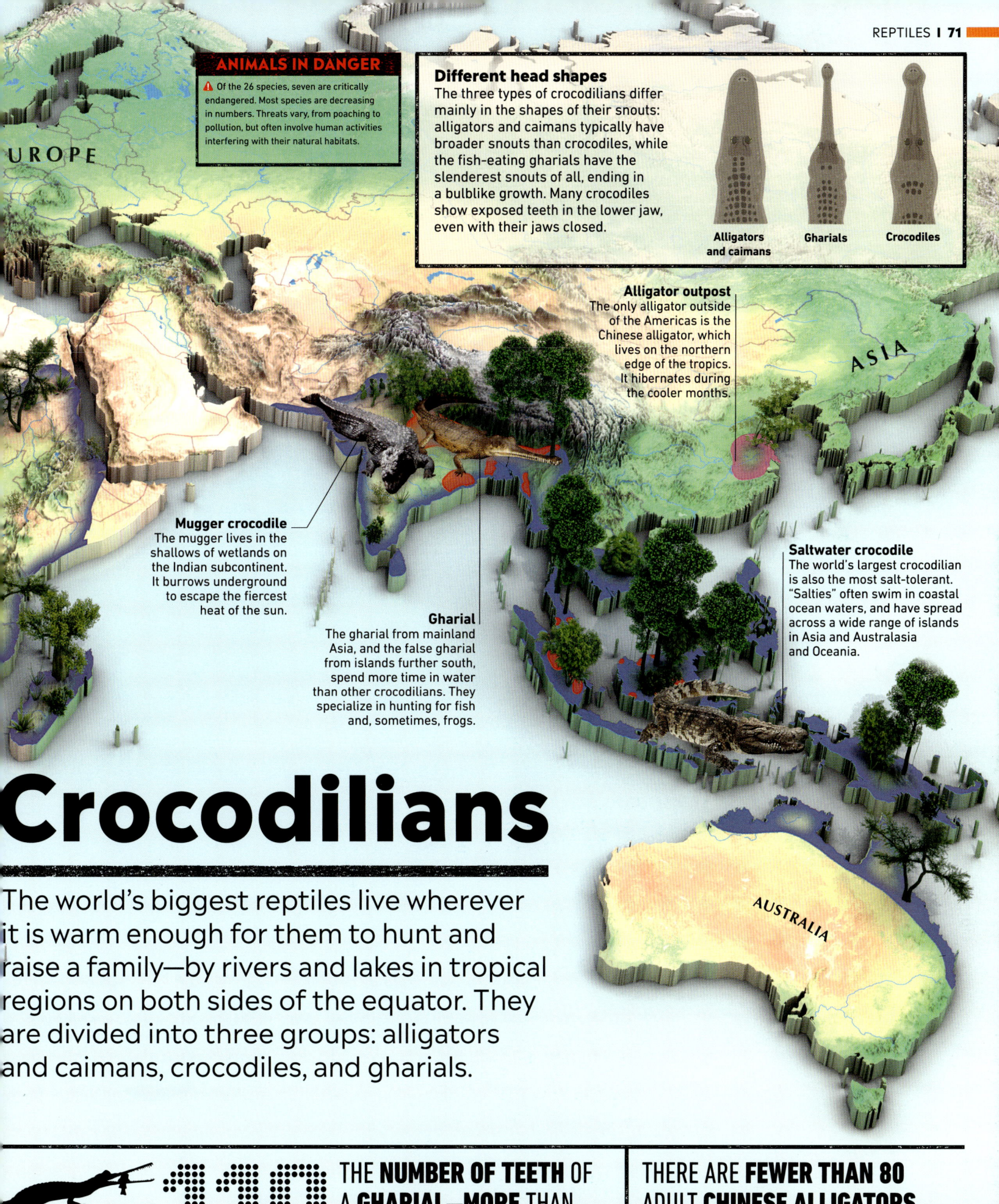

# Crocodilians

The world's biggest reptiles live wherever it is warm enough for them to hunt and raise a family—by rivers and lakes in tropical regions on both sides of the equator. They are divided into three groups: alligators and caimans, crocodiles, and gharials.

### ANIMALS IN DANGER
Of the 26 species, seven are critically endangered. Most species are decreasing in numbers. Threats vary, from poaching to pollution, but often involve human activities interfering with their natural habitats.

### Different head shapes
The three types of crocodilians differ mainly in the shapes of their snouts: alligators and caimans typically have broader snouts than crocodiles, while the fish-eating gharials have the slenderest snouts of all, ending in a bulblike growth. Many crocodiles show exposed teeth in the lower jaw, even with their jaws closed.

**Alligators and caimans** | **Gharials** | **Crocodiles**

### Alligator outpost
The only alligator outside of the Americas is the Chinese alligator, which lives on the northern edge of the tropics. It hibernates during the cooler months.

### Mugger crocodile
The mugger lives in the shallows of wetlands on the Indian subcontinent. It burrows underground to escape the fiercest heat of the sun.

### Gharial
The gharial from mainland Asia, and the false gharial from islands further south, spend more time in water than other crocodilians. They specialize in hunting for fish and, sometimes, frogs.

### Saltwater crocodile
The world's largest crocodilian is also the most salt-tolerant. "Salties" often swim in coastal ocean waters, and have spread across a wide range of islands in Asia and Australasia and Oceania.

**110** THE **NUMBER OF TEETH** OF A **GHARIAL**—**MORE** THAN ANY OTHER CROCODILIAN

THERE ARE **FEWER THAN 80** ADULT **CHINESE ALLIGATORS** LEFT IN THE WILD

# Chameleons

Strange-looking, slow-moving lizards with conical eyes and grasping tails, chameleons live in the tropics of Africa and southern Asia. Over half of the 200 chameleon species are found on the island of Madagascar and nowhere else. The island is home to the biggest and smallest of them all.

**KEY**
- Madagascan giant chameleon
- Labord's chameleon
- Elongate leaf chameleon
- Panther chameleon
- Parson's chameleon

**Madagascan giant chameleon**
The world's biggest species of chameleon—growing nearly 27½ in (70 cm) long—is one of the most widespread in Madagascar. It survives equally well in dry and wet forests all over the island.

**Labord's chameleon**
In the dry west of Madagascar, Labord's chameleon lives just five months before laying eggs during brief rains, and then dies. No other land vertebrate has such a short life.

**Catching prey**
Like all chameleons, the Madagascan giant chameleon catches insects and other prey by shooting out its long projectile tongue, which has a sticky end to trap the target.

**Elongate leaf chameleon**
One of many species of short-tailed leaf chameleons, this one lives in the branches of low bushes, and mimics a dead leaf to hide from predators.

**Madagascar chameleons**
Almost all chameleons live in forests. Some climb the trees while others live on the ground. This map shows five of the chameleon species that live on Madagascar. The island is drier in the west and wetter in the east, and it is in the rich rainforests of eastern Madagascar that most species occur, but many are now threatened by deforestation.

A CHAMELEON'S **TONGUE** CAN EXTEND **TWICE THE LENGTH** OF ITS **BODY**

### Armored lizard
The dragon-like armadillo girdled lizard is covered by protective spiny plates—except on its underside. To shield its soft belly from predator attacks, it grabs hold of its tail and curls up in a ball, like an armadillo (see p.109). This lizard lives in large family groups inside rock crevices in South Africa's western deserts.

# Green anaconda

All snakes prey on other animals, but the biggest kill by constriction, rather than venom. The green anaconda, at home in South America, is the heaviest of all constrictors, and can tackle animals the size of small deer.

**River snake**
More than 1,000 rivers run through the Amazon Basin, making it the perfect habitat for the green anaconda, which can swim faster than it crawls on land.

**Big meal**
Loosely connected jaw bones and a stretchy body help an anaconda swallow prey whole. Large prey, such as deer or caimans, can take weeks to digest.

**KEY**
Green anaconda range

**ANACONDAS GIVE BIRTH TO UP TO 50 YOUNG AT A TIME**

**Squeezed prey**
Constrictors such as anacondas kill not by crushing, but by suffocation. The snake squeezes tighter each time its victim exhales, so breathing becomes impossible, and the heart stops.

**Wetland giant**
The green anaconda grows so heavy that adult snakes tend to stick to rivers and wetlands, where their bodies are supported by water. The river-filled Amazon Basin merges with grasslands in the south, where much of the land is flooded during the rainy season, making a large part of South America prime anaconda habitat.

**Top vision**
The eyes of a green anaconda are set higher on the head than those of many other snakes. This helps it keep watch at the water's surface, while its body is submerged.

**Scaly skin**
As it grows, the anaconda needs to shed its scaly skin several times a year, but the pattern of black oval spots on a muddy green background doesn't change.

**Chunky waist**
At its thickest, an anaconda's body can have a diameter of up to 12 in (30 cm).

## OTHER LARGE CONSTRICTORS

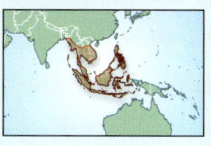

**Reticulated python**
The green anaconda is the heaviest, but the longest snake is likely to be the reticulated python from Southeast Asia, with recorded lengths of more than 23 ft (7 m).

**African rock python**
The biggest snake in Africa, growing to 20 ft (6 m) long, the African rock python has the strength to prey on large crocodiles.

**Burmese python**
Weighing around 400 lb (180 kg), the Burmese python from Southeast Asia is the heaviest recorded snake after the green anaconda.

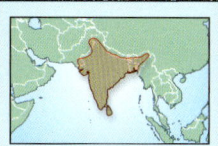

**Indian rock python**
Only slightly smaller than the Burmese and African rock pythons, this snake swims well and is common in wetlands and forests of India and Sri Lanka.

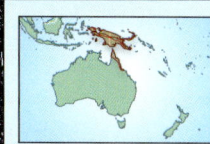

**Amethystine python**
Australia's largest snake hunts possums and wallabies, and sometimes slides into human homes. It is also widespread in New Guinea and nearby islands.

## Deadly snakes

The warm tropics are home to the greatest number of snake species. The most dangerous venomous types belong to two groups: vipers, with large, hinged fangs, and elapids, with shorter fangs that are always raised. This map shows seven of the world's deadliest snakes.

**Western diamondback rattlesnake**
One of the largest venomous snakes found in North America, this rattlesnake hunts desert rodents, but is also responsible for many human injuries in the US.

**Common lance head**
A relative of the rattlesnakes, the common lance head moves about at night, and is one of the most dangerous vipers found in the tropical forests of South America.

**Fangs**
Rattlesnakes are vipers, and have some of the biggest fangs of any snake. The largest rattlesnakes can have fangs more than 2 in (5 cm) long.

**Warning rattle**
The tail tip rattle is made up of special scales that produce a warning sound when shaken if predators come too close.

**Black mamba**
Named for the black lining of its mouth, this elapid is one of the longest and fastest of the venomous snakes in Africa and quickly inflicts multiple dangerous bites.

Western diamondback rattlesnake

### Snake venom
Venom is a poisonous fluid that flows from glands in the snake's upper jaw. When the snake bites, a muscle squeezes venom out through the fangs. Viper fangs reach further forward than those of elapids.

**Elapid** — Elapids have small, fixed fangs at the back of the jaw

**Viper** — Viper fangs swing forward as the jaw opens

### KEY
- Western diamondback rattlesnake
- Common lance head
- Black mamba
- Saw-scaled viper
- Indian cobra
- Many-banded krait
- Tiger snake

# Venomous snakes

There are around 3,850 species of snakes around the world, and about 20 percent of these are venomous. They use their venom to kill their prey—but some also strike in self-defense and, when they do so, some species can be dangerous to humans, such as the ones shown here.

**Saw-scaled viper**
With a dangerous bite, and often found living close to humans, this snake is probably responsible for more human deaths than any other. Similar saw-scaled vipers occur elsewhere on the Arabian Peninsula and in parts of Africa.

**Indian cobra**
The Indian cobra is an elapid that warns anyone approaching that it will strike in self-defense. It extends ribs close to its neck to produce a flat hood, while rising up to appear bigger.

**Many-banded krait**
Kraits are boldly patterned elapid snakes found across Asia. Living near water, the many-banded krait hides during the day and hunts at night, preying on fish. If surprised, it uses its deadly bite in self-defense.

**Tiger snake**
The tiger snake is one of many highly venomous elapid snakes found in Australia. Individuals vary in color and not all have the stripes that give the species its name.

ABOUT **200** SNAKE SPECIES HAVE **VENOM** THAT IS HARMFUL TO **HUMANS**

AROUND **138,000** PEOPLE DIE FROM A SNAKE BITE EVERY YEAR

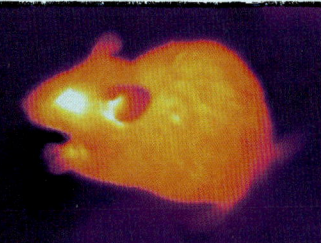

**Hunting by heat**
Vipers have an extra sense that helps them locate prey. Heat-sensitive pits on their head allow them to "see" the body heat of warm-blooded animals, in the same way that the mouse shows up against a cold background in this thermal image.

# BIRDS

# Bird facts

Evolving from two-legged dinosaurs, the first birds took flight about 140 million years ago. Today, birds are found on every continent and in a diverse range of habitats, from grasslands to deserts. Many birds migrate incredibly long distances to breed or find food.

## WHAT IS A BIRD?

**Vertebrates**
Birds have thin and lightweight, yet strong, internal skeletons made of bone.

**Warm-blooded**
From humid rainforests to chilly mountaintops, birds generate and maintain a stable body temperature.

**Lay eggs**
Birds breed by laying hard eggs, which chicks crack open when ready to hatch.

**Most fly**
Using their wings, most birds can take to the skies, however some birds are flightless.

**Feathered**
Feathers are important for retaining body heat and helping birds fly.

## BIRD TYPES

**ESTIMATED NUMBER OF BIRD SPECIES: 11,500**

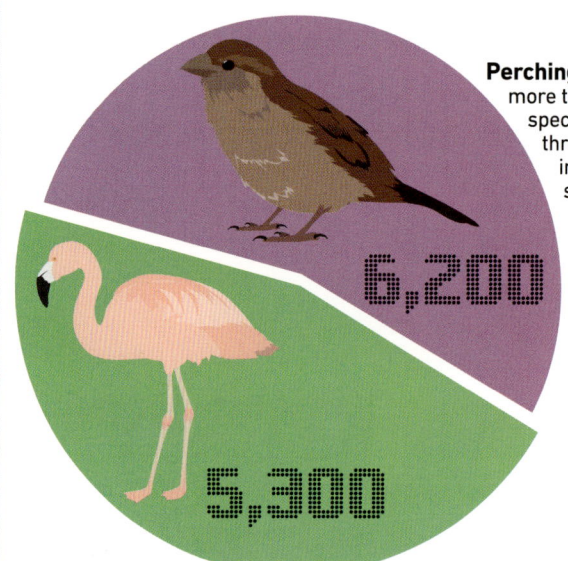

6,200

5,300

**Perching birds** account for more than half of all bird species. Their feet have three unwebbed toes in the front and one strong, flexible toe on the back, allowing them to perch on tree branches. Found globally, they include sparrows, lyrebirds, and birds of paradise.

**Non-perching birds** account for all other species. They include a wide range of birds located across the world including parrots, owls, flamingos, and birds of prey, as well as flightless birds, such as ostriches, emus, and penguins.

**COLOMBIA** HAS OVER **1,850** BIRD SPECIES—**MORE THAN ANY OTHER COUNTRY** IN THE WORLD.

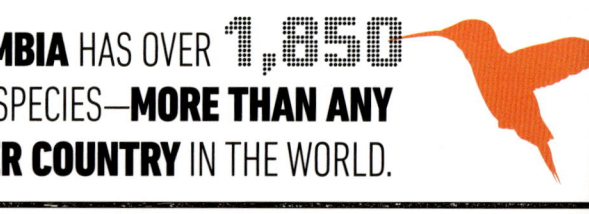

## LONGEST MIGRATION

**ARCTIC TERNS** FLY AN AMAZING **59,650** MILES (96,000 KM) FROM THEIR BREEDING GROUND IN THE **NORTH ATLANTIC** TO **ANTARCTICA** AND BACK AGAIN.

## HIBERNATING BIRD

**The common poorwill,** seen here on a roof, is the only bird species known to hibernate. Its diet of insects rapidly declines during winter, so it goes into a state of hibernation for weeks or even months. This bird is found in the grassy areas of North America.

## BIGGEST GATHERING

Flocks of more than 1.5 billion red-billed quelea have been witnessed flying over the African savanna. In such great numbers, this small bird is a constant threat to crop farmers. In fact, it is such a pest, it is often called the "feathered locust."

## BILL SHAPES

Over millions of years, birds have evolved many different bill shapes. Here are five of them, each designed to help the bird eat or catch its prey.

**Seed-eater**
Birds such as crossbills have strong bills for eating seeds. The crossbill can extract seeds from pine cones with its overlapping bill.

**Water-sifter**
Flamingos have long, wide bills that they sweep from side to side in shallow waters, sifting out animals to eat.

**Nectar-gatherer**
The pointed bills are designed for precision. Sunbirds' bills also curve downward, which is ideal for extracting flower nectar.

**Mud probe**
Birds with long, sensitive bills can explore soft mud in search of prey. The snipe looks for snails and small crustaceans.

**Butchery tool**
This hooked bill, as seen on a golden eagle, is perfect for stripping meat from the bones of fish, birds, or mammals.

---

## THE LARGEST FLYING BIRD IS THE WANDERING ALBATROSS, WITH A WINGSPAN OF 12 FT (3.6 M).

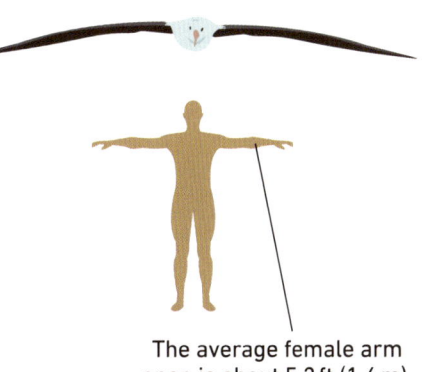
The average female arm span is about 5.2 ft (1.6 m).

## BIGGEST BIRD AND EGGS

THE OSTRICH, A FLIGHTLESS BIRD FROM SUB-SAHARAN AFRICA, IS THE WORLD'S TALLEST BIRD.

IT ALSO BEARS THE LARGEST EGGS, UP TO 6 IN (15 CM) LONG—NEARLY THREE TIMES LONGER THAN A HEN'S EGG.

## SMALLEST BIRD

THE **BEE HUMMINGBIRD** IS JUST 2.4 IN (6 CM) LONG. THIS TINY BIRD IS NATIVE TO **CUBA**.

---

## FASTEST BIRD

Found throughout the world, peregrine falcons are formidable hunters. They swoop in on prey, such as other birds and bats, at a record-breaking speed.

**SWOOPING SPEED = 200 MPH (320 KPH)**

**RÜPPELL'S VULTURE**
**35,000 FT (10,670 M)**

## HIGHEST-FLYING BIRD

**RÜPPELL'S VULTURE** CAN REACH AN ALTITUDE OF **37,000 FT** (11,280 M), HIGHER THAN THE CRUISING ALTITUDE OF AN AIRPLANE.

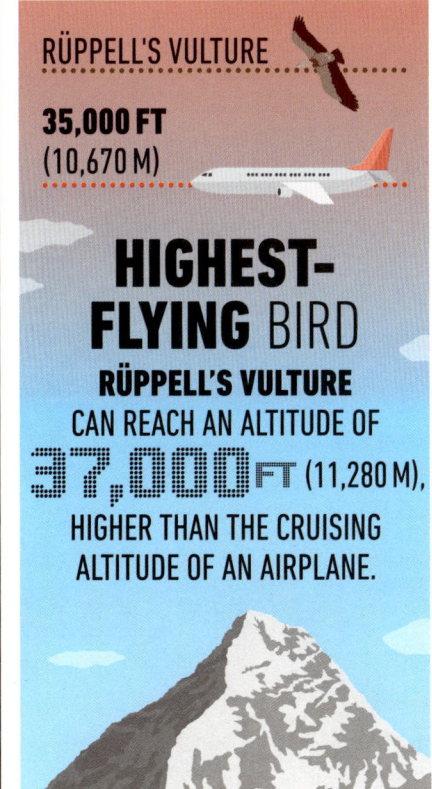

## BIGGEST NEST

**SOCIABLE WEAVERS** MAKE AND MAINTAIN NESTS THAT CAN HOUSE UP TO **500** BIRDS.

## SMART BIRD

Found in the remote Pacific islands after which it is named, the New Caledonian crow can manipulate and use twigs to dig out prey, such as grubs, from trees. These intelligent forest-dwelling birds are the first to be observed making and using tools in this way.

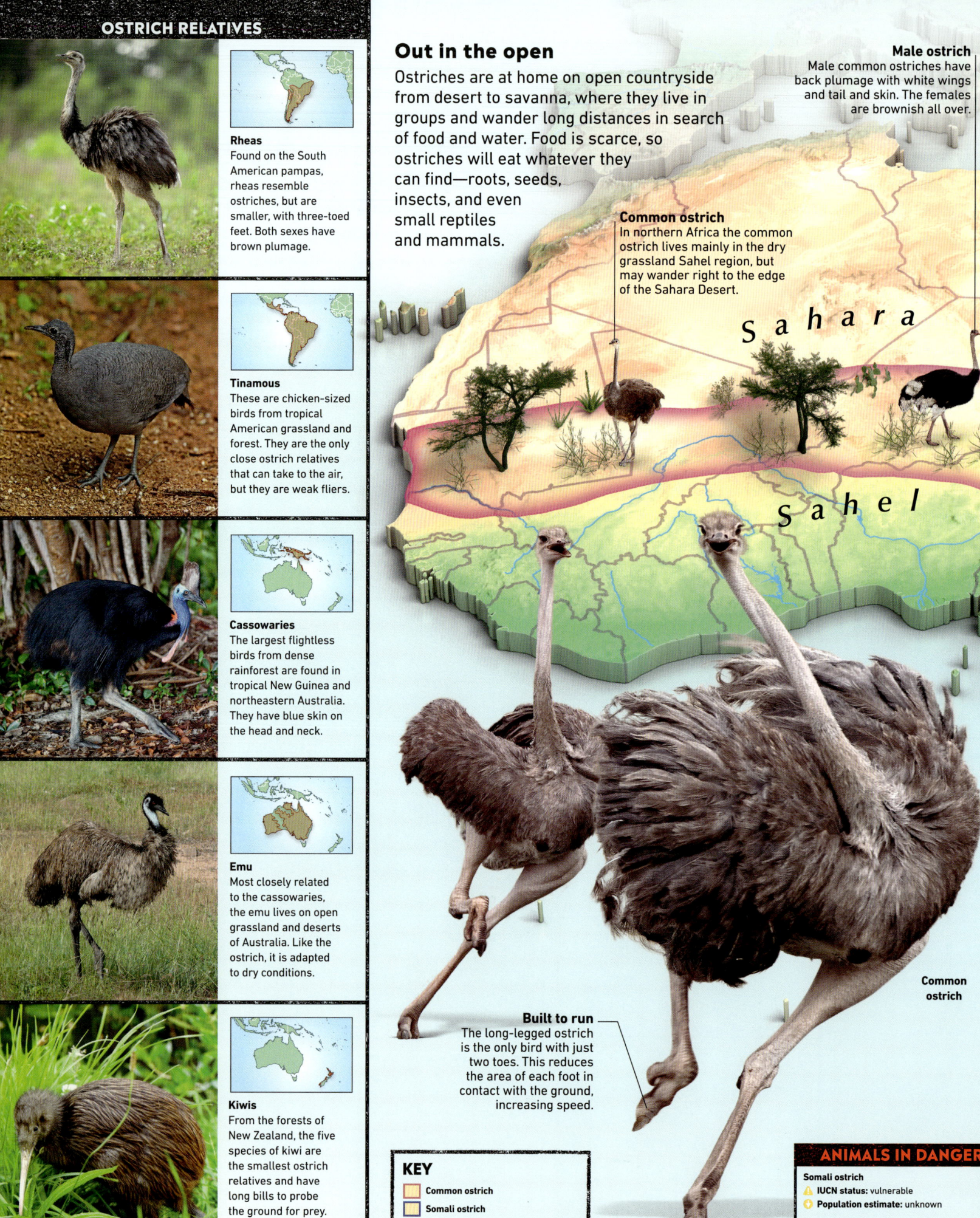

# Ostriches

A bird that can't fly, and roams where there is very little cover, has to run fast to escape predators. The flightless ostrich does just that. As well as being the world's biggest bird it is the fastest animal on two legs. There are two species and both live in open habitats in Africa.

**Ostrich chicks**
All female ostriches in the group lay their eggs in a communal nest, so adults may end up guarding large crèches of chicks.

**Somali ostrich**
This species lives in the eastern horn of Africa—in Somalia, Ethiopia, and Kenya. Males have a gray head, neck, legs, and feet, and a deeper black plumage than the common ostrich.

**Masai region**
In the Masai region of east Africa, common ostriches have a reddish-tinge to their neck but are more closely related to the gray-necked ostriches further south.

**Rift Valley**
The two species of ostrich are separated by the Great Rift Valley (pictured below). On the eastern side, the Somali ostrich has split away from common ostriches and evolved into a separate species.

**Desert dweller**
In the southernmost part of their range, common ostriches live in hot, dry desert.

**MALE OSTRICHES STAND UP TO 9 FT (2.7 M) TALL**

**AT TOP SPEED** AN OSTRICH CAN RUN ABOUT 43 MPH (70 KPH)—THAT'S **FASTER THAN A RACEHORSE**

### Changing colors

Each year, thousands of Caribbean flamingos are born in one of the world's largest flamingo colonies, Mexico's Ría Lagartos Biosphere Reserve. The chicks' gray feathers turn pink when they eat shrimp and other invertebrates containing a dye. This bird's population is rising, from the Caribbean to South America.

ON **ANTARCTIC COASTS** THE **WINTER WINDS** CAN BLOW UP TO **200 MPH** (320 KPH)

 EMPEROR PENGUINS ARE **UNDER THREAT FROM CLIMATE CHANGE,** AS RISING TEMPERATURES **MELT THE WINTER SEA ICE**

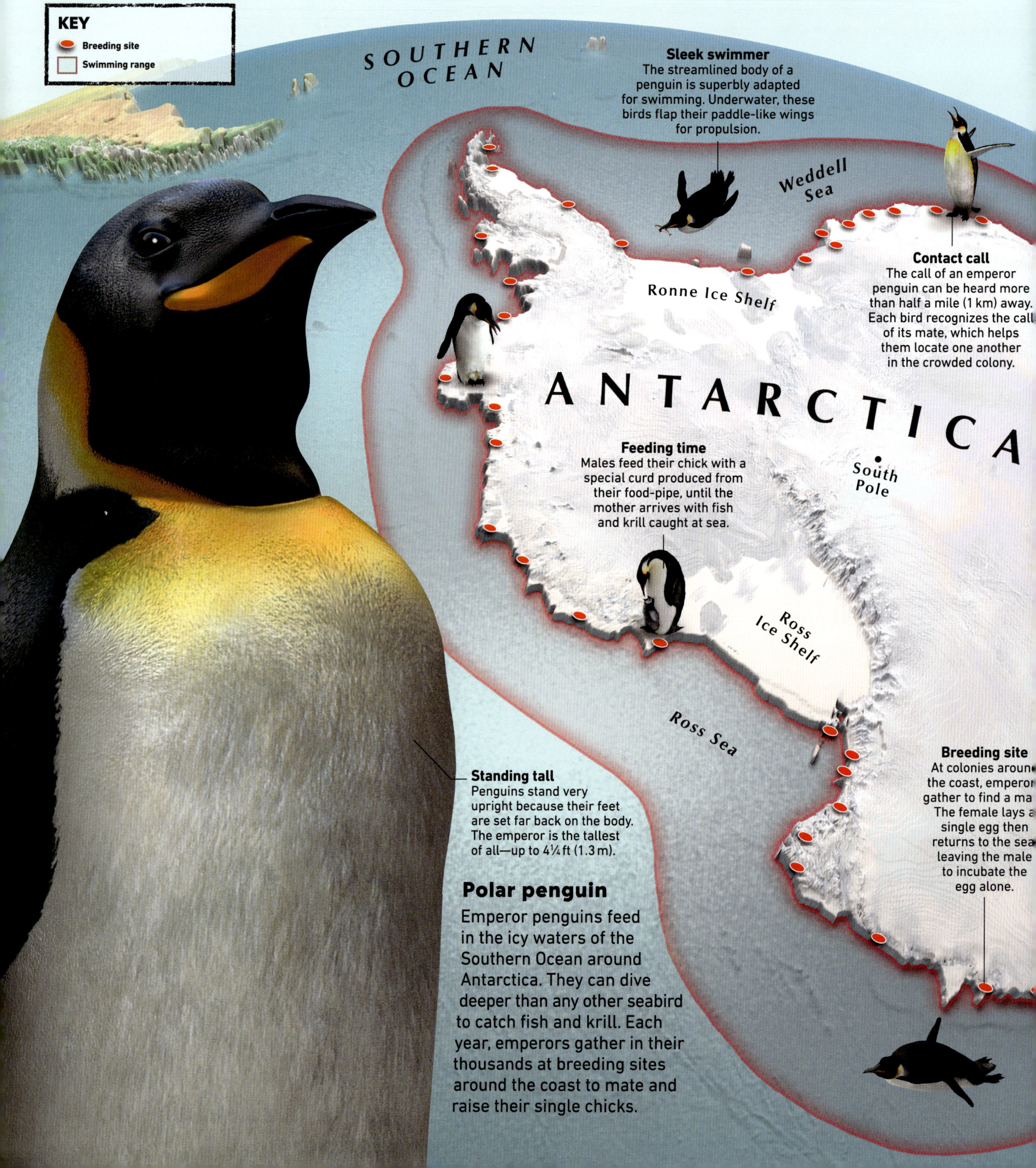

**KEY**
- Breeding site
- Swimming range

SOUTHERN OCEAN

Weddell Sea

Ronne Ice Shelf

ANTARCTICA

South Pole

Ross Ice Shelf

Ross Sea

**Sleek swimmer**
The streamlined body of a penguin is superbly adapted for swimming. Underwater, these birds flap their paddle-like wings for propulsion.

**Contact call**
The call of an emperor penguin can be heard more than half a mile (1 km) away. Each bird recognizes the call of its mate, which helps them locate one another in the crowded colony.

**Feeding time**
Males feed their chick with a special curd produced from their food-pipe, until the mother arrives with fish and krill caught at sea.

**Breeding site**
At colonies around the coast, emperors gather to find a mate. The female lays a single egg then returns to the sea, leaving the male to incubate the egg alone.

**Standing tall**
Penguins stand very upright because their feet are set far back on the body. The emperor is the tallest of all—up to 4¼ ft (1.3 m).

## Polar penguin

Emperor penguins feed in the icy waters of the Southern Ocean around Antarctica. They can dive deeper than any other seabird to catch fish and krill. Each year, emperors gather in their thousands at breeding sites around the coast to mate and raise their single chicks.

# Emperor penguin

The life of the world's biggest penguin is a story of surviving extremes. It is one of the very few animals to live and breed on the Antarctic continent—the coldest place on Earth. Emperor penguins raise their chicks in the dark, bitter Antarctic winter, when the temperature can drop to -76°F (-60°C).

### Fluffy chicks
Emperor penguin chicks have downy gray feathers. They stay on the ice, dependent on their parents, until they molt into their adult plumage and set off to sea to fish for themselves.

### Speedy sliders
Penguins waddle around slowly on land, but they have a way of speeding up—"tobogganing" over snow and ice on their bellies.

**ANIMALS IN DANGER**
Emperor penguin
- IUCN status: near threatened
- Population estimate: 595,000 in 2009

### Keeping warm
Thousands of males huddle together to stay warm in the harsh Antarctic winter. Each is incubating a single egg under his belly, on top of his feet. The males stay on the ice with their egg all winter, until the females return.

SOUTHERN OCEAN

## PENGUINS

**Galápagos penguin**
All 18 species of penguin live in the southern hemisphere. The most northerly one lives on the Galápagos Islands at the equator, nesting in crevices in the volcanic rock.

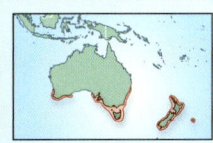

**Jackass penguin**
The only African penguin nests and feeds mainly on and around offshore islands, but is also sometimes found on the coasts of Namibia and South Africa.

**Little penguin**
This is the world's smallest penguin, at only 16 in (40 cm) tall. It lives on southern Australian, Tasmanian, and New Zealand coasts, nesting on the dunes.

**Macaroni penguin**
Like most penguin species, the macaroni penguin lives on islands in the Southern Ocean, between Antarctica and warmer waters further north.

**Adélie penguin**
The Adélie penguin is the only other penguin species restricted to Antarctica. Unlike the emperor, it breeds on ice-free shores during the summer months.

# Snowy owl

Few predatory birds are found as far north as the snowy owl. Many other owl species live in cold northern forests, but only the snowy can survive on the treeless tundra, where the ground is frozen solid and covered in snow for much of the year.

**Ground nester**
Unlike other owls, the snowy owl must nest on the ground in its open tundra habitat. It chooses an elevated site to give it a view of approaching danger.

**Variable clutch**
The number of eggs a snowy owl lays depends upon how much food is available. When there are plenty of prey animals to hunt, the owl may lay eight or more.

**Non-breeding range**
Snowy owls breed in the northerly parts of their range and migrate further south during the winter. They will also sometimes move south at other times if food becomes scarce.

### ANIMALS IN DANGER
Snowy owl
- IUCN status: vulnerable
- Population estimate: 28,000

**Blending in**
The snowy owl is the only owl with an all-white plumage. This helps disguise it against the snowy ground, especially during the Arctic summer when there is almost continuous daylight and the bird is breeding and hunts at all hours.

**Hunting**
The snowy owl has such good hearing it can detect the position of prey burrowing beneath a blanket of snow. It swallows small rodents whole, but will tear larger animals, such as hares and rabbits, to pieces first.

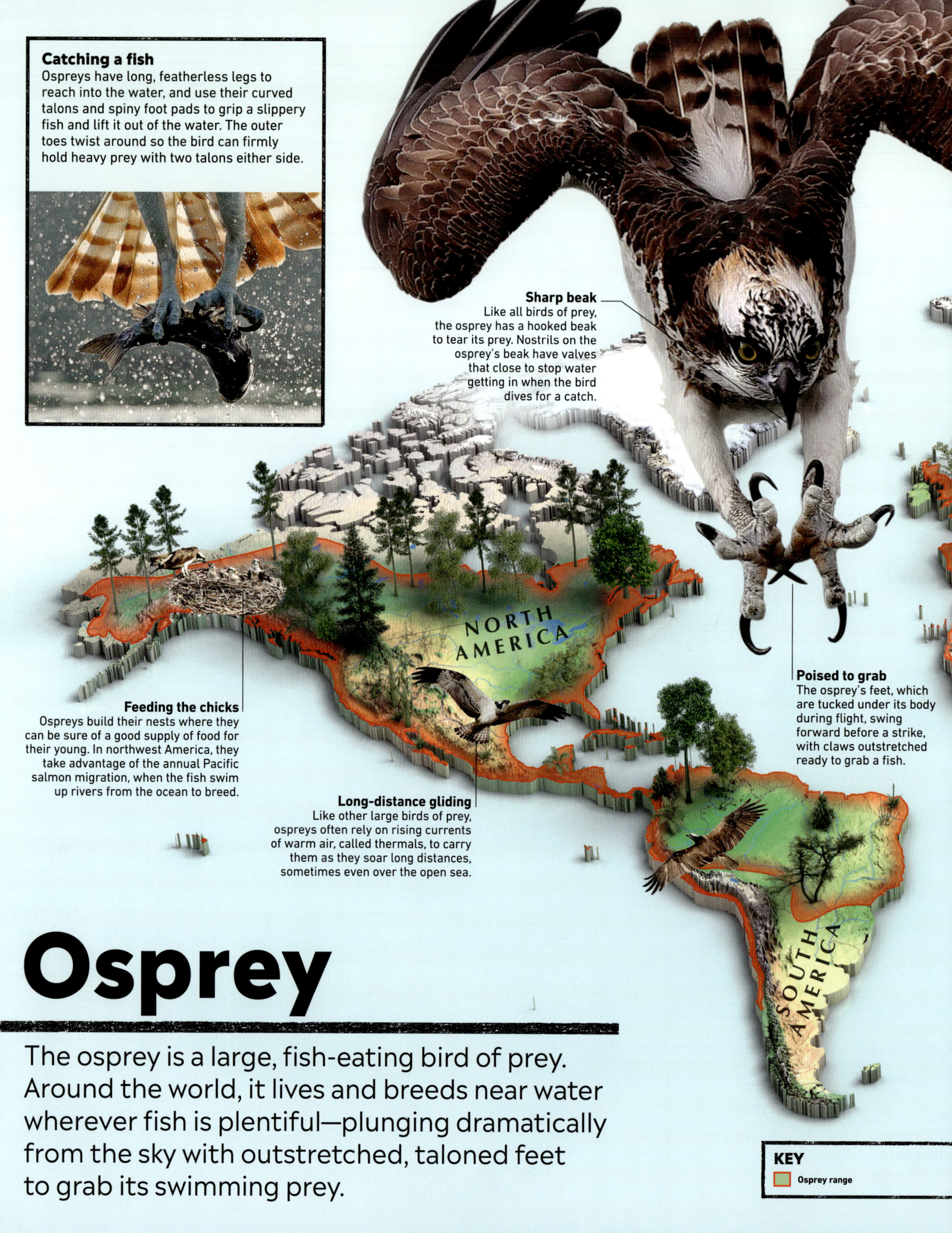

**Catching a fish**
Ospreys have long, featherless legs to reach into the water, and use their curved talons and spiny foot pads to grip a slippery fish and lift it out of the water. The outer toes twist around so the bird can firmly hold heavy prey with two talons either side.

**Sharp beak**
Like all birds of prey, the osprey has a hooked beak to tear its prey. Nostrils on the osprey's beak have valves that close to stop water getting in when the bird dives for a catch.

**Feeding the chicks**
Ospreys build their nests where they can be sure of a good supply of food for their young. In northwest America, they take advantage of the annual Pacific salmon migration, when the fish swim up rivers from the ocean to breed.

**Long-distance gliding**
Like other large birds of prey, ospreys often rely on rising currents of warm air, called thermals, to carry them as they soar long distances, sometimes even over the open sea.

**Poised to grab**
The osprey's feet, which are tucked under its body during flight, swing forward before a strike, with claws outstretched ready to grab a fish.

# Osprey

The osprey is a large, fish-eating bird of prey. Around the world, it lives and breeds near water wherever fish is plentiful—plunging dramatically from the sky with outstretched, taloned feet to grab its swimming prey.

**KEY**
Osprey range

**Passing through**
In the northern parts of their range, ospreys are seasonal visitors, arriving to hunt and breed in spring and summer, before migrating south to avoid the bitter winters.

**Breeding pair**
Ospreys start breeding at around three years old. Typically, a male mates with a single female, but if he can defend two nests, he might have a second partner.

**Year-round residents**
In warmer parts of the world, such as southern Asia, some populations of osprey are resident throughout the year and do not migrate.

**Smaller birds**
The ospreys in Southeast Asia, New Guinea, and Australia are slightly smaller than those in the rest of the world. Some scientists think that they belong to a different species.

**Winter visitors**
Across sub-Saharan Africa, ospreys are winter visitors, traveling from Europe at the end of the northern summer. Only in Egypt and other parts of northeastern Africa are they resident all year.

**Waterside nests**
Ospreys nest along the shores of lakes and rivers or by marshes, typically choosing an exposed tree in which to build a platform of sticks before laying a clutch of three eggs. The first-born chicks are the strongest—younger ones may be left to starve if food is scarce.

## Worldwide raptor

The osprey is one of the world's most wide-ranging birds. It lives almost everywhere there is water to fish, except for the cold polar regions and the remotest islands. Birds in the northern hemisphere migrate south for the winter, but ospreys around the equator tend to stay in the same place all year round.

AN OSPREY CAN **CARRY PREY** WEIGHING AROUND **2 LB (1 KG)**—HALF ITS OWN BODY WEIGHT

AN OSPREY'S **WINGSPAN** MAY BE UP TO **6 FT (2 M)** WIDE

OSPREYS **MIGRATING** FROM **AFRICA** TO **EUROPE** IN SUMMER TRAVEL UP TO **5,000 MILES (8,000 KM)**

**A committee of vultures**
From a rocky peak in the Eastern Rhodope Mountains, Bulgaria, a group of griffon vultures survey their surroundings for food. These large birds of prey are scavengers—they feed on carrion (dead animals). Using their huge wings, they soar on thermal air currents while scanning the ground for fresh carcasses.

# Blue-and-yellow macaw

This spectacular bird is one of the biggest of the world's 405 parrot species. The blue-and-yellow macaw flies in noisy flocks over the canopy of the world's largest forest, the Amazon, which covers much of northern South America.

**Colorful plumage**
Like other species of macaw, this parrot has bright colors—blue above and yellow below—but it is surprisingly difficult to spot it when foraging high in the forest canopy.

**Long tail**
As well as their large size, reaching up to 34 in (86 cm) in length, macaws are also distinguished from other parrots by their long, tapering tail.

**Amazonian parrot**
The blue-and-yellow macaw is found throughout the Amazon forest. Here, tall trees provide fruit and nuts for feeding, while the trunks of dead palms offer comfortable holes to nest. This parrot is still common throughout much of the region, but it is becoming threatened by deforestation and the pet trade.

**Tools for dining**
Like all parrots, the blue-and-yellow macaw is equipped to pick up and crack open hard-shelled nuts. It uses its clawed feet and a very powerful, but sensitive, beak to grasp and break open nuts. Sometimes, one macaw may try to steal the seed from another.

BLUE-AND-YELLOW MACAWS ARE **NOT ENDANGERED**, BUT THEIR **NUMBERS ARE DECLINING** DUE TO **SHRINKING HABITATS**

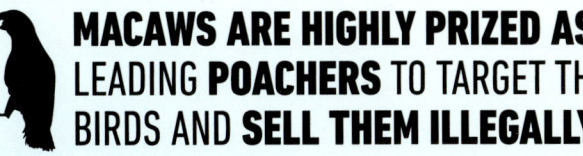 MACAWS ARE HIGHLY PRIZED AS PETS, LEADING **POACHERS** TO TARGET THESE BIRDS AND **SELL THEM ILLEGALLY**

### Flooded forests
In the central Amazon, the blue-and-yellow macaw lives in a type of forest called várzea. This region gets flooded during the rainy season, but the birds can stay feeding in the canopy high above the rising waters.

### Dry forests
In some parts of its range, the blue-and-yellow macaw lives in woodlands very different from the wet rainforest. Here, the trees are deciduous and lose their leaves during the dry season.

**KEY**
- Blue-and-yellow macaw range

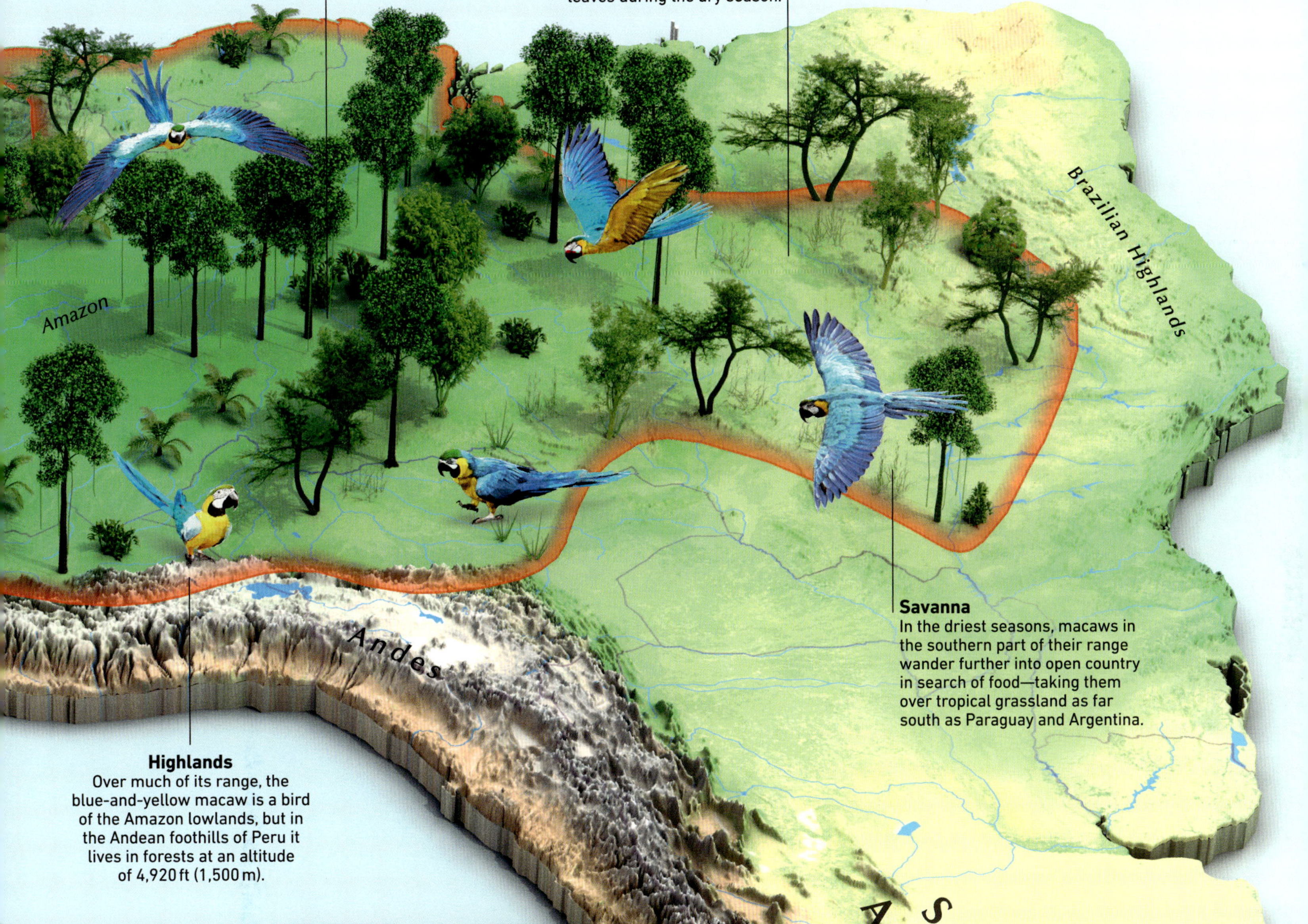

### Savanna
In the driest seasons, macaws in the southern part of their range wander further into open country in search of food—taking them over tropical grassland as far south as Paraguay and Argentina.

### Highlands
Over much of its range, the blue-and-yellow macaw is a bird of the Amazon lowlands, but in the Andean foothills of Peru it lives in forests at an altitude of 4,920 ft (1,500 m).

### Salt lick
Salt is scarce in the rainy Amazon rainforest, so macaws and other animals are attracted to exposed mineral-rich mud banks. Here they nibble the clay, which supplies much of the salt and other nutrients that keep them healthy. Macaws and other parrots are among the few kinds of birds to participate in this unusual feeding behavior.

## Crossing the globe

Barn swallows are found across much of the world, and each year most cross the equator in their migrations—between North and South America or the wildest stretches of Asia. Swallows from Europe even travel across Africa's Sahara Desert to reach their wintering grounds.

**North America**
Barn swallows in North America breed from May to August. The swallows here—like those in far eastern Siberia—have reddish-brown, rather than pure white, underparts.

**Caribbean passage**
Swallows migrating south from North America either island-hop through the Caribbean, or follow the path of land through Central America.

**Europe**
Throughout summer, barn swallows breed across Europe, and as far south as northern Africa. Most of those from northern and central Europe start their migration south in September or October.

**South America**
Barn swallows arriving in South America reach Colombia and the Guianas by late August, and Brazil, Paraguay, and Argentina by September.

**Africa**
Barn swallows overwinter across vast regions of Africa: birds arriving from western Europe tend to head to the west, and those from eastern Europe to the east. The longest distance traveled between Europe and Africa is an incredible 7,245 miles (11,660 km).

# Barn swallow

More than half of all bird species are small perching birds, or passerines. Many are expert at hunting insects on the wing. Barn swallows nest and raise their young in the northern summers, when the skies are buzzing with life. But they must migrate to the warmer tropics before winter comes and insect numbers fall.

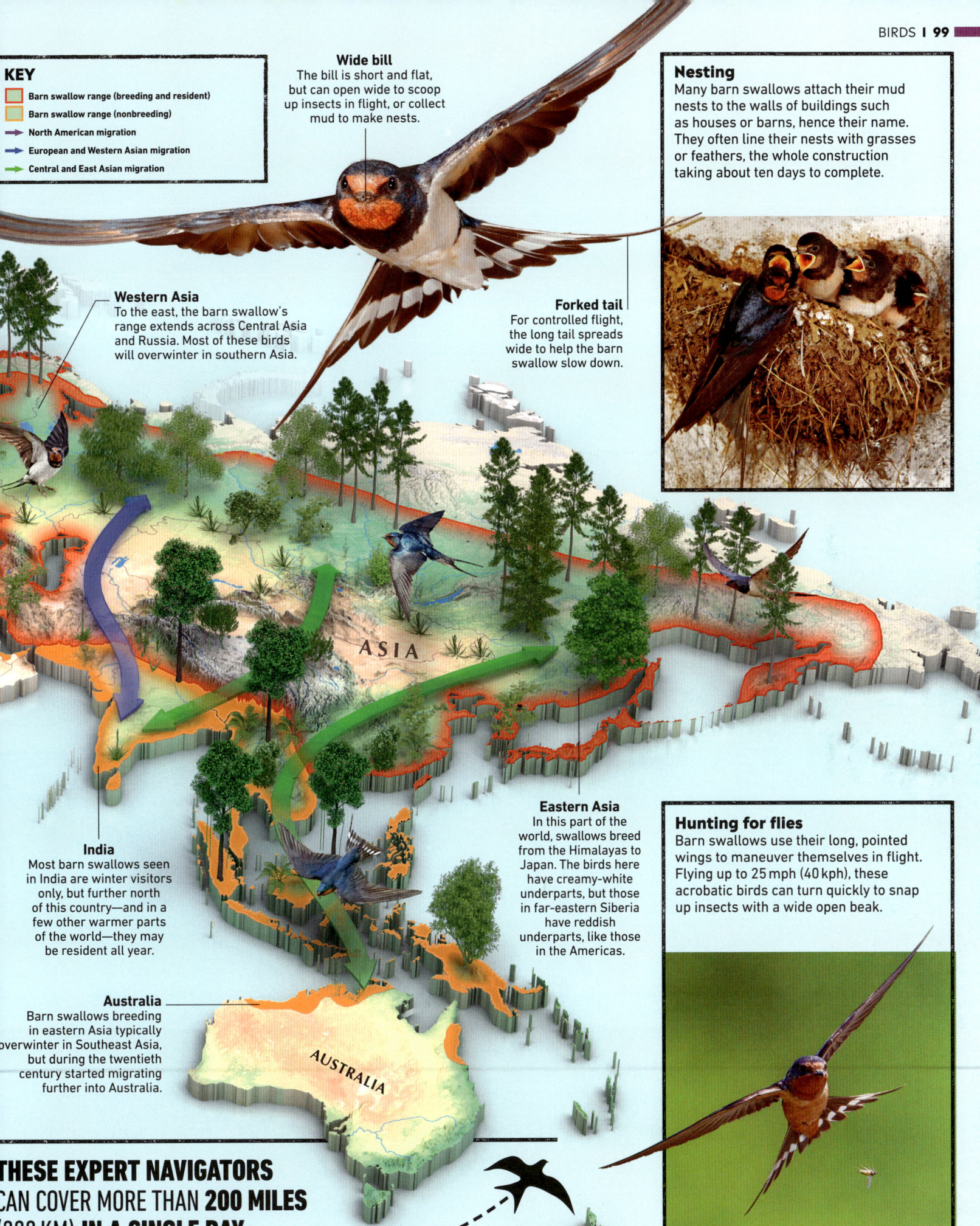

# MAMMALS

# Mammal facts

The first mammals evolved 220 million years ago, when dinosaurs dominated the Earth. Today, mammals have adapted to live almost everywhere and are spread all over the world, from grasslands and rainforests to icy poles and deep oceans.

## WHAT IS A MAMMAL?

**Vertebrates**
Although they may look different, all mammals have an internal skeleton that is made of bone.

**Warm-blooded**
Mammals maintain a stable body temperature, whether they are in a hot or cold environment.

**Live young**
Most mammals give birth to live young, rather than hatching from eggs like birds.

**Drink milk**
Young mammals feed on milk from their mother, which provides vital nutrients for their growth.

**Hair**
Mammals have fur, spines, or scales to trap heat. Marine mammals have insulating blubber.

## MAMMAL TYPES

**ESTIMATED NUMBER OF MAMMAL SPECIES: 6,550**

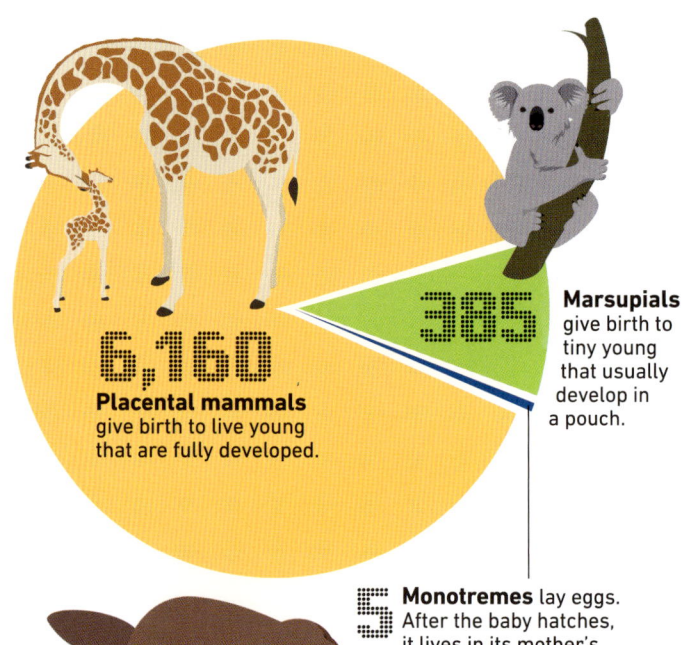

**6,160 Placental mammals** give birth to live young that are fully developed.

**385 Marsupials** give birth to tiny young that usually develop in a pouch.

**5 Monotremes** lay eggs. After the baby hatches, it lives in its mother's pouch for several weeks as it continues to develop.

THE **TAILLESS TENREC** OF **MADAGASCAR** CAN HAVE UP TO **32 BABIES** IN ONE LITTER.

## EXTREME HABITATS

Some hardy mammals have adapted to survive in extremely hot, cold, or rather odd places.

**Musk oxen** use their hooves to dig through snow and find edible plants in temperatures below freezing. They live mainly in the tundra regions of Greenland and Arctic North America.

**Kangaroo rats** have adapted to live in the extreme heat of the deserts in the western US and Mexico. This rodent does not drink water, instead getting moisture from desert grass seeds.

**Goats** can grip tiny crevices with their hooves, allowing them to ascend a vertical cliff safely. These rock-climbing goats are in Greece, but this mammal can be found all over the world.

## INDONESIA IS HOME TO

**291 MAMMAL SPECIES**

MORE THAN ANY OTHER **COUNTRY.**

# BIGGEST MAMMAL

**Blue whales** are the largest animal ever to have lived on Earth. They swim in all of the world's oceans, except the Arctic.

A BLUE WHALE CAN GROW **108 FT** (33 M), THE LENGTH OF 17 ADULT DIVERS.

# SMALLEST MAMMAL

The **Kitti's hog-nosed bat** lives in limestone caves near rivers in parts of Thailand and Myanmar.

ITS HEAD–BODY LENGTH IS UP TO **1 3/8 IN** (34 MM)—TWICE AS LONG AS A BUMBLEBEE.

# FASTEST MAMMALS

Whether on water, land, or in the air, these mammals are some of the fastest in the animal kingdom.

- IN WATER: ORCA AT **55 MPH** (88 KPH)
- ON LAND: CHEETAH AT **70 MPH** (113 KPH)
- IN THE AIR: BRAZILIAN FREE-TAILED BAT AT **100 MPH** (160 KPH)

This speedy bat is found in parts of North, Central, and South America.

# LONGEST OVERLAND MIGRATION

CARIBOU MIGRATION IS A RETURN TRIP OF MORE THAN **745 MILES** (1,200 KM)

**Caribou** are native to North America, and spend summer months in the north of the continent feeding on grasses. This is also where females give birth. When winter snow falls, they head south in search of grazing.

# DEEPEST DIVE

**Cuvier's beaked whales** are found worldwide. The record-breaking dive of this mammal reached a depth equal to the height of **3.5 Burj Khalifa** buildings.

The **Burj Khalifa** in Dubai, UAE, is the world's tallest building, at a height of **2,720 ft** (830 m).

**CUVIER'S BEAKED WHALE 9,816 FT** (2,992 M)

# SMART MAMMALS

**Bottlenose dolphins** in Shark Bay, Australia, use protective marine sponges (an invertebrate) to disturb sandy seafloors filled with potential prey, such as spothead grubfish. It is thought that only females do this, and they pass on this useful fishing skill to their daughters.

# LONG JUMPER

**WHITE-HANDED GIBBONS** OF **SOUTHEAST ASIA** CAN JUMP **40 FT** (12 M) FROM BRANCH TO BRANCH.

# Egg-laying mammals

Some mammals lay eggs instead of giving birth to live young. These are the monotremes, found only in Australia and the island of New Guinea. They include the duck-billed platypus and four species of spiny-coated echidnas.

**Sir David's long-beaked echidna**
This species lives in a tiny area of a mountain range in Indonesia. Only one specimen has ever been found in the wild.

**Western long-beaked echidna**
Long-beaked echidnas from hotter lowlands look spinier because they have less insulating fur than those that live in cooler highlands.

## Highly adaptable
Monotremes inhabit a wide variety of habitats, from Australia's arid deserts to the snow-covered mountains of Papua New Guinea. Short-beaked echidnas are the most adaptable and have the largest range, while the other monotremes are limited to smaller areas.

**Eastern long-beaked echidna**

**Spiny coat**
An echidna's coat is made up of protective spines interspersed with fur. If threatened, the echidna can roll into a spiky ball.

**Toothless feeding**
All monotremes lack teeth, and instead have sensitive beaks for catching invertebrate prey. Echidnas dig through soil with sharp claws to expose prey and use their long, sticky tongue to trap them. The platypus uses its sensitive bill to find shellfish buried in the mud, then crushes them with horny plates inside its bill.

**Short-beaked echidna**
This adaptable monotreme is the only species that lives in the dry, arid interior of Australia, known as the "outback."

**Forest dwellers**
In the forests of western Australia, short-beaked echidnas make their homes among rocks, in the spaces between tree roots, and inside hollow logs.

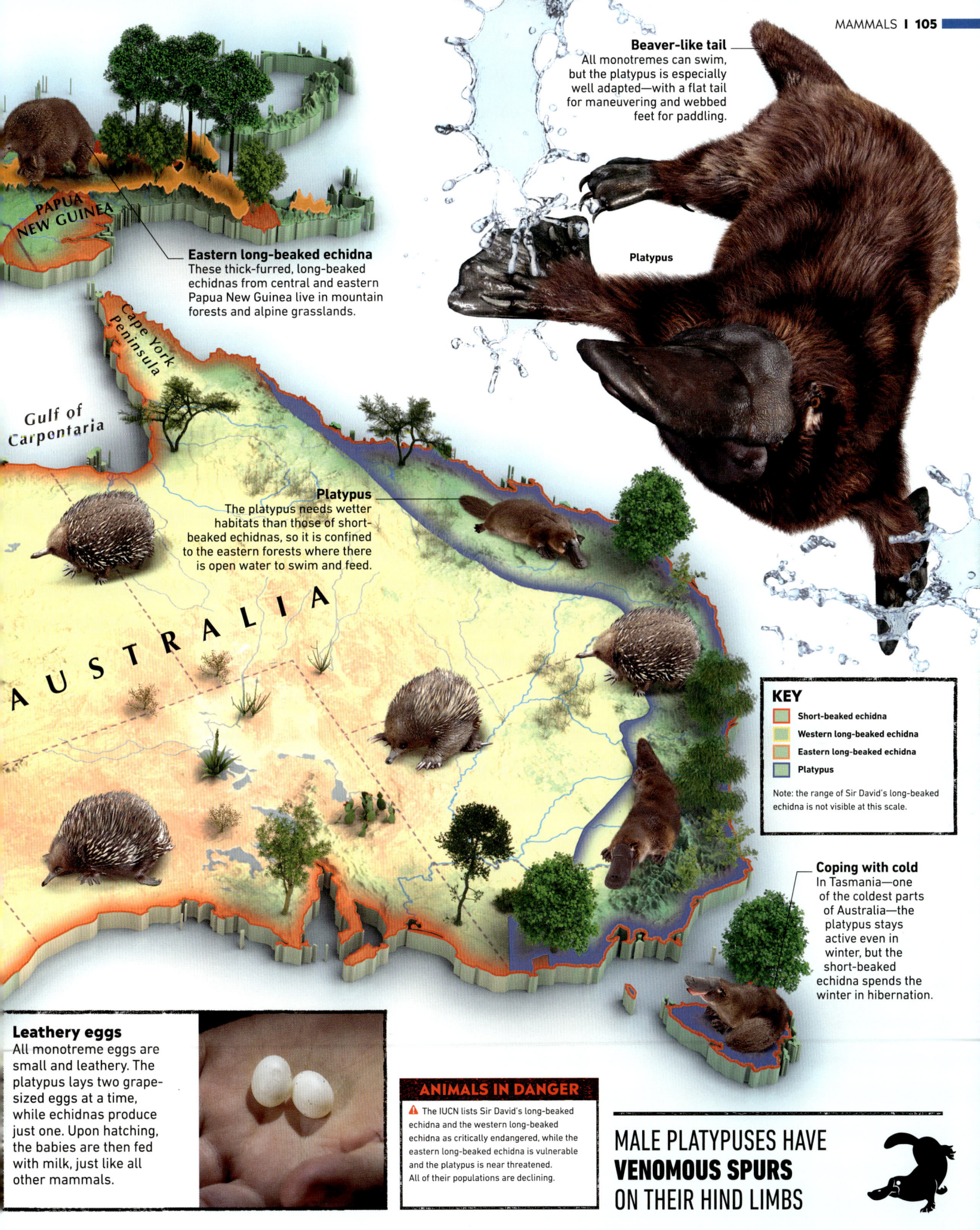

**KOALAS SLEEP UP TO 20 HOURS EACH DAY** (18–20 HRS)

**KEY**
- Koala range

**Keeping cool**
In northeastern Australia, where the climate is very hot, koalas have shorter, paler, fur to help keep them cool.

**ANIMALS IN DANGER**
Koala
- IUCN status: vulnerable
- Population estimate: 100,000–500,000

**Facing forward**
The koala is the only marsupial with forward-facing eyes. This makes it a better judge of distance, which is important for clambering through branches without falling.

**Following eucalyptus**
Though koalas are found in a range of habitats, from subtropical forests to grasslands and savannas, their range is dependent on the presence of eucalyptus trees, the leaves of which make up the large majority of their diet. Much of their habitat has been lost due to logging, forest clearing, and bushfires, putting many koala populations at risk of extinction.

**Tough digestion**
The leaves of eucalyptus are hard and fibrous, making them very difficult to digest. They quickly fill the stomach of a browsing koala, but provide little nutrition, meaning that when they are not eating or sleeping, koalas spend their time resting to conserve energy.

# Koala

Found only in the eucalyptus forests of Australia, koalas belong to a group of mammals called marsupials. Unlike most other mammals, marsupials give birth to tiny young that do most of their growing outside their mother's body—usually in a pouch.

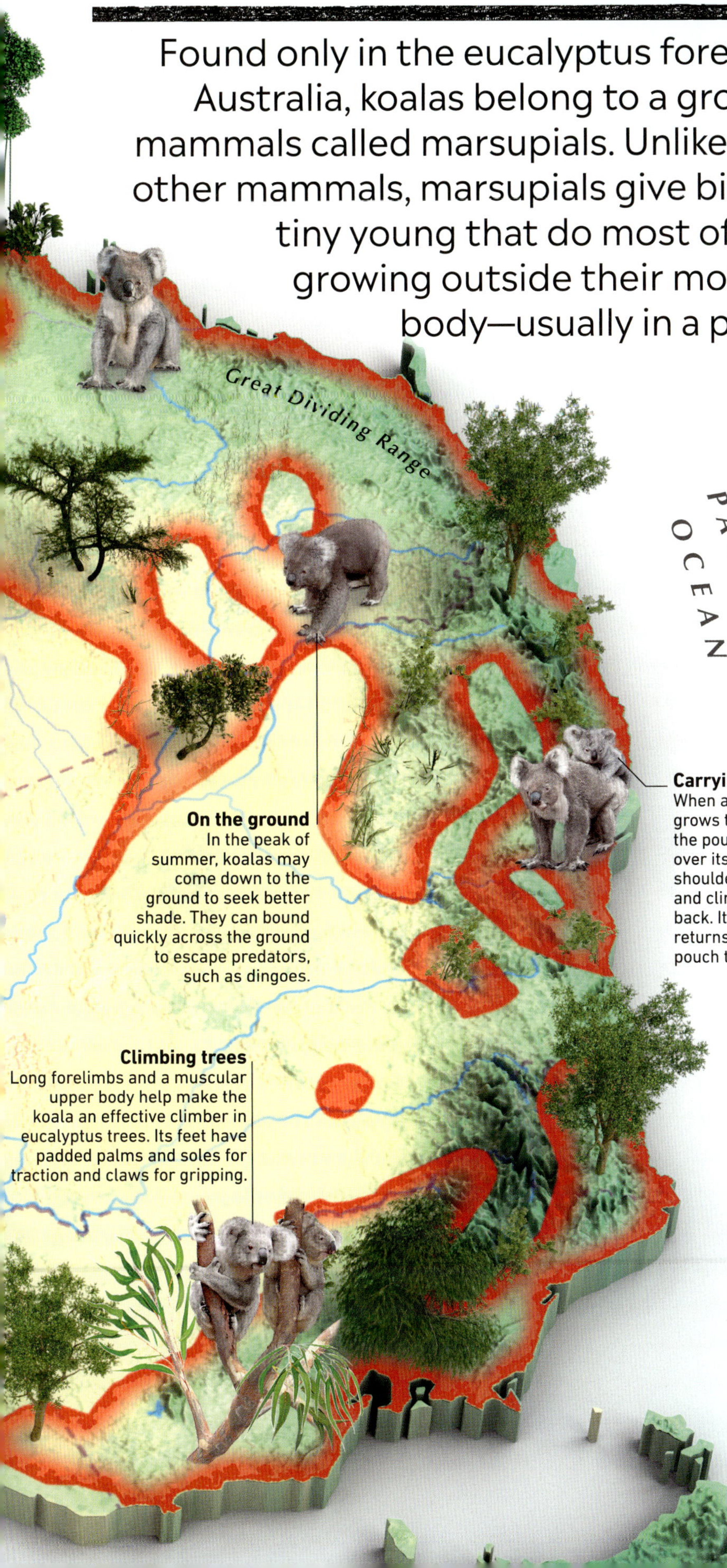

**On the ground**
In the peak of summer, koalas may come down to the ground to seek better shade. They can bound quickly across the ground to escape predators, such as dingoes.

**Carrying babies**
When a baby koala grows too big for the pouch, it climbs over its mother's shoulder or head and clings to her back. It only returns to the pouch to feed.

**Climbing trees**
Long forelimbs and a muscular upper body help make the koala an effective climber in eucalyptus trees. Its feet have padded palms and soles for traction and claws for gripping.

## OTHER MARSUPIALS

**Red kangaroo**
The largest species of kangaroo is well adapted to cope with Australia's dry interior, and ranges widely over the semi-deserts of the country.

**Goodfellow's tree kangaroo**
In the tropical rainforests of New Guinea, Goodfellow's tree kangaroos have evolved to climb through the branches.

**Virginia opossum**
There are 120 species of opossums, mostly found in tropical South and Central America. Only the Virginia opossum ranges into temperate North America.

**Tasmanian devil**
The carnivorous Tasmanian devil used to be widespread across all of Australia, but is now restricted to the southern island of Tasmania.

**Bear cuscus**
Living in tropical lowland forests on the Indonesian island of Sulawesi, the bear cuscus is the most western-dwelling marsupial in Australasia and Oceania.

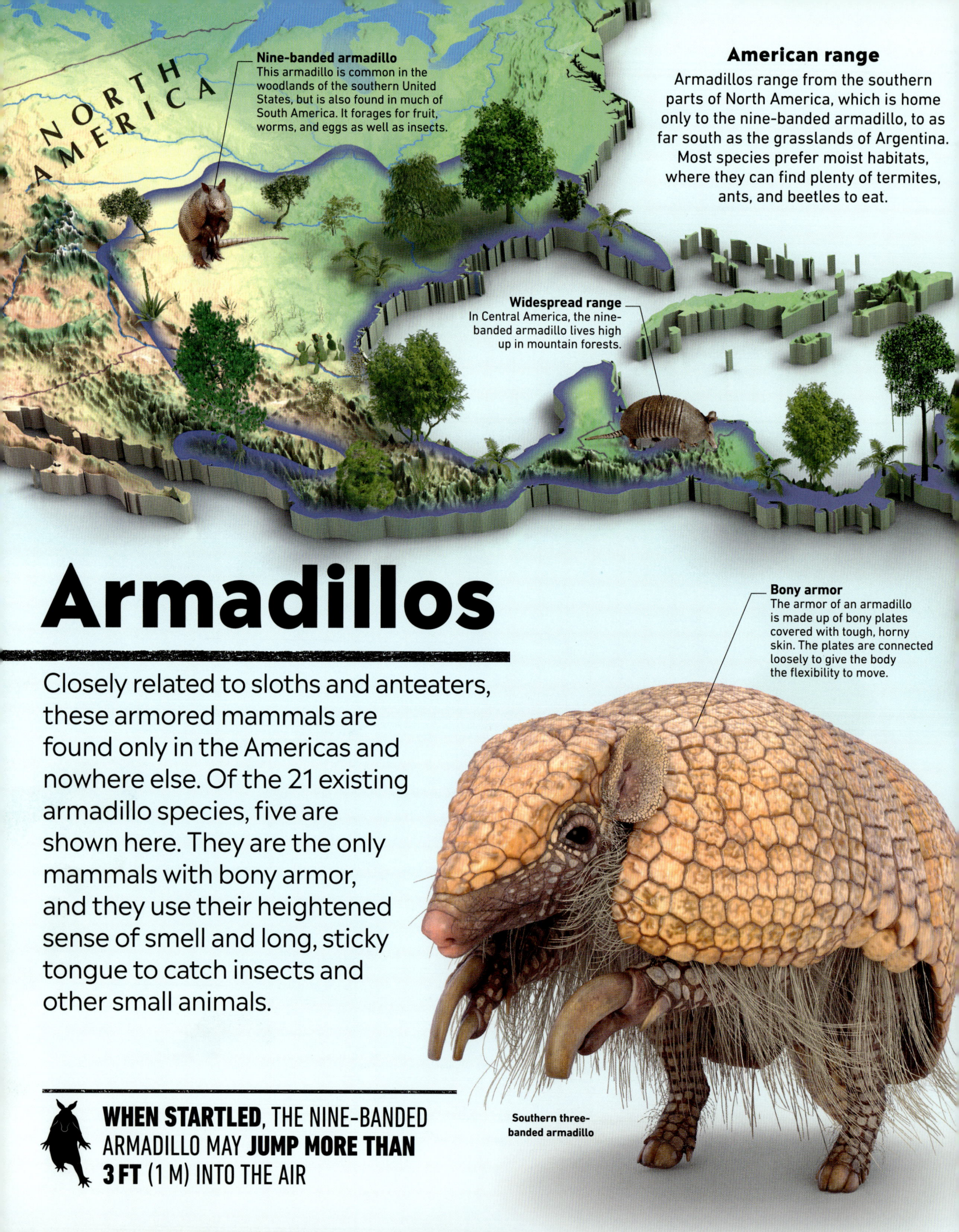

**Nine-banded armadillo**
This armadillo is common in the woodlands of the southern United States, but is also found in much of South America. It forages for fruit, worms, and eggs as well as insects.

**American range**
Armadillos range from the southern parts of North America, which is home only to the nine-banded armadillo, to as far south as the grasslands of Argentina. Most species prefer moist habitats, where they can find plenty of termites, ants, and beetles to eat.

**Widespread range**
In Central America, the nine-banded armadillo lives high up in mountain forests.

# Armadillos

**Bony armor**
The armor of an armadillo is made up of bony plates covered with tough, horny skin. The plates are connected loosely to give the body the flexibility to move.

Closely related to sloths and anteaters, these armored mammals are found only in the Americas and nowhere else. Of the 21 existing armadillo species, five are shown here. They are the only mammals with bony armor, and they use their heightened sense of smell and long, sticky tongue to catch insects and other small animals.

**WHEN STARTLED**, THE NINE-BANDED ARMADILLO MAY **JUMP MORE THAN 3 FT** (1 M) INTO THE AIR

Southern three-banded armadillo

# Brown-throated sloth

Few animals are so tied to life in trees as the sloth. These plant-eaters climb the branches with slow, deliberate movements and have long arms and claws that act as grappling hooks. There are six species of sloths living in tropical forests of the Americas, but the brown-throated sloth is the most common.

**Afternoon activity**
Sloths are most active in the mid-afternoon, when the warmth of the sun helps power their slow bodies, and they often move to sunnier branches to sunbathe.

**Living upside down**
In most mammals, hanging upside down puts pressure on the lungs. But sloths have adapted to this position, allowing them to move more easily through their habitat. They have fibers that attach their inner organs to their lower ribs, holding the organs in place so they don't crush the lungs.

**Ground crawler**
On the rare occasions when the brown-throated sloth leaves the safe haven of the trees, it is able to crawl across the ground by pulling forward with one forearm and the opposite hind foot at the same time.

**KEY**
Brown-throated sloth range

**Trips to the toilet**
The brown-throated sloth descends from the trees for just one reason: to poo. Once a week, it makes its way down to the forest floor, digs a small depression with its short tail, and defecates. It then covers the dung with leaf litter and climbs back up. If forced to do so, a sloth can crawl along the ground using the soles of its front and back feet, but will soon make for the nearest tree to return to the safety of the canopy.

**Living together**
Algae that grow on the fur of the brown-throated sloth tinge its fur green, helping disguise it among the leaves. The algae are fertilized by the droppings of a species of moth that lives only in the sloth's fur. When the sloth descends to the ground to poo, the moths briefly leave the sloth's fur to lay their eggs, and their larvae feed on the dung.

**18 HRS** SLOTHS **SLEEP** FOR UP TO **18 HOURS** PER DAY | IT CAN TAKE AS MANY AS **50 DAYS** FOR A SLOTH TO **DIGEST EACH MEAL** | THE **BROWN-THROATED SLOTH** MOVES ONLY AROUND **130 FT (40 M) IN A DAY**

**Climbing trees**
Sloths climb up and down trees by hugging the tree trunk. When moving horizontally, they hang upside down from the branches.

**Leafy diet**
Sloths move slowly because the rainforest leaves of their diet don't contain many nutrients. The little energy they gain from their diet is needed for both getting around and digestion.

**Water absorbent**
The dense fur of a sloth absorbs a lot of water when it rains. It is thought that a water-soaked coat helps protect it from extreme temperatures.

Brazilian Highlands
Paraguay
Paraná
Atacama Desert
SOUTH AMERICA

**Life in trees**
These slow-moving tree dwellers live in the dense tropical rainforest canopies of Central and South America. They are able to eat the leaves of around 50 species of rainforest tree, but individuals tend to spend most of their time in a single tree that contains their favorite leaves.

MAMMALS | 113

**0,000 AFRICAN ELEPHANTS RE KILLED EACH YEAR FOR THE LLEGAL IVORY TRADE**

**THE AFRICAN ELEPHANT POPULATION HAS DROPPED BY 90% OVER THE LAST 100 YEARS**

### ANIMALS IN DANGER

**African forest elephant**
- IUCN status: critically endangered
- Population estimate: less than 100,000

**African savanna elephant**
- IUCN status: endangered
- Population estimate: less than 315,000

**Asian elephant**
- IUCN status: endangered
- Population estimate: 48,000–52,000

## Habitats at risk

From the savannas, open woodlands, and shrublands of Africa to the grasslands and humid forests of Asia, elephants are a key part of their ecosystems. But human intervention is leading to the destruction of their natural habitats, putting them at risk of extinction.

**Asian elephant**
In mainland Asia—including India—elephants live in grassland or forest. Their natural ranges are shrinking, leaving them access to only 15 percent of their original range.

**Domed head**
Asian elephants are smaller than their African cousins and have a two-domed, rather than single-domed, forehead. Their skin is also smoother and hairier than the rough skin of African elephants.

**Smaller sizes**
Asian elephants living in forests in Borneo are shorter than those on the mainland. They are sometimes called Bornean pygmy elephants.

**KEY**
- African forest elephant
- African savanna elephant
- Asian elephant

**Spreading seeds**
Elephant herds can flatten foliage and tear down trees, but they also help scatter seeds. They eat ripe fruit from their favorite trees, and the seeds pass out in piles of fertilizing dung.

**Tree browsers**
Elephants are not picky eaters—they browse on leaves, seeds, fruit, flowers, grass, and tree bark. They will even push over trees to get to the nutritious roots deep underground.

# Eurasian red squirrel

Around 90 species of tree squirrel live in forests around the world. Among them is the Eurasian red squirrel, which dwells in cool northern forests. Unlike most rodents, bushy-tailed squirrels are active during the day and they can often be spotted climbing trees.

**Competing squirrels**
In Britain, the introduced eastern gray squirrel has displaced the red squirrel from most of its original range (see panel below). It now survives only in places where gray squirrel numbers are controlled.

**Raising babies**
In spring, female squirrels give birth litters of up to six kit in tree holes or drey (nests) made from twigs and leaves in the forest canopy.

**Expansive forests**
Red squirrels survive best in big expanses of forest. In places where forests are fragmented, their numbers drop.

**Outcompeted**
In parts of Europe, such as the UK and Italy, the eastern gray squirrel, introduced from North America, has driven out the native red squirrel because it is stronger and spreads a virus that can be lethal to its red cousins.

**Squirreling nuts away**
In fall, the red squirrel stores pine cones, acorns, nuts, and seeds by burying them. It uses memory and a good sense of smell to find them, even under snow in winter, helping it stay active and keep feeding.

**Bushy-tailed rodent**
The Eurasian red squirrel has a wide rang from western Europe to Siberia. It feeds o tree seeds, especially pine nuts. Its long, bushy tail can be used as a windbreak when the squirrel is feeding, or as shelter from rain or hot sun.

MAMMALS | 115

**A RED SQUIRREL CAN JUMP UP TO 6½ FT (2 M) BETWEEN TREES— 10 TIMES ITS OWN BODY LENGTH**

**IN BRITAIN, THERE ARE AN ESTIMATED 140,000 RED SQUIRRELS, COMPARED TO 2.5 MILLION GRAY SQUIRRELS**

**Social dynamics**
Red squirrels spend most of their time alone, but will huddle in groups in nests on cold nights, or gather together when food is plentiful.

**Cold taiga habitat**
Across Siberia, the red squirrel lives in the great taiga forest: a vast expanse of pine and spruce trees on the edge of the cold Arctic region.

ASIA

**Coniferous habitats**
Pine seeds are a favorite of red squirrels, so they are especially abundant in pine forests. They hoard pine cones, seeds, and nuts as a winter store—particularly when food crops are low during the coldest months.

**Tufted ears**
Red squirrels have distinctive tufts of fur on their ears, which grow longer in winter months.

**Staying active**
Even in the coldest winters, red squirrels do not hibernate for long periods, as many small mammals do. Instead, they may stay snug in their nests in bitter weather.

**Chisel-like teeth**
Like other rodents, red squirrels have chisel-like front incisor teeth. They use these to bite into the woody shells of nuts to reach the nutritious seed inside.

**Colorful fur**
Most red squirrels have reddish-brown fur with a white underside, but some individuals are black, brown, gray, or even blueish.

**KEY**
▢ Eurasian red squirrel range

## Desert rodent

The elusive long-eared jerboa inhabits the deserts and shrublands that stretch between southern Mongolia and northern China. Its elongated feet help it hop around the desert sand and leap into the air to catch insects. The large surface area of the jerboa's ears helps keep it cool by radiating heat from its body.

# Star-nosed mole

With its hyper-sensitive nose and lightning fast reflexes, this unique North American mole is a highly successful hunter of small invertebrates such as worms, insects, and spiders. It spends most of its life in its intricate system of burrows, where it rests, builds nests for rearing young, stores food, and traps prey.

**Western barrier**
The star-nosed mole relies on wet habitats to feed and survive, so the western border of its range ends where the drier central prairies of North America begin.

**Wet habitats**
The star-nosed mole lives in a range of habitats across eastern North America, including coniferous and deciduous forests, swamps, peat bogs, and along the banks of streams, lakes, and ponds. It prefers to build its burrows in water-logged ground, and relies on its sense of smell to detect prey underground.

**KEY**
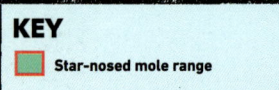
Star-nosed mole range

**Semi-aquatic mammals**
Star-nosed moles are excellent swimmers, and many of their burrows open underwater. They use their highly sensitive nose to hunt for prey—such as aquatic insect larvae, snails, and shrimp—in the waterbed. The rest of their burrow system is built above the water level to prevent flooding.

Mole hill

Some burrows have underwater exits

Nest chamber for rearing young

**Mole hill**
Most of its life is spent in underground burrows, but occasionally the star-nosed mole heads to the surface through mole hills in order to hunt prey at night.

THERE ARE **25,000 TOUCH SENSORS** ON THE **TENTACLES** OF A **STAR-NOSED MOLE**

STAR-NOSED MOLES EAT **50% OF THEIR BODY WEIGHT** IN PREY ANIMALS **EACH DAY**

# Lemurs

There are more than 100 species of lemur, and all of them are found only on the island of Madagascar and nowhere else. The five ranges on this map represent a small sample of these isolated primates, and they all heavily depend on their forest habitats for survival.

**50 SILKY SIFAKAS ARE LEFT IN THE WILD—THEY ARE ONE OF THE RAREST PRIMATES IN THE WORLD**

**Red-tailed sportive lemur**
Despite its name, this species is not very active. Restricted to a tiny area of dry deciduous forest between two rivers, individuals rarely travel more than ⅗ mile (1 km) from their home range. When their habitats are deforested, they are unlikely to move to distant trees.

**Verreaux's sifaka**
The powerful thighs of a sifaka—good for leaping from tree to tree—are also used for bounding across the ground or along horizontal branches. They live in forest habitats, including tropical rainforest and spiny dry forest.

**Fat-tailed dwarf lemur**
This dwarf lemur endures Madagascar's dry winter season by entering a hibernation-like state and surviving on the stores of fat in its tail. Though its range is small, it is one of the few lemur species with an abundant population.

**Ring-tailed lemur**
The ring-tailed lemur is found only in Madagascar's dry southern forests and arid open areas. It spends 70 percent of its time on the ground, more than any other lemur species.

**Spiny tree habitat**
Thorny forests in the dry south of Madagascar—where spiny trees grow like giant cacti—are home to particular kinds of lemurs, such as Verreaux's sifaka. They have padded palms and soles on their hands and feet, allowing them to leap from trunk to trunk without injury.

### ANIMALS IN DANGER
⚠ IUCN lists 34 lemur species as critically endangered, including the red-tailed sportive lemur and Verreaux's sifaka, and 45 as endangered, including the ring-tailed lemur and aye-aye. Most others are vulnerable.

**KEY**
- Verreaux's sifaka
- Red-tailed sportive lemur
- Fat-tailed dwarf lemur
- Ring-tailed lemur
- Aye-aye

INDIAN OCEAN

MADAGASCAR

## Lemurs in danger
Each species of lemur is adapted to live in a different type of forest habitat, from the ring-tailed lemur in the dry forests of the south to the rainforest-dependent aye-aye. Because many lemurs are restricted to tiny areas of habitat, they are increasingly vulnerable to threats such as deforestation.

**WEIGHING ONLY 1 OZ (31 G), MADAME BERTHE'S MOUSE LEMUR IS THE SMALLEST PRIMATE IN THE WORLD**

**Tail flag**
The long, striped tail of a ring-tailed lemur is a visual signal. When traveling in their group, lemurs wave their tails like a flag to help keep members together.

**Aye-aye**
This nocturnal lemur can be found in the rainforests of eastern Madagascar. Despite being rare wherever it occurs, the aye-aye could be one of the widest-ranging lemur species.

**Wet nose**
Lemurs have forward-facing eyes like related monkeys, but differ from monkeys in having a more pointed, wet nose—good for sniffing scents, especially at night.

### Hunting for woodworm
The aye-aye is a highly specialized feeder. It preys on invertebrates, such as fleshy wood-boring grubs, which live inside tree branches. By tapping a branch and listening to the echo, it can detect if a grub is inside. It gnaws a hole in the wood and hooks the grub out with a specially adapted spindly finger.

Ring-tailed lemur

# Japanese macaque

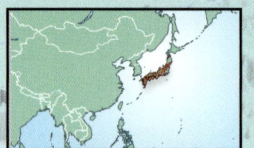

Most of the more than 330 species of monkeys around the world live in the hot tropics, but the Japanese macaque tolerates the cold. In Japanese forests, it lives further north than any other nonhuman primate, sometimes ranging high up into cold mountains with heavy winter snowfall.

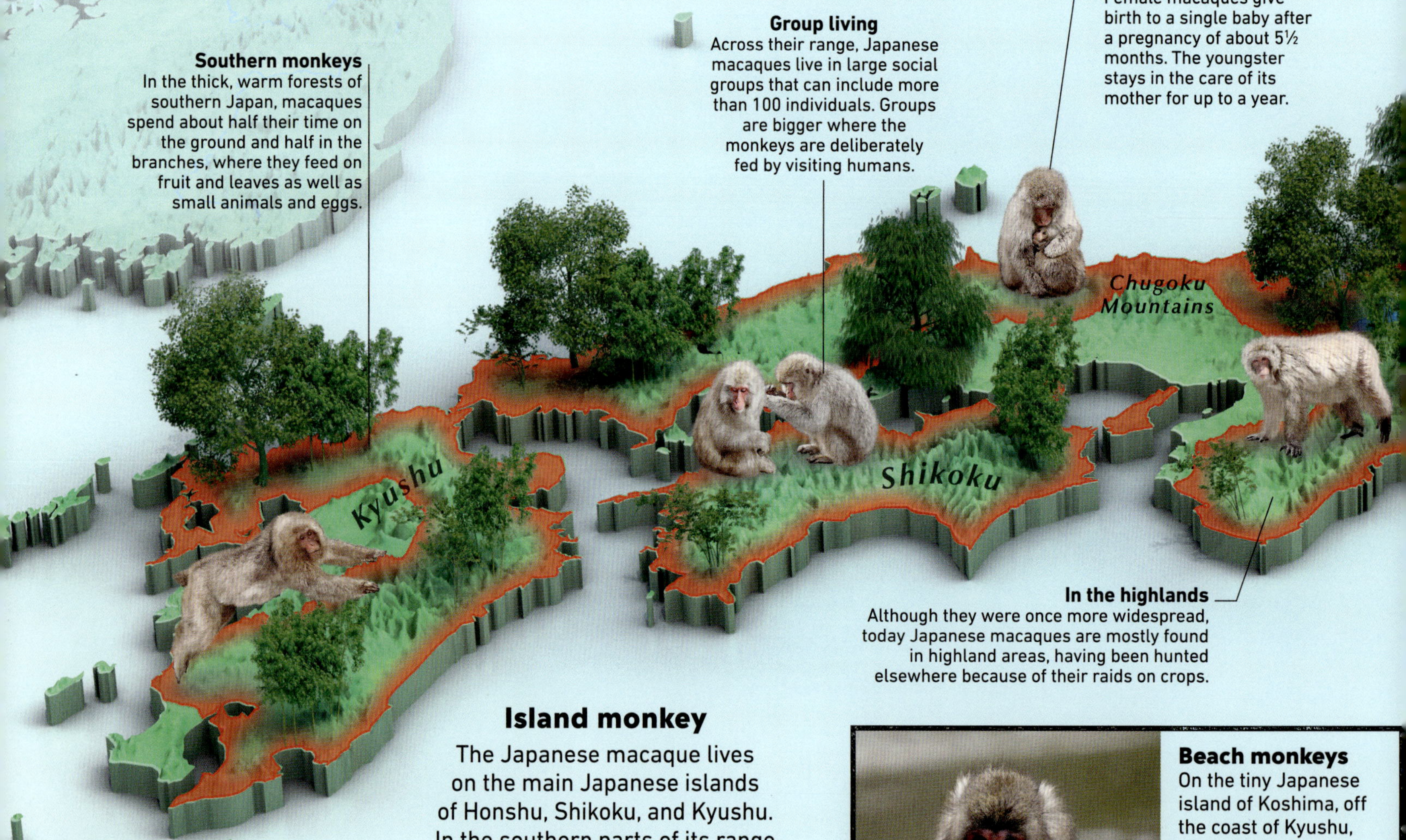

**Southern monkeys**
In the thick, warm forests of southern Japan, macaques spend about half their time on the ground and half in the branches, where they feed on fruit and leaves as well as small animals and eggs.

**Group living**
Across their range, Japanese macaques live in large social groups that can include more than 100 individuals. Groups are bigger where the monkeys are deliberately fed by visiting humans.

**Motherly care**
Female macaques give birth to a single baby after a pregnancy of about 5½ months. The youngster stays in the care of its mother for up to a year.

**In the highlands**
Although they were once more widespread, today Japanese macaques are mostly found in highland areas, having been hunted elsewhere because of their raids on crops.

**Island monkey**
The Japanese macaque lives on the main Japanese islands of Honshu, Shikoku, and Kyushu. In the southern parts of its range this monkey lives in warm, temperate evergreen forest, but it also inhabits temperate deciduous forest further north.

**Beach monkeys**
On the tiny Japanese island of Koshima, off the coast of Kyushu, Japanese macaques have learned skills that get passed down as youngsters copy adults. On beaches, the monkeys wash food such as sweet potatoes in the sea, and separate lighter grains of wheat from heavier sand by letting the grains float upward in the water.

**THE JAPANESE MACAQUE CAN SURVIVE IN TEMPERATURES AS LOW AS 5°F (-15°C)**

# MAMMALS | 123

**Northernmost range**
No wild monkey in the world lives further north than the Japanese macaque. Like macaques in the central mountains, they keep warm by bathing in hot springs.

**Snow monkey**
Japanese macaques living in the snowy mountains of central Honshu—close to ski resorts—have become a popular tourist attraction.

**Hot springs**
In the mountains of central Honshu, temperatures plunge below freezing in the winter. Here, Japanese macaques survive the cold by regularly bathing in thermal pools that are common in this volcanic region.

**Naked face**
Pink skin shows through a very fine coating of fur on the face of an adult macaque, encircled by long, pale whiskers.

**Deciduous forests**
In the northern parts of their range, Japanese macaques range into mountainous areas with deciduous trees—trees that lose their leaves during the winter. At this time of year, macaques move to lower elevations, where there is more food.

**Thick fur**
The grayish fur grows especially long and thick on its back and sides, which helps trap body heat. The monkey molts its coat in late spring so its fur is shorter in the summertime.

**KEY**
Japanese macaque range

BETWEEN 1995 AND 2000, THE **EBOLA VIRUS KILLED THREE-QUARTERS** OF THE WESTERN GORILLA POPULATION

GREAT APES LIVE IN **LARGE FAMILY GROUPS**—ONE EASTERN GORILLA GROUP HAD A RECORD **65 MEMBERS**

### ANIMALS IN DANGER

**Chimpanzee**
- IUCN status: endangered
- Population estimate: 340,000–430,000

**Bonobo**
- IUCN status: endangered
- Population estimate: unknown

**Western gorilla**
- IUCN status: critically endangered
- Population estimate: 316,000

**Eastern gorilla**
- IUCN status: critically endangered
- Population estimate: fewer than 5,000

### KEY
- Chimpanzee
- Bonobo
- Western gorilla
- Eastern gorilla

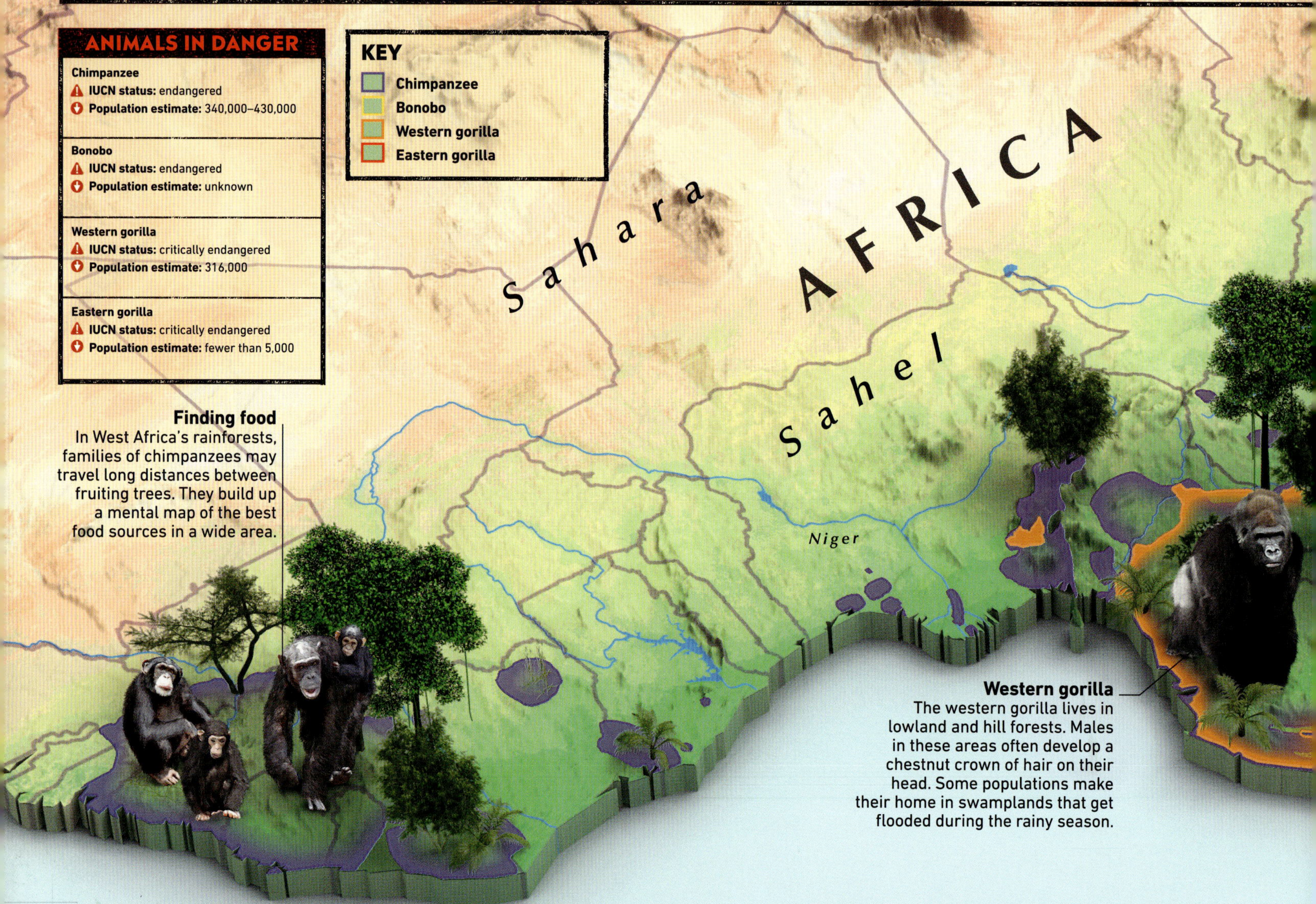

**Finding food**
In West Africa's rainforests, families of chimpanzees may travel long distances between fruiting trees. They build up a mental map of the best food sources in a wide area.

**Western gorilla**
The western gorilla lives in lowland and hill forests. Males in these areas often develop a chestnut crown of hair on their head. Some populations make their home in swamplands that get flooded during the rainy season.

**Green living**
Great apes use branches and foliage to build nests for sleeping at night, and sometimes for resting during the day. Chimpanzee and bonobo nests are built high in trees but gorillas, who are heavier, often nest on the ground, like the one seen here.

# Great apes

The great apes are our closest animal relatives. All great ape species, except the orangutans (see pp.126–127), are found on the continent of Africa. Living in sociable groups in forests around the equator, chimpanzees and bonobos spend more time in trees, while gorillas stay mainly on the ground.

MAMMALS | 125

**Horn of Africa**

**Chimpanzee**
Like other great apes, the chimpanzee walks on its knuckles when on all fours. In the eastern part of its range, it roams central highland forests as high up as 9,155 ft (2,790 m).

**Eastern gorilla**
Eastern gorillas have thicker, blacker fur than western gorillas. Some live in lowland habitats, but eastern mountain gorillas live at heights of up to 12,470 ft (3,800 m); they are the stockiest, furriest gorillas.

**Using tools**
Gorillas and bonobos mainly eat plants and fruit, but chimpanzees are more carnivorous, and even use tools to help catch prey or collect food. They use twigs to pull termites from holes, sharpened sticks to spear tiny primates, and stones or clubs to crack nuts. Young chimpanzees watch older ones to learn how it is done.

White Nile

Congo

Great Rift Valley

**Threat display**
Adult male gorillas intimidate rivals by standing upright to look bigger, while rhythmically beating their chest with cupped hands and hooting or roaring loudly. Older males are known as silverbacks.

**Male eastern mountain gorilla**

**Bonobo**
Also called the pygmy chimpanzee, the bonobo is more lightly built than the chimpanzee. Its range is separated from that of its bigger cousins, who live on the other side of the great Congo River.

Congo

**Shrinking habitats**
The chimpanzee has the widest range of any great ape and can survive in drier, more open woodland than bonobos and gorillas. But all great ape species are threatened with extinction as the cutting down of rainforest continues to shrink their natural habitats, while poaching kills large numbers every year.

# Indian flying fox

With more than 1,400 species, bats make up the second-biggest order of mammals after the rodents, and live in most parts of the world except the poles and remote islands. The Indian flying fox is one of the world's largest bats, and is found in tropical forests and swamps across the Indian subcontinent.

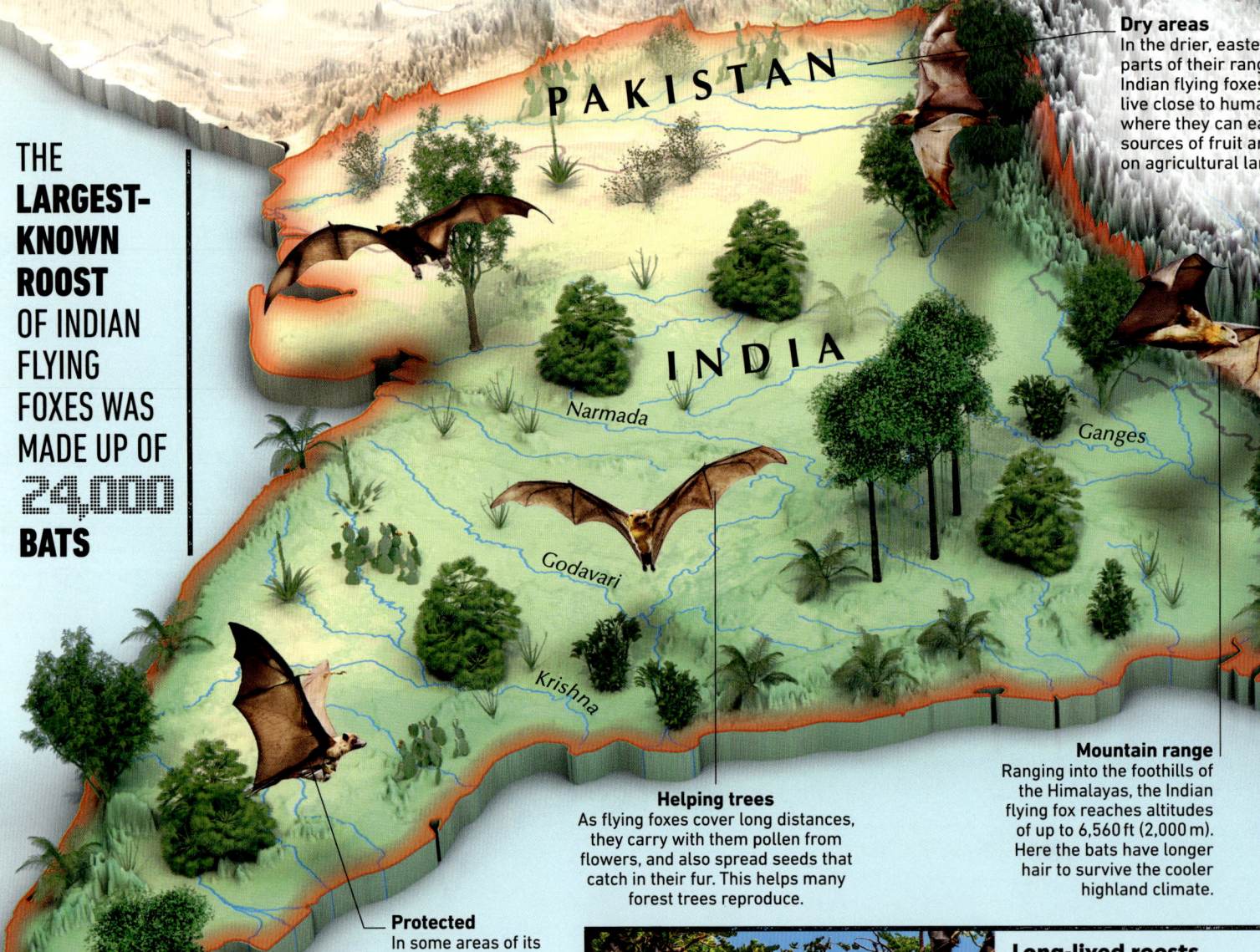

THE **LARGEST-KNOWN ROOST** OF INDIAN FLYING FOXES WAS MADE UP OF **24,000 BATS**

**Dry areas**
In the drier, eastern parts of their range, Indian flying foxes often live close to humans, where they can easily find sources of fruit and water on agricultural land.

**Mountain range**
Ranging into the foothills of the Himalayas, the Indian flying fox reaches altitudes of up to 6,560 ft (2,000 m). Here the bats have longer hair to survive the cooler highland climate.

**Helping trees**
As flying foxes cover long distances, they carry with them pollen from flowers, and also spread seeds that catch in their fur. This helps many forest trees reproduce.

**Protected**
In some areas of its range, this bat is treated as a pest for eating farmers' fruit, but in southern India it is considered sacred and is protected.

**Long-lived roosts**
After nighttime foraging, bats return to their roost at dawn to sleep. A colony can contain thousands of bats and may occupy the same location over generations. One roosting site in southern India was used for more than 75 years.

**KEY**
▬ Indian flying fox range

**Forest colonies**
In Bangladesh, the biggest colonies of Indian flying foxes live in the densest forest—where there is a richer supply of fruiting trees and less disturbance from humans.

Himalayas

**Handy wing**
The wings of all bats are made of thin sheets of skin that extend out from the sides of the body and stretch between the long finger bones of their hands.

## Finding fruit
The Indian flying fox lives across India, Pakistan, Bangladesh, and Sri Lanka. These large, fruit-eating bats sleep through the day and wake at dusk to seek out food. They are known to fly up to 90 miles (150 km) in search of the best sources of food—especially fig trees that are heavy with fruit—which they locate with their highly sophisticated senses of sight and smell.

THE **WINGSPANS** OF INDIAN FLYING FOXES CAN REACH **UP TO 6 FT** (2 M)

## OTHER BATS

**Ghost bat**
Northern Australia is home to one of the world's biggest predatory bats. The ghost bat hunts mice, lizards, birds, and other bats.

**Greater horseshoe bat**
Like many other bats, this species tracks insects in flight by homing in on the sound of echoed clicks. This is called echolocation.

**New Zealand lesser short-tailed bat**
Having evolved on islands originally free of predators, this bat crawls along the ground more than any other species.

**Madagascar sucker-footed bat**
This bat clings to the smooth surfaces in between folds of palm leaves using tiny suckers on its wrists and ankles.

**White-winged vampire bat**
This tropical South American bat mainly targets birds—biting and lapping the blood of a sleeping victim.

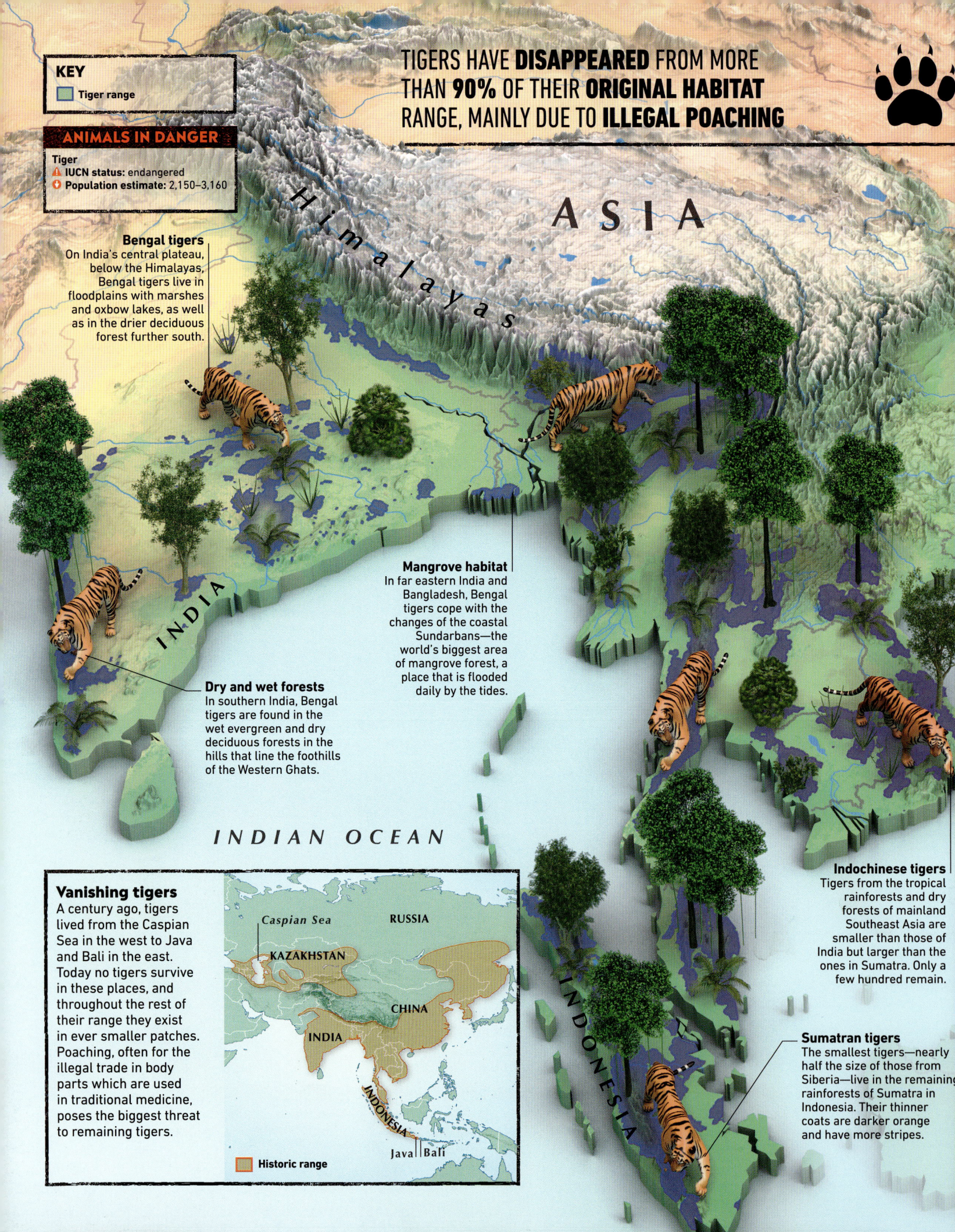

MAMMALS | 131

THERE ARE **MORE** TIGERS KEPT **IN CAPTIVITY** THAN THERE ARE IN THE **WILD**

A TIGER CAN **EAT** MORE THAN **80 LB (35 KG)** OF MEAT IN **ONE MEAL**

**Siberian tigers**
Tigers of Russia's Siberian pine forests are among the largest of all cats, with paler coloring, fewer stripes, and thick fur that keeps out the bitter cold of winter.

**Tiger territories**
There are local populations of tigers in different regions of Asia, but they all belong to the same species. Adult tigers only come together to mate and otherwise live alone, patrolling territories to protect their own supply of prey. Since prey is scarcer for Siberian tigers, they need to roam territories four times bigger than those of the Bengal tigers on the Indian subcontinent.

**Top cat**
A tiger has massive forelimbs, needed to strike with enough strength to bring down large prey. Its fiery-colored coat helps conceal it in sun-dappled forests.

# Tiger

The tiger is the world's biggest cat. But this formidable hunter is also hunted: across Asia, tiger numbers are falling as more become victim to poachers, or lose their habitat to farming, logging, and ever greater numbers of humans needing space.

**Lone hunter**
Adult tigers hunt alone, stalking their prey from the cover of vegetation. Blending in, a tiger can sneak close to its prey before ambushing it. Grabbing the prey with its broad forepaws, and with its long claws extended, the tiger kills its victim by a bite to the neck.

## ANIMALS IN DANGER
**Lion**
- IUCN status: vulnerable
- Population estimate: 20,000–32,000

**KEY**
- Lion range

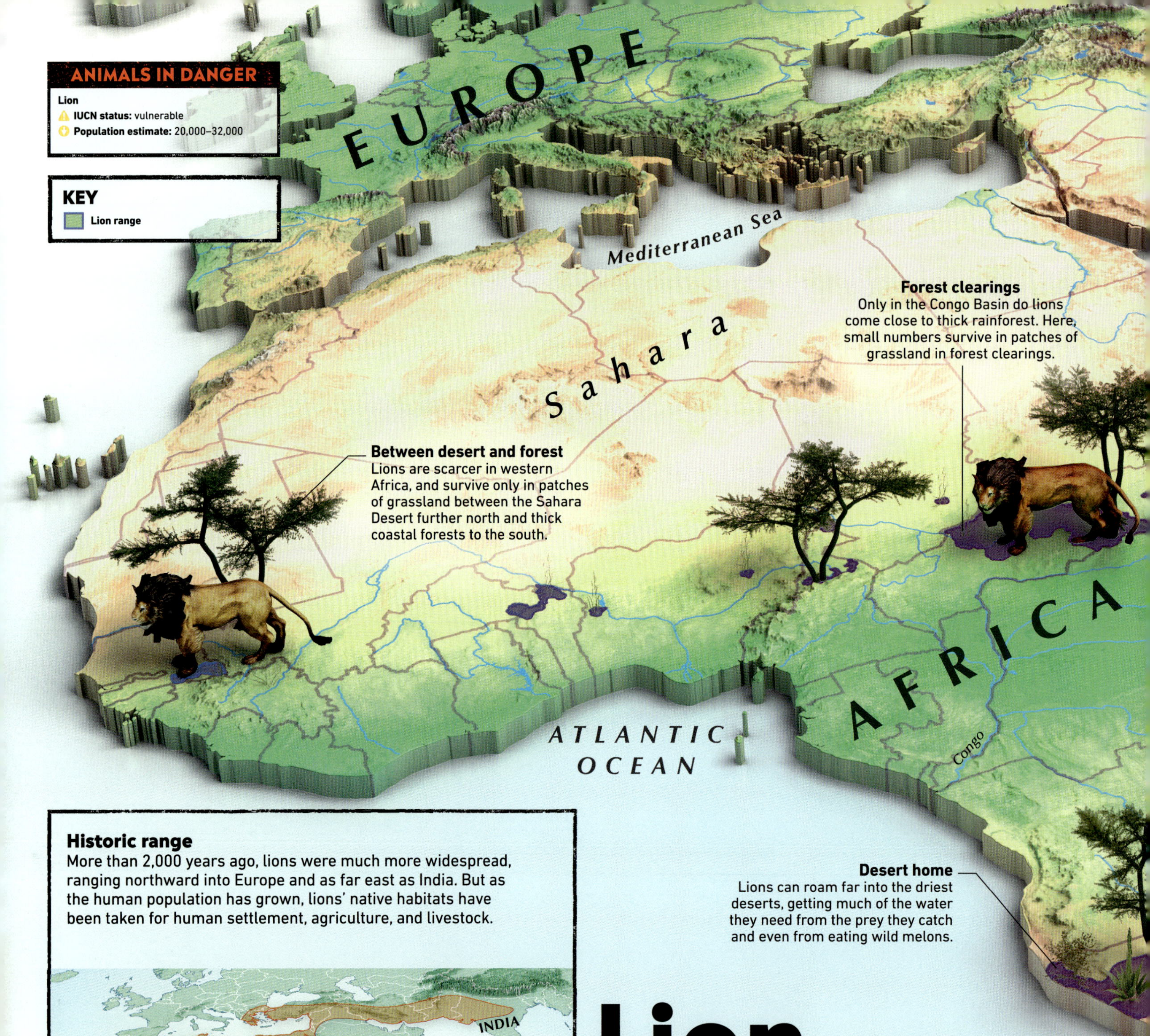

**Mediterranean Sea**

**EUROPE**

**Sahara**

**Forest clearings**
Only in the Congo Basin do lions come close to thick rainforest. Here, small numbers survive in patches of grassland in forest clearings.

**Between desert and forest**
Lions are scarcer in western Africa, and survive only in patches of grassland between the Sahara Desert further north and thick coastal forests to the south.

**AFRICA**

**ATLANTIC OCEAN**

Congo

**Desert home**
Lions can roam far into the driest deserts, getting much of the water they need from the prey they catch and even from eating wild melons.

**Historic range**
More than 2,000 years ago, lions were much more widespread, ranging northward into Europe and as far east as India. But as the human population has grown, lions' native habitats have been taken for human settlement, agriculture, and livestock.

INDIA

AFRICA

Historic range

# Lion

This big cat is second in size only to the tiger. It is known as the king of the jungle, but in fact lives in the open grasslands and savannas of Africa, where it is superbly adapted to hunting. Unlike most cats, which are solitary hunters, lions work together a a group, or pride, to bring down prey.

**THE ROAR OF AN ADULT MALE LION** IS SO LOUD THAT IT CAN BE HEARD CLEARLY UP TO **5 MILES** (8 KM) AWAY

## Asiatic lions
The only wild lions left outside of Africa live in the dry scrublands and deciduous forests of India's Gir National Park.

### Savanna trees
Although lions hunt in open grassland, a pride often gathers under shady trees during the heat of the day and climbs into branches to reach cool breezes. This vantage point also helps them spot prey animals traveling through the grasslands.

## Fragmented habitats
Lions once freely roamed the savannas, grasslands, scrub, and open woodlands of the African continent, but much of their natural habitat has been lost. They are now largely limited to game reserves and national parks.

### Mane
The thicker and darker a male lion's mane is, the more attractive he is to females.

**Male lion**

**Female lion**

### Camouflage
By matching the color of the surrounding grassland of the African savanna, females can get close to prey—including targets as big as buffalo and giraffe—before giving chase.

### Retractable claws
Like those of all cats, the long claws of a lion are pulled back when not in use. They are only extended when needed—such as for attacking prey.

**Stealthy lynx**
Recognizable by the pointy tufts of hair on their ears, these Iberian lynxes are hunting European rabbit—their favorite prey. Once common across the Iberian Peninsula, these cats are now found in only two small areas in southern Spain. A drop in rabbit populations and the spread of human settlements have led to their decline.

**Finding prey**
Wolves from North America live in plains and forests where there is plenty of prey, including beavers, white-tailed deer, and moose. Packs work as a team when hunting big prey, but they hunt alone for smaller meals.

**Arctic tundra**
Arctic wolves are especially adapted to survive in the far-north regions of Greenland and North America.

**Local populations**
In different parts of the wolf's huge range, local populations have habitat-specific adaptations and even look different, from the northern Arctic wolf to the southern dingo. But they all belong to the same species—gray wolf. Packs control and hunt in vast territories, and they communicate with each other by howling and scent-marking.

**Padded feet**
The feet of wolves and dogs have soles with protective pads and clawed toes. Unlike those of cats, their claws are blunt and not retractable.

**Fur**
In most wolves the fur is mottled gray, but some wolves are born white or black. Wolves living in the coldest climates grow thicker fur.

# Gray wolf

This wide-ranging canine is a highly social animal, living and hunting in family groups, known as packs. It is found across vast areas of the globe in many different habitats, from the frozen Arctic to hot, dry deserts.

**Eurasian wolf**
Wolves that live in the forests of Scandinavia and Russia prey on anything from red deer and wild boar to hares and voles. They may also attack livestock and raid human garbage.

**Himalayan habitat**
Found in a variety of alpine habitats, from high-altitude mountains to temperate forests, wolves living here hunt yaks and goats and shelter in alpine caves.

**Siberian tundra**
Living on the open frozen ground across northern Siberia, the large tundra wolf develops a thicker, darker coat in winter and hunts some of the largest prey, including caribou and musk ox.

**KEY**
Wolf range

**Dingo**
Dingoes are highly adaptable and can be found in every habitat in Australia, even deserts—as long as they have access to drinking water.

**Australian dingoes**
All domesticated dogs, which we keep as pets, are descended from the gray wolf and belong to the same species. Dingoes originated from domesticated dogs that were brought to Australia from Asia by humans 4,000 years ago and then returned to the wild.

**Arctic wolves**
Found in the Arctic tundras of Greenland and North America, the Arctic wolf is one of the biggest types of wolf. It survives freezing conditions by having long, thick fur and a thick layer of body fat, and stays white throughout the year as effective camouflage against the snow.

SOME WOLF **TERRITORIES** EXTEND UP TO **1,000 SQ MILES** (2,600 SQ KM)

THE **LARGEST-KNOWN PACK** WAS MADE UP OF **36** WOLVES

WOLVES CAN **ROAM** UP TO **12 MILES** (30 KM) IN A **SINGLE DAY**

# Bears

| ANIMALS IN DANGER |
|---|
| **Sun bear** ⚠ IUCN status: vulnerable ⊕ Population estimate: unknown |
| **Giant panda** ⚠ IUCN status: vulnerable ⊕ Population estimate: 1,800 |
| **Asiatic black bear** ⚠ IUCN status: vulnerable ⊕ Population estimate: unknown |

There are eight different species of bear across the world. They include the largest land carnivores with the power to bring down the biggest prey. But not all bears are ferocious hunters—some eat mainly insects, while others prefer plants and berries.

**Asiatic black bear**
The Asiatic black bear lives in oak and beech forests where there are plenty of nuts and berries. It also feeds on fruit and occasionally hunts small mammals.

**Sloth bear**
In tropical Asia, the sloth bear has a fondness for ants, termites, and fruit. It lives in tropical lowland forests and occasionally can be found in tall grasslands.

**Sun bear**
The smallest bear with the shortest coat lives in tropical forests, where it climbs trees for fruit, insects, and honey.

**Giant panda**
Living in bamboo forests in the mountains of central China, this bear lives almost entirely on bamboo. Loss of their habitat means they are restricted to a very small area.

**KEY**
- Brown bear
- Andean bear
- American black bear
- Polar bear
- Sloth bear
- Sun bear
- Giant panda
- Asiatic black bear

**Different diets**
Most bears are omnivorous—which means they eat both meat and plants. Some bears will eat anything available, while others are specialists that slurp insects or crunch bamboo. The sun bear uses its 10-in- (25-cm-) long tongue to lick up ants from logs.

**POLAR BEARS** ARE THE **BIGGEST SPECIES** AND CAN WEIGH **UP TO 1,760 LB (800 KG)**

THERE ARE FEWER THAN **2,000** GIANT PANDAS LEFT IN THE WILD

# Honey badger

**Caspian badgers**
On the dry, grassy plains of southwest Asia, the honey badger reaches the northernmost limits of its range around the Caspian Sea.

**KEY**
☐ Honey badger range

**Arabian badgers**
Honey badgers survive the dry deserts of the Arabian Peninsula by catching venomous prey, including scorpions and snakes. They shelter under rocks during the hottest part of the day.

**Indian badgers**
The honey badger is widespread across the Indian subcontinent, but is most common in forests and grasslands, where it may share its territory with tigers and sloth bears.

## Opportunistic living
Few animals can survive such a wide range of habitats as the honey badger. Across Africa, India, and the Arabian Peninsula, it lives in forests, savanna, marshes, and deserts—wherever this nocturnal animal can dig a burrow. It is not found in the very driest parts of the Sahara.

Six species of badgers live across North America, Africa, and Eurasia—and all are stocky, strong-bodied animals. The honey badger has a particular reputation for toughness. With a strong bite, thick skin, and sharp claws, it is a fierce hunter that braves stinging bees to satisfy its taste for honey.

**Digging for prey**
As well as excavating burrows, the strong front paws with their long claws can rip open bee hives and dig out animal prey such as rodents from underground. Food is found by smell and sound.

**Quagga**
A subspecies of the plains zebra with fewer stripes, called the quagga, was once common in southern Africa, but was hunted to extinction by about 1883. Today scientists are breeding zebra with quagga-like characteristics to try to bring the animal back.

**African grazers**
Zebras graze on the grasses of a variety of habitats, from the plains zebra in open grasslands and savannas, to the Grevy's zebra in semi-arid scrub, and the mountain zebra on mountainous slopes and plateaus. During the dry season, the Grevy's and mountain zebras spread out further in their range to find better sources of food and water, but the plains zebra follows seasonal rains—to wherever the grass is greener—in large migrations.

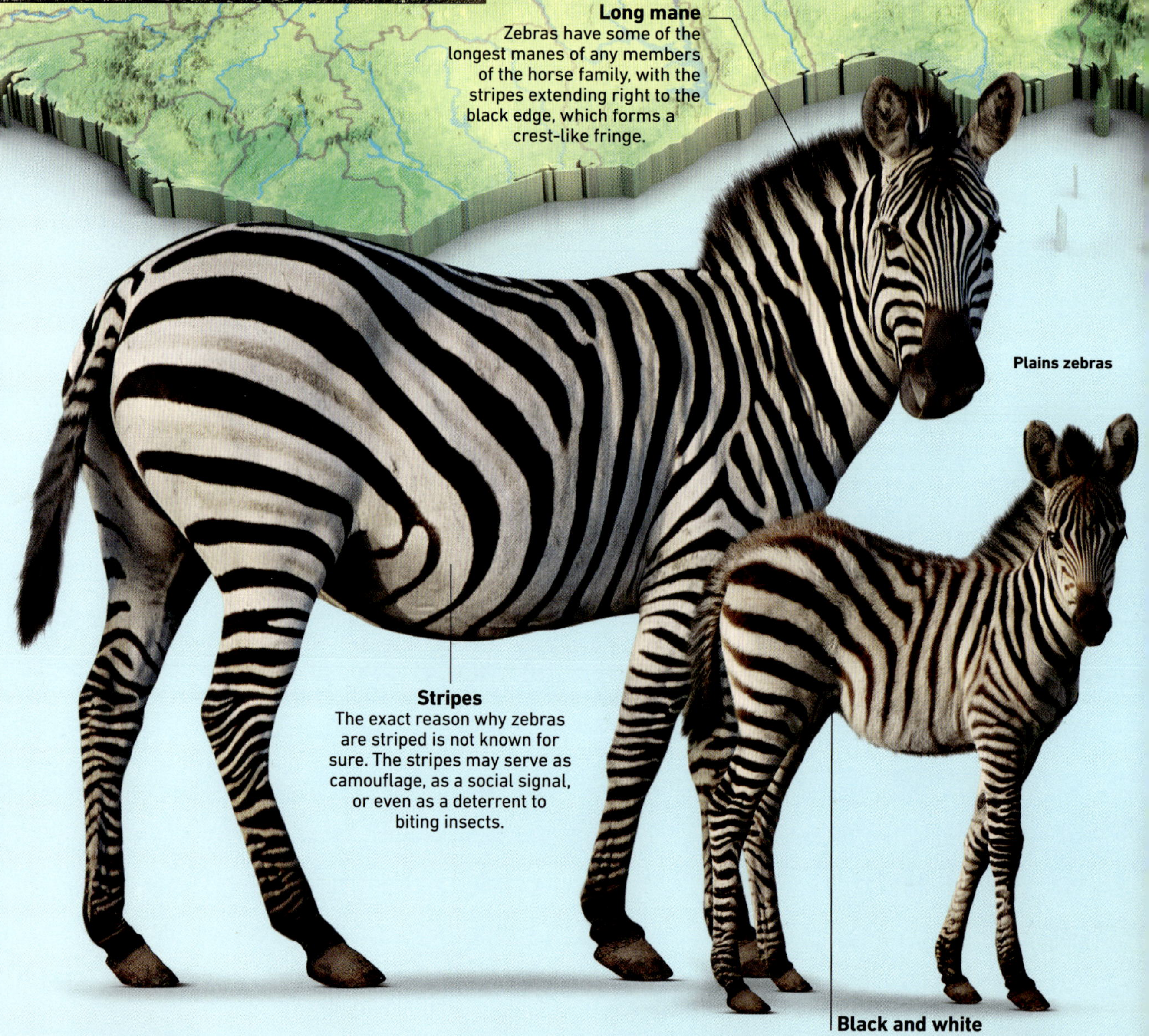

**Long mane**
Zebras have some of the longest manes of any members of the horse family, with the stripes extending right to the black edge, which forms a crest-like fringe.

THE **PATTERN OF STRIPES** OF EVERY INDIVIDUAL ZEBRA IS AS **UNIQUE AS A HUMAN FINGERPRINT**

A **GROUP OF ZEBRAS** IS SOMETIMES CALLED A **DAZZLE**

**Plains zebras**

**Stripes**
The exact reason why zebras are striped is not known for sure. The stripes may serve as camouflage, as a social signal, or even as a deterrent to biting insects.

**Black and white**
Underneath their fur, zebras actually have dark skin. Their stripes develop as white over black rather than vice versa.

# Zebras

Zebras are the most distinctive members of the horse family. Three species live on the grassy savannas in the eastern and southern parts of Africa, each with their own species-specific pattern of stripes.

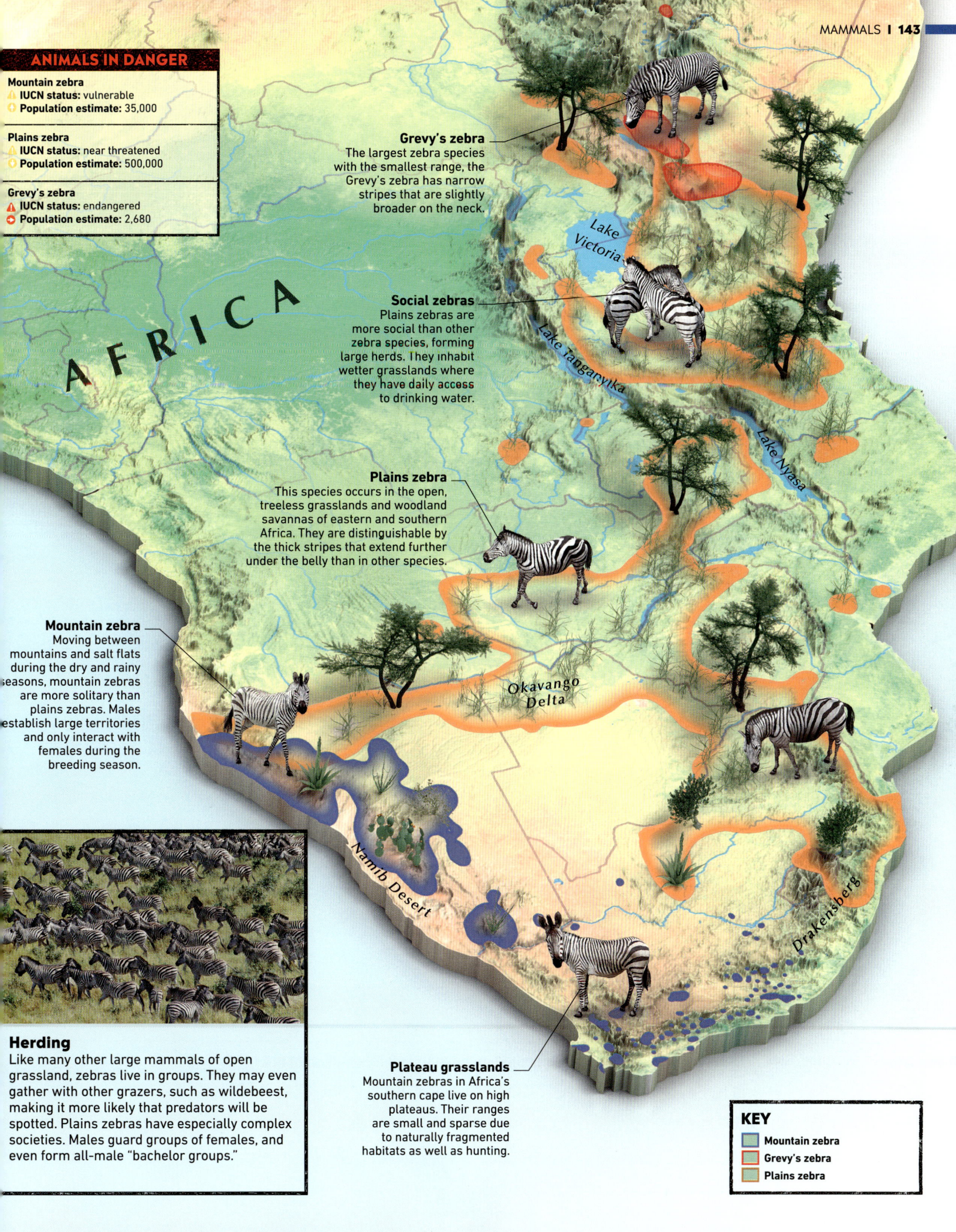

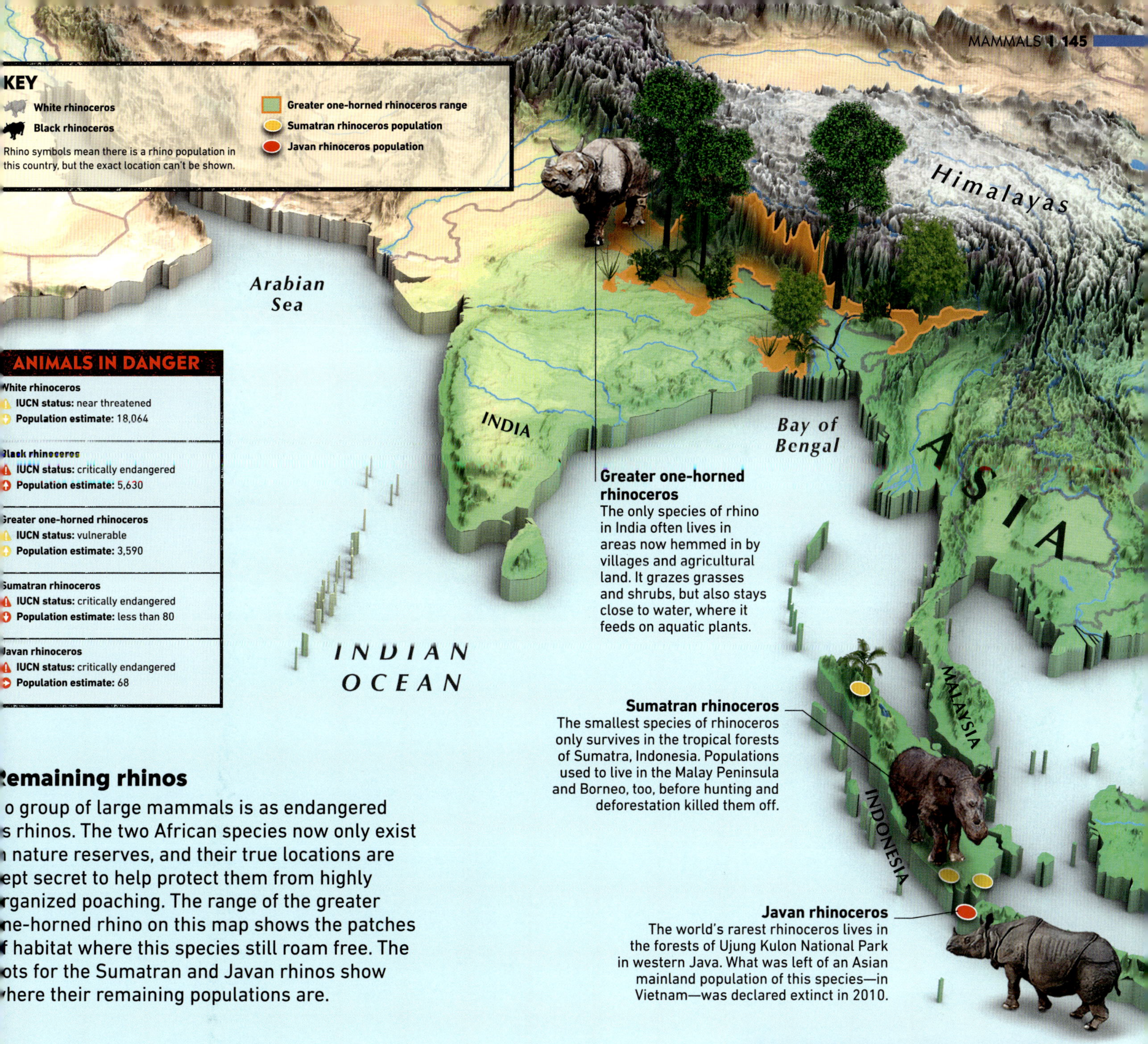

# MAMMALS | 145

## KEY

- White rhinoceros
- Black rhinoceros

Rhino symbols mean there is a rhino population in this country, but the exact location can't be shown.

- Greater one-horned rhinoceros range
- Sumatran rhinoceros population
- Javan rhinoceros population

Himalayas

Arabian Sea

INDIA

Bay of Bengal

ASIA

MALAYSIA

INDONESIA

INDIAN OCEAN

## ANIMALS IN DANGER

**White rhinoceros**
- IUCN status: near threatened
- Population estimate: 18,064

**Black rhinoceros**
- IUCN status: critically endangered
- Population estimate: 5,630

**Greater one-horned rhinoceros**
- IUCN status: vulnerable
- Population estimate: 3,590

**Sumatran rhinoceros**
- IUCN status: critically endangered
- Population estimate: less than 80

**Javan rhinoceros**
- IUCN status: critically endangered
- Population estimate: 68

### Greater one-horned rhinoceros
The only species of rhino in India often lives in areas now hemmed in by villages and agricultural land. It grazes grasses and shrubs, but also stays close to water, where it feeds on aquatic plants.

### Sumatran rhinoceros
The smallest species of rhinoceros only survives in the tropical forests of Sumatra, Indonesia. Populations used to live in the Malay Peninsula and Borneo, too, before hunting and deforestation killed them off.

### Javan rhinoceros
The world's rarest rhinoceros lives in the forests of Ujung Kulon National Park in western Java. What was left of an Asian mainland population of this species—in Vietnam—was declared extinct in 2010.

## Remaining rhinos
No group of large mammals is as endangered as rhinos. The two African species now only exist in nature reserves, and their true locations are kept secret to help protect them from highly organized poaching. The range of the greater one-horned rhino on this map shows the patches of habitat where this species still roam free. The dots for the Sumatran and Javan rhinos show where their remaining populations are.

# Rhinos

In prehistoric times, rhinoceroses ranged across large areas of the globe. Today, five species survive on savannas in Africa and in forests and grassland in Asia, but poaching and habitat destruction have edged these unique creatures to the brink of extinction.

### Guarded treasure
Rhinos are poached for their horns, which some people wrongly believe have medicinal qualities. Armed guards help protect some rhinos, including this white rhino in Kenya.

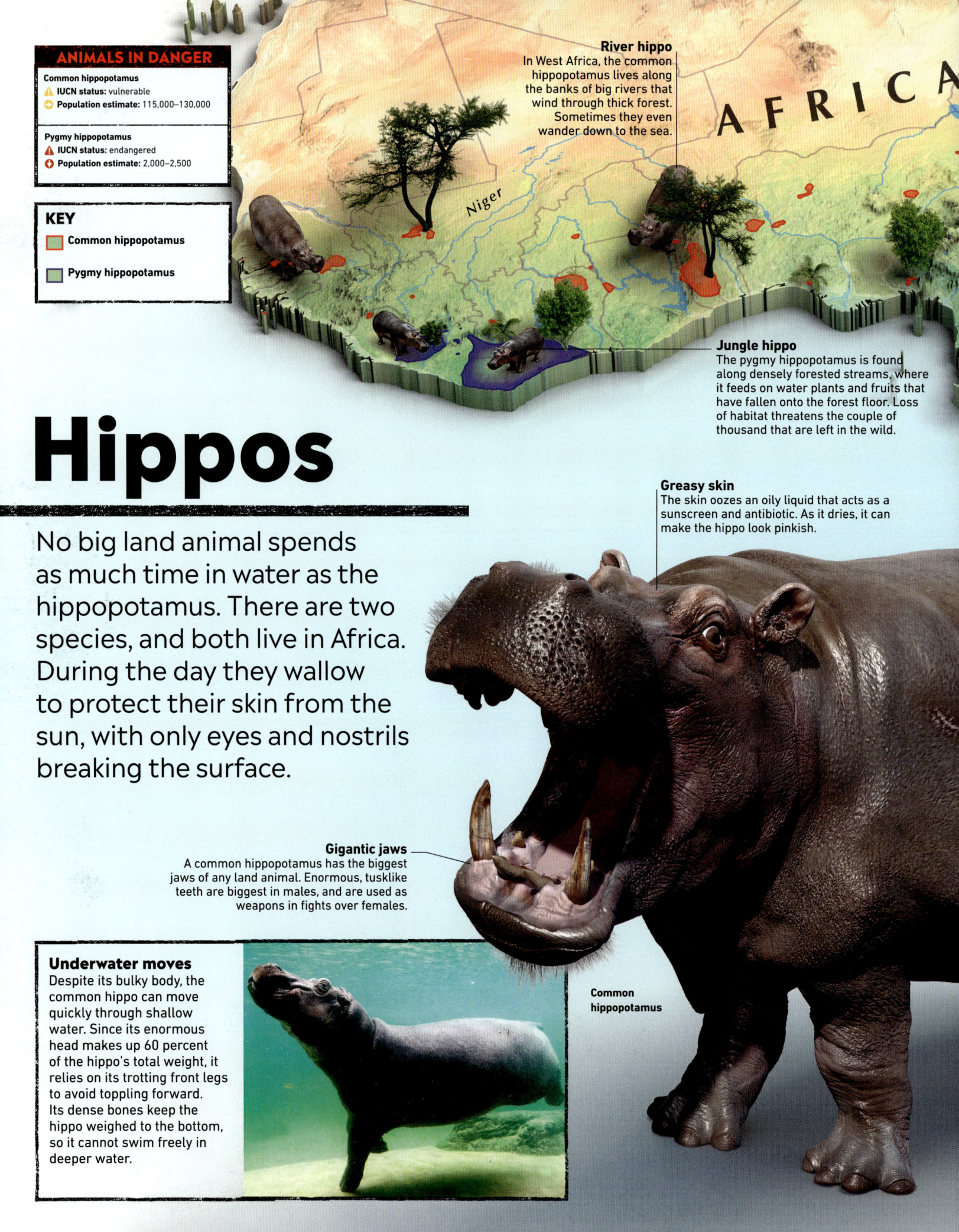

# Hippos

**ANIMALS IN DANGER**

**Common hippopotamus**
- IUCN status: vulnerable
- Population estimate: 115,000–130,000

**Pygmy hippopotamus**
- IUCN status: endangered
- Population estimate: 2,000–2,500

**KEY**
- Common hippopotamus
- Pygmy hippopotamus

**River hippo**
In West Africa, the common hippopotamus lives along the banks of big rivers that wind through thick forest. Sometimes they even wander down to the sea.

**Jungle hippo**
The pygmy hippopotamus is found along densely forested streams, where it feeds on water plants and fruits that have fallen onto the forest floor. Loss of habitat threatens the couple of thousand that are left in the wild.

**Greasy skin**
The skin oozes an oily liquid that acts as a sunscreen and antibiotic. As it dries, it can make the hippo look pinkish.

**Gigantic jaws**
A common hippopotamus has the biggest jaws of any land animal. Enormous, tusklike teeth are biggest in males, and are used as weapons in fights over females.

No big land animal spends as much time in water as the hippopotamus. There are two species, and both live in Africa. During the day they wallow to protect their skin from the sun, with only eyes and nostrils breaking the surface.

**Underwater moves**
Despite its bulky body, the common hippo can move quickly through shallow water. Since its enormous head makes up 60 percent of the hippo's total weight, it relies on its trotting front legs to avoid toppling forward. Its dense bones keep the hippo weighed to the bottom, so it cannot swim freely in deeper water.

Common hippopotamus

MAMMALS | 147

A HIPPO CAN **OPEN ITS** ENORMOUS MOUTH UP TO AN ANGLE OF

**180**

DEGREES— WIDER THAN ANY OTHER **LARGE MAMMAL**

**ADULT MALE** COMMON HIPPOS CAN WEIGH UP TO **4,400 LB (2,000 KG)**

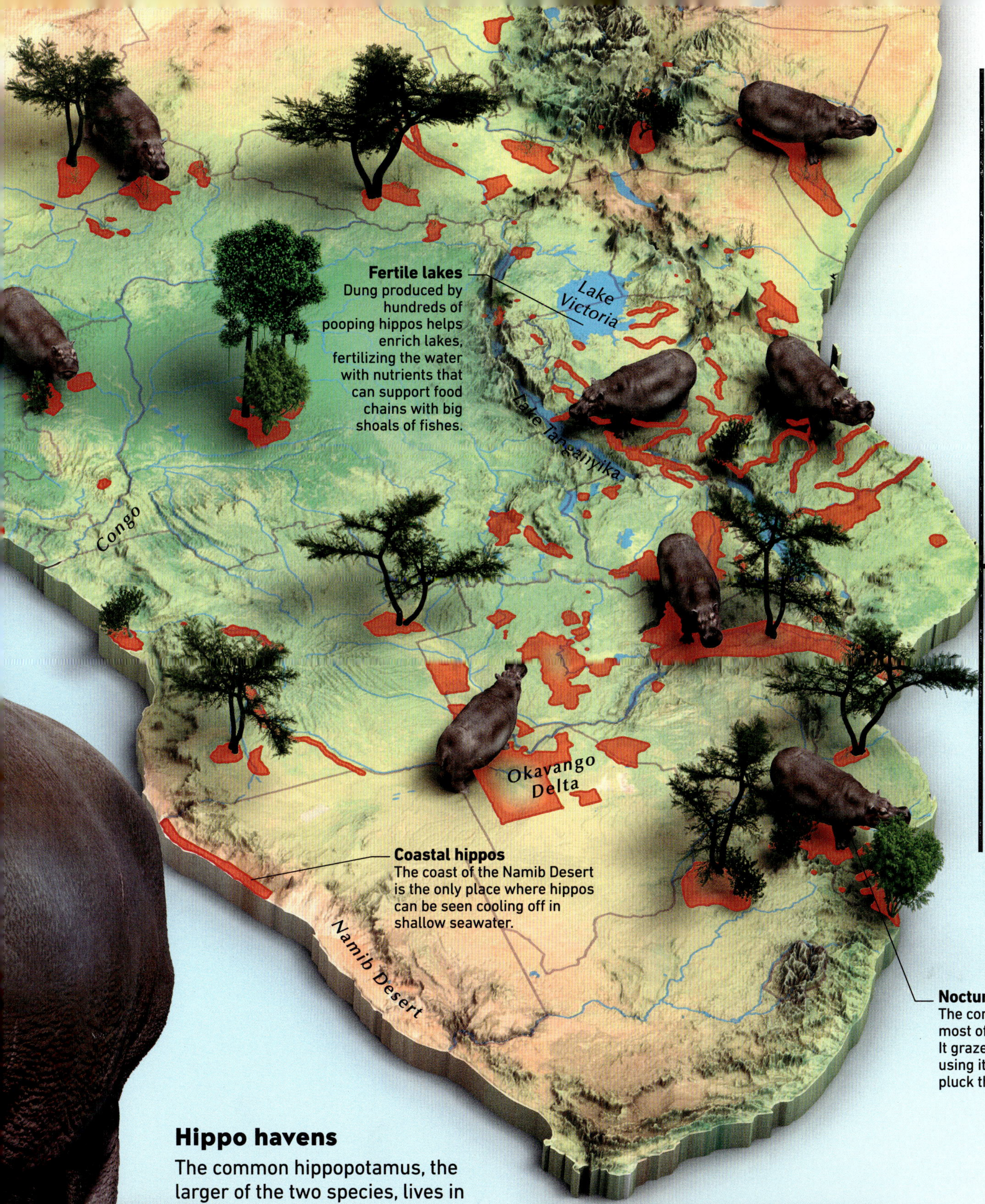

**Fertile lakes**
Dung produced by hundreds of pooping hippos helps enrich lakes, fertilizing the water with nutrients that can support food chains with big shoals of fishes.

Lake Victoria
Lake Tanganyika
Congo
Okavango Delta
Namib Desert

**Coastal hippos**
The coast of the Namib Desert is the only place where hippos can be seen cooling off in shallow seawater.

**Nocturnal grazer**
The common hippo gets most of its food on land. It grazes on grass at night, using its fleshy lips to pluck the blades.

## Hippo havens
The common hippopotamus, the larger of the two species, lives in patches of woodland and grassland around rivers across sub-Saharan Africa. The pygmy hippopotamus only survives in a few fragments of rainforest in West Africa.

HIPPOS CAN **HOLD THEIR BREATH FOR** **5** MINUTES SUBMERGED IN WATER

**Mini hippo**
The forest-dwelling pygmy hippopotamus is about half as tall as its bigger cousin. Shaded by over-hanging trees, it probably spends more time out of water during the day than the common hippo, but its habits are little known.

**1,700 LB (770 KG) IS THE HEAVIEST RECORDED WEIGHT OF AN ADULT MALE MOOSE**

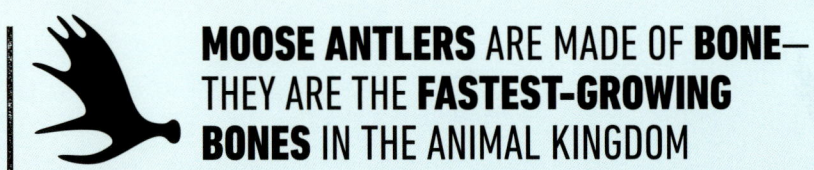

**MOOSE ANTLERS ARE MADE OF BONE—THEY ARE THE FASTEST-GROWING BONES IN THE ANIMAL KINGDOM**

**Alaskan giants**
The biggest moose occur in Alaska and Siberia. Calves born in Alaska can weigh nearly twice as much as those born in Europe.

**Migration**
In the parts of their range with the coldest winters—in North America and Siberia—moose migrate south during the bitter months in search of better food. North American moose may travel up to 125 miles (200 km).

**KEY**
Moose range

**Antler**
A male's antlers start growing in April and are fully formed by summer. Antlers are covered in a nourishing layer of skin, called velvet, that gets rubbed off before the antler is shed in December.

**Marshes and wetlands**
Moose favor the damp, boreal forests that stretch across North America, Europe, and northern Asia, where the snow does not get too deep in winter and temperatures remain cool in summer. They stick to wetland areas, where their favorite food plants—birch, alder, and willow trees—grow in abundance.

# Moose

The world's biggest species of deer also has one of the widest ranges. The moose is an animal of marshy forests and is found across temperate regions of the northern hemisphere—where there is plenty of vegetation to browse and cover for females to raise their calves.

**Motherly care**
A female moose gives birth to one or two calves and feeds them with milk for up to five months. The thick cover of the northern forests helps protect them from predatory gray wolves and brown bears.

**Bellowing bull**
During the breeding season, most male moose defend a female by bellowing loudly and thrashing the vegetation aggressively with their antlers to warn other males to stay away.

**Mountain forests**
In Asia, moose are widespread throughout the forests of Siberia. They are found at their highest altitude in central Asia, including up to 5,580 ft (1,700 m) above sea level in the Altai Mountains.

**Shrinking range**
In prehistory, moose were found as far west as the British Isles and the Pyrenees. Hunting restricted them to Scandinavia and eastern Europe, but their numbers here have increased in the last 50 years.

**Northern tundra**
In the northernmost parts of their range—in the open Arctic tundra—food is scarcer and more scattered. Here, dominant males compete to mate with groups of females called harems.

**Giant antlers**
Like almost all other deer, only male moose grow antlers. These enormous bony weapons—each more than 3 ft (1 m) long—grow new each year as males defend their mates and territories, before being shed at the end of each breeding season.

**A HUMPBACK WHALE** CAN SWALLOW **UP TO 4 TONS OF PREY** EACH DAY

**WHALE SONGS** CAN BE HEARD UP TO **20 MILES (30 KM) AWAY**

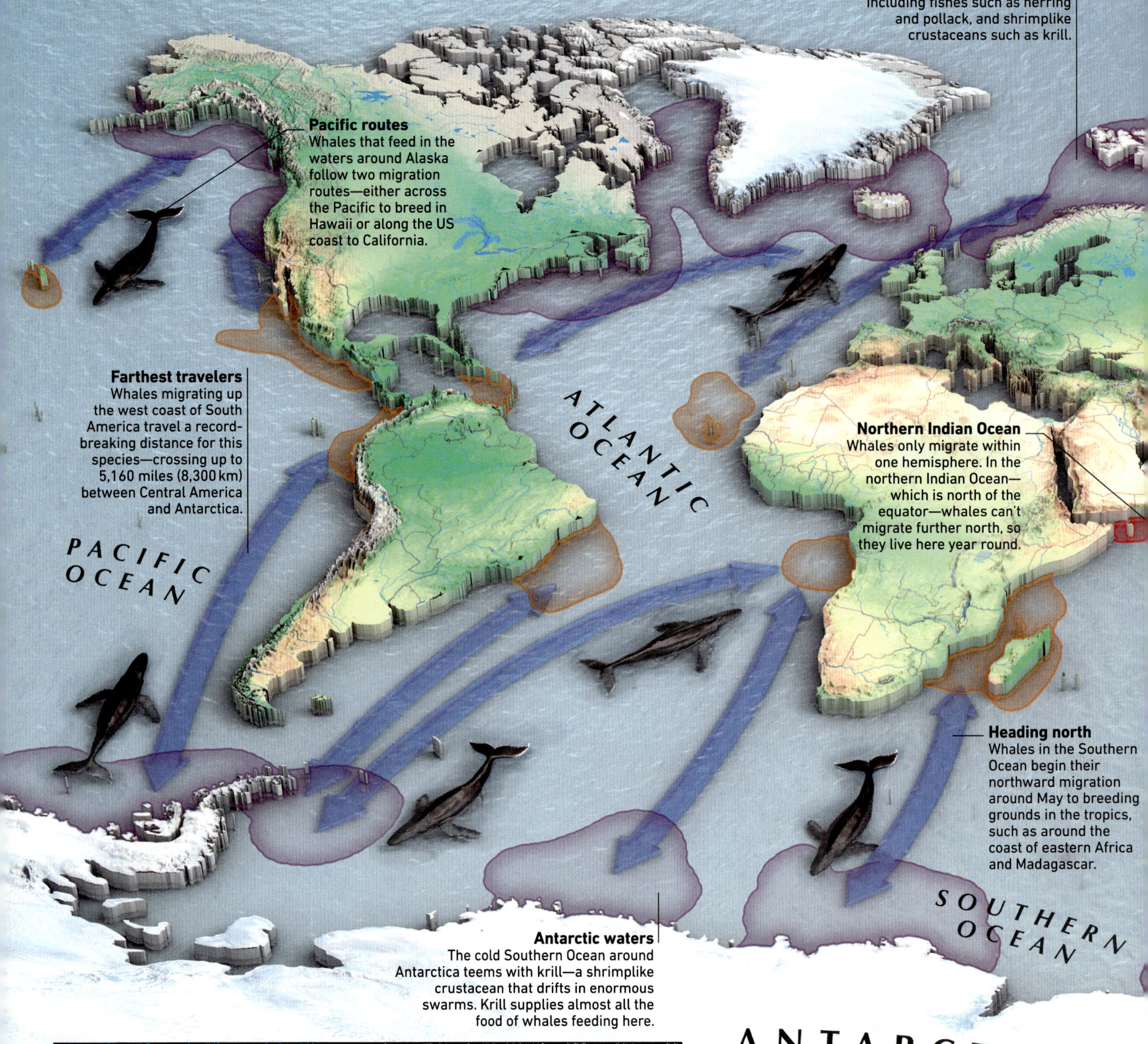

**Icy feeding grounds**
In the cold waters around the Arctic, humpback whales feed on a mixture of small animals—including fishes such as herring and pollack, and shrimplike crustaceans such as krill.

**Pacific routes**
Whales that feed in the waters around Alaska follow two migration routes—either across the Pacific to breed in Hawaii or along the US coast to California.

**Farthest travelers**
Whales migrating up the west coast of South America travel a record-breaking distance for this species—crossing up to 5,160 miles (8,300 km) between Central America and Antarctica.

**Northern Indian Ocean**
Whales only migrate within one hemisphere. In the northern Indian Ocean—which is north of the equator—whales can't migrate further north, so they live here year round.

PACIFIC OCEAN

ATLANTIC OCEAN

**Heading north**
Whales in the Southern Ocean begin their northward migration around May to breeding grounds in the tropics, such as around the coast of eastern Africa and Madagascar.

SOUTHERN OCEAN

**Antarctic waters**
The cold Southern Ocean around Antarctica teems with krill—a shrimplike crustacean that drifts in enormous swarms. Krill supplies almost all the food of whales feeding here.

ANTARCTICA

**Raising young**
After a pregnancy lasting nearly a year, a humpback whale gives birth to a single calf that already weighs almost a ton. The baby grows quickly on more than 90 lb (40 kg) of milk every day, and stays with its mother for up to a year.

**KEY**
- Feeding grounds
- Breeding grounds
- Year-round population
- Migration routes

# Humpback whale

Along with dolphins and porpoises, whales are cetaceans—aquatic mammals that have evolved to swim in the oceans. Together with 14 other species, the humpback whale is a filter feeder—it gulps huge mouthfuls of water and strains out zooplankton (tiny drifting animals) and small swimming fishes.

### Crossing oceans
More plankton live in colder waters around the poles, so humpback whales spend their summers feeding in the far north or south. As winter sets in, they migrate toward the warmer waters of the tropics where they breed and give birth to their calves.

### Northwest Pacific
In the cold Pacific waters around Russia, whales feed mainly on fishes in shallower waters near the coast, and on zooplankton in deeper water offshore.

### Polar front
In the Southern Ocean, many whales gather to feed where cold polar waters meet warmer waters from the north. This zone encircling Antarctica, called the Polar Front, is especially rich in zooplankton.

### Baleen plates
Instead of teeth, strips of horny material called baleen hang down from the roof of the whale's mouth. As the whale closes its mouth, water is forced out through the baleen. The frayed, hairy edges of the baleen trap small animals.

### Unicorns of the sea
Related to whales and dolphins, the narwhal spends much of its time under the thick winter ice of the Arctic seas, only surfacing between ice sheets to breathe. Males grow a distinctive tusk up to 10 ft (3 m) long that is actually a long, sensitive tooth. The tusk is likely used to show dominance or during mating rituals.

# Glossary

**Adaptation**
The way in which a living species has evolved its appearance or behavior, to fit in with its environment.

**Alpine**
Refers to something that lives or grows in mountainous areas.

**Aquatic**
Describes organisms that live in water.

**Arctic Circle**
The imaginary line that encircles the Arctic regions of Eurasia and North America.

**Biome**
A large area that has a particular climate, type of vegetation, and animals living in it.

**Browse**
Describes when animals feed on leaves and twigs from shrubs and trees, higher above ground.

**Bycatch**
Fish or other animals caught by mistake in nets laid out to catch other species.

**Canopy**
The topmost branches of the trees in a forest.

**Carnivorous**
Describes an animal that only eats meat.

**Carrion**
The remains of dead animals that scavengers feed on.

**Cartilage**
The tough, flexible material that makes up the skeleton of animals such as sharks.

**Climate**
The average weather conditions of an area over time.

**Climate change**
The process of gradual change to Earth's climate due to human activity.

**Cold-blooded**
Describes an animal whose body heat depends on the temperature of its surroundings, such as reptiles.

**Colony**
A group of animals—usually, but not always, of the same species—that live together.

**Coniferous**
A type of tree or shrub, such as pine, fir, or juniper, that has needles instead of leaves.

**Conservation**
The saving or protecting of animals or natural habitats.

**Continent**
One of the seven large landmasses on Earth: North America, South America, Europe, Africa, Asia, Australasia and Oceania, and Antarctica.

**Continental shelf**
The submerged edge of a continent that lies beneath shallow coastal seas.

**Coral reef**
A colony of corals growing in a rocklike formation on the seabed, home to a diverse range of marine life.

**Crustacean**
An animal with a hard external skeleton and paired, jointed legs, such as lobsters, crabs, and shrimp.

**Deciduous**
A type of tree, such as oak or birch, that loses leaves each year during a cold or dry season.

**Deforestation**
The cutting down of forests for timber or to clear land for farming or roads.

**Delta**
A low-lying, fan-shaped area at a river mouth, usually where the river flows into the sea.

**Domesticated**
Refers to an animal species that has been bred to be tamed and lives alongside people.

**Echinoderm**
One of a group of animals that includes spiny-skinned marine species, such as starfish and sea urchins.

**Endemic**
An animal or plant that is native to one specific area and found nowhere else.

**Equator**
An imaginary line, at 0° latitude, that divides Earth into the northern and southern hemispheres.

**Estuary**
The part of a river where it flows out into the sea, affected by tides.

**Evolution**
How animals and plants change over many generations as they survive and adapt.

**Exoskeleton**
The tough external skeleton of an animal such as an insect.

**Extinct**
Refers to an animal species that no longer exists because the last remaining individuals have died out.

**Fertilization**
The joining of male and female cells so they develop into seeds or a new organism. Also when dung or chemical fertilizers are spread on fields to make crops grow better.

**Gills**
The organ used by fish and other animals for breathing underwater.

**Glands**
Organs that produce hormones, or substances such as mucus, venom, or poison.

**Habitat**
The environment or place in which an animal normally lives.

**Hemisphere**
The northern hemisphere is the half of Earth north of the equator; the southern hemisphere is the half of the globe to the south of it.

**Hibernation**
When an animal hibernates, or goes into a deep, long sleep, to preserve energy during the cold season.

**Incubate**
To keep eggs warm so they can develop and hatch.

**Intertidal zone**
The part of the shore affected by tides. This area is covered by water when the tide comes in, and emerges when the tide goes out.

**Invertebrate**
An animal without a backbone, for example an insect, worm, or crustacean.

## Ivory
The hard substance from which elephant tusks are made.

## Jet propulsion
The act of pushing forward by jetting out water, used by squids and octopuses.

## Keratin
A tough material that makes up body parts such as hair, feathers, scales, and claws.

## Krill
Tiny marine crustaceans that many animals, such as fish, whales, and seabirds, depend on for food.

## Larva
The immature stage of animals that hatch from eggs and undergo metamorphosis (complete change) to become adults.

## Mangrove
Trees that grow along muddy shores and river banks, often in salty water, and with many of their roots exposed.

## Marine
Relating to the ocean or sea.

## Metamorphosis
When an animal goes through a major change in body shape during its life cycle, such as when a caterpillar turns into a butterfly.

## Microscopic
Something that is very small and can be seen only through a microscope.

## Migration
The regular movement of animals from one place to another, often to find food or breed.

## Mimicry
When an animal has evolved to look or act like another animal, in order to attract prey, or avoid getting eaten.

## Mollusk
One of a group of invertebrates that includes snails, clams, and octopuses.

## Monotreme
A group of mammals that lay eggs.

## Molt
The way an animal sheds part of its outer skin, coat, or exoskeleton. In crustaceans, the regular shedding of the hard outer skeleton (exoskeleton) to allow the animal to grow.

## Nectar
A sugar solution produced by flowers to attract pollinating animals such as bees and butterflies.

## Nocturnal
When an animal is active at night.

## Nutrition
The process of eating and processing food to absorb substances necessary for life.

## Omnivorous
Refers to an animal that eats plants and meat.

## Oxbow lake
A U-shaped lake formed from a river bend cut off from a river that over time has changed its course.

## Pampas
Wide-stretching, grass-covered plains in temperate parts of South America.

## Parasite
An organism that feeds on another, called the host, weakening it, and sometimes eventually killing it.

## Pesticide
Chemicals used to kill insects and other pests that eat or damage crops.

## Pigment
A substance that gives something color.

## Plankton
Small organisms that drift in water.

## Poaching
Illegal hunting and killing of wild animals.

## Pollination
When insects and other animals carry pollen from one flower to another so that fertilization takes place and new plants can grow.

## Prairie
Large, flat grasslands, with very few trees, in North America.

## Prehensile
Able to coil around an object and grip it, like the tail of a monkey or chameleon.

## Primate
One of a group of animals that includes lemurs, monkeys, apes, and humans.

## Proboscis
A long snout, or similar organ.

## Protein
A type of complex chemical found in all living things.

## Range
Referring to the territory, or area, within which an animal lives.

## River basin
The land in which water gathers from one or more rivers.

## Roost
To settle for the night, or a place where birds, bats, and butterflies do this.

## Savanna
Open grasslands in tropical regions, with only a few trees.

## Scavenger
An animal that feeds on the remains of dead animals or other organic waste from living organisms.

## Spawning
Releasing eggs and sperm into water so that fertilization can take place.

## Species
A group of similar organisms than can interbreed and produce fertile offspring.

## Subcontinent
A large landmass that is part of a bigger continent.

## Subspecies
A variant of a species, usually only found in one particular area.

## Subtropical
An area or climate that is nearly tropical, located at the northern or southern edge of the tropics.

## Taiga
The vast coniferous forests covering the northern parts of Eurasia and North America.

## Talons
The large, hooked claws of a bird of prey.

## Temperate
The mild, variable climate found in areas between the tropics and the cold polar regions.

## Thermals
Currents of rising warm air.

## Tropical
Referring to the climate or habitats in the region around the equator, known as the tropics.

## Tundra
A treeless habitat in the cold, northernmost parts of North America, Europe, and Asia, in which the ground is frozen for much of the year.

# Index

Page numbers in **bold** refer to a main topic

## A
adders 66
Adélie penguins 89
Africa **15**, 34-35, 44, 51
   birds 93, 84-85, 89, 98
   Madagascar 72-73, 120-121, 129
   mammals 112, 140
      apes 124-125
      hippopotamuses 146-147
      lions 132-133
      rhinoceroses 144-145
      zebras 142-143
   reptiles 70, 75, 77, 78
Alaska 148
albatrosses 83
algae 110
alligators 70, 71
Amazon region **16**
   rainforest habitats 35, 96, 109
   river habitats 31, 50-51, 76
Amethystine pythons 77
amphibians 11, **54-55**
amphiumas 56
anacondas **76-77**
Andes Mountains 30, 97, 138
Antarctica 24, 88-89, 150-151
antennae 28
antlers 148, 149
apes **124-125**
Appalachian Mountains 57, 119
aquatic
   mammals 150-151, 152-153
Arabian Peninsula 79, 141
Arctic region 36-37, 40, 54, 66
   birds 82, 91
   mammals 150, 152-153
      polar bears 18-19, 138
      wolves 136, 137
armadillo girdled lizards **74-75**
armadillos **108-109**
arthropods 24
Asia **15**
   birds 91, 93, 99
   mammals 137, 141
      bats 128-129
      black bears 139
      elephants 113
      lions 133
      rodents 115, 116-117
   reptiles 71, 77, 79
   *see also* India; Indonesia; Japan
Atlantic Ocean 36-37, 150
   fish 42, 45, 51
Australia
   birds 84, 89, 93, 99
   fish 45, 48
   mammals **104-105**, **106-107**, 129, 137
   snakes 77, 79
   tarantulas 35
aye-ayes 121
Azores, The 28, 36

## B
babies *see* offspring
badgers **140-141**
Baltic Sea 37
Bangladesh 129
barn swallows **98-99**
bats 103, **128-129**
beaks 48, 83, 96, 104
bear cuscuses 107
bears **138-139**
bees **32-33**
beetles 25
Bengal tigers 130
big cats 130-131, 132-133, 134-135
bills 48, 83, 96, 104
biodiversity 16
biomes **12-13**
birds 10, **82-83**
   of prey 90-91, 92-93, 94-95
black mambas 78
black rhinoceroses 144, 145
blacktip reef sharks 46-47
blue-and-yellow macaws **96-97**
blue whales 21, 103
bonobos 124, 125
Borneo 113, 126-127
breeding 57, 63, 149
   birds 88, 90, 93
   *see also* eggs; offspring
brown bears 138
brown-throated sloths **110-111**
Bulgaria 94
bullfrogs 55
Burmese pythons 77
burrows 109, 118
butterflies **30-31**

## C
caecilians 54, 55
caimans 70, 71
camouflage 90, 133, 137, 142
Caribbean 45, 86-87, 98
caribou 103
carnivorous fish 50-51
cartilaginous fish 40
Caspian Sea 141
cassowaries 84
caterpillars 30
catfish 40
cats 130-131, 132-133, 134-135
Central America 30, 98, 108
   amphibians 56, 61
cetaceans 151
chameleons **72-73**
cheetahs 103
chimpanzees 124, 125
China 71, 116, 130
claws 28, 92, 96
   mammals 107, 133, 141
climate change 17, 18, 33
cnidarians 24
cobras 79
cod 40
coelacanths 41
Colombia 82
colonies 88, 119, 128
colors 30, 37, 73, 96
   amphibians 57, 60
   fish 44, 49, 50
   mammals 115, 142
condors 21
Congo tetras 51
conservation **20-21**
continents 14-15
coral reefs 48-49
corvinas 40
crocodiles 67, 70, 71
crocodilians 66, **70-71**
crossbills 83
crows 83
crustaceans 28

## D
deer 149
deforestation 17
desert habitats **13**, 34, 66, 84-85
   mammals 102, 116, 132, 140-141
dingoes 137
dolphins 103
dragonflies 25

## E
ears 112, 115, 116
echidnas 104, 105
echinoderms 24, 36-37
echolocation 129
egg-laying mammals **104-105**
eggs 27, 36, 42, 70
   amphibians 57, 60, 63
   birds 83, 85, 88, 90
   mammals 105
elapids 78-79
elephantnose fish 41
elephants **112-113**
elk 149
emperor penguins **88-89**
emus 84
endangered species **20**
endemic species 41
eucalyptus trees 106
Eurasian wolves 137
Europe
   amphibians 56, 62-63
   birds 91, 93, 94, 98-99
   European lobsters 28-29
   mammals 114, 129, 137, 149
      Iberian lynx 134-135
   starfish 37
extinction 20, 21
eyes 37, 63, 77, 91
   mammals 106, 121

## F
fangs 34, 78
feathers 87, 91, 96
feet 73, 105, 107, 136
filter feeding 42, 151
fins 43
fire salamanders 56
fish 11, 17, **40-41**
flamingos 83, **86-87**
flightless birds **84-85**
flooding 15
flying foxes **128-129**
forelimbs 107, 110, 131, 141
forest habitats **12**, **13**, 72, 97
   mammals 104, 107, 109, 130
   flying foxes 128-129
   lemurs 120-121
   moose 148-149
   primates 122-123, 124
   red squirrels 114-115
   *see also* rainforest habitats
froghoppers 25
frogs 11, 54, 55, 58-59
   strawberry poison frogs **60-61**
fur 106, 115, 123, 127, 136
   brown-throated sloths 110, 111
   manes 133, 142

## G
Galápagos Islands 68-69, 89
gharials 71
ghost bats 129
gills 56, 57
goats 102
Goliath tarantula 34
gorillas 124
grassland habitats 12, 109, 140, 147
   elephants 112
   great apes 124-125
   lions 132
   zebras 142-143
gray wolves **136-137**
Great Lakes 42, 56-57
Great Rift Valley 85
great white sharks **44-45**
green anacondas **76-77**
Grevy's zebras 142, 143
grizzly bears 138
Guyana 30

## H
habitats **12-13**, 18-19
hairy long-nosed armadillos 109
harems 149
herds 143
hibernation 62, 82, 115
Himalayan Mountains 128, 137
hippopotamuses **146-147**
honey badgers **140-141**
honeyeaters 11
horses 21
hot springs 123
hummingbirds 83
humpback whales **150-151**

## I
Iberian lynx **134-135**
India 99, 113, 141
   big cats 130, 133
   cobras 79
   flying foxes 128-129
   rock pythons 77
   tree tarantula 35
Indian Ocean 46, 48, 150-151
Indonesia 77, 102, 104, 107
   orangutans 126-127
   rhinos 145
   tigers 130
invertebrates 11, **24-25**

## J
jackass penguins 89
Japan 26, 44, 56

# INDEX | 157

macaques 122-123
jawless fish 40, **42-43**
jaws 42, 51, 146
jerboas **116-117**

## K
kangaroo rats 102
kangaroos 107
kestrels 21
kites 83
kiwis 84
koalas **106-107**
kraits 79
krill 88, 150

## L
lake habitats 43, 93, 118, 147
    mudpuppies 56-57
lampreys **42-43**
lance heads 78
larvae 36, 42, 43
lemurs 20, **120-121**
limbs 35, 36, 84
    forelimbs 107, 110, 131, 141
lions **132-133**
lizards 66, 67, **74-75**
lobsters **28-29**
locusts 25
lungfish 40
lynx **134-135**

## M
macaques **122-123**
macaroni penguins 89
macaws **96-97**
Madagascar 72-73, 120-121, 129
Maldives 46-47
mammals 11, **102-103**
manes 133, 142
mangrove habitats 130
Mariana Trench 41
marsupials 102, **106-107**
Mediterranean region 12, 29, 43, 44
metamorphosis 55, 56
Mexican red-kneed tarantula 34, 35
midges 24
migration 26, 28, 148
    birds 93, 98-99
    humpback whales 150-151
    toads 62, 63
mimicry 31, 72
mining bees **32-33**
moles **118-119**
mollusks 24
Mongolia 116
monotremes 102, **104-105**
moose **148-149**
mountain habitats **13**, 30, 57, 97
    mammals 102, 108, 119, 137
    flying foxes 128-129
    macaques 123
    moose 149
    zebras 142, 143
mudpuppies **56-57**
mudskippers 40
mugger crocodiles 71
musk oxen 102
mussels 37

## N
Namib Desert 147
Namibia 89
narwhals **152-153**
nectar 31

neon tetras 51
nests 83, 90, 93, 99
New Guinea 39, 48, 55, 77, 105
newts 54, 56
New Zealand 45, 84, 89, 129
Nicaragua 60
North America **14**
    birds 90, 92, 98
    invertebrates 34, 36
    lampreys 42
    mammals 107, 108, 136, 148
        bears 138
        star-nosed moles 118-119
    reptiles 70, 78
    salamanders 56-57
North Atlantic Ocean 42
North Pacific Ocean 26-27, 45, 150-151
North Sea 28, 37
Norway 37
Norwegian Sea 29
noses 73, 119, 121

## O
ocean habitats **12**, 24, 43
    invertebrates 26-27, 28-29, 36-37
    mammals 150-151, 152-153
    sharks 44-45, 46-47
offspring
    birds 86-87, 89, 92
    invertebrates 27, 36
    mammals 114, 140, 149, 150
        marsupials 107
        primates 122, 126
    *see also* breeding; eggs
olms 54
opossums 107
orangutans **126-127**
orcas 103
ospreys **92-93**
ostriches 83, **84-85**
otters 21
owls **90-91**

## P
Pacific Ocean 26-27, 45, 48-49, 150-151
packs 136, 137
pacus 51
Pakistan 128, 129
Panama 61
pandas 139
panther chameleons 73
Papua New Guinea 48, 55, 77, 105
parrotfish **48-49**
parrots **96-97**
patterns *see* colors
penguins **88-89**
peregrine falcons 83
pink fairy armadillos 109
piranhas **50-51**
placental mammals 102
plains zebras 142, 143
plants 33
platypuses 104, 105
poaching 17
poison frogs **60-61**
poisonous animals 30, 59, 61, 62
    *see also* venom
polar bears 18-19, 138
pollination 33
Polynesia 48, 49
poorwills 82
postman butterflies **30-31**
praying mantises 11
prides 132
primates 120-121, 122-123, 124-125, 126-127

proboscis 31
pygmy hippopotamuses 147
pythons 67

## Q
quaggas 142
Queensland whistling spider 35
quelea 82

## R
rabbits 135
rainforest habitats **13**, 30, 34, 60, 96
    mammals 109, 132, 140
        primates 124, 127
    *see also* forest habitats
rattlesnakes 78
red-bellied piranhas **50-51**
red squirrels **114-115**
reptiles 10, **66-67**
rheas 84
rhinoceroses **144-145**
ring-tailed lemurs 120
river habitats 56-57, 110, 146
    fish 40, 43, 50-51
    reptiles 70, 76
rodents 114-115, 116-117
roosts 128
rotifers 25
Russia 91, 114-115
    Siberia 131, 137, 149

## S
sailfish 41
salamanders 54, 55, **56-57**
savannas *see* grassland habitats
saw-scaled vipers 79
scavengers 94, 138, 140
sea habitats *see* ocean habitats
semi-aquatic mammals 118
senses 36, 79
    ears 112, 115, 116
    noses 73, 119, 121
    tongues 63, 72
    *see also* eyes
Seychelles 55
sharks **44-45**, 46-47
shells 68, 69
shoals 46-47, 50
Siberia 131, 137, 149
sifakas 120
skin 27, 36, 77
    amphibians 57, 59, 61
    mammals 129, 140, 145, 146
sloth bears 138
sloths **110-111**
snailfish 41
snakes 66-67, **76-77**, **78-79**
snipes 83
snowy owls **90-91**
Solomon Islands 55
Somali ostriches 85
South Africa 75, 89
South America **14-15**, 16
    birds 84, 87, 89, 92, 98
        macaws 96-97
    Galápagos Islands 68-69, 89
    invertebrates 30-31, 34
    mammals 109, 110-111, 129, 138
    piranhas 50-51
    reptiles 70, 76-77, 78
South Atlantic Ocean 45
South Pacific Ocean 45, 48-49, 150
Southern Ocean 150
Spain 135
spiders 25, **34-35**
spines 36, 104

sponges 24
squids 25
squirrels **114-115**
Sri Lanka 128, 129
starfish **36-37**
star-nosed moles **118-119**
steephead parrotfish **48-49**
strawberry poison frogs **60-61**
Sumatra 126, 130, 145
sun bears 139
sunbirds 83
swallows **98-99**
swamp habitats 56, 118, 124, 128
swimming 26, 41, 88, 146
symmetry 25

## T
tadpoles 55, 60
taiga habitats **12**, 110, 115
tails 43, 73, 78
    birds 96, 99
    mammals 105, 114, 121
Tapanuli orangutans 126
tarantulas **34-35**
Tasmania 105, 107, 109
Tasmanian Devils 107
teeth 42, 51
    fangs 34, 78
    mammals 115, 136, 151
tenrecs 102
tentacles 119
tetras 51
theraphosids 34
tiger fish 51
tiger snakes 79
tigers **130-131**
tinamous 84
toads 54, 55, **62-63**
tongues 63, 72
tortoises 66, 67, **68-69**
tracking devices 26, 45
tuatara 66
tundra habitats **12**, 91, 136, 137, 149
turtles 66
tusks 153

## V
vampire bats 129
várzea forests 97
venom 34, 55, 105, 141
    snakes 78-79
Vietnam 58-59, 145
vipers 11, 78-79
vultures 83, **94-95**

## W
wetland habitats 31, 70-71, 76, 139
    *see also* lake habitats; river habitats
whales 21, 103, **150-151**
whale sharks 41
white rhinoceroses 144, 145
wild dogs 140
wildebeests 143
wings 31, 91, 129
wolves **136-137**
woodland habitats **12**, 108, 112, 125, 147
worms 24
wrasses 11

## Z
zebras **142-143**
zooplankton 151

# Acknowledgments


Dorling Kindersley would like to thank: Sheila Collins for design assistance; Georgina Palffy for editorial assistance; Hazel Beynon for proofreading; Elizabeth Wise for indexing.

**The publisher would like to thank the following for their kind permission to reproduce their photographs:**

(Key: a-above; b-below/bottom; c-center; f-far; l-left; r-right; t-top)

**2 FLPA**: Greg Basco, BIA / Minden Pictures. **4 Alamy Stock Photo:** Narint Asawaphisith (crb). **Getty Images:** Martin Harvey / The Image Bank (tr); James L. Amos / Corbis Documentary (cr). **5 Alamy Stock Photo:** David Carillet (tr). **Dreamstime.com:** Toldiu74 (cl). **Getty Images:** jopstock (clb); Paul Starosta (tl). **6-7 FLPA:** Ralph Pace / Minden Pictures (b). **8-9 Getty Images:** Martin Harvey / The Image Bank. **10-11 Alamy Stock Photo:** National Geographic Image Collection (c). **12 Alamy Stock Photo:** Jelger Herder / Buiten-Beeld (tr); Val Duncan / Kenebec Images (cr); franzfoto.com (cb); Sheila Haddad / Danita Delimont (br); National Geographic Image Collection (tc). **naturepl.com:** Matthias Breiter (cla). **13 Alamy Stock Photo:** John Bennet (bc); Anatoliy Lastovetskiy (bl); Michal Sikorski (crb); Eric Dragesco / Nature Picture Library (cr). **14 Alamy Stock Photo:** Urbach, James / Superstock (c). **Dreamstime.com:** Svetlana Foote (crb). **naturepl.com:** Jane Burton (br). **15 Alamy Stock Photo:** Nobuo Matsumura (cr). **Getty Images:** uzairabdrahim (cra). **naturepl.com:** Cyril Ruoso (clb). **16 Dreamstime.com:** Sandamali Fernando (cra). **17 Alamy Stock Photo:** Ryhor Bruyeu (cl); Allen Galiza (tr). **Getty Images / iStock:** DaveThomasNZ (cr). **Getty Images:** Caroline Pang (bl); UniversalImagesGroup (tl). **18-19 Getty Images:** Ralph Lee Hopkins. **20 Getty Images:** Picture by Tambako the Jaguar. **21 Alamy Stock Photo:** Kevin Elsby (clb); Alex Mustard / Nature Picture Library (cla). **Getty Images:** Arterra (cr); Don Smith (tr); Michael Mike L. Baird flickr.bairdphotos.com (bl); Sandra Standbridge (br). **22-23 Getty Images:** James L. Amos / Corbis Documentary. **24 123RF.com:** Igor Serdiuk (bc); Anna Zakharchenko (c). **Richard E. Lee:** (crb). **Science Photo Library:** Woods Hole Oceanographic Institution, Visuals Unlimited (br). **25 Alamy Stock Photo:** Philip Dalton (br); Fiedler, W. / juniors@wildlife / Juniors Bildarchiv GmbH (tr). **naturepl.com:** Gavin Maxwell (cb). **26 naturepl.com:** Fred Bavendam (clb). **27 naturepl.com:** Fred Bavendam (tr). **28 naturepl.com:** Doug Perrine (bc). **29 Alamy Stock Photo:** Marevision / agefotostock (tr). **30 Dreamstime.com:** Cosmin Manci (tl). **30-31 Dreamstime.com:** Lee Amery (cb). **31 Dreamstime.com:** Maria Shchipakina (br). **Getty Images / iStock:** Merrimon (tr). **32-33 naturepl.com:** Phil Savoie. **34-35 Natural History Museum Bern,. 34 Alamy Stock Photo:** Razvan Cornel Constantin (br). **35 Alamy Stock Photo:** FLPA (bl). **36 Alamy Stock Photo:** FLPA (bl). **37 Alamy Stock Photo:** blickwinkel / H. Baesemann (br). **38-39 Alamy Stock Photo:** Narint Asawaphisith. **40 Alamy Stock Photo:** Jezper (bl). **naturepl.com:** Piotr Naskrecki (bc/ Lungfish). **Shutterstock.com:** Rachasie (bc). **41 Alamy Stock Photo:** blickwinkel / F. Teigler (c); WaterFrame_sta / :WaterFrame (ca); Paulo Oliveira (crb). **Getty Images:** torstenvelden (clb). **42 Alamy Stock Photo:** Marevision / agefotostock (cl); Paulo Oliveira (bl). **45 123RF.com:** Sergei Uriadnikov (br). **Alamy Stock Photo:** Nature Picture Library (tc). **46-47 Getty Images / iStock:** E+ / FilippoBacci. **48 123RF.com:** Richard Whitcombe (tr). **Alamy Stock Photo:** Stephen Frink Collection (tl). **48-49 Shutterstock.com:** Rich Carey (bc). **49 Alamy Stock Photo:** Adam Butler (b). **50 Dreamstime.com:** Chee-Onn-Leong (c). **51 Dreamstime.com:** Tatiana Belova (tr, crb); Slowmotiongli (cra); Gorodok495 (cr); Valeronia (br). **52-53 Getty Images:** Paul Starosta. **54 Alamy Stock Photo:** Pablo Méndez / agefotostock (bc/Frog); Wild Wonders of Europe / Hodalic / / Nature Picture Library (bc). **naturepl.com:** D. Parer & E. Parer-Cook (bl). **55 Alamy Stock Photo:** Odilon Dimier / PhotoAlto (clb); Anton Sorokin (cb). **Getty Images / iStock:** AdrianHillman (c). **naturepl.com:** Fred Olivier (fclb). **Shutterstock.com:** Arun Kumar Anantha Kumar (crb). **56 Alamy Stock Photo:** blickwinkel / W. Pattyn (bl). **Ardea:** Phil A. Dotson / Science Source / ardea.com (cla). **Dreamstime.com:** Slowmotiongli (clb); Martin Voeller (tl); Kevin Wells (cl). **58-59 Alamy Stock Photo:** Chris Mattison / Nature Picture Library. **60 123RF.com:** Dirk Ercken (cb, bc/below). **Alamy Stock Photo:** MYN / JP Lawrence / Nature Picture Library (crb). **Dreamstime.com:** Dirk Ercken (br); Dirk Ercken / Kikkerdirk (fbr). **naturepl.com:** Paul Bertner (fcrb); Michael & Patricia Fogden (clb). **61 naturepl.com:** Lucas Bustamante (b). **63 Alamy Stock Photo:** Rich Bunce (tc). **naturepl.com:** Cyril Ruoso (tr). **64-65 Dreamstime.com:** Toldiu74. **66 123RF.com:** Shakeel SM (bc). **Getty Images:** imageBROKER / Michael Weberberger (bc/Sea snake). **Shutterstock.com:** Grzegorz Lukacijewski (bl). **67 Alamy Stock Photo:** A & J Visage (cla); Mike Robinson (cra); Ken Gillespie Photography (tl); Rweisswald (crb). **Vladimir Dinets:** (br). **69 Alamy Stock Photo:** Krystyna Szulecka Photography (tc). **70 Alamy Stock Photo:** Anthony Pierce (bl). **Getty Images:** Mark Deeble and Victoria Stone (br). **73 Alamy Stock Photo:** Claude Thouvenin / Biosphoto (cra); imageBroker / Thorsten Negro (bl). **Science Photo Library:** Frans Lanting, Mint Images (c). **74-75 Shutterstock.com:** NickEvansKZN. **76 Avalon:** Tony Crocetta (bc). **77 Alamy Stock Photo:** Horizon / Horizon International Images Limited (tr); Arco / G. Lacz / Imagebroker (crb); Sibons photography (br). **naturepl.com:** Jen Guyton (cra); Barry Mansell (cr). **79 Dorling Kindersley:** Daniel Long (bl). **Science Photo Library:** Edward Kinsman (clb). **80-81 Getty Images:** jopstock. **82 Alamy Stock Photo:** blickwinkel / McPHOTO / PUM (crb). **Shutterstock.com:** Rachel Portwood (clb). **83 Alamy Stock Photo:** Christine Cuthbertson (crb); Kike Calvo / Alamy Stock Photo (cr); Bob Gibbons (c). **SuperStock:** Jean Paul Ferrero / Pantheon (br). **84 Alamy Stock Photo:** Neil Bowman (cla); imageBROKER / Konrad Wothe (cl). **Dreamstime.com:** Gerfriedscholz (clb). **Getty Images:** Its About Light / Design Pics (tl); Oliver Strewe (bl). **85 Getty Images:** Lisa Mckelvie (br). **86-87 naturepl.com:** Claudio Contreras. **89 Alamy Stock Photo:** Auscape International Pty Ltd / Ian Beattie (cr); Stefano Paterna (tr); NSP-RF (cra); David South (crb). **Dreamstime.com:** Willtu (br). **naturepl.com:** Stefan Christmann (bc). **90 Alamy Stock Photo:** Nature Picture Library / Markus Varesvuo (bl); Prisma by Dukas Presseagentur GmbH / Bernhardt Reiner (br). **91 Getty Images:** DanielBehmPhotography.Com (cb). **92 Taiwanese Photographer Wilson Chen:** (cla, tr). **93 Getty Images:** 500px / David Gruskin (bc). **94-95 Shutterstock.com:** Ondrej Prosicky. **96 Alamy Stock Photo:** Ger Bosma (tl). **Getty Images / iStock:** RNMitra (bl). **97 Alamy Stock Photo:** Blue Planet Archive AAF (bc). **98 Alamy Stock Photo:** Tierfotoagentur / T. Harbig (bl). **99 Alamy Stock Photo:** blickwinkel / H. Kuczka (cra); VWPics / Mario Cea Sanchez (tc). **naturepl.com:** Phil Savoie (br). **100-101 Alamy Stock Photo:** David Carillet. **102 Alamy Stock Photo:** Arco / C. Hütter (bc); Peter M. Wilson (bc/Goats); Robert Haasmann / imageBROKER (bl); Zoonar / Artush Foto (crb). **Dreamstime.com:** Godruma (cra). **103 Alamy Stock Photo:** Sciepro / Science Photo Library (tr); Nature Picture Library (clb). **Shutterstock.com:** Yann hubert (bl); Lab Photo (cb). **104 Ardea:** D. Parer & E. Parer-Cook (clb). **105 Dreamstime.com:** Valentyna Chukhlyebova (tr). **naturepl.com:** Doug Gimesy (bl). **106 Alamy Stock Photo:** Rawy van den Beucken (br). **Dreamstime.com:** Zcello (bl). **107 Alamy Stock Photo:** National Geographic Image Collection (cra). **Dreamstime.com:** Carolina Garcia Aranda (tr); Holly Kuchera (cr); Hotshotsworldwide (crb). **naturepl.com:** Nick Garbutt (br). **109 naturepl.com:** Gabriel Rojo (cra). **110 naturepl.com:** Suzi Eszterhas (bc, br). **111 123RF.com:** vilainecrevette (r). **112 Alamy Stock Photo:** Cathy Withers-Clarke (br). **TurboSquid:** mohannadhisham / Dorling Kindersley (elephant models). **113 Alamy Stock Photo:** AfriPics.com (br); Friedrich von Hörsten (bc). **TurboSquid:** Skazok / Dorling Kindersley (elephant models). **114 123RF.com:** Dmitry Potashkin (bc). **Alamy Stock Photo:** Giedrius Stakauskas (bl). **115 Dreamstime.com:** Isselee (br). **116-117 naturepl.com:** Klein & Hubert. **119 Science Photo Library:** Ken Catania / Visuals Unlimited, Inc (crb). **120 Alamy Stock Photo:** Michele Burgess (clb). **121 Alamy Stock Photo:** Life on white (crb); Nick Garbutt / RGB Ventures / SuperStock (bl). **Dorling Kindersley:** Jerry Young (br). **122 naturepl.com:** Hiroya Minakuchi (br). **123 Alamy Stock Photo:** Diane McAllister / naturepl.com (tr). **naturepl.com:** Konrad Wothe (b). **124 Alamy Stock Photo:** Arco Images / Vnoucek, F / Imagebroker (bl). **125 Dreamstime.com:** Daniel Bellhouse / Danox (tr). **126 naturepl.com:** Thomas Marent (bc). **127 Alamy Stock Photo:** RDW Environmental (clb). **Dreamstime.com:** Sergey Uryadnikov (br). **128 Alamy Stock Photo:** Marius Dobilas (bc). **129 Alamy Stock Photo:** FLPA (cr); Daniel Romero / VWPics (br). **Dreamstime.com:** Kyslynskyy (tl); Slowmotiongli (cra). **131 Alamy Stock Photo:** Andy Rouse / Nature Picture Library (bc). **133 Dorling Kindersley:** Roman Gorielov (bl). **Getty Images:** David Chen / EyeEm (tc). **134-135 naturepl.com:** Laurent Geslin. **136 Getty Images:** Jim Cumming (b). **137 Alamy Stock Photo:** Arco / TUNS / Imagebroker (cb); Werner Layer / mauritius images GmbH (bc). **138 Dreamstime.com:** Outdoorsman (bc). **139 Alamy Stock Photo:** Genevieve Vallee (crb). **140-141 Dreamstime.com:** Matthijs Kuijpers (bc). **140 naturepl.com:** Suzi Eszterhas (bc). **141 FLPA:** Vincent Grafhorst / Minden Pictures (br). **142 Alamy Stock Photo:** Steve Bloom / Steve Bloom Images (c); Photo Researchers / Science History Images (tl). **143 Alamy Stock Photo:** Mint Images / Mint Images Limited (clb). **144 Alamy Stock Photo:** Denis-Huot / Nature Picture Library (bl). **145 Alamy Stock Photo:** Ann & Steve Toon / Nature Picture Library (br). **146 Alamy Stock Photo:** Lena Ivanova (bc). **147 Alamy Stock Photo:** Juniors Bildarchiv / F300 / Juniors Bildarchiv GmbH (bc). **148 Alamy Stock Photo:** Doug Lindstrand / Alaska Stock RF / Design Pics Inc (bl). **149 Getty Images:** Doug Lindstrand / Alaska Stock RF / Design Pics Inc (bc). **Paul Williams:** Paul Williams (tr). **150 Dreamstime.com:** Seanothon (bl). **151 Alamy Stock Photo:** blickwinkel / AGAMI / M. van Duijn (br). **152-153 naturepl.com:** Flip Nicklin.

All other images © Dorling Kindersley
For further information see: www.dkimages.com

**Map data sources:**

**IUCN 2020. The IUCN Red List of Threatened Species. Version 2020-2. https://www.iucnredlist.org:**

**28–29** Butler, M., Cockcroft, A., MacDiarmid, A. & Wahle, R. 2011. *Homarus gammarus*. The IUCN Red List of Threatened Species 2011: e.T169955A69905303. https://dx.doi.org/10.2305/IUCN.UK.2011-1.RLTS.T169955A69905303.en (Common lobster). **42–43** NatureServe. 2013. *Petromyzon marinus*. The IUCN Red List of Threatened Species 2013: e.T16781A18229984. https://dx.doi.org/10.2305/IUCN.UK.2013-1.RLTS.T16781A18229984.en (Sea lamprey). **44–45** Rigby, C.L., Barreto, R., Carlson, J., Fernando, D., Fordham, S., Francis, M.P., Herman K., Jabado, R.W., Liu, K.M., Lowe, C.G, Marshall, A., Pacoureau, N., Romanov, E., Sherley, R.B. & Winker, H. 2019. *Carcharodon carcharias*. The IUCN Red List of Threatened Species 2019: e.T3855A2878674. https://dx.doi.org/10.2305/IUCN.UK.2019-3.RLTS.T3855A2878674.en (Great white shark). **56–57** IUCN SSC Amphibian Specialist Group. 2015. *Necturus maculosus*. The IUCN Red List of Threatened Species 2015: e.T59433A64731610. https://dx.doi.org/10.2305/IUCN.UK.2015-4.RLTS.T59433A64731610.en (Mudpuppy). **56** Geoffrey Hammerson. 2004. *Amphiuma means*. The IUCN Red List of Threatened Species 2004: e.T59074A11879454. https://dx.doi.org/10.2305/IUCN.UK.2004.RLTS.T59074A11879454.en (Amphiuma); IUCN SSC Amphibian Specialist Group. 2020. *Bolitoglossa mexicana*. The IUCN Red List of Threatened Species 2020: e.T59180A53976360. https://dx.doi.org/10.2305/IUCN.UK.2020-1.RLTS.T59180A53976360.en (Mushroom-tongued salamander); Sergius Kuzmin, Theodore Papenfuss, Max Sparreboom, Ismail H. Ugurtas, Steven Anderson, Trevor Beebee, Mathieu Denoël, Franco Andreone, Brandon Anthony, Benedikt Schmidt, Agnieszka Ogrodowczyk, Maria Ogielska, Jaime Bosch, David Tarkhnishvili, Vladimir Ishchenko. 2009. *Salamandra salamandra*. The IUCN Red List of Threatened Species 2009: e.T59467A11928351. https://dx.doi.org/10.2305/IUCN.UK.2009.RLTS.T59467A11928351.en (Fire salamander); Yoshio Kaneko, Masafumi Matsui. 2004. Andrias japonicus. The IUCN Red List of Threatened Species 2004: e.T1273A3376261. https://dx.doi.

rg/10.2305/IUCN.UK.2004.RLTS. T1273A3376261.en (Japanese giant salamander); Jan Willem Arntzen, Sergius Kuzmin, Robert Jehle, Trevor Beebee, David Tarkhnishvili, Vladimir Ishchenko, Natalia Ananjeva, Nikolai Orlov, Boris Tuniyev, Mathieu Denoël, Per Nyström, Brandon Anthony, Benedikt Schmidt, Agnieszka Ogrodowczyk. 2009. *Triturus cristatus*. The IUCN Red List of Threatened Species 2009: e.T22212A9365894. https://dx.doi.org/10.2305/IUCN.UK.2009.RLTS.T22212A9365894.en (Great crested newt). **60–61** IUCN SSC Amphibian Specialist Group. 2015. *Oophaga pumilio*. The IUCN Red List of Threatened Species 2015: e.T55196A3025630. https://dx.doi.org/10.2305/IUCN.UK.2015-4.RLTS.T55196A3025630.en (Strawberry poison dart frog). **62–63** Aram Agasyan, Aziz Avisi, Boris Tuniyev, Jelka Crnobrnja Isailovic, Petros Lymberakis, Claes Andrén, Dan Cogalniceanu, John Wilkinson, Natalia Ananjeva, Nazan Üzüm, Nikolai Orlov, Richard Podloucky, Sako Tuniyev, Uğur Kaya. 2009. *Bufo bufo*. The IUCN Red List of Threatened Species 2009: e.T54596A11159939. https://dx.doi.org/10.2305/IUCN.UK.2009.RLTS.T54596A11159939.en (Common toad). **68–69** Cayot, L.J., Gibbs, J.P., Tapia, W. & Caccone, A. 2017. *Chelonoidis donfaustoi*. The IUCN Red List of Threatened Species 2017: e.T90377132A90377135. https://dx.doi.org/10.2305/IUCN.UK.2017-3.RLTS.T90377132A90377135.en (Eastern Santa Cruz giant Tortoise); Rhodin, A.G.J., Gibbs, J.P., Cayot, L.J., Kiester, A.R. & Tapia, W. 2017. *Chelonoidis phantasticus* (errata version published in 2018). The IUCN Red List of Threatened Species 2017: e.T170517A128969920. https://dx.doi.org/10.2305/IUCN.UK.2017-3.RLTS.T170517A1315907.en (Fernandina giant tortoise); Caccone, A., Cayot, L.J., Gibbs, J.P. & Tapia, W. 2017. *Chelonoidis becki*. The IUCN Red List of Threatened Species 2017: e.T9018A82426296. https://dx.doi.org/10.2305/IUCN.UK.2017-3.RLTS.T9018A82426296.en (Wolf Volcano giant tortoise); Cayot, L.J., Gibbs, J.P., Tapia, W. & Caccone, A. 2018. *Chelonoidis vandenburghi* (errata version published in 2019). The IUCN Red List of Threatened Species 2018: e.T9027A144766471. https://dx.doi.org/10.2305/IUCN.UK.2018-2.RLTS.T9027A144766471.en (Volcán Alcedo giant tortoise); Cayot, L.J., Gibbs, J.P., Tapia, W. & Caccone, A. 2017. *Chelonoidis porteri*. The IUCN Red List of Threatened Species 2017: e.T9026A82777132. https://dx.doi.org/10.2305/IUCN.UK.2017-3.RLTS.T9026A82777132.en (Western Santa Cruz giant tortoise); Caccone, A., Cayot, L.J., Gibbs, J.P. & Tapia, W. 2017. *Chelonoidis chathamensis*. The IUCN Red List of Threatened Species 2017: e.T9019A82688009. https://dx.doi.org/10.2305/IUCN.UK.2017-3.RLTS.T9019A82688009.en (San Cristóbal giant tortoise); Cayot, L.J., Gibbs, J.P., Tapia, W. & Caccone, A. 2017. *Chelonoidis hoodensis*. The IUCN Red List of Threatened Species 2017: e.T9024A82777079. https://dx.doi.org/10.2305/IUCN.UK.2017-3.RLTS.T9024A82777079.en (Española giant tortoise). **72–73** Jenkins, R.K.B., Andreone, F., Andriamazava, A., Anjeriniaina, M., Brady, L., Glaw, F., Griffiths, R.A., Rabibisoa, N., Rakotomalala, D., Randrianantoandro, J.C., Randrianiriana, J., Randrianizahana, H., Ratsoavina, F. & Robsomanitrandrasana, E. 2011. *Furcifer oustaleti*. The IUCN Red List of Threatened Species 2011: e.T172866A6932058. https://dx.doi.org/10.2305/IUCN.UK.2011-2.RLTS.T172866A6932058.en (Oustalet's chameleon); Jenkins, R.K.B., Andreone, F., Andriamazava, A., Anjeriniaina, M., Brady, L., Glaw, F., Griffiths, R.A., Rabibisoa, N., Rakotomalala, D., Randrianantoandro, J.C.,

Randrianiriana, J., Randrianizahana, H., Ratsoavina, F. & Robsomanitrandrasana, E. 2011. *Calumma parsonii*. The IUCN Red List of Threatened Species 2011: e.T172896A6937628. https://dx.doi.org/10.2305/IUCN.UK.2011-2.RLTS.T172896A6937628.en (Parson's chameleon); Jenkins, R.K.B., Andreone, F., Andriamazava, A., Anjeriniaina, M., Brady, L., Glaw, F., Griffiths, R.A., Rabibisoa, N., Rakotomalala, D., Randrianantoandro, J.C., Randrianiriana, J., Randrianizahana, H., Ratsoavina, F. & Robsomanitrandrasana, E. 2011. *Furcifer pardalis*. The IUCN Red List of Threatened Species 2011: e.T172955A6947909. https://dx.doi.org/10.2305/IUCN.UK.2011-2.RLTS.T172955A6947909.en (Panther chameleon). **72** Jenkins, R.K.B., Andreone, F., Andriamazava, A., Anjeriniaina, M., Brady, L., Glaw, F., Griffiths, R.A., Rabibisoa, N., Rakotomalala, D., Randrianantoandro, J.C., Randrianiriana, J., Randrianizahana, H., Ratsoavina, F. & Robsomanitrandrasana, E. 2011. *Palleon nasus*. The IUCN Red List of Threatened Species 2011: e.T172773A6915062. https://dx.doi.org/10.2305/IUCN.UK.2011-2.RLTS.T172773A6915062.en (Elongated leaf chameleon); Jenkins, R.K.B., Andreone, F., Andriamazava, A., Anjeriniaina, M., Brady, L., Glaw, F., Griffiths, R.A., Rabibisoa, N., Rakotomalala, D., Randrianantoandro, J.C., Randrianiriana, J., Randrianizahana , H., Ratsoavina, F. & Robsomanitrandrasana, E. 2011. *Furcifer labordi*. The IUCN Red List of Threatened Species 2011: e.T8765A12929754. https://dx.doi.org/10.2305/IUCN.UK.2011-2.RLTS.T8765A12929754.en (Laborde's chameleon). **77** Stuart, B., Nguyen, T.Q., Thy, N., Grismer, L., Chan-Ard, T., Iskandar, D., Golynsky, E. & Lau, M.W.N. 2012. *Python bivittatus* (errata version published in 2019). The IUCN Red List of Threatened Species 2012: e.T193451A151341916. https://dx.doi.org/10.2305/IUCN.UK.2012-1.RLTS.T193451A151341916.en (Burmese python); Stuart, B., Thy, N., Chan-Ard, T., Nguyen, T.Q., Grismer, L., Auliya, M., Das, I. & Wogan, G. 2018. *Python reticulatus*. The IUCN Red List of Threatened Species 2018: e.T183151A1730027. https://dx.doi.org/10.2305/IUCN.UK.2018-2.RLTS.T183151A1730027.en (Reticulated python); Tallowin, O., Allison, A., Parker, F. & O'Shea, M. 2017. *Morelia amethistina*. The IUCN Red List of Threatened Species 2017: e.T177501A1489667. https://dx.doi.org/10.2305/IUCN.UK.2017-3.RLTS.T177501A1489667.en (Amethystine python). **78–79** Spawls, S. 2010. *Dendroaspis polylepis*. The IUCN Red List of Threatened Species 2010: e.T177584A7461853. https://dx.doi.org/10.2305/IUCN.UK.2010-4.RLTS.T177584A7461853.en (Black mamba); Frost, D.R., Hammerson, G.A. & Santos-Barrera, G. 2007. *Crotalus atrox*. The IUCN Red List of Threatened Species 2007: e.T64311A12763519. https://dx.doi.org/10.2305/IUCN.UK.2007.RLTS.T64311A12763519.en (Diamond-backed rattlesnake); Ji, X., Rao, D.-q. & Wang, Y. 2012. *Bungarus multicinctus*. The IUCN Red List of Threatened Species 2012: e.T191957A2020937. https://dx.doi.org/10.2305/IUCN.UK.2012-1.RLTS.T191957A2020937.en (Many-banded krait); Michael, D., Clemann, N. & Robertson, P. 2018. *Notechis scutatus*. The IUCN Red List of Threatened Species 2018: e.T169687A83767147. https://dx.doi.org/10.2305/IUCN.UK.2018-1.RLTS.T169687A83767147.en (Tiger snake). **84–85** BirdLife International. 2018. *Struthio camelus*. The IUCN Red List of Threatened Species 2018: e.T45020636A132189458. https://dx.doi.org/10.2305/IUCN.UK.2018-2.RLTS.T45020636A132189458.en (Common

Ostrich, Somali ostrich); BirdLife International. 2016. *Struthio molybdophanes*. The IUCN Red List of Threatened Species 2016: e.T22732795A95049558. https://dx.doi.org/10.2305/IUCN.UK.2016-3.RLTS.T22732795A95049558.en (Common Ostrich, Somali ostrich). **84** BirdLife International. 2020. *Rhea tarapacensis*. The IUCN Red List of Threatened Species 2020: e.T22728206A177987446 (Puna rhea); BirdLife International. 2017. *Casuarius unappendiculatus*. The IUCN Red List of Threatened Species 2017: e.T22678114A118134784. https://dx.doi.org/10.2305/IUCN.UK.2017-3.RLTS.T22678114A118134784.en (Northern cassowary); BirdLife International. 2018. *Dromaius novaehollandiae*. The IUCN Red List of Threatened Species 2018: e.T22678117A131902466. https://dx.doi.org/10.2305/IUCN.UK.2018-2.RLTS.T22678117A131902466.en (Common emu). **88–89** BirdLife International. 2018. *Aptenodytes forsteri*. The IUCN Red List of Threatened Species 2018: e.T22697752A132600320. https://dx.doi.org/10.2305/IUCN.UK.2018-2.RLTS.T22697752A132600320.en (Emperor Penguin). **89** BirdLife International. 2018. *Pygoscelis adeliae*. The IUCN Red List of Threatened Species 2018: e.T22697758A132601165. https://dx.doi.org/10.2305/IUCN.UK.2018-2.RLTS.T22697758A132601165.en (Adelie penguin); BirdLife International. 2018. *Spheniscus mendiculus*. The IUCN Red List of Threatened Species 2018: e.T22697825A132606008. https://dx.doi.org/10.2305/IUCN.UK.2018-2.RLTS.T22697825A132606008.en (Galapagos penguin); BirdLife International. 2018. *Spheniscus demersus*. The IUCN Red List of Threatened Species 2018: e.T22697810A132604504. https://dx.doi.org/10.2305/IUCN.UK.2018-2.RLTS.T22697810A132604504.en (Jackass penguin); BirdLife International. 2018. *Eudyptula minor*. The IUCN Red List of Threatened Species 2018: e.T22697805A132603951. https://dx.doi.org/10.2305/IUCN.UK.2018-2.RLTS.T22697805A132603951.en (Little penguin); BirdLife International. 2018. *Eudyptes chrysolophus*. The IUCN Red List of Threatened Species 2018: e.T22697793A132602631. https://dx.doi.org/10.2305/IUCN.UK.2018-2.RLTS.T22697793A132602631.en (Macaroni penguin). **90–91** BirdLife International. 2017. *Bubo scandiacus* (errata version published in 2018). The IUCN Red List of Threatened Species 2017: e.T22689055A127837214. https://dx.doi.org/10.2305/IUCN.UK.2017-3.RLTS.T22689055A119342767.en (Snowy owl). **92–93** BirdLife International. 2019. *Pandion haliaetus* (amended version of 2016 assessment). The IUCN Red List of Threatened Species 2019: e.T22694938A155519951. https://dx.doi.org/10.2305/IUCN.UK.2019-3.RLTS.T22694938A155519951.en (Osprey). **96–97** BirdLife International. 2018. *Ara ararauna*. The IUCN Red List of Threatened Species 2018: e.T22685539A131917270. https://dx.doi.org/10.2305/IUCN.UK.2018-2.RLTS.T22685539A131917270.en (Blue-and-yellow macaw). **98–99** BirdLife International. 2019. *Hirundo rustica*. The IUCN Red List of Threatened Species 2019: e.T22712252A137668645. https://dx.doi.org/10.2305/IUCN.UK.2019-3.RLTS.T22712252A137668645.en (Barn swallow). **104–105** Leary, T., Seri, L., Flannery, T., Wright, D., Hamilton, S., Helgen, K., Singadan, R., Menzies, J., Allison, A., James, R., Aplin, K., Salas, L. & Dickman, C. 2016. *Zaglossus bartoni*. The IUCN Red List of Threatened Species 2016: e.T136552A21964496. https://dx.doi.org/10.2305/IUCN.UK.2016-2.RLTS.

T136552A21964496.en (Eastern long-beaked echidna); Leary, T., Seri, L., Flannery, T., Wright, D., Hamilton, S., Helgen, K., Singadan, R., Menzies, J., Allison, A., James, R., Aplin, K., Salas, L. & Dickman, C. 2016. *Zaglossus bruijnii*. The IUCN Red List of Threatened Species 2016: e.T23179A21964204. https://dx.doi.org/10.2305/IUCN.UK.2016-2.RLTS.T23179A21964204.en (Western long-beaked echidna); Aplin, K., Dickman, C., Salas, L. & Helgen, K. 2016. *Tachyglossus aculeatus*. The IUCN Red List of Threatened Species 2016: e.T41312A21964662. https://dx.doi.org/10.2305/IUCN.UK.2016-2.RLTS.T41312A21964662.en (Short-beaked echidna); Woinarski, J. & Burbidge, A.A. 2016. *Ornithorhynchus anatinus*. The IUCN Red List of Threatened Species 2016: e.T40488A21964009. https://dx.doi.org/10.2305/IUCN.UK.2016-1.RLTS.T40488A21964009.en (Platypus). **106–107** Woinarski, J. & Burbidge, A.A. 2020. *Phascolarctos cinereus* (amended version of 2016 assessment). The IUCN Red List of Threatened Species 2020: e.T16892A166496779. https://dx.doi.org/10.2305/IUCN.UK.2020-1.RLTS.T16892A166496779.en (Koala). **107** Salas, L., Dickman, C., Helgen, K. & Flannery, T. 2019. *Ailurops ursinus*. The IUCN Red List of Threatened Species 2019: e.T40637A21949654. https://dx.doi.org/10.2305/IUCN.UK.2019-1.RLTS.T40637A21949654.en (Bear cuscus); Ellis, M., van Weenen, J., Copley, P., Dickman, C., Mawson, P. & Woinarski, J. 2016. *Macropus rufus*. The IUCN Red List of Threatened Species 2016: e.T40567A21953534. https://dx.doi.org/10.2305/IUCN.UK.2016-2.RLTS.T40567A21953534.en (Red kangaroo); Pérez-Hernandez, R., Lew, D. & Solari, S. 2016. *Didelphis virginiana*. The IUCN Red List of Threatened Species 2016: e.T40502A22176259. https://dx.doi.org/10.2305/IUCN.UK.2016-1.RLTS.T40502A22176259.en (Virginia opossum); Hawkins, C.E., McCallum, H., Mooney, N., Jones, M. & Holdsworth, M. 2008. *Sarcophilus harrisii*. The IUCN Red List of Threatened Species 2008: e.T40540A10331066. https://dx.doi.org/10.2305/IUCN.UK.2008.RLTS.T40540A10331066.en (Tasmanian devil); Leary, T., Seri, L., Wright, D., Hamilton, S., Helgen, K., Singadan, R., Menzies, J., Allison, A., James, R., Dickman, C., Aplin, K., Flannery, T., Martin, R. & Salas, L. 2016. *Dendrolagus goodfellowi*. The IUCN Red List of Threatened Species 2016: e.T6429A21957524. https://dx.doi.org/10.2305/IUCN.UK.2016-2.RLTS.T6429A21957524.en (Tree kangaroo). **108–109** Anacleto, T.C.S., Miranda, F., Medri, I., Cuellar, E., Abba, A.M. & Superina, M. 2014. *Priodontes maximus*. The IUCN Red List of Threatened Species 2014: e.T18144A47442343. https://dx.doi.org/10.2305/IUCN.UK.2014-1.RLTS.T18144A47442343.en (Giant armadillo); Loughry, J., McDonough, C. & Abba, A.M. 2014. *Dasypus novemcinctus*. The IUCN Red List of Threatened Species 2014: e.T6290A47440785. https://dx.doi.org/10.2305/IUCN.UK.2014-1.RLTS.T6290A47440785.en (Nine-banded armadillo); Superina, M. & Abba, A.M. 2014. *Dasypus pilosus*. The IUCN Red List of Threatened Species 2014: e.T6291A47441122. https://dx.doi.org/10.2305/IUCN.UK.2014-1.RLTS.T6291A47441122.en (Hairy long-nosed armadillo); Superina, M., Abba, A.M. & Roig, V.G. 2014. *Chlamyphorus truncatus*. The IUCN Red List of Threatened Species 2014: e.T4704A47439264. https://dx.doi.org/10.2305/IUCN.UK.2014-1.RLTS.T4704A47439264.en (Pink fairy armadillo); Noss, A., Superina, M. & Abba, A.M. 2014. *Tolypeutes matacus*. The IUCN Red List of Threatened Species 2014: e.T21974A47443233. https://dx.doi.org/10.2305/IUCN.UK.2014-1.RLTS.T21974A47443233.en (Southern three-banded armadillo).

**110–111** Moraes-Barros, N., Chiarello, A. & Plese, T. 2014. *Bradypus variegatus*. The IUCN Red List of Threatened Species 2014: e.T3038A47437046. https://dx.doi.org/10.2305/IUCN.UK.2014-1.RLTS.T3038A47437046.en (Brown-throated sloth). **112–113** Blanc, J. 2008. *Loxodonta africana*. The IUCN Red List of Threatened Species 2008: e.T12392A3339343. https://dx.doi.org/10.2305/IUCN.UK.2008.RLTS.T12392A3339343.en (African forest elephant & African savannah elephant); Choudhury, A., Lahiri Choudhury, D.K., Desai, A., Duckworth, J.W., Easa, P.S., Johnsingh, A.J.T., Fernando, P., Hedges, S., Gunawardena, M., Kurt, F., Karanth, U., Lister, A., Menon, V., Riddle, H., Rübel, A. & Wikramanayake, E. (IUCN SSC Asian Elephant Specialist Group). 2008. *Elephas maximus*. The IUCN Red List of Threatened Species 2008: e.T7140A12828813. https://dx.doi.org/10.2305/IUCN.UK.2008.RLTS.T7140A12828813.en (Asian elephant). **114–115** Shar, S., Lkhagvasuren, D., Bertolino, S., Henttonen, H., Kryštufek, B. & Meinig, H. 2016. *Sciurus vulgaris* (errata version published in 2017). The IUCN Red List of Threatened Species 2016: e.T20025A115155900. https://dx.doi.org/10.2305/IUCN.UK.2016-3.RLTS.T20025A22245887.en (Eurasian red squirrel). **118–119** Cassola, F. 2016. *Condylura cristata* (errata version published in 2017). The IUCN Red List of Threatened Species 2016: e.T41458A115187740. https://dx.doi.org/10.2305/IUCN.UK.2016-3.RLTS.T41458A22322697.en (Star-nosed mole). **120–121** Louis, E.E., Sefczek, T.M., Randimbiharinirina, D.R., Raharivololona, B., Rakotondrazandry, J.N., Manjary, D., Aylward, M. & Ravelomandrato, F. 2020. *Daubentonia madagascariensis*. The IUCN Red List of Threatened Species 2020: e.T6302A115560793. https://dx.doi.org/10.2305/IUCN.UK.2020-2.RLTS.T6302A115560793.en (Aye-aye); LaFleur, M. & Gould, L. 2020. *Lemur catta*. The IUCN Red List of Threatened Species 2020: e.T11496A115565760. https://dx.doi.org/10.2305/IUCN.UK.2020-2.RLTS.T11496A115565760.en (Ring-tailed lemur); Louis, E.E., Sefczek, T.M., Bailey, C.A., Raharivololona, B., Lewis, R. & Rakotomalala, E.J. 2020. *Propithecus verreauxi*. The IUCN Red List of Threatened Species 2020: e.T18354A115572044. https://dx.doi.org/10.2305/IUCN.UK.2020-2.RLTS.T18354A115572044.en (Verreaux's sifaka); Louis, E.E., Bailey, C.A., Frasier, C.L., Raharivololona, B., Schwitzer, C., Ratsimbazafy, J., Wilmet, L., Lewis, R. & Rakotomalala, D. 2020. *Lepilemur ruficaudatus*. The IUCN Red List of Threatened Species 2020: e.T11621A115566869. https://dx.doi.org/10.2305/IUCN.UK.2020-2.RLTS.T11621A115566869.en (Ring-tailed lemur); Blanco, M., Dolch, R., Ganzhorn, J., Greene, L.K., Le Pors, B., Lewis, R., Louis, E.E., Rafalinirina, H.A., Raharivololona, B., Rakotoarisoa, G., Ralison, J., Randriahaingo, H.N.T., Rasoloarison, R.M., Razafindrasolo, M., Sgarlata, G.M., Wright, P. & Zaonarivelo, J. 2020. *Cheirogaleus medius*. The IUCN Red List of Threatened Species 2020: e.T163023599A115588562. https://dx.doi.org/10.2305/IUCN.UK.2020-2.RLTS.T163023599A115588562.en (Fat-tailed dwarf lemur). **122–123** Watanabe, K. & Tokita, K. 2020. *Macaca fuscata*. The IUCN Red List of Threatened Species 2020: e.T12552A17949359. https://dx.doi.org/10.2305/IUCN.UK.2020-2.RLTS.T12552A17949359.en (Japanese macaque). **124–125** Fruth, B., Hickey, J.R., André, C., Furuichi, T., Hart, J., Hart, T., Kuehl, H., Maisels, F., Nackoney, J., Reinartz, G., Sop, T., Thompson, J. & Williamson, E.A. 2016. *Pan paniscus* (errata version published in 2016). The IUCN Red List of Threatened Species 2016: e.T15932A102331567. https://dx.doi.org/10.2305/IUCN.UK.2016-2.RLTS.T15932A17964305.en (Bonobo); Maisels, F., Bergl, R.A. & Williamson, E.A. 2018. *Gorilla gorilla* (amended version of 2016 assessment). The IUCN Red List of Threatened Species 2018: e.T9404A136250858. https://dx.doi.org/10.2305/IUCN.UK.2018-2.RLTS.T9404A136250858.en (Western gorilla); Plumptre, A., Robbins, M.M. & Williamson, E.A. 2019. *Gorilla beringei*. The IUCN Red List of Threatened Species 2019: e.T39994A115576640. https://dx.doi.org/10.2305/IUCN.UK.2019-1.RLTS.T39994A115576640.en (Eastern gorilla); Humle, T., Maisels, F., Oates, J.F., Plumptre, A. & Williamson, E.A. 2016. *Pan troglodytes* (errata version published in 2018). The IUCN Red List of Threatened Species 2016: e.T15933A129038584. https://dx.doi.org/10.2305/IUCN.UK.2016-2.RLTS.T15933A17964454.en (Chimpanzee). **126–127** Ancrenaz, M., Gumal, M., Marshall, A.J., Meijaard, E., Wich, S.A. & Husson, S. 2016. *Pongo pygmaeus* (errata version published in 2018). The IUCN Red List of Threatened Species 2016: e.T17975A123809220. https://dx.doi.org/10.2305/IUCN.UK.2016-1.RLTS.T17975A17966347.en (Bornean orangutan); Singleton, I., Wich, S.A., Nowak, M., Usher, G. & Utami-Atmoko, S.S. 2017. *Pongo abelii* (errata version published in 2018). The IUCN Red List of Threatened Species 2017: e.T121097935A123797627. https://dx.doi.org/10.2305/IUCN.UK.2017-3.RLTS.T121097935A115575085.en (Sumatran orangutan); Nowak, M.G., Rianti, P., Wich, S.A., Meijaard, E. & Fredriksson, G. 2017. *Pongo tapanuliensis*. The IUCN Red List of Threatened Species 2017: e.T120588639A120588662. https://dx.doi.org/10.2305/IUCN.UK.2017-3.RLTS.T120588639A120588662.en (Tapanuli orangutan). **128–129** Molur, S., Srinivasulu, C., Bates, P. & Francis, C. 2008. *Pteropus giganteus*. The IUCN Red List of Threatened Species 2008: e.T18725A8511108. https://dx.doi.org/10.2305/IUCN.UK.2008.RLTS.T18725A8511108.en (Indian flying fox). **129** Armstrong, K.D., Woinarski, J.C.Z., Hanrahan, N.M. & Burbidge, A.A. 2019. *Macroderma gigas*. The IUCN Red List of Threatened Species 2019: e.T12590A22027714. https://dx.doi.org/10.2305/IUCN.UK.2019-3.RLTS.T12590A22027714.en (Ghost false vampire bat); Bates, P., Bumrungsri, S. & Francis, C. 2019. *Craseonycteris thonglongyai*. The IUCN Red List of Threatened Species 2019: e.T5481A22072935. https://dx.doi.org/10.2305/IUCN.UK.2019-3.RLTS.T5481A22072935.en (Hog-nosed bat); Piraccini, R. 2016. *Rhinolophus ferrumequinum*. The IUCN Red List of Threatened Species 2016: e.T19517A21973253. https://dx.doi.org/10.2305/IUCN.UK.2016-2.RLTS.T19517A21973253.en (Greater horseshoe bat); O'Donnell, C. 2008. *Mystacina tuberculata*. The IUCN Red List of Threatened Species 2008: e.T14261A4427784. https://dx.doi.org/10.2305/IUCN.UK.2008.RLTS.T14261A4427784.en (New Zealand (lesser) short-tailed bat); O'Donnell, C. 2008. *Mystacina robusta*. The IUCN Red List of Threatened Species 2008: e.T14260A4427606. https://dx.doi.org/10.2305/IUCN.UK.2008.RLTS.T14260A4427606.en (New Zealand (greater) short-tailed bat); Monadjem, A., Cardiff, S.G., Rakotoarivelo, A.R., Jenkins, R.K.B. & Ratrimomanarivo, F.H. 2017. *Myzopoda aurita*. The IUCN Red List of Threatened Species 2017: e.T14288A22073303. https://dx.doi.org/10.2305/IUCN.UK.2017-2.RLTS.T14288A22073303.en (Madagascar sucker-footed bat); Barquez, R., Perez, S., Miller, B. & Diaz, M. 2015. *Diaemus youngi*. The IUCN Red List of Threatened Species 2015: e.T6520A21982777. https://dx.doi.org/10.2305/IUCN.UK.2015-4.RLTS.T6520A21982777.en (White-winged vampire bat). **130–131** Goodrich, J., Lynam, A., Miquelle, D., Wibisono, H., Kawanishi, K., Pattanavibool, A., Htun, S., Tempa, T., Karki, J., Jhala, Y. & Karanth, U. 2015. *Panthera tigris*. The IUCN Red List of Threatened Species 2015: e.T15955A50659951. https://dx.doi.org/10.2305/IUCN.UK.2015-2.RLTS.T15955A50659951.en (Tiger). **132–133** Bauer, H., Packer, C., Funston, P.F., Henschel, P. & Nowell, K. 2016. *Panthera leo* (errata version published in 2017). The IUCN Red List of Threatened Species 2016: e.T15951A115130419. https://dx.doi.org/10.2305/IUCN.UK.2016-3.RLTS.T15951A107265605.en (Lion). **136–137** Boitani, L., Phillips, M. & Jhala, Y. 2018. *Canis lupus* (errata version published in 2020). The IUCN Red List of Threatened Species 2018: e.T3746A163508960. https://dx.doi.org/10.2305/IUCN.UK.2018-2.RLTS.T3746A163508960.en (Grey wolf). **138–139** Garshelis, D.L., Scheick, B.K., Doan-Crider, D.L., Beecham, J.J. & Obbard, M.E. 2016. *Ursus americanus* (errata version published in 2017). The IUCN Red List of Threatened Species 2016: e.T41687A114251609. https://dx.doi.org/10.2305/IUCN.UK.2016-3.RLTS.T41687A45034604.en (American black bear); Wiig, Ø., Amstrup, S., Atwood, T., Laidre, K., Lunn, N., Obbard, M., Regehr, E. & Thiemann, G. 2015. *Ursus maritimus*. The IUCN Red List of Threatened Species 2015: e.T22823A14871490. https://dx.doi.org/10.2305/IUCN.UK.2015-4.RLTS.T22823A14871490.en (Polar bear); Swaisgood, R., Wang, D. & Wei, F. 2016. *Ailuropoda melanoleuca* (errata version published in 2017). The IUCN Red List of Threatened Species 2016: e.T712A121745669. https://dx.doi.org/10.2305/IUCN.UK.2016-2.RLTS.T712A45033386.en (Giant panda); McLellan, B.N., Proctor, M.F., Huber, D. & Michel, S. 2017. *Ursus arctos* (amended version of 2017 assessment). The IUCN Red List of Threatened Species 2017: e.T41688A121229971. https://dx.doi.org/10.2305/IUCN.UK.2017-3.RLTS.T41688A121229971.en (Brown bear); Garshelis, D. & Steinmetz, R. 2016. *Ursus thibetanus* (errata version published in 2017). The IUCN Red List of Threatened Species 2016: e.T22824A114252336. https://dx.doi.org/10.2305/IUCN.UK.2016-3.RLTS.T22824A45034242.en (Asiatic black bear); Scotson, L., Fredriksson, G., Augeri, D., Cheah, C., Ngoprasert, D. & Wai-Ming, W. 2017. *Helarctos malayanus* (errata version published in 2018). The IUCN Red List of Threatened Species 2017: e.T9760A123798233. https://dx.doi.org/10.2305/IUCN.UK.2017-3.RLTS.T9760A45033547.en (Sun bear); Dharaiya, N., Bargali, H.S. & Sharp, T. 2020. *Melursus ursinus* (amended version of 2016 assessment). The IUCN Red List of Threatened Species 2020: e.T13143A166519315. https://dx.doi.org/10.2305/IUCN.UK.2020-1.RLTS.T13143A166519315.en (Sloth bear); Velez-Liendo, X. & García-Rangel, S. 2017. *Tremarctos ornatus* (errata version published in 2018). The IUCN Red List of Threatened Species 2017: e.T22066A123792952. https://dx.doi.org/10.2305/IUCN.UK.2017-3.RLTS.T22066A45034047.en (Spectacled bear). **140–141** Do Linh San, E., Begg, C., Begg, K. & Abramov, A.V. 2016. *Mellivora capensis*. The IUCN Red List of Threatened Species 2016: e.T41629A45210107. https://dx.doi.org/10.2305/IUCN.UK.2016-1.RLTS.T41629A45210107.en (Honey badger). **142–143** Rubenstein, D., Low Mackey, B., Davidson, ZD, Kebede, F. & King, S.R.B. 2016. *Equus grevyi*. The IUCN Red List of Threatened Species 2016: e.T7950A89624491. https://dx.doi.org/10.2305/IUCN.UK.2016-3.RLTS.T7950A89624491.en (Grevy's zebra); King, S.R.B. & Moehlman, P.D. 2016. *Equus quagga*. The IUCN Red List of Threatened Species 2016: e.T41013A45172424. https://dx.doi.org/10.2305/IUCN.UK.2016-2.RLTS.T41013A45172424.en (Plains zebra); Gosling, L.M., Muntifering, J., Kolberg, H., Uiseb, K. & King, S.R.B. 2019. *Equus zebra* (amended version of 2019 assessment). The IUCN Red List of Threatened Species 2019: e.T7960A160755590. https://dx.doi.org/10.2305/IUCN.UK.2019-1.RLTS.T7960A160755590.en (Mountain zebra). **144–145** Emslie, R. 2020. *Diceros bicornis*. The IUCN Red List of Threatened Species 2020: e.T6557A152728945. https://dx.doi.org/10.2305/IUCN.UK.2020-1.RLTS.T6557A152728945.en (Black rhino); Emslie, R. 2020. *Ceratotherium simum*. The IUCN Red List of Threatened Species 2020: e.T4185A45813880. https://dx.doi.org/10.2305/IUCN.UK.2020-1.RLTS.T4185A45813880.en (White rhino); Ellis, S. & Talukdar, B. 2019. *Rhinoceros unicornis*. The IUCN Red List of Threatened Species 2019: e.T19496A18494149. https://dx.doi.org/10.2305/IUCN.UK.2019-3.RLTS.T19496A18494149.en (One-horned rhino). **146–147** Lewison, R. & Pluháček, J. 2017. *Hippopotamus amphibius*. The IUCN Red List of Threatened Species 2017: e.T10103A18567364. https://dx.doi.org/10.2305/IUCN.UK.2017-2.RLTS.T10103A18567364.en (Hippopotamus); Ransom, C, Robinson, P.T. & Collen, B. 2015. *Choeropsis liberiensis*. The IUCN Red List of Threatened Species 2015: e.T10032A18567171. https://dx.doi.org/10.2305/IUCN.UK.2015-2.RLTS.T10032A18567171.en (Pygmy hippo). **148–149** Hundertmark, K. 2016. *Alces alces*. The IUCN Red List of Threatened Species 2016: e.T56003281A22157381. https://dx.doi.org/10.2305/IUCN.UK.2016-1.RLTS.T56003281A22157381.en (Moose). **150–151** Cooke, J.G. 2018. *Megaptera novaeangliae*. The IUCN Red List of Threatened Species 2018: e.T13006A50362794. https://dx.doi.org/10.2305/IUCN.UK.2018-2.RLTS.T13006A50362794.en (Humpback whale).

**Other Data Credits:**
**26–27** Food and Agriculture Organization of the United Nations.
**30–31** The Genetics Society of America (GSA): The Functional Basis of Wing Patterning in Heliconius Butterflies: The Molecules Behind Mimicry, Marcus R. Kronforst and Riccardo Papa, GENETICS May 1, 2015 vol. 200 no. 1 1-19; https://doi.org/10.1534/genetics.114.172387 / Copyright Clearance Center - Rightslink.
**34–35** World Spider Catalog (2020). World Spider Catalog. Version 21.5.
**36–37** Aquamaps: Computer generated distribution maps for Asterias rubens (common starfish), with mode lled year 2050 native range map based on IPCC RCP8.5 emissions scenario. www.aquamaps.org, version 10 / 2019. Accessed 12 Oct. 2020.
**42–43** This map was retrieved, with permission, from www.fishbase.org/summary/Petromyzon-marinus.html.
**48–49** Aquamaps: Scarponi, P., G. Coro, and P. Pagano. A collection of Aquamaps native layers in NetCDF format. Data in brief 17 (2018): 292-296.
**50–51** Multidisciplinary Digital Publishing Institute.
**68** Rune Midtgaard, RepFocus (www.repfocus.dk)
**70–71** Rune Midtgaard, RepFocus (www.repfocus.dk).
**76–77** Rune Midtgaard, RepFocus (www.repfocus.dk).
**79** Rune Midtgaard, RepFocus (www.repfocus.dk).
**88–89** Elsevier.
**132–133** PLOS Genetics.
**137** Wikipedia: (Dingo).
**150–151** NOAA.

# DK WHERE ON EARTH? ATLASES

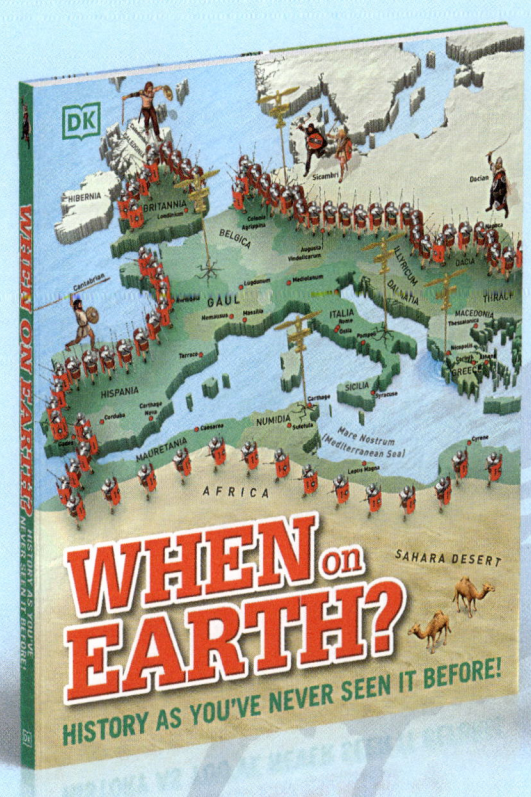
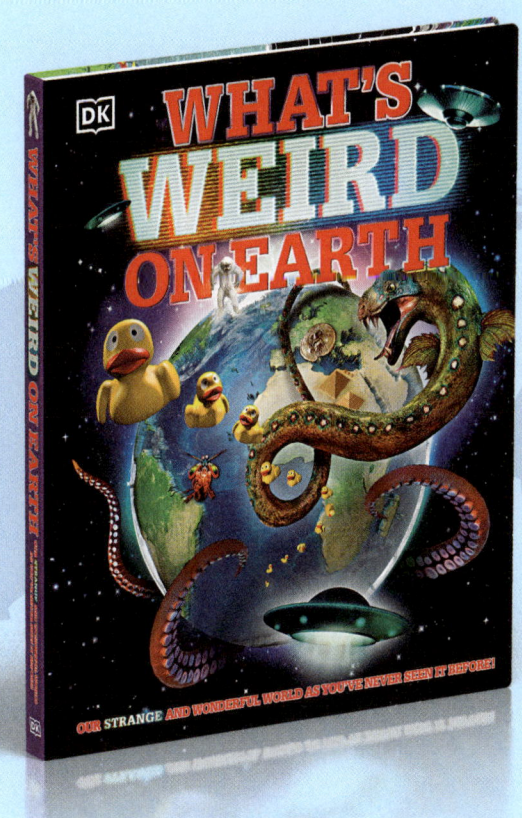